GREAT BRITAIN

A. Taverner/MICHELIN

"Heavens! What a goodly prospect spreads around,
Of hills, and dales, and woods, and lawns, and spires,
And glittering towns, and golded streams, till all
The stretching landscape into smoke decays!
Happy Britannia!"

The Seasons, James Thomson 1700-48

Executive Editorial Director David Brabis

Chief Editor Cynthia Clayton Ochterbeck

THE GREEN GUIDE — GREAT BRITAIN

Editor	Gwen Cannon
Principal Writer	Paul Murphy
Production Coordinator	Allison Michelle Simpson
Cartography	Alain Baldet, Michèle Cana, Peter Wrenn
Photo Editor	Brigitta L. House
Researcher	Lydia B . Dishman
Proofreader	Margo Browning
Layout	Allison Michelle Simpson, Nicole D. Jordan
Cover Design	Laurent Muller
Interior Design	Agence Rampazzo
Production	Pierre Ballochard, Renaud Leblanc

Contact Us :

The Green Guide
Michelin Travel Publications
One Parkway South
Greenville, SC 29615
USA

☎ 1-800-423-0485
www.michelintravel.com
michelin.guides@us.michelin.com

or

Hannay House, 39 Clarendon Road
Watford, Herts WD17 1JA, UK
☎ 01923 205 240 - Fax 01923 205 241
www.ViaMichelin.com
TheGreenGuide-uk@uk.michelin.com

Special Sales :

For information regarding bulk sales, customised editions
and premium sales, please contact our Customer
Service Departments:

USA	1-800-423-0485
UK	(01923) 205 240
Canada	1-800-361-8236

Note to the reader

One Team: A Devotion to Quality

There's just one reason our team is dedicated to producing quality travel publications—you, our reader. We want you to get the maximum benefit from your trip—and from your money. In today's multiple-choice world of travel, the options are many, perhaps overwhelming.

In our guidebooks, we try to minimise the guesswork involved with travel. We scout out the attractions, prioritise them with star ratings, and describe what you'll discover when you visit them.

To help you orient yourself, we provide colourful and detailed, but easy-to-follow maps. Floor plans of some of the major museums help you plan your tour.

Throughout the guides, we offer practical information, touring tips and suggestions for finding the best views, good places for a break and the most interesting shops.

Lodging and dining are always a big part of travel, so we compile a selection of hotels and restaurants that we think convey the feel of the destination, and organise them by geographic area and price. We also highlight shopping, recreational and entertainment venues, especially the popular spots.

If you're short on time, driving tours are included so you can hit the highlights and quickly absorb the best of the place.

For those who love to experience a destination on foot, we add walking tours, often with a map. And we list other companies who offer boat, bus or guided walking tours of the area, some with culinary, historical or other themes.

In short, we test and retest, check and recheck to make sure that our guidebooks are truly just that: a personalised guide to help you make the most of your visit. After all, we want you to enjoy traveling as much as we do.

The Michelin Green Guide Team

PLANNING YOUR TRIP

WHEN AND WHERE TO GO

KNOW BEFOE YOU GO

GETTING THERE

WHERE TO STAY AND EAT

WHAT TO DO AND SEE

BASIC INFORMATION

INTRODUCTION TO GREAT BRITAIN

NATURE

HISTORY

ART AND CULTURE

THE COUNTRY TODAY

SYMBOLS

	Tips to help improve your experience
	Details to consider
	Entry fees
	Walking tours
	Closed to the public
	Hours of operation
	Periods of closure

CONTENTS

DISCOVERING GREAT BRITAIN

How to Use this Guide

Orientation

To help you grasp the "lay of the land" quickly and easily, so you'll feel confident and comfortable finding your way around, we offer the following tools in this guide:

- Detailed table of contents for an overview of what'll you find in the guide, and how it is organized.
- Map of Principal Sights showing the starred places of interest at a glance.
- Detailed maps of city centres, regions and towns.
- Floor and site plans of museums and cathedrals.
- Principal Sights ordered alphabetically for easy reference.

Practicalities

At the front of the guide, you'll see a section called "Planning Your Trip" that contains information about planning your trip, the best time to go, getting to and getting around the destination, basic facts and tips for making the most of your visit. You'll find driving and themed tours and suggestions for outdoor fun. There's also a calendar of popular annual events in the country. Information on shopping, sightseeing, activities for children, sports and recreational opportunities is also included.

LODGINGS

We've made a selection of hotels and arranged them within the cities, categorised by price to fit all budgets (& see the Legend at the back of the guide for an explanation of the price categories). For the most part, we selected accommodations based on their unique quality, their regional feel, as it were. If you want a more comprehensive selection of lodgings, see the red-cover Michelin Guide Great Britain & Ireland.

RESTAURANTS

We thought you'd like to know the popular eating spots in selected cities and towns described in this guide. So we try to feature restaurants that capture the flavour of the area. Many of them feature regional specialties, though we're not rating the quality of the food per se. As we did with the hotels, we organised the restaurants within the Principal Sights and categorised them by price to appeal to all wallets (see the Legend at the back of the guide for an explanation of the price categories). If you want a more comprehensive selection of local eateries, see the red-cover Michelin Guide Great Britain & Ireland.

Attractions

Contact information, admission charge and hours of operation are given for the majority of attractions. Unless otherwise noted, admission prices shown are for single adult only. Discounts for OAPs, students, etc. may be available; be sure to ask. If no admission charge is shown, entrance to the attraction is free.

Within each Principal Sight, attractions within a town or city are described first, sometimes in the form of a walking tour. Then come outlying sights and Excursions. If you're pressed for time, we recommend you visit the three- and two-starred sights first—the stars are your guide.

STAR RATINGS

Michelin has used stars as a rating tool for more than 100 years:

★★★	Highly recommended
★★	Recommended
★	Interesting

SYMBOLS IN THE TEXT

Besides the stars, other symbols in the text indicate tourist information ⓘ; wheelchair access ♿; on-site parking 🅿; and sights of interest to children Kids.

See the box appearing on the Contents page for other symbols used in the text.

See the Maps explanation below for symbols appearing on the maps.

Throughout the guide you will find peach-coloured text boxes or sidebars containing anecdotal or background information. Green-coloured boxes contain information to help you save time or money.

Maps

All maps in this guide are oriented north, unless otherwise indicated by a directional arrow.

See the map Legend at the back of the guide for an explanation of map symbols.

A complete list of the maps found in the guide appears at the back of this book.

Addresses, phone numbers, opening hours and prices published in this guide are accurate at press time. We welcome corrections and suggestions that may assist us in preparing the next edition. Please send your comments to:

Michelin Travel Publications
Editorial Department
P.O. Box 19001
Greenville, SC   29602-9001
Email: michelin.guides@us.michelin.com
Web site: www.michelintravel.com

Edinburgh Military Tattoo

D. Corance/STILL MOVING

Principal sights

MOUSA BROCH

Jarlshof

SHETLAND ISLANDS

ATLANTIC OCEAN

NORTH SEA

ORKNEY ISLANDS

Skara Brae   Mass Howe   Kirkwall

Stromness

ORKNEY ISLANDS

Duncansby Head

Wick

Grey Cairns of Camster

Duff House

Fyvie Castle   Haddo House

ABERDEEN

Pitmedden

Dunnottar Castle

Sueno's Stone

Elgin

Spey

Kildrummy Castle   Castle Fraser

Crathes

Edzell Castle

Deeside

Dornoch

Dunrobin

Cromarty

Inverness

Cairngorm Mountains

Aviemore

Glamis

Dundee

Blair

Pitlochry

Perth

Falls of Measach

LOCH MAREE

WESTER ROSS

Ullapool

Loch Broom

Glen

Loch Ness

Great

Eilean Donan

Dunkeld

Tay

Drummond

THE TROSSACHS

INVEREWE

Portree

SKYE

THE CUILLINS

Glen Coe

Loch Awe

Oban

Stornoway

Lewis

Callanish Standing Stones

Harris

HEBRIDES

Dunvegan

SEA OF THE HEBRIDES

MULL

Iona

WESTERN ISLES

Uist

THE

WHEN AND WHERE TO GO

Driving Tours

👢 *See pp 12–15*

Themed Tours

HISTORIC PROPERTIES

Many country houses, gardens, historic monuments and ruins are owned or maintained by the following organisations which offer free admission to their members. The **Great British Heritage Pass** (valid for 4, 7, 15 days or one month, and valid for 6 months from date of purchase) gives access to over 550 properties throughout Great Britain. It is available from over 50 tourist information centres and through agents in the USA and UK, see www.visitbritain.com for a full list.

Cadw (Welsh Historic Monuments)

Over 125 properties: Cadw, Plas Carew, Unit 5/7 Cefn Coed, Parc Nantgarw, Cardiff CF15 7QQ, Wales, ☎ 01443 336 000; www.cadw.wales.gov.uk

English Heritage

Over 400 properties: Customer Services Department, PO Box 569, Swindon SN2 2YP, ☎ 0870 333 1181; www.english-heritage.org.uk

Historic Scotland

Over 300 properties: Longmore House, Salisbury Place, Edinburgh EH9 1SH, Scotland, ☎ 0131 668 8600; www.historic-scotland.gov.uk

Manx National Heritage

Eight principal sites and 4000 acres: Douglas, Isle of Man, IM1 3LY, ☎ 01624 675 522; Reciprocal arrangements between some of the above organisations entitle members of one organisation to discounted admission to sites owned by another.

National Trust –

England and Wales:

PO Box 39, Warrington WA5 7WD, ☎ 0870 458 4000; www.national trust.org.uk

Scotland:

28 Charlotte Square, Edinburgh EH2 4ET, ☎ 0131 243 9300; www.nts.org.uk

There are reciprocal arrangements between these Trusts and similar overseas Trusts.

The Royal Oak Foundation

American public charity affiliated with the National Trust to promote the preservation of the Anglo-American heritage. Royal Oak members automatically receive the rights and privileges of full Trust members. The Royal Oak Foundation, 26 Broadway, Suite 950, New York, NY 10004, USA, ☎ 1-800-913-6565, 212-480 -889; www.royal-oak.org

SPECIAL INTERESTS

Campaign for Real Ale

230 Hatfield Road, St Albans, Herts, AL1 4LW, ☎ 01727 867 201; www.camra.org.uk.
Protects traditional draught beer and traditional pubs, organises beer festivals and produces the annual *Good Beer Guide*.

British Arts Festivals Association

5th Floor, 12-14 Mason's Avenue, London EC2V 5BB.
☎ 020 7796 4904; Fax 020 7796 4959; www.artsfestivals.co.uk.

Provides advance information on leading annual arts festivals in the United Kingdom.

The Sealed Knot

PO Box 2000, Nottingham NG2 5LH; www.sealedknot.org.
Organises re-enactments of the engagements of the English Civil War.

GARDENS

Formal gardens attached to grand country houses to delightful cottage gardens, all attest to the British passion for gardening. Plants for sale are sometimes on offer.

The National Gardens Scheme

Hatchlands Park, East Clandon, Guildford, Surrey GU4 7RT, ☎ 01483 211 535; www.ngs.org.uk.
Publishes an annual guide – *Gardens of England and Wales* – to private gardens that open to the public for a limited period in aid of charity.

When to Go

SEASONS

There is no season of the year when the weather is too inclement to permit visitors to enjoy the sights, but the changeable British climate lives up to its reputation. Spring and autumn are the best seasons for visiting parks and gardens when the flowers are in bloom or the leaves are turning colour; most stately homes and other country sights are closed from October to Easter. In **spring** as the days grow longer and warmer, the light is glorious, but showers are frequent. **Summer** is unpredictable with moderate temperatures; in July and August there may be occasional heat waves in the southern areas, when the thermometer tops 30°C, or the days may be cloudy and cool. **Autumn** can start dry and sunny, with clear skies and beautiful sunsets; the air is crisp and invigorating. But as the days grow shorter, the temperature usually lowers. In **winter**, southern areas can remain fairly mild until Christmas; there may be cold snaps, but the temperature rarely drops below the freezing point. However, wind and dampness can make it feel very cold. Autumn and winter are the best time for visiting museums or for shopping, as places are less crowded, except in the weeks before Christmas.

CLIMATE

To comment on the weather is a British tradition because change is frequent and "the rain that raineth every day" is rarely unaccompanied by brighter spells. The moist and breezy oceanic climate has many compensations. Stressful extremes of either heat or cold are rare, so that outdoor activity of some kind is almost always possible. Although the western mountains receive the highest amount of precipitation, which on some summits reaches an astonishing 200in/5 000mm, it is in the west that the tempering effects of the **Gulf Stream** are felt and where sub-tropical plants can flourish in sheltered locations. The drier, sunnier climate of the east and south is more continental in character, with colder winters and warmer summers.

WHAT TO PACK

Year-round, it is advisable to have a raincoat or hooded coat, and umbrella, in view of the fickle weather. Warmer wear, including a hat, neck scarf and gloves, is necessary in early spring, late autumn and, of course, winter. In summer it can be cool in the evening, so taking some warmer clothes is recommended. As there will be many times when walking is the ideal means of transport in Great Britain, comfortable footwear is essential, especially for strolling in the countryside and for sightseeing. It's a good idea to take along an extra tote bag for shopping at outdoor markets, carrying a picnic, and for bringing purchased items back home with you.

KNOW BEFORE YOU GO

Useful Web Sites

The web site of **Visit Britain,** the country's official tourist authority, is www.visit.britain.com.

REGIONAL TOURIST BOARD WEB SITES ARE:

- www.visitscotland.com
- www.visitwales.com
- www.visitsoutheastengland.com
- www.visitheartofengland.com
- www.visiteastofengland.com
- www.westcountrynow.com

The **starting point** for all visits to the capital is www.visitlondon.com.
Edinburgh's official web site is: www.edinburgh.org.

Tourist Offices

Visit Britain, formerly known as the British Tourist Authority**,** provides assistance in planning a trip to Great Britain and an excellent range of brochures and maps. It works in cooperation with the three National Tourist Boards (England, Wales and Scotland), the Regional Tourist Boards and other tourist organisations. .

British Travel Centre is located at 1 Lower Regent Street, London SW1Y 4NS (personal callers and written enquiries only).

There are **Tourist Information Centres** in all parts of the country with information on sightseeing, accommodation, places to eat, transport, entertainment, sports and local events. They are usually well signed, but some are open only during the summer season; the address and telephone number of the local tourist office can be found after the introductory paragraph(s) for the majority of Principal Sights.

The **British Tourist Authority** (BTA) has over 40 offices worldwide including Belgium, Brazil, Denmark, Germany, Hong Kong, Ireland, Italy, Japan, the Netherlands, Norway, Spain, Sweden and Switzerland as well as those listed on the opposite page.

International Visitors

EMBASSIES AND CONSULATES

Australia

Embassy:

High Commission: Australia House, The Strand, London WC2B 4LA, ☎ 020 7379 4334, www.australia.org.uk

Consulate:

69 George Street, Edinburgh EH2 2JG
☎ 0131 624 3333

Canada

High Commission: Macdonald House, 1 Grosvenor Square, London WIXK 4AB, ☎ 020 7258 6600; www.dfait-maeci.gc.ca

England

Consulate:

55 Colmore Row, 3rd Floor, Birmingham, B3 2AS
☎ 0121 236 6474.

Japan

Embassy:

101 Piccadilly, London, W1J 7JT
☎ 020 7465 6543

Consulate:

2 Melville Crescent, Edinburgh EH3 7HW ☎ 0131 225 4777; www.uk.emb-japan.go.jp

British Tourist Authority Offices	
United States:	551 5th Avenue, Suite 701, New York, NY 10176, ☎ 212-986-2266, 1-800-462-2748. www.travelbritain.org
Canada:	5915 Airport Road, Suite 120, Toronto, Ontario, L4V 1T1, ☎ 905-405-1835. www.visitbritain.com/ca
France:	BP 154-08 , 75363 Paris Cedex 08 ☎ 01 58 36 50 50. www.visitbritain.com/fr
Australia:	Level 2, 15 Blue Street, North Sydney, NSW 2060, ☎ 2 90 21 44 00 or 1 300 85 85 89. www.visitbritain.com/au
New Zealand:	17th Floor, 151 Queen Street, Auckland 1, ☎ 09-3031-446.

New Zealand

High Commission: New Zealand House, 80 Haymarket, London SW1Y 4TQ ☎ 020 7930 8422; www.nzembassy.com

Scotland

Consulate:
Standard Life House, 50 Lothian Road, Festival Square, Edinburgh EG3 9WJ ☎ 0131 473 6320

South Africa

High Commission: South Africa House, Trafalgar Square, London WC2N 5DP ☎ 020 7451 7299; www.southafricahouse.com

USA:

Embassy:
24-31 Grosvenor Square, London W1A 1AE, ☎ 020 7499 9000; www.usembassy.org.uk

Consulate:
3 Regent Terrace, Edinburgh EH7 5BW ☎ 0131 556 8315

Wales:

Consulate:
c/o St John Cymru Wales, Beignon Close, Ocean Way, Cardiff CF24 5PB ☎ 0292 044 9635

DOCUMENTS

Despite the law, which came into force on 1 January 1993, authorising the free flow of goods and people within the European Union, it is nonetheless advisable for EU nationals to hold some means of identification, such as a **passport**. Non-EU nationals must be in possession of a valid national passport. Loss or theft should be reported to the appropriate embassy or consulate and to the local police.

A visa to visit the United Kingdom is not required by nationals of the member states of the European Union and of the Commonwealth (including Australia, Canada, New Zealand, and South Africa) and the USA. Nationals of other countries should check with the British Embassy and apply for a visa if necessary in good time.

The brochure *Safe Trip Abroad* provides useful information for US nationals on obtaining a passport, visa requirements, customs regulations, medical care etc for international travel; it is published by the government printing office and can be ordered by telephone ☎ 1-202-512-1800 or online, www.access.gpo.gov.

CUSTOMS

Tax-free allowances for various commodities are governed by EU legislation except in the Channel Islands and the Isle of Man which have different regulations. Details of these allowances and restrictions are available at most ports of entry to Great Britain.

It is prohibited to import into the United Kingdom any drugs, firearms and ammunition, obscene material featuring children, counterfeit merchandise, unlicensed livestock (birds or animals), anything related to endangered species (furs, ivory, horn, leather) and certain plants (potatoes, bulbs, seeds, trees).

A Guide for Travellers outlines British customs regulations and "duty free" allowances; it is available from **HM Customs and Excise** ☎ 0845 010 9000, www.hmce.gov.uk.

A booklet *Know before you go* is published by the US Customs Service; its offices are listed in the phone book in the Federal Government section under the US Department of the Treasury or can be obtained online, www.customs.ustreas.gov.

HEALTH

Visitors to Britain are entitled to treatment at the Accident and Emergency Departments of National Health Service hospitals. For an overnight or longer stay in hospital payment will probably be required. It is therefore advisable to take out adequate insurance cover before leaving home.

Visitors from EU countries should apply to their own National Social Security Offices for a **European Health Insurance Card (EHIC)** – the replacement for Form E111 – which entitles them to medical treatment under an EU Reciprocal Medical Treatment arrangement.

Nationals of non-EU countries should take out comprehensive insurance. American Express offers a service, "Global Assist", for any medical, legal or personal emergency – see www.americanexpress.com, or in Great Britain ☎ 0845 456 6524.

In case of an emergency, dial the free nationwide emergency number (999) and ask for Fire, Police or Ambulance.

Accessibility

Many of the sights described in this guide are accessible to disabled people; they are designated by the ♿ symbol in the Admission Times and Charges for the attractions. The *Michelin Guide Great Britain & Ireland* indicates hotels with facilities suitable for disabled people; it is advisable to book in advance.

The **Royal Association for Disability and Rehabilitation (RADAR)** publishes an annual guide with detailed information on hotels and holiday centres as well as sections on transport, accommodation for children and activity holidays. Apply to RADAR, 12 City Forum, 250 City Road, London EC1V 8AF, ☎ 020 7250 3222, www.radar.org.uk.

Holiday Care

7th Floor, Sunley House, 4 Bedford Park, Croydon, Surrey CR0 2AP; ☎ 0845 124 9971, (outside UK) 0044 208 760 0072; www.holidaycare.org.uk.

Other organisations such as Visit Britain, the National Trust and the Department of Transport publish booklets for disabled travellers.

GETTING THERE

By Air

The various national and other independent airlines operate services to London (Heathrow, Gatwick, Luton, Stansted and London City) and to the major provincial airports (Aberdeen, Birmingham, Cardiff, Edinburgh, Glasgow, Liverpool, Manchester, Newcastle, Prestwick). Information, brochures and timetables are available from the airlines and from travel agents.

By Sea

There are numerous cross-Channel (passenger and car ferries, hovercraft) and other ferry or shipping services from the continent. For details apply to travel agencies or to the ferry companies.

Brittany Ferries

The Brittany Centre, Wharf Road, Portsmouth, Hants PO2 8RU. ☎ 08703 665 333*(from within UK only)*; www.brittany-ferries.com

Hoverspeed

Marine Parade, Dover, Kent CT17 9TG. ☎ 0870 240 8070; www.hoverspeed.co.uk

Irish Ferries

PO Box 19, Alexandra Road, Dublin 1; ☎ 08705 17 17 17; www.irishferries.com

P&O Ferries

Channel House, Channel View Road, Dover, Kent CT17 9TJ. ☎ 08705 980 333; www.poferries.com

Stena Line

1 Suffolk Way, Sevenoaks Kent TN13 1YL. ☎ 08705 70 70 70; www.stenaline.com

By Rail

The **Channel Tunnel** provides a direct rail link between London (Waterloo until 2007 when the terminus moves to King's Cross) and Paris and Brussels and a road/rail link between Folkestone and Calais.

Eurostar

Eurostar House, Waterloo station, London SE1 8SE, ☎ 0870 518 6186 (ticket sales and bookings); ☎ 020 7928 0660 (arrival times and lost property); ☎ 01777 77 78 79 (international customer relations); www.eurostar.com.

BritRail Passes or Eurailpasses

are available to visitors from North America and certain Asia-Pacific countries including Australia, New Zealand and South Africa. BritRail Passes allow travel on consecutive days for various periods and Eurailpasses allow travel on a number of days within a given month. These concessions can be obtained only outside Britain and

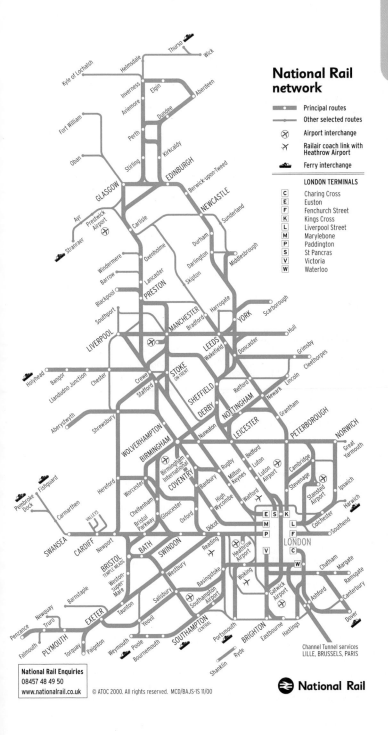

National Rail network

- Principal routes
- Other selected routes
- ⊗ Airport interchange
- ✈ Railair coach link with Heathrow Airport
- ⛴ Ferry interchange

LONDON TERMINALS

C	Charing Cross
E	Euston
F	Fenchurch Street
K	Kings Cross
L	Liverpool Street
M	Marylebone
P	Paddington
S	St Pancras
V	Victoria
W	Waterloo

Channel Tunnel services
LILLE, BRUSSELS, PARIS

National Rail Enquiries
08457 48 49 50
www.nationalrail.co.uk   © ATOC 2000. All rights reserved. MCD/BAJS-1S 11/00

National Rail

23

should be purchased from appointed agents before the beginning of the journey in question; they are worth considering by those who intend to travel extensively in Britain by rail. For information before you arrive see www.raileurope.co./us.

For information on rail services and on other concessionary tickets, including combined train and bus tickets once you are in Great Britain ☎ 08457 48 49 50; www.nationalrailenquiries.co.uk. From overseas ☎ 0044 207 278 5240.

To buy train tickets either go to the station or buy online, www. thetrainline.com.

By Coach/Bus

National Express in association with other bus operators run express coach services covering the whole country. ☎ 0875 808 080 (National call centre) For comprehensive public transport information in the UK ☎ 0870 608 2608; www.traveline.org.uk

Driving in Britain

DOCUMENTS

Nationals of EU countries require a valid **national driving licence;** US driving licence valid for 12 months; a permit is available from your local branch of the American Automobile Association, www.csaa.com
Other nationals require an international driving licence.
For the vehicle it is necessary to have the **registration papers** (log-book) and a nationality plate of the approved size.

INSURANCE

Insurance cover is compulsory and although an **International Insurance Certificate** (Green Card) is no longer a legal requirement in Britain, it is the most effective proof of insurance cover and is internationally recognised by the police and other authorities. Certain UK motoring organisations offer accident insurance and breakdown service plans for members. Europ-Assistance has special plans for members. The American Automobile Association publishes a free brochure *Offices to Serve You Abroad* for its members.

MOTORING ORGANISATIONS

The major motoring organisations in Great Britain are the Automobile Association and the Royal Automobile Club. Each provides services in varying degrees for non-resident members of affiliated clubs.

Automobile Association

Fanum House, Basingstoke, Hants, RG21 2EA; ☎ 0870 600 0371 (general), 0800 085 2721 (breakdown cover); www.theaa.com

Royal Automobile Club

Great Park Road, Bradley Stoke, Bristol BS32 4QN; ☎ 020 8917 2500 (general), 08000 966 999 (breakdown cover); www.rac.co.uk

ROAD REGULATIONS

The **minimum driving age** is 17 years old. Traffic drives **on the left** and overtakes on the right. Headlights must be used at night even in built-up areas and at other times when visibility is poor. There are severe penalties for driving after drinking more than the legal limit of alcohol.

Important **traffic signs** are shown at the end of the **Michelin Guide Great Britain and Ireland,** and in general correspond to international norms.

Seat belts

In Britain the compulsory wearing of **seat belts** includes rear seat passengers when rear belts are fitted and all children under 14.

Speed limits

Maximum speeds are:

- 🚗70mph/112kph, Motorways or dual carriageways
- 🚗60mph/96kph, other roads
- 🚗30mph/48kph, in towns and cities.

PARKING

Off-street parking is indicated by blue signs with white lettering (Parking or P); payment is made on leaving or in advance for a certain period. There are also parking meters, disc systems and paying parking zones; in the last case tickets must be obtained from ticket machines (small change necessary) and displayed inside the windscreen. Illegal parking is liable to fines and also in certain cases to the vehicle being clamped or towed away.

The usual restrictions are as follows:

- Double red line = no stopping at any time (freeway)
- Double yellow line = no parking at any time
- Single yellow line = no parking for set periods as indicated on panel
- Dotted yellow line = parking limited to certain times only.

ROUTE PLANNING

The whole of Great Britain is covered by the **Michelin map series 501-504** (scale 1: 400 00) and the **Michelin Road Atlas of Great Britain and Ireland** (scale 1: 300 00). In addition to the usual detailed road information, they indicate tourist features such as beaches or bathing areas, swimming pools, golf courses, race courses, scenic routes, tourist sights, country parks etc. These publications are an essential complement to the annual **Michelin Guide Great Britain & Ireland,** which offers an up-to-date selection of hotels and restaurants. Traffic in and around towns is heavy during the rush-hour (morning and evening). It is also very heavy on major roads at the weekend in summer, particularly bank holiday weekends.

CAR RENTAL

There are car rental agencies at airports, railway stations and in all large towns throughout Great Britain. European cars usually have manual transmission but automatic cars are available on demand. An international driving licence is required for non-EU nationals. Most companies will not rent to drivers aged under 21 or 25.

Avis	0181 848 8733
Budget	0800 181 181
Eurodollar	01895 256 565
Europecar	0345 222 525
Hertz	0181 679 1799

The following firms operate on a national basis:

Avis ☎ 0870 0100 287 enquiries; 0870 6086 363 customer service; www.avis.co.uk

Budget ☎ 0870 1539 170 pre-rental enquiries; 0161 868 2671 post-rental enquiries; www.budget.co.uk

National Car Rental ☎ 0870 400 4552; www.nationalcar.co.uk

Europcar ☎ 0870 607 5000; www.europcar.co.uk

Hertz ☎ 020 8570 5000, 0870 599 6699, 0870 844 8844; www.hertz.co.uk

EasyCar ☎ 0906 333 3333 (60p/min); www.easycar.com

PETROL/GAS

In service stations dual-pumps are the rule with unleaded pumps being identified by green pump handles or a green stripe.

TOLLS

Tolls are rare; they are levied only on the most recent bridges (Severn, Humber and Skye) and a few minor country bridges as well as road tunnels (Dartford, Tyne).

WHERE TO STAY AND EAT

Hotel and restaurant listings can be found in the Address Books featured in many of the Principal Sights in the guide.

Where to Eat

RESTAURANTS

A selection of places to eat in the different locations featured in this guide can be found in the Address Books appearing in the section entitled *Discovering Great Britain*. The Legend at the back of the book explains the symbols used in the Address Books.

Dining out in the UK has undergone a revolution in the last two decades and now ranks among the very best in the world. Thanks to its colonial past and its cosmopolitan nature, the UK offers authentic tastes from all over the world, often cooked by native chefs, or collected magpie-like by celebrity chefs from culinary tours of the world. Restaurants are becoming less and less formal with only the top hotel dining rooms and traditional establishments stipulating dress codes. Hours too have become more flexible though many places still serve lunch from around 12 noon to around 2.30pm and dinner from around 7pm to 10pm, and close in between. Only in London and the more buzzing metropolises will you find a good selection of late-dining restaurants.

Prices tend to be high compared to many other parts of the world though eating at lunchtime from set menus can save you a small fortune.

Making a reservation for weekend nights and Sunday lunchtime is recommended and if you want to eat in Britain's top restaurants you may need to book weeks in advance (though it's always worth checking at the last minute for cancellations).

BISTROS, BRASSERIES AND CAFES

These European-style establishments, usually serving a variety of relatively simple, pan-European dishes, are the places for snacks, informal meals and drinks in trendy upbeat surroundings right throughout the day and night. The UK now has a profusion of US-style cafés, (most notably Starbucks) on the high streets of most large towns. Less common these days is the traditional English cafe, sometimes called a transport cafe, and more lightheartedly "a greasy spoon." This is traditionally the place for a good old-fashioned fry-up washed down with a mug of strong tea.

PUBS (PUBLIC HOUSES)

Gastropubs

Eating out in public houses—long known as "pubs"—has changed enormously over the last decade or so with more and more establishments putting the emphasis on serving food rather than merely serving drinks. This has led to the rise of the so-called "gastropub," originally only found in London and the Home Counties (the regions around the capital) but now spreading to all parts of the country. The typical gastropub is stylish, blending modern with traditional, and serves a relatively short menu of modern European/modern British food. Prices vary. Some gastropubs offer excellent value for money while in others you may spend as much as you would in a smart restaurant. Beware that the pub-food revolution means that many pubs with no history of serving food have jumped onto the bandwagon, many with little expertise or knowledge, consequently serving poor quality overpriced food. Steer clear of pubs offering complicated sounding dishes, unless they have a particular expertise and long menus. Don't be afraid to ask if ingredients are fresh; in many pubs they won't be.

Pub Hours and Regulations

Pubs' statutory maximum licensing hours have until recently been: Mondays to Saturdays, 11am to 11pm, and Sundays, 12:30pm-10:30pm, with many closing during the afternoon. In 2005, "24-hour drinking laws" came into operation allowing the country's pubs, clubs and bars to open, in theory, around the clock. In practice however relatively few premises have applied for a licence to extend their hours, most opting to open a couple of extra hours later on Thursday, Friday and Saturday nights.

Pubs that serve meals (now the majority) normally allow children on the premises as long as they remain within the eating area and even more traditionally inclined pubs may allow children in before a certain time (say 8pm or 9pm). The best policy is to ask someone behind the bar before simply marching in *en famille*.

You must be 18 to be served with alcohol and you may be asked for some form of identification.

ETHNIC RESTAURANTS

Every town in the UK has its share of Indian and Chinese establishments and in places where large immigrant communities have settled (eg. Bradford or Birmingham) Indian restaurants are ubiquitous. After years of simply being the cheap option after the pubs closed, many ethnic restaurants have now moved upmarket to enjoy critical acclaim.

FURTHER INFORMATION

The **Michelin Guide Great Britain & Ireland** not only celebrates the very best chefs and cuisine that Great Britian has to offer but also reflects the trend towards informal eating with its Bib Gourmand award to restaurants and other establishments offering good food at moderate prices.

The guide **Eating out in Pubs,** also published by Michelin, selects 500 of the best dining pubs in England, Scotland, Wales and Ireland.

Where to Stay

FINDING A HOTEL

The **Michelin Guide Great Britain & Ireland** is an annual publication which presents a selection of hotels and restaurants. All are classified according to the standard of their amenities and their selection is based on regular on-the-spot visits and enquiries. Pleasant settings, attractive décor, quiet or secluded locations and a warm welcome are identified by special symbols. This information is also available at www.ViaMichelin.com. Places listed in the Michelin Guide are underlined in red on the **Michelin map series 501-504** (scale of 1: 400 000). The Michelin Guide includes the addresses and telephone numbers of local tourist offices and tourist information centres, which also appear in this guide for many of the Principal Sights.

RESERVATION SERVICES

Most Tourist Information Centres will provide, free of charge, an information booklet listing all hotels, bed and breakfast and other accommodation. Many will arrange accommodation for a small fee. Room prices are normally just that—the price per room—however even for a double room, they may be quoted per person.

British Hotels Reservation Centre, 13 Grosvenor Gardens, London SW1W 0BD ☎ 020 7340 1616; www.justbookit.com.

BED AND BREAKFAST (B&B)

Many private individuals take in a limited number of guests. Prices include bed and breakfast, usually the cooked variety. Some offer an evening meal though the menu will of course be short. Local Tourist Information Centres usually have a list of the bed and breakfast establishments in the area and book if necessary for a fee. Many houses advertise with a B&B sign.

Bed & Breakfast GB

PO Box 47085, London SW18 9AB ☎ 0871 781 0834 (from UK); www.bedbreak.com.

RURAL ACCOMMODATION

An interesting way of spending a holiday is to stay on one of the many different types of working farm – arable, livestock, hill or mixed – set in the heart of glorious countryside. For information apply for the booklet **Stay on a Farm** supplied by the British Tourist Authority or by The Farm Holiday Bureau based at the National Agricultural Centre, Stoneleigh Park, Warwickshire CV8 2LG, ☎ 02476 696 909, 0870 241 3746 (bookings), 01271 336 141 (brochures); www.farmstayuk.co.uk.

UNIVERSITIES AND COLLEGES

During student vacations many universities and colleges offer low-cost accommodation in the halls of residence. If interested, apply to The Workstation, Paternoster Row, Sheffield S1 2BX ☎ 0114 249 3090; www.venuemasters.co.uk.

YOUTH HOSTELS

The 250 youth hostels in Great Britain are open to members of the **Youth Hostel Association,** or to those with an international membership card. Trevelyan House, Dimple Road, Matlock, Derbyshire DE34 3YH ☏ 0870 770 6127; www.yha.org.uk.

Scottish Youth Hostels Association, 7 Glebe Crescent, Stirling FK8 2JA ☏ 01786 891 400, 0870 155 3255; www.syha.org.uk.

International Youth Hostel Federation ☏ 01707 324 170; www.hihostels.com.

CAMPING

The British Tourist Authority publishes **Camping and Caravanning in Britain** and local Tourist Information Centres supply lists of camping and caravan sites.

The **Camping and Caravanning Club of Great Britain and Ireland,** Greenfields House, Westwood Way, Coventry CV4 8JH, ☏ 02476 694 995; www.campingandcaravanningclub. co.uk.

WHAT TO DO AND SEE

Outdoor Fun

The temperate climate of Great Britain has helped to make it the home of many outdoor sports and games. There are few days in the year when outdoor activities are impossible and the long coastline, the rivers and lakes, the mountains and lowlands provide opportunities for a great variety of sports.

The mild and moist climate has fostered the development of many games played on a flat grass surface – football (both association and Rugby), hockey and lacrosse in winter and croquet, bowls, lawn tennis and cricket in summer. Every weekend from May to September cricket matches are played on club fields and village greens.

The English Tourist Board publishes an annual guide listing contact addresses for many sports.

CYCLING

The Cyclists Touring Club (CTC) publishes brochures with detailed itineraries, useful maps and addresses, main sights etc. Air lines, ferry companies and the rail network will transport accompanied bicycles. Most local Tourist Information Centres will give advice on bicycle hire and provide leaflets on local cycling routes.

Cyclists' Touring Club Cotterell House, 69 Meadrow, Godalming, Surrey GU7 3HS, ☏ 0870 873 0060; www.ctc.org

HORSEBACK RIDING

Trekking and trail riding are good ways of discovering the countryside. There are some 600 approved

Wales Tourist Board

Pony trekking

establishments throughout the country, which offer hacking and pony trekking, usually in groups.

Association of British Riding Schools, Queens Chambers, Office No 2, 38–40 Queen Street, Penzance, Cornwall TR18 4BH, ☎ 01736 369 440; www.abrs.org.

GOLF

Great Britain is well supplied with golf courses which range from the links courses on the coast to the inland park courses. Most are privately owned and accept visitors. Municipal courses are usually very heavily used, with long queues at the first tee. In Scotland green fees are less expensive and queues are rare.

Michelin Maps 501 to **504** and the annual **Michelin Guide Great Britain & Ireland** give information about golf courses.

For more choices see:
www.uk-golfguide.com

English Golf Union
National Golf Centre, The Broadway, Woodhall Spa, Lincolnshire LN10 6PU.
☎ 01526 354 500;
www.englishgolfunion.org

English Ladies Golf Association
Edgbaston Golf Club, Church Road, Birmingham B15 3TB,
☎ 0121 456 2088;
www.englishladiesgolf.org

GAME SHOOTING

Game shooting takes place all over Great Britain but the famous grouse moors are in Scotland and the shooting season opens on 12 August.

British Association of Shooting and Conservation
Marferd Mill, Rossett, Wrexham, Wales LL12 0HL, ☎ 01244 573 000;
www.basc.org.uk

SKIING

Only Scotland has ski resorts – at Lochaber, Glenshee, Lecht and Aviemore in the Cairngorms and the Nevis Range near Fort William. All have ski schools and Aviemore is the most fully developed resort. Forest trails have been opened up for cross-country skiing. The best snow conditions are usually found in March and April but up-to-the minute snow reports are essential.
Information available from **Ski Scotland;** http//:ski.visitscotland.com.

There are dry ski slopes all over the country.

HIKING AND CLIMBING

Throughout the country there are many miles of bridleways and official footpaths, including way-marked **Long Distance Footpaths** which give access to some of the best hill and coastal scenery. Some of the best walking and hikling is provided by the National Parks. For fell-walkers and mountaineers the Lake District, Wales and Scotland provide the most challenging ascents.

All hikers and climbers should be aware of potential dangers and be properly equipped. Climbers are also advised to inform the police or someone responsible of their plans before venturing on hazardous climbs.

Ramblers' Association
2nd Floor, Camelford House, 87-90 Albert Embankment, London SE1 7TW
☎ 020 7339 8500;
www.ramblers.org.uk.

British Mountaineering Council
177-179 Burton Road, West Didsbury, Manchester, M20 2BB.
☎ 0870 810 4878; www.thebmc.co.uk.

WATER SPORTS

Britain boasts miles of coastline, many estuaries, rivers, lakes and canals, which offer facilities for water sports of all kinds.

Boating, Sailing and Cruising

Great Britain provides various opportunities for amateur and professional sailors – a cabin cruiser on the Norfolk Broads, a narrow boat on the canal network, a punt or a rowing boat on the river.

On the rivers, lakes and reservoirs there are marinas and moorings for cruisers, yachts and sailing boats; along the coast there are facilities for ocean-going yachts.

Most of the **canal network** has been rescued from dereliction, to offer angling, pleasant towpath walks and cruises and holidays on narrow boats.

Association of Pleasure Craft Operators
British Marine Authority, Marine House, Thorpe Lea Road, Egnam, Surrey TW20 8BF ☎ 01784 473 377;
www.britishmarine.co.uk

Norfolk Broads Authority
18 Colegate, Norwich, Norfolk NR3 1BQ.
☎ 01603 610 734;
www.broads-authority.gov.uk

Wales Tourist Board

Salmon fishing

British Waterways
Willow Grange, Church Road, Watford,
Hertfordshire WD1 3QA.
☎ 01923 201 101;
www.waterscape.com

British Canoe Union
John Dudderidge House, Adbolton Lane,
West Bridgford, Nottingham NG2 5AS.
☎ 0115 982 1100;
www.bcu.org.uk

British Water Ski Federation
Thorpe Park, Chertsey
☎ 01932 570 885; www.bwsf.co.uk

Windsurfing

Schools and changing facilities for
wind surfers are available on many
inland waters and at the best places
along the coast.

British Surfing Association
The International Surfing Centre,
Fistral Bay, Newquay, Cornwall TR7 1HY
☎ 01637 876 474; www.britsurf.co.uk

FISHING

In Britain there are well over 3.7 million
fishermen. The coarse fishing season
runs from 16 March to 16 June; permits
and advice on local waters can be
obtained from any tackle shop.
The waters around Britain provide
ample opportunity for anglers to test
their skills. Salmon and trout fishing,
for which licences are required, is
found in Scotland, England and Wales.
Sea angling is popular, particularly
along the southwestern and
Northumbrian coastlines. Sea angling
festivals are regular features in some
resorts.

National Federation of Anglers
National Watersports Centre, Adbolton
Lane, Holme Pierrepont,
Nottingham, NG12 2LU
☎ 0115 981 3535;
www.nfadirect.com

National Federation of Sea Anglers
Hamlyn House, Mardle Way,
Buckfastleigh, TQ11 0NS
☎ 01364 64463; www.nfsa.org.uk

Salmon and Trout Association
Fishmongers Hall, London Bridge,
London EC4R 9EL. ☎ 020 7283 5838;
www.salmon-trout.org

Calendar of Events

25 JANUARY

January 25 Mostly Scotland – Burns Night when haggis and whisky are consumed.

LAST TUESDAY IN JANUARY

Lerwick, Shetland – Up Helly Aa: great torchlit procession, burning of Viking longship, night-long celebrations.

APRIL

River Thames – Oxford-Cambridge Boat Race: from Putney to Mortlake.

EARLY MAY

Spalding – Flower Parade and Festival: street procession of floats decorated with tulip heads.

8 MAY OR PREVIOUS SATURDAY IF 8TH FALLS ON SUNDAY OR MONDAY

Helston – Flora Day Furry Dance: five processional dances are performed at 7am, 8.30am, 10am, noon and 5pm. Most spectacular are at 10am and noon.

LAST WEEKEND IN MAY

Blair Castle – Atholl Highlanders Annual Parade.

MAY

London – Chelsea Flower Show: The Royal Hospital.

EARLY MAY-AUGUST

Peak District – Well Dressing: in such Peak villages as Eyam, Monyash, Warksworth and Youlgreave.

MAY-AUGUST

Glyndebourne – Festival of Music and Opera.

MAY-OCTOBER

Pitlochry – Pitlochry Festival Theatre Season.

LATE MAY-EARLY JUNE

Isle of Man – TT Races: motor cycle races.

JUNE

Ascot – Royal Ascot (horseracing)

Doune – Doune Hill Climbs.

2ND OR 3RD SATURDAY IN JUNE

London – Trooping the Colour: the Queen's official birthday parade on Horse Guards Parade.

JUNE-JULY

Wimbledon – Lawn Tennis Championships.

FIRST WEEK IN JULY

Henley – Henley Royal Regatta: England's premier amateur regatta

EARLY JULY

River Thames – Swan-Upping.

JULY

Llangollen – International Eisteddfod.

Ladies' Day at Ascot

A Taverner/MICHELIN

JULY–SEPTEMBER

London – Henry Wood Promenade Concerts: Royal Albert Hall.

JULY

King's Lynn – Festival of Music and the Arts.

THIRD WEEKEND IN JULY – END OCTOBER

Fountains Abbey – Floodlit evenings: Fridays and Saturdays only, dusk to 10.30pm with background Gregorian chant.

AUGUST

Jersey – Battle of Flowers.

AUGUST

Aboyne – Highland Games.

3 WEEKS IN AUGUST

Edinburgh – Edinburgh International Festival: arts festival including the Military Tattoo and the Fringe.

AUGUST

Gloucester, Hereford and Worcester – Every third year each cathedral is the setting for The Three Choirs Festival.

Snape Maltings – Aldeburgh Festival: music festival inaugurated by the late Benjamin Britten.

FIRST SATURDAY IN SEPTEMBER

Braemar – Highland Gathering.

SEPTEMBER

Oban – Argyllshire Highland Gathering.

SEPTEMBER AND OCTOBER

Blackpool – Blackpool Illuminations.

1ST SUNDAY IN NOVEMBER

London-Brighton – Veteran and vintage car rally.

5 NOVEMBER

Throughout the country – Torchlight processions, tar-barrel rolling, fireworks and giant bonfires commemorate Guy Fawkes and the Gunpowder Plot.

NOVEMBER

London – State Opening of Parliament.

2ND SATURDAY IN NOVEMBER

London – Lord Mayor's Procession and Show.

Ludlow – Festival: performances of Shakespeare in castle's inner bailey

DECEMBER

London – Christmas Lights in Regent Street (www.regent-street.co.uk) and Oxford Street (www.visitlondon.com). Carol singing and lighted Christmas tree in Trafalgar Square.

Shopping

OPENING HOURS

Traditional British shopping hours are Mondays to Saturdays from 9am to 5.30pm or 6pm. Many larger shops, particularly in out-of-town locations, also open Sundays from 10am or 11am to 4pm. There is late-night shopping in most large cities on Wednesdays or Thursdays; supermarkets usually close later than other shops. Smaller individual shops may close during the lunch hour; on the other hand some stay open until very late. Many towns have an early closing day (ECD) when shops are closed during the afternoon (*see the Michelin Guide Great Britain & Ireland*).

The winter sales at Christmas and New Year and the summer sales in June and July are a popular time for shopping, as prices are reduced on a great range of goods.

WHAT TO BUY

Great Britain is a good place to buy clothes. There is a wide choice of woollen articles in cashmere or lambswool, particularly in Scotland; classic styles are sold by well-known names such as Jaeger, Burberry, Marks and Spencer, John Lewis, Debenhams and House of Fraser. Made to measure clothing for men is available in London in Savile Row (tailors) and Jermyn Street (shirt-makers).

The best makes of porcelain – Wedgwood, Royal Worcester, Royal Doulton – are available in London and elsewhere; seconds can be bought at the factory or in "reject shops."

Great Britain is also well known for antiques, recorded music, new and second-hand books (Hay-on-Wye for the latter). There are craft shops all over the country.

Popular food souvenirs are Scotch whisky, smoked salmon, tea and marmalade.

Sightseeing

NATURAL SETTINGS

The 12 National Parks in England and Wales and four forest parks in Scotland are areas of scenic attraction for recreation. In addition to marked trails there are picnic sites, visitor centres and facilities for various activities (boating, sailing, canoeing, pony trekking, rambling).

Council for National Parks
6/7 Barnard Mews, London SW11 1QU
☎ 020 7924 4077; www.cnp.org.uk.
The parks provide some of the best walking and rambling country.

Forestry Commission
Headquarters, 231 Corstorphine Road, Edinburgh, Lothian EH12 7AT. ☎ 0131 334 0303; www. forestry.gov.uk

Conservation is the main aim of the **national reserves** (wildfowl sanctuaries, sand dunes, moorland). In general visitors are welcome and amenities include visitor centres, nature trails, observation hides. Most reserves have a warden. The reserves provide visitors with a good chance of observing wildlife. In some cases there are restrictions.

Vale of Rheidol Narrow Gauge Train

Wales Tourist Board

Royal Society for the Protection of Birds
The Lodge, Sandy, Bedfordshire SG19 2DL.
☎ 01767 680 551; www.rspb.org.uk

Wildfowl and Wetlands Trust, National Centre
Slimbridge, Gloucestershire GL2 7BT,
☎ 0870 334 4000; www.wwt.org.uk

Scottish Wildlife Trust
Cramond House, Kirk Cramond,
Cramond Glebe Road, Edinburgh EH4 6NS.
☎ 0131 312 7765; www.swt.org.uk

Scottish Natural Heritage
12 Hope Terrace, Edinburgh EH9 2AS.
☎ 0131 447 4784; www.snh.org.uk

STEAM TRAINS

The hobby of maintaining and operating steam trains is very popular and there are several museums which recapture some of the aura of the Steam Age. The **Association of Railway Preservation Societies Ltd,** www.ukhrail.uel.ac.uk, publishes an annual free guide to steam railways and museums.

The first standard-gauge track to pass into private ownership was the **Bluebell Line** (5mi/8km), near East Grinstead in Sussex, in 1960. The **Romney, Hythe and Dymchurch Railway** (13mi/20km) was built as a miniature line in 1927 and is the longest fully equipped 15in gauge line in the world.

The **West Somerset Railway** (20mi/32km) from Minehead up into the Quantock Hills is the longest preserved line in Britain. No line has more main-line engines than the **Severn Valley Railway** (16mi/26km) between Bridgnorth and Kidderminster.

The **Nene Valley Railway,** near Peterborough (7mi/11km) has locomotives from ten countries. The **Keighley and Worth Valley** line continues to be a vital part of local life. The **North Yorkshire Moors Railway** (18mi/29km) runs through beautiful moorland country from Pickering to Grosmont. The **Ravenglass and Eskdale Railway** (7mi/11km) climbs from Ravenglass up the Esk Valley. In Wales there are many such railways. The narrow-gauge **Vale of Rheidol Railway** (23mi/37km) offers a round trip from Aberystwyth up to Devil's Bridge and the Munach Falls. The **Ffestiniog Railway** (13mi/20km) passes through magnificent mountain scenery between Porthmadog on the coast and Blaenau Ffestiniog. The **Snowdon Mountain Railway**, opened in 1896, offers the easiest ascent to the summit of Snowdon. In Scotland the **Strathspey Railway** (5mi/8km) runs from Aviemore to Boat of Garten, famed as one of the nesting sites of the osprey in the British Isles. On the **Isle of Man** there are 15mi/24km of the three-foot gauge line which used to cover the island. Trains run from Douglas to Port Erin and the line has been in almost continuous operation since 1874.

UNESCO World Heritage List

In 1972 the United Nations Educational, Scientific and Cultural Organization (UNESCO) adopted a Convention for the preservation of cultural and natural sites. To date, more than 150 States Parties have signed this international agreement, which has listed over 500 sites "of outstanding universal value" on the World Heritage List. Each year a committee of representatives from 21 countries, assisted by technical organizations (ICOMOS – International Council on Monuments and Sites; IUCN – International Union for Conservation of Nature and Natural Resources; ICCROM – International Centre for the Study of the Preservation and Restoration of Cultural Property, the Rome Centre), evaluates the proposals for new sites to be included on the list, which grows longer as new nominations are accepted and more countries sign the Convention. To be considered, a site must be nominated by the country in which it is located.

The protected cultural heritage may be monuments (buildings, sculptures, archeological structures etc) with unique historical, artistic or scientific features; groups of buildings (such as religious communities, ancient cities); or sites (human settlements, examples of exceptional landscapes, cultural landscapes) which are the combined works of man and nature of exceptional beauty. Natural sites may be a testimony to the stages of the earth's geological history or to the development of human cultures and creative genius or represent significant ongoing ecological processes, contain superlative natural phenomena or provide a habitat for threatened species.

Signatories of the Convention pledge to co-operate to preserve and protect these sites around the world as a common heritage to be shared by all humanity.

Some of the most well-known places which the World Heritage Committee has inscribed include: Australia's Great Barrier Reef (1981), the Canadian Rocky Mountain Parks (1984), The Great Wall of China (1987), the Statue of Liberty (1984), the Kremlin (1990), Mont-Saint-Michel and its Bay (Great Britain and Ireland, 1979).

UNESCO World Heritage sites in Great Britain are:

Durham Castle and Cathedral

Ironbridge Gorge

Studley Royal and Fountains Abbey

Stonehenge, Avebury and associated sites

Castles and Town Walls of King Edward in Gwynedd

St Kilda

Blenheim Palace

City of Bath

Hadrian's Wall

Palace of Westminster, Abbey of Westminster and St Margaret's Church

Tower of London

Canterbury Cathedral, St Augustine's Abbey and St Martin's Church

Old and New Towns of Edinburgh

Maritime Greenwich

Heart of Neolithic Orkney

Blaenavon Industrial Landscape

Dorset and East Devon Coast

Derwent Valley Mills

New Lanark

Saltaire

Royal Botanical Gardens

Liverpool Maritime Mercantile City

BASIC INFORMATION

Electricity

The electric current is 240 volts AC (50 HZ); 3-pin flat wall sockets are standard. An adaptor or multiple point plug is required for non-British appliances.

Public Holidays

The table below gives the public (bank) holidays in England and Wales, when most shops and municipal museums are closed.

> 1 January
> Good Friday (Friday before Easter Day)
> Easter Monday (Monday after Easter Day)
> First Monday in May (May Day)
> Last Monday in May (Spring Bank holiday)
> Last Monday in August
> 25 December (Christmas Day)
> 26 December (Boxing Day)

In addition to the usual school holidays in the spring and summer and at Christmas, there are mid-term breaks in February, May and October.

Post (Mail)

Post Offices are generally open Mondays to Fridays, 9.30am to 5.30pm and Saturday mornings, 9.30am to 12.30pm. Stamps are also available from many newsagents and tobacconists. Poste Restante items are held for 14 days; proof of identity is required. Airmail delivery usually takes 3 to 4 days in Europe and 4 to 7 days elsewhere in the world.

Within GB	first class post 30p; second class post 21p
Within EU	letter (20g) 42p (+ 18p for each extra 20g)
	postcard 30p
Non-EU Europe	letter (20g) 42p (+ 18p for each extra 20g)
	postcard 30p
Elsewhere	letter (20g) 68p (+ 37-44p for each extra 20g)
	postcard 47p
	aerogramme 42p

Metric System

Britain uses both imperial and metric terms. Some equivalents ((see also the Conversion chart at the end of this chapter):

1 gram = 0.04 ounces	
1 meter = 1.09 yards	
1 kilogram = 2.20 pounds	
1 kilometer = 0.62 miles	
1 litre = 0.53 pints	

Money

BANKS

Banks are generally open from Mondays to Fridays, 9.30am to 3.30pm; some banks offer a limited service on Saturday mornings; all banks are closed on Sundays and bank holidays. Most banks have cash dispensers (ATMs) that accept international credit cards.

Exchange facilities outside these hours are available at airports, currency exchange companies, travel agencies and hotels.

Some form of identification is necessary when cashing travellers cheques or Eurocheques in banks. Commission charges vary; hotels usually charge more than banks.

CREDIT CARDS

The main credit cards (American Express; Access/Eurocard/Mastercard; Diners Club; Visa/Barclaycard) are widely accepted in shops, hotels, restaurants and petrol stations. Most banks have cash dispensers which accept international credit cards. In case of loss or theft, phone:

Amex	01273 696933
Barclay Card	01604 230 230

CURRENCY

The official currency in Great Britain is the pound sterling, not the euro. The decimal system (100 pence = £1) is used throughout Great Britain; Scotland has different notes including £1 and £100 notes, which are legal tender outside Scotland, though you may well have difficulty getting English shopkeepers to accept them; the Channel Islands and Isle of Man have different notes and coins, which are not valid elsewhere.

The common currency – in descending order of value – is £50, £20, £10 and £5 (notes); £2, £1, 50p, 20p, 10p, 5p (silver coins) and 2p and 1p (copper coins).

Telephones

Prepaid phonecards, of varying value, are available from post offices and many newsagents; they can be used in booths with phonecard facilities for national and international calls. Some public telephones accept credit cards. Since deregulation a number of telephone operators have set up in competition with the previous state-run British Telecommunications (BT). Rates vary enormously between operators. For calls made through BT daytime rates are Mon-Fri, 6am-6pm; evening, Mon-Fri, before 6am and after 6pm; weekend midnight Friday to midnight Sunday.

100	Operator
118 505	BT Directory Enquiries in the UK (£1.50/minute, £1.50 minimum charge)
999	Emergency number (free nationwide); ask for Fire, Police, Ambulance, Coastguard, Mountain Rescue or Cave Rescue.

International Calls

To make an international call dial 00 followed by the country code, followed by the area code (without the intitial 0) followed by the subscriber's number. The codes for direct dialling to other countries are printed at the front of telephone directories and in codebooks.

00 61	Australia
00 1	Canada
00 353	Republic of Ireland
00 64	New Zealand
00 44	United Kingdom
00 1	United States of America
155	International Operator
155	International Directory Enquiries; there is a charge for this service

Time

In winter standard time throughout the British Isles is Greenwich Mean Time (GMT). In summer clocks are advanced by an hour to give British Summer Time (BST). The actual dates are announced annually but always occur at the weekend in March and October.

Time may be expressed according to the 24-hour clock or the 12-hour clock.

12.00	noon	19.00	7pm
13.00	1pm	20.00	8pm
14.00	2pm	21.00	9pm
15.00	3pm	22.00	10pm
16.00	4pm	23.00	11pm
17.00	5pm	24.00	midnight
18.00	6pm		

Conversion tables

Weights and measures

1 kilogram (kg)	2.2 pounds (lb)	2.2 pounds
1 metric ton (tn)	1.1 tons	1.1 tons

to convert kilograms to pounds, multiply by 2.2

1 litre (l)	2.1 pints (pt)	1.8 pints
1 litre	0.3 gallon (gal)	0.2 gallon

to convert litres to gallons, multiply by 0.26 (US) or 0.22 (UK)

1 hectare (ha)	2.5 acres	2.5 acres
1 square kilometre (km²)	0.4 square miles (sq mi)	0.4 square miles

to convert hectares to acres, multiply by 2.4

1 centimetre (cm)	0.4 inches (in)	0.4 inches
1 metre (m)	3.3 feet (ft) - 39.4 inches - 1.1 yards (yd)	
1 kilometre (km)	0.6 miles (mi)	0.6 miles

to convert metres to feet, multiply by 3.28. kilometres to miles, multiply by 0.6

Clothing

Women							Men
	35	4	2½	40	7½	7	
	36	5	3½	41	8½	8	
	37	6	4½	42	9½	9	
Shoes	38	7	5½	43	10½	10	**Shoes**
	39	8	6½	44	11½	11	
	40	9	7½	45	12½	12	
	41	10	8½	46	13½	13	
	36	4	8	46	36	36	
	38	6	10	48	38	38	
Dresses &	40	8	12	50	40	40	**Suits**
Suits	42	12	14	52	42	42	
	44	14	16	54	44	44	
	46	16	18	56	46	48	
	36	08	30	37	14½	14,5	
	38	10	32	38	15	15	
Blouses &	40	12	14	39	15½	15½	**Shirts**
sweaters	42	14	36	40	15¾	15¾	
	44	16	38	41	16	16	
	46	18	40	42	16½	16½	

Sizes often vary depending on the designer. These equivalents are given for guidance only.

Speed

kph	10	30	50	70	80	90	100	110	120	130
mph	6	19	31	43	50	56	62	68	75	81

Temperature

Celsius (°C)	0°	5°	10°	15°	20°	25°	30°	40°	60°	80°	100°
Fahrenheit (°F)	32°	41°	50°	59°	68°	77°	86°	104°	140°	176°	212°

To convert Celsius into Fahrenheit, multiply °C by 9, divide by 5, and add 32.
To convert Fahrenheit into Celsius, subtract 32 from °F, multiply by 5, and divide by 9

Little Red Riding Hood

But Little Red Riding Hood had her regional map with her, and so she did not fall into the trap. She did not take the path through the wood and she did not meet the big bad wolf. Instead, she chose the picturesque touring route straight to Grandmother's house, and arrived safely with her cake and her little pot of butter.

The End

Snowdon Horseshoe

NATURE

The exceptionally diverse geological foundation of Britain has given rise to landscapes of great variety, a natural heritage enhanced by a continuous human presence over several millennia which has shaped and reshaped the material to form the present uniquely rich pattern of fields and fells, woods and parks, villages and farmsteads. Celebrated in literature and art, this densely textured landscape, usually domesticated but with its wilder beauties too, has become a kind of national emblem, lived in lovingly and vigorously defended against change by its inhabitants.

Landscape

The complexities of rock type and structure and of relief can be reduced to a broad division into **Upland** and **Lowland** Britain. The former, generally of older, harder material, comprises much of the north and southwest of England and virtually the whole of Wales and Scotland. As well as rolling, open moorlands where the eye ranges freely over vast expanses of coarse grass, bracken or heather, there are mountain chains, modest in elevation but exhibiting most of the features of much higher and more extensive systems and thus attracting serious climbers as well as walkers.

To the south and east the gentler relief of Lowland Britain is mostly composed of less resistant material of later date. Much is "scarp and vale" country where elegantly undulating chalk and limestone hills terminate in steep escarpments commanding grand panoramas over broad clay vales.

Most of the course of the Earth's history can be traced in these landscapes. From the unimaginably distant Pre-Cambrian, more than 600 million years ago, came the Torridonian sandstone and Lewisian gneiss of northwest Scotland as well as the compact, isolated uplands of Charnwood Forest in Leicestershire and the Malvern Hills in Worcestershire. The violent volcanic activity of Ordovician times left the shales and slates of **Snowdonia** and the **Lake District.** Extreme pressure from the southeast in the Caledonian mountain-building period produced the northeast/southwest "grain" of ridges and valleys so evident in much of Wales and Scotland. Most of the abundant reserves of coal originated in the tropical vegetation of Carboniferous times.

Except for the extreme south, the whole country was affected by the action of the often immensely thick ice sheets of the series of Ice Ages. The characteristically sculpted forms of the high mountains testify to the great power of the glaciers as they advanced and retreated, eroding and transporting vast quantities of material, much of which was spread over the lowlands by the mighty ancestors of today's rivers. As the last of the ice melted, the sea level rose, the land bridge joining Britain to the continent of Europe was flooded, and a truncated **Thames**, hitherto a tributary of the Rhine, acquired its own outlet to the sea.

Domestication

The taming and settling of the landscape can be traced back to the fifth millennium BC when Neolithic farmers began to clear the wildwood, the dense forests which had spread northwards in the wake of the retreating ice. The imprint of each succeeding age may be traced, not only in the obvious features of prehistoric stone circles, burial mounds and hill-forts, the planned network of Roman roads or the countless medieval churches, but also in the everyday fabric of the working countryside, where a track may first have been trodden in the Bronze Age or a hedge planted by Saxon settlers.

The many-layered landscape is now characterised by **enclosure**, a web of fields bounded by hedges in the lowlands, by drystone walls in the uplands and by dykes in areas reclaimed from the sea. Small fields with irregular boundaries are likely to be ancient in origin; a regular chequerboard of hawthorn hedges is the result of agricultural "Improvement" in the 18C and 19C.

In spite of conditions which are ideal for tree growth, only 8% of the land surface is wooded. About half of this consists of recent coniferous plantations, mostly in the uplands. In many parts of the lowlands, the lack of great forests is compensated for by an abundance of small woods and by the countless individual trees growing in parks and gardens, and above all, in the hedgerows.

Standing out from this orderly pattern are the "commons", rough open tracts of grass and scrub. Once the villager's

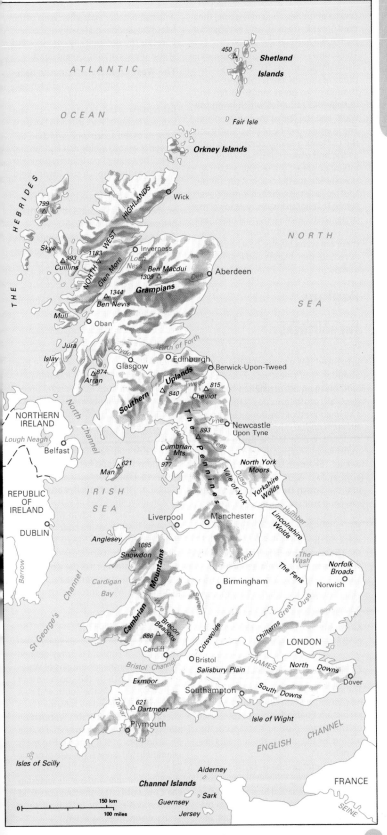

ATLANTIC

OCEAN

450
Shetland
Islands

Fair Isle

Orkney Islands

THE HEBRIDES

799

Wick

NORTH

SEA

Skye
Cuillins
993

NORTH WEST HIGHLANDS

1183
Glen More
Loch Ness
Inverness

Ben Macdui
1309
Grampians
Dee
Aberdeen

1344
Ben Nevis

Mull
Oban

Jura

Islay

Clyde
Firth of Forth

Glasgow
Edinburgh
Berwick-Upon-Tweed

874
Arran

Southern Uplands
Tweed
815
840
Cheviot

NORTHERN
IRELAND

North Channel

Tyne
Newcastle
Upon Tyne

Lough Neagh
Belfast

Eden
893
Tees

Cumbrian
Mts.
977

The Pennines

REPUBLIC
OF
IRELAND

DUBLIN

Man
621

IRISH

SEA

Vale of York
Ouse
North York
Moors
Yorkshire
Wolds

Barrow

Liverpool
Manchester

Humber

Anglesey

1085
Snowdon

Cambrian Mountains

Lincolnshire
Wolds

The
Wash

Norfolk
Broads
Norwich

St George's Channel

Cardigan
Bay

Trent

The Fens

Birmingham

Severn

Wye
Brecon
Beacons
886
Cardiff

Cotswolds

Chilterns

Great Ouse

LONDON

THAMES

Bristol

Salisbury Plain

North
Downs

Dover

Bristol Channel

Exmoor

Southampton

South
Downs

Tamar
621
Dartmoor

Isle of Wight

Plymouth

ENGLISH
CHANNEL

Isles of Scilly

Alderney

Channel Islands
Sark
Guernsey
Jersey

FRANCE

SEINE

0   150 km
       100 miles

source of fodder, food and game, they now provide fresh air and exercise for both town and country people.

The country is well-watered. The abundant rainfall, carried off the hills by a multitude of streams, feeds the rivers which, though of no great length, often end in splendid estuaries which bring salt water and the feel of the sea far inland. The irregular outline of the country and the complex geology combine to form a long and varied coastline. Where the mountains meet the sea there is exceptionally fine coastal scenery, such as the spectacular chalk-white cliffs near Dover, symbol of English insularity. Many of the better stretches of sand and shingle have been appropriated by seaside resorts but there are some quieter beaches as well as remote marshlands and lonely sand dunes.

Regions

THE SOUTHEAST

"London's Countryside" is highly urbanised but its varied relief and an abundance of trees, woods and parkland make an attractive habitat for its generally prosperous population.

The inland rim of the basin containing Greater London is formed by gracefully sculpted chalk hills. The **Chiltern Hills** (northwest) are famous for their beechwoods. The **North Downs** (south) define a great east-west arc. Between them and the **South Downs** lies the **Weald** (deriving from *wald*, the German word for forest), a tract (100 mi/160km) of dense oakwoods, sandy hills and clay vales. To the east is the great estuary of the **Thames**, flanked by creeks and inlets and by orchards and market gardens.

The coastal fringe, facing continental Europe with which it has many links, has changed in outline over the centuries; erosion by the sea has been balanced by the gain of such tracts of rich pastureland as Romney Marsh.

CENTRAL SOUTHERN ENGLAND

The high and airy chalklands centred on Salisbury Plain were the heart of prehistoric England. Innumerable lesser earthworks and other traces form the setting for the greater monuments like Stonehenge.

Later populations have settled in the gentle river valleys and in the ports and resorts of the coast. The great arms of the sea, which are sheltered from the Channel by the pretty Isle of Wight, are an amateur sailor's paradise. West of the beautiful woods and heaths of the New Forest is the geologically complex and scenically fascinating Dorset coast.

The West Country – A granite backbone runs through Devon and Cornwall, showing itself in rugged high moorlands topped by wind-blasted "tors." The Exmoor National Park in North Devon is formed of red sandstone, which in the Devon lowlands yields rich agricultural soils. The county's particularly luxuriant version of the English patchwork field pattern gives way in the harsher environment of Cornwall to smaller fields often of ancient origin, bounded by earthen hedge-banks or stone walls.

The long coastline of the peninsula is unsurpassed; most varieties of coastal scenery are represented; spectacular rocky bastions under fierce attack from Atlantic rollers contrast with sheltered bays and beautifully wooded inlets running far inland.

EAST ANGLIA

England's most extensive area of low relief is a region of great individuality; densely populated in medieval times, it is unequalled in its wealth of ancient villages and small towns. Its dry climate and generally good soils mean that much of its gently undulating farmland is in arable cultivation; fields are large and many trees and hedges have been removed. East of Norwich, the regional capital, are the **Norfolk Broads**, extensive shallow stretches of water formed by peat extraction, rich in wildlife and thronged with pleasure craft.

Building styles express past links with the Netherlands; it was Dutch engineers who carried out much of the work which transformed the marshes and fens around the Wash into the country's richest tract of arable land.

THE MIDLANDS

The centre of England is firmly defined to the west by the mountains of Wales and to the north by the southern end of the Pennines. To the south and east a less marked boundary is formed by a succession of broad vales watered by slowly moving rivers overlooked by the escarpments of hill ranges. The most prominent hill range is the belt of oolitic limestone, which extends from Dorset to the River Humber, and is at its widest in the **Cotswolds**. It is the fine Cotswold stone which gives the built landscape such a distinctive character.

Elsewhere there is a less coherent pattern of modest blocks of hill country, in mixed farming except for heath and woodland tracts such as Cannock Chase (Staffordshire), Charnwood Forest (Leicestershire) and the **Royal Forest of Dean** (Gloucestershire).

The regular pattern of ancient county towns set at the centre of their shires (Gloucester, Northampton, Lincoln) is overlaid by the later one of the Industrial Revolution. Heavy industry began at Ironbridge and was fuelled by the diverse mineral resources of the region. It caused Birmingham to swell to metropolitan size and engendered the chaotic urban sprawls of the Black Country and the Potteries. The derelict land caused by recent industrial decline is being transformed into parkland.

NORTHERN ENGLAND

At a certain latitude not easy to define the personality of the English landscape changes decisively. A less kindly climate, high moorlands and rugged mountains predominate; building stones lend themselves to bold rather than refined treatment; the impact of industry is widespread. These factors combine to give a distinct and strong identity to "The North".

The long mountain chain of the Pennines is the region's central feature, though it is flanked by extensive lowlands; to the west lie the Cheshire and Lancashire plains, the former as lush and tidy as any southern county, the latter much built over but growing horticultural crops on its reclaimed "mosses".

To the east, beyond the densely populated Yorkshire coalfield, is equally fertile country, prolonged northwards by the **Vale of York** and bounded along the coast by chalk wolds divided by the great estuary of the **Humber**.

The **Pennine Chain**, with its three National Parks, is far from homogeneous in character. In the far North, the wild and lonely **Cheviots** of the Northumberland National Park are the well-rounded remains of ancient volcanoes. In the **Yorkshire Dales** the characteristic features of limestone country are well developed tablelands rising to high, flat-topped eminences like **Pen-y-Ghent** (2273ft/693m), gorges, cliffs, caves and underground streams. Here and in that part of the **Peak District** where pale car-

Derwentwater and Stable Hills

R. Thrift/The National Trust

boniferous limestone occurs the rock has been used to build a harmonious landscape of stone, sterner than but similar to the Cotswold Country. Between the Peak District, the mountain playground for much of industrial Lancashire, and the Yorkshire Dales lie many upland miles of even more severe country, underlain by the sombre millstone grit. The abundant rainfall pours off the mountains in fast-flowing streams, which drove the mills and factories in the densely built-up valleys or fed the unspoilt rivers of Dales and Peak. East of the Pennines, the **North York Moors** National Park forms a vast heather-covered tableland which reaches the sea in an undeveloped coastline of great beauty. To the west is the **Lake District**, where the highest peaks in England (**Scafell Pike** 3 206ft/978m) dominate an inexhaustible variety of mountain scenery ranging from the wildest of storm-blasted crags to the exquisite park and scenery reflected in Lake Windermere.

In Northumbria, the northernmost province in England, where the fells draw ever closer to the coast, the windy farmlands contrast with deep wooded denes and the trio of riverside conurbations flanking the Tyne, Wear and Tees.

WALES

The principality is approached from the east via the English **Marches,** attractive farming country interspersed with hill ranges anticipating the mountains beyond. In the south, marking the border near Chepstow, is the luxuriantly wooded gorge of the Wye. To the west lies Cardiff, the capital, flanked by the other former coal ports of the coast which were supplied by the immense coalfield of South Wales, a high plateau deeply cut by valleys filled with mining settlements. North of the mining country is the great bastion of the red sandstone escarpment of the **Brecon Beacons**. Further west the scene is rural, rolling country ending in the cliffs and rocks of the **Pembrokeshire Coast National Park.** The gentle swelling forms of the sheep-grazed uplands of Mid-Wales contrast with the drama of the mountains of **Snowdonia**, true highlands of great grandeur. To the west extends the remote Lleyn Peninsula. The narrow coastal plain of North Wales abounds in seaside resorts. Offshore across the Menai Strait is the Isle of Anglesey.

Scotland – While many elements of the English landscape – enclosed fields, parklands – are repeated in Scotland, often in a neater, simplified form, the country's scenic personality is quite distinct; mountains and moorlands predominate; the climate is noticeably more rigorous (albeit with many compensations, mild winters in the west, sparkling air in the east); human activity is highly concentrated in the lowlands and parts of the coast, leaving much of the surface of the land free from urban intrusions and exhilaratingly open to the influences of Nature. This rich and varied landscape can be broken down into three main regions.

The **Southern Uplands**, sparsely inhabited borderlands, consist of gently rounded moors penetrated in the west by deep, narrow dales, in the east by the broader, cultivated valleys of the **Tweed** and its tributaries.

The **Central Lowlands**, dramatically pierced by the great firths of **Tay, Clyde** and **Forth**, are densely populated and the focus of the urban and industrial life of Scotland. The area is rich in minerals and has a prosperous agriculture. The region, which is low-lying only in contrast to the mountains to the north and south, is enlivened by numerous hill ranges, the Pentland Hills and Campsie Fells forming a background to Edinburgh and Glasgow, the high **Ochils** seeming to bar the way northwards.

The **Highlands and Islands,** the third main region of Scotland, includes the highest peak in Britain, **Ben Nevis** (4 406ft/1 344m) and the **Cairngorm Mountains,** dominated by **Ben Macdui** (4 296ft/1 309m). Much of the area lies above 2 000ft/610m and rises above 4 000ft/1 220m. A complex geological history has left landforms as varied as the smoothly rounded **Grampians**, the towering **Cuillins** of the Isle of Skye and the spectacular mountain and cliff scenery of **Wester Ross.** Water is everywhere; tumbling peat-tinted burns feed fine rivers; there are salt- and fresh-water lochs and in the west, the sea defines an extraordinarily indented coastline.

Cotton grass and heather clothe the mountains; tree cover becomes ever sparser northwards, though there are magnificent remains of the ancient Caledonian pine forest at Glenmore.

The thinly spread human presence favours wildlife; the coast is thronged with seabirds, including puffins; there are grey and common seals; inland the red deer is abundant, and in the wilder places live the wild cat, the eagle, and the recently re-established osprey.

Beyond the mainland lie nearly 800 islands, many uninhabited, each with its own character, like wind-swept **Islay**, almost in sight of Ireland; **Skye**, with its unsurpassed mountain and coastal scenery; **Orkney**, rich in prehistoric remains, and far-off **Shetland**, stern and treeless.

Conservation

Urban pressure in such a densely populated country is resisted by a system of town and country planning which exercises strict control over building development.

NATIONAL PARKS

The 12 National Parks, which comprise the finest upland scenery in England and Wales, much of it farmed and in private ownership, are controlled and managed by each National Park authority to conserve the characteristic landscape and make it accessible to the public.

The first National Park was established in 1951 to preserve the distinctive characteristics of certain rural areas of England and Wales. The scheme was not extended to Scotland where pressure on open countryside was less intense and the law of trespass was different, enabling people to walk where they wished provided they did no damage. According to their individual locations and features the National Parks offer extensive facilities for rambling and walking, pony trekking, pot-holing and caving, freshwater and sea-angling, boating, sailing, windsurfing and canoeing.

Northumberland – Cheviot sheep graze the open moorland, mostly above 1 000ft/305m, which makes up most of this Park. A part of Hadrian's Wall runs along the southern edge of the Park. Kielder Water, just beyond the western boundary, is a much-visited recreational area.

Lake District – Largest of the National Parks, it is a combination of mountain and lake, woodland and farmland. Ice shaped the troughs and corries and glacial rubble dammed the valleys but the underlying rock dictated whether the hills were softly rounded, like Skiddaw, or wildly rugged, like Scafell and Helvellyn.

Yorkshire Dales – Nearly half of the Dales is farmland. Over four centuries the monasteries' sheep walks developed into the start of a road system across the fells, the best known today being the green lane between Kilnsey and Malham Cove and Tarn. The unique limestone pavement "grykes" provide sheltered habitats for lime- and shade-loving plants. The "Dales" themselves, (Ribble-, Swale-, Wensley- and Wharfe-) have welcoming villages in rich valley pastures, while the limestone peaks of Ingleborough and Pen-y-Ghent present a more rugged face.

North York Moors – A relatively quiet Park. The moors are clearly defined, rising sharply from Tees in the north to Pickering and the Vale of York in the south. The eastern boundary is the sea. The Park contains Staithes, home of Captain Cook, and Whitby, famous for jet – a fossilised black amber – so popular with the Victorians, also Rievaulx and Rosedale Abbeys.

Peak District – The deep dales and stone-walled fields of the White Peak are surrounded to east, west and north by the dramatic moors and peat bogs of the Dark Peak. In addition to walking, people come to fish and to cycle. Rock climbing on the gritstone edges has been joined by gliding, hang-gliding and wind-surfing as leisure activities.

Snowdonia – The Snowdon massif, heartland of the Park, and Cader Idris are the most popular areas – with half a million people reaching Snowdon Summit each year and only a quarter of them admitting to using the railway. The Aran Mountains in the south and the rugged Rhynogydd are less crowded. Harlech Castle lies on part of the Park's sweeping sandy coastline.

Pembrokeshire Coast – Second smallest of the Parks, for much of its length it is less than three miles wide. Steep cliffs display spectacularly folded and twisted rock formations; sheltered bays invite bathing and scuba-diving. Offshore islands such as Skomer and Skokholm support huge colonies of seabirds.

Brecon Beacons – High red sandstone mountains divide the ancient rocks of mid-Wales from the coalfields and industrialisation farther south. Along the southern edge of the Park a limestone belt provides a dramatic change in scenery and there are hundreds of sink-holes and cave systems, the most spectacular being the Dan-yr-Ogof Caves at the head of the Tawe valley.

Exmoor – Rising to 1 500ft/460m, from Chapman Barrows to Dunkery Beacon, the heartland is still the windswept haunt of falcon and hawk; cliffs, broken by deep valleys with waterfalls, make protected breeding sites for seabirds. With the Quantocks, Exmoor is the last secure habitat in the south of England for the red deer and a small breeding herd has been established to maintain the declining numbers of Exmoor ponies.

Dartmoor – Largest and wildest stretch of open country in southern Britain. Two plateaux, rising to over 2 000ft/610m and covered with blanket bog and heather moorland, are divided by the River Dart. Ponies – descendants of those turned out in the Middle Ages – still graze much of the lower-lying heather moorland and there are hundreds of ancient sites – chambered tombs, hillforts, stone circles, medieval crosses and waymarks.

New Forest – The most recent of the National Parks, designated in 2005, the New Forest was originally the royal forest of William I (the Conqueror). Today it comprises woodland, marshland and heath where ponies, donkeys, deer and cattle wander, often perilously close to the roadside.

Norfolk and Suffolk Broads – Established as a Park in 1989. The Broads are peat-diggings from the 9C, which flooded and became part of the river system in the 14C. Strenuous efforts by the Broads Authority in the 1980s partly halted environmental degradation, due to nutrients from effluents and fertilisers. The water is recovering its life but care is still needed from all who use and enjoy this Park.

NATURE RESERVES

Other areas of countryside and coast, where the flora and fauna are conserved in their natural habitat, are protected by designations such as Sites of Special Scientific Interest (SSSI), Environmentally Sensitive Areas (ESA), National Nature Reserves (NNR) or Areas of Outstanding Natural Beauty such as the Chiltern Hills and the Cotswolds, stretches of Heritage Coast and the Green Belt round London.

There are also numerous nature reserves and bird sanctuaries set up to preserve the habitat of rare or endangered species, indigenous or migratory. The **Royal Society for the Protection of Birds** (RSPB) administers several bird sanctuaries which are provided with hides. The **Wildfowl and Wetlands Trust** has pioneered work in bringing large numbers of people into contact with the natural environment, where birds, endangered in the wild, will feed from the hand. Their national centre is at Slimbridge but there are others, in the London suburb of Barnes, in Sussex near Arundel, in East Anglia near Wisbech, in Lancashire inland of Southport, in Sunderland near Washington, in Wales at Llanelli and in Scotland near Dumfries.

Many historic houses and gardens, inland and coastal areas belong to the National Trusts of England and Wales and of Scotland, which successfully marry conservation with public access.

HISTORY

Great Britain is positioned at the western edge of Europe, from which it has received successive waves of immigrants who have merged their cultures, languages, beliefs and energies to create an island race which has explored, traded with, dominated and settled other lands all over the world.

Time Line

6 000 BC – Britain detached from continental Europe by the rise in sea level caused by retreating glaciers

5 000 BC – Arrival of agriculturalists whose actions shaped the landscape

4 000 BC-

1800 BC – Construction of Stonehenge and other stone alignments

700 BC – Arrival of the "**Beaker**" people who brought a knowledge of metal working and the Aryan roots of the English language – words such as father, mother, sister and brother

700 BC – Arrival of Celtic settlers whose lifestyle and customs were well established in Britain by 100 BC

The **Celts** brought their language, their chariots, the use of coinage and a love of finery, gold and ornaments. Iron swords gave them an ascendancy in battle over the native Britons, estimated at around a million, who were pushed westwards. The different groups of Celts had only a dialect in common and their lack of any idea of "nationhood" made them vulnerable to the might of Rome.

ROMAN OCCUPATION

55 BC – Julius Caesar landed in Britain

AD 42 – Roman invasion of Britain under the Emperor Claudius

61 – Revolt of the Iceni under Queen **Boadicea**

122 – Beginning of the construction of **Hadrian's Wall**

410 – Roman legions withdrawn from Britain following the sack of Rome by Alaric the Goth

The **Romans** had no strategic interest in the offshore island of Britannia but the lure of corn, gold, iron, slaves and hunting dogs was enough to entice them to invade. By AD 70 much of the north and Wales had been subdued and 50 or more towns had been established, linked by a network of roads. Rome gave Britain its law and extended the use of coinage into a recognised system, essential to trade in an "urban" society. In 313 Christianity was established as the official religion.

ANGLO-SAXONS AND VIKINGS

449 – First waves of Angles, Saxons and Jutes land in Britain; Hengist and Horsa land at Ebbsfleet in east Kent

597 – **Augustine**, sent by Pope Gregory to convert the British to Christianity, founded a Benedictine monastery in Canterbury

627 – Conversion to Christianity of Edwin, King of Northumbria

664 – **Synod of Whitby** which accepted the practices of the Roman Church rather than those of the Celtic Church

731 – The Venerable **Bede**, a monk at Jarrow monastery, completed his *Ecclesiastical History of the English People*

779 – Offa, King of Mercia regarded as the overlord of all England

827 – King Egbert of Essex became first king of England

851 – Viking raiders wintered regularly in Britain and became settlers

871-899 – Reign of **Alfred the Great,** King of Wessex, who contained the Viking advance in 871

876 – York founded by the Danes who had founded Dublin c 840

911 – Kingdom of Normandy founded by Rollo, a Viking

978-1016 – Reign of Ethelred II, the Unready (the "Redeless" which means lacking wise counsel)

1016-35 – Reign of **Canute** (Cnut), first Danish king of England

1035-40 – Reign of Harold I, the younger of Canute's two sons

1040-42 – Reign of Hardicanute (Hardecnut), Harold's half-brother

1042-66 – Reign of **Edward the Confessor**

Saxons in the form of Germanic mercenaries had manned many of the shore forts of Britain before the final withdrawal of regular Roman troops. As pay became scarce they seized tracts of good farming land and settled permanently. When St Augustine arrived in Kent in 597, he found that Christianity was already established at the court of King Ethelbert of Kent, whose wife Queen Bertha was a Christian princess. Until the Synod of Whitby in AD 664 the practices of the Roman church existed side by side with those of the Celtic church, which had a different way of calculating the date of Easter and a strong and distinctive monastic tradition. The Saxon kingdoms of Britain, which traded as far afield as Russia and Constantinople, were constantly engaged in power struggles not only with one another but also with the Angles and Jutes.

Under the **Vikings**, who took to trading and barter instead of their former piracy, London again became a great trading port as it had been during the Roman period. By AD 911 eight vassal kings paid homage to King Edgar for almost the whole country. During the disastrous reign of Ethelred, the "Redeless" – lacking wise counsel, England was attacked by Norsemen; in 1013 Swein, King of Denmark, invaded and briefly became king. Ethelred fled to Normandy. His son, Edmund "Ironside", was left to battle against the invaders. After his murder the parliament (Witenagemot), preferring strength to weakness, elected the Danish invader **Canute** (Cnut) as his successor. Seven years after Canute's death Edward, son of Ethelred and his Norman wife, Emma, was chosen to be King.

Edward the Confessor, as he became known owing to his saintly character, gave land and positions to Normans who viewed the easy-going English with scarcely concealed contempt. To guard the southeast shoreline against invasion and pillage Edward the Confessor established the maritime federation known as the **Cinque Ports** (5 ports) in which Sandwich, Dover, Romney, Hythe and Hastings grouped together to supply ships and men for defence. His great-nephew, **Duke William of Normandy**, is said to have made Harold, son of Earl Godwin, swear an oath to help William claim the English throne on Edward's death. On 5 January 1066, only days after the consecration of his abbey church at Westminster, the gentle Confessor died. Harold Godwinson was elected King.

NORMANS (1066-1154)

1066 – Harold Godwinson defeated at the **Battle of Hastings** by Duke William of Normandy, who was crowned William I in Westminster Abbey on Christmas Day

1086 – Domesday Survey made by William I to reassess the value of property throughout England for taxation purposes

1100-35 – Reign of **Henry I** whose marriage to Matilda of Scots united the Norman and Saxon royal houses

1128 – Marriage of Henry I's daughter, Matilda, to Geoffrey , heir of Anjou

1135-54 – Reign of **Stephen**. Henry of Anjou acknowledged as heir to the throne by the Treaty of Winchester

The **Normans** were descendants of Norsemen, Vikings, who had settled in northern France in 876. Following the death of Edward the Confessor, Duke William of Normandy, accompanied by some 5 000 knights and followers, invaded England and defeated Harold at the **Battle of Hastings** on 14 October 1066, the last time the country was successfully invaded and so traditionally regarded as the beginning of English history. Duke William, better known as William the Conqueror, overcame a nation of 1.5-2 million people – descendants of Celts, Romans, Vikings and Saxons – and imposed a strong central authority on a group of kingdoms which ranked among the richest in western Europe.

By the time of the **Domesday Survey** only a handful of English names feature amongst the list of "tenants in chief", revealing a massive shift in ownership of land, and only one of 16 bishops was an Englishman; by 1200 almost every Anglo-Saxon cathedral and abbey, reminders for the vanquished English of their great past, had been demolished and replaced by Norman works – "He destroys well who builds something better". Forty years after the conquest, however, English soldiers fought for an English-born king, **Henry I**, in his French territories.

PLANTAGENETS (1154-1485)

1154 – Accession of **Henry II**, Count of Anjou (Plantagenet)

1170 – Murder of Thomas Becket in Canterbury Cathedral

1189 – Henry II defeated in battle by his son Richard

1189-99 – Reign of **Richard I** (the **Lionheart**)

1199-1216 – Reign of **King John**. Most of Normandy, Maine, Anjou and Brittany lost to the French

1215 – John forced to sign **Magna Carta** by the Barons

1216-72 – Reign of **Henry III**, who married Eleanor of Provence in 1236

1267 – Treaty of Montgomery recognising the territorial gains of Llywelyn the Great (1173-1240) and his grandson, Llywelyn ap Gruffydd (d 1282)

to create a united principality and ap Gruffydd's claim to the title **Prince of Wales**

1271-1307 – Reign of **Edward I**

1277 – English campaign against Wales

1278 – Charter legalising the Confederation of the **Cinque Ports** which supplied 57 fully manned ships for 15 days a year to defend the coast

1282 – English campaign against Wales; death of Llywelyn ap Gruffydd in battle; beginning of the military resettlement of Wales by the English

1284 – Statute of Wales issued at Rhuddlan Castle; Prince Edward born at Caernarfon

1296-98 – North of England ravaged by Scots under **William Wallace**, who was defeated at Falkirk; he was executed in 1305

1307-27 – Reign of **Edward II**, who married Isabel of France

1314 – Edward II defeated at Bannockburn by Robert I, King of Scotland

1327 – Edward II murdered at Berkeley Castle

1327-77 – Reign of **Edward III** with Isabel and Roger Mortimer as Regents

1328 – Robert I recognised as king of an independent Scotland

1330 – Regents deposed from power by Edward III; execution of Roger Mortimer

1337 – Beginning of the **Hundred Years War** with France; Aquitaine and the French throne claimed by Edward; English victories at Crécy and Calais

1348 – Beginning of the plague known as the **Black Death**

1376 – Death of the Black Prince, heir to the throne

1377-99 – Reign of **Richard II**, younger son of the Black Prince with John of Gaunt as Regent

1381 – Peasants' Revolt, in part provoked by the government's attempt to control wages by the Labourers' Statute (1351)

1396 – Treaty of Paris – peace between France and England

1398 – Richard II deposed by Henry Bolingbroke

1399-1414 – Reign of **Henry IV**

1400 – Death of Richard II, probably murdered

1409 – Capture of Harlech by the English; disappearance of Owen Glyndwr

1413-22 – Reign of **Henry V**

1415 – Battle of Agincourt – English victory

1420 – Treaty of Troyes making Henry V heir to the French throne

1422-61 – Reign of **Henry VI** with Duke of Gloucester and Duke of Lancaster as Regents

1455-85 – **Wars of the Roses**, 30 years of sporadic fighting and periods of armed peace, between the houses of Lancaster and York, rival claimants to the throne

1461-83 – Reign of **Edward IV**

1465 – Henry VI captured and imprisoned in the Tower of London

1470 – Restoration of Henry VI by Warwick and flight of Edward

1471 – Murder of Henry VI and Prince Edward by Edward IV following his victory at Tewkesbury

1483 – Reign of **Edward V** ending in his and his brother's imprisonment in the Tower of London

1483-85 – Reign of **Richard III**

1485 – Battle of Bosworth Field at which Richard was defeated and killed by Henry Tudor

Henry II, Count of Anjou, married Eleanor whose dowry brought Aquitaine and Poitou to the English crown. His dispute over the relative rights of Church and State with Thomas Becket, whom he himself had appointed as Archbishop of Canterbury, led to Becket's murder. Henry's reign deserves to be remembered for the restoration of order in a ravaged country, the institution of legal reforms, which included the establishment of the jury, the system of assize courts and coroners' courts, two reforms of the coinage and the granting of many town charters. He also encouraged the expansion of sheep farming as English wool was of high quality; the heavy duties levied on its export contributed to England's prosperity.

The despotic manner of ruling and of raising revenue adopted by Henry's son, **King John**, caused the barons to unite and force the king to sign **Magna Carta** which guaranteed every man freedom from illegal interference with his person or property and the basis of much subsequent English legislation.

The ineffectual reign of John's son, **Henry III**, was marked by baronial opposition and internal strife.

His son, **Edward I**, a typical Plantagenet, fair haired, tall and energetic, was for much of his reign at war with France and

Wales and Scotland; on the last two he imposed English administration and justice. During his reign the constitutional importance of Parliament increased; his Model Parliament of 1295 included representatives from shire, city and borough.

His son, **Edward II**, cared for little other than his own pleasure and his reign saw the effective loss of all that his father had won. His wife, Isabel of France, humiliated by her husband's conduct, invaded and deposed Edward.

The throne passed to his son, **Edward III**, who sought reconciliation with the barons and pursued an enlightened trade policy. He reorganised the navy and led England into the **Hundred Years War**, claiming not only Aquitaine but the throne of France. He rebuilt much of Windsor Castle, where he founded the Order of the Garter in 1348. In that year the Black Death reached England and the labour force was reduced by one-third. As the Black Prince died before his father, the throne passed from Edward III to his grandson, **Richard II**, with his uncle, John of Gaunt, acting as Regent. In time Richard quarrelled with the barons. John of Gaunt was exiled together with his son Henry Bolingbroke, who returned to recover his father's confiscated estates, deposed Richard and became king.

Henry IV was threatened with rebellion by the Welsh and the Percys, Earls of Northumberland, and with invasion from France.

Henry V resumed the Hundred Years War and English claims to the French throne. On his death his infant son was crowned **Henry VI** in 1429 in Westminster Abbey and in 1431 in Notre Dame in Paris. The regency and Henry's recurrent bouts of insanity allowed the counter-claims of York and Lancaster to develop into the **Wars of the Roses**; the Lancastrians – **Henry IV, Henry V** and **Henry VI**, represented by the red rose of Lancaster – claimed the throne by direct male descent from John of Gaunt, fourth son of Edward III; the Yorkists – **Edward IV, Edward V** and **Richard III**, represented by the white rose of York – were descended from Lionel, Edward's third son, but in the female line. The first engagement, the Battle of St Albans, was won by the Yorkists. In 1461 **Edward IV** became king. In 1467 Warwick plotted unsuccessfully against the king and fled to France, where he was reconciled with the Lancastrians; he returned to England and restored Henry VI, causing Edward to flee. Edward however also returned to England; he defeated and killed Warwick

at Barnet and, after a further victory at Tewkesbury, he murdered Henry VI and Prince Edward. The dispute ended when Elizabeth of York married Henry Tudor, a Lancastrian.

Edward V and his younger brother, Richard, known as the **Little Princes in the Tower**, were imprisoned by their uncle Richard, Duke of Gloucester. His claim to the throne by virtue of their alleged illegitimacy was upheld by Parliament. Gloucester was proclaimed **Richard III** and the princes were probably murdered.

TUDORS (1485-1603)

1485-1509 – Reign of **Henry VII**, whose marriage to Elizabeth of York ended the Wars of the Roses

1503 – Marriage of Henry VII's daughter Margaret Tudor to James IV of Scotland

1509-47 – Reign of **Henry VIII** who married Catherine of Aragon in 1509, originally betrothed to his elder brother who died

1513 – Defeat and death of James IV of Scotland at the Battle of Flodden

1520 – Field of the Cloth of Gold with François I of France

1521 – Title "Defender of the Faith" conferred by Pope Leo X upon Henry VIII for his book attacking the teachings of Martin Luther

1533 – Divorce of Henry VIII from Catherine of Aragon through Cranmer, newly appointed Archbishop of Canterbury, and secret marriage to Anne Boleyn; birth of Princess Elizabeth

1535 – Execution of Sir Thomas More, Chancellor, for refusing to sign the Act of Supremacy, acknowledging Henry VIII as head of the Church in place of the Pope

1536-39 – Dissolution of the Monasteries. Excommunication of Henry VIII

1547-53 – Reign of **Edward VI**, son of Henry VIII and Jane Seymour, Henry VIII's third wife

1549 – First Book of Common Prayer

1553-58 – Reign of **Mary I**; Roman Catholicism re-established

1554 – Marriage of Mary to Philip II of Spain

1558-1603 – Reign of **Elizabeth I**

1558 – Marriage of Mary Queen of Scots, who was born at Linlithgow in 1542, to François, Dauphin of France

1559-60 – Anglicanism re-introduced in England; Calvinism established in Scotland

1561 – Return to Scotland of Mary Queen of Scots (aged 19) on the death of her husband

1565 – Marriage of Mary Queen of Scots to Darnley and then to Bothwell

1567-1625 – Reign of James VI, King of the Scots, with Moray as Regent

1580 – Excommunication of Elizabeth I by the Pope

1580 – Circumnavigation of the world by **Francis Drake**

1586 – Babington Plot to assassinate Elizabeth I and use Spanish help to put Mary Queen of Scots on the English throne

1587 – Execution of Mary Queen of Scots.

1588 – Defeat of the Spanish Armada by Drake and the weather

1600 – Incorporation of the East India Company

Henry VII ruled shrewdly and his control of finances restored order and a healthy Treasury after the Wars of the Roses.

His son, **Henry VIII**, was a "Renaissance Man", an accomplished musician, linguist, scholar and soldier. He was an autocratic monarch of capricious temper and elastic conscience, who achieved union with Ireland and Wales and greatly strengthened the Navy. Thomas Wolsey, appointed Chancellor in 1515, fell from favour for failing to obtain papal approval for Henry to divorce Catherine of Aragon; his palace at Hampton Court was confiscated by the King. The Dissolution of the Monasteries caused the greatest redistribution of land in England since the Norman conquest. Wool, much of which had been exported raw in the previous century, was now nearly all made into cloth at home.

The popularity of **Mary**, daughter of Henry VIII and Catherine of Aragon, was undermined by her insistence on marrying Philip II of Spain, who was a Roman Catholic, the burning of 300 alleged heretics and war with France, which resulted in the loss of Calais, England's last possession in continental Europe.

Elizabeth I, daughter of Henry VIII and Anne Boleyn, restored a moderate Anglicanism, though potential Roman Catholic conspiracies to supplant her were ruthlessly suppressed. She sought to avoid the needless expense of war by diplomacy and a network of informers controlled by her Secretaries, Cecil and Walsingham. Opposition to Elizabeth as Queen focused on Mary Queen of Scots

and looked to Spain for assistance. The long struggle against Spain, mostly fought out at sea, culminated in the launch of the Spanish Armada, the final and unsuccessful attempt by Spain to conquer England and re-establish the Roman Catholic faith; its defeat was the greatest military victory of Elizabeth I's reign. **Elizabeth I** presided over a period of exploration and enterprise, a flowering of national culture and the arts; most of William Shakespeare's greatest plays were produced between 1592 and 1616.

STUARTS (1603-1714)

1603-25 – Reign of **James I** (also James VI of Scotland)

1605 – Gunpowder Plot intended to assassinate the King in Parliament

1620 – Pilgrim Fathers set sail for America

1625-49 – Reign of **Charles I**

1626 – Dissolution of Parliament by the King owing to its refusal to grant him subsidies

1640-53 – "Long Parliament" which passed the Triennial Act ensuring regular Parliaments

1642-49 – Civil War

1649 – Trial and execution of Charles I

1649 – Beginning of the **Commonwealth,** during which England was ruled not by a monarch but by Oliver Cromwell, a commoner, who died in 1653.

1651 – Coronation at Scone of Charles II who was defeated at the Battle of Worcester and fled to France

1652-54 – War against the Dutch

1656-59 – War against Spain

1660-85 – Reign of **Charles II**

1661 – Anglican Church re-established by the Clarendon Code

1665-67 – War against the Dutch

1665 – Great Plague in which more than 68 000 Londoners died

1666 – Great Fire of London which destroyed 80% of the City of London but caused only 20 deaths

1672 – Declaration of Indulgence relaxing penal laws against Roman Catholics and other dissenters

1672-74 – War against the Dutch

1673 – Test Act excluding Roman Catholics and other non-conformists from civil office

1677 – Marriage of Charles II's sister, Mary, to William of Orange

1679 – Habeas Corpus Act reinforcing existing powers protecting individuals against arbitrary imprisonment

1685-88 – Reign of **James II**

1685 – Monmouth Rebellion – unsuccessful attempt to claim the throne by the Duke of Monmouth, illegitimate son of Charles II

1687 – Dissolution of Parliament by James II

1688 – William of Orange invited to England. Exile of James II to France

1689-94 – Reign of **William III and Mary II**

1689 – Defeat of Scottish Jacobites at Killiecrankie. Londonderry besieged by James II; Grand Alliance between England, Austria, the Netherlands and German states in war against France

1690 – Battle of the Boyne and defeat of James II and the Irish Jacobites

1694-1702 – Reign of **William III** following the death of Mary II

1694 – Triennial Act providing for Parliament to meet at least once every three years and to sit for not more than three years

1694 – Foundation of the Bank of England

1695 – Foundation of the Bank of Scotland

1702-14 – Reign of **Queen Anne**

1702-14 – War of the Spanish Succession; French invasion of the Spanish Netherlands

1704 – Gibraltar captured by the English; English victory at Blenheim

1707 – Act of Union joining the parliaments of England and Scotland

1714 – Treaty of Utrecht ending the War of the Spanish Succession

The economy was still largely based on agriculture and on wool. Despite an average life expectancy of only 35 years, the increase of population – from 2.5 million in the 1520s to over 5 million by 1650 – posed problems of availability of work and food. Manufacturing increased, production of iron quadrupled in the century to 1650 but small workshops producing high quality woollen cloth were still the mainstay of commerce.

Elizabeth, the last of the Tudors, was succeeded by **James I** of England and VI of Scotland. The **Gunpowder Plot** was a conspiracy of Roman Catholics who attempted to assassinate James in Parliament, despite his willingness to extend to them a measure of toleration.

Charles I inherited his father's belief in an absolute monarchy – the "divine right of kings" – and attempted to rule without Parliament from 1626 to 1640. His marriage to a Roman Catholic, Henrietta Maria of France, was not popular with the people. He was however finally forced to recall Parliament, which condemned his adviser, the Earl of Strafford, to death for treason, refused to grant the King money until he discussed their grievances and passed a Bill preventing dissolution without the consent of Parliament. Early in 1642 Charles I attempted to arrest five members of Parliament.

The **Civil War** broke out in August 1642. Charles I established his headquarters in Oxford but the balance was tilted against him by Scots support for the Parliamentarians. The North was lost after the Battle of Marston Moor in 1644 and, following the formation of the New Model Army by Cromwell and Fairfax and its victory at Naseby in 1645, the Royalists surrendered at Oxford the following year. The King surrendered to the Scots who handed him over to Parliament in 1647. A compromise was attempted but Charles wavered. He played off one faction in Parliament against another and sought finance and troops from abroad. In 1648 the war resumed. The Scots, to whom Charles promised a Presbyterian England in return for their help, invaded England but were defeated in August at Preston and Charles I was captured. The army demanded his death.

Under the **Commonwealth and Protectorate** the monarchy and the House of Lords were abolished and replaced by a Council of State of 40 members. Attempts by the "Rump" Parliament to turn itself into a permanent non-elected body caused Cromwell to dissolve it and form the Protectorate in 1653, in which he, as Lord Protector, ruled by decree. He was accepted by the majority of a war-weary population but, on his death in 1653, the lack of a competent successor provoked negotiations which led to the Restoration.

The **Restoration** in May 1660 ended ten years of Puritan restriction and opened a period of sensuality and a flourishing of theatre, painting and the arts. In the Declaration of Breda Charles II appeared to promise something for almost every political faction. The **Navigation Acts,** specifying that English goods must be carried in English ships, did much to develop commerce.

In 1685, just after the death of Charles II, his illegitimate son, the Duke of Monmouth, whom he had refused to legiti-

Simplified diagram of the succession to the Throne

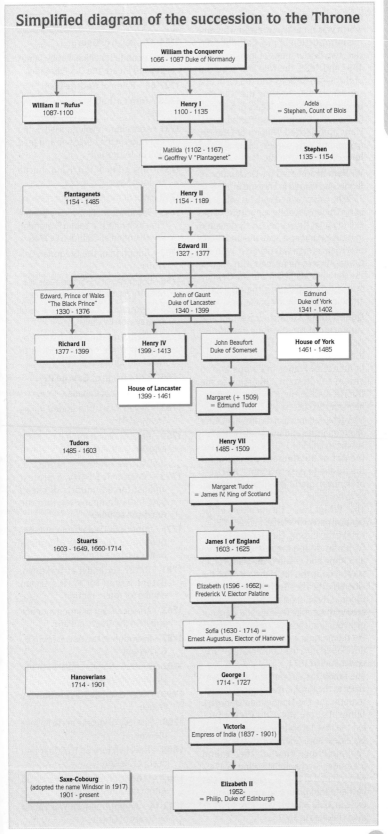

mise, led a rebellion against James II, which was brutally repressed. This and the introduction of pro-Catholic policies, two Declarations of Indulgence in 1687 and 1688, the trial and acquittal of the Seven Bishops and the birth of a son James, who became the "Old Pretender", all intensified fears of a Roman Catholic succession. Disaffected politicians approached William of Orange, married to Mary, James' daughter, and he accepted the throne.

William III accepted the Declaration of Rights and landed in England in 1688. In 1689 he was crowned with his wife Mary as his Queen. Jacobite supporters of the exiled James II were decisively defeated in both Ireland and Scotland and much of William's reign was devoted, with the Grand Alliance he formed with Austria, the Netherlands, Spain and the German states, to obstructing the territorial ambitions of Louis XIV of France.

Queen Anne, staunch Protestant and supporter of the Glorious Revolution (1688), which deposed her father, James II, also strove to reduce the power and influence of France in Europe and to ensure a Protestant succession to the throne. Marlborough's victory at Blenheim and his successes in the Low Countries achieved much of the first aim. After 18 pregnancies and the death of her last surviving child in 1701, Anne agreed to the **Act of Settlement** providing for the throne to pass to Sophia, Electress of Hanover, grand-daughter of James I, or to her heirs.

The **"Whigs"** were the members of the political party which had invited William to take the throne. They formed powerful juntas during the reigns of William and Anne and ensured the Hanoverian succession. In the 1860s they became the Liberal Party. The **"Tories"** accepted the Glorious Revolution but became associated with Jacobite feelings and were out of favour until the new Tory party, under Pitt the Younger, took office in 1783. They developed into the Conservative Party under Peel in 1834.

The **Jacobites**, supporters of the Stuart claim to the throne, made two attempts to dethrone the Hanoverian George I. James II's son, the "Old Pretender", led the first Jacobite rising in 1715 and his eldest son, Charles Edward Stuart, "Bonnie Prince Charlie", the "Young Pretender", led a similar rising in 1745, which ended in 1746 at Culloden, the last battle fought on British soil. He died in exile in 1788 and his younger brother died childless in 1807.

HANOVERIANS (1714-1837)

1714-27 – Reign of **George I**

1715 – Jacobite rebellion, led by James Edward Stuart, the Old Pretender

1727-60 – Reign of **George II**

1728 – Irish Catholics deprived of the vote

1731 – Agriculture revolutionised by the invention of the horse hoe and seed drill by Jethro Tull

1733 – Invention of the flying shuttle by John Kay

1740 – War of the Austrian Succession

1745 – Jacobite rebellion led by Bonnie Prince Charlie, the Young Pretender, which ended at Culloden in 1746

1752 – Adoption of the Gregorian Calendar

1756 – Beginning of the Seven Years War. Ministry formed by Pitt the Elder

1757 – Recapture of Calcutta. Battle of Plassey won by Clive

1759 – Defeat of the French army by General Wolfe on the Heights of Abraham, Quebec

1760-1820 – Reign of **George III**

1760 – Conquest of Canada

1763 – Seven Years War ended in the Treaty of Paris

1769 – Patents issued for Watt's steam engine and Arkwright's water frame

1773 – Boston Tea Party, a protest against forced imports of cheap East India Company tea into the American colonies

1776 – American Declaration of Independence; *The Wealth of Nations* published by Adam Smith

1781 – British surrender at Yorktown. Patent issued for Watt's steam engine for rotary motion

1783 – American War of Independence ended in the Treaty of Paris

1787 – Invention of the power loom by Cartwright

1792-93 – McCartney's embassy to the Emperor of China

1793 – War against Revolutionary France

1799 – First levy of income tax to finance the war

1805 – Naval victory at Trafalgar and death of Nelson

1807 – Abolition of the slave trade within the British Empire

1812-14 – Anglo-American War ended by Treaty of Ghent

1815 – Battle of Waterloo; final defeat of Napoleon; Congress of Vienna

1820-30 – Reign of **George IV**

1823 – Reform of criminal law and prisons by Peel

1825 – Opening of the Stockton and Darlington railway. Completion of the Menai Bridge by Telford

1829 – Catholic Emancipation Act. Formation of the Metropolitan Police

1830-37 – Reign of **William IV**

1832 – First parliamentary Reform Act

1833 – Factory Act. Abolition of child labour

1834 – Tolpuddle Martyrs transported to Australia for forming an agriculture Trade Union

1837-1901 – Reign of **Victoria**

1840 – Marriage of Victoria to Prince Albert. Introduction of the penny post

1842 – Campaign by the Chartist movement for parliamentary reform

1846 – Repeal of the Corn Laws

1848 – Cholera epidemic. Public Health Act

1851 – Great Exhibition in the Crystal Palace in Hyde Park

1854-56 – Crimean War which ended in the Treaty of Paris

1856 – Invention of the Bessemer process

1857 – Indian Mutiny

1858 – Government of India transferred from the East India Company to the Crown

1861 – Death of Prince Albert

1863 – Opening of the first underground railway in London, the Metropolitan Railway

1871 – Introduction of bank holidays

1876 – Victoria adoptes the title Empress of India. Elementary education obligatory

1884 – Invention of the turbine by Parsons

1888 – Local Government Act establishing county councils and county boroughs

1895 – First Motor Show in London

1899-1902 – Boer War ending in the Peace of Vereeniging and leading to the Union of South Africa in 1910

1900 – Formation of the Labour Party

1901-10 – Reign of **Edward VII**

1903 – Women's suffrage movement started by Mrs Pankhurst

1905 – First motor buses in London. Opening of Piccadilly and Bakerloo tube lines

1909 – Introduction of old age pensions

1910-36 – Reign of **George V**

1914-18 – First World War

1914 – Formation of Kitchener's "Volunteer Army"

1916 – Easter Rising in Dublin

When **George I** ascended the throne, the United Kingdom was a European power, which through its economic and naval strength had played a major part in weakening the influence of France in Europe.

Although as Prince of Wales, **George II** quarrelled with his father, he retained the services of Walpole as Prime Minister. He took an active part in the war of the Austrian Succession and was the last monarch to command his forces personally in battle, at Dettingen in 1743. At the end of his reign he virtually withdrew from government business.

He was succeeded by his grandson, **George III**, who was unable to reverse the trend towards constitutional monarchy but he did try to exercise the right of a king to govern, causing great unpopularity, and was forced to acknowledge the reality of party politics. Foreign policy was dominated by the King's determination to suppress the American Revolution and the **Napoleonic Wars** which arose from the threat posed by the Revolution in France to established European powers.

George IV had supported the Whig cause as a symbol of opposition to his father's Tory advisers and was much influenced by the politican Charles James Fox.

William IV was 65 when he succeeded his unpopular brother. Dissatisfaction with parliamentary representation was near to causing revolutionary radicals to join forces with the mob. Reform of the franchise, however, was not possible until the King reluctantly agreed to create 50 new Peers to ensure passage of the Reform Act (1832) through the House of Lords. As William's two daughters had died as infants, he was succeeded on his death by his niece, Victoria.

The **Industrial Revolution** was favoured by the relative political stability which followed the Glorious Revolution and encouraged the growth of a strong banking and credit system, and by the overseas empire which supplied both raw materials and markets for manufactured goods. Vast social changes occurred as the labour force moved from the land into town; overcrowding often bred unrest between worker and employer. The Napoleonic Wars both stimulated this industrialism and aggravated the unrest but by the mid 19C it was clear that in Britain at any rate industrial revolution would not be followed by political revolution.

Queen Victoria

Queen **Victoria**, the last monarch of the House of Hanover, was only 18 when she came to the throne, to become Britain's longest-reigning Sovereign and to give her name to an illustrious age. Her husband, the Prince Consort, Albert of Saxe-Coburg, was her closest adviser until his premature death in 1861. He persuaded her that the Crown should not be aligned with any political party – a principle that has endured. He was the instigator of the **Great Exhibition** which took place between May and October in 1851. It contained exhibits from all nations and was a proud declaration of the high point of the Industrial Revolution, celebrating the inventiveness, technical achievement and prosperity which are the hallmarks of the Victorian Age.

Her son, **Edward VII**, who was excluded from royal duties and responsibilities until 1892, greatly increased the prestige of the monarchy by his own charm and by reviving royal public ceremonial.

HOUSE OF WINDSOR

1917 – Name of the royal family changed to Windsor by George V

1918 – Vote granted to women over 30

1919 – Treaty of Versailles

1921 – Creation of the Irish Free State

1924 – British Empire Exhibition

1926 – General Strike

1928 – Vote extended to women over 21

1931 – Depression – many people out of work; Britain comes off the gold standard

1936 – Accession and abdication of **Edward VIII**

1936-52 – Reign of **George VI**

1939-45 – Second World War

1939 – Winston Churchill becomes Prime Minister on 10 May

1940 – Evacuation of Dunkirk; **Battle of Britain**

1944 – Normandy landings

1944 – Education Act establishing free secondary education

1946 – National Insurance and National Health Acts introduced by Labour Government under Attlee

1947 – Independence and partition of India. Nationalisation of railways and road transport

1949 – Independence of the Republic of Ireland. Foundation of the North Atlantic Treaty Organisation (NATO). Nationalisation of iron and steel industries

1952 – Accession of **Elizabeth II**

1956 – Commissioning of Calder Hall, first nuclear power station

1958 – Treaty of Rome creating the European Economic Community (now the European Union)

1959 – Discovery of oil in the North Sea

1963 – First veto of UK membership of the Common Market by de Gaulle

1965 – Death of Sir Winston Churchill

1967 – Second veto of UK membership of the Common Market by de Gaulle

1969 – Investiture of Prince Charles as Prince of Wales at Caernarfon Castle
Beginning of the troubles in Northern Ireland

1971 – Introduction of decimal currency

1973 – United Kingdom admitted to membership of the European Economic Community

1978-91 – Margaret Thatcher elected first woman Prime Minister

1982 – Falklands War

1995 – 50th Anniversary of Victory in Europe National Lottery established

1997 – Election of a Labour Government by a landslide
50th Anniversary (Golden Wedding) of the marriage of Queen Elizabeth II and Prince Philip, Duke of Edinburgh
Referenda approve Scottish and Welsh Assemblies

1998 – Good Friday Agreement followed by referendum and meeting of Northern Ireland Assembly

1999 – Opening of Scottish Parliament and Welsh Assembly

2002 – Golden Jubilee of Queen Elizabeth II

2005 – Terrorist bombs explode in London killing 52 people

It was **George V** who began the tradition of the Sovereign's Christmas broadcast to the peoples of the Commonwealth and exercised the Sovereign's new restraining influence over politics. He and Queen Mary made many tours of the Empire together, visiting India in 1911, to hold a memorable Coronation in Durbar. In 1917, during the First World War, he changed the name of the royal family to **Windsor**. The First World War was the beginning of many familiar modern developments. Britain's sea power was challenged. The export of one-third of the national industrial output ceased to be sufficient to maintain a favourable balance of trade, and revenue from shipping, overseas investment and insurance no longer made up the difference. Foreign competitors were driving British goods out of many traditional overseas markets and out of the national markets of those same competitors.

The liberal ideas of the 1890s gave rise to industrial unionism and to the Labour movement. The intense pride in Empire, which had marked the same decade, turned in the 1920s to increasing self-consciousness.

Edward VIII's popularity relied on his charm and his concern for the unemployed during the Depression but his desire to marry Wallis Simpson, an American divorcee, led to his abdication.

His younger brother became **George VI.** Both he and his Queen – Elizabeth Bowes-Lyon, whom he had married in 1923 – became beloved and respected symbols of British determination and resistance during the Second World War. After the evacuation from Dunkirk in 1940, Great Britain endured the **Battle of Britain;** from July to October many towns and cities experienced massive aerial bombardment – "the Blitz". British and Commonwealth forces fought world-wide, actively supported by the United States, which came into the conflict after the Japanese attack on Pearl Harbor in December 1941. In 1944 Britain became the springboard for the invasion of Europe and victory.

After 1945 key industries were nationalised and the **Welfare State** was born, providing the National Health Service and improved pension and unemployment benefits. After 1945 the self-governing Dominions, which had stood by Britain during two World Wars, changed into the **British Commonwealth of Nations,** starting with India in 1947; within the ten years to 1957 virtually all Britain's overseas dependencies achieved independence.

Elizabeth II, who succeeded to the throne in 1952, together with her husband, Prince Philip, Duke of Edinburgh, have done much to strengthen the role of monarchy both at home and abroad.

Since 1945 Britain has adjusted to the realities of the modern world. Despite reduced economic strengths, Britain retains her traditional role in international affairs while forging new economic links within the European Union.

The creation of the Scottish Parliament and the Welsh Assembly marked a new stage in the relationships between the constituent parts of the United Kingdom though most of the real power has remained firmly rooted in Whitehall and Westminster.

In 2001 the country was rocked by the devastating events at the World Trade Centre in the USA (which claimed many

Mary Evans Picture Library/EXPLORER

OUR SKIPPER

Winston Churchill

British lives) and the aftermath. The nation mourned the death of Queen Elizabeth the Queen Mother in her daughter's jubilee year of 2002.

The war in Iraq in 2003 divided the nation with the government's credibility questioned, leading to high profile ministerial resignations. Nonetheless in 2005 Tony Blair led his Labour Party to a third general election victory. Joy for the nation in July 2005 as a result of being nominated to host the 2012 Olympics was extinguished the very next day as terrorist bombs exploded across London, killing 52 people.

Scientific Progress

Between 1760 and 1850 the **Industrial Revolution** turned Britain into the first industrial nation of the world. Power-driven machines replaced human muscle and factory production replaced medieval craft work carried out in the home. New methods supplied expanding markets – new machines were invented to satisfy growing demand.

POWER

In 1712 **Thomas Newcomen** designed the first practical piston and steam engine and his idea was later much improved by **James Watt**. Such engines were needed to pump water and to raise men and ore from mines and soon replaced water wheels as the power source for the cotton factories which sprang up in Lancashire. Then **Richard Trevithick** (1771-1833), Cornish tin miner, designed a boiler with the fire box inside which he showed to **George Stephenson** (1781-1848) and his son, **Robert** (1803-59) and this became the basis of the early "locomotives".

Without abundant coal, however, sufficient iron could never have been produced for all the new machines. By 1880, 154 million tons of coal were being transported across Britain. Cast iron had been produced by Shropshire ironmaster **Abraham Darby** in Coalbrookdale in 1709 and was used for the cylinders of early steam engines and for bridges and aqueducts. Wrought iron with greater tensile strength was developed in the 1790s, allowing more accurate and stronger machine parts, railway lines and bridging materials. In 1856 **Sir Henry Bessemer** devised a system in which compressed air is blown through the molten metal, burning off impurities and producing a stronger steel.

TRANSPORT

"Turnpike trusts" had laid the foundation of a coherent road network between 1751 and 1772. **Thomas Telford** (1757-1834) built roads and bridges for the use of stage coaches and broad-wheeled wagons transporting people and goods. By the 1830s there were 20 000 miles of roads but these were often impassable in winter. Cheap transport for bulk goods was by canal; there were 4 000 miles of canals, pioneered by **James Brindley** (1716-72). Eventually heavy goods and long-distance passenger traffic passed to the railways.

Engineered by **George Stephenson** in 1825, the Stockton and Darlington Railway was the first passenger-carrying public steam railway in the world. By 1835, with twin tracks and a timetable, the railway had become the vital element of the Industrial Revolution – swift, efficient and cheap transport for raw materials and finished goods all over the country. The success of Stephenson's *Rocket* proved the feasibility of locomotives. **Isambard Kingdom Brunel** (1806-59), Chief Engineer to the Great Western Railway, designed the Clifton Suspension Bridge and also the first successful trans-Atlantic steamship, the *Great Western,* in 1837. His father Sir Marc Isambard Brunel (1769-1849) was responsible for the first tunnel under the Thames, between 1825 and 1843.

William Henry Morris – Lord Nuffield, the most influential of British car manufacturers, began with bicycles and made his first car in 1913. He is probably best remembered, along with his philanthropic foundations in medicine, for his 1959 "Mini". **John Boyd Dunlop** started with bicycles too. In 1888 this Scottish veterinary surgeon invented the first pneumatic tyre. It was **John Loudon McAdam**, an Ayrshire engineer, who devised the "Tarmacadam" surfacing for roads.

More recently **Christopher Cockerell** patented a design for the first hovercraft in 1955. The Sinclair C5, a battery-powered electric tricycle built by Sir James Sinclair, appeared in 1985 but failed to find favour.

AVIATION

The names of **Charles Rolls** and **Henry Royce** will always be associated with the grand cars they pioneered although their contribution to aviation is arguably even greater. A Rolls-Royce engine powered Sir Frank Whittle's Gloster E28/29, the first jet aircraft, and the De Havilland Comet, the world's first commercial passenger-carrying jet airliner which made its maiden flight in 1949. British aerospace designers worked with their French counterparts in the development of Concorde, the world's first supersonic airliner.

SCIENCE

In 1660 Sir **Francis Bacon** (1561-1626) founded the Royal Society; it was granted a Charter by Charles II in 1662 "to promote discussion, particularly in the physical sciences". **Robert Boyle** and **Sir Christopher Wren** were founder members and Sir Isaac Newton was its President from 1703 to 1727. **Michael Faraday** was appointed assistant to Sir Humphrey Davy, inventor of the miners' Safety Lamp, in 1812. It was Faraday's work with electromagnetism which led to the development of the electric dynamo and motor. An early form of computer, the "difference engine" was invented by **Charles Babbage** in 1833 and can be seen in the library of King's College, Cambridge. **Edmond Halley,** friend of Newton, became Astronomer Royal in 1720. He is best remembered for the comet named after him, and for correctly predicting its 76-year cycle and return in 1758. When Halley's Comet returned in 1985, it was a British Aerospace probe – Giotto – which intercepted it and relayed much information about its composition and nature.

The radio telescope at Jodrell Bank, set up by **Sir Bernard Lovell** in 1955, is still one of the largest in the world and contributes to our widening knowledge of our Universe. In 1968 **Antony Hewish**, a British astronomer at Cambridge, first discovered pulsars, cosmic sources of light or radio energy. Professor Stephen Hawking studied black holes and wrote an influential treatise, *A Brief History of Time.*

MEDICINE

It was **William Harvey,** physician to James I and Charles I, who discovered the circulation of the blood. More recent British achievements in medicine have been those of Dr Jacob Bell who, with Dr Simpson from Edinburgh, introduced chloroform anaesthesia, which met with public approval after Queen Victoria used it during the birth of Prince Leopold in 1853. **Sir Alexander Fleming** discovered the effects of penicillin in killing bacteria in 1928, though large-scale production did not start until 1943. The "double-helix" structure of DNA (deoxyribonucleic acid) – the major component of chromosomes which carry genetic information and control inheritance of characteristics – was proposed by Francis Crick working at the Cavendish Laboratory in Cambridge, with his American colleague, James Watson, in 1953. The cloning of Dolly the sheep by the Roslin Institute in Scotland marks a new era in genetic engineering.

NATURAL HISTORY

John Tradescant and son, who were gardeners to Charles I and planted the first physic garden in 1628, are commemorated in the Museum of Garden History in London. The Chelsea Physic Garden founded in 1673 has a remarkable record in plant propagation: cotton seeds from the South Seas, tea from China, quinine and rubber from South America. James Hutton (1726-97) wrote a treatise entitled *A Theory of the Earth* (1785) which forms the basis of modern geology.

Sir William Hooker, the first director of Kew Gardens, was a distinguished botanist. **Sir Joseph Banks** (1743-1820), botanist and explorer, accompanied James Cook's expedition round the world in *Endeavour* (1768-71) and collected many previously unknown plants. Together with the biologist Thomas Huxley (1825-95), they supported the pioneering research of **Charles Darwin** (1809-1882), the father of the theory of evolution outlined in his famous work, *On the Origin of Species*, which had a great impact on the study of natural sciences. His round the world voyage aboard *HMS Beagle* is meticulously documented.

The geologist and naturalist **John Muir** (1838-1914) is commemorated as the founder of the American National Parks. The British passion for gardening has led to the domestication of exotic species such as azaleas, rhododendrons, orchids among others. The role of Kew Gardens, which has accumulated a seed bank of some 5 000 species over the past 200 years, is vital in the conservation of endangered plant species. The zoologist Desmond Morris has propounded provocative theories on human behaviour based on animal studies. The ornithologist Sir Peter Scott, and the naturalists Gerald Durrell, David Bellamy and Sir David Attenborough have increased public awareness of conservation and other environmental issues.

EXPLORATION

Maritime exploration spurred on by the enquiring spirit of the 16C led to the discovery of new worlds. Following the voyages of Portuguese explorers, **John Cabot**, a Genoese settled in Bristol, discovered Nova Scotia and Newfoundland. Rivalry between England and Spain and other European nations in search of trade as well as scientific advances in navigational aids (charting of winds and currents and astronomical study) and improvements in ship construction led to an explosion of maritime exploration. English mariners, mostly Devon men, included: John Hawkins (1532-95), who introduced tobacco and sweet potatoes to England; **Sir Francis Drake** (c 1540-96), the first Englishman to circumnavigate the world; **Sir Walter Raleigh** (1552-1618), who discovered Virginia; Martin Frobisher, who explored the North Atlantic in search of the Northwest Passage and discovered Baffin Island (1574). Hudson Bay in Canada is named after the explorer Henry Hudson (1610). Captain **James Cook** (1728-79) explored the Pacific, and charted the coasts of Australia and New Zealand and surveyed the Newfoundland coast.

Other famous explorers include **Mungo Park** (1771-1806), who explored West Africa and attempted to trace the course of the Niger river; **David Livingstone** (1813-73), a doctor and missionary who campaigned against the slave trade and was the first to cross the African mainland from east to west and discovered the Victoria Falls and Lake Nyasa (now Lake Malawi); Alexander Mackenzie (1755-1820), the first man to cross the American continent by land (1783); and John McDouall Stuart (1815-66) who explored the Australian desert.

ART AND CULTURE

Architecture

ECCLESIASTICAL ARCHITECTURE

Saxon towers

EARL'S BARTON, Northamptonshire – Late 10C

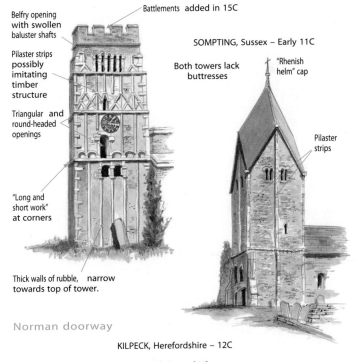

Belfry opening with swollen baluster shafts

Battlements added in 15C

Pilaster strips possibly imitating timber structure

Triangular and round-headed openings

"Long and short work" at corners

Thick walls of rubble, narrow towards top of tower.

SOMPTING, Sussex – Early 11C

Both towers lack buttresses

"Rhenish helm" cap

Pilaster strips

Norman doorway

KILPECK, Herefordshire – 12C

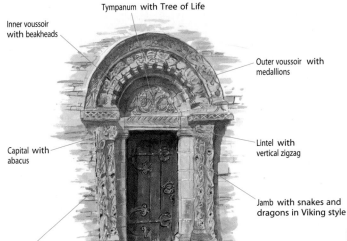

Tympanum with Tree of Life

Inner voussoir with beakheads

Outer voussoir with medallions

Capital with abacus

Lintel with vertical zigzag

Jamb with snakes and dragons in Viking style

Shaft with superimposed figures

R. Corbel/MICHELIN

Norman cathedral

Durham Cathedral was largely completed between 1095 and 1133. It exemplifies the grandeur and solidity of Norman architecture. The characteristic rounded arch prevails, but the pointed-rib vaults anticipate the structural achievements of Gothic architecture.

The side elevation of the nave is divided into: triforium/clerestory and arcade

Corbel

Rounded crossing arch

Diagonal ribs

Pointed-rib vault

Blind arcade

Round pier with incised chevrons

Compound pier

Pier with lozenge decoration

Nave

Choir

Cushion capital

18C rose window

19C rood screen

R. Corbel/MICHELIN

Gothic

WINDOWS

Simple 5-lancet
Early English
window c 1170,
tall, narrow
and with acutely-
pointed arch

Space between
lancets
enlivened by
addition of
quatrefoil
c 1270

Window in
Decorated style
with fully
developed flowing
tracery c 1350

Large window in
Perpendicular style with
4-centred arch and
horizontal emphasis
through use of
transoms

SALISBURY CATHEDRAL (1220-58)

Of great length and highly compartmentalised in layout like most English cathedrals, Salisbury is exceptional in having been completed in a single style –Early English – in a short space of time. The only major addition was the tall crossing tower and spire (404ft) built c 1334.

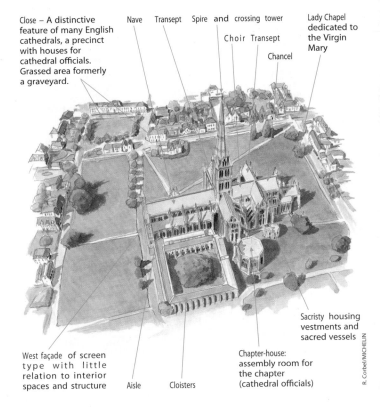

Close – A distinctive feature of many English cathedrals, a precinct with houses for cathedral officials. Grassed area formerly a graveyard.

Nave   Transept   Spire and crossing tower

Choir Transept

Chancel

Lady Chapel dedicated to the Virgin Mary

Sacristy housing vestments and sacred vessels

West façade of screen type with little relation to interior spaces and structure

Aisle   Cloisters

Chapter-house: assembly room for the chapter (cathedral officials)

R. Corbel/MICHELIN

VAULTING

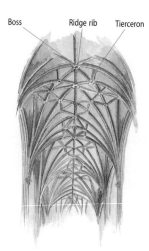

Boss | Ridge rib | Tierceron

Nave vault with liernes (linking ribs not joined to central boss or springer) Canterbury Cathedral c 1390 - 1405

Fan vault with pendants: the ultimate development of this highly ornamental, non-structural vault Henry VII's Chapel, Westminster 1503-12

English Baroque

ST PAUL'S CATHEDRAL, City of London, West façade

Built by Sir Christopher Wren between 1675 and 1710, the cathedral combines Renaissance and Baroque elements in a masterly way. The dome, inspired by St Peter's in Rome, is in three parts: the lightweight and beautifully shaped outer dome, an inner dome, and between them an (invisible) brick core carrying the heavy lantern which helps hold the outer dome in place.

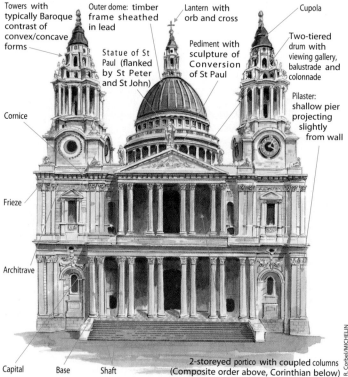

Towers with typically Baroque contrast of convex/concave forms

Outer dome: timber frame sheathed in lead

Lantern with orb and cross

Cupola

Statue of St Paul (flanked by St Peter and St John)

Pediment with sculpture of Conversion of St Paul

Two-tiered drum with viewing gallery, balustrade and colonnade

Pilaster: shallow pier projecting slightly from wall

Cornice

Frieze

Architrave

Capital | Base | Shaft

2-storeyed portico with coupled columns (Composite order above, Corinthian below)

R. Corbel/MICHELIN

MILITARY ARCHITECTURE

Medieval castles

Norman motte and bailey

In the immediate post-Conquest years the Normans built timber castles, using an artificial or natural earthen mound ("motte"). A stockaded outer enclosure combined stables, storehouses etc ("bailey"). From c 1150 rebuilding took place in stone.

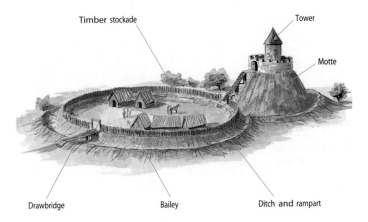

Timber stockade

Tower

Motte

Drawbridge

Bailey

Ditch and rampart

CAERPHILLY CASTLE, South Wales

A late 13C concentric castle which served as a model for Edward I's strongholds in North Wales

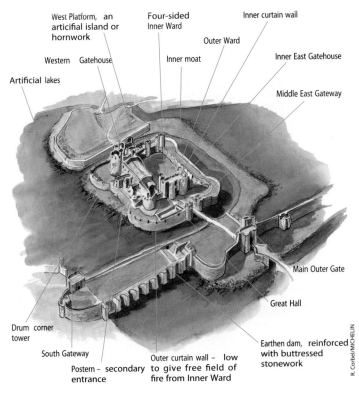

West Platform, an articifial island or hornwork

Four-sided Inner Ward

Inner curtain wall

Outer Ward

Western Gatehouse

Inner moat

Inner East Gatehouse

Artificial lakes

Middle East Gateway

Main Outer Gate

Great Hall

Drum corner tower

South Gateway

Postern – secondary entrance

Outer curtain wall – low to give free field of fire from Inner Ward

Earthen dam, reinforced with buttressed stonework

R. Corbel/MICHELIN

CAERNARFON – A bastide town and castle of the late 13C, North Wales

English kings laid out numerous planned towns ("bastides") to attract settlers and control territory in areas like Gascony and Wales. Though the medieval houses of the English colonists have long since disappeared, Caernarfon retains its castle, its walls and its rectangular street layout.

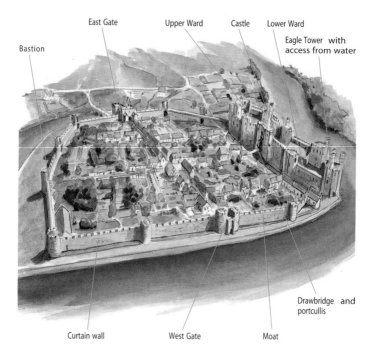

East Gate

Upper Ward

Castle

Lower Ward

Bastion

Eagle Tower with access from water

Drawbridge and portcullis

Curtain wall

West Gate

Moat

BODIAM CASTLE, Sussex

Based on French and southern Italian strongholds of the previous century, Bodiam (late 14C) is a perfectly symmetrical square castle, surrounded by a moat and with an array of well-preserved defensive features.

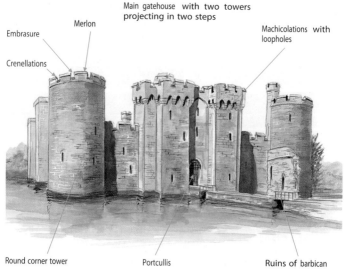

Main gatehouse with two towers projecting in two steps

Merlon

Embrasure

Machicolations with loopholes

Crenellations

Round corner tower

Portcullis

Ruins of barbican

R. Corbel/MICHELIN

COUNTRY HOUSES

LITTLE MORETON HALL, Cheshire

A moated manor house built between the mid-15C and c 1580 with elaborate timber-framing and carved decoration characteristic of the Welsh Marches, Cheshire and Lancashire. Despite its date, this, and many other houses like it, is still medieval in character.

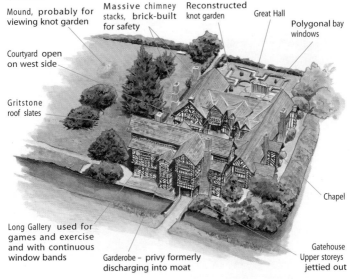

Mound, probably for viewing knot garden

Massive chimney stacks, brick-built for safety

Reconstructed knot garden

Great Hall

Polygonal bay windows

Courtyard open on west side

Gritstone roof slates

Chapel

Long Gallery used for games and exercise and with continuous window bands

Garderobe – privy formerly discharging into moat

Gatehouse Upper storeys jettied out

BLENHEIM PALACE AND PARK, Oxfordshire

Built 1705-22 by Sir John Vanbrugh, the Palace with its vast scale, heroic proportions and rich profusion of forms represents the culmination of the Baroque style in England. The park was transformed between 1764-74 by Lancelot "Capability" Brown, whose masterpiece it is.

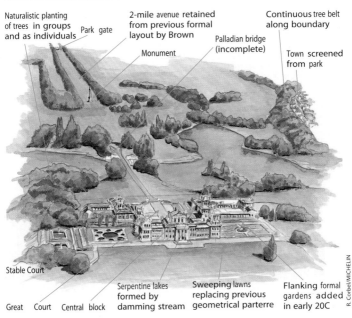

Naturalistic planting of trees in groups and as individuals

Park gate

2-mile avenue retained from previous formal layout by Brown

Continuous tree belt along boundary

Palladian bridge (incomplete)

Monument

Town screened from park

Stable Court

Great Court Central block

Serpentine lakes formed by damming stream

Sweeping lawns replacing previous geometrical parterre

Flanking formal gardens added in early 20C

R. Corbel/MICHELIN

GEORGIAN HOUSING AND PLANNING

In the 18C and early 19C, extensions to inland spas, and later to seaside towns saw a fusion of urban planning and landscape design. In Bath, John Wood the Elder and John Wood the Younger built the splendidly urbane sequence of Queen Square (1736), Gay Street (1734-60), The Circus (1754) and Royal Crescent, the latter a palace-like composition made up of relatively small terraced houses facing out to parkland.

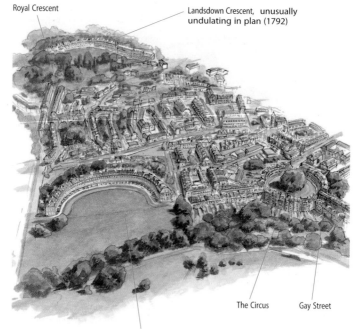

Royal Crescent

Landsdown Crescent, unusually undulating in plan (1792)

The Circus

Gay Street

Ha-ha sunken wall permitting uninterrupted view

In London, strict regulations governed the design of terraced houses which were rated 1-4 according to their size and value.

Sash-windows with thin wooden glazing bars help unify façades. Small or square windows of top floor act as visual stop. Classical appearance aided by low-pitched roofs (sometimes partly concealed by parapet) and lack of emphasis on chimneys. Tall windows emphasize importance of first floor reception rooms.

First-rate house

Second-rate house

Third-rate house

Fourth-rate house

VICTORIAN ARCHITECTURE

ST PANCRAS STATION, London

The Midland Hotel, completed in the Gothic Revival style in 1876 by Sir George Gilbert Scott, conceals the great train shed whose iron and glass arch was the widest (249ft) in the world at the time. Marrying Venetian, French, Flemish and English Gothic in a triumphal synthesis, Scott's building was also a functional masterpiece, housing the myriad activities of a railway terminus on a restricted, triangular site.

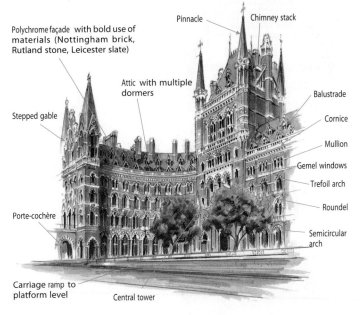

Pinnacle

Chimney stack

Polychrome façade with bold use of materials (Nottingham brick, Rutland stone, Leicester slate)

Attic with multiple dormers

Balustrade

Stepped gable

Cornice

Mullion

Gemel windows

Trefoil arch

Roundel

Porte-cochère

Semicircular arch

Carriage ramp to platform level

Central tower

EARLY MODERN ARCHITECTURE

GLASGOW SCHOOL OF ART

In touch with continental Art Nouveau and looking forward to 20C functionalism, Charles Rennie Mackintosh was also inspired by the robust forms of Scottish baronial architecture. Rising castle-like from its steeply sloping site, his Glasgow School of Art (1897-1909) combines strict utility of purpose with innovative, near-abstract forms and decorative Art Nouveau elements.

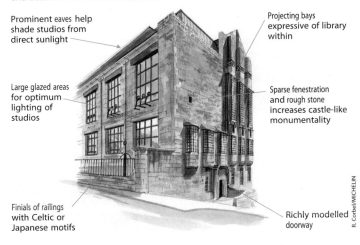

Prominent eaves help shade studios from direct sunlight

Projecting bays expressive of library within

Large glazed areas for optimum lighting of studios

Sparse fenestration and rough stone increases castle-like monumentality

Finials of railings with Celtic or Japanese motifs

Richly modelled doorway

VERNACULAR ARCHITECTURE

CRUCK COTTAGE, HEREFORDSHIRE
Late medieval

The simplest form of timber construction, using the two halves of a massive, curving branch or tree-trunk

HOUSE AT CULROSS, SCOTLAND 16C

Crow-stepped gable

Rubble walls covered in rough cast ("harling") and colour-washed

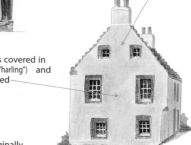

WEALDEN HOUSE, KENT c 1500

Upper floor jettied out

Hipped roof, originally thatched, now tiled

Close-studded vertical timbers

Smoke vent, later replaced by chimney stack

TIMBER-FRAMED HOUSE, Kent 17C

Timber frame clad in contrasting materials: upper floor with hung tiles, ground floor in weather-boarding

STONE COTTAGES, Gloucestershire

Built of oolithic limestone, possibly as a 14C monastic sheephouse and converted into cottages in 17C

Steep-pitched roof with graded stone slates

SEMI-DETACHED SUBURBAN HOUSES
Urban outskirts anywhere in Britain c 1930

Picturesque Arts and Crafts outline and detail. Contrasting treatment: pebble-dash on left, applied "half-timbering" on right

R. Corbel/MICHELIN

ARCHITECTURAL TERMS

Aisle lateral divisions running parallel with the nave in medieval and other buildings, usually churches.

Ambulatory passage giving access between the choir and apse of a church.

Apse rounded or polygonal end of a church or chapel.

Arcade a series of arches, resting on piers or columns.

Architrave the beam, or lowest portion of the entablature (*see below*), extending from column to column. Also used as the moulded frame around the head and side of a window or door opening.

Archivolt concentric mouldings on the face of an arch resting on the impost.

Baldachin canopy supported by pillars set over an altar, throne or tomb.

Baptistery building, separate from the church, containing the font.

Barbican outwork of a medieval castle, often with a tower, defending a gate or bridge.

Barrel vaulting continuous arched vault of semicircular section.

Battlements parapet of medieval fortifications, with a walkway for archers or crossbowmen, protected by merlons (*see below*), with embrasures (*see below*) between them.

Broach spire octagonal spire rising from a square tower without a parapet, having pyramidal broaches at the angles.

Buttress vertical mass of masonry built against a wall, so strengthening it and resisting the outward pressure of a vaulted roof (*see Flying buttress*).

Capital crowning feature of a column or pillar.

Chancel part of the church set aside for clergy and choir, to the east of the nave.

Chantry chapel chapel endowed for religious services for the soul of the founder.

Chapter-house place of assembly for the governing body of a monastery or cathedral. In medieval England, often multi-sided, with vaulting supported on a central pillar.

Chevron Norman decoration of zig-zag mouldings used around windows and doorways.

Choir western part of the chancel, used by the choir, immediately east of the screen separating nave and chancel.

Clerestory upper storey of the nave (*see below*) of a church, generally pierced by a row of windows.

Corbel stone bracket, often richly carved, projecting from a wall to support roof beams, the ribs of a vault, a statue or an oriel window (*see below*).

Cornice crowning projection, the upper part of the entablature in classical architecture. Also used for the projecting decoration around the ceiling of a room.

Crossing central area of a cruciform church, where the transepts cross the nave and choir. A tower is often set above this space.

Crypt underground chamber beneath a church, used as place of burial or charnel-houses. They often also housed the bones or relics of a saint or martyr.

Cupola hemispherical roof.

Drum vertical walling supporting a dome, sometimes with windows.

Embrasure the space between two merlons (*see next page*), on a battlement, through which archers could fire, whilst protected by the merlons.

Entablature in classical architecture, the entire portion above the columns, comprising architrave, frieze (*see next page*) and cornice (*see above*).

Fan vaulting system of vaulting peculiar to English Perpendicular architecture, all ribs having the same curve, resembling the framework of a fan.

B. Kaufmann/MICHELIN

Finial top or finishing portion of a pinnacle, gable, bench end or other feature.

Fluting narrow concave channelling cut vertically on a shaft or column.

Flying buttress external arch springing over the roof of an aisle and supporting the clerestory wall, counteracting the thrust of the nave vault (💧 *see Buttress*).

Frieze central division of the entablature – horizontal decorative design at high level.

Gable triangular end section of a wall of a building, enclosed by the line of the roof.

Hammerbeam roof late Gothic form of roof construction with no tie-beam. Wooden arches rest on corbels and beams bracketed to the walls and eaves.

Harling wall plastered with roughcast. Often painted or with colour incorporated.

Jamb upright side of a window or door opening.

Keep inner tower and strongest part of a medieval fortress (💧 *see Donjon*).

Keystone central, wedge-shaped stone which locks an arch together (💧 *see Voussoir*).

Lancet Early English (13C) sharp-pointed arch.

Lantern glazed construction, for ventilation and light, often surmounting a dome.

Lierne short intermediate rib in Gothic vaulting.

Loggia open-sided gallery or arcade.

Machicolation in medieval military architecture, a row of openings below a projecting parapet through which missiles could be rained down on the enemy.

Merlon upstanding portion between two embrasures on a battlement.

Misericord tip-up seat in choir stalls, with a small projection on the underside, to support a person having to stand through a long service. Often fancifully and grotesquely carved.

Mullions vertical ribs dividing a window into a number of lights.

Narthex western portico at the entrance to early Christian churches.

Nave central main body of a church, west of the choir, into which lay persons were admitted, chancel and choir being reserved for the priests.

Ogee arch used in late Gothic period, combining convex and concave curve, ending in a point.

Oriel window projecting from a wall on corbels.

Pediment triangular termination above the entablature, in classical architecture sometimes "broken" in Renaissance designs.

Pilaster rectangular pillar, projecting from the wall.

Rose window circular window with mullions converging like the spokes of a wheel.

Screen partition, often richly carved, separating nave from choir and chancel.

Skewputt gable's corner stone.

Spandrel triangular space between the curves of arches and the frame in which they are set.

B. Kaufmann/MICHELIN

Squinch arch placed diagonally across the internal corner angles of a square tower, converting the square into an octagonal form.

Tierceron secondary rib in Gothic vaulting.

Transept arms of a cruciform church set at right angles to nave and choir.

Transom horizontal cross-bar or division of a window (💧 see Mullions).

Tympanum space between the flat lintel and the arch of a doorway.

Undercroft vaulted chamber partly or wholly below ground, in a medieval building.

Volute spiral scroll used at the corners of Ionic, Corinthian and Composite capitals.

Voussoir wedge-shaped stones of an arch, their sides tapering towards the imaginary centre of the circle of the arch.

STYLES

Roman – The Roman invasion began in Kent; **Richborough Castle** was part of the Roman system of coastal defences, a series of forts in the southeast under the control of the "Count of the Saxon Shore". Their capital was St Albans linked by military roads to other major settlements in Bath, Chester, Lincoln and York.

London was a trading post near a river crossing on the Thames.

Examples of domestic Roman architecture in Britain are the theatre at St Albans and the ruined **villas** at Chedworth, Fishbourne, Bignor and Brading with their mosaics.

Their greatest military enterprise was **Hadrian's Wall**, a defensive wall reinforced by military camps stretching from Wallsend on the Tyne to Bowness on the Solway Firth (73mi/117 km) to guard the northern boundary of the Empire.

Pre-Romanesque – Few buildings survive from this period, AD c 650 to the Norman Conquest. Much Saxon work, in timber, was destroyed in Viking raids. **All Saints, Brixworth** (c 680) in Northamptonshire makes use of Roman brick and the apse was surrounded by an external ring-crypt, a feature first found in St Peter's in Rome (c 590). **All Saints, at Earl's Barton** nearby, has a late Saxon tower. Saxon crypts survive at **Hexham, Repton** and **Ripon**.

Romanesque or Norman – These bold, massive buildings continued to be erected until after the death of Henry II in 1189 and nowhere else in Europe

is there such a richness or variation of Norman work, nor such an abundance of surviving examples. In English cathedrals, the naves tend to be much longer than on the Continent, for example **Ely** (13 bays) and **Norwich** (14); the eastern end was usually shorter. **Durham Cathedral**, begun in 1093, where the whole interior is one Romanesque scheme, is a fine example of Norman work in Britain, though externally only the lower parts of the tower and nave and the choir show true Romanesque work. Its stone vaulting, completed in 1133, survives in its original form. **Southwell Minster** has a west front c 1130, with later Perpendicular windows. The eastern end of **Norwich** cathedral is tri-apsidal. Its spire and clerestory are later Gothic, but the remainder is Norman. **Rochester, Gloucester, Peterborough, Lincoln, Exeter, Hereford, St Albans,** and the abbey churches of **Tewkesbury** and **Waltham**, are all part of England's heritage of Norman work.

Every county boasts many parish churches with a Norman nave or tower, west doorway, or south porch or chancel arch. **Iffley Church**, Oxfordshire, west front (c 1170), **St Mary and St David, Kilpeck**, Herefordshire (c 1140) with Scandinavian influence in the carving, and **St Nicholas, Barfreston**, Kent, are just some of the hundreds well worth visiting. Most secular buildings are fortifications. The **White Tower**, the keep of the Tower of London, was the first work (1080) of William the Conqueror; it had four storeys (over 90ft/30m high), massive walls (over 20ft/6m thick at the base) and small well-protected openings. **Rochester Castle** c 1130, though ruined, gives an impression of living conditions, with passages, garderobes and bedchambers in the thickness (12ft/3.5m) of the walls. **Chepstow Castle** (1067) is one of the earliest secular stone buildings in Britain.

Gothic – The style evolved in northern France; the Abbey of St Denis outside Paris is the earliest example. Gothic designs resulted in larger and higher buildings, flooded with light. Heavy columns were replaced by slimmer clustered column shafts; towers became taller and more slender.

In England Gothic architecture remained in use much longer than elsewhere in Europe, as it evolved through four distinct phases and retained its distinctive English characteristics.

Transitional (1145-89) – Transitional buildings have both pointed and round arches, especially in windows and vaults. **Ripon Cathedral** (1181) is a good example but the most outstanding is the choir of **Canterbury Cathedral.**

Early English (c 1190-1307) – Distinctive features are the ribbed vaults, narrow pointed arches and lancet windows. **Salisbury Cathedral**, built, apart from tower and spire, between 1220 and 1258, is the only English cathedral to have been built virtually in one operation, hence in a single style. See also **Wells**, the façades of **Peterborough** and **Ripon**, much of **Lichfield**, and the Abbeys of **Tintern** and **Fountains**, and **Bolton Priory**.

Decorated (c 1280-1377) – **Ely Cathedral,** with its octagon and lantern (1323-30), was one of the early experiments in new spatial form and lighting. Other examples include the west façades of **Exeter** and **York**.

Perpendicular – The last – and longest – phase of Gothic architecture in Britain is uniquely English in style. There is an emphasis on vertical lines but the principal features are panelled decoration all over the building, an increase in window area and the consequent development – very much later than in France – of the flying buttress. Fan-vault roofing, a peculiarly English design, can best be seen in **King's College Chapel,** Cambridge (1146-1515), **Eton College Chapel** (1441) and **St George's Chapel,** Windsor (1475-1509).
Contemporary with the fan-vault, and equally English, was the development of the **timber roof**. Tie and collar designs from the 13C and 14C developed into more complex 15C and 16C **hammerbeam** roofs over churches and

White Tower

guildhalls, of which **Westminster Hall** (Hugh Herland, c 1395) is an example. Others are the Great Hall at **Hampton Court** (1535) and **Rufford Old Hall,** near Ormskirk, Lancashire (1505). England also has a wealth of medieval timber-framed houses, built in areas where stone was scarce – **Rufford Old Hall**, the **Guildhall** at Lavenham and the **Feathers Hotel** in Ludlow.

Tudor-Jacobean – This period began with the accession of Henry VII in 1485 and covers the transition from Gothic to Classicism. Tudor Gothic, both ecclesiastical and secular, can be seen in **Bath Abbey** and the brick-built **Hampton Court Palace.**
From 1550 to 1620 building was largely domestic, for a thriving middle class and a wealthy aristocracy. **Longleat House** (1550-80) in Wiltshire, **Monta-**

Wells Cathedral

cute **House** (1588-1601) in Somerset, and Bess of Hardwick's **Hardwick Hall** (1591-97) in Derbyshire are outstanding examples. The courtyard layout of medieval days was abandoned for the E or H shaped plan, a central rectangular block with projecting wings. The **Long Gallery** – used for exercise on winter days – became a feature of all the great houses of the Elizabethan period.

Half-timbered houses were built in areas where stone was scarce – **Little Moreton Hall** (1559) in Cheshire and **Speke Hall**, near Liverpool, begun in 1490 and still being added to in 1612. The staircase began to assume an importance in the design of Elizabethan houses and by Jacobean times had become, in many houses, the focus of the whole interior – Ham, Hatfield, Knole and Audley End. The architectural ideas of the **Renaissance** were brought to England by **Inigo Jones** (1573-1652). His two most outstanding public buildings are the **Banqueting Hall** (1619-22) in London and the **Queen's House** (1616-35) in Greenwich.

He also rebuilt part of **Wilton House** (1647-53) in Wiltshire, where his adherence to Classical proportions is evident in the "double cube" room. Architects in England who had never seen an ancient Classical building based their work on "Pattern Books" published by Renaissance designers.

Tudor Forts – In 1538, faced with the threat of invasion to re-establish the Pope's authority, Henry VIII had to construct a chain of forts and batteries to prevent an enemy invasion fleet from making use of the principal anchorages, landing places and ports.

The first forts built in 1539-40 – Deal, Walmer and Dover in Kent, Calshot and Hurst, overlooking Southampton Water and The Solent, and St Mawes and Pendennis in Cornwall – were squat with thick walls and rounded parapets. In most a central circular keep was surrounded by lower round bastions or enclosed by a circular curtain wall. They were designed to be defended by cannon mounted on carriages and sited on several tiers of platforms to compensate for the limited vertical traverse of each cannon. Lateral traverse was limited only by the splay of the gun ports.

Classicism – Though Classicism was introduced by Inigo Jones, it was in the reign of Charles I (1625-49) that the style really began to make its mark on the English scene. The dominant figure was Sir **Christopher Wren** (1632-1723).

Welsh Marcher Castles

The four best-preserved – Conwy, Caernarfon, Harlech and Beaumaris – are among the most remarkable group of medieval monuments to be seen in Europe.

Between 1276 and 1296 17 castles were built or re-fortified by Edward I and his Marcher lords – Denbigh, Ruthin, Hawarden and Holt – to consolidate English power in North Wales.

The major castles were the work of the greatest military architect of the day, **Master James of St George**, brought by Edward from Savoy. Most were built to be supplied from the sea, as land travel in Snowdonia was impossible for Edward's forces. Square towers were replaced by round, which were less vulnerable to undermining; concentric defences, the inner overlooking outer, made their appearance. The garrisons of these massive stone fortifications were small – only some 30 men-at-arms plus a few cavalry and crossbowmen. Planned walled towns, similar to the "bastides" of southern France, housed the settlers who helped hold the territory. Documents detailing the conscription of labour from all over England, the costs of timber, stone, transport, a wall, a turret, even a latrine, can still be read.

After the Great Fire of London, he was responsible for 53 churches and the new **St Paul's Cathedral**, as well as the **Royal Naval College** at Greenwich and a new wing for **Hampton Court Palace**, which harmonises well with the Tudor brickwork. The **Sheldonian Theatre** (1669) at Oxford, and the **Library** of **Trinity College**, Cambridge (1676-84) are two of his best-known works outside London.

Sir John Vanbrugh (1664-1726), soldier and playwright, who turned architect in 1699, was one of the chief exponents of the **Baroque** in England; his masterpieces, produced in collaboration with **Nicholas Hawksmoor** (1661-1736), are **Castle Howard, Blenheim Palace** and **Seaton Delaval**. Hawksmoor, under a commission of 1711, designed six London churches. **St Mary Woolnoth** in the City of London survives to show his style.

Baroque architecture brought fantasy and movement to the classical order but found little favour in England. It was replaced in the 1720s with **Palladianism**, also a foreign "implant" but one with a symmetry which was eagerly adapted by architects such as **Colen Campbell (Houghton Hall)** and **William Kent (Holkham Hall)**. Palladian houses were set carefully in landscaped parks – many by **Capability Brown** – a far cry from the formality of French and Italian gardens of the period.

Robert Adam (1728-92), son of a Scottish architect, returned from the Grand Tour, having absorbed the principles of ancient architecture and learnt much neoclassical theory. He and his brothers set up in practice in London in 1758, introducing a lighter, more decorative style than the Palladian work then in vogue. Most of Adam's buildings are domestic and he also had great flair as an interior designer.

19C and 20C Architecture – The 19C was predominantly an age of stylistic revivals. The Industrial Revolution and the movement of people into towns stimulated the construction of factories and mills and housing. Iron and glass played a part in the mass-production of these buildings. At first individual craftsmanship was evident in mouldings, decoration and furniture but by 1900 much of this had vanished.

John Nash (1752-1835), builder of many terraces round Regent's Park and down Regent Street in London, also designed the **Royal Pavilion** at Brighton. **Sir John Soane** (1753-1837), probably the last of the original designers, is represented by his house at Lincoln's Inn Fields, now the **Sir John Soane Museum.**

From 1840 the trend was towards the Gothic revival which reached its height between 1855 and 1885. **Sir Charles Barry** (1795-1860) rebuilt the **Palace of Westminster** after the 1834 fire. Alfred Waterhouse (1830-1905) designed the Natural History Museum and built Manchester Town Hall.

The 19C was also the Railway Age. **Isambard Kingdom Brunel** (1806-59), Chief Engineer to the Great Western Railway in 1833, also designed the Clifton Suspension Bridge. **Thomas Telford** (1757-1834) built roads, bridges and canals throughout the country. He was responsible for the London-Holyhead road and for the bridge (1826) which carries it over the Menai Strait. In the 20C Art Nouveau had little influence on architecture but there was passing interest in interior decoration, fabrics and stained glass in the new style. Reinforced concrete was the main structural development.

Between the Wars, the outstanding figure was **Sir Edwin Lutyens** (1869-1944), who adapted Classicism to the needs of the day, in civic and housing design as well as ecclesiastical. His was the genius behind New Delhi in India and he also designed the **Cenotaph** in Whitehall,

and **Hampstead Garden Suburb** in London. **Sir Giles Gilbert Scott** (1880-1960), grandson of Sir George, the 19C architect, built the last great cathedral in the Gothic style, the red sandstone **Anglican Cathedral** of Liverpool. He also set the pattern for power stations with his 1929 design for **Battersea Power Station**.

"Urban planning" was not a 20C idea. Haussmann re-designed much of Paris in the 1860s and the Italian Renaissance painter Martini has left us his picture, painted in 1475, of *The Ideal City*. In Britain, **Welwyn Garden City**, built near St Albans in 1920, was the first of the New Towns, an extension of the idea of the Garden Suburb. The planned layout of streets, cul-de-sacs and closes, romantically named and lined with semi-detached and detached houses, was copied all over the country after the 1939-45 war, in an attempt to check the "urban sprawl" in London, Lancashire, the Clyde Valley and South Wales. The 1946 New Towns Act provided for 28 such New Towns; **Harlow New Town** by Gibberd was built in 1947, **Cumbernauld**, near Glasgow, in the 1950s and **Milton Keynes** in rural Buckinghamshire in the 1970s. As costs escalated and concern grew over the decay of city centres the building of complete new towns was halted. Pedestrian zones and the banishing of traffic have helped to conserve both the fabric and spirit of established town and city centres. **Poundbury** village in Dorchester, Dorset (1993-94), which stresses the importance of architecture on a human scale and is sponsored by the Prince of Wales, represents the latest trend in urban planning.

Outstanding among examples of 20C architecture is **Sir Basil Spence's Coventry Cathedral** (1956-62), remarkable in itself and in the way it blends with the older buildings around it. The imaginative circular design of **The Metropolitan Cathedral of Christ the King** (1926-27) in Liverpool was the work of **Sir Frederick Gibberd**. In the secular sphere, education – established and new universities – and the arts provided good opportunities for pioneering work: Sainsbury Centre for the Visual Arts, East Anglia, Norman Foster 1991; Downing College library, Cambridge, Quinlan Terry 1987; St John College Garden Quad, Oxford, 1993. Custom-built galleries were designed for the Sainsbury Collection (1970s) at Norwich (Norman Foster), Burrell's donation in Glasgow (B Gasson) and the Tate Gallery at St Ives (1993, Evans and Shalev).

Other areas which have provided great scope for exciting modern architecture over the last few years are sports venues – the new Wembley Stadium and Lords' Cricket Ground stand (Michael Hopkins); opera houses – Glyndebourne and Covent Garden, Royal Opera House refurbishment and extension; London office developments – Lloyd's Building, Canary Wharf, Broadgate, The Ark, Swiss Re Tower ("the Gherkin") and City Hall. Major commissions (bridges, community and other projects approved by the Millennium Commission) heralded an explosion of original design for the turn of the century. Many of these are now hugely popular visitor attractions: the Eden Project, Cornwall; Dynamic Earth, Edinburgh; the Great Glasshouse at the National Botanic Garden of Wales; The Lowry, The Imperial War Museum of the North and Urbis, all Manchester; the Glasgow Science Centre and the Armadillo, also in Glasgow. All break new ground in structural and materials technology.

The most controversial have been the Millennium Dome, London, which has remained empty for much of its brief and unhappy existence (though it will probably fulfil an important role in the 2012 Olympics) and the Scottish Parliament building in Edinburgh, finally completed in 2004 three years late and ten times overbudget.

The regeneration of derelict industrial sites and obsolete docks has met with considerable success in Liverpool, Cardiff and particularly the massive London Dockland scheme of the 1990s (still ongoing).

The conservation and re-use of existing indistrial buildings is most apparent in two huge and stunning art galleries at opposite ends of the country, Tate Modern, in London (formerly a power station) and the Baltic Centre for Contemporary Art, in Gateshead (formerly a flour mill).

The Lloyd's Building

Ph. Gajic/MICHELIN

VERNACULAR BUILDINGS

From the end of the medieval period, relative civil peace meant that security was no longer of paramount importance and that the fortified castle could give way to the rural residence designed as a setting for that distinctive culture which at its best combined artistic patronage and a degree of learning with a stylish social round, field sports with progressive farm management. The results are impressive, each generation of the rich and powerful seeking to establish or consolidate its status by building or rebuilding in accord with the dictates of national or international architectural fashion.

It is however in the everyday architecture of cottage, farmhouse and barn that an intimate dialogue takes place between local materials and local skills and which expresses most strongly the individuality of particular places. The range of materials used is enormous, a reflection of man's ingenuity and geological diversity. Every type of stone has been quarried and shaped, from the most intractable of Scottish Aberdeen, Peterhead and Cornish granites to the crumbling, barely suitable chalk of the south. The limestones are often exploited to wonderful effect, as in the **Cotswolds** or the **Yorkshire Wolds**. Where stone is lacking, timber is used – structurally, as in the **cruck-built cottages** of Weobley near Hereford and the elaborate half-timbered houses of much of the Midlands, or as cladding in the tarred or painted **"weather-boarding"** of the southeast coast. In the claylands, most villages once had their own brickfield, producing distinctive tiles as well as bricks, while reedbeds provided thatch for roofing. Less favoured areas, with no one material of particular merit, now have some of the most delightful townscapes, an amalgam of timber, tile and brick, stones and slate, even flints from the fields or pebbles from the beach (Lewes).

Building forms vary as much as materials; few contrasts could be greater than that of the solid **timber-framed house** of a Kentish yeoman (Weald and Downland Open Air Museum) with the humble one-roomed dwelling of a crofter in northwest Scotland **(Black House)**. Settlement patterns are also almost infinitely varied. In the uplands, the isolated farm, sheltered perhaps by a wind-break of sycamores, is characteristic; in the well-watered west, a few cottages and farms may be loosely grouped to form a hamlet; elsewhere, true villages may predominate, street villages accompanying a road for part of its way, others clustered sociably around a green (Long Melford and Dalmeny). Many, having occupied their sites for centuries, are the very image of timeless tranquillity; others are tougher, like the fishing villages on the sea coast (Craster, Polperro and Crail) or the 19C industrial villages, long blank-eyed terraces stretching from pub to chapel, in the shadow of mine or factory (Pontypool and Longton).

PARKS AND GARDENS

A keen appreciation of country life and the pleasures of Nature goes back to the Middle Ages when Royal Forests covered much of the land and every person of consequence had a deer park. It was in the 18C, however, that the face of lowland Britain was transformed in pursuit of the aesthetic ideals of the country's "greatest original contribution to the arts", the **English Landscape Movement**. Ruthlessly sweeping away the grand avenues, parterres and topiary of the previous century, the grandees and lesser gentry of the Georgian age, aided by professionals like **Lancelot "Capability" Brown** (1716-83) and **Humphry Repton** (1752-1818), swept away the boundaries separating house, garden and surrounding countryside to make ambitious compositions fusing buildings and statuary, lawns and woodland, lakes and rivers into a picturesque vision of an idealised Nature. As well as their grander creations (Blenheim, Stourhead), there are many lesser achievements in the field of landscape beautification, which has bequeathed a national passion for landscaping and horticulture.

Britain has a wonderful heritage of gardens, many of which are open to visitors. Owing to the vagaries of the climate, particularly the closeness of the Gulf Stream, conditions have proved favourable to many of the plant collections brought back from all over the world, particularly in the 18C and 19C. The chief name in garden design in the late 19C and early 20C was Gertrude Jekyll (Knebworth and Broughton Castle), who often worked in collaboration with the architect Sir Edwin Lutyens.

Plant trials and serious **horticultural study** are conducted at Kew Gardens in London, at Wisley in Surrey, the gardens of the Royal Horticultural Society, at Harlow Carr and the Botanic Gardens in Edinburgh (17C) and Glasgow. A few of the earliest **medicinal gardens** are still in existence, such as the Botanic Gardens (1621) in Oxford and the Chelsea Physic Garden (1673) in London.

A Museum of **Garden History** occupies Lambeth parish church and graveyard, where John Tradescant, gardener to King Charles I, is buried. Examples of the early knot garden have been created here and at Hampton Court. Formal gardens with geometric layout can be seen at Hampton Court, Ham House and Pitmedden. The most prevalent style is the famous English Landscape, promoted by Capability Brown and Humphry Repton – Stourhead and Castle Howard.

The art of **topiary** is practised at Levens Hall and Earlshall in Scotland. The vogue for follies, usually an artificial ruin at the end of a vista, produced Studley Royal which achieves its climax with a view of the ruins of Fountains Abbey.

Less contrived gardens incorporate the natural features of the site, such as **Glendurgan**, which occupies a deep combe on the Cornish coast.

Gardens range from the most southerly, Tresco **Abbey Gardens** in the Scilly Isles, created and maintained since 1834 by successive generations of the same family, to the most northerly, **Inverewe** in Wester Ross, where, despite the northern latitude, the gardens are frost-free, owing to the warm North Atlantic Drift.

Sissinghurst and Crathes Castle are examples of themed gardens, where the different enclosures are distinguished by colour, season or plant species.

Sculpture

The idea of erecting statues, in stone and bronze, introduced largely by the Romans, fell into disuse in Britain in the Dark Ages. Gradually, however, pagan influences and Celtic scroll-work were put to Christian service, in standing crosses and in church decoration. Massive carving in Norman churches gave way to glorious tracery, windows, ribs and vaults in Early English and Perpendicular churches and cathedrals, complemented by carved wooden misericords, bench ends, altar screens and font covers. Impressive statuary such as that on the west front of Wells Cathedral has survived Reformation and Puritan depredations, to give an idea of the skills of early craftsmen.

Until the early 18C, statuary tended to be confined to tombs and memorials. The fashion for portrait busts was introduced by those who made the "Grand Tour" of Europe.

First Classical and then Baroque memorials began to grace both cathedrals and churches in the flowering of British sculpture which took place between 1720 and 1840. In the Victorian age in many towns and cities statues were erected to the memory of industrialists and benefactors, municipal worthies and military heroes. There are also some very fine sculpted memorials executed in commemoration of those who died in battle.

In the 20C British sculpture has been enlivened by the sometimes controversial works of **Jacob Epstein** and also of **Henry Moore**, whose technique of "natural carving" allowed the grain and shape of the material to dictate the final form. **Barbara Hepworth**, who settled in St Ives in 1943, **Reg Butler** and **Kenneth Armitage** are among other famous modern sculptors.

Monumental sculptures by Jacob Epstein, Eric Gill, Frank Dobson, Henry Moore, Barbara Hepworth and Eduardo Paolozzi among others set the standard for public art in cities, by the sea and in the countryside. Spectacular modern schemes – Broadgate in London, Herne Bay Sculpture Park, Brighton seafront, sculpture at Goodwood near Chichester, Stour Valley Art Project, Yorkshire Sculpture Park, the Gateshead Riverside Sculpture Park, the Northern Arts Project, Glenrothes in Scotland – have inspired major artists to create large-scale outdoor sculptures and promote interest in art in a wider public.

On the contemporary scene the trend is a break with the past as many artists (Damien Hirst, Anish Kapoor, Richard Deacon, Cornelia Parker, Alison Wilding, Stephen Hughes, Tony Cragg, Rachel Whiteread among others) invent new idioms which are sometimes provocative. The Turner Prize awarded by the Tate Gallery is often controversial. Installations which aim to engage the viewer's preconceptions are increasingly popular.

Painting

Early Art – The Celtic peoples loved rhythm and curvilinear scroll patterns, which they used in jewellery and later in manuscripts. The Romans brought their wall paintings and mosaics and both later inspired the medieval church murals – allegories to impress and instruct – which are some of Britain's earliest paintings. Surviving painting from the Saxon and medieval periods consists largely of exquisite work on illuminated manuscripts, such as the **Lindisfarne Gospels** from Holy Island, though the drawings of **Matthew Paris** are notable departures from this stylised work. One of the earliest English paintings is the **Wilton Diptych** (c 1400), now in the National Gallery.

16C-18C – British artists never enjoyed that scale of patronage given to European artists by absolute monarchs and the Papacy. Much early portraiture, other than

St Ives, Cornwall by Ben Nicholson

Courtesy of the Tate Gallery, London

the **Holbein** pictures of Henry VIII and his court, tend to be flat and stiff but the art of the miniature flourished at the court of Elizabeth, where **Nicholas Hilliard** and **Isaac Oliver** created their masterpieces, capturing both the likeness and something of the spirit of the sitters.

The Dutchman **Sir Anthony van Dyck**, knighted by Charles I, enjoyed his patronage and was the first to record the atmosphere of the Stuart Court, in full size paintings, before the Civil War. Canaletto, a Venetian, enjoyed some aristocratic support in the 1740s, as did **Sir Peter Lely** and **Godfrey Kneller,** both of German origin, who worked in England for long enough to be considered founders of the English portrait painting school. **William Hogarth,** English-born and bred, famous for his vivid commentaries on the life of his day, started the idea of public exhibitions of painting, leading ultimately to the founding in 1768 of the **Royal Academy**. **Sir Joshua Reynolds,** its first President, and his contemporary, **Thomas Gainsborough,** raised the status of English painting, especially portraiture, though it was still much influenced by Dutch and Italian example.

Richard Wilson, founder Member of the Royal Academy, was much inspired by the French masters, Claude and Poussin, and founded the English school of **landscape painting,** a fashion which developed in England and spread to include marine scenes as well as country houses and estates.

The Romantic Movement – The visionary, **William Blake**, heralded the dawn of English Romanticism. Portraiture by **Sir Thomas Lawrence** and the works of **Sir Henry Raeburn** in Scotland added Romanticism to the traditions of Reynolds. **John Crome** founded the Norwich School in 1803, a regional treatment of landscape painting which was uniquely English. It was continued after his death by **John Sell Cotman. John Constable** and **Joseph MW Turner** carried this tradition and its studies of the effects of ever-changing light into the 19C. From 1840 to 1850 **Dante Gabriel Rossetti's** group, the **Pre-Raphaelites** and **Sir Edward Burne-Jones**, made a short-lived return to primitive values and religious and moral subjects. Their designs inspired Art Nouveau, best expressed in England by the work of **William Morris** and **Aubrey Beardsley.**

19C trends – **Alfred Sisley,** born in Paris of English parents, was an Impressionist whose sense of colour and tone owed much to the founder of the movement, Claude Monet. The **Camden Town Group,** around **Walter Sickert,** returned to the realism of the Post-Impressionists, whose work **Roger Fry** had exhibited in 1911 and the next 20 years saw many short-lived and loose "movements" such as the **Bloomsbury Group. Augustus John** was known for his fashionable portraits in an almost Impressionist style.

20C – Post-war artists include **Paul Nash** (landscapes infused with symbolism); **Graham Sutherland**, painter of religious themes, landscapes and portraits; **Sir Stanley Spencer** who painted Biblical scenes in familiar British settings. In the 1950s **Ben Nicholson** was the major abstract artist. The optimistic 1960s brought Pop Art: **Peter Blake, David Hockney, Bridget Riley** ("op art"). The portraits and figures of **Francis Bacon** and **Lucian Freud** show a darker, more pessimistic outlook.

Contemporary artists who have won acclaim include Gilbert and George, Paula Rego, Beryl Cooke, Ken Currie, Adrian Wizniewski, Stephen Conroy, Peter Howson, Lisa Milroy, Richard Wentworth, Julian Opie, Damien Hirst among others. The Goldsmith College of Art and the Glasgow School of Art are two of the well-known educational establishments which nurture young talent. Hirst himself was partially responsible for founding The Young British Art group (Angela Bulloch, Michael Landy, Gary Hume etc), the country's most recent art phenomenon. Their work is still championed by the Saatchi Gallery, though many YBAs have now been assimilated into the mainstream.

Music

From Polyphony to instrumental composition – As with painting and sculpture, early and medieval English music was largely inspired by religion. The **Chapel Royal** – an institution, not a building – has fostered English music since 1135. **Thomas Tallis** (c 1505-85), organist at Waltham Abbey near London (until it was dissolved) and later at Queen Elizabeth's Chapel Royal, can be credited with beginning the particularly rich tradition of **church music** for which England is famous. He arranged the harmony for the plainsong responses of Merbecke's English church service (Festal Responses in four and five parts) which are still widely in use and also arranged a setting of the Canticles in Dorian Mode, composed numerous anthems, Latin mass settings, lamentations and motets, of which his most famous is the magnificent *Spem in Alium* for forty voices, and of course his equally famous Canon (c 1567). Together with **William Byrd** (1542/3-1623), himself a prolific composer of high quality church music with whom Tallis was joint organist at the Chapel Royal, he was granted a monopoly on music printing in England (1575).

From the end of the 16C to c 1630, **madrigals**, originally an Italian form, with amorous or satirical themes, were being produced in large numbers by English composers, such as Byrd and **John Dowland** (1562-1626), a talented lute player. Folk music dating back much further accompanied the country dance, which survives today as the **Morris Dance**. Composers such as Byrd and **Thomas Morley** (1557-1602), who wrote settings for several of Shakespeare's plays, spread music into the theatre. **John Bull** (1562-1628), a skilled performer and composer for the virginals, ranks for many as one of the founders of the English keyboard repertoire. He is also sometimes linked with the original tune for *God Save The Queen*. **Ben Jonson** (1573-1637) and **Henry Lawes** (1596-1662) among others were leading exponents of the **masque**, which became popular in the 17C, combining music, dance and pageantry.

Orlando Gibbons (1583-1625), organist of the Chapel Royal under James I and one of the finest keyboard players of his day, wrote quantities of superb church music, madrigals and music for viols and virginals. **Henry Purcell** (1659-95), considered the greatest British composer of his generation (and by some of all time), wrote much splendid church music, stage music (opera *Dido and Æneas*), music for State occasions and harpsichord and chamber music.

Music Applied to Drama – Chamber music (music not intended for church, theatre or public concert room) truly came into its own in the 18C, which also saw great strides taken in the development of English **opera** and the emergence of a new form, the **oratorio**, under the German-English composer **George Frideric Handel** (1685-1759), perhaps its greatest exponent. His vast output included more than 40 operas, 20 or so oratorios, cantatas, sacred music, and numerous orchestral, choral and instrumental works. In 1719-28 the **Royal Academy of Music** was founded as an operatic organisation linked with Handel. The following century (1822) it became an educational institution, later to be joined by the Royal College of Music (1883) and the Royal School of Church Music (1927).

Post-Romanticism and the Modern Age – The composer Thomas Arne (1710-78) set to music the words of James Thomson, *Rule Britannia,* in a masque for Alfred, Prince of Wales in 1740. The late 18C to early 19C was rather a fallow period for Britain in terms of musical composition, although the Romantic movement that swept through Europe made itself felt in other arts such as literature (Wordsworth, Coleridge, Scott), and Romantic song cycles were fashionable with the British public in the 19C.

The next British composer of note was **Sir Edward Elgar** (1857-1934), the first to win international acclaim in almost 200 years. His love of the English countryside (he lived near the Malvern Hills) shaped his music, which is infused with an Englishness that captures the spirit of a nation in its heyday as a world power. Works such as *The Enigma Variations* and *The Dream of Gerontius* placed him on the world stage, and his many orchestral works exhibit the composer's masterly orchestration (Symphonies in A flat and E flat, Cello Concerto). **Frederick Delius** (1862-1934), championed by the conductor Sir Thomas Beecham, composed orchestral variations, rhapsodies, concerti and a variety of other orchestral and choral works stamped with his very individual, chromatic approach to harmony. The compositions of **Ralph Vaughan Williams** (1872-1958) were influenced by his study of English folk songs and Tudor church music; throughout his life he took an active interest in popular movements in music. **Gustav Holst** (1874-1934), prevented from becoming a concert pianist by neuritis in his hand, studied music at the Royal College of Music under Sir Charles Villiers Stanford (1852-1924), an Irish composer of church music and choral works. Holst, an ardent socialist, influenced by his love of the works of Grieg and Wagner as well as a certain innate mysticism, produced his most famous work, the seven-movement orchestral suite *The Planets*, in 1914-16.

Sir William Walton (1902-83) rose to fame with his instrumental settings of poems by Edith Sitwell (*Façade*, 1923) and went on to compose symphonies, concerti, opera, the Biblical cantata *Belshazzar's Feast* and film music (Laurence Olivier's *Henry V, Hamlet* and *Richard III*). **Sir Michael Tippett** (1905-98) won recognition with his oratorio *A Child of Our Time,* reflecting the unrest of the 1930s and 1940s, and went on to produce a rich and varied output, including operas *(The Midsummer Marriage, King Priam)*, symphonies and other orchestral works in which he exhibits formidable powers of imagination and invention, combining inspiration from earlier sources such as Purcell with his interest in popular modern music such as blues and jazz.

Sir Benjamin Britten (1913-76) studied under John Ireland (1879-1962) at the Royal College of Music and after a couple of years in the USA returned to England where he produced mainly vocal or choral works (one exception being his *Variations and Fugue on a Theme of Purcell*, or *Young Person's Guide to the Orchestra)*, notably the operas *Peter Grimes, Billy Budd* and *A Midsummer Night's Dream, A Ceremony of Carols* and the immensely moving *War Requiem*. **John Tavener** (b. 1944), whose haunting *Song for Athene* ended the funeral service of Diana, Princess of Wales, at Westminster Abbey in September 1997, draws the inspiration for his predominantly religious music from his Russian Orthodox faith.

Still popular since their inception by **Sir Henry Wood** (1869-1944) in 1895 are the **Promenade Concerts,** which are held at the Royal Albert Hall every summer *(mid-July to mid-September)*. The chorus *Jerusalem* sung as an unofficial anthem at the end of each season of Promenade concerts is perhaps the best known work of Sir Hubert Parry (1848-1918). Conductors and composers such as Sir Peter Maxwell Davies, Sir Neville Mariner, Sir John Eliot Gardner, Sir Colin Davis, Sir Simon Rattle, Christopher Hogwood and Andrew Davies ensure the continuation of healthy and creative British music. Eisteddfods in Wales and Mods in Scotland carry on a tradition of the Celtic bards. Festivals, such as the **Three Choirs** at Hereford, Worcester and Gloucester Cathedrals and – in completely different spheres – opera productions at **Glyndebourne** and the **English National Opera** contribute to the aim of maintaining public interest in live classical music.

Coda – On a lighter note, the meeting in 1875 of **Sir William Gilbert** (1836-1911) and **Sir Arthur Sullivan** (1842-1900) produced an enduring and well-loved English musical tradition in the form of "Gilbert and Sullivan" operas, staged by Richard D'Oyly Carte. **Musical comedy,** an English development of the European operetta, was born in the 1890s at the Gaiety Theatre in London, with shows like *The Gaiety Girl*. Another typically British institution, the **music hall**, also became popular – variety entertainment with the audience being able to eat and drink while watching the performance. Two names, **Ivor Novello** (1893-1951) and **Sir Noël Coward** (1899-1973), will always be associated with British musical comedy between the World Wars. The tradition of British musicals has since been continued most notably by **Sir Andrew Lloyd Webber** (b. 1948).

Literature and Language

LITERATURE

Middle Ages – **Geoffrey Chaucer** (c 1340-1400), the first great English poet, was influential in the evolution of "standard" English from cruder medieval dialects. The language of the *Canterbury Tales* is consequently as recognisable to us today as are Chaucer's vividly etched characters. **William Langland** (c 1330-1400) in the *Vision of Piers Plowman*, and **Sir Thomas Malory** (d 1471) in *Le Morte D'Arthur* also brought a new depth and expressiveness to literature.

The English Renaissance and the Elizabethan Age – The sonnet was introduced and blank verse became the regular measure of English dramatic and epic poetry. The supreme achievement of this dynamic, expansive period was in the theatre. Ambitious dramatic forms developed by the fiery **Christopher Marlowe** (1564-94) were perfected by the protean genius of **William Shakespeare** (1564-1616), the greatest dramatist and poet of this or any age. His monumental 37 plays appealed to all classes, from the groundlings to the nobility. **Ben Jonson** (1572-1637) created the English comedy of humours.

Seventeenth Century – John Donne (1572-1631), courtier, soldier and latterly Dean of St Paul's, was the most important of the Metaphysical poets whose "witty conceits" were concerned with the interaction between soul and body, sensuality and spirit. **John Milton** (1608-74), after Shakespeare arguably England's greatest poet, was also a powerful pamphleteer for the Puritan cause. He overcame blindness and political disappointment to write his epic masterpiece *Paradise Lost* in 1667. Puritan control was responsible for closing the theatres for nearly 20 years until the Restoration of

Charles II in 1660. Restoration drama primarily reflected the licentiousness of the Court by the use of broad satire, farce, wit and bawdy comedy.

In prose, the language of the Bible – particularly the Authorised Version of 1611 – exerted a strong influence, most notably in the work of **John Bunyan** (1628-88) whose *Pilgrim's Progress* was more widely read than any book in English except the Bible itself. Enormously popular too, but in a very different vein, was *The Compleat Angler* by **Izaak Walton** (1593-1683), which not only gave instruction on fishing but also offered a personal contemplation of Nature. The diaries of **John Evelyn** (1620-1706) and **Samuel Pepys** (1633-1703) detailed the minutiae of everyday life at the time.

Eighteenth Century – The early development of the novel is probably best exemplified in the work of Daniel Defoe (1660-1731). While his *Journal of the Plague Year* is a lively but primarily factual piece of journalism, *Robinson Crusoe*, though it utilises similar reporting techniques, is entirely fiction. Defoe's style was imitated and developed by **Samuel Richardson** (1689-1761), **Henry Fielding** (1707-54) and **Laurence Sterne** (1713-68) in *Tristram Shandy*.

Though the rise of the novel (together with the newspaper) and the expansion of a newly literate middle class were signposts for future developments, the Age of Reason was as notable for other literary achievements. **Alexander Pope** (1688-1744), the finest satirical poet of the time, was matched in both poetry and prose by **Jonathan Swift** (1667-1745), famous for the incisive political and social satire of *Gulliver's Travels*. The age was dominated, however, by the influence of **Samuel Johnson** (1709-84), now best remembered as the subject of Boswell's famous biography and the author of the first *English Dictionary* in 1755.

Nineteenth Century – The French Revolution was a primary inspiration for the Romantic movement, which stressed intensity of emotion rather than elegance and art, freedom of expression rather than stylistic rules. The rebellious spirit of the movement was epitomised in the life of **Lord Byron** (1788-1824) though perhaps a better representative of Romantic poetry is **William Wordsworth** (1770-1850), whose best poems reflect his belief that intense joy could arise from deep harmony with Nature. **Percy Bysshe Shelley** (1792-1822) wrote more directly of the power of joy as a reforming influence, while the intense, lyrical verse of **John Keats** (1795-1821) stressed the power of beauty. Though lyricism, nature and the exotic continued to attract Victorian poets such as **Robert Browning** (1812-89), faith in joy and the senses waned and the verse of **Alfred, Lord Tennyson** (1809-1902) is noble but sombre.

The novel, meanwhile, had continued to develop in range and appeal. The carefully structured domestic comedies of **Jane Austen** (1775-1817) are at once amusing and deeply serious, though the historical novels of her contemporary, **Sir Walter Scott** (1771-1832), were at the time more popular. Popular too were Scott's Victorian successors, **William Makepeace Thackeray** (1811-63), **Anthony Trollope** (1815-82) and, above all, **Charles Dickens** (1812-70), whose sentimental but funny and sometimes despairing vision of city life in the Industrial Revolution struck a deep chord with the reading public. Mary Ann Evans (1819-80), under the pseudonym **George Eliot,** wrote realistic works about the problems of the provincial middle class. Her novels are notable as much for the development and interplay of character as for plot and action. The **Brontë** sisters, **Charlotte** (1816-55) and **Emily** (1818-48), took inspiration from their upbringing on the wild moors of Yorkshire to write their respective masterpieces, *Jane Eyre* (1846) and *Wuthering Heights* (1847). Most important of the writers of the century is **Thomas Hardy** (1840-1928), whose novels express a passionate feeling for man's tragic involvement in Nature and estrangement from it.

National Portrait Gallery

Charles Dickens

Influenced by the new drama in Europe, **George Bernard Shaw** (1856-1950) brought a new purpose and seriousness to the English theatre which had, for nearly two centuries, failed to find a clear direction. The witty comedies of **Oscar Wilde** (1854-1900) were less profound but equally well crafted. They reflected the aims of the Decadent movement which stressed flagrantly amoral beauty – a direct reaction against the undue moral earnestness of the Victorian Age.

Twentieth Century – The early modern masters of the **novel – Henry James** (1843-1916), **Joseph Conrad** (1857-1924) and **EM Forster** (1879-1970) – were still working in a recognisably Victorian tradition. The need for new forms of self-expression, able to encompass a growing awareness of the unconscious, gave rise to a strong individualistic movement. The Dubliner **James Joyce** (1882-1941) used the stream-of-consciousness technique in the highly experimental *Ulysses* (1922) and *Finnegans Wake* (1939). This insistent excavation of personal experience is also found in the very different novels of **Virginia Woolf** (1882-1941) and of **DH Lawrence** (1885-1930) who challenged the taboos of class and sex, particularly in his novel *Lady Chatterley's Lover*. Concurrent with the serious "literary" novel, there developed a growing market for lighter fiction – entertainments – to serve the needs of an increasingly literate public; from the adventure novels of **Robert Louis Stevenson** (1850-94) and the *Sherlock Holmes* stories of **Arthur Conan Doyle** (1859-1930) to the spy thrillers of John Le Carré and Len Deighton in our own time. **George Orwell's** (1903-59) dark political novels *(Animal Farm, 1984)* condemned the evils of communism.

Throughout the century there have been a number of important and stylish writers – less iconoclastic than their more innovative peers – who have continued to work with more traditional subjects and themes. The novelists **Aldous Huxley** (1894-1963), **Evelyn Waugh** (1903-66), and **Graham Greene** (1904-91) achieved considerable critical as well as commercial success, while **Somerset Maugham** (1874-1965) and **JB Priestley** (1894-1984) triumphed equally as playwrights and novelists.

The novel has, in all its forms, become the dominant vehicle of literary expression in the modern age. Eminent contemporary writers range from Anthony Powell who portrays society in crisis owing to political events *(A Dance to the Music of Time)*; Paul Scott writing on the nostalgia of Lost Empire (1920-78, *The Raj Quartet, Staying On)*; Anthony Burgess with his masterly use of language and provocative novels *(A Clockwork Orange* and *Earthly Powers);* Lawrence Durrell who wrote the evocative *Alexandria Quartet* (1957); William Golding, author of *Lord of the Flies* (1954) and *Rites of Passage* (1980), studies of human behaviour; the prolific writer Iris Murdoch (1919-99; *Under the Net; The Sea, The Sea)* who explores complex psychological issues; to John Fowles' haunting stories *(The French Lieutenant's Woman, The Magus)*. Doris Lessing *(The Golden Notebook)*, Muriel Spark *(The Prime of Miss Jean Brodie)*, Daphne du Maurier *(Rebecca, Jamaica Inn)* and Olivia Manning *(The Balkan Trilogy)* are also distinguished authors.

Among the new generation of writers who have won acclaim are Martin Amis *(London Fields, The Information)*, Julian Barnes *(The History of the World in 10 1/2 chapters)*, JG Ballard *(The Empire of the Sun, Crash, Cocaine Nights)*, Angela Carter *(Wise Children, The Magic Toyshop)*, AS Byatt *(Possession)*, Anita Brookner *(Hotel du Lac)*, Beryl Bainbridge *(Every Man for Himself)*, Jeanette Winterson *(Oranges Are Not the Only Fruit)*, Graham Swift *(Last Orders)*, Pat Barker *(Regeneration Trilogy)*, Irvine Welsh *(Trainspotting)*.

The English language tradition is continuously enriched by writers from the Commonwealth and other countries who bring different perceptions into play: VS Naipaul, Caryl Phillips from the Caribbean, Nadine Gordimer, André Brink, JM Coetzee, Ben Okri from Africa; Peter Carey, Thomas Keneally, JG Ballard from Australia, Keri Hume from New Zealand, Salman Rushdie, Vikram Seth, Arundhati Roy from the Indian sub-continent, Timothy Mo from Hong Kong, Kazuo Ishiguro from Japan to name but a few.

Poetry, comparatively speaking, is less widely read than in previous times. The Romantic decadence of the early 20C was swept aside by the modernist poets **Ezra Pound** (1885-1972) and **TS Eliot** (1888-1965) whose *The Waste Land* (1922) is a dense and highly literary meditation on the situation of modern man. Less dramatically modern but equally influential was the slightly earlier poetry of **Thomas Hardy** and **WB Yeats** (1865-1939). The poets of the First World War, particularly **Wilfred Owen** (1893-1918) and **Siegfried Sassoon** (1886-1967), voiced their horror of mass warfare in realistic, pungent images which also looked forward not back. **WH Auden** (1907-73) led a prominent group of intellectual left-wing poets in the 1920s, though it was the exuberant imagery and lyrical rhetoric of **Dylan Thomas** (1914-53) that caught the public's imagination. Only **John Betjeman** (1906-84), with his sympathetic eulogies to the mundane and everyday, has achieved comparable popularity in recent times. Philip Larkin (1922-91) was the leading figure of the group known as the Movement; the cool tone and tight form of his poetry expressing his melancholy sensibilities was in reaction to the romantic excesses of the 1940s. Stevie Smith's instinctive, tender and humorous style captured the spirit of the mid 20C. Poet Laureate Ted Hughes (1930-98), best known for his violent and symbolic nature poems, is one of the most influential contemporary poets. Tom Paulin, Andrew Motion, Roger McGough, Benjamin Zephaniah, Carol Ann Duffy, Wendy Cope, and Helen Dunmore are also notable figures.

The **theatre** of the first half of the century was dominated by well-crafted "traditional" plays and the sophisticated comedies of Noël Coward. In the 1950s however, new voices started to be heard. The Theatre of the Absurd, which saw man as a helpless creature in a meaningless universe, was explored by the Irish writer **Samuel Beckett** (1906-89) and, later in the decade, disillusionment with contemporary Britain was vented by **John Osborne** (1929-94) in his play *Look Back In Anger*. The pithy "comedies of menace" by **Harold Pinter** (b 1930) and the socialist plays of writers such as **Arnold Wesker** (b 1932) were also highly influential and subsequently led to the development of a diverse and challenging contemporary theatre which reflected the fragmentation and problems of modern society. Trenchant plays by Edward Bond, Peter Shaffer, Alan Ayckbourn, David Hare and Tom Stoppard are highlights of the British theatre season. The Edinburgh Festival and The Fringe provide a stage for avant-garde plays by aspiring playwrights which often transfer successfully to mainstream theatres.

LANGUAGE

The English language is a mighty river, fed and enriched by streams of words from many tongues; it owes its rich vocabulary to the many peoples who have settled in Great Britain or with whom the British have come into contact through overseas exploration and conquest.

In 1600 there were about 2 million English speakers. The number is now nearer 400 million, including not only the population of countries such as Australia and New Zealand, Canada and the United States of America, but also of those where English is the only common and therefore the official second language.

Celtic – Celtic-speakers were pushed westward by the invading Anglo-Saxons and their language was relegated to "second class" status. Gaelic, as some of the various branches of the Celtic language are now known, is however still spoken to some extent in Scotland, Wales and Ireland. One major reason for the suppression and decline of the Gaelic tongue in both Scotland and Ireland was the fact that they supported the losing side in England's quarrels with the Pope.

Cornish – This branch of the Celtic languages was the only language of the Cornish peninsula until towards the end of the reign of Henry VIII. Although Dolly Pentreath, who was born in Mousehole in 1686 and died in December 1777, is claimed to be the last speaker of Cornish, there were no doubt other Cornish speakers, none of whom would have outlived the 18C.

Welsh – In the Statute of Rhuddlan in 1284 Edward I recognised Welsh as an official and legal language. After the Battle of Bosworth in 1485 Welsh nobles hopefully followed the Tudors to London but Henry VIII decreed that "no person shall hold office within the Realme except they exercise the English speech".

The tradition of poetry and literature in the Welsh language, guarded by the **bards** and **eisteddfodau**, dates from Taliesin in the 7C. In 1588 the Bible was published in Welsh by Bishop Morgan and it was largely the willingness of the Church in Wales to preach in Welsh which saved the language from extinction. Reading in Welsh was encouraged by the Sunday School Movement, begun in Bala in 1789. The University of Wales was established in 1893. Teaching in Welsh was introduced in primary schools in 1939 and in secondary schools in 1956. Channel 4 – S4C – broadcasts many hours of television in Welsh to speakers of an everyday living language.

Manx – The language spoken in the Isle of Man was similar to the Gaelic of the Western Isles of Scotland but there has been no viable Manx-speaking community since the 1940s. The present Manx dialect of English shows much influence from Lancashire owing to fishing and tourism in the 19C.

Scots Gaelic – In Scotland the Gaelic-speaking area, the **Gàidhealtachd**, is mostly confined to the Western Isles. The language, which was the mother tongue of 50% of the population in the 16C, is now spoken by less than 2%. The "Normanised" kings of Scotland, particularly David I (1124-53) introduced the Anglo-Norman language and later contact with the English court led to English becoming the language of the aristocracy. After the Union of the two kingdoms in 1603, the Statute of Iona attempted to impose the teaching of English on the sons of the chiefs and in 1616 the Westminster Parliament decreed – "that the Inglishe tongue be universallie plantit and the Scots language, one of cheif and principalle causis of the continewance of barbaritie and incivilitie amongst the inhabitantis of the Ilis and Heylandis, may be abolisheit and removeit".

In 1777 a Gaelic Society was formed in London, the first of many all over the world which maintain and encourage Gaelic language and literature. The percentage of Gaelic speakers in Scotland is increasing slowly, particularly in Lowland areas.

Norn – This Viking language, akin to Icelandic, survived in Orkney and Shetland, until the 18C. It was the dominant tongue in Orkney until the Scottish-speaking Sinclairs became Earls of Orkney in 1379 and it remained the language of Shetland until well after the pledging of the Northern Isles to James III of Scotland in 1468-69. Modern dialects of both Shetland and Orkney still contain a sizeable body of words of Norn origin – types of wind and weather, flowers, plants and animals, seasons and holidays. A high percentage of place names throughout the islands are Norn.

Old English, Anglo-Saxon and Norman French – Old English, a Germanic dialect spoken in AD 400 from Jutland to northern France, was established in Britain by AD 800 and by the 16C had taken on the syntax and grammar of modern English. Although Norman French was made the official language after the Norman Conquest, Anglo-Saxon eventually gained precedence and Norman French survives in a few formal expressions used in law and royal protocol. It continued to be spoken in the Channel Islands long after it became obsolete in England.

Modern English – English is a very flexible language which has readily absorbed a considerable inheritance from Celtic, Roman, Anglo-Saxon, Viking and Norman-French origins. Although the spoken language owes most to Anglo-Saxon, the written language shows the influence of Latin, which for many centuries formed the major study of the educated classes.

Immigration over the past hundred years or so has brought many other languages into everyday use by sizeable communities in Britain. Yiddish-speaking Jews came from Russia in the 19C and early 20C and their German-speaking co-religionists fled from Nazi persecution in the 1930s. The largest immigrant communities in Britain today are from Europe – mainly Germany, Italy, Poland and Spain – and from the Caribbean Islands, Africa, Hong Kong, India and Pakistan. Generations born here are often bilingual, speaking the mother tongue of their community and current English with the local accent.

Wales Tourist Board

Chairing the Bard

THE COUNTRY TODAY

The Economy

AGRICULTURE AND FISHING

Until the 18C, the economy of Great Britain was agriculturally based. In the 18C a combination of social and economic conditions led to landowners devoting their wealth and attention to improving land and methods of cultivation, giving rise to the **Agricultural Revolution.** Rapid population growth made it necessary to increase domestic agricultural productivity, as this was before the days of overseas exports. Land enclosure became increasingly widespread, with even common land being suppressed by acts of Parliament, landowners arguing that the system of enclosure was better for raising livestock, a more profitable form of agriculture than arable farming. Landowners enlarged their estates by taking over land abandoned by people leaving the countryside for the town, or emigrating to the New World, and developed a system based on maximising profit by introducing many efficient new farming methods. Milestones in this evolution include the use of fertiliser, abandoning the practice of leaving land to lie fallow every three years, and the introduction of new crop varieties (root crops for fodder and cultivated pasture) which in turn fostered the development of stock raising, itself becoming more selective.

Nowadays, the average size of a British farm is 168 acres/68ha, one of the highest figures in Europe. Agriculture, mechanised as much as possible, employs only 2.3% of the workforce. The practice of mixed farming, combining stock raising and crop farming, means that modern Britain meets its domestic needs in milk, eggs and potatoes, and almost totally in meat (with a national flock of about 29 million head, the United Kingdom is ninth in the world for farming sheep). The European Union's Common Agricultural Policy has hit British farmers hard, the imposition of quotas forcing them to cut production of milk and adopt less intensive farming methods.

The **fishing industry,** once a mainstay of the island's economy, has declined considerably mainly because of modifications to national fishing boundaries and their attendant fishing rights. Arrangements drawn up for the Anglo-Irish zone and the approved quotas have stabilised the annual catch for UK vessels at around 800 000 tons, but have not succeeded in arresting the decline of once-great fishing ports such as Kingston-upon-Hull or Grimsby after the departure of the canning factories. Peterhead in Scotland is now Britain's main fishing port.

ENERGY SOURCES

Coal was mined well before the 18C (Newcastle was exporting 33 000 tons of coal as early as the mid 16C), but became a large-scale industry only after the invention of the steam engine. Since the industry's heyday in the early 20C, production has been dropping steadily, despite a brief revival in the 1950s. Nowadays, in the wake of sweeping pit closures, in which deposits were exhausted or where it was felt extraction was no longer profitable, production remains constant at about 50 million tons annually, mainly concentrated in Yorkshire and Nottinghamshire. Production figures have not been helped by the fact that the high cost of exploiting most mines means that Britain can import coal more cheaply from countries such as Australia, nor by competition from oil and gas.

In the 1960s, prospecting in the North Sea gave rise to sufficiently promising results for the countries bordering the sea to reach an agreement, under the Continental Shelf Act of 1964, on zones for extracting natural gas. Thanks to deposits along the Norfolk and Lincolnshire coasts, Britain is the world's fifth producer, however domestic demand is so great that gas nonetheless has to be imported from Norway. Further north, off Scotland and the Shetland Islands, oil deposits place Great Britain in eighth place worldwide (production: 127 million tons in 1994).

Like the majority of developed countries, the United Kingdom converts a large proportion of its primary energy sources into electricity. About 70% of the electricity currently produced is thermal in origin (the Drax power station in Yorkshire is the most powerful in Europe). Hydroelectricity is negligible, as the relatively flat relief makes it impossible to build any sizeable hydroelectric power stations (those that there are, are located in Scotland and Wales). Nuclear energy, which has evolved since the construction of the experimental reactor at Calder Hall inaugurated in 1956, is produced by a dozen or so nuclear power stations, nearly all of which are to be found on the coast so

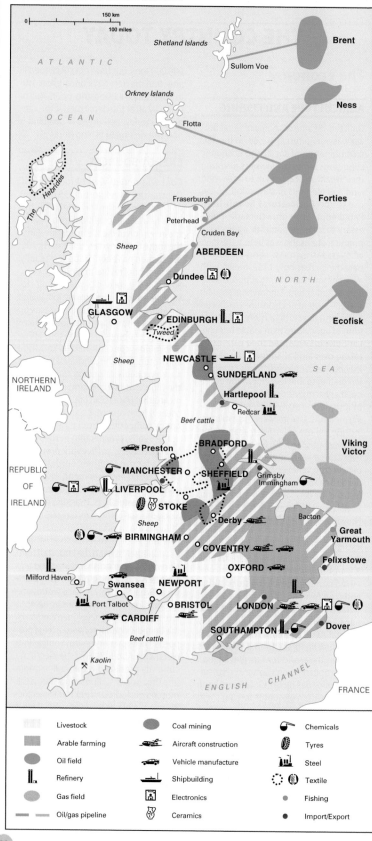

0   150 km
100 miles

Brent

Shetland Islands

ATLANTIC

Sullom Voe

Ness

OCEAN

Orkney Islands

Flotta

Forties

The Hebrides

Fraserburgh

Peterhead

Cruden Bay

NORTH

Sheep

ABERDEEN

Dundee

Ecofisk

GLASGOW

EDINBURGH

Tweed

SEA

Sheep

NEWCASTLE

SUNDERLAND

NORTHERN
IRELAND

Hartlepool

Redcar

Beef cattle

**Viking
Victor**

Preston

BRADFORD

REPUBLIC

MANCHESTER

SHEFFIELD

Grimsby
Immingham

OF

LIVERPOOL

IRELAND

STOKE

Derby

Bacton

Sheep

**Great
Yarmouth**

BIRMINGHAM

COVENTRY

Felixstowe

OXFORD

Milford Haven

NEWPORT

Swansea

Port Talbot

BRISTOL

LONDON

Dover

CARDIFF

SOUTHAMPTON

Beef cattle

Kaolin

ENGLISH   CHANNEL

FRANCE

	Livestock		Coal mining		Chemicals
	Arable farming		Aircraft construction		Tyres
	Oil field		Vehicle manufacture		Steel
	Refinery		Shipbuilding		Textile
	Gas field		Electronics		Fishing
	Oil/gas pipeline		Ceramics		Import/Export

that they can be cooled adequately. More recently, the wind has been harnessed to produce energy at Burgar Hill in the Orkneys, among other places.

INDUSTRY

In the second half of the 18C, hot on the heels of the Agricultural Revolution, capital began to flow from the land into industry, with new industrialists using the money from their family's success as cultivators of the land to set up factories, mills and businesses.

The presence of iron ore in Yorkshire, the Midlands and Scotland gave rise to the **iron and steel industry** (♻ *see IRONBRIDGE GORGE MUSEUM*) which at its peak in the 19C was one of the industries at the core of the country's economy. However, by the beginning of the 20C the mineral deposits were exhausted, and Great Britain found itself importing ore from abroad, effectively bringing about the decline of its own inland iron and steel regions (Durham, the Midlands) in favour of those located on the coast (Teesside) and in South Wales (Port Talbot, Newport), which produce about 12 million tons of cast iron and 17 million tons of steel per year. Metal processing industries have suffered gravely in the face of competition from abroad: the Clyde shipbuilding yards, once the largest in the world and nowadays reduced to manufacturing drilling platforms, have ensured that Great Britain remains ninth in the world for shipbuilding, although less than 2% of global production is assured here (eight ships in 1994), overshadowed by world leader Japan (45%).

The **car industry,** with production levels of 2.3 million vehicles in the mid 1960s, made Great Britain the European leader in this domain. It included some prestigious national companies, such as Austin, Morris, Triumph, Rover, Jaguar, grouped under British Leyland, or Bentley and Rolls Royce. Industrial disputes gave rise to a management crisis, however, culminating in nationalisation (British Leyland in 1975) and privatisation. Japanese firms have been encouraged to set up business in Britain, both building their own assembly plants (Nissan in Sunderland), and collaborating (Rover manufactures Honda cars at Longbridge). In 1994, British production, more than half of which was in the hands of foreign companies, reached almost 1.7 million vehicles (compared with 1.6 million in 1990), placing Great Britain eighth in the world.

In a completely different sphere of activity, Great Britain has provided the brain power behind, if not the actual setting for, the rapid evolution of the **electronics and computer industries**. Foreign companies such as Honeywell, Burroughs, IBM, Hewlett-Packard and Mitsubishi have set up business in Scotland, providing a much-needed economic impetus in the wake of the disappearance of the region's traditional industries.

Great Britain developed a flourishing **textile industry**, thanks to its large numbers of resident sheep and the groundbreaking inventions of the Industrial Revolution, and maintained its position as world leader until the mid 20C. Yorkshire, with Bradford as capital, was home to 80% of wool production. Lancashire, with Manchester as its centre, specialised in cotton. However, this national industry has declined, overtaken by artificial fibres, illustrating the preponderant role that the **chemical industry** now plays in Great Britain's economy. Some of Britain's largest industrial groups are chemical-based: Coats Viyella, whose business is largely concentrated outside Europe, is sixth in the world for synthetic fibres; Courtaulds, originally also in synthetic fibres, has diversified into paint and varnish production, an area in which it occupies seventh position worldwide; ICI, second in the world for paint and varnish and fourth for fertilisers. The largest British chemicals firm is British Petroleum, and two other giants in the field of petrochemicals are supported by an Anglo-Dutch financial association: Shell and Unilever.

TRADE

Great Britain imports more primary materials than it exports, as the majority of its exports are products: foodstuffs (eg. whisky, confectionery); machinery; transport equipment and chemical products. A slight reduction in trade with North America has been offset since 1968 by an increase in volume of trade with European Union member-states, which now counts for half British export trade. Much of this trade was plied for many years by the merchant fleet, world leader until 1939, and some trade is carried out by British Airways which, since privatisation, is world leader for passenger numbers and financial results and seventh for freight.

Settlement markets, marine and air insurance brokers (Lloyd's, the world's leading marine risk insurers), life insurance, bank loans and deposits combine to make the City of London the world's third-ranking **financial centre.** The huge profits generated by this business sector and the interest from investments abroad guarantee an income for the United Kingdom.

Great Britain was the first European country to emerge from the economic crisis of the late 1980s/early 1990s; and during the second half of the decade and the early part of the Millennium continued to outperform its European neighbours and most other world economies in terms of unemployment rate, inflation and other indicators of economic growth.

Imperial State Crown

Government

Great Britain is composed of England, Wales, Scotland, the Channel Islands and the Isle of Man. The first three countries are part of the United Kingdom, which also includes Northern Ireland but does not include the Channel Islands and the Isle of Man, which have their own parliaments and are attached directly to the Crown.

Monarchy – The United Kingdom is a **Constitutional Monarchy**, a form of government in which supreme power is vested in the Sovereign (the King or Queen). The origins of monarchy lie in the seven English kingdoms of the 6C to 9C – Northumbria, East Anglia, Mercia, Essex, Wessex, Sussex and Kent. The most powerful and charismatic king was acknowledged by the others as overlord. Alfred the Great (871-899) began to establish effective rule, which was consolidated by Athelstan in 926 but it was Canute (Cnut), a Danish king, who achieved political unification.

The Norman conquest of Wales, which took place gradually over two centuries, was completed with the conquest of Gwynedd by Edward I in 1283.

The **Coronation** ceremony gave a priestly role to the anointed monarch, especially from the Norman conquest (1066) onwards. The monarchy became hereditary only gradually. The Wars of the Roses, which dominated the 15C, were about dynastic rivalry and the Tudors gained much from their exploitation of the mystique of monarchy. They manipulated anti-clericalism into a doctrine of royal supremacy and the earlier form of address "Your Grace" was replaced by "Your Majesty." Although the kingdoms of England and Scotland were united in 1603, the parliaments were not united until the Act of Union in 1709. The stubborn character of the Stuarts and the insistence of Charles I on

the "Divine Right" of Kings was in part responsible for the Civil War and the King's execution, which was followed by the **Commonwealth** (1649-60) under Oliver Cromwell, the only period during which the country was not a monarchy. At the **Restoration** (1660) the monarch's powers were placed under considerable restraints which were increased at the Glorious Revolution (1688) and the accession of William of Orange.

When Queen Anne died without issue, the desire to maintain the Protestant succession caused the crown to pass to the Hanoverians. The last vain attempt made by the Stuarts to regain the crown was crushed in the Jacobite risings in 1715 and 1745.

During the reign of Queen Victoria (1837-1901) the monarch's right in relation to ministers was defined as "the right to be consulted, to encourage and to warn", although Victoria herself clung tenaciously to her supervision of the Empire and foreign affairs.

The independent nations of the former Empire still have many and important links which are fostered through the Commonwealth of Nations.

Parliament – The United Kingdom has no written constitution. The present situation has been achieved by the enactment of new laws at key points in history. **Magna Carta** was sealed by a reluctant King John at Runnymede on

15 June 1215; copies are held in the British Library and in Salisbury and Lincoln Cathedrals. Clause 39 guarantees every free man security from illegal interference in his person or his property. Since the reign of Henry VII "Habeas Corpus" – known as "you may have the body" – has been used to protect people against arbitrary arrest by requiring the appearance in Court of the accused person within a specified period.

The supreme legislature in the United Kingdom is Parliament, which consists of the **House of Commons** and the **House of Lords**. Medieval parliaments were mainly meetings between the king and his lords. The Commons were rarely summoned and had no regular meeting place nor even the right of free speech until the 16C. The monarch had, however, to summon Parliament to raise money, so frequent Parliaments were unpopular. Regular Parliaments were assured after the Glorious Revolution (1688) but both Houses were dominated by the landed aristocracy until well into the 19C.

Between 1430 and 1832 the right to vote was restricted to those possessing a freehold worth 40 shillings. The Reform Act of 1867 enfranchised all borough householders; county householders were included in 1884. In 1918 the franchise was granted to all men over 21 and women over 30; in 1928 the vote was extended to women over 21. Today all over the age of 18 are entitled to vote provided they have entered their names on the electoral roll. Since 1949 the parliamentary constituencies have been organised on the principle that each should contain about 65 000 voters, which produces 659 Members of the House of Commons. The member elected to represent a constituency is the candidate who receives the largest number of votes. The government is formed by the party which wins the greatest number of seats.

The **House of Lords**, at whose meetings the sovereign was always present until the reign of Henry VI, consists of the **Lords Spiritual** (the senior bishops of the Church of England) and the **Lords Temporal** (Dukes, Marquesses, Earls, Viscounts and Barons). The Lords of Appeal (the Law Lords) have been **Life Peers** since 1876; since 1958 this honour has been bestowed on other men and women of distinction. The Parliament Act (1911) reduced the power of the House of Lords to simple delay of legislation, allowing time for reflection; their power to delay financial legislation was ended in 1949.

Under the Crown, the country is governed by laws which are enacted by the **Legislature** – the two Houses of Parliament – and enforced by the **Judiciary** – the High Court, Criminal Court and Crown Courts.

Traditions and Customs

Folk traditions and customs reach back to the earliest records and beyond into the mists of time. Many rural traditions have declined in observance owing to population mobility, the building over of land once dedicated to festivals and the adoption of new farming methods which have made shearing and harvest ceremonies obsolete. On the other hand the popularity of outdoor activities, particularly those connected with sport and horses, has led to many of them evolving into fashionable events in the social calendar.

Morris Dancing – The origins of Morris dancing are uncertain. According to some the word Morris derives from Moorish. The dancers are traditionally men, dressed in white shirts and trousers, with bells tied below the knee and sometimes colourful hats. Their dances are energetic; for some they carry two handkerchiefs and for others a stout stick which they knock against their partner's stick. The music is played on an accordion, fiddle, or pipe and tabor.

Maypole – Until the 17C many parishes had permanent maypoles, pagan fertility symbols belonging to a spring festival, tacitly accepted and tamed by the Christian church. In 1644, however, under the Puritans, the Maypole was banned throughout England but returned at the Restoration (1660), marking both May Day and Oak Apple Day, 29 May, anniversary of Charles II's entry into London. Permanent maypoles still stand at Barwick-in-Elmet, Yorkshire (80ft/24m) and at Welford-on-Avon (70ft/21m). The church of St Andrew Undershaft, in Leadenhall Street in the City of London, is named after the maypole ("shaft") which stood before the south door until torn down by apprentices rioting against foreign traders in 1517.

Pancake Day – Shrove Tuesday, the day preceding the first day of Lent, is the occasion for cooking, tossing and eating sweet pancakes, which are served with sugar and lemon juice. Pancake races are held in which the competitors have to run a certain distance tossing a pancake in a frying pan on the way.

Cheese rolling – *Parish of Brockworth, Gloucestershire*. A Whit Monday/Spring Bank Holiday festival. A cheese is rolled down a steep slope, with the youth of the village allowed to chase it after a count of three. Cheese used to be paraded around the church in Randwick, Gloucestershire, on May Day.

Furry dance – *Helston*. The sole remaining example of a communal spring festival dance in Britain, this dance has taken place in Helston, Cornwall, for centuries, on 8 May, feast day of St Michael the Archangel, patron saint of the church. The young folk of the town dance in the morning, but the main dance of the day, with the Mayor in chain of office, starts at noon. The song which is sung shows very clearly the origin of the event – *"For Summer is a-come-O and Winter is a-gone-O."* The dancers go in and out of all the houses, shops and gardens of the town, in one door and out of the other, to bring luck and summer. Despite the thousands of tourists who come to see the dance, it has not changed in character and would be recognisable to any pre-Christian inhabitant of the town.

Well dressing – Even in the damp climate of northern Europe a well or spring providing water, the basic necessity of life, has long been venerated as the home of a mysterious power to whom sacrifice and propitiation were due. Christianity forbade the worship of water spirits but many wells were simply "purged" and re-dedicated to the Blessed Virgin or one of the saints. In Derbyshire the custom of decking wells or springs with flowers still continues, under the auspices of the church. Large pictures are formed on boards covered with clay, the design being picked out in flowers, pebbles, shells or any natural object; manufactured materials are not used. It is said that well dressing at Tissington in its present form started either after a prolonged drought in 1615 when only the wells of Tissington continued to give water or in thanksgiving for deliverance from the Black Death (1348-49). St Anne's Well near Buxton, which is dressed on the Thursday nearest Midsummer Day, is named after a statue, possibly a Roman votive offering, found in the spring in the Middle Ages and enshrined in a chapel which was swept away by one of Thomas Cromwell's agents in 1538, together with "all the crutches, shifts, shirts" offered by grateful pilgrims.

Eisteddfodau – Wales is famous for its international cultural festivals offering song, music and dance (Builth Wells, Llangollen). Many contestants perform in their national costumes.

Highland Games – The games, which originated in 11C contests in the arts of war, are held in Scotland between June and September. The heavy events include putting the shot, throwing the hammer and tossing the caber as straight as possible. Other events are athletics, dancing, piping and massed pipe bands.

Outdoor Events – Many regular outdoor events have become part of the season, social occasions associated with high fashion and corporate entertaining. The main events are the Chelsea Flower Show in May, horse racing at Royal Ascot in June, lawn tennis during Wimbledon fortnight at the end of June, rowing at Henley Regatta early in July, sailing during Cowes Week in August on the Isle of Wight, which features the Admiral's Cup every other year and ends with the Fastnet Race.

Equestrian Events – Horses figure largely in British life, particularly in the country and at royal ceremonial occasions. The Household Cavalry are involved in the Changing of the Guard at Horse Guards in London and in Trooping the Colour in June. State visitors usually ride in an open horse-drawn carriage to Buckingham Palace. A horse and carriage plies daily between St James's Palace and Buckingham Palace carrying official communications. Horse racing, the sport of kings, goes on throughout the year with flat racing from March to November and steeple chasing from May to September. The highlight of the calendar is Royal Ascot in June. Fox hounds meet in most English counties, although their future is in doubt following recent anti-fox hunting legislation. The show-jumping competitions, held in indoor arenas in London and the three-day events at Badminton and Hickstead, featuring dressage, cross-country and show jumping, have a good following, both live and on television. Polo matches are played in Richmond Park, at Ham Common, Smith's Lawn, Windsor and at Cowdray Park in Sussex.

Historic battles – The British penchant for nostalgia is evident in the activities of the **Sealed Knot**, a society whose members regularly re-enact the engagements between Cavaliers and Roundheads during the Civil War. The staff of the Commandery in Worcester can always provide up-to-date information on all battle re-enactments and similar events. Many of the battlefields of Britain are marked with museums, maps and guided tours. There is a visitor centre and museum at **Battle** in Sussex, site of the Battle of Hastings (1066), at **Bannockburn** (1314) near Stirling, at **Culloden** (1746) outside Inverness and at **Killiecrankie** (1689) near Pitlochry.

Food and Drink

Great Britain provides a cosmopolitan choice of food but also has a rich tradition of regional dishes, all using local fish, game, fruit and dairy products to best advantage. Some of the treats listed below are now hard to find and do not appear on the tourist menu. You may need to enlist the services of local specialists, such as independent butchers and food shops and farmers markets in order to track them down.

SOME REGIONAL SPECIALITIES

London and the South East – **Steak and kidney pie** is chief among the many varieties of pie found. The Kentish marshes nurture fine **lamb** while Whitstable is famous for its **oysters; Dover sole** and other fresh fish are available along the coast. Sussex produces a range of **hotpots** and **pies**, mostly lamb and mutton based and excellent **smoked mackerel**. An **"Arnold Bennett omelette"**, made with haddock and cheese, is a London dish, as are **Chelsea Buns,** dough buns folded round dried fruit and enjoyed since Georgian days. **Maids of Honour** are small puff pastry tarts with ground almond, served almost exclusively at the eponymous tea rooms in Kew, next to the famous Royal Botanical Gardens.

The West Country – Devon and Cornwall are known for **clotted cream,** served on scones with strawberry jam. It is equally delicious on the **apple pies**, richly flavoured with cinnamon and cloves, for which the region is renowned. **Devon junket** is made with rum or brandy – a reminder of smugglers' tastes from the past. **Dorset jugged steak**, cooked with sausage meat and port, could be followed by **Widecombe gingerbreads** or by a **Taunton cider cake**, made with raisins and a large apple, the cider reduced to concentrate the apple flavour. **Fresh and potted mackerel** are a coastal delicacy, as are **pilchards. Cheddar cheese** is named after the caves in which it is ripened. Cornwall has given its name to the **Cornish pasty**, a mixture of beef (skirt), turnip or swede, potatoes and onion baked in a pastry case, shaped like a half-moon, so that it could be carried down the mine to be eaten at midday; sometimes fruit was put in at one end to provide a sweet.

Heart of England – The Vale of Evesham is England's fruit growing area – **plums** and **greengages** are a speciality, with **apples** and **pears**. Herefordshire raises fine **beef**; the local **cider**, a refreshing but deceptively potent drink, is skilfully combined in local dishes, including a **pigeon casserole**, with cider and orange. Gloucestershire produces excellent **cheeses**. Worcestershire **asparagus**, in season, rivals any in flavour and **Worcestershire sauce,** a blend of anchovies, garlic, treacle and spices, has been enjoyed worldwide since 1839.

Thames and Chilterns – **Brown Windsor soup** made with beef, mutton, carrots and onions is delicious. **Aylesbury duck** and green peas, Hertfordshire **pork puffs**, and **harvest rabbit** with forcemeat balls, could be followed by **Bucks cherry bumpers**, cherries in shortcrust pastry, or some **Banbury**

Brigitta L. House/MICHELIN

apple pie. Breakfasts should always finish with chunky **Oxford marmalade** on toast.

East Midlands – Lincolnshire grows fine **potatoes** and these feature in many dishes particularly with delicate pink, green and white slices of **stuffed chine of pork,** a piece of back of fat pig, stuffed with green herbs. Three regional cheeses enjoyed countrywide are **Stilton, Red Leicester** and **Derby sage.** **Bakewell tarts** are made of shortcrust pastry with an almond and jam filling. Ashbourne produces a **gingerbread** as does Grantham, and **pikelets,** a cross between a crumpet and a pancake, are a regional speciality. **Melton Mowbray pies,** succulent lean pork in jelly, with a little anchovy flavouring in a pastry case, vie with **Sherwood Venison pie,** eaten hot or cold with redcurrant jelly. **Veal collops with orange** are said to have been a favourite dish of Oliver Cromwell.

East Anglia – Norfolk is famed for its **dumplings.** Another delicacy is **mussels in cider and mustard.** During the summer **samphire,** "poor man's asparagus", grows wild along the salt marshes and is eaten with melted butter. In Suffolk they serve a **spicy shrimp pie,** cooked with wine, mace and cloves in a puff pastry case. **Black caps** are large baked apples with the space from which the cores have been removed filled with brown sugar, citrus peel and raisins. **Cromer crabs** are full of flavour and Colchester **oysters,** introduced by the Romans, are the equal of the best from France.

Yorkshire, Humberside and the Northeast – **Roast beef** and **Yorkshire pudding** – a succulent batter pudding on which the juices of the roasting meat have been allowed to drip – rivals **York ham** and **parkin** – a dark oatmeal cake made with cinnamon, ginger, nutmeg and treacle – as Yorkshire's greatest contribution to British gastronomy. **Wensleydale cheese** goes well after any of the many **game pies** or **potted grouse** for which the area is renowned. Humberside offers many fish dishes. Newcastle has **potted salmon** and along the Northumberland coast **baked herrings,** cooked with mint, sage and pepper, are a delicacy, hot or cold.

Cumbria, the Northwest and the Isle of Man – Fish of all sorts from the Irish Sea, **cockles, scallops,** the smaller flavourful **"Queenies"** from the Isle of Man, **potted shrimps in butter,** from Morecambe Bay, and **Manx kippers** are the glory of this region. **Char,** a fish from the deepwater lakes of the Lake District, is eaten fresh-caught or potted; **Goosnargh cakes** are the local gingerbread. Cheshire produces two fine **cheeses,** one white and one a **blue vein. Cumberland sauce** is not to be missed as an accompaniment to ham or game pies.

Wales – In Britain lamb is traditionally eaten with mint sauce, mutton with redcurrant jelly. **Welsh honey lamb** is delicious, cooked in cider, with thyme and garlic, basted with honey. Caerphilly produces a light, crumbly **cheese. Leeks,** the national emblem of Wales, appear in many dishes, including **cawl cenin,** a tasty leek soup. **Baked crab and cockle pie** is a speciality of the Gower peninsula and the local sea trout – **sewin** – is stuffed with herbs before being cooked. Welsh cakes, griddle scones with currants, and **crempog,** small soft pancakes, are best eaten hot with butter. **Bara brith** is a rich moist cake bread, full of raisins, currants, sultanas and citrus peel.

Scotland – **Scottish beef** and **lamb** are deservedly renowned, as is Scottish **venison, grouse** (in season) and **salmon. Partan Bree** is a tasty **crab soup** and there are **Arbroath smokies** and **kippers** to rival kedgeree, made with salmon, haddock or other fish, with rice, hard-boiled eggs and butter. **Haggis** served with swede – the Scots refer to this as turnip – hence **"haggis and neeps",** is a tasty meal traditiionally accompanied by a wee dram of whisky. **Mutton pies** are made with hot water pastry and **oatmeal bannocks** may be spread with local honey. Dundee makes an **orange marmalade** as rich, dark and chunky as that from Oxford. **Raspberries** from this part of the world are a treat too. **Aberdeen buttery rowies** are flaky pastry rolls.

BEVERAGES

Beer – It is one of the oldest and most popular alcoholic drinks in the world. Traditional draught beer is made by grinding malted barley, heating it with water and adding hops which add the familiar aroma and bitterness. Beers in Britain can be divided into two principal types: **Ales** and **Lagers** which differ principally in their respective warm and cool fermentations. Beer can also be divided into **keg** or **cask**; there are several different beer styles in Britain and Ireland.

Keg beer is filtered, pasteurised and chilled and then packed into pressurised containers from which it gets its name.

Cask beer or "Real Ale" as it is often referred to, is neither filtered, pasteurised nor chilled and is served from casks using simple pumps. It is widely considered to be a more characterful, flavoursome and natural beer.

Bitter is the most popular traditional beer in England and Wales. Bitters vary enormously, though most are usually a ruddy brown colour with a slightly bitter taste imparted by hops. Some bitters however are quite fruity in taste and the higher the alcoholic content the sweeter the brew.

There are three classic styles of English Bitters: "Ordinary", the weakest; "Special", moderate strength; "Extra Special", high in alcohol.

Mild is normally only found in Wales, the West Midlands and the North West of England. The name refers to the hop character as it is a gentle, sweetish and full flavoured beer. It is generally lower in alcohol and darker in colour than Bitter, caused by the addition of caramel or by using dark malt.

Stout – The great dry stouts are brewed in Ireland and are instantly recognisable by their black colour and creamy head, Guinness being the standard bearer. They have a pronounced roast flavour with plenty of hop bitterness. Sweet stouts, including milk or cream stouts are sweetened with sugar before being bottled.

In addition there are Pale Ales (like Bitter), Brown Ales (Sweet, like Mild) and Old Ales (sweet and strong) whilst the term Barley Wine is frequently used by English breweries to describe their strongest beer.

In Scotland the beers produced are full bodied and malty and are often known simply as 60/- (shillings), 70/-, 80/- or even 90/-. This is a reference to the now defunct shilling which indicated the barrel tax in the late 1800s calculated on alcoholic strength. The 60/- and 90/- brews are now rare. Alternatively the beers may be referred to as Light, Heavy, or Export which refers to the body and strength of the beer.

Although Ireland is most famous for its stouts, it also makes a range of beers which have variously been described as malty, buttery, rounded and fruity with a reddish tinge.

Pubs are usually tied to a brewer but there are several successful independent brewers who supply free establishments. CAMRA (Campaign for Real Ale) publishes a *Good Beer Guide* with listings of good local pubs.

Whisky (Whiskey) – The term whisky is derived from the Scottish Gaelic *uisage beatha* and the Irish Gaelic *uisce beathadh*, both meaning "water of life". When spelt without an e it usually refers to **Scotch Whisky** which can be produced only in Scotland by the distillation of malted and unmalted barley, maize, rye, and mixtures of two or more of these. It can be divided into 2 basic types: malt whisky and grain whisky.

Malt whisky is produced only from malted barley which is traditionally dried over peat fires. The malt is then milled and mixed with hot water before mashing turns the starches into sugars and the resulting liquid, called wort, is filtered out. Yeast is added and fermentation takes place followed by two distilling processes using a pot still. The whisky is matured in oak, ideally sherry casks, for at least three years which affects both its colour and flavour. All malts have a more distinctive aroma and more intense flavour than grain whiskies and each distillery will produce a completely individual whisky of great complexity. A single malt is the product of an individual distillery. Malt whiskies can be divided into 4 classic regions: the Lowlands, the Highlands, Campbeltown and the Isle of Islay. There are approximately 100 malt whisky distilleries in Scotland.

Grain whisky is made from a mixture of any malted or unmalted cereal such as maize or wheat and is distilled in the Coffey, or patent still, by a continuous process. It matures more quickly than malt whisky. Very little grain whisky is ever drunk unblended.

Blended whisky is a mix of more than one malt whisky or a mix of malt and grain whiskies to produce a soft, smooth and consistent drink. There are over 2000 such blends which form the vast majority of Scottish whisky production.

De Luxe whiskies – These are special because of the ages and qualities of the malts and grain whiskies used in them. They usually include a higher proportion of malts than in most blends.

Many of Scotland's distilleries welcome visitors, and offer not only tours but presentations and lectures. *See ELGIN.*

Irish Whiskey differs from Scotch whisky both in its spelling and method of production. It is traditionally made from cereals, distilled three times and matured for at least seven years. The different brands are as individual as straight malt and considered by some to be smoother in character.

Cider – According to tradition, cider has been brewed from apples since Celtic times. Only bitter apples are used for "real" West Country cider which is dry in taste, flat (non-sparkling) and with an alcoholic content of 5.5% to 5.8%. Full-bodied draught cider is available in pubs. A sparkling cider is produced by fermenting the brew a second time in the bottle. There is also a small production of a strong cider brandy. Genuine **perry** is made with bitter perry pears. Consult the *CAMRA Good Cider Guide* for more detailed information.

Wine – Britain's wine industry has improved by leaps and bounds and there are notable wine makers mostly in the south of the country where the conditions are most favourable. White wines are often blended from one or more varieties of grape to produce ranges of light, dry, fruity wines similar to German wines; red wines are fairly light. Fruit wines and fruit flavoured liqueurs (such as sloe gin) may also be found in specialist outlets.

a. **Meals served in the garden or on the terrace**

b. **A particularly interesting wine list**

c. **Cask beers and ales usually served**

Find out all the answers in the Michelin Guide "Eating Out in Pubs"!

A selection of 500 dining pubs and inns throughout Britain and Ireland researched by the same inspectors who make the Michelin Guide.

- for good food and the right atmosphere
- in-depth descriptions bring out the feel of the place and the flavour of the cuisine.

The pleasure of travel with Michelin Maps and Guides.

The Palladian Bridge and Pantheon, Stourhead

ABERDEEN★★

City of Aberdeen, SCOTLAND

POPULATION 204 885

MICHELIN ATLAS P 69 OR MAP 501 N 12

The dignified and prosperous "Granite City," set roughly halfway along Scotland's eastern coast, developed from two fishing villages on the Dee and the Don and has a rich agricultural hinterland. 🏛 *23 Union Street, Aberdeen AB11 5PP ☎ 01224 288 800, 01224 288 828; www.agtb.org*

▶ **Orient Yourself**: Most of the major attractions are clustered in Old Aberdeen and the City Centre.

🕭 **Don't Miss**: The heraldic ceiling in St Machar's Cathedral; Aberdeen Art Gallery; Pitmedden Gardens, Grampian Castles; a Highland Games gathering.

🕐 **Organizing Your Time**: Allow about 1hr to stroll around Old Aberdeen. Allow another 2 hours to see the sights of the City centre.

Kids Especially for Kids: The maze at Hazlehead (🕭 *See sidebar*)

🖐 **Also See**: Follow the signed routes of the Victorian Heritage Trail, Scotland's Castle Trail, the Coastal Trail and the Malt Whisky Trail which includes famous distilleries and cooperages (barrel makers).

ABERDEEN		Alford Pl.	X	2	Back Hilton Rd	V
		Argyll Pl.	VX		Back Wynd	YZ
Albert St	X	Aschgrove Rd	V		Beach Boulevard	Y
Albyn Pl.	X					

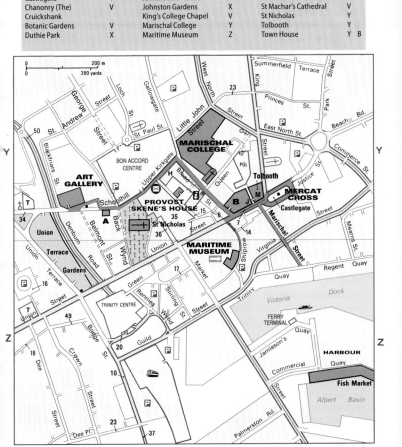

Aberdeen "The Flower of Scotland"

Aberdeen's parks and gardens are justly worthy of a mention: **Union Terrace Gardens** *(YZ – off Union Street)* with their celebrated floral displays including Aberdeen's coat of arms; the unrivalled **Winter Gardens** in Duthie Park (X); the Rose Garden and Maze at **Hazlehead**; the delightful **Johnston Gardens,** and the university's **Cruickshank Botanic Gardens** (V).

A Bit of History

An episcopal city by the 12C, Old Aberdeen had a large secular community outside its precincts; in the late 15C Bishop Elphinstone founded a University. A second distinct burgh grew around the King's Castle and became an active trading centre based on the coastal and Baltic trades. As the city expanded the streets were lined with impressive buildings in a dignified but simple style by the native architect, Archibald Simpson (1790-1847), who gave Aberdeen its **Granite City** nickname and its distinctive character by his masterly use of the local stone. Aberdeen has a strong **maritime tradition** with its shipbuilding industry: vessels for whaling, the Clipper ships which gave Britain supremacy in the China tea trade, wooden sailing vessels and iron steam ships. The North Sea has brought prosperity with the growth of fisheries – whaling from the 1750s, herring boom in the 1870s and white fishing in the present day. More recently Aberdeen has become the "offshore capital of Europe" for the North Sea oil industry and exploration and supply base activities continue to play an important role.

Old Aberdeen★★

Walk through the medieval streets to appreciate the essential character of the old town which became a burgh of barony in 1489, a status retained until 1891.

King's College Chapel★ – ♿ ⏰ *25 High Street. Open Mon-Fri, 9am-4.30pm and by appointment. Access to Chapel by door in Quadrangle (left hand side on entering Quadrangle from street);* ☎ *01224 272 137; chaplaincy@abdn.ac.uk; http://abdn.ac.uk/ chaplaincy.* **Visitor Centre** – ♿ ⏰ *Open Mon-Sat, 9.30am (11am Sat) to 5pm (4pm Sat).* ⏰ *Closed 2 weeks over Christmas and New Year.* ☎ *01224 272660; Fax 01224 276246.* The only original building left of Bishop Elphinstone's University is the beautiful chapel in its campus setting. Outstanding features are a delicate Renaissance **crown spire★★★**, the tinctured arms on the west front buttresses (including those of James IV and his Queen, Margaret Tudor) and rare, richly carved **medieval fittings★★★**.
At the crossroads stands the **Old Town House** (Y), an attractive 18C Georgian house. Beyond is The Chanonry, a walled precinct for the residences of the bishop and other clerics.

St Machar's Cathedral★★ – ♿ *The Chanonry.* ⏰ *Open daily, 9am-5pm.* ⏰ *Closed 1 Jan. Brochure (6 languages).* ☎ *01224 485 988; Fax 01224 483 688; office@stmachar. com; www.stmachar.com.* The twin spires have long been one of the landmarks of Old Aberdeen. The cathedral which dates from the 14C and 15C was built "overlooking the crook of the Don" in compliance with instructions from St Columba. The impressive exterior is complemented by the splendid 16C **heraldic ceiling★★★**. The brightly coloured coats of arms present a vision of the European scene around 1520, the year of the Field of Cloth of Gold, and strongly assert the place of Scotland in a united Europe and a united Church.
Proceed to the early 14C **Brig o'Balgownie★** *(approach via Don Street – V)* with its pointed Gothic arch and a defensive kink at the south end; it is one of Aberdeen's most important medieval structures.

City Centre

Maritime Museum★ (Z) – ♿ ⏰ *Provost Ross's House, Shiprow. Open Mon-Sat, 10am (noon Sun) to 5pm (3pm Sun).* ⏰ *Closed 25-26, 31 Dec, 1-2 Jan.* ☎ *01224 337 700; Fax 01224 213066; www.aagm.co.uk info@aagm.co.uk.* The museum is located in two 16C town houses bordering Shiprow, a medieval thoroughfare winding up from the harbour. It exhibits ship models, paintings and artefacts to trace the story of the fishing, shipping and oil industries, and features interactive displays.
The medieval market place was situated on **Castlegate (Y)**, the gait or way up to Castle Hill. Notable features are the Mannie Fountain (1706), a reminder of the city's first water supply, and the splendid **Mercat Cross★★ (Y)** dating from 1686 and decorated with a unicorn, a frieze, and royal portrait medallions and coats of arms. The cross marked the focal point of the burgh and was the place for public punishment and proclamations.

Behind the 19C **Town House (Y)** on Castle Street rises the tower of the 17C **Tolbooth,** (☞ *Closed until further notice.* ☎ *01224 621 167*) which houses Aberdeen's **museum of civic history,** with a fine model of the city as it was in 1661.

Marischal Street (YZ) – A street laid out in 1767-68 with houses built to a uniform design of three storeys and an attic.

Marischal College★ (Y) – The college was founded in the 16C by the 5th Earl Marischal in the buildings of Greyfriars Monastery and amalgamated with the older King's College to form Aberdeen University; it has a striking 20C granite façade. **Marischal Museum** (🕐 *Broad Street. Open all year, Sun-Fri, 10am-5pm, Sun, 2pm-5pm.* ☎ *01224 274 301; Fax 01224 274 302; museum@abdn.ac uk; www.abdn.ac.uk/marischal_museum*) relates the history and prehistory of Northeast Scotland and displays fine ethnographical collections.

Crown spire, King's College

B. Kaufmann/MICHELIN

Provost Skene's House★ (Y) – ♿(ground floor only) 🕐 *Guestrow (between Broad Street and Flourmill Lane) Open Mon-Sat, 10am-5pm, Sun, 1-4pm.* 🕐 *Closed 1-2 Jan and 25-26 Dec.* ⊜ *£2.50, £1.50 (concessions), £6 (family).* 🔍 *Guided tour by appointment. Coffee shop.* ☎ *01224 641 086; info@aagm.co.uk; www.aagm.co.uk.* This 17C town house contains tastefully furnished period rooms with elaborate plasterwork ceilings, panelling and stone flagging. The chapel boasts an outstanding 17C painted **ceiling**★★ of New Testament scenes within a geometrical framework.

Art Gallery★★ (Y) – ♿🕐 *Schoolhill. Open daily, 10am (2pm Sun)-5pm.* 🕐 *Closed 1 Jan and 25-26 Dec.* ⊜ *No charge.* 🔍 *Guided tour by appointment. Gift shop. Coffee shop.* ☎ *01224 523 700 fax 01224 632133; info@aagm.co.uk; www.aagm.co.uk.* The permanent collection has a strong emphasis on contemporary art. The **Scottish collection** includes important works by two local artists, the 17C portraitist George Jamesone and the 19C William Dyce, a precursor of the Pre-Raphaelites *(Titian's First Essay in Colour, A Scene in Arran)*; by William McTaggart *(A Ground Swell)* in his original "impressionist" style, the Scottish Colourist SJ Peploe and Joan Eardley (20C). The **Macdonald Collection**★★ of British artists' portraits is a highly revealing survey of the art world in the 19C.

Excursions

Deeside★★ – *About 64mi/103km southwest by A 93. Allow at least a whole day.* The splendid valley of the salmon-rich Dee penetrates deep into the Grampian Mountains. where there are many fine castles (🏰 *See GRAMPIAN CASTLES*). The green at **Aboyne** forms the setting for colourful **Highland Games** in August.

Balmoral Castle – ♿ *Exhibitions, gardens, pony trekking and carriage rides:* 🕐 *Open Apr-Jul, daily, 10am-5pm..* ⊜ *Adults £6, Seniors £5, Children (6-15) £1 . Guide book (3 languages). Parking. Cafeteria.* ☎ *013397 42334; Fax 013397 42034; info@balmoralcastle. com; www.balmoralcastle.com*) has been the summer residence of the Royal Family since Queen Victoria's reign. **Braemar** too has its castle, but the village is better known for the **Braemar Highland Gathering** held annually in September and normally attended by royalty. At the road's end is the famous beauty spot of **Linn o'Dee**, where salmon may be seen leaping.

Pitmedden Garden★★ – (NTS) *14mi/22km north by A 92 (V).* ♿(Wheelchairs available) 🕐 *Open May-Sep, daily, 10am-5:30pm. Grounds: open daily.* ⊜ *£5, £4 (child/concessions). Information sheets (5 languages). Parking. Tea room.* ☎ *01651 842 352; Fax 01651 843 188; www.nts.org.uk.* Sir Alexander Seton (c 1639-1719), possibly influenced by designs of Le Nôtre or the gardens of Sir William Bruce at Holyrood, laid out the original formal gardens. The garden is seen at its best in July and August, when some 30-40 000 annuals are in bloom. Within this walled garden a belvedere provides the best viewing point. The Museum of Farming Life adjoins the Great Garden.

ABERYSTWYTH★★

Ceredigion, WALES

POPULATION 8 636

MICHELIN ATLAS P 24 OR MAP 503 H 26

From the front of the National Library of Wales, on top of Penglais Hill, there is a magnificent view★ across this seaside town, set roughly halfway along the west coast of the Principality. The University College of Wales was founded here, in 1872, in a hotel building which still stands on the sea front. *Terrace Road, Aberystwyth SY23 2AG /Fax 01970 612 125; aberystwythtic@ceredigion.gov.uk; www.aberystwyth-online.co.uk*

- **Don't Miss:** A ride on the Vale of Rheidol Light Railway to the Devil's Bridge Falls.
- **Especially for Kids:** The beaches at Aberystwyth North and South, Clarach Bay, Borth (North), Llanrhystud (South); and the Vale of Rheidol Light Railway.
- **Also See:** Cardigan (Aberteifi), Pembrokeshire Coast, Portmeirion, St David's, Snowdonia.

Sights

National Library of Wales – *Open Mon-Sat, 9.30am-6pm (5pm Sat). Exhibitions: 10am-5pm. Closed Bank Hols and first full week in Oct. Parking. Refreshments. 01970 632 800; Fax 01970 615 709; holi@llgc.org.uk; www.llgc.org.uk.* One of the United Kingdom's legal deposit libraries, the National Library houses a priceless collection of manuscripts and treasures of Welsh and Celtic literature. Changing exhibitions present a selection from these riches, while the texts and works of art on display in the **Permanent Collection**★ form an excellent introduction to the history of Wales.

Seafront★ – There are few modern intrusions to mar the Victorian harmony of Marine Terrace, a sinuous line of three- and four-storey hotels and boarding houses facing seawards. To the north, the Cliff Railway of 1896 still scales the heights of Constitution Hill. On the promontory beyond the sadly shortened Pier to the south are the ruins of the Castle, which was begun in 1277 by Edward I on the site of an earlier stronghold; it was taken by Owain Glyndwr in 1414 and it was from here that this Welsh prince proposed the founding of an independent Welsh church and the establishment of two universities.

Vale of Rheidol Light Railway★ – *Operates from Aberystwyth to Devil's Bridge late-Jul to Aug, Mon-Thu, 4 trains per day; Fri-Sun, 2 trains per day; Apr-Jun and Sep-Oct, 2 trains per day (some exceptions). Return journey 3hrs (including 1hr stop at Devil's Bridge); single journey 1hr (approx 12mi) Single Fare £9, Return £12. Parking. Café and WCs at Devil's Bridge. 01970 625 819; Fax 01970 623 769; www.rheidolrailway.co.uk.* This narrow-gauge steam railway hauls its trainloads of tourists from Aberystwyth through the wonderfully wooded Vale of Rheidol to the waterfalls at Devil's Bridge (*see below*). The journey (12mi/19km) takes an hour as the train climbs slowly up to the terminus (639ft/195m). The line was built in 1902 to service the lead mines in the Vale of Rheidol, and the engines and rolling stock (1ft 11.5in gauge) are all originals.

Excursions

Elan Valley★★ – *34mi/55km by A44 east to Rhayader; circuit of lakes 25mi/40km.* Reservoirs were built in the Elan Valley, 1892-1904, to supply water to Birmingham, 73mi/116km away. The Claerwen Dam, built to increase the supply, was opened in 1952. The **Elan Valley Visitor Centre** (*Open mid-Mar to Oct, daily, 10am-5.30pm. Parking £1. Café. 01597 810 898, 810 880 in winter; info@elanvalley.org.uk; www.elanvalley.org.uk) at* the foot of the Caban Coch dam has displays explaining the construction and operation of this great engineering feat, as well as introducing visitors to the ecology of the surrounding woodlands and high moorlands, habitat of the rare red kite. The design of the reservoirs and their attendant structures as well as the passage of a century has resulted in a landscape of great beauty, justifying the title given to the whole region of "The Welsh Lake District" (70 sq mi/180sq km). Submerged under the waters are the remains of Nantgwyllt, the house where the poet Shelley and his young bride spent some time in 1811-12.

Near the junction of the Elan and Claerwen valleys the road crosses the Caban Coch reservoir on a viaduct over the Garreg-ddu dam; it is here that the water is drawn off for the Midlands. The four dams are best seen in flood conditions when huge waterfalls cascade over them.

Devil's Bridge★ (Pontarfynach) – *12mi/19km east by A 4120. If intending to travel to the Falls by rail, visitors should plan their journey allowing at least an hour for the visit.* The rivers Rheidol and Mynach join here and form a spectacular waterfall (300ft/90m), Mynach Falls. The original bridge was probably built by the monks of Strata Florida in the 12C, though legend says it was the Devil who built it to enable a local woman to take her cattle across the torrent. There are now three bridges, one above the other, the second one being built in 1753 and an iron one on top of this, in 1901, to level off the roadway and allow motor cars to cross on an easier gradient.

Strata Florida Abbey★ – (CADW) *16mi/26km southeast of Aberystwyth by B 4340 to Pontrhydfendigaid – Bridge of the Blessed Ford – then on minor road.* ○ *Open Apr-Sept, daily, 10am-5pm.* ∞ *£2, £1.50 (children and concessions), free when unstaffed.* ☎ 01974 831 261 www.cadw.wales.gov.uk. Little more than the Norman arch of the west door and the lines of the walls remains of this Cistercian abbey founded in 1164. Cistercian ideals of simplicity and poverty, rather than the Benedictine Rule, appealed to the Welsh temperament. Strata Florida, completed by 1201, became a centre of Welsh culture and influence. It was here that Llywelyn the Great assembled all the Welsh princes to swear allegiance to his son Dafydd. Many of those early princes are buried here, in the angle between the presbytery and the south transept. The abbey suffered at the hands of Edward I and Henry IV; at the Dissolution the monks took with them their most precious possession, an olive-wood cup, believed to be the Holy Grail.

St Padarn's Church, Llanbadarn Fawr★ – *Eastern outskirts of Aberystwyth by A 44.* ○ *Open daily, dawn-dusk. Guide book (2 languages).* ☎ 01970 623 368. This austere 13C church was built on the monastic site established by Padarn, a 6C contemporary of St David. The antiquity and importance of the parish is celebrated in the south transept, where modern fittings and furnishings provide an impeccable setting for two Celtic crosses which probably date from the 9C or 10C.

ALNWICK★

Northumberland, ENGLAND

POPULATION 7 419

MICHELIN ATLAS P 51 OR MAP 502 O 17

The attractive grey stone town (pronounced Annick), 30 mi/50km north of New-castle-upon-Tyne, in the far north east of England, grew up around the great medieval castle whose stern walls still seem to bar the route from Scotland. *The Shambles, Alnwick NE66 1TN* ☎ *01665 510 665; Fax 01665 510 447; alnwicktic@alnwick. gov.uk; www.northumberland.gov.uk/vg.*

Sights

The Castle★★ – ○ *Open daily Easter-Oct, 11am-5pm (4.15pm last admission). Grounds and tea rooms open 10.00AM.* ∞ *£7.95 concessions £7.50. Guide book (4 languages). Parking. Refreshments.* ☎ *01665 510 777; 01665 511 100 (information line); enquiries@alnickcastle. com; www.alnwickcastle.com.* Among the many fortifications of this much contested border country Alnwick's castle is the most formidable. Begun in Norman times, it was acquired in 1309 by the **Percys**, the region's greatest family, and has remained in their hands ever since. Though much remodelled in the 19C, its basic features are all intact and, in an exquisite setting by the River Aln, it epitomises the romantic ideal of a mighty medieval fortress and recently featured in the first two *Harry Potter* films.

The approach from the town is defended by an impressive early 14C **gatehouse** and **barbican**; the battlements, here as elsewhere around the castle, are guarded by 18C stone warriors. Beyond, the extensive walls enclose the broad lawns of the outer and middle baileys. These are separated by the imposing **keep**, largely rebuilt by the 4th Duke in the mid 19C. The baronial Gothic of its courtyard conceals a sequence of sumptuously furnished rooms decorated in a lavish Renaissance style by a team of Italian designers and master craftsmen. Among the many good **paintings** (Titians, Tintorettos, a Turner) there is a Van Dyck portrait of the 10th Earl. From the north-facing terrace there are fine **views** over the castle's extensive parklands. These were landscaped in the mid 18C by Lancelot Capability Brown and are enlivened by a number of follies such as the sham castle on Ratheugh Crags *(2.5mi/4km northeast).* **Alnwick Garden –** ⏰ *Denwick Lane, ♿To book a wheelchair ☎ 01665 511350. Open daily from 10am. Closing times vary with seasons, from 4pm Nov-Jan to 7pm June-Sep. ⬚ Adult £6, concessions £5.75, children free. Car park: garden visitors: £1.50 non-garden Visitors: £3.00. Café. Shop ☎ 01665 511350; Fax 01665 511351, info@alnwickgarden.com, www.alnwickgarden.co.uk).* Part of the castle estate, the 12-acre walled garden was rescued from dereliction in 2000 and is one of the most exciting contemporary gardens to be developed in the last century in Great Britain. Officially opened in October 2002 by its patron, the Prince of Wales, it was halfway to completion in 2005 and features spectacular water displays, rose gardens and one of the largest tree houses in the world. Alnwick is both notable and unusual among British gardens for being very child friendly. The Garden's Pavilion and Visitor Centre is an impressive contemporary ensemble designed by leading international architect Sir Michael Hopkins.

To the northwest, Hulne Park contains the ruins of Hulne Priory as well as the 18C Brislee Tower which offers wide prospects over the country.

The Town★ – Though its streets were laid out in the Middle Ages, Alnwick's present sober and harmonious appearance dates from the 18C when much dignified rebuilding in stone took place. It is still compact, with countryside everywhere close at hand and, as the market centre for a wide area, has a busy life of its own. Even so, there are many reminders of the Percys' dominating presence; their emblem, a poker-tailed lion, stands on the bridge over the Aln to the north and atop the tall **Tenantry Column** to the south; and the only surviving fragment of the town walls, the 15C **Hotspur Gate,** is named after Harry Hotspur, celebrated in Shakespeare's *Henry IV.*

Excursions

The skeletal ruin of **Dunstanburgh Castle** ★*(8mi/13km northeast of Alnwick by B 1340; after 3mi/5km turn right to Craster.* ⏰ *Open late-Mar to Oct, daily, 10am-6pm (5pm Oct); Nov-Mar, Wed-Sun, 10am-4pm.* ⏰ *Closed 1 Jan, 24-26 Dec. ⬚ £2.60, £2 (child), £1.30 (concessions). Refreshments. ☎ 01665 576 231; www.english-heritage. org.uk)* on its lonely crag of volcanic rock is one of the most stirring sights of the Northumbrian coast.

Seen from the south the long wall and its lesser towers are dominated by the substantial remains of two massive **gatehouse towers.** Beyond is an immense grassy space, the outer bailey, protected on the west by a wall and tower topping the steep slope and on the north and east by the sea itself; the breakers crash against cliffs alive with sea-birds. There are long **views** up and down this wonderfully unspoiled coastline of rocky headlands and sweeping sandy bays backed by dunes. Nearby **Craster** is a tough little fishing village built in dark stone and noted for its kippers (cured herrings).

Warkworth – 7.5mi/12km east of Alnwick by A 1068. Within the easily defended site formed by a loop in the River Coquet is a remarkable sequence of castle ruin, dependent township, church and fortified bridge.

Warkworth Castle★ – ♿. ⏰ *Open late-Mar-Oct, daily, 10am-6pm (5pm Oct); Nov-Mar, daily, 10am-4pm weekends and Mondays only.* ⏰ *Closed 24-26 Dec, 1 Jan. ⬚ £3.00, concessions £2.30. Free tours of the Duke's rooms on Wednesdays, Sundays and Bank Holidays from April to September. Audio guide (40min). Parking. ☎ 01665 711 423; www.english-heritage.org. uk.* The castle, which perches high above the river, dates from the 12C and since 1332 has belonged to the Percys. Its general layout can be appreciated from the upper floor of the fine 13C **gatehouse.** The outer walls, punctuated by towers, enclose a compact area divided into an inner and an outer ward by the foundations of the castle church. The tower entrance to the **Great Hall** on the west is decorated with an odd, dog-faced version of the Percy lion. The most prominent feature is the exceptionally beautiful restored **keep,** designed for comfort and convenience as much as for defence.

From the castle the single street of the little planned town runs steeply downhill to the Norman **church of St Lawrence** and to the river crossing with its rare medieval bridge tower.

Warkworth Hermitage – *0.5mi/1km upstream by hired boat or by footpath and then ferry.* ⏰ *Open 11am-5pm Wed, Sun and Bank Hols 24 Mar to 30 September.* ⏰ *Closed 24-26 Dec, 1 Jan. ⬚ £2, £1.10 (concessions), 80p (child). Access by rowing boat; ☎ Warkworth Castle (♿ see above), www.english-heritage.org.uk.* In its peaceful riverside setting, this extraordinary late medieval retreat, partly hewn into the sandstone cliff, accommodated its hermit in some style, with a chapel and living quarters on two levels.

Rothbury – *11.5mi/18km southwest of Alnwick by B 6341.* The road climbs up over the fells. After 4.5mi/7km there are good **views** northwestwards towards the rounded hills building up to the summit of the Cheviots (2676ft/816m).

Cragside House★ – ⌖ ⏰ *House: Open 22 Mar to 25 September, Tue-Sun, 1-5.30pm, last admission 1hr before closing. Estate and gardens: 22 March to 30 October: 10.30am-7pm (5pm last admission); also 2 Nov to 18 Dec, Wed-Sun, 11am-4pm. ⊕ House, £8.50; estate and gardens £5.70. Parking (near house and in grounds). Restaurant, picnic places. ☎ 01669 620 333; 620 150; 620 448 (visitor centre). Fax 01669 620 066; cragside@national-trust.org.uk; www.nationaltrust.org.uk*

The stupendous success of his engineering and armament works at Newcastle enabled **Lord Armstrong** (1810-1900), perhaps the greatest of Victorian inventor/industrialists, to build this extraordinary country house in which Old English and Germanic styles are romantically combined. The many rooms of its well-preserved **interior★** give a fascinating insight into the comforts and pretensions of late-Victorian domestic life.

Rothbury – Population 1 694. The pleasant little stone town on the River Coquet is overlooked to the south by the crags of the Simonside Hills and is a good centre for exploring the **Northumberland National Park** *(National Park Once Brewed Visitor Centre: ⏰ Open mid Mar-end Oct, daily, 9.30am-5pm ; Nov-Mar, Sat-Sun, 10am-3pm. ☎ 01434 344 396; tic.oncebrewed@nnpa.org.uk; visitorservices@nnpa.org.uk; www. nnpa.org.uk. Ingram Visitor Centre: ⏰ Open Easter to 31 Oct, 10am-5pm; ☎ 01665 578 890; ingram@nnpa.org.uk. Rothbury Visitor Centre: ⏰ Open Easter to 31 Oct, daily, 10am-5pm ; Nov-Mar, Sat-Sun, 10am-3pm.. ☎ 01669 620 887. tic.rothbury@nnpa.org. uk; www.nnpa.org.uk).* This vast tract of wild and sparsely populated upland extends from the Cheviots in the north to Hadrian's Wall in the south.

Chillingham Castle – *12mi/19km northwest by B 6346; after 4mi/6.4km fork right into minor road to Chillingham. Allow at least 1hr 30min. ⏰ Open 1 May to 30 Sep, daily except Sat, 1-5pm last entry 4:30pm. ⊕ £4.50, £3.75 (senior), children free if accompanied by an adult. Tea room. ☎ 01668 215 359; info@chillingham-castle.com; www.chillingham-castle. com.* The 13C-14C castle, which retains its medieval character although it was remodelled in the 18C-19C, is still lived in by the descendants of the Earls Grey who were of Norman origin. Dungeons, torture chambers and **decorative interiors** – furniture, tapestries, arms – bear out the ancient history of the castle, in particular its strategic importance during border feuds; it also enjoyed royal patronage. The splendid **gardens** and avenues were laid out by the royal architect, Sir Jeffry Wyatville. The walk to the lake affords superb **views** of woodlands and of the Cheviot mountains.

Chillingham Wild Cattle – ⏰ ⌖ *Guided tour (1hr) Apr-Oct, Wed-Mon, 10am-noon and 2-5pm Sun 2 - 5pm ⊕ £4.50, £3 (concessions), £1.50 (child), £10 (family). Parking. ☎ 01668 215 250; www.chillingham-wildcattle.org.uk.* A herd of wild white cattle, last of the species which once roamed free through the forest stretching from the North Sea to the Clyde, still remains at Chillingham. Pure bred, uncrossed with domestic cattle, they have been in the park for the past 700 years. Their genetic survival is attributed to the fact that only the "king" bull sires the calves, thus breeding from strength.

Isle of **ANGLESEY**★★

YNYS MÔN – Anglesey, WALES

MICHELIN ATLAS P 32 OR MAP 503 G, H 23, 24

Anglesey, also known in Welsh as Môn or Mam Cymru (Mother of Wales), is an island off the north west tip of Wales, separated from the mainland by the Menai Strait; its landscape of low undulating hills, rich in prehistoric remains, is unlike anywhere else in the Principality. Anglesey and the Strait offer walkers and yachtsmen marvellous opportunities to follow their pastimes. ⊞ *Station Site, Llanfairpwllgwyngyll LL61 5UJ ☎ 01248 713 177; llanfairpwll@nwtic.com; www.anglesey. gov.uk* ⊞ *Port Terminal, Holyhead LL65 1DQ ☎01407 762 622; holyhead@nwtic.com*

▶ **Orient Yourself:** Base yourself in Beaumaris if you intend staying on Anglesey. Holyhead is an islet off Anglesey.

⌖ **Don't Miss:** Beaumaris Castle

Kids Especially for Kids: Beaches on the east coast at Beaumaris, Penmon, Llanddona, Benllech and St David's, and lots more all along the west coast; Beaumaris Castle.

Also See: Caernarfon, Conwy, Llandudno, Snowdonia

Sights

Llanfairpwllgwyngyllgogerychwyrndrobwllllantysiliogogogoch – *The church of St Mary by the white hazel pool, near to the fierce whirlpool by the red cave near St Tysilio's church.* The village name, Llanfair PG for short, was almost certainly strung together in the 19C to amuse – and baffle – English tourists. Rising on its hill above the village is the column and statue (112ft/34m) erected in memory of William Henry Paget, 1st Marquess of Anglesey (1768-1854), one of the Duke of Wellington's most trusted commanders.

Menai Bridge – Thomas Telford (1757-1834) built the suspension bridge to carry his road to Holyhead. The Admiralty insisted upon a clearance of 100ft/30m between water and roadway, and the bridge, with its span of 579ft/176m between towers, was the longest iron bridge in the world when it was opened in 1826.

Britannia Tubular Bridge – Designed by Robert Stephenson it carried the railway across the Strait, in 1850. The railway ran in two separate tubes; these were badly damaged by fire in 1970 and separate decks, between the original towers, now carry both road and rail.

Plas Newydd★★ – ♿ *wheelchair available* ⊙ *Open mid Mar to early Nov, Sat-Wed and Good Friday, noon (11am garden) to 5pm (5.30pm garden). Rhododendron garden: Open mid Mar to early-Jun ⊕ £5.00; garden only, £3.00. Woodland walk, marine walk, boat trip, children's adventure playground. Parking. Licensed tearoom, picnic area. Braille guide.* ☎ *01248 714 795; Fax 01248 713 673; plasnewydd@nationaltrust.org.uk; www.nationaltrust.org.uk.* This magnificently sited late 18C mansion in parkland and gardens (169 acres/68ha) looking over the Strait to the mountains of Snowdonia, and home of the Marquess of Anglesey, was given to the National Trust in 1976. During alterations to the house in 1936, the artist **Rex Whistler** was commissioned to decorate the long dining room. His whimsical masterpiece of trompe l'œil includes frequent references to the Paget family and contains a small portrait of himself, as a gardener sweeping up leaves.

Beaumaris★★ – One of the fortress towns founded in the late 13C by Edward I, Beaumaris is now the most peaceful of little resorts, with a wonderful prospect across the Menai Strait to Snowdonia. The **Castle**★, *(CADW* ⊙ *mid Mar-May and Oct, daily, 9.30am-5pm (6pm Jun to late-Sep); 1 Nov – 31 Mar , daily, 9.30am (11am Sun) to 4pm.* ⊙ *Closed 24-25 Dec.* ⊕ *£3* ☎ *01248 810 361, www.beaumaris.com)* was the last as well as the largest of Edward's Welsh strongholds. Though never finished, it is the finest example in Britain of a concentric castle. A moat surrounds it and there was a defended dock, capable of taking ships of up to 40 tons. The gatehouses were planned to have lavish accommodation; the **Great Hall,** impressive enough as it stands, would have risen to twice its present height, dominating the inner ward.

St Nicholas Church – This 14C church was built to serve the new town which grew up around the castle. In the porch is the stone coffin of Princess Joan, daughter of King John and wife of Llywelyn the Great, who died in 1237.

Court House and Gaol – ♿ *Limited wheelchair access, no charge* ⊙ *Open (except when the court is in session) Easter to late-Sep, daily, 10.30am-5pm.* ⊕ *Court House £1.50, £1 (concessions), family £4.25; Gaol £1.50 £1 (concessions)), family £4.25.* ☎ *01248 810 921 (gaol), 01248 811 691 (court); BeaumarisCourtandGaol@anglesey.gov.uk; www.anglesey. gov.uk/* The quaint Court House dates from 1614 and contrasts with Beaumaris Gaol, in use from 1829-75 and a grim reminder of the Victorian penal system, with stone floors, shackles and treadmill.

Oriel Ynys Môn★ – *On the outskirts of Llangefni.* ♿ ⊙ *Open Tues-Sun and bank holiday Mon, 10.30am-5pm; Guide book and text (2 languages). Café. Shop.* ☎ *01248 724 444; Fax 01248 750 282; rbjlh@anglesey.gov.uk; www.anglesey.gov.uk.* This modern museum and gallery on the outskirts of the market town succeeds admirably in explaining the island's special identity. As well as imaginative displays evoking Anglesey's rich past, there are explanations of current issues and a reconstruction of the Malltraeth studio of **Charles Tunnicliffe** (1901-79), perhaps the foremost wildlife painter of the 20C in Britain.

Welsh Historic Monument ©Crown

Beaumaris Castle

Holyhead – Holyhead Harbour has long been the main port of embarkation for Dublin from England and Wales. It is reached from the mainland of Anglesey by the causeway built in 1822 by Telford to Holy Island, whose coastline more than matches that of the rest of Anglesey for dramatic cliffscapes.

At **South Stack Cliffs**★ the teeming birdlife of the spectacularly folded cliffs can be viewed from the **RSPB reserve** (🕐 *Reserve open at all times. Ellins Tower information centre and Lighthouse visitor centre Open daily, Easter-Sept, 10.30am-5pm daily, 11am-5pm. No charge.* 🐾 *Guided tour of tower available from first Tuesday in May, Tues-Sat, at 2pm. Parking. Refreshments at South Stack Kitchen.* ☎ *01407 764 973; www.rspb.org. uk*) – through closed-circuit TV from the cliff-top **Bird Centre**, from the **Seabird Centre**, housed in the former lighthouse keeper's accommodation on the island, or in live close-up from **Ellin's Tower** on the cliff edge.

Isle of **ARRAN**★★

North Ayrshire, SCOTLAND

POPULATION 4 726

MICHELIN ATLAS P 53 OR MAP 501 E 17

ACCESS: SEE THE MICHELIN GUIDE GREAT BRITAIN AND IRELAND

Arran is the largest of the islands in the Firth of Clyde, just off Scotland's south west corner. Measuring some 20mi/32km long by 10mi/16km wide, and cut in two by the Highland Boundary Fault, Arran presents "Scotland in miniature". A mountainous northern part (Goat Fell 2 866ft/874m) has deep valleys and moorlands, whilst the southern half consists of more typically lowland scenery.

Sheltered bays and sandy beaches, together with ample facilities for yachting, swimming, golf, sea angling and fishing, make tourism the principal industry on Arran today. 🏛 *The Pier, Brodick KA27 8AU* ☎ *0845 225 5121; Fax; 01292 471 832; info@ ayrshire-arran.com; www.ayrshire-arran.com*

- 🔵 **Don't Miss:** Brodick Castle's rhododendron garden in bloom (late spring).
- 🔵 **Especially for Kids:** Sandy beaches.
- 🔵 **Also See:** Ayr, Glasgow.
- 🔵 Make sure the petrol tank is full before setting out on a tour of the island as there are few filling stations.

Tour of the Island

56mi/90km – about 1/2 day, not including visiting time. Mainly a coastal route, the road affords views of the diversity of scenery; but as well as the coast road, try the 10mi/16km String Road across the waist of the island, between Blackwaterfoot and Brodick.

Brodick Castle★★ – & ○ *Castle: Open Good Friday to 31Oct, daily, 11am-4.30pm (3.30pm Oct). Grounds open all year daily 9.30am to dusk. ⊙£10 (including garden). Guide book (2 languages); Information sheet (9 languages). ☎ 01770 302 462; Fax 01770 302 312; brodickcastle@nts.org.uk; www.nts.org.uk.* Historic stronghold of the Hamiltons, Earls of Arran, the 13C castle in red sandstone was extended by Cromwell's troops in 1652 and again in the baronial style by Gillespie Graham in 1844. The Hamilton and Beckford treasures comprise a fine collection of silver, porcelain, furniture and family portraits as well as paintings by Watteau, Turner and Herring. The gilded heraldic ceiling in the Drawing-Room is remarkable.

There is a formal walled garden from 1710 and a 65 acre/26ha **rhododendron garden**, one of the finest in Britain, which benefits from the mild climate.

Machrie Moor Stone Circles – *1.5mi/3km inland off the road north of Blackwaterfoot.* Moorland backed by mountains makes an impressive setting for these remnants of Bronze Age stone circles, built about the same time as the later parts of Stonehenge. Arran was on the main migration route for Neolithic agriculturalists up the western seaboard of Scotland.

As the road swings round Arran's southern tip the granite island of **Ailsa Craig** (1 000ft/300m high) can be seen to the south. The road from Lamlash Bay, sheltered by Holy Island, to Brodick gives a spectacular view of Brodick Castle dominated by Goat Fell.

AYR

South Ayrshire, SCOTLAND

POPULATION 47 872

MICHELIN ATLAS P 48 OR MAP 501 G 17

TOWN PLAN IN THE CURRENT MICHELIN GUIDE GREAT BRITAIN AND IRELAND

This pleasant market town, which has grown around its medieval core, is a thriving resort on Scotland's south west coast with splendid sandy beaches as well as a famous racecourse and golf courses which host international competitions. It is probably most notable, however, as the hub of **Burns Country**. ▯ *22 Sandgate, Ayr KA7 1BW ☎ 0845 225 5121; info@ayrshire-arran. com; www.ayrshire-arran.com*

A moving landmark

According to tradition **Auld Brig** (13C), a narrow cobbled bridge immortalised by the Scottish bard, Robert Burns, was financed by two sisters who lost their fiancés, drowned while trying to ford the river in spate.

Visit

Alloway★ – *3mi/5km south by B 7024.* Alloway is famed as the birthplace of the poet Robert Burns (1759-96), whose birthday on 25 January is celebrated by Scots (and others) throughout the world.

The spartan **Burns Cottage and Museum**★ (○ *Open daily, Apr-Sep, 9.30am-5.30pm; Oct-Mar, 10am-5pm. ○ Closed 1 Jan and 25 Dec. ⊙ £5 including Tam O'Shanter Experience and Monument. Parking. Refreshments. ☎ 01292 443700; Fax 01292 441 750; info@burnsheritagepark.com; www.burnsheritagepark.com)* evoke his humble origins and display an extensive collection of manuscripts and relics. To the south stands the **Burns Monument** overlooking the River Doon and the 13C **Brig o'Doon.** The **Tam o'Shanter Experience** (*All details as Burns Cottage and Museum ⊙ £1.50, or £5 Combined ticket with Burns Cottage and Museum*) presents the bard's life and times as well as an introduction to southwest Scotland. **Alloway Kirk** also has Burns associations.

Excursion

Culzean Castle★ – (NTS) *16mi/25km southwest of Ayr by A 719.* *Castle and visitor center: Open Easter/1 Apr (whichever earliest) to 31 Oct, daily, 10:30am-5pm. Country Park: Open daily, 9.30am-dusk.* *Castle and country park £12; country park only £8 Family and group tickets available. Guide book (3 languages and Braille). Leaflet (7 languages). Woodland Walks. Adventure playground. Parking. Restaurants.* ☎ *01655 884 455; Fax 01655 884 503; culzean@nts.org.uk; www.culzean-castle.net.* The coast road leads through Dunure, an attractive fishing village and on to the **Electric Brae,** where a curious optical illusion, caused by the lie of the surrounding countryside, makes the road appear to be descending, when it is, in fact, going uphill.

Robert Burns

Burns Cottage, Alloway

Culzean Castle (pronounced Cullane) in its dramatic clifftop **setting**★★★, was the work of **Robert Adam** (1728-92). Though a classicist, Adam added arrow slits and battlements to this his most spectacular castle, to complete the mock-medieval touch. The harmonious interior is enhanced by friezes, chimney-pieces and delicately patterned ceilings. The elegant **Oval Staircase**★★ and **Saloon** are good examples of the architect's original style. He also designed the splendid furnishings. The Eisenhower exhibition traces the castle's connection with the former American President.

BANFF★

Aberdeenshire, SCOTLAND

POPULATION 4 402

MICHELIN ATLAS P 69 OR MAP 501 M 10

Set on the coast at the mouth of the River Deveron, some 40mi/65km north of Aberdeen, the small town which became a royal burgh in the 12C boasts attractive 18C buildings (Low St, High Shore, Boyndie St, High St).

Visit

Duff House★★ – *Open daily 11am-5pm.* *£5.50. Shop. Tearoom.* ☎ *01261 818 181; Fax 01261 818 900; duff.house@aberdeenshire.gov.uk; www.duffhouse.org.uk.* The splendid Baroque mansion designed by William Adam, which was used as a military camp during the Second World War, has recently been restored to its former glory and enhanced by a rich array of furnishings, fittings and paintings (from the Scottish National Gallery collections). A double curving staircase rises up to the great central block framed by trees – the wings were never built – and Corinthian pilasters support a richly decorated pediment. Small intimate rooms surround the spacious Vestibule dominated by a grandiose painting by William Etty, and the Great Drawing-Room hung with Gobelins tapestries and pastoral paintings by Boucher. Fine paintings adorn the Great Staircase, where a porphyry lion's paw and marble wine cooler has pride of place, as well as other rooms.

Excursions

Banff is an excellent base for excursions along the splendid coastline, with magnificent views of cliffs and headlands, to the picturesque fishing villages of Portsoy, Cullen, Buckie (west) and Macduff, Gardenstown, Crovie, Pennan (east).

Museum of Scottish Lighthouses – Fraserburgh. *40mi/64km east by B 9031.* *Kinnaird Head, Stevenson Road. Open daily, 11am (10-6 Jul- Aug, noon Sun) to 5pm (4pm Nov-Mar).* *Closed 25 Dec.* *£4.75. A/V display.* *Guided tour. Parking. Cafe.* ☎ *01346 511*

Hall, Duff House

022; enquiries@lighthousemuseum.co.uk; www.lighthousemuseum.co.uk. Scotland's first lighthouse (1787) was located on the top floor of a mansion on Kinnaird Head overlooking the harbour which witnessed the heyday of the herring fishery in the 19C and early 20C. The museum tells the fascinating story of the "Northern Lights" and related technological advances, and evokes the lives of the dedicated keepers as well as the achievement of the Stevenson family who built some hundred lighthouses in all.

BATH★★★

Bath and North East Somerset, ENGLAND

POPULATION 85 202

MICHELIN ATLAS P 17 OR MAP 503 M 29

Bath combines the grace and elegance of the 18C with a long and varied past.
🛈 *Abbey Church Yard ☎ 0906 7112 000 (50p/min), from overseas 0044 870 444 6442; Fax 01225 477 787; www.visitbath.co.uk* 🛈 *Bradford-on-Avon: 50 St Margaret's Street BA15 1DE ☎ 01225 865 797; Fax 01225 868 722; tic@bradfordonavon.co.uk; www.bradfordonavon.co.uk*

▶ **Orient Yourself:** The centre is compact and most of the major sites are within walking distance of each other. The city is best seen on foot; there are numerous elegant street vistas and a wealth of attractive details. City Sightseeing/Guide Friday operate an open-top hop-on hop-off bus tour daily, *(9.15am-5.25pm, every 12min. £8 including discounted rates on entrance fees to most attractions. ☎ 01225 444 102; info@guidefriday.com; www.guidefriday.com, www.cityseeing.co.uk).*

🅿 **Parking:** A Park and Ride system is in operation (follow the signs).

🅐 **Don't Miss:** The Baths, Royal Crescent and by way of contrast (out of town) the American Museum.

🕓 **Organizing Your Time:** Allow at least two full days.

Kids **Especially for Kids:** The Baths, if they are studying the Romans at school. The American Museum.

🖐 **Also See:** Bristol, Cheltenham, The Cotswolds, Devizes, Glastonbury, Gloucester, Lacock, Longleat, Stonehenge, Stourhead, Wells.

🚶 **Walking Tours:** Jane Austen Walking Tour – 🕓 *daily at 11am from the Tourist Information Centre, tours last 1 ½ hours.* 🖙 *£4.50. ☎ www.janeausten.co.uk/centre/walking_tours.html;* Ghost Walks of Bath – 🕓 *Apr-Oct, Mon-Sat 8pm; Nov-Mar, Fri at 8pm, tours last about two hours.* 🖙 *£6. ☎ 01225 463 618; www.ghostwalksofbath.*

co.uk; Mayor's Guides walking tours – ⏱ *daily 10.30am and Sun-Fri 2pm., also May-Sep Tue, Fri, Sat 7pm, depart from outside the Roman Baths entrance, tours last 2 hours.* For more tours ☎ *www.greatbathpubcrawl.com* and *www.bizarrebath.co.uk.*

A Bit of History

Britain's only hot springs surfaced here c100 000 years ago. In 500 BC, according to legend, **Prince Bladud** (the father of King Lear), was cured of his leprosy by wallowing in the mud here. The **Romans**, in the 1C AD, made Bath England's first spa resort with baths, a temple, possibly a gymnasium or theatre... Later, the Saxons took Bath and built a town within the Roman walls and an abbey near the site of the Roman temple.

In the 11C **John de Villula** of Tours, Bishop of Wells and physician, bought Bath for £500. He began a vast Benedictine cathedral priory, and built a palace, new baths and a school. His cathedral was never completed: the present abbey stands on the site of the nave. Bath became a prosperous wool town, but at the Dissolution the monks were forced to sell off parts of the abbey. In 1574 Queen Elizabeth I had a fund set up to restore the abbey and enhance the town, and by the early 18C it had become a fashionable city, though dull and unorganised.

In 1704 **Beau Nash** (1673-1762) came to Bath and, as Master of Ceremonies, he opened the first Pump Room for taking the waters and meeting in polite society; he organised concerts, balls, gambling... Bath prospered – as did Nash – and became the most fashionable city in England. While Nash structured Bath society, **Ralph Allen** (1694-1764) and John Wood (1700-54) transformed its architecture and urban plan. Allen, a Cornish postmaster, made his fortune by creating an efficient postal service in Bath. He then bought quarries nearby in order to build a new city. John Wood, a Yorkshireman, had settled in Bath by 1728. He and his son John Wood (1728-81) were classicists, inspired by Bath's Roman past; they built in the Palladian style with the local honey-coloured stone, now known as **Bath Stone.**

Sights

Roman Baths★★ **(BX)** – ♿ ⏱ *Pump Room, Stall Street. Open Jan – Feb & Nov-Dec 9:30 am to 5:30 pm Mar – Jun, Sep, Oct 9am – 5 pm, Jul and Aug 9am – 9 pm; last entry 1hr after closing ⏱ Closed 25-26 Dec. ⬙ £9.50; combined ticket with Museum of Costume £12.50. Audio guide (7 languages). Guidebook (2 languages). Refreshments.*

Great Bath, Roman Baths

S. McBride/Bath of Northeast Somerset Council

Address Book

For coin ranges, see the Legend at the back.

WHERE TO EAT

Fishworks, *6 Green Street.* ☎ *01225 448707; bath@fishworks.co.uk; www.fishworks.co.uk.* A bustling place set above its own fish shop serving an extensive range of unfussy fish and seafood dishes.

No. 5, *5 Argyle Street.* ☎*/ Fax 01225 444 499.* Classical French cooking underpins this reasonably priced buzzing little bistro which is personally run by the cheery owner.

Hope and Anchor, *Midford* ☎*/Fax 01225 832 296; www. hopeandanchormidford.co.uk.* This cosy traditional pub 5 mi/8km south of Bath serves up hearty English classics such as roast veal chop, venison in sloe gin, and smoked duck, plus an impressive selection of real ales.

WHERE TO STAY

Leighton House, *139 Wells Road* ☎ *01225 314 769; Fax 01225 440 379; welcome@leighton-house.co.uk, www. leighton-house.co.uk.* This former Victorian gentleman's residence enjoys views over Bath, and offers eight individually designed floral bedrooms a ten minute stroll from the city centre.

Athole *33 Upper Oldfield Park* ☎ *01225 334 307; Fax 01225 320 009; info@ atholehouse.co.uk; www.atholehouse.co. uk.* This large Victorian home has been restored to give four quiet and spacious bedrooms contemporary styling and sleek furnishings. Quiet location away from main streets, but only 12 minutes' walk from the city centre.

☎ *01225 477 785; Fax 01225 477 743; romanbaths_bookings@bathnes.gov.uk; www. romanbaths.co.uk.* The baths are fed by a spring which pours out approximately 250 000 gallons/1 136 500 litres of water per day at a temperature of 116°F/46.5°C. Archeological exploration has recovered Mesolithic flints from the waters which indicate that the area was frequented by early man, long before it was inhabited by the Celtic tribe called the Dobunni who regarded the spring as a sacred site. The Roman complex consisted of the Great Bath, a large warm swimming pool, now open to the sky, and two baths of decreasing heat; later a *frigidarium* was built on the west side with openings at the north, overlooking the sacred spring, and two more heated chambers (*tepidarium and caldarium*). The east end was subsequently enlarged, the baths were elaborated and the *frigidarium* transformed into a cold plunge circular bath.

After the Romans had left, the drains soon clogged through lack of attention and mud covered the site. In the early Middle Ages the Normans constructed the King's Bath around the tank which the Romans had lined with Mendip lead. In the 1680s, bathing attire consisted of yellow linen shifts and caps for women, knee-length drawers for men, and birthday suits for children. In 1727 workmen building a sewer along Stall Street found the gilded bronze head of **Minerva**, the goddess of the spring. Since

Georgian terrace architecture, Bath

A. Tavener/MICHELIN

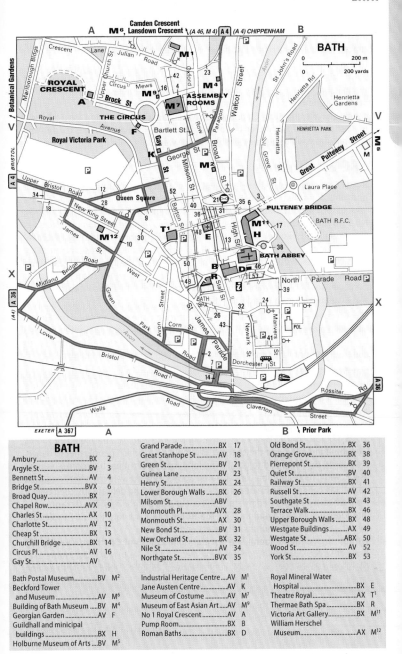

then excavations have revealed the temple and baths complex and a wide variety of artefacts now on display in the **museum**.

Bath Abbey★ (BX) – ♿ *13 Kingston Buildings* ⏱*Open Mon-Sat, 9am-6pm (4.30pm Nov-Easter), Sun, 1-2.30pm and 4.30-5.30pm.* ⏱ *Closed Good Friday, 24-25 Dec (except for services).* ☜ *Donation £2.50.* ☎ *01225 422462; Fax 01225 429990; office@bathabbey. org; www.bathabbey.org.* The present sanctuary, on the site of an abbey founded early in the reign of King Offa (757-96), was begun in 1499 by Bishop Oliver King. From the pillars of the Norman church arose the pure late Perpendicular abbey. At the Dissolution, the incomplete building fell into disrepair, but restoration was begun in the late 16C. Further, more substantial alterations were carried out under Sir Gilbert Scott in 1864-76. Outside, five-light windows stand between flying buttresses, crocketed pinnacles and a castellated pierced parapet. The **west end** has a Perpendicular window, 17C door and, in the stone, tall ladders with angels ascending and descending. Inside, the nave, chancel and narrow transepts soar to **fan vaulting** by Robert and William Vertue (designers of the fan vaulting in the Henry VII Chapel, Westminster Abbey).

Pump Room★ (BX) –   *Open daily for lunch and light refreshments.* *Closed 25-26 Dec.* ☎ *01225 444477 (table reservations); www.romanbaths.co.uk.* The present Pump Room, built in 1789-99, after Nash's death, is nonetheless presided over by his **statue**. The interiors are now elegantly furnished with ornamental pilasters, gilded capitals, a coffered ceiling, Chippendale-style chairs, a Tompion long-case clock and a glass chandelier. The rounded bay overlooking the King's Bath contains the drinking fountain, from which people can still take the waters.

18C Elegance

Royal Crescent★★★ (AV) – The great arc of thirty terrace houses, in which the horizontal lines are counterbalanced by 114 giant Ionic columns rising from the first floor to the pierced parapet, was the great achievement of John Wood II, in 1767-74. **No 1 Royal Crescent★★** (*Open mid-Feb to Nov, Tue-Sun and Bank Hol Mon and Mon during Bath Festival, 10.30am-5pm (4pm Nov).* *Closed Good Fri* ⊛ *£4. Leaflet (11 languages).* ☎ *01225 428 126; Fax 01225 481 850; admin@bptrust.demon.co.uk; www.bath-preservation-trust.org.uk)* has been authentically restored, providing a perfect setting for Chippendale, Sheraton and Hepplewhite furniture and for porcelain and 18C glassware. **Brock Street,** which links the Crescent to the Circus, was also built by John Wood II in 1767.

The Circus★★★ (AV) – The King's Circus, although one of John Wood the Elder's earliest concepts, was built in 1754. It is a tight circle of identical houses, pierced by three equidistant access roads. The houses of pale Bath stone, decorated with coupled columns, rise three floors to a frieze and acorn-topped balustrade.

Gay Street (AV), linking the Circus to Queen Square (AV), was the work of the two Woods, father and son, from 1734 to 1760, while Queen Square was the elder Wood's first example of urban planning.

Assembly Rooms★ (AV) –   *Bennett Street. Open (pre-booked functions permitting) daily, 10am-5pm.* *Closed 25-26 Dec. No charge. Audio guide (7 languages)* ☎ *01225 477 789; Fax 01225 444 793; www.nationaltrust.org.uk.* These elegant rooms were built in 1769-71 for the evening assemblies – at which people met to dance, play cards, drink tea and to gossip. The long, pale green-blue ballroom is as high as it is wide, its decoration concentrated above, at window level, where engaged Corinthian columns rise to support a deep entablature and delicate stuccoed ceiling from which are suspended five magnificent crystal chandeliers. The **Octagon** was intended as a small card room. The **Tea Room** has a rich interior with a splendid two-tiered screen of columns at its west end.

Within the Assembly Rooms the fascinating **Museum of Costume★★★** (*Bennett Street. Open daily, Jan, Feb, Nov, Dec, 11 am to 4 pm Mar – Oct 11am-5 pm.* *Closed 25-26 Dec.* ⊛ *£6.25, concessions £5.25; combined ticket with Roman Baths £12.50. Audio guide (7 languages).* ☎ *01225 477 785; Fax 01225 477 743; costume_bookings@bathnes.gov.uk; www.museumofcostume.co.uk)* presents a colourful and elegant display of the rich range of styles, textures and patterns used in every sort of garment from the Stuart period to the present day. Note in particular the museum's oldest complete attire, the **Silver Tissue Dress** (1660s), and its selection of superb gloves.

Pulteney Bridge★ (BV) – *Same opening times as the Assembly Rooms, above.* ⊛ *£3.80, £2.70 (child).* The bridge, built in 1769-74 to Robert Adam's design, has small shops on both sides, domed end pavilions and a central Venetian window.

Jane Austen Centre – *40 Gay Street , Queens Square.* *Open daily, Summer 10am to 5.30pm 30 Oct to early Mar 11am*

Jane Austen (1775-1817)

Jane visited Bath when staying with her aunt and uncle, the Leigh Perrots, at No 1 The Paragon, and it was in Bath that she set much of *Northanger Abbey.*

In May 1799, the Austen family took lodgings at 13 Queen Square; later, they resided at 4 Sydney Place; it was during their time at 27 Green Park Buildings, that Jane's father died in January 1805; on two further occasions, the remaining ladies of the family lived both at 25 Gay Street and in Trim Street.

It is from Jane's letters to her sister Cassandra, however, that the most vivid portrait of Bath is gleaned.

to 4.30pm. 🖾 *£5.95* ☎ *01225 443 000; Fax 01225 443 018; info@janeausten.co.uk; www.janeausten.co.uk.* The exhibition is devoted to Jane Austen, who knew Bath, both as a visitor and a resident. Every place in Bath associated with Jane or her novels is identified.

Excursions

Dyrham Park★ – *8mi/15km north on A 46. House and garden:* ♿ 🕐 *House: Open late-Mar to early-Nov, Fri-Tue, 12 – 4pm (3:30pm last admission). Garden: Open late-Mar to early-Nov, Fri-Tue, 11am-5pm Park year round 11am - 5pm.* 🖾 *House and grounds £8.80; garden and park only £3.40). Parking. Restaurant, picnics in the park* ☎ *0117 937 2501 Fax 01179 372 501; dyrhampark@nationaltrust.org.uk; www.nationaltrust.org.uk.* The 17C-18C mansion was built for William Blathwayt (1649-1717), whose first architect took back the existing Tudor house to the Great Hall and built instead a formal regular entrance front of local stone. In 1698 the second phase began with "the ingenious **Mr Talman**" as architect. Talman's façade of Cotswold stone, 130ft/40m long, with two storeys rising to an attic topped by the same balustrades and urns as on the other side, is lightened by touches of Baroque ornament. The house contains various 17C and 18C furnishings, objects and works of art, mainly from England and the Low Countries. The **garden** and **park** were designed by Talman and George Wise, but were later replanned by **Humphry Repton** (1752-1818).

American Museum in Britain, Claverton★★ – *3mi/5km east on A 36* ♿ 🕐 *Open mid-Mar – Oct, mid Nov – mid Dec, Tue – Sun 12.00 – 5.30 pm ; Bank Hol Mon and Mon in Aug.* 🖾 *Museum, grounds and galleries £6.50; grounds and galleries £4.* ☎ *01225 460 503; Fax 01225 480 726; info@americanmuseum.org; www.americanmuseum.org.* The museum is housed in Claverton Manor, a Classical country house. The nucleus of its collection is a series of furnished rooms dating from the late 17C to the middle of the 19C presenting 200 years of American life and styles. Besides special galleries, there are also various exhibits in the spacious grounds, including a colonial herb garden and an arboretum.

Bradford-on-Avon★★ – *8mi/13km on A 4, then A 363 southeast.* The houses rising up the hillside from the River Avon give the town its charm and character. The larger houses built in the local creamy-yellow ochre limestone reflect the affluence of the 17C-18C clothiers when the town prospered as a wool centre. The nine-arched **bridge**★, built in 1610 with a small square, domed chapel topped by a weather-vane, is the best starting point for the walk to the top of this attractive town.

The Saxon **church of St Laurence**★★, (♿ 🕐 *Open all year, daily, 10am-7pm (4pm winter).* ☎ *01225 865 797)* may date from the 7C-8C when, as William of Malmesbury records, St Aldhelm built a church here. Having served as a school, cottage and charnel house, the church was re-discovered in 1856. The minute stone building, tall and narrow with steeply pitched roofs and **blind arcading**, is believed to have been erected in a single phase. Windows were inserted in the west end in the 19C. The vast early 14C stone **tithe barn**★ (♿ 🕐 *Open daily, 10.30am-4pm. Parking.* ☎*01345 090 899; www.english-heritage.org.uk)* has gabled doorways and a superbly constructed wooden roof.

BERWICK-UPON-TWEED ★★

Northumberland, ENGLAND

POPULATION 13 544

MICHELIN ATLAS P 57 OR MAP 502 O 16 – LOCAL MAP TWEED VALLEY

As a result of its location right on the border – north east to the English, south east to the Scots – the seaside town of Berwick has been held alternately by the two nations since the 12C. *Castlegate Car Park.* ☎ *01289 330 733; Fax 01289 330 448; tourism@berwick-upon-tweed.gov.uk; www.berwick-upon-tweed.gov.uk/guide.*

A Bit of History

From 1558 onwards the **Walls**★ were replaced with ramparts and bastions in the style just being introduced in Verona, Antwerp and other European cities. The elegant 15-arch **Old Bridge**, built in 1611, is the fifth known structure to have been built between Berwick and Tweedmouth. The castle, where on 17 November 1292 **Edward I** heard the petitions of 13 contenders for the throne of Scotland and gave his decision in favour of John Baliol, has largely been demolished and the railway station was built on part of the site in the 19C. Some of the stone was used for Holy Trinity Church (1651), one of the few to have been built during the Commonwealth, and the remainder was "quarried" in 1720 to build **Berwick Barracks**, which now houses two museums.

🚶 **Don't Miss:** Holy Island.

Especially for Kids: Bamburgh Castle, especially its arms and armour.

Also See: Alnwick, Edinburgh, Tweed Valley.

Cycling: Follow the marked Coast & Castle Cycle Route.

Sights

Burrell at Berwick Collection – *Berwick Barracks, Clock Block, Ravensdowne ◷ Open daily, 10am-6pm. ◷ Closed 1 Jan, 24-26 Dec. ☎ 01289 304 493 (English Heritage); 01289 301 869 (Borough Museum and Art Gallery); museum@berwick-upon-tweed.gov.uk; www.english-heritage.org.uk.* The excellently crafted pieces collected by the "magpie millionaire" **Sir William Burrell** include Imari ware, brassware, medieval religious art, Chinese bronzes and glassware.

Kings Own Scottish Borderers Museum – *Berwick Barracks. The Parade ◷ Open 1 Apr – 30 Sept Mon-Sat, 10am-6pm; 1 Oct – 31 Mar 10am – 4pm. ◷ Closed 1 Jan, 24-26 Dec. ☞ £3. ☎ 01289332 817; Fax 01289 331928; kosbmus@ milnet.uk.net; www.kosb.co.uk.* The history of the regiment, one of the five "numbered" regiments which have never been amalgamated, is traced from its formation in 1689.

Excursions

Lower Tweed Valley★★ – *See TWEED VALLEY.*

Holy Island★ – *13mi/21km south by A 1 and a minor road east; the causeway to Holy Island can be crossed only at low tide. Accessible by a causeway at low tide only; time tables posted at either end of the causeway; Is@ berwick-upon-tweed.gov.uk.*

Saint Cuthbert (AD 635-87), hermit monk from Holy Island, who became Bishop of Lindis-

The Lindisfarne Gospels (detail)

The Bridgeman Art Library

farne in AD 685, is buried in Durham Cathedral. Here were written and magnificently illuminated in Celtic tradition the **Lindisfarne Gospels,** now preserved in the British Museum.

Lindisfarne Priory★ – ⏱ *Open daily, 10am-6pm (4pm, Oct-late Mar).* ⏱ *Closed 24-26 Dec.* 🎟 *£2.70, £1.40 (child), £2 (concessions). Parking. Shop.* ☎ *01289 389 200.* The ruins visible today are those of a Benedictine house, founded from Durham in 1093.

Lindisfarne Castle★ – (EH) ⏱ *Open daily, 10am-6pm (5pm Oct, 4pm Nov-late-Mar); access to the island is restricted by tides, opening times vary accordingly.* ⏱ *1 Jan and 24-26 Dec.* 🎟 *£3 Public car park 1mi from the castle, additional parking on the approach road (charge).* ☎ *01289 389 200; 01289 330 733; www.english-heritage.org. uk.* 16C castle, restored in 1902 by Edwin Lutyens as a holiday home for the founder of *Country Life* magazine, Edward Hudson. The austere but beautifully designed interior is in the inimitable "Lutyens" style.

Bamburgh Castle★ – *20mi/32km south by A 1 and B 1342 east.* ⏱ *Open mid Mar-31 Oct, daily, 11am-5pm.* 🎟 *£5.50. Parking £1. Tearooms.* ☎ *01668 214 515; Fax: 01668 214 060; bamburghcastle@aol.com; www.bamburghcastle.com.* The **Norman keep** still dominates this castle, which was restored in the Victorian era. Bought by Lord Armstrong in 1894, it houses a fine collection of arms and armour from the Tower of London and much Sèvres, Crown Derby, Worcester and Chelsea porcelain. There are exquisite small collections of silver vinaigrettes, Fabergé carvings and jade, and in what was probably the Norman guard room, now the Court Room, a number of family portraits, including one of the present Lady Armstrong by Annigoni.

Farne Islands★ – *15mi/24km south by A 1 and B 1342/1340 east to Seahouses.* ♿ ⏱ *Open May-Jul, daily, 10.30am-1.30pm (Staple Island), 1.30pm-5pm (Inner Farne); late-Mar and Aug-Sep, daily, 10.30am-6pm* 🎟 *Landing fee: May-Jul (breeding season) £5; Apr, Aug-Sep £5. Fee does not include boatmen's charges; access by boat (weather permitting) from Seahouses Harbour.* 👒 *Hats should be worn.* ☎ *01665 721 099 (infoline); 01665 720 651 (warden).* The islands, 15 to 28 of them, depending upon the tide, provide nesting sites for 18 species of seabirds, and are home to the largest British colony of the grey seal. On Inner Farne, where landing is permitted dependent on the breeding dates, is a small chapel, dedicated to St Cuthbert, who lived on the islands from AD 676-685. The islands were home to **Grace Darling,** who, on 7 September 1838 with her father, the keeper of the lighthouse, rowed to the rescue of nine persons from the paddle-steamer *Forfarshire,* aground on Harcar's Rock.

BEVERLEY★

East Yorkshire, ENGLAND

POPULATION 23 632

MICHELIN ATLAS P 41 OR MAP 502 S 22

Georgian façades hide the ancient timber buildings of a town which in 1377, with 5 000 inhabitants, was half the size of York (some 28 mi/45km west) and twice as big as Hull (7 mi/11km south). Behind its 1832 façade, the Guildhall (not open to the public) built in 1762 has a fine courtroom, with a glorious stucco ceiling by Cortese. 🛈 *The Guildhall, Register Square* ☎ *01482 867 430; Fax 01482 863 913.*

Sights

Beverley Minster★★ – ⏱ *Open Mon-Sat, 9am-5pm (5:30 pm May-Aug ; 4pm Nov-Feb), Sun noon -4pm. Services: Sun at 8am, 10.30am, 6.30pm.* 🎟 *Donation £2.* 🔍 *Guided tour by appointment (2 languages)* ☎ *01482 868 540; Fax 01482 887 520; rogershaw@ beverleyminster.co.uk; www.beverleyminster.co.uk.* John of Beverley, Bishop of Hexham and York, sought seclusion in his old age and died here in 721. He was buried in the church he had founded 30 years before. Today's Minster was begun about 1220, an earlier church having been burnt down on 20 September 1188. The Minster is of almost "Cathedral" proportions (332ft/101m long).

Building began at the east end and the Early English style with shafted lancet windows is carried back to the transepts. The nave is Decorated, early 1300s, with the clerestory transitional between Decorated and Perpendicular. The west front is wholly Perpendicular, being completed by 1420.

The great east window, a Perpendicular nine-lighted window containing all the fragments of medieval glass the Minster once possessed, was bequeathed in 1416.

The ornate double staircase in the north wall of the chancel once led to the chapter-house (no longer extant). The Snetzler organ (1769) has 4 000 pipes, 70 stops and four consoles. It was restripped in 1995. The gilding and Sir George Gilbert Scott screen date from 1880.

The Percy Tomb (1340-49) and its canopy, with angels, symbolic beasts, and leaf carvings, is the most splendid of funerary monuments from the Decorated period. It probably commemorates Lady Eleanor Percy, who died in 1328. Sixty-eight misericords in the choir stalls, work of the Ripon school of woodcarvers early in the 16C, are some of the finest in Britain.

St Mary's Church★ – *Open Apr-Sep, Mon-Fri, 9.15am-noon and 1.30-5pm (6.30pm Fri, Jun-Aug), Sat, 10am-5.30pm, Sun, 2pm-5pm; Oct-Mar, Mon-Fri, 9.15am-noon and 1pm-4.15pm. Brochure (4 languages). ☎ 01482 865 709 (church); 01482 860 889 (secretary); www.stmarysbeverley.org.uk.* Founded c 1120, St Mary's was soon adopted by the trade Guilds, and transepts and nave aisles were quickly added. The tiny (36x18ft/11x5.5m) Chapel of St Michael with its ingenious "telescopic" spiral staircase is contemporary with the Percy Tomb in the Minster. The Perpendicular west front with slim shafts and fine mouldings is comparable with King's College Chapel in Cambridge. By 1524 the addition of the tower completed what is one of the finest parish churches.

An extensive collection of carvings of medieval musical instruments is shared between the Minster and St Mary's at Beverley. All told there are 140 represented. Three of the musicians on the brightly painted Minstrels' Pillar in the nave, donated by the Guild of Musicians in 1524, have, unfortunately, lost their instruments, but there are many others, on pew ends, choir stalls, ceiling bosses and in the south porch. The chancel ceiling, painted in 1445, with its pictorial record of 40 English kings, is unique. The keen observer will see a portrait of George VI, which, in 1939, replaced one of the legendary kings in the original design. Twenty-three misericords with extraordinary carvings of animals and men adorn the choir stalls. A "Pilgrim Rabbit" carved about 1325, on a doorway to the sacristy, may have influenced Sir John Tenniel when he drew the "White Rabbit" in his illustrations for *Alice in Wonderland*.

Excursion

Burton Agnes Hall★ – *18mi/29km – north on A 164 to Great Driffield and A 166 towards Bridlington. ♿ Open Apr (Good Fri if earlier) to Oct, daily, 11am-5pm;☞ £5.20. Leaflet (4 languages). ☞ Guided tour (75min). Parking. Licensed cafeteria. Wheelchair access to ground floor. ☎ 01262 490 324; Fax 01262 490 513; burton.agnes@farmline.com; www.burton-agnes.co.uk.* An outstanding example of late Elizabethan architecture, a mellow red brick house, started in 1598, finished in 1610 and little altered since.

In the Great Hall are a screen and alabaster chimneypiece, crowded with fantastic and allegorical carvings, unmatched in Britain. A Dance of Death carving, gruesome but magnificently detailed, is above the fireplace in the Drawing Room. The Staircase allowed generous scope for the Elizabethan woodcarvers to display their talents. The Long Gallery, with its restored plasterwork tunnel-vault ceiling, looks as it did in 1610 and houses many of the Impressionist and post-Impressionist paintings collected by the family.

BIRMINGHAM★

West Midlands, ENGLAND

POPULATION 965 928

MICHELIN ATLAS P 27 OR MAPS 403 OR 404 O 26

The second city of the Kingdom, the geographical heart of England, and one of the centres of the Industrial Revolution, Birmingham still produces a high proportion of Britain's manufactured exports.

▶ **Orient Yourself**: Birmingham is a large city and its attractions are spread over a wide area. Discuss public transport options at the nearest tourist information office.

Don't Miss: Birmingham Museum and Art Gallery, especially its Pre-Raphaelite collection; Black Country Living Museum, Dudley.

Organizing Your Time: Allow 2 days.

Especially for Kids: Cadbury World, Bourneville; Thinktank; National Sea Life Centre.

A Bit of History

Industrialisation began in the mid 16C, the city "swarming with inhabitants and echoing with the noise of anvils" (William Camden) By the mid 17C, in keeping with its radical tradition, it was supplying the Parliamentarians with swords and guns, which provoked Prince Rupert to sack the city. Its 18C growth, marked by the miles of canals radiating from the centre (Birmingham has more miles of canal than Venice) attracted **James Watt** (1736-1819), inventor of the double-action steam engine, **William Murdock** (1754-1839), inventor of coal-gas lighting, and **Matthew Boulton** (1728-1809), whose Soho factory was the first to be lit by gas.

Reaction to the grim conditions caused by the city's phenomenal growth in the 19C came in two ways: a radical approach to civic improvement, pioneered by Joseph Chamberlain (1869-1940), many times mayor and father of Neville Chamberlain, mayor in his time, but ill-fated as Prime Minister; it came also in the private philanthropy of the cocoa manufacturer, George Cadbury (1839-1922), responsible for one of the world's first garden suburbs, Bournville.

The face of the modern city owes much to the ambitious development projects following the Second World War. Expressways, underpasses and high-rise buildings have not created the most attractive of townscapes, but the indoor shopping centres are convenient and there are striking new landmarks like the huge Central Library and the International Convention Centre. Though much was demolished in the course

Address Book

OUT AND ABOUT IN BIRMINGHAM

Tourist Information Centre –

🖥 *Convention & Visitor Bureau 2 City Arcade B2 4TX* ☎ *0121 643 2514; Fax 0121 616 1038; www.beinbirmingham.com* 🖥 *Visitor Information Centre, 130 Colmore Row* ☎ *0121 693 6300 ; Fax: 0121 693 9600.* 🖥 *National Exhibition Centre Convention & Visitor Bureau* ☎ *0121 780 4321.* 🖥 *Birmingham Airport Information Desk.*

Pubs and Restaurants – Visit the Water's Edge and Brindley Place developments in the Gas Street Basin area for lively wine bars, café bars, restaurants and traditional English pubs. There is a wide choice of cuisine on offer in Birmingham but the town is famous for its Chinese and Indian restaurants. The Balti curry houses are renowned.

Shopping – The Pallasades and The Pavilions shopping complexes house most of the major department stores and High Street brands. Explore the Jewellery Quarter for shops selling hand-made gold and silver jewellery.

Entertainment – The Water's Edge quarter offers fine jazz music at the Ronnie Scott's Club and dancing in the nightclubs.

The National Exhibition Centre (NEC) hosts major shows such as the Motor Show, Crufts and the BBC Clothes Show. The Symphony Hall at the NEC holds concerts of classical music while pop and rock concerts and major sporting events are staged in the NEC arena.

of enthusiastic redevelopment, enough fine late 19C/early 20C buildings remain to evoke the atmosphere of the city's civic heyday. The **Bull Ring (KZ)**, an icon of insensitive mid-20C architecture, has now been redeveloped into a new shopping centre boasting spectacular buildings and large-scale public art.

The position of the city and its West Midland hinterland at the hub of industrial Britain is emphasised by its centrality in the national motorway network; a particularly elaborate interchange is known with perverse pride as **Spaghetti Junction**. Especially well served by transport links of all kinds, including Birmingham's international airport, are the vast modern halls of the **National Exhibition Centre (NEC).**

After a century of city status Britain's second city is determined to acquire a new image as a European business and cultural centre. Parts of the townscape have been transformed; the total redesign of **Victoria Square** and its decoration with modern sculpture is generally held to be more successful than the layout of **Convention Square**, graced by the heroically-scaled *Forward* by local sculptor Raymond Mason (b 1922). A superb symphony hall in the International Convention Centre is home to the City of Birmingham Symphony Orchestra (CBSO), the refurbished Birmingham Hippodrome Theatre is the new headquarters for the Birmingham Royal Ballet, formerly Sadler's Wells, and the NEC and the National Indoor Arena (NIA) host myriad sporting events.

Museums and Galleries

Birmingham Museum and Art Gallery★★ (JZ) – ♿ 🕐 *Chamberlain Square. Open daily, 10am (10.30am Fri, 12.30pm Sun) to 5pm.* 🕐 *Closed 1 Jan and 25 Dec.* ☎ *0121 303 2834, 0121 303 1966; www.bmag.org.uk.* The pride of a city whose coat of arms is flanked by a masculine Industry and a feminine Art, Birmingham's gallery is famed for its outstanding collection of **pre-Raphaelite paintings**. At the top of the entrance stairs is a charming fresco, a street scene of 1914 by the local artist Joseph Southall; next is the superb Sultanganj Buddha, the right hand offering peace, the left a blessing. The spacious round room, the original gallery, is crowded with 18C and 19C paintings, among them Leader's *February Fill Dyke,* presided over by Jacob Epstein's *Lucifer*. The elaborate ironwork of the two-tiered Industrial Gallery is a late-Victorian marvel, a fascinating setting for the well-displayed ceramics and stained glass. Beyond it is the surprise of the **Edwardian Tea Room** (restored).

Among the extensive holding of European paintings are outstanding works like the *Madonna and Child* by Bellini, a Claude *Landscape near Rome* and a *Roman Beggar Woman* by Degas. English paintings include works by Wright, Hogarth, Gainsborough and Constable, and by the Birmingham landscape painter, David Cox. At the heart of the collection are the pre-Raphaelites: mostly key works like *The Last of England* by Ford Madox Brown, *The Blind Girl* by Millais, **Beata Beatrix** by Rossetti and *Two Gentlemen of Verona* by Hunt. Another famous 19C work is Augustus Leopold Egg's *The Travelling Companions,* sitting timelessly in their Italian railway carriage, while a selection of 20C paintings includes Sickert's *Miner*.

Birmingham Museum and Art Gallery, Birmingham

Two Gentlemen of Verona by William Holman Hunt

Other rooms are devoted to local history, archaeology and natural history; there is a spectacular **fossilised skull** of a triceratop. The Pinto Gallery contains an extraordinary array of wooden objects from medieval times onwards.

Barber Institute of Fine Arts★★ (HX) – *University of Birmingham Edgbaston. 2.5mi/4km south of the city centre on A 38. From the Bristol Road turn right up Edgbaston Park Road to the University south car park. By train: from New Street station to University station.* ♿ ⊙ *Open daily, 10am (noon Sun) to 5pm.* ⊙ *Closed 1 Jan, Good Friday, 25-26 Dec. Parking.* ☎ *0121 472 0962 (24hr Information), 0121 414 7333 (enquiries), Fax 0121 414 3370; info@barber.org.uk; www.barber.org.uk.* The Institute is part of the sprawling campus of England's archetypal "red-brick" university, a civic foundation which achieved full university status in 1900. Brick of a most uncompromising redness was used in the crescent of ponderous edifices around Chancellor's Court and in the extraordinary Sienese campanile (328ft/100m high), known as Chamberlain Tower.

The gallery itself is in a severe stone and brick building begun in 1935. Within is a small but lovingly chosen and representative collection, built up with the bequest of Lady M C H Barber (d 1933) and displayed together with furniture and other objets d'art. As Sir Henry Barber did not appreciate modern art and stipulated that all works had to be pre-1900, there is a predominance of Old Masters. Among the Italian works there are several Venetians, a *Portrait of a Boy* by Bellini, a *Crucifixion* by Cima, and a *Regatta* by Guardi. Flemish paintings include Brueghel the Younger's *Two Peasants Binding Faggots*, and the wonderfully fresh, "pure" *Landscape near Malines* by Rubens.

The French School is well represented, with works by Poussin, Watteau, Delacroix, Ingres, Corot and Courbet. There is a bright portrait of the Countess Golovine by Elisabeth Vigée-Lebrun and an outstanding group of Impressionists and Post-Impressionists, including Bonnard, Degas, Gauguin, Manet, Monet, Renoir, Vuillard and Van Gogh. Among the English painters are the *Harvest Wagon* by Gainsborough, a *View near Harwich* by John Bernay Crome, Turner's *Sun Rising through Vapour* and Whistler's sensitive study of two girls, *Symphony in White*.

Thinktank – ♿ ⊙ *Open every day, 10am-5pm (4pm last admission).* ⊙ *£6.95; joint ticket with IMAX £11. Parking (charge). Café.* ☎ *0121 202 2222; www.thinktank.ac.* Ten themed galleries chart scientific and technological invention. Testimonies from people involved in the various activities which account for Birmingham's industrial progress give an historical perspective.

Additional Sights

Aston Hall★★ (HV) – *2mi/3km north of the city centre on A 38 (M).* ⊙ *Open Easter to 31 Oct Tue-Sun and Bank Hol Mon, 11:30am- 4pm. Parking. Tearoom. No stiletto heels. No unaccompanied children under 16* ☎ *0121 327 0062; www.bmag.org.uk.* The "noble fabric which for beauty and state much exceedeth anything in these parts" was built (1618-35) by John Thorpe for Sir Thomas Holte, besieged by the Parliamentarians in 1643 (shot marks punctuate its staircase balustrade of sea monsters), used as the setting for Washington Irving's novel *Bracebridge Hall* (1822), leased 1819-48 to James Watt's son.

The typically Jacobean **interior** ("uniformed without, though severely partitioned within": Francis Bacon) is characterised by splendidly ornate ceilings and fireplaces. Its most gorgeous rooms are the long gallery, with its strapwork ceiling, arcaded oak panelling and de la Planche tapestries of the *Acts of the Apostles*, and the great dining room, with more extravagant strapwork, a frieze of the Nine Worthies (Alexander, Hector, Caesar, Joshua, David, Judas Maccabeus, Arthur, Charlemagne and Godfrey of Bouillon) and paintings by Romney and Gainsborough.

For a week in early December Aston Hall by Candlelight re-creates the atmosphere of a Jacobean Christmas with evening tours around the house lit only by candles. Costumed musicians perform period music in the Great Hall with its vast, banked fire (*advance booking is essential*).

St Philip's Cathedral (KYZ) – Thomas Archer's first major commission was built 1711-25 in a very English classical Baroque; its exterior is saved from severity by its exuberant west tower (concave-sided with dome and lantern) and its west door (a baroque joke incorporating as many styles as possible).

The nave, arcades and galleries make a moving contrast to Burne-Jones' gigantic **stained glass portrayals**★ of the Nativity, Crucifixion, Ascension and Last Judgement.

Canal Walk (JYZ) – *1mi/1.6km.* The walk between Gas Street Basin **(JZ)** and the Museum of Science and Industry **(JY)** passes the canals, locks, bridges and buildings spawned by the city's 19C expansion.

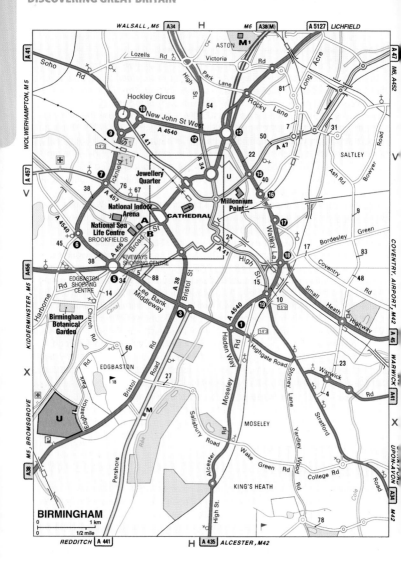

BIRMINGHAM

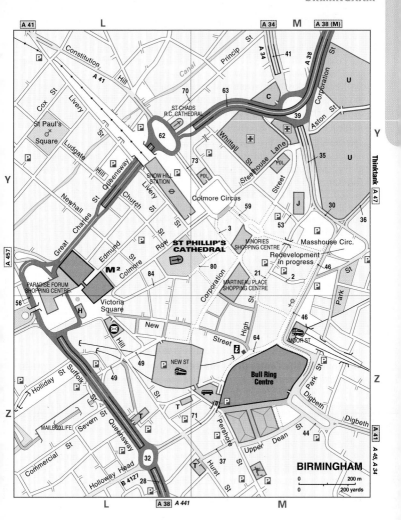

BIRMINGHAM

The **Gas Street Basin (JZ)** is surrounded by both new and restored 18C and 19C buildings, including a 23-storey hotel and Matthew Boulton's factory, known as the Brasshouse in Broad Street, refurbished to accommodate a restaurant and pub. The gaily painted narrow boats moored along the quay are typical of the craft which once plied the Midlands' canal network.

On the east bank is the **International Convention Centre,** a modern structure providing comprehensive facilities: 11 major halls around a central mall and a custom-built Symphony Hall for the City of Birmingham Symphony Orchestra.

At the junction of the two canals stands the National Indoor Arena.

Jewellery Quarter (JY) – *1mi/1.2km northwest.* Something of the atmosphere of early industrial Birmingham with its countless workshops and specialist craftspeople survives in this densely built-up area just outside the city centre. The **Museum of the Jewellery Quarter,** (& *75 - 79 Vyse Street. ◷ Open Mon-Fri, 11.30am-4pm, Sat, 11am-5pm. Tearoom. ☎ 0121 554 3598; Fax 0121 554 9700; www.bmag.org.uk)* set up in the former premises of a jewellery business, tells the story of the area as well as demonstrating traditional skills and techniques. The splendid Georgian **St Paul's Church** forms the centrepiece of St Paul's Square, the only remaining 18C square in Birmingham.

Soho House – *2mi/3km northwest.* & *Soho Avenue (off Soho Road). ◷ Open Easter – 31 Oct Tue-Sun and Bank Hol Mon, 11:30am (noon Sun) to 4pm. Guide book, Braille guide. Refreshments. ☎ 0121 554 9122; www.bmag.org.uk.* In 1761 Matthew Boulton acquired the Georgian house overlooking his Soho Manufactory and with the help of James and Samuel Wyatt made it into the most technologically advanced building of the age, with central heating, metal windows, flush toilet and hot and cold running water. A fit setting for the meetings of the Lunar Society which brought together Birmingham's leading thinkers, Soho House has been fully restored and serves as a museum honouring Boulton and his progressive contemporaries.

National Sea Life Centre (HV) – *Brindleyplace.* & ◷ *Open daily, 10am-5pm (last admission) ◷ Closed 25 Dec.* ✉ *Email for most current admission prices. Refreshments. ☎ 0121 633 4700; 0870 840 5678 (information); slcbirmingham@merlin-entertainments. com; www.sealife.co.uk.* While boasting the usual features of this nationwide group of marine life centres, including SeaLab and the Kingdom of the Seahorse, this large new aquarium concentrates on the specific story of the River Severn. A zig-zagging pathway climbs up through the displays of sea and freshwater fish as the landscape changes from the oceans to the estuary and upriver to its source. From the top, with a view over the canals below, a lift takes visitors down to the "seabed" and an impressive transparent tunnel to walk beneath rays and sharks.

Birmingham Botanical Gardens & Glasshouses (HX) – *Westbourne Road, Edgbaston.* ◷ *Open daily, 9am (10am Sun) to 7pm/dusk; telephone* to confirm hours for Bonsai Collection ✉ *£5.90. Children's discovery garden; sculpture trail. Parking. Tearoom, gallery, shop. ☎ 0121 454 1860; admin@birminghambotonicalgardens.org.uk; www.birminghambotanicalgardens.org.uk.* First opened in 1832, the 15 acres/6ha of ornamental gardens still largely follow JC Loudon's original design. Exotic birds are displayed in aviaries and the elegant 19C glasshouses include the steamy Tropical House where pineapple, banana, sugar cane and appropriately, so near Bournville, cocoa plants grow in rainforest humidity. One relatively recent addition is the **National Bonsai Collection,** arrayed behind bars.

Excursions

New Art Gallery Walsall – *Gallery Square.* ◷ *Open Tue-Sun and Bank holidays, 10am (noon Sun) to 5pm. No charge. Restaurant. Café. ☎ 01922 654 400; 01922 637 575 (Infoline); Fax 01922 654 401; info@artatwalsall.org.uk; www.artatwalsall.org.uk.* At the head of the canal basin, the tall 5-storey building rising opposite St. Matthews Church and near the Town Hall forms the focal point of the Black Country town as part of a major regeneration scheme of Walsall Town Wharf. In contrast to the terracotta tiled facade with its irregular pattern of windows, the interior is wood-panelled with interesting, intimate spaces. Masterpieces on display include paintings by Matisse, Picasso, Van Gogh and Degas. Go up to the roof terrace to enjoy fine **views** of the Black Country.

National Motorcycle Museum, Bickenhill – *9mi/13km east of Birmingham on A 45, at junction with M 42.* & ◷ *Open daily, 10am-6pm. ◷ Closed 24-26 Dec.* ✉ *call for admission fee. Parking. Cafeteria (no wheelchair access). ☎ 01675 443 311; Fax 01675 443 310; admin@nationalmotorcyclemuseum.co.uk; www.nationalmotorcyclemuseum.co.uk.* The West Midlands were the heartland of the once mighty British motorcycle industry. The hundreds of exhibits in this museum-cum-conference complex enable the enthusiast to appreciate the evolution of the British motorbike from its ungainly beginnings at the turn of the century to the purposeful machines of the heyday of motorcycling in the 1950s and 1960s.

Bournville★ – *4mi/6km southwest of city centre on A 38 and A 441.* In 1879 the Quaker **Cadbury brothers** moved their cocoa factory from the cramped conditions of the city centre to the rural surroundings of the Bournbrook estate. Cottages and community facilities for their workers were built around the **Village Green** where the stone **Rest House,** presented to Mr and Mrs George Cadbury in 1914 as a Silver Wedding Anniversary gift from Cadbury employees worldwide, is now an information centre. To one side the Bournville School tower houses the **Bournville Carillon** (occasional tours and ringing demonstrations) installed by George Cadbury after hearing the old Carillon in Bruges. To the northeast of the green, **Selly Manor** (*Open Tue-Fri, 10am-5pm; also Apr-Sep, Sat-Sun and Bank Hol, 2-5pm. £3. Limited disabled access. 0121 472 0199; sellymanor@bvt.org.uk; www.bvt.org.uk/sellymanor)* and Minworth Greaves are half-timbered houses rescued by George and Laurence Cadbury. Transported and restored here they are now home to a fine collection of 13C-1750 vernacular furniture. South of the green the famous chocolate factory itself can be visited. **Cadbury World** (*Open at variable times; telephone for details; reservation advised. £10.50, children £7.90. Play area. Parking. Restaurant; picnic areas . 0121 451 4159 (bookings) or 0121 451 4180 (information line). www.cadbury.co.uk)* is particularly popular with school parties and other younger visitors as it not only tells the story of chocolate and cocoa and gives an insight into production and packing methods past and present but also offers the "Cadabra" ride through fairytale Beanville, and several tasting opportunities.

Avoncroft Museum of Historic Buildings – *Stoke Heath, Bromsgrove, 13mi/21km southwest on A 38 (signposted from Bromsgrove). Jul-Aug, daily and bank holidays, 10.30am-5pm ; Apr-Jun, Sep-Oct, Tue-Sun, 10.30am-4.30pm ; Mar 10.30am-4.30pm, Nov Sat-Sun, 10.30am-4pm. Parking. Tearoom. Children's play area £6. 01527 831 363; Fax 01527 876 934; avoncroft1@compuserve.com; www.avoncroft.org.uk.* Rescued buildings from throughout the Midlands have been reconstructed at this 15-acre/6ha open-air museum to create a collage of agricultural, industrial, domestic and social life spanning 700 years. Many include working demonstrations; particularly unusual is the **National Telephone Kiosk Collection** with working examples of police boxes and all kiosks since the 1920s. At the heart of the collection a modern building, the New Guesten Hall, now incorporates the superb 14C roof from the Prior's Guest Hall at Worcester.

Black Country Living Museum, Dudley★ – *Tipton Road, 10mi/15km northwest of Birmingham on A 4123 or 3mi/4km from Junction 2 on the M 5. Open Mar-Oct, daily, 10am-5pm; Nov-Feb, Wed-Sun, 10am-4pm. Telephone for Christmas closing times £9.95. Parking. Refreshments. Disabled visitors are requested to book in advance. b 0121 557 9643 (info) ; Fax 0121 557 4242; info@bclm.co.uk; www.bclm.co.uk.* The sprawling landscape of the South Staffordshire coalfield may have given rise to the name Black Country, which comprises Wolverhampton, Walsall, Dudley and Sandwell. The museum (26 acres/11ha) presents the rich heritage of this fast-growing revitalised industrial region. Coal mining is represented by a reconstructed pit head and an impressive underground display of the conditions in a "Thick Coal" mine in the 1850s. Nearby is a working replica of the world's first steam engine (1712). The heart of the display, reached by an electric tramway and flanked by two canal arms, is an industrial village: houses, a grocery, hardware shop, baker's, chemist's, sweet shop, glasscutter's, chainmaker's, nail shop, rolling mill, anchor forge, boatdock, Methodist chapel and pub. The spectacular limestone caverns beneath the adjacent Castle Hill can be visited by boat.

Lock Museum, Willenhall – *54 New Road, 15mi/24km northwest on M 6 and A 454 (signposted from junction 10). Open Wed – Sat 12pm - 4pm. 0121 557 9643; Fax 0121 557 4242; info@bclm.co.uk; www.lockmuseum.net.* Just as brewing was to Burton, so was lockmaking to Victorian Willenhall, with hundreds of backyard workshops producing locks and padlocks for the world. Not only has the Hodson family's workshop at number 54 New Road survived in working order *(telephone for dates of demonstration days)*, but the house from which Edith and Flora Hodson ran their drapers shop gives a glimpse of domestic life throughout this century. The collection of historic locks is displayed upstairs.

Ironbridge Gorge Museum★★ – *35mi/56km northwest. See IRONBRIDGE GORGE.*

BLACKPOOL

Lancashire, ENGLAND

POPULATION 146 297

MICHELIN ATLAS P 38 OR MAP 502 K 22

TOWN PLAN IN THE MICHELIN ATLAS P 108

Since 1846 when the railway first made seaside holidays a possibility for the masses, Blackpool has been one of the most popular and most typical of British seaside resorts in all bar its north west location. Thousands of holidaymakers have flocked from the industrial towns of the north of England *(Liverpool lies 55 miles/88km due south)* for their annual holiday, although short breaks are now more popular. About a third of visitors to Blackpool come in autumn to see the famous Blackpool **illuminations**. For many years the **Winter Gardens** have played host alternately to the main political parties for their annual political conferences.

Blackpool is known for "fresh air and fun," the former found on the miles of beach and promenade (7mi/11km) and in Stanley Park with its gardens and sporting facilities. Fun in the form of man-made entertainment is provided principally by the three 19C piers, the Pleasure Beach and the famous Blackpool Tower (🕯 *see below)*. A tramway runs the length of the Promenade and continues north to the port of Fleetwood.

Visit

Blackpool Tower★ – 🚸 🕐 *Feb-Nov, daily, 10am-11pm; Dec-Easter, Sat-Sun, 10am-11pm.* 🎫 *£10* ☎ *01253 622 242; Fax 01253 625 194; www.blackpooltower.com.* Since it opened in 1894, the tower (518ft/158m high), which was inspired by the Eiffel Tower in Paris, has been the trademark of the resort. There is a splendid view from the top and the intervening levels provide a variety of entertainment.

Address Book

OUT AND ABOUT IN BLACKPOOL

Tourist Information Centre – *1 Clifton Street Blackpool FY1 1LY* ☎ *01253 478 222; Central Promenade* ☎ *01253 478 222; Fax 01253 478 210; www.visitblackpool.com*

Public Transport – **Travelcards** for unlimited bus and tram travel are available from Blackpool Bus Station, tourist information centres, transport offices and selected hotels and newsagents, and are valid for one, three, five and seven-day periods. ☎ *01253 473 000 (Blackpool Transport Bus & Tram Enquiries).*

Sightseeing – Holders of a valid Travelcard are entitled to a reduction on tramcar tours of the Illuminations which depart from North Pier.

Shopping – The main shopping centre is **Hounds Hill** Shopping Centre, but there is also a variety of shops in **Red Bank Road, Ocean Boulevard** and **Waterloo Road**.

Entertainment – Not to be missed is Blackpool's **Pleasure Beach**, home to the "Pepsi Big Max", one of the world's tallest (235ft/71m) and fastest (87mph/140kmph) rollercoasters, and boasting a total of over 140 rides and attractions, including 11 rollercoasters. **Blackpool Tower** houses a hi-tech theme park: ballroom, circus, aquarium, animatronic journey through the history of the world, assault course for children, scientific exploration and history of the tower.

The **Golden Mile** offers traditional seaside entertainment – candyfloss, hamburgers and slot machines abound, and there is also a range of discos and cabarets. For theatre or other shows visit the **North Pier.** Aquariums, waxworks, a zoo, a model village, ice skating, go karts, bowling and golf are also on offer.

Illuminations – 🚸 🕐 *early Sep to early-Nov, every evening dusk until late. Leaflet (6 languages).* ☎*01253 478 222; Fax 01253 478 210; tourism@blackpool.gov.uk; www. blackpooltourism.com.* Spectacular lights and tableaux stretch along the seafront (over 5mi/8km) every autumn.

Excursions

Lytham St Anne's – *South of Blackpool by the coast road.* Lytham offers a tranquil and leisurely atmosphere of beaches and sand dunes near the mouth of the River Ribble. There are four superb championship golf courses, including The Royal, and many good walks and beauty spots. The white **windmill** (🕐 *– Lytham Green. Open Jun-Sep, Tue-Thu and Sat-Sun, 10.30am - 4:00pm.* ☎ *01253 794 879 ext 3710; vivw@ fyle.gov.uk; www.fylde.gov.uk)* is the sole survivor of the many which used to work along the foreshore.

Preston – *16mi/26km east by M 55 and A 6.* This busy town, the administrative centre of Lancashire, was transformed in the 18C from a fashionable Georgian town into a centre of the cotton industry.

National Football Museum ♿ 🕐 *– Sir Tom Finney Way. Open Tue-Sun and Bank Hol Mon, 10am (11am Sun) to 5pm.* 🕐 *Closed 25 Dec. No charge.* ☎ *01772 908 400 (24hr information), 01772 908 403 (enquiries); Fax 01772 908 433; enquiries@nationalfootball-museum.com; www.nationalfootballmuseum.com.* Showcased here are the history and highlights of the game and celebrated through interactive exhibits and the FIFA collection of 20 000 pieces of football memorabilia.

The **Harris Museum and Art Gallery** (♿ 🕐 *– Open Mon-Fri (except Bank Hols), 10am-5pm, Sun 11am - 4pm.* 👟 *Guided tour by appointment. Café.* ☎ *01772 258 248, 01772 257 112 (information line); Fax 01772 886 764; harris.museum@preston.gov. uk; www.preston.gov.uk)* tells the story of Sir Richard Arkwright (1732-92), who was born in Preston, and of his invention of the spinning frame which made cotton spinning into a factory industry. There are also interesting collections of ceramics, glass and costumes.

Samlesbury Old Hall – *Preston New Road, 19mi/31km east of Blackpool by M 5, 6 and A 677.* 🕐 *Open every day except Saturday 11am-4.30pm.* 🍽 *Tearoom* ☎ *01254 812 010; Fax 01254 812 174; enquiries@samlesburyhall.co.uk; www.samlesburyhall.co.uk.* The well-restored example of a timber-framed manor house was begun in 1325 but is mainly 15C and 16C; it was twice saved from dereliction in 1875 and 1924 and is now used to display antique furniture.

Hoghton Tower – *21mi/34km by M 55, M 6 and A 675.* 🕐 *Open Jul-Sep* 👟 *Guided tour (1hr) Sun and Bank Hols, 1pm-5pm;, Mon-Thur, 11am-4pm.* 🕐 *1 Jan and 25 Dec.* 🍽 *House and gardens* 🎫*£5. Parking. Refreshments.* ☎ *01254 852 986; Fax 01254 852 109; mail@hoghtontower.co.uk; www.hoghtontower.co.uk.* A spectacular approach, a long straight drive (550ft/170m), leads to the hilltop site of this fortified mansion, which was built by Sir Thomas Hoghton in 1565; there are 17C additions and a walled garden. According to tradition it was here in 1617 that James I (VI of Scotland) "knighted" a loin of beef so that it has been known as sirloin ever since.

BLENHEIM PALACE★★★

Oxfordshire, ENGLAND

MICHELIN ATLAS P 18 OR MAP 504 P 28

This greatest building of the English Baroque, residence of the Dukes of Marlborough, is matched in splendour by the sublime landscape of its vast park. At the park gates is the elegant town of **Woodstock**, built of mellow Cotswold stone, where old coaching inns and antique shops cluster round the Classical town hall.

A Bit of History

"Royall and National Monument" – The Royal Manor of Woodstock (8 mi/13km north west of Oxford) once the hunting ground of Saxon kings, was the birthplace of Edward the Black Prince (b 1330), also known as Edward of Woodstock. In the 18C the royal manor was given by Queen Anne to **John Churchill, Duke of Marlborough** (1650-1722), to mark his victory in 1704 over the armies of Louis XIV at Blenheim in

Blenheim Palace

A. Touy/EXPLORER

Bavaria. Seemingly limitless funds were made available for a "**Royall and National Monument**" to be erected in celebration of this decisive check to France's pan-European ambitions. Leading architects and craftsmen were employed, foremost among them **Sir John Vanbrugh**, one of England's most original architects, whose inventiveness and sense of drama found full expression here. Alas, court intrigues led to Marlborough's fall from the Queen's favour; the flow of money was cut off and building stopped. When it resumed it was at the Duke's own expense. His disputatious Duchess, Sarah, her sense of value for money now sharpened, quarrelled constantly over supposed extravagance, provoking Vanbrugh's resignation. The grandiose project, truly a monument rather than a home, was completed only after the first Duke's death in 1722. A century and a half later, on 30 November 1874, his direct descendant, **Winston Churchill**, was born here. This most illustrious of Englishmen is now buried in the churchyard in Bladon *(3mi/4.8km south).*

The Palace

🚻🕐 *Park: Open daily (except 25 Dec and one Sat in Nov), 9am-4.45pm. Palace: Open mid Feb-mid Dec, daily (🕐 closed Mon-Tue during Nov-Dec), 10.30am-4.45pm (4.45pm last admission).* 🎫 *Palace and park (including garden attractions) £13, Park and gardens only £8.* 🎧 *Guided tour (1hr,4 languages) every 10min; Guide book (£4; 6 languages). Parking. Restaurant, cafeteria.* ☎ *01993 811 325 (24hr recorded information); admin@blenheimpalace.com; www.blenheimpalace.com.* The palace's huge scale and fortress-like character are relieved by dynamic, almost theatrical composition and exuberant detail. Thus its silhouette has a romantic, even medieval air, with an array of turrets, pinnacles and disguised chimney-pots, and the Great Court (450ft/137m long) is like a stage set, a succession of colonnades, towers and arcades, leading the eye inexorably to the main façade with its imposing portico. Symbols of military prowess and patriotism abound, from heaped-up trophies to centurions standing proudly on the parapet; over the courtyard gateway the unfortunate cockerel of France is mauled by the haughty English lion.

Interior – A series of splendidly decorated rooms continues the monumental theme. In the **Great Hall** (67ft/20m high) the ceiling is painted with an allegory of Marlborough's victory. Sir Winston Churchill's life is celebrated in a suite of rooms, including the one in which he was born. State apartments are furnished with original pieces, many of the highest quality. There are portraits by Reynolds, Romney, Van Dyck and one, by Sargent, of the ninth Duke with his family and American-born wife Consuelo. The vast **Saloon** has a great painted colonnade, apparently open to the sky, thronged with figures representing the four continents. The main axis of the park runs through this room, terminating in the spire of Bladon church. The **Long Library**, with a magnificent stucco ceiling, runs the entire length (180ft/55m) of the west front. In the Chapel is the overwhelming marble **tomb** of the first Duke.

Grounds★★★

The ancient hunting park, with its venerable trees and deer-proof wall (9mi/15km long), was worked upon in the early 18C by the royal gardeners. The **Italian Garden** to the east of the palace and the spectacular Water Garden to the west are modern, as is the symbolic maze of trophies, cannon and trumpets in the walled garden, but they capture something of the spirit of the formal avenues and geometrical parterres which were mostly swept away by **Lancelot Capability Brown**, the greatest of English landscape architects. The redesigned park is his masterpiece, offering from the Woodstock Gate what has been described as "the finest view in England". Sweeping grassy slopes, noble groves of trees and the curving outline of the great lake, crossed by Vanbrugh's **Grand Bridge**, combine to "improve upon Dame Nature" and provide a more than worthy setting for the palace.

A huge **Doric column** (134ft/41m high), topped by a statue of the first Duke with Victory in his grasp, forms one focal point of the recently replanted axis which on the north side of the palace runs to the Ditchley Gate (2mi/3km). By the lake is the site of old Woodstock Manor, long demolished, and Fair Rosamund's Well, a reminder of this favourite of Henry II. Downstream, Brown's water engineering terminates in his **Grand Cascade**, over which the little River Glyme foams to rejoin its former bed.

In the Pleasure Grounds (the area nearest the House) are a maze, a butterfly house and various exhibitions.

BOSTON

Lincolnshire, ENGLAND

POPULATION 34 606

MICHELIN ATLAS P 37 OR MAP 504 T 25

Lying just north of East Anglia, Boston was the second largest port in England in the 13C; in the 17C it was a centre of Puritanism and prison of the Pilgrim Fathers (1607), a group who sailed from Boston and founded the eponymous American colony. There are many elegant Georgian houses, such as Fydell House *(South Street)*; old warehouses line the bank of the River Witham. Boston is now a sleepy market town *(open air auction on Wednesdays, market on Saturdays)* making a living from light industry, agriculture and the docks. ⓘ *Market Place PE21 6NN ☏/Fax 01205 356 656; tic@boston.gov.uk; www.boston.gov.uk/tourism*

Sights

St Botolph's Church★ – *Market Place.* ♿ ⏰ *Open daily, 9am-4.30pm. Tower: Open daily except during inclement winter weather.* ⌛ *Tower: £2.* 🔊 *Guided tour (30-45min), no charge but donation requested. Leaflet (10 languages).* ☏ *01205 362 864 (office); 01205 354 670 (Verger); parish.office@virgin.net.* When it was built in the 14C St Botolph's was the largest church in England and its tower, known as the **Boston Stump**, may have been intended to carry a spire. The building possesses a rare unity of style, the body being Decorated and the stump and octagonal lantern being Perpendicular. Note the 14C misericords – two men squeezing cats like bagpipes with the animals' tails in their mouths, a schoolmaster threatening three boys with a birch, and a hunter chased by his wife. The southwest chapel is dedicated to John Cotton (1584-1652), vicar of St Botolph's before sailing to Boston, Massachusetts. The tower (272ft/83m – 365 steps) was designed in the style of Flemish churches. On a fine day the view embraces Hunstanton *(40mi/64km east)* and Lincoln *(32mi/50km northwest).*

Guildhall Museum – *South Street* ♿ ⏰ *Closed until 2007.* ☏ *01205 365 954; heritage@originalboston.freeserve.co.uk.* This brick building (1450), which has a 16C stained glass window over the door, was once the hall of St Mary's Guild, later the town hall. On the ground floor are old kitchens with copper pots and ranges; more interesting are the barred cells where the Pilgrim Fathers were imprisoned in 1607. On the first floor is the Court Room where they were tried. Other rooms display the history of Boston – reminders of its seafaring past are shown in the Maritime Room; a portrait of Sir Joseph Banks, botanist and former Recorder of Boston, hangs in the Council Chamber where china and glass are displayed. The Banqueting Hall (with its original roof) and Minstrels' Gallery contain an archeological collection and memorabilia of local worthies.

Maud Foster Mill – *Willoughby Road.* ⏰ *Open Wed, 10am-5pm, Sat and Bank Hols, 11am-5pm, Sun, 1pm-5pm; also Jul-Aug, Thu-Fri, 11am-5pm.* ⏰ *Closed Christmas and New Year* ☎ *01205 352 188; www.lincolnshire.gov.uk/windmills.* Visitors can see the workings and buy the flour at this handsome, seven-storey windmill overlooking a canal near the town centre.

Excursions

Skegness – *22mi/35km northeast on A 52.* This coastal town has all the trimmings of a traditional British seaside resort: seafront promenade, games arcades, big dippers, themed swimming pools, fish and chip shops, pubs, a large sandy beach... and a famously bracing climate. The **Church Farm Museum** *(Church Road South west of town centre –* ⏰ *Open Apr-Oct, daily, 10.30am-5.30pm.* ⏰ *Closed Good Friday.* 💰 *£1, 50p (child).* ☎ *01754 766 658.)* is home to a well-presented display of domestic and farming implements, set out in the buildings of an old farm, illustrating the way of life on a local farm in the 19C. It includes a fine example of a traditional Lincolnshire "Mud and Stud" thatched cottage moved here from a nearby village and re-erected on site. There is a programme of exhibitions and events (sheep-shearing demonstrations etc) throughout the season.

South of the town centre is the Gibraltar Point Nature Reserve, a must for keen bird-watchers and those interested in the flora and fauna of coastal dunes.

Tattershall Castle★ – *15mi/24km northwest on A 1121, B 1192 and A 153 (signs).* ♿⏰ *Open (functions permitting) early Mar– Easter Sat-Sun, noon-4pm; Easter–Oct, Sat-Wed , 11am-5.30pm (4pm Oct); Nov to mid-Dec, Sat-Sun, noon-4pm.* 💰 *£3.70. Free audio guide, Braille guide. Parking. Refreshments.* ☎ *01526 342 543; tattershallcastle@ ntrust.org.uk; www.nationaltrust.org.uk.* Built by Ralph, Lord Cromwell (veteran of Agincourt and Lord Treasurer), Tattershall is closer to a French château than a 15C castle, heralding the Renaissance castle-as-status-symbol such as Oxburgh Hall (note Tattershall's elegant, traceried windows). Well fortified, nevertheless, with double moat and thick walls (16ft/5m), the striking **Great Tower**, a masterpiece of medieval English brickwork, is built of red brick laid in English bond interspersed with diaper patterns in bluish brick, with white stone window surrounds and machicolations, and stands out 110ft/33.5m above the Lincolnshire flatlands. Its four floors contain exceptional mid-15C **chimney-pieces**, carved with the coats of arms of families connected with Cromwell and symbols of his office, and the battlements provide panoramic **views**. There are explanatory panels explaining the castle's history and architecture in the turret rooms. By the early 20C the castle was in ruins and the site about to be sold off to speculators. It was saved by Lord Curzon, Viceroy of India, an intervention that led to the Ancient Monuments Act of 1913. On his death in 1925, the property was bequeathed to the National Trust.

The path from the car park to the entrance of the castle takes visitors past the **Collegiate Church of the Holy Trinity,** built at the behest of Cromwell in c 1465-85 (after Cromwell's death) in place of a Norman chapel. This attractive Perpendicular building in limestone is one of the largest parish churches in the county. There are some interesting memorial brasses in the north transept.

Battle of Britain Memorial Flight, RAF Coningsby★ – *14mi/22.5km northwest on A 1121, B 1192 and A 153.* ⏰ *Guided tour (1hr) Mon-Fri, 10:30am-5pm (3.30pm last tour; 3pm Nov-Feb).* ⏰ *Closed Sat-Sun, bank holidays and for 2 weeks over Christmas.* 💰 *Call for charges* ☎ *01526 344 041; Fax 01526 342330; bbmf@lincolnshire.gov.uk; www. raf.mod.uk/bbmf/bbmfhome.html* The Battle of Britain Memorial Flight was formed in 1957 at Biggin Hill, Kent, in order to preserve some of the famous aircraft which had been active in the Second World War. It now numbers five Spitfires, two Hawker Hurricanes, a Lancaster, a Douglas Dakota DC-3, two Chipmunks (used for training) and a Devon (in storage but still in condition to be flown). These historic aircraft (display duties permitting) can be viewed as part of a fascinating tour conducted by guides who mostly have first hand experience of the aircraft on show. The visit provides a wealth of technical details about the aircraft, as well as considerable nostalgic interest from accounts of when and where they were flown. A group of 18 technicians and mechanics maintains the Flight's aircraft, often working irregular hours voluntarily to support them during the Display season (April to late September, the climax of which is usually the Battle of Britain commemoration events in mid September). Some of the aircraft have starred in films, such as The Battle of Britain in 1968 (the Mk II Spitfire P7350 used in this is the oldest plane of its kind still flying in the world).

Spalding

16mi/26km south on A 16. The town, which is as Georgian as Boston, stands on the northern edge of The Fens beside the River Welland; during the **Bulb Festival** each spring it comes ablaze with a million flowers.

Ayscoughfee Hall Museum – *Churchgate. Museum and Information Centre* – ♿ ○ *Open Mar – Oct Mon – Sat 10 am – 5 pm (Sun 11am) Nov – Feb closed weekends.Gardens – ○ Open all year, daily, 8am (10am Sun)-5pm (or 30min after dusk). ○ Closed 25 Dec. Parking. Refreshments, garden café, picnic area.* ☎ *01775 725 468; Fax 01775 762715.* The museum covers local history, the draining of the Fens and the history of the Hall, which was built in 1430 but much altered in the 18C and 19C. It was the home of Maurice Johnson, founder of the Spalding Gentlemen's Society (1710), the second oldest antiquarian society in England, which counted Newton, Pope, Addison and Gray among its members.

Springfields World of Flowers – *Camelgate, off Holbeach Road.* ♿ ○ *Open year round. Parking. Restaurant. Wheelchairs available.* ☎ *01775 724 843; Fax 01775 711 209; info@springfields.net; www.springfields.mistral.co.uk.* The gardens (25 acres/10ha) are at the centre of the British bulb industry; they are famous for their tulips and roses and have changing displays of 250 000 bedding plants.

BOURNEMOUTH

Dorset, ENGLAND

POPULATION 155 488

MICHELIN ATLAS P 9 OR MAP 503 O 31

The Grand Old Lady of England's south central coast, Bournemouth has been a popular summer and winter resort since the late 19C. Its amenities include two piers, the pavilion (now a theatre), the always colourful public gardens and numerous hotels, shops and leisure facilities.

Address Book

OUT AND ABOUT IN BOURNEMOUTH

Tourist Information Centre – Visitor Information Bureau, Westover Road. ☎ 01202 451 700; Fax 01202 454 799; info@bournemouth.co.uk; www.bournemouth.co.uk.

Public Transport – "Buzzcards", giving unlimited travel on various bus routes, either for one day or longer periods, are available from bus drivers. Ask the drivers for further details, or telephone the Bus Information Line ☎ 01202 636 000.

Sightseeing – The Visitor Information Bureau runs free guided walks from late May to late September. These depart from the Visitor Information Bureau, late-May to late-Sep, Mon-Tue and Thu-Fri at 10.30am, Sun at 2.30pm (Town centre); Wed at 10.30am (West Cliff area). The walks are free of charge and last approximately 90min. ☎ 01202 451 700; www.bournemouth.co.uk.

Guide Friday Bus Tours operate late-Apr to late-Sep, daily, 10am-4.30pm (5pm in peak summer season), every 30min. ☎ £6.50. Round trip (30min; with commentary) from Bournemouth Pier via the cliffs, art gallery and museum. Collapsible wheelchairs accepted. ☎ 01273 540 0893; info@city-sightseeing.com; www.guidefriday.com.

Alternatively take a boat trip around the bay – details are available from the offices along the seafront. Or look out for "The Shoreline Scenic", a land-train which runs for 6mi along the promenade from Boscombe to Southbourne, giving views of the bay, the Purbecks and the Isle of Wight.

Shopping – Wimborne Market with over 400 stalls is open on Fridays, Saturdays and Sundays.

Entertainment – Bournemouth which has a lively student population is packed with theatres, pubs and clubs. Every Friday in summer there is a firework display from the pier. There are also facilities for ballooning, go-karting, bungee jumping, clay shooting, sky diving, rambling and watersports.

Sights

Russell-Cotes Art Gallery and Museum★★ – *Eastcliff, Russell-Cotes Road.* ♿ ○
Open Tue-Sun, 10am-5pm. ○ *Closed Good Friday, 25-26 Dec.* ⊙*No charge. Cafe. Shop.*
☎ *01202 451 858; Fax: 01202 451851; diane.edge@bournemouth.gov.uk; www.russell-
cotes.bournemouth.gov.uk.* Housed in **East Cliff Hall**, decorated in archetypal ornate
High Victorian taste, with inlaid furniture, painted ceilings, decorative windows and
coloured wallpaper, the collections include numerous paintings (William Frith, Landseer, Leighton, Birket-Foster, Rossetti, Alma-Tadema, Edwin Long), fine English china,
gold and silver plate, and souvenirs from abroad (the Orient, Germany, Egypt).

Christchurch★ – This small Hampshire village is now separated from its larger neighbour only by modern leisure centres and shopping malls. The prosperous little coastal
town features at its epicentre a Norman **priory**★ and Norman castle grouped around
a harbour filled with fishing and pleasure craft.

Excursions

Compton Acres★★ – *164 Canford Cliffs Road, 2mi/3km west by A 338.* ♿ ○*Open
daily, 9am-6pm (5pm last admission).* ○ *Closed 25-26 Dec.* ⊙ *£5.95 summer £2.00
winter.Parking. Licensed cafe, terrace brasserie, restaurant.* ☎ *01202 700 778; sales@
comptonacres.co.uk; www.comptonacres.co.uk.* This series of nine distinct **gardens**
(Italian, rock, water and Japanese) spreads over 15 acres/6ha in a rift in the sandstone
cliffs; it is famous for having flowers in bloom throughout the year. The **English
Garden** lies open to sunsets and a westerly **view**★★★ of Poole harbour, Brownsea
Island and the Purbeck Hills.

Poole★ – *4mi/6km west by A 338.* Poole with its fine sandy beach at Sandbanks,
situated on one of the largest harbours in the world, is both a popular yachting
haven and a major roll-on-roll-off port. By the quay, dominated by an Anthony Caro
sculpture, is the **Waterfront Museum** (♿ ⊶ *Due to reopen Autumn 2006. Open
daily, 10am (noon Sun) to 5pm (3pm Nov-Mar).* ☎ *01202 262 600; Fax 01202 262 622;
museums@poole.gov.uk; www.poole.gov.uk)* telling the history of the port and town
Scaplen's Court (*4 High Street.*○ *Open Aug, daily, 10am (noon Sun)-5pm.* ☎ *01202
262 600; Fax 01202 262 6221; museums@poole.gov.uk; www.poole.gov.uk),* a domestic
building from the late medieval period, the **Aquarium Complex** (*Hennings Wharf.*
♿ ○ *Open July-Aug, daily, 9am-9pm; Sept-June, daily, 10am-5:30pm.* ○ *Closed 24-25
Dec.* ⊙ *Aquarium/Serpentarium £3.95; Aquarium/Serpentarium/Model railway £4.95.
Refreshments.* ☎ *01202 686 712; pooleaquarium@2crfm.net),* the renowned **Poole
Pottery** (*Sopers Lane.* ○ *Open daily, 9:30am to 4.30pm* ⊙ *£2.50 Coffee shop.* ☎ *01202
666 200; www.poolepottery.co.uk)* and the **RNLI Lifeboat Museum** (*West Quay Road*
♿ ○ *Open Mon-Fri except Bank Hols, 9.30am-4.30pm.* ☎ *01202 663 000, Fax 01202
663 167; info@rnli.org.uk www.lifeboats.org.uk).* The attractive, largely 18C **Old Town**,
focusing on St James' Church, and the fine 18C Guildhall building are also of note.

Poole Harbour from Studland Heath

A. Tavernier

Brownsea Island★ – ⅀ ⏰ *Access by boat from Poole, Sandbanks and Bournemouth. mid Mar-late Jul 10am - 5pm, late Jul- early Sep 10am - 6pm , early Sep-30 Sep 10am - 5pm, Oct 10am-4pm; check time of last boat.* ⌂ *Landing fee £4.20. Braille guide.* ⏱ *Guided tour of nature reserve* ☏ *01202 709 445). Open-air theatre and other events in summer (*☏ *01985 843 601). Audio guide, mobility vehicles, all-terrain baby buggies (*☏ *01202 707 744). Refreshments near landing quay until 30min before departure of last boat.* ☏ *01202 707 744, Fax 01202 701 635; brownseaisland@nationaltrust.org.uk; www. nationaltrust.org.uk/brownsea.* This 500-acre island, covered in heath and woodland and fringed by inviting beaches along its south shore, consists of two nature reserves, either side of **Middle Street** along the central spine of the island. The north reserve is a sanctuary for waterfowl and other birds, and the south reserve, where visitors can wander at will, is likewise home to numerous birds, including peacocks. There is a good **view**★★ across Poole Bay to the Purbeck Hills from **Baden-Powell Stone,** which commemorates the first experimental Boy Scout camp held here in 1907.

Corfe Castle★ – *18mi/29km southwest by A 35 and A 351.* ⅀ ⏰ *Open daily, 10am-6pm (5pm Mar, 4pm Nov-Feb)* ⏰ *Closed 25-26 Dec and 1 day mid-Mar (tel for details).* ⌂ *£5. Parking. Refreshments.* ☏/*Fax 01929 481 294; corfecastle@nationaltrust.org.uk; www. nationaltrust.org.uk.* Corfe Castle has dominated the landscape since the 11C, first as a towering stronghold and since 1646 as a dramatic ruin. From the high mound on which it stands, the **views**★★ are spectacular. In 987 the 17 year-old King Edward, son of Edgar, visiting his half-brother at the castle, was murdered by his stepmother, Queen Aelthfryth; in 1001 he was canonised as **St Edward, King and Martyr.** It was the home of Sir John Bankes, Chief Justice to King Charles I. His wife resolutely defended it from 1643-45 and when it fell, owing to the treachery of one of the garrison, it was looted and blown up by the Parliamentarians.

Lulworth Cove★ – *8mi/14km west of Corfe Castle by B 3070.* The road (B 3070) passes **Blue Pool**★, a beautiful blue-green lake (3 acres/1.2ha) fringed by silver birch and pine woods, gorse and heather through which sandy paths meander, giving views of the Purbeck Hills. The circular sweep of Lulworth Cove is almost enclosed by the downland cliffs. From here, the Dorset Coast Path leads to the striking cliff archway of **Durdle Door** to the west, a dramatic climax to the whole of this spectacular area of headlands and bays, which has been likened to a crash course in geology.

Swanage★ – *5mi/8km east of Corfe Castle by A 351.* A scenic stretch of road leads to this quarry town and harbour, from which stone and marble were shipped to build Westminster Abbey and the cathedrals of Exeter, Lincoln and Salisbury. Swanage also boasts a good beach and a range of seaside leisure facilities.

Take the Dorset Coast Path east of Swanage to discover the **Old Harry Rocks**★★, two stacks of gleaming chalk once part of an unbroken shoreline from The Needles but now separated from the mainland and each other (Old Harry is the larger and his wife the slimmer).

Address Book

WHERE TO EAT

⌂⌂ **Noble House,** *3-5 Lansdowne Road.* ☏ *01202 292 277.* This friendly and smoothly run family operation in the city centre offers a comprehensive choice of Chinese dishes carefully prepared from fresh ingredients.

⌂⌂⌂ **John B's,** *20 High Street, Poole.* ☏/*Fax 01202 672 440; mark@markroberts. co.uk.* Fish and seafood are the specialities at this long established friendly traditional place presided over by Mark Roberts (one of the region's finest chefs) and his wife.

⌂⌂ **Salathal,** *106 Christchurch Road, Boscombe East.* ☏ *01202 420 772.* You will be charmed by the friendly welcome and the range and quality of authentic Thai dishes served up at this neighbourhood restaurant.

WHERE TO STAY

⌂⌂⌂ **Tudor Grange,** *31 Gervis Road, East Cliff, Bournemouth.* ☏ *01202 291 472; Fax 01202 311 503;info@ tudorgrangehotel. co.uk; www.tudorgrangehotel.co.uk.* This smart black-and-white country house-styled 11-room hotel features beautiful old oak panelling and the main stairway is 300 years old yet it is very central, with a trendy bar attached, and offers excellent value.

⌂⌂⌂ **Druid House,** *26 Sopers Lane, Christchurch.* ☏*01202 485615; Fax 01202 473 484; reservations@druidhouse.co.uk; www.druidhouse.co.uk.* Overlooking a quiet park in the centre of Christchurch, this 1930s house is bright and airy with a cottagey ambience and 8 spacious bedrooms (two with balconies).

BRADFORD ★

West Yorkshire, ENGLAND

POPULATION 289 376

MICHELIN ATLAS P 39 OR MAP 402 O 22

TOWN PLAN IN THE CURRENT MICHELIN ATLAS (UNDER LEEDS)

Bradford, like Leeds its northern neighbour, prospered through the wool trade. In 1500 it was a bustling market town "which already standeth much by clothing". The Bradford canal opened in 1774 to improve communications and trade. By 1850 there were 120 mills and Bradford had become the world's worsted capital. Among its famous sons are the author JB Priestley (1894-1984), composer Frederick Delius (1862-1934) and the contemporary painter David Hockney (b 1937). It is essentially a Victorian city, which grew rather than was planned. ■ *Central Hall, Centenary Square, Bradford BD1 1HY* ☎ *01274 433 678; Fax 01274 739 067; touristinformation@bradford.gov.uk; www.visitbradford.com* ▯ *City Hall* ☎ *01274 433 678; Fax 01274 739 067.*

Sights

National Museum of Photography, Film and Television★ – *Prince's View.* ○ *Museum: Open Tue-Sun and Bank Hol Mon and half term holidays, 10am-6pm. Cinemas: Open 10am-late. Shop. Café. Restaurant.* ☎ *01274 202 030; Fax 01274 723 155; talk.nmpft@nmsi.ac.uk; www.nmpft.org.uk.* An offshoot of London's famous Science Museum, this houses Britain's largest cinema projector and a curved screen (52ft/16m high and 64ft/20m wide), designed to show IMAX films. The displays trace the history and practice of photography, the cinema and television.

Wool Exchange – *Market Street.* ○ *Open normal shopping hours).* Built 1867 in Italian style, it was the centre of the world's wool trade. Brokers still meet here once a week. The statues at the entrance are those of St Blaize, patron saint of wool combers, and of Edward III, who did much to encourage the wool industry. It now serves as a bookshop.

Bradford Cathedral – *Church Bank, 1 Stott Hill.* ♿ ○ *Open daily, 8am-3pm.* ☙ *Guided tour (45min): Guide book (5 languages).* ☎ *01274 777 720; Fax 01274 777 730; cathedral@bradford.anglican.org; www.bradfordcathedral.co.uk.* The battlemented exterior does not give the impression of a building which, in parts, dates back to the 1440s; the west tower with battlements and pinnacles dates from 1493. The church, which is dedicated to St Peter, was raised to cathedral status in 1919 and the chancel has some fine stained glass, c 1862, by William Morris, Rossetti and Burne-Jones.

Little Germany – *Near the cathedral.* This merchants' district, named after the booming mid-19C export trade with Germany, has been cleaned and restored to show the high Victorian architecture, much of it the work of Eli Milnes (1830-99), at its best.

Colour Museum – *Grattan Road, northwest of the city centre.* ○ *Open Tue-Sat, 10am-4pm.*☜ *£2. Lunch room. Shop.* ☎ *01274 390 955; Fax 01274 392 888; museum@sdc.org. uk; www.colour-experience.org/index.htm.* This fascinating little museum with its

---

Address Book

OUT AND ABOUT IN BRADFORD

Tourist Information Centre – *Central Hall, Centenary Square, Bradford BD1 1HY* ☎ *01274 433 678; Fax 01274 739 067; touristinformation@bradford.gov.uk; www.visitbradford.com* ▯ *City Hall* ☎ *01274 433 678; Fax 01274 739 067.*

Public Transport – For local bus and rail times ☎ 0113 245 7676.

Pubs and Restaurants – A booklet listing places to eat in Bradford City Centre is available free of charge from the Tourist Information Centre. Bradford is famous for its curry houses.

Entertainment – A booklet containing all the information you will need for a night out in Bradford, including pubs, clubs, cinemas and theatres, is also available free of charge from the Tourist Information Centre. Three cinemas at the National Museum of Photography show the latest releases and host film festivals. Bradford festival is held in summer.

intriguing interactive exhibits is housed in the headquarters of the Society of Dyers and Colourists and is the only one in Britain which sets out to explain the theory and use of colour.

Excursions

Saltaire – *3mi/5km north of Bradford.* The model village (49 acres/20ha), a planned complex offering employment, housing, education and recreation, was built (1851-71) by Sir Titus Salt (1803-1876), who made a fortune weaving Alpaca and other unusual fibres in Bradford. So that his workers could escape from the appalling housing conditions, he built a new mill (1851) north of the city on a site served by the River Aire, the Leeds and Liverpool Canal (1774) and the Colne extension of the Leeds and Bradford Railway (1846). The adjoining village contained several different sizes of house to match the hierarchy of the workers, a High School, a hospital, alms houses, the United Reformed Church, built in the Classical Roman style, an institute, a park and a boathouse on the river; there was, however, no pub.

The **1853 Gallery** *(Victoria Road ⊙ Open daily, 10am-6pm. ⊙ Closed 1 Jan and 25-26 Dec. No charge. ☎ 01274 531 163; www.saltsmill.org.uk)* displays a collection of works by David Hockney, distributed over the three floors of the impressive old Weaving Shed, which also houses a bookshop, furniture shop and clothes shop and the Salts Diner.

The Victoria Hall, the old institute, now houses the **Reed Organ and Harmonium Museum** *(⊙ Open all year, Sun-Thur, 11am-4pm. ⊙ Closed Jan and Dec. ⊜ £2.50. ⟿ Guided tour available. ☎ 01274 585 601, 07976 535 980; phil@harmoniumservice. demon.co.uk);* the mouth organ invented in China in 2800 BC evolved into the instrument which was greatly in vogue in the 19C. This collection contains a great variety – designed for churches and chapels, for parlours, as portable models, with transposing keyboards, with a system for playing by numbers for the unskilled – together with a collection of music and a display of wall posters and publicity.

Shipley Glen Tramway – *From Saltaire across the River Aire to Prod Lane, Baildon.* ⧉ ⊙ *Schedule varies call ahead.* ⊙ *Closed 1 Jan and 25–26 Dec.* ☎ *01274 589 010 , 01274 492 026; info@glentramway.co.uk; www.glentramway.co.uk.* The oldest cable-hauled tram in the country, built in 1895 and known locally as the Cape to Cairo Railway, travels from the little station at Baildon through woodland to the Shipley Glen funfair and aerial ride.

Brooks Mill – *Elland; 9mi/14km southwest of Bradford off M 606 and A 646.* ⧉ ⊙ *Open daily 10am to 5pm.* ⊙ *Closed 24–26 Dec.* ☎ *01422 377 337.* At the back of this large mill-turned-retail outlet, Walkleys, the clog manufacturers, run a shop and factory where customers can choose from a range of ready-made clogs or be fitted for a pair and then watch them being made. Wood-turners work downstairs, leather-cutters and stitchers in the shop itself.

Halifax – *8mi/13km west of Bradford via A 6036.* Although medieval in origin, this manufacturing town, set in a great bowl among the hills, is now overwhelmingly Victorian in character, its streets lined with dignified buildings in local stone. Foremost among these 19C structures is Sir Charles Barry's **Town Hall** (1862) with its spire (180ft/51m). The most extraordinary edifice however is the Georgian **Piece Hall**★ (1779), where clothiers once brought their "pieces" of cloth for sale; its blank exterior walls give little hint of the magnificence within, a sloping colonnaded piazza of Renaissance grandeur; the galleries where traders once haggled now house a range of speciality shops. Even vaster in scale is **Dean Clough,** a complex of 19C former carpet mills, which now contains an array of business and cultural facilities including art galleries. **Eureka! The Museum for Children** *(⧉ ⊙ Open daily, 10am-5pm. ⊙ Closed 24-26 Dec. ⊜ £6.50, Parking (pay and display). Café. Shop. Lift. Audio-guide. ☎ 07626 983 191; info@eureka.org.uk; www.eureka.org.uk),* an ultra-modern structure, offers hundreds of brightly coloured interactive exhibits designed to stimulate and satisfy the under-12s.

BRECON BEACONS★★

Carmarthenshire, Merthyr Tydfil, Monmouthshire, Powys, Rhondda Cynon Taff, WALES

MICHELIN ATLAS PP 15, 16 OR MAP 503 I, J, K 28

These red sandstone mountains culminate in a spectacular north-facing escarpment overlooking the lesser uplands of mid-Wales. South from this great barrier (highest point Pen-y-Fan, 2 907ft/886m) extend high rolling moorlands cut by lush valleys, the broadest of them formed by the River Usk. Downstream from Brecon, centrally placed for exploring the Brecon Beacons National Park, the river is accompanied by the most delightful of waterways (33mi/53km), the Monmouthshire and Brecon Canal. *Cattle Market Car Park, Brecon ☎ 01874 622 485; brectic@powys.gov.uk Mountain Centre (National Park Visitor Centre), Libanus, Brecon, Powys LD3 8ER ☎ 01874 623 366; Fax 01874 624 515; www.brecon-beacons. com/mountain-centre.htm.*

▶ **Orient Yourself:** The best starting point is the Brecon Beacons Mountain Centre at Libanus (*5mi/8km southwest of Brecon by A470 and a minor road. ♿ ⏰ Open daily, 9.30am-5pm (6pm Jul-Aug; 5.30pm Sat-Sun, Apr-Jun and Sep; 4pm Nov-Feb). ⏰ Closed 25 Dec. Parking (pay and display). Tearoom. Picnic Area. ☎ 01874 623 366; Fax 01874 624 515; www.brecon-beacons.com/mountain-centre.htm*), which provides a wide range of information and other facilities. Although walking is the best way to discover the Brecons you should be aware that these are real mountains and take sensible precautions.

⊙ **Don't Miss:** Dan-yr-Ogof Caves; hire a narrowboat on the Monmouthshire and Brecon Canal (details from tourist office).

Kids Especially for Kids: Dan-yr-Ogof Caves, especially the "Dinosaur Park."

�🚲 **Bicycle trails:** Routes are marked out at the Garwnant Forestry Commission Visitor Centre (6mi/9km north of Merthyr Tydfil by A 470 and a long winding side road - brown signs

The National Park

Brecon (Aberhonddu) – *Population 7 166*. The Normans constructed a castle here, the ruins of which overlook the meeting of the rivers Honddu and Usk, and a priory too: its church is now the Cathedral. The stone-built former county town has kept its intricate medieval street pattern and numerous dignified 18C houses. The **Brecknock Museum** (♿ ⏰ *Open Apr-Aug, Mon-Fri, 10am-5pm, Sat 10am-1pm and 2pm-5pm, Sun noon-5pm; Sep-Mar, Mon-Sat, 10am-5pm (4pm Sat Nov-Feb). ⏰ Closed Sun Sept-Mar, 1 Jan, Good Friday, 25 Dec. ☞ £1, 50p (concessions), children free. Limited parking. Assistance available to people in wheelchairs. ☎ 01874 624 121.*) has good local displays and there is also the museum of the South Wales Borderers (24th Foot).

Dan-yr-Ogof Caves★ – *19mi/30km southwest of Brecon by A 40 and A 4067. ⏰ Open Apr-Oct, 10am-3pm (last admission). ☞ £9.50. Parking. Coffee shop, under-cover picnic areas. ☎ 01639 730 801; Fax 01639 730 293; info@showcaves.co.uk; www.showcaves. co.uk.* The underground complex includes the largest as well as the longest single chamber cave open to visitors in Britain. There are archaeological displays, a "Dinosaur Park" and an interpretive exhibition. The caves have been formed in the permeable limestone which underlies this southern part of the Beacons. The action of water on the soft rock gives rise to many other typical features of limestone scenery, including swallow holes and underground rivers, examples of which can be seen in the "waterfall country" around the village of **Ystradfellte**★.

Hay-on-Wye – *Population 1 578. 16mi/30km northeast of Brecon by A 470, A 438 and B 4350*. The quiet market town at the northern end of the Black Mountains has become internationally known for its numerous second-hand bookshops and its annual Literary Festival.

South of the town is **Hay Bluff★★** (*4mi/6km by B 4423 and a single track road*), an escarpment of the Black Mountains offering imcomparable **views** over the Wye Valley and far into central Wales.

Llanthony Priory★★ – *8mi/13km south of Hay-on-Wye by B 4423. ⏰ Open all year, daily, 9am-6pm. Parking. Licensed premises (pub closed Nov-Easter, midweek except at*

Christmas). ☎ *01873 890 487.* In the Vale of Ewyas beside the River Honddu stand the ruins of a late-12C Augustinian priory. Eight splendid arches, topped by the ruined triforium, still stand beside the remains of the crossing tower and the east end of the church; parts of the monastic quarters now house a small hotel. The monks, whose numbers had sunk to four by the Dissolution, lasted longer than later communities who were attracted by the seclusion and tranquillity – the poet, **Walter Savage Landor,** who vainly tried to restore the ruined priory, the charismatic preacher, **Father Ignatius** and his adherents at the turn of the 19C, and **Eric Gill** and his followers in the 1920s.

Address Book

For coin ranges, see the Legend at the back of the guide.

WHERE TO EAT

The Pear Tree, *Hay-on-Wye.* ☎ *01497 820777; info@peartreeathay.co. uk; www. peartreeathay.co.uk.* Enjoy the pick of the daily local produce sitting on the outdoor terrace in the garden of this charming 18C stone house.

Usk Inn, *Talybont-on-Usk.* ☎ *01874 676251; Fax 01874 676 392; stay@ uskinn.co.uk; www.uskinn.co.uk.* A changing menu of seasonal dishes is served in the large dining room of this comfy country pub 6m/10km southeast of Brecon. 11 well-maintained bedrooms.

The White Swan, *Llanfrynach.* ☎ *01874 665276; Fax 01874 665 362*

A characterful village pub 3m/5km southeast of Brecon with open fires, exposed brickwork and beams serving modern and classic dishes.

WHERE TO STAY

The Old Post Office, *Llanigon.* ☎ *01497 820 008; www.oldpost-office.co. uk.* This beautifully converted characterful former 17C inn, 2 miles/3km from Hay-on-Wye, mixes smart modern ambience with exposed beams and antique fittings in its 3 rooms.

Plough Inn, *Rhosmaen, Llandeilo.* ☎ *01558 823 431; Fax 01558 823 969; enquiries@ploughrhosmaen.co.uk; www.ploughrhosmaen.co.uk.* This former farmhouse is well furnished with picture windows offering fine views of the countryside. The Italian patron/chef serves local and Continental meals.

BRIGHTON★★

East Sussex, ENGLAND

POPULATION 200 168 (INCLUDING HOVE)

MICHELIN ATLAS P 11 OR MAP 504 T 31

TOWN PLAN IN THE CURRENT MICHELIN GUIDE GREAT BRITAIN AND IRELAND

With its south-facing beach punctuated by piers and backed by a wide promenade, its elegant Georgian, Regency and Victorian architecture, the labyrinthine lanes of the old fishing town contrasting with lavishly planted open spaces and parkways, Brighton is where the English seaside tradition was invented and brought to a pitch of perfection. Just 55 miles (88km) due south of the capital it is a popular summer weekend haunt of Londoners.

▶ **Orient Yourself:** Brighton is a very compact town which is best explored on foot.

Don't Miss: Royal Pavilion, The Lanes for their shops and eating places.

Organizing Your Time: In summer you'll want to spend one night here at least to catch the evening buzz.

Especially for Kids: Brighton Pier, the Bowlplex Centre, Sea Life Centre.

A Bit of History

Modern Brighton began in the mid 18C with the promotion by Dr Richard Russell of the healthy effect of drinking and bathing in seawater. The new modishness of the once decayed fishing town of Brighthelmstone was confirmed by the allure it exercised

A.F. Kersting

Royal Pavilion, Brighton

throughout his lifetime on the Prince of Wales, following his first visit in 1783. From the 1840s the London, Brighton and South Coast Railway brought ever-increasing numbers of holidaymakers of all classes to what had truly become "London-by-the-Sea". Today's mature town has remained young, stage-managing its raffish appeal to attract successive generations of visitors from home and abroad, while acquiring the ingredients of a miniature metropolis: specialist shops, uncountable restaurants, entertainments of all kinds, and even, on its outskirts, the modern University of Sussex. *10 Bartholomew Square, BN1 1JS. ☎ 0906 711 255 (50p/min, within UK only); brighton-tourism@brighton-hove.gov.uk; www.visitbrighton.com*

Royal Pavilion★★★ *1hr*

Open daily, Apr-Sep, 9.30am-5.45pm, Oct-Mar, 10am-5.15pm. Closed 25-26 Dec. £5.35. Leaflet (8 languages). Guide book (3 languages) £6.10. Mini guides: 6 languages, 75p. Guided tour (4 languages). Wheelchair acces to ground floor only. ☎ 01273 290 900; Fax 01273 292 871; royalpavilion@brighton-hove.gov.uk; www. royalpavilion. org.uk. This fantastic oriental confection in stucco and stone reflects the brilliant personality of **George Augustus Frederick, Prince of Wales** (1762-1811), later Regent (1811-20), finally King George IV. A year after his clandestine marriage in 1785 to the young and attractive commoner and Catholic, Mrs Fitzherbert, "Prinny" rented Brighton House, and this "superior farmhouse" he successively enlarged and transformed until, between 1815 and 1824, in genial collaboration with the architect John Nash and with inspired interior designers, he created a uniquely flamboyant setting for the extravagant festivities of his seaside court, a pleasure palace which is the representative monument of the Regency Age.

Address Book

OUT AND ABOUT IN BRIGHTON

Tourist Information Centre – 10 Bartholomew Square, BN1 1JS. ☎ 0906 711 255 (50p/min, within UK only); brighton-tourism@brighton-hove.gov.uk; www. visitbrighton.com

Pubs and Restaurants – For a wide selection of pubs and restaurants head towards the town centre, or take a walk through the North Laine or the Lanes.

Shopping – North Laine, running parallel with Queens Road, is an area of quirky, specialist shops, cafés, restaurants and pubs, with a bohemian feel to it. Many of the main High Street shops run along North Street, East Street, Churchill Square

and Western Road, and just behind North Street are the Lanes lined with elegant clothes shops, antique and jewellery shops, as well as bistros, restaurants, pubs and cafés.

Entertainment – There is a wealth of pubs and clubs to choose from. For up-to-date information consult *The Latest* or *Impact* magazines.

The Brighton Festival runs for three weeks every May, and is the biggest mixed arts festival in England. The festival brochure is published in March each year, and can be requested from the Brighton Dome Ticket Office, New Road, Brighton BN1 1VE. ☎ 01273 709 709; www. brighton-festival.org

The Pavilion is approached via two exotic gateways. Its extraordinary silhouette, all bulbous domes, pinnacles, turrets and spikes pricking the skyline, is a free interpretation of "Hindoo" architecture. Within, throughout a series of gorgeously furnished and decorated interiors, Chinoiserie prevails, taken to astonishing lengths in the **Music Room**, lit by lotus-shaped gaseliers, where painted serpents and dragons writhe beneath the gilded scales of a great dome. Equally sumptuous is the great **Banqueting Room**; from its dome (45ft/14m high) hangs a one-ton crystal lighting device, at its apex a huge winged dragon in silver outlined against enormous trompe l'oeil plantain leaves. The deliciously refurbished **royal apartments** on the first floor are reached by a staircase whose cast-iron banister is cunningly disguised as bamboo.

All this exuberance is set in restored **gardens**, which have been remodelled and replanted to correspond as closely as possible to their state in Regency times. The grounds are bounded on the northwest by the former royal stables, a massive building in subdued Oriental style housing a municipal library and museum and the Dome concert hall.

Seafront★★

The meeting of Victorian Brighton and the sea is marked by a broad **promenade**, carried on massive brick vaults and with generous ramps and stairs leading to a roadway at beach level. A wealth of light-hearted detail, from splendid decorative ironwork to jaunty little kiosks and shelters, sets the holiday mood, and is extended into the sea on the **West Pier** of 1866 and the later Palace Pier, a lively place of fun and refreshment.

Close to the Palace Pier, now restyled Brighton Pier, at the meeting point of the upper and lower promenades is the **Sea Life Centre** (& ⏱ *Marine Parade Open daily, 10am-5pm (4pm winter); last admission 1hr before closing.* ⏱ *Closed 25 Dec.* ⊞ *£6.75. Leaflet; guide book £2.50.* ☎ *01273 604 234; brightonslc@freeserve.co.uk; www.sealife.co.uk.)* offering a variety of ways to view marine life at close quarters, including tropical and freshwater fish displayed in the original Victorian vaulted aquarium – the largest in the world when it opened in 1872. The pioneering electric **Volks Railway** of 1883 runs eastward along the foot of the rising chalk cliff to the somewhat remote modern **Marina**.

Within the continuous wall of seafront building is a succession of architectural set-pieces, designed to enhance the status of early visitors and offer at the very least a glimpse of the waves. Of these, the most distinguished, just in the adjoining borough of Hove, is **Brunswick Square** of 1825-27, with stucco, bow windows, Classical details and elegant ironwork; the earliest, **Royal Crescent** of 1798-1807, in black mathematical tiles; and the grandest, far to the east, the vast expanse of **Lewes Crescent/Sussex Square**, core of Thomas Reid Kemp's ambitiously planned Kemp Town, developed from 1823 onwards. Victorian building, exemplified in the many-storeyed and richly decorated Grand and Metropole hotels, stresses panache as much as elegance.

Address Book

WHERE TO EAT

🍴🍷 **Havana**, *32 Duke Street.* ☎ *01273 773 388; Fax 01273 748 923.* Once the late 18C Theatre Royal, buzzing Havana is still a theatrical experience with mock Colonial styling and a Cuban theme which carries through to the food and drinks, alongside classic international dishes.

🍴🍷🍷 **One Paston Place**, *1 Paston Place, Kemp Town.* ☎ *01273 606 933; Fax 01273 675 686; info@onepastonplace.co.uk; www.onepastonplace.co.uk.* Just off the seafront in the town centre this is the place in to sample modern European haute cuisine in very elegant and relaxed surroundings.

WHERE TO STAY

🏠🍷🍷🍷 **Hotel du Vin**, *Ship Street.* ☎ *01273 718 588; Fax 01273 718 599; info@ brighton.hotelduvin.com; www.hotelduvin. com.* Style is the keyword in this 19C neo Gothic building, with 37 striking minimalist rooms plus a first-class bohemian bistro (alc28) where booking is essential.

🏠🍷🍷🍷 **Ainsley House**, *28 New Steine.* ☎ *01273 605 310; Fax 01273 688 604; rooms@ainsleyhotel.com; www. ainsleyhotel.com.* This comfortable Regency terraced house is in the centre of town just off the seafront; 11 rooms furnished in traditional style.

🏠🍷🍷 **The Dove**, *18 Regency Square.* ☎ *01273 779 222; Fax 01273 746 912; enquiries @ thedovehotel.co.uk; www. thedovehotel.co.uk.* Centrally located Regency terrace house with bright unfussy bedrooms, two of which have appealing views onto the pleasant square.

Town Centre

The Lanes★ – This maze of animated alleyways in the old town, lined with countless boutiques and antique shops, focuses on **Brighton Square**.

St Bartholomew's★ – *Ann Street* ⏰*Open Mon-Sat, 10am-1pm and 2pm-4.30pm. Services: Mon-Fri, 12.15pm (Low Mass); Sat, 9.30am; Sun, 9.30am (Family Mass), 11am (Solemn High Mass).* ☎ *01273 620 491; Fax 01273 572 215; e-mail stbartsfastnet.co.uk; www.brighton.world-guides.com/brighton_churches.html.* Of Brighton's many Victorian churches this large edifice of 1872-74 is outstanding. The sublime simplicity of patterned brick walls carrying the nave to the awesome height of 135ft/41m contrasts with rich **furnishings** (Lady Altar, main altarpiece, giant candlesticks), masterworks of the Arts and Crafts Movement.

Brighton Museum and Art Gallery – ♿ *Church Street.* ⏰*Open Tue-Sun, 10am (2pm Sun) to 5pm (7pm Tue)* ⏰ *Closed 1 Jan, Good Friday, 25-26 Dec.* ☎ *01273 290 900; Fax 01273 292 841; www.museums.brighton-hove.gov.uk.* In addition to its local history collection, Dutch and English paintings, porcelain and pottery, and its fashion and ethnographical gallery, the intimate interior of this section of the Royal Pavilion's former stables also houses a well-presented display of 20C decorative arts, ranging from Art Nouveau to post-war Scandinavian design.

Excursions

Preston Manor – *2mi/3km north by A 23. Preston Drove.* ⏰*Open daily 10am (2pm Sun, 1pm Mon) to 5pm.* ⏰ *Closed Good Friday, 25-26 Dec.* 💷 *£3* ☎ *01273 292 770; Fax 01273 292 771; museums@brighton-hove.gov.uk; www.prestonmanor.virtualmuseum. info.* The Stanford family owed much of their wealth and influence to their extensive landholdings which blocked the northward expansion of Brighton in the 19C. Their 18C house, much remodelled at the beginning of the 20C, is well stocked with **furniture** and **fittings** evoking the life lived here in the balmy days of Edwardian Brighton.

Booth Museum of Natural History – *1.5mi/2km northwest, 194 Dyke Road.* ♿⏰*Open Fri-Wed, 10am (2pm Sun) to 5pm.* ⏰ *Closed 1 Jan, Good Friday, 25-26 Dec. No charge. Wheelchair users advised to use rear entrance to avoid steps.* ☎ *01273 292 777; Fax 01273 292 778; museums@brighton-hove.gov.uk; www.booth.virtualmuseum.info.* Founded in 1874 by Edward Thomas Booth to display his pioneering **dioramas** of stuffed birds in naturalistic settings, this is the country's largest natural history museum outside London, with no fewer than 621 000 items in its zoological, geological and botanical collections. The original Brighton Rock – the Cretaceous chalk that underlies the South Downs – is fully explained and, as well as Booth's original dioramas, there are excellent displays in a more modern style which evoke the richness and variety of bird, animal and insect life.

Devil's Dyke – *5mi/8km northwest by the Dyke Road.* The sweeping expanses of the South Downs, their steep north-facing scarp followed by the Long Distance Footpath of the **South Downs Way**, offer relief from the congestion of the coast. Magnificent northward **views★** over the woods and villages of the Sussex Weald can be enjoyed from the prehistoric earthworks overlooking the **Devil's Dyke**, a deep coombe cutting into the hills.

BRISTOL★★

Bristol, ENGLAND

POPULATION 407 992

MICHELIN ATLAS P 17 OR MAP 503 M 29

🔲 *Colston Centre, 11 Colston Avenue BS1 4UB; Wildwalk-At-Bristol; the Mall Galleries, Broadmead.* ☎ *0906 711 2191 (50p/min), from outside UK 0044 870 444 0654; ticharbourside@bristol-city.gov.uk.*

▶ **Orient Yourself:** take the Bristol (open top) Bus Tour, Easter through Sept, which includes the city centre and Clifton. 🚌 24hr ticket £8. ☎ 0845 408 0474, 0870 608 2608.

⊙ **Don't Miss:** The Georgian House, Clifton.

🕐 **Organizing Your Time:** Allow two days.

Kids Especially for Kids: Bristol Zoo

🖐 **Also See:** Bath, Brecon Beacons, Cardiff, Gloucester, Wells

🚤 **Boat Trips:** The Bristol Packet, located at Wapping Wharf Gas Ferry Road, operates a city docks tour during the summer season. Also river trips to: Beese's Tea Garden; Chequers Inn and Lock and Weir Avon Gorge Cruise (3hr 30min). Day trips to Bath. Call for information. ☎ *0117 926 8157; www.bristolpacket. co.uk.*

A Bit of History

In the 10C Bristol was a settlement at the western limit of Saxon influence, trading with Ireland. Its port flourished and by the Middle Ages Bristol was England's second city. By the 17C its trade had expanded to the Canaries, South and North America, Africa and the West Indies. In the 18C-19C new industries developed locally: iron, brass, copper, porcelain, glass, chocolate and tobacco. To overcome the problems caused in the port by the exceptional tidal range (the second highest in the world), an elaborate system of locks was constructed in 1804-09 to maintain a constant water level along the city's extensive quaysides, so creating the **Floating Harbour**★★. The Industrial Revolution drew interests north, however, and the city declined. Modern docks on the estuary of the Severn now enable virtually all commercial shipping to avoid the difficult passage through the Avon Gorge. Bristol's present affluence and regeneration is underpinned by the electronic age: high-technology research and assembly (Rolls Royce, British Aerospace) continues to maintain Bristol's strong engineering tradition, while the shift of major banking and insurance services away from London provides numerous jobs in the financial sector. The quaysides have become thriving leisure and recreation areas and the setting for the **Arnolfini Arts Centre** and the Watershed media centre along St Augustine's Reach (**CZ**).

Architecturally, Bristol prospered from Domesday to the 18C, or from the Norman, through Gothic – particularly the Perpendicular – to the Jacobean and Palladian periods. Its medieval churches were mostly spared 19C restoration, while the city benefited from the genius of the visionary engineer **Isambard Kingdom Brunel** (1806-59), designer of the Clifton Suspension Bridge and the steamship *Great Britain* and architect of the impeccably planned, broad-gauge Great Western Railway, which reached its terminus here, Station Building (**DZ**), in 1841. In 1940-42 the city was heavily bombed and much of today's centre is the result of post-war rebuilding.

"Shipshape and Bristol fashion"

This expression was coined to describe the many and varied preparations required before a ship sailed up the river. Given the dramatic rise and fall of the tide, ships were often left askew when stranded on the mudflats; if cargo was not properly stowed it was liable to fall or spill. Appropriately enough, it was a Bristol-born man, **Samuel Plimsoll,** who came up with the idea of limiting cargo weight and checking whether it was correctly loaded by means of the elementary concept known as the Plimsoll line.

BRISTOL

Anchor Rd	CZ	
Ashley Rd	BX	
Ashton Ave	AX	4
Avon St	DYZ	
Baldwin St	CY	
Bath Rd	BX	
Bedminster Parade	CZ	5
Berkeley Pl.	AX	7
Black Boy Hill	AX	8
Bond St	DY	
Bristol Spine Rd	BX	
Broad Quay	CYZ	13
Broad St	CY	14
Broad Weir	DY	
Broadmead	DY	
Brunel Way	AX	16
Cheltenham Rd	AX	20
Clarence Rd	DZBX	22
Cliff House Rd	AX	24
Clifton Down Rd	AX	25
Clifton Hill	AX	26
Clifton Park	AX	28
College Green	CZ	30
College St	CYZ	32
Colston Ave	CY	33
Colston St	CY	
Commercial Rd	CZ	
Corn St	CY	
Coronation Rd	AX	
Countership	DY	
Cumberland Rd	CZ	
East St	BX	
Eastgate Shopping Centre	BX	
Easton Way	BX	
Fairfax St	CDY	35
Feeder Rd	BX	
Frog Lane	CY	37
Frogmore St	CY	
Galleries Shopping Centre	DY	
Haymarket	DY	38
High St	CDY	39
Horfield Rd	CY	
Horse Fair	DY	
Hotwell Rd	AX	
King St	CZ	
Lawrence Hill	BX	41
Lewins Mead	CY	
Long Ashton Rd	AX	
Lower Castle St	DY	43
Malago Rd	BX	44
Marlborough St	CDY	46
Merchant St	DY	47
Narrow Plain	DY	50
Nelson St	CY	51
Newfoundland St	DY	
Newgate	DY	
North St	DY	52
Old Market St	DY	54
Park St	CY	
Park Row Perry Rd	CY	
Passage St	DY	55
Pembroke Rd	AX	56
Penn St	DY	
Philip St	BX	57
Portway	AX	
Prewett St	DZ	
Prince St	CZ	
Quay St	CY	58
Queen Charlotte St	CZ	60
Queen's Rd	AX	
Redcliffe Hill	DZ	
Redcliffe Mead Lane	DZ	61
Redcliffe St	DZ	
Redcliffe Way	CDZ	
Regent St	AX	62
Royal York Crescent	AX	63
Rupert St	CY	65
St. Augustine's Parade	CY	66
St. John's Lane	BX	
St. Michael's Hill	CY	
St. Thomas St	DZ	
Sheene Rd	BX	67
Sion Hill	AX	70
Stapleton Rd	BX	
Stokes Croft	BX	72
Temple Gate	DZ	75
Temple Way	DYZ	
Tower Hill	DY	
Trenchard St	CY	77
Union St	DY	
Unity St	DY	
Upper Maudlin St	CY	
Victoria St	DZ	
Wapping Rd	CZ	
Wellington Rd	DY	
Wells Rd	BX	
Welsh Back	CZ	
West St	ABX	
Whiteladies Rd	AX	
Wine St	DY	80
York Rd	DZ	

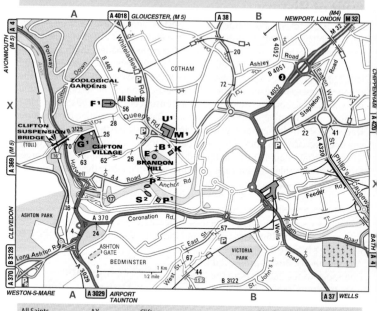

All Saints	AX	
All Saints Centre	CY	A
Arnolfini Arts Center	CZ	
At-Bristol	CZ	
Berkeley Square	AX	B[1]
Brandon Hill	AX	
Bristol University	AX	U[1]
Broadmead Baptist Church	DY	D
Brunel statue	CZ	
Cabot Tower	AX	E
Castle Park	DY	
Cathedral	CZ	
Cathedral of St. Peter and St. Paul	AX	F[1]
Christchurch and All Saints	CY	F[2]
City Museum and Art Gallery	AX	M[1]
Clifton Suspension Bridge	AX	
Clifton Suspension Bridge Visitor Centre	AX	G[1]
Clifton Village	AX	
Com Exchange	CY	G[2]
Council House	CYZ	C
Floating Harbour	CDZ	
Georgian House	ABX	K
Harveys Wine Cellars	CY	M[2]
Hatchet Inn	CY	L
Industrial Museum	CZ	M[3]
John Wesley's New Room	DY	N
Llandoger Trow Inn	CZ	
Lord Mayor's Chapel	CZ	
Maritime Heritage Centre	AX	P[1]
Matthew	AX	P[2]
Merchant Seamen's Almshouses	CZ	Q
Norman Arch	CZ	R
Quakers Friars	DY	
Queen Square	CZ	
Red Lodge	CY	
SS Great Britain	AX	S[2]
St. Augustine's Reach	CZ	
St. John The Baptist	CY	
St. Mary Redcliffe	DZ	
St. Nicholas Church	DY	
St. Stephen's City	CY	S[1]
Temple Church	DZ	
Temple Meads Station	DZ	
Theatre Royal	CZ	T
Watershed	CZ	
Zoological Gardens	AX	

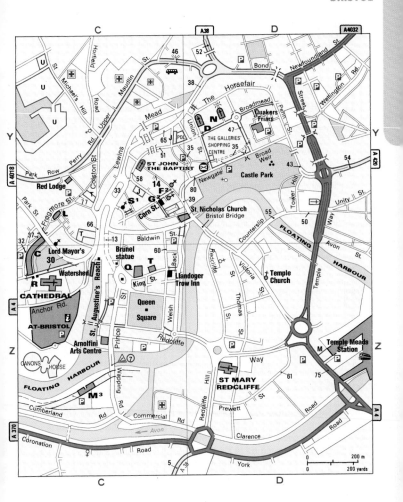

Sights

At-Bristol★★ – *Harbourside.* ◐*Open daily, 10am-5pm; IMAX theatre: Films every 75min. Closed 25 Dec.* ✆ *Explore £7.50; Wildwalk £8; IMAX £6.50; any two attractions £11-£12.50.* ☎*0845 345 1235; information@at-bristol.org.uk; www.at-bristol.org.uk.*

St Mary Redcliffe★★ **(DZ)** – *Redcliff Hill.* ◐*Open daily, 9am-4pm. Services: Sun at 8am, 9.30am, 11.15am, 6.30pm. Brochure (8 languages). Cafe: Open Mon-Fri, 10am-4pm.* ☎*/Fax 0117 929 1487; parish.office@stmaryredcliffe.co.uk; stmaryredcliffe.co.uk.* This pale Dundry stone-faced edifice, "the fairest, goodliest, and most famous parish church in England" according to Queen Elizabeth I, represents the most perfect expression of the Gothic style spanning the 13C to 15C evolution of Early English to Perpendicular. The **spire** (1872) rises 292ft/just under 90m above the city. Crocketed pinnacles adorn the west end, transepts, porches and angles of the tower, while finialled buttresses separate the wide, pointed windows of the nave and chancel before flying to support clerestory windows inserted after the original spire collapsed in 1446. The Decorated hexagonal **north porch** (1290) is the antechamber to the shrine of Our Lady, in an inner, more modest Early English porch (1185).

Inside, slender shafted pillars sweep up to break into **lierne vaulting** in which every one of the 1 200 or more intersections is masked by a different **boss**, each (except those beneath the tower) picked out by gold leaf (1740). The church contains a number of interesting furnishings (late 16C wooden statue of Queen Elizabeth I and armour of Admiral Sir William Penn in the **American** or **St John the Baptist chapel**; medieval octagonal **font** in the south aisle; **effigies** of William Canynges, local MP and benefactor, in the south transept; 18C brass **candelabra** in the ambulatory).

Address Book

For coin ranges, see the Legend at the back of the guide.

The Modern French menu is excellent value at lunchtime.

WHERE TO EAT

🍶🍶🍶 **Fishers**, *35 Princess Victoria Street, Clifton Village.* ☎ 0117 974 7044; diningroom@fishers-clifton.co.uk; www.fishers-restaurant.com. Only the freshest seasonal fish and shellfish is used here, invariably served in a simple classic style. There are nautical fixtures and fittings and an informal and friendly atmosphere.

🍶🍶🍶 **Quartier Vert,** *85 Whiteladies Road, Clifton.* ☎ 0117 973 4482; info@quartiervert.co.uk; www.quartiervert.co.uk. Simple Modern European cooking in a bustling attractive restaurant using local, organic ingredients. There is also a cafe areas serving snacks and tapas.

🍶🍶🍶🍶 **Michael Caines at Bristol Marriot Royal Hotel.** ☎ 0117 910 5309; Fax 0117 910 5330; tablesbristol@michaelcaines.com. Caines is Britain's youngest two-star Michelin chef and this, his signature restaurant, occupies a splendidly opulent Georgian neo-classic vaulted atrium with mellow Bath stone pillars, arches and balconies.

WHERE TO STAY

🍶🍶🍶 **Westbury Park,** *37 Westbury Road.* ☎ 0117 962 0465; Fax 0117 962 8607; www.westburypark-hotel.co.uk. This large Victorian House with original interior stained glass and a pleasant front garden is set on the edge of downlands, a ten-minute drive from the city centre. The rooms have been sympathetically and unfussily restored.

🍶🍶🍶 **Courtlands,** *1 Redland Court, Redland.* ☎ 0117 942 4432; Fax 0117 923 2432; reservations@courtlandshotelbristol.co.uk; www.courtlandshotelbristol.co.uk. Set in a residential suburb near a leafy park, this is a comfy 19C house with 25 spacious well-kept rooms, some overlooking the neat walled garden.

🍶🍶🍶🍶 **City Inn,** *Temple Way,* ☎ 0117 925 1001; Fax 0117 910 2727; bristol.reservations@cityinn.com; www.cityinn.com. Intelligent contemporary design, all mod cons and central location are the City Inn hallmarks; smart brasserie (🍶🍶🍶🍶).

Industrial Museum★★ (CZ) – ♿*Princes Wharf.* 🕐*Open daily, 10am-5pm. Mayflower cabin and engines on view during trips at the weekend in summer. Occasional trips and demonstrations on the Pyronaut.* ☎ 0117 925 1470; www.bristol-city.gov.uk/museums. The museum is contained in a 1950s warehouse on the Floating Harbour quayside, and celebrates the city's long history of manufacturing, in particular transport vehicles: horse-drawn carriages, coaches, railway carriages, cars, motorbikes etc. Upstairs, highly technical displays relate the pioneering developments in the aeronautical industry, particularly engine manufacture. Alongside the many treasures in the collection is the 19C **Mayflower** Steam Tug, restored to working order.

Georgian House★★ (AX) – ♿ 🕐 *Open daily, Sat-Wed, 10am-5pm.* 🕐 *Closed Good Friday.* ☎ 0117 921 1362; karin_walton@bristol-city.gov.uk; www.bristol-city.gov.uk/museums. The house was built c 1790 for the merchant and sugar planter John Pinney. The architect William Paty produced a handsome, typical late 18C-design in Bath stone with a pedimented door and rooms with Adam-style decoration; Pinney himself attended to every detail of the elegant and restrained interior. Among the fine furniture in the house note the mid-18C **bureau-bookcase**, the mahogany standing **desk** and the **long-case clock** (c 1740) in the hall; the many mahogany pieces in the pale blue dining room; the elaborate gilded **girandoles** in the first-floor drawing room; the enormous Sheraton-style **double secretaire bookcase** (c 1800) and the collector's cabinet in the rich green library. The service rooms in the basement include a pantry, a well-equipped **kitchen**, laundry room, the housekeeper's room, and the **cold-water plunge bath** which Pinney used daily.

Bristol Cathedral★ (CZ) – *College Green* 🕐*Open daily, 8am-6pm. (5:30 Sat 7:30am – 5pm Sun). Suggested donation* 🍶 *£2. (2 languages) . Brochure and leaflet.* ☎ 0117 926 4879; Fax 0117 925 3678; administrator@bristolcathedral.co.uk; www.bristol-cathedral.co.uk. The cathedral is a 14C-15C Perpendicular Gothic church with a crenellated and pinnacled crossing tower, tall pointed windows framed by finialled buttresses and pinnacled parapets; the nave and twin west towers are 19C. It was an Augustinian abbey and already 400 years old when dissolved by Henry VIII in 1539; three years later it was reconsecrated as the Cathedral Church.

Of particular interest inside are the screen, the choirstalls (lively **15C misericords**), the 19C reredos and, over the nave, the highly original early 14C vault which is unique in English cathedrals; over the choir the ribbed vaulting sweeps up to form cusp-lined kites at the crest. The east end is a **hall church** with chancel and aisles rising to an equal height. The **Elder Lady Chapel** (off the north transept) of 1210-20 with vaulting of 1270 contains foliated capitals and charming carved figures. The **East Lady Chapel** (added 1298-1330) has a riot of medieval colour highlighting the elaborately carved stone. The **Harrowing of Hell,** a remarkable 1 000 year-old Saxon carved stone coffin-lid, stands in the south transept. The late Norman rib-vaulted **chapter house** and columned vestibule were built 1150-70: the walls have elaborate interlacing, the cross-ribs bold zig-zags.

SS Great Britain and Maritime Heritage Centre★ (AX) – 🚹 ⏰ *Open daily, 10am-5.30pm (4.30pm winter).* ⏰ *Closed 24-25 Dec.* 🎫 *£7.50.* 🔍 *Guided tour (1hr) by appointment. Parking. Refreshments.* ☎ *0117 926 0680.* The *SS Great Britain* was launched in 1843 and was the first iron-built, propeller-driven Atlantic liner. Her vast hulk, 322ft/98m long and 51ft/16m across, is being painstakingly restored here in her original dry dock. The innovations of Brunel's design, and the saga of the great vessel's history and of Bristol shipbuilding since the 18C are described in the museum. The Maritime Heritage Centre (opened 1985) displays collections of ship models and drawings accumulated by shipbuilders, illustrating the transition from sail via steam to diesel and also from wood via wrought iron to steel from 1773-1976.

Additional Sights

Lord Mayor's Chapel★ (CYZ) – ⏰ *Open Tues-Sat, 10am-noon and 1pm-4pm; Sun, for services only. Donation.* ☎ *0117 929 4350.* St Mark's Chapel was once part of the medieval hospital of the Gaunts. The impressive Perpendicular chapel beside the narrow nave contains 15C-17C **tombs**. Note the 16C continental **glass**, the mayors' hatchments, the gilded sword rest (1702) and the fine wrought iron gates.

St John the Baptist★ (CY) Tower Lane – ⏰ *Closed until a new keyholder is found* ☎ *020 7936 2285 (Churches Conservation Trust); publicity@tcct.org.uk; www.visitchurches.org.uk* This 14C church with its battlemented tower and spire stands over a triple arch, one of the six medieval gateways in the city walls. It contains some interesting 17C woodwork (lectern, communion table, hour-glass) and an earlier brass (chancel).

St Stephen's City★ (CY) – St Stephen's Street. Call for information. ☎ *0117 927 7977; enquiries@ststephensbristol.co.uk; www.ststephensbristol.co.uk.* The 15C tower of the city parish church rises 130ft/40m by stages of ogee arched openings to a distinctive crown and two-tier pierced balustrade linking corner turrets adorned with fountains of pinnacles. The interior houses memorials to local merchants, 17C wrought-iron gates and a medieval eagle lectern.

City Museum and Art Gallery★ (AX) – 🚹 Queen's Road ⏰ *Open daily, 10am-5pm.* ⏰ *Closed 25-26 Dec. Café. Free admission. Shop.* ☎ *0117 922 3571; ray_barnett@bristol-city.gov.uk; www.bristol-city.gov.uk.* This museum's substantial and varied collections of artefacts include Antique, oriental and locally produced glassware, pottery, porcelain and silver ware, local archaeology and geology, fine art (works from the Italian, 19C French and 19-20C British Schools), selections from the Hull-Grundy costume jewellery bequest, Assyrian and Ancient Egyptian Antiquities, scale models of locomotives, and maritime history.

Red Lodge (CY) – ⏰ *Open Apr-Oct, Sat-Wed, 10am-5pm.* ☎ *0117 921 1360; karin_walton@bristol-city.gov.uk; www.bristol-city.gov.uk/museums.* The unassuming exterior of this c 1590 house hides glorious 16C woodwork and stone fireplaces inside, notably in the Great Oak Room.

Corn Street (CY) – The four **brass nails,** on which corn merchants struck deals and paid in cash (hence the expression "cash on the nail"), testify to the importance of this street in Bristol trade. Behind them stands the giant pilastered and pedimented **Corn Exchange,** built by John Wood the Elder of Bath in the mid-18C. To the left of the sober 19C Greek Doric Council House is the exuberant Venetian Cinquecento façade of Lloyds Bank, which dates from 1854-58. Note also the 18C Coffee House.

St Nicholas Church (CD) – This proud Georgian church, gutted by fire in 1941 and rebuilt with a soaring white stone spire, houses Hogarth's Ascension altarpiece (from St Mary Redcliffe) and the Bristol Tourist Information Centre.

King Street (CZ) – This cobbled street contains 18C and 19C warehouses at the harbour end, 17C almshouses and pubs and the **Theatre Royal★★ (T),** which opened in 1766 but was granted a royal licence by George III in 1778 and is the oldest playhouse in the country still in use. At the northwest end are the **Merchant Seamen's Almshouses★,** built in 1544 and enlarged in 1696, with the coloured arms of the Merchant Venturers on the outside wall.

Queen Square (CZ) – The square, framed by handsome merchants' houses, dates from the time of Queen Anne. An equestrian statue of **William III** by Rysbrack stands at the centre.

Castle Park (DY) – The park surrounding the ruined church of St Peter encloses the remains of Bristol's 10C motte and bailey and subsequent castle and keep (13C), and is the setting for a small formal garden, a fountain and contemporary sculptures.

Temple Meads (DZ) – Temple Meads is the name of Bristol's railway station, comprising both the modern terminal and the old station.

British Empire and Commonwealth Museum – *Temple Meads, Station Approach. Open daily 10am–5pm. Closed Dec 25-26. £6.50 0117 925 4980; Fax 0117 925 4980; admin@empiremuseum.co.uk; www.empiremuseum.co.uk.* This fascinating collection, housed in the old Temple Meads railway station, represents the first serious attempt in the United Kingdom to present a warts-and-all history of the British empire and to examine its continuing impact on Britain and the rest of the world. It presents a viewpoint from all sides, from explorers to aboriginal peoples, viceroys to freedom fighters, district officers to indentured servants and covers not only the maritime, military and technological triumphs of empire, but also examines issues such as racism, economic exploitation, cultural imperialism and slavery. The starting point is John Cabot's voyage from Bristol to Newfoundland in 1497 and the birth of Britain's trading empire. The exhibition continues through twenty themed galleries which use a mix of authentic objects, costume, film, photographs and sound recordings and concludes with an examination of life in Britain today.

Clifton★★

The elegant suburb of Clifton began to take shape on the heights above the Avon Gorge in the early 1790s, with a mad rush of building abruptly halted by a wave of bankruptcies. When building picked up again in about 1810 a more assured Grecian style was applied, giving birth to distinguished crescents, squares and terraces generously interspersed with greenery. Streets such as The Mall, Caledonia Place, Princess Victoria Street and Royal York Crescent make up the delightful **Clifton Village**★ **(AX)** with terraced houses, small shops and G E Street's 1868 **All Saints Church (AX)** with John Piper windows.

Clifton Suspension Bridge★★ (AX) – *Free guided tours at 3.00pm daily 28 May-11 Sep. £1.90. 0117 974 4664; Fax 0117 974 5255; visitinfo@clifton-suspension-bridge.org.uk; www.clifton-suspension-bridge.org.uk.* The bridge, designed by Brunel (1829-31), is arguably the most beautiful of early English suspension bridges. Unfortunately funds ran out and Brunel never saw his 702ft/214m-long bridge completed; he died five years too soon, in 1859. Close to the suspension bridge on the cliff stands the 1729 Observatory Tower at the top of which is an 18C "camera obscura", affording views for miles around.

A. Taverner/MICHELIN

Clifton Suspension Bridge

Of countless bridge stories, Sarah Ann Henley's is the happiest: in 1885, a lovers' quarrel induced a lover's leap, but Sarah Ann's petticoats opened and she parachuted gently down to the mud below – she subsequently married and lived to be 85...

Cathedral of St Peter and St Paul★★ (AX) – *Clifton Park* ⏰*Open daily, 7am-8pm.* ☎ *0117 973 8411; Fax 0117 974 4897; cathedral@cliftondiocese.com; www.cliftoncathedral. org.uk.* The Roman Catholic cathedral is an impressive hexagonal edifice in white concrete, pink granite, black fibreglass, lead and glass; it was consecrated in 1973. Note the windows and the Stations of the Cross carved in stone.

Bristol Zoological Gardens★★ (AX) – ♿ ⏰ *Open all year, daily, 9am-5.30pm (5pm Sept-May).* ☜ *£9.70.* ☎ *0117 973 8951; Fax 0117 973 6814; e-mail informationbristolzoo. org.uk; www.bristolzoo.org.uk.* The famous zoo (opened 1836) features a large selection of animals – from gorillas in their landscaped compound to "Bugworld" – accommodated in various architect-designed houses (Reptile and Ape Houses in particular).

Excursion

Clevedon Court★ – *11mi/16km west on A 370 (AX), B 3128 and B 3130.* ⏰ *Open late-Mar to late-Sep, Wed, Thu, Sun, Bank Hol Mon 2-5pm.* ☜ *£4.50.* ☜ *Guided tour by arrangement. Tea room.* ☎ *01275 872 257; www.nationaltrust.org.uk.* This well-preserved early 14C house, which had achieved its present appearance by 1570, displays evidence of every period in its interior furnishings. The 14C Great Hall has Tudor windows and fireplaces; the remarkable Hanging Chapel, with its unusual reticulated window tracery, contains 17C prayer desks and 15C and 16C Biblical carvings. The contents of the 14C State Bedroom reflect ten generations of family taste, while the Justice Room displays local Nailsea glass made between 1788 and 1873.

BURY ST EDMUNDS★

Suffolk, ENGLAND

POPULATION 31 237

MICHELIN ATLAS P 22 OR MAP 504 W 27

Set in the heart of East Anglia, Bury St Edmunds boasts the ruins of one of the richest abbeys in Christendom, a cathedral built by John Wastell (architect of King's College Chapel, Cambridge), an 11C grid-shaped town centre, the earliest example of town planning since the Romans, and a wide range of English architectural styles, from secular medieval, The Guildhall, often hidden behind 17C and 18C façades, to grand Victoria, the **Corn Exchange.** Two of the best preserved Georgian buildings are the **Athenaeum,** where Charles Dickens once read excerpts from *The Pickwick Papers,* and the Manor House, now a museum (♿ *see below*) built in 1736 for the Earl of Bristol's family. The Theatre Royal is an elegant legacy from Regency times. 🛈 *6 Angel Hill IP33 1UZ* ☎ *01284 764 667; gill.hawkins@stedsbc.gov. uk; www.stedmundsbury.gov.uk; www.burystedmundstourism.co.uk*

Sights

Abbey Ruins★ – ⏰ *Open daily, Mon-Sat, 7.30am-4/5pm; Sun and Bank Hol 9am-5pm* ☎ *01284 764 667; www.stedmundsbury.gov.uk.* Founded in 633 and later renamed in honour of the Saxon king and martyr Edmund (d 870), rebuilt by Benedictine monks in the 11C, only two of its monumental crossing towers still stand upright (one bearing a plaque to Archbishop Langton and the 20 barons who forced the **Magna Carta** on King John). Remnants of nave, chancel and transepts, together with the **Abbey Gate,** give some idea of its vastness (505ft/154m long with 12 bays).

The **Norman Tower's** richly decorated gateway frames a bronze of St Edmund by Elisabeth Frink and the cathedral precinct houses built into the abbey's west end. The Abbey Visitor Centre provides an interpretation of the ruins which are also identified with explanatory plaques.

St Edmundsbury Cathedral★ – ♿ ⏰ *Open daily, 8.30am-8pm (6pm winter).* ☜ *No charge (£2 donation requested) Treasury 20p. Brochure, leaflet (6 languages).* ☜ *Guided tours by appointment. Licensed refectory (Mon-Sat, 10am-4.30pm). Shop.* ☎ *01284 754 933; Fax 01284 768 655; cathedral@bjcathedral.fsnet.co.uk; www.stedscathedral.co.uk.*

The parish church, which dates from 1530 and was dedicated to St James, changed its name when it was granted cathedral status in 1914. A perfect late Perpendicular composition of nine bays leads the eye to the chancel and transepts (1960) by Stephen Dykes Bower. Note the Flemish stained-glass Susanna window (c 1480) and hammerbeam roof (19C) with angels. The tower (150ft/46m) was completed in 2001.

Moyse's Hall Museum – *Main Square. Open Mon-Fri, 10.30am-4.30pm, Sat-Sun, 11am-4pm. £2.50 01284 706 183; moyses.hall@stedsbc.gov.uk, www.stedmundsbury.gov.uk.*. The old stone building with vaulted undercroft displays a good Bronze Age hoard and other local finds.

Manor House Museum – *Honey Hill. Open Wed-Sun, 11am-4pm. Closed Mon (except Bank Holidays), Good Friday, 25-26 Dec. £2.50 01284 757 072; Fax 01284 747231; manor.house@stedsbc.gov.uk; conman/sebc/visit/manor-house.cfm.* Under ornate plasterwork ceilings the collection concentrates on clocks but also includes costumes, textiles, portraits and objets d'art bequeathed by local families.

St Mary's Church – *Crown Street . Open (subject to staff availability) daily, 10am (2pm Sun) to 4pm; Nov-Easter, Mon-Sat, 11am-3pm. Brochure (4 languages). 01284 754680; hr50@dial.pipex.com; www.stmary_burystedmunds.org.uk.* The 1430 church is famous for its spectacular **nave roof** (alternating arched braces and hammerbeams held up by angels, the spandrels carved with dragons, unicorns, fish and birds), for the wagon roof of the chancel with its many carved bosses and for the grave of Mary Tudor (1496-1533), sister of Henry VIII.

Excursions

Ickworth House★ – *3mi/5km southwest by A 143. The Rotunda, Horringer. House: Open late-Mar to 30- Sep,Fri - Tues , 1pm-5pm (4.30pm Oct). Garden: Open late-Mar to early-Nov, daily, 10am-5pm; Nov to early-Dec, Mon-Fri, 10am-4pm; early-Jan to late Mar, daily, 10am-4pm Park: Open daily, 7am-7pm. House, garden and park £6.70, Braille guide. Guided tour available. P. Licensed restaurant. 01284 735 270; Fax 01284 735 175; www.nationaltrust.org.uk; ickworth@ntrust.org.uk.* A rotunda dominated by ribboned friezes based on Flaxman's Homer, with two wings curving inward and set in one of the first semi-formal Italianate gardens in England, Ickworth was built between 1795 and 1829 by the fabulously rich Frederick Hervey, 4th Earl of Bristol, Bishop of Derry, Irish nationalist and eccentric traveller after whom the Hotel Bristols throughout Europe are named.

In the entrance **hall** four scagliola columns frame Flaxman's *Fury of Athamas.* The **Library** contains Hogarth's Holland House Group and Gravelot's conversation piece of Augustus Hervey, his command Princesa and members of the family. In the **Dining Room** are works by Lawrence, Reynolds and Gainsborough and in the **Smoking Room,** Titian's *Portrait of a Man* and Velazquez's *Infante Balthaser Carlos.* In the West Corridor is an extensive collection of Georgian silver. The beautifully painted neo-classical walls of the Pompeian Room are by JD Crace, who painted the library at Longleat and the staircase in the National Gallery in London.

National Horse Racing Museum, Newmarket – *12mi/19km west by A 45, Market Street. Open Easter to early-Nov, Tue-Sun and Bank Hols, 11am (10am race days) to 5pm; also Jul-Aug, Mon, 11am-5pm. £4.50, Minibus tours depart 9.20am (not Sun). £16.50 (advance booking essential). Licensed café. 01638 667 333; Fax 01638 665 600; www.nhrm.co.uk.* Devoted to the Sport of Kings that embraces all English social classes, the museum tells the story of racing from 2000 BC. Exhibits include fine paintings by Stubbs and Herring, bronzes, the skeleton of Eclipse and video clips of other great racehorses such as Persimmon, Arkle and Red Rum.

Lavenham★ – *11mi/18km southeast by A 134 and A 1141.* This is a medieval wool town crowded with timber-framed houses. The late 15C **Church of St Peter and St Paul★** (*Open Mon-Sun (services permitting), 8.30am-5.30pm (3.30pm in winter). Leaflets (4 languages). Guided tours (1hr) by arrangement. canonstiff@hotmail.com*) is one of the great "wool" churches with a noble tower and porch and enchanting misericords. The Guildhall facing the Market Place dates from c 1520 and houses a **museum (NT)** (*Open Jun-Sep, daily, 11am-5pm; late-Mar to May and Oct, Wed-Sun and Bank Hol Mon, 11am-5pm; early to late-Mar and Nov, Sat-Sun, 11am to 4pm. Closed Good Friday. £3.25. Exhibition. Parking. Tea room. 01787 247 646; lavenhamguildhall@nationaltrust.org.uk; www.nationaltrust.org.uk*) about the East Anglian wool trade and local history.

CAERNARFON★★

Gwynedd, WALES

POPULATION 9 271

MICHELIN ATLAS P 32 OR MAP 503 H 24

The strategic site of Caernarfon, at the southwestern end of the Menai Strait and offering views stretching north to Anglesey and south over the hills and mountains of Snowdonia, has been appreciated from earliest times. It was the most westerly position of the Romans in Wales, who built their fort of Segontium nearby; the Normans chose the castle's present site for their wooden stronghold, which was probably replaced by a stone castle even before Edward I began his mighty structure, bristling with towers and turrets and designed as a seat of power. Caernarfon's name itself derives from the Welsh for "Fort on the Shore."

The town today, still watched over by the castle and partly encircled within its walls, is a centre for visitors to Snowdonia and for yachtsmen eager to make use of the town's proximity to the waters of the strait and Caernarfon Bay. *Oriel Pendeitsh, Castle Street LL55 1ES ☎ 01286 672 232; Fax 01286 678 209; info@visitcaernarfon.com; www.visitcaernarfon.com.*

- **Don't Miss:** Caernarfon Castle, viewed from the water if possible
- **Organizing Your Time:** Allow 2 hours to se the castle and town
- **Especially for Kids:** Beaches at Port Donorwic (*east*) and at Dinas Dinlle (*south west*)

Caernarfon Castle★★★

1hr excluding the Regimental Museum ⊙ Open late-Mar to late-Oct, daily, 9.30am-5pm (6pm Jun to late-Sep); late-Oct to late-Mar, daily 9.30am (11am Sun) to 4pm ⊙ Closed 1 Jan and 24-26 Dec. ☞ £4.75 ☎ 01286 677 617; www.caernarfon.com.

Building work on this impressive structure started in 1283 under Master James of St George (c 1235-1308), who built for his royal patron a castle with walls decorated with bands of coloured stone and polygonal towers like those of Constantinople. Grandiose in design, it was to serve as the seat of English government in the principality.
The appearance of the castle today is due to the vision of the Constable in the 1840s, **Sir Llewelyn Turner** (1823-1903), who cleared, restored, re-roofed and renewed, in the teeth of local opposition.
Massive curtain walls link the towers to form a figure of eight with the lower bailey to the right and upper to the left. The great twin-towered gatehouse, **King's Gate**, was defended by five doors and six portcullises.

Caernarfon Castle

A Williams/MICHELIN

The **Eagle Tower,** crowned by triple turrets, each, as in Constantinople and *The Mabinogion*, crested with an eagle, had accommodation on a grand scale. Currently it houses the exhibition *"A Prospect of Caernarfon"*, re-creating the Investiture of **Charles, Prince of Wales**, in July 1969. It was here that the first English Prince of Wales was born in April 1284, Edward of Caernarfon, later Edward II. The **Queen's Tower** houses the Regimental Museum of the Royal Welch Fusiliers. The Great Hall once stood between this and the Chamberlain Tower.

In **Castle Square**, opposite the balcony from which Charles, Prince of Wales, greeted his subjects, is the statue of **David Lloyd George** (1863-1945), Liberal MP for Caernarfon for 55 years and Prime Minister 1916-22.

Additional Sights

Town walls – The circuit (800yd/734m) of walls and towers encircling the medieval town was built as a single operation at the same time as the castle. The walls are punctuated at regular intervals by eight towers and two twin-towered gates.

Segontium Roman Fort – *Southeast outskirts of Caernarfon on A 487.* ♿ ⏱ *Llanbeblig Road. Open daily and bank hols 12:30pm–4:30pm.* ⏱ *Closed 1 Jan & 24-26 Dec. Parking. No charge. Shop.* ☎ *01286 675 625; www.nmgw.ac.uk.* The Roman auxiliary fort of Segontium overlooks Caernarfon town and the remains of Roman buildings in a large area of the fort are on view to the public. An exhibition in the site **museum** tells of the conquest and occupation of Wales by the Roman army, the military organisation of the day, the garrisons of Segontium and the history of the fort as seen in its remains; it also displays selected finds excavated on the site which reveal much about daily life in this remote Roman outpost.

St. Peblig's Church – ♿ ⏱ *Open by appointment. Services (Welsh only): Sun, at 10am and 6pm, Fri, at 8.30am.* ☎ *01286 674 181. Fax 01286 673 750.* Situated outside the town, near to Segontium, this is the parish church of Caernarfon. Peblig, reputed to have been the son of Magnus Maximus, is said to have returned to introduce Christianity. The church is mainly 14C, and contains a striking 16C alabaster tomb in the Vaynol chapel.

The **CAIRNGORMS**★★

Highland and Moray, SCOTLAND

MICHELIN ATLAS PP 61, 62, 67, 68 OR MAP 501 I, J, K 11 AND 12

This granitic range between the Spey Valley and Braemar has some of Britain's wildest and most dramatic mountain scenery. Lying mainly above 3 000ft/about 900m, with Ben Macdui (4 296ft/1309m) as its highest point, the region is named for Cairn Gorm (4 084ft/1245m). Glacial erosion has worn the summits down to form flat plateaux and at the same time glaciers have gouged out the trough of Loch Avon and the Dee valley.

☺ **Don't Miss:** the view from Cairn Gorm (on a clear day) and perhaps a sunset meal in their award-winning restaurant at 1079m

☺ **Please Consider:** in view of the fickleness of the weather these remote and dramatic mountains can be a treacherous place to all but well-equipped and experienced walkers and mountaineers.

Kids Especially for Kids: The Strathspey Steam Railway.

Fishing: angling centre at Grantown-on-Spey.

Visit

Cairngorms National Park – This park covers 64 000 acres/26 000ha; it is the biggest National Park in Britain, with the largest area of arctic mountain landscape in the UK at its heart. The severe climate of the windswept summits allows only an Arctic-Alpine flora to flourish. They are the home of the golden eagle, ptarmigan, snow bunting, dotterel and of the rare osprey (RSPB observation hide at Loch Garten). ⊞ *National Park Authority 14 The Square, Grantown-on-Spey PH26 3HG* ☎ *01479 873 535; Fax 01479 873 527; enquiries@cairngorms.co.uk; www.cairngorms.co.uk; www.visitcairngorms.com (for Eastern Cairngorms).*

A Highland Experience

The **Highland Folk Museum** (at Kingussie ♿ ◷ Open Easter-Aug, Mon-Sat, 9.30am-5.00pm; (Sept – Oct 4pm) ◷ Closed 1 Jan & 25 Dec. ⬤ £4.Craft demonstrations: summer. £2.50 Information sheet (6 languages). 🚶 Guided tour (1hr). Parking. ☎ 01540 661 307; Fax 01540 661 631; highland.folk@highland.gov.uk; www.highlandfolk.com) relates the life of the Highlanders (dress, musical instruments, farm implements, old crafts) and includes a black house typical of the Western Isles, and a clack mill. Kingussie is also a pony-trekking centre.

At the **Highland Wildlife Park**★ (near Kincraig ♿ ◷ Open (weather permitting) Apr-Oct, daily, 10am-6pm (7pm Jun-Aug); Nov-Mar, 10am-4pm. Visitor Centre: Open Apr-Oct, daily, 10am-6pm; Nov-Mar, restricted hours and limited facilities. ⬤ £8.50. Leaflet (4 languages). Guided tour by appointment. Parking. Coffee shop; picnic areas ☎ 01540 651 270; Fax 01540 651 236; info@highlandwildlifepark.org; www.highlandwildlifepark.org) rare species of wildlife range freely. The **Landmark Visitor Centre** (near Carrbridge ♿ ◷ Open all year, Apr-Oct, 9.30am-6pm (8pm July and Aug); otherwise 9.30am-5pm. ◷ Closed 25 Dec. ⬤ £6.20, £4.35 (child), £19.50 (family 2A+2C). Parking. Licensed restaurant. ☎ 01479 841 613; 0800 731 3446 freephone infoline.) gives an excellent introduction to the Highlands: forest trails, nature centre, audio-visual presentations.

The only reindeer herd in Britain is to be found in the Glenmore Forest Park. The **Speyside Way** winds northwards.

This area is famous for its salmon fishing and there is an exhibition on salmon fisheries at the **Tugnet Ice House** (♿ Spey Bay, near Fochabers. ◷Open May-Sep, daily, 11am-4pm. ⬤ No charge. Audio-visual presentation. Shop. Parking. ☎ 01309 673 701; museums@moray.gov.uk).

Panorama from Cairn Gorm★★★ – The **Mountain Railway** (♿ ◷ Open May-Nov, daily, 10am-5.30pm (last train departs at 4.30pm). Trains run every 15min. Allow 2hr for visit. ⬤ £8.50 (funicular and exhibition). Restaurant. ☎ 01479 861 261; Fax 01479 861 207; www.cairngormmountain.com.) provides summer visitors with an easy way of appreciating something of the magic and beauty of this mountainous region.

Aviemore★ – The northern and western slopes of Cairngorm are ideal for skiing, and the building in the 1960s of the Aviemore Centre – a complex of shops, hotels and entertainment facilities with an "après-ski" flavour – transformed the village into Britain's first winter sports resort. There are ice-rinks for skating and curling, a dry ski slope and a swimming pool. Winter sports facilities are also available at Grantown-on-Spey, an elegant 18C town. The **Strathspey Railway** (♿ Dalfaber Road. Steam trains operate from the main station in Aviemore (15min single journey to Boat of Garten, 40min to Broomhill) Timetable and price varies, check web or phone ahead for schedule, also at Christmas and New Year. 🅿 Refreshments (train). ☎ 01479 810 725; information@strathspeyrailway.co.uk.; www.strathspeyrailway.co.uk) operates a steam service on the five miles of track between Aviemore and Boat of Garten.

CAMBRIDGE★★★

Cambridgeshire, ENGLAND

POPULATION 95 682

MICHELIN ATLAS P 29 OR MAP 504 U 27

England's second oldest university city (after Oxford), Cambridge lies 58 mi/41km due north of London on the western edge of the East Anglian fenlands situated on the River.

▶ **Orient Yourself**: All the main colleges and the Fitzwilliam Museum are tightly clustered in the centre of town. There is a hop-on hop-off bus tour *(see Address Book for details)*.

🅿 **Parking**: Park and ride system in operation. City centre closed to motor vehicles during the week from 10am to 4pm.

👁 **Don't Miss**: St John's College; punting on the river Cam; King's College chapel, particularly when the Choir is in voice.

🕐 **Organizing Your Time**: Allow two full days.

Kids Especially for Kids: Imperial War Museum, Duxford.

🚶 **Walking Tours:** Guided walking tours and ghost tours are organised daily by the tourist information centre ☎ *01223 457 574; tours@cambridge.gov.uk)*. Christian Heritage Walking Tours depart Sun at 2.30pm and Wed at 11am; £3. ☎ 01223 311 602; Fax 01223 306 693; admin@christianheritageuk.org.uk; www. christianheritageuk.org.uk.

A Bit of History

Cambridge established its academic reputation in the early 13C (c 1209), attracting groups of scholars from Oxford and Paris interested in studying theology, church and civil law, and logic. Its advantageous position, at the head of a navigable waterway to the sea not far removed from London, had already drawn a number of monasteries to it. The oldest Cambridge college, **Peterhouse**, was founded in 1284 and by 1352 seven more colleges had been built, all with their characteristic four-sided enclosed monastic courtyard.

The burgeoning academic community was recognised by a Papal Bull in 1318. As with Peterhouse, other colleges were founded to provide lodgings. It is the collegiate system which distinguishes Cambridge (and Oxford) from younger universities with a more centralised administration. Today the 31 colleges are totally independent self-governing bodies while the University undertakes all public teaching and confers the degrees. Cambridge is a showpiece for new architecture, some controversial, both on college sites and on the west side of the city where several faculties have been re-sited; the latest is the mainly glass Law Faculty Building.

In Oxford and Cambridge, before the universities were established, teaching was confined to ecclesiastical schools. The scholars usually lodged with townspeople or lived in hostels known as Halls. By the early 15C all undergraduates had to belong to a hall. The Colleges were founded later and were reserved exclusively for graduates. As with other medieval corporate bodies, the members, in this case graduates, enjoyed separate living quarters but a common hall and chapel. New College, Oxford, founded in 1379 by William of Wykeham, was the first to accommodate both graduates and undergraduates.

Sights

Some colleges make an admission charge from March to September; most are closed during the examination period from mid-April to late June. See the University website *www.cam.ac.uk* for all visiting details

St John's College★★★ (Y)

♿ 🕐 *Open daily, 10am-5.30pm.* 👓 *£2, Dec-Feb no charge.* ☎ *01223 338 600; www. john.cam.ac.uk.*

A walk through St John's (founded 1511) is a walk through architectural history. It is the second-largest college and its turreted gatehouse, decorated with coats of arms, is one of the most beautiful in Cambridge.

Address Book

OUT AND ABOUT IN CAMBRIDGE

Tourist Information Centre – Cambridge Tourist Information Centre, The Old Library, Wheeler Street, Cambridge CB2 3QB. ☎ 0906 586 2526 (general - 60p/min), 01223 457581 (accommodation only); tourism@cambridge.gov.uk; www.visitcambridge.org.

Sightseeing – For daily guided walking tours, ghost tours and trishaw tours contact the Visitor Information Centre ☎ 01223 322 457574; tours@cambridge.gov.uk. Christian Heritage Walking Tours depart Sun at 2.30pm and Wed at 11am ☎ 01223 311 602; admin@christianheritageuk.org.uk; www.christianheritageuk.org.uk.

Guide Friday Tours operate hop-on–hop-off open-top bus tours of the city, with buses running every 10-20 minutes. Tickets can be purchased directly from the driver, or in advance from the Cambridge Tourist Information Centre, or from the Guide Friday Tourism Centre ☎ 01353 663 659.

Riverboat cruises: contact Cambridge Passenger Cruises ☎ 01223 307694; www.georgina.co.uk

Pubs and Restaurants – There is a list of places for eating out available from the Cambridge Tourist Information Centre.

Shopping – Most High Street and department stores can be found in **Petty Cury, Market Square, Lion Yard,** St Andrew's Street and the **Grafton Centre**. Shoppers looking for something slightly different or quirky should try the shops in **King's Parade, Rose Crescent, Trinity Street, Bridge Street, Magdalene Street, St John's Street** and **Green Street.** In **Market Square** there is a general market, open daily except Sundays.

Entertainment – Lists of places for entertainment are compiled by the Cambridge Tourist Information Centre (⚑ *see above*).

The Cambridge Folk Festival, late July, is Britain's best music festival of its kind, ☎ 01223 357 851; www.cam-folkfest.co.uk

Punting – A trip to Cambridge would not be complete without a punt trip.

Cambridge Chauffeur Punts – Chauffeur and self-punting available. ☎ 01223 354 164; www.punting-in-cambridge.co.uk

Trinity Punts – Self-punting from Trinity College. ☎ 01223 338 483.

The Granta Boat & Punt Company – Chauffeur and self-punting available. ☎ 01223 301 845.

Scudamores – Chauffeur and self-punting available. ☎ 01223 359 750; www.scudamores.com. Punt & Pint Tour Sat 2.30pm from Scudamore's Mill Lane.

Tyrell's – Chauffeur and self-punting available. ☎ 01480 413517

First, **Second** and **Third Courts** are predominantly Tudor; Ruskin called the Second the most perfect in Cambridge. Behind Third Court is the 18C Kitchen Bridge, with its view of Hutchinson's exquisite **Bridge of Sighs**. That in turn prepares you for his neo-Gothic **New Court**, so obsessively symmetrical that he once reprimanded a student for leaning out of the window. Beyond is Powell and Moya's 20C **Cripps Building** and the 13C **School of Pythagoras**, the oldest medieval stone house in Cambridge.

Trinity College★★ (Y)

🕐 *Open mid-Mar to Oct, daily, 10am-5pm* ⬡ *£2. Wren Library: Open Mon-Fri, noon-2pm; Sat, 10.30am-12.30pm during Full Term.* ☎ *01223 338 400; Fax 01223 339 209.*

The largest Cambridge college was founded in 1546 by Henry VIII; its oldest buildings surround the **Great Court** – the 1432 **King Edward's Tower** (clock tower) and the **Great Gate**, completed in 1535, topped by a statue of Henry VIII. In the centre of the Great Court stands an ornate stone fountain, provided in the late 16C by Sir Thomas Nevile, the Master who was responsible for the present layout of the buildings. The deliberately conservative **chapel**, built by Queen Mary, is in Late Gothic style with statues of Trinity's most famous men in the ante-chapel.

In cloistered **Nevile's Court** (1612) stands the **Wren Library,** completed in 1695 and named after its designer. The bookcases are decorated with limewood carvings by Grinling Gibbons and crowned with plaster busts of literary figures. The statue of Byron by the Danish sculptor Thorwaldsen is accompanied by marble busts of 17C and 18C Trinity men by Roubiliac and others. Among the manuscripts are the 8C Epistles of St Paul, Shakespeare's First Folio and illuminated 15C French Books of Hours. Outside on the roof stand four statues representing Divinity, Law, Physic (ie Medicine) and Mathematics carved by Gabriel Cibber. On the opposite side of the Court is **Tribune**, also by Wren, an ornamental platform with niches and columns.

Trinity Hall (Y)
Down Senate House Passage. 🕐 *Open daily, dawn-dusk.* 🕐 *Closed mid Apr-late June and 24 Dec-2 Jan. College may be closed at other times without prior notice.* ☎ *01223 332 500; rac44@cam. ac. uk; www.trinhall.cam.ac.uk.*
Behind the 18C ashlar of **Principal Court** are three ranges (best viewed from North Court) which date from 1350, the year of the college's foundation, and beyond the delightful Elizabethan Library is the garden Henry James called "the prettiest corner of the world".

Clare College★ (Y)
Old Court, Hall and Chapel: 🕐 *Open usually all year, daily, 10.30am-5pm.* 🎟 *£2 (including leaflet) from Easter-Sept. Leaflet. Gardens:* 🕐 *Open daily, as above except for bad weather and occasionally maintenance.* ☎ *01223 333 200; Fax 01223 333 219; dph29@ cam.ac.uk; www.clare.cam.ac.uk.*
The college was founded in 1326 as University Hall and refounded in 1338 as Clare Hall. The 17C ranges are the work of **Robert Grumbold** and his father **Thomas** and are among the most serene in Cambridge.
Clare Bridge was built by Thomas Grumbold, before the 17C ranges. Note the missing segment of one of the stone balls on the bridge's parapet. He had vowed never to complete the bridge unless he was paid. He never was.

Old Schools and Senate House
These are the oldest of the university's central buildings. **Old Schools** was the School of Law and Divinity before assuming its Palladian frontage; the **Senate House (Y)** is an 18C blend of Roman Wren and new Palladianism by **James Gibbs.**

King's College★★ (YZ)
🕐 *Grounds: Open daily except mid-Apr to mid-Jun and 25 Dec to 3 Jan. Chapel: Open (functions permitting), termtime, Mon-Sat, 9.30am-3.30pm (3.15pm Sat), Sun, 1.15pm-2.15pm and*

King's College Chapel, Cambridge

A. F. Kersting/MICHELIN

CAMBRIDGE

Barton Rd	Z 2
Bene't St	Z 3
Bridge St	Y 5
Corn Exchange	Z 6
Drummer St	Y 7
Free School Lane	Z 9
Garret Hostel Lane	Y 10
King's Lane	Z 12

King's Parade	YZ 13
Lion Yard Centre	Y
Madingley Rd	Y 14
Magdalene St	Y 15
Maid's Causeway	Y 17
Market Hill	Y 18
Market St	Y 20
New Square	Y 21
Northampton St	Y 22
Parker St	YZ 24

Pembroke St	Z 25
Petty Cury	Y 27
St. John's St	Y 29
St. Andrew's St	Z 28
Senate House Passage	Y 31
Sidney St	Y
Trinity Lane	Y 32
Trinity St	Y 34
Trumpington Rd	Z 35

CAMBRIDGE COLLEGES

Christ's	Y	A
Clare	Y	
Corpus Christi	Z	G¹
Darwin	Z	D
Downing	Z	E¹
Emmanuel	YZ	

Gonville and Caius	Y	G²
Jesus	Y	
King's	YZ	
Lucy Cavendish	Y	O¹
Magdalene	Y	
Newnham	Z	E²
Pembroke	Z	
Peterhouse	Z	O²

Queen's	Z	
St Catharine's	Z	R
St Edmund's House	Y	U
St John's	Y	
Sydney Sussex	Y	P
Trinity	Y	
Trinity Hall	Y	V

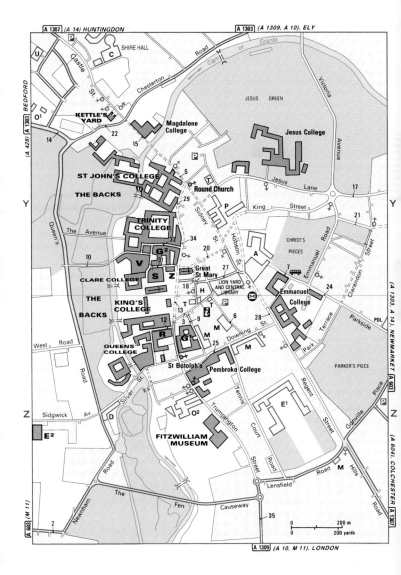

Backs (The)	YZ	
Cockerell Building	Y	S
Fitzwilliam Museum	Z	

Great St. Mary's Church	Y
Kettle's Yard	Y
Round Church	Y

St. Botolph's	Z	
Senate House	Y	Z

Address Book

For coin ranges, see the Legend at the back of the guide.

WHERE TO EAT

◌◍◍ **Bruno's Brasserie,** *52 Mill Road.* ☎/Fax 01223 312 702; brunos@btconnect. com. This converted shop with modern artworks is host to a young buzzing crowd. Try out the zingy Mediterranean flavours in the patio garden with arbour.

◌◍◍ **Crown and Punchbowl,** *Horningsea.* ☎ 01223 860 643; Fax 01223 441 814; info@cambscuisine.com; www. cambscuisine.com. Formerly the 17C village inn (5 miles/8km west of the city centre) and still serving real ale, this is now a full-blown restaurant, given a contemporary makeover and dishing up a mixture of traditional, modern and international favourites.

◌◍◍◍ **Three Horsehoes,** *High Street, Madingley.* ☎ 01954 210 221; Fax 01954 212 043; www.huntsbridge.com. A picture-perfect thatched pub 5 miles/8km west of Cambridge, with a stylish airy interior. The bar does a short well-priced grill menu, the lounge offers innovative cuisine —

salmon with barley couscous and caramelised lemon tart.

WHERE TO STAY

◌◍◍ **Wallis Farmhouse,** *98 Main Street, Hardwick.* ☎ 01954 210 347; Fax 01954 210 988; enquiries@wallisfarmhouse. co.uk; www.wallisfarmhouse.co.uk. Set in a picturesque village 5miles/8km west of Cambridge this late Georgian farmhouse offers b&b in spacious timbered bedrooms in a converted barn. The friendly owners serve hearty breakfasts. There are also four individual self-catering units.

◌◍◍◍ **Arundel House,** *Chesterton Road.* ☎ 01223 367 701; Fax 012223 367 721; info@arundelhousehotels.co.uk; www. arundelhousehotels.co.uk. Beautifully located overlooking the river Cam and open parkland, it is only a short walk across Jesus Green, to the city centre and the wealth of historic buildings for which Cambridge is famous. The hotel is formed from a terrace of late 19C houses whose facade and elegantly proportioned interiors have been carefully preserved.

5pm-5.30pm; summer vacation, out of term-time, Mon-Fri, 9.30am-4.30pm, Sun, 10am-5pm. Grounds and Chapel ⬬£3.50. Brochure (7 languages). ☎ 01223 331 212 (College Tourist Liaison Officer); Fax 01223 331 212; derek.buxton@kings.cam.ac.uk; www.kings@cam.ac.uk.

Founded in 1441 and set back behind **William Wilkins'** Gothic revival **screen** and **gatehouse**, King's is dominated by **Gibb's Building** in the Classical style and the soaring late Perpendicular buttresses of King's College Chapel.

King's College Chapel★★★ – Built between 1446 and 1515 mainly by three Kings (Henry VI, Henry VII and Henry VIII), King's College Chapel is the final and most glorious flowering of Perpendicular. Turner painted its exterior, Wordsworth wrote three sonnets about it, and Wren, marvelling at the largest single-span vaulted roof in existence, offered to make one himself, if only someone would tell him where to lay the first stone.

The dimensions (289ft/88m long, 94ft/29m high, 40ft/12m wide) suggest a cathedral choir rather than a college chapel; the 18 side chapels and door emphasise the height of the 22 buttresses which take the weight of the roof.

The 12-bay nave rises upwards on stonework so slender that it forms a mere frame to the 25 stained-glass windows (16C) illustrating episodes from the Old Testament *(above)* and from the New Testament *(below)*. The vaulting (nearly 2 000 tons), Wordsworth's "branching roofs", appears weightless. The architect was **John Wastell**.

Note the splendid early Renaissance **screen** and **stalls** by foreign craftsmen and **Rubens'** *Adoration of the Magi*. Above the screen is the organ in its 17C case used for services such as the Festival of Nine Lessons and Carols broadcast live on Christmas Eve across the world. King's College Chapel Choir has international repute, and includes boy choristers trained at a special Choir School affiliated to the College.

Corpus Christi College (Z)

Enter via Old Court in Bene't Street; return via New Court. 🕒 *Open (functions permitting) mid-Jun to late-Apr, daily, 2pm-4pm* 🕒 *Closed late-Dec to early-Jan (10 days) and late-Apr to mid-Jun (examination period). No groups larger than 12.* ☎ 01223 338 000; www. corpus.cam.ac.uk.

Founded in 1352, Corpus Christi is the second-smallest college in Cambridge, but nonetheless one of the most historically interesting. **Old Court** still retains its monastery-style ranges (1352-77) of stone rubble with clunch dressings. The Saxon

St Bene't's Church adjoining Old Court is the oldest in Cambridge. **New Court** is by William Wilkins who is buried in the chapel.

Queens' College★ (Z)

Via Silver Street and Queens' Lane. ○ *Open 28 Mar to 1 Apr and 23 Jun to 29 Sep, daily, 10am-4.30pm; 23 Mar to19 May, daily, 11am-3pm.* ○ *Closed 20 May to 22 Jun (examinations).* ⊠ *£1.20 including booklet (6 languages), No charge Nov-Mar.* ☎ *01223 335 551; sf114@hermes.cam.ac.uk; www.quns.cam.ac.uk.*

Named after the patronage bestowed by two successive queens, Margaret of Anjou, wife of Henry VI, and Elizabeth Woodville, wife of Edward IV, the College was granted its first charter in 1446. **Old Court,** completed in 1449, shows late medieval brickwork; in charming **Cloister Court** the half-timbered building is the **President's Lodge**. The Dutch philosopher **Desiderius Erasmus** taught Greek at Queens' but his rooms (Erasmus' Tower) cannot be definitely identified; his name, however, lives on in the brick Erasmus Building (1960) by Basil Spence. Another recent addition is the glass and concrete Cripps' Court (1981) by Powell, Moya and Partners. The wooden **Mathematical Bridge** over the river is a 20C copy (1904), the second, of the original one (1749) designed by James Essex.

The Backs★★ (YZ)

The "Backs" (of the colleges) along the River Cam are as fine as the fronts; they form a wonderful combination of buildings and lawns in a riverside setting and are best viewed from a punt (on hire at Silver Street Bridge).

Fitzwilliam Museum★★ (Z)

Trumpington Street. ⊘○ *Open Tue-Sun, 10am (12pm Sun) to 5pm.* ○ *Closed 24, 25, 26, 31 Dec, 1 Jan.* ⊠ *No charge.* •⌐ *Guided tour (English, 90min) Sun at 2.45pm and by appointment (4 languages). Refreshments. No disabled access for next 18 months, due to refurbishment work.* ☎ *01223 332 900; Fax 01223 332 923; fitzmuseum-enquiries@ lists.cam.ac.uk; www.fitzmuseum.cam.ac.uk.*

The famous University Museum, which opened to the public in 1843, was designed by **George Basevi** in a monumental Neoclassical style verging on Victorian Baroque (1837-75). Some of the museum's particular treasures are 25 watercolours by JMW Turner, donated by John Ruskin in 1861, a selection of some of William Blake's best works, and an outstanding collection of prints by Rembrandt.

Lower Galleries – This section consists of profuse and well-arranged collections of Oriental, Mediterranean and Classical antiquities – West Asiatic Gallery: fine Assyrian reliefs; Second Egyptian Gallery: brightly coloured mummies and sarcophagi including the massive granite tomb lid of Rameses III; Greek Gallery: Attic black and red figure vases and small terracotta figures; Roman Gallery: the priceless marble **Pashley sarcophagus** (AD 130-150) depicting the return of Dionysius from India; Far Eastern Gallery: Chinese ceramics and bronzes, a bronze tripod with black inlay from the early Shang Dynasty (1523-1028 BC) and a large jade buffalo (Ming 1368-1844); Lower Marlay Gallery: English, continental and Far Eastern porcelain; Glaisher Gallery: an incomparable collection of English and European pottery. Textiles, armour and glass (Small Henderson Gallery) have rooms of their own. The Rothschild Gallery glitters with treasures: enamels, jewellery, English miniatures and illuminated manuscripts.

Upper Galleries – Interspersed among the paintings are fine pieces of French and English furniture, Italian maiolica and bronzes, carpets, ceramics and silver, giving the feeling of a stately home.

The paintings include **Old Masters** of exceptional quality – Upper Marlay Gallery: Italian works including fine altar panels by Simone Martini (14C) and Domenico Veneziano (15C Venetian), drawings by Leonardo; Courtauld Gallery: the Founder's Titian and works by Veronese, Canaletto and Palma Vecchio; Flemish and Spanish Gallery: landscapes and portraits by Pieter Brueghel II and Rubens; Dutch Gallery: Cuyp, Hals, Ruisdael, Hobbema and the Founder's Rembrandt; Gallery V: collection of French Impressionists including landscapes by Monet, Seurat and Cézanne as well as studies by Renoir and Degas; Gallery IV: paintings by earlier French artists, Poussin, Vouet and Delacroix; Gallery III: fine array of 18C works by Gainsborough, Reynolds, Stubbs and Hogarth and the devotional *Virgin and Child* by Sir Anthony Van Dyck acquired by public appeal in 1976; Gallery II: works by Constable (Hampstead Heath) and some lively pre-Raphaelite pictures; 20C Gallery: works by Picasso, Nicholson and Sutherland; Broughton Gallery: flower paintings given by Lord Fairhaven; Shiba Gallery: Japanese prints and drawings.

Additional Sights

Kettle's Yard★ (Y) – ♿ *House:* ◷ *House: Open Easter-Aug, Tue-Sun, 1.30pm-4.30pm; Sep-Easter, Tue-Sun, 2pm-4pm. Gallery: Open Tue-Sun and Bank Hol Mon, 11.30am-5pm. No charge.* ☎ *01223 352 124; mail@kettlesyard.cam.ac.uk; www.kettlesyard.co.uk.* In complete contrast to the academic atmosphere of the Fitzwilliam is Kettle's Yard, which, according to its creator Jim Ede is "a living place where works of art can be enjoyed inherent in the domestic setting". This excellent collection of 20C art includes works by Ben Nicholson, Henry Moore, Barbara Hepworth, Eric Gill, Henri Gaudier-Brzeska and Joan Miró, most of whom were friends of Ede; the pieces are disposed about the house among the books and furniture so that visitors may sit down to admire the exhibits or read the books.

Magdalene College (Y) – *College and chapel:* ◷ *Open daily, 9am-6.30pm. Hall:* ◷ *Open daily, 9.30am-12.30pm. Garden:* ◷ *Open daily, 1pm-6.30pm;* ◷ *all closed during exams. Pepys' Library:* ◷ *Open late-Apr to end-Aug, Mon-Sat, 11.30am-12.30pm and 2.30-3.30pm; mid-Jan to mid-Mar, early-Oct to early-Dec, Mon-Sat, 2.30-3.30pm. sjp51@cam.ac.uk; www.magd.cam.ac.uk.* The college was founded in 1542 by Lord Audley of Audley End on the site of a Benedictine college. The First Court is essentially 15C except for the 16C **gatehouse** and hall.

Beyond in the late 16C and early 17C **Second Court** is the **Pepys Building** which contains Samuel Pepys' own library left by him to the college in 1703 and which includes the cipher manuscript of his Diary.

Jesus College (Y) – *Courts and gardens:* ◷*Open most months, daily, 10am-4.30pm.* ◷ *Closed Apr-June and 24-26 Dec.* ♿ *No charge.* ☞ *Guided tour by appointment (Cambridge Tourist Office).* ☎ *01223 339 469; domestic-bursar@jesus.cam.ac.uk.* Founded 1496, Jesus was a former Benedictine Nunnery, growing up around **Cloister Court** and the 12C Priory Chapel; **First Court** with its robust early Tudor **gatehouse** was added in the 16C, **Second Court** and **Chapel Court** in the 19C, **North Court** in the 20C. It is the only college with 3-sided courts occupying a spacious site.

Round Church (Y) – Holy Sepulchre Church is one of only five circular Norman Churches in the country.

Gonville and Caius College (Y) – ◷ *Open without restriction, Oct-Mar; late-Mar to early-May and mid-Jun to Sep, 9am-2pm. Max 6 people.* ◷ *Closed early-May to early-Jun; Sat-Sun and bank hols.* ☎ *01223 332 400 (Porter's Lodge); www.cai.cam.ac.uk.* Founded in 1348 by Edmund Gonville and in 1557 by John Caius (pronounced "keys"), Renaissance scholar and physician to Edward VI and Queen Mary. Its charm is its gates, conceived by Caius to symbolise the scholar's progress. He enters the college through the **Gate of Humility** (now relocated in the Master's Garden) into the **Tree Court;** progresses through the **Gate of Virtue** into **Caius Court**, before finally passing through the **Gate of Honour** to receive his degree at what is today the Senate House. The **Cockerell Building (Y D)** is in the 19C Classicism of CP Cockerell.

Great St Mary's (Y) – ◷ *Open daily, 8am-6pm. Tower: 10am-4.30pm;* ♿ *£2.* ☎ *01223 741716.* The rebuilding of the university church began in 1478 in late Perpendicular style and did not finish until 1608 when **Robert Grumbold's** grandfather, also Robert, built the **tower** that affords such a fine **view**.

St Catharine's College (Z) – ◷ *Open daily Jul-Apr, 11am-5pm.* ◷ *Closed May-Jun, 25 Dec.* ☎ *01223 338 300; www.caths.com.ac.uk.* Founded 1473. The three Restoration ranges were built by Robert Grumbold, the **chapel** clearly influenced by his apprenticeship under Wren.

St Botolph's Church (Z) – Enchanting Perpendicular with nave built 1300-50 and tower added c 1400.

Pembroke College Chapel (Z) – ◷ *Open all year, daily, 2pm-5pm.* ◷ *Closed May and June, 25 Dec.* ☎ *01223 338 100; Fax 01223 338 128; www.pem.cam.ac.uk.* Wren's first completed building and the first classical building in Cambridge, the commission was a gift from his uncle, Matthew Wren, Bishop of Ely. The ceiling is by Henry Doogood who worked on the ceilings of 30 Wren churches.

Emmanuel College (Z) – ♿ ◷ *Open daily, 9am-6pm.* ◷ *Closed 1 Jan and 25 Dec.* ☎*01223 334 200; Fax 01223 334 426; www.emma.cam.ac.uk.* Founded 1584 by Sir Walter Mildmay. "I have set an acorn, which when it becomes an oak, God alone knows what will be the fruit thereof" he told Queen Elizabeth. The only surviving buildings of the Dominican, or Black Friars, priory are the **Hall** and **Old library** (with

Tudor façades) forming the south and east ranges of **New Court**. The **Chapel** was built by Wren (1668-74) in a classical style touching on baroque and has a memorial to John Harvard, 17C founder of Harvard College in Boston, USA.

Newnham College – *Southwest of city centre (Z Q)*. As the second Cambridge college to be founded for women (1871; Girton 1869, now co-educational; New Hall 1954), Newnham has a tradition of active participation in feminist reform as well as a reputation for academic excellence. It was founded by moral philosopher and Cambridge professor Henry Sidgwick, a believer in women's right to be educated, with Anne Jemima Clough as its first Principal. The attractive Queen Anne-style buildings, the work of Basil Champneys (1875), with Dutch red brick gables and white woodwork, are set around beautiful gardens. Newnham was granted a college charter in 1917, and women were finally admitted to university degrees in 1948.

Excursions

Imperial War Museum, Duxford★

9mi/14km south on M 11. ♿ ⏰ *Open daily, 10am-6pm (4pm late Oct-mid Mar).* ⏰ *Closed 24-26 Dec.* ⊛ *£12. Parking. Restaurant. .* ☎ *01223 835 000; duxford@iwm.org. uk; www.iwm.org.uk.* The vast hangars at this Battle of Britain airfield now house a historic collection of civil and fighter aircraft, several of which, including Concorde, you can climb aboard. To celebrate Duxford's Second World War associations with the USAAF it is now also home to the new American Air Museum in Britain; the centrepiece, a B-52 bomber with a wing-span of 185ft/56m, was restored at Duxford before taking up residence in Sir Norman Foster's striking award-winning concrete and glass building. Air shows including historic fighter aircraft take place during the summer months.

Audley End★★

13mi/21km south on the Trumpington Road, A 1309, A 1301 and B 1383. ♿ ⏰ *Open: House, Mar & Oct: Thu - Mon and Bank Hols, 10am – 4pm; late Mar-early Oct, Wed-Mon noon-5pm. Last admission 1 hr before closing. Grounds daily 10 – 5 (6 pm summer)* ⊛ *£8.95; grounds only £4.60. No photography within the house. Guide book (English only). Leaflets (4 languages). Parking. Restaurant.* ☎ *01799 522 399; www.english-heritage.org.uk.*

A Benedictine monastery here was granted to Sir Thomas Audley at the Dissolution of the Monasteries in 1539. The house he built was replaced in 1605-14 by another when the estate came into the possession of Thomas Howard, Earl of Suffolk and Lord High Treasurer. It was one of the greatest Jacobean houses in England and cost £200 000. "Too large for a king, but might do for a Lord Treasurer" said James I who unintentionally helped to finance it and later imprisoned the Earl for embezzlement. Briefly owned by Charles II it was partially demolished in 1721 when the interior was redesigned by **Robert Adam** and the grounds by **Capability Brown**. The present house, vast enough, is but a shadow of its former glory.

Interior – The heart of the house is the **Great Hall,** its two screens, the splendid Jacobean oak screen and Vanbrugh's c 1721 stone screen confronting each other. In total contrast are the Adamesque **Great Drawing Room** (to make such a small room "great", Adam designed the furniture deliberately small, giving the room the impression of a doll's house) and the **Little Drawing Room** (domestic Classicism with lovingly detailed ceiling and wall panels by Biagio Rebecca and unforgettably funny cherubs painted on the inner door panels by Cipriani). Upstairs the outstanding features of the **State Rooms** are the ceilings and the 200-year-old four-poster bed covered in embroidered hangings in the **State Bedroom**, built for a visit by George III which never took place.

CANTERBURY★★★

Kent, ENGLAND

POPULATION 36 464

MICHELIN ATLAS P 13 OR MAP 404 X 30

The ecclesiastical capital of England, rich in medieval atmosphere, is dominated by its renowned cathedral. Long open to influences from the Continent, the city lies on Watling Street, the great Roman thoroughfare linking London (some 56 miles/90 km west) with the port of Dover. It also forms the terminus of the **Pilgrims' Way**, a trackway of prehistoric origin used by some of the worshippers at the shrine of St Thomas, England's best-known martyr. *12/13 Sun Street, The Buttermarket ☎ 01227 378 100 ; Fax 01227 378 101; canterburyinformation@canterbury. gov.uk; www.canterbury.co.uk.*

- **Don't Miss**: The Cathedral, especially the tomb of the Black Prince
- **Organizing Your Time**: allow half to a full day
- **Especially for Kids**: The Canterbury Tales; Howlett's Wild Animal Park
- **Walking Tours**: Canterbury Walks tours *(Apr-Oct)* start from the Visitor Information Centre. *☎01227 459 779; www.canterbury-walks.co.uk*; A Ghostly Tour of Old Canterbury ☎ *07779 575 831; www.greenbard.8m.com*, depart from opposite Alberry's (*8pm Fri, Sat: no booking required*).

A Bit of History

Early settlement – Although certain Neolithic and Bronze Age finds indicate early human occupation, Canterbury's recorded history begins with Emperor Claudius' invasion of AD 43 and the foundation of the walled town of Durovernum. After the Roman withdrawal early in the 5C, the city was settled by Jutish invaders and renamed Cantwarabyrig – "stronghold of the Men of Kent".

A Christian See – In AD 597 **St Augustine** arrived in Kent to convert the pagan population to Christianity. The impact of his mission was decisive; the city became the centre of the English Church and Augustine was consecrated as first archbishop.

In 1170 a later archbishop, **Becket**, was bloodily assassinated in the cathedral by four of Henry II's knights who had taken all too literally their ruler's desire to be rid of "this turbulent priest". Thomas was canonised two years later and his shrine immediately attracted countless pilgrims, many of whose stories are recounted in **Chaucer's** Canterbury Tales. The cathedral's monastery was the largest in the country and by the 13C Grey and Black Friars were established as well. This thriving monastic life came to an end at the Dissolution; the cathedral's treasures were appropriated by Henry VIII, the saint's shrine destroyed, the pilgrimages ended.

A prosperous city – The post-Reformation saw the arrival of French Huguenot refugees at the invitation of Elizabeth I. These skilled craftsmen contributed to Canterbury's prosperity. The city continued to flourish in spite of the depredations of the Puritans in the Civil War.

Greater damage was suffered in the "Baedeker" bombing raids of 1942, when part of the historic centre was reduced to rubble; providentially, the cathedral remained untouched and the rebuilding of the devastated area is now complete. Today Canterbury is the thriving centre of the eastern part of Kent and the seat of a new university. The city exerts as strong a pull on the modern tourist as in medieval times but it remains a religious centre, as the See of Canterbury is the focal point of the Anglican Communion throughout the world.

Canterbury Cathedral★★★ *1hr*

Open (services permitting) Summer 9am – 7pm. (Winter 5pm). The Crypt 10am-7pm (Winter 5pm) Check opening times before visiting. ☎£5. Guided tour (75min): Mon-Sat, £3.50. Audio-visual presentation £1.50. Audio guide (35min; 7 languages) £2.95. Brochure (9 languages). Ramps; lift; wheelchairs; touch and hearing model. ☎ 01227 762 862; Fax 01227 865 222; visits@canterbury-cathedral.org; www. canterbury-cathedral.org.

The original cathedral built by St Augustine was destroyed in a fire in 1067 and replaced by a large-scale building by the first Norman Archbishop, **Lanfranc**. An equally vigorous Archbishop, **Anselm**, replaced his predecessor's choir by an ambitious structure. It too was gutted by fire in 1174, four years after Becket's murder, though the crypt and nave were spared. As the cathedral had become the most important centre of pilgrimage in Northern Europe, the opportunity was seized to rebuild in a manner worthy of the martyr; both the choir and its extension eastwards to the Trinity Chapel and Corona were built in an early Gothic style which was to be of great subsequent influence in the development of English architecture. The work was started by the French architect **William of Sens** and completed by another William – "the Englishman".

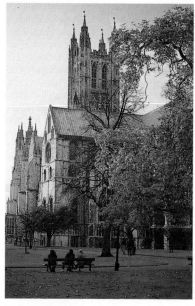

Canterbury Cathedral

R. Kord/Explorer

The nave and cloisters were rebuilt in Perpendicular style in the 14C; the transepts and towers, including **Bell Harry Tower** crowning the entire building, were completed in the 15C. The north-west tower was demolished in 1832 and replaced by a copy of the southwest tower.

Christ Church Gate★ (A), built in the early 16C and decorated with coats of arms, is the main entrance to the cathedral. **Mercery Lane★** (AB 21), a bustling street which has kept its medieval charm, offers an impressive view of Christ Church Gate and the western towers of the cathedral.

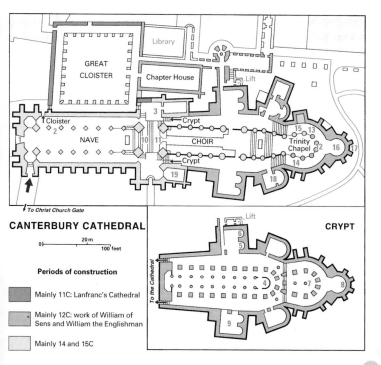

CANTERBURY CATHEDRAL

CRYPT

0 ____ 20 m
   ____ 100 feet

Periods of construction

Mainly 11C: Lanfranc's Cathedral

Mainly 12C: work of William of Sens and William the Englishman

Mainly 14 and 15C

Interior – *Enter through the southwest porch.* In the **nave** built (1392-1404) by Henry Yevele, the slender columns soar majestically to the lofty vault and aisles. The great west window (1) contains 12C glass (note Adam delving). Near the north door stands a 17C classical marble **font** (2) depicting the Four Evangelists and the Twelve Apostles. In the north transept the "Altar of the Sword's Point" and a modern cruciform sculpture commemorate the **site of Becket's martyrdom** (3). Pope John-Paul II and Archbishop Runcie prayed together on this spot on 29 May 1982.

Steps lead down to the 12C vaulted **crypt**. The delicate screens of the **Chapel of Our Lady Undercroft** (4) and the capitals are masterpieces of Romanesque carving. The transept houses the altars of St Nicholas (5) and St Mary Magdalene (6). In the eastern extension (post-1174) with its massive columns and pointed vaults is the site (7) where the body of St Thomas Becket was entombed until 1220. Beyond is located the admirable Jesus Chapel (8). The south transept was the Black Prince's Chantry (9), subsequently the Huguenots' Church; it is still used for services in French today. *Leave the crypt on the south side to return to the upper level.*

Turn right into the crossing to admire the lace-like **fan vaulting underneath the Bell Harry Tower** (10); the bosses are decorated with the coats of arms of those responsible for the tower's construction.

Pass through the iron gates into the choir which contains a mid-15C **screen** (11) with figures of six kings, the High Altar and the 13C marble **St Augustine's Chair** (12) traditionally used for the enthronement of the Archbishop, Primate of All England. From either of the choir aisles the long vistas back to the Perpendicular-style nave reveal the evolution of Gothic style over three centuries.

The wonderful medieval **stained glass** includes one depicting the Miracles (13) wrought by St Thomas in the Trinity Chapel. His shrine, placed here in 1220, has gone, though the fine Roman mosaic pavement in front of it remains. Among the remarkable tombs is that of the **Black Prince** (14) (d 1376); above hang replicas of his helm, crest, shield, gauntlets and sword; the fragile originals are displayed nearby. Opposite is the alabaster **tomb**

Black Prince's effigy

of Henry IV (15) (d 1413) and Queen Joan of Navarre. In the **Corona** (16), a circular chapel said to have housed the top of St Thomas' skull, there is an early 13C **Redemption window** (17) behind the altar.

The **Chapel of St Anselm** (18) – *(southwest corner of Trinity Chapel)* is mostly Norman and contains a rare 12C wall painting (high up in the apse).

Off the south transept *(main exit)* is the **Chapel of St Michael** (19) with Renaissance and Baroque memorials.

Exterior – The great cathedral with its soaring buttresses, pinnacles and towers above which Bell Harry rises to a height of almost 250ft/76m, is an impressive sight. The elaborate vaulting of the galleried **Great Cloister** (rebuilt c 1400) is ornamented with grotesque faces, religious symbols and scenes of everyday life. Off the east walk is the **Chapter House** with its intricately ribbed oak roof and Perpendicular windows with glass depicting characters in the cathedral's history.

City Centre

St Augustine's Abbey★★ (B) – ♿ ◷ *Open daily, 10am-6pm (5pm Oct; 4pm Nov-Mar).* ◷ *Closed 1 Jan and 24-26 Dec.* ◉ *£3. Audio guide. Parking nearby. Some steps.* ☎ *01227 767 345; www.english-heritage.org.uk.* The abbey was founded in AD 597 by St Augustine. Extensive ruins remain of the great Norman abbey church which replaced earlier Saxon buildings. There are also vestiges of Saxon burial places and to the east, of the church of St Pancras (7C), originally a pagan temple; the walls are built of Roman brick.

The extant medieval abbey buildings are occupied by **St Augustine's College (B)**. The early 14C **Great Gateway** is of particular interest.

Roman Museum (A) – ♿ *Longmarket.* ◷*Open Mon-Sat, 10am-5pm (last admission 4pm); June-Oct, Sun, 1.30pm-5pm (last admission 4pm).* ◷ *Closed Good Friday and Christmas week.* ◉*£2.90; combined ticket with West Gate Museum and Heritage Museum £5.90.* ☎ *01227 785 575; Fax 01227 455 047; www.canterbury-museums.co.uk.* Deep below the Longmarket shopping centre, part of Canterbury's excavated Roman levels have been transformed into this modern museum, which uses contemporary techniques not only to bring the Roman city of Durnovernum Cantiacorum to life but also to introduce the visitor to some of the excitements of the archeological process.

The King's School★ (B) – *The Precincts Grounds (within the cathedral precincts):* ◷ *Open daily, 7am-9pm. Admission charge to cathedral precincts.* ☎ *01227 595 501.* ✎ *For guided tour (5 languages) including the school buildings at St Augustine's Abbey, apply in writing to The Headmaster, The King's School, Canterbury CT1 2E* ☎ *01227 595 501; headmaster@kings-school.co.uk; www.kings-school.co.uk.* An ancient foundation remodelled by Henry VIII in 1541, the school occupies buildings of the former cathedral monastery grouped in the main around Green Court. The immense length of the cathedral is best appreciated from this point. In the northwest corner are the Norman Court Gate and the splendid Norman **staircase** (12C).

Address Book

For coin ranges, see the Legend at the back of the guide.

WHERE TO EAT

😊😊 **Tuo e Mio,** *16 The Borough.* ☎ *01227 761 471; Fax 01227 784 924.* Family-run restaurant serving variations on popular Italian dishes using top quality rustic ingredients.

😊😊 **White Horse Inn,** *53 High Street, Bridge.* ☎ *01227 830 249; Fax 01227 832 814; whitehorsebridge@hotmail.com; www.whitehorsebridge.co.uk.* Enjoy pub favourites in the bar of this smart traditional hostelry, or more modern and original dishes (such as Whitstable oysters and oxtail terrine with pickles and chutney) and an outstanding cheeseboard, in the classically styled dining room. 5 miles/8km from Canterbury along the A2.

WHERE TO STAY

😊😊😊 **Clare Ellen Guest House,** *9 Victoria Road.* ☎ *01227 760 205; Fax 01227 784 482; loraine.williams@ clareellenguesthouse.co.uk; www. clareellenguesthouse.co.uk.* Characterful Victorian house, a six-minute walk from the centre, offering 6 smart bedrooms and Victoriana.

😊😊😊😊 **Ebury,** *65-67 New Dover Road.* ☎ *01227 768 433; Fax 01227 459 187; info@ ebury-hotel.co.uk; www. ebury-hotel.co.uk.* This centrally located elegant Victorian house has 15 spacious rooms plus a small indoor pool and spa. It also boasts a good restaurant with a French chef, serving fine Anglo-French cuisine and self-catering flats and cottages.

Blackfriars Monastery (A) – All that remains of a 13C Dominican Friary are the Great Hall and the Refectory (now an arts centre).

West Gate Towers★ (A) – *St. Peter's Street.* 🕐*Open Mon-Sat, 11am-12.30pm and 1.30pm-3.30pm.* 🕐 *Closed Good Friday and Christmas week.* 💷 *£1.15; combined ticket with Heritage Museum and Roman Museum £5.90.* ☎ *01227 452 747; museums@can-terbury.gov.uk; www.canterbury-museums.co.uk.* This is the last of the gatehouses which once formed part of the city walls. It later served as a prison and now houses a museum with an interesting arms collection. From the battlements there are fine **views** of the city dominated by the cathedral.

Canterbury Weavers (A) – This group of picturesque Tudor houses overlooking the River Stour takes its name from the refugee Huguenot weavers who settled in the area.

Hospital of St Thomas, Eastbridge (A) – *25 High Street.* 🕐*Open Mon-Sat, 10am-5pm* 🕐 *Closed 25-26 Dec.* 💷 *£1. Leaflets (3 languages).* ☎ *01227 462 395; eastbridge@freeuk. com; www.thycotic.com/guide/sights/easthosp.html.* The hospital was founded in 1180 and served as lodgings for poor pilgrims to the shrine of St Thomas. After sharing the fate of the monasteries at the Dissolution, it was refounded in the 16C as a boys' school and then as an almshouse, a role it still fulfils today.

The building presents a black flint exterior. The 14C door leads into a vaulted hall (11C). The 12C **undercroft** was originally a pilgrims' dormitory. Upstairs are the **refectory** and the **Chapel** – both 12C – with its fine timber roof.

Greyfriars House (A) – *25 High Street.* 🕐*Open Easter Mon to late-Sep, Mon-Sat, 2-4pm; Wed, 12.30pm Eucharist all year.* 💷 *Donation.* ☎ *01227 471 688; info@eastbridgehospital. org.uk www.eastbridgehospital.org.uk.* This charming 13C building originally housed the Franciscan Friars. The upstairs room is now a chapel open to all.

Museum of Canterbury★ (A) – *Stour Street.* 🕐 *Open Mon-Sat, 10.30am-5pm; also Jun-Sep, Sun, 1.30pm-5pm (4pm last admission).* 🕐 *Closed Good Friday and Christmas week.* 💷 *£3.20, combined ticket with West Gate Towers and Roman Museum £5.90.* ☎ *01227 452 747; www.canterbury-museums.co.uk.* This modern museum is housed in the **Poor Priests' Hospital**, founded in the 13C as an almshouse. It presents the history of Canterbury from prehistoric to modern times: Roman, Anglo-Saxon and Viking artefacts, panoramic paintings of the changing city.

The Canterbury Tales (A) – 🕐 *St. Margaret's Street.* 🕐 *Open daily early-Jul to early-Sep 9.30am-5pm, Jan to early-Jul, 10am-5pm (4.30pm Jan-Feb); early-Sep to Dec, 10am-5pm (4.30pm Oct-Dec).* 💷 *£6.95. Commentary (45min) (7 languages).* ☎ *01227 479 227 (information line); Fax 01227 765 584; info@canterburytales.org.uk; www.canterbu-rytales.org.uk..* The converted interior of St Margaret's Church is the setting for this ingenious, multi-media attempt to popularise some of the vivid characters created by Chaucer as they make their pilgrimage from the Tabard Inn in Southwark to the shrine of St Thomas.

Norman Castle (A) – Only the keep remains of the 11C castle built of flint with bands of stone.

City walls – A walk follows the top of the well-preserved **medieval walls (AB)**, stoutly built on Roman foundations. The **Dane John Mound** overlooks the charming little park and a **memorial (A)** to Christopher Marlowe, Canterbury's famous playwright.

Additional Sights

St Martin's Church★ (B) – ♿ *The Rectory, Roman Road.* ⏰*Open daily, 9am-5pm (dusk in winter).* ☞ *Guided tour, Apr-Sept, by guides on rota as available or by appointment. Limited access for disabled visitors; 7 steps up to church.* ☎ *01233 720 898.* The church built on St Martin's Hill may be the oldest parish church in England. It has Roman brickwork in its walls and a Perpendicular tower. Inside there is a Norman font, a piscina, also Norman, opposite the pulpit and a "Leper Window" at the back of the nave.

St Dunstan's Church (B) – *St Dunstan's Street.* ⏰*Open daily 8am-5pm. Brochure (3 languages). Video.* ☎ *01227 463 654 (Vicar); Closed Good Friday and Christmas week. No charge.* ☎ *01227 452 747; museums@canterbury.gov.uk; www.canterbury-artgallery. co.uk.* The church was founded in the late 11C by Lanfranc. It was used by Henry II in 1174 when he changed into penitential garments for his involvement in the murder of St Thomas Becket. The head of Sir Thomas More is buried in the Roper family vault.

Royal Museum and Art Gallery (A) – ⏰ *Open all year, Mon-Sat, 10am-5pm.* ⏰ *Closed Good Friday and Christmas week.* ☜ *No charge.* ☎ *01227 457 747.* The city's decorative arts and picture collection includes a gallery dedicated to the Victorian cattle painter TS Cooper, born in Canterbury in 1803 and still working in his 99th year. The **Buffs Museum** commemorates the story of the Royal East Kent Regiment named for the buff-coloured facings of their 18C red coats. The exhibits chart English military history from the 16C to the 20C and include the last message from a Captain James Fenwick in the Peninsula War written in his own blood.

Excursions

Isle of Thanet – *Northeast.* For a pleasant excursion along the Kent coast take the A 290 north to **Whitstable** famous for its oysters and proceed east on the A 299 past the resort of **Herne Bay** with its long seafront. Beyond the ruined Roman fort at **Reculver** (nature reserve) standing guard over the exposed "Saxon Shore", are the popular resorts of **Margate** (sandy beaches, theatres, amusement parks), **Broadstairs** (fine bay, Dickens associations) and **Ramsgate** (chalk cliffs, Regency architecture, port). At RAF Manston *(west of Ramsgate by A 253)*, the **Spitfire and Hurricane Memorial Building** *(♿ ⏰ Open daily, 10am-5pm (4pm Oct-Mar).* ⏰ *Closed 1 Jan and 25-27 Dec. ☜ Donations. Parking. Refreshments.* ☎*/Fax 01843 821 940; pete@spitfire752.freeserve. co.uk; www.spitfire-museum.com)* presents an informative and moving tribute to the pivotal role played by the RAF station, the closest airfield to the continent during the Battle of Britain. Continue west and take a local road south to **Minster** (fine 11C-12C Abbey).

Sandwich★ – *13mi/21km east by A 257.* The road runs through the pretty village of **Wingham** with its wide leafy street and attractive old buildings.

This fascinating medieval borough, which was one of the original Cinque Ports, is still largely contained within its earthen ramparts and seems to have changed little since the River Stour began to silt up in the 15C. Its pretty houses of all periods cluster around its three **churches** – St Clement's with a sturdy, arcaded Norman tower; St Peter's with a bulbous cupola reflecting Flemish influence; and St Mary's, much reduced by the collapse of its tower in 1668.

Richborough Roman Fort – *13mi/21km east by A 257 and local road.* ♿ ⏰ *Open late-Mar to Sept, daily, 10am-6pm.* ⏰ *Closed 1 Jan and 24-26 Dec ☜ £3.70. Audio guide. Parking.* ☎ *01304 612 013; www.english-heritage.org.uk.* This is where Emperor Claudius' invading forces probably landed in AD 43. Roman Rutupiae remained one of the province's most important ports and was later the headquarters of the Count of the Saxon Shore, responsible for repelling the ever-growing pressure from Germanic sea-borne raiders. The massive **walls** still impress, though the prospect is no longer of the sea, now 2mi/3km distant, but of the monotonous levels of the River Stour. *Howletts Wild Animal Park - ♿Open summer from 10am to 6pm (4.30pm last admission); winter 10am to dusk (3pm last admission). £12.95. Parking. Restaurant.* ☎*01303 264 647; Fax 01303 264 944; www.howletts.net.*

CARDIFF★★★

CAERDYDD – Cardiff, WALES

POPULATION 262 313

MICHELIN ATLAS P 16 OR MAP 503 K 29

Cardiff, capital city (and also the most southerly part) of Wales, arose around the Roman fort guarding the crossing of the Taff, on the road between Caerleon and Carmarthen. It was the world's principal coal port at the start of the 20C and much of its appearance today can be directly attributed to this era. Rugby football, the national sport of Wales, has its headquarters in the Millennium Stadium (formerly Cardiff Arms Park).

▷ **Orient Yourself**: The sights are spread over quite a large area so the City Sightseeing/Guide Friday (hop on-hop off) bus tour is a good way to get around. Operates Mar to late-Oct, daily. £7. ☎ 029 2038 4291, 01789 284 466; info@guidefriday.com; www.guidefriday.com.

⊙ **Don't Miss**: National Museum of Wales; Cardiff Castle exotic interiors; a major sporting or musical event at the Millennium Stadium if possible.

⊙ **Please Consider:** Be aware that large events at the Millennium Stadium will mean congestion on the roads and may mean city centre accommodation is in short supply.

🕐 **Organizing Your Time**: Allow at least a full day.

Kids **Especially for Kids**: Techniquest for hands-on fun.

City Hall, Cardiff

Sights

Cardiff Castle★ (BZ)

Kings Way. Castle grounds (including Roman Wall, Norman Keep and 2 military museums): Open daily, 9.30am-6pm (5pm Nov-Feb). Closed 1 Jan, 25-26 Dec. Mar-Oct, daily, 10am-5pm. Tours every 20min; Nov-Feb, weekdays, at 10.30am, 11.45am, 12.45pm, 2pm and 3.15pm, weekends, at 10.30am, 11.45am, 12.15pm, 1.30pm, 2pm (possible 2.30pm and 3.15pm). Castle grounds £3.30; guided tour and grounds £6.50. Guided tour (1hr): Mar-Oct, daily, 10am-5pm (last tour), every 20min. Brochure (7 languages). Tearoom. 029 2087 8100; Fax 029 2023 1417; cardiffcastle@cardiff.gov. uk; www.cardiffcastle.com.

After Hastings, William gave Robert FitzHamon a free hand in the southern borderlands, and he built a timber motte and bailey castle within the ruins of the Roman fort. The twelve-sided stone keep is 12C.

It was the third **Marquess of Bute** (1847-1900), reputedly the richest man in Britain at the time, who in 1868 commissioned the architect **William Burges** (1827-81); his romantic imagination was given free rein in an extraordinary series of exotic **interiors** – Arab, Gothic and Greek – to create the unique monument to the Victorian age we see today. Also in the grounds are the **Welch Regiment Museum (M1)** and the Queen's Dragoon Guards Museum.

National Museum and Gallery of Wales★★★ (BY)

Museum Avenue. Open Tue-Sun and most Bank Hol Mon, 10am-5pm. Audio guide and brochure (most European languages). Refreshments. 029 2039 7951; Fax 029 2037 3219; post@nmgw.ac.uk; www.nmgw.ac.uk.

The magnificently refurbished and extended headquarters of the National Museum and Gallery of Wales is situated in **Cathays Park,** the spacious early 20C Civic Centre, which is the outstanding example in Great Britain of Beaux-Arts planning and architecture. There are impeccably arranged displays of archeology, glass, silver and porcelain; the picture galleries and the natural history collections are among the finest in the UK.

The Evolution of Wales★★ – Wales' 600 million years journey through time is told in a stunning series of state-of-the-art displays which are not only informative but succeed in evoking the beauty of the natural world and its often dramatic processes.

Picture galleries★★ – European painting and sculpture from the Renaissance onwards are well represented, with fine works by Italian masters, by **Claude** and **Poussin**, and by moderns such as Kokoschka and Max Ernst, but the great strengths of the gallery lie in its collections of British art and in works by the French Impressionists.

The survey of British art is comprehensive but has a natural emphasis on works by Welsh artists or with Welsh subjects. The fascination felt by **Richard Wilson** (1713-82) for picturesque Welsh scenes was shared by his pupil **Thomas Jones** (1742-1803), who was responsible for the dramatic depiction of *The Bard* about to hurl himself from the cliff in the face of his English persecutors. Many British moderns are represented,

Wales Tourist Board

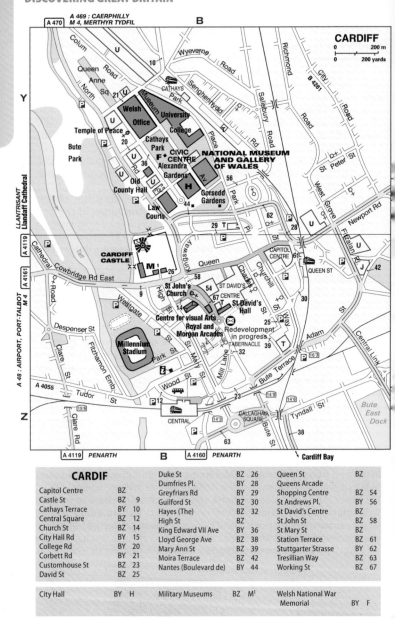

among them the Welshmen **Ceri Richards** (1903-71) and the popular **Kyffin Williams** as well as the flamboyant **Augustus John** (1878-1961) and his sister Gwen.

The vast fortune amassed by the Welsh coal magnate David Davies (1818-90) was used by his grand-daughters to build a superb collection of French art. Beginning with Millet and Corot, the sisters went on to acquire wonderful canvases by **Monet, Manet, Pissarro, Sisley, Degas, Renoir, Cézanne** and **Van Gogh,** making Cardiff an essential stop for any lover of French Impressionism and Post-Impressionism.

Cardiff Bay★

The decline of Cardiff's extensive docklands, once the outlet for much of the coal dug from the South Wales Valleys, is being reversed by an ambitious programme of conservation and restoration and by the creation of major new cultural and recreational facilities. The project's keystone is the barrage constructed across the estuary of the Taff to create a freshwater lake (500 acre/200ha) with a waterfront (8mi/13km). **Butetown**, named after the first promoter of the docks, the Second Marquess of Bute, was the core of the harbour area; its buildings, slowly being rescued from dilapidation,

Address Book

OUT AND ABOUT IN CARDIFF

Tourist Information Centre – Contact the TIC for information and advice, accommodation reservations, street parking vouchers at: The Old Library, The Hayes, CF1 1QY ☎ 0870 909 2005 (UK only), 029 2022 7281; fax 029 2023 9162; visitor@thecardiffinitiative.co.uk; www. visitcardiff.com; Harbour Drive, Cardiff Bay ☎ 029 2046 3833; thetube@ thecardiffinitiative.co.uk.

Sightseeing – A good way to see the major sights is to board the **City Sightseeing hop-on hop-off bus tour** which starts at Cardiff Castle.Operates Mar to late-Oct, daily, every 30min. ☎ £7; ticket valid all day and for discounts at many major attractions, retailers and restaurants ☎ 029 2038 4291, 01789 284 466; info@city-sightseeing.com; www. city-sightseeing.com.

Shopping – The **Capitol Shopping Centre, St David's Centre** and **Queen's Arcade** are modern shopping malls. Elegant Edwardian and Victorian arcades house speciality shops. **Craft in the Bay** (The Flourish, Cardiff Bay) is the shop window for the work of members of the Makers Guild of Wales – ceramics, glass, textiles, jewellery, wood and basketware. ☎ 029 2049 1136.

Pubs and restaurants – Visit the **Café Quarter** (Mill Lane) and the area around Cardiff Bay for a wide choice of establishments.

Entertainment – Cardiff has a lively cultural scene, including the Welsh Proms, Welsh National Opera, the Cardiff Singer of the World competition (June), a Festival of Folk Dancing (June) and a Summer Festival (July and August) comprising comedy, street entertainment, children's events, free open-air concerts and fairground fun. Venues: St David's Hall, New Theatre, Cardiff International Arena (also exhibition venue), Sherman Theatre, Chapter Arts Centre. The Wales Millennium Centre is an international arts centre.

There are also facilities for skating and ice hockey at Cardiff Ice Rink which is a venue for ice spectaculars.

Atlantic Wharf Leisure Village – (Hemingway Road). Themed leisure complex with a multi-screen cinema, bowling arena, restaurants and shops. ☎ 029 2025 6261.

For coin ranges, see the Legend at the back of the guide.

WHERE TO EAT

◒◒◓ **Armless Dragon,** *97 Wyeverne Road.* ☎ 029 2038 2357; Fax 029 2038 2055; paul@thearmlessdragon.fsnet.co.uk. Long-established homely restaurant offering no-nonsense cooking featuring Welsh ingredients – choose from the blackboard.

◒◒◓ **La Fosse,** *9-11 The Hayes.* ☎ 029 2023 7755; Fax 029 2023 8855. This very stylish underground venue was once a fishmarket and specialises in fish and seafood with some fashionable menus.

◒◒◓ **Izakaya Japanese Tavern,** *1st Floor, Mermaid Quay, Cardiff Bay.* ☎ 029 2049 2939; ayakazi@aol.com. Authentic high quality Japanese cuisine is served at this smart bayside restaurant decorated with paper lanterns and traditional banners.

WHERE TO STAY

◒◒◓ **Georgian,** *179 Cathedral Road.* ☎ Fax 029 2023 2594; gmenin@ georgianhotelcardiff.co.uk; www. georgianhotelcardiff.co.uk. Friendly family-run centrally located guesthouse in a very elegant three-storey Georgian redbrick building.

◒◒◓◓ **Lincoln House,** *118 Cathedral Road.* ☎ 029 2039 5558; Fax 029 2023 0537; reservations@lincolnhotel.co.uk; www. lincolnhotel.co.uk. Beautifully renovated and sympathetically furnished 23-bedroom Victorian 1900 house in an ideal central location. The owners are friendly and service is eager to please.

---

include the huge neo-Renaissance pile of the **Coal Exchange,** completed in 1866. More than its equal in impact is the strident red brick and terracotta **Pierhead Building** of 1896, in total contrast to the silver tube of the **Cardiff Bay Visitor Centre**.

Techniquest★

♿ *Stuart Street.* 🕐*Open Mon-Fri, 9.30am-4.30pm, Sat-Sun and bank hols, 10.30am-5pm.* ☎ *£6.90. Guide book (3 languages). Café. Shop.* ☎ 029 2047 5475; Fax 029 2048 2517; info@techniquest.org; www.techniquest.org.

Overlooking the old dry docks, this ultra-modern structure in steel and glass houses a compelling array of hands-on exhibits intended to make the appreciation of scientific principles an enjoyable and stimulating experience.

Llandaff Cathedral★

By A 4119 **(Z)**. 🕐 *Open daily, 7am-7pm; Sun services: 8am, 9am, 11am (Sung Eucharist), 12.15pm (Said Eucharist), 3.30pm (Sung Evensong), 6.30pm (Parish Evensong).* 🔊 *Guided* tour by appointment. ✎£2, details from Administration Office ☎ 029 2056 5445. Parking. Restaurant. ☎ 029 2056 4554; Fax 029 2056 3879; office@llandaffcathedral.org.uk; www. llandaffcathedral.org.uk. Tradition has it that St Teilo founded a community here in about AD 560, naming his church (*Llan*) after the Taff river nearby. The cathedral was built between 1120 and 1280 but fell into decay after the Reformation. The 13C tower and roof collapsed in a storm in 1723 and it was not until the 18C that John Wood was chosen to restore the cathedral. Almost the whole of his work was destroyed by a land-mine which fell to the south of the cathedral on 2 January 1941. The chancel is now divided from the nave by a concrete arch embellished with some of the 19C figures from the choir stalls and by a huge aluminium *Christ in Majesty* by Epstein. In the Memorial Chapel of the Welch Regiment is a triptych – *The Seed of David* – by Rossetti.

Excursions

Museum of Welsh Life, St Fagans★★ – On the western outskirts of Cardiff in the village of St Fagans. ♿ ◷ Open daily, 10am-5pm. ◷ Closed 24-26 Dec. Guide book (6 languages). Parking. Self Service Restaurant. Picnic Area. Refreshments. ☎ 029 2057 3500; Fax 029 2057 3490; www.nmgw.ac.uk. One of the finest collections of vernacular buildings in Britain stands in the parkland of St Fagans Castle, an Elizabethan mansion. These re-erected buildings from all over Wales include cottages, farmhouses, a chapel, bakehouse, school, corn mill, woollen mill, tannery, a village store and unusual edifices like a toll house and a cockpit. A unique collection of coracles, a working farmstead and an award-winning terrace of miners' cottages add to the variety of the exhibits, while a number of traditional craftsmen demonstrate their skills in their craft workshops. Modern galleries present the traditional domestic, social and cultural life of the country and there are displays on costume and on agriculture.

St Fagans Castle itself was built c 1580 on the site of an earlier castle. It has been restored to its 19C appearance and furnished appropriately. Its fine formal gardens include a mulberry grove and there are fishponds, stocked as in the 17C with carp, bream and tench.

Caerphilly Castle★★ (Caerffili) – 7mi/11km north by A 470 (Y) then A 469. ◷ Open late-Mar to late-Oct, daily, 9.30am-5pm (6pm Jun to late-Sep); late-Oct to late-Mar, daily, 9.30am (11am Sun) to 4pm. ◷ Closed 1 Jan and 24-26 Dec. ✎ £3.30 ☎ 029 2088 3143; www.cadw.wales.gov.uk; www.caerphilly.gov.uk. This massive stronghold sits threateningly behind its extensive water defences, reducing to apparent insignificance the busy town gathered round the outer limits of its vast site.

Begun in 1268 by the powerful baron Gilbert de Clare, the castle was the first in Britain to be built from new on a regular concentric plan; the design of its walls, towers and gateways embodied many innovative features too and it served as a model for the castles of Edward I shortly to be built in North Wales (♿ see INTRODUCTION: Architecture). One of its owners was **Hugh Despenser,** favourite of Edward II, who himself made a brief sojourn here in 1326 in flight from his Queen, Isabella, and her lover Mortimer.

The castle's later decay was accelerated in the Civil War by deliberate destruction, of which the half-ruined "leaning tower" in the southeast corner of the main ward is a poignant reminder. The present state of the impressive complex is largely due to the general restoration carried out in the 19C and 20C by the 3rd and 4th Marquesses of Bute.

The visitor's approach to the castle is via the great gatehouse; this is set in the immensely long **East Barbican,** a fortified dam separating the outer moat from the inner moat and its flanking lakes to north and south. Behind these defences is the castle's core, an outer ward with semicircular bastions and an inner ward with drum towers, mighty gatehouses and **Great Hall**, the last rebuilt c 1317 by Despenser. Protecting the western gatehouse, the original entrance, is an extensive western outwork and beyond this, the 17C redoubt on the site of a Roman fort.

Castell Coch★★ – 5mi/8km north by A 470 **(BY)**; signed from Tongwynlais. ◷ Open late-Mar to late-Oct, daily, 9.30am-5pm (6pm Jun to late-Sep); late-Oct to late-Mar, daily 9.30am (11am Sun) to 4pm. ◷ Closed 1 Jan and 24-26 Dec. ✎ £3 ☎ 029 2081 0101; www.cadw.wales.gov.uk. A pseudo-medieval stronghold, created, as was Cardiff Castle, by the wealth of the Marquess of Bute and the imagination of William Burges, who in 1875 started to build a fantasy 13C castle, with turrets inspired by Chillon and Carcassonne in France and complete with drawbridge, portcullis and 'murder holes'. French, Gothic and Moorish influences combine in the interior decorations.

Caerleon Amphitheatre, Barracks and Baths★★ – *12mi/19km east by M 4 (BY) to Junction 25, then follow signs.* ○ *Open Apr to late-Oct, daily, 9.30am-5pm; late-Oct to Mar, Sat-Thu, 9.30am (1pm Sun) to 5pm* ○ *Closed 1 Jan and 24-26 Dec.* ⊛ *£2; joint ticket with Roman Legionary Museum £3.30.* ☎ *01633 422 518.* Isca to the Romans, Caerleon, or 'City of the Legions' in Welsh, was home to the 5-6 000 men of the Legio II Augusta, from AD 75 until AD 300. They built the enormous **Fortress Baths★**, magnificently preserved and presented. The **Roman Legionary Museum★** (& ○ *Open daily, 10am (2pm Sun) to 5pm.* ○ *Closed 1 Jan, 24-26, 31 Dec. No charge.* ☎ *01633 423 134; Fax 01633 422 869; www.nmgw.ac.uk.)* nearby displays other finds from this important site in an exemplary way. The **amphitheatre★** (car park) just outside the fortress walls was built about AD 90. The **barrack buildings,** in pairs, with verandahs onto a central street, eight men to a room and the centurion at the end of the block, are the only remaining Roman Legionary barracks to be seen in Europe.

Tredegar House★★ – *11mi/18km east by M 4.* & ○ *Open Easter to Sep, Wed-Sun and Bank Hols, 11.30am-4pm (last admission). House and garden* ⊛ *£5.10.* *Guided tour (1hr). Guide book. Children's playground. Boating. Parking £1. Restaurant, picnic area. Craft shops. Wheelchairs available.* ☎ *01633 815 880, (opening times); Fax 01633 815 895; http://members.fortunecity.com/tredegarhouse/home.htm.* One of the finest houses in England and Wales to be built in the expansive years following the Civil War, this great mansion of 1664-72 was the residence of the fabulous wealthy Morgan family, landowners, entrepreneurs and the developers in the 19C of the docks in Newport. The house and gardens are being conscientiously restored and already give a fine impression of Tredegar in its heyday, before the Morgan fortune was dissipated on yachts and high living. Many of the interiors have been refurnished, in part with original pieces; among the most striking are the Brown Room with its exuberant carving, the Gilt Room, and the Cedar Closet with its scented panelling. The **grounds★** retain something of their original formal layout, with superb ironwork gates and geometric parterres whose shapes have been filled out once more with the original materials of coal dust, seashells and coloured earths.

South Wales Valleys – Immediately to the north of Cardiff and the other ports of South Wales lie **The Valleys**, once one of Britain's greatest coalfields. The metalworks, pitheads and attendant railways, overlooked by rows of terraced houses interspersed with chapels, occupied the floors of the deep valleys, separated from each other by high green hills. From this place of coexistence between wild nature and heavy industry came Aneurin Bevan, eloquent politician and founder of the National Health Service. His statue, pointing northwards to the coalfield, stands in Cardiff; another memorial to him is on the breezy heights above Ebbw Vale, for which he was MP from 1929 until his death in 1960.

The whole area is rich in the relics of an industrial age but the essence of The Valleys seems particularly concentrated in the Rhondda Fawr and Rhondda Fach. In Pontypridd *(12mi/20km northwest by A 470),* at the outlet of the Rhondda into the Taff Vale, the **Pontypridd Historical Centre** (& ○ *Open Mon-Sat, 10am-5pm.* ⊛ *Free Admission. Craft shop. Book shop.* ☎ *01443 490 748, Fax 01443 490 746; www. pontypriddmuseum.org.uk.)* is housed in a particularly fine example of a chapel. Just upstream, the **Rhondda Heritage Park★**, (& *Lewis Merthyr Colliery* ○ *Open Apr-Sep, daily, 10am-6pm; Oct-Apr, Tue-Sun, 10am-6pm.* ○ *Closed 25 Dec-3 Jan.* *Guided tour: 10.30am-4.30pm (last tour) every half hour. £5.60. Underground tour: A Shift in Time, Black Gold. Audio-visual presentations (7 languages). Leaflet (7 languages). Guide book (2 languages). Children's giant play area. Art gallery. Parking. Licensed restaurant.* ☎ *01443 682 036; Fax 01443 687 420; info@rhonddaheritagepark.com; www.rhonddaheritagepark. com.)* developed around the old Lewis Merthyr mine, tells the fascinating and often poignant story of coal mining in these valleys and includes a dramatic "underground" train ride. Retired miners act as genial guides, as they do in the far east of the coalfield, at **Blaenavon** *(28mi/45km northeast by M 4, A 4042 and A 4043).* Here at **Big Pit★** (& ○ *Open mid-Feb to Nov, daily, 9.30am-5pm (3.30pm last admission)* ○ *Dec-Feb, subject to closure, phone for details and times. Underground tour (1hr; child must be one meter tall) 10am-3.30pm, at frequent intervals. Site guide. Parking. Licensed cafeteria, tearoom; picnic areas. Ramps; underground tour for the disabled by appointment only.* ☎ *01495 790 311; Fax 01495 792 618; bigpit@nmgw.ac.uk; www.nmgw.ac.uk/bigpit.),* where mining ceased in 1980, the former pitmen take visitors deep underground; in the pithead buildings there are comprehensive displays recalling the realities of work in this now largely defunct industry.

CARDIGAN

ABERTEIFI – Cardiganshire (CEREDIGION), WALES

POPULATION 3 758

MICHELIN ATLAS P 24 OR MAP 503 G 27 – LOCAL MAP PEMBROKESHIRE COAST

The remains of the Norman castle still guard the southern approaches to Cardigan, but today the town has a mainly Victorian character. The fine six-arched town bridge, originally Norman, was rebuilt in 1640 after being damaged in the Civil War. There is a fine view from the cliffs at nearby Gwbert. *Theatr Mwldan, Bath House Road ☎ 01239 613 230; Fax 01239 614 853; cardigantic@ceredigion.gov.uk; http://tourism.ceredigion.gov.uk.*

Excursion

Teifi Valley – *20mi/32km south of Cardigan by A 478; turn left towards Cilgerran and follow signs to Welsh Wildlife Centre.* This most delightful of rivers is known for its salmon fishing .

Cardigan Bay Marine Wildlife Centre - ☉ *Open Apr-Oct, daily, 10am-5pm. Donation. Boat trips in Cardigan Bay (2hr-£8; 4hr-£16 and 8hr-£36) and to the Irish coast (5-day; £40 per day for the boat only). ☎ 01545 560032; Fax 01545 560 032; cbmwc@tiscali.co.uk; www.new-quay.com/marinecentre.htm.*

Welsh Wildlife Centre – ♿ *7 Market Street.* ☉*Open daily 10.30am-5pm. Visitor Centre: Open Easter-Nov daily. ☜ £3. Parking. Restaurant; café. Shop. Lift and flat surfaced paths. ☎ 01239 621 600; Fax 01239 613 211; members.aol.com/skokholm/wwc.htm.* An award-winning visitor centre commands extensive views over the varied habitats of this extensive nature reserve located at the point where the Teifi breaks out from its deep wooded gorge into an area of estuarine marshland.

Cilgerran Castle – ♿ ☉ *Open daily, 9.30am-6.30pm (4pm late-Oct to late-Mar).* ☉ *Closed 1 Jan and 24-26 Dec. ☜ £2.50 . ☎ 01239 615 007; www.nationaltrust.org.uk; www.cadw.wales.gov.uk.* The romantic ruins perch on a promontory high above the deep wooded gorge of the Teifi; they were the subject of paintings by Turner, one of which is in the Leicestershire Museum and Art Gallery. This was probably the castle from which, in 1109, Owain, Prince of Powys, abducted the beautiful Nest, wife of Gerald of Windsor. Her sons, Fitzroys, Fitzowens and Fitzgeralds, all founded powerful Anglo-Irish families. **Drum towers**, four storeys high, defended the landward approach and still dominate the scene.

▶ *Follow signs to Llechryd and turn east onto A484.*

Cenarth Falls – Downstream from the attractive falls the river is the setting for an annual coracle race. Pairs of coracles – small boats made from interwoven ash ribs covered with tarred canvas – are still used to trawl for salmon and sea-trout here and on the River Twyi. The history of these frail but amazingly adaptable craft is told in the **Coracle Museum**★ *(♿ ☉ Open Easter-Oct, daily except Sat. 10.30am-5.30pm; otherwise by appointment. ☎ 01239 710 980, 710 507; Fax 01239 710 980; martinfowler@ btconnect.com; www.coracle-centre.co.uk.)* nearby.

▶ *Continue on A 484; 3mi/5km after Newcastle Emlyn turn right into a minor road.*

Museum of the Welsh Woollen Industry★ – ♿ ☉ *Open previously Apr-Sept, Mon-Sat, 10am-5pm; Oct-Mar, Mon-Fri, 10am-5pm. ☉ Closed 1 Jan and 24-26 Dec. ☜ No Charge. Guided tour (1hr) at 11am and 2pm or by appointment. Leaflet. Parking. Café. Wheelchair access to ground floor only. ☎ 01559 370 929; Fax 01559 371 592; www. nmgw.ac.uk.* A branch of the National Museum of Wales, housed in impressive mill buildings at Dre-fach Felindre, tells the story of an important rural industry in Wales from its very early domestic origins to the factory system of this century.

CARLISLE★

CUMBRIA – POPULATION 72 439

MICHELIN ATLAS P 44 OR MAP 502 L 19 – LOCAL MAP HADRIAN'S WALL

TOWN PLAN IN THE MICHELIN GUIDE GREAT BRITAIN AND IRELAND

The centre of Carlisle is marked by the Market Cross, which stands on the site of the Forum of Luguvalium, founded by the Romans, whose occupation lasted 400 years. The following 500 years of decline and decay and 400 years of border warfare and strife between England and Scotland did not encourage the inhabitants to build grandly or for posterity. The Guildhall (1407) is a timber-framed house built by Richard de Redness. ⌂ *Old Town Hall, Green Market* ☎ *01228 512 444; Fax 01228 625 604*

A Bit of History

In 1745 the Young Pretender, Prince Charles Edward, invaded England at the head of a Jacobite army. On 17 November from the Market Cross in Carlisle he proclaimed his father, the Old Pretender, King James III of England and lodged at Highmoor House before continuing south to Derby. On 30 December his adversary, the Duke of Cumberland, captured Carlisle and he too lodged in Highmoor House, before pursuing the Jacobite army back into Scotland.

Sights

Cathedral★ – ♿ ⏰ *Open all year, daily, 7.30am-6.15pm (5pm Sun).* ⌖ *Donation £2. Leaflet (7 languages).* ⌖ *Guided tours (30-90min). Restaurant. Shop. Ramps for disabled visitors; loop system.* ☎ *01228 548 151, 01228 535 169; Fax 01228 547 049; office@carlislecathedral.org.uk; www.carlislecathedral.org.uk.* Henry I gave the responsibility for a Border priory, probably founded by Walter the Priest in about 1100, to the Augustinians in 1122, creating a See of Carlisle in 1133. All that remains of the Norman building is the truncated nave and the south transept. Hugh of Beaulieu became bishop in 1219 and new work was begun in 1225. The new choir was twelve feet broader than the nave. The extension had to be to the north, for the monastic buildings were all on the south side, hence the "offset" between nave and choir. The two most important works from this period are the east window, a fine example of Decorated tracery, containing much original 14C glass in the upper section and the choir, with its set of sculptured capitals, a unique series of 14, 12 of which represent the occupations and pursuits of the months of the year. In the choir, too, is a magnificent **painted ceiling★**, completed in 1360, featuring golden suns and stars on a blue ground, not unlike the later nave ceiling of St Mary's, Beverley. The 16C Brougham Triptych in the north transept is a masterpiece of Flemish craftsmanship.

Tullie House Museum and Art Gallery – ♿ *Castle Street.* ⏰*Open Sat-Sun: Jul-Aug, 10am (11am Sun) to 5pm; Apr-Jun and Sep-Oct, 10am (noon Sun) to 5pm; Nov-Mar, 10am (noon Sun) to 4pm.* ⏰ *Closed 25-26 Dec.* ⌖*£5.20. Public parking 5min on foot. Restaurant.* ☎ *01228 534 781; Fax 01228 810 249; enquiries@tullie-house.co.uk; www. tulliehouse.co.uk.* The original house, which dates from 1689 and contains its original oak staircase, has been extended to house the local museum, which presents the long and often turbulent history of the border town through well-presented and lively displays – Roman occupation and Hadrian's Wall; the border Reivers (audio-visual presentation 10min); Civil War siege; local industries and natural history.

Carlisle Castle – ♿ ⏰*Open late-Mar to Oct, daily, 9.30am (10am Oct) to 6pm (5pm Oct); Oct-Mar, daily, 10am-4pm.* ⏰ *Closed 1 Jan and 24-26 Dec.* ⌖ *£4 .* ⌖ *Guided tours Apr-Oct (small charge). Disabled parking inside the castle, wheelchair access to grounds only.* ☎ *01228 591 922; www.english-heritage.org.uk.* Established by William II in 1092, the castle served to block the passage of Scots raiders. The Norman keep was altered in Tudor times to accommodate cannon in place of archers. Opposite the entrance to the keep is the shell of the medieval hall, which now houses the museum of the King's Own Royal Border Regiment. All that remains of the tower, in which Mary Queen of Scots was held, is the staircase to the east of the museum building. A feature of the outer ward is the Tudor half-moon battery, built in the 1540s for the deployment of cannon.

Church of St Cuthbert with St Mary – *Church:* ⏰*Open daily, 9am-dusk, Tithe Barn: Open most mornings* ☎ *01228 521 982; pratt@primex.co.uk.* The galleried church dates from 1779. The unusual pulpit was installed in 1905 to enable the preacher to speak to the galleries. It was so massive that it completely hid the chancel from the congregation, so it was placed on rails and is moved into position before the sermon. The great**Tithe Barn**★(115ft/34m x 27ft/8m), which now serves as the church hall, was built c 1502 of red sandstone with massive oak tiebeams, near the road leading to the rich corn lands west of the town.

Excursions

Hadrian's Wall★★ – 👍 *See HADRIAN'S WALL.*

Lanercost Priory – *11mi/18km northeast by B 6264 to Brampton and a minor road north.* ⏰ *Open late-Mar to Oct, daily, 10am-6pm (4pm Oct).* 💰 *£2.60. Parking. Audio guide.* ☎ *01697 73030; www.english-heritage.org.uk.* The priory was built between 1200 and 1220, much of the stone being brought from Hadrian's Wall nearby. At the Dissolution, in 1536, the lead was stripped from the roof, apart from the north aisle which was left as the parish church. The west front is a fine example of the Early English style, with a figure of St Mary Magdalene, the Priory's patron saint, in a lancet in the gable end. The nave and north aisle are today roofed over and still serve as the parish church. The choir, transepts and sanctuary, all open to the sky, contain tombs of the Dacre family, including that of Sir Thomas Dacre of Kirkoswald, Lord of the Marches.

CHANNEL ISLANDS★★

POPULATION 146 314

MICHELIN ATLAS P 5 OR MAP 503 P, Q 33

The Channel Islands, west of the Cherbourg peninsula of the Normandy coast, are composed of fertile granite plateaux sloping to open sand dunes.

▸ **Orient Yourself**: Stay on Jersey or Guernsey and use one of these as a base from which to visit the other islands.

⊙ **Don't Miss**: Jersey, especially its Zoo and German Underground Hospital. St Peter Port, Guernsey; the car-free islands of Sark and Herm if you seek peace and quiet.

⏰ **Organizing Your Time**: Allow a few days to relax here.

Kids **Especially for Kids:** Both Guernsey and Jersey have good sandy beaches.

A Bit of History

The islands are rich in prehistoric tombs and monuments indicating human habitation from 7500-2500 BC. Few traces remain of the brief Roman occupation. The islands were annexed by the Normans in 933 and later attached to the English crown by William the Conqueror. Some customs and traditions and the Norman-French dialect heard on these islands, which have only been universally English-speaking since the early 20C, date back to this period. In 1204 King John was forced to cede Normandy to the French, but the Channel Islanders chose to remain loyal to the English Crown in return for certain privileges, one of which was an independent parliament. Despite this, the French tried repeatedly to capture the islands; a papal Bull of Neutrality was issued in

Access by air – Direct to Jersey, Guernsey and Alderney from most airports in the United Kingdom by Aurigny Air Services Ltd (☎01481 822 866; www.aurigny.com), British Airways (☎ 0870 850 9850; www.britishairways.com), bmi baby (☎ 0870 624 2229, www. bmibaby.com), Thomsonfly (☎ 0870 1900 737; www.thomsonfly.com), VLM (☎ 020 7467 6677;www.flyvlm.com) and Rockhopper (☎ 01481 824567;www.rockhopper.aero.com

Aurigny also operate flights from Cherbourg and Dinard

☎ 01534 492 000 (Jersey Airport); ☎ 01481 37682 (Guernsey Airport); ☎ 01481 822 551 (Alderney Airport).

Access by sea – Services operated by Condor Ferries Ltd The Quay, Weymouth, Dorset DT4 8DX ☎ 0845 345 2000, 0870 243 5140; www.condorferries.com).

1483 and remained in force technically until 1689 although it became a dead letter once the islands became Protestant in the 1540s. In the Civil War Jersey was Royalist while Guernsey supported Cromwell. Threats of invasion by Napoleon account for many defence (Martello) towers built along the coasts. The islands were occupied by the Germans from 1940-45, the only British territory to fall to the enemy during the Second World War, and the islanders suffered considerable hardship during this period.

Constitution – The Channel Islands are divided into the **Bailiwick of Jersey** (which includes Jersey and two rocky islets, the Minquiers and the Ecrehous) and the **Bailiwick of Guernsey** (Guernsey, Alderney, Sark and Brecqhou, Herm and Jethou). The original Norman laws and systems enshrined in the first charters granted by King John in the 13C have been renewed by subsequent monarchs, although modifications were introduced in the 20C to separate the judiciary from the legislature. In matters of defence and international relations the islands are subject to decisions made by the Home Office in London.

Modern economy – Being self-governed, the Channel Islanders benefit from a VAT exempt economy and lower rates of income tax; coins, bank-notes and postage stamps are issued locally, but are not legal tender elsewhere. The islands have therefore become a tax haven for British citizens and developed a buoyant industry in **financial services,** including offshore banking, trust management and insurance. Additional income, although small, is generated by international collectors of coinage and the highly decorative special issues of stamps. Blessed by better weather than mainland Britain, the Channel Islands have developed tourist facilities to attract sailors to their marinas, surfers and swimmers to their beaches, bird-watchers, walkers and cyclists to their unspoilt rural countryside. Trade in imported luxury items is boosted by the minimal duty levied on such merchandise. **Farming** still plays an important part in the local economy, reducing, where possible, the needs for importing basic foodstuffs and maintaining a supply to mainland Britain of early vegetables (potatoes, tomatoes, grapes) and cut flowers, not to mention Channel Island milk, so rich in butterfat, produced by the famously pretty local cattle. A characteristic feature of the islands are the "honesty boxes" along the road advertising fresh, home-grown produce.

Jersey★★

Liberation Square, St Helier; ☎ *01534 500 777; Fax 01534 500 808; info@jersey.com; www.jersey.com.* The largest and southernmost of the group, only 12mi/19km from the coast of France and close to the Gulf Stream, is thick with flowers in spring and summer. The sandy bays which characterise the coastline occur even among the steep pink granite cliffs of the sparsely populated north coast. Visitors are greeted by a charming combination of Englishness tinged with Norman-French tradition. Local features echo not only Normandy but also Cornwall.

St Helier

The capital is named after the 6C hermit saint who brought Christianity to the island *(access on foot via causeway at low tide)* stands **Elizabeth Castle,** (Open late-Mar to late-Oct, daily, 9.30am to 6pm (5pm last admission). £5.25; Discount Ticket (also valid for 2 other Jersey Heritage sites: Jersey Museum, Jersey Maritime, La Hougue Bie, Hamptonne, Mont Orgueil) £12.50. Guided tour (1hr 30min). Restaurant. ☎ 01534 23971; Fax 01534 633 301; marketing@ jerseyheritagetrust.org; www.jerseyheritagetrust.org.) begun in the mid 16C on the site of a 12C abbey. In the Civil War it was adapted to resist attacks by the Parliamentarians and during the Second World War the occupying German forces made their own additions. West of the **Militia Museum** (mementos of the Royal Jersey Regiment) the Upper Ward encloses the Mount (keep) affording **views**★ across

Famous sons and daughters

The most famous name connected with Jersey is **Lillie Langtry** (1853-1929), the "Jersey Lily" who became an actress and captivated British high society with her beauty and who was also a close friend of Edward VII – she is buried in St Saviour's churchyard. The fashionable 19C painter, **Sir John Everett Millais** (1829-96), who won acclaim with his painting entitled *Bubbles,* grew up in Jersey and belonged to an old island family. So too did **Elinor Glyn** (1864-1943), who became a novelist and Hollywood scriptwriter. The well-known French firm which makes Martell brandy was founded by **Jean Martell** from St Brelade.

St Aubin's Bay. Today a breakwater leads south to the 12C hermitage chapel on the rock on which St Helier lived *(procession on or about 16 July, St Helier's Day)*. The centre of the town is the charming **Royal Square** with a 1751 statue of George II dressed as a Roman emperor. The pink granite **parish church,** predating the Norman Conquest, was restored in the 19C. Other features are: the **Jersey Museum**★ *(& ◷ Open all year, daily, 10am-5pm (4pm winter). ◷ Closed 25 Dec. ⊕ £5.25; Discount Ticket (also valid at 2 other Jersey Heritage Trust sites: Jersey Maritime, Elizabeth Castle, La Hougue Bie, Hamptonne, Mont Orgueil) £12.50. ☏ Guided tour by appointment. ☎ 01534 633 300; Fax 01534 633 301; marketing@jerseyheritagetrust.org; www.jerseyheritagetrust.org)* containing displays of maritime exhibits and on the story of Jersey;

Fort Regent *(& Fort Regent Road. ◷ Open daily; telephone for times and charges. Parking. Refreshments. ☎ 01534 500 200; Fax 01534 500 225; c.stanier@gov.je; www.esc.gov. je/sport/news/facilities/fortregent.aspx)* built 1806-14 to protect Jersey from invasion by Napoleon, and now used as a leisure centre; and the **Maritime Museum and Jersey Occupation Tapestry** *(& ◷ Open daily, 10am-5pm (4pm Nov-Mar). ◷ Closed 1 Jan and 25 Dec. ⊕ £5.25; Discount Ticket (also valid at 2 other Jersey Heritage Trust sites: Jersey Museum, Elizabeth Castle, La Hougue Bie, Hamptonne, Mont Orgueil) £12.50 ☎01534 811 043; Fax 01534 633 301; marketing@jerseyheritagetrust.org; www.jerseyheritagetrust.org)*, installed in converted 19C warehouses, celebrating the importance to Jersey of the sea and displaying a twelve-panel tapestry (6ft x 3ft/2m x 1m) illustrating the Occupation of Jersey from the outbreak of war to the Liberation, each scene based on archive photographs and film footage and embroidered by a different Jersey parish.

Jersey Zoo★★ – *& ◷ Open daily, 9.30am to 6pm/dusk (4pm last admission) 10am – 5 pm winter ◷ Closed 25 Dec. ⊕ £11.50. ☏ Guided tour (1hr) by appointment. Parking. Refreshments. ☎ 01534 860 000; Fax 01534 860 001; jersey.zoo@ durrell.org; www.jerseyzoo.co.uk.* This famous zoo – full title the Jersey Wildlife Preservation Trust – was founded in 1963 by the naturalist **Gerald Durrell** to preserve and breed rare and endangered species. It is now home to some of the most exotic creatures in the world, which live in an environment as similar as possible to their natural habitat. The high rate of success in the zoo's prime objective has led to exchanges with other zoos (Bristol, Newquay, Paignton) and the reintroduction of a number of threatened species into native habitats. The symbol adopted by the Trust is the Dodo, the great, flightless bird of Mauritius first

Ringed-tailed Lemur, Jersey Zoo

J. Morgan/DWCT Photo Library

identified in 1599 and extinct by 1693. The history and work of the Trust is presented in the Princess Royal Pavilion.

Eric Young Orchid Foundation★ – *Victoria Village, Trinity. & ◷ Open Wed-Sat, 10am-4pm ◷ Closed 1 Jan and 25-26 Dec. ⊕ £3. ☎ 01534 861 963; Fax 01534 863 293; www.ericyoungorchidfoundation.co.uk.* A fabulous show of prize plants appealing to both amateur and professional growers of orchids is presented in a display house. The Foundation's mission is to "promote orchid improvement for all", and it collaborates on a conservation and research basis with the Royal Horticultural Society and the Royal Botanic Gardens at Kew.

La Hougue Bie★

& ◷ Open late Mar-Oct, daily, 10am-5pm. ⊕ £5.25; Discount Ticket (also valid for 2 other Jersey Heritage Trust sites: Jersey Museum, Jersey Maritime, Elizabeth Castle, Hamptonne, Mont Orgueil) £12.50. Parking. ☎ 01534 853 823; Fax 01534 633 301; marketing@ jerseyheritagetrust.org; www.jerseyheritagetrust.org.

La Hougue Bie, northeast of St Helier, is notable for the cruciform **Neolithic tomb**★ dating from 3000 BC, a 33ft/10m passage roofed with granite slabs leading to a 10ft x 30ft/3m x 9m funeral chamber and three side chambers. On top of the mound stand the 12C **Chapel of Our Lady of the Dawn** and the 1520 **Jerusalem Chapel** containing early 16C frescoes of archangels.

Hamptonne Country Life Museum★ – ♿⏰ *Open late Mar-Oct, daily, 10am-5pm.* ☜ *£5.25; Discount Ticket (also valid for 2 other Jersey Heritage Trust sites: Jersey Museum, Jersey Maritime, Elizabeth Castle, La Hougue Bie, Mont Orgueil) £12.50.* ☎ *01534 863 955; Fax 01534 633 301; marketing@jerseyheritagetrust.org; www.jerseyheritagetrust.org.* Hamptonne House, thought to have been completed in 1637, partly thatched and partly slate-roofed and very atmospheric, provides an insight into family life style during the 17C and early 18C with museum staff dressed in period costume.

German Underground Hospital★ – ♿ *Meadowbank, Les Charrieres Malorey.* ⏰ *Open early-Mar to early-Nov, daily, 9.30am-5pm; Nov-Dec, Sun and Thu, 2-5pm; last admission 4.15pm.* ⏰ *Closed early Nov-early Mar.* ☜ *£6.50. Parking. Cafe.* ☎ *01534 863 442, Fax 01534 865 970; www.jersey.co.uk/attractions/ughospital.* This large complex of tunnels is kept as a memorial to the forced labourers who worked on its construction for three and a half years under the harshest conditions. Wartime films, archive photographs, newspaper cuttings, letters and memorabilia document the personal suffering and trauma of those caught up in the events.

Gorey – This charming old port at the north of the Royal Bay of Grouville is dominated by **Mont Orgueil Castle**★ *(⏰ Open daily, 9.30am-6pm (dusk in winter), last admission 1hr before closing.* ☜ *£5.25; Discount Ticket (also valid for 2 other Jersey Heritage Trust sites: Jersey Museum, Jersey Maritime, Elizabeth Castle, La Hougue Bie, Hamptonne) £12.50.* ☎ *01534 853 292; Fax 01534 633 301; marketing@jerseyheritagetrust.org; www.jerseyheritagetrust.org)* which dates back to the 13C. Set on a rocky promontory, its position and defensive strength account for the name (Mount Pride). A spiral network of steps and passages between separate defence systems leads up to excellent **views**★★ at the top. Other sights include the **Jersey Pottery**★, *(♿⏰ Gorey Village Open daily, 9am (10am Sun) to 5.30pm.* ⏰ *Closed 25 Dec - 1 Jan. Parking. Licensed restaurant.* ☎ *01534 850 850; Fax 01534 856 403; jsypot@itl.net; www.jerseypottery. com)* set in a magnificent garden, and the 49ft/15m **Faldouet Dolmen,** dating from 2500 BC, with a 20ft/6m wide funeral chamber.

St Matthew's Church, Millbrook – ♿ ⏰ *Open Mon-Fri, 9am-6pm (4.30pm Oct-Mar), Sat-Sun, for services only. Guide book (2 languages). Parking. Fax* ☎ *01534 502 864.* The church, built in 1840, is remarkable for **René Lalique's** rich **glasswork**★ interior executed in 1934 as a memorial to Lord Trent.

Fishermen's Chapel, St Brelade – The chapel is decorated with delicate medieval **frescoes**★.

Samarès Manor – ♿ *St. Clement Garden:* ⏰*Open Apr-Oct, daily, 10am-5pm. Falconry: Sun-Fri. Carriage and Agricultural Museum. House:* ☚ *Guided tour (40min) Apr-Oct, Mon-Sat at 11.45am, 12.30pm, and 1.30pm.* ☜ *£5.35. Garden talks: Mon-Fri, at 2.30pm. Parking. Refreshments.* ☎ *01534 870 551; Fax 01534 68949; www.information-britain. co.uk/showPlace.cfm?Place_ID=2253.* Although much altered through generations of use, the house is a typical Jersey manor, with a rare 11C dovecote in the grounds.

Guernsey★

🛈 *PO Box 23, North Esplanade, White Rock, St Peter Port GY1 3AN* ☎ *01481 723 552 (general), 01481 723 552 (accommodation); fax 01481 714 951; enquiries@guernseytouristboard.com; www.visitguernsey.com.* The second largest of the islands has many greenhouses except along the wild, dramatic **southern cliffs** and the sandy beaches and rocky promontories of the west and north coasts, excellent for bathing, surfing and exploring rock pools.

St Peter Port★★

The island capital, attractively situated on a hillside on the east coast, overlooks a sheltered harbour. The medieval town was rebuilt after the Civil War in which Guernsey had supported Cromwell. A late 18C building boom produced a delightful Regency town built in local granite. **Castle Cornet**★, *(⏰ Open Apr-Oct, daily, 10am-5pm. Noonday gun fired daily.* ☜ *£5; joint ticket with Guernsey Museum and Fort Grey £7.* ☚ *Guided tour (1hr) morning and afternoon. Parking nearby. Shop. Refreshments.* ☎ *01481 721 657 (Castle); 01481 726 518; Fax 01481 715 177)* dating back to c 1206 and reinforced under Elizabeth I, remained loyal to the king in the Civil War, being the last of the royal strongholds to surrender, after eight years of siege. In 1672 the gunpowder store was struck by lightning and the resulting explosion decapitated the castle, destroying the tower and medieval banqueting hall. The castle had to be rebuilt. It now houses the Royal Guernsey Militia Museum and the Guernsey Maritime History Museum. The Ceremony of the Noonday Gun is performed by two Guernsey Militia men on the saluting platform of the castle's outer bailey; one trains a telescope on the town clock and the other fires the cannon.

Address Book

WHERE TO EAT - JERSEY

🍽🍽🍽 **Borsalino Rocque,** *La Rocque.* ☎ *01534 852 111; Fax 01534 856 404.* This long-established family business, 8 miles/12km from St Helier, is popular with locals and visitors. It specialises in seafood and offers a wide choice of menus.

🍽🍽🍽**Old Court House Inn,** *St Aubin's Harbour.* ☎ *01534 746 433; Fax 01534 745 103.* This atmospheric 15C inn, formerly a court house and a merchant's house offers a cosmopolitan menu with a seafood emphasis.

WHERE TO STAY - JERSEY

🍽🍽🍽🍽 **Au Caprice,** *Route de la Haule, St Brelade.* ☎ *01534 722 083; Fax 01534 280 058; aucaprice@jerseymail.co.uk.* Light and airy white guesthouse close to a large sandy beach; good value, homely rooms.

WHERE TO EAT - GUERNSEY

🍽🍽🍽 **Fleur du Jardin,** *Kings Mills, Castel.* ☎ *01481 257 996; Fax 01481 256 834; info@fleurdujardin.guernsey.net; www. fleurdujardin.guernsey.net.* Set in the heart of the island, the beamed restaurant of this 15C hotel inn has a lovely old granite fireplace, local water colours and offers daily menus of local seafood, while the traditional pub lounge bar is renowned for its excellent value bar meals.

WHERE TO STAY - GUERNSEY

🍽🍽🍽🍽 **La Michele,** *Les Hubits, St Martin.* ☎ *01481 238 065; Fax 01481 239 492; info@lamichelehotel.com; www. lamichelehotel.com.* This 16-room hotel enjoys a quiet country location, a short walk from picturesque Fermain Bay. You can relax in the conservatory lounge or the lovely secluded garden with pool. (Tariff includes evening meal).

St Peter Port **Town Church**★ dates back as far as 1048, when it also served as a fort, and was completed around 1475. It now contains several memorials to famous Guernseymen. The French poet **Victor Hugo** lived on Guernsey in political exile at **Hauteville House**★ (🕐⚓ *Guided tour, 15 persons max, Apr-Sep, Mon (excl bank holidays)-Sat, 10am-11.45am and 2-4.45pm.* ⚓ *£4* ☎ *01481 721 911; Fax 01481 715 913; hugohouse@gtonline.net; www. mairie-paris.fr)* which he decorated in a highly eccentric way. The **Guernsey Museum** (♿🕐 *Open daily, 10am-5pm (4pm winter).* 🕐 *Closed 25 Dec to 1 Jan. Call for ticket prices. Refreshments.* ☎ *01481 726 518, Fax 01481 715 177; admin@museum.guernsey.net; www. museum.guernsey.net)* contains art and archeological collections.

The island boasts a fine house, **Sausmarez Manor** (♿🕐 *Sausmarez Road. Garden: Open daily, 10am-5pm. Subtropical Gardens: Open Feb-Dec, daily, 10.30am-5pm. Art gallery: Open Easter-Oct, daily, 10am-5pm. Art park sculpture garden: Open Mar-Jan, daily, 10.30am-5.30pm. House:*⚓ *Guided tour Jun-Sep, Mon-Thu at 10.30am, 11.30am, 2pm; Mar-May and Oct, Mon-Thu at 10.30am and 11.30am. Dolls' House Collection: Open Easter-Oct, daily, 10am-5pm.* ⚓ *Garden and Art Gallery no charge; Subtropical garden £2.50; Art park £2.50; House £4.90; Dolls' House £2; Pitch and putt; putting green. Parking. Tearoom.* ☎ *01481 35571 (Estate Office), Fax 01481 35572; peter@artparks.co.uk; www. artparks.co.uk)* an elegant, Queen Anne house (1714-18), not to be confused with **Saumarez Park**★ the venue for the annual Battle of Flowers (a parade held on the fourth Thursday in August, originally started in 1902 to celebrate the coronation of Edward VII, after which the floats are traditionally broken up and the crowd pelt each other with flowers). The **Guernsey Folk Museum**★ (🕐 *Open late Mar-late Oct, daily, 10am-5.30pm.* ⚓ *£3 Parking.* ☎ *01481 255 384; folkmuseumntgsy@getonline.co.uk; www.nationaltrust-gsy.org.gg)* is housed in the outbuildings of the manor.

St Sampson

Guernsey's second port. The oldest church on the island was built where the Welsh monk St Sampson came ashore in the 6C; the oldest part of the present church is the early Norman saddle-back tower. The ruined medieval **Château des Marais** crowns a low knoll, first used in the Bronze Age. Excavations in 1975-77 revealed 13C coins in a chapel dedicated to Our Lady of the Marshes.

Prehistoric remains

The most notable are the burial chambers **Déhus Dolmen** *(north)*, **le Trépied Dolmen** *(west)* and **La Gran'mère du Chimquièrea**, a Stone Age figure at the gate to St Martin's churchyard. A similar female figure stands outside the 12C church of **Ste Marie du Câtel** which also contains 13C frescoes of the Last Supper and the Three Living and the Three Dead.

Alderney, Herm and **Sark**★★, the other islands making up the Bailiwick of Guernsey, are well worth a visit. Sark has stayed remarkably remote from modern society, even to the extent of being totally free of cars.

CHATSWORTH★★★

Derbyshire, ENGLAND

MICHELIN ATLAS P 35 OR MAP 502 P 24

The original Chatsworth was begun in 1551 by Sir William Cavendish and Bess of Hardwick, that indomitable Elizabethan who was married four times and multiplied her wealth with each marriage. She first exercised her passion for building at Chatsworth, where she created a Renaissance palace, but, on deciding that her third husband, the Earl of Shrewsbury, was a "knave, fool and beast" and that he had had an affair with his prisoner, Mary Queen of Scots, Bess returned to her Hardwick property fifteen miles away and built another. Chatsworth was transformed between 1686 and 1707 by the first Duke of Devonshire into a Baroque palace, which was greatly extended between 1820 and 1827 by the 6th Duke. In 1854 Charles de Saint-Amant described it as "le second Versailles".

♿ *House only* 🕐 *Open Mar to mid-Dec, daily, 11am-5.30pm (6pm/dusk garden). House and garden* 👓 *House and garden £9.50; garden £5.75.* 👥 *Guided tour by appointment only, £17 per head (minimum 8 people).Brochure (6 languages). Parking. Refreshments.* ☎ *01246 582 204; Fax 01246 583 536; www.chatsworth.org*

House

The Painted Hall is unashamedly Baroque, as only Laguerre can do it; the ceilings and walls are a soaring profusion of colours depicting the triumphs of Caesar.

Beneath the Great Stairs (and acting as a support) is the grotto, with superb stone carvings by Samuel Watson. The bronze Mercury is after Giambologna, the three sculptured figures by Caius Gabriel Cibber (1630-1700) and the ceiling by Verrio.

After her involuntary stay, the Mary Queen of Scots Rooms were rebuilt and clad in Regency Chinoiserie by Sir Jeffry Wyatville; the two coronation chairs in the lobby were used by William IV and Queen Adelaide in 1830. The long landscape by Gaspard Poussin in the Green Satin Dressing Room is "not only among the most beautiful works of the master but among the finest landscapes in the world" (Gustave Waagen); a rare portrait of the architect, William Kent (1685-1748), hangs in the Green Satin Bedroom.

The State Rooms, the grandest in the house, are characterised by unrestrained ceilings by Laguerre and Verrio and Louis XIV furniture; the gilt side tables in the Dining Room are by Kent; the Drawing Room tapestries (c 1635), based on Raphael, were woven at Mortlake; the violin on the inner door of the Music Room is a trompe l'oeil by Jan van der Vaart (c 1653-1727). The China Closet contains the Casting out of the Swine by Breugel the Elder and the Wheel of Fortune (1533) by Hans Schauffen.

The wrought-iron panels on the landings of the West Stairs are by Jean Tijou. The ceiling depicting the Fall of Phaeton is an early work by Sir James Thornhill (1675-1734) and the painting of Samson and Delilah is by Tintoretto (1518-94).

Three more paintings on the stairs, including one of the house in Bess of Hardwick's time, show the changes in Chatsworth up to the mid 18C. In the corridor are two Egyptian memorial tablets which are 3 800 years old.

The chapel has remained unaltered since 1694 when the ceiling was painted by Laguerre; a *Doubting Thomas* by Verrio hangs over the altar; the limewood carving and cedar panels are by Samuel Watson

State Drawing Room, Chatsworth

A. F. Kersting / MICHELIN

and the gloriously Baroque altarpiece by Cibber. *The Adoration of the Magi* by Paolo Veronese hangs in the passage outside.

The Library (90ft/28m) contains 17 000 books and stretches almost the entire length of the east range; the books are almost lost in the splendid gilded stucco ceiling by Edward Goudge (Wren's best pupil) framing Verrio's paintings.

The 6th Duke built the Sculpture Gallery to house an incomparable collection of sculptures, among the finest of which are Hebe, Endymion and Napoleon's Mother by Antonio Canova and Day and Night, low reliefs by Bertel Thorwaldsen. Hanging amid these glories is King Uzziah by Rembrandt.

Park and Garden★★★

The genius of Capability Brown made this one of the grandest of 18C parks. The garden's most majestic feature is the Cascade, designed in 1696 by Grillet, a pupil of Le Nôtre, each step a different height, to vary the sound of the falling water that disappears into pipes, to reappear out of the Sea Horse Fountain on the south lawn. The garden as we see it today, however, is mostly the creation of Joseph Paxton (1803-65), working for the 6th Duke. To the north of the Cascade is his "Conservative Wall" – a pun on "conservatory" – as well as the 1698 Greenhouse and Rose Garden, while to the south are the 1842 rockeries and the 1692 Willow Tree Fountain, later restored, which so intrigued Celia Fiennes. She wrote of it, in 1696, "by turning a sluce it raines from each leafe and from the branches like a shower, it being made of brass and pipes to each leafe, but in appearance is exactly like any willow". A maze now covers the ground plan of Paxton's Great Conservatory, which was demolished in 1920. He built it eleven years before designing the Crystal Palace for the Great Exhibition of 1851.

CHELTENHAM★

Gloucestershire , ENGLAND

POPULATION 91 301

MICHELIN ATLAS P 17 OR MAP 503 N 28

TOWN PLAN IN THE MICHELIN GUIDE GREAT BRITAIN AND IRELAND

The benefits of the waters of this most elegant of English spas were discovered early in the 18C but it was at its most fashionable in the Regency period, when it became a pleasure town of Classical architecture, its squares, terraces and crescents in a delightful setting of trees and gardens which are still its pride. Long favoured for residence, retirement and recreation, it has an animated cultural life, with internationally important musical and literary festivals. It is an excellent centre for exploring the varied landscapes around the Severn Vale, the Wye Valley and the Forest of Dean, the Malvern Hills and the Cotswolds themselves, whose escarpment rears up northwest of the town. The composer **Gustav Holst** was born here in 1874. ◪ *77 Promenade GL50 1PJ ☎ 01242 522 878; Fax 01242 255 848; tic@cheltenham.gov.uk; www.visitcheltenham.gov.uk.*

Sights

Town Centre★ – Of pre-spa Cheltenham there remains the secluded Church of St Mary and the line of the much rebuilt High Street. At right angles to this old thoroughfare is the **Promenade**; its lower part, the most spacious of shopping streets, is lined on one side by the **Municipal Offices**, an imposing terrace of 1823; its upper part, twice as broad, rises gently to the stately stuccoed façade of the **Queen's Hotel** of 1838. To the east are the **Imperial Gardens**, a multicoloured floral cocktail in summer; to the west, behind a double avenue of parkland trees, are some of the refined **Regency houses** with classical details and exquisite balcony ironwork which characterise the town. Farther south is **Montpellier Walk**, whose mid-19C shop-fronts are divided up by Grecian caryatids; it terminates in the colonnade and dome of **Montpellier Spa** (now Lloyds Bank).

Museum and Art Gallery – ⚐ ⊕ *Open Mon - Sat, 10am (11am first Thu in month) to 5.20pm (4.20pm Sun).* ⊕ *Closed bank holidays, Easter and 25 Dec. No charge, donations welcome.* ⬛ *Guided tour (1hr) by prior arrangement. Public parking nearby. Cafeteria. Wheelchair access to all galleries; ramps; lift.* ☎ *01242 237 431; Fax 01242 262 334; artgallery@cheltenham.gov.uk; www.cheltenhammuseum.org.uk..* Among the paintings, porcelain and pottery and many exhibits of local interest is a good **collection of applied art** illustrating the im-portance of the Cotswolds in the Arts and Crafts Movement.

Pittville – This distinguished district of Classical terraces and villas was laid out early in the 19C by Joseph Pitt. It focuses on the romantic landscape of **Pittville Park**, where great trees and sweeping lawns surround the picturesque lake.

Pittville Pump Room★ – ⊕ *Open daily except Tues; May-Sept, 10am-4.30pm; Oct-Apr, 11am-4pm. Closed 25-26 Dec.* ⬛ *Ground floor no charge; museum £1.50, 50p (child).* ⬛ *Guided tour (45min) by appointment: £15 per group of 15 people + 50p per head admission charge. Parking.* ☎ *01242 523 852.* This outstanding Grecian building (1825-30), with its Ionic colonnade and domed interior, was designed by Joseph Pitt and now houses a small gallery of fashion where costumed figures are displayed in historic settings.

Holst Birthplace Museum – *4, Clarence Road.* ⊕*Open Tue-Sat, 10am-4pm.* ⊕ *Closed some Bank Hols and mid Dec – mid- Jan.* ⬛ *£2.50, 50p (child). Public parking nearby.* ☎ *01242 524 846; Fax 01242 580 182; holstmuseum@btconnect.com; www.holstmuseum. org.uk.* Near the park entrance is the Regency house where the composer of *The Planets* was born in 1874.

Excursions

Deerhurst

7mi/12km north of Cheltenham by A 4019, A 38 and a minor road west. The village of Deerhurst (population 100) possesses two important **Anglo-Saxon** buildings. Once part of a flourishing monastery, **St Mary's Church**★ *(⚐⊕ Open daily, 8.30am-dusk. Guide books and brochures. Some small steps.* ☎ *01684 292 562; Fax 01684 273 057)* of which parts may date from as early as the 8C, is strongly Saxon in character – the roughly-built walls contain masonry laid in a herringbone pattern; a curious triangular-headed window opens into the tall nave from the tower; carvings include a Madonna and Child, the heads of beasts and, high up outside, an angel. The fine **font** is Saxon, too. Much later is the 15C **brass**, commemorating not only Sir John Cassey and his wife, but also her pet dog Terri.

Odda's Chapel *(⊕ Open daily, Apr-Sept, 10am-6pm (4pm Oct-Mar).* ⊕ *Closed 1 Jan, 25-26 Dec. Parking.* ☎ *www.english-heritage.org.uk)* which stands on a low knoll rising from the flood plain of the nearby Severn, was dedicated by Earl Odda in 1056 and consists of a nave and chancel, both of touching simplicity. It was re-discovered in the 19C, having once served as the kitchen of the adjoining farmhouse.

Tewkesbury★

8mi/13km north of Cheltenham by A 4019 and A 38. The little town, founded in Saxon times, is dominated by the imposing presence and tower of the great Norman abbey church. As it is hemmed in by the floodlands around the confluence of the navigable rivers Severn and Avon and was bypassed by the railway, Tewkesbury grew little in the 19C and has conserved its historic character almost intact. In 1471 it was the scene of bloody slaughter, both during and after the **Battle of Tewkesbury,** which marked the decisive defeat of the Lancastrian cause in the Wars of the Roses.

Tewkesbury Abbey★★ – ⚐*Church Street.* ⊕*Open daily, 7.30am-6pm. (Sunday 7pm). Evensong: Term time, Mon-Thur, 5pm.* ⬛ *£2 donation requested. Leaflets (6 languages).* ⬛ *Guided tour (£2). Refectory.* ☎ *01684 850 959; Fax 01684 273 113; office@tewkesbu-ryabbey.org.uk; www.tewkesburyabbey.org.uk.* The church, once part of a wealthy and important Benedictine abbey, combines a noble simplicity of structure with great richness of detail. As many of the abbey's noble benefactors are buried here, it has been called "the Westminster Abbey of the feudal baronage". At the Dissolution it was saved from demolition by the townsfolk, who bought it for £453.

The most impressive element is the huge 12C **tower** which impresses most, its solidity relieved by the elaborate patterning of its upper stages. The complex east end of the church with its cluster of chapels contrasts with the grandeur of the **west front**, with its recessed arch (65ft/20m high).

The Norman **nave**★★, composed of eight bays divided by massive cylindrical columns, is covered by a beautiful 14C vault which replaced an earlier timber roof. The church's many monuments are grouped around the choir. Hugh and Elizabeth Despenser lie solemnly side by side, an intricate canopy of delicately carved lime-stone – an early example of fan vaulting – suspended above them. The extraordinary figure of Edward Despenser kneels in prayer on the roof of his chantry chapel. Bishop Wakeman is grotesquely commemorated by a **memento mori,** a decomposing cadaver crawling with vermin.

The 14C **stained-glass windows** of the choir depict local notables as well as Biblical scenes. The choir **vault**★ is a gloriously intricate web of ribs and bosses; a ring of suns, the Yorkist emblem, was added to mark the victory of 1471.

There are two survivals from monastic days – the **Abbey House** and the handsome **Gatehouse**, which is just outside the precinct.

Sudeley Castle★

7mi/11km northeast of Cheltenham by B 4632. The road climbs over the shoulder of Cleeve Hill, one of the highest points in the Cotswolds, before descending to the winding High Street of **Winchcombe**, once an important Saxon town; **St Peter's Church** (& ◐ *Open daily, 8.30am-5pm. Services: Sun, at 8am, 10am, 6.30pm. Brochure; guidebook (5 languages). Loop system.* ☎ *01242 602 067; Fax 01242 602 067)* is a fine example of the Perpendicular style with grotesque exterior carvings.

Sudeley Castle – & Gardens only. *Castle Street.* ◐ *Late Feb-Oct, daily, 10.30am-5.30pm.* ◠ *Castle and gardens: £7.20; Hols and Sun between May and Aug. Parking. Refreshments.* ☎ *01242 604 357 (recorded information); marketing@sudeley.org.uk; www.sudeleycastle.co.uk.* The house is surrounded by the dramatic scenery of the Cotswold escarpment. Once a medieval stronghold, it later was the home of **Katherine Parr,** widow of Henry VIII; it was besieged and largely destroyed in the Civil War. In the 19C the house was restored, although some parts were left in a ruined state.

The interior's fascinatingly varied collection of furniture and relics includes a small number of outstanding **paintings**★ by Constable, Turner, Van Dyck and Rubens, as well as the late 16C Sheldon Tapestry. The nostalgic Victorian landscape scene embraces the pretty Church of St Mary where Katherine Parr is buried, the Romantic ruins of the Tithe Barn and Banqueting Hall, to form a harmonious whole with the formal gardens and great parkland trees. The formal Queen's Garden is flanked by the famous double yew hedges.

CHESTER★★

Cheshire, ENGLAND

POPULATION 80 110

MICHELIN ATLAS P 34 OR MAP 403 L 24

Set on the northeast border of Wales in the green and prosperous countryside of Chesire, Chester has been an important city since Roman times and retains many tangible reminders of this period. The town's lasting impression on most visitors however its its classic black-and-white half-timber buildings which feature prominently in this well preserved highly tended historic walled city. 🛈 *Town Hall, Northgate Street CH1 2HJ* 🛈 *01244 402 111; tic@chester.gov.uk; www.visitchester.com; www.chester.gov.uk* 🛈 *Vicar's Lane, CH1 1QX* ☎ *01244 402 111.*

▸ **Orient Yourself**: Almost everything of interest is inside the old city walls.

⌂ **Don't Miss**: The Rows; horse racing at Chester's historic racecourse ☎ *01244 304 600; www.chester-races.co.uk.*

◐ **Organizing Your Time**: Allow half a day, more if you visit the zoo.

Kids **Especially for Kids**: Chester Zoo.

A Bit of History

Deva (or Dewa), the Roman legionary fortress and naval base built on a sandstone ridge on a loop of the River Dee, was one of the largest (60 acres/c 24ha) in Britain and home to the XX Valeria Victrix Legion for 200 years. 1 900 years ago a Roman surveyor laid out the line of the Via Praetoria, now Bridge Street, and of the Via Principalis, now East Gate Street and Watergate Street, which took over where the

The Rows, Chester

Watling Street entered the fort. The legionary headquarters stood at the junction on the site now occupied by St Peter's Church.

Chester was re-fortified at the start of the 10C by the daughter of Alfred the Great, Aethelflaeda, who extended the Roman walls down to the river, thus creating the present circuit (2mi/3km).

In 1070 William the Conqueror made Hugh Lupus, his alleged nephew, Earl of Chester. The Earldom reverted to the Crown in 1237 and since 1301, when Henry III conferred it upon his son, later Edward I, it has remained one of the titles of the eldest son of the monarch.

Chester port is known to have been used by sea-going vessels during the Roman occupation. The period of the city's greatest prosperity was from the 12C to the 14C; even until the end of the 16C, Chester regarded Liverpool as a "creek of the Port of Chester". By the 15C the Dee estuary was silting up and ships were forced to anchor some 12mi downstream.

The **Roodee**, a name meaning "Island of the Cross" derived from Anglo-Saxon, is a tract of land between the river and the city wall now occupied by Chester racecourse. Horse racing has been held here since 1540, when increasing spectator violence and hooliganism caused the City Fathers to ban the traditional games of football.

The Rows★★ – These shopping arcades, unique in Britain, first appear in the city records for 1331. As they extend no further than the limits of the original Roman fort, they probably originated in the 14C when merchants erected shops at street level against the lower courses of the Roman buildings that had lined the streets or on top of the stone rubble and made steps and walkways to link them; upper storeys were built to provide accommodation for the traders and their families. Shopping in The Rows is pleasantly free from the disadvantages of traffic and inclement weather. A Roman hypocaust system was found beneath one of the shops and excavations beneath the crooked front of a neighbouring house dating from 1664, now a book-shop, revealed a 13C crypt.

Chester Cathedral★ – 🚹🕐 *Open daily, 8am-5pm* 🏷 *£4.* 👣 *Guided tour (1hr) by appointment. Leaflet (8 languages). Refectory. Gift shop. Visitor centre. Assistance for disabled visitors; ramps; induction loop.* ☎ *01244 324 756; Fax 01244 341 110; office@ chestercathedral.com; www.chestercathedral.com.* The 14C gateway leads into Abbey Square, once the outer courtyard of the abbey; ahead are the cloisters on the north side of the cathedral.

The Norman abbey church was replaced between 1250 and 1540 by the present magnificent red sandstone building, which has been carefully restored since 1868. Many of the original abbey buildings still stand round the 16C **cloisters**. The ham-mer-beam roof of the refectory has been magnificently recreated. The Dean and

CHESTER			Handbridge	B	13	Pierpoint Lane	B	31
			Little St John St	B	19	St John St	B	32
Boughton	B	2	Liverpool Rd	B	21	St Martins Way	B	33
Bridge St	B	3	Lower Bridge St	B	23	Vicar's Lane	B	40
Eastgate St	B	7	Nicholas St	B	25	Watergate St	B	
Forum Shopping centre	B		Northgate St	B	26			
Frodsham St	B	9	Parkgate Rd	B	28			
Grosvenor Park Rd	B	10	Pepper St	B	30	Grosvenor Museum	B	M¹
Grosvenor St	B	12				Town Hall	B	H

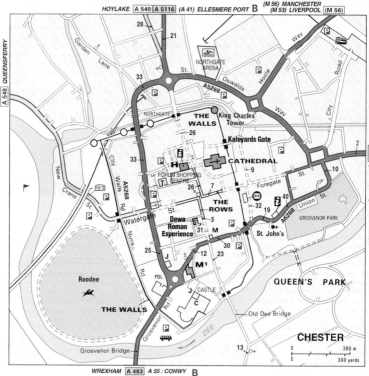

Chapter still meet in the 13C **Chapter House** and the clergy and choir assemble in the vestibule before services.

The north transept contains the oldest part of the cathedral fabric, an 11C round-headed arch and arcade, and the oldest wooden ceiling, the **camber beam** roof (1518-24), which carries a splendid display of Tudor heraldry; on the floor stands the monument to John Pearson, Bishop of Chester (1673-86) and author of the Exposition of the Creed. In the northwest corner of the nave are the Norman arches intended to support a tower above what is now the baptistery.

The stalls and misericords in the choir date from 1390 and are comparable with those at Lincoln and Beverley; the richly carved Victorian tabernacle work over the stalls blends perfectly with the rest of the carvings. The **Lady Chapel** was carefully restored to its 1250 appearance. At the back of the chapel behind the High Altar is the 14C **shrine of St Werburgh**, daughter of the King of Mercia; she died about AD 700.

City Walls★ – No other city in Britain has preserved a continuous circuit of walls. From the Eastgate by the Clock Tower looking west to the spire of Holy Trinity Church (now the Guildhall) one can see the width of the Roman fortress. Parts of the Roman wall are visible between the northgate and **King Charles' Tower** – so called because it is said that it was from this tower that King Charles I watched the defeat of his troops in September 1645.

Grosvenor Museum – 27 Grosvenor Street. ◷*Open daily, 10.30am (1pm - 4pm Sun) to 5pm.* ◷ *Closed 1 Jan, Good Friday, 24-26 Dec.* ☎ *01244 402 008; Fax 01244 347 587; s.rogers@chestercc.gov.uk; www.chestercc.gov.uk.* The history of Chester is traced with particular emphasis on the Roman period; among the displays is an interesting collection of coins, minted in Chester in Saxon and Norman times and during the Civil War.

Dewa Roman Experience – *Pierpoint Lane.* ⏰*Opendaily, 9am-5pm (10 Sun)£4.25.* ☎ *01244 343 407; Fax 01244 347 737; info@dewaromanexperience.co.uk; www.dewa-romanexperience.co.uk.*

Town Hall – ♿ ⏰ *Open (functions permitting) closing in Jan 2007 for refurbishment Mon-Sat, 9am-5.30pm, Sun, 10am-4pm.* ☎ *01244 402111; www.chestercc.gov.uk.* This fine Gothic-style building (1869), in red and grey sandstone, with its tower (160ft/49m) replaced an earlier Town Hall which had been destroyed by fire; the Assembly Rooms are open to view (functions permitting).

St John's Church – *Parkgate Road.* ⏰*Open daily, 9.30am-5.30pm (4pm in winter - except during services). Brochure (6 languages).* ☎*01244 683 585; Fax 01244 674 246; ajohn1@aol.com; www.saintoswaldandsaintthomaschester.org.uk.* Begun in 1075, the unfinished building was left unroofed for a hundred years. Norman drum columns lean deliberately outwards, an unnerving technique seen, apart from here, only at Orvieto and at Rheims. Above the arches, three arcades show clearly the change from Norman to Transitional to Early English work in the clerestory.

Excursion

Chester Zoo★ – *3mi/5km north by A 5116.* ♿⏰ *Open daily (except 25 Dec) from 10am (closing times vary according to season - telephone for details); last admission 90min before closing time* 🍴 *Summer £ 14.50, winter £10.50. Parking. Licensed restaurant, cafés. Wheelchairs and electric scooters available for hire.* ☎ *01244 380 280; Fax 01244 371 273; marketing@chesterzoo.co.uk; www.chesterzoo.org.* A splendid zoo where the animals are housed and displayed in spacious enclosures, separated from the public by moats and flower borders rather than cages. The overhead railway provides a good view and relaxed tour.

CHICHESTER★★

West Sussex, ENGLAND

POPULATION 26 050

MICHELIN ATLAS P 10 OR MAP 503 R 31

TOWN PLAN IN THE MICHELIN GUIDE GREAT BRITAIN AND IRELAND

On the flatlands between the South Downs and the sea, Chichester and its classic cathedral spire present one of the most English of English views.

🅿 **Parking**: Park by the river to enjoy the classic view of the cathedral across the meadows.

👁 **Don't Miss**: Chichester Cathedral, especially its Norman stone panels; a boat trip.

⏰ **Organizing Your Time**: Allow a couple of hours for the city centre but a couple of days to visit the surrounding area.

Kids **Especially for Kids**: The beach at West Wittering.

👓 **Also See**: The pretty villages of Bosham, Fishbourne, Birdham, Itchenor, East and West Wittering along the many channels of Chichester harbour.

⚓ **Sailing**: Bosham Sailing Club ☎ *01243 57234; www.boshamsailingclub.co.uk.*

🎣 **Fishing:** Deep sea fishing with Something Fishy (East Wittering) ☎ *01243 671 153.*

A Bit of History

Many English towns grew up around their cathedral, but Chichester was already a thousand years old before the cathedral was thought about; its North, South, East and West Streets running off the 1501 ornamental **Market Cross** still conform to their Roman plan.

Chichester enjoyed a golden age in the 18C and its domestic architecture is almost wholly of this period; the resulting harmonious Georgian townscape is best seen in **The Pallants**. The 20C is represented, beyond the walls, by Powell and Moya's hexagonal Chichester Festival Theatre of 1962. 🖺 *29a South Street PO19 1AH* ☎ *01243 775 888; Fax 01243 539 449; chitic@chichester.gov.uk; www. chichester.gov.uk*

Sights

Cathedral★★

West Street. Open daily, 7.15am-7pm (6pm Nov-Mar). Donation £2. Guided tour Mon – Sat 11:15am and 2:30pm (45 min) . Brochure (7 languages). Refectory. Loop system; touch and hearing centre. ☎ 01243 782 595; Fax 01243 536 190; vo@chicath.free-serve.co.uk; www.chichestercathedral.org.uk. Work began in 1091 and was completed in 1184. The nave is Norman; porches, retrochoir and clerestories are Early English; tower, side chapels and Lady Chapel are Decorated; and the cloisters, the unique belltower and splendid spire (rebuilt 1861) are Perpendicular.

Interior – It is Romanesque in style and spirit, though every architectural movement of the Middle Ages has left its mark. In spite of its Norman austerity, the **nave** (best viewed looking west) appears small, almost intimate. The splendid **screen** is Perpendicular. In the **south transept,** lit by a Decorated window, are early 16C paintings of the cathedral; in the **north transept** is the grave of the composer Gustav Holst (1874-1934); east of it, a stained-glass **window** by the French painter Marc Chagall (1887-1985).

The Lady Chapel ceiling paintings are notable, too, but the cathedral's greatest treasures are the 12C **stone panels**★★ in the south choir aisle; they depict scenes from the Raising of Lazarus and are among the finest examples of Norman sculpture in England.

St Mary's Hospital★

St Martin's Square. Open by appointment only. Closed Sat-Sun and bank hols. Donation. Guided tour (30min). ☎ 01243 783 377. A medieval hospital (1290) with an aisled infirmary hall prolonged by a chapel. The hall provided accommodation for elderly people "of good character... from within five miles of Chichester". The compartmented **hall** retains its 17C brick chimneys rising up through the medieval roof. The chapel has interesting misericords.

Pallant House★

9 North Pallant. Closed at time of writing, will reopen late Mar 2006. ☎ 01243 774 557; Fax 01243 536 038; pallant@pallant.co.uk; www.pallant.org.uk. The Queen Anne town house was built in 1712 for the wine merchant, Henry Peckham, and the tastefully furnished period rooms are the setting for collections of Bow **porcelain** and **paintings** (Henry Moore, Graham Sutherland, John Piper and Paul Nash).

Excursions

Petworth House★★

14mi/22km northeast by A 27 and A 285. Park: Open daily, 8am-dusk. Grounds: Open 8am- dusk. House: Open late-Mar to early-Nov, Sat-Wed and Good Fri, 11am-5pm. Extra rooms: Open Mon-Wed (not Bank Hol Mon)., £7.50. Park and grounds only £2. Braille guide. Guided tours by appointment. Parking. Licensed restaurant. Wheelchair access to ground floor only. ☎ 01798 342 207, 01798 343 929 (infoline); Fax 01798 342 963; petworth@ntrust.org.uk; www.nationaltrust.org.uk. This grand 17C mansion (1688) is the nearest there is to a French château in England. The restrained west front is the perfect complement to the **grounds**★★, designed by Capability Brown, with their view of the South Downs.

Interior – The rooms contain exquisite carvings by Grinling Gibbons and John Selden, antique statuary and a fine collection of paintings, including many by Turner, who was a frequent guest. The most spectacular feature is the **Grand Staircase** with its painted walls and ceiling by Laguerre. The **Turner Room** contains the largest collection of his works outside the Tate Gallery. Other famous artists represented are Reynolds (Marble Hall), Van Dyck (Square Dining Room) and Kneller (Beauty Room). Lely's *Children of Charles I* hangs in the Oak Hall, Bosch's *Adoration of the Magi* in the Dining Room. **Grinling Gibbons'** carvings adorn the **Carved Room**. Recent restoration work near the chapel has revealed a spiral staircase and a mullioned window from an earlier building probably dating from 14C-15C.

Arundel Castle★★

11mi/18km east by A 27. Open Sun-Fri, Apr-Oct, noon-5pm (4pm last admission). Closed Sat and Good Friday. £8.50. Leaflets (4 languages). Guide books (3 languages). Parking. Self-service restaurant ☎ 01903 882 173; Fax 01903 884 581; info@arundelcastle.org; www.arundelcastle.org. The Castle is the home of the Duke of Norfolk, foremost Catholic layman in England. The original Norman **gatehouse and keep**

(1138) survive after 750 years of assaults and sieges, unlike the lower bailey which was largely rebuilt by the Victorian 15th Duke, 1875-1900.

The ashlared **keep** *(119 steps)* looks out over Arundel Cathedral (by Joseph Hansom, designer of the Hansom Cab), the meeting place of two revivals, the Catholic and the Gothic.

The finest Victorian rooms are the **Chapel** and **Barons' Hall** (paintings by Mytens, Kneller, Van Loo and Van Dyck); in the **Drawing Room** hang portraits by Mytens, Van Dyck, Gainsborough and Reynolds. The **Library** (122ft/70m long), which dates from c 1800 and is in the Gothic Revival style, displays a Fabergé silver icon and a portrait of Richard III.

Fitzalan Chapel – On the boundary of the castle grounds and forming the east end of the parish church stands the Decorated private **Fitzalan Chapel**, crowded with tombs and monuments to the Howards. Originally the church and the chapel were one. The church became Protestant but with the establishment of the Howards' ownership of the east end, the chapel remained Catholic; thus the two denominations worship under one roof.

Weald and Downland Open Air Museum★★

6mi/10km north by A 286. ♿🕐 *Open Mar-Oct, daily, 10.30am-6pm; Nov-Feb, Sat-Sun, 10.30am-4pm; 26 Dec to 1 Jan, daily 10.30am-4pm. Last admission 1 hr before closing.* ✆ *£7.70 Leaflet (4 languages). Parking. Refreshments ☎ 01243 811 348; Fax 01243 811 475; wealddown@mistralco.uk; www.wealddown.co.uk.* Over thirty historic buildings have been re-erected on the beautiful Downland slopes of this attractively located museum, launched in 1967 to rescue vernacular rural buildings in southeast England. They include a cottage, shop, medieval farmhouse, Tudor market hall, working watermill, toll cottage and a school. An excellent introduction to the museum is given in Hambrook Barn and there are demonstrations of activities such as milling and charcoal burning.

Goodwood House

5mi/8km northeast by A 27 and A 285. ♿🕐 *Open Apr-Oct, Sun-Mon, 1-5pm; also Aug, Sun-Thu.* 🕐 *Closed on event days.* ✆ *£7. Parking. Tearoom.* ☎ *01243 755 000, 01243 755 040 (recorded information); enquiries@goodwood.co.uk; www.goodwood.co.uk.* The original Jacobean mansion, extended in the 18C, was the home of George Lennox, Duke of Richmond, the illegitimate son of Charles II. The elegant Regency **interior** is enhanced by 18C French furniture, tapestries (Tapestry Drawing Room) and porcelain. Family portraits and splendid paintings by Canaletto (Entrance Hall), Lely, Stubbs, Reynolds, Romsey and Ramsay hang in the formal rooms. The **Egyptian Dining Room** with its opulent yellow scagliola marbling has been restored to its full glory.

Arundel Castle

B. Kaufmann/MICHELIN

Fishbourne Roman Palace★★

1mi/2km west by A 259. ♿ *92 High Street.* ⏱ *Open daily, 10am-5pm (6pm Aug, 4pm Feb, and Nov to mid-Dec); 16-31 Dec to Jan, Sat-Sun, 10am-4pm.* *Guided tour (1-2hr) Sat-Sun or during school holidays at 11am and 2.30pm.* *£5.40. Leaflet (3 languages). Parking. Cafeteria. Tape tour for blind visitors.* ☎ *01243 785 859; Fax 01243 539 266; adminfish@sussexpast.co.uk; www.sussexpast.co.uk.* This splendid Roman palace built c AD 75 was probably the home of Cogidubnus, a loyal ally of Imperial Rome. The lavish complex which included living quarters, reception rooms, guest lodgings and grand colonnades, burned down in the 3C. Tableaux tracing the history of the palace and richly patterned **mosaics**★ are on view in the north wing, which was discovered in 1960 by a workman digging a pipeline.

Bignor Roman Villa

Pulborough, 13mi/21km northeast by A 27 and A 29. ♿⏱ *Open Mar – Oct , daily closed Mon except Bank Hols., 10am-6pm (5pm May - Oct).* *£3.50.* *Guided tour (45min) £17.50. Guide book for loan (2 languages). Parking.* ☎ *01798 869 259; Fax 01798 869259; bignorromanvilla@care4free.net;www.romansinsussex.co.uk/sussex/bignor_site.asp.* It is less grand than Fishbourne, a farm rather than a palace, but it boasts very fine **mosaics**★ – the **Ganymede Mosaic,** in the piscina, a **Head of Venus** and the chillingly austere **Winter**, in the north range, and a **Medusa Head** in the bathhouse.

CHILTERN HILLS★

Buckinghamshire, ENGLAND

MICHELIN ATLAS PP 18, 19 AND 28 OR MAP 503 Q R 27 AND 28

The chalk downs known as the Chiltern Hills run from southeast to northwest (60mi/96km) between London and Oxford, rising gently to their highest point at Coombe Hill (852ft/260m). In the 1960s the hills were designated an area of outstanding natural beauty and the Chiltern Society was formed to ensure the protection of the area (650 sq mi/1 683km2). Two of Britain's ancient roads, the **Icknield Way** and the **Ridgeway,** follow the line of the hills. Iron-Age man cleared the woodland and grazed sheep on the grassy slopes; medieval man introduced cattle. The beech forests which once supplied the furniture makers of High Wycombe are much reduced but the forest known as **Burnham Beeches** (444 acres/18ha) still provides beautiful colour in early spring and autumn. ▯ *8 Bourbon Street, Aylesbury HP20 2RR ☎/Fax: 01296 330559; tic@aylesburyvaledc.gov. uk; www.visitbuckinghamshire.org;* ▯ *The Old Gaol, Market Hill, Buckingham MK18 1JX ☎ Fax: 01280 823020; buckingham.t.i.c@btconnect.com; www.visitbuckinghamshire. org.*

Sights

Buckinghamshire County Museum – *Aylesbury.* ⏱ *Open daily and Bank Hols, 10am (2pm Sun) to 5pm; telephone for confirmation during half-term.* *£3.50. Refreshments.* ☎ *01296 331 441; www.buckscc.gov.uk.*

The **Dahl Gallery** is a delight for all, especially children, who enjoy the wit and inventiveness of the novels written by Roald Dahl. The main museum traces the history of the locality.

Waddesdon Manor★★ – *5mi/8km northwest of Aylesbury A 41.* ♿ *House:* ⏱ *Open late-Mar to early-Nov, Wed-Sun and Bank Hol Mon, 11am-4pm; timed tickets required, phone for details. Grounds and Aviary: Open late-Feb to mid-Dec, Wed-Sun and Bank Hol Mon, 10am-5pm.* *House and grounds £11, grounds £4. Parking. Licensed restaurants.* ☎ *01296 653 211 (infoline); 01296 653 226 (bookings); Emma.Robinson@ nationaltrust.org.uk www.waddesdon.*

Chiltern Hundreds

When a Member of Parliament wishes to retire from office between elections, he may apply for the stewardship of the Chiltern Hundreds or of the Manor of Northstead of Yorkshire, as such a post is an office of profit under the Crown and cannot be combined with Parliamentary duties. A hundred was a division of a county or a shire, having its own court. There are three Chiltern Hundreds – Burnham, Desborough and Stoke – and the steward's duty is to provide protection for travellers against being attacked by brigands from the forests.

org.uk. The house, which was built in 1874-89 for Baron Ferdinand de Rothschild in French Renaissance style, contains the superb Rothschild **collection** of Dutch, French and English paintings, 18C French furniture, porcelain, carpets and many other works of art. Twenty rooms are furnished with French 18C royal furniture, Sèvres porcelain and Savonnerie carpets. On the walls hang portraits by Gainsborough, Reynolds and Romney. There are also pictures by Rubens (Pink Boy), Cuyp, Van der Heyden, Ter Borch and other Dutch and Flemish masters. In the rooms on the first floor are collections of buttons, lace and fans, besides pastimes and mementoes of the Rothschild family. In the Blue Sèvres Room is a Sèvres dessert service of over 100 pieces. The house is set in 150 acres of grounds laid out by the French landscape gardener, Elie Lainé.

Claydon House★ – *10mi/16km northwest of Aylesbury by A 41 to Waddesdon and a minor road north (signs).* &. ○ *Open late-Mar to early-Nov, Sat-Wed, 1-5pm (4pm on Event days; noon-6pm for grounds).* ◎ *£5. Leaflet (4 languages). Pottery. Secondhand bookshop. Parking. Restaurant (not NT). Wheelchair access to ground floor only (half price).* ☎ *01296 730 349; 01494 755 572 (events); tcdgen@smtp.ntrust.org.uk; claydon@nationaltrust.org.uk; www.nationaltrust.org.uk.* The house boasts extravagant Rococo eccentricities by Hugh Lightfoot ("such work the world never saw"): the parquetry staircase (thin veneers of ebony, ivory, box and mahogany) and the "gothic chinoiserie" woodwork of the Chinese Room. More conventional but equally beautiful are the Mytens and Van Dyck oils. There are mementoes of Florence Nightingale, who was a frequent visitor.

Stowe Gardens★★ – *3mi/5km northwest of Buckingham by a minor road (signs). Gardens* ○ *Open daily Wed-Sun and Bank Hol Mon), 10am-5.30pm; Nov-Dec, Sat-Sun, 10am-4pm. Last admission 1 hr before closing.* ○ *Closed 28 May. House: usually open during school holidays. Gardens* ◎ *£5.80; House £2. Parking. Tearoom, picnics. audio-cassette guides, Braille guide.* ☎*01280 822 850, 01494 755 568 (infoline); Fax 01280 822 437; stowegarden@ nationaltrust.org.uk; www.nationaltrust.org.uk.* The magnificent landscaped gardens, some of the finest in Europe, were created for the Temple family, over a period of 200 years starting in 1700 west of the house with a formal layout and a haha inspired by French military fortifications. In 1733 **William Kent** replaced the straight lines with curves; the developments to the east of the house are the work of **Launcelot "Capability" Brown,** who was appointed head gardener in 1741. The long straight approach up the **Grand Avenue** *(1.5mi/2.5km)* gives glimpses through the trees of the temples, columns and arches and also a full view of the north front of the house *(property of Stowe School).* A full tour of the gardens would take several hours but a shorter walk close to the house provides a visit or a view of the major features. The **Grecian Valley** near the entrance is flanked by the **Temple of Concord and Victory** and the **Queen's Temple.** The **Elysian Fields** descend beside the Alder river, renamed the River Styx, flanked on either bank by a variety of garden monuments - **Temple of British Worthies,** the **Temple of Ancient Virtue** and the **Doric Arch;** from the **Shell Bridge** there is a view *(east)* of the **Gothic Temple.** The **Octagon Lake** is spanned by the **Palladian Bridge** *(east)* and linked by a cascade *(west)* with the **Eleven Acre Lake**. A golf course now surrounds the **Rotondo**, once part of the early formal layout. Near the house are *(southwest corner)* the **old menagerie**, which now houses a shop, and the **parish church**, which is the sole survivor of the medieval village of Stowe.

COLCHESTER

Essex, ENGLAND

POPULATION 96 063

MICHELIN ATLAS P 23 OR MAP 504 W 28

Some 60 miles/100km north east of London, the original settlement of Camulodunum was the ancient British capital of King Cunobelin (Shakespeare's Cymbeline). Colchester became a Roman *colonia* under Claudius in AD 50 and soon established the reputation for **oysters** which it still has. After the Conquest the town became the site of the largest Norman keep and one of the richest priories in Europe. The oyster remained the principal source of wealth until the late Middle Ages when **wool** took over. Colchester continues to prosper today, the epitome of the economically thriving south and east of England. ▯ *1 Queen Street CO1 2PG* ☎ *01206 282 920; vic@colchester.gov.uk; www.visitcolchester.co.uk*

Sights

Roman Walls – *Balkerne Hill, Roman Road, Priory Street and Eld Lane.* Encircling the town centre the 9ft/3m thick walls are built of stone in concrete between brick bonding courses; best **viewed** from Balkerne Hill where **Balkerne Gate,** with arches and flanking towers, extends 30ft/9m in front of the wall.

Castle and Museum★ – ♿ ⏰ *Open Mon-Sat, 10am-5pm; Sun, 11am-5pm.* ⏰ *Closed 1 Jan and 25 Dec.* ⊜ *£3.90.* 🍴 *Guided tour of castle vaults, roof, and chapel, daily (extra charge). Refreshments.* ☎ *01206 282 939; Fax 01206 282 925.* Built with 12ft/4m thick walls on the vaults of the Roman Temple of Claudius, its massive dimensions (151ft/46m by 110ft/34m) make it half again the size of the White Tower at the Tower of London. Gutted and re-roofed, it is now a **museum** housing one of the largest collections in Britain of Roman antiquities gathered from one site.

St Botolph's Priory – *Priory Street.* ♿⏰ *Open any reasonable time. Parking* ☎ *01206 282 939; Fax: 01206 282 925.* Only the skeleton remains of the 12C priory, yet it gives a hint of its grandeur. Built, like the castle, of Roman brick, only the piers, west front (with the earliest circular windows in Britain) and 120ft/37m nave survive.

> ### Oyster Feast
>
> The oyster fishery rights in the Colne estuary were given to the town of Colchester by King Richard I in 1186. To open the dredging season, the Mayor and Council set out in a boat, read a proclamation asserting the rights, toast the Sovereign with gin and gingerbread and ceremonially dredge up the first oysters. The Oyster Feast is held on or about 20 October each year.

CONWY★★

Aberconwy and Colwyn, WALES

POPULATION 3 649

MICHELIN ATLAS P 33 OR MAP 503 1 24

Viewed from the east bank, the River Conwy and bestriding bridges, the walled town and Conwy Castle, massive and bristling with towers, make a breathtaking sight against the mountain background. Llywelyn the Great chose this ideal site, controlling the estuary, for his future burial place and to this end endowed a Cistercian abbey. Later, with the building of Edward I's mighty fortress and garrison town, the monks were moved upstream to Maenan. All of Edward I's castles in Wales – with the exception of Harlech – were built in association with a "bastide", a town laid out on a rectangular grid. The town developed with the castle but remained contained by its circuit of walls. 🛈 *Conwy Castle Visitor Centre LL32 8LD* ☎ *01492 592 248; Fax : 01492 573 545; conwytic@virgin.net.*

▸ **Orient Yourself**: City Sightseeing buses operate a service between here and Llandudno (*mid May-late Sept* ☎ *01708 866 000; www.citysightseeing.co.uk*).

🜂 **Don't Miss**: Conwy Castle; a trip on the Princess Christine northeast.

⏰ **Organizing Your Time**: Allow 2 hours to see town and castle.

📷 **Especially for Kids**: beaches at the Conwy Marina and Penmaenmawr (west); Conwy Butterfly Jungle.

Sights

Conwy Castle★★ – ⏰ *Open daily 9:30am – 5pm (6pm Jun- Sept, 4pm Nov –Mar).* ⏰ *Closed 1 Jan and 24-26 Dec.* ⊜ *£4* ☎ *01492 592 358; www.conwy.com.* This masterpiece of medieval architecture was supplied from the sea, as were Edward's other Welsh castles. Building started in 1283 and was under the direction of Master James of St George (🜂 *see INTRODUCTION: Architecture)*; towards the end of June building was sufficiently advanced for the king and queen to stay here and by 1287 work was almost completed.

Eight massive drum towers with pinnacled battlements protect the two wards of the castle, set on its rocky ridge. The inner ward with the royal apartments was approached by water and the large outer ward from the town. In the outer ward the Great Hall lines the right hand side. Beyond the well the Middle Gate gives access to the inner ward, the heart of the castle, with the King's Hall and King's Tower on the right. The now vanished Water Gate was to the east of the Chapel Tower.

The Town – The 13C **town walls**★★ (35ft/11m high and 6ft/2m thick) girdle the town on three sides, and were built at the same time as the castle. The circuit is defended by 22 towers and three gateways and provides a good wall walk between Upper Church Gate and Berry Street. The original founder of Conwy, Llywelyn the Great, dominates all from his column in Lancaster Square. Further down the High Street at the corner of Crown Lane is **Plas Mawr**★★, (& ○ Open Apr-Oct, daily and Bank Hol 9.30am-5pm (6pm Jun to early-Sep; 4pm Oct). ⊜ £4.50 ☎ 01492 580 167; www.conwy.com/plasmawr. html) a mansion built in 1577 by Robert Wynne, a true "Elizabethan adventurer". Its rooms today still evoke a picture of the more gracious moments of the age in which it was built. At the junction with Berry and Castle Streets is **Aberconwy House**, (NT ○ Open late-Mar to Oct, Wed-Mon and Bank Hol Mon, 11am-5pm. ⊜ £2.60 ☎ 01492 592 246; Fax 01492 585 153) a medieval town house of c 1300. Its ground floor, some two feet below today's street level, houses an interesting "History of Conwy" exhibition. On the quayside nearby is what is claimed to be the "Smallest House in Great Britain".

At **Conwy Butterfly Jungle** you can see many of the worlds most beautiful tropical butterflies in free flight set in a large jungle garden, complete with rainforest sounds. & Bodlondeb Park. ○Open April to early September 10am - 5.30pm; early Sept-Oct 10am - 3pm. ⊜ £4. Refreshments, picnic area. Shop. ☎ 01492 593149, Fax 01492 593149; info@conwy-butterfly.co.uk; www.conwy-butterfly.co.uk.

Conwy Crossing – The estuary of the River Conwy is spanned by no fewer than three bridges. The earliest (1826) is Thomas Telford's elegant suspension bridge, now reserved for pedestrians. The second was added by Robert Stephenson in 1848 to carry his Chester and Holyhead Railway and is a commendable attempt to harmonize with the architecture of the Castle. The third, a far less distinguished structure from the 1950s, failed so completely in its task of relieving the town of its flood of holiday traffic that it was replaced by the tunnel which forms part of the North Wales Expressway (A 55).

Excursions

Bodnant Garden★★ – 8mi/13km south of Conwy by A 470. & ○ Open mid-Mar to early Nov, daily, 10am-5pm. ⊜ £5.50. Parking. Refreshments. Wheelchairs: not bookable.☎ 01492 650 460; Fax 01492 650 448; office@bodnantgarden.co.uk; www.bodnantgarden. co.uk. The garden (99 acres/40ha), laid out largely in the late 19C and early 20C, offers the visitor formal terraces around the house and "The Dell", an area of shrubbery and woodland walks. Noted for rhododendrons, camellias and magnolias, it is also justly famed for the "Laburnum Arch" which produces, in late May and early June, a curved tunnel of golden racemes.

Penrhyn Castle★★ – Bangor, 17mi/27km west of Conwy by A 55. & ○Open late-Mar to Oct, Wed-Mon, noon (11am Jul-Aug) to 5pm. Grounds, museum, and tearooms: Open as castle, 11am (10am Jul-Aug) to 5pm. ⊜ £6; grounds and stableblock £4. Audio tour £1. Adventure playground. Parking (200m). Licensed tearoom; picnicking in grounds. Wheelchair available; access to ground floor; induction loop audiotour; braille guide. ☎ 01248 353 084 and 01248 371 337 (infoline); Fax 01248 371 281; penrhyncastle@nationaltrust. org.uk; www.nationaltrust.org.uk. This extraordinary evocation of the Middle Ages was built in the 1820s and 1830s by Thomas Hopper for George Dawkins Pennant, heir to the enormous wealth produced by the Penrhyn slate quarries. With its keep (124ft/38m high) it is the very image of an impregnable Norman fortress but in fact was a country home of the utmost sumptuousness, providing hospitality to the members of the Anglo-Irish Ascendancy on their way to and from the port of Holyhead. The décor of the interior is a tour-de-force of traditional craftsmanship, filled with furniture of an opulence seldom seen. The paintings on show in the Dining Room include an array of Old Masters (Rembrandt, Canaletto, Jan Steen, Van der Velde ...) unparalleled in North Wales. Part of the grandiose outbuildings houses an Industrial Railway Museum; the extensive parklands shelter a walled garden with many unusual plants.

CORNISH COAST★★★

Cornwall, ENGLAND

MICHELIN ATLAS PP 2, 3 OR MAP
503 D TO H 32, 33

LOCAL MAP UNDER TINTAGEL

Remoteness and wildness are the charms of the Cornwall peninsula with its long rugged coastline. The Cornwall Coast Path – part of the larger South West Way – winds a sinuous course (268mi/430km) above the sheer cliffs and indented coves and is the ideal way to discover the scenic splendours of the peninsula. The footpath is clearly waymarked and there is a wide choice of inland paths as short cuts.

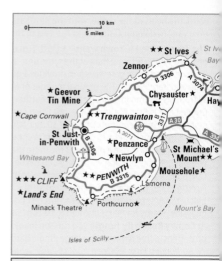

North Coast

From Tintagel to St Ives – 🖑 See TINTAGEL.

Penwith

From St Ives to St Michael's Mount – 🖑 See ST IVES.

South Coast

Between St Michael's Mount and Plymouth – 🖑 See TRURO.

The COTSWOLDS★★★

Gloucester, Hereford and Worcester, ENGLAND

MICHELIN ATLAS PP 17 AND 27 OR MAP 503 O 27 AND 28

Rising gently from the Upper Thames valley in the southeast to a dramatic escarpment overlooking the Severn Vale in the west, the Cotswolds offer the essence of rural England in concentrated form. Airy open uplands, sheltered in places by stately belts of beech trees, alternate with deep valleys enfolding exquisite villages and small towns.

▶ **Orient Yourself**: There are various bus tours of the area, departing from the surrounding towns of Oxford, Stratford, Cheltenham and Bath, including City Sightseeing (*mid May-late Sept* ☎ 01708 866000; www.citysightseeing.co.uk).

⊙ **Don't Miss**: Bibury, Cirencester Chastleton House, Snowshill Manor, Chipping Campden, Hidcote Manor Garden.

⊙ **Organizing Your Time**: Allow 3 days to see the area at a leisurely pace.

Kids **Especially for Kids**: Cotswold Wildlife Park and various attractions at Bourton-on-the-Water.

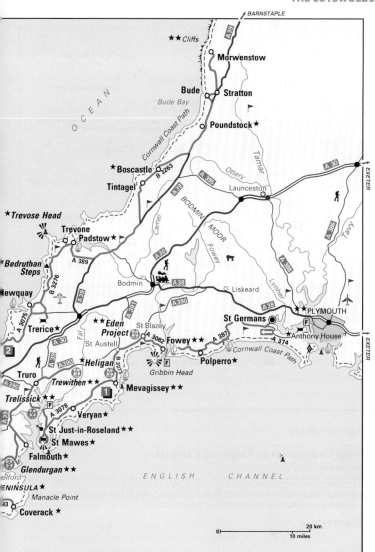

A Bit of History

The region has long been favoured for settlement. The commanding heights in the west are crowned more often than not by the hill-forts of prehistoric man, whose burial places also abound, from the chambered tombs of the Neolithic to the round barrows of the Bronze Age. Great estates were farmed from the Roman villas lying just off the ruler-straight Ermin Street and the Fosse Way. In the Middle Ages it was the wool from countless sheep grazing on the fine pasture of the wolds which gave rise to a trade of European importance and to a class of prosperous merchants, whose monuments are the great "wool" churches which they built from the underlying **oolitic limestone**. Ranging in colour from silver or cream to deepest gold, this loveliest of building stone is inseparable from any definition of "Cotswold character". Yielding the sophisticated masonry of manor house, the "tiles" of cottage roof, rough-dressed wall of barn and even the drystone boundaries of fields, it creates a rare harmony of building and landscape.

Far removed from coalfields and big cities, the area escaped the effects of industrialisation; its rural pattern is intact, an idyllic setting for quiet exploration of the past.
🛈 1 Cotswold Court, Broadway ☎ 01386 852 937 (summer only). 🛈 The Guildhall, Chipping Campden ☎ 01608 644 379. 🛈 Corn Hall, Market Place, Cirencester ☎ 01285 654 180; Fax 01285 641 182; tourism@cotswold.gov.uk; www.cotswold.gov.uk.

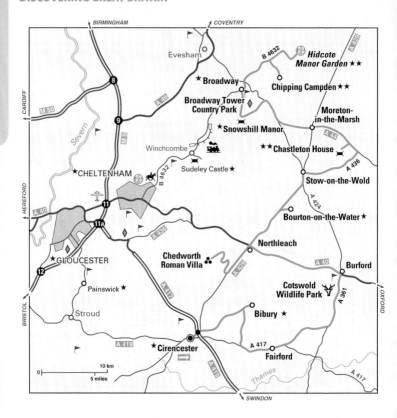

Excursions

From Cirencester to Chipping Campden

40mi/64km; 1 day

Starting in the centre of the Cotswolds, the tour runs northwards through some of the region's most delightful small towns and villages towards the spectacular prospect from the escarpment high above Broadway.

Cirencester★

The "Capital of the Cotswolds," which is still the market town for a prosperous rural region, was founded as a Roman fort, Corinium, established early in the Roman occupation at the junction of three major roads – Ermin Street, Akeman Street and the Fosse Way; by 2C AD it had become a walled city, second only to London in size, the centre of a flourishing countryside of great villa estates.

The confusion and destruction of the Dark Ages was followed by a long period of wool-based wealth which produced the fine parish church.

The old town is compact and has kept a traditional townscape, little marred by incongruous intrusions. It is hemmed in by the green spaces of two ancient estates: the gardens of the abbey sloping down to the pretty River Churn (the abbey buildings were demolished at the Dissolution) and the grandiose formal landscape of **Cirencester Park,** which contains the magnificent length of the **Broad Avenue** (5mi/8km) and the great house concealed from the town by a high wall and even higher yew hedge.

Church of St John the Baptist★ – ◷ *Open daily, 9.30am-5pm (except during services).* ◷ *Closed 25-26 Dec except for services.* ⟿ *Guided tour by arrangement with the Parish Office. Brochure (7 languages).* ☎ *01285 659 317 (Parish office).* This most important example of a Cotswold "wool church" is of great interest and beauty. The lofty tower of 1400-20, supported by powerful spur buttresses, rises grandly above the town. The unusual three-storey porch opening into the market place once served as the town hall.

The nave is exceptionally high and spacious; its immensely tall piers carry angels bearing the coats of arms of those pious townsfolk responsible for the ambitious rebuilding of 1516-30. Throughout the interior there is a wealth of detail: an unusual pre-Reformation pulpit; the **Boleyn Cup**, a gilt cup made for Anne Boleyn; memorial brasses grouped in the Chapel of the Holy Trinity; and, in the Lady Chapel, the charming effigies of Humfry Bridges (d 1598), his wife and their numerous children, their solemn demeanour contrasting with the insouciant air of the semi-reclining figure opposite of Sir Thomas Master (d 1680).

Corinium Museum★ – *Park Street. Open daily 10am (2pm Sun) to 5pm Closed 24-26 Dec. £3.70. Leaflet (3 languages). Café. Ramps; Braille guides. Ramps for disabled visitors. Braille guides. ☎ 01285 655 611; Fax 01285 643 286; museums@cotswold.gov.uk; www.cotswold.gov.uk.* This modern and well-ordered museum explains Cotswold history from geological to recent times. The Roman heritage is emphasised with many local finds, including a series of superb **mosaic pavements★**.

▷ *From Cirencester take A 429 and B 4425 east.*

Bibury★

William Morris' epithet of "the most beautiful village in England" is justified by the combined prospect of the friendly River Coln, stone bridges, weavers' cottages and the gables of Bibury Court against a wooded background. Dating from the 17C **Arlington Mill,** *(Open daily 10am-6pm (5pm Nov-Mar). £2. Restaurant; tea room; gift shop. ☎ 01285 740 368)* has been restored to house a small folk museum with exhibits on corn milling and Victorian agriculture.

▷ *From Bibury return southwest by B 4425; at the crossroads turn left; in Poulton turn left onto A 417.*

Fairford

This old coaching village is famous for the **Church of St Mary★**, harmoniously rebuilt in the late 15C. Sculptures, some humorously grotesque, enrich the exterior. Inside, the screens, stalls and misericords of the choir are of exceptional quality. But the church's glory is its wonderful set of **stained glass windows★★** (c 1500), tracing in colour the Bible story from Adam and Eve to the Last Judgement. The twelve apostles face the twelve prophets and in the clerestory the twelve martyrs afront the twelve wicked enemies of the faith.

▷ *From Fairford take A 417 east and A 361 north.*

Cotswold Wildlife Park

Open daily 10am-6.30pm/dusk (summer 4.30pm last admission, 3:30 winter). £8.50 (child 3 to 16 years, and concessions). Restaurant. Adventure playground and children's farmyard. ☎ 01993 823 006; www.cotswoldwildlifepark.co.uk. The peaceful

N. Meers/The National Trust

Arlington Row, Bibury

Address Book

For coin ranges, see the Legend at the back of the guide.

WHERE TO EAT

⊜⊜⊜ **Jonathan's at the Angel brasserie,** 14 Witney Street, Burford. ☎ 01993 822714; Fax 01993 822 069; jo@theangel-uk.com; www.theangel-uk.com. Splendidly converted 16C coaching inn now serving brasserie dishes ranging from Thai to Mediterranean; south facing courtyard. 3 restful rooms (⊜⊜⊜).

⊜⊜⊜ **Goblets,** High Street, Broadway. ☎ 01386 854418; Fax 01386 858 611. A concise menu of light seasonal dishes is offered in this characterful firelit dining room in rustic dark oak. Booking essential.

⊜⊜⊜ **The Bell,** Sapperton. ☎ 01285 760 298; Fax 01285 760 761; thebell@sapperton66.freeserve.co.uk; www.foodatthebell.co.uk. Charming pub 5 miles/8km west of Cirencester made up of three beamed cottages with log fires inside and a terrace outside. Traditional English and clasic European dishes.

WHERE TO STAY

⊜⊜⊜ **Alderley,** Rissington Road, Bourton-on-the-Water. ☎ Fax 01451822 788; alderleyguesthouse@hotmail.com. Simple guesthouse offering 3 bright homely floral bedrooms and a summer terrace for good quality breakfasts.

⊜⊜⊜ **Cotteswold House,** Arlington, Bibury. ☎/Fax 01285 740 609; cotteswoldhouse@btconnect.com. This Victorian house has been thoroughly converted into a simple spotless guesthouse with 3 bedrooms and a manicured garden, just outside the picturesque village.

⊜⊜⊜ **Windrush House,** Station Road, Broadway. ☎ 01386 853 577; 01386 853 790; richard@broadway-windrush.co.uk; www.broadway-windrush.co.uk. This Edwardian house, a few minutes' walk from the village, offers 5 modern bedrooms and a landscaped garden with countryside views.

⊜⊜⊜ **Nineveh Farm,** Mickleton, Chipping Campden. ☎ 01386 438 923;ninevehfarm@hotmail.com. This Georgian farmhouse extends a warm welcome with 5 comfortable rooms, some with garden views.

and natural habitat of the park (120 acres/49ha) and gardens is home to a wide variety of wildlife – rhinos, zebras and ostriches protected by unobtrusive moats, tigers and leopards in grassed enclosures; monkeys and otters in the old walled garden and tropical birds and plants in the tropical house; there are also a reptile house, aquarium and insect house. When the animals pall there is an adventure playground and narrow gauge railway to rekindle excitement in the young. In the gardens the lawns provide space for picnics, sheltered by various trees and shrubs.

▷ *Continue north on A 361.*

Burford

One of the focal points of the wool trade, later an important coaching town, Burford's growth stopped when the turnpike road (A 40) bypassed it in 1812. With its wealth of beautifully preserved buildings, nearly all of Cotswold limestone, it now welcomes the modern traveller to this beautiful region of which it is so typical.

The single main street descends steeply, then more gently, to cross the pretty River Windrush. About half-way down is the 16C Tolsey, once the courthouse, now the local museum.

Slightly apart from the town is the large **Church of St John the Baptist★**, its tall spire rising gracefully above the watermeadows. Norman in origin, the church exhibits a rich variety of work from many periods; the pinnacled three-storey 15C porch is outstanding. Among the memorials is the exuberant wall-monument to Edward Harman (d 569), decorated with Red Indians and rows of kneeling children.

▷ *From Burford take A 40 west to Northleach.*

Northleach

The market place of this little stone town is dominated by the **Church of St Peter and St Paul★**, a fine example of a "wool" church. The graceful two-storey south porch is adorned with medieval carvings. The remarkable set of **wool merchants' brasses★** recalls former prosperity.

At the crossroads stands the old "House of Correction", which served as prison and courthouse from 1791 to 1974 (*limited public access to building*).

▷ *Take A 429 south and turn right to Chedworth.*

Chedworth Roman Villa

&Yanworth, nr Cheltenham. Open Mar-Nov, Tue-Sun and Bank Hol Mon, 10am-5pm; Mar and Oct-Nov, 11am-4pm. £5. Parking. 01242 890 256, 01684 855 371 (information line); chedworth@nationaltrust.org.uk; www.nationaltrust.org.uk. This large and rich villa stood at the head of a small valley beside its own spring. It was undoubtedly one of the grandest buildings of the Roman Cotswolds. The remains, including good mosaic floors, have been carefully excavated and are well presented. The museum displays items found on the site.

▷ Return to Northleach and continue north on A 429.

Bourton-on-the-Water★

The village owes its special charm to the clear waters of the Windrush which run between well-tended grass banks beside the main street and under elegant stone bridges. It is a focal point of Cotswold tourism with a model village, a motor museum and "Birdland".

▷ Make a detour west of A 429 by a minor road to the Slaughters.

Both **Lower** and **Upper Slaughter** are picturesquely sited by the River Eye.

▷ Take the minor road northeast into Stow-on-the-Wold.

Stow-on-the-Wold

The village, the highest settlement in Gloucestershire, probably developed from a lookout post on the Roman road, known as the Fosse Way, into a Cotswold wool town. It is a regular stop for tourists to browse in the antique shops, admire the 14C cross in the market place or the Crucifixion by Caspar de Crayer (1610) in the church.

▷ From Stow take A 436 northeast; at the crossroads turn left onto A 44.

Chastleton House★★

Chastleton, nr Moreton-in-Marsh Open late-Mar to early Nov, Wed-Sat, 1-5pm (4pm Oct-), last admission 1hr before closing; booking recommended at peak periods as visitors restricted to 175 per day. £6. Parking 250m. Braille guide. 01494 755 585 (advance bookings), 01494 755 560 (infoline); chastleton@nationaltrust.org.uk; www.nationaltrust. org.uk. This perfect example of a Jacobean country house was built in the early 17C by a rich wool merchant and has hardly altered since.

The symmetrical gabled **front**, in grey and gold Cotswold stone, is flanked by two massive towers containing the staircases. The interior decor – panelling and plaster-work – has the rough vitality of the period and is complemented by original furniture. The **Great Hall**, one of the last of its kind to be built, the richly decorated **Great Chamber** and the tunnel vaulted Long Gallery, running the whole length of the top floor, evoke the atmosphere of domestic life in the 17C. Off one of the bedrooms is a secret chamber where Chastleton's owner may have hidden from Cromwell's troops after the battle of Worcester in 1651.

On one side of the forecourt are the 17C stables; on the other the modest little **Church of St Mary**. To the east of the house is a great rarity, a small formal **garden** surviving from about 1700.

▷ Continue west on A 44.

The route passes through **Moreton-in-the-Marsh**, a dignified little town where the Fosse Way broadens out to form the main street.

▷ After 6mi/km turn left onto B 4081.

Snowshill Manor★

& Open late-Mar to Oct, Wed-Sun, noon-5pm (4.20pm last admission); admission by timed ticket. Grounds: 11am-5.30pm; last admission 5pm. Liable to serious overcrowding on Sun and bank holiday Mon. Closed Good Friday. House and garden £7; garden only, £4. No dogs. Parking. Restaurant. 01386 852; snowshillmanor@nationaltrust.org. uk; www.nationaltrust.org.uk. This typical Cotswold manor house (c 1500) is snugly sited below the rim of the escarpment. The house is crammed with a wondrous array of objects acquired during a lifetime of collecting by the eccentric Charles Wade, who also laid out the enchanting **terraced garden**★.

▷ Return northeast on B 4081; turn left onto a minor road.

Broadway Tower Country Park

& Open Apr-Oct, daily, 10.30am-5pm (11am –3pm Sat , Sun). £3.50. Adventure playground. Parking. Restaurant, barbecues, picnic area. 01386 852 390; Fax 01386 858 038; broadway-tower@clara.net; www.broadway-cotswolds.co.uk/tower.html. The

Broadway Tower, a battlemented folly (1800), marks one of the highest points (1 024ft/312m) in the Cotswolds. The vast westward **panorama**★★★ extends over the fertile Vale of Evesham to the jagged line of the Malvern Hills and, in clear weather, beyond to the far distant landmarks of the Welsh border country – the Forest of Dean and the Black Mountains (southwest), Clee Hill and the Wrekin (northwest).

▶ *Continue on minor road; turn left into A 44 which descends a long hill.*

Broadway★

This "show village", set at the junction of two main roads, devotes itself wholeheartedly to the needs of its many visitors with a variety of antique and craft shops, cafés and restaurants, hotels and guest houses. The long, partly tree-lined "broad way" rises gently from the village green at the western end to the foot of the escarpment, flanked by mellow stone buildings which range from picturesque thatched cottages to the stately Lygon Arms.

▶ *Take B 4632 and B 4035 north and east to Chipping Campden.*

Chipping Campden★★

Its long curving High Street, lined with buildings of all periods in the mellowest of limestone, makes Chipping Campden the embodiment of Cotswold townscape at its most refined. Its welcome is warm, yet discreet, with little of the commercialisation to which some less favoured places have succumbed.

The town has been quietly prosperous since the great days of the medieval wool trade and something of its present state of preservation is due to the care and skill of the artists and craftspeople who were attracted to Chipping Camden in the early 20C. Many of the houses in the **High Street** are substantial but, more than individual distinction, it is the overall harmony of the street scene which impresses. The centre of the town is marked by the arched and gabled **Market Hall** of 1627. Further north, distinguished by its two-storeyed bay window, is the **house of William Grevel**, "the flower of the wool merchants of all England", who died in 1401 and is commemorated by a fine brass in the parish church. In Church Street stand the Almshouses built in 1617 by Sir Baptist Hicks, whose own mansion opposite was destroyed in the Civil War. Two pavilions survive, together with pepperpot lodges and the gateway, near the entrance to **St James's Church**, (🕐 *Open daily, 10am (2pm Sun) to 6pm (5pm Sat-Sun; 4pm winter). Services: public worship in the mornings)* one of the noblest Cotswold "wool churches"; it was almost entirely remodelled in the 15C in the Perpendicular style and conveys a great sense of unity and repose.

▶ *Take minor roads north.*

Hidcote Manor Garden★★

Hidcote Bartrim, nr Chipping Campden ♿🕐 *Open Mar – Oct 10:3am – 6pm (5pm Oct); Last admission 1hr before closing.* 👓 *£6.60. Parking. Licensed restaurant; tea room. Wheelchair access to part of the garden.* ☎ *01386 438 333; Fax 01386 438 817 hidcote@ nationaltrust.org.uk; www.nationaltrust.org.uk.* In creating one of the greatest English gardens of the 20C, the horticulturalist Lawrence Johnstone contrived an enchanting variety of effects in a small space (10 acres/about 4ha). Calm expanses of lawns, vistas down avenues or into the countryside beyond contrast with places of luxuriant but carefully controlled wildness. A labyrinth of "garden rooms" encloses an intricate arrangement of herbs, a composition of plants entirely in white, a mysterious pool. The whole is combined into a unified design by trim hedges of yew, beech and holly.

COVENTRY ★

West Midlands, ENGLAND

POPULATION 299 316

MICHELIN ATLAS P 27 OR MAP 504 P 26

Sited at the geographic centre of England, the city is known for its magnificent cathedral, Lady Godiva's ride through the streets, and untold devastation during the Second World War. ⚑ *Bayley Lane CV1 5RN ☎ 02476 227 264; Fax 02476 227 255.*

A Bit of History

Coventry's history stretches back to Saxon times. In 1043 a Benedictine Priory was founded by Leofric, Earl of Mercia, and his wife, **Lady Godiva**, who, according to legend, rode naked through the streets to persuade her husband to relieve the citizens from the burdensome taxes he had imposed. The city grew rich in the Middle Ages through the cloth and wool trade and a new church, St Michael's, was built c 1200. In the 20C light industries brought a new kind of wealth and the population grew from 70 000 in 1900 to 250 000 in 1930.

On 14 November 1940 the biggest bombing raid of its time destroyed most of the city, including the 13C church, which in 1918 had become a cathedral. The new city, planned by Sir Donald Gibson and Arthur Ling, is both a visual and functional success, owing to its human scale and the preservation of the remains of medieval Coventry, the timber-framed properties in **Spon Street (Y)**.

> Miracle plays, now known as Mystery plays, were first performed during the Middle Ages to convey moral teaching. They involved much singing and music and were generally based on events from the New Testament or the story of Christ, told through a cycle of plays. As medieval drama passed from the hands of the clergy into those of the craftsmen's guilds, so the performances moved out of the church on to the steps and the open space before the west door. The two cycles of mystery plays which have been revived in England are performed in outdoor settings at Coventry (every three years 2006, 2009...) and York (every four years 2006, 2010 ...).

The Cathedral ★★★ 1hr

Fairfax Street. ⏱ Open daily, 9am to 5pm. ⊕ *Cathedral £3 donation. Tower £2. Leaflets (8 languages). Guide book (3 languages).* ☎ *024 7622 7597; Fax 024 7663 1448; information@ coventrycathedral.org; www.coventrycathedral. org.uk.* Although regarded by traditionalists as too modern and by modernists as too traditional, the **new cathedral** is one of the few post-war buildings to meet with the approval of the ordinary person. The architect was **Sir Basil Spence.** The success of his design lies in its synthesis of traditional dimensions and structural possibilities and its use of light.

The tower and spire, with restored bells, dominate the city which is well known as the city of the three spires. The flèche on the new cathedral (sometimes described as a TV aerial) has been both criticised and praised. Flanking the entrance steps is *St Michael Defeating the Devil* by **Jacob Epstein.** The majestic porch was designed to link the new cathedral with the ruins of the old and dramatically expresses the meaning of death and resurrection.

The overwhelming impression of the **interior** is of height, light and colour: height from the soaring slender nave pillars supporting the cano-

St Michael Defeating the Devil by Jacob Epstein

MICHELIN

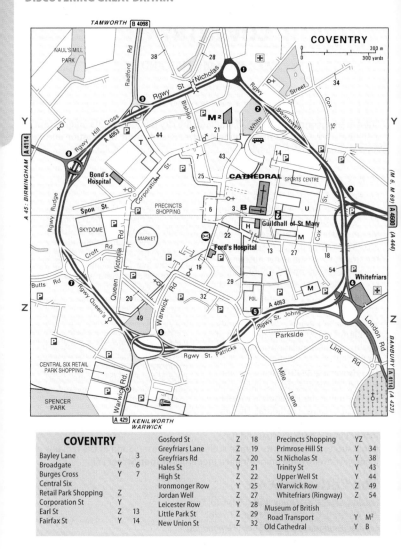

pied roof; light from the great west screen, a wall of glass engraved with patriarchs, prophets, saints and angels by John Hutton; colour from the Baptistery window by John Piper, a symbol of the light of truth breaking through the conflicts and confusions of the world. The font is a great rough boulder from the hillside at Bethlehem. The ten great windows are set in recesses angled southwards to enable the sun to pour into the nave through the beautiful colours. The whole is dominated by the huge tapestry, *Christ in Glory,* designed by **Graham Sutherland** (whose studies for this work are displayed in the Herbert Art Gallery nearby).

An exquisite statue of the Blessed Virgin Mary is to be found in the Lady Chapel; the Chapel of Christ in Gethsemane houses the *Angel with the Shining Chalice;* beyond is the Chapel of Christ the Servant with its unique hanging cross and Crown of Thorns. The Chapel of Unity, under the control of the Joint Council, has many interesting features: the floor is the work of the Swedish artist Einer Forseth, its centrepiece a Dove on a nest of flame, the symbol of the Holy Spirit, surrounded by representations of the five continents as well as traditional Christian symbols; the tall windows are the work of Margaret Traherne and are a beautiful sequence of colour, which casts exciting patterns of light on the floor when the sun shines.

Old Cathedral★ (Y) – The building was late 13C with large-scale Decorated and Perpendicular additions. All that remains are the walls, the crypt and the tower (294ft/90m) and the spire, one of the architectural glories of England, exceeded in height only by Norwich and Salisbury. The east end is marked by a simple cross of charred timbers, a replica of one erected by a fireman out of two roof beams in the aftermath of the firestorm in 1940. The Altar of Reconciliation is the focus of the Friday liturgy.

Additional Sights

Guildhall of St Mary (Z) – &. ⓒ *Open (functions permitting) Easter-Sept, Sun-Thur, 10am-4pm. No charge.* ☎ *024 7683 3041.* Founded in 1342, it was the prison of Mary Queen of Scots in 1569. Its treasures are two tapestries (one Flemish c 1500), showing Henry VII kneeling, the other showing Queen Elizabeth and her courtiers. The **Hall** is ceiled with a splendid timber roof and lit by stained-glass windows portraying the Kings and Queens of England.

Whitefriars (Z) – At the Reformation the Carmelite monastery (1342) became a workhouse; the beautifully vaulted eastern cloisters and the **monks' dormitory** survive.

Ford's Hospital (Z) – ⓒ *Open daily, 10am to 5pm/dusk.* ☎ *02476 223 838.* Much restored after war damage the half-timbered almshouses (1509) form a tranquil courtyard, a picture, with its flowers and creepers, in the heart of the late 20C city.

Bond's Hospital (Y) – Exterior only. The enchanting half-timbered almshouse, forming a courtyard with **Bablake Old School**, looks out on **St John's Church** (14C). The oldest part is the **east range** (c 1500) founded by Thomas Bond "for as long as the world shall endure".

Museum of British Road Transport★ (Y) – &.*Millennium Place, Hales Street.* ⓒ*Open daily, 10am-5pm (4.30pm last admission).* ⓒ *Closed 24-26 Dec. No charge. Guide book; leaflet. Coffee shop.* ☎ *024 7683 2425; Fax 024 7683 2465; museum@mbrt.co.uk; www. mbrt.co.uk.* Appropriately for the city that was the birthplace of the British car industry – with Daimler in 1896 – and subsequently home to over 100 different manufacturers of motor vehicles (Daimler, Standard, Rover, Riley, Humber, Lea & Francis, Singer, Hillman, Triumph...) and motor cycles (Swift, Rudge-Whitworth, Raleigh, Norton...) this display illustrates the industry, its growth and decline in the present century. The earliest models are attractively presented in an authentic turn-of-the-century street scene. In the line-up look for the 1908 Riley with its carbide lighting system as an optional extra, the well loved bull-nosed Morris (1922), the no 1 state car a 1947 Daimler and the latest Jaguar, the epitome of comfort and elegance. The display ends with Thrust 2, former holder of the world land speed record at 633.468mph/1 019.468kmph.

DARTMOOR★★

Devon, ENGLAND

MICHELIN ATLAS P 4 OR MAP 503 H, I 32

A **National Park**, Dartmoor is the largest of the five granite masses which form the core of southwest England. Nearly a third of the land is owned by the Duchy of Cornwall (since 1503 the estate of the monarch's eldest son), the rest by farmers and various government agencies.

Geological Notes

Dartmoor covers an area of 365 sq mi/945km2. The centre is open moorland, approximately 1 000ft/300m high, while the tors, mainly to the north and west, rise to as much as 2 000ft/600m, though the two highest, High Willhays (2 038ft/621m) and Yes Tor (2 030ft/619m), are in the military training area and therefore often inaccessible. To the east and southeast are **wooded valleys**, cascading streams and small villages. Ponies, sheep and cattle graze freely on the moor, buzzards, kestrels and ravens may be sighted above and, beside the streams, woodpeckers, wagtails and dippers.

☺ Because Dartmoor is a National Park, it belongs to the nation as a heritage and cannot be despoiled; the public does not have a universal right of access – on enclosed land, access is by public footpaths and bridleways only (note: it is an offence to drive or park more than 15yd/15m off a road). The number of visitors annually to the moor has been calculated at 8 million.

- 🕭 **Don't Miss**: The South Devon Railway, Castle Drogo, Lydford, views from Brent Tor.
- 🕘 **Organizing Your Time**: Allow two to three days to explore the Moor's highlights.
- 📶 **Especially for Kids**: There are various children's attractions spread around the Moor including ithe Miniature Pony Centre near Moretonhampstead, an adventure centre at Becky Falls and childrens activities at the River Dart Country Park at Ashburton.

The Moor

Ashburton – This former stannary, or coinage, town stands on a tributary of the River Dart at the beginning of the old road (B 3357) across the moor to Tavistock. The church with its tall Perpendicular granite tower was built in the 15C when the town was a wool centre. Slate-hung houses indicate its importance as a slate mining centre from the 16C-18C.

Signposted from the town is the **River Dart Country Park**, a popular country park with a range of outdoor facilities for the family and good birdwatching.

Becky Falls – *Manaton, Newton Abbot.* 🕘*Open Mar-Oct, daily, 10am-6pm/dusk.* 🎟 *£3.25, £1.95 (child). Attended parking. Licensed cafeteria, picnic area.* ☎ *01647 221 259; Fax 01647 221 267; beckyfalls@btconnect.com; www.becky-falls-dartmoor.com.* The Becka Brook tumbles some 70ft/20m from the moor into a wooded glade. The estate is criss-crossed by nature trails, making it a good departure point for walks on the moors.

Bovey Tracey – This small town is a gateway to Dartmoor. Many of its cottages are built of moor granite, mellowed by thatch in Devon fashion. The **church of St Peter, St Paul and St Thomas of Canterbury**★ was founded in 1170 by Sir William de Tracey, in atonement for his part in St Thomas Becket's murder, it is said. The church is largely 15C, although considerably restored, and contains some interesting Jacobean tombs, 15C lectern and beautifully carved pulpit and rood screen. Riverside Mill is home to the **Devon Guild of Craftsmen,** (♿*Riverside Mill.* 🕘*Open daily, 10am-5.30pm. Craft Shop. Café.* ☎ *01626 832 223; Fax 01626 834 220; devonguild@crafts.org.uk; www. crafts.org.uk.)* founded in 1954 largely by craftsmen working in Totnes, Torquay, Exeter and at Dartington Hall. A variety of local craft work is exhibited throughout the year.

Brent Tor – The 1 130ft/344m hill of volcanic stone is crowned by St Michael's, a small 13C stone church with a low stalwart tower affording excellent views★★ for miles around.

Buckfast Abbey – ♿ *Abbey church and grounds:* 🕘 *Open daily, 5.30am-9pm. Visitor Centre: Open daily, 9am-5.30pm (10am-4pm winter). Mass: Sun at 9am, 10.30am, 5.30pm; Monastic services: daily at 5.45am, 6.45am, 1pm, 6.30pm (6.15pm Sat), 9pm.Exhibition (🎟 no charge). Parking. Restaurant, bookshop.* ☎ *01364 645 500; enquiries@buckfast. org.uk; www.buckfast.org.uk.* The present abbey church was consecrated in 1932, some 900 years after the original foundation under King Canute. The new church is

BIDEFORD

★★ LYDFORD

Lyd

Lydford Gorge

Brent Tor
☩ 330

Great Mis Tor
△ 539

ℹ
Tavistock

B 3357

TRURO

A 390

Walkham

B 321

Burrator
Reservoir

Yelverton

✠ BUCKLAND
ABBEY ★★

Meavy

Tavy

Tamerton
Foliot

Plym

Plympton

ℹ
★ PLYMOUTH

★★ SALTRAM HOUSE

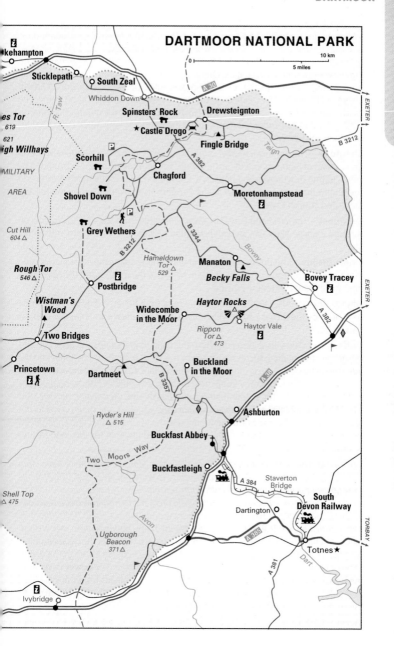

DARTMOOR NATIONAL PARK

Norman in style, following the plan of the Cistercian house dissolved under Henry VIII, and is built of grey limestone relieved by yellow Ham Hill stone. The interior of white Bath stone rises to a plainly vaulted roof, 49ft/15m above the nave floor. Note the ornate **high altar** (gold, enamelwork and jewels) and the modern **Blessed Sacrament Chapel** (1966) with walls of stained glass. An exhibition in the **crypt** retraces the history of the abbey.

Buckfastleigh – This market town on the southeast edge of the moor, which inspired the Sherlock Holmes mystery *The Hound of the Baskervilles,* is best known as the terminus of the **South Devon Railway**, (&⊙ *Open Mar-Oct, daily, 9.30am , 9am Bank Hols, to 6pm. £8.50. Parking. Shop. Refreshments.* ☎*0845 345 1427; www.southdevonrailway. org*) a former Great Western Railway line, one of the most picturesque in England.

Buckland in the Moor – Thatched stone cottages set in a wooded dell and the late medieval moorstone church form a particularly characteristic Devon village.

Castle Drogo★ – (NT) Drewsteignton 👤 House: 🕐Open late-Mar to early-Nov, Wed – Monday and Good Fri, 11am-5pm (4 pm Oct-Nov). Garden: Open daily, 10.30am-dusk. 🎫 Castle, garden, grounds £6.50; garden only £4. Leaflet (7 languages).Parking. Licensed restaurant, tearoom. ☎ 01647 433 306; Fax 01647 433 186; castledrogo@nationaltrust. org.uk; www.nationaltrust.org.uk. On discovering his descent from a 12C Norman nobleman Dru or Drogo, the successful grocer Julius Drewe, commissioned **Edwin Lutyens** (1869-1944) to create an extravagant castle to the glory of his name. The castle was built 1911-30 of granite partly from Drewe's own quarry; the exterior shows Norman and Tudor influences while the interior is very much Lutyens at his best (fine oak fittings).

Chagford – The medieval market town stands high above the Teign Valley, with good views of high tors and of Castle Drogo. The **market square** is surrounded by small granite or whitewashed houses, a 13C-16C inn built as the manor house and the quaint market house known as the Pepperpot, all overlooked by the tall 15C pinnacled **church tower.**

Dartmeet – The West and East Dart Rivers converge from the uplands to flow on through a gorge-like valley between wooded hillsides lively with bird and animal life.

Fingle Bridge – The three-arched 16C granite bridge spans the most picturesque reach of Fingle Gorge. On the 700ft/213m hilltop to the north stand the ruins of an Iron Age hillfort, Prestonbury Castle.

Haytor Rocks – Alt 1 490ft/454m. The by-road from Bovey Tracey to Widecombe runs close by these rocks, from which there is a good **view**★ as far as the coast at Widecombe.

Lydford★★ – The village descends from the main road towards the River Lyd and the gorge, the buildings increasing in age to the 16C oak-timbered cottages and the inn. The castle testifies to Lydford's military importance as a Saxon outpost from the 7C to the 13C; the two-storey **keep**, now in ruins, was built in 1195 to hold prisoners. Alongside is the 16C oak-timbered Tudor **Castle Inn**, (Restaurant. ☎ 01822 820 241/242; Fax 01822 820 454; castleinnltd@aol.com) which at one time served as the rector's house. **St Petroc's Church**, founded in the 6C, was rebuilt and enlarged on Norman foundations in the 13C, the south aisle and tower in the 15C, and further changes were made in the 19C.

Lydford Gorge – 👤The Stables: 🕐Open daily, late-Mar to Oct, 10am-5.30pm (4pm Oct); early-Nov to Mar, 10.30am-3pm (entrance to waterfall only). 🎫 £4.50. Arduous walk (2hr for the joint Upper and Lower Path); unsuitable for the very young or elderly; stout footwear required; easy access path via old Great Western Railway track. Tea room. Shop. ☎ 01822 820320; Fax 01822 822 000; www.nationaltrust.org.uk; lydfordgorge@ nationaltrust.org.uk. The wooded gorge is about 1.5mi/2km long with rock walls in places about 60ft/18m high. There are three marked paths from the main entrance; the **Upper Path** following the northeast – southwest course of the gorge giving excellent views of the river below and glimpses of Dartmoor. The **Lower Path** skirts the northwest bank at the water's edge. The **Third Path** leads from the Pixie Glen to the Bell Cavern via the thundering whirlpool known as the **Devil's Cauldron**. At the south end is the 90ft/30m **White Lady Waterfall.**

Moretonhampstead – Known locally as Moreton this old market town was a coaching stage on the Exeter-Bodmin road. The 14C-15C granite **church** has a commanding west tower but the most remarkable building is the row of thatched, colonnaded granite **almshouses**, dating from 1637.

Two miles (3km) west, set in 20 acres of beautiful parkland, the **Minature Pony Centre** (👤🕐 Open daily from 17th March until 30th October 10.30am-4.30pm (10.00am until 5.00pm in July & August. 🎫£6.50. Daily Birds of Prey display. Shop Cafe. ☎ 01647 432400; enquiries@miniatureponycentre.com; www.minatureponycentre.com) is a great favourite with young children and features a daily Birds of Prey display alongside the Moor's favourite four-legged creatures.

Okehampton – This market town on the northern boundary of Dartmoor is Saxon in origin, but was later refounded as a strongpoint by the Normans. It prospered as a medieval market town during the great wool period. The ruins of **Okehampton Castle** - (EH 👤 Castle Lane. 🕐Open late-Mar to Sept, daily, 10am-5pm (6pm Jul-Aug). 🎫 £3. Audio guide. Parking. Picnic area. ☎ 01837 52844; www.english-heritage.org. uk), initially a Norman motte and bailey and then later rebuilt (13C), include the gatehouses, barbican, outer and inner baileys, keep and stair turret. In town, an 18C mill is home to the **Museum of Dartmoor Life.** *(Museum Courtyard, off 3 West Street* 🐾 🕐 *Open Easter-Oct, Mon-Sat, 10:15am-4:30pm; also Jun-Sep, Sun; Nov-Easter, Mon-Fri, 10am-4pm.*👓 *£2. Leaflet (4 languages). Parking. Refreshments. Shop.* ☎ *01837 52295; Fax 01837 659 330; dartmoormuseum@eclipse.co.uk; www.museumofdartmoorlife. eclipse.co.uk).*

Postbridge – The **clapper bridge** made of large granite slabs is believed to date from the 13C when tin-mining and farming were being developed on the moor. The three openings are spanned by slabs weighing up to 8 tons, each about 15ft/5m long.

Princetown – The town, the highest in England at 1 400ft/425m, is dominated by one of the best-known prisons in England – the least welcoming place in Devon. Originally built in 1806-08 to hold Napoleonic prisoners of war, it already held 5 000 men in 1809 and 9 000 by 1813. After a period as a factory it was re-opened as a convict prison in the 1840s, when the practice of deportation had ceased.

Rough Tor – The 1 791ft/546m tor stands at the centre of the moor north of **Two Bridges,** and **Wistman's Wood.**

Scorhill Circle – *4mi/6km west of Chagford on the Teigncombe road to Batworthy, then 1mi/2km over Teign footbridge.* The path leads to a rare Bronze Age stone circle on the moor.

Shovel Down – *1mi/2km south of Batworthy on foot.* Shovel Down is the site of an interesting Bronze Age group of a monolith and five stone alignments.

Sticklepath – This attractive village with its slate and thatch roof houses is home to the **Finch Foundry,** *(* 🕐 *Open late-Mar to Oct, Wed-Mon , 11am-5.30pm.* 👓 *£3.50. Regular demonstrations. Walks. Parking. Tea Room.* ☎*01837 840 046; www.nationaltrust. org.uk)* a restored 19C edge-tool factory and forge (display includes agricultural hand-tools and working waterwheels).

Two Bridges – The Two Bridges, one a medieval **clapper bridge**, cross the West Dart at the junction of two ancient tracks across the moor (now the B 3357/B 3212).

Widecombe in the Moor – A cluster of white-walled, thatched cottages, grouped around the church, stands in the shallow valley (wide combe) surrounded by granite ridges which rise to 1 500ft/460m. The Perpendicular **Church of St Pancras**, a vast building with an imposing pinnacled 135ft/40m tall tower of red ashlar granite is sometimes known as the **Cathedral of the Moor.** The plain barrel roof is decorated with a series of finely carved **bosses**. The two-storey stone **church house** fronted by a loggia with seven octagonal columns dates back to 1537, when it was the village alehouse.

Wistman's Wood – *3mi/5km on foot, return, north of Two Bridges.* On the steep and rocky slopes of the West Dart River grow stunted mossy oaks, survivors and descendants of the primeval woodland which once clothed these uplands. Nearby are large groups of Bronze Age remains.

DARTMOUTH★★

Devon, ENGLAND

POPULATION 5 676

MICHELIN ATLAS P 4 OR MAP 503 J 32

Dartmouth enjoys one of the most beautiful and unspoiled settings in south west England. It occupies a deepwater haven in a tidal inlet encircled by verdant hills and the waterfront has changed little since the days of the press gang. 🛈 *The Engine House, Mayor's Avenue* ☎ *01803 834 224; Fax 01803 835 631; holidays@ discoverdartmouth.com; www.discoverdartmouth.com* 🛈 *The Old Market House, The Quay, Brixham TQ5 8TB* ☎ *0870 70 70 010 ; Fax 01803 852 939; brixham.tic@torbay. gov.uk; www.theenglishriviera.co.uk* 🛈 *Vaughan Parade, Torquay* ☎ *00870 70 70 010; Fax : 01803 214 885; tourist.board@torbay.gov.uk; www.theenglishriviera.co.uk* 🛈 *The Esplanade, Paignton TQ4 6ED* ☎ *0870 70 70 010 ; Fax: (01803) 551959; paignton.tic@ torbay.gov.uk; www.theenglishriviera.co.uk.*

Dame Agatha Christie (1890-1976)

Agatha Miller was born and brought up in Torquay. At the outbreak of the First World War she enrolled in the Volunteer Aid Detachment, working in the Town Hall while it doubled as a Red Cross Hospital. This experience provided the novelist with inspiration for Hercule Poirot, who was distilled from the many Belgian refugees stranded in Torquay at that time. From nursing, Agatha rose to dispenser and trained thereafter in a pharmacy for the Society of Apothecaries – a perfect source of inside information for concocting her detective stories. Her first marriage ended in divorce; her second husband, Max Mallowan, was an archeologist with whom she travelled extensively to the Middle East. Agatha Christie published several other novels under the pseudonym Mary Westmacott.

▶ **Orient Yourself**: Dartmouth is small, easily covered on foot; you will need a car or public transport to get around the English Riviera towns. The River Link is an open or closed top bus service between Paignton Seafront and Totnes Steamer Quay and Totnes Plains *(Apr-Oct, daily, ten departures to connect with the rail and boat timetables. £8.* ☎ *01803 834 488; Fax 01803 835 248; sales@riverlink.co.uk; www.riverlink.co.uk).*

🅿 **Parking**: Use the park and ride scheme in Dartmouth. The roads and parking areas aroound the English Riviera towns are extremely busy in the summer holidays.

🚂 **Don't Miss**: A trip on the Paignton and Dartmouth Steam railway and a river cruise along the Dart.

🕓 **Organizing Your Time**: Allow two hours in Dartmouth excluding river and rail trips.

🧒 **Especially for Kids**: Torquay and Paignton have a large selection of sandy beaches and typical English seaside attractions – Paignton Zoo is recommended and Kent's Cavern is a perfect rainy day option.

👁 **Also See**: Totnes.

💧 **Sailing**: The English Riviera offers some of the UK's best sailing waters. There is a large marina at Torquay and a smaller one at Brixham.

A Bit of History

Dartmouth grew wealthy on maritime trade and The Quay was constructed in 1548 when it served as the centre of the town's activities. It is lined with elegant merchants' houses, built in the early-mid 17C. The **Butterwalk**★ *(Duke Street)* is a terrace of four shops with oversailing upper floors supported on 11 granite pillars (built 1635-40, restored 1943). In the late 17C, however, when trading concentrated on Bristol and London, Dartmouth became purely a naval port, as the presence of the Britannia Royal Naval College, built at the turn of the century, now testifies.

Sights

Pannier Market – *Victoria Road, continuation of Duke Street*. The general market is on Friday; miscellaneous goods are sold during the rest of the week.

St Saviour's Church – *Anzac Street*. The tall square pinnacled tower has been a landmark for those sailing upriver since it was constructed in 1372. Note especially the south door with its two ironwork lions and rooted Tree of Life, and the medieval altar with legs carved like ships' figureheads.

Higher Street – The Shambles, the main street of the medieval town, is still lined with houses of that period – the early 17C four-storey **Tudor House** and the **Carved Angel**, a late 14C half-timbered merchant's house, now an inn.

Britannia Royal Naval College ⚓ *Guided tour Easter-Oct.* ☎ *01803 832 141 for times and charges (Dartmouth Tourist Office); Fax 01803 677015; webmaster-brnc@a.dii. mod.uk; www.britannia.ac.uk.*

Dartmouth Castle – *1mi/2km southeast by Newcomen Road, South Town and Castle Road.* 🕓 *Open, daily, 10am-5pm (6 pm Jul-Aug, 4pm Oct-Mar); Nov-Mar Sat and Sun only.* 🕓 *Closed 24-26 Dec, 1 Jan.* 🎫 *£3.60. Guide dogs only. Limited parking. Picnic places.* ☎ *01803 833 588; customer@english-heritage.org.uk; www.english-heritage. org.uk.* The fort was begun in 1481 by the merchants of Dartmouth to protect their homes and deepwater anchorage, and modified in the 16C and 18C. It commands

Britannia Royal Naval College, Dartmouth

excellent **views**★★★ out to sea and across and up the estuary. The most interesting fact about the castle is that it is the first in England to have been designed to have guns as its main armament; the gun ports are splayed on the inside to allow a wide sweep without an enlarged opening.

Excursions

Greenway House – ⚬━ *(Not open to the public) Garden: Open Mar– early Oct. Wed- Sat 10:30am – 5pm.* ⊛ *ferry charges £3.75 for pedestrians; £4.50 per person by car; book parking place in advance. Access by ferry from Dartmouth; by ferry from Dittisham (* ☎ *01803 833 206); by steam train to Churston station and walk down Greenway Road; by bus (no 106 from Paignton to Galmpton;* ☎ *09018 802 288) and walk down Greenway Road. Shop, cafe.* ☎ *01803 842 382; greenway@nationaltrust.org.uk; www.nationaltrust.org.*

Paignton and Dartmouth Steam Railway – *Queen's Park Station, Torbay Road.* 🕐 *Operates Jun-Sep, daily; Apr-May and Oct, on selected dates. Telephone for timetable.* ⊛ *Kingswear Return £7, Dartmouth Return £8.50; combined river ticket available.* ☎ *01803 555 872; Fax 01803 664 313; www.paignton-steamrailway.co.uk.*

Dart River Boat Trips – 🕐 *Operate river boat cruises upstream summer, daily, 10.30am-3.30pm, every 30min; early and late season, daily, 11.30am-3.30pm, every 1hr.* ⊛ *£6. Upstream to Totnes. From Totnes to Sharpham Vineyard (3hr) late-Jul, Sun at 6.30pm and early-Aug, Sun at 6.15pm.* ☎ *01803 834 488; Fax 01803 835 248; sales@riverlink.co.uk; www.riverlink.co.uk.*

Coastal Cruises – 🕐 *Operate (weather permitting) Jun-Aug. £6. Wildlife Cruises (2hr): late Jun, 11.30am and 1.30pm; and late Jul, 11.45am and 12.30pm.* ⊛ *Call for price.* ☎ *01803 834 488; Fax 01803 835 248; sales@riverlink.co.uk; www.riverlink.co.uk.*

Totnes★ – *12mi/19km north on B 3207 then A 381.* ♿ *See TOTNES.*

Torbay★ – This area, which markets itself as **"The English Riviera"**, encompasses **Torquay, Paignton** and **Brixham**, originally all fishing villages. These towns have capitalised on natural advantages which include a mild climate, exotic palm-tree vegetation, sea views and wide sandy beaches by adding hotels, promenades, piers, pavilions and public gardens to attract holidaymakers. Tourism is now the main source of income for the resident population.

Torquay – *10mi/16km northeast of Dartmouth. Ferry across the Dart estuary, then A 379 and A 3022.* In this bustling South Devon summer resort, houses extend up the hill behind the shore; large pale Victorian and Edwardian hotels and villas set in lush gardens are being replaced by modern apartment blocks and high-rise hotels, white by day and a spangle of lights by night. Following his visit, Dickens described Torquay as "a compound of Hastings and Tunbridge Wells and bits of the hills around Naples".

Excavations in the group of limestone caves known as **Kents Cavern**★ (Wellswood, *Ilsham Road, right off Babbacombe Road, B 3199* ♿ ⏰ ☎ *Guided tour daily, 10am–5pm (last tour Jul–Aug; 4pm Oct–Mar); also Jul–Aug, 5.30–9pm.* ⏰ *Closed 25 Dec. Book for evening tour by phone.* ☎ *£6.50. Parking. Refreshments.* ☎*01803 215 136; mail@ kents-cavern.co.uk; www.kents-cavern.co.uk),* have shown that they were inhabited by prehistoric animals and by men for long periods from the Paleolithic era, 100 000 years ago, until Roman times. The tour *(0.5mi/800m)* leads through contrasting chambers with petrified "waterfalls", beautiful white, red-brown and green crystals and many **stalactites** and **stalagmites**.

Torre Abbey – *Torbay Road.* ☛ *Closed until summer 2008 for restoration. www. torre-abbey.org.uk)* Set in luxuriant gardens, Tore Abbey consists of an 18C house, the so-called Spanish Barn and the ruins of the medieval abbey. The house, now a museum, contains collections of **English pewter,** 18C-19C glass and a rare set of proof copies of **William Blake's** illustrations for the *Book of Job.*

Paignton Zoo★★ – This is one of Britain's largest zoos, measuring 75 acres/30ha, *(Half a mile/800m west along A 385 to Totnes* ♿⏰ *Open daily, 10am-6pm (4:30pm Nov-Feb).* ⏰ *Closed 25 Dec.* ☎ *£10. Parking. Restaurant.* ☎ *01803 697 500, Fax 01803 523 457; info@ paigntonzoo.org.uk; www.paigntonzoo.org.uk)* with a large collection of animals, as part of a far-reaching conservation programme, and a luxuriant botanical garden.

DENBIGH★

DINBYCH – Denbighshire, WALES

POPULATION 7 710

MICHELIN ATLAS P 33 OR MAP 503 J 24

The market town of Denbigh is clustered on a hillside overlooking the Vale of Clwyd in the far north of Wales. It is dominated by the ruins of the castle★ built by Henry de Lacy in 1282, on the orders of Edward I after he defeated Llywelyn. The three interlinked 14C towers of the gatehouse, similar in plan to Caernarfon, probably show the influence of the King's master mason, James of St George. The town walls, still almost complete, date from the same period, with the Burgess Gate being the main entrance to the town.

Robert Dudley was created Earl of Leicester and Baron Denbigh in 1564. In 1579 work began on Leicester's Church, the first purpose-built Protestant church in Britain, but it was unfinished at his death in 1588. The walls still stand to roof height.

Henry Morton Stanley (1841-1904), African explorer in his own right, but best known for his remark "Doctor Livingstone, I presume," was born in Denbigh and brought up in the workhouse at St Asaph (see below).

Excursion

St Asaph (Llanelwy) – *5mi/8km north by A 525.* ♿⏰ *High Street Open daily, 8am-6pm.* ☎ *Guided tour (1hr). Fact sheet (3 languages). Parking. Braille guide.* ☎ *01745 583 429, 583 597; www.stasaphcathedral.org.uk.* This is the second smallest cathedral city in the country, after St David's. St Kentigern founded the cathedral and a monastic community on the site in AD 560. The present cathedrala, mainly 13C, houses the Bible used at the Investiture of the Prince of Wales in 1969 and the memorial of Bishop William Morgan, translator of the Bible into Welsh in 1588 – "Religion, if not taught in the mother tongue, will lie hidden and unknown."

DERBY

Derbyshire , ENGLAND

POPULATION 223 836

MICHELIN ATLAS P 35 OR MAP 502 P 25

TOWN PLAN IN THE MICHELIN GUIDE GREAT BRITAIN AND IRELAND

The Roman town of Derventio was built in the eastern heartlands of England on the River Derwent. It was one of the five Daneburghs – the others were Leicester, Lincoln, Nottingham and Stamford – and the most southerly point reached by Bonnie Prince Charlie's army before its retreat to Culloden (1746). In 1756 William Duesbury founded the Derby porcelain industry, excelling in tableware and unglazed figures in light neo-Classical mode. Derby is also the home of Rolls-Royce, manufacturers of the world's most luxurious motor cars. 🚹 *Assembly Rooms, Market Place, Derby DE1 3AH ☎ 01332 255 802; Fax 01332 256 137; tourism@ derby.gov.uk; www.visitderby.co.uk.*

Sights

Cathedral – *Queen Street. ♿🕐 Open daily, 8.30am-6pm. Guides (8 languages and large print). 🔊 Pre-boooked guided tours available. Entrance to Tower on certain days. 💶 cathedral visit, donation requested; tower £2. ☎ 01332 341 201; Fax 01332 203 991; visitors@derbycathedral.org; www.derbycathedral.org.* A sublime blending of three eras – early 16C (the high tower), early 18C (James Gibbs' nave) and late 20C (retrochoir). Inside, the impression of classical simplicity is countered by the magnificent Bakewell wrought-iron **screen and gates**, and the pedimented baldachin over the high altar. South of the chancel rests Bess of Hardwick (♿ Hardwick Hall), outshining her neighbours in death as in life.

Museum and Art Gallery★ – *The Strand. ♿ The Strand. 🕐 Open daily, 10am (11am Mon, 2pm Sun and Bank Hol Mon) to 5pm. 🕐 Closed Christmas and New Year. Free Admission. Multi-storey parking nearby. ☎ 01332 716 659; Diane.Peake@derby. gov.uk; www.derby.gov.uk/museums.* Derby Museum and Art Gallery is home to two superb collections. The China Gallery contains the largest **collection of Derby Porcelain★**, some 3 000 covering the different periods of manufacture. Of particular interest are works typical of the early period by André Planché; unglazed biscuit figures and groups by Pierre Stephan dating from the Chelsea Derby period (1770-84); painted scenes from the Crown Derby period (1784-1811) by John Brewer, especially naturalistic flowers and landscapes, George Robertson shipping scenes, Zachariah Boreman's Derbyshire landscapes, as

Derby Candlestick (1756-60)

well as more elaborate items from the Robert Bloor period (1811-48). In addition there is a good selection from the Crown Derby Company production since its foundation in 1876 to the present day.

The Wright Gallery holds many of the finest paintings and drawings of **Joseph Wright of Derby** (1734-97); his early studies in artifical light *(Blacksmith's Shop, A Philosopher Lecturing on the Orrery)*, his portraits *(The Rev d'Ewes Coke Group)* and the romantic masterpieces in natural light *(Landscape with Rainbow, Indian Widow)* of his later life.

Royal Crown Derby Museum★ – ♿ *194 Osmaston Road. 🕐 Open Mon-Sat, 9.30am-5pm, Sun 10am-4pm. Last admission 1hr before closing. 💶 Full tour £4.95; Visitor Centre only tour available; booking recommended. Factory shop. Museum. Parking. Restaurant. ☎ 01332 712 800; Fax 01332 712 899; www.royal-crown-derby.co.uk.* The new works, founded in 1847, house a collection of Derby porcelain, dating from 1756 to the present day. George III accorded royal patronage in 1773 and the **Royal Crown Derby title** was granted by Queen Victoria in 1890. In the **Raven Room** a priceless mint collection of Royal Crown Derby is displayed as it would have been in a Victorian house.

The Silk Mill Derby Industrial Museum – *Full Street.* ♿ 🕒 *Open Mon-Sat, 10am (11am Mon; 2pm Sun and Bank Hol Mon) to 5pm; Christmas-New Year telephone for details. No charge.* ☎ *01332 255 308; www.derby.gov.uk/museums.* Traditional local industries are represented in a Railway Engineering Gallery with displays of beam engines, Rolls-Royce aero-engines and cast-iron goods. The museum is housed in a silk mill whose bell and undercroft are the sole remains of the original 1718 building, claimed to be England's first factory.

Pickford's House – *41 Friar Gate.* ♿ 🕒 *Open Tue-Sat, 10am (11am Mon, 2pm Sun and Bank Hol Mon) to 5pm.* ☎ *01332 255 363; pickfordhouse@derby.gov.uk; www. derby.gov.uk/museums.* This elegant four-storey town house, which was built in 1770 by Joseph Pickford, architect, as his family home and work premises, is furnished as in Pickford's time with displays of 18C and 19C costume and a formal Georgian garden at the rear. There are demonstrations of cooking and laundry and exhibitions on the importance of Joseph Pickford as a Midlands architect and the history of the Friar Gate area.

Excursions

Kedleston Hall★★ – *4mi/6km northwest of Derby on Kedleston Road.* ♿ *House:* 🕒 *Open late-Mar to Oct, Sat-Wed, noon-4.30pm. Garden: as house, 10am-6pm. Park: late-Mar to late-Dec, daily, 10am-6pm (4pm early-Nov); early-Jan to mid-Mar, Sat-Sun, 10am-4pm.* ◉ *£6.30; park and garden only, £2.40; park £2 per vehicle (Thu-Fri). Parking. Licensed restaurant. For wheelchair access contact the Property Office.* ☎ *01332 842 191; Fax 01332 841 972; kedlestonhall@nationaltrust.org.uk; www.nationaltrust.org.uk.* Sir Nathaniel Curzon began to pull down his Restoration house in 1758, employing Matthew Brettingham to replace it with a Palladian mansion connected by curving arcades to four detached wings. James Paine built the north front in the Palladian style and in 1760 Robert Adam, fresh from his Italian Grand Tour, was called in to add the south front, where the movement of the stairs and dome break with the Classical mould, and to design the interior, one of his earliest great works. The disastrous effects which such a triple change of architects might have had was avoided since all three worked in the neo-Classical context, creating one of the grandest 18C houses in England. The Curzons have lived at Kedleston for over 500 years and one, Lord Curzon, was Viceroy of India from 1898 to 1905.

The **rooms** centre on the **Marble Hall**, lit from above so as not to detract from the Greek and Roman splendours of gods and goddesses in the alcoves. The arabesque stucco ceiling is by Joseph Rose, Adam's own plasterer. The **State Drawing Room** shows Adam at his most colourful; note the Cuyp landscape and the Veronese Achilles. As grand as the Marble Hall but as warm as the State Drawing Room is the **Saloon or Rotunda,** reaching to the coffered dome (62ft/19m), which is as surprising as the neo-Classical Scenes from British History by Biagio Rebecca. The final Adam surprise is the **Ante Room** and **Dressing Room**, graced by a neo-Classical screen with a segmental arch above the entablature, in a room hung with 17C and 18C Masters including Van Dyck, Lely, Kneller and Jansen.

Sudbury Hall★★ – *15mi/24km west of Derby by A 516 and A 750.* ♿ *Hall and Museum:* 🕒 *Open mid-Mar to Oct, Wed-Sun, Bank Hol Mon and Good Fri, 1-5pm/dusk. Grounds: Open as hall, 11am-6pm.* ◉ *Hall and museum £9; grounds £1. Parking.* ☎ *01283 585 305; Fax 01283 585 139; sudburyhall@nationaltrust.org.uk; www.nationaltrust.org. uk.* The **Jacobean exterior** (1660-1702) is deliberately conservative, the **interior** a radical combination of late Renaissance Classicism and budding Baroque. The old formal gardens were swept away in the 18C to make way for a naturalistically landscaped park.

The hall, which is densely hung with 18C paintings, is beautified by the work of Grinling Gibbons, Edward Pierce and James Pettifer (all craftsmen who had worked with Wren on many of his London churches) and capped by Louis Laguerre's ceiling paintings. In the **Entrance** and **Great Hall** is a bird's-eye view of Sudbury by Griffier and portraits by Reynolds and Lawrence; the **Staircase** was built by Pierce and the exquisite plasterwork above it is by Pettifer; two Griffiers and a Hoppner hang beneath Pettifer's ceiling of winged cherubs in the **Drawing Room**; the finest ceiling of all is in the **Long Gallery.**

Calke Abbey★ – *Ticknall, 10mi/16km south of Derby by A 514.* ⟨access⟩ ⟨clock⟩ *Open late-Mar to Oct , Sat-Wed and Bank Hol Mon, 1 pmto 5.30pm); last admission 5pm. Park open during daylight hours* ⟨audio⟩ *House and garden £6.30; garden only £3.80. Braille guide. Parking. Restaurant.* ☎*01332 863 822; Fax 01332 865 272; calkeabbey@nationaltrust.org.uk; www. nationaltrust.org.uk.* A long drive through extensive undulating parkland leads to the early 18C house set deep in a valley. The estate remained in the possession of one family from 1622 until 1985 and, owing to the characteristic shyness and even eccentricity of the later generations, the house has scarcely been altered since 1886.

To preserve the unique quality of Calke only two rooms have been redecorated – the Caricature Room, where the walls are papered with the work of caricaturists such as Rowlandson, Gillray and Cruikshank, and the Dining Room, which was designed by William Wilkins the Elder in 1793. The Saloon and several other rooms display the cases of stuffed birds, part of the Natural History collections which introduce the atmosphere of a private museum. One of the treasures of Calke is the **State Bed,** a magnificent Baroque creation, probably made for George I in c 1715 which was found unused in its boxes; the Chinese silk hangings have therefore been preserved with their original colours and detailed design. The kitchen, which dates from 1794, appears as it was when abandoned in the 1920s.

The stables present a selection of old carriages and the harness room. The walled gardens (7 acres/2.83ha) contain the flower garden planted in the 19C "mingled" style, the Auricula Theatre, a physic garden and a conservatory (1777). The pleasure grounds were laid out c 1705 by London and Wise, gardeners to the king. A chain of eight ponds bisects the grounds north of the house.

Denby Pottery – *8mi/13km north of Derby by A 38 and B 6179. Visitor Centre, Derby Road:* ⟨clock⟩ *Open daily, 9.30am (11am Sun) to 5pm.* ⟨clock⟩ *Closed 25-26 Dec.. Glass Studio tour Mon-Fri. Museum. Restaurant. Garden Centre. Parking.* ☎ *01773 740 799; visitorcentre@ denby.co.uk; www.denbyvisitorcentre.co.uk.* During the tour of the factory the visitor is shown the various stages, many done by hand, in the production of the famous Denby earthenware and given the opportunity to mould a figure and decorate a plate. Denby ware is on sale in the shop together with many other excellent kitchen items.

DEVIZES

Wiltshire, ENGLAND

POPULATION 13 205

MICHELIN ATLAS P 17 OR MAP 503 O 29

Devizes developed around an early Norman castle which was rebuilt by Bishop Roger of Sarum in 1120, became Crown property, but being "utterly ruinated and decayed" by 1596, was finally demolished by Cromwell's forces in 1646. The present castle is a 19C fantasy (private). The town, 17 miles/28 km east of Bath, flourished as a cloth market from medieval times to the 19C, specialising in the narrow woollen suiting known as "drugget"; from the 17C it profited from tobacco grown widely in the area and it is now probably best known for its brewery. All this accounts for the number of well-disposed 18C town houses. ▯ *Cromwell House, Market Place, Devizes SN10 1JG ☎01380 729 408; Fax: 01380 730 319; all.dtic@kennet. gov.uk; www. kennet.gov.uk.*

- 🕸 **Don't Miss**: Avebury Stones; at least one of the area's chalk "white horses"; Savernake Forest Grand Avenue.

- 🕐 **Organizing Your Time**: Allow 2-3 hours for Devizes plus half a day per excursion.

- 👃 **Also See**: Bath, Lacock, Salisbury, Stonehenge, Wells.

Sights

St John's★★ – This major Norman parish church has a mighty oblong **crossing tower** with, on the inside, round arches towards the nave and chancel and an early example of pointed arches towards the transepts. Inside, the vaulted east end is typically Norman, decorated with interlaced arches articulated with chevron and zigzag mouldings in contrast with fish-scale filled spandrels. The side chapels (1483) are separated from the chancel and sanctuary by decorative stone screens and have fine lacunar roofs resting on carved corbels.

Wiltshire Heritage Museum★ – 👃 *41 Long Street.* 🕐*Open Mon-Sat, 10am-5pm, Sun, noon-4pm and Bank Hol Mon. Library £3; no charge Sun-Mon.* ☎ *01380 727 369; Fax 01380 722 150; wanhs@wiltshireheritage.org.uk; wiltshireheritage.org.uk.* In addition to geology and natural history collections and an art gallery, the museum has a famous archeological department where models of nearby Stonehenge and Avebury are displayed among a collection of local finds.

Town Centre – The classical-fronted **Corn Exchange,** crowned with the gilded figure of Ceres, dates from the 19C. Facing down onto the broad **Market Place**★, which grew around the flourishing trade in sheep, is the fine **Old Town Hall** (c 1750), open to serve as a market on the ground floor, fronted by Ionic columns rising to a pediment enclosing a clock and putti. The elegant Georgian (1808) **Town Hall** has a rusticated ground floor, arched windows and tall Ionic columns. **St John's Alley** is lined with a complete range of half-timbered, compact Elizabethan houses with jettied upper floors. Among the many old coaching inns, note in particular the 18C **Black Swan** and the early 18C **Bear Hotel**, known for the portrait sketches drawn in the 18C by the landlord's son **Thomas Lawrence** (1769-1830). Note also **Parnella House,** built c 1740 by a doctor who decorated the front with a statue of Asklepios, the Greek god of medicine (modern copy). The old dark street known as **The Shambles** still serves as a market (best on Thursdays and Saturdays).

Kennet and Avon Canal Centre – *The Wharf.* 🕐 *Open Mar-Dec, daily, 10am-4pm.* 🎟 *£1.50 (museum).* ☎ *01380 721 279; Fax 01380 727 870; www.katrust.org.* The exhibition in the old granary (1810) which houses the centre describes the construction (1794-1810) of the waterway which linked Bristol and London and was engineered by John Rennie, who also designed the bridges and aqueducts.

Excursions

Avebury★★

7mi/11km northeast on A 361. Though less famous than Stonehenge, Avebury and the surrounding district is extremely rich in prehistoric monuments and earthworks, the earliest dating from c 3700-3500 BC. The site is the more fascinating as the village lies inside the circle of 30-40 ton sarsen stones within the earth "ramparts". The

Kennet and Avon Canal

In 1792 an advertisement in a Salisbury journal promoted a scheme to build a canal between navigable sections of the River Avon and River Kennet, thereby linking Bristol and Bath with Newbury and Reading: private investors welcome. The project's surveyor and engineer **John Rennie** designed a waterway that could accommodate large barges (13ft 10in/4.2m in the beam) which were considerably bigger than those operating on the Midland canals (6ft 10in/2.08m). Building work began shortly after Royal Assent was granted in 1794; by 1807 the 57mi/92km waterway was in operation; in 1810 the flight of 16 locks up Caen Hill was completed. The bulk of the freight was coal from Radstock and Poulton, but with the advent of the Great Western Railway (1841), traffic dwindled forcing the canal authorities to sell up to GWR, who deliberately abandoned the canal.

Recently restored (1988-90), the canal is once more open to navigation, threading its way through the Avon Valley, the Vale of Pewsey and on into Berkshire: for details of boat trips and the state of the towpath for cyclists, contact the Kennet and Avon Canal Trust, Canal Centre, Couch Lane, Devizes SN10 1EB, ☎ 01380 721 279; www. katrust/org.

village church, St James's, is an interesting juxtaposition of Anglo-Saxon, Norman, Perpendicular and 19C work.

The Stones★ – It is difficult to make out the plan of the stones, since the only vantage points are on the earth banks, reinforced by an inner ditch, around the 28 acre/11ha site. These are broken at the cardinal points of the compass to allow access to the centre (now used by modern roads) and enclose a circle of 100 sarsens from the Marlborough Downs and two inner rings. From the south exit, an avenue of about 100 pairs of stones (only some of which can still be seen, as the site was viewed as a convenient source of building material for the village), alternating square "male" and slender "female" stones in each file, once led to the burial site known as the Sanctuary on Overton Hill (excavated in 1930). The **Barn Gallery and Alexander Keiller Museum** *(NT, EH ♿ ⊙ Open daily, 10am-6pm (4pm Nov-Mar). ⊙ Closed 24-25 Dec. ⊙ £4.20 ☎ 01672 539 250; Fax 01672 539 388; avebury@nationaltrust.org.uk; www. nationaltrust.org.uk)* gives a valuable insight into this and neighbouring sites.

Neighbouring sites

Silbury Hill★ *(2mi/3km south)* is a 130ft/40m high man-made chalk mound, one of the largest of its kind in Europe. The reasons for its construction remain a mystery. The **West Kennet Long Barrow**★ *(3mi/5km south)* is England's finest burial barrow (340ft long x 75ft wide/104m x 23m), dating from 3500-3000 BC. The entrance at the east end is flanked by giant sarsens, and the passage, lateral vaults and chamber at the far end are roofed with massive capstones supported on upright sarsens and drystone walling. Some 50 skeletons from the early Neolithic period were discovered in the vaults.

A. Taverner/MICHELIN

The Stones, Avebury

The Ridgeway Path★★

This ancient trade route was already in use by the nomadic peoples of the Paleolithic and Mesolithic ages, who followed the line of the chalk ridge, as it was easier going than the lower slopes covered in forest or scrub. The modern path, opened in 1973 and waymarked by Countryside Commission acorns, runs from Overton Hill near Avebury via the Uffington White Horse to the Ivinghoe Beacon near Tring in Hertfordshire (85mi/140km). Those planning to walk some distance or the full length will find the 1:50 000 Ordnance Survey maps (nos 173, 174, 175 and 165) useful. The local museum in Devizes illustrates some of the rare downland plants to be found along the path.

Marlborough★

This former market town strategically placed on the London-Bath road (A 4) has been home to a famous public school since the 19C. To the north of the town stretch the **Marlborough Downs**, crossed by the Ridgeway Path and home to flocks of sheep (every town in Wiltshire was originally a wool town). The **High Street** leads from The Green at the east end of town to Marlborough College at the west end. It is lined by attractive houses, no two quite alike, and, at the east end, pent houses supported on pillars. **St Mary's church**, also at the east end, was rebuilt after a fire during the Commonwealth, hence its Puritan austerity. The High Street boasts a couple of interesting 17C **coaching inns** (Castle and Ball, Sun Inn). At the west end, the **church of St Peter and St Paul** (now an arts and crafts centre) is Norman in origin, but was rebuilt in the 15C and extensively restored in the mid 19C. **Marlborough College** (private), founded in 1843 with 200 boys on its register, now has about 900 students (boys and girls).

A couple of miles southeast of Marlborough lies **Savernake Forest**★★, once a royal forest hunted for boar and deer. Its 4 000 acres/1 619ha were replanted by Capability Brown in the 18C and are now home to oak, ash, larch and above all beech trees, present in their thousands. The forest is Crown property, administered by the Forestry Commission and is a wonderful place to explore on foot or by bicycle. Cutting through the forest northwest-southeast is the **Grand Avenue**★★★, lined with superb beeches.

Potterne

2mi/3km south by A 360. The pride of this village is the fine 15C half-timbered **Porch House**★★ (private). In spite of later additions, **St Mary's Church** is still a good example of Early English architecture.

White Horses

Marlborough White Horse – *South of the Bath road (A4), just west of Marlborough College.* The small, elongated white horse (62ft long by 47ft high/19m x 14m) was designed and cut in 1804 by boys from the local town school.

Hackpen – *6mi/10km northwest of Marlborough on B 4041.* Said to have been cut in honour of Queen Victoria's coronation in 1838. It measures 90ft by 90ft/27m x 27m (possibly in an effort to overcome the lack of slope). Best seen from the unnumbered road (off the A 346) from Marlborough to Broad Hinton.

Pewsey Vale White Horses – *7mi/12km south of Marlborough on A 345.* Just beyond Pewsey, the Pewsey Horse (66ft long by 45ft high/20m x 14m) can be seen striding across the hillside. The second figure on this site, it was cut in 1937 to celebrate the coronation of King George VI. Just after Upavon, take the A 342 towards Devizes. The Alton Barnes Horse (160ft long by 166ft wide/49m x 51m) looks south over the Vale of Pewsey from Old Adam Hill. It was cut in 1812.

Cherhill Horse – *9mi/15km west of Marlborough, towards Calne (visible from A 4).* This horse measures 131ft by 123ft/40m x 37m from nose to tail and dates from 1780.

Broad Town Horse – *10mi/17km northwest of Marlborough, visible from the B 4041 from Broad Hinton to Wootton Bassett.* This horse is said to have been cut in 1864 by a farmer, which may explain its more naturalistic appearance and proportions (78ft long by 57ft/24m x 17m).

Uffington White Horse – *20mi/33km northeast of Marlborough on White Horse Hill, Berkshire Downs; visible from the A 420 or B 4508 or B 4507 east of Swindon.* This is one of England's oldest chalk hill figures, cut between 100 BC and AD 100. It is 365ft/111m long and, along with Osmington, is the only horse facing right.

Westbury White Horse – *27mi/45km southwest of Marlborough on Bratton Down, best viewed from B 3098 between Edington and Westbury.* This is Wiltshire's oldest white horse, cut in 1778. It measures 166ft long by 163ft high/51m x 50m.

Bowood House★

10mi/16km northwest by A 342, then A 4 right. ♿🕐 *Open late-Mar to early-Nov, daily, 11am-6pm/dusk (5pm last admssion).* 🅿 *£6.60. Rhododendron walks £3.70. Parking. Coffee Shop.* ☎ *01249 812 102; houseandgardens@bowood.org; www.bowood.org.* The house evolved under a series of famous architects from 1725, when it was begun. It was sold, still incomplete, in 1754 to the first Earl of Shelburne, father of the future Marquess of Lansdowne. In 1762-68, **Capability Brown** laid out the park, including a lake, woodlands and specimen trees such as a cedar of Lebanon (now 140ft/43m tall) in his design. In 1955, the "big house" at Bowood was demolished; the Orangery and its attendant pavilions were retained as a residence and sculpture gallery. Besides beautiful trees, the grounds feature a cascade, an 18C Doric temple, a grotto, Italianate terraces and a woodland garden (resplendent with bluebells, rhododendrons and azaleas in May and June).

The house is entered through the Orangery, classically designed by **Robert Adam** in 1769. To the right is the small room where Joseph Priestley discovered oxygen in 1774 and Jan Ingenhouse (d 1799) the process of plant photosynthesis. From the windows of the end library, designed by CR Cockerell after Robert Adam (beautiful decor and fittings), there is a good **view**★ of the park. The sculpture gallery extending the length of the Orangery displays selected pictures, statuary and tapestries from the Lansdowne collections.

DORCHESTER★

Dorset, ENGLAND

POPULATION 15 037

MICHELIN ATLAS P 8 OR MAP 503 M 31

The Romans built the south west settlement of Durnovaria in the 1C AD on the London-Exeter highway, but Dorchester today is famous for being "Hardy Country", home to the great British novelist, Thomas Hardy (👤 *see below*) and the setting for many of his 19C tales. Architecturally it is notable for its 17C houses, many of them refaced or rebuilt in the 19C, producing façades of infinite variety. 🚩 *11 Antelope Walk, Dorchester, DT1 1BE* ☎ *01305 267 992; Fax : 01305 266 079; dorchester. tic@westdorset-dc.gov.uk; www.dorsetforyou.com.*

Visit

Dorchester Streets – The 17C **King's Arms,** boasting an expansive early 19C front with broad porch on Doric columns, is to be found on High East Street, one of Dorchester's main thoroughfares. South Street, Dorchester's main shopping street, starts with an impressive row of 18C red brick fronts. No 10, where the Mayor of Casterbridge lived in the novel of that name and now a bank, is a distinguished late 18C three-storey house faced with lustred brick headers and red-brick dressings. In High West Street stands the much restored **St Peter's Church** with white stone doorway, white stone tower, battlements and pinnacles. No 6 is the town's only half-timbered building, early 17C with overhangs at two levels; here the notorious Judge Jeffreys stayed during the **Bloody Assizes** when trying over 500 of the men who took part in the Monmouth Rebellion (1605).

Eric Kennington's 1931 **Thomas Hardy Memorial** *(top of High West Street)* is a portrait of the author as an old man, hat on knee, seated on a flowery tree-stump.

Dorset County Museum★ – *High West Street* ♿🕐*Open Mon-Sat, 10am-5pm; also Jul-Sept , Sun.* 🕐*Closed Good Friday, 24-25 Dec.* 🅿 *£5.* ☎ *01305 262 735; Fax 01305 257 180; dorsetcountymuseum@dor-mus.demon.co.uk; www.dorsetcountymuseum.org.* A splendid **Victorian gallery,** with painted cast-iron columns and arches supporting a glass roof, houses **Thomas Hardy** memorabilia: furniture and paintings and papers from **Max Gate,** the house Hardy built for himself in 1885, as well as a reconstruction of his study as it was at his death. Note also the **Maiden Castle Gallery** (👤 *see below*) and the collection of local fossils.

Thomas Hardy (1840-1928)

Born at Higher Bockhampton, near Dorchester, the son of a stonemason, Thomas trained and worked as an architect (1856-72) before deciding to dedicate himself to writing. A number of his interconnected novels are set in Wessex, which he based on the Saxon Kingdom of Britain which then encompassed Dorset, Wiltshire, Hampshire, parts of Somerset, Oxfordshire and Berkshire: in short, the area linked by the chalk uplands. At the heart was Dorchester, which he renamed Casterbridge.

Excursions

Cerne Abbas★ – *8mi/13km north of Dorchester on A 352.* The 180ft/55m high chalk outline of a naked giant, cut out of the turf, has been connected, for obvious reasons, with local fertility rituals, although its origin and date remain unclear. The **village**★ is notable for the beautiful range of timber-fronted 16C houses in Abbey Street, and **St Mary's Church**, a mixture of Early English and Perpendicular, with a spectacular **tower** built in Ham Hill stone.

Milton Abbas★ – *12mi/19km northeast on A 35 and A 354 and by-road.* The **Abbey Church,** (*Open normally all year, daily, in daylight hours*) was rebuilt after a fire in 1309 in the Early English and Decorated styles, but work was stopped by the Black Death in 1348. Although 136ft/41m long (its size reminds us that it was intended to be a great medieval abbey, founded 934), the foreshortened church consists of an aisled presbytery, chancel, crossing and transepts only.

The 18C **house,** *(Burton Road. Open daily, 10am-6pm. Donation £2. Leaflet (4 languages). Parking. Refreshments (summer). 01258 880 489)* with its impressive **staterooms,** was built by Sir William Chambers for Lord Milton in the centre of a park designed by Capability Brown. He had the village rebuilt out of sight of the abbey; twin lines of identical thatched cob cottages marked in the centre by the 1786 church and the **Tregonwell Almshouses**, a rebuilding of the original 16C houses.

Bere Regis Church★ – *11mi/18km east on A 35.* The fine Perpendicular church of **St John the Baptist** is the only building in the village to have survived the last of a series of fires in 1788. Its **roof**★★ is a pure joy: a structure of oak tie beams and braces, posts outlined by cresting, filled with tracery, decorated in rich colours, with bosses masking the meeting points and the not-in-fact hammers disguised by almost life-size, clearly recognisable carved figures of the apostles. Note the capitals in the late 12C arcade with carved figures in agony with toothache and sore throat...

Clouds Hill – *(NT) Wareham, Open late-Mar to late-Oct, Thu-Sun and Bank Hol Mon, noon-5pm. Information Centre; guide book (Braille). £3.50. Parking. 01929 405 616; www.nationaltrust.org.uk.*

Maiden Castle★★ – *(EH) 2mi/3km southwest on A 354. Open daily, dawn-dusk. Parking.* Britain's finest **earthwork ramparts** were begun c 350 BC on the site of a Neolithic settlement dating back to c 3000 BC. There were four main building phases before this massive 47 acre/19ha complex was fully equipped with its defence system c 60 BC. However the hillfort was stormed by the future Roman Emperor Vespasian in AD 43, when his infantry cut through rampart after rampart, reached the inner bay and burnt the huts.

Chesil Beach★★ – *10mi/16km southwest via Martinstown, the Admiral Hardy Monument and Portesham.* Chesil Beach is a remarkable 8mi/13km shingle bank which forms a lagoon; at one end stands the village of **Abbotsbury**, which derives its name from an 11C Benedictine abbey, dissolved in 1541 and now a ruin. The unique **swannery**★ (*New Barn Road Open mid-Mar to early-Nov, daily, 10am-6pm (5pm last admission). £6.80. Guided tour (90min). Parking. Restaurant. Shop. 01305 871 858 (Swannery); 01305 871 130; Fax 01305 871 092; info@abbotsbury-tourism.co.uk; www. abbotsbury-tourism.co.uk),* was founded by the monks c 1390 and now accommodates more than 400 birds and their cygnets. The lushness of the **sub-tropical gardens**★ (*Bullers Way. Open daily 10am-6pm (4pm/dusk Nov-Feb); last admission 1hr before closing. £6.80. Parking. Colonial tea house. Plant centre. Gift shop. 01305 871 387; Fax 01305 871 092; info@abbotsbury-tourism.co.uk; www.abbotsbury-tourism.co.uk),* contrasts with the ruggedness of the wind-blown 14C **St Catherine's Chapel**★ *(EH Open any reasonable time)* on its 250ft/76m downland crest.

DOVER

Kent, ENGLAND

POPULATION 34 179

MICHELIN ATLAS P 13 OR MAP 504 X, Y 30

TOWN PLAN IN THE MICHELIN GUIDE GREAT BRITAIN AND IRELAND

Flanked by the famous white cliffs, Dover has been the south-east gateway to England since Roman times, receiving sailing ships, steam ships and hovercraft. The opening of the Channel Tunnel seems to have had only a marginal effect on the port's intense cross-Channel ferry traffic.

The town was badly damaged during the Second World War and of her two Norman churches, **St Mary's** survived; St James' stands in ruins. Of the other buildings the 14C **Maison Dieu**, the 17C **Maison Dieu House**, both in Biggin Street, and Philip Hardwick's late Regency **Waterloo Crescent**, have survived, giving Dover islands of elegance rare amongst working ports. *Old Town Gaol, Biggin Street ☎ 01304 205 108; Fax 01304 245 409; tic@doveruk.com; www.dover.org.uk.*

Sights

Castle★★ – (EH) Castle Hill Road. *Open daily, 10am-6pm, (5pm Oct, 4pm Nov-Mar). Closed 24-26 Dec, 1 Jan. £8.95. Guided tour of secret wartime tunnels, until one hour before closing. Audio guide (4 languages). Parking. Refreshments. Wheelchair access to grounds and secret wartime tunnels; medieval tunnels and upper floors inaccessible to wheelchairs. ☎ 01304 201 628 (infoline); 01304 211067 (office); www.english-heritage. org.uk.* The high land to the east, commanding town and port, has been fortified since the Iron Age. The Romans built a lighthouse (Pharos) which still stands within the castle walls, and the Saxons a church (St-Mary-in-Castro). The defences were strengthened by William the Conqueror, then by Henry II, who in the 1180s added the splendid **keep**, set within a curtain wall. The spectacular **Constable's Tower** dates from the early 13C.

The warren of tunnels and secret chambers beneath the Castle – the Underground Works – dates from early times but was greatly added to in the Napoleonic period and during the Second World War. Operation Dynamo, the evacuation of the British Expeditionary Force from Dunkirk in 1940 was planned and directed from here.

A guided tour of the **Secret Wartime Tunnels** takes visitors through the dimly-lit chambers and passageways of the underground hospital and communications centre for the Combined Headquarters, known as Hellfire Corner. Realistic sound effects and sometimes gruesome props evoke all the atmosphere of this truly Orwellian world which, in the event of nuclear Armageddon, would have become a Regional Seat of Government.

Town Centre – German bombs and shells from batteries on the French coast devastated Dover more than any other Kent town but, together with postwar redevelopment, helped reveal the archeology of this ancient port. The **Roman Painted House** *(New Street. Open Apr-Sep, Tue-Sun (also Mon and Bank Hols, Jul-Aug), 10am-5pm (last admission 4:30) (2 -5 Sun). Shop. £2. ☎ 01304 203 279; www.romans-in-britain. org.uk),* has the finest Roman wall-decorations to be seen in situ north of the Alps, as well as a section of the wall of the Saxon Shore Fort. The spacious **Dover Museum**, *(Market Square. Open daily, 10am-5.30pm. Closed 1 Jan and 25-26 Dec. £2. Restaurant. ☎ 01304 201 066; Fax 01304 241 186; museumenquiries@dover.gov.uk; www.dovermuseum.co.uk)* presents artefacts from all periods of the town's long history, including the 50ft/9.5m section of the 3 000-year-old **Dover Bronze Age boat** discovered nearby in 1992.

Western Heights – On the chalk downland rising from the harbour towards Shakespeare Cliff are some 2sq mi/5km2 of elaborate defences, among them the **Drop Redoubt** of 1808 and the unique triple staircase of the **Grand Shaft** (140ft/42m in height) to counter the threat of Napoleonic invasion.

Gateway to the White Cliffs *(NT) Upper Road. Open Mar-Oct, 10am-5pm; Nov-Feb, 11am-4pm. Closed 25 Dec. Car park open 8am-5pm (later in summer);. Audio-visual presentation. Coffee shop. Shop. ☎ 01304 202 756; Fax 01304 205 295; whitecliffs@nationaltrust.org.uk; www.nationaltrust.org.uk.*

Excursions

Deal – A modern pier protrudes eastwards from Deal's shingle beach towards the notorious wreck-littered Goodwin Sands. Landward is a long line of mostly Georgian houses, backed by narrow streets of fishermen's cottages. The solid, Tudor-rose shaped **Deal Castle** *(EH. 8.5mi/14km east by A 258. &. Open late-Mar-Sep daily, 10am-6pm. Closed 1 Jan and 24-26 Dec. £3.70 Audio guide (3 languages). Parking. Refreshments. Wheelchair access to groundfloor and courtyards only. ☎ 01304 372 762; 369 576; www. english-heritage.org.uk),* was built in Henry VIII's reign, the 'petals' being bastions from which heavy guns could withstand attack from the sea. In contrast, its twin, **Walmer Castle** *(EH. 1mi/2km south &. Open Mar-Oct, daily, 10am-6pm (4pm Mar and Oct). Closed 1 Jan and 24-26 Dec and during residence of the Lord Warden. Audio tour. £5.95 Parking. Wheelchair access to courtyard and garden only. ☎ 01304 369 576; www.english-heritage.org.uk)* was transformed in the 18C into an elegant house with charming **gardens**, the official residence of the Lords Warden of the Cinque Ports – a confederation of English Channel seaports which came together formally around the 13C. Elizabeth, the late Queen Mother (1900-2002) was a recent Lord Warden. Memorabilia of past wardens includes the original boots of the Duke of Wellington and the chair in which he died in 1852.

Folkestone – *8mi/13km west by A 20*. Once a rival to Dover as a Channel ferry port, Folkestone is now served only by a Seacat link to Boulogne. On the clifftop to the west is a splendid grassy promenade, **The Leas**★, laid out in the mid-19C at the height of the town's heyday as a fashionable resort. The magnificent seaward **panorama**★ extends to the coast of France on clear days. Near **The Bayle,** the site of an ancient castle, is the Church of St Mary and St Eanswyth, founded in the 12C. Immediately to the north of the town at the foot of the North Downs is the English portal of the **Channel Tunnel** and the complex of buildings, loading facilities and railway tracks that make up the terminal.

In the summer of 1940 the Battle of Britain was largely fought in Kentish skies. This epic of the air is commemorated by the **Battle of Britain Memorial** *(Capel, off A 20 between Folkestone and Dover Open Mon-Fri, 10am-5pm (subject to availability of volunteers); at other times entry through side gate with walk to the Memorial. Parking. Guide book. Shop. ☎ 01303 249 292; 276 697),* where the stone figure of a sitting airman gazes seaward from the clifftop, and at the **Kent Battle of Britain Museum** *(Aerodrome Road, Folkestone &. Tue-Sun, 10am-5pm; last admission 1hr before closing. £4.50. No dogs. Parking. No cameras. Ramps. ☎ 01303 893 140; kentbattleofbritain@internet.com; www.kentbattleofbritainmuseum.org.uk).* The impact of the museum's array of artefacts is enhanced by their display in the buildings of the former Fighter Command airfield.

Hythe – *14mi/23km west by A 20 and A 259*. The High Street of this Cinque Port is now half a mile/nearly 1km from the modern seafront promenade, as Hythe Haven silted up centuries ago.

Picturesque alleyways rise steeply to **St Leonard's Church,** *(Oak Walk. Open daily, 8am-5pm. Crypt: Open May-Sept, 10.30am-noon and 2.30pm-4pm. Church: no charge; crypt: 50p. ☎ 01303 263 739; secretary@stleonardschurchhythe.co.uk; www. stleonardschurch.com)* perched imposingly halfway up the former cliff. The beautiful 13C **chancel** is unusually ambitious for a parish church, a reflection of the town's ancient prosperity. In the vault is a macabre ossuary of 500 skulls and countless thighbones. From the church over the roofs to the town may be enjoyed fine **views** of the Channel and of the coastline of Romney Marsh (see RYE) curving away to the remote spit of Dungeness.

The **Royal Military Canal**, linking Hythe and Rye, and three martello towers on the seafront were part of the coastal defences against attacks by Napoleonic forces. The canal banks are the setting for a biennial water carnival, the **Venetian Fête** *(August, odd years)*. Hythe is also the terminus of the famous miniature Romney, Hythe and Dymchurch Railway *(see RYE).*

Howlett's Wild Animal Park – *16mi/26km west by A 20, A 259, B 2067 and local road.* &. Bekesbourne Road. Open daily , from 10am-6pm (4.30pm last admission); winter, 10am-dusk (3.30pm last admission). £12.95. Safari shuttle service around park, (small charge). Parking. Licensed restaurant. ☎ 01227 721 286; Fax 01303 264 944; www.howletts.net. In 1912 Sir Philip Sassoon built the red brick house and laid out the large **gardens** which command extensive **views** over Romney Marsh to the sea. Inside there is a fascinating trompe l'oeil **Tent Room,** painted by Rex Whistler and an Asian animals **mural** by Spencer Roberts. Outside, the rhinos, tigers, lions, elephants and other animals of the Zoo Park disport themselves in enclosures and on the open slopes below.

DUMFRIES ★

Dumfries and Galloway, SCOTLAND

POPULATION 21 164

MICHELIN ATLAS P 49 OR MAP 501 J 18

TOWN PLAN IN THE MICHELIN GUIDE GREAT BRITAIN AND IRELAND

Dumfries, "Queen of the South", has long been the chief town of Scotland's southwest and is probably best known for its historical associations. Robert the Bruce (1306-29) started his long campaign to free Scotland from Edward I in Dumfries by killing John Comyn, one of the Competitors for the crown, and having himself crowned at Scone in 1306. Eight years later, his victory at Bannockburn was crucial in achieving Scotland's independence. The Dervorgilla Bridge commemorates Dervorgilla, wife of the Competitor John Balliol and founder of Sweetheart Abbey (below), who built a wooden bridge across the Nith in the 1270s; it was replaced by the present narrow six-arch bridge in the 15C. The poet Robert Burns, who epitomized the national spirit, was its most famous citizen. *64 Whitesands DG1 2RS ☎ 01387 253 862; Fax : 01387 245 555 64; info@dgtb.visitscotland. com; www.visitdumfriesand galloway.co.uk.*

Excursions

Drumlanrig Castle★★

18mi/29km northwest by A 76. Castle and garden: ☐ Open May-Aug, daily, noon-5pm (4pm last admission). Country Park and Gardens: Open early-May to Sep, daily, 11am-5pm. Castle £7, grounds only, £3 . Audio-visual presentation. Adventure playground. Parking. Licensed restaurant. ☎ 01848 330 248; bre@drumlanrigcastle.org.uk; www. buccleuch.com. The castle was a Douglas stronghold from the 14C until the 18C. In the 17C William, 1st Duke of Queensberry, built a mansion worthy of his station; he was so appalled by the cost, however, that he spent only one night there before returning to the family seat at Sanquhar. James, 2nd Duke, was the High Commissioner who presented the Treaty of Union to Queen Anne in 1707. The property now belongs to the Montagu-Douglas-Scott family.

The castle stands impressively with four square towers quartering – in true native tradition – the courtyard structure. Innovation comes with the main façade and its terraces, horseshoe staircase, dramatic turreted skyline and rich sculptural detail such as the entrance breast with ducal crown aloft.

Interior – There is a varied and superb collection of paintings, including a Holbein, a Leonardo and Rembrandt's *Old Woman Reading* (1655), and fine furniture and clocks can be admired throughout the castle. In the oak-panelled Dining Room, carved panels attributed to Grinling Gibbons alternate with 17C silver sconces and family portraits. The Douglas crest of the "winged heart" appears on plasterwork, on wall hangings and wood carvings and even on picture frames, to remind the visitor that Drumlanrig is a Douglas seat.

Sweetheart Abbey★

(HS) 8mil/13km southwest by the New Abbey Road, A 710. ☐ Open daily, 9.30am - 6.30pm; Oct-Mar 9.30am (2pm Fri, Sun) to 4.30pm (noon Thu). £2. Parking. ☎ 01387 850 397; www.historic-scotland.gov.uk. Sweetheart, which was founded in 1273 by Dervorgilla, was the last Cistercian foundation in Scotland. Its name derives from the fact that the foundress was laid to rest in the presbytery together with a casket containing the embalmed heart of her husband. The beauty and charm of the ruins are enhanced by the contrast between the warm red sandstone and the clipped green of the surrounding lawns.

▶ *On the way back to Dumfries turn left just out of New Abbey.*

Shambellie House – *(New Abbey. ☐ Open Apr-Oct, daily, 11am-5pm. £3. Room guide (3 languages). Parking. Tearoom, picnic area. ☎ 01387 850 375; Fax 01387 850 461; www. nms.ac.uk)* Don't miss the delightfully presented **costume collection**★, donated to the Royal Scottish Museum in 1977 by Charles Stewart. Both historical and modern costumes are displayed in the charming setting of a small country house.

Robert Burns (1759-96)

The bard lived and farmed in and around the town. A statue stands at the north end of the High Street. The **Robert Burns Centre** *(Mill Road ♿ ◷ Open Apr-Sep, Mon-Sat, 10am-8pm, Sun, 2-5pm; Oct-Mar, Tue-Sat, 10am-1pm and 2-5pm. Audio-visual theatre Free admission. Leaflet (6 languages). Parking. ☎ 01387 264 808; Fax 01387 265 081; info@ dumfriesmuseum.demon.co.uk; www.dumfriesmuseum.demon.co.uk)*, is an excellent introduction to Burns who spent the last few years of his life at **Burns House**, *now a museum, (◷ Open Apr-Sep, daily, 10am (2pm Sun) to 5pm; Oct-Mar, Tue-Sat, 10am-1pm and 2-5pm Sun. Leaflet (7 languages). Free admission ☎ 01387 255 297; www.dum-friesmuseum.demon.co.uk)* after giving up his farm at **Ellisland**, *(◷ Hollywood Road. Open Apr-Sep, daily, 10am-1pm and 2-5pm (Sun 2-5pm); Oct-Mar, Tue-Sat, 10am-5pm; otherwise by appointment. ⬟ £2.50. Audio-visual presentation. ☎ 01387 740 426; www. ellislandfarm.co.uk)* outside Dumfries, and taking up a post with the Excise. Behind the Old Red sandstone church is a **mausoleum** where Burns, his wife Jane Armour and several of their children are buried. **Alloway** *(3mi/5km south of Ayr)*, his birthplace, is also on the **Burns Trail** *(leaflets from local tourist information centres)*.

Caerlaverock Castle★

(HS) 9mi/15km southeast by B 725; bear right at Bankend. ♿ ◷ *Open daily, 9.30am (2pm Sun Nov-Mar) to 6.30pm (4.30pm Nov-Mar). ⬟£4. Audio-visual presentation. Parking. Restaurant, tearoom. Picnic area. ☎ 01387 770 244; www.historic-scotland. gov.uk.* Overlooking the Solway Firth, this imposing medieval castle is girt by a moat and earthen ramparts. Its formidable machicolated exterior with a keep gatehouse and curtain walls is in sharp contrast to the harmonious **Renaissance courtyard façade★★**. The castle, which was besieged by Edward I in 1300 and later became the principal seat of the Maxwells, was abandoned in the 17C.

Ruthwell Cross★

(HS) 16mi/26km by B 725; fork left at Bankend. ◷ Key available from the modern bun-galow on B 724 or from the old manse (now a small country hotel). In the church stands the 7C Ruthwell Cross which depicts the Life and Passion of Christ; it is an outstanding example of **early Christian art**. The tracery, animals and birds, together with runic inscriptions are a credit to the artistry and skill of the sculptor. The cross was demol-ished in 1642 on orders from the General Assembly; the pieces were re-assembled in the 19C by the Rev Dr Henry Duncan and installed in the church in 1887. Duncan's other claim to fame was the founding, in Ruthwell in 1810, of the first Savings Bank, forerunner of today's widespread movement.

DUNDEE★

City of Dundee, SCOTLAND

POPULATION 165 873

MICHELIN ATLAS P 62 OR MAP 501 K, L 14

TOWN PLAN IN THE MICHELIN GUIDE GREAT BRITAIN AND IRELAND

Dundee enjoys an almost perfect situation on the northern shore of the River Tay on Scotland's east coast, with the Sidlaw Hills as a backdrop. As Scotland's fourth city, it is a busy seaport, an educational centre and the capital of the Tayside region. Prosperity accrued from the three "j"s – jute, jam (Mrs Keiller first made her re-nowned **marmalade** in 1797) and journalism in the Victorian era. The adhesive postage stamp was invented by **James Chalmers** (1823-53), a local man, and the Thomson publishing empire originated in Dundee. The town became Britain's chief whaling port in the 1860s. Traditional activities (whaling, jute milling) have now given way to modern, high-technology industries.

The railway bridge, built in 1878 to replace the world's first train ferry (1850) across the Tay estuary, collapsed on a stormy winter night in December 1879 with the loss of 75 lives. Ten years later the Tay and the Forth estuaries were successfully bridged. ⬚ *21 Castle Street, Dundee DD1 3AA ☎ 01382 527 527; Fax 01382 434 665; enquiries@angusand dundee.co.uk; www.angusanddundee.co.uk.*

Sights

The Frigate Unicorn★ – *Victoria Dock.* &⊘ *Open Apr-Oct, daily, 10am-5pm; Nov-Mar, Wed-Sun, noon-4pm (10am Sun).* ⊘ *Closed 1 Jan and 24-26 Dec.* ⊛ *£3.50. Parking. Tearoom, picinic areas.* ☎ *01382 200 900; frigateunicorn@hotmail.com; www.frigateu-nicorn.org.* The Unicorn was launched in 1824 as a 46-gun frigate for the Royal Navy. She is now the oldest British-built ship still afloat. Visitors can explore the main gun decks, with their 18-pounders and the Captain's and officers' quarters and discover the flavour of life in the Royal Navy in the golden age of sail.

Discovery Point★ – *Discovery Quay, Craig Harbour.* &⊘ *Open daily, 10am (11am Sun) to 6pm (5pm Nov-Mar).* ⊘ *Closed 25 Dec, 1-2 Jan.* ⊛ *£6.45 (joint ticket available with Verdant Works).* ⟷ *Guided tour by appointment. Parking. Café. Shop. Wheelchairs available.* ☎ *01382 201 245; Fax 01382 225 891; info@dundeeheritage.sol.co.uk; www.rrsdiscovery.com.* The **RRS Discovery★**, which was custom-built in Dundee in 1901 for scientific exploration, is the pride of the city. It forms the centrepiece of an exciting exhibition, with a spectacular audio-visual presentation devoted to Captain Scott's Antarctic Expedition (1901-04), the vessel's dramatic rescue and other journeys.

McManus Galleries★ – *Albert Square.* &⊘ *Open Mon-Sat, 10.30am-5pm (7pm Thu), Sun, 12.30-4pm.* ⊘ *Closed 25-26 Dec, 1-3 Jan. Café.* ☎ *01382 432084; Fax 01382 432052; mcmanus.galleries@dundeecity.gov.* A fine Victorian Gothic building houses the city's art gallery and museum. There are excellent displays on the city's traditional activities, portraits and **Scottish paintings** and an original array of arts and crafts in the splendid **Albert Hall.**

Verdant Works★ – *West Henderson's Wynd.* &⊘ *Open daily, 10am (11am Sun) to 6pm (5pm Nov-Mar).* ⊛ *£5.95 (joint ticket with Discovery Point). Audio-visual presentation. Leaflet. Parking. Café. Shop.* ☎ *01382 225 282; Fax 01382 221 612; info@dundeeheritage. sol.co.uk; www.verdantworks.com.* A jute mill which has been converted into a museum tells the story of the jute industry which expanded worldwide.

Behind the impressive new **Dundee Contemporary Arts Centre** on Nethergate is **Sensation,** (&*Greenmarket.* ⊘*Open daily Apr-Oct 10am-6pm, Nov-Mar 10am-5pm* ⊛ *£6.50. Shop. Cafe.* ☎ *01382 228800; staff@sensation.org.uk; www.sensation.org. uk)* an award-winning hands-on science centre.

Excursions

Broughty Ferry – *3mi/5km east by A 930.* Leaving Dundee along the coast, the road passes some of the substantial houses built by the 19C jute "barons". Broughty Ferry was the ferry terminus in the 1850s and has become Dundee's own seaside resort today. **Broughty Castle Museum**, located in the restored 15C fort, (⊘ *daily, 10am (12.30pm Sun) to 4pm; early-Oct to Mar, Tue-Sun, 10am (12.30pm Sun) to 4pm.* ⊘ *Closed 1 Jan and 25-26 Dec.* ☎ *01382 436916; Fax 01382 436951; broughty@dundeecity.gov.uk; www.dundeedcastle.gov.uk/broughtycastle)* has an interesting section on whaling. Just to the north is **Claypotts Castle,** *(HS Arbroath Road.* ⊘*Limited opening hours; check by phone.* ☎ *01786 450 000)* a perfect example of a 16C Z-plan tower house, with rounded towers at the opposite corners of the rectangular centrepiece.

Arbroath★ – *16mi/26km east by A 94.* This fishing port on the Angus coast is famous for its abbey, although there are those who remember it also for its "smokies" – flavourful smoked haddock. The **Abbey,** *(HS* ⊘ *Open daily, Apr-Sep, daily, 9.30am-6.30pm; Oct-Mar, daily, 9.30am (2pm Fri, Sun) to 4.30pm, Closed 25, 26 Dec and 1,2 Jan.* ⊛*£3.30 Parking.* ☎ *01241 878 756; www.historic-scotland.gov.uk)* was founded by William the Lion, in 1178, in memory of his childhood friend, Thomas Becket, murdered in Canterbury eight years previously. William died before the abbey was finished and is buried before the High Altar. The **Declaration of Arbroath** was drawn up and signed here on 6 April 1320, asserting Scotland's independence. Even as they are now, these "fragments of magnificence", as Dr Johnson called them, give some idea of its former splendour.

DUNFERMLINE ★

Fife, SCOTLAND

POPULATION 29 436

MICHELIN ATLAS P 56 OR MAP 501 J 15

Dunfermline, the former capital of Scotland, lies immediately north of the present capital, Edinburgh, across the Firth of Forth. It figures frequently in Scottish history, largely in association with its great abbey and royal palace. It has long been a thriving industrial centre, with coal mining and linen weaving, and new industries maintain this tradition today. *1 High Street, Dunfermline (Easter-Oct) KY12 7DL ☎ 01383 720 999; Fax 01383 730 187.*

A Bit of History

Royal residence – Malcolm Canmore (c 1031-93) sheltered the heir to the English throne, **Edgar Atheling** and his family, fleeing from William the Conqueror after Hastings (1066). Edgar's sister **Margaret** married the Scots king in 1070. She was a devout Catholic and was largely responsible for introducing the ideas which gradually supplanted the rituals of the Celtic church. The Benedictine abbey was founded by **David I**, son of Queen Margaret. It grew in importance with the revenues from coal, salt panning, land and ferry dues and the town prospered with it until, following the untimely deaths of Alexander III and Margaret of Norway, Edward I of England was called in as mediator in the struggle for succession. On his departure in 1304 the monastic buildings were a smouldering ruin.

Robert the Bruce (1274-1329) helped with the reconstruction and is buried in the abbey – although his heart is in Melrose Abbey, in the Borders.

The guest house was refurbished for James V's French wife, but it was James VI (James I of England) who gave the palace to his Queen, Anne of Denmark, and it was here that Charles I was born, together with his sister, the Winter Queen. There were fleeting royal visits, after the Union of the Crowns in 1603, under the Stuarts, but the palace was never again a royal residence for long.

Sights

Dunfermline Abbey★ – (HS) ♿ ◷ *Open daily, 9.30am-6.30pm (4:30 Oct-Mar).* ⊸ *£2.50.* ⚬ *Guided tour. Parking.* ☎ *01383 739 026; www.historic-scotland.gov.uk.* The 11C Benedictine abbey was founded on the site of a Celtic church. The Norman nave of the **abbey church★★** with its massive pillars and round-headed arches is one of the finest in Scotland. The east end (rebuilt in the early 19C) serves as the parish church; a memorial brass marks the tomb of Robert the Bruce. There are few remains of the great monastic ensemble. **Abbot House** (♿◷ *Maygate. Open daily, 10am-5pm (4.15pm last admission).* ◷ *Closed 1 Jan and 25 Dec.* ⊸ *£3. Parking. Refreshments.* ☎ *01383 733 266; Fax 01383 624 908; dht@abbothouse.fsnet.co.uk; www.abbothouse.co.uk)* is now a heritage centre.

Andrew Carnegie Birthplace – *Moodie Street.* ♿◷ *Open Apr-Oct, daily, 11am (2pm Sun) to 5pm.* ⊸ *£2.* ⚬ *Guided tour by appointment. Weaving demonstration: May-Oct, first Friday of month. Brief guide (7 languages).* ☎ *01383 724 302; Fax 01383 721 862; carnegiebirthplace@hotmail.com; www.carnegiemuseum.com; www.carnegiebirthplace. com.* The self-made steel baron and great philanthropist, Andrew Carnegie (1835-1919) was born in this house before emigrating to America with his family in 1848. An exhibition traces his life and work.

Excursions

Loch Leven Castle

(HS)12mi/19km north by M 90. Ferry service from Kinross. ◷*Open Apr-Sep, daily, 9.30am-6.30pm.* ⊸ *£3.50 including ferry trip. Parking. Picnic area.* ☎ *07778 040 483; www. historic-scotland.gov.uk.* Mary Queen of Scots was imprisoned on this island stronghold from June 1567 until her escape the following May. The Douglas fortress comprises a 14C tower with its entrance at second-floor level, and a later curtain wall.

Culross★★

13mi/21km east by A 944 and B 9037. According to legend St Mungo, patron saint of Glasgow was born in this small burgh on the north shore of the Firth of Forth. A Cistercian house was founded here in the 13C. Trade with the Low Countries, salt panning and coal mining brought prosperity to the town which was accorded the status of Royal Burgh by James VI in 1588.

Culross (pronounced Coo' ross) is justly famous for its fine examples of Scottish vernacular architecture of the 16C and 17C in all its rich detail. The small buildings in the **village**★★★ feature inscribed lintels, decorative finials, skewputts, crow-stepped gables, forestairs, harling and rubble stonework with door and window trims. The **Town House** *(NTS – same ticket to Study and Palace* ♿🕑 *Open late-Jun to early Sep, daily, 10am - 6pm; late-Mar to Sep, daily, noon-5pm, garden all year 10am - dusk.* ☞ *£8. Parking. Shop. Refreshments.* ☎ *01383 880 359; Fax 01383 882 675; cwhite@nts.org.uk; www.nts.org.uk)* is a stone and slate building erected in 1625 in Flemish style; it contrasts with the white harling and red pantiles of the surrounding buildings. The Back Causeway, behind, has a central line of raised paving stones for the exclusive use of local notables. Opposite **The Study**★, which has a 17C painted ceiling (restored) and original panelling, is the oldest house in Culross with a replica of the 1588 mercat cross in front of its gable end.

The **Palace**★★, a comfortable house built (1597-1611) by George Bruce, a rich merchant and coalmine owner, boasts pine-panelled rooms and 21 fireplaces which burnt coal rather than logs. Dutch tiles carried as ballast in his ships were used for flooring and roofing.

Falkland★

31mi/48km northeast by M 90, A 91 and A 312. The ancient royal burgh has retained its original character; the wynds and streets around the palace are lined with mansions decorated with carved lintel and marriage stones, harled and red-pantiled buildings and single-storey cottages built in vernacular style by court officials, servants and tradesmen.

Falkland Palace★ – **(NTS)** ♿ 🕑 *Open Mar to late-Oct, daily, 10am (1pm Sun) to 6pm (5:30pm Sun). Last admission 1 hr before closing. Palace and gardens* ☞ *£10;. Leaflet (8 languages). Guide book (3 languages).* ☞ *Guided tour (45min).* ☎ *01337 857 397; Fax 01337 857 980; www.nts.org.uk.* The hunting-seat of the earls of Fife passed to the crown in 1425 and became one of the Stewarts' favourite royal palaces. The gatehouse and street façade built in Gothic style by James IV, a Renaissance monarch who entertained a splendid court, is in sharp contrast with the Renaissance ornament of the courtyard façade of the south range added by his son, James V who took a French bride. A tour of the interior includes the Keeper's apartments in the gatehouse adorned with royal portraits, coats of arms and elegant furnishings. The east range contained the royal apartments. The first floor affords a good view of the south range front. At the far end of the attractive **gardens**★ is a Real (Royal) Tennis court.

The Palace, Culross

B. Kaufmann/MICHELIN

DURHAM★★★

Durham , ENGLAND

POPULATION 36 937

MICHELIN ATLAS P 46 OR MAP 501 P 19

TOWN PLAN IN THE MICHELIN GUIDE GREAT BRITAIN AND IRELAND

The quiet streets of the little medieval city with its castle are the perfect foil for the great sandstone mass of the Norman cathedral rising above the deep wooded gorge of the River Wear in a sublime fusion of architecture and landscape, in what is a truly remarkable setting★★★. 🞂 2 Millennium Place, Durham, DH1 1WA ☎ 0191 384 3720; Fax 0191 386 3015; touristinfo@durhamcity.gov.uk; www. durhamcity.gov.uk

▶ **Orient Yourself**: You can see this compact little city quite easily on foot; for an alternative view, boat trips are available and rowing boats are for hire.

🞂 **Don't Miss**: The Cathedral's Chapel of the Nine Altars; the riverside views from or near Prebend's Bridge.

🕚 **Organizing Your Time**: Allow half a day.

A Bit of History

Christianity flourished early in the Saxon Kingdom of Northumbria but conditions were rarely stable in this border country with its coastline exposed to raiders from the east. In 875 the monks of Lindisfarne fled south from Danish attacks, carrying with them the body of **St Cuthbert**

> ### 🞂 Touring Tip 🞂
> It is advisable to use the car parks on the edge of the city centre, as parking is difficult near the Cathedral and Castle.

(d 687) but it was not until more than 100 years later that his much venerated remains found their final resting place on easily defended bluffs carved out by the Wear. From the 1070s the site's natural advantages were strengthened by the Normans, who built their castle to command the peninsula's narrow neck. In 1093 the cathedral's foundation stone was laid. Uniquely in England, Durham's bishop was not only spiritual leader but lay lord, the powerful Prince Palatine of a long-troubled province.

The city has remained compact, physically unaffected by the once intense industrial activity all around it. Its scholarly character was confirmed with the foundation in 1832 of the University, after Oxford and Cambridge England's oldest. It is also the county town, an important administrative and shopping centre. On the second Saturday in July, it is thronged with the thousands attending one of Britain's great popular festivals of modern times, the famous Miners' Gala.

Cathedral★★★ 1hr

♿🕚 Open daily, mid-Jun to early-Sep, 9.30am-8pm; early-Sep to mid-Jun, Mon-Sat, 7.30am-6.15pm, Sun, 7.45am-5pm. 🕚Closed during recitals and concerts. 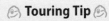 Guided tour (1hr): Sat 1 Jun to Sat 8 Jun, daily (except Sun 2 Jun) at 11am and 2.30pm; mid-Jun to mid-Jul, Sat at 11am and 2.30pm; late-Jul to late-Sep, Mon-Sat, at 11am and 2.30pm; also late-Jul to late-Aug, Sat at 6.15pm, Sun at 5pm. Monks' dormitory: Apr to late-Sep, daily, 10am (12.30pm Sun) to 3.30pm, (3.15pm Sun). Tower: 🕚Open (services and weather permitting) Apr to late-Sep, Mon-Sat, 9.30am-4pm; late-Sep to late Mar, Mon-Sat, 10am-3pm. Services: Sun at 8am (Holy Communion), 10am (Choral Matins), 11.15am (Sung Holy Communion), 3.30pm (Choral Evensong). ☞ Donation £3; Treasury £2; A/v presentation 80p; Dormitory 80p; ☞ guided tour £3.50; tower £2. Guide (7 languages). No photography within the cathedral. Bookshop. Restaurant. ☎0191 386 4266 (Chapter Office); Fax 0191 386 4267; enquiries@durhamcathedral.co.uk; www.durhamcathedral. co.uk. Durham's beauty lies in its unity: its fabric was mostly completed in the short period between 1095 and 1133 and though added to since, it remains a supremely harmonious achievement of Norman architecture on the grandest possible scale.

Exterior – The calm and level space of **Palace Green**, bounded to the north by the castle wall and to the east and west by a mixture of university buildings, is dominated by the imposing north elevation of the Cathedral running its entire width. The solemn rhythm of nave and chancel is set off by the two west towers, richly decorated, by the high central tower, mostly 15C and, to the east, by the great Early English Chapel of the Nine Altars.

Durham Cathedral

B. Kaufmann/MICHELIN

The usual entrance is the northwest portal, which has many arches and is embellished with the celebrated lion's head **Sanctuary Knocker**★, a 12C masterpiece of expressive stylisation.

Interior – In the **nave**★★★ the first impression is one of overwhelming power. Huge deeply-grooved columns alternate with massive many-shafted piers to form an arcade supporting a gallery and clerestory. The pointed ribs of the beautiful vault are an important technical and aesthetic innovation, heralding the lightness and grace of Gothic architecture. The great weight of masonry, its arches enriched with various zig-zag patterning, is however so well proportioned that the final effect is one of repose, of great forces held in equilibrium.

From the crossing there is a stupendous view up into the vault under the central tower, while in the south transept is an extraordinary brightly painted 16C clock. In the choir there are fine **stalls** and the splendidly vain **throne** and **tomb** of the 14C Bishop Hatfield. Beyond the 14C **Neville Screen** with its delicate stonework is the **shrine of St Cuthbert**.

The 13C **Chapel of the Nine Altars**★★★, an earlier example of which is to be found at Fountains Abbey, is an Early English addition to the cathedral. The sunken floor, designed to gain as much height as possible, and the extravagantly tall lancet windows, which are separated by columns of clustered shafts, reveal a new preoccupation with lightness and verticality. The carved stonework of the bosses and capitals is extremely rich.

At the extreme western end of the building, perched on the very edge of the ravine, is the **Galilee Chapel**. Twelve slender columns, their arches profusely decorated with zig-zag carvings, subdivide the interior, which contains the tomb of the **Venerable Bede** (d 735), England's first historian.

From the top of the cathedral's central tower *(a long climb of 325 steps: access from south transept)* spectacular **views**★ reinforce the full drama of Durham's site.

Monastic buildings – Around the much rebuilt cloisters are grouped the buildings of the former abbey. They include the monks' dormitory and the **Cathedral Treasury**★, with its collection of Anglo-Saxon embroideries, precious objects and manuscripts and, above all, the evocative relics associated with St Cuthbert – his tiny portable altar, his pectoral cross, fragments of his oak coffin... To the south is the tranquil precinct of **The College**, its mellow, mostly 18C buildings resting on medieval foundations.

Additional Sights

Castle★ – *Guided tour (45min) during university vacations. Open daily, late Mar–Sept, 10am-noon and 2-4.30pm; in term time, Mon, Wed, Sat-Sun, 2-4pm. Closed Christmas* *vacation.* ☎ *£5. Guide book £2.50.* ☎ *0191 374 3800; Fax 0191 374 7470; j.a.marshall@ durham.ac.uk; www.durhamcastle.com.* The Norman architecture of the castle was much modified by successive Prince Bishops. The building now forms part of Durham University, the **keep** having been converted into student residences as early as 1840.

From the courtyard, protected by the much rebuilt gatehouse and overlooked by the keep on its great earth mound, the visitor is taken via the 15C **kitchen** into the imposing **Great Hall,** then to galleries built around the original castle wall, whose fine arched doorway is still intact. The upper floors are reached by the broad steps of the spectacular **Black Staircase** of 1662. There are two chapels, one of the 16C with humorous misericords including a bagpipe-playing pig and a nagging wife in a wheelbarrow. The **Norman chapel**★, deep below, dates from the castle's earliest days and evokes a more primitive world, with its close-set columns hewn from a strangely patterned sandstone and capitals crudely ornamented with weird figures and savage faces.

City and riverside – Most traffic has been removed from the centre and some streets have been attractively repaved. From the **Market Place**, sited at the very neck of the peninsula and mostly 19C in character, streets descend steeply to the sloping Elvet Bridge on the east and to **Framwellgate Bridge** on the west. From here there is a fine **view**★★ upstream of the Cathedral with the stern walls of the Castle in the foreground.

North Bailey and **South Bailey**, with their many pleasant 18C houses, follow the line of the town wall. Near the church of St Mary-le-Bow, now housing the Durham Heritage Centre, a lane leads downhill to Kingsgate footbridge of 1963, elegantly spanning the gorge to link the city with the uncompromisingly modern building of the University Students' Union, **Dunelm House**. South Bailey ends at the Watergate, from which a track leads down to **Prebends' Bridge**. From here, from the path on the far bank and from the riverside itself are those **views**★★★ which have long captivated writers and artists; a perfect composition is created by the elements of water, massed trees and humble mill buildings enhancing the grandeur of the noble architecture above.

Oriental Museum★★ **(Durham University)** – *From the city centre take A 1050 and A 167 south towards Darlington.* ♿ *Elvet Hill, off South Road.* ⏰*Open daily, 10am (noon Sat-Sun) to 5pm.* ⏰ *Closed 24 Dec-1 Jan.* ☎ *£1.50. Parking. Refreshments.* ☎ *0191 334 5694 Fax 0191 374 7911; oriental.museum@durham.ac.uk; www.dur.ac.uk/oriental. museum.* In a leafy setting among other buildings of the University of which it forms part is this modern museum, a treasure house of oriental art and artefacts. Its changing displays range from Ancient Egypt via India and South East Asia to Japan, but of outstanding interest are ceramics, a range of jade and other hardstone pieces and an extraordinary room-like bed, all from China.

Durham Light Infantry Museum – *Aykley Heads, 1.5mi/2.5km northwest on A 691 and B 6532.* ⏰ *Open daily, 10am-5pm (4pm Nov-Mar).* ☎ *£3.* ☎*0191 384 2214; dli@durham. gov.uk; www.durham.gov.uk/dli.* A modern building set in an attractive park near a river houses exhibitions tracing the 200-year history of the county regiment, using weapons, uniforms and photographs. Other displays include a hands-on exhibition about life in County Durham during the Second World War. Crafts and sculpture are displayed in an upper-floor gallery.

Excursions

Hartlepool Historic Quay★ – *Jackson Dock, 14mi/23km southeast. Maritime Avenue.* ⏰*Open daily, 10am-5pm.* ⏰ *Closed 25-26 Dec, 1 Jan.* ☎ *£5.50.* ☎ *01429 860 006; hartlepool.quay@hartlepool.gov.uk.* The masts of HMS *Trincomalee*, an 1817 frigate, tower above the smartly restored quayside off the road towards Hartlepool's modern docks. Re-created 19C buildings include a prison for French POWs, Cornelius Mumford's printers' shop and a ships' chandlers, and galleries house displays on naval life and the empire and ship surgery among other related themes. The **Museum of Hartlepool,** on the same site, has remains of an Anglo-Saxon monastery and a medieval sea port.

Killhope The North of England Lead Mining Museum – *28mi/45km west on A 689, beyond Cowshill.* ⏰ *Open late Mar -Oct, daily, 10.30am-5pm; Oct, Sat-Sun and at half term.* ☎ *£4.50; £6 including trip down Park Level Mine.* ☎ *01388 537 505; killhope@ durham.gov.uk; www.durham.gov.uk/killhope.* There are marvellous **views** of the remote North Pennine countryside on the approach road to Killhope, which sits low in a valley surrounded by sheep farms. This was prime lead-mining country in the 19C and the stone mine buildings, tramways and huge water wheel illustrate the harsh working conditions of the time. An exhibition explores the area's history through the lives of two past inhabitants, William and Phoebe Millaun.

EASTBOURNE

East Sussex, ENGLAND

POPULATION 94 793
MICHELIN ATLAS P 12 OR MAP 504 U 31
TOWN PLAN IN THE GUIDE GREAT BRITAIN AND IRELAND

An unassuming farming village sheltered by the South Downs was transformed into England's most gentlemanly resort by William Cavendish, Duke of Devonshire (1808-91). Careful development of his estates from the 1850s onward created a decorous seaside town of dignified hotels and picturesque villas in tree-lined roads. Eastbourne is no longer as gracious as it once was and is now better known as a retirement haven. It continues to attract visitors – who, like Claude Debussy who wrote part of *La Mer* while here, appreciate a place "where the sea displays herself in strict British correctness." *3 Cornfield Road BN21 4QL ☎ 01323 411 400; Fax 01323 649 574; www.eastbourne.org/tourism.*

Visit

Seafront★ – Eastbourne's long southeast-facing promenade is backed by trim lawns and carefully tended flower beds. The holiday mood is set by the spick and span pier of 1870 and continued by the remarkable bandstand of 1935 on the lower promenade. This central part of the seafront is defined by defence works of Napoleon's time; eastwards the great **Redoubt** (military museums); to the west, on rising ground and giving good views, the **Wish Tower.** Beyond, the clifftop rises via King Edward's Parade to the foot of the Downs, while the lower promenade leads to gardens with fine views across the bay to Hastings.

Eastbourne Heritage Centre – *Near the Congress Theatre. 2 Carlisle Road.* ◔*Open Apr -Oct, Sun-Fri, 2-5pm.* ∞ *£1. Audio visual presentation (20min).* ☎ *01323 721 825; owenboydell@tinyworldco.uk; www.eastbourne.org.* The displays in this quaint little tower give a good explanation of the town's development since 1800. Nearby is the entertainment complex adjoining Devonshire Park, the Victorian theatre of that name, the historic Winter Garden and the modern Congress Theatre.

Excursion

Beachy Head★★★ – *4mi/6km south by B 2103. Turn left at the top of the rise outside the town.* Few prospects are more exhilarating on a sunny day than that of the blue sea washing against the toy-like lighthouse at the foot of the dazzling white 500ft/150m cliffs. West of this wonderful viewpoint extends a "Heritage Coast" of sweeping downland ending in lesser, but still spectacular, chalk headlands, the **Seven Sisters,** mostly accessible only on foot.

Address Book

OUT AND ABOUT IN EASTBOURNE

Tourist Information Centre – Tourist Information Centre, Cornfield Road, Eastbourne BN21 4QL ☎ 01323 411 400; Fax: 01323 649 574. www.eastbourne.org/tic.

Public Transport – For local bus information ☎ 01323 416 416. For unlimited travel visitors can purchase a Travelcard (2, 3 or 4 week), or a twelvecard, which entitles the traveller to 12 single journeys for the price of 10.

Pubs and Restaurants – A free booklet entitled Dining Out is available from the Tourist Information Centre (◔ *see above*), and contains details of numerous restaurants and some pubs along the seafront and in the town.

Shopping – There are three indoor shopping centres, the **Arndale Centre** for many of the High Street names, the **Enterprise Centre** for a more specialist range of shops and the **Crumbles centre** with a large supermarket and various other retail outlets. Other shops are located in Terminus Road, The Labyrinth, Seaside Road, Pevensey Road, Susan's Road, Langney Road, Cavendish Place, South Street and Grove Road. Collectors of antiques should visit Cornfield Antiques Market. ☎ 01323 733 345.

Entertainment – A free list of nightclubs and discotheques is available from the Tourist Information Centre (◔ *see above*). For cinema goers there is a three-screen Curzon cinema located in the town centre.

There are facilities for rambling and walking, riding, bowling, golf, angling, watersports and a miniature railway.

EDINBURGH★★★

City of Edinburgh, SCOTLAND

POPULATION 418 914

MICHELIN ATLAS P 56 OR MAP 401 K 16

Edinburgh, capital of Scotland, lies on the Firth of Forth, a deep inlet gouged into the east coast. The city is spectacularly located on a series of volcanic hills, each giving a different and often spectacular vantage point. Perhaps the best known is Arthur's Seat (823ft/251m), overlooking Holyrood Park. Edinburgh boasts a past rich in history; the Old Town, huddled for years on the ridge running down from the Castle Rock, contrasts with the New Town, with its elegant Georgian streets and squares.

▶ **Orient Yourself**: Edinburgh is compact. You can visit all the Old Town and much of the New Town on foot (there are several guided walking tours (see below); bus tours of the city depart from Waverley Bridge next to the station (www.citysightseeing.co.uk).

🅿 **Parking**: Difficult and expensive; don't drive in central Edinburgh.

Don't Miss: The Royal Mile; an underground tour; the Scottish Parliament Building; the views from the Nelson Monument and Arthur's Seat; Charlotte Square; the Festival Fringe; Royal Museum and Museum of Scotland; Royal Yacht Britannia; Forth Bridges view from South Queensferry.

🕐 **Organizing Your Time**: Allow at least three days.

Especially for Kids: a (not too scary) ghost tour; Edinburgh Zoo, Our Dynamic Earth; Deep Sea World (at North Queensferry).

Walking Tours: The Edinburgh Literary Pub Tour (☎/ Fax 0131 226 6665; www.edinburghliterarypubtour.co.uk); Mercat Tours; City of the Dead Tours (not recommended for children or the faint hearted).

A Bit of History

The Castle Rock had been a secure refuge for generations when in the late 11C Malcolm Canmore and his Queen Margaret chose the site for their residence. Their son, David I, favoured the site by founding the Abbey of the Holy Rood. During the reign of the early Stuarts Edinburgh gradually assumed the roles of royal residence, seat of government and capital of Scotland. With the Union of the Crowns (1603) and subsequent departure of James VI of Scotland and I of England for London, Edinburgh lost much of its pageantry, cultural activity, and in 1707 with the Union of the Parliaments, its parliament.

It was in the late 18C during the Enlightenment, a period of intellectual ferment, that plans were mooted for a civic project of boldness and imagination: the creation of the Georgian New Town.

The town has gained further status as the seat of the Scottish Assembly, approved by the 1998 referendum, which sits in the controversial award-winning Parliament building next to the Palace of Holyroodhouse.

The Royal Mile★★

🕐 *Allow a whole day, including Castle and Palace visits*

The principal thoroughfare of Old Edinburgh runs from the Castle down the ridge to the Abbey and Palace of Holyroodhouse. For two centuries the city's Flodden Wall (16C)

Edinburgh International Festival★★★

This prestigious festival *(3 weeks in August)* has provided a quality programme of performances in all the art forms since its inception in 1947. The **Military Tattoo** presents a spectacle rich in colour, tradition, music and excitement, under the floodlights of the Castle Esplanade. Also a part of festival time, **The Fringe** spills out onto the streets and squares of Edinburgh, with performers from all over the globe presenting over a thousand productions, often avant-garde, sometimes just plain eccentric. Also part of the festival are the **Jazz** and **Film Festivals**.

Address Book

OUT AND ABOUT IN EDINBURGH

Tourist Information Centre – 3 Princes Street, south of Waverley Station. ☏ *0845 2255 121 (in UK), 0044 1506 832 121 (outside UK); Fax 01506 832 222; info@visitscotland.com.* The centre offers an accommodation and theatre booking service. There is also a bureau de change, a tourist information service, a bookshop and a souvenir shop.

Public transport – Bus services are frequent and on time. Visit the Tourist Information Centre or the Transport Information Centre at 1 Cockburn Street. The two main operators are Lothian Buses ☏ 0131 555 6363 and First Buses ☏ 08708 72 72 71.

Shopping - Princes Street boasts Edinburgh's famous department store, Jenners, and popular UK high-street names such as John Lewis (St James Shopping Centre) and Marks and Spencer. The best-quality shops however are now to be found on George Street.

Fashion boutiques and music shops are to be found in Rose Street (parallel to Princes Street). Antique shops are mainly in the area around the Royal Mile, Victoria Street and Grassmarket in the Old Town and in Dundas and Thistle streets in the New Town.

Quality garments in tweed, tartan, cashmere and wool are sold in Jenners, Burberrys, the Scotch House, Romanes Patterson (Princes Street) and Kinloch Anderson. The Cashmere Store in the Royal Mile and Kinloch Anderson's Retail Shop on the corner of Commercial Street and Dock Street in Leith are also worth a visit. Edinburgh Crystal in Penicuik (free shuttle bus from Waverley Bridge) has a huge array of crystal articles on sale in its factory shop.

In the Royal Mile there are gourmet food shops selling smoked salmon, kippers, cheese, haggis, oatcakes, shortbread and Dundee cake as well as malt whiskies.

Pubs and Restaurants - The best way to sample the local brews is on a pub crawl starting at the **Abbotsford** in Rose Street or the **Café Royal**, the haunt of literary celebrities, in Register Place. The latter boasts an oyster bar. **Deacon Brodie's** in Lawnmarket or **Greyfriars Bobby** in Candlemaker Row are also popular establishments. There are pubs with a lively atmosphere popular with students in Grassmarket, and fashionable pubs and wine bars by the riverside in Leith. These establishments all offer simple meals at reasonable prices.

Edinburgh has a wide range of restaurants; those offering Scottish fare are identified by the Taste of Scotland logo.

Entertainment – *The List,* a fortnightly magazine, lists films, plays and concerts on offer in town. Certain hotels hold "Scottish Evenings" including traditional entertainment, and pubs like the Ensign Ewart in Lawnmarket and Bannerman's in Niddry Street are reguar venues for jazz, folk, Scottish and world music.

---

restricted the spread of Edinburgh, confining expansion to the ten-and twelve-storey "tenements", with narrow wynds and closes, so typical of the Old Town.

Defoe, in the 18C, called it "perhaps the longest, largest and finest street, not in Britain only, but in the world". The few original buildings which remain can still today give the impression of what medieval and 17C Edinburgh must have looked like.

Castle★★ **(AYZ)** – *(HS)* ♿🕐 *Open (subject to state and military events and the Tattoo) daily, 9.30am-6pm (5pm Oct-Mar); last admission 45mins before closing. Closed 25-26 Dec.* ⊙ *£9.80.* 🔊 *Guided tour. Parking (charge; not available Jun-Oct). Restaurant.* ☏ *0131 225 9846; www.historic-scotland.gov.uk.* The impressive silhouette of the castle and its **rock**★★ is probably the best known feature of views of Edinburgh. Though a royal residence since the 11C, the castle and most of the buildings today are basically those resulting from its use as a military garrison over recent centuries.

The esplanade, an 18C parade ground, is the setting for the Festival's most popular event, the Military Tattoo. The fortifications afford splendid **views** across Princes Street to the New Town. The one o'clock salute is fired from one of the batteries. The main points of interest include the **Honours of Scotland**★★★ (the Scottish Crown Jewels), the **Stone of Destiny** on display in the Crown Room, **Mons Meg**, one of the oldest and most spectacular cannons in the world, and the **Royal Scots Regimental Museum**, the senior regiment in the British Army, raised in 1633, *(*♿🕐 *Open Apr-Sep, daily, 9.30am-5.30pm; Oct-Mar, Mon-Fri, 9.30am-4pm.* 🕐 *Closed 1 Jan and 25-26 Dec.* ⊙ *same ticket as Castle.* ☏*0131 310 5014; Fax 0131 310 5019; rhqroyalscots@edinburghcastle.fsnet.co.uk; www.theroyalscots.co.uk).* The small 12C St Margaret's Chapel is dedicated to Malcolm's Queen Margaret. Around Crown Square are: the Scottish National War Memorial *(north side)*; the Scottish United Services Museum *(west side)*; the 16C **Great Hall** with its hammerbeam roof, and 15C Palace containing the royal apartments.

Proceed down the Royal Mile past the **Scotch Whisky Heritage Centre** (⅏ 354 *Castlehill*. 🕐 *Open daily, 10am-6pm (6:30 summer)*. 🕐 *Closed 25 Dec.* ⚲ *£8.50 including tasting and discount voucher for gift shop.* ⚲ *Guided tour (45min). Commentaries (8 languages). Restaurant, bar. Gift shop.* ☎0131 220 0441; Fax: 0131 220 6288; enquiry@ whisky-heritage co uk; www.whisky-heritage.co.uk) with an exhibition and film on whisky distilling and the Outlook Tower and **Camera Obscura,** (⅏🕐 549 *Castlehill. Open Apr-Oct, daily, 9.30am-6pm, Nov-Mar, daily 10am-5pm.* ⚲ *£6.45* ☎ 0131 226 3709; info@camera-obscura.demon.co.uk; www.camera-obscura.co.uk) which affords a fascinating ever-changing "live" view of the city.

Gladstone's Land★ (BY) – *(NTS) 477B Lawnmarket.* 🕐*Open late-Mar to late-Oct, daily, 10am - 5pm (1pm Sun, 7pm Jul-Aug).* ⚲ *£5. Translation (8 languages).* ☎ *0131 226 5856; Fax 0131 226 4851; www.nts.org.uk.* This narrow six-storey tenement is a typical building erected within the Flodden Wall in the 17C; in 1617 it was acquired and extended by Thomas Gledstanes, a wealthy merchant. The restored premises comprise a shop with living quarters above. The first floor is a good example of a 17C town house with original painted ceilings and furnishings.

The **Writers' Museum (BY M1),** *(Lady Stair's Close, off Lawnmarket.* 🕐 *Open Mon-Sat, 10am-5pm; also during the Festival, Sun, 2-5pm. Free Admission* ☎ *0131 529 4901; Fax 0131 220 5057; enquiries@writersmuseum.demon.co.uk)* located in Lady Stair's House, presents an exhibition on three of Scotland's greatest literary figures: Robert Burns (1759-96), Sir Walter Scott (1771-1832) and Robert Louis Stevenson (1850-94).

St Giles' Cathedral★★ (BY) – *Royal Mile.* 🕐*Open Mon-Sat, 9am-7pm (5pm mid-Sep to Apr), Sun, 1pm-5pm.* ⚲ *Donation. Thistle Chapel: leaflet (7 languages).* ☎ *0131 225 9442; Fax 0131 225 9576; stgiles@hotmail.com; www.stgiles.net.* The High Kirk of Edinburgh is probably the third church to occupy this site. Alterations and restorations have, however, drastically changed its character since its rebuilding in the 14C. The only original exterior feature is the crown **spire★★★** dating from 1495. Inside, it is the monuments and details that provide much of the interest. The Thistle Chapel was designed by **Robert Lorimer** in 1911 in Flamboyant Gothic style for the Most Noble Order of the Thistle, founded in 1687. There are monuments to John Knox and to Covenanter-turned-Royalist, the Marquess of Montrose.

To the south of Parliament Square is **Parliament Hall (BYZ),** (⅏🕐 *Open Mon-Fri, 10am-4pm.* 🕐 *Closed Bank Hols. Restaurant.* ☎ *0131 225 2595; Fax 0131 240 6755; supreme.courts@scotcourts.gov.uk; www.scotcourts.gov.uk)* the 17C hall decreed by Charles I, now behind a Georgian façade, in which the Scottish Parliament met from 1693 to 1707. Nearby is a 17C equestrian statue of Charles II. At the east end of the square stands the **Mercat Cross**, formerly the hub of Edinburgh life, meeting place of traders and merchants and scene of royal proclamations, demonstrations and executions.Opposite are the **City Chambers (BY)**, formerly the Royal Exchange built in 1753. Adjacent, though part of the same complex. is the entrance to the **Real Mary King's Close** *(Warriston's Close.* 🕐*Tours Apr-Oct 10am-9pm; Nov-Mar Sun-Fri 10am-4pm; Sat 10am-9pm* 🕐 *25 Dec.* ⚲ *£8. No children under the age of 5. Children under 16 must be accompanied by an adult. Shop. Cafe. Advance booking advisable.* ☎ *08702 430160; www.realmarykingsclose.com)* Hidden beneath the Royal Mile lies one of Edinburgh's secrets; a warren of "closes" (narrow alleyways) where people lived, worked and died. As the Old Town expanded ever upwards these closes became built over, or as legend has it, deliberately sealed up, inhabitants and all, whenever the dreaded plague visited (which it did frequently). For centuries they lay forgotten and abandoned until the late 1990s when tours were licensed to reintroduce them to the general public. The Real Mary King's Close is the most popular of the tours which guide visitors through these labyrinthine passageways but also the most commercialised (with mannequins, sound effects etc) . Paranormal activity has been recorded frequently down here.

The picturesque **John Knox House (BY),** (⅏🕐 Open Mon-Sat, 10am-5pm; (7pm Aug), Sun, noon-4pm. 🕐 *Closed 25-26 Dec, 1-2 Jan.* ⚲*£2.25.* ⚲ *Guided tour (30min) by appointment. Café.* ☎ *0131 556 2647, 9579; netherbow-admin@dial.pipex.com)* built in about 1490, is associated with both John Knox, the religious reformer, and with James Mossman, the goldsmith to Mary Queen of Scots. An exhibition incorporates details on both men and re-creates the atmosphere of 16C Edinburgh.

On the south side of the Royal Mile, the **Museum of Childhood (BY),** (⅏ 42 *High Street, Royal Mile.* 🕐*Open Mon-Sat, 10am-5pm; also Jul-Aug, Sun, noon-5pm.* 🕐 *Closed 1-2 Jan and 25-26 Dec.* ⚲*No charge.* ☎ *0131 529 4142; Fax 0131 558 3103; admin@ museumofchildhood.fsnet.co.uk; www.cac.org.uk)* presents an unusual collection of exhibits devoted to anything and everything to do with childhood.

Just before Canongate Church stands the attractive 16C **Canongate Tolbooth**★ **(BY) (People's Story Museum)** (&*163 Canongate.* ⏱*Open daily, 10am-5pm (noon Sun).* ⊗*No Charge.* ⏱ *Closed 1 Jan and 25-26 Dec.* ☎ *0131 529 4057; Fax 0131 557 3346; www.cac.org.uk)* with its turreted steeple; opposite stand three 16C mansions known as Huntly House **(BY)** occupied by the **Museum of Edinburgh,** (& *142 Canongate.* ⏱*Open Mon-Sat, 10am-5pm; also during the Festival, Sun,noon-5pm.* ⊗*No charge.* ☎ *0131 529 4143; Fax 0131 557 3346; www.cac.org.uk)* offering some very interesting local exhibits.

The independent burgh of Canongate was where the nobility and officers of the Royal Household resided in proximity to the palace.

Abbey and Palace of Holyroodhouse★★ **(BY)** – &*Palace:* ⏱*Open Apr-Oct, daily, 9.30am-5.15pm (3pm Jun –Jul); Nov-Mar (*☞ *by guided tour - 1hr), daily, 9.30am-3.45pm. Abbey:* ⏱*Open (unguided visit following the tour of the Palace) same times as Palace. Gardens:* ⏱*Open summer only.* ⏱ *Closed during Royal and State visits.* ⊗ *£8.50 (on line booking). Guide book (5 languages).* ☎ *0131 556 7371; holyroodhouse@royalcollection. org.uk; www.royal.gov.uk.* At the east end of the Royal Mile, amid the green slopes of Holyrood Park, leading up to Arthur's Seat, stands the Palace of Holyrood, official residence of the monarch in Scotland. The abbey was founded by David I, in 1128. James IV started to transform the guesthouse of the abbey into a royal palace but it was Charles II, though he never set foot in the palace, who had his architect Sir William Bruce draw up designs; influenced perhaps by the work of Inigo Jones in Whitehall, Bruce created a magnificent building in the Palladian style.

The inner court elevations are outstanding Renaissance work of the Stuart period and among Scotland's earliest examples. The decoration of the **State Apartments** is lavish, the craftsmanship outstanding. Particularly noteworthy are the **plasterwork ceilings**★★★, the fruit of ten years' labour by "gentlemen modellers" who had worked for the Lauderdales, patrons of Sir William, at Ham House in London and also for Charles II at Windsor.

The **Historic Apartments** in the 16C round tower, which have close associations with Mary Queen of Scots, contain tapestries from the Mortlake workshop founded by her son; the painted ceilings are magnificent. It was in the small room adjoining the bedchamber that Mary's Italian secretary, Rizzio, was murdered in 1566.

Abbey – ⏱ ☞ *Same opening times as the palace. Visitors are free to visit on their own at the end of the guided tour.* The roofless nave is all that is left of this once great abbey, dating from the late 12C and early 13C. Here are buried the remains of David II, James II, James V and also of Lord Darnley, father of James VI of Scotland, who united the Crowns in 1603.

Scottish Parliament – &⏱ *Meetings in the Chamber are normally held on Wednesday afternoons, Thursday mornings and Thursday afternoons. It is advisable to book tickets for the public gallery in advance.* ☞ *Guided tour every 15 mins Mon, Fri Apr-Oct 10.15am-5.15pm, (Nov-Mar 3.15pm); Sat-Sun 10.15am-3.15pm. Note these only operate on non-business days (i.e all weekends, Mondays and Fridays when Parliament is sitting, all weekdays when Parliament is in recess; main summer recess Jul-Sep, see website for other breaks).* ⊗ *Public Gallery no charge.* ☞ *guided tours £3.50. Shop, café, crèche, Visitor Information Desk.* ☎ *0131 348 5200; 0131 348 5601; sp.bookings@scottish.parliament. uk; www. scottish.parliament.uk.* Britain's most controversial post-Millennium building was designed by the Spanish architect Enric Miralles (1955-2000) who died before its completion in 2005, four years late and ten times over budget. Its unusual design and outlandish features make it a must-see for students of modern architecture and recommended viewing for anbody else.

New Town★★ *1767-1830*

When the decision had been taken to extend the Royalty of Edinburgh, the development was organised by a then unknown architect, James Craig, whose design had won the competition. The North Bridge was thrown across the valley and the New Town was laid out on a gridiron pattern, with vistas and focal points. It was not until 1782 that regulations were introduced to control uniformity of façades and storeys. The wealthy soon took up residence in these splendid squares and elegant streets.

Charlotte Square★★★ **(AY)** – It was Robert Adam who was commissioned in 1791 to design what is New Town's most elegant square. No 5 is occupied by the National Trust for Scotland, who have also refurbished No 7, the **Georgian House**★ **(AY)** *(NTS. 7 Charlotte Square.* ⏱*Open late-Jan to late-Dec, daily, 11am (10am to 6pm late-Mar to late-Oct) to 4pm; last admission 30mins before closing.* ⊗ *£5. Audio-visual presentation.*

EDINBURGH

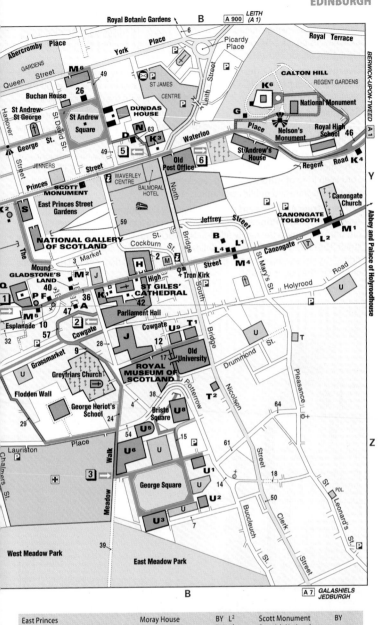

Room summaries (various languages). ☎/Fax 0131 226 3318; thegeorgianhouse@nts.org. uk; www.nts.org.uk.); its lower floors now give a delightful impression of domestic life in the period 1790-1810.

George Street (ABY) – The principal street of Craig's plan is closed at either end by Charlotte and St Andrew squares. From the street intersections there are good views away to the Forth or down to Princes Street Gardens with the castle as backdrop.

St Andrew Square (BY) – It has none of the unified elegance of its counterpart, Charlotte Square, but its houses have great charm and individuality; they are now occupied by banks and insurance companies.

New Register House (BY) – The building, which is enclosed by fine wrought-iron gates, houses the offices of the Registrar General for Scotland and the Court of the Lord Lyon King of Arms. Lord Lyon regulates all heraldic matters in Scotland, and officiates at state and public ceremonies.

Princes Street and Gardens (ABY) – Originally the southern boundary of the New Town development, **Princes Street** has grown from a totally residential street, looking out onto gardens in the newly filled-in Nor'Loch, into Edinburgh's prime shopping street. The railway came in 1845-46, followed by commercial development. The south side of the street was protected from building by Act of Parliament and the gardens opened to the public in 1876.

Y. Travert/Photononstop

Princes Street

Following Sir Walter Scott's death in 1832, a public appeal was launched and the foundation stone of the **Scott Monument**★ **(BY),** *(Princes Street.* 🕐*Open daily, 9am-6pm (10am Sun, 9am-3pm Mar – Oct).* 👝 *£3.* ☎ *0131 529 4068; www.cac.org.uk)* was laid in 1840. The 200ft/61m tall Gothic spire, as well as sheltering a Carrara marble statue of **Scott,** is surrounded by statuettes of 64 characters from his novels and by the busts of 16 Scottish poets. For the agile *(287 narrow stairs to the top)* a viewing platform affords a magnificent **view**★ over central Edinburgh.

Dividing Princes Street Gardens into East and West are two imposing classical buildings, the National Gallery (♿ *see below)* and the Royal Scottish Academy.

In West Princes Street Gardens, nearby, is the **Floral Clock (BY)** composed of 20 000 annuals.

East of Princes Street, beyond the elegant Waterloo Place, rises **Calton Hill (BY)** crowned by Classical monuments which gave rise to the name "Edinburgh's acropolis": the porticoed **National Monument**, a Greek **temple (BY)** and the 18C **Old Observatory (BY).** There are wonderful views from here but for the very best **panorama**★★★ climb to the top of the **Nelson Monument**, a folly in the shape of an upturned telescope (🕐 *Apr-Sep Mon 1pm-6pm; Tue -Sat 10am-6pm; Oct-Mar Mon-Sat 10am-3pm.* ☎ *0131 556 2716; Fax: 0131 529 3977; cac.admin@edinburgh.gov.uk; www.cac.org.uk).*

The harmonious sweep of **Regent, Calton** and **Royal Terraces** (19C) is enhanced by attractive architectural and ironwork features.

Address Book

For coin ranges, see the Legend at the back of the guide.

WHERE TO STAY

🍽🍽🍽🍽 **Balmoral,** *1 Princes Street.* ☎ *0131 556 2414; Fax 0131 557 8740; reservations@thebalmoralhotel.com; www. thebalmoralhotel.com.* The haunt of visiting royalty, rock stars and presidents who enjoy richly furnished rooms in baronial style at this most central of all city landmarks.

🍽🍽🍽🍽 **The George Intercontinental,** *19-21 George Street.* ☎ *0131 225 1251; Fax; 0131 226 5664; www.ichotelsgroup.com.* Beautifully appointed classic New Town Hotel which makes the most of Robert Adams listed 18C design. Carvers restaurant (🍽🍽🍽🍽) sits beneath a magnificent glass dome.

🍽🍽🍽 **The Glasshouse,** *2 Greenside Place.* ☎ *0131 525 8200 ; Fax; 0131 525 8205; resglasshouse@theetongroup.com; www. theetongroup.com.* The city's most unusual and trendy boutique hotel mixes ultramodern styling (glass themes with great views onto park and city) and all the latest gadgets with the facade of a 19C church.

🍽🍽🍽 **The Scotsman,** *20 North Bridge Street.* ☎ *0131 556 5565; Fax 0131 652 3652; reservations@the scotsmanhotelgroup.co.uk; www. the scotsmanhotelgroup.co.uk.* Occupying the grand marble former offices of Edinburgh's principal newspaper this stunning hotel has impressive lesiure facilities and very well equipped modern bedrooms. Its beautiful North Bridge Brasserie (🍽🍽🍽🍽) is recommended.

🍽🍽🍽🍽 **Prestonfield,** *Priestfield Road.* ☎ *0131 225 7800; Fax 0131 220 4392;* reservations@prestonfield.com. This superbly restored elegant 17C country house on the edge of Holyrood Park is just a few minutes walk from the city centre and offers 22 rooms. Excellent restaurant (🍽🍽🍽🍽).

WHERE TO EAT

🍽🍽 **Atrium,** *Traverse Theatre, 10 Cambridge Street.* ☎ *0131 228 8882; eat@atriumrestaurant.co.uk; www. atriumrestaurant.co.uk.* Ultra stylish, beautifully furnished friendly restaurant with an adventurous food repertoire, set inside a popular modern theatre.

🍽🍽 **Le Café Saint-Honoré,** *34 North West Thistle Street Lane.* ☎ *0131 226 2211.* A bustling atmospheric, typically French bistro celebrating the Auld Alliance between Scotland and France. Booking essential.

🍽🍽 **Marque Central,** *Lyceum Theatre, 30b Grindley Street.* ☎ *0131 229 9859; Fax 221 9515.* This modern restaurant, part of the Lyceum Theatre, draws on contemporary Scottish and Italian influences for its reasonably priced dishes.

🍽🍽 **Rogue,** *67 Morrison Street,* ☎ *0131 228 2700; Fax 0131 228 31299; info@ rogues-uk.com.* Stylish bright venue with beautiful wooden-stripped bar and contemporary fittings. Modern international menu with substantial choice and value.

🍽🍽 **The Tower,** *Museum of Scotland, Chambers Street.* ☎ *0131 225 3003; Fax 0131 225 4392; mail@tower-restaurant.com; www. tower-restaurant.com.* Expect top-class game, grills and seafood at this very stylish contemporary restaurant on the top floor of the Museum of Scotland; stunning views from window tables and the terrace.

Museums and Galleries

The city is justly proud of its museums with rich collections of international standard and fine holdings of Scottish art.

Royal Museum of Scotland★★ (BZ) – *Chambers Street. Open daily, 10am (noon Sun) to 5pm (8pm Tue). Closed 25 Dec. No charge. Guided Audio tour. Restaurant, cafes. ☎ 0131 247 4219; Fax 0131 220 4819; www.nms.ac.uk.* The elaborate Venetian Renaissance-style façade of the main building contrasts with the interior. The spacious, well-lit Main Hall is a masterpiece of Victorian cast iron and plate glass construction. The collections devoted to the arts and sciences range from natural history and geology to sculpture, decorative arts and Asiatic, European and Middle Eastern art.

A sandstone drum tower highlights the innovative design of the new **Museum of Scotland** intended to trace the story of the country from 3 500 years ago to the present day with the unique collections placed in their historical perspective and with the help of an interactive computer system. The exhibits *(start in the basement galleries)* explain the natural landscape and geological foundation, the peopling of the country, the independent kingdom (1100–1707), the modern state (18C–19C) and various other aspects of Scotland.

National Gallery of Scotland★★ (BY) – *The Mound. Open daily, 10am (noon Sun) to 5pm (7pm Thurs, later during the Edinburgh Festival). Closed 25-26 Dec. Limited parking. Shop. ☎ 0131 624 6200, 0131 332 2266 (recorded information); enquiries@nationalgalleries.org; www.nationalgalleries.org.* An imposing Classical building houses the collection of paintings displayed in elegant octagonal rooms with connecting arches and enhanced by period furniture. The museum presents masterpieces of European art (15C–19C) including Raphael, Rembrandt, Vermeer, Poussin, Claude Lorrain, Boucher, Monet, Van Gogh. The British tradition is represented by Turner, Gainsborough and Constable among others. There is a fine collection of **Scottish paintings**, in particular by Jamesone, Ramsay, Raeburn, McTaggart and the Glasgow School.

Scottish National Gallery of Modern Art★ – *Belford Road. Open daily, 10am-5pm (later during the Edinburgh Festival). Closed 25-26 Dec. No charge for permanent collection. Parking. Café. Shop. ☎ 0131 624 6200, 0131 332 2266 (recorded information); enquiries@nationalgalleries.org; www.nationalgalleries.org.* In a garden setting with sculptures by Epstein, Hepworth and Moore among others, the museum has fine examples of 20C art ranging from Fauvism, Cubism and Russian Primitivism to Nouveau Réalisme and Pop Art, and a comprehensive collection of Scottish art, in particular by the Scottish Colourists and the Edinburgh school.

Scottish National Portrait Gallery★ (BY) – *1 Queen Street. Open daily, 10am-5pm (7pm Thur; later during the Edinburgh Festival). Closed 25-26 Dec. No charge for permanent collection. Cafe. Limited parking. ☎ 0131 624 6200, 0131 332 2266 (recorded information); enquiries@nationalgalleries.org; www.nationalgalleries.org.* The museum, which is housed in a building provided by a donation from the proprietor of The Scotsman in 1882, "illustrates Scottish history by likeness of the chief actors in it". On display are masterpieces of portraiture of royalty, statesmen, politicians and literary figures.

Excursions

Dalmeny★★ – *6mi/10km west by A 90.* The village is famous for its parish **St Cuthbert's Church★**, *(Open Apr-Sept, Sun, 2-4pm; otherwise key obtainable at post office or 5 Main Street, opposite church. ☎ 0131 331 1479)* an exceptionally fine example of Norman ecclesiastical architecture, with an intricately carved south **doorway★★**. To the east of the village is **Dalmeny House★**, *(South Queensferry. Open Jul-Aug, Sun-Tue, 2-5.30pm. £5. Guided tour available. Guide book, leaflet. Tearoom. ☎ 0131 331 1888; Fax 0131 331 1788; events@dalmeny.co.uk; www.dalmeny.co.uk)* home of the earls of Rosebery. Archibald the 4th Earl commissioned William Wilkins to build the Gothic revival house which was completed in 1817. Archibald the 5th Earl married Hannah de Rothschild and it was he who succeeded Gladstone as Prime Minister in 1894. Of particular interest are the Rothschild collection of 18C French furniture, porcelain and tapestries and the memorabilia of the Napoleon Room collected by the Prime Minister 5th Earl.

Forth Bridges★★ – *Best viewed from the esplanade at South Queensferry, 9mi/15km west by A 90.* The first ferry across this, the narrowest part of the Forth, was instituted by Queen Margaret in the 1070s, and was operated by the monks of Dunfermline, for pilgrims travelling to the abbey. By the 17C it was the busiest ferry crossing in Scotland.

Forth Bridge

The **Forth Rail Bridge** was begun in 1883 – an intrepid endeavour so soon after the Tay Bridge disaster of 1879 – and was opened in 1890. The **Road Bridge,** a slim-line elegant suspension bridge, with its amazing "curve", was built from 1958 to 1964. It carries two carriageways (24ft/7m wide), cycle tracks and footpaths.

On the north side of the bridge stands **Deep Sea World,** (&🕐 *Open daily, 10am-6pm;* 🕐 *Closed 25 Dec .☞£8.55. Presentations. Parking, Café.* ☎ *01383 411 880; 0906 9410077 (information 10p per minute); Fax 01383 410 514; info@deepseaworld.com; www. deepseaworld.com)* a spectacular aquarium which is a popular attraction.

Hopetoun House★★ – *11mi/18 km west by A 90 and A 904.* &🕐 *South Queensferry. Open Easter-Sep, daily, 10am-5.30pm (last admission 4.30pm); Oct 11am-5:30pm (last admission 4.30pm).* ☞ *House and grounds £7. Parking. Restaurant, picnic area.* ☎ *0131 331 2451; Fax 0131 319 1885; dayvisits@hopetounhouse.com; www.hopetounhouse. com.* Hopetoun House is a mansion of contrasts set in beautiful landscaped grounds. The original house (built 1699-1707) displays the mature classicism of **Sir William Bruce**, its main staircase richly embellished with carving leading the eye upward to the painted cupola – a unique survival of decorative art of the Baroque period. The later flamboyant extensions and frontage (1721-67) are the work of William Adam, completed by his son John. The grandeur of the State Apartments is complemented by the original furnishings, magnificent plaster ceilings and a notable art collection. An interesting exhibition covering the architects and craftsmen at Hopetoun includes advice from Robert Adam, while on the Grand Tour with the Hope family.

The Binns – *(NTS) 15mi/24km west by A 8 and M 9.* &🕐 *House:* 👣 *Guided tour (40min) Jun-Sep, Sat-Thu, 2-5pm.* ☞ *£8. Parkland: Open daily, Leaflet (9 languages). Parking. Picnic area.* ☎ *01506 834 255; www.nts.org.uk.* The home of the Dalyell family has interesting **plasterwork ceilings** in the Drawing Room and the King's Room. The history of the house is dominated by the colourful personality of **General Tam** (1615-85), a staunch Royalist who refused to cut his hair or beard until the monarchy was restored, and the founder of the Royal Scots Greys.

Linlithgow Palace★★ – *(HS) 19mi/31km west by A 8 and M 9.* 🕐 *Open daily, 9.30am (2pm Sun Oct-Mar) to 6.30pm (4.30pm Oct-Mar).* ☞ *£2.80. Parking. Picnic areas.* ☎ *01506 842 896; www.historic-scotland.gov.uk.* The history of the town is that of its royal palace around which it grew from the 12C. Following the rebuilding of the palace in 1424 it enjoyed over a century of grandeur as the centre of Scotland's court until the Union of the Crowns (1603). The roofless and forbidding four-square ruin still shelters several delicate features, notably the 1530s **fountain**★ in the courtyard and a superbly carved **fireplace** at the dais end of the Great Hall. Alongside the palace stands the 15C-16C late Gothic **St Michael's Church**★, *(Cross House.* 🕐*Open May-Sep, daily, 10:30am) to 4pm; Oct-Apr, Mon-Fri, 10:30am-3pm.* 👣 *Guided tour (30min) by appointment. Leaflet (4 languages). Parking.* ☎ *01506 842 188; Fax 01506 206 140; info@stmichaelsparish.org.uk; www.stmichaelsparish.org.uk)* with its controversial defiantly modern spire (1964).

Cairnpapple Hill★ – *(HS) 24mi/39km west by A 8, M 9 to Linlithgow and A 707 to Torphi-chen. Cairnpapple is a mile beyond.* 🕐 *Open Apr-Sep, daily, 9.30am-6.30pm.* ☞ *£2.50. Parking.* ☎ *01506 634 622; www.historic-scotland.gov.uk.* The site is unique in that five distinct phases in prehistoric evolution are represented. The earliest consists of cremation burials of the late Neolithic (c 3000-2500 BC). A henge with a bank and ditch and a stone circle were built c 2500-2000 BC. Within and slightly overlying this are two successive burial cairns, the first dating to c 1600 BC (now reconstructed with a concrete dome) and the second, larger, cairn to c 1300 BC. The final phase is represented by four Iron Age burials.

Rosslyn Chapel★★ – *7mi/11km south near the village of Roslin.* ◷ *Open Mon-Sat, 9:30am- 6pm, Sun, noon-4.45pm.* ✆ *£6. Guide book. Leaflet.* ☎ *0131 440 2159; Fax 0131 440 1979; rosslynch@aol.com; www.rosslynchapel.org.uk.* Rosslyn Chapel stands on the edge of the Esk Valley and is a bewildering example of craftsmanship. It was built at the orders of Sir William St Clair, third and last Prince of Orkney (1396-1484). Work lasted from 1446 until 1486, just after Sir William's death. By then, only the choir of the planned collegiate church had been completed; this was damaged in 1592, and used as a stable for the horses of General Monck's men in 1650. Amongst the intricate, rich decoration, perhaps the best known single item is the **Apprentice Pillar**★★★. Legend has it that whilst the master mason was abroad, his apprentice carved the pillar. The enraged master mason, on his return, is said to have killed his too-gifted apprentice.

ELGIN★

Moray, SCOTLAND

POPULATION 11 855

MICHELIN ATLAS P 68 OR MAP 501 K 11

Elgin stands on the banks of the Lossie just off the northeast coast. The original town plan has been well preserved, with the main street linking the two mainstays of a medieval burgh – the cathedral and castle. ▯ *17 High Street* ☎ *01343 542 666; Fax 01343 552 982; www.elginscotland.org.*

Visit

Cathedral★ – *(HS)* ♿◷ *Open Apr-Sep, daily, 9.30am-6pm; Oct-Mar, 9.30am (closed Thur, Fri) to 4.30pm (noon Thu).* ✆ *£3.30.* ☎ *01343 547 171; www.historic-scotland.gov. uk.* The ruins stand as a monument to that period of intensive church building, the 13C. The diocese dates back to 1120, but the ruins here are those of a cathedral built in 1270, replacing one destroyed by fire. In 1390 Alexander Stewart, known as the **Wolf of Badenoch,** second son of King Robert II, destroyed both cathedral and town. Both were repaired, and the 13C **chapter house**★★ was reconstructed in the 15C, but the cathedral suffered further deterioration after the Reformation since it was no longer

The Whisky Trail

The subtle flavours of pure **malt whisky** distilled according to age-old methods are greatly appreciated throughout the world. A signposted tour *(70mi/112km)* through the glens of Speyside includes famous distilleries (Cardhu, Glenfarclas, Strathisla, Glen Grant, Tamnavulin, The Glenlivet) which offer a fascinating experience of the production of the "sovereign liquor" from its monastic beginnings to the warehouses where the spirit matured, "losing some flavours, gaining others". An excellent introduction to the art of whisky distilling is given at **Glenfiddich Distillery** *(♿◷ Guided tour (1hr 30min) Easter-Oct, daily, 9.30am (noon Sun) to 4.30pm.* ◷ *Closed 2 weeks at Christmas and New Year. Leaflet (7 languages). Audio-visual presentation (6 languages). Parking.* ☎*01340 820 373; Fax 01340 822 083; www.glenfiddich.com)* in Dufftown, the capital of the malt whisky industry, and at the picturesque **Dallas Dhu Distillery** *(HS 1.25mi/2km south of Forres* ♿ ◷ *Open Apr-Sep, daily, 9.30am-6.30pm; Oct-Mar, 9.30am (closed Thu -Fri) to 4.30pm . Audio-visual presentation.* ✆ *£4 Parking. Picnic area.* ☎ *01309 676 548).* **Speyside Cooperage** *(♿ Dufftown Road.* ◷*Open early-Jan to mid-Dec, Mon-Fri, 9.30am-4pm.* ✆ *£2.95. Audio-visual presentation (6 languages). Guided Tour. Tastings. Parking. Picnic area.* ☎ *01340 871 108; Fax 01340 881 437; info@speyside-coopers.co.uk; www.speysidecooperage.co.uk.)* relates the story of this ancient craft. Apply to the local tourist offices for detailed brochures.

used as a place of worship. After the collapse of the tower in 1711, the ruins became a quarry for building materials. Conservation was begun in the early 19C.

Excursions

Sueno's Stone★★ – *Forres. 12mi/19km west by A 96 and B 9011*. This superbly carved Pictish stone, which is probably a funerary monument commemorating a battle, stands on the outskirts of the ancient burgh of Forres. The large sandstone slab (20ft/6m high), which dates from the 9C, is unique in Britain. Three sides are decorative – one carved with a wheel cross. The fourth side, the most spectacular, is narrative, and shows horsemen, warriors and headless corpses.

A short detour to the scenic **Findhorn area** and **Culbin Forest** north of Forres is very rewarding.

Brodie Castle★ – *(NTS) 20mi/32km west by A 96.* 🔴 *Forres, Moray Grounds:* 🕐*Open daily, 9.30am/dusk. Castle: Open late-Mar to late-Sep, Thu-Mon, noon-4pm; open by appointment throughout the year for groups.* ☜ *Castle £8; grounds, donation. Adventure playground, woodland walks. Parking. Tearoom.* ☎ *01309 641 371; Fax 01309 641 600; brodiecastle@nts.org.uk; www.nts.org.uk.* The seat of the Brodies since the 11C, the castle developed over the centuries from a 16C house to the present building. Interiors of various periods are the setting for a splendid collection of paintings (Van Dyck, Romney, Scottish works), exquisite timepieces and French **furniture**. The ornate **plasterwork ceilings** date from the 17C. Brodie is also famous for its collection of daffodils to be admired in spring.

ELY

Cambridgeshire, ENGLAND

POPULATION 10 329

MICHELIN ATLAS P 29 OR MAP 504 U 26

Once called Elig or Eel Island because of the abundance of eels, Ely lies on the River Ouse on a rise (70ft/21m) above the flat fenland in the east of England 13 miles/21 km north of Cambridge. It has been a place of worship since St Etheldreda, a Saxon queen, founded a religious community and built an abbey here in the 7C. The small town is still dominated by the cathedral and monastic buildings and retains many medieval houses. Its citizens showed a rebellious streak in 1066 when Hereward the Wake made his last stand against the Normans in Ely. In the 17C Oliver Cromwell lived in the town. 🛈 *29 St Mary's Street, ELy CB7 4HF* ☎ *01353 662 062; Fax 01353 668 518; tic@east-cambs.gov.uk; http://tourism.eastcambs.gov.uk, www.ely.org.uk/tic.htm.*

Cathedral★★

🔴🕐 *Open Apr-Oct, daily, 7am-7pm; Nov-Mar, daily, 7.30am-6pm (5pm Sun). Octagon: Open Apr-Oct, Mon-Sat at 10.30am, 11.45am, 2.15pm, 3.30pm, Sun at 12.30pm, 2.15pm. West Tower: Open Jul-Aug, Mon-Sat at 10.45am, noon, 2.30pm and 4pm; Sun at 12.45pm and 2.30pm. Stained Glass Museum: Open Easter-Oct, daily, 10.30am (noon Sun) to 5pm (5.30pm Sat, 6pm Sun); Nov-Easter, daily, 10.30am (noon Sun) to 4.30pm (5pm Sat). Cathedral* ☜ *£4.80; Octagon £4; West Tower £3.50; reduction for those with a cathedral ticket; Museum £3.50.* ☜☜ *Guided tour (1hr) of ground floor; check times for seasonal variations.*

A. Williams/MICHELIN

Ely Cathedral

Guide book (3 languages). Mini guides (7 languages). Parking (4min on foot from Cathedral). Restaurant, tea room. ☎01353 667 735; Fax 01353 665 658; receptionist@cathedral. ely.anglican.org; www.cathedral.ely.anglican.org.

The superb Norman nave and transepts contrast with the surprises beyond: the wonderful Decorated east end and Lady Chapel, and that 14C masterpiece, the Octagon. After the sacking of Etheldreda's abbey by the Danes in 870, a second religious community was founded by the Benedictines in 970. The present church was begun in 1083; in 1250 the east end of the original Norman building was reconstructed, using Purbeck marble. In 1321 work started on the Lady Chapel under the monastery surveyor Alan de Walsingham. The following year the great Norman crossing tower fell down. Alan did not know "where to turn or what to do". What he did was a triumph of medieval engineering. He cut off the four Norman corners of the crossing and built on the eight points an octagonal space three times the size of the Norman tower.

Exterior – The cathedral is best viewed from the northwest to appreciate its length (537ft/164m), castellated west tower (215ft/66m), Early English Galilee Porch, the Decorated **Octagon** (170ft/52m) and the wooden lantern above it.

Interior – The visitor is instantly overwhelmed by rich colours emanating from ceilings, stained glass windows and stone pillars. The **southwest transept** (c 1200) is an outstanding example of the Romanesque period. The relentless rhythm of the long and slender Norman nave, with arcades, triforium and clerestory of almost similar height, is broken only by the ornate Norman work of the **Prior's Door.** The panelled ceiling of the nave was painted by local Victorian artists (1858-61). The eye is led to the **Octagon**; its eight pillars support 200 tons of glass, lead and timber; below its high windows are panels decorated with angels. The Octagon is separated by a 19C **screen** by George Gilbert Scott from the beautifully vaulted choir, with its splendid 14C **choir stalls**; the first three bays were built at the same time as the Octagon and are in mid-14C Decorated style, the rest of the choir is 13C Early English. In front of the High Altar lies the shrine of St Etheldreda. The ceilings of both transepts are painted and decorated with 15C carved angels. The light and spacious **Lady Chapel** was the largest single span of vaulting in its time, above niches, canopies and windows; most of its statues and windows were destroyed in 1541 during the Dissolution of the Monasteries. The ornate stone Perpendicular chapels of **Bishop Alcock** and **Bishop West** were built as chantries.

The **Stained-Glass Museum** in the triforium, reached by a steep winding staircase, shows stained-glass and lead-cutting processes by means of diorama models. It is a joy to examine the rich colours at close range; the earliest glass is 13C, most is 19C and 20C from Britain and other European countries.

The group of medieval domestic buildings, together with the ruined cloisters, is the largest in England; some form part of The King's School or are in private hands. Prior Crauden's Chapel with 14C wall paintings can be visited *(ask at the South Door)*. The 14C **Ely Porta** was the monastery gateway.

Oliver Cromwell's House★ –   *29 St Mary's Street.* ⏰*Open Apr-Oct, daily, 10am-5:30pm; Nov-Mar, Mon-Sat, 10am-5pm (11:15 – 4 Sun).* 🚌 *£3.75; £11 joint ticket for 4 main sights in Ely (Cathedral, Oliver Cromwell's House, Stained Glass Museum, Ely Museum).* ☎ *01353 662 062; tic@eastcambs.gov.uk; www.ely.org.uk/tic.htm.* The history of this ancient house (13C) and of its most illustrious resident is clearly explained by means of room commentaries, videos and tableaux. The furnished rooms are few – kitchen, bedroom, study – but the flavour of the age is superbly captured. Children may find trying on period hats more fun than viewing armour and weapons in the Civil War Room. A video is also shown.

Excursion

Wicken Fen★ – (NT) *Take A 10 south; in Stretham turn left on A 1123. Lode Lane Reserve.* ⏰*Open (weather permitting) daily, dawn-dusk.* ⏰ *Closed 25 Dec. Visitor Centre: Open Tue-Sun and Bank Hol, 10am-5pm (sometimes closed in winter). Fen Cottage: Open Apr-Oct, Sun and Bank Hol Mon, 2-5pm.* 🚌 *£4.10* ☎/*Fax 01353 720 274; wickenfen@ntrust. org.uk; www.wicken.org.uk.* The oldest nature reserve in Britain is a wilderness of swamp and scrub which harbours the characteristic plant and animal species of the primeval fenland in a landscape little changed since the time of Hereward the Wake.

The Fens, which stretch from Cambridge to Boston, are now a very fertile agricultural region. The swamps and marshes, mostly below sea level, were comprehensively drained by Dutch engineer Cornelius Vermuyden in the 17C.

EXETER★★

Devon, ENGLAND

POPULATION 94 717

MICHELIN ATLAS P 4 OR MAP 503 J 31

A visit to Exeter, the regional centre of this part of the south west, is rewarding for the charm of its crescents and terraces and in particular for its cathedral, standing out in elephant grey against the red sandstone of the city churches and the city wall, and the red-brick Georgian houses. ▯ *Civic Centre, Paris Street, EX1 1JJ, Exeter ☎ 01392 265 700; Fax 01392 265 260; tic@exeter.gov.uk; www.exeter.gov.uk/tourism.*

▶ **Orient Yourself**: The city centre is compact and can be covered on foot.

☻ **Don't Miss**: Cathedral nave vaulting and misericords; Royal Albert Memorial Museum's Devon Gallery and ethnography collection.

◔ **Organizing Your Time**: Allow 2-3 hours.

🔍 **Walking Tours**: Redcoat walking tours programme available from the Tourist Information Centre.

A Bit of History

In the 1C AD the Romans captured the settlements of the Isca Dumnoniorum tribe on the western bank of the River Exe, making it their most westerly strongpoint. The Saxon town which succeeded it was largely devastated by Danish invaders from 876 to 1003, but was rebuilt enough for the bishop's see to be transferred from Crediton to Exeter in 1050. In the Middle Ages trade prospered thanks to the city's position at the head of the navigable waters of the River Exe and it became one of the chief markets of country woollens. With the advent of steam power and machinery, however, Exeter's share of the woollen trade declined and the city settled down to the calm life of a county town. Heavy bombing in 1942 destroyed much of the city's medieval fabric.

Sights

Cathedral★★ (Z) – ♿◔ *Open daily, 9.30am-5pm. Donation ⊕ £3.50.* 🔍 *Guided tour: Apr-Oct, daily at 11am (Sat only), 2.30pm (except Sat) and 4pm (Sun only). Leaflet (13 languages). Guide book (3 languages). ☎ 01392 285 983 (cathedral office), 01392 214 219 (guided tour); Fax 01392 498 769; admin@exeter-cathedral.org.uk; www.exeter-cathedral.org.uk.* The **Norman transept towers** are the earliest part of the cathedral, since the majority of the building was remodelled and improved in the 13C by Bishop Bronescombe

---

Address Book

For coin ranges, see the Legend at the back of the guide.

WHERE TO EAT

⊖⊖ **Rodean,** *The Triangle, Kenton. ☎ 01626 890 195; Fax 01626 891 781; excellence@rodeanrestaurant.co.uk.* This former 1900s butcher's shop enjoys a pretty location 7 miles/11km southeast of Exeter. The menu employs good use of local ingredients. Dinner only and Sunday lunch.

⊖⊖⊖ **Jack in the Green Inn,** *Rockbeare. ☎ 01404 822 240; Fax 01404 823 445; info@jackinthegreen.uk.com; www.jackinthegreen.uk.com.* This traditional whitewashed pub 6 miles/10km east of Exeter serves accomplished and sophisticated Modern British meals in the oldest part of the premises.

WHERE TO STAY

⊖⊖⊖⊖ **The Edwardian,** *30-32 Heavitree Road. ☎ 01392 276 102; Fax 01392 253 393; michael@edwardianexeter. co.uk; www.edwardianexeter.co.uk.* Traditional decor and antiques make for a complete period-piece atmosphere in this city centre private hotel; some of the 12 rooms have four-poster beds.

⊖⊖⊖⊖ **St Andrews,** *28 Alphington Road. ☎ 01392 276 784; Fax 01392 250 249; standrewsexeter@aol.com.* This converted Victorian house with 17 rooms is traditionally English but unfussy. The large bay-windowed dining room is a highlight

⊖⊖⊖⊖ **Silversprings,** *12 Richmond Road. ☎/Fax 01392 494 040; reservations@ silversprings.co.uk; www.silversprings.co. uk.* This charming Georgian townhouse hotel offers ten luxury bedrooms and a sunny south-facing garden where guests may take breakfast or enjoy a coffee.

and finally completed a century later by Bishop Grandisson. Set in its Close, an island of calm amid the city's traffic, and surrounded by buildings from many periods, the west front of the cathedral rises through tier upon tier of carved angels, bishops and monarchs, through Decorated tracery to castellated parapets. The towers, twin but not identical (the northern one being earlier), mount solidly through tiers of blind arcading and intersecting arches to castellations and the angle turrets with pepperpot roofs, substituted in the 15C for the traditional Norman pyramids. At the west end the upper gable window is half-hidden by the main window which in turn is masked at the base by the pierced parapet edging the splendid late 14C-early 15C **image screen.**

Interior – The most striking feature is the tierceron **nave vaulting,** extending 300ft/91m from west to east in an uninterrupted line of meeting ribs, with huge gilded and coloured bosses studding the intersections. Also impressive are the 14C **corbels** between the pointed arches of the arcade, supported on piers of sixteen clustered columns with plain ring capitals. Note the 14C **minstrels' gallery** (north side) with 14 angels playing instruments and the west rose window with reticulated tracery (20C glass).

Behind the high altar stands the **Exeter Pillar,** the prototype of all the others in the cathedral. Through the two barely pointed arches behind the high altar can be seen the clustered pillars of the ambulatory and beyond them the Lady Chapel with its bosses and corbels. Sir Gilbert Scott's canopied choir stalls (1870-77) incorporate the oldest complete set of **misericords** in the country, carved in 1260-80. The exquisite

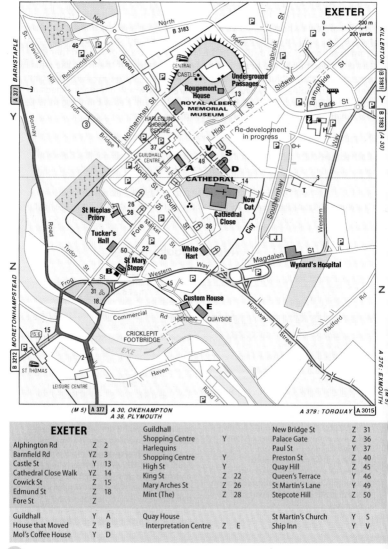

Gallery of the Kings, Exeter Cathedral

bishop's throne was carved in oak in 1312. Above the high altar the late 14C east window contains much original glass. In the north transept note the 15C clock with the sun and moon revolving around the earth.

Cathedral Close (Z) – The Close is diamond-shaped with the cathedral at its centre, almost abutted to the east by the gabled red sandstone bishop's palace. Marking the limits are the old **city wall (YZ)**, **St Martin's Church (Y S)**, **Mol's Coffee House (Y D)** – the four-storey timber-framed house dated 1596 – the cathedral choir school and a curving line of tall 17C-19C shops and houses ending in a white, four-storey Georgian house (now a hotel).

Royal Albert Memorial Museum★ (Y) – *(NACF)*   *Queen Street. Open Mon-Sat, 10am-5pm; Bank Hols, telephone for times. Closed 25-26 Dec. Free Admission. Café. ☎ 0139 265 858; www.exeter.gov.uk.* This dynamic, purpose-built museum contains superb collections of artefacts covering four main areas of interest – natural history, archeology, ethnography and fine and decorative arts – as well as pursuing an active educational policy. The Devon Gallery presents local **geology and ecology** and one of the most comprehensive collections of animal, vegetable and mineral specimens, from all five continents, to be found outside London. The museum is also the depository for some of the most important **prehistoric material** found in Devon, as well as large numbers of **Roman artefacts** left over from the city's occupation by Roman legions (AD 55-75) and some medieval fragments. The **ethnography** display reflects the number of Exeter families with far-flung trade contacts, especially in West Africa and the Pacific. The specimens of tribal art include artefacts collected by Captain Cook. Local **decorative arts** are represented by the fine displays of 18C-19C clocks and watches from Exeter and Bristol, 16C-19C silver (church plate, coffee, chocolate and tea pots etc) including a bequest of 60 **West Country spoons** (16C-17C), and examples of Devon pottery and glass ware. The museum's **fine art** collection spans the 17C-20C, concentrating particularly on artists associated with Devon.

Guildhall (Y) – *Open Mon-Fri mornings and afternoons, civic functions permitting (call for opening times). Closed public holidays. Donation. Guided tour available. ☎ 01392 665 500; guildhall@exeter.gov.uk; www.exeter.gov.uk.* The more striking parts of this ancient municipal building are the decorated Tudor portico added in 1593 and the Chamber which has a timber roof of 1468-70 and ornate Elizabethan oak panelling.

St Nicholas Priory (Z) – *Closed for renovation, reopens Summer 2006 ☎ 01392 665 858 (Royal Albert Memorial Museum); Fax 01392 421 252.* The sandstone building was the former guest wing of a small Benedictine priory founded in 1087 which later became an Elizabethan merchant's home. In the Norman undercroft-crypt massive round columns support low ribbed vaulting. The Guest Hall and Prior's Room have handsome timber roofs and contain 16C-17C furniture.

Quayside (Z) – *Access via the Butts ferry or the Cricklepit footbridge. Open Easter-Oct, daily, 10am-5pm. No charge. ☎ 01392 265 213.* The quay dates from the days when Exeter was a tidal river port, during a period of prosperity which was brought to an abrupt end in the 13C, when Isabella, Countess of Devon, built a weir across the river and successfully diverted all trade from Exeter to Topsham. By the 16C, the river was no longer navigable, so the first **ship canal** in England was dug (1563-66). The **Quay**

House Interpretation Centre (K) (🕐 *Open Easter-Oct, daily, 10am-5pm.* ☎ *01392 265 213*) presents models, paintings and artefacts and an audio-visual history of Exeter.

Exeter University (Y) – *2mi/3km north of city centre via Queen Street and New North Road.* The university campus is mostly situated in new buildings, including the Northcott Theatre, on the undulating 350 acre/140ha Streatham estate. The grounds are recognised as the most beautiful and botanically interesting of any British university.

Excursions

Bicton Gardens★ – *8mi/13km southeast on B 3182 then B 3179 and a minor road.* ♿ 🕐 *Open daily, 10am-6pm (5pm winter).* 👓 *£5.95. Woodland railway £1.30. Licensed restaurant.* ☎ *01395 568 465; Fax 01395 568 374; info@bictongardens.co.uk; www.bictongardens.co.uk.* The grounds of Bicton house, now an agricultural college, have been designed (formal Italian gardens after Le Nôtre) and planted with specimen trees over the last 200 years. Among other features are an **American Garden** (started in the 1830s), a secluded **Hermitage Garden,** the James Countryside Collection of tools and implements used on the land over the centuries and the Woodland Railway running through the grounds and by the lake.

Ottery St Mary★ – *12mi/19km east on B 3183, A 30 and B 3174.* The town, attractively situated on the River Otter and surrounded by green hills, has winding streets and small squares with 17C and Georgian houses. At the top of the hill stands the twin-towered parish church of **St Mary's★,** consecrated in 1260 and converted into a collegiate foundation in 1336: the chancel, nave, aisle and Lady Chapel were remodelled in the Decorated style and many of the furnishings belong to this period, including **Grandisson's clock** in the south transept and the gilded wooden **eagle lectern**, one of the oldest and grandest in England. A special feature of the church is its varied **vaulting**, superb coloured **bosses** and **corbels**.

EXMOOR★★

Somerset and Devon, ENGLAND

MICHELIN ATLAS PP 6, 7 OR MAP 503 8 I, J 30

The great southwest moor (267 sq mi/692km2) which bestrides the boundary between North Devon and Somerset and slopes down to the Bristol Channel is one of Britain's National Parks. The upland ridges of the Brendon Hills, covered in blue moor-grass, bracken or heather, ripple away as far as the eye can see, while to the north lies the Exmoor Forest, until 1818 a Royal Forest where game was reserved for the royal hunt. Red deer, wild Exmoor ponies (a protected species directly descended from prehistoric horses), sheep and cattle still roam the moor which is vividly described in RD Blackmore's famous novel *Lorna Doone* (1869). Exmoor's rugged coastline also provides sanctuary to a large variety of seabirds. 🗊 *There are several tourist information centres and five National Park Visitor Centres spread around the region: www.visit-exmoor. info is the official tourism portal site and has details of all these.*

▶ **Orient Yourself**: The National Park Visitor Centres give information on public rights of way, cycle routes, bridleways, guided walks and nature trails.

👓 **Don't Miss**: The views from Dunkerry Beacon; Dunster Castle; Watersmeet; Tarr Steps.

🕐 **Organizing Your Time**: Allow 2-3 days excluding activities.

🔢 **Especially for Kids**: Beaches at Porlock Weir (shingle) and Lynmouth (rocky). Nearby Minehead is a fully fledged seaside resort with a long sandy beach.

The Moor

Although Exmoor is one of the smallest of the National Parks, its many varied sights invite exploration.

Dulverton★ – The "capital" village of the area is sited 450ft/137m above sea level amid beautiful scenery and boasts a solid church (rebuilt in the 19C) with a 13C west tower and pretty cottages along the main street and market square.

Dunkery Beacon★★★ – At 1 705ft/519m the Beacon is the highest point on the Moor, visible for miles around and commanding **views★★★** of the moor.

Dunster★★ – The beautiful old town of Dunster on the northeast edge of Exmoor enjoyed a flourishing coastal and continental trade with Bordeaux, Spain, Italy and Wales until the sea retreated in the 15C-16C, whereupon it became a wool market and weaving centre.

Literary associations

The 14C thatched pub, the **Rising Sun Inn** on Mars Hill, is said to have sheltered **RD Blackmore** while he wrote his novel *Lorna Doone*. From here it is a steep climb up the Lyn valley to Watersmeet.

In 1797, the poets **Wordsworth** and **Coleridge** arrived here on foot, having walked 30 miles from Nether Stowey in the Quantock Hills. While staying at Culbone nearby (now called Ash Farm), Coleridge began his poem *Kubla Khan* before being rudely awakened from an opium-induced reverie by the "person from Porlock".

Years later, in 1812, the disowned young poet **Shelley** came to Lynmouth accompanied by his 16-year-old "bride" Harriet Westbrook, her sister Eliza, a former governess and an Irish servant. During his stay, Shelley distributed his revolutionary pamphlet, the *Declaration of Rights* he had had printed in Ireland: some he sealed inside bottles which were wrapped in oiled cloth and packed into crates fitted with a sail before being launched from the beach; others he despatched in miniature hot-air balloons from Countisbury Hill.

It is now a popular tourist destination in season. The red sandstone **castle**★★, (*NT & Castle: Open late-Mar to early-Nov, Sat-Wed and Good Friday, 11am-5pm (4pm late-Sep to early-Nov). Exhibition. Garden and Park: Open daily, 11am-5pm (4pm Oct-Mar). Closed 25 and 26 Dec. Castle, garden and park £7.20; garden and park £3.90. 01643 821 314, 01643 823 004 (information line); Fax 01643 823 000; wdugen@smtp.ntrust.org.uk; www. nationaltrust.org.uk*) dominates the town from the tor on which a fortification has stood since Saxon times. The castle was begun by the Norman baron William de Mohun, but by 1374 the de Mohun line was dying out and the castle was sold to Lady Elizabeth Luttrell. When George Fownes Luttrell inherited the property in 1867 he commissioned the architect **Anthony Salvin** to transform the castle to its present appearance of a fortified Jacobean mansion. The **water mill**★, (*NT & Mill Lane. Open late-Mar to early-Nov, daily, 10.30am-5pm. £2.20. Tearoom. Wheelchair access free of charge to ground floor only in mill. 01643 821 759; www.nationaltrust.org.uk*) on the River Avill, rebuilt and improved since Domesday, ground corn until the late 19C, came back into use during the 1939-45 war and was rebuilt and restored to working order in 1979-80. The long, wide **High Street** lined by 17C-19C houses is graced by the unique 17C octagonal, dormered **Yarn Market**. Many of the buildings along **Church Street** are related to the priory founded in 1090 and dissolved in 1539: 14C Nunnery and Priest's House (restored 19C); 20ft/6m high early medieval **dovecote**★ (beyond the gate in the end wall of the Priory Garden). **St George's church**★ was originally built by the Normans in the 12C then rebuilt by the monks in the 14C. Its 110ft/34m **tower**, dating from 1443, houses a carillon (*which plays daily at 9am, 1pm, 5pm and 9pm*). Inside are **wagon roofs**, a splendid 54ft/16m carved **screen**, a 16C Perpendicular **font** and the **Luttrell tombs.**

Lynton and Lynmouth★ – These complementary towns in a hollow at the top and at the foot of 500ft/152m North Devon cliffs rejoice in glorious **views**★ across the Bristol Channel to the distant Welsh coast. Lynton is predominantly Victorian-Edwardian while Lynmouth remains a traditional fishing village with small stone cottages and houses. The **Valley of the Rocks**★ (1mi/2km west) is a group of rocks rising from the wide grass-covered valley to crests of bare sandstone and shale spectacularly carved by the wind.

Oare – This tiny village in a green valley only a couple of miles from the sea owes its fame entirely to *Lorna Doone* (see above). The Doone family is said to have lived here and it was in the restored 14C-15C church that Lorna was married to John Ridd. A path leads to **Doone Valley**★ (*6mi/9km*) which came to fame with the publication of Blackmore's novel, based on tales of a group of outlaws and cut-throats who settled in Badgworthy Valley in the 1620s.

Porlock★ – This is an attractive, though much visited, village – rendered infamous by "the man from Porlock" who interrupted Coleridge as he was writing Kubla Khan. The 13C **St Dubricius Church**★ with its truncated shingle-covered spire, is a reminder of Dubricius, a legendary figure who died aged 120 and is said to have been a friend of King Arthur (see GLASTONBURY and TINTAGEL). Inside is a remarkable canopied tomb with alabaster effigies.

Tarr Steps★★ – The finest **clapper bridge**★★ in the country, dating back to the Middle Ages or earlier, crosses the River Barle at this point.

Watersmeet★ – A beauty spot where the Rivers East Lyn and Hoaroak meet in a deep wooded valley, the riverbed strewn with boulders around which the water swirls endlessly.

Winsford★ – With its seven bridges within yards of each other, Winsford's oldest is the **packhorse bridge** over the River Exe.

FOUNTAINS ABBEY★★★

North Yorkshire, ENGLAND

MICHELIN ATLAS P 39 OR MAP 502 P 21

Set in the wooded valley of the little River Skell 3 miles/5km west of Ripon, in the glorious North Yorkshire countryside, these Cistercian ruins are wonderfully evocative of monastic life in the Middle Ages.

A Bit of History

In 1132 a small band of Benedictines, in revolt against slack discipline at their abbey in York, were granted land in this "place remote from all the world." Accepted by St Bernard into his austere order, the monks set about transforming the northern wilderness into the flourishing and productive countryside characteristic of Cistercian endeavour. Within a century, Fountains was the centre of an enormous enterprise, managing fish-farms and ironworkings, as well as forests and vast tracts of agricultural land, the profits from which paid for an ambitious building programme.

The great complex fell into decay following the Dissolution but in 1768 it was bought by the Aislabie family, who had long desired it as the ultimate in picturesque ruins to complete their lavish landscaping of the adjacent Studley Royal estate.

Visit

Visitor Centre – The Centre provides information on the history of the abbey, the Cistercian rule and the construction of the gardens of Studley Royal.

▶ *From the Visitor Centre take the minibus or take the steep and direct path (5min) or the longer less steep path with view points (10min); at the gate fork right to Fountains Hall or left to the* **abbey ruins and the gardens**. ♿ ◷*Open Mar-Oct, daily, 10am-5pm (3pm, 12-13 Jul, and Oct); Nov-Jan, Sat-Thu, 10am-4pm/dusk); Feb-Mar, daily, 10am-4pm. Deerpark open daily during daylight hours. Last admission 1 hr before closing.* ◷ *Closed 1 Jan and 24-25 Dec.* ⊙ *£5.50.* ⟵ *Guided tour of abbey, water garden and mill. Deer park £2. Licensed restaurant. 01765 608 888 (infoline); Fax 01765 601 002; www.fountainsabbey.org.uk.*

Fountains Hall – Stone from the abbey was used to build the splendid five-storey Jacobean mansion (1598-1611). Behind the striking **facade**★ with its Renaissance details, the interior is laid out to the conventional medieval plan.

Fountains Abbey – The grassy levels of Abbey Green extend to the west front of the roofless abbey church and the monastic buildings adjoining the south side. The scale and diversity of the monastic buildings suggest the varied activities of the great community of monks and lay brothers.

Fountains Abbey

B. Kaufmann/MICHELIN

The church's tall tower (c 1500) rises above the stately Norman nave. At the east end is the spectacular 13C **Chapel of the Nine Altars**, an unusual feature later repeated at Durham Cathedral, with soaring arches and a huge Perpendicular window.

The most complete and beautiful remains are those of the buildings grouped round the cloister in accordance with the standard Cistercian plan: in the western range is the **cellarium**, with its astounding 300ft/90m vaulted interior below the lay brothers' dormitory; in the south range is the **great refectory**, its single doorway a masterpiece of elaborate moulding; in the east range is the **chapter house**, entered through three fine Norman arches. To the east are the foundations and lower walls of the monks' infirmary and the abbot's house. The guest house and the lay brothers' infirmary are outside the precinct in the southeast corner of Abbey Green. All the dormitories ended in latrines (reredorters) constructed over the river, which acted as a drain.

The abbey museum contains a large-scale model of the abbey.

Studley Royal – The gardens were designed to be visited starting from the Canal Gates: short walk *(45min)*, medium route *(1hr 45min)*, complete tour *(2hr excluding the Seven Bridges Walk)*.

John Aislabie, then Chancellor of the Exchequer, began to create a garden at his Yorkshire estate in 1716. From 1720 – when he retired in disgrace as a result of the South Sea Bubble – until his death in 1742, he devoted his vast personal fortune to remodelling the floor of the sinuous valley of the Skell into a spectacular landscape consisting of a series of formal water features and contrived views, embellished with garden buildings and flanked by woodland on the steeper slopes.

The canalised river, emerging from a dark grotto, is led past the **Moon Pond**, which is overlooked by a Classical **Temple of Piety**, and finally discharges into a lake over a grand cascade flanked by symmetrical pavilions, known as fishing tabernacles.

Along the east side of the valley is a high-level walk which passes through a twisting tunnel, past the **Gothic Tower** and the elegant **Temple of Fame** to **Anne Boleyn's Seat** and the surprise view of the east end of the abbey ruins.

The **Seven Bridges Walk** follows the course of the Skell downstream from the lake zigzagging from bank to bank.

In the deer park, north of the Visitor Centre, stands **St Mary's Church**, a masterpiece of High Victorian Gothic by William Burges, on the axis of a long avenue which extends east to the original entrance to the park from the village of **Studley Royal** and aligned on the twin towers of **Ripon Cathedral**.

GLAMIS ★

Angus, SCOTLAND

POPULATION 648

MICHELIN ATLAS P 62 OR MAP 501 K, L 14

This pleasant village, famous for its Macbeth associations, is set in the rich agricultural Vale of Strathmore in the Angus glens countryside of eastern Scotland. An attractive row of 19C cottages houses the Angus Folk Museum★ *(♿ Kirkwynd, Glamis.* ◷*Open Mar-late Sept, Fri-Tues, noon-5pm (Jul-Aug 11am-5pm).* ⊚ *£5.* ☎ *01307 840 288; www.nts.org.uk).* **A fascinating collection of domestic and agricultural items gives an insight into rural life in bygone days.**

Sights

Glamis Castle★★

♿*Dundee Road.* ◷ *Open late-Mar to mid-Dec, daily 10am - 6pm (4.30pm last admission).* ⊚*£7. Grounds only, £3.50.* ◷ *Guided tour (50min) every 10-15min (translations available). Parking. Restaurant. Picnic area.* ☎ *01307 840 393; admin@glamis-castle.co.uk; www.glamis-castle.co.uk.* Glamis (pronounced Glarms) is the epitome of a Scottish castle; the massive sandstone pile bristles with towers, turrets, conical roofs and chimneys; it has a ghost (Lady Glamis, burnt as a witch), literary associations (Macbeth was Thane of Glamis) and has been the home of the Lyon family (forebears of the recently deceased Queen Mother) since 1372.

Exterior – The 15C L-shaped core of the castle has been added to and altered, apparently at random through the centuries, giving the present building its impressive appearance.

Glamis Castle

Interior – Family and other portraits, Jacobean armour and furniture, and interiors of many periods, form the charm of the guided tour. The chapel has a series of paintings of the Apostles and scenes from the Bible by Jacob de Wet (1695-1754), a Dutch artist who also worked at Blair and Holyroodhouse. The splendid **Drawing Room** is adorned by a **plasterwork ceiling** (1621) and a magnificent fireplace. Here, as in Holyroodhouse, hang tapestries from the workshop founded at Mortlake by James VI and I, after his accession to the English throne.

Statues of James and his son, Charles I, flank the driveway. To the side is a beautiful Italian Garden.

Excursions

Pictish Stones – The area around Glamis is rich in carved stones of the Picts. Their enigmatic carvings, some dating from the 7C and boasting Christian symbols incorporated in later centuries, vividly illustrate their life and art. The Pictish Kingdom and its distinctive art lasted for some 500 years, but faded away after Kenneth MacAlpine unified the thrones of Picts and Scots in AD 843.

Aberlemno Stones★ – *12mi/20km northeast by A 94 and B 9134. ◷ Open May-Oct. The stones are boarded up from Nov-Apr.* Four sculptured stones, with animal and abstract symbols, hunting and battle scenes and a cross with flanking angels, stand at the roadside and in the churchyard.

Meigle Museum★★ – *7mi/11km west by A 94. ♿ ◷ Open daily late Mar - Sep, 9.30am (2pm Sun, Oct-Mar) to 6.30pm). ⊜ £2.20. ☎ 01828 640 612; www.historic-scotland.gov.uk.* In the former village school behind the church is displayed an outstanding collection of early **Christian monuments★★** in the Pictish tradition, all found locally. The carving is full of vitality and shows a high degree of skill.

Edzell Castle★ – *(25mi/40km northeast by A 94 and B 966 to Edzell village. ♿ ◷ Open Apr-Sep, daily, 9.30am-6.30pm; Oct-Mar, Sat-Wed, 9.30am to 4.30pm (12.30pm Thu). ⊜ £3.30. Parking. Picnic area. ☎ 01356 648 631; www. historic-scotland.gov.uk.* The ruined castle, the former seat of the Lindsay family, comprises the early 16C tower house – view of the

Pictish Stones

Pleasance from the top of the great hall – a traditional L-shaped building with decorative corbelling and a later 16C extension. The highlight is a formal walled garden, **The Pleasance**★★★ which is without equal in Scotland. Sir David Lindsay (c 1550-1610) created this garden in 1604; it is a product of the Renaissance ideas he had absorbed on his wide travels. The blaze of summer colour against the rich red of the walls may divert the attention from the heraldic and symbolic **sculptures** on the walls, but these, too, reward closer inspection.

GLASGOW★★★

City of Glasgow, SCOTLAND

POPULATION 662 853

MICHELIN ATLAS P 55 OR MAP 501 H 16

Glasgow, Scotland's most populous city, is an important industrial centre and port, lying 44 miles/70km west of Edinburgh, just a few miles inland of the east coast. It is currently enjoying a renaissance as a cultural centre.

▶ **Orient Yourself**: Since Glasgow's main sights are well scattered about, it is advisable to use public transport. The underground stations are indicated on the town plan below. City tours in open-topped buses leave from George Square. Contact Scotguide Tours Services for further information. ☎ 0141 204 0444; www.scotguide.com.

⊘ **Don't Miss**: The Burrell Collection, Glasgow Cathedral; Hunterian Art Gallery Mackintosh wing; Museum of Transport, an excursion to New Lanark.

⊙ **Organizing Your Time**: Allow at least three days in the city itself.

Kids Especially for Kids: Glasgow Science Centre.

A Bit of History

It was to this part of the embattled Kingdom of Strathclyde that **St Mungo** came in the mid 6C: he set up his wooden church on the banks of the Molendinar Burn, and became the first bishop, then patron saint of the city. In the 17C, Glasgow – always a radical city – became the centre of the Protestant cause. By the 18C the city was rich from trade in textiles, sugar and tobacco, her wealth increasing in the 19C through banking, shipbuilding and heavy industry.

The arts prospered amid the wealth: neither the **Glasgow Boys** (WY MacGregor, James Guthrie, George Henry and John Lavery who advocated realism in an age of romanticism), nor the pioneer modern movement led by Charles Rennie Mackintosh, could have so flourished in any other city. The realist and radical traditions have been adopted by the Glasgow painters of the 1980s (Steven Campbell, Ken Currie, Peter Howson, Adrian Wisniewski and Stephen Conroy). Today Glasgow is the home of the Scottish Opera, Scottish Ballet and several notable art collections.

Burrell Collection★★★

3mi/5km southwest by M 77 **(AZ)** ♿ *Pollok Park.* ⊙*Open daily, 10am (11am Fri and Sun) to 5pm.* ⊙ *Closed 1-2 Jan and 25-26 Dec.* 🚶 *Guided tour (1hr). Parking. Restaurant.* ☎ *0141 649 2550; Fax 0141 289 2579.* The collection of one man, the shipowner **Sir William Burrell** (1861-1958) who gifted it to his native city in 1944, it is now on display in a custom-built gallery which is surrounded by parkland and is "as simple as possible" as Burrell wished.

The collection is spaciously laid out in six sections. The **Ancient Civilisations** section includes items from Egypt, Mesopotamia, Italy and Greece, notably the 2C AD **Warwick Vase** and the porphyry **Head of Zeus** or **Poseidon** dating from the 4C AD. The section **Oriental Art** incorporates ceramics, bronzes and jades from the 3rd millennium BC to the 19C, and features the enamelled Ming figure of a **lohan**, or disciple of Buddha, which is dated to 1484. Burrell's particular interest was in **Medieval and Post-Medieval European Art** and two delightful specimens are the 15C Tournai tapestry *Peasants Hunting Rabbits with Ferrets* and the fragment of 12C stained glass depicting the **Prophet Jeremiah**. Of the early works to be found in

Address Book

OUT AND ABOUT IN GLASGOW

Tourist Information Centre – The Glasgow City Marketing Bureau at 11 George Square (☎0141 204 4400; Fax 0141 221 3524; www.seeglasgow.com) offers an accommodation and theatre booking service. It also has a bureau de change, a tourist information service, a bookshop and a souvenir shop. There is an office at Glasgow Airport ☎ 0141 848 4440; Fax 0141 849 1444.

Public Transport – The Travel Centre, St Enoch's Square ☎ 0141 332 7133 gives information on travel passes for the metro, bus and trains. The SPT **Discovery** ticket valid for one day allows visitors to discover the varied aspects of Glasgow starting from different metro stations.

The **Charles Rennie Mackintosh Trail Ticket** (£12) gives users combined entry to all paying Mackintosh attractions in the city, the Hill House in Helensburgh as well as unlimited travel on Subway and FirstBus services in Greater Glasgow.

Sightseeing – **Clyde Helicopters,** (City Heliport, SECC, Glasgow ☎ 0141 226 4261) offer helicopter rides which afford spectacular views of the city and of Loch Lomond.

Boat trips "doon the watter" along the Firth of Clyde are also very popular.

Pubs and Restaurants – The lively atmosphere of Glasgow pubs is famous: **Rab Ha's** in Hutcheson Street, **Times Square** in St Enoch's Square, **Curlers** and **Bonhams** in Byres Road and **Dows** in Dundas Street among many other venues are well worth a visit. Glasgow also offers a wide range of restaurants to suit all tastes.

For a light meal or afternoon tea visit the delightful Willow Rooms at 217 Sauchiehall Street, designed by CR Mackintosh for Miss Cranston.

Shopping – Sauchiehall, Buchanan and Argyle Streets are pedestrian shopping precincts. The glass-roofed Princes Street shopping centre in Buchanan Street is a pleasant haven where Scottish items are on offer. The Italian Centre on the corner of John and Ingram Streets has on sale the finest Italian fashion and also offers bars, brasseries, restaurants and cafés in a beautiful decor.

Scottish Crafts in Princes Street displays fine items by Scottish craftsmen.

The Barras, a large indoor and outdoor market, is the place to visit not only for a bargain but also for the spectacle.

Entertainment – Glasgow has a dynamic cultural scene with avant-garde theatre staged by the Citizens Theatre, the Centre for Contemporary Arts, the Tramway Theatre and the Tron Theatre. Other venues include The Mitchell Theatre, the King's Theatre and the Theatre Royal. Exhibitions are held at the McLellan Galleries, The Third Eye Centre, The Lighthouse and The Gait - recently converted at great expense from The Old Fruitmarket and City Hall.

The List magazine, published fortnightly, is the best guide to what's on in the Greater Glasgow area. Tickets for many events are on sale at the Ticket Centre, City Hall, Candleriggs. Football is a city passion, and it is essential to book well in advance for the "Old Firm" matches between Rangers and Celtic, but be warned that strong sectarian feelings are aroused at these engagements.

Paintings, Drawings and Bronzes Bellini's *Virgin and Child* is notable. There is an important group of 19C French works with the pastel Jockeys in the Rain by Degas among them.

The Hutton Castle Rooms, once part of Burrell's own home, are complete with medieval and antique furnishings.

Pollok House★ – ♿ Pollokshaws Road. ◷Open daily, 10am-5pm. ◷ Closed 1-2 Jan and 25-26 Dec. 👝 £8;. Leaflet (5 languages). Parking. Restaurant. ☎ 0141 616 6410; Fax 0141 616 6521; pollokhouse@nts.org.uk; www.nts.org.uk.. The highlight of this 18C mansion is the representative collection of **Spanish paintings★★** acquired by Sir William Stirling Maxwell (1818-78). The paintings, including portraits by El Greco, etchings by Goya as well as works by Tristan, Alonso Cano and Murillo, are displayed in tastefully furnished rooms.

Medieval Glasgow

Cathedral★★★ (CY) – ♿◷ Open daily, 9.30am (2-4pm Sun) to 6pm (5pm Sun; 4pm Oct-Mar). ◷ Closed 1-2 Jan and 25-26 Dec. ☎ 0141 552 6891; www.glasgowcathedral.org.uk. The Gothic cathedral, fourth church on the site of St Mungo's original building, is best viewed from the heights of the nearby Necropolis. The cathedral is mostly 13C and 14C with 15C additions (chapter house, Blacader Aisle, central tower and stone spire). The **nave** is late Gothic; its elevation of richly moulded and pointed arches, more numerous at each level, rises to the timber roof. Beyond the 15C stone screen

– unique in Scotland – is the **choir**, mid-13C in finest early pointed style, the triple lancets of the clerestory echoed in the lines of the east window. Beyond the ambulatory, through one of the four chapels leading off from it, is the upper chapter-room (rebuilt in the 15C) where the medieval university held its classes.

The lower church is another Gothic delight, where light and shade play effectively amidst the piers enshrining the **tomb of St Mungo**, Glasgow's patron saint, whose legend is illustrated on the St Kentigern Tapestry (1979). The 15C **Blacader Aisle** is an extension by Glasgow's first archbishop and has decorative ribbed vaulting and carved bosses.

Cathedral Square (CY) – The pre-Reformation heart of the ecclesiastical city; of the original buildings only the Cathedral and **Provand's Lordship** (1471) (&. *3 Castle Street.* ⏰*Open Mon –Thu and Sat , 10am (11am Fri and Sun) to 5pm.* ⏰ *Closed 1 Jan and 25 Dec. Parking.* ☎ *0141 552 8819; www.glasgow.gov.uk)* survive. The 20C Royal Infirmary replaces an earlier Adam brothers' one (1792), built now the site of the medieval Bishop's Castle. The visitor centre houses the **St Mungo Museum of Religious Life and Art**, (&. *2 Castle Street.* ⏰*Open daily, 10am (11am Fri and Sun) to 5pm.* ⏰ *Closed 1-2 Jan and 25-26 Dec.* ➴ *Free guided tours. Parking. Refreshments. Shop.* ☎ *0141 553 2557; www.glasgow. gov.uk)* devoted to a comparative presentation of religious creeds.

Glasgow Cross (CZ) – The heart of Glasgow until Victorian times; the **Tolbooth Steeple**★ is the last reminder of its faded elegance.

Bridgegate (CZ) – Once a fashionable thoroughfare to Glasgow's first stone bridge (1345); all that is left of its better days is the steeple (164ft/50m) of Glasgow's Merchants Hall (1659), which served as a look-out for homecoming ships.

Glasgow Green (CZ) – A place used for grazing, jousting, parades, public hangings and above all free speech; the most historic piece of common land in the city.

The People's Palace, (&. *Glasgow Green.* ⏰*Open daily, 10am (11am Fri and Sun) to 5pm.* ⏰*Closed 1-2 Jan and 25-26 Dec. Parking. Restaurant.* ☎ *0141 554 0223; www. glasgow.gov.uk)* is a social history museum with exotic winter gardens.

The Barras (CZ) – A weekend market, providing some of the most attractive and colourful street scenes in the city.

University District

The University was founded in 1451 and its nucleus is George Gilbert Scott's neo-Gothic **Gilmorehill Building** (completed by his son John Oldrid). It houses two fine collections.

Hunterian Museum – *First floor, main building, East Quadrangle.* &.⏰ *Open Mon-Sat, 9.30am-5pm.* ⏰ *Closed Easter, Sat in Sep, local Bank Hols. Wheelchair access (telephone from main Gatehouse).* ☎ *0141 330 4221; Fax 0141 330 3617; hunter@museum.gla.ac.uk; www.gla.ac.uk/Museum.*

The collection of William Hunter (1718-83), anatomist and pioneer obstetrician, is now divided between the museum and art gallery. The geological, anatomical, archeological and ethnographical collections are complemented by a fine **coin and medal collection**★.

Hunterian Art Gallery★★ – &.⏰ *Open Mon-Sat, 9.30am-5pm.* ⏰ *Closed Sun and local Bank Hols.* ➴*No charge. Refreshments. Shop.* ☎ *0141 330 5431; Fax 0141 330 3618; hunter@ museum.gla.ac.uk; www.hunterian. gla.ac.uk.* The University's art collection includes an important holding of works by **James McNeill Whistler** (1843-1903) – *Rose et Argent, La Jolie Mutine, Red and Black, The Fan and Blue and Silver, Screen with Old Battersea Bridge* – as well as portraits and 19C and 20C Scottish art.

The **Mackintosh Wing**★★★ is a reconstruction of the home of Charles Rennie Mackintosh (1869-1928), the Glasgow architect and designer.

Art Gallery and Museum Kelvingrove★★ – &.⏰ *Closed until Feb. 2006.* ☎ *0141 287 2699; Fax 0141 287 2690; www.glasgowmuseums.com.*

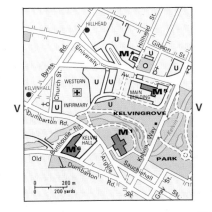

The building, which opened in 1902 financed by the 1888 Glasgow International Exhibition, houses the various donations by local captains of industry. The European art section is displayed in the first-floor galleries. The Dutch and Flemish holding includes works by Jordaens, Rubens, Bruegel the Elder, Rembrandt *(A Man in Armour)* as well as Ruisdael landscapes. French 19C and early 20C movements are represented by Millet *(Going to Work)*, Fantin-Latour, Courbet; and Monet, Pissarro, Renoir and Sisley for the Impressionists. Van Gogh's 1887 portrait depicts the Glasgow art dealer, Alexander Reid, with whom he shared a flat in Paris.

The British section includes portraits by Ramsey, Raeburn, Reynolds and Romney and the work of the Pre-Raphaelites. Also of note is the luminous quality of William McTaggart's outdoor scenes, precursors of the late 19C Glasgow Boys, a school contemporary with the Barbizon and Hague Schools. Henry's *A Galloway Landscape* is typical of the Scottish movement, while the combined compositions of Henry and Hornel show a strong Japanese influence. The highly distinctive works of the Scottish Colourists (Peploe, Hunter, Cadell and Fergusson) are enjoying a growing reputation.

The newly refurbished **Glasgow Style** gallery provides a permanent home for the city's extensive collection of Charles Rennie Mackintosh exhibits, including the spectacular interior of Kate Cranston's Ingram Street Tea Rooms.

Museum of Transport★★ – & *1 Bunhouse Road.* ○*Open daily, 10am (11am Fri and Sun) to 5pm.* ○ *Closed 1-2 Jan and 25-26 Dec. Parking. Restaurant.* ☎ *0141 287 2720; Fax*

GLASGOW

Albert Bridge	CZ	2
Anderson Quay	BZ	
Arcadia St	CZ	3
Argyle St	BCZV	
Bain St	CZ	4
Baird St	CY	
Ballater St	CZ	
Bath St	BY	
Bells Bridge	AZ	
Berkeley St	BY	
Binnie Pl.	CZ	6
Bridge St	BZ	7
Bridgegate	CZ	9
Broomielaw	BZ	
Buccleuch St	BY	10
Buchanan Galleries	CY	
Buchanan St.	CYZ	12
Bunhouse Rd	V	
Byres Rd	V	
Caledonia Rd	AV	14
Cambridge St	BY	15
Castle St	CY	17
Cathedral Square	CY	
Cathedral St	CY	
Church St	V	
Clyde St	CZ	
Clydeside Expressway	BY	
Commerce St	BZ	18
Cook St	BZ	
Cowcaddens Rd	CY	
Craighall Rd	CY	
Dobbie's Loan	CY	
Duke St	CZ	
Dumbarton Rd	V	
Eglinton St	BZ	
Eldon St	BY	
Finnieston St	BYZ	21
Gallowgate	CZ	
Garscube Rd	BY	
George Square	CY	
George V Bridge	BZ	22
Gibson St	V	
Glasgow Bridge	BZ	25
Glassford St.	CZ	26
Gorbals St	CZ	
Gordon St	BY	27
Govan Rd	ABZ	
Gray St	V	
Great Western Rd	BY	
Greendyke St	CZ	
High St	CZ	
Hillhead St	V	
Hope St	BY	
Hospital St	CZ	
Ingram St	CZ	
Jamaica St	BCZ	28
John Knox St	CZ	29
Kelvin Way	V	
Kilbirnie St	BZ	31
Killermont St	CY	32
King's Drive	CZ	
Kingston St	BZ	33
Kyle St	CY	
Lancefield Quay	BZ	
Laurieston Rd	CZ	35
London Rd	CZ	
Maryhill Rd	BY	
Morris Pl.	CZ	36
Morrison St	BZ	38
Nelson St	BZ	
Norfolk St	BCZ	
North Canalbank St	CY	
North Hanover St	CY	
Old Dumbarton Rd	V	
Oswald St	BZ	39
Oxford St	BCZ	40
Pinkston Rd	CY	
Pitt St	BY	42
Port Dundas St	CY	43
Queen St	CZ	45
Renfield St	CY	46
Renfrew St	BCY	
St. Enoch Shopping Centre	CZ	47
St. Vincent St.	BCY	
St George's Rd	BY	
Saltmarket	CZ	
Sauchiehall St	BY	
Scotland St	BZ	
Scott St	BY	48
Seaward St	BZ	
South Portland St	CZ	49
Springburn	CY	
Stirling Rd	CY	50
Stockwell St	CZ	52
Trongate	CZ	
Union St	CYZ	
University Ave	V	
Victoria Bridge	CZ	54
Waterloo St	BYZ	
West George St	CYZ	
West Graham St	BY	55
West Nile St	CY	56
West Paisley Rd	ABZ	
West St	BZ	
Woodlands Rd	BY	
Art Gallery and Museum Kelvingrove	V	
Barras (The)		CZ
Burrell Collection		AZ
Cathedral		CY
City Chambers		CY
Gallery of Modern Art		CZ
Glasgow Cross		CZ
Glasgow Green		CZ

0141 287 2692; www.glasgow.gov.uk. The museum has comprehensive displays of trams and trolley buses from 1872-1967, vintage cars with the emphasis on **Scottish-built cars**★★★ (Argyll, Albion and Arrol-Johnston), fire vehicles and bicycles. In the Kelvin Street exhibit there is a reminder of the subway prior to modernisation. The **Clyde Room of Model Ships**★★★ displays the varied and impressive output of Scottish shipyards, in particular those of Clydeside.

City Centre

George Square – Though started in 1782 George Square is magnificently Victorian. Of special interest are the 1869 **Merchants' House (CY A)** and, opposite, the **City Chambers**★ **(CY)** (&⏱ 📷 *Free Guided tour (45min; official functions permitting) Mon-Fri at 10.30am and 2.30pm. ⏱ Closed Bank Hols.* ☎*0141 287 4017, 287 4018; Fax 0141 287 5666; www.glasgow.gov.uk*) where the grandeur and opulence of the loggia, council and banqueting halls are reminders that Glasgow was the second city of the Empire in Victorian times.

Hutchesons' Hall – & *158 Ingram Street.* ⏱*Open (functions permitting) late-Jan to late Dec, Mon-Sat, 10am-5pm. ⏱ Closed Bank Hols. Access to gallery is free, charge for special exhibits Audio-visual presentation.* ☎ *0141 552 8391; Fax 0141 552 7031; hutchesonshall@nts.org.uk; www.nts.org.uk.* The original hospital was endowed in 1639 by the Hutcheson brothers, whose statues adorn the frontage of the 1802-05 hall. It is now a National Trust for Scotland visitor centre.

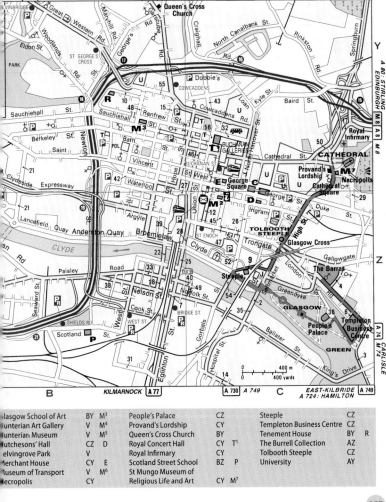

Gallery of Modern Art★ – ♿ *Queen Street.* 🕐*Open daily, 10am (11am Fri and Sun, Thur until 8 pm) to 5pm.* 🕐 *Closed 1-2 Jan and 25 Dec.* ☎ *0141 229 1996; Fax 0141 636 0086; www.glasgow.gov.uk.* A great 18C neo-Classical mansion with a massive Corinthian portico and a magnificent main hall with a barrel-vaulted ceiling houses a collection of contemporary art ranging from paintings, sculpture and graphic works to photographs, mobiles and installations. Among the British works are *Karaoke* by Beryl Cook, *Illustrations from "Fourteen Poems by CP Cavafy"* by David Hockney and *Arrest III* by Bridget Riley while European artists include Vasarely (pioneer of Op Art), Nicky de Saint-Phalle *(Autel du Chat Mort),* Eduard Bersudsky *(The Great Idea, Karl Marx).* Also on display are intriguing Aboriginal paintings by Robert Campbell Jr and Paddy Jalparri Sims.

Glasgow School of Art★ – ♿ *167 Renfrew Street. Mackintosh Gallery.* 🕐*Open Mon-Fri at 10 am,5pm, Sat 10am – 2pm. Newberry Gallery Mon-Fri 10am-5pm.* 🕐 *Closed 23 Dec-4 Jan.* 💷 *£5. Refreshments.* ☎ *0141 353 4526; Fax 0141 353 4746; design@gsa. ac.uk; www.gsa.ac.uk.* The building was designed by Charles Rennie Mackintosh when he was only 28, and this unique working educational institution remains his masterpiece. It was built in 1897-99 and 1907-09 and holds his acclaimed library with its three-storey-high windows and suspended ceiling, and the furniture gallery with items from Miss Cranston's Tea Rooms.

Address Book

For coin ranges, see the Legend at the back of the guide.

WHERE TO EAT

◖◗◖◗ **Bouzy Rouge,** *111 West Regent Street.* ☎ *0141 221 8804; Fax 0141 221 6941; res@bouzy-rouge.com; www. bouzy-rouge. com.* An unusual but vibrant city centre restaurant with furnishings hand-crafted from Scottish elm and intricate iron work. The menu is similarly eclectic with Modern Scottish and Mediterranean-influenced "casual gourmet" dishes.

◖◗◖◗ **Cafe Ostra,** *The Italian Centre, 15 John Street.* ☎ *0141 552 4433; Fax 0141 552 1500; info@cafeostra.com; www. cafeostra.com.* Attractive city centre restaurant on two levels with a snappy art deco interior, serving Modern Scottish and Mediterranean dishes with a seafood emphasis.

◖◗◖◗ **The Cook's Room,** *13 Woodside Crescent.* ☎ *0141 353 0707; Fax 0141 332 0088; info@thecooksroom.co.uk; www. thecooksroom.co.uk.* Simple small dining room with charmingly mismatched wooden chairs and tables serving an eclectic but accomplished Scottish-Mediterranean influenced menu.

◖◗◖◗ **The Dhabba,** *44 Candleriggs.* ☎ *0141 553 1249; Fax 0141 553 1730; info@ thedhabba.com; www.thedhabba.com.* Large modern North Indian restaurant with bold colours and huge wall photos, serving authentic and accomplished dishes.

◖◗◖◗ **Mao,** *84 Brunswick Street.* ☎ *0141 564 5161; Fax 0141 564 5163; info@ cafemao.com.; www.cafemao.com.* Bright funky buzzy two-floor establishment serving tasty south east Asian food.

◖◗◖◗ **Stravaigin 2,** *8 Ruthven Lane.* ☎ *0141 334 7165; Fax 0141 357 4785; stravaigin@btinternet.com.* This lilac painted cottage with a simple unfussy bistro interior offers a contemporary menu with an eclectic range of original dishes.

WHERE TO STAY

◖◗◖◗ **Bewley's,** *110 Bath Street.* ☎ *0141 353 0800; Fax 0141 353 0900; gla@ bewleyshotels.com; www.bewleyshotels. com.* «One price every room every night» is the motto of this excellent value hotel chain. Bedrooms are attractive clean and modern with a glass-walled restaurant for people watching.

◖◗◖◗ **Jury's Inn,** *70-96 Jamaica Street.* ☎ *0141 314 4800; Fax 0141 314 4888; jurysinnglasgow@jurydoyle.com; www. jurydoyle.com.* Attractive modern chain hotel on the riverside with spacious interiors and modern comfy bedrooms.

◖◗◖◗ **Malmaison,** *278 West George Street.* ☎ *0141 572 1000; Fax 0141 572 1002; glasgow@malmaison.com; www. malmaison.com.* Visually striking former Masonic chapel with ultra-stylish rooms in bold patterns and colours. The French themed Brasserie is recommended.

◖◗◖◗ **Sherbrooke Castle,** *11 Sherbrooke Avenue, Pollokshields.* ☎ *0141 427 4227; Fax 0141 427 5685; mail@ sherbrooke.co.uk; www.sherbrooke.co.uk.* A celebration of late 19C Baronialist style with rich imposing furnishings, country house refinement and a panelled dining room.

◖◗◖◗ **The Town House,** *4 Hughenden Terrace.* ☎ *0141 339 1559; Fax 0141 339 9605; hospitality@ thetownhouseglasgow.com; www. thetownhouseglasgow.com.* Elegant personally run townhouse with nice Victorian touches, spacious rooms and an inviting lounge with a real fire.

Charles Rennie Mackintosh (1868–1928)

The famous architect and decorator developed his original style combining the Scottish vernacular tradition and Art Nouveau influences. Glasgow takes great pride in its legacy of fine buildings and interiors by Mackintosh: **Glasgow School of Art, Mackintosh Wing** at the Hunterian Art Gallery (Glasgow University), The **Willow Rooms** *(217 Sauchiehall St)* **Queens Cross Church** *(270 Garscube Rd)*, **Scotland Street School** *(225 Scotland St)* as well as the offices of the *Daily Record (Renfield Lane)* and the **Glasgow Herald** *(Mitchell St)*. **Hill House** in Helensburgh is a must for amateurs. An unusual recent addition is the **House for an Art Lover** *(Bellahouston Park)* built to Mackintosh's original design for a competition. See also the redesigned **Kelvingrove** collection.

Tenement House – ⌖ *145 Buccleuch Street.* 🕐*Open Mar to late-Oct, daily, 1pm-5pm.* ⌗ *£4. Guidebook (4 languages).* ☎ *0141 333 0183; tenementhouse@nts.org.uk, www. nts.org.uk.* This is a piece of social history. The flat, consisting of two rooms, kitchen and bathroom complete with original fittings, portrays turn- of-the-century tenement life, at once private and centred on the back court and its community.

Glasgow Science Centre – ⌖🕐 *Open daily 10am-6pm, Tower (8pm Fri-Sat).* ⌗ *£6.95. Planetarium £2.00 with a Science Mall ticket IMAX: noon-5pm (8pm Fri-Sat). Opening hours and show times are subject to change. Parking. Cafés.* ☎ *0141 420 5010; Fax 0141 420 5011; admin@gsc.org.uk; www.glasgowsciencecentre.org.*

Excursions

Hill House, Helensburgh★ – The road follows the north shore of the Clyde Estuary. At the entrance to the town of Dumbarton are the bonded warehouses and distillery (left) guarded by geese in the Roman style. Perched on the basaltic Dumbarton Rock (240ft/73m), once the capital of the Kingdom of Strathclyde, **Dumbarton Castle** provides panoramic views of the Clyde from its 18C fortifications.

Hill House★ (1902-04) rises on a hillside overlooking the Clyde. It is a first-rate example of pioneer modern architecture and interior design by Mackintosh. *(NTS) 21mi/34km northwest by A 82 and A 814. Upper Colquhoun Street.* 🕐*Open late-Mar to late-Oct, daily, 1.30-5.30pm; access may be restricted at peak times.* ⌗ *£8. Room guides (6 languages). Tea room.* ☎ *01436 673 900; Fax 01436 674 685; thehillhouse@nts.org. uk; www.nts.org.uk.*

Bothwell Castle★ – *9mi/15km southeast by A 74.* ⌖🕐 *Open Apr-Sep, daily, 9.30am-6.30pm; Oct-Mar, Sat – Wed , 9.30am to 4.30pm.* ⌗ *£2.50. Parking.* ☎ *01698 816 894; www.historic-scotland.gov.uk.* The vast red sandstone fortress, now in ruins, dominates the Clyde Valley as it has since it was built in the late 13C. The massive circular keep is 13C while the great hall, chapel and southeast tower are 15C.

Hill House

NTS, Edinburgh

In nearby Blantyre an 18C mill tenement, Shuttle Row, houses the **David Livingstone Centre**★ (⛄ *165 Station Road.* ⏱*Open late-Mar to late-Dec, daily, 10am (Sun 12.30pm;) to 5pm.* ⌦ *£5. Park. Parking. Café.* ☎ *01698 823 140; Fax 01698 821 424)* presenting the life and work of the missionary-cum-explorer (1813-73). The displays trace his pioneering journeys through the "dark continent" and his encounter with Stanley (⛄ *see DENBIGH).*

New Lanark★★ – *20mi/32km southeast by M 74 and A 72.* ⛄ *Visitor Centre:* ⏱*Open daily, 11am-5pm.* ⏱ *Closed 1-2 Jan and 25 Dec.* ⌦ *£5.95.* ⟿⟲ *Guided tour (2hr) by appointment. Audio-visual presentation (6 languages). Parking. Tearoom, picnic areas.* ☎ *01555 661 345; Fax 01555 665 738; visit@newlanark.org; www.newlanark.org.* In the deep gorge of the River Clyde, an 18C planned industrial village comprising four cotton mills, housing and amenities for the workforce was the acclaimed achievement of the Glasgow manufacturer and banker David Dale and his son-in-law Robert Owen, a social reformer. In 1986, the village was nominated a World Heritage Site. Among the interesting buildings are the Nursery Buildings for pauper apprentices, the store, the counting house and tenements *(Caithness Row)*, and the Institute – a social centre. **Mill no 3 (Annie McLeod Experience, exhibition, visitor centre)** is the most handsome of the four units sited between the river and the lade. The riverside **Dyeworks** has displays on the wildlife of the Falls of Clyde Reserve. The **Falls of Clyde** framed by woods are a popular beauty spot which has inspired painters (Turner) and poets (Scott, Wordsworth) alike.

GLASTONBURY★★

Somerset

POPULATION 7 747

MICHELIN ATLAS P 8 OR MAP 503 L 30

Though Glastonbury has been a ruin for centuries its name still conjures up the great abbey, one of the richest in the land and famous as a centre of learning. The town, which grew up around the abbey, has become an important centre of spiritualism and alternative lifestyle which finds its most public expression in the hugely successful open-air Glastonbury Festival for contemporary music.
🛈 *The Tribunal, 9 High Street, Glastonbury BA6 9DP* ☎ *01458 832 954 ; Fax: 01458 832; Glastonbury.tic@ukonline.co.uk.*

- 🔍 **Don't Miss**: The Abbey Ruins; the view from Glastonbury Tor.
- 🔍 **Please Consider:** in summer thousands of pilgrims flock to Glastonbury so book well ahead to be sure of a room.
- 🕐 **Organizing Your Time**: Allow three hours, to include the Tor.

A Bit of History

Glastonbury Tor and the Polden Hills were once islands in the marshes which were connected to the open sea by tidal channels; by the Iron Age (450 BC) the hilltops were occupied by forts enclosing hut settlements. According to the Grail legends an abbey was founded by Joseph of Arimathea, who caught the blood of the crucified Christ in the cup of the Last Supper; when he planted his staff in the ground it sprouted and became the famous **Glastonbury Thorn**, a tree which flowers at Christmas and in May.

Another legend links **King Arthur** with Glastonbury: mortally wounded by his stepson Mordred, Arthur sailed to the Isles of Scilly or to the Isle of Avalon, held to be near Glastonbury. He and Guinevere were supposedly buried in Glastonbury, and their bodies "discovered" in the abbey cemetery in 1191.

The historian William of Malmesbury, in his ecclesiastical history of Glastonbury begun in 1120, gives us the first solid date: 688, when Ine, King of the West Saxons, having driven the Celts from Somerset, built, with **Aldhelm's** guidance, an additional church to that already on the site. Although **Dunstan**, Abbot of Glastonbury from 943 to 959, enlarged and rebuilt the abbey, the abbot appointed after the Norman Conquest considered the church inadequate for the richest abbey in the land and began to rebuild it. After a fire entirely destroyed the buildings in 1184, rebuilding began with the Lady Chapel, completed within two years, and continued over the next two centuries. Having acquired vast manorial holdings, it was annihilated at the Dissolution in 1539.

Sights

Abbey Ruins★★ – &🕐 *Open
daily, 9.30am (9am Jun-Aug; 10am-
4:30 Dec-Jan, 5pm Feb and Oct) to
6pm/dusk.* 🕐 *Closed 25 Dec.* ⊚ *£4.
Audio guide (5 languages). Brochure
(5 languages). Fax*☎ *01458 832 267;
glastonbury.abbey@dial.pipex.com;
www.glastonburyabbey.com.* The
ruins extend far across the lawns,
standing tall amidst majestic trees.
The Lady Chapel in Doulting stone
has a corner turret, decorated
walls, and rounded doorways,
with that to the north enriched
by carved figures of the Annunciation, the Magi and Herod. East
on the impressive Gothic transept
piers remain the chancel walls and
beyond them the site of the Edgar
Chapel, a mausoleum for the Saxon
Kings. The 14C **Abbot's Kitchen**★,
the sole building to survive intact,
is square with an eight-sided roof
rising to superimposed lanterns,
which served to draw the smoke

Abbot's Kitchen, Glastonbury Abbey

from the corner fires in the kitchen up the flues in the roof. North of the abbey stands
the **Glastonbury Thorn Tree**.

Town – The two main streets, **Magdalene Street,** lined with attractive little 17C-19C
houses, and **High Street**, overlooked by the 15C **George and Pilgrims Hotel** and the
14C **Tribunal**, both once connected with the abbey, intersect at the Victorian-Gothic
market cross. The Tribunal houses the tourist information centre and **Lake Village
Museum** (*EH 9 High Street.* 🕐*Open daily, 10am-5pm (4pm Oct-Mar; 30min later Fri-Sat
all year).* ⊚ *£2.* ☎ *01458 832 954; glastonbury.tic@ukonline.co.uk; www.somerset.gov.
uk)* of excavated artefacts from an **Iron Age Lake Village** northwest of town. The
134.5ft/41m tower of the 15C **church of St John the Baptist**★★ is one of the finest in
Somerset with its crown of crocketed pinnacles (St Katherine's chapel inside survives
from the 12C building). The **Somerset Rural Life Museum**★, (& *Bere Lane.* 🕐 *Open
Apr-Oct, Tue-Fri and Bank Hol Mon, 10am-5pm, Sat-Sun, 2pm-6pm; Nov-Mar, Tue-Sat,
10am-3pm. Free admission. Parking. Refreshments (summer only).* ☎ *01458 831 197;
county-museums@somerset.gov.uk; www.somerset.gov.uk/museums)* illustrates daily
life on a Somerset farm in the 19C; the outstanding exhibit is the 14C "home" barn
of Glastonbury Abbey with its exceptional roof and stonework.

Glastonbury Tor★ – The tor, 521ft/159m high, is a landmark for miles around. The
tower at its summit is the last remnant of a Church to St Michael, built in the 14C. On a
fine day, the **view**★★★ embraces the Quantocks, Bristol Channel and the Mendips.

GLOUCESTER★

Gloucestershire, ENGLAND

POPULATION 114 003

MICHELIN ATLAS P 17 OR MAP 503 N 28

TOWN PLAN IN THE MICHELIN GUIDE GREAT BRITAIN AND IRELAND

Gloucester (pronouced Gloster) is a busy centre of administration, manufacturing
and commerce, dominated by its glorious cathedral; only traces remain of its 2
000 years of history, a fragment of which is endearingly captured in *The Tailor of
Gloucester* by Beatrix Potter (& *see LAKE DISTRICT).* 🔖 *28 Southgate Street, Gloucester Gl1
2DP*☎ *01452 396 572; Fax 01452 504 273; tourism@gloucester.gov.uk; www.gloucester.
gov.uk* 🔖 *Merchant Quay. Gloucester Docks.*

▶ **Orient Yourself**: Gloucester ciy centre is compact and the docks are closeby, for a guided tour of the docks ☎ 01452 501 666, 01452 311 190.

Don't Miss: Gloucester Cathedral; excursions to Berkeley Castle, Painswick and the Wildfowl & Wetlands Trust.

Organizing Your Time: Allow 3-4 hours for the city centre and docks.

Especially for Kids: Little ones will love The House of the Tailor of Gloucester shop.

A Bit of History

The Roman fort of Glevum was situated at the lowest crossing point on the River Severn, right on the south east border of Wales, commanding the approaches. The plan of the legionary fort is reflected in the four "gates" of the medieval city which still meet at the central Cross.

The Cathedral★★ *1hr*

Open daily, 8am-6pm. Donation £3. Guided tour on request. Tower Tours Wed-Fri 2:30pm, Sat and Bank Hols 1:30pm and 2:30pm. £2.50. Brochure (8 languages). Restaurant. Induction loop; touch and hearing model. ☎ 01452 528095; Fax 01452 300469; office@gloucester2001.demon.co.uk; www.gloucestercathedral.org.uk. The present structure is essentially the creation of the Norman Benedictine abbot, Serlo, and of his 14C successors, who pioneered the Perpendicular style and adorned the transepts and choir using funds provided by royal patronage or by pilgrims visiting the tomb of Edward II, who was murdered in 1327 in Berkeley Castle.

The building was extended in the 15C by the addition of the Lady Chapel.

In the nave, massive Norman columns, reddened at the base by a fire in 1122, give an impression of enormous strength. Further east Perpendicular elegance prevails: in the exquisite tracery of the high **vault** (92ft/28m); in the magical **east window**, the largest of its kind in medieval glass, commemorating the Battle of Crecy; and in the wonderfully light **Lady Chapel** of about 1500.

Edward's effigy, north of the choir, is protected by a 14C stonework canopy of rare delicacy.

The **cloisters** contain the **lavatorium** where the monks washed their hands at the entrance to the refectory; the 14C fan vaulting, the earliest of its kind, is of exceptional richness. William the Conqueror is said to have ordered the Domesday Survey from the adjoining chapter house.

The mid-15C **tower** (225ft/69m), with its unmistakable crown of parapet and pinnacles, rises gracefully above **College Green**, a pleasant combination of mainly 18C houses, replacements of earlier monastic buildings. **St Mary's Gate** is an impressive medieval survival.

Every three years in August the city welcomes the choirs of Worcester and Hereford cathedrals as part of the Three Choirs Festival which began in the 18C. It not only features the three cathedral choirs but has an accompaning fringe festival too which has a very wide remit of sport and entertainment. Gloucester is host again in 2007.

Additional Sights

Gloucester Docks★ – The fine 19C inland port and warehouses have been conserved. The **National Waterways Museum,** (*Llanthony Warehouse, Gloucester Docks. Open daily, 10am-5pm. Closed 25 Dec. £5.95. River and canal cruises available: Easter-Oct. Private boat hire all year. Parking. Café. Lifts, ramps, wide doorways. ☎ 01452 318 054; Fax 01452 318 066; info@nwm.demon.co.uk; www.nwm.org.uk*) explores the long history of river and canal navigation in Britain through models, displays, text panels, video simulations and a variety of historic vessels moored at the quayside.

City Centre – The point where the Roman streets intersect is marked by the central Cross and **St Michael's Tower**. There are two excellent examples of late medieval timber buildings: in Northgate Street the **New Inn** and in Westgate Street **Bishop Hooper's Lodging★**, now **Gloucester Folk Museum** (*Open Tues-Sat, 10am-5pm. Closed 1 Jan, Good Friday and 25-26 Dec. No charge. Wheelchair access ground floor only. ☎ 01452 396 868; Fax 01452 330 495; www.glos-city.gov.uk*) where the lively exhibits include the history of fishing on the River Severn, a toy and games gallery and a huge stuffed Gloucester old spot pig.

Via Sacra – This distinctively-paved pedestrian route roughly follows the line of the Roman walls and links the cathedral with a modern shopping centre and with other points of interest, notably **Blackfriars**, a medieval Dominican friary.

The House of The Tailor of Gloucester
– *The Tailor of Gloucester,* published 1903, was Beatrix Potter's personal favourite among her Peter Rabbit Books. In 1897 when Beatrix Potter was on holiday, she sketched a little shop at 9 College Court, which was known as The Tailor's House. She became fascinated by a local folk tale about John Pritchard, a tailor who had been commissioned to make a fine suit of clothes for the Mayor of Gloucester, and so the story was born. The shop still exists today, selling a full range of Beatrix Potter merchandise (🕐 *Open Mon - Sat (excluding bank holidays), Apr-Oct 10am-5pm, Nov-Mar 10am-4pm* ☎ *01452 422856*).

Severn Bore

The village of Minsterworth *(4mi/6.5km west of Gloucester by A 40 and A 48)* is a good place from which to observe the phenomenon known as the Severn Bore, a roaring wall of water (up to 6ft/2m high) advancing up the Severn estuary, which occurs at the time of the equinoxes. In fact it occurs at every tide but it is usually imperceptible.

Excursions

East of Gloucester★ – *From Gloucester take A 417 east; at the roundabout at the summit of the hill turn left and follow signs to Crickley Hill Country Park.*

Crickley Hill Country Park – *Visitors Centre:* 🕐*Open daily, 12.30pm (10am Sun) to 5pm. Parking. Picnic and barbecue areas.* ☎ *01452 863 170.* The dramatic promontory of the Cotswold escarpment is the site of successive Neolithic and Iron Age settlements (explanatory information available; annual excavations). There are extensive **views**★ west of the Severn Valley, the Forest of Dean and the Black Mountains in Wales. *Return to the roundabout; take A 417 south to Birdlip; follow the signs to Painswick.*

Painswick★ – The streets of the hilltop village contain many old buildings of golden Cotswold stone. The elaborate Baroque tombstones in the parish churchyard are accompanied by 99 clipped yew trees.

Painswick Rococo Garden – *North of Painswick by B 403 – signs Butt Green.* 🕐*Open early-Jan to Oct, daily, 11am-5pm.* 🎫 *£4 . Parking. Refreshments.* ☎*01452 813 204; info@ rococogarden.co.uk; www.rococogarden.co.uk.)* has been restored to its original 18C plan, a rare example of the fashion for gardens to combine the informal, such as the famous Snowdrop Grove, with more formal vistas, interspersed with temples and grottoes.

Westonbirt Arboretum★ – *Tetbury, 20mi/32km south of Gloucester via Stroud and Nailsworth by A 46, B 4014 and A 433.* ♿ 🕐 *Open daily, 10am-8pm/dusk.* 🕐 *Visitor Centre closed Christmas week.* 🎫 *£5 Jan-May, £6.50 Jun-early Sep, £7.50 Oct-mid Nov, mid Nov-Dec , no charge . Plant centre. Café.* ☎ *01666 880 220; www.westonbirtarboretum. com.* The road passes through **Tetbury**, an elegant town built of silver-grey stone round a quaint Market House (1655) and St Mary's Church, a refined 18C interpretation of medieval motifs. Outside the town stands Highgrove *(right)*, the country residence of the Prince of Wales.
The arboretum was first planted in 1829 by Robert Halford. Since then this most important plant collection has grown steadily to comprise some 14 000 trees and shrubs from all over the world maintained by the Forestry Commission which conducts scientific research. There are many miles of signed walks and a modern visitor centre. Some trees are the largest of their species in Britain. The many varieties of maple guarantee a spectacular autumn display.

The Wildfowl & Wetlands Trust, Slimbridge★ – *15mi/24km southwest of Gloucester by A 38 and a minor road west.* ♿🕐 *Open daily, 9.30am-5.30pm (4pm in winter).* 🕐 *Closed 25 Dec.* 🎫 *£6.75. Parking. Licensed restaurant. Gift shop. Wheelchair hire.* ☎ *01453 890 333; Fax 01453 890 827; info.slimbridge@wwt.org.uk; www.wwt.org.uk.* Bordering the extensive wetlands of the tidal Severn, this water-bird sanctuary, created over a period of 40 years by the late Sir Peter Scott, has acquired an international reputation for research and conservation and as a place where the public can observe at fascinatingly close quarters a great variety of native and exotic wildfowl. The hides and observatories permit experienced and amateur birdwatchers alike to enjoy the spectacular winter arrival of thousands of wild ducks, geese and swans; exhibits such as Pond Zone bring other wildlife inhabitants of the wetlands under the microscope.

Berkeley Castle★★ – *20mi/32km southwest of Gloucester by A 38 and a minor road west.* 🕐 *Open Jul-Aug, daily, 11am (2pm Sun) to 5pm; Jun and Sep, Tue-Sun, 11am (2pm Sun) to 5pm; Easter and Apr-May, Tue-Sun, 2-5pm; Oct, Sun, 2-4.30pm; Bank Hol Mon, 11am-5pm; last admission 30min before closing.* 🎫 *£7.50; gardens £4; Butterfly house £2.* 🚶 *Guided tour (1hr) available. Parking. Refreshments.* ☎ *01453 810 332; info@berkeley-castle.com;*

www.berkeley-castle.com. This archetypal medieval stronghold commanded the narrow strip of lowland between the Cotswolds and the Severn; its defences could be strengthened by flooding the surrounding water meadows. The outer wall still displays the breach made by Cromwellian cannon in the siege of 1645 and the inner courtyard is dominated by the great drum of the **keep** of 1153.

The **interior** is a confusion of twisting passages and stairways, vaulted cellars, ancient kitchens and deep dungeons. Through a grille in the King's Gallery can be seen the chamber, simply and evocatively furnished, where the deposed **Edward II** was kept prisoner and then foully murdered. Other rooms are richly furnished with reminders of the castle's continuous occupation since the 12C by the Berkeley family. The **Great Hall** presents a timber roof (32ft/10m high) and a printed screen; the decoration of the ceiling in the **Morning Room**, once a chapel, incorporates lines from the 14C Norman French translation of the Bible, which was worked on here by the castle chaplain, John Trevisa.

Berkeley in USA

William Berkeley was the first Governor of Virginia from 1641 to 1677. Part of the library of the famous metaphysician Bishop Berkeley passed on his death in 1753 to Yale University and then to the California university which bears his name. The naming of Berkeley in California was inspired from his line – "Westward the course of empire takes its way". **George Berkeley** (1684-1753) was born in Thomastown in Ireland and became Bishop of Cloyne in County Cork, where there is a memorial to him in the north transept of the 14C cathedral.

GRAMPIAN CASTLES★★

Aberdeenshire, SCOTLAND

MICHELIN ATLAS P 69 OR MAP 401 L, M AND N 12 AND 13

Aberdeen's hinterland is rich in castles, from Norman to the Scottish baronial style which characterises the golden age of castle building (16C-17C). The masterpieces of the latter are representative of a flourishing native tradition revelling in both an imaginative and an inventive approach.

Sights

Haddo House★ – *26mi/42km north of Aberdeen by A 92 and B 9005. House: Open Good Friday to Easter Mon 11am-4.30pm; May to Jun, Sat-Sun only 11am-4.30pm; 1 Jul to 31 Aug, daily 11am-4.30pm; Sep, Sat-Sun only 11am-4.30pm. Garden: Open year round, daily. Stables Shop and Tearoom: Good Fri to 30 Jun, Fri-Mon 11-5; 1 Jul to 31 Aug, daily 11-5; Sep to Christmas Fayre (1st weekend in Nov), Fri-Mon 11-5. Country park: Open daily, 9.30am-dusk. £8 Concession £4. Guided tour every 45 minutes. Guide book. Leaflet (6 languages). Parking. Tearoom. Plant Sales. 01651 851 440; Fax 01651 851 888; haddo@nts.org.uk; www.nts.org.uk.* On the estate acquired by the Gordons in 1469, William 2nd Earl of Aberdeen (1679-1745) commissioned William Adam to design the present house. George Hamilton Gordon (1784-1860), Prime Minister during the Crimean War, still found time to repair the house, by then derelict, and to landscape the parkland. The interior was transformed when his youngest son refurbished it in the Adam Revival style. Elegant rooms with coffered ceilings and wood panelling are a perfect setting for family portraits (Battoni, Lawrence) and mementoes. The country park offers splendid vistas.

Fyvie Castle★ – *26mi/42km north of Aberdeen by A 947. Castle: Good Fri to 30 Jun and Sep, Sat-Wed (closed Thu and Fri except on bank hol weekends when open Fri) 12pm-5pm; 1 Jul to 31 Aug, daily 11am-5pm. Last admission 4.15pm. Grounds: open year-round daily. £8, concessions £5. Guide books (3 languages). Leaflet (7 languages). Tea room; picnic area. 01651 891 266; Fax 01651 891 107; www.nts.org.uk.* Alexander Seton, Lord Chancellor (c 1639-1719), creator of Pitmedden Garden, remodelled Fyvie incorporating the Preston and Meldrum towers, thus creating the spectacular **south front** (150ft/46m long), an impressive example of 17C baronial architecture, and the **wheel stair**, dating from 1603. In the late 19C Fyvie was purchased by Lord Leith and refurbished in an opulent Edwardian manner. He also collected, in the manner of other American millionaires, in particular portraits by the Scottish master of the art, **Henry**

Raeburn. The paintings (by Lawrence, Reynolds, Gainsborough among others) are displayed in the fine rooms, some of which are adorned with stuccowork.

Crathes Castle★★ – *15mi/24km southwest of Aberdeen by A 93.* ♿ ⏱ *Garden and grounds: Open daily, 9am-dusk. Castle and visitor center: Open Good Friday to 30 Sept, daily, 10am-5.30pm (4.30pm Oct)1 Nov through 31 Mar for guided tours only 10 am- 3:45; last admission 45 min. before closing. Admission by timed ticket.* ∞ *£10; Information (17 languages). Adventure playground. Parking* ∞ *£2. Plant sales. Licensed restaurant; picnic area. Wheelchairs available; access to ground floor only.* ☎ *01330 844 525; Fax 01330 844 797; crathes@nts.org.uk; www.nts.org.uk.* The wonderfully crowded and detailed skyline of this 16C tower house is a striking example of the inventive baronial tradition. The interiors include some fine early vernacular furniture as well as some outstanding examples of **painted ceilings** (Room of the Nine Nobles and the Muses Room). This lively form of decoration, peculiar to the east coast, may well have been copied from Scandinavian contacts. By the mid-17C decorative painting was eclipsed by ornate plasterwork ceilings. Stone pendants and armorial paintings adorn the barrel-vaulted **High Hall** where the **Horn of Leys** – the original token of tenure dating from 1322 – has pride of place above the fireplace. The oak-panelled roof decorated with armorial devices and the horn motif is a unique feature of the **Long Gallery**. The whole is enhanced by the delightful **gardens**, the lifetime achievement of the late Sir James and Lady Burnett. The visitor is lured through a series of distinct and **separate gardens★★★**, each a delight in the wealth and colour of the planting.

Castle Fraser★ – *15mi/24km west of Aberdeen by A 944 and B 993 at Dunecht.* ♿ *Castle:* ⏱ *Open Good Friday to 30 Jun daily (closed Fri and Mon*) 12-5; 1 Jul to 31 Aug daily 11-5; 1 to 30 Sep daily (but closed Fri and Mon*) 12pm-5pm. Property open at weekends preceeding Bank Holidays Fri-Mon. Last admission 45 mins before closing. Shop also open 1 Nov to 18 Dec, Sat, Sun 12pm-4pm. Castle, garden and grounds* ∞ *£8. Brochure (7 languages). Woodland trails. Adventure playground. Parking. Tea room, picnic area.* ☎ *01330 833 463; Fax 01330 833 819; castlefraser@nts.org.uk; www.nts.org.uk.* Castle Fraser, built between 1575 and 1636, is one of the grander Castles of Mar, a traditional tower house with highly individual decoration. The **exterior★★** is remarkable. The local style with its harmonious combination of traditional features – turrets, conical roofs, crow-stepped gables, chimney stacks, decorative dormers and gargoyles – was Scotland's unique contribution to Renaissance architecture. The **central block** of this Z-plan castle is distinguished by a magnificent heraldic achievement. The refurbished interiors bring to life the simple lifestyle of a 17C laird.

Kildrummy Castle★ – *38mi/61km west of Aberdeen by A 944 and A 97 at Mossat.* ♿ ⏱ *Open late Mar-Sep daily 9:30am to 6:30pm; last entrance at 6pm.* ∞ *Adult £2.50. Child £1 Concession £1.90. Shop. Parking. Limited access for disabled visitors.* ☎ *01975 57133; www.historicscotland.gov.uk.* The extensive ruins of this 13C courtyard castle, the "noblest of northern castles", incorporate two different concepts of defensive design. The late 13C-14C **gatehouse**, which may have been built for King Edward I of England, displays striking similarities with the gatehouse at Harlech Castle in Wales, while the circular **Snow Tower** resembles the keep of the great castle of Coucy in France, which was built by the father of Alexander II's queen. Although these important elements

Ceiling (detail), Crathes Castle

are no more than foundations, substantial fragments of the castle (Great Hall, solar, chapel) still survive and the overall layout is clearly visible.

Dunnottar Castle★★ – *18mi/29km south of Aberdeen by A 92.* ○ *Open Easter-Oct, Mon-Sat, 9am-6pm, Sun, 2-5pm; Nov-Easter, Fri-Mon, 9am-dusk.* ○ *£4. Children under 16, £1. Unsuitable for disabled visitors.* ☎ *01569 762 173; info@dunechtestates.co.uk; www.dunechtestate.com.* Legend has it that St Ninian founded a Christian settlement here in the 5C. Sir William Keith built the present castle on the site in the 14C and was excommunicated for building on consecrated ground. It is set on an almost inaccessible **promontory**★★★ with sheer cliffs on three sides and it was the last castle remaining in Royalist hands during the Commonwealth. Here the Honours of Scotland (royal regalia) were held during an eight-month siege by Cromwell's troops in 1651-52, being finally smuggled out and hidden in nearby Old Kinneff church. The fortifed **gatehouse** and L-shaped **keep** contrast with the 17C **Waterton's Lodging** and the **16C-17C buildings** arranged around a quadrangle.

Drum Castle – *10 mi/16km west of Aberdeen by A 93. NTS.* ⚹ *(Wheelchairs available – very limited supply) Castle, Tearoom and Shop* ○*Open 1 Apr through 30 Sep, daily 1 Apr – 30 May and 1 Sep – 30 Sep 12:30pm – 5:30 p.m., 1 June – 31 Aug 10am – 5:30pm. Garden of Historic Roses: Open 25 Mar to 30 Sep, daily, 10am-6pm. Grounds Open daily, 9.30am/dusk.* ○ *adults £8, £2.70(child/concessions), Family (2 adults and up to six children) £20; garden and grounds only £2.50, £1.30 (child/concessions). Car Park Charge of £2 for non-members of the Trust . Guide sheet (8 languages). Playground. Woodland walk. Tea room; picnic area. Parking. Tearoom.* ☎ *01330 811 204; Fax 01330 811 962; drum@nts.org.uk; www.drum-castle. org.uk).* Sited high on a ridge, Drum Castle has been occupied continuously from at least 1323 to the present day and for 652 years, until 1975, it was the seat of the Irvine family, before passing into the care of the National Trust for Scotland. Its shape and character has evolved with the additions made to the building over the years, from the original medieval tower, to a Jacobean mansion house and several later additions by Victorian lairds. Its Garden of Historic Roses is a peaceful corner.

GUILDFORD

Surrey, ENGLAND

POPULATION 65 998

MICHELIN ATLAS P 19 OR MAP 504 S30

Guildford grew up at the convergence of trading routes, 30 miles/50km west of London, which crossed the chalk ridge of the North Downs through the gap cut by the River Wey. From the Middle Ages until the 17C the town's wealth was based on the wool industry.

The prospect of Guildford's elegant cobbled **High Street** descending towards the River Wey and of the green slopes of the Mount beyond is essentially that of the prosperous 18C town, when it was crowded with coaching inns and travellers breaking their journey between Portsmouth and London. Since the mid 20C Guildford has also been a university town. Today it is the quintessential wealthy middle class regional centre.

▶ **Orient Yourself**: The town centre is small (though hilly) and can easily be covered on foot.

ⓐ **Don't Miss**: Clandon Park's Marble Hall, Painshill, Wisley Garden.

ⓒ **Organizing Your Time**: Allow two hours for Guildford centre.

▦ **Especially for Kids**: Thorpe Park and Chessington World of Adventures are major theme parks; Birdworld.

⌁ **Walking Tours**: Guildford Town Tour (May-Sep, Mondays at 11.30am, Sun, and Wed at 2.30pm, Thu (except Sep) at 7.30pm. Meet at Tunsgate Arch, High Street, no charge. ☎ 01483 444 333; tic@guildford.gov.uk; www.guildford.gov.uk. Ghost Tour of Guildford, Mar-Oct Fri 8pm ☎ 01483 506 232; www.ghosttourofguildford.co.uk.

Sights

Town Centre – Just as in olden times, the High Street is dominated by the **Guildhall**, (⌁ *Tours Tue and Thu at 2pm and 3pm* ☎ *01483 444 035)* with its ornate projecting clock.

Nearby **Guildford House Gallery** *(155 High Street ⊙Open Tue-Sat, 10am-4.45pm. Tearoom. ☎ 01483 444 740; guildfordhouse@remoteguildford.gov.uk; www.guildfordborough.co.uk)* is an elegant late 17C townhouse whose handsome carved staircase leads to a display of paintings from the Borough's art collection and a changing programme of exhibitions. The fine vaulted **stone undercroft**, *(⊙ Open May-Sep, Tue and Thu, 2-4pm, Sat, noon-4pm. ☎ 01483 444 751; museum@remote.guildford.gov.uk; www.guildfordborough.co.uk)* built by a 13C wool merchant beneath a shop on the High Street, can be visited on the town's guided tour, which also includes the Tudor-style **Abbot's Hospital,** founded by Archbishop Abbot in 1619 and still in use as a home for the elderly.

Guildford Castle and Grounds – ♿ *Grounds: ⊙Open daily. No charge. Castle keep closed for refurbishment. ☎ 01483 444 702.* Beneath the solid sandstone walls of the 12C keep, almost all that remains of Surrey's royal castle, banks of flowerbeds provide spectacular seasonal colour. Jeanne Argent's 1990 sculpture *Alice Through the Looking Glass* commemorates writer Lewis Carroll, a frequent visitor to Guildford who rented a nearby house for his sisters. He died while visiting them and is buried in the Mount Cemetery.

Guildford Museum – *Quarry Street. ⊙Open Mon-Sat, 11am-5pm. ⊙ Closed Good Fri, 25-26 Dec. Parking for disabled visitors. ☎ 01483 444 750; museum@remote.guildford.gov. uk; www.guildfordborough.co.uk.* Mementoes of Lewis Carroll and of gardener and writer Gertrude Jekyll are included in this history of the town, which traces earlier inhabitants of Guildford via the things they left behind – paleolithic hand-axes, a Roman priest's headdress, Saxon coins and jewellery,17C glass and Victorian needlework.

Guildford Cathedral – ♿⊙ *Open daily, 8.30am-5.30pm. ⟶ Guided tour 9.40am-4pm. Parking. Shop. Refreshments. ☎ 01483 565 287; visits@guildford-cathedral.org; www.guildford-cathedral.org.* Designed by Sir Edward Maufe and built between 1936 and 1961, the cathedral overlooks the town from its dramatic setting on Stag Hill, an illuminated beacon at night.

Excursions

Wisley Garden – *6mi/9km northeast of Guildford by A 3. ♿⊙ Open daily, Mar-Oct 10am-6pm/dusk, Nov-Feb 10am-4:30pm (Sat-Sun, 9am). ⊙ Closed 25 Dec. ⊛ £7. Parking. No dogs. ☎ 020 7834 4333; info@rhs.org.uk, www.rhs.org.uk.* The gardens of the Royal Horticultural Society are a beautiful experience at all seasons. In the setting of an old site, with many fine trees, there is a great range of different sorts of gardens – pinetum, alpine house, rock garden, small model gardens, gardens for the disabled, which attract visitors of all types, – trial grounds of various kinds and practical display areas, of more interest to the amateur gardening enthusiast, who can also seek information from the advisory service. The plants for sale in the nursery garden are of high quality and some are very unusual; the shop offers a great range of gardening books.

Chessington World of Adventures – *17mi/27km northeast of Guildford by A 3, A 244 and B 280 (12mi/18km southwest of London by A 3 and A 243). ♿ ⊙ Opening times vary, call for info. ⊛ £28. Parking. Restaurants. Wheelchairs available in advance. ☎ 0870 444 7777; gservices@chessington.com; www.chessington.com.* In the same family as Alton Towers, this traditional theme park is popular both with families and older thrillseekers, combining several hair-raising rides, such as "Rameses Revenge", "The Vampire" and the "Rattlesnake" with children's rides, stage entertainment and a collection of wild animals, birds and reptiles best seen from the Safari Skyway.

Birdworld – *12mi/20km southwest of Guildford by A 31 and A 325. ♿ Holtpound, Farnham. ⊙Open daily 10am-6pm (4.30pm Nov-Mar), mid-Feb to late-Oct and mid-Dec to early-Jan; open Sat-Sun late-Oct to mid-Dec and early-Jan to mid-Feb; last admission 1hr before closing. Closed ⊙ 25-26 Dec. ⊛ £9.95. Parking. Refreshments. ☎ 01420 22140; bookings@ birdworld.co.uk; www.birdworld.co.uk.* This extensive bird collection is displayed in 28 acres of landscaped gardens and includes a free-flight parrot aviary which is the largest of its kind in Britain. A breeding programme is undertaken at the incubation research centre and the park also features Underwater World, with crocodiles, invertebrates, freshwater and marine fish, and the Jenny Wren children's farm.

Thorpe Park – *13mi/20km north of Guildford by A 320 (21mi/34km southwest of London by M 3, M 25 and A 320). Staines Road. ⊙Open early-Apr to early-Nov, times vary, call for info. ⊛ £30, online discount £15 . Parking. Restaurants. ☎ 0870 444 4466; www.thorpe-park.com.* Set around the landscaped lakes of former gravel pits, it is no surprise that this theme park's top attractions are water rides – rafting on Thunder River and the stomach-churning drop of Logger's Leap (remember to smile for the camera halfway down). Waterbuses glide across the lake to 1930s Thorpe Farm and there are plenty of gentler rides for smaller children – and plenty of opportunities to get wet.

HADDINGTON★

East Lothian, SCOTLAND

POPULATION 7 342

MICHELIN ATLAS P 56 OR MAP 501 L 16

This handsome market town, 18 mi/29km east of Edinburgh, grew up in the 12C around a royal palace; by the 16C it was the fourth-largest town in Scotland, and in the 18C entered a golden age based on agricultural wealth.

The Town

Town centre – The 14C-15C **St Mary's Parish Church** (♿ ⊙ *Open Good Friday-Oct, Mon-Sat, 11am-4pm, Sun, 2pm-4.30pm. ⟡ Guided tour. Audio tour. Leaflet (several languages). Coffee shop. Brass Rubbing. Exhibitions. ☎ 01620 823 109; StMarys.Haddington@btinternet.com)* enjoys a peaceful riverside setting. Its impressive dimensions are a reminder that it was built as one of the great burgh churches. Inside, note the Burne-Jones window in the south transept and the four recumbent effigies of the Maitland family in the 17C **Lauderdale Aisle**.

Follow The Sands past the 16C **Nungate Bridge** with its pointed cutwaters up to the **High Street**★ and its continuous line of frontages, often gable-ended. This type of colourful and varied streetscape was typical of Scottish burgh architecture. Beyond, in Lodge Street, a pend leads to the childhood home of Jane Welsh, the wife of Thomas Carlyle. At the junction of High and Market Streets is William Adam's dignified 18C town house.

Excursions

Tantallon Castle★ – *(HS) 13mi/21km northeast by A 1 and A 198. ⊙ ♿ Open Apr-Sep, daily, 9.30am-6.30pm; Oct-Mar, 9.30am (2pm Fri, Sun) to 4.30pm (noon Thu). ⟡ £3.30. Parking. Picnic area. ☎ 01620 892 727; www.historic-scotland.gov.uk.* The scenic road passes the pretty village of **Tyninghame**★ – nearby are **Preston Mill**★, a 16C working watermill with red pantiled roof, and the beehive-shaped Phantassie Dovecot – and the tiny village of **Whitekirk**, formerly a pilgrimage centre, with its 15C Church of St Mary's, an old red sandstone building with crow steps and a squat tower with corbelled parapet.

The formidable ruin of this Douglas stronghold clings to its clifftop site defying both waves and winds, as so aptly described by Scott in his narrative poem *Marmion*. Ditches and earthen ramparts defend the landward side of this gaunt Old Red Sandstone ruin, now attractively weathered.

Lennoxlove★ – *1mi/0.5km south by B 6369. ♿⊙ ⟡ Guided tour (1hr 15 min) Mar - Oct, Wed-Thu and Sun, noon-4.30pm; Sun by appointment. ⟡ £4.50. Guide book (3 languages). Parking. Garden Room. Café. ☎ 01620 823 720; Fax 01620 825 112; enquiries@lennoxlove.com; www.lennoxlove.com.* This historic home has been the seat of Maitlands and latterly the Dukes of Hamilton and it houses some of the family collections from the now demolished Hamilton Palace. There are numerous historic associations with such personalities as Mary Queen of Scots, Frances Teresa Stewart or La Belle Stewart, the Duke of Lauderdale sometimes referred to as the "King of Scotland", as well as that other personality, "El Magnifico", the 10th Duke of Hamilton. The many **portraits** bring these and other figures to life and there is a fine collection of **furniture**.

Gifford★ – *4mi/6km south by B 6369.* This late 17C-early 18C estate village is one of the several attractive villages (East Saltoun, Pencaitland, Garvald and Stenton) nestling in the rolling countryside of the northern foothills of the Lammermuir Hills. The T-shaped church (1710) has an emblazoned laird's loft and in the churchyard a monument to John Witherspoon, the only clergyman signatory of the American Declaration of Independence.

HADRIAN'S WALL★★

Cumbria, Northumberland, ENGLAND

MICHELIN ATLAS PP 50 AND 51 OR MAP 502 L 19 M, N AND O 18

In AD 122, during a tour of the western provinces of the Empire, the Roman Emperor Hadrian visited Britain. He ordered the building of a defensive wall across the northernmost boundary of the Empire from Wallsend on the Tyne, to Bowness on the Solway Firth (73mi/117km). Although Hadrian's Wall has come to represent the frontier between England and Scotland it is well south of the modern border between the countries. Parts of this wall can still be seen today and museums, camps and settlements give a picture of military and civilian life on Rome's "Northwest Frontier". *Wentworth Car Park, Hexham, Northumberland, NE46 1QE ☎ 01434 652220; hexham.tic@tynedale.gov.uk; www.hadrians-wall.org.*

A Bit of History

The Wall – The wall was built by legionaries, citizens of Rome, and garrisoned by as many as 24 000 auxiliaries from conquered territories. It was defended by a ditch on the north side; on the south side it was paralleled by a military road and "vallum", defining the military zone. The wall was built in stone and turf, with forts, milecastles and turrets at regular intervals along its length. It follows the best strategic and geographical line and, at places such as Cawfields and at Walltown Crags, commands splendid **views. Arbeia Fort** *(South Shields)* guarded the entrance to the estuary of the River Tyne – the reconstructed West Gate, the excavated ruins and a museum give a glimpse of military life. Milecastles along Hadrian's Wall have been numbered, from east to west, starting at Wallsend (0), and finishing at Bowness (80). The Roman mile was about 1 620yd/1 481m, somewhat shorter than today's mile of 1 760yd/1 609m. Many of the guidebooks specific to the wall refer to this system.

The **Museum of Antiquities**★ *(at the University in Newcastle-upon-Tyne)* – scale models and artefacts – provides a good introduction to the wall and its different elements *(for detailed description & see NEWCASTLE-UPON-TYNE)*.

Main Sights and Landmarks

Follow the B 6318 which is hilly. The main sites all have car parks and are indicated by light brown signposts. They are listed below in topographical order from east to west *(local map below)*.

Corbridge – *Population 2 757.* The attractive town of Corbridge had its origins in the settlement of civilians and camp followers which grew up alongside the Roman station of Corstopitum. In Saxon times it was relocated here. Corbridge has an interesting Vicar's Pele, a 14C fortified dwelling within the churchyard, three storeys high, built of Roman worked stones.

Corbridge Roman Camp★ – *(EH) West of Corbridge. ♿ ⏱ Open Apr-Oct, daily, 10am-6pm (5pm Oct); Nov to late-Mar, Sat-Sun, 10am-4pm. ⏱ Closed 21 Jan and 24-26 Dec. ☎ £3.60. Audio guide. Parking. Wheelchairs available. ☎ 01434 632 349; www.english-heritage.org.uk.*

> ☺ **Touring Tip** ☺
>
> Police warning: Beware of car thieves, leave no valuables.

This site was occupied for longer than any other on the wall. The township sprang up around the fort and supply-base which lay north of the bridge carrying Dere Street and it also marked the junction with the east-west Stanegate. The wall runs along the rise to the north. The **museum** of the Corbridge Roman Camp presents the layout of the site with its **granaries**, fountain, headquarters building and temples. From the elevated viewpoint there is a good overall **view** of the visible remains which represent only a small central part of the supply-base and settlement.

▶ *Beyond the Planetrees roadside fragment of the Wall and once down in the valley turn left onto A 6079.*

Almost immediately on the left is **Brunton Turret.**

Hexham Abbey★ – *Hexham. ♿ ⏱ Open daily, 9.30am-7pm (5pm Oct-Apr). ⏱ Closed Good Fri. ☎ Donation. 🔊 Guided tour (1hr) by appointment. Leaflet (6 languages). ☎ 01434 602 031; Fax 01434 606 116; hexhamabbey@ukonline.co.uk; www.hexhamabbey.*

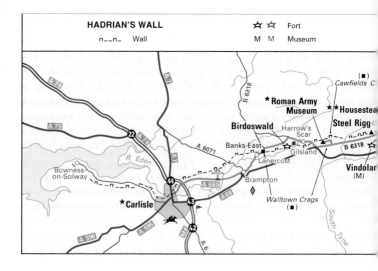

HADRIAN'S WALL ☆ ☆ Fort
ᴨ__ᴨ_ Wall M M Museum

★ **Roman Army Museum** ★★Houstea
Cawfields C
Birdoswald Harrow's Scar **Steel Rigg**
Banks-East Gilsland
Lanercost B 6318
Vindolar
(M)
Bowness-on-Solway
R. Eden **Brampton**
★**Carlisle**
Walltown Crags
(■)

org.uk. Stones from the Roman settlement of Corbridge (Corstopitum) were used in the construction of Hexham Abbey, which was founded in AD 674 and dedicated to St Andrew. The founder was Wilfrid, the Northumbrian churchman who had been responsible for the adoption of the Roman rite at the Synod of Whitby in 664, and the land was granted to him by Queen Etheldreda.

All that remains of Wilfrid's abbey is the **Saxon Crypt**★★. The fine Early English choir with imposing transepts belongs to the later church (1180-1250). The stone staircase in the south transept was the Night Stair, which led to the canons' dormitory. The **Leschman Chantry**★ (1491) has amusing stone carvings on the base and delicate woodwork above.

Chesters Roman Fort★ – *(EH) Near Chollerford.* ♿🕐 *Open daily, 9.30am (10am Oct-Mar) to 6pm (4pm Oct -Mar).* 🕐 *Closed 1 Jan and 24-26 Dec.* ⊗ *£3.60. Parking. Refreshments (summer only).* ☎ *01434 681 379; www.english-heritage.org.uk.* The fort lies just west of the point where the wall crossed the River Tyne and remains of the bridge can still be discerned on the far bank. The four gateways, headquarters building and barrack blocks of this fort can still be traced from their foundations. Down by the river are the fascinating remains of a **bath house**★. The **museum** contains a selection of sculptured stones collected among and around the wall in the 19C.

Temple of Mithras – *Carrawburgh. 5min walk from the car park.* The temple is an unexpected find in such a desolate stretch of moorland. This compact mithraeum is the only one visible of the three discovered in the vicinity of the Wall. Inside the lobby is a statue of the mother goddess; beyond, earth benches for worshippers flanked a narrow nave with three altars at the end. The originals can be seen in a reconstruction of the temple in the Museum of Antiquities in Newcastle. The temple was destroyed early in the 4C, probably by the Christians, who saw, in the Mithraic ritual of taking bread and water, a caricature of their own sacrament.

Housesteads Roman Fort★★ – *(EH)* ♿🕐 *Open daily, 10am-6pm (4pm Oct -Mar).* 🕐 *Closed Jan 1 and 24-26 Dec.* ⊗ *£3.60. Informations panels (4 languages). Parking. Refreshments.* ☎ *01434 344 363; www.english-heritage.org.uk.* The fort (5 acres/2ha) is perched high on the ridge and is the most complete example on the Wall. Still clearly visible are the foundations of the large courtyard house of the commandant, the granaries, barracks, headquarters building, the four main gateways, the **hospital** and 24-seater **latrine block** as well as part of the civilian settlement, clustering round the south gate.

The Wall is visible to east and west as it undulates over the whinsill ridge.

Steel Rigg – The car park high up on the sill gives a good **view**★ of and access to Wall sections winding east to Peel Crags and west to Winshields Crags. The section of the Wall from Steel Rigg to Housesteads is popular with walkers.

Vindolanda – ♿ *Chesterholm.* 🕐*Open daily, 10am-6pm (5pm Apr-Mar and Sep-Oct;* 🕐 *Closed mid-Nov to mid-Feb.* ⊗ *£3.50 ; saver ticket (valid for Vindolanda and Roman Army Museum) £6.50. Trail. Archaelogical excavations, Apr-Aug, Sun-Fri (weather permitting). Parking. Refreshments.* ☎ *01434 344 277; Fax 01434 344 060; info@vindolanda.com;*

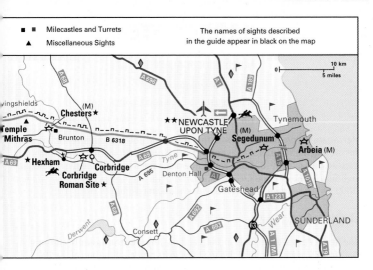

■ ■ Milecastles and Turrets
▲ Miscellaneous Sights

The names of sights described
in the guide appear in black on the map

www.vindolanda.com. The fort and civilian settlement on the Stanegate to the south
of the Wall date from the period before the building of the wall. Full-scale replicas
have been built of a stretch of the Wall with a stone turret, as well as of the turf wall,
which was the earliest barrier, with a timber milecastle. As well as objects of metal,
bone and stone, there is an interesting collection of writing tablets (unique), leather
goods, textiles and wooden objects in the **museum**★. These records, stores accounts
and letters add significantly to information about the Roman settlement.

▶ *Take the road to the right in the direction of Whiteside; park in the quarry car park.*

A short climb gives access to the precariously-perched Cawfields Milecastle 42. These
fortlets could accommodate from 8 to 32 soldiers.

Roman Army Museum★ – *Carvoran.* ♿🕐 *Open daily, as for Vindolanda.* 🕐 *Closed
mid-Nov to mid-Feb.* 💷*£3.50; saver ticket (valid for Roman Army Museum and Vindolanda): £6.50. Hadrian's Wall leaflet (3 languages). Parking. Refreshments.* ☎ *01697 747
485; Fax 01697 747 487; vindolanda.com; www.vindolanda.com.* With an audio-visual
presentation and examples of Roman armour, dress and weapons, this is the largest
and most modern of the Wall museums and presents a lively picture of the Wall and
its garrison.

The adjoining unexcavated fort of Carvoran was on the pre-Hadrianic frontier. To the
east the quarry viewing-point provides a good view of one of the finest sections of
the Wall, **Walltown Crags.**

▶ *At the end of B 6318 take A 69.*

Birdoswald Roman Fort – 🕐 *Open Mar-Oct, daily, 10am-5.30pm.* 💷 *£3.60. Parking. Visitor centre. Tearoom.* ☎*01697 747 602; birdoswald@dialpipex.com; www.
birdoswaldromanfort.org.* Of this fort, fine sections of gateways and granaries have
been excavated. To the west is the **Banks East** section of the Wall.

HARROGATE★

North Yorkshire, ENGLAND

POPULATION 66 178

MICHELIN ATLAS P 40 OR MAP 502 P 22

TOWN PLAN IN THE MICHELIN GUIDE GREAT BRITAIN AND IRELAND

Harrogate is a pleasant town with fine shops and hotels and is an excellent base for touring the Yorkshire Dales and Moors. Its growth from a town which scarcely existed on a map in 1821 to a well-known spa town has left a legacy of elegant buildings. 🛈 *Royal Baths Crescent Road, Harrogate, HG1 2RR. ☎ 01423 537300; Fax: 01423 537305; tic@harrogate.gov.uk; www.harrogate.gov.uk.*

A Bit of History

The **Royal Pump Room,** built in 1842, and the **Royal Baths Assembly Rooms**, built in 1897, were the hub of this spa town in its heyday at the end of the 19C when some 60 000 people a year came to "take the waters." There are 36 springs within an area of an acre, less than half a hectare, mostly sulphurous, but no two with water of identical chemical composition. An interesting aspect of the town is the **Stray**, 200 acres/80ha of grassland surrounding the town centre.

Sight

Royal Pump Room Museum – &*Crown Place.* ⏲*Open daily, 10am (noon Sun) to 5pm (4pm Nov-Mar).* ⏲*Closed 1 Jan and 24-26 Dec.* ✆ *£2.80. ☎ 01423 556 188; Fax 01423 556 130; www.harrogate.gov.uk/museums.* Here you can taste the strongest sulphur water in Europe, wonder at the old spa treatments and discover how Harrogate became a spa town.

Excursions

Harewood House★★ – *8mi/13km south by A 61. Harewood House –* &⏲ *Open Apr-Nov, daily, 10am (11am house) to 6pm (4.30pm last admission to bird garden; 4pm last admission to house).* ✆ *Grounds, bird garden, terrace gallery, Mon-Fri £8.25; Sat-Sun/Bank Hol: £10.25 . All attractions Mon-Fri £11; Sat, Sun/Bank Hol £13.00 .* ☎*Guided tour (1hr) on request. Parking. Refreshments. Wheelchairs available. ☎ 0113 218 1010 (24hr recorded information); business@harewood.org; www.harewood.org.* **Edwin Lascelles** started to construct Harewood House in 1759. The building is an essay in Palladian architecture by John Carr of York; most of its interiors are neo-Classical, lighter in spirit, one of the greatest achievements of Robert Adam, recently returned from Italy. Lascelles chose **Thomas Chippendale** (1718-79), born at nearby Otley, to make the furniture, and **Capability Brown** to develop the grounds.

The **Entrance Hall** is the only room to retain John Carr's original form. The fine plaster-work ceiling, like all the ceilings in the house, is the work of York craftsman Joseph Rose. Old Master paintings are hung throughout, mostly English and Italian, but note the superb El Greco *A Man, a Woman and a Monkey* in the Green Drawing Room; there is much rare Chinese porcelain, as well as Sèvres pieces collected at the beginning of the 19C. **The Gallery**★ is perhaps the pinnacle of Adam's work at Harewood. The wooden curtain swags were "carved and painted under the direction of Mr Chippendale, in so masterly a manner as to deceive any beholder". In the **Music Room,** the ceiling and the Axminster carpet were designed by Adam, to give an illusion of "roundness" in a square room.

In the grounds is the **Bird Garden.** The **Tropical House** has been refurbished to simulate one of the earth's rapidly disappearing natural wonders, the Rain Forest. River Bank and Waterfall display plants, birds and butterflies, all in authentic environments.

CRAFT SHOP

Darley Mill Centre – *7mi/10km west by A 59.* ⏲ *Open daily, 9.30am (11am Sun) to 5.30pm (5pm Sun). ☎ 01423 780 857.* A well restored flour mill in the Nidder valley has been converted into a craft shop selling glassware, gifts, household goods and linen. Its water wheel is still in good working order.

Knaresborough – *2mi/3km east of Harrogate by A 59.* Knaresborough is a small market town set on the north bank of the river Nidd. The castle **keep**, (♿ *Castle Yard. ○Open Good Friday-Sep, daily, 10.30am-5pm. ∞ £2.50 including Museum and Sallyport. ⚓ Guided tour through the Sallyport (underground tunnel) at 11am, 12pm, 2:30pm, 3:30pm. Parking (charge). Limited wheelchair access by appointment. ☎ 01423 556 188; www.harrogate.gov.uk/museums)* now in ruins, was started in about 1130; within the precinct are the sallyport (an underground tunnel) and the Old Courthouse Museum. After murdering Thomas Becket in Canterbury Cathedral in December 1170, the four murderers – the Constable, Hugh de Morville, and his three companions – took refuge in the castle before setting out for Jerusalem on a pilgrimage for pardon; three died there and the fourth on his way home.

Beside the river is **Mother Shipton's Cave,** (○ *Open daily 10.00am -5.30pm 1 Mar to 31 Oct (Weekends only until start of Easter School Hols). ∞ £5.50. Woodland Walk. Tea rooms, picnic area. Shop. Adventure playground. Parking. ☎ 01423 864600; Fax 01423 868888; info@mothershiptons.co.uk; www.mothershiptonscave.com)* where Mother Shipton, England's most famous prophetess, born c 1488, was reputed to have lived and prophesied. Adjacent is the **Petrifying Well**, a geological phenomenon whose cascading waters seem to turn items into stone. In fact they are covering it with a stalactite deposit. It is said to be England's oldest visitor attraction, first opening its gates in 1630 (entrance included in Mother Shipton's Cave ticket).

Harlow Carr Botanical Gardens – *2mi/3km west by B 6162.* ♿ *Crag Lane. ○Open daily, 9.30am-6pm(4pm Nov-Feb). ∞ £5.50. Guided walks during summer, Sat-Sun (1hr 30min). Parking. Licensed restaurant; café. Plant and gift shop. ☎ 01423 565 418; Fax 01423 530 663; debbiela@rhs.org.uk; www.rhs.org.uk.* The ornamental gardens (68 acres/28ha), the trial grounds of the Northern Horticultural Society, occupy an exposed site, bisected by a stream, descending from the road to a reclaimed bog (carr). Old gardening tools are presented in the Museum. The Bulb Garden *(Apr and early May)*, the Rose Garden *(July to Sep)*, the Island Beds of herbaceous perennials *(late summer)*, the heather beds *(all year colour)* and the Winter Garden contrast with the less formal Streamside (for plants which prefer moist soil and boggy conditions) the Peat Terraces providing partial shade, the Tarn Meadows around two ponds and the Arboretum and Woodland.

HAWORTH

North Yorkshire, ENGLAND

POPULATION 4 956

MICHELIN ATLAS P 39 OR MAP 502 O 22

Haworth is an unpretentious Yorkshire hill village, its dark, gritstone cottages crowded together on the edge of the Pennine moors. The long, steep main street is lined with souvenir shops and tea rooms, all enjoying the benefits of association with the Brontë family, who lived in the parsonage at the top of the hill. 🗓 *2-4 West Lane, Haworth BD22 8EF. ☎ 01535 642 329; Fax 01535 647 721; haworth@ytbtic. co.uk; www.visithaworth.com, www.visitbrontecountry.com.*

Sights

Brontë Parsonage Museum – ♿○ *Open daily, Apr-Sep, 10am-5.30pm; Oct-Mar, 11am-5pm (last admission 1/2hr before closing) ○ Closed 24-27 Dec and 2-31 Jan. ∞ £4.90. Brochure. Parking. ☎ 01535 642 323; Fax: 01535 647 131; christine.fox@bronte. org.uk; www.bronte.info.* The parsonage, where the Reverend Patrick Brontë and his family lived, conserves their furniture, books and paintings and fascinating memorabilia, such as the children's drawings and home-made books. Here the children invented the elaborate imaginary kingdoms of Angria and Gondal; later they wrote poetry and the three younger sisters created their masterpieces; here their brother, Branwell, painted a picture of these three sisters, which now hangs in the National Portrait Gallery in London.

A gateway *(now marked by a stone)* led directly from the parsonage garden to the church, where five of the six Brontë children and their mother are buried in the vault.

Brontë Family

Patrick Brontë was born Patrick Brunty in Northern Ireland and studied for Holy Orders at St John's College in Cambridge. He came to Haworth as curate in 1820, bringing his wife, Maria and their six children. His wife, who was consumptive, died the following year. In 1825 the two eldest girls, Maria and Elizabeth, fell ill at boarding school in Cowan Bridge and died. In 1846 appeared the first publication by the three surviving sisters, a joint volume of poems by "Currer, Ellis and Acton Bell", names chosen to preserve their initials but conceal that they were women. There followed *Wuthering Heights* (1847), *The Tenant of Wildfell Hall* by Anne, who also drew on her experience as a governess for *Agnes Grey* (1847), and *Jane Eyre* (1847) by Charlotte. All died young: their brother, Branwell, aged 31 in September 1848, Emily (at 30) three months later and Anne (at 29) the following summer in Scarborough, where she is buried. Charlotte married her father's curate in 1854 and died in 1855, aged 39. Patrick Brontë outlived his wife and all six children.

Brontë Weaving Shed: Townend Mill – *Town End Mill , North Street.* ⊙*Open Mon-Sat 10am-5.30pm, Sun 11am-5pm.* ⊙ *Closed Easter Sunday, 25 Dec.* ⊛ *No charge.* ☏ *01535 646 21.* Haworth was originally a weaving village, with over 1 200 handlooms in action at its peak in the 1840s. Here Victorian looms produce "Brontë tweed" and visitors can try their hand at operating them; there is also an exhibition about Timmy Feather, known as Yorkshire's last handloom weaver. A shop sells knitwear made at the mill.

Excursions

Top Withens – *3mi/5km west; 1hr.* A walk through open moorland leads to the ruined stone farmhouse, thought to have been the inspiration for Wuthering Heights.

Keighley and Worth Valley Railway – *Oxenhope. 2mi/3km south on A 6033.* ♿⊙ *Operates between Keighley and Oxenhope via Ingrow, Oakworth, Haworth (5mi/30min) late-Jun to Sep, daily; Oct to late-Jun, Sat-Sun, Bank Hols.* ⊛ *£8 return ticket; £12 Day Rover. Parking. Refreshments at Oxenhope and Keighley, buffet car on some trains in summer.* ☏ *01535 647 777 (24hr recorded information), 01535 645 214 (office); Fax 01535 647 317; admin@kwvr.co.uk; www.kwvr.co.uk.* A re-created Edwardian station is the terminus of this railway, whose steam engines travel through moor scenery along a complete branch line linking Oxenhope on Penistone Hill with Haworth, Oakworth (where the film *The Railway Children* was set), Damems, Ingrow and Keighley. At Ingrow is a **Museum of Rail Travel** *Halifax Road.* ⊙*Open daily, 11am-4.30pm.* ⊙*Closed 25-26 Dec.* ⊛ *£1.50.* ☏ *01535 680 425; Fax 01535 610 796; admin@vintagecarriagestrust.org; www.vintagecarriagestrust.org).*

Hebden Bridge – *7mi/11km south by A 6033.* For hundreds of years this was just a crossing point, where packhorses laboured over the Calder River. Between 1750 and 1850 the packhorse trails gave way to railway and canal, as the textile industry boomed.

The village takes its name from a 1510 stone bridge spanning Hebden Water, which replaced an earlier wooden version. Now the redundant stone mills and the Rochdale Canal have been restored, and the narrow streets are busy with walkers en route to the Pennine countryside. Beside the canal *(east of town centre on A 646 Burnley Road)* stands **Walkleys Canalside Mill**, *(♿Canal Wharf, Sawmills, Burnley Road.* ⊙*Open daily, 10am-5pm (5.30pm Sat, Sun and bank holidays).* ⊙ *Closed 1 Jan and 25-26 Dec. Shop.*

Brontë Country

The Brontë sisters drew on their local knowledge for descriptions of the places in their novels. Two houses which appear in *Shirley* under other names can be visited near Batley. In the 19C the family of Mary Taylor, one of Charlotte's close friends, lived in an 18C red-brick house, now the **Red House Museum** *(Oxford Road, Gomersal, near Batley* ⊙ *Open daily, 11am (noon Sat-Sun) to 5pm.* ☏ *01274 335 100; Fax 01274 335 105);* the house appears in *Shirley* as Briarmains and is now furnished as it would have been in the 1830s. **Oakwell Hall**, *(Nutter Lane, Birstall, near Batley, on A 638* ⊙♿ *Open daily, 11am-5pm, Sat-Sun, noon-5pm.* ⊛ *£1.40 Information centre. Shop. Tearoom.* ☏ *01924 326 240)* is a dark-stone Elizabethan manor, with impressive latticed windows, furnished as it was for the Batt family in the 1690s; it is surrounded by traces of a moat and a country park with a wildlife garden, willow maze and nature trails.

Tea room. ☎ *01422 844868 (Mill); 01422 842 061; www.caldervalley.co.uk) a Victorian* building, which now houses craft shops (gifts, knitwear, stationery) and exhibitions on clog-making, minting and 'the world of the honey bee', and sells a range of clogs with fashionable touches.

From Hebden Bridge *(1.5mi/2.5km northwest off A 6033 at the end of Midgehole Road)* a narrow hillside road winds up to **Hardcastle Crags,** *(NT Hollin Hall, Crimsworth Dean, Hebden Bridge.* ◷*Open daily.* ♿ *Parking £2 per car.* ☎*/Fax 01422 844 518; hardcastlecrags@nationaltrust.org.uk; www.nationaltrust.org.uk) covering the two steep,* wooded valleys of Hebden Dale and Crimsworth Dean. Trails lead into the woods, landscaped in the 19C as an approach to Lord Savile's shooting estate, and remnants of the valley's past industries include an 1801 cotton mill.

Ponden Mill – *Colne Road, Stanbury, 2mi/3km west on B 6144.* ◷ *Open daily, 9.30am (11am Sun) to 5.30pm (5pm Sun).* ☎ *01535 643 500.* In an attractive setting overlooking a stream and hills criss-crossed with dry-stone walls sits a mill-turned-craft shop, selling a wide selection of household goods, gifts and linen. A track leads to 17C Ponden Hall, the model for Thrushcross Grange in *Wuthering Heights*.

Wycoller Country Park – *6mi/10km west along minor roads to A 6068.* A stone clapper bridge and a 700-year-old packhorse bridge span the river, yards apart; fragments survive of Wycoller Hall, described as Ferndean Manor in *Jane Eyre*. The local field boundaries are marked by "Vaccary walls" made of upright stone slabs – an ancient system used by cattle-breeding farms. From the park one can walk *(550yd/500m)* to the pretty riverside village of **Wycoller**, which traces its origins to the Anglo-Saxon era; it evolved from agricultural settlement to weaving village in the 18C but the industrial age, in the main, passed it by.

HEREFORD ★

Herefordshire, ENGLAND

POPULATION 48 277

MICHELIN ATLAS P 26 OR MAP 503 L 27

TOWN PLAN IN THE MICHELIN GUIDE GREAT BRITAIN AND IRELAND

Seat of a bishop in AD 676, Hereford was a flourishing city and became capital of Saxon Mercia, with its own mint. In 1070 William Fitzosborn, builder of Chepstow castle, established a new market where the roads converged north of the town. Today Hereford is the flourishing centre for a rich agricultural region on the border with Wales. Outstanding among the many half-timbered buildings preserved in the city is the **Old House**★, dating from 1621, a fine example of Jacobean domestic architecture.

Hereford is unique in possessing two chained libraries, one in the Cathedral and one in All Saints Church.

Every third year the Cathedral is the setting for the Three Choirs Festival, which it has shared with Gloucester and Worcester since the 18C. ⟐ *1 King Street, Hereford HR4 9BW* ☎ *01432 268 430; Fax 01432 342 662; tic-hereford@herefordshire.gov.uk*

Cathedral ★★

♿*Cathedral:* ◷*Open for visitors Mon-Sat 9.15am-5pm.* 🕭 *Guided tour: weekdays at 11am and 2pm* ♿ *£2.50. Brass rubbing £2.50. Leaflet (7 languages). Refreshments.* ☎ *01432 374 212. Mappa Mundi Exhibition and Chained Library:* ◷*Open Mar-Sep, daily, 10am (11am Sun) to 4.15pm, (3.15 Sun) (last admission); Oct-Feb, Mon-Sat, 11am - 3.15pm (last admission).* ♿ *£4. Café.* ☎ *01432 374 209; www.herefordcathedral.org.* The red sandstone building is mainly of the 12C. The massive tower was added in the 14C, largely funded by offerings from pilgrims to the shrine of St Thomas Cantilupe, Bishop from 1275-82. His shrine, minus effigy, stands in the north transept. The chantry to John Stanbury, Bishop from 1453-74, is a fine example of Perpendicular architecture. Among the treasures is the **Mappa Mundi**★, a map of the world with Jerusalem at its centre, made by Richard of Haldingham in Lincolnshire. The **Chained Library**, one of the finest in the country, contains 1400 books and over 200 manuscripts, dating from the 8C to the 15C, including the "Cider Bible" in which the "strong drink" of the Authorised version has been translated as "cidir". There is a small 13C Limoges enamel reliquary, which used to contain a relic of St Thomas Becket, whose murder is depicted on the side.

Cider Museum and King Offa Distillery – *21 Ryelands Street. ⚐ ⏱ Open Apr-Oct, daily, 10am-5pm; Nov -Mar, noon-4pm. ⚐ £3 . Parking. ☎ 01432 354 207; info@cidermuseum. co.uk; www.cidermuseum.co.uk.* An old cider factory houses the museum which tells the story of cider making through the ages, particularly during its heyday in the 17C when Herefordshire landowners took bottled ciders to their London houses for the season. Here the techniques of racking, dropping, fining and keeving are explained and you can learn the difference between an Upright French and a Black Huffcap and admire the display of cider bottles from all over the world. The distillery is licensed to produce cider brandy, which is on sale in the shop together with many other apple and pear beverages.

Excursions

Kilpeck Church★★ – *8mi/13km southwest of Hereford by A 465 and a minor road (right). ⏱ Open daily, dawn-dusk. Services: check board for times. ⚐ Donation. Tea/coffee generally available. Parking. ☎ 01981 570 315; j.p.bailey@ btinternet.com.* The Church of St Mary and St David was built in 1135 in place of a Saxon church dating from AD 650. Nowhere else in Britain has such rich Norman **carving** and decoration survived. The south door with its portal and columns is particularly fine. Only two of the 70 grotesques around the corbel have any religious significance. The gargoyle heads on the west wall are pure Viking in inspiration, as if they had been lifted straight from the prows of longships.

According to the Domesday book, at that time in the 11C the manor of Kilpeck was held from the king for "fifteen sesters of honey and ten shillings annually".

South Door, Kilpeck

Abbey Dore – 12mi/20km southwest of Hereford by A 465 and an unmarked road (left). The village church (1180), originally part of the abbey founded in 1147, is one of the few Cistercian churches in England regularly used for worship. In 1632 Lord Scudamore commissioned its restoration by John Abel who carved the magnificent screen from Hereford oak. 204 tons of timber were required to re-roof the nave and presbytery. The church was reconsecrated on Scudamore's birthday, Palm Sunday 1634.

ILFRACOMBE

Devon, ENGLAND

POPULATION 10 941

MICHELIN ATLAS P 6 OR MAP 503 H 30

This is the most popular resort on the North Devon coast, its fine coves and cliff scenery set against a backdrop of attractive wooded hills and valleys. Originally a fishing and trading port, Ilfracombe became a magnet for holidaymakers in the 19C when steamship day outings from South Wales and the arrival of the railway made the town more widely accessible.

The hills around the town provide good vantage points for surveying the area: **Capstone Hill**★ (156ft/47m) offers a good **view**★ of the town, the harbour mouth, the rock-enclosed bays and beaches; **Hillsborough**, at the centre of the pleasure ground, rises to 447ft/136m and affords an even more extensive **view**★★ along the coast; Lantern Hill is the site of a beacon to guide night shipping in the Bristol Channel. *The Landmark, The Seafront, Ilfracombe EX34 9BX ☎ 01271 863 001; Fax 01271 862 586; info@ ilfracombe-tourism.co.uk; www.ilfracombe-tourism.co.uk*

- **Don't Miss:** Clovelly, Lundy Island.
- **Especially for Kids:** Beaches *(below)*; Watermouth Castle.
- **Also See:** Dartmoor, Exmoor, Exeter.
- **Bicycle Trails:** The Tarka Trail is a flat and scenic cycling trail which follows old railway lines between Appledore, Bideford, Instow and other small North Devon seaside towns, ask at the nearest tourist office for details.
- **Beaches:** Tunnels Beaches *(below)*; east of the harbour at Reparee Cove, Hele Bay and Barricane; west at Woolacombe , Croyde and Saunton; east at Braunton.

Sights

Holy Trinity – The parish church dates from the Norman period (enlarged in the 14C) and has an ancient, elaborately carved **wagon roof**★★.

St Nicholas' Chapel – *Lantern Hill.* ⓘ *Open late May-mid Oct, daily, 10am-1pm and 2.30pm-5pm; also May-Aug, 7.30pm-dusk.* In the early 14C the beacon set as a marker on Lantern Hill was replaced by this mariners' chapel which, though much altered, still shines a red light to guide shipping.

From the rock platform on which the chapel stands there is a good **view**★ over the almost land-locked harbour and out to sea.

Tunnels Beaches – *Granville Road.* ⓘ *Open (subject to tide) May-Oct, daily 10am-6pm (7pm Jul-Aug).* £1.75. Refreshments, picnic area. ☎ www.tunnelsbeaches.co.uk. In the 19C the hill between the road and the sea was tunnelled and the rock cove, on the far side, made accessible. The cove was then equipped with a sea wall to prevent the tide running out and so provide all day bathing.

Excursions

Watermouth Castle – *1mi/1.6km southeast on A 399.* ⓘ *Open Easter-Oct 11am-5pm; 10am-6pm during school hols.* £9.50, Cafe, picnic site. Parking. ☎ 01271 867474; Fax 01271 865 864; www.watermouthcastle.com. Overlooking picturesque Watermouth Cove, this Victorian folly castle is a handsome sight. Its beautifully landscaped gardens now hosts a theme park for young children.

Chambercombe Manor – *1mi/1.6km southeast on A 399. Chambercombe Road* ⓘ*Open Easter-Oct, Sun-Fri, 10am (2pm Sun) to 5.30pm.* Guided tour (45min). £4. Parking. Refreshments. ☎ 01271 862 624; www.chambercombemanor.co.uk. The attractive white-painted and slate-roofed stone house (15C-17C) lying in a wooded dell was once thatched. Inside, interesting features include 200-300 year old polished **lime ash floors**; a 13C Peter's Pence **almschest; barrel vaulting**; a robustly carved Elizabethan **four-poster bed** made from Spanish oak timbers; a Cromwellian oak cradle; a Jacobean chest of drawers; a William and Mary yew **tallboy**; and a Victorian room.

Barnstaple★ – *13mi/21km south.* The town was one of the first in the country to receive a charter, in 930, and has been the regional centre for trade, agriculture and industry since: the 19C cast-iron and glass-roofed **Pannier Market**, adjoining **Butchers' Row,** is still used on Tuesday, Friday and Saturday to sell local produce (Devon cream, fruit, vegetables, preserves; also a cattle market on Friday).

Long Bridge★ (520ft/158m) was first built c 1273; three of its 16 stone arches were replaced around 1539. The 13C **Parish Church,** (🕐 *Open Mon-Fri, 9am-3pm. Sun services: 10.30am (3rd Sun in month also 6pm).* ☎ *01271 344 589)* is notable for the memorial monuments within and for its 17C lead-covered broach spire. The 17C **Horwood Alms-houses** and **Alice Horwood School** *(Church Lane)* have attractive wooden mullioned windows. The 19C **Guildhall,** *(High Street.* ☜ *Guided tour Fri-Sat (30min). Apply to the Tourist Information Centre, Boutport Street.* ☎ *01271 375 000)* contains the Dodderidge Parlour, panelled in 17C oak, in which the town's famous collection of corporation plate is displayed. The **Museum of North Devon,** *(NACF ♿ The Square.* 🕐*Open Mon-Sat, 9:30am-5pm.* 🕐 *Closed Bank Hols.* ☎ *01271 346 747; Fax 01271 346 407; museum@northdevon.gov.uk; www.devonmuseums.net/barnstaple)* traces regional history. Downriver from the bridge is the colonnaded **Queen Anne's Walk** (1609, rebuilt 1708), built as a merchant's exchange and crowned by a statue of Queen Anne.

Northeast of Barnstaple *(8mi/13km on A 39)* is **Arlington Court**★★, *(NT ♿ House, carriage collection and Victorian garden:* 🕐*Open late-Mar to early-Nov, Sun-Fri, 11am (10.30am garden) to 5pm (4.30pm last admission). Park: Nov-Mar, during daylight hours. Bat Cave: as garden.* ☜ *House and gardens £6.50; gardens and carriage collection £4.20. Parking. Refreshments.* ☎ *01271 850 296; Fax 01271 850 711; arlingtoncourt@ nationaltrust.org.uk)* a Classically-styled house (1820-23, altered 1865) containing the varied collections of *objets d'art* accumulated by its former owner, Miss Rosalie Chichester (1865-1949), perhaps the most remarkable of which is her collection of **model ships** including 36 made by Napoleonic prisoners of war.

Clovelly★★ – *30mi/50km southwest of Ilfracombe.* This picture-postcard village, which was mentioned in the Domesday Book, is now privately owned and can only be entered via a **Visitor Centre,** *(♿🕐 Open Jul-Sep, daily, 9am (9.30am Oct-Jun) to 6pm/dusk.* 🕐 *Closed 25 Dec.* ☜ *£4.50 includes Audio-visual show (15min) and entrance to museums. Landrover shuttle £1.60 (from Red Lion at the bottom up to the Visitor Centre); 80p (from Red Lion at the bottom up to the white railings just below Visitor Centre). Parking. Refreshments.* ☎ *01237 431 781; www.clovelly. co.uk)* which outlines the history of this charming, fishermen's community and its preservation.

Clovelly

The steep, stepped and cobbled **High Street,** known as **Down-a-long** or **Up-a-long** depending on the direction being faced, is lined with small, whitewashed 18C and 19C houses decked with bright flowers. Donkeys and mules are still the only form of transport up and down the High Street. At the bottom of the High Street lies **Quay Pool**, the small, restored 14C harbour protected from the open sea by a curving breakwater which offers a **view** extending from Lundy to Baggy Point. The pebble beach is backed by stonebuilt cottages and balconied houses, the old harbour lime kiln, the inn and the lifeboat store. The square, unadorned tower of Clovelly **church**, on the outskirts of the village, rises in three parts to a crenellated top within a lush, tree-shaded cemetery. The Perpendicular building contains some particularly interesting monuments (a 16C brass, 17C epitaphs, 18C sculptures) as well as a Norman font and Jacobean pulpit. **Hobby Drive,** *(🕐 Open to pedestrians only, Easter-mid Oct, daily, 10am-6pm.* ☎ *01237 431 200)* a 3-mile/5km toll road *(closed to vehicles)* from the A 39 to the outskirts of the village, meanders 500ft/152m above sea-level through the woods, affording lovely views of the coast and cliffs.

Braunton★ – *8mi/13km south on A 361.* The older, prettier part of this village lies at its northeast end around the largely 13C **St Brannock's Church**★, with its solid Norman tower topped by a lead-covered spire. The church contains some interesting carving (bosses on the wagon roof, 13C font, 16C bench ends). Southwest of the village lies one of the few remaining examples of open-field cultivation in Britain, the **Great Field**. Beyond Braunton Marsh, by the coast, are the **Braunton Burrows**★, *(For* *leaflets on Nature Trails apply to the Tourist Information Centre, The Bakehouse Centre, Caen Street, Braunton, North Devon, EX33 1AA, ☎ 01271 816 400; brauntontic@visit.org. uk)* one of the largest sand dune systems in Britain (about 2 400 acres/971ha), two thirds of which is now a National Nature Reserve.

Lundy Island★★ – 🕐 *2hr crossing by MS Oldenburg (267 passengers) operates (according to tide) from Bideford Quay all year, also from Ilfracombe Pier summer only.* 🚢 *£3.50 (landing fee included in ferry fare from Bideford and Ilfracombe. Coach service to port of embarkation when the return service disembarks at a different harbour. Also private launches from Clovelly (90min).* ☎ *01271 863 636 (sailing details), 01237 470 422 (Lundy Island Manager); info@lundyisland.co.uk; www.lundyisland.co.uk.* Lundy Island derives its name from the Icelandic word for puffin, *Lunde.* The attraction of the island is its fascinating bird, marine and wild life, in a peaceful setting free of many of the trappings of modern life (no cars, no telephones, no newspapers). Despite the island's name, there are reportedly only thirty breeding pairs of puffins on it (May to July); other resident bird life includes razorbill, guillemot, fulmar, Manx shearwater, shag, kittiwake and various species of gull. Lundy has been designated a **Marine Nature Reserve** since 1986, with grey seals, basking shark and porpoise. The clear waters and numerous wrecks offer excellent diving.

The island is formed by a granite mass, three miles long and less than a mile wide, rising 400ft/122m out of the Atlantic-Bristol Channel breakers. It was settled by Bronze and Iron Age man and Celts, before the Norman-Somerset Marisco family arrived in the 12C (the island was seized by the Crown in the 13C, in retaliation for the Marisco's lawlessness). The island's position in the Channel made it the ideal lair for pirates during the centuries of Bristol's trade with Europe, America and the West Indies. The modern era dates from the 19C, when the quarries were worked industrially, the road laid up from the beach and the church built. The island's last private owners introduced the Lundy ponies (a New Forest-Welsh Mountain cross), the rarely seen Sika deer and the wild Soay sheep, also the island's own puffin stamps, in the 1930s. Lundy is now the property of the National Trust, financed and managed by the Landmark Trust.

A complete circuit of the island is 11mi/18km and takes about 4hr *(on foot)*. From Landing Beach, overlooked by 12-13C **Marisco Castle**, the track leads uphill to Lundy village, past the Classical-style granite **Millcombe House** (1830s). The strangely urban-looking village church, **St Helena's**, dates from 1896. Take the footpath west to the **Old Light** (1819), replaced in 1896 by the **North Light**, now automated. The path along the west coast leads past a **battery** which was used as a fog warning station, the site of a landslip, named after an earthquake in the 19C, past **Jenny's Cove** (good viewing point for gulls, auks and puffins) and **Devil's Slide** (rock-climbing). From North Light, you can either take the path back along the east coast (past the quarries), or the more popular route along the spine of the island.

Mortehoe★★ – The late 13C tower added to the original 12C Norman **St Mary's Church**★ was saved from ruin in 1988 by an anonymous benefactor. Inside, note the Norman or Early English font, the finely carved 16C bench ends and the angel mosaic adorning the early chancel arch. **Morte Point**★ marks the western end of the spectacular Somerset-North Devon coast and offers good **views** over the coastline and the impressive landscape inland.

INVERARAY★★

Argyll and Bute, SCOTLAND

MICHELIN ATLAS P 54 OR MAP 501 E 15

The whitewashed township lies roughly halfway along Scotland's west coast on the shores of Loch Fyne.

The original 15C seat of Clan Campbell with its attendant settlement was replaced in the 18C and a new planned village was rebuilt at a distance. The 3rd Duke of Argyll commissioned Roger Morris as architect and William Adam as clerk of works for this ambitious project. *Front Street ☎ 01499 302 063; info@inveraray.visitscotland.com; www.inveraray-argyll.com.*

Inveraray Castle★★

Open Jun-Sept, daily, 10am (1pm Sun) to 5.45pm; Apr-May and Oct, Mon-Sat, 10am-1pm and 2-5.45pm, Sun, 1-5.45pm; last admission 12.30pm and 5pm. £5.90. Guided tour (1hr). Guide book (5 languages). Parking. Tearoom. ☎ 01499 302 203; Fax 01499 302 421; enquiries@inveraray-castle.com; www.inveraray-castle.com. The exterior remains a good example of Gothic Revival in spite of 19C alterations (dormers and conical roofs). The façades are adorned with Gothic windows and a tiered keep rises above the roof line.

Interior – The 5th Duke refurbished the interiors in the neo-Classical style after the fashion of Carlton House in London. In particular, the **dining room** is a masterpiece of delicately detailed plasterwork and painting. The Tapestry Drawing Room reveals an Adam-designed compartmented ceiling, decorative panels and overdoors by Girard. The **armoury hall** with its decorative display of pole-arms, Lochaber axes and broadswords is where the duke's personal piper plays a medley of Campbell tunes to awaken the household.

In the Saloon Pompeo Batoni's 8th Duke of Hamilton faces Gainsborough's Conway. Among the portraits in the northwest hall and staircase note the rebuilding 3rd Duke (Allan Ramsay), the redecorating 5th Duke (Gainsborough) and his Duchess Elizabeth Gunning.

Excursions

West shore of Loch Fyne to Crinan – *3mi/53km by A 83*. The great sea loch of **Loch Fyne**★★ stretches from the heart of the Argyll mountains down the arm of Loch Gilp where it turns due south to reach the open sea. In the 19C this was the scene of a successful herring fishery.

Auchindrain★ – *Open Apr-Sep, daily, 10am-5pm. £3.80. Tour (1hr). Parking. Picnic area. ☎ 01499 500 235.* This open-air folk museum evokes life in the communal-tenancy farms. Once the commonest kind of Scottish farming, they survived longest in the Highlands. Farming methods, domestic interiors, barns and byres are among the many aspects of life presented here.

▶ *Continue along A 83 to Lochgilphead then follow A 816 to Cairnbaan. B 841 leads westwards to Crinan.*

The rocky eminence, Dunadd Fort *(access from A 816)*, rising abruptly out of the flat lands to the right, was a Dark Age fortification and capital of the Scots Kingdom of Dalriada from AD 498 to 843.

Crinan★ – A delightful hamlet at the western end of the Crinan Canal, linking the Sound of Jura with Loch Fyne.

Loch Awe★★ – Picturesque roads (A 819 north to Cladich and the lochside B 840) lead to the scenic loch which is hemmed in by forests. *(For the northern tip of the loch see OBAN, Excursions)*

INVERNESS★

Highlands, SCOTLAND

POPULATION 62 186

MICHELIN ATLAS P 67 OR MAP 501 H 11

TOWN PLAN IN THE MICHELIN GUIDE GREAT BRITAIN AND IRELAND

Inverness, standing at the northern end of the Great Glen, astride the River Ness flowing from Loch Ness, is the traditional capital of the Scottish Highlands and the legendary Loch attracts many boating visitors. *Castle Wynd, Inverness IV2 3BJ ☎ 01463 234 353; Fax 01463 710 609.*

A Bit of History

Inverness was strategically important from the days of the Picts; St Columba visited King Brude in the vicinity, and King Duncan (murdered by Macbeth in the 11C) had his castle here. Its strategic value was its downfall, and fought over by Scottish monarchs, Highland clans, Jacobites and English, the town now has few significant buildings dating from before the 19C.

▶ **Orient Yourself:** in Inverness with a City Sightseeing open-top hop-on hop-off buses tour late May-Sept ☎ www.citysightseeing.co.uk

⊙ **Don't Miss:** a cruise on Loch Ness – "monster hunting" trips depart from Inverness and Fort Augustus.

Especially for Kids: Loch Ness 2000 Visitor Centre at Drumnadrochit; a short trip on the Loch.

Walking Tours: walking tours depart from the tourist office in Inverness usually at 11am and 2pm most days in summer, check with the tourist office.

Sights

Inverness Castle – The 19C castle is the most recent of a series of castles and it now serves as a courthouse and administrative building. A good **view** of the town and the River Ness may be enjoyed from the esplanade (statue of Flora MacDonald).

Museum and Art Gallery★ – *Castle Wynd.* ⸝ ⊙ *Open Mon-Sat, 9am-5pm.* ⊙ *Closed 25-26 and 31 Dec, 1-2 Jan. Brochure. Coffee shop.* ☎ *01463 237 114; Fax 01463 225 293; inverness.museum@highland.gov.uk; www.highland.gov.uk.* On the first floor an imaginative and well-presented exhibition "Inverness, Hub of the Highlands" interprets the region's rich heritage. Exhibits on the Great Glen, the Picts, General Wade's roads and Telford's Caledonian Canal are of special interest. The Highlanders' way of life is presented on the upper floor.

St Andrew's Cathedral – *Ardross Street.* ⊙*Open daily, 9.30am (2pm Sun Oct-Mar) to 6.30pm (4.30pm Oct-Mar). Guide book. Leaflet (5 languages).* ☎/*Fax 01463 233 535; www.inverness-cathedral.org.uk.* A richly decorated neo-Gothic church of 1866-69, its nave piers are of polished Peterhead granite, the reredos and pulpit of carved stone. Both choir screen and rood cross are by Robert Lorimer.

Excursions

Cawdor Castle★ – *13mi/21km northeast by A 96 and B 9090.* ⸝ ⊙ *Open May to mid-Oct, daily, 10am-5:30 pm.* ⸙ *£6.80. Brochure (5 languages). Parking. Licensed restaurant.* ☎ *01667 404 615; Fax 01667 404 674; info@cawdor.castle.com; www.cawdorcastle.com.* Built in the late 14C by the Thanes of Cawdor (this was the title Shakespeare's witches promised Macbeth), the central tower was the 14C keep. The castle was added to in the 17C. During a visit to this historic home note the lovely 17C Flemish and English tapestries and amidst the many portraits one of the 18th thane, resplendently attired in an assortment of tartans refuting the idea of "one clan one sett."

Fort George★ – *(HS) 20mi/32km northeast by A 96 and B 9006.* ⸝ ⊙ *Open daily, 9.30am to 6.30pm (4.30pm Oct-Mar); last admission 45min before closing time.* ⸙ *£6. Parking. Restaurant (Apr-Sep); picnic area.* ☎ *01667 462 777.* Set on a peninsula jutting out into the Moray Firth, this impressive artillery fortress was built (1745-46), on the orders of George II, to prevent once and for all Hanoverian law and order from being disrupted by the Highland clans. The fort, its elaborate defences as well as several exhibitions bring to life the lot of the troops in the 17C and 18C.

Cromarty★ – *26mi/42km northeast by A 9 and A 832.* On the northern tip of the Black Isle at the mouth of the Cromarty Firth guarded by the Sutors Stacks, the tiny port of Cromarty has been aptly described as "the jewel in the crown of Scottish vernacular architecture". The fine 18C **Cromarty Courthouse,** *(Church Street.* ◷*Open Mar-Oct, daily, 10am5pm.* ⊜ *£3 (includes audio tour 3 languages). Guide sheets (6 languages).* ☎ *01381 600 418; info@ cromarty-courthouse.org.uk; www.cromarty-courthouse.org.uk)* is noteworthy.

Dornoch★ – *55mi/88km northeast by A 9.* The scenic route cuts across the Black Isle, passes along the north bank of the Cromarty Firth, near the pretty little town of **Tain** built in honey-coloured stone, which was formerly an important pilgrimage centre, and crosses the Dornoch Firth to reach the charming burgh which boasts miles of sandy beaches and famous championship golf courses. The medieval cathedral with its square tower and broach spire dominates the town.

Dunrobin Castle – *12mi/19km north from Dornoch.* ◷ *Open Apr to mid-Oct, daily, 10.30am (noon Sun, Apr-Jun, and Sep to mid-Oct) to 4.30pm (5.30pm Jun-Sep).* ⊜ *£6.50 including museum, garden and falconry displays. Falconry Display: at 11.30am, 1.30pm, 3.30pm; smaller displays at other times. Parking. Tea room.* ☎ *01408 633 177, 01408 633 268; Fax 01408 634 081; info@dunrobincastle.net.* The ancestral seat of the earls and dukes of Sutherland, stands on a natural **terrace** overlooking the sea. Later additions surround the original tower of 1400. The interior remodelled by Charles Barry (1850s) and Robert Lorimer (early 20C) is enhanced by a fine collection of **paintings** including family portraits by masters of the art such as Jamesone, Ramsay, Reynolds, Hoppner, Lawrence and Wright. The attractive formal **gardens** may be admired from the terrace. In the Hunting Trophy House massed antlers look down on local archeological specimens. The museum displays fine Pictish stones.

The Mound causeway, built by Thomas Telford carries the road across the head of Loch Fleet which attracts wintering wildfowl to the pretty town of **Golspie** where St Andrews Church (finely carved Sutherland loft and canopied pulpit) and the Geological and mineralogical exhibition at the **Orcadian Stone Company Ltd**, *(Main Street.* ◷*Open Mon-Sat, 9am-5.30pm; also summer, Sun, 10am-4pm.* ◷ *Closed 25 Dec, 1 Jan.* ⊜ *£1.* ☎*/Fax 01408 633 483; www.orcadianstone.co.uk)* is worth a visit.

Culloden – *(NTS) 6mi/10km east by A 9 and B 9006.* ♿*Culloden Moor Site:* ◷*Open daily. Visitor Centre:* ♿ ◷*Open late-Mar to late-Oct, daily, 9am-5:30pm; late-Jan to late-Mar and late-Oct to late-Dec, daily, 10am-4pm.* ⊜ *£5.* ⟿ *Guided tour (1hr) in summer. Audio-visual presentation (6 languages). Guide book (3 languages). Parking. Restaurant.* ☎ *01463 790 607; Fax 01463 794 294; www.nts.org.uk.* Here on 16 April 1746 the Jacobite army under Bonnie Prince Charlie was slaughtered by Government troops under "Butcher Cumberland", George II's younger son, finally ending the hopes of a Stuart restoration to the British throne. On the Battlefield site are the Memorial Cairn and the Clan Graves. Footpaths demarcate the front lines. The **visitor centre** has an audio-visual programme and exhibition area explaining the battle. The restored Old Leanach Cottage can also be viewed.

Clava Cairns★ – *Continue on B 9006 and turn right at the Cumberland Stone.* Of the three Neolithic cairns, girdled by stone circles and a small ring of boulders in a unified design, the middle one was always open to the sky while the other two had roofed entrance passages leading to burial chambers.

Great Glen★ – *65mi/105km southwest by A 82 – allow 3-4hr.* The geological fault of the Great Glen, running southwest to northeast, cuts across the Highlands, linking the Atlantic Ocean with the North Sea through a series of narrow lochs joined together by part (22mi/35km) of Thomas Telford's **Caledonian Canal** (1803-22). The lochs and canals are now used principally for pleasure craft; some operators offer "Monster Hunting" trips on Loch Ness.

The initial stretch of lochside road provides good views of the loch.

Loch Ness★★ – The dark waters of this loch (754ft/230m deep) are renowned the world over as the home of the elusive

Nessie

The initial sighting of a large snake-like, hump-backed monster with a long thin neck in Loch Ness was made in the 8C by a monk. Despite various expeditions, some highly equipped with submarines, helicopters and sonar electronic cameras, the loch has failed to reveal its secret (the true identity of Nessie). The tradition is hardly surprising in a country where the kelpie or water-horse was common in the tales and legends of the past.

Loch Ness

Nessie. First espied in the 8C by a local monk, Nessie has continued to captivate and mystify and, despite modern technology, preserve her true identity. A roadside monument commemorates the death of the racing driver John Cobb in 1952, while attempting to break the water speed record.

Urquhart Castle – *(HS)* ⓒ *Open daily, 9.30am to 6.30pm (4.30pm Oct-Mar); last admission 45min before closing.* ⊛ *£6. Parking.* ☎ *01456 450 551; hs.urquhart@scotland.gsi. gov.uk; www.historic-scotland.gov.uk.* The ruins are strategically set on a promontory jutting out into the loch and the stronghold was one of a chain controlling this natural route. The landward gatehouse leads to a double bailey courtyard. The viewing platform in the tower house affords good **views** of the castle's layout and of the loch in its mountain setting. A fairly steep path and stairs lead down to the loch.

Drumnadrochit – This pretty little village's **Loch Ness 2000**★ (⧖ⓒ *Open Jun-Sep, daily, 9am-pm (6pm Jun and Sep); Oct, daily, 9.30am-5.30pm (5pm Easter-May); Nov-Easter, daily, 10am-3.30pm.* ⓒ *Closed 25 Dec.* ⊛ *£5.95. Parking. Coffee shop. Restaurant.* ☎ *01456 450 573; Fax 01456 450 770; brem@loch-ness-scotland.com; www. loch-ness-scotland.com)* is an entertaining multi-media visitor centre which tell you all about the Loch and of course the Nessie enigma.

Fort Augustus – *Population 575.* Sitting astride the Caledonian Canal at the southern end of Loch Ness, this busy little town becomes a bottleneck in summer as traffic negotiates the swing bridge. On the site of General Wade's 18C fort stands Fort Augustus Abbey, known for its Catholic school.

Beyond Fort Augustus the road runs east of the Caledonian Canal then skirts Loch Oich. Past Invergarry the road crosses to the east side of the glen at Laggan where pleasure boats negotiate the **Laggan Locks** built to overcome the 13ft/4m difference between Loch Oich and the shallow waters of Loch Lochy (10mi/16km long) flanked by forests. The road then descends past a Second World War Commando memorial to Fort William.

Fort William★ – Fort William lies on the shore of Loch Linnhe in the shadow of Britain's highest mountain, **Ben Nevis** (4 406ft/1 344m). The town makes an ideal touring centre from which to discover the beauty of the surrounding countryside. At Torlundy, **cable cars,** (⧖ⓒ *Open daily (weather permitting), 10am-5pm; longer hours Jul-Aug.* ⊛ *Return trip £8. Restaurant, bar, café.* ☎ *01397 705 825; Fax 01397 705 854; nevisrange@sol.co.uk; www.nevis-range.co.uk)* rise to the Nevis Range ski resort providing wonderful **views**★★ on the way.

Isle of **IONA** ★

Argyll and Bute, SCOTLAND

POPULATION 268

MICHELIN ATLAS P 59 OR MAP 501 A 14 AND 15

ACCESS: SEE THEMICHELIN GUIDE GREAT BRITAIN AND IRELAND.

The remote and windswept tiny Isle of Iona lies immediately west of the Isle of Mull at the southern end of the Great Glen fault line (⏱ *see Loch Ness*). St Columba established his monastic settlement here 1 400 years ago, and this is one of the most venerated places in Scotland. The Saint's community flourished (the intricately carved crosses and grave slabs are a testament to its artistic accomplishments) until brought to an end by the Norse raids of the 8C and 9C. A monastery was re-established in the early 13C, this time Benedictine, disappearing at the Reformation. In 1938 a third religious brotherhood – now an ecumenical community – came to the isle and a major restoration programme was completed in 1966. The abbey is a place of hospitality, reflection and worship. A small community of crofters inhabits the fertile island.

😊 **Please Note:** Cars are not permitted on the island.

Visit

Take the road from the old Benedictine **Nunnery** (restored late 19C) with its medieval church and conventual buildings. Go through the gate past the intricately carved 15C **Maclean's Cross**★ and the early Christian burial ground, **Reilig Odhrian** (where Scotland's kings from Kenneth MacAlpine to Malcolm III were buried) to the 12C **St Oran's Chapel**★, the oldest building on the island, with a fine Norman west door. Walk down the **Street of the Dead**, where three **High Crosses** catch the eye (an 8C **Cross of St Martin**★, a 9C-10C truncated shaft of St Matthew and a replica of the 8C St John's Cross). On the other side of the Street of the Dead is St Columba's cell, Tor Abb.

The **abbey**, (♿⏱ *Open daily, subject to ferries, 9.30am (2pm Sun, Oct-Mar) to 6.30pm (4.30pm Oct-Mar).* ✆ *£3.30 including admission to Infirmary Museum.* 📣 *Guided tour available.* ☎ *01681 700512; ionacomm@iona.org.uk; www.iona.org.uk/abbey*) stands on the site of its Columban predecessor; the original 13C church was enlarged in the 15C with a tower at the crossing and a south aisle to the choir. Fragments of the 13C Benedictine church include the north transept and arcade of the choir's north wall.

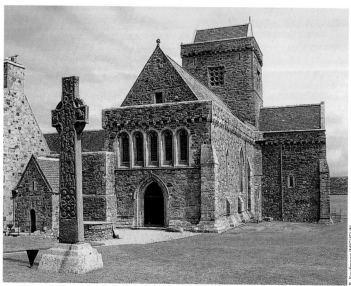

High Crosses, Iona

The elaborate trefoil-headed doorway below was inserted when the north aisle was converted into a sacristy (15C). The twin-columned arcade of the cloisters is noteworthy. To the north of the west front is St Columba's shrine.

Beyond the abbey is the **Infirmary Museum**★, (🕐 *Open all year, daily, 9am-5pm. Brochure (French, German, Italian).* ☎ *01681 700 404.)* with an outstanding collection of early Christian and medieval stonework including the ornate 8C **Cross of St John**★ (restored), medieval effigies and grave slabs.

IPSWICH

Suffolk, ENGLAND

POPULATION 130 157

MICHELIN ATLAS P 23 OR MAP 504 X 27

TOWN PLAN IN THE MICHELIN GUIDE GREAT BRITAIN AND IRELAND

This bustling country town, set at the head of the Orwell estuary on the south East Anglian coast, is mostly Victorian and modern in character. All that remains of the distant past is its Anglo-Saxon street layout and about a dozen medieval churches, some just towers, built when the town was a rich port and trading centre. The Tower Ramparts exist in name only and a large pedestrian area includes the Buttermarket shopping precinct. The glass Willis Corroon building (1975) by Norman Foster is one of the temples to the insurance industry, of which Ipswich is now a centre. The Victorian Wet Dock, once the largest in the world, with its warehouses, merchant's houses and maltings, makes an interesting walk. ▯ *St Stephen's Church, St Stephen's Lane, Ipswich IP1 1DP ☎ 01473 258 07; Fax: 01473 432017; tourist@ipswich.gov.uk; www.visit-ipswich.com.*

Sights

Christchurch Mansion – ♿ *Christchurch Park.* ⊙*Open Tue-Sat and Bank Hol Mon, 10am-5pm (4pm/dusk Nov-Mar); Sun 2.30-4.30pm/dusk.* ⊙ *Closed Good Friday, 1 Jan and 24-26 Dec. Pedestrian access from Soane Street; cars via Bolton Lane. Access for disabled visitors to ground floor.* ☎ *01473 433 554.* This much-restored Tudor manor house, set in pleasant parkland, is full of treasures from Ipswich and the surrounding countryside, displayed in period settings. It holds a good collection of paintings by 17C Suffolk-born artists, including several by **John Constable** (*Mill Stream, Willy Lott's House,* and two Stour Valley landscapes of his father's kitchen and flower gardens) and **Thomas Gainsborough** (*Portrait of William Wollaston of Finborough Hall, Crossing the Ford, Cottage Door with Girl and Pigs and View Near the Coast).* Other items of interest include the *Painted Closet* by Lady Drury (early 17C), Lowestoft porcelain and an authentic period kitchen. In the "Tudor Hall" (added 1924) hangs a colourful 16C French tapestry of King Arthur.

St Margaret's Church – *Bolton Lane, near the entrance to Christchurch Park.* The 14C parish church with elaborate stone and flint exterior contains a double hammerbeam roof and 13C coffin lid.

Ancient House – *Buttermarket.* ⊙ *Open normal shop hours, Mon-Sat 9am-5.30pm.* The exterior of this 15C house, abounds in Restoration plasterwork, pargeting and stucco reliefs of nymphs, pelicans and the then-known continents: Europe (a Gothic Church), Asia (an Oriental dome), Africa (an African with a sunshade astride a crocodile) and America (a tobacco pipe). The coat of arms is that of Charles II who visited the building in 1668. Although it is now a shop, visitors can view several panelled rooms (c 1603) with wall pargeting, ornamental ceilings and 18C ceramic tilework. The Museum Room *(first floor)* has muted Rococo wall paintings and finds related to the house. The 15C double hammerbeam roof can be seen from the Chapel.

Excursions

Stour Valley★ – "I associate my careless boyhood to all that lies on the banks of the Stour", wrote **John Constable** (1776-1837), "They made me a painter and I am grateful". The lower Stour is **Constable Country**; the upper Stour is **Gainsborough Country**; in between is Sudbury, where Gainsborough was born and where Constable went to school.

▶ *Take A 12 south for 8mi/13km, turn left on B 1070 and follow signs.*

Flatford Mill★ – *Apply to Field Studies Council, Flatford Mill, East Bergholt, Suffolk, CO7 6UL. Interpretation Centre and guides at Bridge Cottage (♿ see below).* ☎ *01206 298 283; Fax 01206 298 892; enquiries.fm@field-studies-council.org; www.field-studies-council.org.* The mill (1773) was the home of John Constable, whose father was a miller. Together with **Bridge Cottage,** formerly known as **Willy Lott's Cottage,** (⊙ *Open May-Oct, daily, 10am (11am Oct) to 5.30pm; Mar-Apr and Nov-Dec, Wed-Sun, 11am-3.30pm.* ⊙ *Closed 1 Jan and 25 Dec.* *Guided tour of the area when available*

(☞ £2): Easter, Bank Hols and May-Sep, every afternoon. ☞ Parking £1. Refreshments. No dogs. ☎ 01206 298 260; Fax 01206 299 193; flatford@ntrust.org.uk; www.nationaltrust. org.uk) and the river valley, the mill inspired some of his best-loved landscapes – *The Haywain, Boatbuilding* and *Flatford Mill.*

▶ *Take the road west or the riverbank path.*

Dedham – This quintessentially English village, where "there is nothing to hurt the eye" (Pevsner), was the subject of many Constable landscapes.
Pass under the A 12 and take the B 1068 and the B 1087 for 6mi/10km.

Nayland – **St James' Church** (15C) (☉ *Open daily, 9am-5pm/dusk. Services: Sun at 8am and 9.30pm.)* contains *The Last Supper* by Constable.

▶ *Continue on the B 1087; in Bures take the B 1508.*

Sudbury – Sudbury, a silk-weaving centre and market town, boasts several half-timbered cottages among the rows of Georgian houses and three monumental Perpendicular churches – St Gregory's, St Peter's and All Saints.

Gainsborough's House★ – *46 Gainsborough Street. ☉ Open Tue-Sun, 10am (2pm Sun and Bank Hols) to 5pm (4pm Nov-Mar). ☉Closed Good Friday, 24 Dec-1 Jan. ☞ £3.50. Brochure (3 languages). Wheelchair access to ground floor only. ☎ 01787 372 958; Fax 01787 376 991; mail@gainsborough.org; www.gainsborough.org.* The late medieval building behind an elegant 18C façade was the birthplace of Thomas Gainsborough (1727-88). On display are Gainsborough memorabilia, a display of Gainsborough's work from the 1740s and 1750s (in the Parlour on the ground floor), including his earliest extant portrait of an unknown boy and girl which has been cut into two, and the **Portrait of Abel Moysey**, one of his finest portraits from the late 1760s (in the Aubrey Herbert Room).

▶ *Take the A 134 north for 3mi/5km.*

Long Melford – The long main street *(2mi/3km)* is lined with 16C, 17C and 18C timbered and pink-plastered houses. It terminates in a green and spacious triangle, overlooked by **Trinity Hospital** (1573) and **Holy Trinity Church** (late 15C), one of the great "wool churches" of East Anglia, which contains a 14C alabaster relief of the Adoration of the Magi and 15C stained glass.

Melford Hall★ – *(NT) ☉ Open May-Sep, Wed-Sun and Bank Hol Mon, Oct to early-Nov and late-Mar to Apr, Sat-Sun and Bank Hol Mon, 2-5.30pm. ☞ £4.70 . Leaflet (5 languages). ☎ 01787 880 286; melford@nationaltrust.org.uk; www.nationaltrust.org. uk.* Although the house is early Elizabethan, built around three sides of a courtyard, only the **Main Hall** has preserved its Elizabethan features. The Drawing Room is splendidly Rococo and the staircase (1813) is by Thomas Hopper in the Greek Revival style. The West Bedroom contains the original Jemima Puddle-Duck and watercolours by **Beatrix Potter** (☞ *see LAKE DISTRICT)* who was a frequent visitor.

Snape Maltings – *20mi/32km northeast on A 12 and A 1094.* The early 19C malthouses standing serenely on the River Alde are now a musical arts complex, home of Benjamin Britten's **Aldeburgh Festival.**

IRONBRIDGE GORGE★★

Shropshire, ENGLAND

MICHELIN ATLAS P 26 OR MAP 503 M 26 – 12MI/19KM EAST OF SHREWSBURY

The densely-wooded, mineral-rich Severn Gorge is widely accredited as the birthplace of the Industrial Revolution. In the autumn of 1708 **Abraham Darby** (1678-1717), Bristol ironmaster, came to Coalbrookdale; he was the first to use coke in 1709 as a fuel for smelting iron, replacing traditional charcoal. His experiments revolutionised the industry, making possible the use of iron in transport (wheels, rails), in engineering (steam engines, locomotives and ships), and in construction (buildings and bridges, including the famous Iron Bridge).

A number of sites along the gorge now form an important industrial museum. ▣ *The Wharfage, Ironbridge TF8 7AW ☎/Fax 01952 884 391; tic@ironbridge.org.uk; www. ironbridge.org.uk, www.shropshiretourism.info/ironbridge.*

Ironbridge Gorge Museum★★

Museum sites – &♿🕐 *Open daily Mar-Oct, 10am-5pm; Nov to mid-Mar, some sites closed.* 🚌 *Passport ticket valid for all sites £13.25 . Parking free at all sites except in Ironbridge town. Refreshments. Wheelchairs available at Blists Hill; access guide and large print text available on request.* ☎ *01952 432 166; 0800 590 258 (freephone for complimentary visitor guide); Fax 01952 432 204; www.ironbridge.org.uk.*

Museum of Iron★ – The museum illustrates the history of ironmaking and the story of the Coalbrookdale Company. It is housed in the great warehouse, built in 1838, which has cast-iron windows, sills and lintels. By the time of the Great Exhibition in 1851, the Coalbrookdale Company employed 4 000 men and boys and produced 2 000 tons of cast iron a week, for railway stations, bridges, fireplaces and a multitude of other uses.

Beyond the car park is the restored cast-iron Boy and Swan fountain, designed by John Bell and produced by the Coalbrookdale Company for the Great Exhibition in 1851. It was re-cast in 1994 by craftsmen at the Jackfield Museum.

Darby Furnace – This is the place where in 1709 Abraham Darby pioneered his techniques using coke rather than charcoal as fuel; smelting continued until c 1818. The Upper Furnace Pool, along with five other pools, provided power for five iron-works.

Further to the north the fine houses of the ironmasters stand close to the cottages of the workers (Carpenters Row). On the opposite or west side of the valley are two of the Darby family homes. Rosehill House, built in 1734 to supersede neighbouring Dale House *(restoration in progress)*, is furnished as it might have been in Victorian times with items from other family homes. An exhibition presents the various members of the Darby family. Further uphill is the Quaker burial ground.

Museum of the Gorge and Visitor Centre★ – An 1840s wharf and warehouse have been restored and now house an exhibition and audio-visual introduction to Ironbridge Gorge.

The Iron Bridge★★ – A bridge across the Severn Gorge at Coalbrookdale was needed to replace the hazardous ferry crossing, the only other bridges being at Buildwas and Bridgnorth. A design by Shrewsbury architect, Thomas Pritchard, was chosen and the Act of Parliament obtained in February 1776. Work began under **Abraham Darby III** in November 1777 and the Iron Bridge was opened on New Year's Day 1781. The bridge's single graceful span was a triumph of the application of new technol-

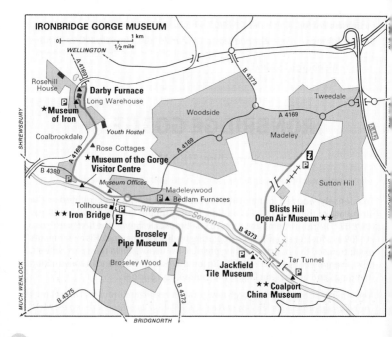

IRONBRIDGE GORGE MUSEUM

ogy to the solution of a difficult problem. The ironwork weighs over 378 tonnes – the builders, unfamiliar with the new technology, undoubtedly erred on the side of caution. In the old **Tollhouse** is an information centre with a display illustrating the history of the bridge.

The **Bedlam Furnaces** (1757) were among the first to be custom-built for coke smelting.

Iron Bridge (c 1845)

The Ironbridge Gorge Museum Trust

▶ *Take the roadbridge beyond Bedlam Furnaces over the Severn.*

Jackfield Tile Museum – *Restoration of building in progress.* The former tilery contains a small museum of the colourful wall and floor tiles once manufactured here in immense quantities in the 19C. Visitors can see the reconstructed offices of its heyday and view tile-manufacturing and decoration. A geology gallery explains the background of the tile-making industry.

▶ *Return over the bridge; turn right into B 4373.*

Coalport China Museum★★ – Coalport china was made here from 1792 until the works moved to Stoke-on-Trent in 1926. The old works, including the interior kiln of a bottle oven, have been restored as a museum of china, showing techniques of manufacture and particularly the products of Coalport.

Nearby is the **Tar Tunnel,** cut in 1786 to aid drainage from the Blists Hill Mine. It was found to ooze bitumen through the mortar of the brick lining.

Blists Hill Open Air Museum★★ – On this site (50 acres/20ha) step back into a working community of the 1890s, with bank, pub, butcher's shop, school, mason's yard, mine and candle factory, as well as the inclined plane which carried boats from Blists Hill to the Severn and Coalport. Many of the buildings have been brought from elsewhere and rebuilt on site.

JEDBURGH★

Borders, SCOTLAND

POPULATION 4 053

MICHELIN ATLAS P 50 OR MAP 501 M 17

The royal burgh of Jedburgh, spanning the Jed Water with a mid-12C triple-arched bridge was once a much fought-over border town. Today it is a peaceful market town on one of the main routes into Scotland. ▪ *Murray's Green, Jedburgh TD8 6BE ☎ 0870 6080404; Fax: 01750 21886; bordersinfo@visitscotland.com; www. scot-borders.co.uk.*

Sights

Jedburgh Abbey★★ – *(HS)* ⚐ ⏱ *Open daily 9.30am (2pm Sun) to 6.30pm (4.30pm Oct-Mar).* ⚐ *£3.30. Parking. Picnic area.* ☎ *01835 863 925; www.historic-scotland.gov. uk.* The abbey, founded in 1138 for the Augustinian order, was one of the many Border abbeys founded by David I to spread monasticism in 12C Scotland. The mellow stone church took 75 years to build and witnessed the coronation of Malcolm IV in the 12C and many royal events; it was often plundered and attacked before the final destructive raid in 1545. The ruined abbey church is a majestic example of 12C architecture and has a powerful **west front**, while the rhythm and design of the **nave** display the assurance of an art well-mastered. The mid-12C **east end** is notable for the massive pillars rising to the clerestory and buttressing the arches of the main arcade as well as for the Norman rounded arches and chevron decoration. From the south aisle a Norman doorway leads to the cloisters; although only the foundations of the cloister buildings survive, their layout can be clearly distinguished following the usual pattern.

Mary Queen of Scots House★ (Visitor Centre) – ⏰ Open Easter to mid-Nov, daily 10am (11am Sun) to 4.30pm. ⚲ £2.50. Brochure (6 languages). ☎ 01835 863 331; Fax 01450 373 457. This is the attractive 16C tower house where Mary Queen of Scots stayed when she made her 20mi/32km ride to **Hermitage Castle** (below). Engraved glass panels, paintings and documents relate the life of this hapless queen.

Jedburgh Castle Jail and Museum – ⏰ Open year-round daily 10am to 4.30pm (1-5pm Sun). ⚲ 80p. ☎ 01835 863 254; Fax 01450 378 506. The prison with its strict reforming ethic, built in 1823 on the site of the original castle, was considered one of the most modern jails of its day. It centred around the governor's block which overlooked the three centrally-heated cell blocks and was linked to them by first-floor gangways. There are exhibits interpreting Jedburgh's local and industrial history.

Excursions

Bowhill★★ – 19mi/31km northwest by A 68, A 699, A 7 and A 708. ♿House: ⏰Open Jul, daily, 1-4.30pm; Aug-Jun, by appointment. ☛ Guided tour (1hr 15min). Country Park: Open mid-Apr to late-Aug, Sat-Thu (also Fri in Jul), noon-5pm. House ⚲ £4.50; park £2. Guided walks. Adventure playground. Parking. Refreshments. ☎/Fax 01750 22204; bht@buccleuch.com; www.buccleuch.com. Among the many treasures which grace Bowhill, the Border home of the Duke of Buccleuch (pronounced Buckloo) and Queensberry, are fine pieces of French **furniture**, Mortlake tapestries, relics of the Duke of Monmouth and an important collection of paintings including works by Leonardo da Vinci, Canaletto, Claude, Wilkie (George IV in Highland Dress), Reynolds (Winter, The Pink Boy), Gainsborough and other masters. There is also an outstanding collection of **miniatures** (Cooper, Hilliard, Oliver, Holbein) as well as portraits and mementoes of Sir Walter Scott.

Hermitage Castle★ – 26mi/42km southwest by the B 6358, the A 698 and the B 6399. ⏰ Open Apr-Sept, daily, 9.30am-6.30pm. ⚲ £1.50. In its isolated moorland setting this massive ruin evokes the Borders' troubled past. A strategic stronghold of the Wardens of the March, it guarded the old reivers' routes. It was here that Mary Queen of Scots came on her dash to the injured Earl of Bothwell, her future husband.

The uniform appearance of Hermitage is deceptive as the original fortified manor-house dating from the mid 14C was converted into a late 14C tower house with four corner towers added at a later stage. The castle is enclosed by tall outer walls with loopholes, parapet and pointed arches.

The Border Abbeys were part of King David I's main achievement, the widespread development of monasticism in 12C Scotland: Kelso 1128 (original foundation 1113), Melrose 1136, Jedburgh 1138 and Dryburgh 1150.

KING'S LYNN

Norfolk, ENGLAND

POPULATION 41 281

MICHELIN ATLAS P 30 OR MAP 504 V 25

Situated on the River Ouse at the mouth of the Wash in nothern East Anglia, the town dates from the Norman Conquest (1066) and was mentioned in the Domesday Book in the early 12C. The Saturday Market dates from this time and the Tuesday Market from about 50 years later. Bishop's Lynn, as it was called in the Middle Ages, was then a bustling port and member of the Hanseatic League, exporting cloth and wool. In the 13C the town was protected by **walls**, part of which can be seen in Wyatt Street, off Littleport Street; the **South Gate** is the sole surviving entrance gate. The fine townscape is especially rich in medieval merchants' houses; many with their own well-constructed warehouses line the River Ouse. 🛈 The Custom House, Purfleet Quay, PE30 1HP ☎ 01553 763 044, Fax 01553 777 281; kings-lynn.tic@west-norfolk.gov.uk; www. west-norfolk.gov.uk

Don't Miss: At least one of the area's opulent stately halls; if you are around in July, the King's Lynn Arts Festival.

Organizing Your Time: Allow 4-6 hours for King's Lynn and a day or two for excursions.

Especially for Kids: Wells-Walsingham Light Railway, operates daily, late Mar – early Nov. £6.50. *01328 711 630; www.wellswalsinghamrailway.co.uk.*

Walking Tours: *Depart 2pm from the Old Gaol. May, Jun, Oct: Tue, Fri, Sat, Sun. Jul, Aug ,Sept: Mon, Tue, Fri, Sat, Sun, including Easter and Bank Hols.* £3. *01553 774297.*

Visit

Town Centre – In Queen Street, which is mainly Georgian in character, stands Thorseby College, founded in 1502 for training priests but later converted into a merchant's house with a 17C courtyard. The dignified Dutch-inspired Custom House (17C) is destined to become the Tourist Information Centre.

King's Staithe Lane, which leads to the quayside on the River Ouse, contains 16C and 17C warehouses; in cobbled King's Staithe Square stands a grand double-fronted red brick house, crowned with a statue of King Charles I and marked by a plaque commemorating Samuel Cresswell, explorer of the North-West Passage.

King Street, further north, presents a delightful succession of houses of varied dates and materials including **St George's Guildhall**, the largest surviving medieval guild-hall in England, where Shakespeare is supposed to have acted; it is now the King's Lynn Arts Centre where the annual Arts Festival is held.

The top of King Street opens into **Tuesday Market**, a large open space surrounded by well-preserved Georgian and Victorian buildings.

Tales of the Old Gaol House – *Saturday Market.* Open Easter-Oct, daily 10am-5pm (4.15pm last admission); Nov-Easter, daily except Sun and Mon 10am-4pm. £2.60. Audio tour. *01553 774 297; Fax 01553 772 361; gaolhouse@west-norfolk.gov.uk.* Occupying the chequered flint **Guildhall** (1421), visitors pass through the old police station with its tiny cells and fearsome instruments of torture (unconnected with the police!). In the Regalia Room are town charters, mayoral robes, civic silver and the **King John Cup** (1340); also on display is the Red Register (first entry 1307), recording business between Lynn and other Hanseatic towns.

The nearby **Town House Museum of Lynn Life,** (*Open May-Sep, daily, 10am (2pm Sun) to 5pm; Oct-Apr, Mon-Sat, 10am-4pm.* *Closed Bank Hols.* £1.80. Wheelchair access to ground floor only. *01553 773 450; townhouse.museum@norfolk.gov.uk*) displays an appealing set of period rooms.

St Margaret's Church – *Open daily, 7.45am-5.45pm (7.45pm Sun). Sun services 8am, 10am, 6.30pm.* *01553 772 858; www.stmargaretskingslynn.org.uk.* This twin-towered church originally built in the 13C on unsound foundations now exhibits examples of most architectural styles. Surviving glories include 14C screens, a Georgian pulpit and a 17C moon clock. Two 14C mayors and their three wives are com-memorated in huge brasses; one illustrates a peacock feast given for Edward III.

True's Yard – *North Street* *Open daily, 9.30am-3.45pm.* *Closed 25 Dec to 3 Jan.* £1.90. *Guided tour by appointment. Tearoom. Gift shop.* *01553 770 479; truesyard@virgin.net; http://freespace.virgin.net/trues.yard.* Two cottages have been converted to form a small museum illustrating the daily hardships of the former fishing community.

Excursions

Holkham Hall★★ – *31mi/50km north and east by A 149.* *Open Jun to Sep, Sun-Thur 1pm (11.30am Bank Hol Sun and Mon) to 5pm.* £6.50 ; combined ticket with Bygones museum £10 . Parking. Refreshments. Wheelchair access to ground floor. *01328 710 227; Fax: 01328 711 707; www.holkham.co.uk.* Seat of the Earls of Leicester and Coke of Norfolk (1754-1842), the inventor of modern agriculture, Holkham Hall is palatial Palladian designed by **William Kent**. Most monumental of the interiors is the Marble Hall (photograph below), faced with polished pink alabaster, carrying a gallery of pink Ionic columns, and dramatically setting off the surrounding neo-Classical sculpture (more of which can be seen in the Statue Gallery). Almost as grand are the Drawing Room (with works by Claude and Poussin) and the Saloon (works by Rubens and Van Dyck). In the South Sitting Room hang Titian's *Unknown Lady*, Guido Reni's *Joseph Taking Leave of Potiphar's Wife,* a Gainsborough and Battoni's *Coke of Norfolk*; the Landscape Room is devoted to Poussin and Claude.

Houghton Hall★★ – *13mi/21km east by A 1076 and A 148 and a minor road (left).* ♿ ○ *Open Easter to Sep, Thu, Sun and Bank Hol Mons, 11am (house 1:30pm) to 5.30pm.* ⊚ *£7. Grounds and park only, £4.50. Parking. Tearoom, picnic area.* ☎ *01485 528 569; Fax 01485 528 167; houghton@houghtonhall.com; www.houghtonhall.com.* The house, which is transitional between Baroque and Palladian and inspired by Colen Campbell, was built (1722-35) for Sir Robert Walpole, Britain's first Prime Minister. Its main rooms by William Kent are dedicated to "taste, expense, state and parade". Its joys are its ceilings and Kent furniture, the Sèvres porcelain in the Marble Parlour, the thrones by Pugin and 17C Mortlake tapestries of the Royal Stuarts in the Tapestry Dressing Room and Oudry's *White Duck* in the White Drawing Room.

Oxburgh Hall★★ – *(NT) 18mi/29km southeast by A 10, A 134 and a minor road (signs).* ♿ *House:* ○ *Open late-Mar to early-Nov, Sat-Wed and Bank Hols, 1pm (11am Bank Hols) to 5 pm. Garden: Open late-Mar to early-Nov, Sat-Wed, 11am-5.30pm (also Thu-Fri, Aug); early to late-Mar, Sat-Sun, 11am-4pm.* ⊚ *£6; garden only, £3 . Parking. Licensed restaurant.* ☎ *01366 328528; Fax 01366 328 066; oxburgh@ntrust.org.uk; www.nationaltrust.org.uk.* This was one of the first fortified manor houses (1482) to be built as status symbols. Its **gatehouse** – "one of the noblest specimens of domestic architecture in the 15C" (Pugin) – and flanking ranges are 15C; the hall range is 19C. The interior presents elaborate **embroideries** depicting mammals, fish and plants by Mary Queen of Scots and Bess of Hardwick (♿ *see Hardwick Hall*) in the Marian Needlework Room; letters from Henry VIII, Queen Mary and Queen Elizabeth I, and woodcarvings by Grinling Gibbons in the King's Room; a priesthole under the floor in the adjoining octagonal chamber; the Sheldon tapestry map of the Heart of England (1647) in the Queen's Room. The walls of the staircases are covered in 17C Cordova leather.

Sandringham★ – *8mi/13km northeast by A 1076 and A 149.* ♿ ○ *Open Easter to mid-Jul and early-Aug to late-Oct, daily, 10.30am-5pm (house 11am-4.45pm).* ⊚ *£7.50; grounds and museum only, £5. Brochure (3 languages). Parking. Visitor Centre. Restaurant, tea room. Flower stall. Braille guide; ramps, land train for those with walking difficulties.* ☎ *01553 772 675; Fax 01485 541 571; visits@sandringhamestate.co.uk; www.sandringhamestate.co.uk.* "Dear old Sandringham, the place I love better than anywhere else in the world", wrote George V of the Royal Family's country home, a neo-Jacobean house acquired in 1862. The Saloon, the largest room in the house, is hung with family portraits by Von Angeli and Winterhalter, and 17C tapestries of *Emperor Constantine* by Brier of Brussels. The corridor is adorned with intricately-wrought Oriental arms and armour. In the main Drawing Room – "a very long and handsome drawing room with painted ceiling and panels and two fireplaces" (Queen Victoria) – is Russian silver and Chinese jade. And in the Ballroom, bedecked with armour, is a photo exhibition about the owners.

Castle Rising – *(EH) 4mi/6km northeast by A 149.* ♿ ○ *Open late Mar-Oct, daily, 10am-6pm (dusk Oct); Nov to late-Mar, Wed-Sun, 10am-4pm.* ○ *Closed 1 Jan and 24-26 Dec.* ⊚ *£3.85 (including audio tour guide). Parking. Picnic site.* ☎ *01553 631 330; Fax 01553 631 724; thecastle@castlerising.com; www.english-heritage.org.uk.* Extensive earthworks and thick walls (8ft/2m) protect Castle Rising (1138), which was built by William d'Albini, Earl of Sussex, for his wife, widowed queen of Henry I. In 1331 it became home to another dowager queen, the disgraced Isabella, lover of Roger Mortimer and murderer of her husband Edward II.

The Norman gatehouse leads to the unusually intricately decorated keep forebuilding with stairs leading to the portal (converted into a fireplace in the 16C). Apart from the figured corbels for the hall roofbeams only the gallery and chapel (Early English doorway and Norman arcading) have survived.

Castle Acre – *(EH) 18mi/29km east by A 47 and A 1065.* ♿ ○ *Castle ruins: Open any reasonable time, no charge. Priory: Open late-Mar to Oct, daily, 10am-6pm (5pm Oct); Nov-Mar, Wed-Sun, 10am-4pm.* ○ *Closed 1 Jan and 24-26 Dec.* ⊚ *£4.30 , includes audio guide. Parking. Wheelchair access to ground floor and grounds.* ☎ *01760 755 394; www. english-heritage.org.uk.* Here are the twin supports of the medieval nobility: a castle for security in this world, a priory for salvation in the next. The **castle** built by William de Warenne, one of William the Conqueror's most trusted supporters, is unusual in originally being a fortified stone manor house enclosed by earthworks.

The keep was not built until the c 1140 civil wars. Of the **Cluniac priory** the west front of the church, prior's lodgings and late 12C porch still stand, though there are remnants of the "bare ruin'd choirs", chapter house, dormitories, kitchens and latrines south of the church.

Four Fenland Churches★ – The glories of the Fens (📖 *see ELY*) are its churches and sunsets, both admirably complemented by the flat and featureless landscape.

▶ *From King's Lynn take A 17 west for 5mi/8km; then turn right.*

Terrington St Clement – **St Clement's Church**, (🕐 *Church accessible at all reasonable times. Keys available at times listed on the porch gate.* ☎ *01553 828 430)* big and Perpendicular, boasts a splendid west window and northwest tower. The interior has exquisite Georgian panelling at the west end and a 17C **font cover** with paintings of New Testament scenes inside.

▶ *Take the minor road southwest, crossing A 17, via Walpole St Andrew.*

Walpole St Peter – **St Peter's Church,** (🕐 *Open daily 9.30am-4pm.* 💷 *Donation)* built in the 14C transition between Decorated (west window and tower) and Perpendicular (nave windows and chancel stalls) is known as the Cathedral of the Fens. Among its charms are its raised altar (to provide space for a groined right of way underneath), 17C woodwork and embossed south porch. Huge plain glass windows illuminate a magnificent interior.

▶ *From Walpole St Andrew take the road south to Wisbech.*

West Walton – **St Mary's Church** (🕐 *Open daily, 9.30am-3.30pm. Keyholders indicated on the gate.* ☎ *01945 582 693; www.ely.anglican.org/parishes/westwalton)* is mid-13C Early English at its most profuse and extravagant: beautifully ornate arcading and doorways, and wall paintings in the clerestory.

▶ *Continue south towards Wisbech.*

Walsoken – **All Saints' Church** – 🕐 *Open Sat. Key available from the Rectory, Church Road, Walsoken or Whyte Lodge, Grimmers Road, Walsoken.* ☎/*Fax 01945 461291.* Dating from 1146, "the grandest Norman parish church in Norfolk" (Pevsner) presents zig-zag mouldings on arcade arch and chancel arch, a hammerbeam and cambered tie-beam roof, an eight-sided **font** portraying the Seven Sacraments and Crucifixion, a 16C wall painting of the Judgement of Solomon and a 20C stained glass window.

Marble Hall, Holkham Hall

A. F. Kersting/MICHELIN

KINGSTON-UPON-HULL

ENGLAND

POPULATION 310 636

MICHELIN ATLAS P 41 OR MAP 502 S 22

TOWN PLAN IN THE MICHELIN GUIDE GREAT BRITAIN AND IRELAND

Kingston-upon-Hull, commonly known as Hull, has a long maritime history. It was an important centre for fishing and particularly for whaling, and is still a major seaport. The **Old Town**, contained between the River Humber and the west bank of its tributary, the Hull, was once surrounded by walls and a moat and still presents the narrow cobbled lanes and ancient inns of medieval and 17C Hull. In the Georgian period a number of docks were built below the east wall; the first of them was Queen's Dock (1778-1920), now Queen's Gardens.

Here stands a statue of Hull's most celebrated citizen, William Wilberforce (see below), whose Bill to abolish the slave trade became law in 1807; he lived to see the abolition of child labour in British territories in 1833. A more recent famous resident was Philip Larkin (1922-91), the poet and librarian of Hull University, which is situated north of the town centre. *1 Paragon Street, Hull, HU1 3NA ☎ 01482 223 559; Fax 01482 613 959; Tourist.Information@hullcc.gov.uk; www. hullcc.gov.uk.*

Sights

Hull Maritime Museum – *Queen Victoria Square.* ⏱ *Open Mon-Sat, 10am-5pm, Sun, 1.30-4.30pm.* ⏱ *Closed Good Friday, 25-26 Dec, 1 Jan.* ✪*No charge.* ☎ *01482 613 902; www.hullcc.gov.uk/museums.* The museum, which is housed in the old Town Docks Office (1871), presents Hull's maritime heritage, dating back over seven centuries, by means of models, miscellaneous artefacts and a collection of paintings.

Ferens Art Gallery – *Queen Victoria Square.* ♿ *Queen Victoria Square.* ⏱*Open daily 10am (1.30pm Sun) to 5pm (4.30pm Sun).* ⏱ *Closed Good Friday, 25-26 Dec, 1 Jan.* ✪*No Charge.* ☎ *01482 300 300; Fax 01482 613 710; museums@hullcc.gov.uk; www. hullcc.gov.uk/museums.* The city art collection ranges from European Old Masters to contemporary art, including works by such artists as Franz Hals, Canaletto, David Hockney and Henry Moore. There is also a selection of works representing Hull's maritime history.

Visitors wanting to call home from Hull should look out for the city's telephone boxes which are just like the traditional British red ones, except that they are white, reflecting the fact that the city of Hull is unique in Britain in owning its own telephone company (from time to time the object of bids from foreign telephone operators).

Wilberforce House Museum – *High Street.* ♿⏱*Closed until 2007* ☎ *01482 300 300; Fax 01482 613 710; museums@hullcc.gov.uk; www.hullcc.gov.uk/museums.* The birthplace of **William Wilberforce** (1758-1833) houses a museum about slavery – the triangular trade and the plantations – and on the life and work of the man who was instrumental in achieving its abolition. There is period furniture in certain rooms, as well as collections of costumes, clocks and Hull silver.

Streetlife – Transport Museum – ♿ *High Street.* ⏱*Open daily, 10am (1.30pm Sun) to 5pm (4.30pm Sun).* ⏱ *Closed Good Friday, 25-26 Dec, 1 Jan.* ✪*No Charge.* ☎ *01482 300 300; museums@hullcc.gov.uk; www.hullcc.gov.uk/museums.* Exhibits include a bumpy stage coach simulator, a hobby-horse bicycle without pedals, a penny-farthing, motorcycles, trams, early cars of the horseless carriage type and a railway signal box.

Hull and East Riding Museum – *36 High Street.* ⏱*Open Mon-Sat, 10am-5pm; Sun, 1.30-4.30pm.* ⏱ *Closed Good Friday, 25-26 Dec, 1 Jan.* ✪*No Charge.* ☎ *01482 613 902; Fax 01482 613 710; museums@hullcc.gov.uk; www.hullcc.gov.uk/museums.* This museum traces local geology, archeology and natural history from prehistoric times using the latest technology in its exciting displays.

Holy Trinity Church – ⏱ *Open Mon-Fri, 11am-3pm (2pm Oct-Mar); Sat, 9.30am-noon.* ☎ *01482 324 835; office@holytrinityhull.fsnet/co/uk; www.holy-trinity.org.uk.* This is the largest of all parish churches in Britain (285ft/87m long). The lower stage of the tower (150ft/46m high) and the transepts (c 1330) are remarkable for being built partly in brick, for Hull had a municipal brickyard as early as 1303.

Hands on History – *South Church Side.* ⓞ*Open daily, 10am (1.30pm Sun) to 5pm (4.30pm Sun).* ⓞ *Closed Good Friday, 25-26 Dec, 1 Jan.* ⓢ*No Charge.* ☎ *01482 613 902; Fax 01482 613 710; museums@hullcc.gov.uk; www.hullcc.gov.uk/museums.* The old red-brick Grammar School building, the oldest secular building in the city (1583-5), now houses a resource centre for schools. On the ground floor is an interactive exhibition on Victorian Britain, and on the first floor a presentation of the Story of Hull and its People, as well as a small display on Tutankhamun.

Trinity House – *Trinity House Lane.* The stuccoed and pedimented building dates from 1753-54. A religious Guild, founded 1369, became a Mariners' Guild by royal charter in 1541 and took on the control of navigation and shipping in the 17C and 18C.

Spurn Lightship – *Hull Marina.* ⓞ*Open daily, Apr-Sep, 10am (1.30pm Sun) to 5pm (4.30pm Sun). No Charge.* ☎ *01482 613 902; Fax 01482 613 710; museums@hullcc.gov. uk; www.hullcc.gov.uk/museums.* This former navigation aid to shipping approaching the River Humber, built in 1927, is now open to visitors, who can find out how her crew lived and worked from the present crew.

The Deep – ♿ⓞ *Open 10am-6pm (5pm last admission).* ⓞ *Closed 24-25 Dec.* ⓢ *£7.50. Tickets can be reserved one day in advance for fast track entry. Limited parking; park and ride advisable. Restaurant.* ☎ *01482 381 000; Fax 01482 381 010; info@the deep.co.uk; www.thedeep.co.uk.*

Excursions

Humber Bridge – *West of city centre.* ⓢ *Toll £2.50 per car;* ☎ *www.humberbridge. co.uk.* Construction started in 1972 and the bridge was opened by HM the Queen on 17 July 1981. At that time it was the longest single-span suspension bridge in the world (4 626ft/1 410m), but it has subsequently been exceeded.

Burton Constable★ – *16mi/27km east on A 165, B 1238 and a minor road north in Sproately. Skirlaugh Grounds.* ♿ⓞ *Grounds open 12.30-5pm. House:* ⓞ*Open Easter Sun to Oct, Sat-Thur, 1-5pm.* ⓢ *£5.50; grounds only, £1.00. Parking. Refreshments.* ☎ *01964 562 400; Fax 01964 563 229; enquiries@burtonconstable.com; www.burtonconstable. com.* The house was built by Sir Henry Constable about 1600. The **east front**, brick with mullion windows and two projecting wings, still gives the first and strongest impression. The **Entrance Hall**, the Great Hall of the Elizabethan house, is by Thomas Lightoller (1760), as is the portal with Tuscan columns and window above, by which the visitor enters.

In the **Muniment Room,** the remodelling of the house in Georgian times can be followed from documents of the period. A **Long Gallery,** of noble proportions and decoration, was designed by William Constable in the mid 18C and contains many family portraits. The marble **fireplace**, the work of a Beverley master-mason, is inlaid with flowers and birds by **Domenico Bartoli.**

In the Chapel, Ballroom and Dining Rooms the delicate plasterwork is by Giuseppe Cortese, the Italian master who created the courtroom ceiling in Beverley. In these rooms and in the **Chinese Room** many fine pieces of Chippendale furniture are displayed.

National Fishing Heritage Centre – *28mi/45km south on A 15 and A 180 to* **Great Grimsby.** ♿ *Alexander Dock.* ⓞ*Open late-Mar-Oct, Mon-Fri, 10am-4pm, Sat-Sun, 10.30am-5.30pm. Nov – Easter 10-4 (Sat, Sun 11-3).* ⓢ *£6.* ☎ *01472 323 345; Fax 01472 323 555; www.nelincs.gov.uk.* Grimsby is England's main fishing port, a trade it has plied since the 11C. The hardships of the fisherman's life are brought to life in an extensive and detailed display about working on a trawler, including simulations of sailing at freezing temperatures and standing on a heaving deck at night when the catch is landed. The tour *(45min)* of the trawler, *Ross Tiger,* where retired fishermen act as guides, includes the hold, where the gutted fish were stored in ice, the engine room, the crew's quarters and the galley, the bridge and the skipper's cabin.

Just south of Grimsby is **Cleethorpes**, now a suburb, which has developed into a popular seaside resort.

LACOCK★★

Wiltshire, ENGLAND

POPULATION 1 068

MICHELIN ATLAS P 17 OR MAP 503 – N 29

This peaceful picturesque stone and brick village on the route from London to Bath has always been under special patronage, first of the Augustinian canonesses resident at the abbey, then the Talbots and now the National Trust. It comprises little more than four streets laid out in a square and has provided the film set for numerous period televison and movie dramas *(Pride and Prejudice and Moll Flanders, for example).*  *Town Hall, Market Lane, Malmesbury, SN16 9BZ ☎ 01666 823748; Fax 01666 826 166; malmesbury@northwilts.gov.uk; www.northwilts.gov.uk.*

Visit

Village streets – The wide **High Street**★ leading to the abbey is lined with cottage-shops and houses of various heights, sizes and designs, some of which date from as long ago as the 14C and 16C. **West Street** and **East Street** are also enclosed by interesting old houses and inns (the George Inn, or "The Inn", is the oldest inn in the village – 1361). **Church Street** (note the 14C Cruck House and 15C Sign of the Angel Inn) runs parallel to the High Street, leading into the village's original Market Place on the *right.*

St Cyriac★ – ⏲ *Open daily, 10am-5pm. Sun services 8am, 10.30am, 6.30pm. ☎ 01249 730 272.* The Perpendicular church is a "wool church" from the days of Lacock's prosperity as a wool and cloth market in the 14-17C. It was extensively restored in 1861. Distinctive features include the large pinnacled **porch** and older **tower**, the Perpendicular tracery of the north aisle west window, an early 17C mullion-windowed **cottage** on the south side, and the 15C lierne vaulting and 16C tombchest in the **Talbot** or **Lady Chapel.**

Fox Talbot Museum of Photography★ – ♿ ⏲ *Open daily, 11am-5pm (5pm last admission). ⊚ £3.80. ☎ 01249 730 459; www.r-cube.co.uk/fox-talbot.* This museum is housed in a 16C barn at the abbey gate. It is devoted to the achievements of **William Henry Fox Talbot** (1800-77), pioneer of modern photography *(on the ground floor),* and the work of contemporary photographers *(on the first floor).*

Lacock Abbey★ – *(NT)* ♿ *Abbey:* ⏲*Open late-Mar to Oct , Wed-Mon , 1-5pm. Museum, cloisters and garden: Open mid-Mar to early-Nov, daily, 11am-5pm; early-Nov to mid-Mar, (4m Sat-Sun). Closed Good Friday and 21-29 Dec. ⊚ Abbey, cloisters, grounds, museum £6.20; abbey and garden only, £5. Guide (7 languages and Braille). ☎ 01249 730 227 (abbey), 01249 730 459 (museum); Fax 01249 730 501; www.r-cube.co.uk.* To the east of the village lies the abbey, founded in the 13C and converted into a stately home following the Dissolution (the cloisters, sacristy and chapter house survive) in 1539, when it was purchased by an ancestor of the Talbot family, **William Sharington**. Successive generations of **Talbots** added decorative features following tastes of their day: Ivory Talbot added Gothick style embellishments, such as the entrance hall, in the mid 18C; William Henry Fox Talbot added three oriels to the south front in 1827-30, the central one of which was the subject of his first successful photograph (1835). This same Talbot, also a well-respected botanist, mathematician, astronomer, Egyptologist, MP for Chippenham and Fellow of the Royal Society, was responsible for planting the grounds with exotic trees.

Inside the **house**, note the fine continental-style stone table (c 1550) in Sharington's Tower, the prints from Fox Talbot's original negatives of the oriel window (now in the Science Museum, London) in the South Gallery, examples of early 18C and 19C English and Continental furniture, numerous portraits (including a Van Dyck of Charles I's children) and Aubusson and Wilton carpets.

Excursions

Corsham Court★★

5mi/8km north. ♿ ⏲ *Open late-Mar to Sep, Tue-Sun and Bank Hol Mon, 2-5.30pm; Oct-Nov and Jan to mid-Mar, Sat-Sun, 2-4.30pm. ⊚ £5; gardens only, £2. ⌕ Guided tours available. Parking. ☎/Fax 01249 701 610; www.corsham-court.co.uk.* This Elizabethan

South porch, Malmesbury Abbey

mansion built in 1582 was bought by Paul Methuen in the mid 18C. Corsham was altered and enlarged on several occasions (by architects such as "Capability" Brown in the 1760s, John Nash in 1800 and Thomas Bellamy in 1845-49) to house the extensive Methuen collection of master **paintings** (16C and 17C Italian and 17C Flemish), **statuary, bronzes** and **furniture**.
The excellent collection in the elegant, triple-cube **Picture Gallery** includes works by Caravaggio, Reni, Tintoretto, Veronese, Rubens and Van Dyck, as well as pier-glasses and tables by the Adam brothers, girandoles attributed to Chippendale and a splendid white marble fireplace. The **Cabinet Room** contains Fra Filippo Lippi's Annunciation (1463), Chippendale side tables and pier-glasses by the Adam brothers, while the highlight of the **Octagon Room,** designed by Nash, is Michelangelo's *Sleeping Cupid* (1496). Note also fine family portraits by Reynolds in the **Dining Room** and the beautiful furniture in the **State Bedroom** and **Music Room**.

Malmesbury★

12mi/20km north. The centre of this small market town, with its attractive terraces of stone tiled roofs, is graced by a **market cross★★,** one of England's finest, built of local stone in 1490, when the town was known for its tanning, wool weaving and other textile industries. The ornately carved 40ft/12m cross rises in a riot of buttresses, crocketed pinnacles, castellations and flying arches to a spirelet, crowning pinnacle and cross.

Abbey★ – *Open daily 10am-6pm; 10am-4pm Nov-Easter ☎ 01666 826 666.*
Famous figures connected with the abbey, founded in the 7C, include St Aldhelm (639-709), one the first abbots, the great historian William of Malmesbury (1095-1143), Elmer the "Flying Monk" who launched himself from the top of the tower in 1010 and "flew" 250yd/230m before crashing but remained convinced it was only the lack of a tail which had brought him down, and the philosopher Thomas Hobbes (1588-1679).
The present church, in which gaunt ruins are strikingly juxtaposed with living architecture, was begun in the 12C and by the 14C extended 320ft from east to west. In 1479, the spire and central crossing tower were brought down by a fierce storm, destroying the east end transepts and crossing in their fall; a century later, the west tower collapsed, bringing down the three adjacent bays of the nave. Six majestic bays are still standing. In between times, the abbey had been suppressed by Henry VIII and sold to a local clothier, who presented the remains to the village people as their parish church in 1541.
The masterpiece of the abbey is the **south porch,** an outstanding example of Norman sculpture and decoration featuring geometrical patterning and magnificent carved figures in a style reminiscent of that found in churches of southwest France (Moissac, Souillac) on the pilgrimage route to Santiago de Compostela. The massive Norman pillars inside have scalloped capitals supporting just-pointed arches and a triforium of rounded bays and zig-zag carving. On the south side is the watching loft from where the abbot or a monk could follow the service beyond the chancel screen. The medieval stone screen at the end of the south aisle marks the chapel of St Aldhelm, who was buried in an earlier abbey destroyed by fire in 1050.

LAKE DISTRICT★★★

Cumbria, ENGLAND

MICHELIN ATLAS P 44 MAP 502 K, L 20

"I do not know of any tract of country in which, in so narrow a compass, may be found an equal variety in the influences of light and shadow upon the sublime and beautiful". The words of the poet William Wordsworth express something of the attraction that draws vast numbers of visitors to the Lake District. Most of the area is incorporated in the **Lake District National Park** (880sq mi/2 280km2) of which one quarter is conserved by the National Trust. The Lake District can be appreciated in many ways – exploring the narrow and often congested lanes by car, taking a trip in a launch, sailing or windsurfing on the lakes and best of all by walking or climbing in the fells.

Hawkshead LA22 0NT ☎ 015394 36525; Fax 015394 36349; HawksheadTIC@lake-district. gov.uk. Beckside Car Park (Ullswater), Glenridding, Penrith, CA11 0PD ☎ 017684 82414; Fax 017684 82414; ullswatertic@lake-district.gov.uk Bowness on Windermere LA23 3HJ ☎ 01539 442 895; Fax 01539 488 005; bownesstic@lake-district.gov.uk. Website for all offices: *www.lake-district.gov.uk.*

▶ **Orient Yourself**: Visit the Brockhole National Park Visitor Centre to get an overall view of the district; **Ambleside and Windermere make good touring bases;** half-day and full-day guided tours in mini-coaches are available from several companies including Lakes Supertours, (*1 High Street, Windermere ☎ 01539 442 751, 01539 488 133; www.lakes-supertours.com*) and **Mountain Goat tours** (*Victoria Street, Windermere, ☎ 01539 445 161; www.lakes-pages.co.uk*).

Don't Miss: A boat trip; a walk (for as long as you can manage!);

Please Consider: Motorists should note that **some mountain roads are narrow with sharp bends and severe gradients, sometimes over 1:3/30%.**

Walkers and fell climbers are advised to choose routes suited to their experience; to tell someone of their intended route and time of return; to take the necessary maps and equipment; to wear appropriate footwear and clothing; not to set out in failing daylight or deteriorating weather conditions: Hill Top (Beatrix Potter's cottage) is hugely popular, and you may well have to wait to get in *(timed ticket system).* **Try to avoid peak periods when you may not get in at all.**

Organizing Your Time: Allow at least three days if you want to get a flavour of the area.

Especially for Kids: Hill Top (Beatrix Potter's cottage) for little ones.

Lake Windermere

A. Williams/MICHELIN

Walking Tours: There are many guided walks and rambles, ask at your nearest TIC. Advance registration essential. Park in Grange and take the train to Arnside. Those who grow tired during the walk (8mi/13km; at least 3hr) can be picked up by a tractor and trailer. Sturdy shoes are advised as the foreshore is at the start is rocky; Wellington boots or jeans are not advised as you will get wet during the river crossing (approx 2ft deep); at any time of year wear several layers rather than one thick covering; in summer suntan lotion and hats are necessary but it may also be windy; bring water and a towel for cleaning the mud off your feet at the end. ☎ *01539 534 026; Fax 01539 534 331; info@morecambebay.org.uk; www. morecambebay.org.uk.*

Bicycle Trails: Cycles are available for hire from many places, including Windermere railway station.

Sailing: Lake Windermere has many sailing and watersports options. A popular venue is Coniston Boating Centre, Coniston Water ☎ *015394 41366; conistonbc@ lake-district.gov.uk*

Geological Notes

The area takes its name from the beautiful stretches of water which occupy many of the glaciated valleys radiating out from a high central core of volcanic rocks, presenting abrupt cliffs, crags and precipices. Among the many famous peaks are the stony wastes of **Scafell Pike** (3 206ft/977m), the highest point in England. Elsewhere, much of the landscape has been formed by slate: to the north, in the gently-rounded but majestic heights of the Skiddaw group; to the south, in the more broken country reaching its highest point in the commanding presence of **The Old Man,** looming over Coniston Water. The most austere scenery is near the head of Wasdale, where awesome screes plunge to the shore of Wast Water, the deepest and most forbidding of the lakes. The wild drama of the fells is set off by the gentler, pastoral character of much of the lowland, particularly in the park-like surroundings of Lake Windermere.

Rainfall is high and the many tarns and tumbling becks are well-fed. The peaks are often capped in cloud and the slopes shrouded in mist but the air is soft and the changing light plays continuously with the rich and subtle colour-mix of rock and vegetation: coarse grasses, heathers and bracken clothing the mountainsides, bright-berried rowans and white-stemmed birches sheltering in mossy clefts, dark pines standing elegantly by the lakeside and bright green pastures interspersed with the luxuriant foliage of oak and sycamore.

The rocks are used in the man-made structures of the countryside – in ancient bridges, in the drystone walls which climb high into the fells, in the rough-hewn stone of sturdy barns, cottages and whitewashed farmhouses with massive roofs of slate. Even the towns are mostly built of stone and slate.

Until well into the 20C mining was an important activity in Cumbria – coal, iron-ore, lead, copper and graphite – some of which was transported to the coast by rail and caused the coastal fishing villages to develop into thriving ports. Slate and granite are still quarried on a limited scale compatible with the conservation of the environment.

1 Lakeland Poets Tour

30mi/48km

The more frequented area round Windermere evokes the memory of the Lakeland poets – **Wordsworth, Coleridge** and **Southey** – who were variously inspired by the landscape.

Lake Windermere★★ – The longest lake in England (10mi/16km), attractively framed by wooded slopes and bare fells, is particularly lively and popular for water sports. On the east shore stands the town of **Windermere**, a railhead town, built mostly of slate, which was created in the 19C tourist boom. **Windermere Lake Cruises, (** *Cruises daily, between Lakeside (Newby Bridge) and Bowness and between Bowness and Waterhead (Ambleside) with seasonal conections for Fell Foot Country Park, Ferry House (connecting bus service for Hilltop, Hawkshead and Coniston), Brockhole and Wray Castle. Telephone for price details. Leaflet (2 languages). Parking at Lakeside (300 spaces), Bowness (600 spaces) and Ambleside (350 spaces). On board catering. Steamers and larger launches suitable for wheelchairs. ☎ 01539 531 188; Fax: 01539 531 947; w.lakes@virgin. net; www.windermere-lakecruises.co.uk)* pass close to the many islets, including Belle Isle, and the unspoilt west bank.

Swallows and Amazons for ever!

Arthur Ransome (1884-1967) worked in publishing, then as a war correspondent during the Russian Revolution and continued to work as a freelance political journalist for *The Manchester Guardian* while writing critical and travel books, before finally making his name as a writer of children's fiction with *Swallows and Amazons* (1931) and its sequels. The holiday adventures of the Walker children – sailing, camping, hunting for treasure and escaping from pirates... – are set on and around Coniston Water and Lake Windermere, which have been fused in Ransome's fiction. Several local landmarks are nonetheless clearly identifiable in his stories: Peel Island on Coniston Water and Blake Holme on Windermere become Wild Cat Island; the Old Man of Coniston becomes Kanchenjunga; Bowness-on-Windermere –Rio; Silver Holme – Cormorant Island; Belle Isle – Long Island; Allen Tarn – Octopus Lagoon; Bank Ground Farm – Holly Howe.

The **Windermere Steamboat Centre,** (♿*Rayrigg Road.* ⏱*Open mid-Mar to Oct, daily, 10am-5pm.* ∞ *£4.75. Model boat pond. Refreshments, picnic area.* ☎ *01539 445 565; post@steamboat.co.uk ; www.steamboat.co.uk)* on the lake shore, has a collection of steam, motor and sail boats, some afloat, including the 19C Dolly, claimed as the world's oldest mechanically powered boat.

Bowness-on-Windermere – The pretty village is known for its promenade skirting the bay. A **ferry** (⏱ *Operates Bowness to Far Sawrey (5min) late-Mar to early-Nov,; early-Nov to late-Mar, daily, call for schedule.* ∞ *Single £3.20* ☎ *01228 606 744; Fax 01228 606 755)* carries cars and pedestrians across the lake to Sawrey.

The **Aquarium of the Lakes,** (♿*Lakeside, Newby Bridge.* ⏱*Open daily, 9am-6pm (5pm winter); last admission 1hr before closing time. Closed 25 Dec.* ∞ *£6.25. Parking (charge). Café.* ☎ *015395 30153; Fax 015395 30152; aquariumofthelakes@reallive.co.uk; www.aquariumofthelakes.co.uk)* reveals the fascinating aquatic and animal life of the rivers, streams and lakes.

▶ *In Newby Bridge turn right to Sawrey.*

Hill Top – *(NT) Near Sawrey.* ⏱ *Open late-Mar to Oct, Sat-Wed 10.30am to 4.30pm; last admission 30min before closing; timed entry.* ∞ *£4.50. Parking.* ☎ *01539 436 269; Fax 01539 436 118; hilltop@nationaltrust.org.uk; www.nationaltrust.org.uk.* The tiny 17C house was the home, unchanged since her death in 1943, of **Beatrix Potter** who created Peter Rabbit, Benjamin Bunny, Jemima Puddle-Duck and many more favourite characters. It attracts thousands of visitors seeking the inspiration for their childhood delight. Inside are Beatrix Potter's watercolours, her dolls' house and mementoes. She saw herself primarily as a sheep farmer and was embarrassed at the acclaim conferred on her for her children's books.

Hawkshead★ – The narrow slate-walled lanes and paths of this traditional Lakeland village are bordered by flower-decked cottages. Wordsworth attended the local grammar school from 1779 to 1787.

The **Beatrix Potter Gallery,** *(NT* ♿ *Main Street.* ⏱*Open late-Mar to Oct, Sat - Wed and Good Friday, 10.30am-4.30pm. Admission by timed ticket.* ∞ *£3.50. Braille guide. Village car park 200m.* ☎ *01539 436 355; Fax 01539 436 187; beatrixpotter@nationaltrust. org.uk; www.nationaltrust.org.uk)* covers her work as artist, author and local farmer, and a selection of her watercolours are displayed in the old offices of her husband, William Heelis, a solicitor.

Coniston Water★ – The road from Hawkshead provides a fine view of the lake and the surrounding fells dominated by the form of **The Old Man of Coniston** (2 631ft/801m). It was on this stretch of water that **Donald Campbell** died in 1967 trying to beat the world water speed record.

Brantwood★ – *East shore of Coniston Water.* ♿⏱ *Open mid-Mar to mid-Nov, daily, 11am-5.30pm; mid-Nov to mid-Mar, Wed-Sun, 11am-4.30pm.* ⏱ *Closed Dec 25,26.* ∞ *£5.50; grounds only, £3.75 . Video presentation. Craft gallery; exhibitions in the studio. Guide book (4 languages). Parking. Licensed restaurant, tearoom. Wheelchair access to ground floor.* ☎ *01539 441 396; Fax 01539 441 263; enquiries@brantwood.org.uk; www. brantwood.org.uk.* This house was the home of **John Ruskin**, one of the greatest figures of the Victorian age. On the walls are exquisite watercolours by himself and by Pre-Raphaelite contemporaries whom he championed. His study turret provides a splendid **view**★ of Coniston in its attractive lakeside setting with the form of The Old Man to the left, perfectly mirrored in the tranquil waters of the lake.

Coniston – The little slate-grey town is known for its associations with the author, artist and social reformer John Ruskin (1819-1900) who came to live at nearby Brant-wood in 1872. He is buried in the local churchyard.

Nearby, a small **Ruskin Museum,** (⛅🕐 *Open Easter to mid-Nov, daily, 10am-5.30pm;* ∞ *£3.75 . Audio-guide (4 languages).* ☎ *01539 441 164; Fax 01539 441 132; vmj@ ruskinmuseum.com; www.ruskinmuseum.com)* with drawings, manuscripts and other mementoes illustrates his many talents.

▷ *From Coniston take A 593; in Skelwith Bridge turn left to Grasmere.*

Grasmere – The village would be beautiful even if **Wordsworth** had never existed. It was here that the family lived in two different dwellings between 1799 and 1850 – Dove Cottage and Rydal Mount. The churchyard of 13C St Oswald's is where Wordsworth, various members of the family and Coleridge's son David Hartley are buried.

> *"Not raised in nice proportion was the pile.*
> *But large and massy; for duration built.*
> *With pillars crowded, and the roof upheld.*
> *By naked rafters intricately crossed."*

(Wordsworth)

Dove Cottage★ – *Town End just off the A 591.* 🕐 *Open daily, 9.30am-5.30pm (5pm last admission).* 🕐 *Closed 24-26 Dec, second week in Jan-first week in Feb.* ∞ *£6.* ☎ *01539 435 544; Fax 01539 435 748; enquiries@wordsworth.org.uk; www.wordsworth.org.uk.* An early 17C converted inn (The Dove and Olive Bough) and home of William and his sister Dorothy from 1799 to 1808, Dove Cottage became a magnet for the early 19C literary Romantics: Coleridge, Southey and De Quincey. In the kitchen where Dorothy cooked the inhabitants' two meals per day (both porridge) are three chairs embroidered by the poet's daughter, Dora Wordsworth, Sara Coleridge and Edith Southey, while the room off it was first Dorothy's, then William's. Upstairs is the sitting room, looking out over the waters of Grasmere (in Wordsworth's time the cottage stood on its own), the main bedroom (first William's, then Dorothy's), the Newspaper Room, wallpapered in newspaper to keep it warm, and the pantry-cum-spare room. The cottage was for a short period home to De Quincey. Behind is a museum containing manuscripts, memorabilia and Lakeland paintings.

Rydal Mount and Gardens – *Windermere-Keswick Road.* 🕐 *Open Mar-Oct, daily, 9.30am-5pm; Nov-Feb, daily except Tue, 10am-4pm.* ∞ *£4. Guide board (34 languages and Braille). Parking.* ☎ *01539 433 002; Fax 01539 431 738; rydalmount@aol.com.* In the hamlet of Rydal overlooking Rydal Water. A c 1574 cottage extended in the 18C into a farmhouse, Rydal Mount was the home of William Wordsworth (1770-1850) from 1813, through his decline from revolutionary poet to reactionary Poet Laureate, to his death in 1850. Here he wrote his most financially successful book, *Guide to the Lakes.* Inside, his library now forms part of the drawing room, and the study ceiling is still painted with the Renaissance design he copied from a visit to Italy.

Ambleside – North of Windermere this attractive town makes a good touring base.

2 Eskdale via Wrynose Pass

50mi/80km

This route leads to the less-frequented, wilder and at times desolate expanses of Ulpha Fell and Furness Fell and goes over two high passes *(severe bends and gradients).*

▷ *From Windermere take A 591 north.*

Brockhole National Park★ – A comprehensive and imaginatively-run **visitor centre**, (⛅🕐 *Open Apr-Nov, daily 10am-5pm. Parking (charge). Café. Adventure playground* ☎ *01539 446 601; Fax 01539 445 555; infodesk@lake-district.gov.uk; www.lake-district. gov.uk)* with displays on the ecology and history of Lakeland, a Beatrix Potter exhibition and lakeside walk.

▷ *South of Ambleside turn left on A 593. Beyond Skelwith Bridge turn right.*

At first the road is enclosed by dykes and then starts to climb up the V-shaped valley between the bare slopes which are grazing grounds for hill sheep.

Wrynose Pass★★ – From the pass (1 280ft/390m) there is a **view** back down to Little Langdale.

Wrynose Bottom – The road runs parallel with the River Duddon along Wrynose Bottom through the wild splendour and gently rounded forms of the fells, which rarely exceed 3 280ft/1 000m but are scarred by steep scree slopes.

Hardknott Pass★★ – At the southern end of the pass (1 289ft/393m), which looks west over the more pastoral valley of **Eskdale**, are the ruins of **Hardknott Fort**, an outstanding example of a Roman auxiliary fort built of stone in the 2C AD.

Ravenglass and Eskdale Railway – ♿ ⏱ *Operates late-Mar to early-Nov daily; Nov to late-Mar, reduced service, call for schedule. Single journey (40min) Ravenglass-Eskdale (Dalegarth).* ☎ *01229 717 171; Fax 01229 717 011; steam@ravenglass-railway.co.uk; www.ravenglass-railway.co.uk.* The narrow-gauge railway (7mi/11.3km), which was laid down in 1875 to carry iron ore and granite, now carries passengers in closed, semi-closed or open carriages drawn by one of twelve locomotives, six of which are steam engines. The line passes from the high fells and tributary waterfalls down the Esk valley, through the heather, bracken or tree-clad lower slopes to Ravenglass, where

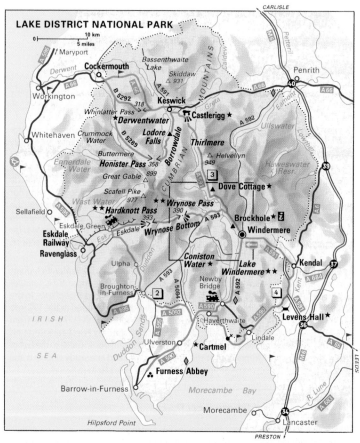

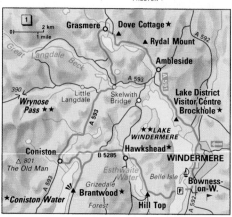

Other National Parks described in the Guide

Brecon Beacons
Dartmoor
Exmoor
Norfolk and Suffolk
Broads
Northumberland
North York Moors
Peak Distrit
Pembrokeshire Coast
Snowdonia
Yorkshire Dales

seabirds gather in the estuary. The tiny museum at Ravenglass station is devoted to the history of the railway and the local mines.

▶ *Either return by the same route or make a long detour via Ulpha, Broughton-in-Furness and Newby Bridge at the southern end of Lake Windermere.*

3 Keswick and Northern Lakes

29mi/47km

The first part of the tour is described in tours 1 *and* 2*.*

North of Dove Cottage the road runs parallel to the Rothay up to Dunmail Raise before descending into the valley overshadowed by "the dark brow of mighty" **Helvellyn** (3 114ft/949m). Wordsworth used to walk this route to visit Coleridge and Southey in Keswick.

Thirlmere – The lake enclosed by mountains and forests is in fact a reservoir, raised 50ft/15m by a dam, surrounded by plantations.

Castlerigg Stone Circle★ – *Signposts.* The circle is older than Stonehenge and its purpose is unknown. It is set on a grassy outcrop offering far-flung **views** south towards Thirlmere and Helvellyn and west to Derwentwater and Keswick.

Keswick – Keswick, a lakeland town of medieval origin, claims the world's first pencil factory (1832), using the graphite which was mined in Borrowdale as early as the mid-16C. The small but interesting **Pencil Museum,** (⌖ ◷ *Open daily, 9.30am-4pm (last admission); longer hours during peak periods.* ◷ *Closed 1 Jan and 25-26 Dec.* ⌖ *£3 . Parking.* ☎ *01768 773 626; museum@acco-uk.co.uk; www.pencils.co.uk)* recounts the process of high-quality pencil making. The local **museum,** (⌖ *Station Road.* ◷ *Open Good Friday to Oct, daily, 10am-4pm. No charge.* ☎ *017687 73263; Fax 017687 80390; keswick.museum@allerdale.gov.uk; www.allerdale.gov.uk/keswick-museum)* contains a 500-year-old cat, the famous musical stones and manuscripts by both Wordsworth and Southey. Wordsworth used to visit Southey and Coleridge when they and their extended families lived together at Greta Hall (*private*).

▶ *From Keswick take B 5289 south.*

Derwentwater★ – This lake is 3mi/5km long, 1mi/0.5km wide and flanked by clere-stories of crags. Southey called it the most beautiful of English lakes.

Lodore Falls – The most literary cascade of the lakes, according to Southey "it comes thundering and floundering, and thumping and plumping and bumping and jumping and whizzing and hissing and dripping and skipping and grumbling and rumbling and tumbling and falling and brawling and sprawling" (but only after heavy rain).

Borrowdale – The attractive valley, where graphite was first mined in the mid 16C, leads to the tiny hamlet of Rosthwaite set in a clearing in characteristic Lakeland scenery.

Honister Pass – The road climbs over the pass (1 175ft/358m). To the south are two of the region's most prominent summits – **Great Gable** (2 949ft/899m) and **Scafell Pike** (3 206ft/977m).

Beyond the pass the road descends to Buttermere, which is separated by a glacial delta from Crummock Water, and continues to Cockermouth.

Wordsworth House – *(NT) Cockermouth. Main Street.* ◷ *Open daily late Mar to early-Nov, 11 am-4.30pm (4pm last admission).* ⌖ *£4.50. Braille guide. Tearoom.* ☎ *01900 820884; Fax 01900 824 805; wordsworthhouse@nationaltrust.org.uk; www.nationaltrust. org.uk.* The elegant Neoclassical Georgian house (1745), in which the poet, **William Wordsworth**, was born in 1770 and spent his early years, is furnished with his own or contemporary pieces of furniture and exhibits some of his work, related documents and the Wordsworth family tree. The garden leads down to the River Derwent.

▶ *From Cockermouth return to Keswick EITHER by A 66, the quicker route, OR by B 5292 the slower and steeper route.*

The quicker route skirts the west shore of **Bassenthwaite Lake** whereas the slower road climbs over **Whinlatter Pass** (1 043ft/318m) revealing extensive and magnificent views of typical lakeland scenery.

4 Kendal and Furness

40mi/64km

▶ *From Windermere take A 591 east.*

Kendal – The "Auld Grey Town", built out of the local limestone, is the thriving centre for a wide area. It was the birthplace of Henry VIII's sixth wife, Catherine Parr, but long before her day was already famous for its wool trade.

Address Book

For coin ranges, see the Legend at the back of the guide.

WHERE TO STAY

⊜⊜🛌 **Fair Rigg Guest House,** *Ferry View, Bowness on WIndermere,* ☎ 015394 43941; stay@Fairrigg.co.uk; www.fairrigg.co.uk. A traditional 19C property with views over the lake to the hills; all six rooms are modern light and cheery, taking advantage of the vista.

⊜⊜⊜🛌 **Riverside Hotel,** *Under Loughrigg, Ambleside.* ☎ 015394 32395; Fax 015394 32440; info@riverside-at-ambleside.co.uk; www.riverside-at-ambleside.co.uk. Beautiful Victorian country house beside the river on a quiet lane a short stroll from the village , with five attractive bedrooms, one with a four-poster bed and two with spa baths; all have views of river or garden.

WHERE TO EAT

⊜🍴 **Black Bull Inn,** *1 Yewdale Road, Coniston* ☎ 015394 41335; Fax 015394 41168; theblackbullconiston@easicom.com.

A large 16C coaching inn of great character which takes its beers very seriously (there's a microbrewery on site) and produces honest-to-goodness traditional Lakeland dishes such as trout with almonds and plum pudding.

⊜⊜🍴 **The Weary Sportsman**, *Castle Carrock* ☎ 01228 670230; Fax 01228 670 089; relax@theweary.com; www.theweary.com. The traditional whitewashed pub exterior hides a thoroughly contemporary interior with striking modern lighting and chic furnishings and fittings; the menu is similarly eclectic, from toffee pudding to vegetable tempura.

⊜⊜🍴 **Masons Arms,** *Strawberry Bank, Cartmell Fell* ☎ 015395 68486; Fax 015395 68780; info@strawberrybank.com; www.strawberrybank.com. This cosy warren-like pub with its snugs and parlours also has broad canopied parasols and outdoor heaters that bring a hint of cafe culture to the lakes; the food is mostly easy-going international and British favourites.

Abbot Hall Art Gallery and Museum of Lakeland Life, (🕐 *Open mid-Feb to Dec, Mon-Sat, 10.30am-5pm (4pm mid-Feb to Mar and Nov-Dec).* 🎟 *£4.75. Admission to Art Gallery or Museum includes discount on admission to the other.* ☎ 01539 722 464; Fax 01539 722 494; info@abbothall.org.uk; www.abbothall.org.uk) occupies an 18C country house built on a medieval site. It features changing exhibitions and a collection of drawing-room paintings by George Romney (1734–1802). The museum section has a room devoted to the children's author **Arthur Ransome** (of Swallows and Amazons fame, 🕮see box above). From the castle there is a fine view of the town in its setting of foothills. Kendal is also famous for its Mint Cake, an essential energy-boosting item for the backpack of any walker.

▸ *Take A 591 and then A 590 south.*

Levens Hall and Garden★ – 🕐 *Open late-Mar to late-Oct, Sun-Thur and Bank Hol Mon, 10am (noon house) to 5pm.* 🎟 *£8 ; gardens only, £5.90. Brochure (4 languages). Parking. Refreshments. Wheelchair access to gardens.* ☎ 01539 560 321; Fax 01539 560 669; houseopening@levenshall.fsnet.co.uk; www.levenshall.co.uk. An Elizabethan manor has been added to a 13C pele tower to give the present graceful residence. The Great Hall, with its panelling of local oak and ornate ceiling, is an introduction to equally outstanding carving and **plaster-work**, Elizabethan and later, throughout the rest of the rooms. The dining room, covered in Cordova leather in 1692, has a magnificent set of Charles II walnut dining chairs. The **Topiary Gardens** are unique in that the 1690 design has been preserved intact. They are the only surviving examples of the work of Monsieur Beaumont, who also worked for James II at Hampton Court.

▸ *Take A 590 west to Lindale and then minor roads (signs) to Cartmel.*

Cartmel Priory★ – ♿🕐 *Open daily, 9am-5.30pm (3.30pm in winter). No visiting during services.* ☎/Fax 01539 536 261; vicar.cartmel@virgin.net. The priory church, which survived the Dissolution of the Monasteries (16C) to become the parish church, is the grandest medieval building in the Lake District, being mostly 12C. Its curious tower is in fact a double tower, one set diagonally upon the other. Inside there is a fine Perpendicular east window and, above the droll misericords in the choir, a beautifully carved screen (1620). The **Priory Gatehouse,** (🕐 (NT) Cavendish Street. Open Easter-Oct, Wed-Sun, Nov-Easter, Sat-Sun, 10am-4pm. 🎟 £2. ☎ 01539 536 874; Fax 01539 536 636; cartmelpriory@nationaltrust.org.uk; www.nationaltrust.org.uk) and the 17C and 18C houses give the market square an urbane air.

▶ *Take B 5278 north; in Haverthwaite turn left on A 590.*

Furness Abbey – EH ♿ 🕐 *Open Apr-Oct, daily, 10am-6pm 4pm Nov-Mar, Thur-Sun ,* 🕐 *Closed 1 Jan and 24-26 Dec; phone for confirmation of winter opening hours.* ⊸ *£3.30 Audio guide. Parking.* ☎ *01229 823 420; www.english-heritage.org.uk.* Stephen, Count of Boulogne, later King of England, gave a site near Preston to the Order of Savigny, for a convent, in 1123. The group moved to a more secluded site in Furness in 1127 and became part of the Cistercian Order. The red sandstone ruins of the abbey sit in a secluded vale. The transepts and choir walls stand almost to their original height, as does the western tower. In the south wall of the Presbytery are four seats (sedilia) and basin (piscina), with relatively little damage to their canopied heads. The mid-13C vestibule and chapter house have the graceful simplicity associated with Cistercian building of the period.

LANCASTER

Lancashire, ENGLAND

POPULATION 44 497

MICHELIN ATLAS P 38 OR MAP 502 L 21

Set on England's north west coast just south of the Lake District the name Lancaster is most famous for its dynasty of English kings (descended from John of Gaunt), notably being one of the opposing factions in the Wars of the Roses.

The Castle and the Priory Church of St Mary share the same hill on which the Romans established their fort guarding the crossing of the River Lune. The town prospered in the 18C from trade with the West Indies and contains many fine buildings from this period, including the Georgian Customs House. 🛈 *29 Castle Hill LA1 1YN* ☎ *01524 32878; Fax 01524 382 849; lancastertic@lancaster.gov.uk; www. visitlancaster.co.uk.*

Sights

Lancaster Castle★ – 🕐 ⊸ *Open daily, guided tour only, telephone for times, 10.30am-4pm.* ⊸ *Guided tour £4.* ☎ *01524 64998; Fax 01524 847 914; christine.goodier@property. lanscc.gov.uk; www.lancashire.gov.uk/resources/ps/castle/index.htm.* The massive John of Gaunt Gatehouse, which dominates the uphill approach, was built c 1407-13 by Henry IV, John of Gaunt's son. Much of the rest of the medieval castle, which was begun in the 11C – the **Great Keep** and **Hadrian's Tower** – was incorporated into the substantial additions made to the structure in the late 18C, in accordance with an Act of Parliament requiring the improvement of prisons; the walls were also rebuilt following the original 14C alignment.

The Gothic **Shire Hall** presents a fine ceiling of carved stone and a display of heraldic shields of monarchs and sheriffs.

The site of the Great Hall, the seat of the Assizes since 1176, is now occupied by the **Crown Court** and the **Drop Room**, from which the condemned prisoners were led out to execution. All three are fine examples of the late 18C.

Priory Church – 🕐 *Open daily, 10am-4.30pm.* ⊸ *Guided tour by appointment. Refreshments.* ☎ *01524 65338; lancasterpriory@yahoo.co.uk; www.priory.lancaster. ac.uk.* A priory dedicated to St Mary was founded nearby in 1094 but the present building is predominantly Perpendicular in style. The south porch doorway dates from c 1180 but the glory of the church is the late-medieval **chancel stalls** with elaborate carvings of foliage.

Maritime Museum – *St George's Quay.* ♿🕐 *Open daily, Easter-Oct, 11am-5pm; Nov-Easter, 12.30-4pm. Brochure (5 languages).* ☎ *01524 64 637; Fax 01524 841 692; museums@ lancaster.gov.uk.* The Customs House, designed by a member of the Gillow family in 1764, now houses the Maritime Museum which illustrates various aspects of local maritime history – the packet boat for canal travel, the hazards of "crossing the sands" and the exhibit on the growth of the nearby seaside towns such as Morecambe and Heysham (🕐 *see below*).

Excursions

Morecambe and Heysham – *5mi/8km west by A 589.* These are two traditional seaside holiday resorts which overlook the broad sweep of Morecambe Bay to the Furness peninsula and the mountains of the Lake District.

Morecambe offers a long promenade (5mi/8km), indoor and outdoor swimming pools, a Wild West theme park and model village for children.

Heysham, now a port for the Isle of Man and Ireland, is the site of a **nuclear power station** (🕐 🛈 *Guided tour by appointment.* ☎ *0800 376 0676; Fax 01294 826 008; be.ps-tours@british-energy.com; www.british-energy.com*) comprising two advanced gas-cooled reactors (1983 and 1988). Below the headland stands **St Peter's Church**, a Saxon foundation much rebuilt, which contains an Anglo-Norman hogback tombstone (*south aisle*), decorated in a mixture of Norse mythology and Christian symbols. Above on the headland stand the ruins of **St Patrick's Chapel**, a Saxon building, adjoining six graves, cut into the rock, probably the work of 8C Irish monks.

LEEDS ★

West Yorkshire, ENGLAND

POPULATION 424 194

MICHELIN ATLAS P 40 OR MAP 502 P 22

TOWN PLAN IN THE MICHELIN GUIDE GREAT BRITAIN AND IRELAND

Set in the heart of northern England, Leeds is above all a great Victorian city; its population multiplied tenfold between 1800 and 1900 and it now ranks third in size among England's provincial cities. Moreover it is Britain's fastest growing city. Heavy industry has been replaced by light engineering and offices, and clothing manufacture by retail trade; the precincts and arcades attract shoppers from all over the North. The rich cultural life of a provincial capital ranges from the fine productions of Opera North to the night-time attractions which bring in multitudes of weekend revellers. Long separated from the city centre by the railway, the once industrialised banks of the River Aire are attracting new cultural and recreational uses, foremost among them the superb Royal Armouries Museum. Headingley, northwest of the city centre, is the home of Yorkshire cricket.

Sights

Royal Armouries Museum ★★★ (GZ) – *on south bank of the River Aire. Armouries Drive.* 🕐*Open daily, 10-5pm,. Last admission 1hr before closing.* 🕐*Closed 24-25 Dec. No charge.* ☎ *0113 220 1940 (recorded inormation); enquiries@armouries.org.uk; www.armouries. org.uk.* Although larger than the multi-storey 19C warehouses on the opposite bank of the Aire, this citadel in grey brick and marble sits comfortably on the waterfront, overlooking weir, lock and the Clarence Dock. It was inaugurated in 1996 to provide a worthy setting for part of the superlative collection of weaponry, formerly housed and partially displayed in the Tower of London. The quality of the exhibits is matched by an array of advanced and imaginative display techniques which set the items in their context and encourage interaction by the visitor: interactive computers and video screens chatter and hum, and live demonstrations provide movement and drama. A splendid central space, the **Street**, rises between the six floors of the main part of the building to the glazed roof. It terminates in the **Hall of Steel** (over 100ft/30m high), a glazed keep; its interior walls are hung with a stunning assortment of weaponry arranged in decorative patterns.

Five spacious galleries are devoted to **War, Hunting, the Tournament, Self-defence** and to the weaponry of **Asia**. The countless treasures include a grotesque grinning face-mask presented to Emperor Maximilian (the museum's emblem), gorgeously inlaid sporting guns, a set of Japanese armour presented to King James I in 1614 and a near-complete set of elephant armour. Among the curiosities is a tiny cyclist's revolver designed to discourage dogs and a monumentally unwieldy punt gun once used by wildfowlers to fell dozens of ducks at a single discharge.

The **Tiltyard**, the first to be built in Britain for hundreds of years, is the setting for thrilling performances of jousting and combat of all kinds.

Address Book

OUT AND ABOUT IN LEEDS

Tourist Information Centre – Gateway Yorkshire, Regional Travel and Tourist Information Centre, Station Arcade, Leeds City Station. The centre is open Mondays to Saturdays, 9am to 5.30pm, and Sundays, 10am to 4pm. ☎ 0113 242 5242; tourinfo@leeds.gov.uk; www.leeds.gov.uk

Public Transport – For regional bus and train travel information ☎ 0113 245 7676 (Metroline).

Sightseeing – During the summer months guided walks leave from Gateway Yorkshire on Wednesdays and Sundays at 2pm. Further details can be obtained from Gateway Yorkshire (👜 see above). Boat trips on Leeds Canal are a leisurely way of exploring the area.

Pubs and Restaurants – Leeds Waterfront, once derelict, is now home to a vast array of restaurants, pubs and shops. The traditional Ancestor Pub is at Tetley's Brewery Wharf (brewery tour and museum of local brewing). Down hill past the Corn Exchange is one of the busiest areas for evening dining. Worth a mention are the *Pool Court at 42* and *Anthony's*, both with a high Michelin rating. For further information on restaurants, contact the tourist information centre

for a copy of *Leeds On* for a detailed description of different places to eat around the city.

Shopping – Many of the main high street stores are to be found in **Briggate**, and the elegant **Victoria Quarter** which boasted the first Harvey Nichols store outside London. For hand-made goods head for **Granary Wharf**, which is open daily. For something special or eclectic pay a visit to the slightly bohemian **Corn Exchange,** which has over 50 outlets. The Sunday Festival Market, or Kirkgate market, is said to be the largest covered market in Europe and the site where, in 1884, Michael Marks launched his Penny Bazaar, leading to the founding of Marks & Spencer in 1890.

Entertainment – Leeds is renowned for its club culture, and has a vast array of clubs to choose from. For details contact the TIC (👜 see above). The Varieties Music Hall, the West Yorkshire Playhouse, the Grand Theatre and the Opera House cater to all tastes in music. Outdoor concerts ranging from opera, ballet, pop, jazz and classical music are held in the summer. Leeds also hosts an International Film Festival and an International Piano Competition.

Town Hall and Victoria Square (FY) – The town hall was the winning design in a competition in 1853. External Corinthian columns, the Baroque tower (225ft/69m) and the splendour of the interior made it a symbol of civic pride when opened by Queen Victoria in 1858. On fine days, chess enthusiasts can be seen playing 'Giant Chess' on the boards marked out in Victoria Square.
Millennium Square extending to Civic Hall gives a new focus to the town.

Briggate (GZ) – Since the main spine of the planned town was laid out around 1200, Briggate has been the principal shopping street. Opening into it at right angles are numerous arcades, the most splendid being the opulent **County Arcade** *(GZ 20, next to Victoria Quarter)* with mahogany shopfronts, faience decoration and mosaic figures of the arts and industries beneath a glazed dome. Just to the east are the almost equally ornate and splendidly spacious covered **Kirkgate Market** as well as the oval **Corn Exchange** of 1864, now home to a variety of specialist shops.

St John's Church, (GY) (🕐 *Open Tue-Sat, 9.30am-5.30pm.* ☎ *0113 244 1689)* is the oldest church in central Leeds. A sensitive restoration in 1868 left the interior virtually unchanged since the church was built in 1632-34. Sumptuous screen and pulpit.

The Grand Theatre (GY), (👜🕐 *Closed through Summer 2006.* ☎ *0113 222 6222; Fax 0113 246 5906; www.leeds.gov.uk)* completed in 1878 in the Gothic style and modelled on La Scala, Milan, is the home of "Opera North".

★City Art Gallery (FG) – 👜 *The Headrow.* 🕐 *Open Mon-Sat, 10am-5pm (8pm Wed); Sun, 1-5pm.* 🕐 *Closed 1 Jan and 25-26 Dec. Leaflet. No charge.* ☎ *0113 247 8248; Fax 0113 244 9689; www.leeds.gov.uk.* The gallery's strength lies in its collection of **19C and 20C British art,** particularly in its holdings of paintings of the early to mid 20C, virtually all major artists of the period being represented. A selection from its rich collection of British watercolours is normally also on display.
Dominating a limited number of Pre-Raphaelite paintings is the striking *The Shadow of Death* by Holman Hunt. There are several of the large narrative paintings so popular in the 19C, among them Lady Butler's *Scotland for Ever!* and some characteristically atmospheric scenes by the local painter Atkinson Grimshaw.

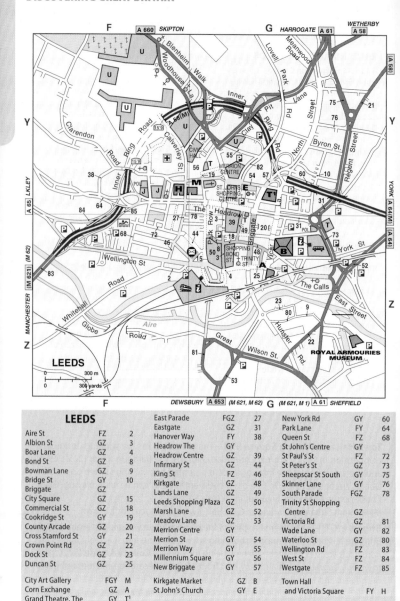

LEEDS

Aire St	FZ	2
Albion St	GZ	3
Boar Lane	GZ	4
Bond St	GZ	8
Bowman Lane	GZ	9
Bridge St	GY	10
Briggate	GZ	
City Square	GZ	15
Commercial St	GZ	18
Cookridge St	GY	19
County Arcade	GZ	20
Cross Stamford St	GY	21
Crown Point Rd	GZ	22
Dock St	GZ	23
Duncan St	GZ	25

East Parade	FGZ	27
Eastgate	GZ	31
Hanover Way	FY	38
Headrow The	GY	
Headrow Centre	GZ	39
Infirmary St	GZ	44
King St	FZ	46
Kirkgate	GZ	48
Lands Lane	GZ	49
Leeds Shopping Plaza	GZ	50
Marsh Lane	GZ	52
Meadow Lane	GZ	53
Merrion Centre	GY	
Merrion St	GY	54
Merrion Way	GY	55
Millennium Square	GY	56
New Briggate	GY	57

New York Rd	GY	60
Park Lane	FY	64
Queen St	FZ	68
St John's Centre	GY	
St Paul's St	FZ	72
St Peter's St	GZ	73
Sheepscar St South	GY	75
Skinner Lane	GY	76
South Parade	FGZ	78
Trinity St Shopping Centre	GZ	
Victoria Rd	GZ	81
Wade Lane	GY	82
Waterloo St	GZ	80
Wellington Rd	FZ	83
West St	FZ	84
Westgate	FZ	85

City Art Gallery	FGY	M
Corn Exchange	GZ	A
Grand Theatre, The	GY	T¹

Kirkgate Market	GZ	B
St John's Church	GY	E

Town Hall and Victoria Square	FY	H

Most of the early 20C painting is arranged around the grand stairway and on the upper floor. At the top of the stairs is a stunning Vorticist portrait, *Praxitella* by Wyndham Lewis. The more muted work of the Camden Town School includes a Charles Ginner landscape of 1914, *The Leeds Canal*, and there is a range of the highly individual work of Stanley Spencer. Native surrealism is well represented, with canvases by Paul Nash, John Armstrong, Tristram Hillier and Edward Wadsworth; the later strain of neo-Romanticism is present too, in the work of John Minton, Graham Sutherland and John Piper. Post-war trends, international as well as British, are illustrated as well in, for example, the disturbing *Painting* of 1950 by Francis Bacon.

The dominance of British art is relieved by the presence of some French paintings: a Courbet, several Impressionists and a brilliant Derain of 1905, Barges on the Thames. The greatest British sculptor of the 20C, **Henry Moore** (1898-1986), was a Yorkshireman; the range of his achievement, from exquisite small-scale studies to the *Reclining Figure* of 1929 and the powerful post-war *Meat Porters,* is shown in the gallery and in the neighbouring **Henry Moore Institute** (Open daily, 10am-5.30pm (9pm Wed). ☎ 0113 246 7467. www.henry-moore-fdn.co.uk.

Kirkstall Abbey★ – *2mi/3km northwest of the city centre by A 65.* ♿ *Abbey Ruins:* 🕐*Open daily, dawn-dusk, no charge. Abbey House Museum: Open Tue-Sun 10am (noon Sat) to 5pm.* ➔ *£3.* ☎ *0113 230 5492; www.leeds.gov.uk/kirkstallabbey.* The austere ruins, which still stand almost to roof height, are dominated by the crossing tower, which was raised in height between 1509 and 1528. Kirkstall was a traditional Cistercian Abbey, started in 1152 by monks from Fountains Abbey.

Excursions

Temple Newsam★ – *Near Whitkirk, 5mi/8km east by A 63.* ♿🕐 *Open Tues – Sun and Bank Hol Mons. 10:30am – 5pm (4pm winter).* ➔ *House £3.50, Farm £3, combined ticket £5.50.* ☎ *0113 264 7321; Fax 0113 260 2285; www.leeds.gov.uk.* This was the birthplace of Lord Darnley, husband of Mary Queen of Scots. The brick Jacobean-style house, forming three sides of a court, was begun in the late 15C and substantially rebuilt in the first part of the 17C. An inscription from this latter period, praising God, honouring the King and calling for prosperity for those within the house, runs round the balustrade.

The house makes an appropriate and attractive setting for a collection of English, European and oriental **decorative arts★** and for many of the Old Master paintings owned by the City of Leeds.

The park, which is composed of a variety of gardens, was once landscaped by Capability Brown.

Nostell Priory★ – *(NT) 18mi/29km southeast by A 61 and A 638.* ♿ *Doncaster Road. House:* 🕐*Open late-Mar to early-Nov, Wed-Sun and Bank Hol Mon, 1-5pm; First week of Dec noon-4pm. Grounds: late-Mar to early-Nov, Wed-Sun and Bank Hol Mon, 11am-6pm; early to late-Mar and early-Nov to mid-Dec, Sat-Sun, 11am-4.30pm.* ➔ *£6; garden only, £3.50.* ☎ *01924 863 892; Fax 01924 865 282; nostellpriory@nationaltrust.org.uk; www. nationaltrust.org.uk.* A Palladian mansion near the site of a 12C priory dedicated to St Oswald, the house, started in 1733 by James Paine, then only nineteen years old, is in *piano nobile design*, all the chief rooms being on the one floor approached by an external flight of steps.

Robert Adam was commissioned in 1765 to complete the State Rooms and they are amongst his finest interiors. **Thomas Chippendale,** once an apprentice on the estate, designed furniture especially for the house. The **Library Table** and the green and gold **Chinoiserie** furniture of the State Bedroom are some of his finest pieces. The **Dolls' House**, complete with original furniture and fittings, is probably also by him.

National Coal Mining Museum for England – *South of Leeds and 6mi/10km west of Wakefield by A 642.* ♿🕐 *Open daily, 10am-5pm (last tour 3:15).* 🕐 *Closed 1 Jan and 24-26 Dec. No charge. Underground tour (1hr; 6 languages). Audio tours. Nature Trail. Parking. Cafeteria. Induction loop. Wheelchair access to underground tour (telephone to arrange).* ☎ *01924 848 806; Fax 01924 840 694; info@ncm.org.uk; www.ncm.org.uk.* Until its closure in the 1980s Caphouse Colliery contributed significantly to Britain's industrial might. There is an array of machinery around the pithead buildings as well as displays and exhibits evoking mining and the life of its dependent communities but the highlight of a visit is the donning of helmet and lamp and the descent (450ft/140m) into the old workings in the company of a former miner.

Yorkshire Sculpture Park★ – *20mi/32km south by M 1 to Junction 38 and 1mi/1.5km north off A 637. West Bretton.* 🕐*Open daily, 10am-6pm (4pm winter).* 🕐 *Closed 1 Jan and 24-25 Dec.* ➔ *Parking £3 . Galleries. Café.* ☎ *01924 830 302 (information); Fax 01924 830 044; office@ysp.co.uk; www.ysp.co.uk.* Bretton Hall accommodates part of the University of Leeds while the great trees and swelling slopes of its parkland make a fine setting for an outstanding array of modern sculpture which includes works by Henry Moore and Barbara Hepworth, both of Yorkshire origin. There are temporary exhibitions and an Access Sculpture Trail.

Lotherton Hall – *16mi/26km northwest by A 63, A 1 and B 1217.* ♿*Abeford.* 🕐*Open Apr-Oct, Tue-Sun and Bank Hol Mon, 10am (1pm Sun) to 5pm; Nov-Dec and Mar, Tue-Sat, 10am (noon Sun) to 4pm; last admission 45min before closing Garden and park 8am-8pm (6pm winter).* 🕐 *Closed 1 Jan and 25 Dec.* ➔ *£3. Parking. Café.* ☎ *0113 281 3259; www. leeds.gov.uk.* The Hall was given to Leeds City Council in 1968 by the Gascoigne family, who have lived in the area since the 14C. It now houses items from the art collections belonging to the City of Leeds. There is furniture, sculpture and fine silver from the Gascoigne family treasures, much of it collected during "Grand Tours" between 1720 and 1780. Historical costume from the 18C onwards is well represented and there is a large collection of ceramic and pottery work from the 1700s to the 1920s.

In the grounds is a tiny but well preserved **Norman chapel** and a **Bird Garden** containing over 200 species from all the continents.

Brodsworth Hall★ – *(EH) 25mi/40km southeast of Leeds by M 1 to Junction 40, A 638 and a minor road (right) in Upton.* ⚐ *House:* ⏰ *Open late-Mar to late-Oct, Tue-Sun and Bank Hols, 15pm. Gardens: late-Mar to late-Oct, daily, 10am-5:30pm;.* ⚐ *House and gardens £6.60; gardens only, £4.60 (£2 in winter). Guide. Parking. Tearoom.* ☎ *01302 722 598; michael.constantine@english-heritage.org.uk; www.english-heritage.org.uk.* This solid country house was built in the 1860s for Charles Thelusson by the Chevalier Casentini, an Italian architect, and furnished according to the grand High Victorian fashion. After the First World War, as the family requirements and domestic staff diminished, parts of the house were shut off: as a result, a tour of the rooms (restored by English Heritage) traces the changes down the generations, from the perfectly preserved Victorian sections such as the billiards room and kitchen with its cast-iron ranges, to partially modernised bathrooms and discarded mountains of family clutter: ancient roller skates, a rowing machine, a saddled toy horse. The extensive grounds are currently being restored, including the unusual quarry garden.

LEICESTER

Leicestershire, ENGLAND

POPULATION 318 518

MICHELIN ATLAS P 28 OR MAP 504 Q 26

The East Midlands town of Leicester was once the capital of King Lear's kingdom, the seat of the 8C East Mercian bishops and one of the five Danelaw towns – with Derby, Lincoln, Nottingham and Stamford. Among the tenants of the castle, built by William I, have been Simon de Montfort, Earl of Leicester, and John of Gaunt. The wealth of Leicester was based on the manufacture of hosiery from the medieval period until the mid 20C. 🛈 *7-9 Every Street, Town Hall Square* ☎ *LE1 6AG* ☎ *0906 294 1113 (25p per min); info@goleicestershire.com; www.goleicestershire.com/visit*

Jewry Wall and Archeology Museum (B M¹) – *(EH)* ⚐⏰ *Open Feb-Nov, Sat-Sun 11am to4.30pm. Guide book. Parking in the street.* ☎ *0116 247 3021; www.english-heritage. org.uk, www.leicestermuseums.ac.uk.* On the site of the excavated Roman baths the museum contains excellent Roman relics, including the Blackfriars Mosaic and the Peacock Pavement mosaic.

St Nicholas Church (B A) – The oldest church in Leicester, begun in late Saxon times, incorporates re-used Roman bricks. The present length of the church dates from then (see the small nave windows and chancel wall). The tower is 11C and 12C, restored 1905; the attractive south chancel chapel c 1220.

★Guildhall (B) – ⚐ *Guildhall Lane.* ⏰ *Open Sat-Wed , 10am (1pm Sun) 4:30pm Feb-Nov.* ⏰ *Closed 1 Jan and 24-26 Dec. No charge.* ⚐ *Guided tour by appointment. Guide book and leaflet (3 languages). Wheelchair access to ground floor only.* ☎ *0116 253 2569.* The oldest part built in the 14C, the remainder in the 16C and forming a courtyard, the Guildhall was the site of the last stand of the Leicester Parliamentarians in the Civil War. Note the robust timber roof and uprights in the Hall, the c 1500 glass depicting the Four Seasons in the Mayor's parlour and upstairs one of the earliest public libraries in England.

St Martin's Cathedral (B) – ⚐*St Martins.* ⏰*Open daily, 8am-5.30pm.* ⚐ *Guided tour by appointment. Leaflet.* ☎ *0116 262 5294; leicestercathedral@leccofe.org; www. cathedral.leicester.anglican.org.* A cathedral since 1927, the first St Martin's was Norman. The church that replaced it is Early English, with a Perpendicular clerestory and east end and a very "correct" Victorian interpretation of an Early English exterior (including the tower and spire). Note the Robert Herrick family memorials in the north choir aisle dating back to 1589, the Richard III memorial stone in the chancel and the rare 15C oak-vaulted roof of the north porch.

St Mary de Castro Church★ (B) – ⚐⏰ *Open Easter-Oct, Sat and Bank Hol Mon, 2-5pm. Otherwise key available from 15 Castle Street, Leicester.* ☎ *0116 262 8727.* The shadowy and attractive interior, a "pattern book of architectural styles" (Pevsner), goes back to 1107. The best Norman work is the sedilia. The south aisle and tower are 13C, the **chancel roof** 14C.

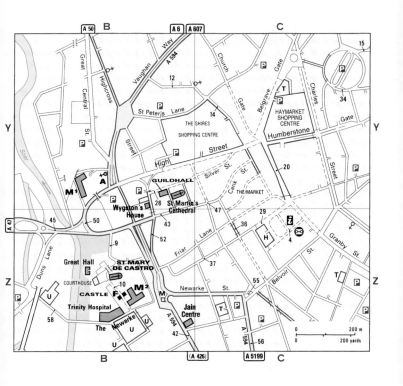

Leicester Castle – ◷ *Open only on special event days and for privately booked groups.* ☎ *0116 253 2569.* The **Great Hall**, which dates from c 1150, acquired a new brick façade in 1695 when it became the Courthouse and no longer resembles a castle in any sense. The **Turreted Gateway** (1423), which was gutted during pro-Reform riots in 1832, leads into the **The Newarke** ("new work"), a walled extension added to the castle in the 14C by Henry, Earl of Lancaster.

Trinity Hospital – The hospital was founded in 1331 as an almshouse within The Newarke; much of it was rebuilt early in the 20C as an old people's home. The **chapel** *(◷ By appointment only. ☎ 0116 250 6090)* is said to contain the grave of Mary Bohun (d 1394), mother of Henry V.

Newarke Houses Museum (B) – *The Newarke.* ⊶*Closed through 2006.* ☎ *0116 255 4900; www.leicestermuseums.ac.uk.* The Leicestershire Museum of Social History is set in two 16C houses.

★Museum and Art Gallery (A) – ♿ *53 New Walk.* ◷*Open daily, 10am (11am Sun) to 5pm.* ◷ *Closed 1 Jan, 24-26 Dec, 31 Dec.* ☎ *0116 255 4100; Fax: 0116 247 3057; shaunknapp@yahoo.co.uk; www.leicestermuseums.ac.uk.* An excellent collection of works by English painters, including Wright of Derby, Hogarth, Bacon, Stanley Spencer and LS Lowry; and the country's largest collection of German Expressionist works.

Leicester Abbey (A) – *Abbey Park, St Margaret's Way.* ♿◷ *Open daily, dawn-dusk. Guided walks. Parking. Cafe. Ramps.* ☎ *0116 222 1000; Fax 0116 222 1003; www. leicester.gov.uk/parks.* Founded in 1132, it became the second richest Augustinian Abbey in England. It was here that the dying Cardinal Wolsey came in 1530 – "an old man, broken with the storms of state". At the Reformation, its stones were used to build the now ruined Cavendish House next door, headquarters of Charles I before the Battle of Naseby (1645).

National Space Centre★ – ♿◷ *Open Tue-Sun, 10am-5pm (3:30 last admis*sion); *also during Leicestershire School Hols, Mon, noon-4.30pm.* ☎ *£9 .95, including Space Theatre show. Parking. Cafe. Induction loop; wheelchairs available (☎ 0116 258 2111).* ☎ *0116 261 0261; Fax 0116 258 2100; info@spacecentre.co.uk; www.spacecentre. co.uk.*

Excursions

Snibston Discovery Park★ – *Ashby Road, Coalville. 16mi/26km northwest by A 50.* ♿◷ *Open daily, 10am-5pm.* ◷ *Closed 1 week in Jan and 25-26 Dec.* ☎ *£5.70.* ⊶ *Guided tour of pit-top buildings (1hr), daily;* ☎ *£1.30. Parking. Refreshments. Wheelchairs available.* ☎ *01530 510 851; snibston@leics.gov.uk; www.leics.gov.uk.* Coalville was a mining town from 1832 until the closure of its colliery in 1986. The derelict pit land has now been transformed into landscaped grounds and an impressive exhibition hall, with hands-on science displays, working steam engines and a collection of vehicles which includes an unusual 19C two-in-one-hearse, with mourners' car and coffin set on the same chassis.

Bosworth Battlefield and Visitor Centre – *Sutton Cheney, Market Bosworth. 14mi/22km west, near A 447.* ♿◷ *Open daily, dawn-dusk. Visitor Centre: late-Mar to-Oct, daily, 11am-5pm; Nov-Dec, Sun, 11am/dusk; Mar, Sat-Sun, 11am-5pm.* ☎ *£3. Parking £1. Guided walks. Special events.* ☎ *01455 290 429; Fax 01455 292 841; bosworth@leics. gov.uk; www.leics.gov.uk.* In 1485 Richard III was killed at the Battle of Bosworth and the first Tudor monarch, Henry VII, took the throne, ending years of dynastic war. A visitor centre on the edge of the rollling fields where the battle took place has displays on medieval history; information boards indicate the route of Richard's fleeing troops. A short distance away is the part-Norman Church of St James, where Richard heard his last mass.

LEWES

East Sussex , ENGLAND

POPULATION 15 376

MICHELIN ATLAS P 11 OR MAP 504 T, U 31

The downland spur on which the long High Street of this attractive south eastern country town (9 mi/14km north east of Brighton) is built, drops abruptly to the gap cut through the surrounding hills by the River Ouse.

Beyond the chalk massif of Caburn, looming over the town to the east, is **Glyndebourne**, the country house internationally famous for its annual opera festival. Lewes itself is renowned for its exuberant Bonfire Night (November 5) celebrations and its architectural heritage, named among the top 50 towns in England by the Council for British Archaeology. 🗗 *Corn Exchange Building, 187 High Street, Lewes, BN7 2DE ☎ 01273 483 448; Fax 01273 484 003.*

A Bit of History

The site's strategic value was appreciated by William de Warenne who built his castle here soon after the Conquest. With his wife Gundrada, he also established a great priory of which little remains. In 1264 Simon de Montfort's rebellion against Henry III led to the defeat of the royal forces at the **Battle of Lewes**, fought on nearby Mount Harry. The religious conflicts of the 16C were marked by the burning at the stake of 17 Protestant martyrs commemorated along with Guy Fawkes and the Gunpowder Plot on 5 November (torchlit processions, tar-barrel rolling, fireworks and giant bonfires).

Castle – *(EH) 169 High Street.* 🕐*Open:, daily 10am (11am Sun, Bank Hols) to 5.30pm; Jan, Tue-Sun, 10am (11am Sun) to 5.30pm; last admission 5pm.* 🕐 *Closed 25-26 Dec.* 💷 *£4.40 (ticket also valid for The Story of Lewes Town and Museum); joint ticket with Anne of Cleves House £6.20.* ⟶ *Guided tour by appointment.* ☎ *01273 486 290; Fax 01273 486 990; castle@sussexpast.co.uk; www.sussexpast.co.uk.* Entry to the castle remains is via Barbican House, a fine 16C timber-framed building with a late-Georgian façade. It contains good displays on Sussex archeology. A perfect flint-built 14C **barbican** guards the castle precinct in which, unusually, there are two mounds, on one of which, high above the rooftops, is perched the **keep**. From one of its towers there are fine **views**⋆ of the town and the gracefully-sculpted outlines of the chalk hills all around.

The **Lewes Living History Model,** *(*🕐 *Open as for castle (see above).* 💷 *£4.20, ticket also valid for castle and museum. Leaflet in 12 languages)* is housed nearby; the town's history is brought to life by an audio-visual show accompanying a detailed scale model.

⋆**Town** – In the well-preserved **High Street**⋆ there is a delightful variety of traditional building materials: flint, stone, brick, timber, stucco, hung tiles, and the local speciality, "mathematical tiles", which in the 18C were used on older timber buildings to simulate a fashionable brick façade. Cobbled **Keere Street**⋆ is very pretty, dropping steeply downhill to a fragment of the old town walls and to **Southover Grange**, built of stone taken from the priory. In Southover High Street is the timber-framed **Anne of Cleves' House,** *(*🕐 *Open mid-Feb to early-Nov, daily, 10am (noon Sun) to 5pm; late-Nov to Dec, Tue-Sat , 10am to 5pm.* 🕐 *Closed 24-28 Dec.* 💷 *£3* ☎ *01273 474 610; anne@sussexpast.co.uk; www.sussexpast.co.uk)* a museum of local history; it has a particularly interesting gallery devoted to the iron industry which once flourished among the deep oak forests of the Sussex Weald.

Excursions

Sheffield Park Garden⋆ – *9.5mi/15km north by A 275.* ♿🕐 *Open Mar to mid-Dec, Tue-Sun and Bank Hol Mon, 10am-6pm/dusk (4pm Nov-Dec); Jan-Feb, Sat-Sun, 10.30am-4pm; last admission 1 hr before closing.* 💷 *£4.80. Parking.* ☎ *01825 790 231; Fax 01825 791 264; sheffieldpark@ntrust.org.uk; www.nationaltrust.org.uk.* This large 18C and 19C landscaped park with its four **lakes** linked by cascades was enriched early in this century with thousands of trees and shrubs from all over the world.

As a **plant collection** it is outstanding and the effects obtained by waterside planting are dramatic; the varied shapes of conifers contrast with each other and with the exotic outline of the Gothicised mansion *(*⟶*not open to the public),* half-hidden in drifts of shrubs; azaleas and rhododendrons give magnificent colour effects in spring and the autumn leaf show has few equals.

Bluebell Railway – ⚐🕐 *Operating May-Sep, daily; Oct-Apr, Sat-Sun.* 🚃 *Return ticket (round trip) £9.20. Bus shuttle between East Grinstead station and Kingscote station on the Bluebell line. Parking.* ☎ *01825 722 370 (24hr recorded information re timetable); 01825 723 777 (general enquiries); 01825 720 801 (Golden Arrow Pullman reservations); www.bluebell-railway.co.uk.* Five miles/8km of former London Brighton and South Coast Railway track now carry the **steam trains** of Britain's first full-scale preserved railway between Sheffield Park and Horsted Keynes. Everything – trim stations, uniformed staff, carriages and locomotives in authentic livery – evokes the atmosphere of yesterday's country railway.

Charleston Farmhouse – *9mi/14km southeast by A27.* ⚐🕐 *Open late-Mar to Oct, Wed-Sun and Bank Hol Mon, 2-6pm.* 🚃 *£6; garden only, £2.50; Connoisseur's tour Fri, 2-4.30pm £7.* 🔍 *Guided tour (except Sun and Bank Hol Mon). Parking. Gallery. Tearoom.* ☎ *01323 811 265; info@charleston.org.uk; www.charleston.org.uk.* This traditional Sussex farmhouse was home to **Bloomsbury Group** members Clive and Vanessa Bell and Duncan Grant from 1916 until Grant's death in 1978. The house and garden overflow with their distinctive decorative style, from textiles and ceramics to hand-painted walls, furniture and fireplaces, and paintings by the artists and their friends who included Derain, Sickert and Augustus John.

LICHFIELD ★

Staffordshire, ENGLAND

POPULATION 28 666

MICHELIN ATLAS P 27 OR MAP 502 O 25

This predominantly Georgian town lies just north of the Midlands industrial conurbation; "a place of conversation and good company" according to Daniel Defoe, it is graced by one of the most beautiful and most picturesquely sited cathedrals in England.

"Every man has a lurking wish to appear considerable in his native place", wrote **Samuel Johnson** (1709-84) whose statue stands in the Market Place opposite the house where he was born. 🛈 *Donegal House, Bore Street, Lichfield WS13 6NE* ☎ *01543 252 109; Fax 01543 308 211; tic@lichfieldtourist.co.uk; www.lichfield-tourist.co.uk*

Cathedral ★★

⚐🕐 *Open daily, 7.30am-6.30pm. Lea-flet (3 languages).* 🔍 *Guided tour by appointment (* ☎ *01543 306 240). Restaurant.* ☎ *01543 306 100; Fax 01543 306 109; enquiries@lichfield-cathedral. org.uk; www.lichfield-cathedral.org. uk.* Although the site has been Christian since at least the 7C, the present building, which replaced an earlier Norman church, was begun in 1195 and is a fine synthesis of the Early English and Decorated styles with some Perpendicular work.

During the Civil War the close was besieged three times, the cathedral was bombarded and the central spire collapsed in 1646. Repairs were made during the 1660s and the interior of the building was changed substantially by Wyatt in the 18C. The medieval grandeur of the cathedral was however restored by the thorough and sensitive work carried out by Sir George Gilbert Scott from 1857-1901.

Lichfield Cathedral

Exterior – The three spires – no other English cathedral has three – are known as the **three sisters** of the vale.

On the west front the mellow red sandstone is richly carved with saints; some date from the 13C but most are the work of Scott.

Interior – Lichfield is the smallest and narrowest of England's cathedrals. The perfectly proportioned nave, adorned with wooden roof **bosses** and decorated capitals, leads the eye past the Transitional crossing and western choir to the Lady Chapel and the fine 16C Flemish glass at the east end.

Among the monuments are *(west end)* Anna Seward, an 18C writer *(The Swan of Lichfield)*, and Lady Mary Wortley Montagu, the diplomat and orientalist, *(south transept)* Samuel Johnson and David Garrick and *(south choir aisle)* Erasmus Darwin and *Sleeping Children,* a tender carving by Sir Francis Chantrey. The display of modern silver shows how it is used, together with the vestments, in church services.

The Close – The cathedral precinct is situated beside the water of the Minster Pool and enclosed by Georgian, early Victorian and neo-Georgian buildings, including *(north side)* the **Deanery** (1704) and the **Bishop's Palace** (1687), now a school, by Edward Pierce, a pupil of Wren.

Samuel Johnson Museum

Market Street. ⏰*Open daily, 10.30am (noon Oct-Mar) to 4.30pm.* ⏰ *Closed 1 Jan and 25-26 Dec.* ⬛ *£2.50 Audio-visual presentation.* ☎ *01543 264 972; Fax 01543 414779; sjmuseum@lichfield.gov.uk; www.lichfield.gov.uk.* Samuel Johnson (1709-84), the famous **lexicographer**, was born in this house (1708), built by his father. The exhibits illustrate Johnson's life from childhood to marriage, through his move to London, the Dictionary and his friendship with Boswell.

Excursion

The Bass Museum of Brewing – *Burton upon Trent. 15mi/24km northeast on A 38 (signposted).* ♿ *Horninglow Street.* ⏰*Open daily, 10am-5pm (4pm last admission).* ⏰ *Closed 1 Jan and 25-26 Dec.* ⬛*£6 . Parking. Refreshments.* ☎ *08456 000 598; Fax 01283 513 613; enquiries@bass-museum.com; www.bass-museum.com.* Burton became the brewing capital of Britain through good transport links, an excellent supply of naturally-filtered water (though not from the River Trent) and the enterprise of many small brewing companies, most of which are now long forgotten. **William Bass** established his brewery in 1777, and the 19C buildings in Horninglow Street now house a lively and extensive collection which charts both the history of Bass in Burton and follows the process of brewing itself, from malting and mashing to delivery by the shire horses and drays or the early steam-driven lorries, which can often be seen giving demonstrations.

LINCOLN★★

Lincolnshire, ENGLAND

POPULATION 80 281

MICHELIN ATLAS P 36 OR MAP 502 S 24

The city of Lincoln is visible for miles around the Eastern England countryside, set high on a limestone plateau beside the River Witham and dominated by the triple towers of the cathedral. The name Lincoln is an Anglo-Saxon corruption of the Roman Lindum, itself derived from the earlier Lindon. Much of the lower part of the town is a pedestrianised shopping area dotted with the occasional medieval church; steep narrow streets lead to the upper town with its imposing Cathedral, Castle and Roman remains. *9 Castle Hill, Cathedral Quarter, Lincoln LN1 3AA* ☎ *01522 873 213; tourism@lincoln.gov.uk; www.lincoln.gov.uk* *21 The Cornhill, High Street, LN5 7HB;* ☎ *01522 873256 Fax: 01522 541447; tourism@lincoln.gov.uk; www.lincoln.gov.uk.*

▶ **Orient Yourself**: It's easy to cover the city centre on foot though open top City Sightseeing hop-on hop off buses operate in the summer ☎*www.citysightseeing. co.uk.*

☺ **Don't Miss**: The Cathedral, especially the roof tour on a clear day (Sat only); the High Bridge; Belvoir Castle (excursion).

🕐 **Organizing Your Time**: Allow a full day to see the cathedral and town.

🚶 **Walking Tours**: City walks are operated in the summer by the tourist office.

A Bit of History

Lindum Colonia, a settlement established since the Bronze Age and occupied by the Ninth Legion in about AD 60, was turned into a colonia in about AD 96 and confined to the plateau top (42 acres/17ha) surrounded by a wooden palisade. In the 3C Lincoln, now one of the four provincial capitals of Roman Britain, doubled in size. The city spread down the southern slopes to the river and was encased in a stone wall (4.5ft/1.5m thick) with six gates – offering a good view from the Bishop's Old Palace or East Bight. The surviving **Newport Arch**, the only Roman arch in England through which traffic still passes, was the north gate of the Roman city.

Lincoln survived the Roman decline, emerging as the capital of the Anglo-Saxon kingdom of Lindsey and converted to Christianity in c 630. It became one of the five

Lincoln Cathedral

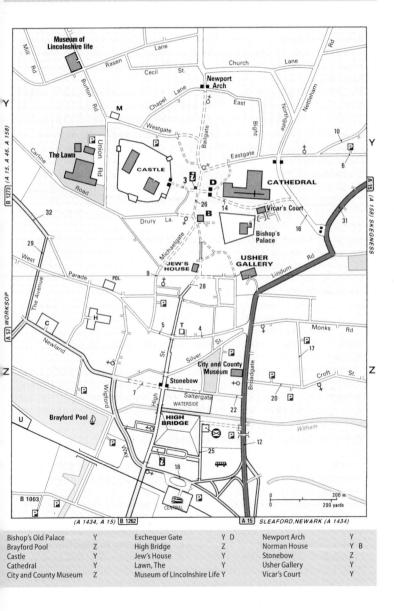

Danish burgh towns – the others were Derby, Leicester, Nottingham and Stamford. After the Conquest, it gained in importance, with the building of the castle and cathedral, and became one of the most prosperous cities in medieval England, shipping its wool direct to Flanders from Brayford Pool on the River Witham. Many half-timbered buildings survive from this time.

The Cathedral ★★★ 1hr

&⊙ *Open daily, 7.15am-8pm (6pm winter).* ⌐ *£4.* ✎ *Guided tour (1hr) daily at 11am, 1pm (May-Sep only), 2pm (Jan-Mar only), 3pm (May-Sep only). Roof tour (90min; max 12) Sat at 11am, 2pm (children under 14 not admitted unless accompanied by an adult). Leaflet (13 languages). Coffee shop. Ramps; audio guide for visually impaired visitors.* ☎ *01522 544 544; visitors@lincolncathedral.com; www.lincolncathedral.com.* The first cathedral, built by Remigius, was early Norman, the result of a short and decisive programme between 1072 and 1092. Alexander, Lincoln's third bishop, builder of Newark Castle, re-roofed the cathedral following a fire in 1141. Hugh of Avalon, a French monk, built the present Early English cathedral following the earthquake of 1185 which virtually destroyed the original Norman building.

Exterior – Few cathedrals have achieved such even proportions: the chancel is as long as the nave, the west towers almost as high as the crossing tower. The **west front**, the most famous view, consists of early Norman central sections, surrounded by a cliff-face of Early English blind arcading.

The south side is graced by the intricate carving inside the **Galilee Porch** and **Judgement Porch** and the north side provides a splendid and varied view of the buttressed Decorated **east end,** the north transept and the flying-buttressed chapter house.

Interior – Lincoln limestone and Purbeck marble shafts combine to create piers of contrasted texture which support the triforium, clerestory and vaults, showing Early English architecture at its best.

The **nave** is composed of seven bays; an exceptional font of Tournai marble stands in the second south bay; the windows are filled with Victorian stained glass. The crossing is flooded with light from the windows of the **Dean's Eye** (13C glass) in the north transept and the **Bishop's Eye** (14C leaf-patterned tracery, filled with fragments of medieval stained glass) in the south.

East of the magnificent 14C stone screen is **St Hugh's Choir**, furnished with 14C oak **misericords** and covered with the so-called "crazy vault of Lincoln", the first rib-vault of purely decorative intentions in Europe, curiously asymmetrical yet "easier to criticise than improve" (Pevsner).

The **Angel Choir** is geometrical (late Early English), rich, light and spacious, so called after the 28 carved stone angels in the spandrels beneath the upper windows.

The soaring **East Window** of Victorian glass depicts Biblical scenes in the earliest Gothic eight-light window (1275). High on the first pier from the east end on the north side, the **Lincoln Imp**, the grotesque that has become the city's emblem, looks down on the shrine of St Hugh.

The 13C **cloister** is vaulted in wood (note the bosses: a man pulling a face, a man sticking out his tongue). Forming the north range is Christopher Wren's **Library**, above a classical loggia. East of the cloister is the **Chapter House** (early 13C) – the vaulting springing from a central shaft and externally supported by flying buttresses – where Edwards I and II held some of the early English Parliaments.

Precincts – Amidst the mostly Georgian and Victorian houses are two of particular note.

The **Vicar's Court (Y)** dates from 1300 to 1400; the four ranges and mid-15C barn behind are a rare survival of medieval domestic architecture and one of the prettiest examples of their kind in England.

Though in ruins, the **Bishop's Old Palace (Y),** (⊙ *Open late-Mar to Oct, daily, 10am-6pm (5pm Sep-Oct); Nov-Mar, Mon, Thur, Fri, Sat-Sun, 10am-4pm.* ⊙ *Closed 1 Jan and 24-26 Dec, .* ⌐ *£3.60* ☎ *01522 527 468; www.english-heritage.org.uk)* built on the plateau's slopes, is redolent of its former grandeur and gives an idea of the richness of Lincoln's medieval prelates. The East Hall is Norman, the West Hall, built by St Hugh, Early English. According to a description before its destruction in the Civil War, "the great hall is very fair, lightsome and strong... one large middle alley and 2 out alleys on either side with 8 grey marble pillars bearing up the arches and free-stone windows very full of stories in painting glass of the Kings of this land."

Additional Sights

Castle Hill (Y) – The street, which is lined by houses dating from the 16C to the 19C, links the 14C **Exchequer Gate** and the East Gate leading to the castle.

Castle★ (Y) – ⏱ *Open daily, 9.30am (11am Sun) to 5.30pm (4pm in winter).* 👓 *£3.70.* 🚶 *Guided tour Apr-Sept, daily. Leaflet (6 languages). Tearoom.* ☎ *01522 511 068; Fax 01522 512 150; www.lincolnshire.gov.uk.* The construction of the Norman keep and wooden stockade (13 acres/5ha) was begun by William the Conqueror in 1068 and required the demolition of 166 houses; nothing remains of the original. The keep's mound is now crowned by the late 12C **Lucy Tower**, once surrounded by a ditch (20ft/6m deep) and a drawbridge. At the top is a circular Victorian burial ground for prisoners, marked by rows of small gravestones. The **East Gate** was added in the 12C, **Cobb Hall** in the 13C. This was a defensive tower and in the 19C the roof was the scene of public hangings. Iron rings, still fixed to the walls, were used to attach prisoners' chains. A Norman tower was enlarged in the 14C and heightened in the 19C when it became known as the Observatory Tower from which there is a splendid **view** of the Cathedral and the surrounding countryside. It is possible to walk round the walls along the east, north and west sides *(not recommended for vertigo sufferers)*. Although besieged in the wars of 1135-54 and 1216-17, the castle gradually lost its military significance but became a centre for the administration of justice which continues to this day; the Crown Court (1822-26) is at the west end of the complex.

The Georgian **Prison Building,** constructed between 1787 and 1791, is now used to display one of the four surviving copies of **Magna Carta** (1215) in a darkened room accompanied by a voice intoning its contents in medieval Latin. The vellum document is preceded by a small exhibition explaining the document's history and importance to democracy. In the **Victorian Prison Building** (1845/6), where prisoners were kept in solitary confinement, is a tableau showing oakum picking and the tiered **Prison Chapel** where a preacher addressed prisoners in their separate pews.

Jew's House★ (Y) – The house and its beautifully designed Norman windows and doorway and original chimney buttress date from c1170; the adjoining **Jews' Court** was once used as a synagogue.

Usher Gallery★ (YZ) – ♿⏱ *Open Tue-Sat, 10am-5pm, Sun, 1-5pm.* ⏱ *Closed 1 Jan and 25-26 Dec.* 👓 *No charge. Leaflet. Junior guidebook and activities for children. Café. Craft sales.* ☎ *01522 527980; Fax: 01522 560 165; usher.gallery@lincolnshire.gov.uk; www.lincolnshire.gov.uk.* The gallery was financed from a legacy by James Ward Usher (who made a fortune at the turn of the century selling replicas of the Lincoln Imp), to house his collections of 16C-19C **miniatures**, 17C and 18C French and English clocks, Chinese, Sèvres, Meissen and English **porcelain** and English and Continental glass. There is also an impressive coin gallery. A room is devoted to the watercolours of **Peter de Wint** (1784-1849) who painted views of the Lincolnshire countryside and of Lincoln Cathedral. The Gallery has paintings by local artists, such as William Logsdail. In the Tennyson room are many of the poet's personal items including hats, pens, the warrant appointing him Poet Laureate, and photos of his funeral.

Stonebow (Z) – Stonebow is a replacement of an earlier 14C gate, built on the site of the southernmost Roman gate. The east range is late 14C, the west early 16C. The gate and **guildhall** (⏱🚶 *Guided tour, Fri and first Sat of the month, at 10.30am and 1.30pm.* ☎ *01522 873 507)* above it were built between the two. The niches in the flanking towers contain statues of the Virgin Mary and the Archangel Gabriel.

High Bridge★★ (Z) – Medieval (though much restored), with the River Witham flowing through its Norman vaults (the Glory Hole), its timber-framed houses are a unique reminder of what Old London Bridge must have looked like. The projection on the other side of the bridge once carried the Chapel of Thomas Becket.

Upstream is **Brayford Pool (Z)**, Lincoln's medieval port, while downstream are two historic inns, the 14C "Green Dragon" and the 15C "Witch and Wardrobe."

Museum of Lincolnshire Life (Y) – Burton Road. ⏱ *Open May-Sep, daily, 10am-5pm;* ⏱ *Closed Oct-Apr: Sun.* 👓 *£2.10. Tearoom.* ☎ *01522 528 448; Fax 01522 521 264; lincolnshirelife.museum@lincolnshire.gov.uk; www.lincolnshire.gov.uk.* Housed in the former barracks of the Royal North Lincoln Militia is an interesting display on local domestic, social and industrial life over the last two centuries, using authentic re-creations of room settings, craftsmen's workshops, stores and an exhibition of agricultural and other vehicles, all in working order.

The Lawn (Y) – The buildings and grounds of the old Lincoln Asylum (1820), later known as the Lawn Hospital, now contain an exhibition on the work of the hospital, the **Archaeology Centre,** (♿🕐 *Open daily, 10am-5pm (4pm Oct-Mar; 4.30pm Fri, Apr-Sep).* 🕐 *Closed 25-26 Dec, 1 Jan. Cafe.* ☎ *01522 873 627)* where visitors can experience something of the work of archaeologists through hands-on activities, and the **Sir Joseph Banks Conservatory,** a small hothouse recalling the work of the Lincolnshire botanist who accompanied Captain Cook on his first voyage to Australia.

Excursions

Skegness – *42mi/67km east on A 158.* ♿ *See BOSTON: Excursions.*

Tattershall Castle and Battle of Britain Memorial Flight (Coningsby)★ – *26mi/42km southeast on A 158 east to Horncastle, then A 153 south.* ♿ *See BOSTON: Excursions.*

Belvoir Castle★★ – *35mi/56km southwest on A 607 via Grantham; in Denton turn right (signs).* ♿🕐 *Open May-Sep, daily (closed Mon and Fri except bank hols), 11am-5pm; Oct, Sun only.* 🎫 *£10 . Garden only £5. Guide book (5 languages). Parking. Refreshments.* ☎ *01476 871 000; Fax 01476 870 443; info@belvoircastle.com; www.belvoircastle.com.* Built by John Webb (pupil of Inigo Jones) in 1654-68, Belvoir (pronounced "Beever") was romanticised by James Wyatt into an early 19C "castle on a hill." The interior is part Gothic fantasy, part Baroque fantasy; the Ballroom contains Thomas Becket's illuminated breviary. The ceiling of the Elizabeth Saloon depicts Jupiter, Juno, Mercury and Venus. In the picture gallery are miniatures (Hilliard and Oliver) and paintings, including *Grace before Meat* (Jan Steen), the *Earl of Southampton, Shakespeare's patron* (Cornelius Janssen), *Proverbs* (David Teniers II), *Seven Sacraments* (Poussin) and *Woodcutter's Return* (Gainsborough). The Regent's Gallery (131ft/40m long) is hung with vast Gobelins tapestries recording the *Adventures of Don Quixote.*

Belton House★ – *26mi/42km south on A 607 towards Grantham.* ♿🕐 *Grantham House: Open late-Mar to early-Nov, Wed-Sun, Good Fri and Bank Hol Mon, 12.30-5pm. Garden and park: same hours as house 11am (10.30am Aug) to 5.30pm.* 🎫 *£5.60. Adventure playground. Braille guide. Parking. Licensed restaurant.* ☎ *01476 566 116; Fax 01476 579 071; belton@nationaltrust.org.uk; www.nationaltrust.org.uk.* A late 17C mansion crowned by balustrade and cupola with late 18C neo-classical alterations by James Wyatt, Belton is the fulfilment of the golden age of English domestic architecture from Wren to Adam. Inside, the classical simplicity of the Marble Hall provides the setting for the paintings by Reynolds, Hoppner and Romney; the exquisite woodcarvings in the Salon are possibly the work of Grinling Gibbons; the Red Drawing Room is graced by Fra Bartolomeo's *Madonna and Child*; the Tyrconnel Room boasts a rare Greek Revival painted floor; the two glorious 1681 "oriental" tapestries in the Chapel Ante Room are by John Vanderbanc (partly copied from Mogul miniatures); the Chapel ceiling is by Edward Goudge and the wood carvings by Edmund Carpenter.

Grantham – *29mi/47km south on A 607.* 🚹 *The Guildhall Centre, St Peter's Hill* ☎ *01476 406166.* Owing to its importance as a staging point on the road north from London, Grantham thrived in the Middle Ages and continues to prosper. St Wulfram's is one of England's most beautiful parish churches. The town was the birthplace of Sir Isaac Newton (1643-1727) and Lady Margaret Thatcher, Britain's first woman Prime Minister.

The spire of **St Wulfram's Church**★, (🕐 *Open (weddings and functions permitting) Apr-Sep, daily, 9am-5.30pm; Oct-Mar, Mon, Thu-Sat, 9am-12.30pm and 2-5.30pm; Tue, 9am-12.30pm.* ☎ *01476 561 342)* is not only one of the tallest spires in Britain (272ft/83m) but is so beautiful that Ruskin is said to have swooned at its sight. The church is largely Early English, the Lady Chapel dates from c 1340 and the rare **chained library** contains over 300 books (south porch). Facing the churchyard is the Grammar School (c1500) where Isaac Newton was educated. The stone front of the **Angel and Royal Inn** *(High Street)* belongs to one of the great medieval inns of England established by the Knights Templar; it has played host to monarchs from King John to Richard III. It was here that the latter signed the death warrant for the Duke of Buckingham.

Doddington Hall★ – *5mi/8km south and west of Lincoln on A 1434 and B 1190 and from the A 46 bypass (Z).* ♿🕐 *House and Gardens: Open May to late-Sep, Wed, Sun and Bank Hol Mon, 2-6pm. Gardens: Open also mid-Feb to Apr, Sun 2-6pm.* 🎫 *£5.30, gardens only, £3.65. Parking. Refreshments. Wheelchair access to gardens and ground floor.* ☎ *01522 694 308; Fax 01522 685 259; www.doddingtonhall.com.* Built by Robert Smythson, who had worked on Longleat, Hardwick Hall and Wollaton Hall, Doddington Hall is late Elizabethan, E-shaped and outward-looking, abandoning the traditional internal courtyard, a sign of a self-confident age.

With the exception of the Parlour, all the interior was refurbished in 1764 by Thomas Lumby, a local builder. The **Parlour** itself is in Queen Anne style, its walls graced with paintings, including Sir Thomas Lawrence's Mrs Sarah Gunman, Sir Peter Lely's *Cymon and Iphegenia* and Ghaerardt's portrait of *Meg of Meldon*, a local witch. The Stairs are Lumby's masterpiece. The superb **Long Gallery** has displays of paintings and porcelain.

Gainsborough Old Hall★ – *18mi/29km west on A 57 (Z) and north on A 156. ♿🕐 Open Easter Sun to Oct, daily, 10am to 5pm (1-4:30 pm Sun); Nov- Easter, Mon-Sat 10am-5pm. 🕐 Closed 1 Jan, Good Fri and 24-26 Dec. 🎫 £3.20. 🎧 Guided tour (90min) by appointment. Taped guide. Leaflet (4 languages). Tea shop. Book shop. Audio tour with induction neck loops; ramps on ground floor. ☎ 01427 612 669; officialfoha@hotmail.com; www.gainsborougholdhall.co.uk.* One of the best-preserved late medieval manor houses in England, the striking timber-framed hall with two flanking ranges was built by Sir Thomas Burgh between 1460 and 1480. Richard III visited it in 1483. It was originally all timber-framed, except for the brick kitchen, brick tower and stone bay window, but Elizabethan features were added to the two ranges. The Hall itself has a sturdy single-arched braced roof; the **kitchen** gives an unforgettable impression of medieval life in the servants' quarters. The east wing contains great chambers, while the west wing, in contrast, is a unique example of 15C lodgings. The tower is furnished as a late 15C bedchamber. There is a permanent exhibition about the Old Hall and the Mayflower Pilgrims.

LIVERPOOL★

Merseyside, ENGLAND

POPULATION 481 786

MICHELIN ATLAS P 34 OR MAP 502 L 23

Though its days of mercantile splendour are long over, Liverpool remains an eminently handsome city, with some glorious architecture and fine civic buildings, reflecting the energy, taste and philanthropy of the Victorian age. Today leisure developments lead the way in the revival of the city's fortunes, from the country's first Garden Festival in 1984, to the more recent Albert Dock revival and brand new Tate Liverpool gallery; in 2008 Liverpool will be celebrating its role as European Capital of Culture.

Liverpool waterfront

LIVERPOOL

CROSBY [A 565]   C   (A 65, A 59) [A 5038]

MERSEY

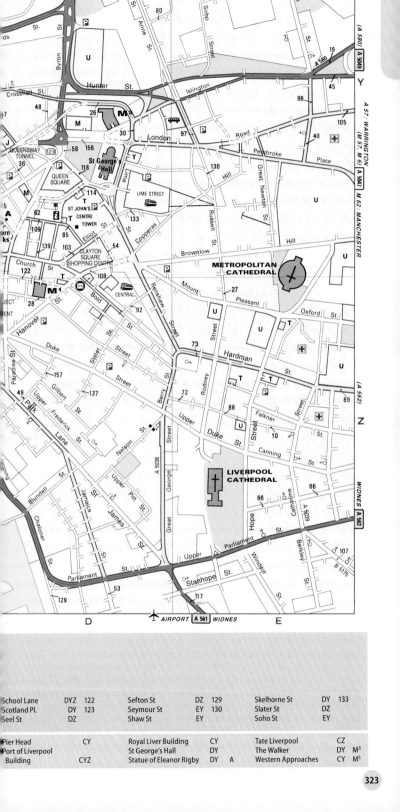

The city's most famous sons, the Beatles, gave the city a new reputation in the 1960s; the Liverpool sound and the Mersey beat and their career are celebrated in Albert Dock and throughout the city. ⓘ *Queen Square, L1 1RG* ⓘ *Albert Dock Centre, Merseyside Maritime Museum, Albert Dock, L3 4AE. General information* ☎ *0906 680 6886 (premium rate line); accommodation (from within the UK)* ☎ *0845 601 1125, (from overseas)* ☎ *0044 151 709 8111; info@visitliverpool.com; www.visitliverpool.com.*

▶ **Orient Yourself**: Get to know the city by way of an amphibious tour that includes the river Mersey and the city streets: *Liverpool Duck Tours,* ♿ 🕐 *Gower Street Bus Stop. Operates mid-Feb to Christmas, departures every hour, daily, 11am-6pm.* 🌐 *Peak £11.95, Off-peak £9.95.* ☎ *0151 708 7799; www.theyellowduckmarine.co.uk).* Conventional open-top bus tours run every hour (*11am-2pm Mar-Oct, also 3pm in July*) starting at Albert Dock.

😊 **Don't Miss**: The Walker Gallery; Liverpool Anglican Cathedral; Albert Dock museums.

🕐 **Organizing Your Time**: Allow at least 2 days, (to include one excursion).

🧒 **Especially for Kids**: Hands-on fun at World Museum; sharks at Blue Planet Aquarium; animals at Knowsley Safari Park.

👣 **Also See**: Blackpool, Bradford, Isle of Man, Manchester.

🚶 **Walking Tours**: Guided walking tours with a Blue Badge guide depart daily from the tourist office in summer.

A Bit of History

On 28 August 1207 King John granted a Charter for settlers to establish a port on the Mersey. Gradual silting up of the Dee estuary and the attendant abandonment of Chester, a port since Roman times, turned the new village of Liverpool into England's second port. It centred around seven streets, which still exist today – Castle and Old Hall, Water and Dale, Chapel and Tithebarn, up to Hatton Garden – and the "Pool", an inlet following today's Canning and Paradise Streets and Whitechapel. Liverpool started to expand when trade with the West Indies – sugar, rum, cotton and, until 1807, slaves – brought such prosperity that by 1800 there were more than 80 000 "Liverpudlians". In the 19C Liverpool, home to the Cunard and White Star liners, was Britain's gateway to the empire and the world. The Mersey Docks and Harbour Company handled the cargo traffic, employing some 20 000 men in the immediate post-war period. Today with container ships and mechanical handling, only just over 2 500 men now work in the docks.

Sights

Pier Head (CY)

The spirit of Liverpool and the Mersey is best appreciated by standing on the corner of Water Street and the Strand. The ferries on the Mersey have been part of the scene since the monks of Birkenhead Priory began rowing travellers across in about 1150. The green-domed **Port of Liverpool Building** (1907) and its neighbour, the **Cunard Building** (1913), reflect the city's maritime connections but the **Royal Liver Building** (1908), with its "Liver Birds" (pronounced "Lyver") on the cupolas, is probably the best known symbol of Liverpool.

Albert Dock★ (CZ)

Massive brick warehouses enclose a dock basin (7 acre/3ha). Completed in 1846, finally closed in 1972, the complex has now been revitalised with shops, cafés and apartments, a maritime museum and the northern extension of the Tate Gallery.

Merseyside Maritime Museum★ – *Albert Dock.* ♿🕐 *Open daily, 10am-5pm.* 🕐 *Closed 1 Jan, 25-27 Dec. (Edmund Gardner - open 11am-4pm summer only.) Ships and Quayside also closed Nov-Apr.* 🌐 *No charge. Fact sheet (4 languages). Parking. Restaurant, coffee shop.* ☎ *0151 478 4499; Fax 0151 478 4590; www.liverpoolmuseums.org. uk/maritime.* The many facets of Liverpool's intimate involvement with the sea are recounted on five floors *(start on the fourth floor and work down).* Liverpool's seafaring past is presented through displays on the history of shipbuilding, the evolution of the port, navigation and the growth of maritime insurance, ship models and paintings. The poignancy of the story of the nine million emigrants to the New World who passed through Liverpool between 1830 and 1930 is exceeded only by the history of the slave trade (basement).

HM Customs & Excise National Museum – *Albert Dock. ⏰ Open daily, 10am to 5pm. ⏰ Closed 1 Jan and 23-26 Dec. ∞ No charge. ☎ 0151 478 4499; Fax 0151 478 4590; www.liverpoolmuseums.org.uk.* The museum charts the fight against smuggling over the centuries as well as modern detection methods. The complex includes a maritime park with hisotirc vessels and boat displays, the piermaster's house and the pilotage buildings, now occupied by the **Museum of Liverpool Life** (*⏰ Albert Dock Open daily, 10am-5pm. ⏰ Closed 23-26, and 1 Jan. ∞ No charge. ☎ 0151 478 4080; www.museumofliverpoollife.org.uk.*) The museum traces the life and aspirations of the people of this hardworking city associated with the docks, the railways or car manufacturing.

Tate Liverpool★ – ♿ *Albert Dock. ⏰ Open Tue-Sun and Bank Hol Mon, 10am-5.50pm. ⏰ Closed 1 Jan, Good Fri and 24-26 Dec. ∞ No charge; special exhibitions £4; details by phone. ⏺ Guided tour (30min) daily at 2pm. Parking at King's Dock. Licensed café: Open gallery hours. ☎ 0151 702 7400; 0151 702 7402 (recorded information); Fax 0151 702 7401; liverpoolinfo@tate.org.uk; www.tate.org.uk/liverpool.* The Tate family originated in Liverpool and the choice of the city to house part of the national collection of 20C art was a happy one. The architect James Stirling, who also designed the Clore Gallery at the Tate in London, has created unobstructed display areas by retaining the cast-iron supports and perimeter wall. The transformed warehouse will eventually offer as much space as the parent gallery for semi-permanent exhibitions from the primary collections of 20C art and for temporary exhibitions.

The Beatles Story – ♿ *Britannia Vaults, Albert Dock. ⏰ Open daily, 10am-6pm (5pm last admission); ⏰ Closed 25-26 Dec. ∞ £8.99 . Parking. ☎ 0151 709 1963; www.beatlesstory. com.* Relive or discover the decade of the Beatles, the 1960s, the new phenomena of rock'n'roll, teenagers, the Merseybeat and Beatlemania. The original Beatles group consisted of **John Lennon** (1940-1980), **Paul McCartney** (b. 1942), **George Harrison** (1943-2001) and **Ringo Starr** (b. 1940); their manager was the late Brian Epstein. The places (the basement cellar club The Cavern, Strawberry Fields, Penny Lane, Hamburg) and the hits *(Strawberry Fields, Magical Mystery Tour, Sergeant Pepper's Lonely Hearts Club Band, Yellow Submarine among others)* are presented in a lively

Paul McCartney by Sam Walsh

National Portrait Gallery

and entertaining manner in this walk-through presentation.

20 Forthlin Road, Allerton – *⏰ Open late-Mar to late-Oct, Wed-Sun ⏺ Guided tours only. Access by minibus from Albert Dock and Speke Hall; call to check times and pick-up points. No photography. ∞ £6 (£12 joint ticket with Mendips). ☎ 0870 900 256 (infoline); 0151 427 7231 (bookings); 20forthlinroad@nationaltrust.org.uk; www.nationaltrust.org.uk.* The most popular Beatles tour is the two-hour **Magical Mystery Tour** (*⏰ daily from Tourist Information Centre at Queen Square at 2.10pm or at The Beatles Story at Albert Dock at 2.30pm ∞ £11.95. Advance reservations are recommended. ☎ 151 236 9091; www.cavern-liverpool.co.uk).*

Liverpool Anglican Cathedral★★ (EZ)

Although the cathedral is not oriented east-west, the cardinal points are used here as though it were. St James Mount. ⏰ Open daily, 8am-6pm. ∞ General admission: no charge, donations welcome; Tower & Embroidery Gallery, £2. ⏺ Guided tour (1hr) 10am-3pm. Leaflet (17 languages). Parking. Refectory; function room. Lift. ☎ 0151 709 6271; Fax 0151 709 7292; www.liverpoolcathedral.org.uk. On its ridge overlooking the Mersey, this monumental edifice in red sandstone is the largest Anglican church in the world. Work on it began in 1904 and it has taken most of the century to build, a triumphant reinterpretation of the Gothic tradition by its architect **Sir Giles Gilbert Scott** (1880-1960). On entering the nave one's first impression is that of the poet Sir John Betjeman – vastness, strength and height no words can describe. From the **nave bridge** one can admire Carl Edwards' west window; its Old Testament theme of the Benedict – *O all ye works of the Lord, bless ye the*

Lord is balanced by the New Testament Te Deum window at the east end. Scott's unusual design includes double western and eastern transepts and a **central space** (15 000sq ft/1 400m²) under the tower, giving an uninterrupted view of altar and pulpit. The tower (331ft/100m) extends the full width of the building and houses the heaviest ringing peal of bells in the world (31 tonnes). Set in the floor immediately below is the memorial to the architect, who once said of his design: "Don't look at my arches, look at my spaces." A Roman Catholic, he is buried just outside the west door.

In the western of the two south transepts is the **Baptistery**, with its marble font and a baldachin and font cover containing some of the finest wood carving in the cathedral. In the **choir** there are Liver Birds on the steps leading into the stalls. Beyond is the **Lady Chapel**★ which served as the cathedral from its completion in 1910 until the consecration of the main building in 1924; it has a notable reredos and a 15C Madonna by Giovanni della Robbia. In the south choir aisle is a memorial to Bishop Chavasse, who inspired the building of the cathedral. The foundation stone was laid in 1904 by King Edward VII; in 1978, at the service of dedication, his great-granddaughter Queen Elizabeth II unveiled a commemorative stone, fulfilling the hopes of three generations in the completed cathedral.

Metropolitan Cathedral of Christ the King★★ (EYZ)

♿ *Mount Pleasant.* 🕐 *Open daily, 8am-6pm (5pm Sun in winter). Donation. Parking.* ☎ *0151 709 9222; met.cathedral@boltblue.com; www.liverpoolmetrocathedral.org.uk.* It stands on Brownlow Hill, occupied from 1771 to 1928 by the Poor Law Institute, haven for Liverpool's destitute; the site seemed to the Diocesan authorities an apt one for the new cathedral. In 1930 **Sir Edwin Lutyens** was chosen as the architect and the foundation stone was laid on Whit Monday, 1933.

Building stopped in 1941; the crypt was completed after the war but inflation had raised the cost of the cathedral as planned to over £27 million. Architects were invited to submit plans which would make use of the existing crypt, cost no more than £1 million and be completed in five years. Sir Frederick Gibberd's design was chosen; building began in October 1962 and the completed cathedral was consecrated on the Feast of Pentecost, 14 May 1967.

The **exterior** is distinctive, an extraordinary buttressed circular structure in concrete, culminating in the lantern (290ft/88m high) with its crown of pinnacles. The main entrance, with its bronzed fibreglass doors carrying the emblems of the Evangelists, is set into the wedge-shaped belltower.

From the inner porch the High Altar is immediately visible, at the centre of the circular nave (194ft/60m in diameter). The **tower**, its stained glass in the colours of the spectrum with three bursts of white light representing the Trinity, rises above the **High Altar,** architectural as well as liturgical focal point. The baldachin is suspended from above; the candlesticks are short; the Crucifix is purposely narrow – all to ensure an uninterrupted view of the celebrant at the altar for every member of a full 2300-strong congregation. Near the entrance is the circular **Baptistery**. The font, with its dull silver cover, is a simple design in white marble, matching the High Altar.

The largest of the chapels around the circumference is the **Lady Chapel**, almost feminine in its gentleness and elegance.

In the crypt Lutyens' massive brick vaults now form four main areas, including a parochial hall, a venue for regular concerts and a museum recounting the story of the building of the cathedral.

This last area also has the **Chapel of Relics**, burial place of the Archbishops, which has as its door a fretted six-tonne marble disc, which rolls back as did the stone sealing the tomb of Christ.

World Museum

♿ *William Brown Street.* 🕐 *Open daily 10am-5pm.* 🚫 *1 Jan and 25-26 Dec.* ⊘ *No charge. To visit the planetarium you need to collect a timed ticket (no charge) from the information desk on the ground floor. Cafe. Shop.* ☎ *0151 478 4393; www.museumofliverpoollife.org. uk.* This eclectic new museum whose subjects range from live bugs to space exploration, combines historic treasures from across the globe with the latest interactive technology. Its internationally important collections include archaeology, ethnology and the natural and physical sciences as well as Britain's only free Planetarium. Its origins are the old Liverpool Museum and includes the major part of the collection of Joseph Mayer (a mid-19C local goldsmith and antiquarian) featuring Anglo-Saxon treasures, Egyptian mummies and Wedgwood china.

The Walker★★ (DY)

♿ *William Brown Street.* ⏰ *Open daily, 10am to 5pm.* ⏰ *Closed 1 Jan and 23-26 Dec. Cafeteria.* ☎ *0151 478 4199; Fax: 0151 478 4190; thewalker@nmgm.org.uk; www.thewalker.org.uk.* The gallery's collection of paintings, British and European, is among the best in the country.

Numerous painters of the Italian school are represented, from the 14C to the Renaissance and after, among them an exquisite Simone Martini *Christ Discovered in the Temple* and a Salvator Rosa *Landscape with Hermit.* There is a fine precisely-constructed Poussin, *Landscape with the Ashes of Phocion,* while the extensive holdings of Northern European art include works by Rembrandt, Elsheimer and the invitingly drowsy *Nymph of the Fountain* by Cranach.

The range of British work is particularly complete, extending from Elizabethan and later portraits to key works by Stubbs *(Horse Frightened by a Lion)*, Wright of Derby *(Easter Sunday at Rome)* and Richard Wilson *(Snowdon from Llan Nantlle)*; there are typically uncanny works by Fuseli and many **Pre-Raphaelites**, including Millais' *Lorenzo and Isabella* and Ford Madox Brown's *Coat of Many Colours* and narrative paintings like WR Yeames' *When did you last see your Father?* The gas-lit murk of Victorian Liverpool is evoked by Atkinson Grimshaw's *The Custom House,* a world away from the rustics and fisherfolk of Stanhope Forbes and George Clausen.

A small number of French Impressionists, Degas, Seurat and Monet, are juxtaposed with their British contemporaries like Sickert, whose Bathers at Dieppe are observed as through a camera's telephoto lens.

The good selection of modern British artists includes Gilman, Ginner and Bevan of the **Camden Town School**, Stanley Spencer and Lucian Freud, with a townscape, Villas at Cookham and Interior near Paddington respectively, both paintings of disturbing intensity. Paul Nash's surreal Landscape of the Moon's Last Phase contrasts with the cheerful townscape of Dame Laura Knight's Spring in St John's Wood or with the meticulously-detailed rural scenes of James McIntosh Patrick and Stanley Badmin.

St George's Hall (DY)

"One of the finest neo-Grecian buildings in the world" (Pevsner) was completed in 1854; it contains a circular Concert Room with caryatid gallery and a vast tunnel-vaulted Great Hall of more than Roman opulence.

The hall dominates the neighbouring neo-classical civic buildings which constitute the landward focal point of the city.

Statue of Eleanor Rigby (DY)

Stanley Street. The statue is the work of Tommy Steele, a contemporary of The Beatles, who created Eleanor; as in the song, she sits on a bench with shopping bag and headscarf, sharing her few crumbs with the sparrows; a plaque behind her dedicates the statue "To all the lonely people."

Round the corner in Mathew Street is the site of the Cavern Club, where the Beatles first performed, now marked by a modern precinct, Cavern Walks.

Bluecoat Arts Centre (DZ)

♿ *School Lane.* 🔒 *Closed for refurbishment.* ☎ *0151 709 5297; admin@bluecoatartcentre.com; www.bluecoatartscentre.com.* A Queen Anne building set round a cobbled court, founded 1717 as a charity school, now houses the Merseyside Arts Trust and series of exhibitions.

Western Approaches Museum

1 Rumford Street . ⏰ *Open Mar-Oct, Mon-Thu and Sat, 10.30am-4.30pm (3.30pm last admission).* 💷 *£4.75.* ☎ *0151 227 2008.* During the Second World War, the underground command headquarters for the battle of the Atlantic played a vital role. The labyrinth of rooms includes the main operations room and the Bombed-out room.

Sefton Park Palm House

Sefton Park, South Liverpool ♿⏰ *Open daily, usually 10.30am-4.30pm but enquire about special events* ☎ *0151 726 2415; Fax: 0151 726 2419; info@palmhouse.org.uk; www.palmhouse.org.uk.* This magnificent 3-tiered octagonal Grade II-listed Victorian glasshouse showcases the Liverpool Botanical collection.

Excursions

Southport – *20mi/32km north by A 565.* 🛈 *112 Lord Street, Southport* ☎ *01704 533 333* This elegant and dignified seaside resort is distinguished by its tree-lined streets, attractive flowerbeds and famous gardens; the Flower Show is held annually in late August. Broad and spacious **Lord Street,** where the shops have wrought-iron and glass-roofed canopies extending over the pavements, is the epitome of a Victorian promenade.

Children delight in the great stretches of sand (6mi/9km) and amusement parks. **Royal Birkdale** (south), the championship course, is one of several first-class golf courses in the locality.

Rufford Old Hall★ – *20mi/32km north A 59 (DY).* ♿ 🕐 *House: Open late-Mar to late-Oct, Sat-Wed, 1-5pm. Garden: Open as house, 11am-5.30pm.* ⬢ *£4.70; garden only, £2.60. Parking. Licensed restaurant. Wheelchairs available; braille guide.* ☎/*Fax 01704 821 254; ruffordoldhall@nationaltrust.org.uk; www.nationaltrust.org.uk.* Built by Sir Thomas Hesketh, who held the manor between 1416 and 1458, this is one of the finest 15C houses in Lancashire. The **Great Hall**★ has a magnificent **hammerbeam roof** and ornate carved screen. The Carolean wing was reconstructed in brick in 1662. There is much original furniture, arms and armour, and a folk museum.

Martin Mere Wildfowl and Wetlands Centre – *20mi/32km north by A 59 (DY) to Rufford and west by B 5246.* ♿ 🕐 *Open daily, 9.30am-5.30pm (5 pm in winter).* 🕐 *Closed 25 Dec.* ⬢ *£5.95 . Parking. Refreshments.* ☎ *01704 895 181; Fax 01704 892 343; info@ martinmere.co.uk; www.martinmere.co.uk.* The sanctuary, which provides hides and nature trails for birdwatchers, is a protected habitat (350 acres/140ha) for wildfowl. The mere is home to flamingos, black swans, geese and a winter haven to thousands of pink-footed geese, Icelandic Whooper swans and Bewick swans from Russia.

Wigan Pier – *19mi/31km northeast by A 59 (DY) and M 58.* ♿ 🕐 *Open Sun -Thu and Good Fri, 10am (11am Sun) to 5pm.* 🕐 *Closed 25-26 Dec, 1 Jan.* ⬢ *£5.25 . Parking. Refreshments.* ☎ *01942 323 666; Fax 01942 701 927; wiganpier@wiganmbc.gov.uk; www.wiganpier.net.* In 1936 when **George Orwell** was preparing *The Road to Wigan Pier* he had set his heart on seeing the celebrated Pier but he had to admit "Alas! Wigan Pier has been demolished, and even the spot where it used to stand is no longer certain." The canal warehouses (1770) have been restored and turned into a Heritage Centre, showing life as it was at the turn of the century.

Knowsley Safari Park – *8mi/13km east by A 5047* **(EY)** *and the east-bound carriageway of the A 58 (Prescot by-pass).* ♿🕐 *Open Mar-Oct, daily, 10am-4pm (last admission); Nov-Feb, 10.30am-3pm (last admission.* ⬢ *£9.50 . Parking. Amusement rides. Refreshments.* ☎ *0151 430 9009; Fax 0151 426 3677; www.knowsley.com.* It was in the menagerie, established at Knowsley in the 19C by the Earl of Derby, that **Edward Lear** made many of his animal drawings; the tales he told to Lord Derby's grandchildren became his Book of Nonsense. Today 30 species of mammal roaming 200 hectares of land, plus a few birds, reptiles and invertebrates make this one of the most interesting of private collections.

The National Wildflower Centre – *Just off junction 5 of the M62 (follow the brown tourist signs) or a short drive from Knowsley Safari Park (see directions above).* ♿🕐 *Court Hey Park. Apr-Sep 10am-5pm.* ⬢ *£3. Shop. Cafe. Play Area.* ☎ *0151 738 1913; Fax 0151 737 1820; info@nwc.org.uk; www.nwc.org.uk.* Set in a Victorian park within 35 acres of parkland this bucolic Millennium Commission attraction features seasonal wildflower displays, demonstration areas with events and activities, and a mix of old and award-winning new buildings.

The World of Glass – *12mi/18km east by A 5047 (EY) and A 57 to St Helens.* ♿🕐 *Open Tue-Sun, 10am-5pm and Bank Hol.* 🕐 *Closed 25-26 Dec, 1 Jan.* ⬢ *£5.30. Parking. Café.* ☎ *08707 444 777 (hotline); Fax 01744 616 966; info@worldofglass.com; www. worldofglass.com.* Pass through an inverted brick cone recalling the old furnaces into the modern building on the site of the pioneering Pilkington factory. As the story of glass unfolds from ancient Egypt and the glories of Venice, discover the magic of glass manufacture and its myriad uses; explore the tunnels of a Victorian furnace and admire the craftsmanship of modern artists.

Speke Hall★ – *Near the Airport, 8mi/13km southeast by A 561 (EZ).* ♿ *The Walk. House:* 🕐 *Open late-Mar to late-Oct, Wed-Sun and Bank Hol Mon, 1-5.30pm; late-Oct to early-Dec, Sat, 1-4.30pm. Garden and grounds: Open daily 11am-5.30pm (4pm mid-Oct to Mar).* 🕐 *Closed 24-26 Dec and 31 Dec-1 Jan. House and garden* ⬢ *£6.25; garden only, £3.25 . Guide book. Parking. Restaurant, picnic area. Wheelchair access to all areas except upper floor.* ☎ *0151 427 7231, 08457 585 702 (infoline); Fax 0151 427 9860; spekehall@ nationaltrust.org.uk; www.nationaltrust.org.uk.* This "black and white" Elizabethan manor house was built between 1490 and 1612 by successive generations of the

Norris family. The **Great Hall** is the oldest part of the building; its panelling, including the Great Wainscot of 1564, is particularly fine. The many smaller rooms reflect the Victorian preference for privacy and comfort. In the courtyard are two ancient yews, possibly pre-dating the house.

The Wirral

Under the Mersey by the Queensway Tunnel **(DY)***, then south by A 41*

The Wirral peninsula is a tongue of land bounded by the River Mersey and the River Dee.

Birkenhead – On the west bank of the Mersey, Birkenhead with its sweeping Victorian terraces and imposing stone houses grew rapidly in the 19C, following the starting of a regular ferry service in the 1820s and the opening of the docks in 1847.
4mi/6km south by A 41.

Port Sunlight – The model village was established in the late 19C by William Hesketh Lever for the workers of his soap factory, giving them a style of life very different from that of the crowded slums of the period. Lord Leverhulme's company became Unilever, one of the largest manufacturers of consumer goods.
The **Lady Lever Art Gallery**, *(&* *Open Mon-Sat, 10am-5pm, Sun noon-5pm.* *Closed 1 Jan and 25-27 Dec. Parking. Restaurant. Ramp, lift. ☎ 0151 478 4136)* also founded by Lord Leverhulme and opened in 1922, contains British paintings including Pre-Raphaelite works, period furniture, and a fine Wedgwood collection.
Take minor roads west via Junction 4 on M 53 and by B 5136 to Neston.

Ness Botanic Gardens – *&* *University of Liverpool Environmental & Horticultural Research Station.* *Open daily, 9.30am-5pm (4pm Nov-Feb).* *Closed 25 Dec.* *£4.70.* *Guided tour (90min). Parking. Licensed refreshments. Picnic area. Gift shop; plant sales. Wheelchair route. ☎ 0151 353 0123; ejs@liv.ac.uk; www.merseyworld.com/nessgardens.* The University of Liverpool Botanic Gardens, which are set on the south-facing slope of a sandstone hill overlooking the Dee Estuary and the Welsh Hills, have an extensive collection, particularly of rhododendrons, azaleas, alpines and heathers. Ness was the birthplace of Emma Hamilton, Lord Nelson's mistress.
Return east by minor road via Willaston; take M 53 south as far as Junction 9.

Ellesmere Port – *&* *Open Apr-Oct, daily, 10am-5pm; Nov-Mar, Sat-Wed, 11am-4pm.* *Closed 24-26 Dec.* *£6.45. Parking. Refreshments. ☎ 0151 355 5017; Fax 0151 355 4079; info@boatmuseum.freeserve.co.uk; www.boatmuseum.org.uk.* The **Boat Museum**, located where the Shropshire Union Canal meets the Manchester Ship Canal, has over 50 historic canal boats.
Visitors can make canal trips and, in the workshops, see restoration work being carried out.

Blue Planet Aquarium – *From the M6, join the M56 at J20, then head towards Ellesmere Port and turn onto the M53 at junction15. Follow the brown tourist information signs.* *&* *Cheshire Oaks.* *Open daily 10am-6pm during school holidays, and all weekends, 10am-5pm other times.* *£9.95. Scuba diving with sharks, e-mail for details. ☎ 0151 357 8804, ticket line 0906 941 0088; info@blueplanetaquarium.co.uk; www. blueplanetaquarium.co.uk.* This claims to be the largest "aquarium adventure" and to have more more types of shark (10 different species) than anywhere else in Britain. As you walk through the Aquatunnel, one of the longest in the world at 70m/230ft, large sand tiger sharks glide by, sometimes within inches of your head.

LLANDUDNO

Aberconwy and Colwyn, WALES

POPULATION 13 202

MICHELIN ATLAS P 33 OR MAP 503 I 24

TOWN PLAN IN THE MICHELIN GUIDE GREAT BRITAIN AND IRELAND

Safe sandy beaches make Llandudno a popular family summer holiday resort on the north coast. *1-2 Chapel Street, LL30 2YU ☎ 01492 876 413; Fax 01492 872 722; llandudno.tic@conwy.gov.uk; www.llandudno-tourism.co.uk.*

▶ **Orient Yourself**: City sightseeing buses operate a service between Llandudno and Conwy (*mid May-late Sept ☎ 01708 866 000; www.citysightseeing.co.uk*).

☺ **Don't Miss**: The Great Orme tramway; Bodelwyddan castle.

Kids **Especially for Kids**: The beach on the North Shore; for little ones The Alice in Wonderland Centre.

Seafront and Pier, Lllandudno

Visit

The **Pier**★ of 1875, a delicious confection in the Anglo-Indian style, is, unlike many contemporary structures of its kind, splendidly ship-shape. The family of Alice Liddell, inspiration for Lewis Carroll's immortal *Alice in Wonderland,* spent most of their holidays in Llandudno. A delightful statue of the White Rabbit stands on the West Shore and there are animated tableaux featuring the characters of *Wonderland* and *Through the Looking Glass* to be enjoyed in **The Alice in Wonderland Centre** (& *3&4 Trinity Square.* ◷ *Open daily, 10am-5pm (Mon-Sat Nov-Easter).* ◷ *Closed Christmas, New Year and Sun in winter. Audio guide (5 languages). Transcript (5 languages). Shop. ☎/Fax 01492 860 082; alice@wonderland.co.uk; www.wonderland. co.uk.*

The **Great Orme** (679ft/207m), reached by the **Tramway**★ which dates from 1903, by road or cabin lift, offers superb views of the coast and mountains of Snowdonia. The energetic can even walk up! Far underground are the caves and passageways of the **Great Orme Ancient Copper Mines,** (&◷ *Open Feb-Oct, daily, 10am-5pm.* ☞ *£5. Self guided tour available (1hr). Audio visual presentation. Parking. Refreshments. ☎/Fax 01492 870 447; gomines@greatorme.freeserve.co.uk; www.greatorme.freeserve. co.uk)* first worked by Bronze Age miners.

Excursions

Bodelwyddan★★ – *11mi/18km east by A 470 and A 55.* ⚅ 🕒 *Open Jul-Aug, daily, 10.30am-5pm; Apr-Jun and Sep-Oct, Sat-Thu and Good Fri, same times; Nov-Mar, Sat-Sun, 10.30am-4pm; last admission 1hr before closing.* ⚅ *£4.50. Audio guide, guide book and leaflet (4 languages); Braille guide.* ☎ *01745 584 060; Fax 01745 584 563; www.bodelwyddan-castle.co.uk.* Transformed in the course of the 19C to resemble a medieval stronghold, **Bodelwyddan Castle** has become a superb setting for a magnificent selection of **Victorian portraits** from the **National Portrait Gallery.** The paintings are hung in rooms whose fittings and furniture have been carefully and entertainingly chosen and arranged to evoke various themes. Thus the Billiard Room celebrates the masculine life of field, turf and boxing ring, the Library highlights eminent intellectuals and men of science, while the Drawing Room has many female portraits. The gardens have been restored to their Edwardian character.

On the opposite side of the road (A 55) stands **St Margaret's Church,** (♿🕒 *Open daily, 9am-5pm (later in summer). Services: Sun, 11am, 6pm (5pm in winter); Wed, 10am. Ramps.* ☎ *01745 583 034)* the "Marble Church," equal in its Victorian grandiloquence to the Castle. It was built in 1860 as a memorial to Baron Willoughby de Broke and its sumptuous interior incorporates no fewer than 13 different varieties of marble.

Rhuddlan Castle★★ – *16mi/26km east by A 470, A 5 and A 547. Castle Street.* 🕒 *Open late-Mar to late-Sep, daily, 10am-5pm.* ⚅ *£2.75.* ☎ *01745 590777; www.rhyl.com/rhuddlan.html.* Diggers from the Fens and elsewhere laboured for three years during the war of 1277 to divert the River Clwyd, so that a castle which could be supplied from the sea could be built. A town grew up which, in the war of 1282, replaced Chester as the main base of operations against the Welsh in Snowdonia. In 1284 the "Statute of Wales" was issued here, as the plaque on the so-called "Parliament House" in the High Street records, "securing to the Principality of Wales its judicial rights and independence." A few beam holes, foundations and roof creases are all that remain today of the splendour of the black-and-white timber-framed buildings around the Inner Ward, which rang then with laughter and music, and no trace at all remains of the little garden made for the Queen. It is likely that Edward presented his Welsh-born son, the future Edward II, to the assembled princes of Wales at Rhuddlan, rather than at Caernarfon, as tradition has it. The castle was partly demolished after the Civil War. Entry to the remains is by the **west gatehouse**, the best surviving feature. First and second floors provided comfortable apartments with fireplaces. Similar suites must have existed in the east gatehouse. The concentric plan of the castle within its wide dry moat, with lower walls to the outer ward and a defended river wall and dock, can still be traced on the ground.

St Asaph Cathedral★ – *15mi/24km east by B 5155 and A 55.* ♿ *High Street.* 🕒 *Open daily, 8am-6pm . Guided tour (1hr). Fact sheet (3 languages). Parking. Braille guide.* ☎ *01745 583 429, 583 597; www.stasaphcathedral.org.uk.* This is the second smallest cathedral city in the country, after St David's. St. Kentigern founded the cathedral and a monastic community on the site in AD 560. The present **cathedral**★, mainly 13C, houses the Bible used at the investiture of the Prince of Wales in 1969 and the memorial of Bishop William Morgan, translator of the Bible into Welsh in 1588 - "Religion, if not taught in mother tongue, will lie hidden and unknown."

Henry Morton Stanley (1841-1904), African explorer in his own right, but best known for his remark "Doctor Livingstone, I presume," was brought up in the workhouse at St Asaph but born in Debigh.

Denbigh - *10.5 mi/8km south by A 525.* The market town is clustered on a hillside overlooking the Vale of Clwyd and dominated by the ruins of the **castle**★ built by Henry de Lacy in 1282, on the orders of Edward I after he defeated Llywelyn. The three interlinked 14C towers of the gatehouse, similar in plan to Caernarfon, probably show the influence of the King's master mason, James of St George. The town walls, still almost complete, date from the same period, with the Burgess Gate being the main entrance to the town.

LLANGOLLEN ★

Denbighshire, WALES

POPULATION 2 546

MICHELIN ATLAS P 33 OR MAP 503 K 25

The verdant Vale of Llangollen and the valley of the Dee have long formed a convenient route for travellers from England on their way to North Wales; the little market town, dominated by the dramatically sited ruins of the 12C Castle Dinas Brân, is still a popular stopping place.

Llangollen hosts the **International Eisteddfod** (Festival) and many other events in and around the spectacular tent-like structure of the **Royal International Pavilion** and the town's international standing is reinforced by the presence of the International Centre for Traditional and Regional Cultures, **ECTARC.** 🖪 *Town Hall, Castle Street, Llangollen, LL20 5PD* ☎ *01978 860 828 ; Fax : 01978 861 928: contact@ llangollen.org.uk; www.llangollen.org.uk*

Visit

Plas Newydd★ – *10min on foot from the town centre.* 🚻 🕓 *Open Easter to October 10am-5pm.* 👓 *£5. Guide book (5 languages). Parking (7min from house); limited parking close to house. Tearoom. Access for disabled visitors to ground, first floor (stair climber) and grounds.* ☎ *01978 861314 www.llangollen.com/plas.html.* From 1780, when they arrived from Ireland and set up house together, it was the home of **The Ladies of Llangollen.** Lady Eleanor Butler and Miss Sarah Ponsonby caused considerable comment at the time but entertained a constant stream of distinguished visitors at their home. They began the transformation of a humble cottage into the eccentric "black and white" building it is today. They are buried in the nearby St Collen's Church, under a roof believed to have been taken from Valle Crucis Abbey at the Dissolution.

Excursions

Llangollen Railway

🚻 🕓 *Operates May-Oct, Mon-Fri at 11am, 1pm, 3pm; Sat at 11am, 12.40pm, 2.20pm, 4pm; Sun, 11am-4pm (hourly); Sep-Oct, Sat-Sun at 10.45am, 12.30pm, 2.15pm, 4pm.* 👓 *£8 return. Refreshments.* ☎ *01978 860 951 (24hr talking timetable), 01978 860 979 (enquiries); Fax 01978 869 247; office@llangollen-railway.co.uk; www.llangollen-railway. co.uk.* This is the only standard-gauge preserved steam railway in Wales; the regular services are perhaps the best way of exploring the Vale of Llangollen upstream as far as Glyndyfrdwy.

Canal Trips – *Llangollen Wharf.* 🕓 *Open late-Mar to Oct, daily.* 🕓 *Sometimes closed Oct, Thu-Fri, except in school hols.* 👓 *£7.* ☎ *01978 860 702; sue@horsedrawnboats.co.uk; www.horsedrawnboats.co.uk.* A more relaxing way of enjoying the scenery around Llangollen is to take a ride on a **horse-drawn barge** on the winding Llangollen branch of the Shropshire Union Canal built by Telford mainly as a feeder supplying water to the system from the River Dee; the towpath follows the narrowing canal westward to join the Dee at Telford's **Horseshoe Falls**, a curving weir of great elegance in a romantic setting. You can also hire a barge from here to cross the spectacular Pont Cysyllte "stream in the sky" (🕯 *see below*).

Valle Crucis Abbey – *2mi/3km north by A 542.* 🚻 🕓 *Open Mar-Sept 10am-5pm, grounds open year round.* 👓 *£2.* ☎ *01978 860 326; www.llangollen.com/valle.html.* Beautifully sited ruins of an important Cistercian abbey, founded 1201, whose name is taken from the **Pillar of Eliseg**, a 9C cross commemorating the ancient Kings of Powys. The abbey was well known for its patronage of the bards; Iolo Goch, a 14C poet from Dyffryn, is buried here. The Early English west front still stands and the vaulted and ribbed 14C **chapter house** is intact.

Wrexham (Wrecsam) – *13mi/21km northeast by A 539 and A 483.* Wrexham is the largest town in North Wales; its long-standing prosperity stems from its position between profitable coal seams and rich agricultural land. In the churchyard of the fine Perpendicular Gothic **St Giles Church** ★ (🚻 🕓 *Open Apr-Oct, Mon-Fri, 10am-4pm.* ☎ *01978 355 808; Fax 01978 313 375; wrexhamparish@aol.com.)* is buried **Elihu Yale** (1649-1721). His gifts to Newhaven College in America caused it to be named Yale

University in his honour. His family had come from near Wrexham, returning to Britain when Elihu was two years old. He spent much of his life in the East India Company and his epitaph starts: "Born in America, in Europe bred, in Africa travelled, and in Asia wed, where long he liv'd and thriv'd: in London dead." The **Royal Welch Fusiliers** have their Memorial Chapel, Roll of Honour and Colours in St Giles.

Erddig★★ – *2mi/3km south of Wrexham (see above), off A 525.* ♿ 🕐 *House: Open late-Mar to Oct, Sat-Wed and Good Fri, noon-5pm (4pm Oct); last admission 1hr before closing. Garden: Open Mar-Oct, Sat-Wed and Good Fri, 11am (10am Jul-Aug) to 6pm (5pm Oct-Nov). House, outbuildings and gardens ⊜ £7.40; garden and outbuildings only, £3.80. Parking. Licensed restaurant. Access to the house difficult for wheelchairs; boarded walk in the park. ☎ 01978 355 314; 01978 315 151 (infoline); Fax 01978 313 333; erddig@nationaltrust.org.uk; www.nationaltrust.org.uk.* This late 17C house was rescued in 1973 from dereliction due to mining subsidence. It contains much furniture of outstanding quality, supplied for it in the 1720s, as well as magnificent porcelain, tapestries and paintings. There is also a unique collection of portraits, photographs and poetic descriptions of staff. The restored joiner's shop, sawpit, laundry, bakehouse, kitchen and servants' hall all furnish an insight into the complex running of a country estate.

The **State Bedroom** with 18C Chinese wallpaper contains the magnificently restored bed from 1720.

The early 18C formal garden survived, at least in outline, and has now been restored.

Chirk Castle★★ – *7mi/11km east by A 5.* ♿ *Castle:* 🕐 *Open late Mar to Oct, Wed-Sun and Bank Hol Mon, noon-5pm (4pm Oct). Gardens: Open same hours as castle, 11am-6pm (5pm Oct). ⊜ £6.40, castle and gardens; £4, gardens only. Parking 200yds/180m from castle; courtesy coach from car park to castle. Licensed tearoom. Stairclimber. ☎ 01691 777 701; Fax 01691 774 706; chirkcastle@nationaltrust.org.uk.* Chirk Castle, or Castell y Waun, was built to a design similar to that of Beaumaris (👆 *see Isle of ANGLESEY*), started the same year, 1295. It is unique in having been in continuous occupation from then until the present day and shows the adaptation of a great fortress to the changing needs of later times. The **State Rooms** in the north wing are the great glory of Chirk today.

Chirk stands in a landscape park of great splendour and extent, in part laid out in the late 18C by William Emes, a follower of Capability Brown. Close to the house, topiary and hedging recall the formal gardens swept away by Emes but the most distinctive feature of the grounds are the **wrought-iron gates**★, a Baroque masterpiece made at the nearby Bersham iron works.

Pont Cysyllte★★ – *4mi/7km east by A 539.* One of the great monuments of the industrial age, this magnificent aqueduct was built 1795-1810 by the great engineer Thomas Telford to carry the Ellesmere Canal over the River Dee. Throughout its length (1007ft/307m) it is accompanied by a towpath protected from the drop (121ft/23m) by iron railing.

LONDON

POPULATION 6 679 699

MICHELIN ATLAS P 19-21 AND MAP 504 T 29

London is the commercial, political and artistic capital of the United Kingdom, and one of the great financial centres of the world. Although the one city plays several roles, it has twin centres – the City of London, known as **The City**, for trade and commerce, and the City of Westminster, known as the **West End**, for royal palaces and parliament, theatres and entertainment, art and fashion.
For tourist information, see the Address Book.

▶ **Orient Yourself**: Most sightseeing and tourist activites are confined to Westminster, the West End and Kensington. The underground is the most effective way of getting around town, though buses will allow you to see more. Taxis are expensive. Always catch a (licensed) black taxi cab unless your hotel recommends another taxi company. Short distances are best covered on foot. There are various bus sightseeing tours, of which The Big Bus Company (*www.bigbustours.com*) is among the best.

⊙ **Don't Miss**: The BA London Eye, British Museum, National Gallery, Covent Garden, Westminster Abbey, Tower of London, Kew Gardens, Hampton Court Palace, Greenwich by river boat.

⊙ **Organizing Your Time**: Allow at least 4 days.

▦ **Especially for Kids**: Natural History Museum; hands-on fun in the Science Museum; buskers and toyshops in Covent Garden; London Zoo; London Dungeon (teens only).

➥ **Walking Tours:** There are many walking tour operators, the best is the Original London Walks (*http://london.walks.com*).

A Bit of History

Although the name London is of Celtic origin, the city only began to take shape under the Romans, who made it the hub of their road system, enclosed it with walls and built the first London Bridge. Remains of the Roman walls, together with medieval additions, are still visible in the street called London Wall and near the Tower of London.

It was Edward the Confessor (1042-66) who established the rival centre at Westminster, when he built a royal palace and founded an abbey, the minster in the west as opposed to St Paul's Cathedral, the minster in the east.

In fact London did not become the official capital of England until the mid 12C, as until then Winchester had been more important administratively. The City and its busy

Tower Bridge

Brigitta L. House/MICHELIN

port gained considerable freedom and independence from the crown, which was often dependent on the City merchants for raising money for military expeditions. The City did not encroach on Westminster and, with few notable exceptions, citizens held no office under the Crown or Parliament but there was however much traffic between the two centres, originally by water – later by road. The great houses of the nobility lined the Strand along the north bank of the Thames and city merchants built elegant mansions in the less crowded West End or the villages such as Islington, Holborn and Chelsea.

The overcrowding in the City was somewhat reduced by the ravages of the **Great Plague** (1665), in which 75 000 out of 460 000 people died, and of the **Great Fire** (1666) which destroyed 80% of the buildings. Within six days of the end of the fire, Christopher Wren, then 33 years old, submitted a plan to rebuild the City with broad straight streets. It was not accepted and, although the authorities stipulated that the buildings should be of brick and slate, rebuilding took place round the tiny courts and along the narrow streets of the medieval city. Wren was however commissioned to build the new St Paul's Cathedral and the majority of the city churches, which demonstrate his great ingenuity in fitting them into narrow and awkward sites.

As the population continued to expand, the parish vestries, who were responsible for drainage, paving, lighting and the maintenance of the streets, proved unable or unwilling to control the proliferation of poor quality housing, to limit the increase in traffic and to provide sanitation. The appalling conditions of the 18C are strikingly illustrated in the work of **William Hogarth**; there are vivid descriptions of the poverty of the 19C in the journalism and novels of **Charles Dickens** and in Henry Mayhew's Survey of the London Poor, 1850.

Address Book

OUT AND ABOUT IN LONDON

Tourist Information Centre – The main tourist information point is the Britain and London Visitor Centre, 1 Lower Regent Street, SW1Y 4NS. ☎ 0870 156 6366; www. visitlondon.com. For what is happeneing specifically in the City (London's ancient square mile), go to the City of London Information Centre, St Paul's Churchyard, EC4. ☎ 020 7332 1456; www.cityoflondon. gov.uk. There are also information centres at Richmond and Greenwich.

Public Transport – Transport for London is the body responsible for running the tube (underground), buses, overground trains including the Docklands Light Railway (DLR) and Thames riverboats. There are individual and combined tickets, available by the journey, day, multiple days or longer, suitable for every kind of travel. Most types of ticket can be bought in advance at bus and main underground stations. There are travel information offices at Heathrow Airport, Euston railway station, Liverpool Street underground station and Victoria (train station and coach station) ☎ 020 7222 1234; www.tfl.gov.uk.

Sightseeing – Tours on open-topped buses start from Victoria, Green Park, Piccadilly, Coventry Street, Trafalgar Square, Haymarket, Lower Regent Street, Marble Arch, Baker Street, Tower Hill. Some tours are non-stop; some allow passengers to hop on or off and continue on a later bus. Ticket prices vary. For guided walking tours consult the Britain and London Visitor Centre or press listings (*Time Out*).

Thames cruises start from Westminster Pier, Charing Cross Pier, Tower Pier, Greenwich Pier. Evening cruises with music and/or a meal are also available.

The **London Waterbus Company** operates a regular service along the Regent's Canal ☎ 020 7482 2550; www. londonwaterbus.com. Also Jason's Trip ☎ 020 7286 3428; www.jasons.co.uk, and Jenny Wren ☎ 020 7485 6210.

Pubs and Restaurants – There is a wide choice of traditional pubs and wine bars in all areas. Restaurants specialising in all kinds of cuisine abound. See the Michelin Red Guide to London for detailed information and prices. Afternoon tea at some of the large hotels or at Fortnum and Mason is a great treat.

Shopping – Visit Knightsbridge (Harrods, Harvey Nichols), Bond Street (fashion, antiques), Oxford and Regent Streets (department stores), King's Road (boutiques, antiques), Kensington High Street (large stores and boutiques), Covent Garden (boutiques and crafts), Piccadilly (gentlemen's outfitters, sportswear)

Entertainment – Theatres, cinemas, nightclubs and music venues are to BE found in the area around Leicester Square, Piccadilly and Covent Garden. Consult the daily press (*Evening Standard*) or *Time Out* (published Wednesdays) for listings.

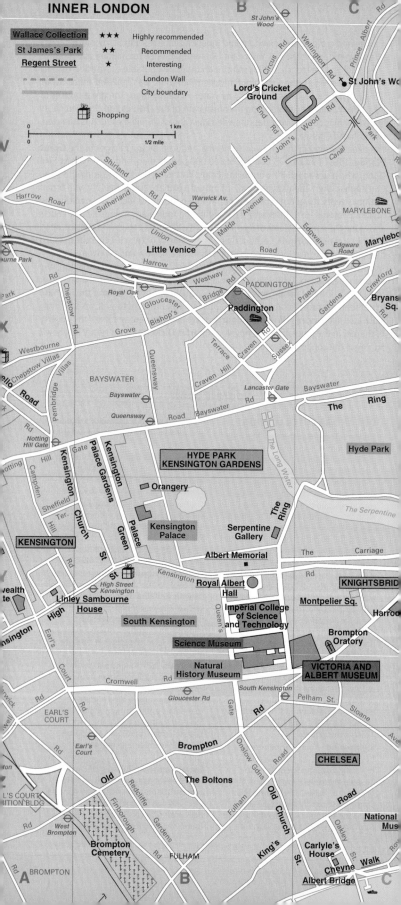

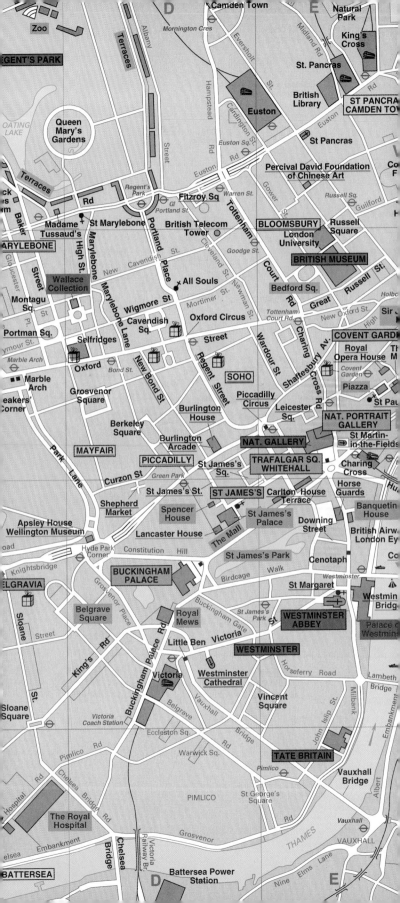

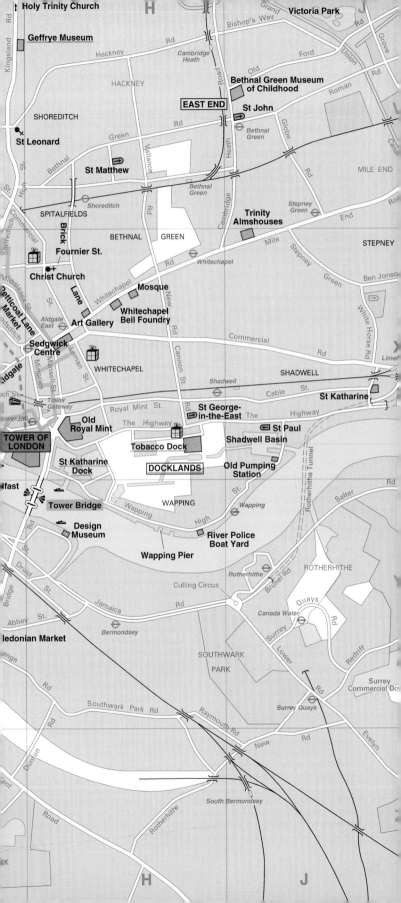

Address Book

For coin ranges, see the Legend at the back of the guide.

WHERE TO EAT

INNER LONDON

Cigala, *54 Lamb's Conduit Street, WC1N 3LW,* ☎*020 7405 1717; tasty@cigala. co.uk; www.cigala.co.uk.* This smart Spanish restaurant is simply furnished with large windows and an open-plan kitchen offering an authentic taste of robust cooking; informal tapas bar downstairs.

Fino, *33 Charlotte St (entrance on Rathbone St), W1T 1RR,* ⊖ *Goodge Street,* ☎*020 7813 8010; www.finorestaurant.com. Closed Sun, bank hols.* This new-wave Spanish tapas bar in a trendy basement offers a wide range of authentic dishes and is acclaimed as the probably the best Iberian restaurant in London.

Hakkassan, *8 Hanway Place, WT1 IHD,* ⊖ *Tottenham Court Road,* ☎*020 7907 1888.* Beautifully lit and styled, this is London's most distinctive modern interpretation of Cantonese cooking (specials include Dim Sum, Peking Duck with Beluga caviar), set in a cavernous basement.

Incognico, *117 Shaftesbury Ave, WC2H 8AD* ⊖ *Covent Garden* ☎ *020 7836 8866; www.incognico.com. Closed Sun.* Situated in the heart of theatreland, Incognico (named after proprietor and superchef Nico Ladenis) has the atmosphere and look of a classical French brasserie, serving top-class, pared-down French and English classics.

Mela, *152-156 Shaftesbury Ave, WC2H 8HL,* ☎*020 7836 8635; Fax* ☎*020 7379 0527; info@ melarestaurant.co.uk; www. melarestaurant.co.uk.* Tasty Indian "country-style" food in a bright modern buzzing environment in the heart of Theatreland.

Archipelago, *110 Whitfield Street,W1T 5ED,* ☎*020 7383 3346. Closed Sat lunch, Sun, bank hols.* Eccentric in both menu (reindeer carpaccio, cricket and locust salad, blackened kangaroo) and décor this is not for the faint hearted but does offer a taste of food from around the world.

Crazy Bear, *26-28 Whitfield St, WT1 2RG,* ⊖ *Goodge Street,* ☎*020 7631 0088; www.crazybeargroup.co.uk. Closed Sat lunch, Sun, bank hols.* Sleek and savvy this new hyper-chic restautant is a mixture of Orient Express and New York style with art deco inspired fittings and an Asian menu with strong Thai leanings –very much for the smart set.

CHELSEA AND EARL'S COURT

Eight Over Eight, *392 Kings Rd, SW3 5UZ,* ⊖ *Sloane Square,* ☎*020 7349 9934; www.eightovereight.nu. Closed Sun. lunch.* Enjoy inventive unusual combinations of Pan Asian (mostly Chinese, Japanese, Thai) dishes in chic, comfortable Chelsea surroundings with bargain lunchtime deals and Dim Sum available all day.

Hollywood Arms, *45 Hollywood Rd, SW10 9HX,* ⊖ *Earl's Court.* ☎*020 7349 7840.* Stylish period gastro-pub popular with the Chelsea set, offering a concise menu with Mediterranean influences and flavours.

Langan's Coq D'Or Bar and Grill, *254-260 Old Brompton Rd, SW5 9HR,* ⊖ *Earl's Court.* ☎*020 7259 2599; www. langansrestaurants.co.uk. Closed bank hols.* This classic buzzy brasserie incorporates a bar and grill, an outdoor terrace and offers excellent value classic and Modern British cooking.

Le Cercle, *1 Wilbraham Place, SW1X 9AE,* ⊖ *Sloane Square,* ☎*020 7901 9999; Closed Sun, Mon.* This discreetly designed basement restaurant in residential Chelsea offes accomplished tapas-style French menus.

Mao Tai, *96 Draycott Avenue, SW3 3AD* ⊖ *South Kensington,* ☎*020 7225 2500; Fax* ☎*020 7225 1965; info@maotai.co.uk; www. maotai.co.uk.* Excellent MSG-free Chinese food in a buzzy brasserie environment, featuring Dim Sum until 8pm, unique Szechuan menus and some highly original dishes.

Brasserie St Quentin, *243 Brompton Road, SW3 4NX,* ⊖ *Sloane Square,* ☎*020 7589 8005; Fax* ☎*020 7584 6064; reservations@brasseriestquentin.co. uk; www.brasseriestquentin.co.uk.* This long established Parisian-style brasserie serves simple classic dishes at an affordable price in a lively atmosphere with banquettes and rows of closely set tables.

Daphne's, *112 Draycott Avenue London, SW3 3AE,* ☎*020 7589 4257; www. daphnes-restaurant.co.uk.* A long-time favourite with the Chelsea set the food here is classic Italian inspired while the terracotta tones in the bricked dining room is resonant with rustic Tuscan charm

Le Colombier, *145 Dovehouse St, SW3 6LB,* ⊖ *South Kensington,* ☎*020 7351 155.* A fiercely Gallic restaurant with bright and cheerful surroundings including an attractive enclosed terrace, serving traditional French cooking.

Manicomio, *85 Duke of York Square, SW3 4LY,* ⊖ *Sloane Square,* ☎*020 7730 3366.* Choose from the main restaurant or the café next door, both serving rustic Italian food; perfect venue for outdoor dining on a delightful terrace overlooking the square.

⊜⊜ **Rasoi Vineet Bathia**, *10 Lincoln St, SW3 2TS, ☎020 7225 1881; www. vineetbhatia.com. Closed Sat lunch, Sun, bank hols.* Owned and run by the first Indian chef to be awarded a Michelin Star, this is London's top Indian restaurant of the moment set in an elegant mid-19C Chelsea townhouse.

CITY

⊜ **Almeida,** *30 Almeida Street, N1 1AD,* ⊖ *Old Street, ☎020 7354 4777; www.conran-restaurants.co.uk.* A member of the Conran Group this spacious open-plan restaurant serves high quality classic French dishes in a contemporary setting next to Islington's Almeida Theatre.

⊜ **Brasserie La Trouvaille,** *353 Upper St., N1 0PD,* ⊖ *Angel, ☎020 7704 8323. Closed Mon; lunch Tue.* Near Camden Passage this appealing brasserie offers classic cooking (cassoulet, escargot) in two rooms with warm yellow walls and simple furniture.

⊜ **Drapers Arms,** *44 Barnsbury St, N1 1ER,* ⊖ *Highbury & Islington, ☎020 7619 0348.* This impressive Georgian gastropub features rough wooden floors, leather sofas, tables and booths along walls made over with a contemporary palette and serves modern British and international dishes.

⊜ **Smiths of Smithfield,** *Top Floor, 67-77 Charterhouse St, EC1M 6HJ,* ⊖ *Barbican, ☎020 7251 7950. Closed Sat lunch.* The higher you go the more formal it gets at this ever popular bustling three-storey shrine to Modern British cooking with good views of Smithfield Market from the top terrace.

⊜⊜ **Bonds,** *5 Threadneedle Street, EC2R 8AY,* ⊖ *Bank, ☎020 7657 8090; www. theetongroup.com. Closed Sat, Sun.* This beautifully appointed and modernized grand 19C City building holds a vast dining room with high pillars offering Modern French Cuisine in a relaxing yet exciting environment

⊜⊜ **Club Gascon,** *57 West Smithfield, EC1A 9DS,* ⊖ *Barbican, ☎020 7796 0600; Closed Sat lunch, Sun, bank hols.* The rich flavours of South West France, specifically Gascony and its many variations on foie gras are the forte of this acclaimed intimate and rustic restaurant on the edge of Smithfield Market.

⊜⊜ **Coq d'Argent,** *1 Poultry, EC2R 8EJ* ⊖ *Bank, ☎020 7395 5000; www.conran-restaurants.co.uk. Closed Sun. dinner.* Regional French food, highlighted by popular shellfish dishes, is served in a spectacular dining room which, like its spacious lawned al fresco roof terrace, offers a unique rooftop site and views over the City of London.

⊜⊜ **Metrogusto,** *13 Theberton St, NI 0QY,* ⊖ *Highbury & Islington, ☎020 7226 9400; www.metrogusto.co.uk. Closed Sun; lunch Mon-Thu.* Progressive Italian cooking is the theme at this stylish, smart contemporary Islington restaurant adorned with striking modern art.

⊜⊜ **Rhodes Twenty Four,** *Tower 42, 25 Old Broad St, EC2N 1HQ,* ⊖ *Liverpool Street, ☎020 7877 7703; www.rhodes24.co. uk. Closed Sat, Sun, bank hols.* On the 24th Floor of the City's tallest tower block the quality of the modern Classic British cuisine (e.g. braised oxtail cottage pie) served by one of the country's best known chefs, is as elevated as the views.

COVENT GARDEN, SOHO, CHINATOWN

⊜ **Aurora,** *49 Lexington St, W1F 9AJ,* ⊖ *Piccadilly Circus.* An informal Bohemian bistro with a languid atmosphere, a small but pretty walled garden terrace and a short but balanced menu of simple fresh food.

⊜ **L'Escargot,** *48 Greek St, W1D 4EF,* ⊖ *Tottenham Court Road, ☎020 7437 6828; www.whitestarline.org.uk. Ground Floor closed Sat lunch, Sun; Picasso Room closed Saturday lunch, Sun, Mon.* This old favourite, now under Marco Pierre White, features a chic vibrant brasserie while upstairs the Picasso Room is famed for its artworks and provides a more intimate and discreet ambience for fine French dining.

⊜ **Vasco & Piero's Pavilion,** *15 Poland St, W1F 8QE,* ⊖ *Tottenham Court Road, ☎020 7437 8774. Closed Sun, Sat lunch, bank hols.* A longstanding family-run Italian restaurant with a loyal local following, offering a warm welcome and traditional cooking.

⊜ **Bank,** *1 Kingsway, WC2B 6XF,* ⊖ *Covent Garden, ☎020 7379 9797; www. bankrestaurants.com. Closed Sun, Sat lunch and bank hols.* Set in the heart of theatreland this is a stylish bustling brasserie featuring a sweeping chandelier with almost three thousand glass shards, and a vast mural stretches from bar to restaurant. The open-plan kitchen provides an extensive array of modern dishes.

⊜⊜ **J Sheekey,** *28-32 St Martin's Court WC2N 4AL,* ⊖ *Leicester Square, ☎020 7240 2565.* One of London's oldest traditional fish restaurants, festooned with photos of thespians, its wood panels and alcove tables create a famed intimate atmosphere.

⊜⊜ **St John,** *26 St. John St, EC1M 4AY,* ⊖ *Barbican, 020 7251 0848; www. stjohnrestaurant.com. Closed Sun.* This very popular converted 19C smokehouse specializes in hearty English fare including offal and an original mix of traditional and rediscovered dishes.

⊜⊜ **Yauatcha,** *15 Broadwick Street W1F 0DL,* ⊖ *Tottenham Court Road, 020 7494 8888.* This upmarket Chinese restaurant is a conversion of a Soho post office; below is a smart cool tea room, above a spacious dining room serving unusual refined authentic dishes including quail and venison.

KENSINGTON, SOUTH KENSINGTON

Notting Hill Brasserie, *92 Kensington Park Rd, W11 2PN,* Notting Hill Gate, ☎*020 7229 4481. Closed Sun.* Modern comfortable restaurant with quiet formal atmosphere set over four rooms serving contemporary European dishes

The Waterway, *54 Formosa St, W9 2JU,* Warwick Avenue, ☎*020 7266 3557; www.thewaterway.co.uk.* Pub (though hardly recognizable as such) with a thoroughly modern metropolitan ambience right on the waterfront in leafy Maida Vale; the young and trendy tuck into Modern British favourites on a large decked terrace.

Wódka, *12 St Alban's Grove, W8 5PN,* High Street Kensington, ☎*020 7937 66513; www.wodka.co.uk. Closed Sat lunch, Sun.* Some of London's best Polish and East European food (plus vodkas) served in a simple mellow setting in a former dairy retaining its old tiles and panelled walls. Good value lunch

Assaggi, *39 Chepstow Place (above Chepstow Pub), W2 4TS,* Bayswater, ☎*020 7792 5501. Closed two weeks Christmas, Sun, bank hols.* Polished wood floorings, tall windows and modern artwork provides the bright surroundings for this perennially popular establishment serving a concise menu of robust Italian dishes with favourites including tagliolini alle erbe and fritto misto.

Babylon, *(at the Roof Gardens) 7th Floor, 99 Kensington High St, W8 5SA (entrance on Derry Street),* High Street Kensington, ☎*020 7368 3993; www. roofgardens.com. Closed Sat lunch, Sun dinner.* In a stunning roof top garden setting with an al fresco option in warm weather, this stylish modern dining room offers contemporary British cooking. Good value lunch.

Belvedere, *off Abbotsbury Rd, Holland Park, W8 6LU,* Holland Park, ☎*020 7602 1238; www.whitestarline.org. uk. Closed Sun dinner.* Dating back to the 17C this was once the summer ballroom to the Jacobean mansion that was Holland House, then the orangery, set in the middle of one of London's most beautiful parks, in one of the capital's most fashionable areas. Modern take on classic dishes.

Clarke's, *122-4 Kensington Church St,W8 4BH,* Notting Hill Gate, ☎*020 7221 9225; www.sallyclarke.com. Closed 10 days Christmas to New Year.* One of London's top restaurateurs, Sally Clark, personally oversees the kitchen providing modern British cooking in comfortable bright neighbourhood surroundings.

Kensington Place, *201 Kensington Church St, W8 7LX,* Notting Hill, ☎*020 7727 3184.* This long established restaurant set the trend for large bustling informal eating and still attracts the crowds with its modern cooking.

Notting Grill, *123 Clarendon Rd, W11 4JG,* Holland Park, ☎*020 7229 1500. Open dinner only and lunch Sat and Sun.* This converted rustic-style pub specializes in well-sourced quality meats, particularly steaks.

KNIGHTSBRIDGE, ETC

Cross Keys, *1 Lawrence St, SW3 5NB,* Sloane Square, ☎*020 7349 9111; www. thexkeys.co.uk. Closed bank hols.* Behind a 200-year old pub façade lies a spacious bar with tall windows that goes up to a gallery with large mirrors, a huge curly chandelier and rustic tools that have coined the tongue-in-cheek term Chelsea Ironic-Rustic. Flavoursome generous Modern British food.

The Ebury Brasserie, *11 Pimlico Rd, SW1W 8NA,* Sloane Square, ☎*020 7730 6784; www.theebury.co.uk.* Typical new-wave London brasserie with walnut bar, simple tables, a large seafood bar and a very high standard of modern cooking with a wide-ranging menu from snacks to full meals.

Amaya, *Halkin Arcade, 19 Motcomb St, SW1X 8JT,* Knightsbridge, ☎*020 7823 1166; www.realindianfood.com.* London's Indian restaurant of the moment, Amaya specializes in different Indian grilling methods in full view of diners in a specially designed open show kitchen which turns out light, piquant and aromatic dishes. Modern subtly exotic surroundings.

Mango Tree, *46 Grosvenor Place, SW1X 7EQ,* Victoria, ☎*020 7823 1888; www.mangotree.org.uk.* Authentic and traditional Thai dishes become works of art in this sleek contemporary minimalist Belgravia dining room.

Olivo, *21 Eccelston St, SW1W 9LX,* Victoria, ☎*020 7730 2505.* Simple, unfussy Italian cuisine which relies on the quality of seasonal ingredients is the key at this welcoming rustic informal establishment.

La Poule au Pot, *231 Ebury St, SW1W 8UT,* Sloane Square, ☎*020 7730 7763.* Subdued lighting and friendly informality make this one of London's more romantic restaurants serving a classic French menu with extensive *plats du jour.*

MARYLEBONE, ETC

The Abbey Road, *63 Abbey Rd, NW8 0AE,* St John's Wood, ☎*020 7328 6426. Closed Mon lunch.* Grand gastropub with a patio terrace for summer, a snazzy duck-egg blue dining room with French posters, high ceilings and ornate mirrors, plus large windows that let you see and be seen. Modern Mediterranean style menus.

Sardo Canale, *42 Gloucester Ave, NW1 8JD,* Chalk Farm, ☎*020 7722 2800; www.sardocanale.com. Closed Mon.* Next to the Regent's Canal, sit indoors in one of five snug modern dining rooms or out on the terrace by the 200-year old olive tree; Sardo Canale specialises in Sardinian cuisine.

Caffe Caldesi, *118 Marylebone Lane, W1U 2QF,* ⊖ *Bond Street,* ☎*020 7935 1144; www.caldesi.com. Closed Sun evening.* Drop in to this attractive converted pub for a cappuccino, pizzas and pastas or full meals featuring robust and authentic dishes with Tuscan specialities.

Locanda Locatelli, *8 Seymour St, W1H 7JZ,* ⊖ *Marble Arch; www. locandalocatelli.com. Closed Sun and bank hols.* Giorgio Locatelli is probably the best Italian chef in town and the quality of food at this stylishly appointed restaurant (banquettes and cherry wood with glass dividers) attracts the rich and famous.

No. 6, *6 George St, W1U 3QX,* ⊖ *Bond Street,* ☎*020 7935 1910. Open Mon-Fri lunch only.* To the front is a charming deli, behind is a simple well kept dining room.

Roka, *37 Charlotte St, W1T 1RR,* ⊖ *Tottenham Court Road,* ☎*020 7580 6464. Closed Sun lunch.* Behind the striking glass and steel frontage lies an airy interior of teak, oak and paper wall screens where authentic flavoursome Japanese cuisine with a variety of grill dishes is served.

Rosmarino, *1 Blenheim Terrace, NW8 0EH,* ⊖ *St John's Wood,* ☎*020 7328 5014.* Enjoy robust Italian dishes a la carte or from a carefully balanced *prix-fixe* menu in this friendly modern and understated establishment.

MAYFAIR

Chor Bizarre, *16 Albemarle St, W1S 4HW,* ⊖ *Green Park,* ☎*020 7629 9802; www.chorbizarrerestaurant.com. Closed Sun lunch, bank hols.* The London branch of one of New Delhi's most innovative and popular restaurants has a vibrant kaleidoscopic interior and scores highly for romantic atmosphere and fine authentic noth Indian and Kashmiri cuisine in a unique atmosphere.

Teca, *54 Brooks Mews, W1Y 2NY,* ⊖ *Bond Street,* ☎*020 7495 4774. Closed Sun, Sat lunch, bank hols.* A glass-enclosed cellar is one of the features of this slick modern Italian establishment which offers a set price menu with an emphasis on seasonal produce.

The Greenhouse, *27a Hays Mew, W1X 7RJ,* ⊖ *Hyde Park Corner,* ☎*020 7499 331; www.greenhouserestaurant.co.uk. Closed Sun, Sat lunch.* A pleasant courtyard off a quiet mews leads to this long-established restaurant offering original inventive one Michelin-starred British cooking, complemented by an exceptional wine list.

The Square, *6-10 Briton St, W1J 6PU,* ⊖ *Green Park,* ☎*020 7495 7100; www. squarerestaurant.com. Closed lunch Sat, Sun, bank hols.* Marble flooring and bold abstract canvasses add an air of modernity to this stylish sophisticated two-Michelin star restaurant offering French-influenced dishes of the highest order.

Umu, *14-16 Bruton Place, W1J 6LX,* ⊖ *Bond Street,* ☎*020 7499 8881; www. umurestaurant.com. Closed bank hols.* The only Kyoto-style restaurant in the UK, this exclusive one Michelin-star restaurant has a central sushi bar and uses the highest quality ingredients.

PICCADILLY, ST JAMES'

The Avenue, *7-9 St James' St, SW1A 1EE,* ⊖ *Green Park,* ☎*020 7321 2111; www. egami.co.uk.* This attractive and stylish bar and restaurant is a local favourite, serving progressive Modern European fresh seasonal food with an unfussy approach.

Brasserie Roux, *8 Pall Mall, SW1Y 5NG,* ⊖ *Piccadilly Circus,* ☎*020 7968 2900.* Informal smart classic brasserie with large windows, serving classic French dishes, many daily specials and a comprehensive wine list.

Alloro, *19-20 Dover St, W1S 4LU,* ⊖ *Green Park,* ☎*020 7495 4768. Closed Sun, Sat lunch, bank hols.* One of the new breed of stylish modern Italian restaurants with contemporary art and leather seating plus a separate bustling bar.

The Wolseley, *160 Piccadilly, WIJ 9EB,* ⊖ *Green Park,* ☎*020 7499 6996; www. thewolseley.com.* One of London's most popular recent openings, set in a former car showroom this has the feel of a grand European coffee house with pillars, high vaulted ceiling, mezzanine tables, Japanese lacquer screens and friezes and food ranging from caviar to a hot dog. Open for breakfast and throughout the day.

SOUTH BANK, ETC

Anchor & Hope, *36 The Cut, SE1 8LP,* ⊖ *Southwark,* ☎*020 7928 9898. Closed Sun, Mon lunch, Tue lunch after bank hols.* One of London's most talked about dining pubs, plain from without, bare floorboards and simple wooden furniture within, offering cooking with a French regional rustic base.

The Hartley, *64 Tower Bridge Rd, SE1 4TR,* ⊖ *Borough,* ☎*020 7394 7023 www. thehartley.com. Closed Sunday dinner.* This small but classic 19C red-brick pub has had a gastro pub makeover complete with rickety bistro tables, an open kitchen and a quirky taste in décor.

Tate Restaurant, *Tate Modern, Bankside, SE1 9TG,* ⊖ *Southwark,* ☎*020 7401 5020; www. www.tate.org.uk. Open Sun-Thu lunch only, Fri-Sat dinner.* The Restaurant, on level 7, at the top of the building, has spectacular views over London and offers an eclectic menu based around fresh seasonal food and an innovative wine list.

Tentazioni, *2 Mill St, Lloyds Wharf, SE1 2BD,* ⊖ *Bermondesy,* ☎*020 7237 1100. Closed Sun, Mon, Sat lunch.* This former warehouse provides a bright and lively setting (with an open staircase between the two floors) for a meal of simple carefully prepared Italian food.

Wapping Food, *Wapping Wall, E1W 3ST,* ⊖ *Wapping,* ☎ *020 7680 2080. Closed Sunday dinner.* An unlikely but winning combination of dining in a former hydraulic power station which also serves as a gallery; enjoy the modern menu surrounded by turbines and TV screens.

OUTER LONDON

North West

Bradley's, *25 Winchester Rd, NW3 3NR,* ⊖ *Swiss Cottage,* ☎ *020 7722 3457. Closed Sat lunch, Sun dinner, Mon, bank hols.* Warm pastel colours and modern artwork give a Mediterranean ambience to this neighbourhood restaurant, which is complemented by the cooking.

Eriki, *4-6 Northways Parade, Finchley Rd, NW3 5EN,* ⊖ *Swiss Cottage,* ☎ *020 7722 0606. Closed Sat lunch, bank hols.* Despite the vivid red interior this Indian restaurant is a relaxing venue with good service of carefully presented flavoursome dishes from southern India.

The Wells, *30 Well Walk, NW3 1BX,* ⊖ *Hampstead,* ☎ *020 7794 3785; www. thewellshampstead.co.uk.* Satisfyingly in between a restaurant and a pub the attractive 18C Wells comprises a smart modern Hampstead bar downstairs and linen-covered formal tables upstairs where the menu is from a classical French repertoire.

North East

Cru, *2-4 Rufus St Hoxton, N1 6PE,* ⊖ *Old Street,* ☎ *020 7729 5252; www.cru.uk.com.* This bar-deli-restaurant complex in a trendily converted 19C warehouse caters for all tastes and pockets with bar food as well as full meals from all over Europe.

Real Greek, *14-15 Hoxton Market, N1 6HG,* ⊖ *Old Street,* ☎ *020 7739 8212; www.therealgreek.co.uk. Closed Sun.* Set in the heart of super-trendy Hoxton in an old Victorian pub, the food here is regional home-style cooking, with many of the dishes on the menu never previously seen in the UK before. Unaffected, pleasant service.

South Battersea

Le Petit Max, *Chatfield Rd, Battersea Reach, SW11 3SE,* ☎ *020 7223 0999. Closed Sun dinner.* Good value robust Gallic cooking can be enjoyed al fresco on the decked terrace at this riverside apartment-based restaurant.

South-South West

The Farm, *18 Farm Lane, SW6 1PP,* ⊖ *Fulham Broadway,* ☎ *020 7381 3331; www. thefarmfulham.co.uk.* This converted pub with leather sofas and contemporary open fireplaces is ultra stylish and the menus are Modern British with a French accent.

The Fire Stables, *27-29 Church Rd, Wimbledon, SW19 5DQ,* ⊖ *Wimbledon,* ☎ *020 894 6101.* There's a high vaulted ceiling in this very popular old pub diner, a startling abstract painting on the wall,

modern and retro furniture and a nice unfussy menu that borders on the Modern British.

South West

Ma Cuisine, *The Old Post Office, Station Approach, TW9 3QB,* ⊖ *Kew Gardens,* ☎ *020 8332 1923.* This "petit bistrot" complete with red gingham tablecloths and pavement tables used to be the Kew post office – it now delivers good value classic French food.

WHERE TO STAY

BLOOMSBURY

The Montague, *15 Montague St, WC1 5BJ,* ☎ *0207637 1001; www. montaguehotel.com.* Located near the British Museum, this charming hotel features a host of amenities and friendly staff. Rooms, each individually decorated, are elegantly comfortable, with rich furnishings and modern conveniences. Spacious grounds, an on-site restaurant and lovely tea service are added benefits.

Myhotel Bloomsbury, *11-13 Bayley St, Bedford Square,* ☎ *020 7667 6000; www.myhotels.co.uk.* This very trendy dynamic mix of east meets west features Mybar, a state-of-the-art spa, a library and Yo Sushi! conveyor belt diner; rooms are based on minimalist feng-shui principles.

CHELSEA, EARLS' COURT

Draycott, *26 Cadogan Gardens, SW3 2RP,* ☎ *020 7730 6466; www. draycotthotel.com.* Charming 5-star Victorian house in a residential area with an elegant sitting room which overlooks tranquil gardens; individually decorated rooms in country-house style.

CITY

Great Eastern Liverpool St, *EC2M 7QN,* ☎ *020 7618 5000; www.great-eastern-hotel.co.uk.* Behind the classic Victorian railway hotel façade is one of London's best post-Millennium hotels with bright spacious bedrooms (all mod cons), three highly fashionable bars and four restaurants plus gym and treatment rooms.

Threadneedles, *5 Threadneedle St, EC2R 8AY,* ☎ *020 7657 88080; www.theetongroup.com.* The self-styled "City's boutique hotel," Threadneedles occupies a magnificent classic 1856 banking hall with stained glass cupola; rooms are stylish with CD players and Egyptian cotton sheets.

CLERKENWELL, ISLINGTON

Malmaison, *Charterhouse Square, EC1M 6AH,* ☎ *020 7012 3700; www. malmaison.com.* Hidden behind a Victorian-brick façade in the cobbled courtyard of leafy Charterhouse Square are stylish comfy public areas, bedrooms in vivid bold colours with lots of cutting-edge extras and luxury touches, a gym, an excellent brasserie and contemporary bar.

The Zetter, *St John's Square, 86-88 Clerkenwell Road, EC1M 5RJ, ☎020 7324 4444; www.thezetter.com.* An old five-storey warehouse in fashionable Clerkenwell has been converted into a small luxury hotel and restaurant opened in 2004, featuring discreetly trendy modern design with extras ranging from old paperbacks to plasma screen TVs.

COVENT GARDEN, SOHO

The Soho, *4 Richmond Mews, W1D 3DH, ☎020 7559 3000; www.firmdale. com.* Opened in 2004 this very stylish small-medium luxury hotel has two large drawing rooms, up-to-the-minute bedrooms, all boasting hi-tech extras plus a contemporary bar and restaurant.

KENSINGTON

Holland Court, *31-33 Holland Rd, W14 8HJ, ☎020 731 1133.* Privately owned hotel set in a terrace house with a pretty little garden next to the conservatory. Well kept bedrooms benefit from large windows.

Mornington, *12 Lancaster Gate, W2 3LG, ☎020 7262 7361.* The classic portico belies the cool modern Scandinavian-influenced interior and modern spacious bedrooms.

The Milestone, *1 Kensington Court, W8 5DL, ☎020 7917 1000; www. milestonehotel.com.* Behind a glorious Victorian façade this luxury boutique hotel and apartments has a charming oak-panelled lounge and snug bar , meticulously decorated English country-style bedrooms with period detail and a charming little oratory for privacy seekers.

KNIGHTSBRIDGE BELGRAVIA ETC

Knightsbridge, *10 Beaufort Gardens, SW3 1PT, ☎020 7584 6300; www. firmdale.com.* A very artfully renovated town house drawing on many influences from the UK and abroad including two drawing rooms with an African feel, a romantic Library, original British artwork and bedrooms in fresh modern English style.

The Halkin, *Halkin St, SW1X 7DJ, ☎020 7333 1000; www.halkin.co.uk.* A London favourite, the Halkin was one of the first minimalist hotels in town. Its cool marbled reception has an understated charm and spacious bedrooms have every facility.

MARYLEBONE, ETC

St George, *49 Gloucester Place, W1U 8JE, ☎020 7486 8586; www.stgeorge-hotel. net.* The A charming grade II listed Town House with nineteen en-suite, a short walk from Oxford Street and Baker Street offering a warm welcome and spotless attractive bedrooms.

Charlotte Street, *15-17 Charlotte Street, W1T 1RJ, ☎020 7806 2002; www.firmdale.com.* Another very artistic townhouse conversion by the same company behind the Knightsbridge Hotel (*see above*) and The Soho Hotel (*see above*) with a charming and understated English feel.

PICCADILLY

22 Jermyn Street, *22 Jermyn Street, SW1Y 6HL, ☎020 7734 2353; www.22jermyn.com.* A discreet entrance on London's most famous gentlemen's clothing street leads to this exclusive boutique hotel where stylishly decorated bedrooms more than compensate for the lack of lounge space.

Eventually in 1855 the Government established the Metropolitan Board of Works, a central body with special responsibility for main sewerage and to act as co-ordinator of the parish vestries. In 1888 the County of London was created with an area equivalent to the present 12 inner London boroughs. In 1965 it was superseded by the Greater London Council which controlled an area of 610sq mi/1 508km2 containing a population of 6 700 000. In 1986 the GLC was abolished and its functions devolved to the borough councils and various new statutory bodies. In a referendum of 1998, Londoners voted in favour of having their own elected mayor, as distinct from the Lord Mayor of the City of London.

The many bomb sites resulting from the Second World War (1939-45) provided opportunities for modern and imaginative re-development such as the Festival Hall, which forms the nucleus of the **South Bank Arts Centre**, and the **Barbican**, a residential neighbourhood incorporating schools, shops, open spaces and an arts centre. The most recent re-development project is the regeneration of the Docklands, several square miles of derelict warehouses and dock basins east of the City, north and south of the Thames, which have been converted into innovative office accommodation such as Canary Wharf, modern flats, adjoining new low-rise housing and even water sports facilities.

London Today

The City, which is thronged with thousands of business men and women during the day, tends to be deserted in the evenings and at weekends, when the commuters, some of whom travel up to 100mi/160km a day, have returned to the suburbs and farther afield.

The West End however is lively at all hours – by day with shoppers and office workers and by night with people going to the theatre, to a pub or restaurant, to a disco or club.

Although few people live in the centre of London, many live in what was a belt of "villages" which have become completely absorbed into the metropolis but have retained their own particular character of which their inhabitants are proud. It is worth exploring such districts as Southwark, Hampstead, Chiswick, Kensington or Chelsea to trace this evolution.

The cosmopolitan atmosphere of London has been greatly reinforced in the latter half of the 20C by easier foreign travel, higher standards of living, immigration from the Commonwealth and Britain's membership of the European Union, resulting in a more international outlook and an increase in the number of foreign restaurants and food stores.

Traditional London

Tradition still plays an important role in London life. The ceremonial **Changing of the Guard** at Buckingham Palace *(daily at 11.30am in summer; otherwise every other day)* and **Horse Guards** *(daily at 11am; Sundays at 10am)* still draw the crowds. There is a fine display of brilliant pageantry and military precision when the Queen attends **Trooping the Colour** on Horse Guards Parade *(2nd or 3rd Saturday in June)* and the **State Opening of Parliament** *(November)*.

In the **Lord Mayor's Show** *(second Saturday in November)* the newly elected Lord Mayor of London proceeds through the City in the golden state coach before taking his oath at the Royal Courts of Justice in the Strand. The famous **London to Brighton Rally** begins with a parade of veteran and vintage cars in Hyde Park *(first Sunday in November)*. A more recently introduced event is the annual **London Marathon** *(third week in April)*, in which thousands compete, running from Greenwich to Westminster Bridge along streets lined with tens of thousands shouting their support.

The text below is divided into those districts containing the sights of major interest in Inner and Outer London. The major museums and galleries are listed under a separate heading. For a more detailed description see the Michelin Green Guide London.

City of London and Environs★★★

St Paul's Cathedral★★★ (FX)

🔶🕐 *St Pauls Churchyard; Open for visitors Mon-Sat, 8.30am-4pm (last admission); Sun for services only (admission free) at 8am (Holy Communion), 10.15am (Matins), 11.30am (Sung Eucharist), 3.15pm (Evensong), 6pm (evening service).* 🔶 *Galleries: 9.30am-4pm,*

Gwen Cannon/MICHELIN

View of St. Paul's and Millennium Bridge

£8. Guided tours (90-120min) at 11.30am, 1.30pm, 2pm. Audio guide (6 languages). Leaflets (9 languages). Guide book (6 languages). ☎ 020 7246 8348; visits@stpaulsca-thedral.org.uk; www.stpauls.co.uk. The present cathedral, the fourth or fifth on a site dating back to AD 604, is considered to be the masterpiece of **Sir Christopher Wren** (1632-1723), though it is worth visiting some of his other churches in the City (eg St Stephen Walbrook, St Margaret Lothbury) to gain a fuller impression of the flexibility and ingenuity of Wren's art. After the Great Fire Old St Paul's was a sad ruin; Wren submitted plans for a new cathedral to the authorities before going ahead as Surveyor General to the King's Works. The foundation stone was laid on 21 June 1675. 33 years later Wren saw his son set the final stone in place – the topmost in the lantern. When Wren died 15 years later he was buried within the walls; beneath the dome his own epitaph reads in Latin: "Reader, if you seek his monument, look around you."

Exterior – The most striking feature is the **dome**, even today a dominant feature of the City skyline. Unlike the dome of St Peter's, which fascinated and influenced Wren, it is not a true hemisphere. The drum below it is in two tiers, the lower encircled by columns and crowned by a balustrade, the upper recessed behind the balustrade so as to afford a circular viewing gallery, the **Stone Gallery.** On top of the dome, the lantern is restrained English Baroque with columns on all four sides and a small cupola serving as a plinth to the 6.5ft/2m-diameter golden ball.

The **west end,** which is approached by two wide flights of steps, is composed of a two-tier portico of Corinthian and composite columns below a decorated pediment surmounted by the figure of Saint Paul. On either side rise Wren's most Baroque spires as a foil to the dome. A notable feature of the exterior is the profuse carving by Gibbons and others.

Interior – The immediate impression is one of space, of almost luminescent stone and, in the distance, gold and mosaic. In the **nave** the entire space between two piers in the north aisle is occupied by the Wellington monument; in the south aisle hangs Holman Hunt's *The Light of the World*. From the **Whispering Gallery** in the dome (259 steps) there are impressive views of the concourse below, the choir, arches and clerestory, and close views of the interior of the dome, painted by Thornhill. A whisper spoken close to the wall can be clearly heard on the diametrically opposite side. The **views**★★★ from the **Golden Gallery** at the top of the dome are better than from the Stone Gallery *(543 steps).* The **transepts** are shallow, that to the north serving as baptistery with a font carved in 1727 by Francis Bird, that to the south including Flaxman's fine statue of **Nelson**. In the **choir** the dark oak stalls are the exquisite work of **Grinling Gibbons**. The iron railing, the gates to the choir aisles and the great gilded screens enclosing the sanctuary are the work of Jean Tijou. The graceful sculpture of the Virgin and Child in the north aisle is by Henry Moore (1984). In the south aisle is a rare pre-Fire relic, a statue of **John Donne**, the great poet and Dean of St Paul's 1621-31. The **Crypt** contains tombs of many illustrious individuals and memorials to the dead of many wars and to others, too numerous to list.

Barbican★ (FGX)

The project (1962-82) combines residential accommodation with schools, shops, open spaces, a conference and arts centre, a medieval church and the Museum of London (& see below). The rounded arch motif, used vertically in the arcades and on the roofline and horizontally round the stairwells, gives a sense of unity to the various elements which are linked by high and low level walkways and interspersed with gardens and sports areas.

Tower of London★★★ (GHX)

Open Mar-Oct, daily, 9am (10am Sun) to 6pm; Nov-Feb, daily, 9am (10am Sun-Mon) to 5pm; last admission 1hr before closing. Chapel of St Peter-ad-Vincula: Services: Sun at 9.15am (Holy Communion), 11am (Matins and sermon). Closed 24-26 Dec, 1 Jan. £11.50. Tickets are also available from London Underground stations. Guided tour (1hr) by Yeoman Warders from the Middle Tower (exteriors plus Chapel of St Peter-ad-Vincula). Jewel House: queues tend to be shorter early in the day. Audio guide (Prisoners' Trail - 5 languages). Guide book and leaflet (7 languages). Royal Fusiliers Regimental Museum 50p. 020 7709 0765 (Tower of London); www.hrp.org.uk; 020 7488 5611 (Regimental Museum). William I constructed a wooden fortress in 1067, replacing it by one in stone (c 1077-97) in order to deter Londoners from revolt; its vantage point beside the river also gave immediate sighting of any hostile force coming up the Thames. Norman, Plantagenet and Tudor successors recognised its value and extended it until it occupied 18 acres – 7ha.

From 1300-1810 the Tower housed the Royal Mint; because of its defences it became the Royal Jewel House and served as a grim prison.

The **Jewel House** displays the **Crown Jewels**★★★ which date from the Restoration to the present day, almost all of the earlier regalia having been sold or melted down by Cromwell. The **Chapel of St Peter ad Vincula**, consecrated in the 12C, rebuilt in the 13C and 16C, is the burial place of several dukes and two of Henry VIII's queens, beheaded in the Tower. Note the carvings on the organ casing by Grinling Gibbons.

Traitors' Gate was the main entrance to the Tower when the Thames was still London's principal thoroughfare; later, when the river served only as a secret means of access, the entrance acquired its chilling name. The Bloody Tower gained its name in the 16C and was perhaps the place where the little Princes in the Tower were murdered in 1483. Sir Walter Raleigh was imprisoned in it from 1603-15 and wrote his *History of the World* there.

The keep, known as the **White Tower**★★★, is one of the earliest fortifications on such a scale in western Europe, begun by William I in 1078 and completed 20 years later by William Rufus. The 100ft/31m high stone walls form an uneven quadrilateral, its corners marked by one circular and three square towers. The **Armour Collection**, one of the world's greatest, was started by Henry VIII and increased under Charles II. On the second floor **St John's Chapel**★★ remains much as it was when completed in 1080, a 55ft/17m long stone chapel rising through two floors. An inner line of great round columns with simply carved capitals bear circular Norman arches which enfold the apse in an ambulatory and are echoed above in a second tier beneath the tunnel vault.

Beauchamp Tower★, built in the 13C, has served as a place of confinement since the 14C. The walls of the main chamber are inscribed with dozens of carved graffiti.

Tower Bridge★★ (HY)

Tower Bridge Road. Open daily, Apr-Sept 10am-6.30pm (5.30pm last admission). Oct-Mar 9.30am-6pm (5pm last admission). £5.50. Audio-guide (6 languages). Guide book (5 languages). 020 7940 3761; Fax 020 7357 7935; enquiries@towerbridge.org.uk; www.towerbridge.org.uk. Access: by bus 15, 42, 47, 78, 100, D1, P11; River boat to Tower Pier. Tower Hill, London Bridge. The familiar Gothic towers, high-level walkways *(lift or 200 steps)* and the original engine rooms form part of the tour which traces the design of the bridge by Sir John Wolfe-Barry and Horace Jones, its construction (1886-94) and explains the functioning of the hydraulic mechanism which, until 1976, raised the 1100t bascules (now operating by electricity).

St Katharine Docks★ (HX)

In 1828, on the site of the 12C Hospital of St Katharine by the Tower, **Thomas Telford** developed a series of basins and warehouses; the dock was the nearest to the City and prospered for over a hundred years. After wartime bombing the dock was abandoned until 1968, when moorings were organised for private yachts. Telford's Italianate building was restored as Ivory House with apartments above a shopping arcade.

HMS Belfast (GY)

Morgan's Lane, Tooley Street. 🕐*Open daily, 10am-6pm (5pm Nov-Feb); last admission 45min before closing.* 🕐 *Closed 24-26 Dec.* 🎫 *£8. Brochure (4 languages). Snack bar.* ☎ *020 7940 6300; Fax 020 7403 0719; mail@iwm.org.uk; www.iwm.org.uk.* The cruiser (1938) moored against the south bank of the Thames saw service with the North Atlantic Convoys and on D-Day in 1944.

Southwark★ (FGY)

The Borough of Southwark, also known familiarly as "The Borough," takes its name from the defence at the south end of London Bridge. It became both famous and infamous in the 16C as a location, outside the jurisdiction of the City, for brothels and theatres. Near the site of the original **Globe Theatre**, where Shakespeare's plays were performed, now stands the **International Shakespeare Globe Centre** (*21 New Globe Walk.* ⚐🕐*Open daily, May-Sep, 9am-noon (theatre tour every 30min); exhibition noon-4pm; Oct-Apr, 10am-5pm (tours and exhibition).* 🕐 *Closed 24-25 Dec.* 🎫 *£9. Cafe, restaurant.* ☎ *020 7902 1500; Fax 020 7902 1515; exhibit@shakespearesglobe. com; www.shakespeares-globe.org. Access: by bus 11, 15, 17, 23, 26, 45, 63, 76, 149, 344, P11;* ⊖ *Mansion House, London Bridge)*, constructed with 16C techniques, to promote an appreciation of Shakespeare's plays in an authentic setting. One of the few medieval buildings to survive is the George Inna (GY), built round three sides of a courtyard, although only one of the galleried ranges has survived. The old warehouses have been converted to new uses – **Hays Galleria** with its shops, pubs and modern sculpture, and the **Bramah Tea and Coffee Museum (HY)** (*40 Southwark Street;* ⚐🕐*Open daily, 10am-6pm.* 🕐 *Closed 25-26 Dec.* 🎫 *£4. Tearoom.* ☎*/Fax 020 7403 5650; bramah@btconnect.com; www.bramahmuseum.co.uk),* which traces the history and fashions in these beverages. The river front boasts the **Design Museum (HY)** (*Shad Thames.* ⚐🕐*Open daily, 10am-5.45pm (last entry 5.15pm)* 🎫 *£7. Cafe, restaurant* ☎ *0870 833 9955; Fax 020 7378 6540; www.designmuseum.org. Access: U Tower Hill, London Bridge, bus 100 to Tower Gateway; 42, 47, 78, 188, 381 to Tooley Street, 225 to Jamaica Road),* which illustrates the evolution of contemporary design, and also some fine restaurants with a view of the City. Under the arches of London Bridge Station is the **London Dungeon (GY)** (⚐🕐 *Open Apr-Oct, daily, 10am-5.30pm (8pm mid-Jul to early-Sep); Nov-Mar, daily, 10.30am-5pm (last admission). Closed 25 Dec.* 🎫 *£17.50. Leaflet (3 languages). Refreshments.* ☎ *020 7403 7221; Fax 020 7378 1529; www. thedungeons.com. Access: London Bridge: main line and underground (Northern and Jubilee): Monument, Bank Station: Docklands Light Railway and underground (District & Circle, Central and Northern); by bus: 21, 35, 40, 43, 47, 48, 78, 133, 149, 381),* a gruesome spectacle of death, disease, disaster and torture in past centuries, which is popular with teenagers but unsuitable for young children.

Winston Churchill's Britain at War

64-66 Tooley Street. ⚐🕐*Open daily, 10am-6pm (5pm Oct-Mar).* 🕐 *Closed 24-26 Dec.* 🎫 *£8.50.* ☎ *020 7403 3171; Fax 020 7403 5104; britainatwar@dial.pipex.com; www. britainatwar.co.uk.* ⊖ *London Bridge.*

Southwark Cathedral★★ (GY)

⚐🕐 *Open daily, 7.30am-6pm. Guide book. Suggested Donation £4. Restaurant. cathedral@dswark.org.uk; www.dswark.org. Access: by bus 17, 21, 35, 40, 43, 47, 48, 133, 149, 344, 501, 521, D1, P11* ⊖ *London Bridge.* The earliest work is the fragment of a Norman arch in the north wall. The massive piers supporting the central tower and the intimately proportioned Early English **chancel** date from the 13C. The **altar screen**, presented by Bishop Fox in 1520, appears in sumptuous Gothic glory; it remained empty until 1905 when statues were carved to fill the niches. The nave was rebuilt in 1890-97 to harmonise with the chancel. Notable features are the **Harvard Chapel** *(north chancel aisle),* the 1616 **monument** to Alderman Humble and his wives *(north of altar screen)* and the 12 **bosses** rescued from the 15C wooden roof which collapsed in 1830 *(on west wall at end of north aisle).*

Westminster★★★

Westminster Abbey★★★ (EY)

⚐🕐 *Open Mon-Sat, 9.30am-3.45pm (1.45pm Sat).* 🎫 *£8. Leaflet (8 languages). Audio-guide (£2; 7 languages).* ☎ *020 7222 5152; Fax 020 7233 2072; info@westminster-abbey. org; www.westminster-abbey.org.* 🎧 *Guided tours by Vergers (£4; maximum 90min):*

Westminster Abbey

Apr-Sept, Mon-Fri at 10am, 10.30am, 11am, 2pm, 2.30pm, Sat at 10am, 10.30am, 11am; Oct-Mar, Mon-Fri at 10am, 11am, 2pm, 2.30pm, Sat at 10am, 10.30am, 11am. ☎ *020 7222 7110. Sunday Services: 8am (Holy Communion), 10am (Matins), 11.15am (Sung Eucharist), 3pm (Evensong), 5.45pm (Organ recital), 6.30pm (Evening Service); Cloister: Open daily, 8am-6pm. Chapter House: Open (State occasions permitting) daily, 10am (9.30am Apr-Sep) to 5pm (4pm Nov-Mar).* 🕐 *Closed 24-26 Dec, 1 Jan.* ☎ *020 7222 5897. Chapel of the Pyx and Westminster Abbey Museum: (EH) Open daily, 10.30am-4pm. Reduced charge for those who have paid Abbey admission charge.* ☎ *020 7233 0019. College Garden: Open Tue-Thu, 10am-6pm (4pm Oct-Mar). Donation. Brass Band concerts: Jul-Aug, 12.30pm-2pm.* ☎ *020 7222 5152.* The abbey, in which William the Conqueror was crowned as **William I** on Christmas Day 1066, was built by **Edward the Confessor** in the Norman style; only after the rebuilding by the Plantagenet Henry III in 1220 did it acquire its Gothic appearance. Inspired by the style of Amiens and Reims, Henry III began with the Lady Chapel, to provide a noble shrine for the Confessor, who had been canonised in 1163. Gradually the existing building was demolished as new replaced the old; progress halted after the construction of the first

Palace of Westminster

bay of the nave and it was another two centuries before the nave was finished. When Henry VII constructed his **chapel** at the east end (1503-19), Perpendicular Gothic was still the ecclesiastical style and he produced the jewel of the age. The west towers by Wren and Nicholas Hawksmoor (1722-45) and repairs by George Gilbert Scott kept to the Gothic spirit. The Dissolution in 1540 meant the confiscation of the abbey's treasure, forfeiture of its property, the disbanding of the 600-year-old Benedictine community of 50 monks, but not the destruction of the buildings. In 1560 Queen Elizabeth I granted a charter establishing the Collegiate Church of St Peter with a royally appointed Dean and chapter of 12 canons and the College of St Peter, generally known as Westminster School.

Interior – The vaulting is glorious, the carving on screens and arches delicate, often beautiful, sometimes humorous; the ancient tombs in **Henry VII's, St Edward's** and the ambulatory chapels are dignified and sometimes revealing in expression (some being derived from death masks). The transepts and aisles abound with sculpted monuments, particularly in the famous **Poets' Corner**★ *(south transept)* where there are monuments to many great poets though few are actually buried here; the tomb of Geoffrey Chaucer was the first in this corner, others interred here include ALfred Lord Tennyson and Robert Browning.

The **Sanctuary** beyond the **Choir** is where the **Coronation ceremony** is performed. To the right hangs a 16C tapestry behind a large 15C altarpiece of rare beauty. Beyond is an ancient 13C sedilia painted with full length royal figures (Henry III, Edward I).

The **Henry VII Chapel**★★★ with its superb fan-vaulted roof is the most glorious of the abbey's many treasures. The banners of the Knights Grand Cross of the **Order of the Bath** hang still and brilliant above the stalls patterned with the heraldic plates of former occupants and those of their esquires, with inventive 16C-18C misericords.

The **Chapel of Edward the Confessor**★★ is rich in history, with the Confessor's shrine ringed with the tombs of five kings and three queens. In the centre against a carved stone **screen** (1441) stands the Coronation Chair which until recently contained the Stone of Scone beneath the seat (👆 *see EDINBURGH and PERTH*).

The **Chapter House**★★ (1248-53) is an octagonal chamber (60ft/18m in diameter) with vaulting springing from a slim central pier of attached Purbeck marble columns. Its walls are partially decorated with medieval paintings.

Palace of Westminster★★★ (EY)

🔎 *Guided tour (75min) Aug-Sep (Summer Recess) starting from The Victoria Tower.* 🎫 *£7; £2 surcharge on foreign language tours.* ☎ *020 7219 4272; Firstcall 0870 906 3773; www.firstcalltickets.com. When Parliament is in session - see website or call for*

times - the general public are allowed into the Visitors' Gallery free of charge to watch the proceedings in the House of Commons. Be prepared to queue for popular sessions such as Prime Ministers Question Time. The palace built by Edward the Confessor was enlarged and embellished by the medieval English kings but most of the surviving buildings, by then occupied by Parliament, were destroyed in a disastrous fire in 1834. The oldest remaining part is **Westminster Hall**★★ which William Rufus added to his father's palace between 1097 and 1099. This scene of royal banquets and jousts in the Middle Ages was altered and re-roofed by command of Richard II between 1394 and 1399. For this the upper parts were rebuilt and what is perhaps the finest timber roof of all time was built, a superb **hammerbeam**★★★ designed by the king's master carpenter, Hugh Herland, carved with flying angels. After the 1834 fire which, fortunately, did not damage Westminster Hall, **Charles Barry** and **Augustus Pugin** won a competition for a new design for the Palace, which became known as the Houses of Parliament. These ardent Gothicists created a masterpiece of Victorian Gothic architecture. It was completed in 1860, with over 1000 rooms, 100 staircases and 2mi/3km of corridors spread over 8 acres/3ha.

The Clock Tower (316ft/96m) – the most famous feature of this distinctive building, was completed by 1859. The name **Big Ben**★ applied originally to the great bell, probably so called after Sir Benjamin Hall, the Commissioner of Works and a man of considerable girth. The clock, which has an electrically wound mechanism has proved reliable, except for minor stoppages for 117 years until it succumbed to metal fatigue in 1976 when it required major repairs. Big Ben was first broadcast on New Year's Eve 1923 and its chimes have subsequently become the most famous in the world. The light above the clock remains lit while the House of Commons is sitting.

The **House of Commons**★, rebuilt after being bombed in 1941, seats 437 of the 659 elected Members of Parliament; at the end of this simply decorated chamber is the canopied Speaker's Chair. Red stripes on both sides of the green carpet mark the limit to which a Member may advance to address the House – the distance between the stripes is reputedly that of two drawn swords.

The **House of Lords**★★ is a symphony of design and workmanship in encrusted gold and scarlet. The throne and steps, beneath a Gothic canopy mounted on a wide screen, all in gold, occupies one end of the chamber. The ceiling is divided by ribs and gold patterning above the red buttoned leather benches and the Woolsack, seat of the Lord Chancellor since the reign of Edward III, adopted as a symbol of the importance to England of the wool trade.

British Airways London Eye★★ (EY)

On the opposite side of the river the giant London Eye observation wheel is a spectacular Millennium landmark on the Thames. Sightseers are accommodated in glass pods to enjoy unparalleled **views**★★★of London 443ft/135 metres high during their 30-minute ride. *South Bank; ticket office in County Hall.* ♿ 🕐 *Daily. Oct - May 10am - 8pm, June - Sept 10am - 9pm. Due to the huge popularity of this ride it is recommended that visitors book a time slot in advance; only a limited allocation of tickets are sold on site on the day of the flight.* 🕐 *Closed one week January for annual maintenance* ✆ *£12.50. Cafe next to ticket office.* ☎ *0870 5000 600; www.londoneye.com.*

Whitehall★★ (EY)

The wide street, which leads north from Parliament Square and Parliament Street, is lined by government offices. In the middle stands the Cenotaph, the austere war memorial designed by Sir Edwin Lutyens. On the left is Downing Street, where a modest Georgian house (no 10) has been the residence of the Prime Minister since it was rebuilt for Sir Robert Walpole in 1732.

The **Banqueting House**★★ *(Whitehall.* ♿🕐*Open (government functions permitting); Mon-Sat, 10am-5pm.* 🕐 *Closed Good Fri, 24-26 Dec, 1 Jan and all Bank Hols. £4 (including audio guide).* ☎ *0870 751 5178; val.jarvis@hrp.org.uk; www.hrp.org.uk. Access: by bus 3, 11, 12, 24, 29, 53, 77A, 88, 159)*, the only part of Whitehall Palace to survive, was designed by Inigo Jones, begun for James I in 1619; the north entrance and staircase were added in 1809 and the exterior refaced in 1829. The hall is a double cube (110 x 55 x 55ft/33.5 x 16.75 x 16.75m) with a delicate balcony on gilded corbels; the ceiling is divided by richly decorated beams into compartments filled with magnificent paintings (1634-35) by Rubens. It was on a platform erected in front of this building that Charles I was executed in January 1649.

Opposite stands **Horse Guards**★ **(EY)**, an unadorned mid-18C building by William Kent and John Vardy, distinguished by the statue-like presence of the **House-**

hold **Cavalry sentries** (*Ceremonial mounting of the Queen's Life Guard daily by the Household Cavalry at 11am (10am Sun) in summer on Horse Guards Parade; dismount ceremony daily 4pm in the Front Yard of Horse Guards. The Cavalry rides along the Mall between Horse Guards and their barracks in Hyde Park. ☎ 020 7414 2353; www. army.mod.uk).* At the rear of the shallow forecourt a central arch beneath a clock tower leads to the parade ground, where Trooping the Colour takes place in June, and to St James's Park.

St James's Park★★ (DEY)

The oldest and most beautiful royal park in London dates from 1532 when Henry VIII had **St James's Palace (DY)** built in place of an old hospital for lepers. The park was landscaped in the 19C by John Nash who was also responsible for the majestic **Carlton House Terrace**★ (EY) in the northeast corner. From the bridge over the water there is a fine **view** of Whitehall and Buckingham Palace. Look out too for the park's famous pelicans, the first one was a gift to Charles I from a Russian Ambassador - it promptly flew off and was shot while over Norfolk. Another resident, Peter from Karachi stayed for 54 years before emigrating without leaving a forwarding address. The present pair came from Prague Zoo.

Buckingham Palace★★ (DY)

Sentry duty at Horse Guards

🚻🕐 *Open early-Aug to late-Sep, daily, 9.30am-5.30pm (4.15pm last admission); timed ticket. Joint ticket with Royal Mews and Queen's Gallery. £11.50. Brochure (6 languages). ☎ 020 7321 2233; buckinghampalace@royal-collection.org.uk; www.royal.gov.uk.* The house built by the newly-created Duke of Buckingham in 1703 on land granted to him by Queen Anne was purchased in 1762 by George III for his bride Charlotte. Under George IV it was converted into a palace (1825-37) by John Nash and Edward Blore; the east front containing the famous balcony was added in 1847.

The tour includes the Throne Room, the Drawing Rooms, the Dining Room and the Picture Gallery, hung with Royal portraits and old masters from the Royal Collection (*Charles I*, Van Dyck; portraits by Rembrandt and Frans Hals; seascapes by Van de Velde; *A Lady at the Virginals*, Vermeer; pastoral and religious scenes by Rubens...) and furnished with many pieces collected by George IV.

When the Sovereign is in residence, the Royal Standard flies over the Palace.

Changing of the Guard★★ (🕐 *Takes place usually May to early-Aug, daily at 11.30am; otherwise, alternate days at 11.30am. ☎ 020 7414 2497*) takes place in the forecourt. The **Queen's Gallery**★★ (🚻🕐 *Open daily, 8am-6pm (4.30pm last admission). Timed ticket, ☎ £7.50. ☎ 020 7321 2233; Fax 020 7930 9625; buckinghampalace@royalcol-lection.org.uk; www.royal.gov.uk*) presents exhibitions of the portraits, paintings, drawings and furniture in the superb Royal Collection.

West End★

Trafalgar Square★★ (EX)

The square was laid out by Nash in 1820 as part of a north-south communication between Bloomsbury and Westminster. Begun in 1829, the square was completed in the 1840s, when Charles Barry levelled it and built the north terrace for the National Gallery (🕐 *see below*). In 1842 **Nelson's Column** was erected; the monument is 185ft/56m tall, with the pedestal, fluted granite column, bronze capital and a 17ft/4.5m statue of the great admiral who lost his life winning the Battle of Trafalgar.

The church of **St Martin-in-the-Fields**★ (*Trafalgar Square; 🚻🕐 Open daily, 8am-6pm. Brochure (6 languages). Choral services: Sun at 10am, 12noon, 5pm; Wed at 1.05pm, 5pm. Lunchtime recitals: Mon-Tue and Fri at 1.05pm; no charge. ☎ 020 7766 1100 (church* *office); Fax 020 7839 5163; clergyoffice@smitf.co.uk; www.stmartin-in-the-fields.org. Outdoor market: daily. Evening concerts: Thu-Sat at 7.30pm; tickets available from the Crypt box office (Mon-Sat, 10.00am-5pm) or by telephone. ☎ 020 7839 8362 (ticket office); Fax 020 7839 5163; boxoffice@smitf.co.uk. Café in the Crypt: Open daily, 10am (noon Sun) to 8pm (10.30pm Thu-Sat). ☎ 020 7839 4342. Bookshop in the Crypt: Open daily, 10am (noon Sun) to 7.30pm (7pm Sun) ☎ 020 7766 1122)* was built by James Gibbs in 1722-26, with a Corinthian portico and elegant spire. Note the equestrian statue *(south)* of **Charles I** cast by Le Sueur in 1633. A plaque in the road next to it marks the spot from where all road distances from London are measured. **Canada House,** *(west),* is a classical building of Bath stone (1824-27) by Robert Smirke.

The Inns of Court

The area around High Holborn and Fleet Street has been the centre of legal London since the 14C, housing some of the world's oldest surviving legal training establishments, Lincoln's Inn, Gray's Inn, Inner Temple and Middle Temple, known collectively as the Four Inns of Court, comprising. Each inn (which meant house in Old English) resembles a small university campus, comprising rooms for practising barristers, a dining hall, a library and a chapel. They are oases of calm, little known to most Londoners, and the grounds and some buildings are open to the public from Monday to Friday.

Covent Garden★★ (EX)

Covent Garden Piazza, the first London square, was designed by Inigo Jones in 1631 for the 4th Earl of Bedford who had been granted the land, once the property of Westminster Abbey, by Henry VIII. It was originally surrounded by colonnades, long demolished; **St Paul's Church** however, still stands, its elegant portico dominating the west side of the square.

At the centre are the **Central Market Buildings,** designed in 1832 by Charles Fowler, to house the fruit and vegetable market which moved out in 1974. The tiny shops and market stalls which now occupy it sell a great variety of goods – books, cooking pots, fashion, jewellery, crafts and refreshment – and musicians and street artists perform on the open cobblestones.

Covent Garden has long been synonymous with opera, and its **Royal Opera House** has recently been magnificently refurbished. Its design incorporates the original iron framework of the old Floral Hall. Across the Piazza from here the old flower market now houses the **Theatre Museum** *(Russell Street.* &⏰ *Open Tue-Sat, 10am-6pm. Last admission 5.30pm. Closed Bank Hols. Visitor notes (6 languages). Free admission. Guided tour, make-up demonstrations, costume workshops: daily. ☎ 020 7943 4700; tmenquiries@vam.ac.uk; www.theatremuseum.org ⊖ Covent Garden),* an annexe of the Victoria and Albert Museum, and **London' s Transport Museum** *(*&⏰ *closed for renovation until 2007. ☎ 020 7565 7299 (24hr information); 020 7379 6344; Fax 020 7565 7254; contact@ltmuseum.co.uk; www.ltmuseum.co.uk).*

It is well worth exploring the narrow side streets in and around Covent Garden, particularly **Neal's Yard** (off Shorts Gardens, a two-minute walk from Covent Garden underground station) complete with period hoists, dovecotes, trees in tubs, geranium filled window boxes and a whole raft of eco-friendly shopkeepers, vegetarian and wholefood restaurants and food outlets. It's a particularly attractive spot in summer when everyone eats outside.

Soho★ (DX)

This very cosmopolitan district, where immigrants once tended to congregate, is the home of the music and film trades, evening entertainment (theatres and restaurants) and night life (clubs of every kind). In the latter decades of the 20C it became synonymous with sex-clubs, prostitution and low life. Today although a few sex clubs and sex shops can still be found the night scene is more reputable (and safe), including some of London's best places to eat and drink. Soho is also particularly popular with the gay community. There are dozens of excellent restaurants, including many French, Italian, Greek and Chinese. Many of the latter can be found in and around Gerrard Street, London's small **Chinatown** district. This colourful area is marked by oriental gates and other exotic street furniture and abounds in eating places, supermarkets selling eastern foodstuffs and oriental goods. At Chinese New Year this is the scene of one of London's most colourful street festivals. Gerrard Street leads onto **Old Compton Street**, the spiritual heart of this bohemian area lined with pubs, wine merchants, pastry shops and Italian food stores. In summer many office workers and locals grab a sandwich or snack and retreat to delightful **Soho Square**, between Greek Street and Frith Street, laid out in 1680. It is adorned by a statue of Charles II by Caius Cibber and a charming polygonal rustic little hut right in the centre of the square, which excites a lot of curiosity among visitors. In fact is a relatively modern structure that houses the gardener's tools!

At **Leicester Square**★ the Bohemian character of Soho dissipates with the huge crowds that traverse this tree-shaded pedestrian precinct, made garish by the lights of cinemas and cheap food outlets. At the **Society of London Theatres' Half-Price Ticket Booth** you can buy tickets for leading West End shows - though tickets for the really popular ones are rarely if ever available - at half price *(🕐 Open Mon-Sat, noon-6.30pm for matinée and evening shows; Sun noon-around 3.30pm, matinées only. 💷 Cash only; service charge £2.50 per ticket, maximum 4 tickets per person)* and a statue of Charlie Chaplin, who was born in Lambeth on the south bank. Beware there are other non-officai reduced-price theatre ticket booths around the Square. These are not illegal but may not offer the best service either and are therefore not recommended. The **Trocadero Complex** is composed of the original Trocadero, a 19C music-hall, and the London Pavilion (1885), first a theatre and then a cinema, which together have been converted to house shops and restaurants and a large and loud amusement complex which draws a host of multinational teenagers into the small hours.

Piccadilly Circus★ (EX)

This famous road junction, once considered the hub of the British Empire, is still dominated by **Eros**, the Angel of Christian Charity, surmounting the fountain erected in memory of the philanthropist, **Lord Shaftesbury,** in 1892. Shaftesbury Avenue (1886), created as a slum-clearance measure, is now at the heart of theatreland. It is best known for its advertising hoardings, spelled out in lights, and as a meeting place.

Mayfair★ (DX)

The most luxurious district of London takes its name from a cattle and general fair held annually in May until it was closed in 1706 for unruly behaviour. It contains what are probably the most elegant hotels and the greatest concentration of smart shops in all of London: **Burlington Arcade**★ **(DX)** (1819) where the bow-fronted boutiques sell fashion, jewellery, leather goods; **Bond Street**★ famous for art auctioneers and dealers (Sotheby's, Phillips, Agnew's, Colnaghi), jewellery (Asprey, Cartier) and fashion (Fenwick, Yves St Laurent); **Regent Street** well known for elegant stores (Austin Reed, Aquascutum, Burberry, Jaeger and Liberty); **Oxford Street** lined with the more popular department stores (John Lewis, Debenhams, DH Evans, Selfridges and Marks & Spencer). Less well known is **Shepherd Market**, a charming maze of lanes, alleyways and paved courts linked by archways with a village atmosphere. It is named after Edward Shepherd, an architect, who in 1735 took out a 999-year lease on the site and opened a food market. Today you will find Victorian and Edwardian pubs and houses, antique shops and small inserted shop fronts which serve in summer as pavement cafés. You will find it hard to hear a nightingale singing in **Berkeley Square** these days but it is still a very impressive plane-tree lined ensemble which was laid out in 1737 - the trees are not much younger, many dating from the late 1780s. Look for the late 18C houses on the west side with ironwork balconies, lamp holders at the steps and torch snuffers. The famous ill-fated governor, Clive of India lived at no 45.

Holborn★ (EFX)

The medieval manors at this former crossroads have been transformed into Lincoln's Inn and Gray's Inn, two of the four Inns of Court (👆 *see below*). The fields where beasts once grazed are less in extent but still open; on the north side stands the remarkable time capsule of **Sir John Soane's Museum**★★ **(EX** ♿ 🕐 *13 Lincoln's Inn Fields. Open Tue-Sat, 10am-5pm; first Tue of each month, 6pm-9pm. 🕐 Closed Bank Hols, Good Fri and 24 Dec. Free admission. 🔊 Guided tour: Sat at 2.30pm (💷 £3; no booking; 22 tickets given out from 2pm). Library and drawings collection available to scholars by appointment. ☎ 020 7405 2107; Fax 020 7831 3957; www.soane.org***).** This presents the highly individual collection of Classical sculpture, architectural fragments, drawings, prints and paintings, assembled by Soane, the architect, in his own house and left virtually untouched as stipulated in his will in 1833. The highlight is the **collection of pictures** mostly assembled on folding and sliding planes which make the most of the very limited available space. There are drawings by Piranesi, paintings by Canaletto, Reynolds and Turner and 12 of Hogarth's minutely observed paintings of London's underbelly including the *Election* and the *Rake's Progress.*

Lincoln's Inn★★ **(FX** *Grounds:* ◷*Open Mon-Fri. Closed Sat-Sun and Bank Hols. Chapel: Open Mon-Fri, noon-2.30pm. Old Hall, New Hall and Library:* ⟶ *Guided tour (minimum 15;* ⊗ *£2 per head) on written application to the Assistant Under Treasurer, Lincoln's Inn, London WC2A 3TL. Fax 020 7831 1839; mail@lincolnsinn.org.uk; www.lincolnsinn.org.uk***)** is the grandest of the four Inns of Court, and as we see it today dates back to the late 15C with its buildings of brick with stone decoration, organised on the self-contained collegiate plan of inter-communicating courts. The Old Hall dates from 1490, the Old Buildings are Tudor, refaced in 1609, while the Chapel was rebuilt in 1620-23.

The **Temple,** a remarkable ancient complex comprises two of the four Inns of Court, Inner Temple and Middle Temple. The Tudor Inner Temple Gateway, gabled, half-timbered 3 storeys high, leads into the Temple past 19C buildings and the houses (right) where Dr Johnson (of Dictionary fame) lived in the 1760s, to Temple Church (◷ *Open Wed-Sun 11am-4pm* ✉ *verger@templechurch.com; www.templechurch.com)* built in the 12C in the round style of the Church of the Holy Sepulchre in Jerusalem. On the stone floor lie 10 effigies of knights in armour dating from the 10C to the 13C. The highlight of Middle Temple is the magnificent Middle Temple Hall (♿◷ *Open Mon-Fri (functions permitting) 10am-11.30am, 3-4pm.* ✉ *library@middletemple.org. uk; www. middletemple.org.uk).* The Elizabethan Great Hall has ancient oak timbers, panelling and fine carving, heraldic glass, helmets and armour and a remarkable double hammerbeam construction roof (1574). The splendid dining table is reputedly made from the hatch of Sir Francis Drake's flagship *Golden Hinde*, and the suits of armour standing guard around the hall are of similar vintage

On High Holborn **Gray's Inn**★ **(FX** *Gardens:* ◷*Open Mon-Fri, noon-2.30pm. Closed Bank Holidays. Squares: Open Mon-Fri, 9am-5pm; www.graysinn.org.uk***)** dates from the 14C in its foundation, from the 16C in its buildings, many of which, however, have had to be renewed since the war. On the opposite side of the road, a remarkable survival from the late 16C is the row of **half-timbered houses** (1586-96), forming the front of **Staple Inn**★ **(FX)** which was also once a legal training establishment though it was never an Inn of Court. Just around the corner is another remarkable little half-timbered house, known as the **Old Curiosity Shop (**EX) (*Portsmouth Street, southwest corner of Lincoln's Inn Fields)* immortalised by Dickens in his eponymous novel (1841). It is a rare example of an Elizabethan building (c 1567) to survive intact in London.

Bloomsbury★ (EVX)

The once residential area with its many squares is dominated by two learned institutions, the British Museum *(⟲ see p365)* and the ever-expanding London University. The development of Bloomsbury Square in 1661 brought a new concept in social planning; the 4th Earl of Southampton erected houses for the well-to-do around three sides of a square, a mansion for himself on the fourth, northern side and a network of service streets all around with a market nearby. A century later, in 1775, the elegant **Bedford Square**★★ **(EX)** was developed by Gertrude, widow of the 4th Duke of Bedford. It is still complete, with its three-storey brick terrace houses with rounded doorways and first-floor balconies. Other squares, now partly incorporated into the University precinct, followed in the 19C. The most famous residents of these squares were the **Bloomsbury Group** of writers, artists and philosophers, loosely centred around the figures of Virginia Woolf, Vanessa Bell, Roger Fry and others in the 1920s.

Kensington★★

Kensington Palace★★ (BY)

♿◷ *Open daily, 10am-6pm (last admission); Nov-Mar, Wed-Sun, 10am-5pm (last admission).* ◷ *Closed Good Fri, 24-26 Dec, 1 Jan.* ⊗ *£10* ⟶ *Guided tour.* ✆ *020 7937 9561; www.hrp.org.uk. Access: by bus 9, 10, 33, 49, 52, 52A, C1;* ⊖ *Queensway, High Street Kensington.* Since its purchase in 1689 by William III this early 17C Jacobean house has passed through three phases: under the House of Orange it was the monarch's private residence, with **Wren** as principal architect; under the early Hanoverians it became a royal palace, with Colen Campbell and William Kent in charge of decorative schemes; since 1760 it has been a residence for members of the royal family, most notably the late **Diana**, Princess of Wales.

The **State Apartments** are approached by the Queen's Staircase designed by Wren. The **Queen's Gallery** has carving by Grinling Gibbons and portraits by Kneller and Lely; in the Queen's Drawing Room hangs a painting by Kneller of the first Royal Gardener, Henry Wise, who was in charge of Kensington Gardens. The **Privy** and lofty **Presence Chamber, Cupola** and **Drawing Rooms**, added for George I in 1718-20, were decorated by William Kent during 1722-27. The staircase, built by Wren in 1689, was altered in 1692-93 and again when Kent covered the walls and ceiling with *trompe l'œil* paintings including a dome and gallery of contemporary courtiers. The gallery was built to house William's finest pictures. Kent's ceiling depicts scenes from the story of Ulysses.

For many visitors the highlight is the **Court Dress Collection** which is displayed in period room settings on the ground floor and shows the dresses and uniforms which have been worn at the select court occasions spanning 12 reigns from 1750.

Kensington Gardens★★ (BXY)

The gardens (originally 26 acres/10ha and extended finally to 275 acres/110ha) were at their prime under the Queens Mary, Anne and Caroline (George II's consort) and the royal gardeners, Henry Wise and his successor in 1728, Charles Bridgeman. In the 18C the **Round Pond** was dug, facing the State Apartments, as the focal point for avenues radiating northeast, east and southeast to the **Serpentine** and **Long Water,** which terminates at its northernmost point in the 19C Italian Gardens and Queen Anne's Alcove. Other features of the period are the **Broad Walk** and the early 18C **Orangery**★, Hawksmoor's splendidly Baroque centrepiece (1705) which now houses a pleasant restaurant. At the weekends the Park is a favourite walk with Kensington locals, most famously nannies with their small charges.

Beyond the Flower Walk on the south side of the gardens stands the **Albert Memorial**★ (1876), designed by George Gilbert Scott. Four wide flights of steps lead up to the neo-Gothic spire, which is ornamented with mosaics, pinnacles and a cross. At the centre, surrounded by allegorical statues and a frieze of 169 named figures of poets, artists, architects and composers, sits a bronze statue (14ft/4.25m) of the Prince Consort who did so much to further the arts and learning, until his premature death in 1861.

Opposite stands the **Royal Albert Hall**★ (1867-71), a popular venue for meetings, conferences and concerts, notably the eight-week summer season of **Promenade Concerts.**

Farther south are the Science Museum (💧 *see below*), The Natural History Museum (💧 *see below*) and the Victoria and Albert Museum (💧 *see below*), all part of the great educational centre established by Prince Albert with the profits (£2 000 000) from the Great Exhibition which was organised by Prince Albert in 1851 and took place in Hyde Park. To house it, Joseph Paxton designed the **Crystal Palace** (19 acres/7.5ha), a metal and glass structure, which was re-erected at Sydenham but destroyed by fire in 1936.

Hyde Park★★ (CXY)

This less formal park extends east of the Serpentine to Park Lane. Pitt the Elder called it and Kensington Gardens "the lungs of London"; 250 years later the park still enables office-workers and tourists to enjoy the fresh air and feed the ducks.

Speakers' Corner (CX) is a relatively modern feature of the park; not until 1872 did the government recognise the need for a place of public assembly and free discussion. Anyone can stand up and speak here as they frequently do on a Sunday morning, as long as they are not blasphemous, nor must they incite a breach of the peace. To its north stands **Marble Arch (CX)**, the triumphal arch of Italian marble which was designed by John Nash in 1827 as a grand entrance to Buckingham Palace in commemoration of the battles of Trafalgar and Waterloo. Embarrasingly it was never used as it was too narow to accommodate the royal Gold Stage Coach and so was moved to this rather incongruous setting.

LONDON

Banqueting House	EY	Courtauld Institute	EFX	Kensington	ABY
Barbican	GX	Covent Garden	EX	Kensington Palace and	
Bedford Square	EX	Cutty Sark	UY	Gardens	BXY
Bloomsbury	EVX	Dulwich Picture Gallery	UZ	Kenwood House	TX
British Museum	EX	Fenton House	TX	Kew Palace and Gardens	TY
Buckingham Palace	DY	Gray's Inn	EFX	Leicester Square	EX
Burlington Arcade	DX	Greenwich	UY	Lincoln's Inn	FX
Carlton House Terrace	EY	Ham House	TZ	London Zoo	CV
Chelsea	CZ	Hampton Court Palace		Madame Tussaud's	CV
Chiswick House	TY	and Gardens	TZ	Marble Arch	CX
County Hall	EY	Horse Guards	EY	Mayfair	DX
		Hyde Park	CXY	Museum of London	FGX
		Imperial War Museum	FY	National Army Museum	CZ

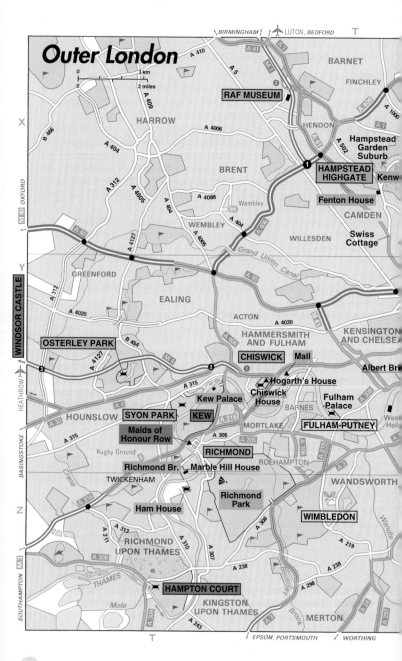

National Gallery	EX	Sir John Soane's Museum	EX	Tate Modern	FX
National Maritime Museum	UY	Soho	DX	Tower Bridge	HY
National Portrait Gallery	EX	Somerset House	EX	Tower of London	GHX
Natural History Museum	BY	South Bank Arts Centre	FX	Trafalgar Square	EX
New Bond Street	DX	Southwark	FGY	Victoria and Albert Museum	CY
Osterley Park	TY	Southwark Cathedral	GY	Wallace Collection	DX
Palace of Westminster	EY	St James's Park	DEY	Westminster Abbey	EY
Piccadilly Circus	EX	St Katharine Dock	HX		
Richmond	TY	St Martin in the Fields	EX		
Richmond Park	TYZ	St Paul's Cathedral	FX		
Royal Albert Hall	BY	Staple Inn	FX		
Royal Hospital	CZ	Syon Park	TY		
Science Museum	BY	Tate Britain	EZ		

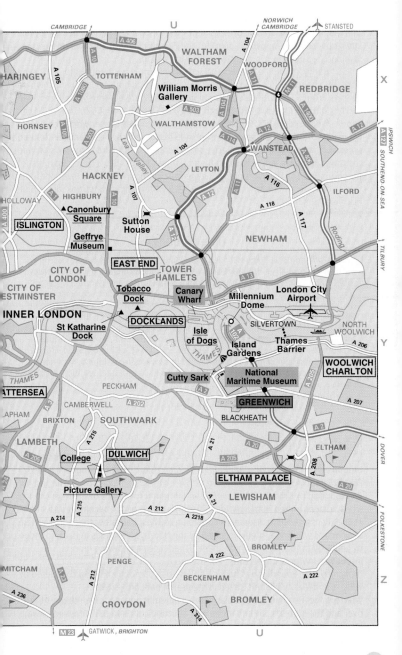

Chelsea★★

Although the completion of the Embankment in 1874 removed the atmosphere of a riverside community evoked in paintings by Rowlandson, Turner and Whistler, Chelsea continued to attract artists, architects, writers, actors and gained a reputation for fashionable Bohemian living. Oscar Wilde lived at 34 Tite Street, the Pre Raphaelite poets and painters Dante Gabriel Rosetti, his sister Christina, Burne-Jones, William and Jane Morris, Holman Hunt, Walter Sickert, Swinburne, Millais all lived and worked here. Other artists include William de Morgan, John Singer Sargent and Augustus John. Henry James, Mark Twain, TS Eliot, AA Milne (author of Winnie the Pooh) and Ian Fleming all found writing inspiration here (Fleming created James Bond while in Chelsea). In 1955 the opening of Bazaar by the young up and coming designer Mary Quant led to a radical change in dress with the launch of the mini skirt. King's Road Chelsea became "the navel of swinging London" in the 1960s and Mick Jagger, among many pop stars, lived here (on Cheyne Row). In 1971 Chelsea fashion was reinvigorated by Vivienne Westwood who opened her clothes shop at 430 Kings Road. Five years later it became the launching point for the Punk movement and even today punk fashions are still seen sporadically on the King's Road.

In 1537 Henry VIII built a riverside palace on a site now occupied by 19-26 Cheyne Walk. His chancellor, Sir Thomas More, had built a large house near the river where he lived from 1523 until his execution in 1535. A figure of More seated has been erected outside **Chelsea Old Church (CZ** ⏱ *64 Cheyne Walk; Open Tue-Fri, 2-5pm, Sun, 1.30-6pm.* ☎ *020 7352 5627; Fax 020 7795 0092; www.chelseaoldchurch.org.uk*) where he remodelled the south transept in 1528; the church dates from pre-Norman times and has a 13C chancel but, after being bombed during the Second World War, the tower and nave were rebuilt in their original style of 1670. A few yards west of the church, also on the riverfront, is Cheyne Walk (pronounced Chainey), a handsome terrace of houses, rich with memories of artists, writers and royalty; look for the blue plaques along here.

Blue Plaques

You will find Blue Plaques affixed to buildings where famous people have lived all over the capital, in total there are over 760 in London including actors, authors, politicians, painters, scientists, sportsmen, campaigners and reformers – people from different countries, cultures and backgrounds – have all been commemorated in this way. In order to be eligible for a plaque there are a number of criteria to be met: the person must have been dead for 20 years, or have passed the centenary of their birth, whichever is the earlier; be considered eminent by a majority of members of their own profession or calling; have made an important positive contribution to human welfare or happiness; be recognisable to the well-informed passer-by; deserve national recognition; have resided in a locality for a significant period, in time or importance, within their life and work. To illustrate their diversity, in Mayfair there is a plaque to George Frederick Handel at 25 Brook Street and next door at no. 23 a plaque to Jimi Hendrix.

Royal Hospital★★ (CZ)

⏱ *Open daily, 10am-noon and 2-4pm; and Apr-Oct, closed Sun (Oct-Mar) and bank hols. Grounds: Open usually daily, 10am-4pm. Free admission. Leaflet (8 languages).* ☎ *020 7881 5204; info@chelsea-pensioners.org.uk; www.chelsea-pensioners.co.uk.* The hospital was founded by King Charles II in 1682 as a retreat for veterans of the regular army who had been retired from duty, after 20 years' service, or had become unfit for duty, as a result of wounds or disease. The provision of a hospital, rather than some system of pensions was undoubtedly inspired by the Hôtel des Invalides in Paris, founded by Louis XIV in 1670 about which Charles II had received glowing reports. The Latin inscription in Figure Court reads: "For the succour and relief of old soldiers and men broken by War. Founded by Charles II enlarged by James II and long completed by William and Mary, King and Queen in the year of our Lord – 1692."

Wren produced a quadrangular plan with a main court open to the south towards the river and the grounds,; he expanded it by abutting courts to east and west, always leaving one side open. The main entrance is beneath the lantern-crowned octagon porch in the north range of the original **Figure Court**, after the classical statue of

Tyburn Gallows

The spot now marked with a small brass plaque at the junction of Bayswater Road and Edgware Road (adjacent to Marble Arch) was for nearly 400 years the deadliest site in England. The first recorded execution took place here in 1196, but it became the principal place of public executions in 1388. In 1571 the "Tyburn Tree," London's first permanent gallows, was erected. It was a triangular structure some 12ft (4m) high with three 9ft (3m) cross beams on which up to 24 people could be hanged at one time. Although public executions were intended as a deterrent they degenerated into riotous carnivals more analagous to modern-day fairs or sports event. Temporary grandstands were ercted and "Tyburn Fairs" attracted enormous crowds. In 1714 an astonishing 200,000 people turned out to witness the hanging of the legendary highwayman Jack Sheppard. By the time of the last execution here in 1783 it is estimated that around 50,000 people had perished on this spot.

Charles II by **Grinling Gibbons** at the centre. From the octagon porch, steps rise to the **Chapel** and **Great Hall,** both panelled beneath tall rounded windows. The Chapel has a barrel vault decorated with plasterwork and, at the end, a domed, painted apse by Ricci. The Hall is decorated with an 18C mural of Charles II on horseback before the hospital.

The "Old Soldiers" themselves can be seen in their blue un-dress and on more formal occasions in their scarlet full-dress uniforms, out and about on the nearby streets.

Every summer, the **Chelsea Flower Show** is held in the hospital grounds, attracting thousands of visitors over three days. It is one of the highlights of the British summer showing off flowers gardens and all related matters to the nation.

Carlyle's House (CZ)

(NT) ⏰ *24 Cheyne Row. Open late-Mar to Oct, Wed-Sun and Bank Hol Mon, 2pm (11am Sun and Bank Hol Mon) to 5pm. Closed Good Fri.* ⊜ *£4.* ☎ *020 7352 7087; 01494 755 559(infoline); Fax 020 7352 5108; carlyleshouse@nationaltrust.org.uk; www.nationaltrust. org.uk. Access: by bus 11, 19, 22, 49, 239, 249, 319.* The modest Queen Anne house was the home of the historian and writer Thomas Carlyle from 1834 to 1881; it contains portraits, personal relics, books and furniture.

OUTER LONDON

River cruise downstream

In fine weather it is pleasant to make an excursion to Greenwich by river cruiser from Westminster, Charing Cross or Tower Pier, returning by the foot tunnel under the Thames to Island Gardens, Docklands Light Railway (DLR) and the underground, or by train to Charing Cross Station or London Bridge Station. The scenic ride on the elevated track of the DLR is highly recommended. ☎ *020 7222 1234 (London Travel Information Service - 24hrs); travinfo@tfl.gov.uk; www.tfl.gov.uk.* The cruise passes a number of famous landmarks, old and new. Opposite Westminster Pier stands **County Hall**★ **(EY)** opened in 1922 and designed by Ralph Knott. The **Royal Festival Hall**★ (1951) is the earliest of the **South Bank Arts Centre**★★ **(EFXY)** buildings; later additions are the **Queen Elizabeth Hall** and the **Purcell Room** (1967), the **Hayward Gallery** (1968) and the **National Theatre**★ (1976) by Denys Lasdun, comprising three theatres seating audiences of 400, 890 and 1 100. Opposite is the river façade of **Somerset House**★ **(EX)** designed by Sir William Chambers in 1777. Further along the Victoria Embankment are *HMS Wellington,* a Second World War frigate converted into the floating hall of the Honourable Company of Master Mariners, and *HMS Chrysanthemum,* the headquarters of the London Division of the Royal Naval Volunteer Reserve, backed by the gardens of the Inner Temple. Below Blackfriars Bridges, Southwark Bridge and Cannon Street Bridge is the Kathleen May a 1900 trading schooner, moored near to **Southwark Cathedral** (👆 *see p349*). London Bridge (1973) is the latest structure; its predecessor was sold for £1 000 000 and is now in Arizona. Above **Tower Bridge**★★ (👆 *see p348*) is the **Tower of London**★★★ facing *HMS Belfast* (1938) a Second World War cruiser (11 500t), moored beside **Hays Galleria** (👆 *see p349*). Below the bridge are **St Katharine Docks**★. The river loops north round the old Surrey Docks (south bank) and then south opposite the **Canary Wharf Tower** (1992) on the Isle of Dogs *(north bank)* before passing Deptford Creek *(south bank)* upstream from Greenwich.

Greenwich ★★★ (UY)

Maritime Centre

Greenwich has been in the royal domain since King Alfred's time. Henry V's brother, Humphrey, Duke of Gloucester, first enclosed the park and transformed the manor into a castle which he named Bella Court. The Tudors preferred Greenwich to their other residences and Henry VIII, who was born there, extended the castle into a vast palace with a royal armoury; he also founded naval dockyards upstream at Deptford and downstream at Woolwich. During the Commonwealth the palace became derelict. The only building to survive was the Queen's House (☉ see below).

After the Restoration, Charles II commissioned John Webb, a student of Inigo Jones, to build a King's House. William and Mary, who preferred Hampton Court (☉ see below), granted a charter for the foundation of a Royal Hospital for Seamen at Greenwich, with **Wren** as surveyor. In 1873 the Webb and Wren buildings were transformed into the Royal Naval College, while the Queen's House, extended by two wings in 1807, became the National Maritime Museum in 1937.

Queen's House ★★

Romney Road, Greenwich. ♿ ⏱ *Open daily, 10am-5pm (6pm summer).* ⏱ *Closed 24-25 Dec.* ☎ *020 8858 4422; 020 8312 6565 (24hr recorded information); www.nmm.ac.uk.* This elegant white Palladian villa, which is part of the **National Maritime Museum** ★★ (☉ *see Museums and Galleries below*), was commissioned by James I for his queen, Anne of Denmark, from Inigo Jones, who designed it in 1615 as the very first Classical mansion in England. Although work ceased on Anne's death it was resumed when Charles I gave the house to his Queen, Henrietta Maria, whose name and the date 1635 appear on the north front. Distinctive features include its colour, the beautiful horse-shoe shaped staircase descending from the terrace on the north front and the loggia on the south front facing the park. The ground floor rooms illustrate the architecture of the house, famous associations and its historical importance in relation to Greenwich. On the first floor are displayed naval portraits and paintings.

Greenwich Park and Royal Observatory ★

♿ ⏱ *Opening times and charges the same as for the National Maritime Museum.* The Park, the oldest enclosed royal domain, extends for 180 acres/72ha, rising to a point 155ft/47m above the river, crowned by the Old Royal Observatory and the **General Wolfe** Monument. In 1675 Charles II directed Wren to "build a small observatory within our park at Greenwich, upon the highest ground at or near the place where the castle stood" for the "finding out of the longitude of places for perfect navigation and astronomy." Until the inauguration of the annual Nautical Almanack in 1767 map makers fixed the zero meridian where they chose; thereafter they began to base their calculations on Greenwich and by 1884 75% of the world's charts were based on the Greenwich Meridian.

Inside Wren's brick **Flamsteed House** is the lofty Octagon Room, beautifully proportioned, equipped with what John Evelyn called "the choicest instrument." It is from this building that the new Millennium celebrations will be inaugurated. The **Meridian Building** was added in the mid 18C to house the growing **collection** ★★ of telescopes.

The Millennium Dome

Riverside walks, parkland and lakes to attract wildlife have transformed the Greenwich peninsula where the site of a former gas works has been extensively developed to include roads, housing and other local amenities. The most striking building and focal point is the Millennium Dome originally built for the Millennium celebrations. Sited right on the Meridian Line, the Dome is the largest single roofed structure in the world. Its external appearance is that of a huge (365m diameter) white marquee held up by twelve 95m-high towers. its circumference exceeds 1km and the floorspace is large enough to park 18,000 London buses. To celebrate the Millennium it held the Millennium Experience, a multi-media attraction that received a lot of hostile criticism from the press and did not attract the visitor numbers it hoped. The huge cost of the project and the fact that it has lain mostly empty since then has made it one of the most derided projects in the country. However with the announcement that London is going to host the 2012 Olympics it has been thrown a lifeline. The Dome will be transformed into a 20,000 seat venue that will host Gymnastics and the finals of the Basketball competition. Meanwhile the World Gymnastics Championships will take place at the Dome in 2009.

Note Airey's Transit Circle, through which the meridian passes and outside, the brass meridian of 0°, the clocks showing world times and the 24hr clock.

Old Royal Naval College★★

Painted Hall and Chapel and Greenwich Gateway Visitor Centre. ◷*Open daily, 10am (Sun 11am service) to 5pm. Free admission.* ☎ *020 8269 4791; Fax 020 8269 4757; info@ greenwichfoundation.org.uk; www.greenwichfoundation.org.uk.* After demolishing the Tudor Palace (⌚ *see above),* Wren retained the King Charles Block to which he added three symmetrical blocks named after King William, Queen Mary and Queen Anne. For the Queen's House (⌚ *see above)* he provided a river vista (150ft/46m) flanked by twin cupolas over the Chapel and the Painted Hall down to a new river embankment.

The **Painted Hall**★ in the domed refectory building is the work of **Sir James Thornhill,** exuberant Baroque representations of William and Mary, Anne, George I and his descendants, in an allegorical celebration of British maritime power, painted 1708-27. The ceiling is covered by the largest painting in Great Britain, the Triumph of Peace and Liberty by Sir James Thornhill. It measures 106ft/32m by 51 ft/15m and has been descibed as the finest example of Eglish baroque decorative painting, The rate of pay was £3 per square yard for the ceiling (and £1 per yard for the walls). Thornhill and his assistants worked on it for 20 years finally completing it in 1727. They received, what was for then, the princely sum of £6685, which at the time made it the world's most expensive painting.

The **Chapel**★ by Wren was redecorated after a fire in 1779 by **"Athenian" Stuart** and **William Newton** as a Rococo interior in Wedgwood pastels. In contrast to such delicate patterns, at the apse is *St Paul after the Shipwreck at Malta* by **Benjamin West,** who designed the stone medallions for the pulpit which is made from the top of a three-decker.

Cutty Sark★★

King William Walk. ◷*Open daily, 10am-5pm.* ◷ *Closed 24-26 Dec.* ᐧ *£4.50. Leaflet (22 languages); guide book (3 languages).* ☎ *020 8858 3445; Fax 020 8853 3589; info@ cuttysark.org.uk; www.cuttysark.org.uk.* Emphasising Greenwich's maritime importance, this splendid clipper, launched in 1869 for the China tea trade, stands in a dry dock by the river. Famous in her heyday as the fastest clipper afloat, her best day's run, with all 32 000sq ft/3 000m2 of canvas fully spread, was 363mi/584km.

There is a fine **view**★★ of Greenwich Palace from Island Gardens on the north bank, which can be reached via the foot tunnel (lift or 100 steps). Canaletto painted this scene in 1750 and and his work hangs in the National Maritime Museum.

Kew and Hampton Court★★★

Kew Gardens★★★ (TY)

♿◷ *Open daily, late-Mar-Oct, 9.30am-6.30pm (7.30pm Sat-Sun and Bank Hol); Sep-Mar 9.30am-6pm (4.15pm late-Oct to early-Feb, 5.30pm early-Feb to late-Mar).* ◷ *Closed 25 Dec, 1 Jan. Glasshouses, museum and galleries close earlier than the Gardens.* ᐧ *£10. Visitor Centre at Victoria Gate.* ᐧ *Guided tour from Victoria Gate: daily at 11am and 2pm. Maps available (5 languages). Restaurants. Shops.* ☎ *020 8332 5655; info@kew.org; www.kew.org.* The **Royal Botanic Gardens,** the finest in the land, are a treat at any time of year. The layman will spot commonplace flowers and shrubs and be amazed by exotics, while experienced gardeners can check their knowledge against the well labelled specimens. For this 300 acre/1200 ha garden is not just a pleasure garden but the offshoot of laboratories engaged in the identification and conservation of plants from from every corner of the earth, for economic, medical and other purposes. It also contains the biggest herbarium in the world, a library of over 100,000 volumes and a "university of botany" training students over a three-year course.

The gardens were begun in 1756 by **Sir William Chambers** at the behest of Augusta, Princess of Wales. The same architect designed the **Orangery**★, the three small classical temples and in 1761 the 163ft/50m high ten-storey **Pagoda**★. As the gardens grew, more buildings were added, notably Decimus Burton's **Palm House**★★ in 1848, which has recently been completely refurbished. In 1899 Burton completed the **Temperate House**★, which contains camellias, rain forest and dragon trees. In 1987 Diana Princess of Wales opened the **Princess of Wales Conservatory,** a steel and glass diamond-shaped structure in which ten different tropical habitats ranging from mangrove swamp to sand desert are created and maintained by computer. Other buildings to visit include the **Alpine House** which sits beneath a glass pyramid from which rainwater drains in to the surrounding moat; the **Marianne North Gallery**

Royal Botanic Gardens, Kew

which exhibits the beautiful paintings of Marianne North made during her botanically inspired travels between 1871 and 1874.

Close to the river stands **Kew Palace**★★ built for the London merchant Samuel Fortrey in 1631. The dark-red brick building with distinctive Dutch attic gables was leased by George II for Queen Caroline in about 1730 and purchased by George III in 1781. The interior is, therefore, that of a small country house of George III's time, with panelled rooms downstairs and intimate family portraits by Gainsborough, Zoffany and others upstairs. It served as a location in the 1994 film *Madness of King George*.

Hampton Court Palace and Gardens★★★ (TZ)

East Moseley, Surrey; &Open daily, 9.30am (10.15am Mon) to 6pm (4.30pm mid-Oct to mid-Mar). Closed 24-26 Dec. Guided tour. Family trails. Audio guide. £11. Privy Garden or Maze only, £3.50. Parking £3.50. Restaurant, café. Carriage rides (summer only). 020 8781 9500; www.hrp.org.uk. Tudor Tennis Court and Banqueting House: Open in summer as for palace. Chapel Royal: Services: Sun at 8.30am (Holy Communion); 11am (Sung Eucharist on 1st Sun; Choral Matins on other Sun); 3.30pm (Choral Evensong); Visitors 12.45-1.45pm. Gardens: Open daily free, 7am-dusk (9pm summer; 4pm winter).

This magnificent Tudor palace was begun (1514-29) by **Cardinal Wolsey**, son of an Ipswich butcher. He rose to high office but his failure to obtain papal approval for Henry VIII's divorce from Catherine of Aragon and the size and sumptuousness of his palace angered the King. He died in disgrace in 1530 a year after his fall from favour; Hampton Court was appropriated by the King.

Henry VIII then set about enlarging the palace; he built wings on the imposing west front, the splendid Great Hall with its hammerbeam roof and lavishly transformed the chapel. The remarkable Astronomical Clock in Clock Court, though made for him in 1540, was brought here from St James's Palace in the 19C.

150 years after Henry's death, William and Mary had plans to rebuild the palace (which had survived Cromwell, having been reserved for him), but instead Wren began alterations in 1688. He rebuilt the east and south fronts, the **State Apartments** and the smaller royal apartments. These rooms were decorated with carvings by **Grinling Gibbons** and painted ceilings by **Verrio**. The apartments and rooms contain a superb collection of **paintings** and **furniture**, while the **Kitchens** and the **King's Beer Cellars** and the **Wine Cellars** offer a glimpse of life in Tudor times, all enhanced by costumed actors who interact with visitors while taking great care to stay within their "own" time period! The **Gardens**★★★ as seen today are the results of various schemes. Charles II had the mile-long canal dug and William III created the Great Fountain Garden. The famous triangular **maze** north of the palace was planted in 1690. Further north, outside the palace walls, lies Bushy Park with its **Chestnut Avenue,** particularly colourful in May. In 1768 under George III, Capability Brown planted the **Great Vine**★, now a plant of remarkable girth which usually produces an annual crop of around 500-600 bunches of grapes *(on sale late August/early September).*

Museums and Galleries

British Museum★★★ (EX)

Great Russell Street. ♿🕐*Open daily, 10am-5.30pm (8.30pm Thu-Fri).* 🕐 *Closed Good Friday, 24-26 Dec, 1 Jan. No charge to main galleries, variable rates for temporary exhibitions.* ✎ *Various guided tours - a charge is made for this ; lectures, gallery talks and films. Guide (8 languages). Restaurant, café. Wheelchairs for hire.* ☎ *020 7323 8299; 020 7637 7384 (recorded information for disabled visitors); 020 7323 8181 (bookings); Fax 020 7323 8614; information@thebritishmuseum.ac.uk; www.thebritishmuseum.ac.uk.*

When Sir Hans Sloane's collection was bequeathed to the nation in 1753 Parliament was encouraged to found the British Museum.

Already in the vaults in Westminster lay Sir Robert Cotton's (1570-1631) priceless collection of medieval manuscripts and the old Royal Library of 12 000 volumes assembled by monarchs since Tudor times. As more and more collections were presented a separate building became necessary. Montagu House was bought with money raised in a lottery and the Museum opened in 1759. Exhibits were displayed unlabelled, causing Cobbett to call the museum "the old curiosity shop."

To house the burgeoning collection Smirke produced plans which culminated in the replacement of Montagu House by the present building and its later additions. The early sequence of acquisitions, increased in the 19C and 20C by finds by archeologists attached to the museum, brought the BM its reputation as one of the greatest centres of world antiquities. Notable among the Egyptian antiquities are the **mummies** and the **Rosetta Stone**. The latter is part of a 6ft block of black basalt found in the Western Egyptian Delta region by French troops. With the capitualtion of Alexandria in 1801 the French were compelled to hand the stone to the British. Its significance rests in the parallel transcriptions in Ancient Greek and two written forms of Egyptian, one being pictorial heiroglyphics, the other Demotic text, forming a decree passsed 27 March 196 BC. For the first time Egyptologists were therefore provided with the key to decipher heiroglyphics which had been in use since the third millenium BC and Demotic texts which dated back to 643 BC. No less fascinating is **"Ginger"** (so-named after the colour of his hair) a 5000-year old corpse naturally preserved intact by dehydration after being buried in the hot sands around 3300 BC.

The collection of Western Asiatic antiquities is particularly wide-ranging, while the Greek and Roman antiquities include the **Elgin Marbles** (sculptures from the Parthenon). These are the museum's most contentious exhibit. The Museum correctly argues that had the British, specifically Lord Elgin, not removed them from Athens at the time then they would have been destroyed. However the Greek governement mounts a continuous lobby for their return. The British Museum, and British government, fearing that such a move would signal the beginning of the end for its collections from all over the world have so far resisted. Look closely at the tiny but exquisite Roman **Portland Vase** and you can see that it has been carefully pieced back together again after a madman smashed it into 200 pieces with a hammer in 1845.

The Oriental collection with its fine T'ang horses is no less significant. In the Prehistoric and Romano-British and Medieval sections admire the craftsmanship of the shields,

Changes post-Millennium

The British Museum has undergone large-scale re-organisation since the year 2000 and if you have not visited recently you wil be amazed by the changes: the **British Library** has moved into new purpose-built premises in Euston Road (next to St Pancras Station) and the ethnographic collections formerly displayed in the Museum of Mankind (on Piccadilly) have been moved here to three permanent galleries that exhibit ethnographic material : the Sainsbury African Galleries, the Chase Manhattan North American Gallery, and the Ancient Mexico Gallery. The African galleries are open daily but the Mexican and North American galleries are subject to closure, so do check prior to visiting.

The **Great Court Project**, designed by Sir Norman Foster is now the hub of the museum and makes for a stunning entrance foyer adorned with an enigmatic Easter Island statue. This glass and steel roof spans the space to the Round Reading Room (which is now used for research as a high-tech information centre) and creates the largest covered square in Europe. Work in progress or to be completed in the near future includes: The Grand Rooms will be restored to their former glorious Regency decorative schemes; the King's Library will provide displays relating to the Age of Enlightenment and connoisseurship; Classical sculpture will be displayed in the Manuscripts Saloon.

helmets and delicate golden torcs. Less appealing is **Lindow Man** (1C AD) garroted and with his throat cut, preserved in a peat bog, evidence of human sacrifice. Reminders of Roman Britain abound in the Weston Gallery of Roman Britain, most notably the 4C silver set of tableware known as the **Mildenhall Treasure**, found in Mildenhall, Suffolk, and considered to be the finest pieces of their kind anywhere in the Roman Empire. Even this was eclipsed however in 1994 by the **Hoxne Hoard** which comprises thousands of coins, jewellery and silver plate, also found in Suffolk.

In the Medieval. Renaissance and Modern Collections is the **Sutton Hoo Ship Burial** which shows the rich variety of artefacts retieved from a royal tomb including fabulous gold jewellery, weapons and armour. Note too the beautifully carved mid-12C walrus ivory **Lewis Chessmen** found on the Isle of Lewis in the Outer Hebrides and, nearby, the **Royal Gold Cup** of the kings of France and England, made in Paris c.1380.

The Western Asiatic section covers the ancient lands of Mesopotamia and Asia Minor and the collection of **Assyrian sculptures** from the cities of Nimrud, Khorsabad and Nineveh are breathtaking. From ancient Iran the rich artistic tradition of the Persian Empire shines through in the **Luristan Bronzes** c.1200BC, and the fabulous **Oxus Treasure** (5C-4C BC). In the Ancient Turkey and Iraq section is the **Flood Tablet** telling a story from the Epic of Gilgamesh.

The circular, domed **Reading Room** (40ft/12m wide) dates from 1857, and was designed by Principal Librarian Antonio Panizzi and architect Sydney Smirke (younger brother to Robert) to ensure that the "poorest student" as well as men of letters should be able to have access to the library, the King's Library, a splendid room by Smirke, being too small to provide sufficient seating or to house the Grenville Library, bequeathed in 1847. The Reading Room has accommodated 400 readers and 25mi/40km of shelving (1 300 000 books). The restored blue and gold decoration of the dome recreates the original setting, where Karl Marx, Lenin and George Bernard Shaw, among thousands of luminaries once sat and studied

British Library

*96 Euston Road. Exhibition Galleries: ♿ ◷ Open Mon-Sat, 9.30am-6pm (8pm Tue; 5pm Sat), Sun, 11am-5pm. Reading rooms: Open only to readers with a Readers Pass. Cafe. ☎ 020 7412 7332 (Visitor Services); visitor-service@bl.uk; www. bl.uk.*The British Library was designed by Professor Sir Colin St John Wilson and is a free-form, asymmetric building of red brick, Welsh slate roofs, metal and granite weatherings, which has provoked a mixed response from the public (and a famously negative one from the Prince of Wales, a lover of Classical rather than Modern architecture). The entrance piazza is dominated by a monumental bronze statue of Newton (after Blake) by Sir Eduardo Paolozzi. Naturally, it is not only the building's aesthetic appeal, but also its practicality as a place to read and think which must be the criteria for judging its success. The Library aims to improve its services to readers with the aid of automated systems for the catalogue, requests and bookhandling.

The Library's most famous treasures include a copy of Magna Carta, the Lindisfarne Gospel, Codex Sinaiticus the Gutenberg Bible, Diamond Sutra, Essex's death warrant, Nelson's last letter, Shakespeare's signature and First Folioo (1623), the Beatles manuscripts) are on display in the John Ritblat Gallery. Advanced technology makes it possible to turn the pages of rare books (if only virtually) at the touch of a button. The Pearson Gallery of Living Words, organised in five themes, reflects the diversity of the Library's collection through books, manuscripts, interactive displays etc. The Workshop of Words, Sound and Images is a hands-on gallery tracing the story of book production from the earliest written documents to the 20C digital revolution (interactive displays, demonstrations).

National Gallery★★★ (EX)

Trafalgar Square; ♿ ◷ Open daily, 10am-6pm (9pm Wed). ◷ Closed Good Fri, 24-26 Dec, 1 Jan. No charge to main galleries. Micro Gallery: Open daily, 10am-5.30pm (8.30pm Wed). ⬤ Guided tour (1hr): daily at 11.30am and 2.30pm (6.30pm Wed); meet in Sainsbury Wing Vestibule. Gallery Guide Soundtrack for hire (6 languages). Welcome sheet (6 languages). Restaurant, café. ☎ 020 7747 2885; Fax: 020 7747 2423; information@ng-london. org.uk; www.nationalgallery.org.uk. Access: by bus 3, 6, 9, 11, 12, 13, 15, 23, 24, 29, 53, X53, 77A, 88, 91, 109, 139, 159, 176. ⊖ Charing Cross, Leicester Square, Embankment, Piccadilly Circus. After more than a century of discussion the collection was founded by Parliamentary purchase in 1824, its nucleus being 38 pictures collected by City merchant and banker **John Julius Angerstein** (1735-1823). Only in 1838 was the new gallery completed, its pedimented portico of Corinthian columns forming a climax to Trafalgar Square. The sixth and latest extension to the original building by William Wilkins is the Sainsbury Wing (1991) by R Venturi.

There are now more than 2 000 paintings in the collection; they represent the jewels in the public domain from Early to High Renaissance Italian painting, early Netherlandish, German, Flemish, Dutch, French and Spanish pictures and masterpieces of the English 18C. (The fuller representation of British art, particularly the more modern and 20C work of all schools is in the Tate Gallery.)

The galleries are arranged chronologically starting with the period 1260-1510 in the **Sainsbury Wing**. Leonardo's fragile prparatory "cartoon" of *Virgin and Child with St Anne and John the Baptist* is spectacular while his *Virgin on the Rocks* is similarly enigmatic and engaging. Ucello exploits strong lines and colour in his epic *Battle of San Romano*. Haunting realism and solemn stillness are the keywords in the works of Van Eyck and Van der Weyden particularly in the former's legendary *Arnolfini Portrait*. Boticelli is represented by *Venus and Mars* and *Portrait of a Young Man* while other Italian masters in this gallery are Raphael, Mantegna and Bellini whose perfect use of oils is encapsulated in his *Madonna and Child*. Earlier German and Netherlandish work is also represented by Dürer, Cranach, Bosch and Memlinc.

Paintings in the **West Wing** range from 1510 to 1600. *The Ambassadors* by Holbein is a wonderful large scale historical portrait and its famous *trompe l'oeil* skull is a great favourite with gallery visitors. TIntoretto, El Greco, Michelangelo and Veronese are also here.

In the North Wing are paintings by the French School, the Spanish School and from the Low Countries. Works by Claude and the great British landscape artist JMW Turner are exhibited together and should not be missed. Rembrandt and Rubens, Caravaggio, Velazquez and Van Dyck (his huge *Equestrian Picture of Charles I* is unmissable) also star here.

Paintings from 1700 to 1900 are exhibited in the **East Wing**. The British School is exemplified by classics such as *The Haywain* by Constable, *The Fighting Temeraire* and *Rain Steam and Speed*, by JMW Turner. There are works by Canaletto, Goya , Tiepolo and Delacroix but many visitor's favourites are the Impressionist collection starring Pisarro, Renoir, Monet, Manet, Degas and Cézanne. Van Gogh is probably the most easily recognised artist with *Van Gogh's Chair* and *Sunflowers* (once the world's most expensive painting) standing out as crowd pleasers. Seurat's *Bathers at Asnière* is another favourite. Another distinctive and well liked artist is Henri Rousseau whose *Tiger in a Tropical Storm* is a classic.

Science Museum★★★ (BY)

Exhibition Road, South Kensington. &*Open daily, 10am-6pm.* *Closed 24-26 Dec. Brochure (6 languages). Free Admission. Bookshop. Restaurant; picnic area.* 0870 870 4868; sciencemuseum@nmsi.ac.uk; www.sciencemuseum.org.uk. This factory-laboratory of Man's continuing invention extends over 7 acres/nearly 3ha. There are innumerable working models, handles to pull, buttons to push as well as a hands-on experience area, the Launch Pad. The Wellcome Galleries on the History of Medicine were opened in the early 1980s.

Tate Britain★★★ (EZ)

Millbank. &*Open daily, 10am-5.50pm.* *Closed 24-26 Dec. No charge for permanent collection; variable fee for temporary exhibitions. Guide book (6 languages). Restaurant: Open daily noon-3pm (4pm Sun). Self-service café: Open daily, noon-5.40pm (4pm Sun). Audio guide* £3. 020 7887 8000 (recorded information), 020 7887 8000; 7887 8687 (minicom); Fax 020 7887 8007; information@tate.org.uk; www. tate.org.uk. Access: by bus 2, 3, 36, 77A, 88, 159, 185, 507, C10; Pimlico, then 5min walk (follow the signs); BR Vauxhall Station. The gallery developed because within 50 years of the founding of the National Gallery in 1824 the nation had acquired a large number of pictures – notably through the Turner bequest of 282 oils and 19 000 watercolours (1856), the Chantrey bequest for the purchase of works by living artists as well as early masters and through two major collections. These pictures were variously exhibited in the National Gallery, the Victoria and Albert and Marlborough House until, in 1891, Henry Tate, sugar broker and collector of modern art, offered his collection to the nation and £80 000 for a building, if the government would provide a site.

The site of the former Millbank prison was offered and in 1897 the Tate opened as the Gallery of Modern British Art. Tate and the Duveens funded extensions, Sir Hugh Lane bequeathed 39 paintings, including some superb Impressionists, in 1923 Samuel Courtauld funded the purchase of modern French paintings and in 1955 the Tate became legally independent of the National Gallery.

Tate Modern★★

Bankside. ♿🕐 *Open daily, 10am (galleries 10.15am) to 6pm (10pm Fri-Sat).* 🕐 *Closed 24-26 Dec. No charge for permanent collection; variable fee for temporary exhibitions. Parking for the disabled only. Restaurants. 020 7887 8000 (exhibitions), 020 7887 8008 (recorded information); 0870 166 8283 (ticketmaster); www.tate.org.uk. Access: by bus: 45, 63, 100, 381, 344* ⊖ *Southwark, Blackfriars.*

Victoria and Albert Museum★★★ (CY)

Cromwell Road; ♿🕐 *Open daily, 10am-5.45pm (10pm Wed and last Fri of month).* 🕐 *Closed 24-26 Dec. Brochure/map (26 languages).* 🔊 *Guided tours (1hr; no charge): daily at 10.30am, 11.30am, 12.30pm. 1.30pm, 2.30pm and 3.30 (also Wed at 4.30pm and 7.30pm) from the Main Entrance. Gallery talks daily, 1pm (no charge). Demonstrations Sat, 2-5pm (no charge). Photography permitted (no flash, no tripods). Restaurant. Entrances in Cromwell Road and Exhibition Road. Print Study Room: Tue-Fri, 10am-4.30pm.* ☎ *020 7942 2000; 0870 442 0809 (recorded information on current exhibitions); www.vam.ac.uk. Access: by bus C1, 14, 74,* ⊖ *South Kensington.* This fabulously rich and varied collection was started, in part, with the purchase of contemporary works manufactured for the Great Exhibition of 1851. It includes the national collection of furniture, British sculpture, textiles, ceramics, silver and watercolours, as well as world-famous displays of fashionable dress, jewellery, Italian Renaissance sculpture, and art from India and the Far East. Since 1909 the Museum has been housed in Aston Webb's idiosyncratic building of brick, terracotta and stone, fittingly adorned with a figure of Prince Albert. Even among London museums this is a huge rambling collection and for the one-time visitor its size is overwhelming. It is best to head for those areas that you take a special interest in and then perhaps meander back through other collections. The following are a few highlights.

Renaissance Sculptures. There are works by Donatello and Bernini but the most highly prized is Michelangelo's *Slave*, a wax preparatory model for a figure intended for the tomb of Pope Julius II.

Cast Courts. A collection of casts made 1860-1880 for the benefit of art students who could not go abroad to see the real thing, include Trajan's Column (AD 113), bronze doors of the baptistery in Florence by Ghiberti, *St George* by Donatello and *Dying Slave* by Michelangelo.

Prints, Drawings and Paintings. This section covers various media including the National Collection of Watercolours , the National Collection of Portrait Miniatures,the Sheepshank Gift (an important bequest containing works by JMW Turner and William Blake) and the John Constable collection. The most valuable collection however is the **Raphael Cartoons**, seven huge tapestry patterns, commissioned in 1515 by Pope Leo X for the Sistine Chapel.

Furniture and Woodwork. The collection ranges from the Middle Ages to the present day and encompasses just about ever culture. **The Great Bed of Ware,** mentioned by Shakespeare, is the most remarkable piece of ancient British furniture. It is said to have once slept 52 people (26 butchers and their wives). There are some striking Art Nouveau objects in the American and European 1800-1900 section while the Frank Lloyd Wright gallery is pernennially popular with those who want to study or just admire the works of the "greatest American architect to date."

Textiles and Dress. One of the world's most extensive collections of textiles spanning 5,000 years and most of the globe. For general interest the Fashion Gallery will bring a smile to the face of most people who are at all interested in the vagaries of clothing fashions.

Metalworks and Jewellery. This is perhaps the most diverse and eclectic national collection, ranging from the 2C BC to the 21C AD and encompasses a very broad spectrum. The Jewellery Galleries, the Burghley nef (a salt holder in the form of a ship), the Nuremberg beaker and the collection of clocks, sundials and watches displayed with the Musical instruments, are among the finer pieces.

Eastern works of art. Some 60,000 artefacts from China, Korea and Japan make up this collection. The most famous exhibit is **Tipu's Tiger**, a near-lifesize painted wooden tiger mauling its white victim. Within the tiger is an organ that simulates both the tigers roars and its victim's groans. It was captured by the British from their arch enemy Tipu, Sultan of Mysore at the fall of Seringapatam in 1799.

Wallace Collection★★★ (DX)

Oxford Street; Open daily, 10am (noon Sun) to 5pm. Closed Good Fri, May Day Hol, 24-26 Dec, 1 Jan. Guided tour (1hr). Leaflet. Guide book (3 languages). Free Admission. 020 7563 9500; Fax 020 7224 2155; admin@the-wallace-collection.org.uk; www.wallacecollection.org. The gathering of one of the world's finer collections of 18C French art was the life's work of the 4th Marquess of Hertford (1800-70) who lived mostly in Paris at his small château, Bagatelle, in the Bois de Boulogne. He greatly increased the family collection of Italian masters, 17C Dutch painting, 18C French furniture (note the magnificent cabinets by A C Boulle), and Sèvres porcelain and bought extensively the 18C French painters **Watteau, Boucher** and **Fragonard**. His son Richard Wallace (1818-90), founder and benefactor of the Hertford British Hospital in Paris, having added yet more to the collection, finally brought it to England, where his widow subsequently left it to the nation in 1900. Don;t miss the formidable display of European weapons and arms, nor **Gallery 22** hung with the larger 17C pictures and Old Master paintings including works by Rubens, Murillo, Velazquez, Rembrandt, Van Dyck, Gainsborough and the most popular work in the museum, *The Laughing Cavalier* by Frans Hals.

National Maritime Museum★★

Open daily, 10am-5pm (6pm summer). Closed 24-26 Dec. Licensed café- restaurant. Play area. 020 8858 4422; 020 8312 6565 (24hr recorded information). As part of its £20 million transformation, the museum now boasts an impressive single-span glazed roof, the largest in Europe, above a neo-Classical courtyard. It is organised by theme, covering past, present and future aspects in most cases: **Explorers** begins with the stories of Columbus and Cook through to modern sailors and underwater exploration; **Passengers** relates historic stories of migration and also looks at futuristic cruise liners and nautical fashion; **Traders** examines the development of the global economy through maritime trade; the **Global Garden** illustrates how the impact of plants and produce from distant lands has changed our life style; **Trade and Empire** studies the political influences of the travellers; and **Future of the Sea** emphasizes ecology and the environment. The museum's fine collections of art is on display (rotating) in a new **Art and the Sea** gallery. For children, the new **Bridge** feature links with the already popular **All Hands** gallery. Also part of the museum is the Queen's House and the Royal Observatory, Greenwich.

Natural History Museum★★ (BY)

Cromwell Road. Open daily, 10am (11am Sun) to 5.50pm (5.30pm last admission). Free Admission. Map and guide. Changing programme of special events. Activity sheets for children (40-80p). Book shop. Restaurant, café, coffee bar, snack bar and picnic area. 020 7942 5000; www.nhm.ac.uk. Access: bus 14, 49, 70, 74, 345 & C1; South Kensington. Alfred Waterhouse's vast symmetrical palace, inspired by medieval Rhineland architecture, was opened in 1881 to house the British Museum's ever-growing natural history collection, which today illustrates all forms of life, from the smallest bacteria to the largest creatures, fossils and dinosaurs, minerals and rocks as well as an exhibition of Man's place in evolution.

Museum of London★★ (FGX)

London Wall. Open daily, 10am (noon Sun) to 5.50pm (last admission 5.30pm). Closed 24-26 Dec, 1 Jan. £5, Free admission Mon (excl. bank hols) 10am-2pm. 0870 444 3852, recorded info line 0870 444 3851; Fax 020 7600 1058; info@museumoflondon. org.uk; www.museumoflondon.org.uk. In an interesting modern building, the Museum of London - the biggest city history museum in the world - presents the story of London from prehistory to the present day, with exhibits as various as the sculptures from the Roman temple

Natural History Museum

of Mithras, medieval pilgrim badges, the Cheapside Hoard of Jacobean jewellery, a diorama of the Great Fire, the doors from Newgate Gaol, 19C shops and interiors, the Lord Mayor's Coach, souvenirs of the women's suffrage movement... The development of domestic life and public utility services are illustrated as well as political and fashionable London.

Courtauld Institute Galleries★★ (EX)

Somerset House, The Strand. ♿🕐 Open daily, 10am (noon Sun) to 6pm. 🕐 Closed 25-26 Dec. ⊞ £5. Coffee shop. ☎ 020 7848 2526; Fax 020 7848 2589; galleryinfo@courtauld. ac.uk; www.courtauld.ac.uk. Since 1990 the Courtauld Institute Galleries have been housed above the gateway in the Strand Block of Somerset House; the **Fine Rooms**, which are notable for their proportions and handsome plaster ceilings, originally housed three learned societies – the Royal Society, the Antiquaries and the Royal Academy. Somerset House, which was built from 1776-86 of Portland stone, was designed by **Sir William Chambers**, a founder member and treasurer of the Royal Society, as a square of terraced houses overlooking a central courtyard; the south front is supported on a row of massive arches which in the 18C were at the river's edge. The galleries' collection consists of major art bequests to London University: Samuel Courtauld's splendid private collection of **Impressionists** including canvases by Manet *(Bar at the Folies-Bergère)*, Degas, Bonnard, Gauguin (Tahitian scenes), Van Gogh *(Peach Trees in Blossom, Self-Portrait with Bandaged Ear)*, Cézanne *(Lake at Annecy)* and Seurat; the Princes Gate Collection, bequeathed to the nation by Count Antoine Seilern, including 30 oils by **Rubens** and six drawings by **Michelangelo** as well as works by Breugel, Leonardo, Tiepolo, Dürer, Rembrandt, Bellini, Tintoretto and Kokoschka; paintings of the Italian Primitive school and of the Renaissance to the 18C donated by Thomas Gambier-Parry and Viscount Lee of Fareham; paintings by the **Bloomsbury Group** gifted by Roger Fry (1866-1934).

National Portrait Gallery★★ (EX)

♿🕐 St. Martin's Lane. Open daily, 10am-6pm (9pm Thur-Fri). 🕐 Closed Good Fri, 24-26 Dec, 1 Jan. No charge except for special exhibitions. CD-Rom sound guide (4 languages). Restaurant, café. ☎ 020 7306 0055; Fax 020 7306 0056; www.npg.org.uk. Access: ⊖ Leicester Square, Charing Cross. The near neighbour of the National Gallery contains portraits of almost every British man or woman of public or historical interest from the Middle Ages to the present day, some painted, sculpted or photographed by the famous artists of the day. Look out for the raffish picture of **William Shakespeare**, which depicts the Bard at the apogee of his career. It is his only known contemporary portrait and probably the most accurate of his many representations. In **Britain 1960-90**, Sir Winston Churchill - "the greatest Englishman"- is sketched by Graham Sutherland and Margaret Thatcher, the most politically successful Englishwoman of the 20th century is captured on film by Helmut Newton. On the ground floor is **Britain since 1990** where you can expect to see changing portraits of such modern icons as Diana Princess of Wales, David Beckham and the Spice Girls.

Imperial War Museum★ (EFY)

♿🕐 Lambeth Road. Open daily, 10am-6pm. 🕐 Closed 24-26 Dec. No charge except for special exhibitions. Parking for disabled persons. Leaflet (3 languages). Café. ☎ 020 7416 5000, 0900 1600 140 (recorded information); Fax 020 7416 5374; mail@iwm.org.uk; www. iwm.org.uk. The museum, founded in 1917, was transferred in 1936 to the present building, formerly the Bethlem Royal Hospital ("Bedlam"), which was designed in 1812-15, with its dome and giant portico added in 1846 by Sydney Smirke.
It is one of the most sensitive, dignified and thought-provoking exhibitions in London and in no sense glorifies war; instead it honours those who served and also remembers those who stayed at home or were caught up as civilians in the conflicts of the 20th century. A wide range of weapons and equipment is on display: armoured fighting vehicles, field guns and small arms, together with models, decorations, uniforms, posters and photographs, as well as a selection from the museum's outstanding collection based on the work of two generations of Official War Artists.

National Army Museum★ (CZ)

♿🕐 Royal Hospital Road, Chelsea; Open daily, 10am-5.30pm. 🕐 Closed Good Fri, May Day Hol, 24-26 Dec, 1 Jan. Free Admission. ☎ 020 7730 0717; Fax 020 7823 6573; info@ national-army-museum.ac.uk; www.national-army-museum.ac.uk. Access: by bus 11, 19, 22, 211 to King's Road; 137 to Pimlico Road; 239 (Mon-Sat only, stops immediately outside museum). ⊖ Sloane Square; BR to Victoria Station. The display tells the stirring story of the British Army from the formation of the Yeomen of the Guard by Henry

VII on Bosworth Field in 1485 to the present day. Displays trace the evolution from armour via red coats to battledress and from pikes and swords to revolvers and machine guns.

Dulwich Picture Gallery★ (UZ)

&🕐 *Gallery Road, Dulwich; Open Tue-Sun and Bank Hol Mon, 11am (10am Tue-Fri) to 5pm. £4; no charge on Fri. 020 8693 5254; info@dulwichpicturegallery.org.uk; www. dulwichpicturegallery.org.uk. Access: 12min by train from London Bridge to North Dulwich, or from Victoria to West Dulwich; by bus P4 from Brixton underground station.* The building, the oldest public art gallery in England, is located in an elegant suburb which retains some of the rural quality of the small country town where city merchants resided in the 18C and 19C. The building (1811), designed by **Sir John Soane**, houses a collection of Old Masters including works by Rembrandt, Poussin, Murillo, Claude, Rubens, Van Dyck and Cuyp, some 400 pictures assembled by Noel Joseph Desenfans, and the collection made by **Edward Alleyn,** the great Elizabethan actor, which contained 80 likenesses of contemporary authors and players. The neighbouring buildings, the Chapel and College of God's Gift, is a charitable foundation established (1619) by Alleyn, who had married money but had no children; the educational element grew into the famous Dulwich College.

Fenton House★ (TX)

(NT) &🕐 *Windmill Hill, Hampstead. Open late-Mar to Oct, Wed-Sun and Bank Hol Mon, 2pm (11am Sat-Sun and Bank Hol Mon) to 5pm; early to mid-Mar, Sat-Sun, 2-5pm. £4.80. Guide book (4 languages). Braille guide. ☎/Fax 020 7435 3471; 01494 755 563 (infoline); fentonhouse@nationaltrust.org.uk; www.nationaltrust.org.uk. Access: bus 46, 268.* The **Benton Fletcher collection** of early keyboard instruments (harpsichords clavichords...), ranging in date from 1540 to 1805, together with furniture, pictures and 18C porcelain, are displayed in a red brick house (1693), one of the earliest and largest in Hampstead.

Additional Sights

London Zoo★★ (CV) – &🕐 *Outer Circle, Regent's Park. Open daily, 10am-5.30pm (4pm Oct-Feb); last admission 1hr before closing. £14. Restaurant, refreshments. ☎ 020 7722 3333; Fax 020 7586 5743; www.londonzoo.co.uk.* The London Zoological Society opened on a 5 acre/2ha site in Regent's Park in 1828, at the instigation of Sir Stamford Raffles. Today the Zoo has spread to cover 36 acres/14ha and has a staff of more than 100 caring for approximately 8 000 animals of 900 species.

Many new and innovative buildings have been constructed to house the animals, and the emphasis is now placed on breeding endangered animals and on foreign conservation projects, rather than purely entertainment for the masses. The elephants have been transferred to the zoo's outreach at Whipsnade Park where they have more space but there are still family favourites such as lions, tiges, rhinos and giraffes to see. It's best to pick up a programme of activities (talks, feeding times, grooming/bathing the animals, Animal Encounters where you are introduced to small animals by their keepers etc...) as you enter the zoo and base your visit around these.

Kenwood House★★ (The Iveagh Bequest) (TX) – *(EH)* &🕐 *House: Open daily, 10am (10.30am Wed and Fri) to 6pm (5pm Oct; 4pm Nov-Mar). 🕐 Closed 2-26 Dec, 1 Jan. Exhibitions (first floor): admission charge; ☎ 020 8348 1286 for details. Audio-guide (additional charge). Grounds: Open daily, 8am-dusk. Gypsy caravan, by appointment: ☎ 020 7973 3893 (estate office). Lakeside concerts: Jul to early-Sep, Sat evenings (occasionally Sun). Parking. Restaurant, picnic area. ☎ 020 8348 1286; Fax 020 7973 3891. Access: by bus 210 (from Golders Green or Archway).* William Murray, younger son of a Scottish peer, acquired Kenwood, a 50-year-old brick house on the north side of Hampstead Heath, in 1754, two years before becoming Lord Chief Justice and Earl of Mansfield.

In 1764 he invited fellow Scot Robert Adam to enlarge and embellish the house. Adam transformed it, outside and in, leaving a strong imprint of his style. Particularly notable are the Library★★ and the very fine collection of paintings.

Osterley Park★★ (TY) – *(NT)* &🕐 *Jersey Road, Isleworth. House: Open late-Mar to Oct, Wed-Sun and Bank Hol Mon; early to late-Mar, Sat-Sun, 1-4.30pm. 🕐 Closed Good Fri. £4.90. Guided tour by appointment. Park: Open daily, 9am-7.30pm/dusk/early during major events. Parking £2.50 (🕐 closed Good Fri and 25-26 Dec). Tearoom. ☎ 020 8232 5050 (general enquiries), 01494 755 566 (infoline); Fax 020 8232 508; osterley@ nationaltrust.org.uk; www.nationaltrust.org.uk. Access: ⊖ Osterley (Piccadilly Line) then 20min walk.* Osterley is the place to see **Robert Adam** interior decoration at its most complete – room after room just as he designed them, in every detail from ceilings and walls to the furniture. What had started life as a late 15C Tudor brick manor house was transformed into a mansion by Sir Thomas Gresham, founder of the Royal Exchange, in 1562.

In 1711 the mansion was purchased by Francis Child, a clothier's son from Wiltshire who had sought and found his fortune as a City banker. He was 69 when he bought Osterley and never lived there. It was his grandson, Francis, who commissioned Adam to transform the mansion, achieving between 1761 and 1780 the rich interior visitors can admire today.

Syon Park★★ (TY) – ⚐⏱ *Gardens: Open daily, 10:30am-5pm/dusk. House: Open mid-Mar to Oct, Wed-Thur, Sun and Bank Hols, 11am-5pm. Audio-guide. Guide book. Leaflet.* ⏱ *Closed 25-26 Dec.* ⚐ *House and gardens £7.50; gardens £3.75.* ☎ *020 8560 0882; Fax 020 8568 0936; www.syonpark.co.uk.* The colonnaded east front is visible across the river from Kew Gardens. The Lord Protector, Duke of Somerset, built a Tudor mansion on the site of a former monastery, given to him by his nephew Edward VI in 1547; five years later he was charged with treason and executed. During the next hundred years many owners of the house were beheaded and when, in less troubled times, the house passed to Hugh Percy, 1st Earl of Northumberland, in 1762, he felt it needed remodelling. **Robert Adam** richly ornamented and furnished the house, particularly the Great Hall where he is at his most formal. A number of notable Stuart portraits by Van Dyck, Lely and others further embellish the interior. **Capability Brown** re-designed the gardens and extended them to the river; two of his mulberry trees still survive and a vast rose garden is in bloom from May to August. The Great Conservatory, a beautiful semi-circular building of white-painted gun metal and Bath stone, with a central cupola and end pavilions dates from 1827 and is home to cacti and an aquarium.

Ham House★★ (TZ) (NT) – ⚐⏱ *Ham Street. House: Open late-Mar to early-Nov, Sat-Wed and Good Fri, 1-5pm. Garden: Open Sat-Wed, 11am-6pm/dusk.* ⏱ *Closed 25-26 Dec, 1 Jan.* ⚐ *£7.50. Braille guide. Parking. Refreshments.* ☎ *020 8940 1950; Fax 020 8332 6903; hamhouse@nationaltrust.org.uk; www. nationaltrust.org.uk. Access: by bus via Petersham Road, 371 to Royal Oak, Ham or 65 to Fox and Duck, Petersham then 20min on foot; U/train to Richmond. Ferry from Marble Hill House, Twickenham, daily Mar-Oct, 10am-6pm.* ☎ *020 8892 9620 (ferry);* This is an exquisite three-storey brick house dating from 1610 which was enlarged in the 1670s by Elizabeth Dysart and her second husband, the Duke of Lauderdale. Much of their original furnishing has survived, lavish even by the standards of the age. The house is rich in ornate plasterwork on the ceilings and splendid carved wood panelling on the walls. The Great Staircase of 1637, built of oak around a square well and gilded, has a beautiful balustrade of boldly carved trophies of arms. Notable among the many fine Dutch, English and Italian paintings are portraits by Lely, Kneller and Reynolds, including ladies at Charles II's Court – young, fair, delicately complexioned and far from innocent.

Richmond★★ (TY) – Possessing what has been called the most beautiful "urban village" green in England, Richmond grew to importance between the 12C and 17C as a royal seat and, after the Restoration, as the residential area of members of the Court – Windsor, Hampton Court and Kew are all easily accessible. Today private houses stand on the site of Henry VII's Royal Palace (the third on the site) which he had sumptuously rebuilt and in which he died in 1509 – as did his granddaughter, Elizabeth I in 1603. Among other fine Georgian houses in the "village" note the **Maids of Honour Row**★★ on the Green, built in 1724.

Climbing **Richmond Hill's** steep road, lined by 18C houses with balconied terraces, one has excellent views, immortalised by artists such as Turner and Reynolds. At the top **Richmond Park**★★ (TYZ), which had been a royal chase for centuries, was enclosed as a 2 470 acre/1000ha park by Charles I in 1637. It is the largest of the Royal Parks and is known today for its wildlife, including badgers and herds of red and fallow deer. From the top of Henry VIII's Mound, near Pembroke Lodge and the Richmond Gate, on a clear day the panorama★★★ extends from Windsor Castle to St Paul's Cathedral in the City.

Chiswick House★ (TY) – (EH) ⚐⏱ *Burlington Lane; Open late-Mar to Oct, Wed-Sun, 10am-5pm(2pm Sat).* ⏱ *Closed Nov-Mar.* ⚐ *£4.* 🍴 *Guided tour by appointment. Audio guide (3 languages). Picnic area.* ☎ *020 89 950 508; www.english-heritage. org.uk.* A Jacobean mansion was purchased by the 1st Earl of Burlington in 1682. The 3rd Earl, Richard Boyle (1695-1753), a generous host and patron, made the first alterations and additions. On his return from his second Grand Tour (1714-19) he designed a Palladian villa (1727-29) to display his works of art and to entertain his friends. **William Kent** (1686-1748), a follower of Inigo Jones and Burlington's protégé, was responsible for much of the interior decoration and the gardens.

This lass so neat, with smiles so sweet,
Has won my right good-will,
I'd crowns resign to call thee mine,
Sweet lass of Richmond Hill.
Leonard Macnally (1752-1820)

The lower floor – octagon hall, lobbies and library – now displays a video, engravings, sculptures and other material about the creation and restoration of the house and garden. On the principal floor the **Dome Saloon,** its eight walls punctuated by gold-highlighted doors and Classical busts, rises by way of an ochre entablature to a windowed drum and diamond-patterned dome.

Madame Tussaud's★ (CV) – ♿⊙ *Open daily, 10am (9am-6pm Sat-Sun) to 5.30pm (last admission).* ⊙ *Closed 25 Dec.* ⊛ *£23.99 (peak), £15 (off-peak). Brochure (5 languages). Wheelchair users must book in advance.* ☎ *0870 400 3000; Fax 020 7465 0862; www. madame-tussauds.com.* The famous waxworks include Louis XV's mistress, portrayed as Sleeping Beauty, made by Madame Tussaud herself plus statesmen of several ages and countries, modern celebrities in the worlds of sport and entertainment, murderers at the scene of their crimes in the Chamber of Horrors (complete with live actors) as well as a brief dark ride through the history of London.

Down House★ – *Downe Village, Kent. 18mi/29km southeast. Admission by pre-booked ticket only.* ⊙ *Open Wed-Sun, 10am-6pm (or dusk in Oct, 4pm Nov-Jan).* ⊙ *Closed in Feb, and 24-26 Dec.* ⊛ *£5, £3.80 (senior/student), £2.50 (child).* ☎ *0870 603 0145 (ticket reservations).* This Georgian house set in 18 acres/7ha of land became the family home of famous naturalist Charles Darwin (1809-82) in 1842. The Darwins lived there, altering the house and garden extensively to suit their needs, for over forty years until Charles Darwin's death (after which the family moved to Cambridge and used Down House only during the summer).

After his five-year voyage round the world and five years' residence in London, Darwin chose this house as a rural retreat, and it is where he wrote most of his major works, including *On the Origin of Species.* As visitors walk through the rooms and grounds, there is a strong sense of his presence not only as a scientist but also as a family man. The ground floor of the house is mostly as it would have been towards the end of Darwin's life; much of the furniture on display is original and there are quantities of Darwin's books, notebooks and other personal possessions. Visitors are equipped with audio-guides which give explanations of each room, with further details if required on the decor, furniture or paintings. Particularly interesting is Darwin's study, which looks as if he might return to it at any moment. On the first floor is an exhibition on Darwin's life and work, including an outline of his impressive family heritage (grandson of the famous potter Josiah Wedgwood and respected physician Erasmus Darwin), a display on his voyage of discovery on HMS Beagle (1831-36) and some of the vast collection of natural history that he collected, details of the furious controversy provoked by his theory of evolution as elaborated in *On the Origin of Species,* and interactive exhibitions on natural history.

LONGLEAT★★★

Wiltshire, ENGLAND

MICHELIN ATLAS P 8 OR MAP 503 N 30

This grand 16C house, in a glorious wooded lakeside setting, south of Bath, is built in golden stone in early Elizabethan style, designed by Robert Smythson. It rises through three tiers of windows to a skyline of balustrading and ornamental chimneystacks. The grounds consist of a park landscaped by Capability Brown in 1757-62 (short boat trips circumnavigate Gorilla Island giving views of the resident hippos and sea-lions), formal flower gardens, developed since Brown's day, a narrow-gauge railway, the longest maze in the world (over 1.5mi/2.5km of pathways), planted in 1975, a butterfly house, a two-acre adventure playground, King Arthur's Mirror Maze and the Safari Park.

The house is still owned by the descendants of Sir John Thynne, who completed the building in 1580 on the site of an Augustinian priory, purchased from Henry VIII in 1541. Its harmonious "new unmistakable Elizabethan" style is drawn from the indigenous Perpendicular tradition, Early Italian Renaissance, the French taste flourishing in the Loire Valley and the geometric simplicity of Flanders. Its contents reflect the range of interests of the unbroken line of the Thynnes, from Sir John to the present Marquess of Bath – the family tree from 1215 is at the foot of the Grand Staircase. In the 19C, for example, the 4th Marquess had seven rooms along the east front Italianised after his extensive Continental travels.

Tour

House *90min*

 ♿ ⏱ *House Open mid-Mar to Sep, daily, 10am-5.30pm/dusk; Oct-Dec (🗨• by guided tour), daily, 11am-3pm/dusk (telephone to check times). ⏱ Closed 25 Dec. Safari Park: Open mid-Mar to early-Nov, daily, 10am-4pm (5pm Sat-Sun, Bank Hols, school hols); no pets; free kennelling. Other attractions: Open mid-Mar to early-Nov, daily, 11am-5.30pm/dusk. ✈ £15 (Passport including all 12 attractions). Safari bus £3 (booking at Pets' Corner). Coarse fishing all year; permits from water bailiff at lakeside. Parking. Refreshments. ☎ 01985 844 400; enquiries@longleat.co.uk; www.longleat.co.uk.* It was Sir John Thynne's idea that the rooms at Longleat should look out over the park, rather than onto inner courtyards. In the 19C, on his return from a tour of Venice, Florence and Rome, the 4th Marquess ordered that nine rooms along the east and south fronts be remodelled in the Italianate style. On the ground floor, the late 16C Great Hall with its fine hammerbeam roof decorated with the arms of Sir John Thynne (note the Gresham gold grasshopper crest) contains a splendid pillared fireplace. The Ante-Library, the work of John Dibblee Crace, is graced by Italian furniture, marble door frames, inlaid walnut doors and ceiling panels. The Red Library boasts *trompe-l'oeil* ceiling panels echoing

Longleat House

those in Renaissance palazzi of Rome and Venice, while the gilded coffered ceiling of the Lower Dining Room is modelled on one in the Doge's Palace in Venice (note the pair of Indian ebony chairs dating from c 1670-80 and the William IV dining chairs of ebonized beechwood). In the Breakfast Room, hung with yellow damask, family portraits look down on Chippendale-style chairs and japanned gaming tables. Six windows in the passages along the back of the house are inset with 16-17C continental stained-glass panels and the walls hung with modern works of art from Lord Bath's Wessex Collection.

Upstairs, the State Dining Room with its tooled Cordoba leather walls displays a Meissen porcelain table centrepiece (c 1760), the 90ft/27m 17C Long Gallery a massive marble fireplace by Crace copied from one in the Doge's Palace in Venice, the State Drawing Room paintings (mainly Italian) and various pieces of 18C French furniture, and the Apartments a dress collection and cabinets of English and continental porcelain. The ceiling of the State Drawing Room, inspired by that in St Mark's Library in Venice, is set with panels after Titian and Veronese. The Royal Bedrooms comprise an elegant dressing room hung with hand-painted Chinese wallpaper and a Music Room-cum-Sitting Room with a gold Crace ceiling. The Prince of Wales Bedroom takes its name from the portrait of Henry over the fireplace. Go down the stairs and out through the Victorian kitchens. The outbuildings comprise a butchery (model of the house), stable block (eclectic collection of ephemera entitled Lord Bath's Bygones) with its tack room and blacksmith's forge, and a second exhibition area dedicated to the present Lord Bath's father, Henry Frederick Thynne, 6th Marquess (portrait by Graham Sutherland, 1903-80).

Safari Park

▶ *40min. Follow the road that leads from the car park away from the house.*
The "drive-in zoo" is most famous for its lions; it also has enclosures for wallabies, giraffes, zebras, llamas, dromedaries, camels, white rhinos, long-horned cattle, eland, fallow deer, rhesus monkeys (which may climb over the car), Indian elephants, Canadian timber wolves and various types of tiger.

LUDLOW ★

Shropshire, ENGLAND

POPULATION 9 040

MICHELIN ATLAS P 26 OR MAP 403 L 26

Set in the rolling Shropshire hill, close to the mid Wales border, Ludlow is a Norman "planned town." One-time seat of the powerful Mortimer family, the castle passed into royal ownership with the accession of Edward IV. The town prospered in the 16C and 17C because of its role as seat of the Council for Wales and the Marches. The centrepiece of the Ludlow Festival (last week of June and first week of July) is a Shakespeare play performed in the inner bailey of the castle. *Castle Street, Ludlow, SY8 1AS* ☏ *01584 875 053; Fax: 01584 877 931;info@ludlow.org. uk; www.ludlow.org.uk*

Ludlow Castle ★ – ♿ ⏰ *Castle Square, Open daily, 10am-5pm (7pm Aug; 4pm Oct-Mar).* ⏰ *Closed 25 Dec, Mon-Fri in Jan.* ⊛ *£4. Brochure (2 languages). Audio tape guide.* ☏ *01584 873 355 (24hr info line); info@ludlowcastle.com; www.ludlowcastle.com.* The castle, which stands on a fine defensive site protected by the River Teme and low limestone cliffs, was begun by Roger de Lacy shortly after the Domesday survey and built of locally quarried stone. It was from here that Roger Mortimer, the most powerful and perhaps the richest man in all England, virtually ruled the country, after using his power to topple Edward II in 1326. He completed the block of buildings containing the **Great Hall** and Solar, one of the leading palaces of the day. **Arthur, Prince of Wales** brought his young bride **Catherine of Aragon** to honeymoon in Ludlow in the winter of 1501 and it was here that Arthur died early the following year. The chapel with its richly ornamented west door is one of only five round chapel naves still standing in Britain. The first performance of **Milton's** masque *Comus* was given in the Great Hall in 1634.

St Laurence's Church★ – ♿🕐 *Open Apr-late Dec, daily, 10am-5:30pm; (Sun 12.30pm) Dec-Mar 11am-4pm (Sun after morning services).* 🖼 *£1 Donation suggested. Leaflet (6 languages).* 👣 *Guided tour by appointment.* ☎ *01584 872 073; www.stlaurences. org.uk.* The tower dominates the surrounding countryside and is mentioned in the collection of poems *A Shropshire Lad* by **AE Housman** (1859-1936), whose ashes are buried in the churchyard. The church was enlarged in 1199 – a reflection on the prosperity of the town – and parts of it are in a style transitional between Norman and Early English. The north transept has Decorated features and its construction must reflect the recovery of Ludlow from the Black Death, which reduced the population by a third in 1349. Nave and chancel roofs date from about 1440. The decoration of the latter, though 19C, is based on surviving fragments of the original colour. Twenty eight **misericords**★ in the choir stalls date from 1447. Allegorical scenes intermingle with Yorkist and Lancastrian devices, for though the king, Henry IV, was a Lancastrian, the town's manorial lord was Richard, Duke of York; (political expediency was ever wise in troubled times!).

Feathers Hotel★ – ♿🕐 *Open to non-residents daily 11am-11pm.* 👣 *Guided tour (30min) by appointment. Free parking if refreshment is taken.* ☎ *01584 875 261; Fax 01584 876 030; enquiries@feathersat-ludlow.co.uk www.fea-thersatludlow.co.uk* The existing building was enlarged and re-fronted in 1619 to produce what Pevsner described as "the prodigy of timber-framed houses where everything of motifs that was available has been lavished on the façade." The balcony was added for election-eering purposes in the mid-1840s.

Feathers Hotel, Ludlow

Excursions

Stokesay Castle★ – (EH) 6mi/10km north on A 49. ♿🕐 *Open Mar to Oct, daily, 10am-5pm (6pm Jun-Aug); Nov-Mar, Wed-Sun, 10am-4pm.* 🕐 *Closed 24-26 Dec, 1 Jan.* 🖼 *£4.60 Audio guide. Parking. Refreshments (Apr-Sep).* ☎ *01588 672544; www.english-heritage. org.uk.* Stokesay is the best preserved example in England of a 13C fortified manor house. The hall, which has a fine roof of shaped and tapered tree trunks, was built by Lawrence of Ludlow, a wool merchant who bought the property from the Say family in about 1281. The solar is furnished with a notable stone fireplace, peepholes into the hall below and the 17C fittings include a fine Flemish overmantel.

Berrington Hall★ – (NT) 8mi/13km south on A 49. ♿🕐 *Nr. Leominster; House: Open late-Mar to Oct, Sat-Wed and Good Fri, 1-4.30pm. Garden: Open as for house, noon-5pm (4.30pm Nov-Dec). Park walk: Jul to early-Nov, times as for house.* 🖼 *£5; garden only, £3.50. Parking. Refreshments.* ☎ *01568 615 721; Fax 01568 613 263; berrington@ nationaltrust.org.uk; www.nationaltrust.org.uk.* The hall was begun in 1778 by Thomas Harley, a contractor who supplied pay and clothing to the British Army in America. The architect was **Henry Holland**, son-in-law of Lancelot "Capability" Brown who laid out the gardens and lake. When Thomas Harley's daughter married the son of Admiral Lord Rodney in 1781, the original plans for a gentleman's modest country house were much altered. The present interior is a fitting setting for the remarkable collection of French and other furniture, paintings and objets d'art.

Croft Castle – *(NT) 10mi/16km south on A 49 and B 4362.* ♿⏱ *Nr. Leominster; Garden: Open late-Mar to early-Sep, Wed-Sun, Good Fri and Bank Hol Mon, 11am-5pm. Parkland and Croft Ambrey: Open daily. Castle: Open usually May-Sep, Wed-Sun and Bank Hol Mon, 1-5pm (4.30pm Oct); Apr and Oct, Sat-Sun, also Good Fri, 1-5pm. ,* 🚻 *House and Garden £4.60; garden only, £3.20.* ☎ *01568 780 246; Fax 91568 780 462; croftcastle@ nationaltrust.org.uk; www.nationaltrust.org.uk.* This Welsh Marcher castle has been the home of the Croft family since Domesday except for a break of 170 years. The walls and towers are mainly 14C and 15C; the central structure is 18C. The interior is finely decorated Georgian Gothic with notable plasterwork ceilings. The park is famous for its ancient trees.

Offa's Dyke Visitor Centre – *17mi/27km west on A 4113 to Knighton.* ♿⏱ *Knighton, Powys; Open daily, 9am-5.30pm (5pm winter).* ⏱ *Closed Sat-Sun in winter.* 🚻 *Donations welcome. Interactives. Parking.* ☎ *01547 528 753; oda@offasdyke.demon.co.uk; www.offasdyke.demon.co.uk.* The path, which was officially opened in Knighton (Trefyclawdd), the "town on the Dyke" on 10 July 1971, runs from Prestatyn east of Colwyn Bay in the north to the Severn estuary near Chepstow in the south.

This long-distance footpath *(177mi/285km)* offers the walker real moorland country, pastoral landscapes and thickly wooded valleys; some points on it are easily accessible by car for those who want a walk of only a few miles.

The Dyke, which does not always follow the same course as the path, has in some places almost disappeared; in others it consists of an earthen bank (12ft/4m high) with a correspondingly deep ditch. It is unlikely that it was ever "manned" as Hadrian's Wall was garrisoned by Roman legionaries. It was built to consolidate the western (Welsh) border of his kingdom by Offa, who was king of Mercia from 757 to 796 and introduced the penny into English currency; he added East Anglia to his domains and became powerful enough to be in diplomatic contact with both the Pope and Charlemagne.

Address Book

WHERE TO STAY

🛏🛏🛏🛏 **Cliffe Hotel**, *Dinham* ☎ *01584 872 063; Fax 01584 873 991; thecliffehotel@hotmail.com; www. thecliffehotel.co.uk.* This converted 19C house sits among fields and woodlands with a view of the town;s famous castle, a 10 min walk away; its 9 rooms are simple and uncluttered.

🛏🛏🛏🛏 **Ravenscourt Manor**, *Woofferton* ☎ *Fax 01584 711 905; ravenscourtmanor@amserve.com.* A characterful black-and-white timbered 16C manor house set in large lawned grounds 4 mi/6.5km south of Ludlow; rooms are individually decorated in period style.

WHERE TO EAT

🍴🍴🍴🍴 **Merchant House** *(Hill)* Lower Corve Street, ☎ *01584 875 438;* mail@merchanthouse.co.uk; www. merchanthouse.co.uk. Acclaimed gourmet restaurant set in a characterful cosy converted Jacobean house, turning out Modern British dishes using mainly local produce. Booking essential.

🍴🍴🍴 **The Crown Inn**, *Hopton Wafers.* ☎ *01299 270 372; Fax 01299 271 127; www. crownathopton.co.uk.* This handsome foliage clad 16C former coaching inn just outside Ludlow serves modern and traditional British dishes with the choice of more formal restaurant or relaxed bar dining.

🍴🍴🍴 **Koo** *127 Old Street.* ☎ *Fax 01584 878 462.* You'll find a friendly atmosphere in this simply styled Japanese restaurant, decorated with banners and artifacts, and serving authentic good value meals

Isle of MAN ★

POPULATION 69 788

MICHELIN ATLAS P 42 OR MAP 402 G 21

"Whichever way you throw me, I stand" – so says the motto beneath the three-legged symbol of this mountainous island in the Irish Sea. Manx identity is complex: settled by Celts, then by Norsemen, ruled by Scotland then by England. Its own language, Manx, akin to Gaelic, is now extinct, though the famous tailless cat survives. The island, a British dependency but not part of the United Kingdom, has its own laws, presented each year to an open-air parliament of the people; this 1 000-year-old descendant of the Norse *Thingvollr* ("assembly field") is held at a central point on the island, Tynwald Green, a site with prehistoric associations.

The lowland pattern of unspoiled farmland, small fields bounded by stone walls or high hedgebanks, gives way as the land rises to wild open moorland, bright in late summer with gorse and heather. From the highest summit Snaefell (2 036ft/621m), six ancient kingdoms can be seen – England, Scotland, Ireland, Wales, Man itself and the Kingdom of Heaven. Most of the coastline (100mi/160km) is untouched by modern intrusions and much of it is of exceptional beauty, offering breezy clifftop walks or the delights of pretty beaches. *Sea Terminal Building, Douglas Isle of Man IM1 2RG. ☎ 01624 686766; Fax: 01624 627443; tourism@gov.im; www.gov.im/tourism.*

Visit

Manx transport – The island still attracts multitudes of pleasure-seekers, mainly from the north of England. Its halcyon days of mass tourism were, however, the late 19C and early 20C and from this time dates an extensive network of vintage transport. Horse trams – nicknamed "toast racks" – ply the Douglas promenades, narrow-gauge steam railways serve the south and, most remarkable of all, double-track electric tramways lead from Douglas along the high cliffs to the northern resort of Ramsey and to the very summit of Snaefell.

Isle of Man TT Races – Motor cyclists flock to the island each year as they have done since the first Tourist Trophy race was held here in 1907.

Douglas – The great sweep of Victorian and Edwardian hotels facing promenades and the sandy bay give the island's capital an unmistakable identity among British resorts.

The **Manx Museum**, (*Open Tues-Fri 11am-4pm, Sat-Sun10am-5pm. Closed 25-26 Dec, 1 Jan. Free Admission. Parking. Restaurant. ☎ 01624 648 000; Fax 01624 648 001; enquiries@mnh.gov.im; www.gov.im/mnh.*) "the treasure house of the island's story" (RH Kinvig), displays good examples of early Christian sculpture including the unique 9C **Calf of Man Crucifixion**; the Folk-Life Galleries include a reconstructed Manx farmhouse.

Excursions from Douglas

Laxey Wheel★★ – *Take the Manx Electric railway north along the coast. Walk up the valley (0.6mi/1km). Open Easter to late-Oct, daily, 10am-5pm. £3. Parking. ☎ 01624 675 522; www.gov.im/mnh.* The water wheel, a splendid monument of the industrial age and now one of the emblems of the island, was built in 1854 when the Laxey valley was the scene of intense lead and silver mining activity.

The water needed to drive the wheel (75ft/22m in diameter) is collected by an extensive network of artificial channels and fed to the wheel from the top of the tower *(95 steps)*. Power is transmitted by a rod running along a viaduct to the head of the shaft (1 640ft/500m deep) which the wheel used to drain at a rate of 270 gallons/1 225 litres per minute.

Snaefell Mountain Railway★ – *Take the Manx Electric railway via Laxey on the east coast. Operates (weather permitting) Laxey to summit, May-Sep, daily, 10.30am-3.30pm. Return (US round trip) (90min. £6. Parking. Refreshments at the summit. ☎ 01624 663 366; Fax 01624 663 637; businfo@bus-rail.gov.im.* A vintage tramcar climbs up the side of the glen and on to the mountain slopes to the terminus at the café just below the summit. On a clear day there are stupendous **views**★★★ of the lands fringing the Irish Sea.

Southwest of Douglas

20mi/32km approximately southwest of Douglas either by road (A 25 or A 5) or by the Isle of Man Steam Railway to Port Erin.

Castletown – The streets and squares of the little harbour town, the island's capital until 1869, are gathered around the compact and well-preserved **Castle Rushen** (🕐 *Open daily, Easter to late-Oct, 10am-5pm.* ⬛ *£4.25. Parking.* ☎ *01624 675 522; enquiries@mnh.gov.im; www.gov.im/mnh).*

In the boat-cellar of the **Nautical Museum,** (♿🕐 *Open Easter to late-Oct, daily, 10am-5pm.* ⬛ *£3. Parking.* ☎ *01624 675 522; enquiries@mnh.gov.im; www.gov.im/ mnh)* where she was constructed in 1791, is the clinker-built *Peggy.* Above her is the strange Cabin Room, built in imitation of the stern cabin of a large sailing ship of Nelson's time.

Port St Mary – A fishing port with a south-facing sandy beach and room for many pleasure craft.

Port Erin – The terminus of the railway, with a small Railway Museum and the aquarium of the Marine Biological Station. The site is perfect – a curving sandy beach set in the deep bay, protected by high cliffs prolonged on either side to form some of the island's finest coastal scenery.

Cregneash Folk Museum★ – ♿🕐 *Open Easter to late-Oct, daily, 10am-5pm.* ⬛ *£3. Parking.* ☎ *01624 675 522; enquiries@imn.gov.im; www.gov.im/mnh.* Crofting traditions survived longest in the remoter southwest of the island. They are sensitively evoked in this tiny village where a number of buildings have been carefully restored.

Spanish Head – From the most southerly point on the island there is a view across the turbulent waters of the Calf Sound to the **Calf of Man,** an islet inhabited only by lighthouse keepers and bird sanctuary wardens.

MANCHESTER ★

Greater Manchester, ENGLAND

POPULATION 402 889

MICHELIN ATLAS P 39 OR MAP 502 N 23

Though the smoking chimneys of the cotton mills in this north west metropolis have long gone, Manchester still retains many fine historical buildings erected by the Victorian successors to those hard-headed Georgian merchants. Today the city has developed into a major provincial centre of finance.

▶ **Orient Yourself**: The city centre is compact and can be covered on foot. Public transport links to other sights around the centre are good, or take a City Sightseeing hop-on hop-off tour bus ☎ www.citysightseeing.co.uk.

Don't Miss: The Lowry; Imperial War Museum North.

Organizing Your Time: Allow at least two days to visit Manchester.

Especially for Kids: Hands-on fun in the MOSI or at Urbis; a tour of Manchester United's Old Trafford stadium for football-mad kids.

A Bit of History

Manchester grew from a Roman settlement and played a colourful part in both the Civil War and the Jacobite era. By the "Forty Five" (1745), Manchester merchants had discovered that political faction interfered with trade. They paid lip-service to the Stuart cause but enjoyed the prosperity brought by Hanoverian rule.

Owing to trade with the American colonies, Manchester became the centre of the rapidly expanding cotton industry.

The city can be justly proud of its strongly held principles of Free Trade which inspired the construction of the Free Trade Hall on the site of the **Peterloo Massacre**; on 16 August in 1819 a crowd assembled on St Peter's Fields to demand Parliamentary reform and repeal of the Corn Laws; 11 died and many were injured by the cavalry sent in to disperse them.

Castlefield Heritage Park ★

South end of Deansgate – Britain's first urban heritage park, Castlefield traces the development of Manchester from Roman times. The remains of the **Roman fort** became known as "the castle in the field" and the north gate and part of the west wall have been reconstructed on their original site.

In the 18C Castlefield became the centre of a canal system, which started in 1761 with the Duke of Bridgewater's canal. In 1830 the world's first passenger station, Liverpool Road Station, was opened by the Liverpool and Manchester Railway.

The tow-path is open to pedestrians and a walkway (1mi/1.5km) beside the River Irwell links Castlefield with the Ship Canal and Salford Quays.

River and Canal Trips – Several cruises are offered along the waterways that once carried goods across the Pennines: **Manchester Ship Canal Cruises** (& ⓒ *Open May-Oct, Sat-Sun, 10am-4pm; telephone for programme.* ⌇ *return £2.10.* ☎ *0151 330 1444; info@merseyferries.co.uk; www.merseyferries.co.uk)*, along the route opened by Queen Victoria in 1894 (6hr – 36mi/58km), and the **Irwell and Mersey Packetboat Company** (ⓒ *Round trips, call for times* ☎ *0161 736 2108)*, along the River Irwell and Ship Canal to Salford Quays (50min).

Museum of Science and Industry ★ **(CZ)** – *Liverpool Road;* ⓒ*Open daily, 10am-5pm.* ⓒ *Closed 24-26 Dec. Free admission to permanent collections. Brochure (9 languages)* ⌇ *Parking £5. Cafés.* ☎ *0161 832 1830 (24hr information line); marketing@msim.org.uk; www.msim.org.uk.* MOSI, as it is fondly known, gives a fascinating view of Manchester's industrial heritage. The exhibits are grouped thematically in a series of halls. The **Lower Byrom Street Warehouse** contains exhibitions on printing, textiles and machine tools as well as a hands-on science centre, **Xperiment**.

In the **Power Hall** the locomotives such as the HW Garratt no 2352 take pride of place. The **National Gas Gallery** describes the process of making town gas and its uses and the discovery of natural gas and its off-shore extraction. The **National Electricity Gallery** traces the role of electricity in the home and in the development of industry. In the buildings lining Liverpool Road are exhibits on the history of the city and an

Address Book

OUT AND ABOUT IN MANCHESTER

Tourist Information Centre – Manchester Visitor Centre, Town Hall Extension (off St Peter's Square), Lloyd Street, M60 2LA. ☎ *0161 234 3157; Fax 0161 236 9900; touristinformation@ marketing-manchester.co.uk www. manchester.gov.uk.* The centre is open Mon-Fri 10am to 5.15pm.

Public Transport – A modern tram system, **Metrolink**, runs frequent services connecting the main railway stations. For further details ☎ 0161 205 2000. For information on bus timetables and services contact the Greater Manchester Passenger Transport Executive ☎ 0161 228 7811. For 24hr information on train timetables and services ☎ 08457 48 49 50 (National Rail Enquiries). A "Day Saver" ticket gives a day's unlimited travel on trains within Greater Manchester and Metrolink trams after 9.30am. Tickets should be purchased at a train station before travel, or on the train if the ticket office is closed. A "Wayfarer" ticket combining bus, train and Metrolink travel and valid for use on almost all bus, train and Metrolink services must be purchased in advance from rail stations, GMPTE Travelshops, or selected post offices and tourist information centres.

Sightseeing – Walking and coach tours are available, and you can see the city with the help of a qualified Blue Badge guide ☎ 0161 969 5522. For a list of alternative tours contact the Visitor Information Centre.

Pubs and Restaurants – Manchester boasts a wide variety of restaurants, with something to suit every palate.

Chinatown in the city centre has over 30 restaurants. There is a wide range in the **Northern Quarter** and **Princess Street. Rusholme,** outside the city centre, is the area for Indian restaurants. For further details pick up a free copy of the *Manchester Food and Drink Guide,* available from the Visitor Information Centre or by telephoning the Manchester Visitor 24hr Phone Guide.

Shopping – Along **Market Street** and in the **Arndale Centre** you will find all the main High Street department stores. For boutiques and designer shops visit **King Street** and **St Ann's Square**. Bargain hunters should head towards the **Northern Quarter, Afflecks Palace** and the **Coliseum Centre.**

Entertainment – For information on Manchester's nightlife pick up a copy of the Manchester City Guide, available from the Manchester Visitor Information Centre and bookshops or telephone the Manchester Visitor 24hr Phone Guide. *City Life,* published fortnightly, is available from newsagents. *The Manchester Food and Drink Guide (see Pubs and Restaurants, opposite)* gives a small selection of places to go to in the evening.

The Printworks is a new entertainment complex with 24 hour licencing and is home to night clubs, themed bars and restaurants, live music venues and the first Hard Rock Café in the North West of England. There are a range of Theatres (The Palace, the Royal Exchange, the Opera House), Bridgewater Hall, home of the Hallé Orchestra, Manchester's two football clubs (United and City), the Velodrome and the MEN Arena featuring music and sporting events.

---

underground sewer. Beyond in the Liverpool Road Station the first-class booking hall has been recreated displaying an exhibition on the Liverpool and Manchester Railway (1830) and a replica of the *Planet* locomotive.

The **Air and Space Gallery** occupies the former city exhibition hall *(east side of Lower Byrom Street)* and illustrates the history of flight from the exploits of the earliest flying machines to the space age. The enormous four-engined Avro Shackleton reconnaissance aeroplane was only one of the many famous aircraft manufactured by the Manchester aircraft company, Avro.

Additional Sights

Chetham's Hospital and Library (CY) – *Long Millgate; Library: Open 9am-12.30pm and 1.30-4.30pm. Guided tour (45min) by appointment with the Librarian.* ☎ 0161 834 7961; librarian@chethams.org.uk; www.chethams.org.uk. Founded in 1653 as the result of the will of local merchant, Humphrey Chetham, the hospital, originally a school for 40 poor boys, and library, one of the oldest in the country, are housed in the domestic buildings of the former chantry college. It is now a school for young musicians.

Urbis – *Cathedarl Gardens Open Tues-Sun, 10am-6pm; timed entry, last admission 4.30pm. Free admission to permanent collection. Café, restaurant. Shop.* ☎ 0161 907 9099; Fax 0161 907 9001; www.urbis.org.uk. Interactive galleries introduce you to the city.

Cathedral★ (CY) – *Open Mon-Sat 10am-4.30pm, Sun 11.30am-4.30pm. Free Admission. Guided tour. Licensed Restaurant.* ☎ 0161 833 2220; Fax 0161 839 6226;

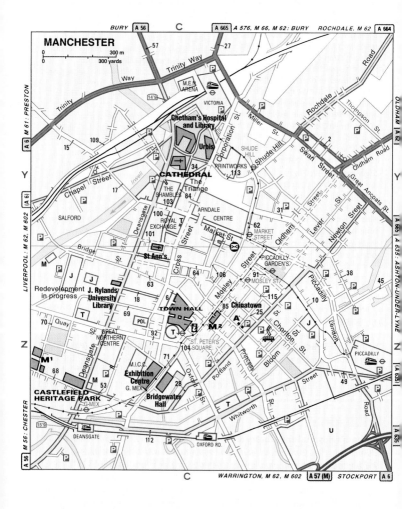

office@manchestercathedral.org; www.manchestercathedral.org. The church, refounded as a chantry college in 1421, became the cathedral of the new diocese in 1847. Six bays form the nave – the widest of any church in England – and six the choir. The **choir screen** is a unique piece of medieval wood carving. In the choir itself the **stalls and canopies**★ are beautifully carved. The **misericords** (c 1500) show a strong similarity in style and in their humorous depiction of medieval life to the contemporary ones in Beverley and Ripon.

Royal Exchange (CY) – Manchester owes its prosperity to "King Cotton". Raw cotton imported via the port of Liverpool and the canal network, a pure water supply from the Pennines, a high degree of humidity in the air and a large available working population were the factors responsible for the rapid growth of the cotton and ancillary industries. English cotton was sold throughout the world and the Manchester cotton exchange was at the very nerve centre of this trade.

Inside the exchange the prices of cotton on the day the Market last traded are still shown on the board high up near the roof *(west end)*. Today this immense hall is partly occupied by the 700-seat Royal Exchange Theatre.

St Ann's Church (CYZ) – *St. Ann's Street;* Open daily, 11.30am-5pm. ☎ 0161 834 0239. Founded 1709 and consecrated 1712, it is a good example of a Renaissance church, returning towards simpler, sterner Classical architecture. Fine Georgian mouldings border the plaster ceiling; in the Lady Chapel is the Queen Anne-style **altar table**, given by the founder, Lady Anne Bland.

John Rylands University Library (CZ) – ⚿ *Closed until late 2005 for major renovations,* ☎ 0161275 3764; *special.collections@manchester.ac.uk*. The John Rylands Library at Deansgate is one of the finest examples of modern Gothic architecture in Europe, designed by Basil Champneys, opened in 1900 and founded in memory of a successful textile manufacturer. The library possesses many early printed books – 3 000 of which are dated before 1501 – and manuscripts from the collections of the Earls Spencer and Crawford.

Free Trade Hall (CZ) – The hall, the third on the site, is the home of the Hallé Orchestra. Among its best known conductors were Sir Thomas Beecham and Sir John Barbirolli; a triptych statue of the latter in action is in the sculpture hall of the Town Hall *(see below)*.

Exhibition Centre (CZ) – The single-span Central Station (1876) designed by Sir John Fowler has been converted into the Greater Manchester International Exhibition and Events Centre (G-MEX).

Rolls and Royce met for the first time nearby in a typical 19C hotel which has been refurbished.

Town Hall★ **(CZ)** – Designed in Gothic style by Alfred Waterhouse and built from 1868 to 1877, it is one of the greatest civic buildings of the Victorian era. Its tower with octagonal top stage rises 286ft/87m above the pedestrian area of Albert Square.

Two staircases lead from the low vaulted entrance hall to the **Great Hall,** with its hammerbeam roof and twelve Pre-Raphaelite style murals of Manchester events, painted by Ford Madox Brown 1876-88.

Manchester Art Gallery★ **(CZ)** – *Moseley Street;* Open Tue-Sun and Bank Hol Mon, 10am-5pm. Closed 1 Jan, Good Friday, 24-26 and 31 Dec. No charge. Audio tour (3 languages). Parking (charge) nearby. Café, restaurant. ☎ 0161 235 8888; Fax 0161 235 8899; www.manchestergalleries.org.uk. The interior, recently restored to its 19C glory, displays an interesting Pre-Raphaelite collection with works by Millais, Hunt and Rossetti and Ford Madox Brown's *Work* (1852) illustrating the various classes of a developing industrial society.

Note the works of Stubbs, Turner and Constable. The industrial landscapes of the North were captured with sensitivity by LS Lowry (1887-1976). His studio has been recreated on the ground floor.

Jewish Museum – *Cheetham Hill Road (CY). Cheetham Hill Road;* Open Mon-Thur, 10.30am-4pm, Sun, 11am-5pm; Fri mornings by appointment. Closed Jewish holidays. Audio guide for visually impaired visitors. Wheelchair access to

Chinatown

Nearly 20 000 Chinese make the Manchester community one of the two largest outside London (the other is Liverpool). They have made the area around Faulkner Street their own with vibrant Chinese decorations, gardens and murals and the huge **Imperial Chinese Archway (CZ)**. The Chinese Arts Centre in Charlotte Street illustrates the art, crafts and customs of the Chinese people.

ground floor. ☎ *0161 834 9879; Fax 0161 834 9801; don@manchesterjewishmuseum. com; www.manchesterjewishmuseum.com.* In the former Spanish and Portuguese synagogue (1874), a Victorian building in the Moorish style, the museum traces the history of the city's Jews, from the 18C to today's 40 000-strong community.

Manchester Museum – *University of Manchester, Oxford Road.* ♿🕐 *Open Mon, Sun and Bank Hols 11am-4pm; Tue-Sat 10am-5pm.* 🕐 *Closed Good Friday day. Free Admission* ☎ *0161 275 2634; Fax 0161 275 2676; museum@manchester.ac.uk; www.museum. man.ac.uk.* This fine modern university collection takes a comprehensive look at the natural worlds and lifes sciences with galleries on Animal Life, Archaeology, Ancient Egypt, Living Cultures, Prehistoric Life, Rocks and Minerals and Science for Life. Their prize exhibit, "Stan" the Tyrannosaurus is the world's second most complete T Rex skeleton yet to be discovered.

Excursions

The Lowry★ – *Pier 8, Salford Quays;* ♿🕐 *Building open Tues-Sat, 10am-8pm, (Sun, Mon 6pm). Galleries Sun-Fri 11am-5pm (Sat 10am) Free Admissions. Parking (charge). Restaurants, cafés, bars. Shops.* ☎ *0870 787 5780, 0161 876 2000 (bookings and information); Fax 0161 876 2001; info@thelowry.com; www.thelowry.com.* This visually stunning arts and entertainment complex graces the docks of Greater Manchester. Attend a show or dine in one of the cafes to see the equally impressive interior.

Imperial War Museum North★ – *The Quays, Trafford Wharf;* ♿🕐 *Open daily, 10am-6pm (Nov-Feb 5pm).* 🕐 *Closed 25-26 Dec. No charge. Parking. Café, restaurant. Shop.* ☎ *0161 836 4000; Fax 0161 836 4012; info@iwmnorth.org.uk; www.iwm.org.uk.* Located on the city's ship canal, this museum features an hourly show titled The War at Home,which depicts how the Second World War affected the homefront.

Manchester United Tour and Museum – *Old Trafford.* 🕐 *Matt Busby Way; Open daily, 9.30am-5pm (or until 30min before kick-off on home match days) Tour 9.40am-4.40pm.* 📷 *Museum and tour £9; museum only, £5.50. Parking. Café. Shop.* ☎ *0161 868 8631; tours@manunited.co.uk; www.manutd.com.* Tucked into the East Stand of Old Trafford football stadium is the entrance to a coffee shop and exhibition room, where past and present stars and matches are commemorated and a display pays tribute to the victims of the Munich air disaster. Tours of the stadium are run on non-match days.

Helmshore Textile Museum – *Near Haslingden; 13mi/21km north of Manchester city centre by M 66, A 56 and B 6232. Holcombe Road;* ♿🕐 *Apr-June & Sept-Oct Mon-Fri 2-5, Sun 1-5. July-Aug Mon-Fri & Sun 1-5pm.* 📷 *£3.* ☎ *01706 226 459; helmshoremuseum@museumoflancs. org.uk.* An extensive display of photographs and machinery is set out in two large former woollen mills: Higher Mill, built to finish cloth in 1789, and the 19C Whitaker's Mill. Working demonstrations are given regularly and panels trace the history of the weaving industry from the days when villagers sold their urine at a penny a pot to be used in the fulling process (hence the expression 'to spend a penny').

British in Indian – *Newton Street.* 🔒 *Closed due to relocation. Open Apr-Sep, Wed and Sat, 2pm-5pm.* 🕐 📷 *£3.* ☎ *01282 613 129; Fax 01282 870 215.* Memorabilia of British life in India, from the days of the East India Company to Independence in 1947. The eclectic collection includes medals, pictures, models, letters and surprises such as a mosque window, a tigerskin and the elaborate Indian clothes worn by EM Forster, author of *A Passage to India*.

Whitworth Art Gallery★ – *Whitworth Park; 1.5mi/2.5km south of the city centre. Denmark Road;* ♿🕐 *Open daily, 10am (2pm Sun) to 5pm.* 🕐 *Closed Good Friday. Free admission.* ☎ *0161 275 7450; whitworth@man.ac.uk; www.whitworth.man.ac.uk.* Collections of past and present knitwear and wallpaper are housed next to a fine display of modern art, including *Snow White and Her Stepmother* by Paula Rego, works by Rossetti, Ford Madox Brown, Millais, and satirical cartoons by Gillray and Cruikshank. Sculpture by Hepworth and Moore are among the pieces displayed in the 1995 Mezzanine Court, one wall of which is the red-brick facade of an Edwardian building.

Quarry Bank Mill★ – *(NT) 10mi/16km south of Manchester, off B 5166; exit 5 from M 56. Quarry Bank Road; Mill:* ♿🕐 *Open late-Mar to Sep, daily, 10.30am-5.30pm; Oct-Mar, Tue-Sun, 10.30am-5pm; last admission 90min before closing. Apprentice House and garden: Tue-Fri, 2-4.30pm; Sat-Sun and school holidays, 11am-4.30pm; entry by timed ticket only.* 📷 *Mill and Apprentice house £8; mill only, £5.50. Ramps and step lift; Braille guide, large-print guide.* ☎ *01625 527 468; Fax 01625 539 267; quarrybankmill. recep@nationaltrust.org.uk; www. nationaltrust.org.uk.* In a wooded country park (284 acres/11ha) beside the fast-flowing River Bollin stands a five-storey cotton mill, built in 1784, powered by a massive water wheel (50t); steam power is due to be introduced with an 1840s beam engine. The production of cotton cloth from the cotton plant to the bolt of calico on sale in the mill shop is traced in a fascinating exhibition – live demonstrations of hand-spinning, the spinning Jenny, hand-loom weaving, machine-loom weaving. The Apprentice House presents the Spartan conditions of life for the pauper children apprenticed to the mill.

Macclesfield – *19mi/31km south of Manchester by A 6 and A 523.* For more than 200 years Macclesfield was synonymous with silk production, carried on in over 100 mills. The story of silk is expertly and entertainingly told in two museums; the **Silk Museum,** (*Park Lane.* ⊙ *Open daily, 11am (1pm Sun) to 5pm.* ⊙ *Closed 25-26 Dec, 1 Jan, Sun Jan-Mar.* ⊛ *£2.95.* ☎ *01625 612 045; Fax 01625 612 048; info@macclesfield.silk.museum; www.silk-macclesfield.org)* is housed in Macclesfield's Georgian Sunday School building, while at **Paradise Mill,** (⊙ *Open Tue-Sun and Bank Hol Mon, 1.15, 2.15, 3.15pm.* ⊙ *Closed Good Friday, 24 Dec to 3 Jan.* ⊛ *£3.* ☎ *01625 618 228; info@macclesfield.silk.museum; www.silk-macclesfield.org)* experienced guides operate Jacquard handlooms with punched card controls which at the very start of the 19C anticipated the workings of the computer. Silk throwing was in the vanguard of the Industrial Revolution, the first textile trade to shift from home to factory production. Prosperity was nevertheless precarious; boom conditions prevailed when French silk was excluded during the Napoleonic wars but a series of slumps followed, forcing some 15 000 Macclesfield people to take their skills to the silk city of Paterson, New Jersey in America.

Jodrell Bank Science Centre – ⊙ *Bomish Lane. Open late-Mar to late-Oct, daily, 10.30m-5.30pm; Nov-Mar, Christmas and New Year, phone for times; last admission 1hr before closing.* ⊛ *£3. Planetarium show (extra charge). Parking. Café, picnic area. Induction loop system; specialist resources for visually impaired visitors.* ☎ *01477 571 339; Fax 01477 571 695; visitorcentre.jb.man.ac.uk; www.jb.man.ac.uk/scicen.* A discovery centre, 3-D theatre, arboretum and outdoor play areas are just some of the fun places you'll find at this science complex. Until 2006, the Planetarium is closed during a general refurbishment of the centre.

Bramall Hall – ♿ ⊙ *13mi/21km southeast by A6 and A 5102. Bramhall Park. Open Good Fri to Sep, Mon-Sat, 1pm-5pm; Sun and Bank Hol Mon, 11am-5pm (last admission 4.15pm); Oct- 1 Jan, 1pm-4pm; Sun and Bank Hol Mon, 11am-4pm (last admission 3.15pm); 2 Jan-Good Fri, Sat-Sun, 1pm-4pm (last admission 3.15pm). |£3.95; gardens no charge. Parking (charge). Tea room.* ☎ *0161 485 3708; Fax 0161 486 6959; bramall.hall@ stockport.gov.uk; www.stockport.gov.uk.* The hall, which was first mentioned in the Domesday Book, is a fine example of a black and white timber-framed manor house dating from 1500 to 1600. Wood panelling, plaster ceilings, furniture and paintings adorn the Tudor Rooms and the Victorian kitchen and servants' quarters give insight into the life of a country mansion.

Isle of **MULL**★

Argyll and Bute, SCOTLAND

POPULATION 2 838

MICHELIN ATLAS P 59 OR MAP 501 B, C 14

This narrow island (nowhere more than 26mi/42km across) sits at the mouth of Scotland's Great Glen, the diagonal fault line that threatens to slice the country in two. It is dominated by the mountain Ben More (3 169ft/966m), with a deeply-indented coastline (some 300mi/480km long) ranging from rocky cliffs to sandy beaches; the sea views are superb. Inland, pastoral crofting landscapes contrast with desolate moorlands. The festivals (Mull Music Festival, Tobermory Highland Games) reflect the island's rich traditions. ⓘ *The Pier, Craignure* ☎ *08707 200 610; Fax 01680 812497; info@mull.visitscotland.com; www.visitscottishheartlands.com.* ⓘ *Main Street, Tobermory* ☎ *08707 200 625; info@tobermory.visitscotland.com; www. visitscottishheartlands.com.*

Sights

⊛ *The roads are twisting and narrow; petrol stations are scarce.*

Tobermory – The main town and ferry port fringes Tobermory Bay, the sea grave of a Venetian treasure galleon that sailed with the Spanish Armada (1588). It is a popular yachting centre.

Torosay Castle – *1.5mi/2.5km south of the ferry port of Craignure.* ♿ ⏰ *Open Easter-Oct, daily, 10.30am-5pm. Gardens: Open Easter-Oct, daily, 9am-7pm; Nov-Easter, dawn-dusk.* 👓 *£5.50; gardens only, £4.50.* 🔦 *Guided tour by appointment. Brochure. Parking. Refreshments.* ☎ *01680 812 421; Fax 01680 812 470; torosay@aol.com; www.torosay.com.* Torosay (1856) is an example of David Bryce's fluency in Scottish baronial style, perfected by Robert Lorimer's delightful **gardens**★, which afford spectacular **views**★.

Duart Castle – *3mi/5km from Craignure.* ⏰ *Apr, Sun-Fri, 11am-4pm; May to mid-Oct, daily, 10.30am-5.30pm.* 👓 *£4.50. Leaflet (5 languages). Walks. Parking. Refreshments.* ☎/Fax 01680 812 309; duartguide@isle-of-mull.demon.co.uk; www.duartcastle.com. Duart, home of the Chief of the **Clan MacLean,** is perched on a rocky crag guarding the Sound of Mull, with magnificent views. The keep dates from c 1250 but the 13C castle was burnt in the late 17C. The Macleans supported the Stuart cause and finally lost the castle and lands to the Campbells after the 1745 rebellion. Sir Fitzroy MacLean, the 26th Chief, restored the stronghold to its present appearance in 1911. Displays in the keep relate clan history and there is an exhibition on Spanish prisoners from the Armada in the dungeons.

Staffa – ⏰ *Open daily. Landing fee.* ☎ *0141 616 2266. Ferry from Iona and Fionnphort* ☎ *01681 700 338 or 01681 700 358; Ferry from Ulva, Mull* ☎ *01688 400 242. Coach link between Craignure and Fionnphort* ☎ *01680 812 313.* The basaltic island, with its amazing rock formations and spectacular caves, on the western seaboard owes its fame to Mendelssohn's overture *Fingal's Cave*, composed following his visit in 1829. Its awesome beauty has also proved a source of inspiration to poets (Keats, Tennyson, Scott) and painters (Turner).

Isle of Iona★ – 🚶 *See Isle of IONA; access from Fionnphort on the Ross of Mull.*

NEWCASTLE-UPON-TYNE★

Tyne and Wear, ENGLAND

POPULATION 189 150

MICHELIN ATLAS P 51 OR MAP 502 P 19

The city is an important hub served by major roads on the busy east coast route to Scotland. Its dramatic site, rich history and the distinctive dialect spoken by its population of hearty and humorous "Geordies" give this undisputed capital of the North East of England an exceptionally strong identity.

Despite recent decline Newcastle retains great vigour as a commercial, educational, entertainment and cultural centre. The city centre shopping complex in Eldon Square was one of the most ambitious of its kind when built, while the gargantuan Metro Centre on the outskirts of Gateshead is billed as the largest shopping and leisure city in Europe. Post Millennium, the Baltic Centre for Contemporary Arts and The Sage music centre are powerful symbols of the city's new cultural ambitions.

No account of Tyneside would be complete without a reference to football's Premier Division team of Newcastle United, whose devoted supporters, the "Toon army," worship at the shrine of St James Park, one of Britain's great soccer stadiums, now comprehensively modernised.

▶ **Orient Yourself**: Newcastle city centre is compact and best seen on foot. Newcastle is divided into four different areas which are colour-coded. On each signpost there is a menuboard listing all the sights, and indicating the colour area of the sight. Signposts around the city correspond to the different colours, making sightseeing easy. The Metro system offers fast, efficient travel around Newcastle and Tyneside.

🚫 **Don't Miss**: The Angel of the North; The Baltic Centre; the views from the city bridges; Beamish open-air museum

All Saints	CZ		Discovery Museum	CZ	M³	Laing Art Gallery		
Baltic Centre	Z		Eldon Square	CY		and Museum	CY	M¹
Bessie Surtees' House	CZ	D	Gateshead Millennium			Life Interactive World	CZ	
Blackfriars	CZ		Bridge		Z	Museum of Antiquities	CY	M²
Black Gate	CZ	E	Grey's Monument	CZ	F	Swing Bridge	CZ	
Castle Keep	CZ		Guildhall	CZ	G	Tyne Bridge	CZ	
Central Station	CZ		High Level Bridge	CZ				

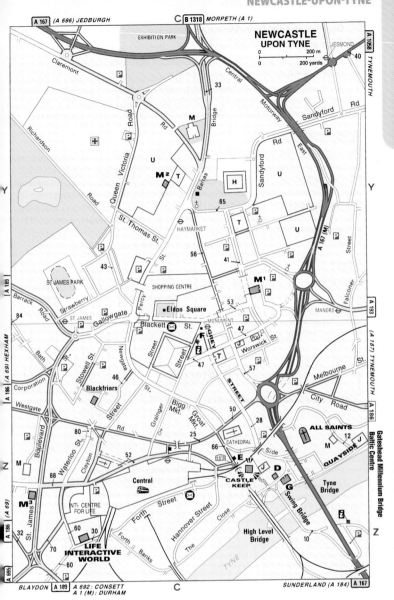

🕐 **Organizing Your Time**: Allow at least two days, plus extra for excursions.

🧒 **Especially for Kids**: Hands-on fun at LIFE; Beamish open-air musem.

👣 **Also See**: Alnwick, Carlisle, Durham, Hadrian's Wall, Lake District

👣 **Walking Tours**: The Association of City Guides runs guided tours of the city; information, programmes and tickets from the Tourist Information Centre. There are also a number of walking City Trails covering different aspects of the city's history. Contact the Tourist Information Office for further details and maps.

A Bit of History

The easily defended bridging point where the Tyne enters its gorge was exploited by the Roman founders of Pons Aelius, one post among many along Hadrian's Wall, then by the Normans, whose "New Castle" dates from 1080. Later abundant mineral resources, particularly of coal, stimulated trade, manufacturing and engineering; **George Stephenson** (1781-1848) was born nearby as was his son Robert, and in the 19C Tyneside became one of the great centres of industrial Britain, dominated by figures like **William Armstrong**, later Lord Armstrong (1810-1900), whose engineering and armament works at Elswick helped equip the navies of the world.

Visit

Site★★ – The approach from the south through the separate borough of **Gateshead** reveals an astonishing **urban panorama**. The city of Newcastle has spread slowly from the north bank of the Tyne via steeply-sloping streets and precipitous stairways up to the flatter land to the north. Buildings of all periods and materials are dominated by the Castle Keep and the lantern tower of the Cathedral (**CZ**).

Address Book

OUT AND ABOUT IN NEWCASTLE

Tourist Information Centre – Main office: 132 Grainger Street, Newcastle b: 0191 277 8000; Fax 0191 277 8009; tourist.info@newcastle.gov.uk. Office also at The Guildhall, Quayside (same contact details).

Public Transport – The Tyne and Wear Metro runs from 5.30am to 11.30pm, linking Newcastle city with Tyneside and the coast. Trains run every seven minutes to the airport and the coast, and every three minutes at peak times within the city. A Metro DaySaver ticket giving unlimited travel for the day is available after 9.30am. A "Day Rover" ticket (available from NEXUS Travelcentres) includes bus travel. For full details on bus and Metro travel contact the NEXUS Travel line ☎ 0870 608 2608

Sightseeing For sightseeing on the River Tyne, regular cruises run from Newcastle Quayside and North and South Shields during the summer months. Contact Tyne Leisure Line for further details ☎ 0191 251 5920; www.tyneleisureline.co.uk. Trips along the river are also run by Nexus ☎ 0870 608 2608.

Pubs and Restaurants – Jesmond Road, Shieldfield Road and Shields Road offer a variety of pubs. The *Evening Chronicle* gives details of pubs with live music, and of what is playing where. The Bigg Market area and Newcastle Chinatown offers a wide range of Indian and Chinese restaurants respectively, but for full

details of restaurants consult *Eating Out*, a pocket-sized guide available from Tourist Information Centres. For nightlife, Bigg Market with over 160 pubs is popular with the youth of Newcastle. A young crowd also flocks to the Quayside area.

Shopping – **Metrocentre** in Gateshead is open daily, and boasts over 300 shops and services. **Eldon Square**, a shopping mall, houses High Street shops and department stores. **Eldon Garden** has a more fashionable range. Also worth a visit is **Northumberland Street. Monument Mall** is accessible directly from Monument Metro station. The Vine Lane Antiques Market, near the top of Northumberland Street, the Newcastle Antiques Centre in Grainger Street, or the southern area of Jesmond are a must. Other traditional markets include the Grainger Market, the Greenmarket *(open Mon-Sat)* and Bigg Market, the city's oldest market, in Bigg Market Street; Sunday shoppers can visit Quayside market, held on the Quayside under Tyne Bridge; or the Armstrong Bridge Arts Market.

Entertainment – Current listings can be found in the *Evening Chronicle, The Crack* and *The North Guide*.

The Sage, the Theatre Royal, Newcastle Playhouse, Tyne Theatre and the Opera House host drama, music, opera and dance. Newcastle Telewest Arena is the venue for major bands and spectacular shows and sporting events. St James' Park stadium, the home of Newcastle United football team, also welcomes visitors.

Quayside★ (CZ) – Newcastle and Gateshead are linked by seven bridges, which make an outstanding **composition**★ extending upstream. The oldest is the unusual **High Level Bridge (CZ)** (1848), designed by **Robert Stephenson** with railway tracks above and roadway below. The **Swing Bridge (CZ)** (1876) designed by Lord Armstrong, brightly painted and nautical-looking, follows the alignment of the original crossing. The monumental stone piers of the great **Tyne Bridge (CZ)** (1928) add drama to the townscape.

BALTIC The Centre for Contemporary Art – &. ○ *Open Mon-Thur, 9.30am-5.30pm (Fri 9am-5pm). Cafe, restaurant. Shop.* ☎ *0191 478 1810; Fax 0191 478 1922; info@balticmill.com; www.balticmill.com.* Among the tightly-packed Victorian commercial buildings are a few much older survivors: the 17C Guildhall (B), the remarkable timber-framed **Bessie Surtees' House** and the 18C Classical **All Saints Church**★ which has an unusual elliptical **interior**★ and a delicately proportioned portico and tower. The riverside walkways enhanced by sculpture, pubs, bars and hotels are a popular place for a stroll.

Castle Keep★ (CZ) – ○*Open daily, 9.30am-5.30pm (4.30pm Oct-Mar).* ○ *Closed Good Friday, 25-26 Dec, 1 Jan.* ☞ *£1.50.* ☎ *0191 232 7938.* The city took its name from the 'new castle' built by William the Conqueror's son, Robert Curthose in 1080. The present keep is all that remains of its 12C successor and is a particularly good example of a Norman keep. From the roof of this massive stone edifice there is an all-embracing panorama of city, river and distant countryside. The complex railway tracks serving the many-arched **Central Station** were driven ruthlessly through the castle precinct in 1848, severing the keep from the picturesque **Black Gate** to the north.

Just over a mile to the east rises the strange outline of the multi-storey flats of the colourful **Byker Wall,** outcome of successful collaboration between architects and the re-housed inhabitants of the old working-class district of Byker.

City Centre★ (CY) – Enlightened planning gave 19C Newcastle a new centre of classical dignity, comprising fine civic buildings, great covered markets and shopping arcades and spacious streets, of which the most splendid is **Grey Street**★ **(CZ)**, curving elegantly downhill from the high column of **Grey's Monument**, past the great portico of the Theatre Royal. Into this heritage of **"Tyneside Classical"** have been inserted new developments such as **Eldon Square (CY)**, one of Europe's largest indoor shopping and recreational centres.

Laing Art Gallery and Museum★ (CY) – *New Bridge Street.* ○*Open daily 10am (2pm Sun) to 5pm.* ○ *Closed Good Friday, 25-26 Dec, 1 Jan. Free Admission. Cafe.* ☎ *0191 232 7734; laing@tyne-wear-museums.org.uk; www.twmuseums.org.uk.* The gallery's collection of English art emphasises the 19C, notably with the apocalyptic works of the visionary **John Martin**. The development of artistic traditions in the region is traced in **Art on Tyneside**. There are good displays of **Tyneside glass** and **silverware**.

Museum of Antiquities★ (CY) – *University, King's Walk.* ○*Open Mon-Sat, 10am-5pm.* ○ *Closed Good Friday, 1 Jan and 24-26 Dec. Free Admission. Brochure (5 languages).* ☎ *0191 222 7846; Fax 0191 222 8561; m.o.antiquities@ncl.ac.uk; www.ncl.ac.uk/antiquities.* Models of the wall, vallum, forts, milecastles and turrets, as well as a wealth of on-site finds

A. Williams/MICHELIN

Grey's Monument, Newcastle

Public Art

A bold initiative to bring art celebrating social history and the natural environment to the people in depressed areas where traditional industries – coal mining, shipbuilding, steel manufacturing, fishing – have declined owing to the economic recession has resulted in fascinating works of modern art, sometimes controversial set in the city, in the countryside or by the sea. The best examples by artists mostly living and working in the North East are in Sunderland (*Pathways of Knowledge*, steel gates and other works by Colin Wilbourn), Darlington (*Train* by David Mach), Middlesbrough (*Bottle of Notes* by Claes Oldenberg), North Shields (*Stan Laurel* by Bob Olley). Artworks in Gateshead include murals, stained glass, mobiles, mosaics, environmental sculptures (*Windy Nook* by Andy Cole) and monumental steel and stone carvings. Marking the southern entry to Tyneside *(near the A 1)* **The Angel of the North** by Anthony Gormley, made from 200 tonnes of steel and with a wing span of 177ft/54m, towers 65ft/20m above its hilltop setting. The **Gateshead Riverside Sculpture Park** has imaginative displays (*The Cone* by Anthony Gormley, *Rolling Moon* by Colin Rose, *Bottle Bank* by Richard Harris, Goats by Sally Matthews). The **Great North Forest** scheme aims to create a sense of place and to develop artistic and cultural links between local people and the countryside. The Four Seasons Project will involve major European artists. The Gateshead Art Map which pinpoints these exciting sculptures is available from the Gateshead Tourist Office.

(altars, tombstones and armour), make an interesting visit for those going on to Hadrian's Wall. The reconstruction of the mithraeum at Carrawburgh boasts the original sculptured stones. Also on display is a set of legionary body armour *(lorica)* alongside two variants.

LIFE Interactive World – ♿ ⏰ *Open daily, 10am (11am Sun) to 6pm. Last admission 4.30pm. £6.95. Parking (charge). Café. ☎ 0191 243 8210 (information), 0191 243 8223 (bookings); www.lifesciencecentre.org.uk. Hands-on fun for children is the order of the day, as they learn about science and nature.*

Blackfriars (CZ) – The much-restored buildings of the Dominican friary, founded in the 13C, now house a craft centre.

Excursions

Hadrian's Wall★★ – ♿ *See HADRIAN'S WALL.*

Beamish★★
10mi/16km south by any of the river bridges and A 692 towards Consett. At Sunniside turn left into A 6076. After 2mi/3km turn right into a picnic area. A path leads via an old waggonway to the Causey Arch (about 600yd/550m).

Causey Arch – One of the deep wooded "denes" characteristic of the area is boldly bridged by this pioneering stone arch of 1726, once part of a regional network of wooden waggonways linking collieries to the Tyne. In the early 18C nearly 1 000 individual waggons (chauldrons) would rumble every day over the bridge on their way down to the river. By the early 19C the horse and gravity powered waggonways had been succeeded by steam railways, one of which, the nearby **Tanfield Railway,** (♿ ⏰ *Engine shed: Open daily, 10am-5pm (4pm Oct-Mar). Trains: Timetable call for info. (North Pole Express; booking essential). £5. ☎ 0191 388 7545; Fax 0191 387 4784; tanfield@ingsoc.demon.co.uk; www.tanfield-railway.co.uk)* has been reopened by enthusiasts.

▶ *Continue south by A 6076; on entering Stanley turn left and left again into A 693 towards Chester-le-Street. After about 1mi/1km turn left and follow signs to Beamish Museum.*

Beamish, The North of England Open-Air Museum★★ – ⏰ *Open late-Mar to late-Oct, daily, 10am-5pm (last admission 3pm); Nov-Mar, Tue-Thu and Sat-Sun, 10am-4pm (last admission 3pm); Christmas times by phone. £15 (5hr); £6 (2hr in winter,Town and Tramway only). Brochure (5 languages). Parking. Licensed period pub; tearoom; picnic areas. ☎ 0191 370 4000; Fax 0191 370 4001; museum@beamish.org.uk; www. beamish.org.uk.* As well as recreating life in the North of England around the turn of the century this popular museum in its attractive countryside setting also evokes the environment of ordinary people at the start of the 19C, as the full effect of the Industrial Revolution began to be felt in the region.

Preserved tramcars, supplemented by a pre-First World War motorbus, take visitors through the extensive site to the **town**, whose shops, houses, bank, working pub, sweet factory, newspaper office and printer's workshop, stocked and furnished authentically, and inhabited by costumed guides, evoke the urban scene of yesteryear. The **railway station** with its goods yard and signal box faithfully reproduces the atmosphere of a country station; the road transport collection boasts old vehicles of every kind, some displayed in an early 20C garage. Near the **coal mine**, overlooked by a carefully recreated spoil heap, is the colliery village with pit cottages and gardens, chapel and school. Visitors can penetrate underground into the old workings of a real "drift" mine. The buildings of **Pockerley Manor** demonstrate the lifestyle of a yeoman farmer of the 1820s, while the Pockerley Waggonway exhibit will have as its centrepiece a superb full-scale working replica of Stephenson's *Locomotion* of 1825.

Seaton Delaval Hall★

11mi/18km northeast by A 189 (CY) and A 190. Open: May-Sep, Wed, Thu, Sun and Bank Hol Mon, 2-6pm. £3. Parking. Tearoom. 0191 237 1493; www.seatondelaval.org.uk. This powerful Northern version of a Palladian villa is a masterpiece (1718-29) designed for Admiral George Delaval by **Sir John Vanbrugh**, the architect of Blenheim Palace and Castle Howard. The ruined mansion looks north across windswept countryside towards the industrial port of Blyth, the bleakness of the scene echoed in the great masses of sombre stonework. The eastern of the two symmetrical flanking wings houses sumptuous **stables**. The interior of the central portion, gutted by fire in 1822 and twice partially restored since, is of Piranesian grandeur and gloom. A fine portico adorns the south front.

The Delaval family were notorious for wild revels but found time in the mid-18C to build extensive harbour works at nearby **Seaton Sluice.**

Wallington House★

20mi/32km northwest by A 696 (CY); after 18mi/29km turn right into minor road and follow the signs. Cambo, Morpeth. House: Open late-Mar to beg Sep, Wed-Mon, 1-5.30pm (4:30 Sep-Oct). Walled garden: Open Apr-Mar, daily, 10am-7pm (6pm Oct, 4pm/dusk Nov-Mar). Grounds: Open during daylight hours. House, garden and grounds £7.30; garden and grounds only, £5.20. Parking. Restaurant. Wheelchairs and self drive powered vehicle available; access to ground floor of house, most of grounds, conservatory and walled garden; Braille guides. 01670 773 600; 01670 773 967 (infoline); Fax 01670 774 420; wallington@nationaltrust.org.uk; www.nationaltrust.org.uk. The original property was bought in 1688 by Sir William Blackett from the bankrupt Sir John Fenwick, most of the £2000 price being paid as an annuity as long as Sir John should live. When Sir John became involved in a plan to assassinate King William III, Sir Walter voted energetically in Parliament for a Bill of Attainder, which eventually took Sir John to the scaffold in 1697 and terminated the annuity! But Sir John had his posthumous revenge. King William had confiscated Sir John's horse White Sorrel and this was the mount which stumbled on a molehill, throwing the King and causing his death – the origin of the Jacobite toast to "the little gentleman in the black velvet coat".

The house rebuilt by Sir William and refurbished by his heir Sir Walter is renowned for its 18C **plasterwork** by an Italian, Francini. The original courtyard, now the hall, is decorated with a series of **painted scenes** from Northumbrian history by William Bell Scott, a reminder of the Pre-Raphaelite connections with Wallington. The large collection of **porcelain** includes many 18C Chinese and Japanese items as well as Bow and Chelsea pieces. The important collection of dolls' houses is another fascinating feature of Wallington.

The **bridge** by James Paine and the **walled garden** as well as the whole village of Cambo are fine examples of the imaginative vision of Sir Walter, who also designed the layout of the parkland with minimal assistance from Capability Brown, who was born just two miles away. Battle Hill beyond is the site of Chevy Chase where Hotspur and Douglas fought, a familiar subject in the Border ballads of this marchland area.

Belsay Hall, Garden and Castle

14mi/23km southwest by A 696. Open 10am-6pm (Thur-Mon, 4pm Oct-Mar). Closed 1 Jan and 24-26 Dec. £5.30. Leaflet. Tearoom. 01661 881 636; Fax 0661 881 043; www.english-heritage.org.uk. The estate of the prominent Northumbrian Middleton family has fascinating features from most periods of its existence.

The stalwart Border castle keep was built by 1460 and a mansion added to it in the early years of the 17C. Both were abandoned in favour of a neo-Classical mansion of the utmost severity completed in 1817, its austerity emphasized by its total lack of furnishings. There are formal gardens and parkland, but the most appealing feature of the grounds are the **gardens** laid out in the quarries formed to build the mansion; sheltered from the bleak northeastern climate, they form a romantic landscape of sandstone cliff faces and exotic plants. The 19C arcaded buildings of Belsay village replaced the village demolished when the park was extended.

Bede's World

In Jarrow, 7mi/11km east by A 184, A 194 and A 108. ♿🕐 *Open Mon-Sat and Bank Hols), 10am (noon Sun) to 5.30pm (4.30pm Nov-Mar).* 🕐 *Closed Good Friday.* 👓 *£4.50. Restaurant. Electric wheelchair vailable.* ☎ *01914 892 106; visitor.info@bedesworld. co.uk; www.bedesworld.co.uk.* Hailed as Britain's first historian, the **Venerable Bede** (AD 672/3-735) was only a child when he entered St Peter's monastery at Wearmouth which had been founded by Benedict Biscop in AD 674. As a young man, Bede moved to St Peter's sister establishment at Jarrow. It was here that he wrote his *Ecclesiastical History of the English People*, and it is here that he is commemorated by this ambitious project which incorporates not only **St Paul's Church** with Saxon tower and chancel (the only surviving part of the monastery) but also the late 18C Jarrow Hall, a modern visitor centre in a style evocative of the Mediterranean world from which Early Christianity had sprung, and an evolving attempt to recreate the Saxon farmlands which would have formed the background to Bede's work – reconstructed timber buildings and rare breeds.

National Glass Centre, Sunderland

♿🕐 *Open daily, 10am-5pm.* 🕐 *Closed 25 Dec and 1 Jan.* 👓 *Tour £5. Parking. Restaurant. Shop.* ☎ *0191 515 5555; Fax 0191 515 5556; www.nationalglasscentre. com.* Watch the stages of glass manufacture and explore the uses of glass in the modern world. The history of glass on Wearside and the town's long glassmaking tradition are vividly illustrated.

Sunderland Churches

12mi/20km southeast by A 184. The Saxon tower and porch of Benedict Biscop's 7C monastery survive, though the rest of **St Peter's Church,** (♿🕐 *Open Easter-Oct, daily, 2-4.30pm. Guide. Leaflet.* ☎ *0191 516 0135; Monkwearmouth. Parish@durham. anglican.org)* is a 19C rebuilding by Sir George Gilbert Scott. The church stands high above the River Wear, once a centre of shipbuilding which made Sunderland a rival to Tyneside. The torch of Christianity rekindled by Benedict and his followers still shone brightly enough in the early years of the 20C to inspire the building of **St Andrew's Church,** (🕐 *Open Mon-Fri, 9am-1pm. Services: Sun at 8am, 9.30am, 6pm; Wed at 10am.* 👓 *Donation. Parking.* 🔎 *Guided tour by appointment. Brochure available.* ☎ *0191 516 0135)* in the suburb of Roker. One of the most extraordinary achievements of modern church architecture, its austere interior is a stunning interpretation, almost Expressionist in its vigour, of the Gothic spirit, relieved by superb fittings and furnishings designed by virtually all the great names of the Arts and Crafts movement.

Washington Old Hall

7mi/11km south in the town of Washington, District 4. ♿🕐 *The Avenue; Open late-Mar to Oct, Sun-Wed and Good Friday, 11am-5pm.* 👓 *£3.80. Limited parking. Tearoom. Wheelchair access to ground floor; partial access to garden; Braille guide.* ☎ *0191 416 6879; Fax 0191 419 2065; washington.oldhall@nationaltrust.org.uk;www.nationaltrust. org.uk.* The hall was the seat of the forebears of George Washington (1732-99), the first president of the United States. A small English manor-house stands on the site of earlier buildings. The ground floor is furnished with items typical of the 17C-18C.

NEW FOREST★★

Hampshire, ENGLAND

MICHELIN ATLAS P 9 OR MAP 503 O, P 31

William I made the area near his castle in Winchester a royal forest for hunting; severe penalties were imposed on poachers or anyone who harmed the deer or trees. The Crown ceded jurisdiction of the forest (144sq mi/373km2) to the Forestry Commission in 1924 and it 2005 it was given the status of National Park. Ponies, donkeys, deer, cattle and occasionally pigs still roam freely in the unspoilt woodland, heath and marshland and not infrequently by the roadside. Motorists should drive slowly and always with extreme care. *High Street. Lyndhurst; ☎ 023 8028 3444; Fax 023 8028 4236; office@newforestmuseum.org.uk; www.newforestmuseum.org.uk, www.newforestnpa.gov.uk.*

▶ **Orient Yourself**: The New Forest Museum and Visitor Centre is the best place to start.

Don't Miss: One of the Ornamental Drives; Beaulieu Motor Museum; Buckler's Hard.

Organizing Your Time: Allow two days.

Especially for Kids: Beaulieu National Motor Museum; Wildlife Conservation Park.

Walking Tours: Ask at the visitor centre.

In the Forest

Bolderwood Ornamental Drive★★ – This is a lovely drive through several enclosures created in the 19C and now containing many fine, mature trees, especially oak and beech. The **Bolderwood Walks**, at the beginning of the drive, enable visitors to see some of the forest deer at close quarters from observation platforms. Further along, some of the oak and beech pollards are at least 300 years old. At the end of the drive just before the A 35 is the venerable **Knightwood Oak** reputedly 375 years old.

Lyndhurst – Capital of the New Forest, this bustling and attractive town was where the forest verderers held court in the 17C **Queen's House**. The bold red-brick Victorian church is notable for its Burne-Jones windows and an 1864 fresco by Lord Leighton. In the churchyard is the grave of Alice Hargreaves, née Liddell, who inspired Lewis Carroll to write *Alice in Wonderland.*

The **New Forest Museum and Visitor Centre,** (*High Street. Open daily 10am-5pm, Closed Christmas Eve from 12 noon, 25-26 Dec. £3. ☎ 023 8028 3444; Fax 023 8028 4236; office@newforestmuseum.org.uk; www.newforestmuseum.org.uk*) offers an excellent introduction to the area with displays on every aspect of life in the New Forest: a film; computer interactives; the 25' long New Forest embroidery; and children's activities.

Minstead – This attractive and largely unspoilt village, just south of the A 31, has a red-brick **All Saints Church** (13C), notable for its two-tiered gallery, 17C three-decker pulpit and two manorial pews. North of the village are the informal **Furzey Gardens,** (*Garden: Open daily, 10am-5pm/dusk. Gallery: Open Mar-Oct, daily, 10am-5pm. Closed 25-26 Dec. £3.50 (Mar-Oct); £1.50 (Nov-Feb). Parking. ☎ 023 8081 2464; Fax 023 8081 2297*) with a 16C thatched cottage showing how New Forest workers lived 400 years ago.

Knightwood Oak

Rhinefield Ornamental Drive★★ – This is a magnificent drive along an avenue of trees planted in 1859 which are today Britain's finest collection of mature conifers. Some of the Douglas Firs and Redwoods stand 150ft/46m high.

Rufus Stone – In a quiet glen, a memorial tablet marks the spot where William II, known as Rufus, was killed by an arrow while hunting in 1100. Historians have never ascertained whether it was an accident or murder.

By the River

Beaulieu★★ – This pretty village at the head of the Beaulieu River is famous for the National Motor Museum (*see below*) one of the world's most comprehensive collections of motor vehicles, set in the grounds of the Cistercian monastery founded in 1204 by King John.

After the Dissolution the **abbey** fell into ruin, its stone being in demand for Henry VIII's coastal forts. Only the footings remain of what was once the largest Cistercian abbey in England. The cloister has partly survived, notably the lay brothers' quarters (now housing an exhibition of monastic life) and the 13C refectory, converted into the parish church; behind a screen of Purbeck marble columns, the staircase leading to what was the lector's pulpit is an interesting feature.

Palace House, the home of the 1st Lord Montagu, is a strange mixture of medieval monastic architecture, Victorian home comforts and mementoes of the Montagu family.

National Motor Museum★★ – *Open daily, 10am-6pm, 10am-5pm Oct-Apr; last admission 40min before closing time. Closed 25 Dec. £11.95 combined ticket with Monastic Life Exhibition and National Motor Museum. Parking. Refreshments. 01590 612 345; Fax 01590 612 624; www.beaulieu.co.uk.* The collection of more than 250 vehicles celebrates the story of motoring from 1895 to the present day. The Classic Car Hall of Fame presents the great motoring pioneers. Veteran and vintage cars (Rolls-Royce Silver Ghost, Ford Model T) recall the exciting beginnings while the 1930s section (Austin Seven) traces the benefits of mass production. Racing heroes are commemorated in the Racing and Record-Breaking Car section (*Bluebird* 1961). There are also displays of commercial vehicles and motorcycles. "Wheels" (ground floor) is a ride in automated pods through 100 years of motoring. Walk through a recreated 1930s country garage and hear the mechanics at work, while upstairs a series of hands-on stations encourage children to explore for themselves how an engine works.

National Motor Museum

1913 Rolls-Royce Alpine Eagle

Buckler's Hard ★
– *2mi/3km southeast of Beaulieu. Open daily, 10am (11am Oct-Easter) to 5.30pm (4pm Oct-Easter). Closed 25 Dec. £4. River cruise (30min) £3. Souvenir shop. Hotel. Cafeteria. Pub, beer garden, picnic area by the river. 01590 616 203.* The charming hamlet comprises one very wide street lined with 18C cottages running down to the Beaulieu River. In the 1740s the village became a shipbuilding centre for the Navy. As iron replaced wood in shipbuilding the industry declined but the Hard has found new patronage among yachtsmen including round-the-world yachtsman Sir Francis Chichester (1901-72). The **Maritime Museum★** illustrates many aspects of life and work in the 18C with the reconstructed interiors of two cottages and the New Inn, furnished in the style of the 1790s. Boat trips from the wharf.

NORTHAMPTON

Northamptonshire, ENGLAND

POPULATION 179 596

MICHELIN ATLAS P 28 OR MAP 504 R 27

TOWN PLAN IN THE MICHELIN GUIDE GREAT BRITAIN AND IRELAND

Most of this important South Midlands medieval town, where in 1164 Thomas Becket stood trial in the castle (c 1100), was destroyed by fire in 1675. The late 17C town which rose from the ruins was described by Defoe as the "handsomest and best town in this part of England". In 1845 the castle was obliterated by the railway.
Guildhall, St Giles Square ☎ 01604 838800 Fax: 01604 604180; tic@northampton.gov. uk; www. northampton.gov.uk.

Sights

Church of the Holy Sepulchre – *Sheep Street.* ⚹ Open May-Sep, Wed, noon-4pm, Sat, 10am-2pm, alternate Fri, 2pm-4pm. Guide book and souvenir. ☎ 01604 754 782 or 231 800, Fax 01604 626 828; www.northampton.org.uk/.heritage. One of only four Norman round churches in England, founded by Simon de Senlis, veteran of the First Crusade, with a **round nave** and circular **ambulatory**.

All Saints Church – *George Row.* Open daily, 8.30am-2.30pm; also Mon-Tue and Thu-Fri, 4-6.30pm. Sevices: Sun at 8am, 10.30am, 6.30pm. Coffee shop. ☎/Fax 01604 632 194; allsaintsnorthampton@freeserve.co.uk; www.allsaintschurchnorthampton. co.uk. The church was built after the 1675 fire in the Classical style with a dome and a beautiful plastered ceiling by Sir Edward Goudge, who worked for Sir Christopher Wren. The portico dates from 1701.

Guildhall – ⚹ St Giles Square; Tour by appointment. Ticket from the Guildhall Office. ☎ 01604 233 500 ext 3400; www.northampton.gov.uk. Victorian Gothic at its most confident by Edward Godwin, c 1860, when he was only around 28. The exterior is ennobled with kings, queens and other neo-Gothic props; the interior is invested with local municipal worthies, almost lost amid the imitation Early English foliage on the cast-iron columns.

Northampton Museum and Art Gallery★ – *Guildhall Road;* ⚹ Open daily, 10am (2pm Sun) to 5pm. Closed 25-26 Dec. Free Admission. Guide (4 languages). ☎ 01604 838 111; Fax 01604 238 720; museums@northampton.gov.uk; www.northampton.gov. uk/museums. Northampton was a shoe-making centre for over 500 years and the museum houses an interesting, if rather cramped, collection of footwear, ranging from the remnants of Romano-British sandals to 16C satin slippers and the shoes of Queen Victoria's household.

Excursions

Anglo-Saxon Church Architecture – Two marvels of pre-Conquest church building survive in the Northamptonshire countryside.

All Saints, Brixworth★ – *8mi/13km north on A 508.* Open Mon-Fri, 8.15am-2.15pm. Services: Sun at 8.30am, 10.30am, 6.30pm, three choirs; Tue-Fri, midday (Communion), Mon-Tue and Thu-Fri, 5.30pm (Evensong). Donation. Coffee shop (8.30am-1.45pm); brixworth.friends@virgin.net. The largest Saxon church to survive almost entire was established by monks from Lindisfarne in the 7C and rebuilt after being sacked by Danes in the 9C; the defensive tower was a useful retreat during Viking raids. Note the Roman tiles and Saxon arches in the nave and chancel.

All Saints, Earls Barton – *8mi/13km east on A 45.* ⚹ Open spring and summer, daily; check times ☎ 01604 810 045. Guide book and brochure (3 languages). ☎/Fax 01604 810 447; michaelc.webber@btinternet.com; www.northamptonshire.co.uk. The fortress **tower** is Saxon, built in the reign of Edgar the Peaceful (959-995), the golden age of Saxon architecture. The patterning is clearly derived from older timber-framed buildings. The tower door and west door are Norman.

Boughton House★★ – *17mi/27km northeast on A 43, turn right in Geddington. House:* Open Aug, daily, 1pm-5pm. Grounds: Open May-Sept, Sat and Thur, also daily in Aug, 1pm-5pm. House and grounds £4, £3 (senior citizens and children); grounds only £1.50, £1 (senior citizens and children); no charge (disabled). Parking. ☎ 01536 515 731; Fax 01536 417 255; e-mail ltboughtonhouse.org.uk. Originally a monastic house owned by the Abbey of

Edmundsbury (⚘ see BURY ST EDMUNDS), it was bought by Edward Montagu in 1528, who made the first extensions. More were made by the first Duke of Montagu, ambassador to Louis XIV, who built the north front, commissioned Chéron's Baroque ceilings, introduced the "parquet de Versailles" floors and embellished the house with furniture, porcelain and paintings. Though the fourth Duke made more additions in the mid 18C, the house has hardly changed since c 1700. The 365 windows, 7 courtyards and 12 entrances match the number of days in the week and days and months in the year.

Amongst the finest paintings are El Greco's Adoration of the Shepherds, and Murillo's John the Baptist in the Low Pavilion Ante Room; Teniers the Younger's Harvest Scene in the Little Hall; the Earl of Southampton by Gainsborough in the Great Hall and numerous Van Dycks, Lelys and Knellers.

Milton Keynes – 17mi/27km south on M 1. This prosperous planned city, midway between London and Birmingham, is the last and most ambitious of Britain's postwar New Towns. Its lavishly landscaped 22 000acre/8 900ha site includes three established towns (Stony Stratford, Wolverton and Bletchley), several ancient villages, trim new residential areas, community facilities and high-tech industries, set in parkland and linked by a web of expressways; shoppers are attracted from a vast catchment area by the gleaming City Centre with 140 stores under its roof and parking for 10 000 cars.

Canal Museum – 6mi/9km south on A 508 at Stoke Bruerne. ⊙ Open summer, daily, 10am-5pm; winter, Tues-Sun, Mon, 10am-4pm. Last admission 30 mins before closing. ⊙ Closed 25-26 Dec. £3.75. Parking. ☎ 01604 862 229; www.thewaterwaystrust.org.uk. The old cornmill beside the lock on the Grand Union Canal now traces the history of the canal age. The display of drawings, photographs, models, old signs and canal furniture illustrates the construction of canals, the operation of locks and inclined planes, the engineers who designed them, the different types of narrow boats, for goods or passengers, their crews and motive power, the traditional brightly-coloured decoration of roses and castles. One may watch the passage of boats up and down the flight of seven locks (gongoozling in canal parlance) or walk along the towpath to the southern end of the Blisworth Tunnel (3 056yd/2 820m), the longest navigable continuous bore tunnel in Britain, opened in 1805.

Sulgrave Manor – 18mi/29km southwest on A 45, B 4525 and minor road. Manor Road; ♿⊙Open: late-Mar to Oct, Thu-Tue, 2pm-5.30pm (last admission 4.30pm). ⊙ Closed 22-26, 31 Dec, and Jan plus special days in June and July - call ahead for details. ⊞ £5.75; special events (telephone for details). Parking. Refreshments. ☎ 01295 760 205; Fax 01295 768 056; enquiries@sulgravemanor.org.uk; www.sulgravemanor.org.uk. The home of the Washington family, from 1539 to their departure to Virginia in 1656, is now a museum of Washingtonia, jointly owned by the American and British peoples. In the Great Hall are the Washington coat of arms (note the resemblance to the Stars and Stripes); the Deed Room and Porch Room contain George Washington's saddle bags, velvet coat, medals and several of his letters. The manor is a good example of a Tudor home at the time of Shakespeare.

Althorp – 5mi/8km northwest on A 428. ⊙ Open Jul-Sep, daily, 10am-5pm (4pm last admission); booking recommended as only a restricted number of entry tickets are on sale. ⊙ Closed 31 Aug. ⊞ £12. Cafe; picnic area. ☎ 0870 167 9000 (booking and information); 01604 770 107; Fax 01604 770 042; mail@althorp.com; www.althorp.com. In view of the number of visitors, parking restrictions apply. This 16C house, remodelled during the 18C, was the family home of **Diana, Princess of Wales**. Following Diana's tragic death in a car accident in Paris in August 1997 at the age of only 36, Earl Spencer has renovated his estate to include a **museum** to the memory of his sister.

The exhibition, devoted to the life of one of the world's most famous women, is housed in a converted Palladian style coach house (c 1740), designed by Russhied Ali Din, an architect identified with clean, modern lines. The museum follows seven themes: Diana as an independent woman, her public works, her impact on the world, her funeral, as wife and mother, her historical links with the monarchy, and her place among Spencer women. Exhibits include many mementoes from Diana's former home at Kensington Palace, such as her wedding dress, as well as a display of some of the outfits she wore, illustrating the development of her unique sense of style over the years, and some of the hundreds of books of condolence signed by the public after her death. There are also photographs and video footage of her as a child from the Spencer family albums, not previously available to the public.

The church of **Great Brington** (parking restrictions) west of Althorp houses the tombs of the Spencer family, with the exception of that of Diana which it was decided for reasons of privacy to place on a small island in the middle of the lake on the estate (⚘ not accessible to the public).

NORWICH★★

Norfolk, ENGLAND

POPULATION 171 304

MICHELIN ATLAS P 31 OR MAP 504 Y 26

Norwich, one of England's best preserved medieval cities, is situated on the river Wensum and is the capital of East Anglia. The city retains its confusing Saxon street grid though its most prosperous period was during the Middle Ages when it was the centre of the East Anglian wool trade; the surviving towers and spires of over 30 flint churches, many now redundant, etch the skyline. The city is dominated by the hilltop castle keep; below is the centre of old Norwich, where cobbled streets, lined with half-timbered houses, lead through stone gateways to the cathedral. 🗓 *Forum, Millennium Plain* ☎ *01603 727927; Fax 01603 765389; tourism@ norwich.gov.uk; www.visitnorwich.co.uk.*

▶ **Orient Yourself**: Start first at the Origins visitor centre; then take an open-top bus hop-on hop-off tour for a good overview of the city (*Apr-Oct* ☎*01708 866 000; www.city-sightseeing.com*).

🐱 **Don't Miss**: the Cathedral; Market Place on a busy day; Blickling Hall (excursion); boating on the Norfolk Broads in the summer.

🕐 **Organizing Your Time**: Allow one-two days for the city.

Kids Especially for Kids: Boating on the Norfolk Broads.

Walking Tours: City tours with a Blue Badge Guide depart from the tourist information centre (Apr-Oct) ☎ 01603 727927. Norwich Ghost Walk, May-Sept, Mon-Thurs 7.30pm.☎ 01953 607262

Cathedral★★ *2hr*

Palace Street. ♿🕐*Open daily, 7.30am-7pm (6pm winter). Donation.* 🔊 *Guided tour (1hr) by appointment. Organised tour Jun-Oct, Mon-Sat, 10.45am, noon, 2.15pm. Leaflet (8 languages). Buffet. Shop. Audio loop; touch and hearing centre.* ☎ *01603 218 321; Fax 01603 766 032; vis-profficer@cathedral.org.uk; www.cathedral.org.uk.* The Norman cathedral was begun in 1096 and consecrated in 1278. Its choir clerestory was rebuilt in Early English style in the 14C and Perpendicular vaults added in the 15C and early 16C. Faced with Caen stone, conveyed to the site via a canal dug from Pull's Ferry, the rich Norman **tower** and 15C **spire** act as a perfect foil to the long low nave and graceful flying buttresses at the east end. The Cathedral has been struck by many disasters – fires, riots and sackings – and the spire fell down in a gale in 1362. The 15C spire (315ft/96m) is the second-tallest in England after Salisbury.

Interior – Above the steadfast Norman nave and transepts the 400 carved and painted bosses on the vaults portray "a strip cartoon of the whole story of God's involvement with man from creation to last judgement" (Dean Alan Webster). Two of the original spiral pillars mark the end of the first phase of building in 1119. Behind the altar are two fragments of carved stone under the Bishop's Throne, thought to have been part of the Saxon Bishop's throne. Note the **misericords** of the choir stalls, the ambulatory, St Luke's Chapel (displaying the famous 14C five-panelled Despenser Reredos) and Jesus Chapel (displaying Martin Schwarz's *Adoration of the Magi*, painted in the 1480s).

Cloisters and Close – The **Prior's Door,** leading from the nave to the cloisters, with its sculptured figures of Christ flanked by two angels, two bishops and two monks, is one of the most beautiful doors of the early Decorated style. The unusual two-storeyed cloisters (the largest in England) were rebuilt (c 1297-1430) and have superb tracery. Coats of arms decorate some of the walls; the 400 roof bosses on the vaulted ceiling illustrate the Book of Revelations. The predominantly Georgian close, entered through **Erpingham Gate** (1420) **(Y)** or **St Ethelbert's Gate** (c 1300) **(Y)** leads to Pull's Ferry, the old watergate.

Additional Sights

Castle (Z) – The castle, which stands at the centre of Norwich, was begun in 1160 and was built on a commanding hilltop. The motifs of the external blind arcading

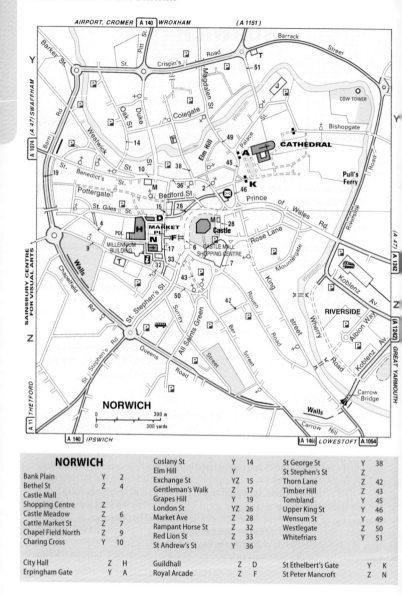

were faithfully reproduced when the building was refaced in Bath stone by Salvin (1833-39). The building was later used as a prison.

Norwich Castle Museum★ – Castle Meadow. *&Open daily, 10am (1pm Sun) to 4.30pm; school holidays until 5.30pm).* ☎ *01603 493 625. Fax 01603 493 623; museums@ norfolk.gov.uk; www.norfolk.gov.uk.* The high-walled stone **keep** has retained many of its original features – Norman arches, windows, chapel niche and the well (110ft/34m deep); the **battlements** and **dungeons** are included in a guided tour. Here the history of Norwich, which in 1066 was the fourth most populous city in England, is traced through Norman and later local finds, such as pots.

The art gallery *(ground floor)* displays an outstanding collection of works by the **Norwich School** of painters, formed at the start of the 19C by local, self-taught painter **John Crome** (1768-1821), whose most talented pupil was **John Sell Cotman** (1782-1842). This school was greatly influenced by Dutch landscape artists and Crome's rural scenes are often suffused with a golden light. Also on display are works by 20C **East Anglian** artists – Alfred Munnings, Edward Seago – as well as Victorian and Dutch works.

The porcelain section contains a fascinating collection of British teapots from 1720 and pretty pieces from Lowestoft. The Ecology gallery shows dioramas of the Norfolk coast and the remains of the 600 000-year-old West Runton Elephant, excavated in 1992, many of whose hyena-chewed bones look much like wood.

Walls (Z) – The stone walls (1294-1320) surrounding the city centre are as long (2.25mi/just under 4km) as the walls of the City of London; the best **view** is from Carrow Bridge and Carrow Hill.

Market Place★ (Z) – The square, which is 900 years old and the largest in East Anglia, is occupied six days a week by market stalls mostly selling local produce. To the north is the chequered flint **Guildhall**, begun in 1407, which now houses the Tourist Information Centre. To the west, at a higher level, is the modern **City Hall**, "probably the foremost English public building of between the wars" (Pevsner).

The Forum – *Open daily 10am (11am Sun) to 5.15pm; £5.95. Info in 4 languages. Parking. Lift. ☎ 01603 727 920; Fax 01603 727 955; info@theforumnorfolk.co.uk; www. theforumnorwich.co.uk.* To the south is Norwich's grandest parish church, **St Peter Mancroft**, Perpendicular par excellence, with a fine hammerbeam roof, a great east window with medieval glass, and a 15C font. To the east is the Art Nouveau **Royal Arcade**.

Elm Hill (Y) – This quaint cobbled street, formerly the centre of the weaving industry, is lined with medieval brick and timber houses. At the northern (Tombland) end stands the late Perpendicular church of **St Simon and St Jude**, now divided horizontally and put to commercial use. Farther along sits the thatched 15C restaurant, **Britons Arms** *(right)*, and then the medieval church of **St Peter Hungate** (rebuilt 1460 *Open Apr-Sept, Mon-Sat, 10am-5pm. No charge. ☎ 01603 667 231*), now an ecclesiastical museum displaying embroidered vestments, church brasses and stained glass. Across the street can be seen the east window of **Blackfriars Hall,** which together with **St Andrew's Hall** once formed the choir and nave of the Convent Church of the Blackfriars who came to Norwich in 1226. Blackfriars' later became a church for Flemish weavers; St Andrew's was an assize court and corn exchange. Both halls, with fine hammerbeam roofs, are now used for public and civic functions. The cloisters, too had many uses and are now occupied by the Norwich School of Art; the 13C brick vaulted crypt survives as a café.

Sainsbury Centre for Visual Arts★ (Z) – *University of East Anglia; 3mi/5km west of the city centre. Closed for refurbishment until late 2006. ☎ 01603 456 060 (recorded information); Fax 01603 259 401; scva@uea.ac.uk; www.scva.org.uk.* The centre, one of the most exciting buildings of the 1970s, was designed by Norman Foster and is constructed out of 37 prismatic steel trusses forming a tube (400ft/122m x 100ft/31m) of interchangeable glass, solid and grilled panels; the intention was to create a non-museum environment in which to look "at works of art from a sensual, not only an intellectual point of view" (Sir Robert Sainsbury).

The 19C and 20C European works by Degas, Seurat, Picasso, Epstein, Bacon, Modigliani, Moore and Giacometti are delightfully juxtaposed with African, Pacific, Oriental and American Indian art and high quality artefacts, both ancient and modern, of bronze, wood and faience. There is a display of Lucy Rie pots in the Mezzanine Gallery and a Reserve Collection in the Crescent.

Excursions

Blickling Hall★★ – *(NT) 15mi/24km north on A 140 (Y). House: Open late-Mar to Oct, Wed-Sun and Bank Hol Mon, 1-5pm (4pm Oct-Nov). Gardens: Open same as house; also Aug, Tue, 10.15am-5.15pm; early-Nov to mid Dec, Thu-Sun, 11am-4pm; early-Jan to Mar, Sat-Sun, 11am-4pm. Park: Open daily, dawn-dusk. House and garden. £7.30; garden £4.20. Braille guide. Parking. Restaurant. Bookshop. Cycle hire. ☎ 01263 738 030 ; Fax 01263 738 035; blickling@nationaltrust.org.uk; www.nationaltrust.org.uk.* This splendid turreted and gabled brick mansion was built 1619-25 by Robert Lyminge, the architect of Hatfield House; it is one of the most intact of great Jacobean houses; the extensive late 18C alterations carried out by Thomas Ivory of Norwich were tactfully "in keeping". There is a staircase of barbarous profusion; a plastered ceiling (120ft/37m) portraying the *Five Senses* and *Learning* in the Long Gallery; a splendid tapestry of Peter the Great defeating the Swedes at Poltava, presented by Catherine the Great to Blickling's owner the Earl of Buckinghamshire, in the Peter the Great Room; and paintings by Reynolds, Gainsborough and Canaletto.

The present parterre and gardens date from the late 19C, the original layout of the grounds having been landscaped away in the late 18C, probably by Humphry Repton. Far away in the park is an extraordinary pyramidal mausoleum (40ft/12m high).

Norfolk Broads

A. Williams/MICHELIN

Knapton – *18mi/29km north on A 1151 (Y) and B 1150 to North Walsham and then B 1145.* The glories of the **Church of St Peter and St Paul,** (Open daily) are the 1504 double hammerbeam roof bearing 138 carved angels, each one different, and its font cover.

Norfolk Broads★

The Broads, one of Britain's premier wildlife habitats, are the home of Chinese water deer, kingfishers, bitterns, herons and great crested grebes, and insect species such as the swallowtail butterfly and the Norfolk hawker dragonfly which are found nowhere else in Britain. Peaceful waterways wind their way through the misty fens, cutting between lush woods and open marshes beneath a seemingly endless sky. The villages are famous for their churches, some of which have hammerbeam and thatched roofs.

This beautiful natural environment is, however, also a fragile one: the delicate eco-logical balance of the water is easily upset, for example by sewage and agricultural fertilisers which encourage the growth of invasive quantities of algae; the banks of the broads are susceptible to erosion as reeds and other plants disappear, leaving them vulnerable to the wash from motor boats; and the fens themselves, no longer maintained by activities such as sedge cutting (thatched roofs being less common), are giving way to woodland, robbing local wildlife of its habitat. The **Broads Authority**, originally set up in 1978, has made strenuous efforts over the years to arrest this decline and oversee a programme of restoration and conservation.

The navigable waterways (over 125mi/200km) and the 14 Broads, large lakes formed out of medieval peat diggings, are best explored by boat.

From Norwich take A 1151 north.

Wroxham – This is a good centre on the River Bure where boats can be hired by the hour, the day or the week.

Take the local roads south to Salhouse and east via Woodbastwick to Ranworth.

Ranworth – The Perpendicular tower and Decorated south porch of **St Helen's Church** (Open daily, 9am-6pm (4pm winter). Tea and coffee shop: Open Sat-Sun, 2pm-5pm; also Easter-Oct, Mon-Fri, 10.30am-4.30pm. Leaflet (3 languages). Ramp into the Church. Audio guide. Aromatic garden for visually impaired visitors) give no hint of the splendour inside: the finest rood screen (15C) in East Anglia, a brightly painted (restored) array of saints, apostles and martyrs.

Take the local road south to South Walsham, B 1140 east to Acle, A 1064 north and, after crossing the Bure, fork left on B 1152.

Potter Heigham – The capital of the northern Broads is on the River Thurne. **St Nicholas' Church** has a Norman tower and a hammerbeam and thatched roof. Potter Heigham is also home to a famously low bridge, so sailors should beware!

NOTTINGHAM
Nottinghamshire, ENGLAND

POPULATION 270 222

MICHELIN ATLAS P 36 OR MAP 504 Q 25

TOWN PLAN IN THE MICHELIN GUIDE GREAT BRITAIN AND IRELAND

This famous East Midlands city evokes Robin Hood's arch enemy, the Sheriff of Nottingham, lace-making and DH Lawrence. It was originally Snotingeham, a settlement peopled by the followers of a Dane called Snot. The town, the gateway to the North, is on the north bank of the Trent and became one of the five Danish burghs; the others were Derby, Leicester, Lincoln and Stamford. *County Hall, Loughborough Road, West Bridgford NG2 7QP, ☎ 0115 977 3558; Fax 0115 977 3886. 1-4 Smithy Row, NG1 2BY ☎ 0115 9155 330; tourist.information@nottinghamcity.gov. uk; www.visitnottingham.com.*

▸ **Orient Yourself**: Nottingham City Centre is compact and can be covered on foot.

◉ **Don't Miss**: Southwell Minster (excursion).

◕ **Organizing Your Time**: Allow one day in Nottingham, one day for excursions.

Especially for Kids: Tales of Robin Hood; World of Robin Hood.

Walking Tours: Ask at the tourist office or see the official website for details of city walking tours.

A Bit of History

The castle, which was begun by William the Conqueror in 1068, saw the surrender of supporters of Prince John to Richard the Lionheart in 1194, the imprisonment by Edward III of Mortimer and Queen Isabella, who assassinated Edward II, the departure of Richard III to defeat and death on Bosworth Field in 1485 and the raising of the standard of Charles I at the beginning of the Civil War in 1642.

Address Book

OUT AND ABOUT IN NOTTINGHAM

Tourist Information Centre – 1-4 Smithy Row, Nottingham, NG1 2BY ☎ 0115 915 5330; tourist.information@ nottinghamcity.gov.uk ; www. visitnottingham.com.

Public Transport – Note that Nottingham City Transport operates an "exact fare/no change" policy on buses; visitors should have the correct fare ready when boarding – fares are displayed at all bus stops. Alternatively purchase a City Rider ticket (one-day) or Easy Rider Travelcard for unlimited travel. Most services run at least every 30min, with buses running at 10min intervals during the day on popular routes.

Sightseeing – Blue Badge Guides run various **sightseeing tours** ☎ 01909 482 503 for further details. Alternatively contact Nottinghamshire County Council, which also runs a programme of guided walks each year ☎ 0115 977 4212. River cruises (with dining facilities, disco evenings) are a relaxing way to explore the area ☎ 0115 910 0400 and 01642 608 038.

Pubs and Restaurants – Traditional bars include The Salutation Inn, The Bell and Ye Olde Trip to Jerusalem.

Shopping – **Victoria** and **Broad Marsh** shopping centres house the major high street stores. The **Flying Horse Walk** and **Exchange Arcade** have fashionable boutiques; antique hunters should go to **Derby Road,** where there is a concentration of antique shops. The **Lace Market** area of Hockley is for the eclectic shopper. Nottinghamshire has a strong market tradition. Newark, to the northeast of Nottingham, is one of the largest market towns, with markets four days a week, held in the market square. The county also boasts over 25 factory shops. A booklet is available from West Bridgeford Tourist Information Centre ☎ 0115 977 3558.

Entertainment – Maypole dancing is held at Wellow in early May. The Annual Robin Hood Festival (song, dance, storytelling and jousting tournaments) is held in Sherwood Forest in early August. The Robin Hood Pageant (jousting and other events) takes place in autumn. The **Goose Fair** *(early October)* is Europe's largest travelling fair.

Nottingham Castle Museum and Art Gallery

Alabaster Altarpiece (15C)

From 1350 to 1530 the city was the home of a school of alabaster carvers specialising in delicately-detailed scenes illustrating the life of Christ, the Virgin and the saints. The early free-standing figures and panels were superseded by altarpieces combining both panels and figures arranged in a wooden framework. The few works which survived the systematic destruction of the Reformation were mostly sold to the Continent. Nottingham was one of the first towns to industrialise when the Spinning Jenny arrived in 1768 and it was shaken by the Luddite riots (1811-16) which inspired Lord Byron's maiden speech in the House of Lords in their defence.

It was again shaken by riots in 1831 during which the Baroque castle, the property of the Duke of Newcastle who was opposed to the Reform Bill, was partially destroyed by fire. In the 19C there was more protest against the industrial society by another local writer, **David Herbert Lawrence** (1885-1930), who was born in Eastwood.

Sights

★Castle Museum – ♿🕐 *Open daily, 10am-5pm. Closed 1-2 Jan and 25-26 Dec.* 💷 *£3 (joint ticket with Museum and Brewhouse). Cave Tours 11am, 2pm, 3pm.* 💷 *£2. Cafe.* ☎ *0115 915 3700; Fax 0115 915 3653; www.nottinghamcity.gov.uk.* Nothing of the original Norman castle survives, save the subterranean passage, **Mortimer's Hole,** from the castle to the **Brewhouse Yard**, and **Ye Olde Trip to Jerusalem** (allegedly the oldest inn in England) below.

The buildings which survived the fire in 1831 now house a **museum and art gallery** displaying Bronze Age, Roman and Greek antiquities, ceramic pieces, jewellery, glass and 16C Italian, 17C Dutch, 17C French and 18C to 20C English paintings. Displays on the lower floors tell the history of Nottingham from prehistory to the present day and include fine examples of medieval Nottingham **alabasters** ★.

Lace Hall – *High Pavement.* ♿🕐*Open daily. Handmade demonstrations: Easter-Oct, 2-4pm. 0115 941 3539.* Displays illustrate Nottingham's leading role in the history of British lacemaking. Both hand and machine lace-making methods are described.

Galleries of Justice Museum – *High Pavement.* 🕐 *Open Tue-Sun and Bank Hol Mon, 10am-5pm; last admission 1hr before closing.* 💷 *£6.95.* 🕐 *Closed 24-28 Dec and 31 Dec-1 Jan.* ☎ *0115 952 0555, 0115 952 0558 (information); info@galleriesofjustice.org. uk; www.galleriesofjustice.org.uk.* Behind the elegant 18C facade the turnkey takes visitors down into the cramped and squalid prison conditions of earlier centuries – some of the cells date from the 15C – and provides a good explanation of the legal and penal system.

Tales of Robin Hood – *Maid Marian Way.* ♿🕐 *Open daily, 10am-6pm (5.30pm Oct-Mar), last admission 90 mins before closing).* 🕐 *Closed 25-26 Dec.* 💷 *£6.50. Licensed restaurant. Audio tape (7 languages).* ☎ *0115 948 3284; Fax 0115 950 1536; robinhoo-dcentre@mail.com; www.robinhood.uk.com.* "Adventure cars" carry visitors through a recreated Sherwood Forest to illustrate the legend of the medieval outlaw, using models, sound and smell effects; archery lessons are also given on the *Shoot the Sheriff* range.

Excursions

Wollaton Hall★ – *2.5mi/4km west by Ilkeston Road, A 609.* ♿🕐 *Open daily, 11am-5pm (4pm Nov-Mar).* 🕐 *Closed 1 Jan and 25-26 Dec.* 💷 *£2 (charge on weekends and Bank Hols only, otherwise free). Refreshments.* ☎ *0115 915 3900; www.nottinghamcity.gov.uk.* The hall, which houses a natural history museum, is an exuberant display of Elizabethan grandeur, built by Robert Smythson, the architect of Longleat and Bolsover Castle, for coal magnate, Sir Francis Willoughby. Instead of an inner courtyard there is a central hall so high it overtops the roof line and is lit through a clerestory.

DH Lawrence Birthplace Museum — *Eastwood, 10mi/16km northwest of Nottingham by A 610. 8A Victoria Street; Open daily, 10am-5pm (4pm Nov-Mar). 24 Dec to 1 Jan. £3. Parking. 01773 717 353; Fax 01773 713 509; www.broxtowe.gov.uk.* This tiny terraced cottage (restored) was the first of four Lawrence family homes in Eastwood. Exhibits and a video presentation in the museum give a useful insight into the writer's early life and influences in this small mining town.

Newstead Abbey★ — *11mi/18km north of Nottingham off A 60. House: Open Apr-Sep, noon-5pm (4pm last admission). Gardens: Open daily. 9am-dusk; Closed last Fri Nov and 25 Dec. £6; gardens only, £3. Parking. Refreshments. Wheelchair access to grounds and ground floor of house; audio guides for the visually impaired. 01623 455 900; Fax 01623 455 904; www.newsteadabbey.org.uk.* As the name implies, the medieval priory was converted in the 16C into a house, which was the ancestral seat of Lord Byron. The 19C rooms include the apartments of Byron and a selection of Byron manuscripts, memorabilia and portraits.

Adjoining the main range is the ruined façade of the priory church, its gabled niche holding a seated figure of the Virgin. Th lakes, gardens and parkland make an attractive setting.

Sherwood Forest – Once one of the 65 Royal Forests which covered much of England, thick with oak, birch and bracken, it was protected from agriculture and development by royal hunting forest laws: in this perfect environment for poaching, the outlaw bands recorded by the chroniclers of Godber, Coterel, Folville and Robyn Hode all became legends, and by the 15C **Robyn Hode** had become a composite folk-tale character embracing all their exploits. Some of the woodland was subsequently cleared and is now heathland; much has been replanted with conifers. There are, however, attractive remnants. The **Sherwood Forest Visitor Centre and Country Park** (*1mi/2km north of Edwinstowe Country Park. Open daily, dawn-dusk. Visitor Centre: Open daily, 10.30am-5pm (4.30pm Nov-Mar). Parking (small charge). Restaurant, picnic site. 01623 823 202; marilyn.louden@nottscc.gov.uk; www.nottinghamshire. gov.uk*) stands where the supposed marriage of Robin Hood and Maid Marian took place; from it paths lead to the 500 year old **Major Oak** (33ft/10m in diameter). At Walesby (*4mi/6km northwest*), **The World of Robin Hood** (*Open mid-Feb to Oct, daily, 10.30am-4pm; Nov to mid-Feb, phone for times. £4.95. Parking. Restaurant, bars, café. Owl Centre £1. 01623 823 202; Fax 01623 836 003); Parking. Refreshments. 01623 860 210*) uses technological effects to convey medieval Nottingham.

Clumber Park – (*NT*) *25mi/40km north of Nottingham by A 60 and A 614. Park: Open daily, dawn/dusk; last vehicle admission 2hr before closing. Closed concert days and 25 Dec. Walled kitchen garden: Open Apr-Sep, Wed-Fri, 10.30am-5.30pm, Sat-Sun and Bank Hol Mon, 10.30am-6pm. £4 per car, £5.20 per minibuses and car with caravan; £1 kitchen garden. Cycle hire. Information Point. Restaurant. 01909 476 592; Fax 01909 500 721; clumberpark@nationaltrust.org.uk; www.nationaltrust.org.uk.* The focus of this extensive stretch of parkland and wooded walks, Clumber House, seat of the Dukes of Newcastle, was demolished in the 1930s; only its vague outline remains facing the lake, together with the chapel, kitchen garden, apiary and vineyard, and decorative "temples" among the trees.

Mr Straw's House★ – (*NT*) *7 Blyth Grove, Worksop, 20mi/32km north of Nottingham; signed from B 6045 (past Bassetlaw Hospital). 7 Blythe Grove; Open, by advanced booking only, late-Mar to early-Nov, Tue-Sat, 11am-4.30pm (timed ticket). Closed Bank Hol Mon, Good Friday. £4.60. 01909 482 380; mrstrawshouse@nationaltrust. org.uk; www.nationaltrust.org.uk.* Forget period furnishings and restored interiors: this is a family home frozen in time, as though the occupants have just stepped out for a moment. Brothers William and Walter Straw lived in this semi-detached Edwardian house virtually all their lives but kept everything much as it had been when their parents died in the 1930s. When William died, aged 92, in 1990, he left the entire contents to the National Trust. The brothers' coats and caps still hang neatly in the hall; jars of ancient home-made jam and tinned vegetables are stacked in the cupboards. It is a fascinating, moving and slightly disturbing experience.

Southwell Minster★★ – *7mi/11km northeast of Nottingham by A 612. Open daily, 8am-7pm/dusk. Donation £3. Guided tour by appointment. Parking. Refreshments. 01636 812 649; Fax 01636 815 904; mail@southwellminster.prestel.co.uk;*

www.southwellminster.org.uk. The "well-built clean town" (John Byng) of Southwell – pronounced Su'thel – is dominated by the Norman Minster, well known for the foliage carving of its late 13C master masons. It is the only cathedral in England to boast a complete set of three Norman towers and dates from c 1108. Smooth lawns and well-spaced graves frame the **west front** which is pierced by a Perpendicular seven-light window. The Norman north porch is covered by rare barrel vaulting.

It was preceded by an earlier Saxon church built on the site of a Roman villa; fragments of its mosaic flooring can be seen in the south transept.

The intimate **interior** combines Norman severity with the glory of the mid-14C **screen**, depicting 286 images of men, gods and devils and the even more glorious Early English **choir** and **chapter house** (1288). The latter is the first single-span stone vaulted chapter house in Christendom decorated with some of the finest medieval naturalism (late 13C) carved in stone.

Newark-on-Trent – *7mi/11km northeast of Nottingham by A 612.* It is mostly a Georgian town, called by John Wesley "one of the most elegant in England". The **castle**, where King John died (1216) and King Charles gave up the struggle, was raised by Alexander, Bishop of Lincoln. It was thrice besieged during the Civil War; the keep overlooking the Trent has not survived but there are traces of a late 12C gateway, 13C west wall and the northwest and central towers. The exhibition in the **Gilstrap Centre** (&🕐 *Open daily, 10am-6pm (5pm Oct-Mar).* 🔎 *Guided tour by appointment.* ☎ *01636 655 765 or 01636 655 738; gilstrap@network-sherwooddc. gov.uk; www.newark-sherwooddc.gov.uk)* traces the history of the castle. The Market Place embraces an endearing mixture of styles. **St Mary Magdalene**★ (&🕐 *Open Mon-Sat, 8.30am-4.30pm; also summer, Sun, 2-4pm. Closed 1hr at lunchtime.* 🔎 *35p (Treasury).* 🔎 *Guided tour (30min) by appointment.* ☎ *01636 706 473)* is topped by a soaring spire (252ft/77m) and lit by a vast area of window in the transepts – "Nothing like it was tried again until the time of the Crystal Palace" (Pevsner). Note the **brass** to Alan Fleming (d 1361) and the **wall painting** (c 1520) of the Dance of Death in the south chantry chapel.

OAKHAM

Rutland, ENGLAND

POPULATION 8 691

MICHELIN ATLAS P 28 OR MAP 501 R 25

This handsome market town is once again the administrative centre of England's smallest county, Rutland, which officially disappeared in the boundary reorganisation in 1974 but was reinstated in 1997. Oakham's L-shaped market place, medieval Butter Cross, with its five-holed stocks, Tudor grammar school and restored 13C church (bearing one of England's oldest weathervanes) form a rough semi-circle around the castle. 🏠 *Flore's House, 34 High Street* ☎ *01572 724 329; www. goleicestershire.com/rutland.*

Sights

Rutland County Museum – *Catmos Street.* &🕐*Open daily, 10am (2pm Sun) 5pm (4pm Sun, late-Oct to late-Mar).* 🕐 *Closed Good Friday, 25 Dec and 1 Jan. Donation.* ☎ *01572 758440; Fax 01572 758445; museum@rutland.gov.uk; www.rutnet.co.uk/rcc/museums.* The exhibits in this museum illustrate the history of this unusual county.

Oakham Castle★ – &🕐 *Open Mon-Sat, 10am-1pm and 1.30-5pm, Sun, 1-5pm (4pm late-Oct to late-Mar).* 🕐*Closed Good Friday, 25 Dec and 1 Jan. Donation.* ☎ *01572 758 440; Fax 01572 758 445; museum@rutland.co.uk; www.rutnet.co.uk/rcc/rutlandmuseums.* Approached through 19C wrought-iron gates set in a 17C gateway, the castle now consists only of a great hall, once part of a fortified manor house built in the 12C for Walkelin de Ferrers. Inside the hall, which is one of the country's best examples of domestic Norman architecture, over 200 horseshoes of all sizes cover the walls. The horseshoe was part of the Ferrers coat of arms and the lord of the manor still demands one as a forfeit from every peer of the realm and member of royalty passing through the manor of Oakham Lordshold.

Excursions

Rutland Water★★ – *2mi/4km west by A 606 or south by A 6003*. This is one of Britain's biggest man-made lakes (3 100 acres/1 254ha), constructed in 1970 to supply the major centres of Peterborough, Corby and Northampton. Cycling and walking trails follow its shores and the **Anglian Water Birdwatching Centre**, *(off A 6003 ⚊ ⏱ Open daily, 9am-5pm (4pm Nov-Mar). ☞ £4; £3 after 1pm. ☎ 01572 770 651)* provides hides and closed-circuit TV for views of the wildlife.

Isolated on the reservoir's southern edge *(near A 606 and A 6121)* is **Normanton Church**★ *(⏱ Open Apr-Oct, daily, 11am-4pm; 11am-5pm Sat-Sun and Bank Hol Mon. ☞ 80p. ☎ 01572 653026)*, now a museum, which traces the local history, but once the focus of Normanton village of which it is the only surviving building. Normanton was abandoned in the 18C but the crumbling church was rebuilt by the landowner in 1764 and again in 1826, when it gained its Classical tower, a copy of St John's, Smith Square in London. When the valley was flooded, local campaigners raised £30 000 to preserve the church; the upper windows now sit at eye-level as the floor level had to be raised to protect it from the water.

OBAN

Argyll and Bute, SCOTLAND

POPULATION 8 203

MICHELIN ATLAS P 60 OR MAP 501 D 14

A busy tourist centre and service town for the hinterland and islands – a far cry from 1773 when Dr Johnson had to content himself with "a tolerable inn" – Oban lies opposite the Isle of Mull at the southern end of the Great Glen. It owes its development to the railways and steamboats; hence the dominating Victorian aspect to the town. The outstanding landmark is **McCaig's Tower** (1897), a replica of the Colosseum, built by an Oban banker to relieve unemployment , but never finished.

☺ There is a traditional piping competition on the opening day of the Argyllshire Highland Gathering, as well as putting the shot, throwing the hammer and tossing the caber (as straight, rather than as far, as possible). ℹ *Argyll Square ☎ 08707 200 630; Fax: 01631 564273; info@oban.visitscotland.com; www.visitscottishheartlands.com.*

The Glens

Loch Awe★★ – *18mi/29km east by A 85*. The road follows the narrow defile of the **Pass of Brander** overlooked to the north by the lower slopes of **Ben Cruachan** (3 689ft/1 126m).

Loch Awe, Scotland's longest lake (over 25mi/40km long), lies in the heart of Campbell country. **Kilchurn Castle** juts out on the northern shore. The 15C stronghold, built by Sir Colin Campbell, with 1693 extensions, was abandoned in the mid 18C. ⚊ *See also INVERARAY – Excursions.*

▸ *Continue along the verdant Glen Orchy with Ben Lui towering to the south as far as Tyndrum and take A 82 north through the harsh landscape to Bridge of Orchy, past Loch Tulla and through the desolation of Rannoch Moor.*

The Glen Coe Massacre

After James VII went into exile (1688) and the Convention offered the Scottish crown to William and Mary, the Highlanders loyal to the Stuart cause won a victory at Killiecrankie but were defeated at Dunkeld (1689); in return for a pardon they were invited to take an oath of allegiance to the British Crown. In 1692 forty members of the pro-Stuart MacDonald clan were treacherously massacred and their homes burnt by the Campbells who were billeted with the clan. "Murder under Trust" was a heinous crime especially as the MacDonald clan chief had met the deadline for taking the oath of allegiance at Fort William but was directed instead to Inveraray. An official enquiry later revealed that the Crown's Scottish minister had exceeded royal orders.

Glen Coe★★ – The dramatic approach to Glen Coe (11mi/18km long) – it was in this stark and grandiose setting that the infamous Glen Coe massacre occurred – is heralded by the **Meall a Bhuiridh** (Hill of the Roaring Stags, 3 636ft/1 108m), the **Buachaille Etive Mor** (Big Herdsman of Etive 3 345ft/1 022m) and the glacial valley, Glen Etive, between them. The flat-topped rock, the Study *(right)* pinpoints the head of Glen Coe. Beyond the waterfall rise mighty rock faces; the **Three Sisters**, the outliers of the **Bidean nam Bian** (Peak of the Bens), soaring to 3 766ft/1 141m, stretch out to the left, and the serrated ridge of **Anoach Eagach** to the right; Loch Achtriochtan spreads out on the valley floor.

Glen Coe

NTS, Edinburgh

Glen Coe Centre *(Site: & ⊙Open daily. Visitor Centre: Open May to late-Oct, daily, 10am to 5.30pm; Nov–Feb 4pm. ⊗ £5. Guided hill walks: Wed and Sat, 10.30am-4pm. Audio-visual presentation. Refreshments, picnic area. ☎ 01855 811 307 (Visitor Centre), 01855 811 729; Fax 01855 811 772 (Ranger Service); glencoe@ nts.org.uk; www.nts.org.uk)* provides information on local walks and climbs.

On the shores of Loch Leven nestles the village of **Glencoe** (Population 315) which houses the small **Glencoe and North Lorn Folk Museum**. *(& ⊙ Open Easter week and mid-May to Sep, Mon-Sat, 10am-5.30pm. ⊗ £2. Parking. ☎ 01855 811 664).*

The picturesque road south *(A 82, A 828)* skirts the south shore of Loch Leven and descends along the east coast of **Loch Linnhe,** the largest sea loch in Scotland, and cuts across to Loch Creran and back to Oban passing the **Scottish Sea Life Sanctuary** *(& ⊙ Open mid-Feb to mid-Nov and 25 Dec school hols, daily, 10am-5pm (4pm Oct-Easter); mid Nov-mid Feb, Sat-Sun, 10am-3pm. ⊙ Closed 1 Jan and 25 Dec. ⊗ £9.50. Adventure playground. Nature trail. Parking. Restaurant, picnic area. Shop. ☎ 01631 720 386; Fax 01631 720529; oban@seallife.fsbusiness.co.uk)* which combines a spectacular aquarium with a busy rescue and rehabilitation facility for both common and grey seal pups.

⊙ *Passing places are provided to allow vehicles to pass one another and to permit overtaking. Do not park in passing places and do not hold up a following vehicle.*

ORKNEY ISLANDS★★

Orkney, SCOTLAND

POPULATION 19 612

MICHELIN ATLAS P 74 OR MAP 501 K, L, M 6 AND 7

Lying off the northeast tip of mainland Scotland, the Orkney archipelago comprises 67 islands of which less than 30 are inhabited. The cliffs are home to countless seabirds, and seals and otters are common. ▯ *6 Broad Street, Kirkwall KW15 1NX* ☎ *01856 872 856; Fax 01856 875056; info@visitorkney.com; www.visitorkney.com* ▯ *Ferry Terminal Building, The Pier Head, Stromness* ☎ *01856 850 716; www.visitorkney.com.*

- ▶ **Orient Yourself**: The main island of Orkney is divided into the Eastern Mainland and the Western Mainland. Orkney Ferries (☎ *01856 872044*) and Loganair (☎*01856 872494)* service the other islands.
- 🚫 **Don't Miss**: St Magnus Cathedral, Kirkwall; Maes Howe; Skara Brae; The Old Man of Hoy.
- 🕐 **Organizing Your Time**: Allow at least three days.
- 👜 **Also See**: Shetland Islands, Wick.
- 🚶 **Walking Tours**: Enquire at the tourist offices.
- 🚲 **Cycling**: Mountain bikes available from Stromness Cycle Hire, Ferry Road, Stromness, (☎ *01856 850 750)* and Orkney Cycle Hire, 54 Dundas Street, Stromness, (☎ *01856 850255).*

A Bit of History

The first Neolithic settlers came in the 4th millennium BC. Some of their dwellings remain and their fine stone tombs can be seen throughout the islands. From the early Iron Age – around the 5C BC – fortified villages grew up round the massive stone buildings known as brochs. The Vikings came to Orkney from the late 8C AD, sweeping away the culture of the Pictish Orcadians. Orkney's culture still has Scandinavian elements, though the islands were pawned to King James III of Scotland in 1468, as part of the dowry of his Danish bride.

Kirkwall★★

A capital since Viking days, Kirkwall stands on the isthmus separating the eastern and western parts of the island. The town houses (now shops), some emblazoned, lining the stone-flagged main street and the pends leading to attractive paved courtyards are noteworthy.

Notable games include the 25 Dec and 1 Jan's Day **Ba Games** when the Uppies play the Doonies, symbolising the old rivalry between the ecclesiastical town and the secular authority represented by the now-vanished castle.

St Magnus Cathedral★★ – 🕐 *Open Apr-Sep, daily, 9am (2pm Sun) to 6pm; Oct-Mar, Mon-Sat, 9am-1pm and 2pm-5pm.* 🚶 *Guided tour. Parking.* ☎ *01856 874 894.* Built by Earl Rognvald from 1137 to 1152 and dedicated to his murdered uncle, Earl Magnus, the cathedral is Norman in character, contemporary with Durham. The red stone exterior is severe and plain, dominated by the tower and steeple. The three west front **doorways** added later show confident originality in their combination of red and yellow sandstone. The interior, though somewhat severe, is pleasingly harmonious, carefully controlled proportions creating a sense of vastness belying the building's modest dimensions. The square pillars on either side of the organ screen enshrine the relics of St Magnus *(right),* and Earl Rognvald *(left).*

Earl's Palace★ – 🕐 *Open Apr-Sep, daily, 9.30am-6.30pm.* 🎫 *£2 combined ticket with Bishop's Palace; £11 joint ticket for all Orkney monuments.* ☎ *01856 871 918.* The remains of this early Renaissance palace have splendid corbelling on the windows, chimney breast and corbel course, and sculptured panels above the main entrance and oriel windows. It was built c 1600-07 by **Earl Patrick Stewart,** whose execution for treason in 1615 was said to have been delayed to allow him time to learn the Lord's Prayer. The vaulted chambers on the ground floor hold exhibitions of Orkney history from the early Middle Ages to the present, while the grand staircase leads to the Great Hall and other princely apartments.

Bishop's Palace – The palace was built in the 12C alongside the cathedral, and it was here that King Haakon of Norway died after the Battle of Largs (1263). Most of what can be seen dates from the rebuildings in the 16C and 17C, the latter by Earl Patrick Stewart.

The Orkney Museum★ – *Tankerness House, Broad Street.* ◷*Open Apr-Sep, Mon-Sat, 10.30am-5pm, Sun, 2pm-5pm; Oct-Mar, Mon-Sat, 10.30am-12.30pm and 1.30-5pm;* ✎ *Admission Charge.* ☎ *01856 873 191; Fax 01856 871 560; museum@orkney.gov.uk; www.orkney.org.* A fine 16C town house with excellent introductory displays on the islands' prehistory.

Excursions

Western Mainland★★

▶ *Leave Kirkwall by A 965.*

Rennibister Earth House – *Behind the farmhouse, access by trapdoor and ladder.* The oval chamber has five wall recesses and an entrance passage. Human bones were found in it, though its original purpose remains uncertain.

▶ *Continue through Finstown on A 965.*

Maes Howe★★ – ◷ *Open Apr-Sep, daily, 9.30am-6.30pm; Oct-Mar, 9.30am (2pm Sun) to 4.30pm.* ✎ *£2.80; £11 (joint ticket for all Orkney monuments). Parking. Restaurant.* ☎ *01856 761 606.* This Neolithic burial cairn is a work of unique skill in stone building from people whose only tools were stones and flint. It dates from pre-2700 BC and was covered by a mound (26ft/8m high and 115ft/35m wide). The cairn was broken into in the 12C by Norsemen, who left an important series of runic graffiti.

Ring of Brodgar – The Stone Age circle, standing on the neck of land between the lochs of Stenness and Harray, still has 27 of its original 60 stones standing. Two entrance causeways interrupt the encircling ditch.

Unstan Cairn – *Park in front of the house; the keys hang in a box by the back door.* The Stone Age chambered tomb, from the mid-fourth millennium, compartmentalised by upright slabs, overlooks the Loch of Stenness.

Stromness★ – Second-largest town and principal port. The town grew, from its original Norse settlement, in the 18C to be a whaling station and the last port of call for the Hudson Bay Company ships sailing to Canada. The **Pier Gallery,** (◷ *Open Jun-Aug, Tue-Sat, 10.30am-5pm; Sep-May 10.30am-12.30pm and 1.30pm-5pm.* ☎ *01856 850 209)* has a permanent collection of abstract art based on the work of the St Ives artists, Ben Nicholson and Barbara Hepworth. Aspects of Orkney's natural and maritime history are presented in the **museum** (♿◷ *Open May-Sep, daily, 10am-5pm; Oct-Apr, Mon-Sat, 10.30am-12.30pm and 1.30pm-5pm.* ✎ *£2.50. Stairlift. Parking.* ☎ *01856 850 025).*

▶ *A 965, A 967 and B 9056 lead northwards to Skara Brae.*

Skara Brae★★ – ♿◷ *Open Apr-Sep, daily, 9.30am-6.30pm; Oct-Mar, 9.30am (2pm Sun) to 4.30pm.* ✎ *£4.50; £3.30 (winter); £11 (joint ticket for all Orkney monuments). Parking. Restaurant. Picnic area.* ☎ *01856 841 815.* The settlement, which is 5 000 years old, was buried in sand for a long period. The seven best-preserved Stone Age dwellings are rectangular with coursed flagstone walls and a hearth in the middle, and are connected by a subterranean sewer system.

Brough of Birsay★ – *Access on foot across causeway at low tide.* ◷ *Open mid-Jun to Sep, 9.30am-6.30pm, when tides permit.* ✎ *£1.50.* ☎ *01858 841 815 or 01858 721 205.* The earliest remains are Pictish. In the 10C Norse farmers occupied the island and **Earl Thorfinn the Mighty** (c 1009-65) built a church after a pilgrimage to Rome. It became a cathedral and was the initial resting place of St Magnus before the construction of Kirkwall Cathedral. Excavations show a small oblong nave, short narrow choir and rounded apse, surrounded by a Norse graveyard. A little to the southwest is a collection of stone and turf-built **Norse long houses** with the living quarters at the upper end and the byre lower down.

▶ *A 966 and A 965 to the left lead back to Kirkwall.*

Scapa Flow

About 10mi/16km south by A 961, past St Mary's. From the **Churchill Barriers**, built in the Second World War by Italian prisoners of war to link the four islands with the mainland, there is a good view of the naval base where the German Grand Fleet scuttled itself in 1919. Beyond the first barrier is the **Italian Chapel**★, built by the same prisoners inside two Nissen huts: a unique and moving testament to faith in adversity.

B. Kaufmann/MICHELIN

The Old Man of Hoy

Pentland Firth Crossing

The crossing (two-hour journey for the roll-on, roll-off car ferry operating between Stromness and Scrabster) is an ideal way of seeing the outstanding cliff scenery of Hoy (the name means high island): the sheer cliffs of St John's Head (1 140ft/347m) and the spectacular **Old Man of Hoy**★★★, a breathtaking red sandstone sea stack (450ft/137m) rising sheer out of the turbulent waters. It is the domain of myriad screeching and hovering seabirds.

OXFORD

Oxfordshire, ENGLAND

POPULATION 118 795

MICHELIN ATLAS P 18 OR MAP 504 Q 28 – LOCAL MAP

The city of Oxford, on the Thames, 58 mi/93km northwest of London, incorporates England's oldest University and smallest cathedral.

▶ **Orient Yourself**: Oxford is compact and can be covered on foot.

- **Don't Miss**: Punting on the river; Christ Church; Bodleian Library; Ashmolean Museum; University Museum of Natural History/Pitt Rivers Museum.

- **Organizing Your Time**: Allow at least three days. Many of the colleges are open only in the afternoon; visiting times are usually displayed at the porter's lodge. All college opening times can be seen on *www. www.ox.ac.uk/visitors*.

- **Kids Especially for Kids**: Family Walking Tour - Children must be accompanied by an adult with a maximum of 4 children per adult. *School hols, daily 2.30pm.* Adults *£5 and children 6-16 years £3*; The Oxford Story.

- **Walking Tours**: City and Colleges Tour – Daily 11am, 2pm, additional tours on Saturday at 10.30am and 1pm. £6.50. City and College Tour including Christ Church – Fri-Sat 2pm. £7.50. Ghost Tour June-Oct, Fri- Sat 7.45pm. £5. Inspector Morse Tour – Sat 1:30pm; advisable to book in advance at TIC or ☎ 01865 726871; £7.

A Bit of History

Oxford developed in Saxon times around the 8C nunnery of St Frideswide, now Christ Church, and still maintains its original street plan and parts of its city walls. Religious foundations sprang up and about 1200 the university emerged; it was essentially a federation of monastic halls and is still a federation of autonomous colleges. During the Reformation Oxford provided martyrs for both sides – Latimer, Ridley, Cranmer and Campion, who are commemorated in the **Martyrs' Memorial** (BY). The organist and composer **Orlando Gibbons** was born here in 1583. It was the headquarters of the Royalists during the Civil War (Charles I staying at Christ Church and Henrietta Maria at Merton College). Matthew Arnold called it the "home of lost causes and... impossible loyalties."

The 18C saw new buildings but few new ideas. Reform came in the 19C, with the Anglo-Catholic Oxford Movement, which revived the Catholic tradition within the Anglican Church, and the growth of scientific research. In the 20C women were

Address Book

OUT AND ABOUT IN OXFORD

Tourist Information Centre – *15-16 Broad Street, Oxford OX1 3AS* ☎ *01865 726 871; Fax 01865 240 261; tic@oxford.gov.uk; www. visitoxford.org.*

Sightseeing – You can participate in various themed guided walks of Oxford city and of the colleges. Further details and tickets can be obtained from Oxford Information Centre (see above). Alternatively you can view the sight of Oxford from an open-top bus. The City Sightseeing hop-on–hop-off tour lasts for one hour ☎ 01865 790522; www. citysightseeingoxford.com. For a boat trip on the Cherwell or the Thames, self-hire or chauffered punts are available by the hour; for longer trips there are electric boats, a steam boat and river cruisers.

Boat houses and punting stations are at Magdalen Bridge, Folly Bridge and Bardwell Road.

Pubs and Restaurants – The *Oxford Food & Drink Guide* is a free leaflet giving details of pubs and restaurants in the area, available from the Oxford Information Centre.

Shopping – Oxford's main shopping streets are **Queen Street, Magdalen Street** and **Cornmarket Street**. Shoppers browsing for books, souvenirs, gifts and antiques should visit **Broad Street, High Street** and **Turl Street**. An open-air market is held in **Gloucester Green** every Wednesday, and an antiques market every Thursday. Also of interest is the **Victorian Covered Market**, open from Monday to Saturday.

admitted and most of the colleges are now co-educational. The essence of Oxford however remains unchanged – "a city where too many bells are always ringing in the rain" (Elmer Davis).

The bicycle shop opened in Longwall Street by **William Morris** in 1902, where he began to make motor cycles, has since developed into a vast motor manufacturing enterprise in the suburb of Cowley.

Walking Tour

Carfax (BZ) – ⏰ *Open daily Apr-Oct, 10am-5.30pm (3.30pm Nov-Mar).* ⏰ *Closed 25 Dec to 1 Jan.* ☎ *018652 770 000.* No child under 5 admitted. The centre of the Saxon and medieval city, the 14C tower is all that remains of St Martin's Church. There are good views of the High Street, known as "the High," from the top of the tower.

▶ *Continue south down St Aldate's.*

Museum of Oxford (BZ) – ⏰ *Open Tue-Sun, 10am (noon Sun) to 4pm (5pm Sat).* £2. ☎ *01865 252 761; museum@oxford.gov.uk; www.oxford.gov.uk.* The museum uses items from local excavations and models to trace the history of the city from the Bronze Age to the present day.

Christ Church★★ (BZ) ⏰ *College: Open daily, 9am (1pm Sun) to 5.30pm. Hall: Open as above daily except noon and 2pm. Cathedral: Open daily, 9am (1pm Sun) to 4.30pm. Picture gallery: Open daily except Sun mornings, 10.30am-1pm and 2-5.30pm (4.30pm Oct-Easter).* Chapter house, cathedral and hall £4; picture gallery £2. For Behind the Scene tours, contact the Head Custodian. Wheelchair ramp for entry to College and Cathedral. Fax ☎01865 276 492; custodian@chch.ox.ac.uk; www.chch.ox.ac.uk. Founded in 1525 by Cardinal Wolsey and refounded in 1532 by Henry VIII after Wolsey's fall from grace, "The House" is Oxford's biggest and grandest Renaissance college. The chapel, originally St Frideswide's rebuilt in Norman times, was consecrated as England's smallest cathedral while remaining also the college chapel in the 16C.

Oxford's largest quadrangle is **Tom Quad**★. The southern ranges are by Wolsey, the northern ranges by Dr Samuel Fell (late 17C), and the fountain statue in the middle a copy of Giovanni da Bologna's *Mercury*. Above Wolsey's gatehouse is Wren's synthesis of Baroque and Gothic, **Tom Tower**★, a fine domed gateway; to the south is the Tudor **Hall**★★, with its magnificent fan-vaulted entrance stairway by James Wyatt, hammerbeam roof and portraits by Kneller, Romney, Gainsborough,

A. Williams/MICHELIN

Radcliffe Camera, Oxford

Lawrence, Millais; to the northeast are the 18C Peckwater Quad and **Picture Gallery** (Italian Renaissance Masters). South of the college Christ Church Meadow stretches from St Aldate's to the River Thames.

Christ Church Cathedral★ – Late Norman with a 16C roof, originally the church of St Frideswide's Priory and now the smallest cathedral in England, its glory is its 15C stellar vaulted **choir roof**★. Note the c 1330 stained glass depicting Becket's martyrdom in the Lucy Chapel, the early Gothic chapter house and late Gothic cloisters.

▶ *Walk through Peckwater Quad to Oriel Square.*

Oriel College (BZ) – ⛔ *The Lodge.* ◷*Open term time.* ☎ *01865 276 555; lodge@oriel. ox.ac.uk; www. oriel.ox.ac.uk.* Founded 1326 but entirely rebuilt in Jacobean-Gothic between 1619 and 1642, a second quadrangle was added in the 18C; the library is by James Wyatt.

▶ *Cross Merton Street.*

Corpus Christi College (BZ) – ◷ *Open daily, 1.30pm-4.30pm.* ◷ *Closed Easter and over Christmas.* ☎ *01865 276 700; college.office@ccc.ox.ac.uk; www.ccc.ox.ac.uk.* Founded in 1517, the gateway (note the fan-vaulted ceiling) and Front Quad are early Tudor. The **Pelican Sundial** in the centre of the quad was designed in 1581, the 16C **Hall** has a splendid hammerbeam roof and the 16C chapel contains an altarpiece of the *Adoration of the Shepherds* attributed to the studio of Rubens.

Merton College★★ (BZ) – ◷ *Open Mon-Fri, 2-4pm; Sun, 10am-4pm.* ◷ *Closed for Easter week and over Christmas.* ☎ *01865 276 310; Fax 01865 276 361; www.merton.ox.ac. uk.* Founded in 1264, boasting the oldest and most picturesque college buildings in Oxford, the oldest quad is **Mob Quad**, a complete 14C quadrangle with the **Library** (1371-78), the first medieval library to put books on shelves, on two sides. Adjacent is the Decorated **Chapel** (1294-97), a naveless chancel with the 14C transepts forming the antechapel, its windows ablaze with original glass.

▶ *Turn left into Logic Lane to High Street.*

The Queen's College★ (BZ) – ◷ *Open by prior appointment only.* ☎ *01865 279 120; lodge@queens.ox.ac.uk; www.queens.ox.ac.uk.* Founded 1340 in honour of Queen Philippa, it was rebuilt 1671-1760 and is the only college in Oxford in one unified style. The entrance, crowned by its cupola, leads into the **Front Quadrangle**, cloistered on three sides with the hall and chapel in the building opposite. The 60ft/18m barrel-vaulted **Hall** shows the influence of Wren; the 100ft/30m classical **Chapel** has a ceiling painting by Sir James Thornhill who also decorated the dome of St Paul's, painted glass of 1635 by Van Linge and a finely carved organ screen as well as a good brass eagle lectern of 1662. Beyond in **North Quad** is Hawksmoor's noble **Library** with a carved pediment representing Wisdom crowned by an eagle.

Magdalen College★★ (BZ) – ◷ *Open daily, 2pm (noon late-Jun to Sep) to 6pm/dusk.* ◷ *Closed 20 Dec - 1 Jan.* ⛔£3. *Refreshments in Old Kitchen usually miday and afternoon.* ☎ *01865 276 050; Fax 01865 276 103; marilyn.simms@magdalen.ox.ac.uk.* Founded 1458 – pronounced "maudlen" – and originally the Hospital of St John the Baptist, the wall running along the High Street is 13C. The chapel, bell tower and cloisters are sumptuous late Perpendicular. The naveless chapel, though Victorianised inside, is magnificently adorned with gargoyles and pinnacled buttresses. The 150ft/46m **bell tower** is still "the most absolute building in Oxford" (James I). The unforgettable gargoyles on the cloister buttresses are a familiar feature of the Great Quadrangle. Beyond the cloister amid the meadows is New Building (1733) between Magdalen's deer park and the River Cherwell.

Botanic Gardens (BZ) – ⛔ *Rose Lane.* ◷*Open daily, 9am-5pm (4.30pm winter); last admission 45min before closing time.* ◷ *Closed Good Friday, 25 Dec.* ⛔ £2.60; *Apr-Aug.* 🔍 *Guided tour (2hr; £5) by appointment.* ☎ *01865 286 690; Fax 01865 286 693; postmaster@botanic-garden.ox.ac.uk; www.botanic-garden.ox.ac.uk.* Established in 1621, these gardens are the oldest in England; they provide a view of both the college towers and spires and the River Cherwell, crowded with punts in the summer; the c 1630 gateways were built by Nicholas Stone, borrowing ideas from Italy.

▶ *Walk up Queen's Lane and New College Lane.*

St Edmund Hall (BZ) – ⛔◷ *Open (functions permitting) daily, dawn-dusk.* ◷ *Closed Easter, Aug Bank Hol and Dec 25. Ramps.* ☎ *01865 279 000; Fax 01865 279 090; www. seh.ox.ac.uk.* Founded c 1220, St Edmund Hall is the last remaining medieval hall; though the oldest parts are only mid-17C, it still maintains its tiny dimensions and English horticultural charm. The adjoining church of St Peter in the East is now the college library, though the c 1150 crypt is open.

OXFORD

Blue Boar St	BY	2
Broad St	BZ	3
Castle St	BZ	5
Clarendon Shopping Centre	BZ	
Cornmarket St	BZ	6
George St	BZ	9
High St	BZ	
Hythe Bridge St	BZ	12

Little Clarendon St	BY	13
Logic Lane	BZ	14
Magdalen St	BYZ	16
Magpie Lane	BZ	17
New Inn Hall St	BZ	20
Norfolk St	BZ	21
Old Greyfriars St	BZ	23
Oriel Square	BZ	24
Park End St	BZ	30

Pembroke St	BZ	31
Queen's Lane	BZ	33
Queen St	BZ	34
Radcliffe Square	BZ	35
St Michael St	BZ	40
Turl St	BZ	41
Walton Crescent	BY	42
Westgate Shopping Centre	BZ	
Worcester St	BZ	47

Ashmolean Museum	BY	M^1
Bodleian Library	BZ	A^1
Botanic Gardens	BZ	
Carfax	BZ	
Christ Church	BZ	
Christ Church Meadow	BZ	
Clarendon Building	BYZ	B^1

Martyrs' Memorial	BY	D^1
Museum of Oxford	BZ	M^5
Museum of the History of Science	BZ	M^2
The Oxford Story	BZ	N^1
Pitt Rivers Museum	BY	M^3
Radcliffe Camera	BZ	P^1

Sheldonian Theatre	BYZ	T
St Mary the Virgin	BZ	S
St Michael	BZ	
University Museum of Natural History	BY	M^4

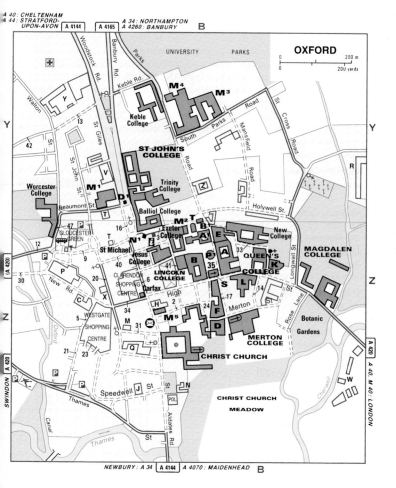

COLLEGES

All Souls	BZ	A
Balliol	BY	
Brasenose	BZ	B
Christ Church	BZ	
Corpus Christi	BZ	D
Exeter	BZ	
Hertford	BZ	E
Jesus	BZ	
Keble	BY	

Linacre	BZ	N
Lincoln	BZ	
Magdalen	BZ	
Merton	BZ	
New	BZ	
Nuffield	BZ	P
Oriel	BZ	F
Pembroke	BZ	Q
Queen's	BZ	
Sommerville	BY	Y

St Catherine's	BY	R
St Cross	BY	V
St Edmund Hall	BZ	K
St Hilda's	BZ	W
St John's	BY	
St Peter's	BZ	X
Trinity	BY	
University	BZ	L
Wadham	BY	Z
Worcester	BY	

New College (BZ) – ⏰ *Open daily, 11am (2pm Oct-Apr) to 5pm (4pm Oct-Apr).* 🎟 *£2 (Easter and summer). Brochure (8 languages).* ☎ *01865 279 590; Fax 01865 279 590; www.new.ox.ac.uk.* Founded by William of Wykeham in 1379 three years before his other foundation, Winchester College. The college still maintains some of its original buildings: the Great Quad is quintessential English Perpendicular, the hall the oldest in Oxford. The 15C **Chapel**★ is vast, naveless like Merton, with 14C glass in the antechapel transepts and Epstein's **Lazarus** rising under Reynolds' 1777 west window. The cloister is a place of calm, offering a view of the 1400 Bell Tower. In the gardens is Oxford's finest section of city walls, including five bastions.

Sheldonian Theatre★ (BZ) – ♿⏰ *Open (university functions permitting) Mon-Sat, 10am-12.30pm and 2-4.30pm (3.30pm mid-Nov to mid-Feb).* ⏰ *Closed Easter and over Christmas.* 🎟 *£1.50.* ☎ *01865 277 299; Fax 01865 277 295; custodian@sheldon.ox.ac.uk; www.sheldon.ox.ac.uk.* Built 1664-69, Oxford's first Classical building and Wren's first work of architecture was designed to accommodate formal University ceremonies. Alongside is Hawksmoor's 1713 Palladian **Clarendon Building (BZ)** built to house the University Press and now also part of the Bodleian Library. On the other side, facing onto Broad Street, is the Old Ashmolean, now a museum of the History of Science.

Bodleian Library★★ (BZ) – ♿*Broad Street.* 👁 *Guided tour (university ceremonies permitting) mid-Mar to Oct, Mon-Fri at 10.30am, 11.30am, 2pm, 3pm, Sat at 10.30am, 11.30am; Nov to mid-Mar, Mon-Fri at 2pm, 3pm, Sat at 10.30am, 11.30pm.* 🎟 *£3.50.* ☎ *01865 277 224; tours@bodley.ox.ac.uk; www.bodley.ox.ac.uk.* One of the world's great libraries, established in the 14C, rebuilt in the 17C, the Bodleian contains almost 5 million books, manuscripts and maps. The entrance leads to **Old Schools Quadrangle**, built in 1439 in the Jacobean-Gothic style so characteristic of Oxford. On the right is the **Tower of the Five Orders**, richly decorated with the five classical orders of architecture. Opposite is the 15C **Divinity School,** famous for the bosses and pendants of its **lierne vaulting**★. Above is Duke Humphrey's Library (1610-12) with its gaily decorated **ceiling**★★. Regular exhibitions of the Library's treasures are held.

Radcliffe Camera★ (BZ) – The Baroque rotunda, designed by James Gibbs, stands at the heart of the University, between the "federal" university buildings around the Bodleian and Sheldonian to the north and the university church to the south.

All Souls College (BZ) – *Entrance in High Street.* ⏰ *Open Mon-Fri, 2-4.30pm (4pm Nov-Mar).* ⏰ *Closed at Easter, Aug and Dec 25-Jan 1. Ramp to entrance.* ☎ *01865 279 379; Fax 01865 279 299; www.all-souls.ox.ac.uk.* Founded in 1438 as a memorial to those killed in the Hundred Years War, the Front Quadrangle is mid-15C and the larger North Quad 18C by Nicholas Hawksmoor. Between them is the 1442 Perpendicular **Chapel**★, with its 15C glass in the antechapel, and magnificent medieval reredos.

St Mary the Virgin (BZ) – Late 15C Perpendicular with a Decorated 13C tower (offering a **view** of the city's domes, spires, quadrangles and the surrounding hills) and a delightfully incongruous Baroque porch (1637) by Nicholas Stone. St Mary's is the University Church and adjoins the earliest rooms used by the University: the early 14C **Congregation House** where the governing body convened, with the first Library above. Inside is the Vice-Chancellor's Throne.

Brasenose College (BZ) – ⏰ *Open daily, 10am-11.30am and 2-4.30pm.* ⏰ *Closed 25-26 Dec. Brochure (2 languages).* ☎ *01865 277 823; Fax 01865 277 822; www.bnc.ox.ac. uk.* Founded 1509, the Gatehouse, Front Quad and Hall are early 16C, the Library and Chapel mid-17C and the old kitchen a 14C relic of Brasenose Hall (the name refers to a doorknocker from the hall).

Lincoln College★ (BZ) – ⏰ *Open daily, 2pm (11am Sun and Bank Hols) to 5pm.* ⏰ *Closed 1 Jan, 25 -26 Dec.* ☎ *01865 279 800; www.linc.ox.ac.uk.* Founded 1427, the Front Quad and Hall were built in 1436 and provide a rare glimpse of what medieval Oxford must have looked like. The 1610-31 Chapel in the Back Quad contains original 17C Flemish stained glass and between the two quads are the oak panelled rooms of **John Wesley**, the founder of Methodism.

Trinity College (BY) – ⏰ *Open (functions permitting) 10.30am-noon and 2-4pm.* ⏰ *Closed at Christmas.* 🎟 *£1.50. Booklet 50p.* ☎ *01865 279 900; www.trinity.ox.ac. uk.* Founded 1555, Trinity was the successor to Durham College suppressed at the Dissolution. Standing well back from Broad Street behind gardens in the Front Quad is the **Chapel**★, with Grinling Gibbons' exquisite cherub and wood carvings, in the Durham Quad the 17C Library and in the Garden Quad, facing **Trinity Gardens**★, a north range by Wren.

Balliol College (BY) – ⏱ *Open usually daily, 2pm-5pm.* ⏱ *Closed at Easter (approx 10 days), Aug (usually last 2 weeks), Sep (first week) and at Christmas and New Year.* ⌨ *£1.* ☎ *01865 277 777; Fax 01865 277 803; www.balliol.ox.ac.uk.* Founded 1282, the college is totally Victorian in appearance, except around the 15C front quad.

The Oxford Story (BZ) – ♿⏱ *Open daily, Jul-Aug 9.30am-5pm; Jan-Jun and Sep-Dec, 10am (11am Sun) to 4.30pm.* ⏱ *Closed 25 Dec.* ⌨ *£6.95. (Commentary 6 languages).* ☎ *01865 728 822 (facilities for disabled visitors* ☎ *01865 790 055); Fax 01865 791 716; info@oxfordstory.co.uk; www.oxfordstory.co.uk.* You'll find this provides a lively and imaginative introduction to the university – its constitution, its history, its role in national events and its relations with the city.

St John's College★ (BY) – ♿⏱ *Open daily, 1-5pm.* ⏱ *Closed Easter, 25-26 Dec.* ☎ *01865 277 300; www.sjc.ox.ac.uk.* Founded in 1555 and stretching out beyond the original 16C front, the gardens are by Capability Brown; the front quad contains the remains of the medieval St Bernard's College (founded 1437), while Canterbury Quadrangle's colonnades (1631-36) give a delightful touch of Italian Classicism to Oxford's predominant Jacobean-Gothic style.

Ashmolean Museum★★ (BY)

♿⏱ *Open Tue-Sat, 10am-5pm; noon-5pm Sun and Bank Hols. June-Aug 10am-7pm on Thur.* ⏱ *Closed Easter, 4-6 Sep (St Giles' Fair) and over Christmas. Free Admission.* ⌨ *Guided tour Sat, 11am or by appointment. Brochure. Café.* ☎ *01865 278 000; Fax 01865 278 018; www.ashmol.ox.ac.uk.* Built by C R Cockerell in free Grecian form (1845), the Ashmolean has grown from "Tradescant's Ark", an array of curiosities assembled by John Tradescant, gardener of Hatfield House, and his son, into the University's museum of archeology. The collections are rich and varied, though their display is sometimes dauntingly old-fashioned.

Ground Floor – The Greek and Roman sculptures of the Arundel Collection include fragments of a frieze from an Athenian temple and a torso of c 480 BC. Among the Egyptian antiquities is an Eighteenth Dynasty fresco of a princess, showing for the first time in the history of art a rounded body on a flat surface. The decorative and fine arts of China, Japan, Tibet, India and Persia are well represented. The outstanding object in the Medieval Room is the exquisite late 9C Alfred Jewel, assumed to have been made for Alfred the Great. There is a good collection of Worcester porcelain.

First Floor – Part of Tradescant's original "twelve cartloads", including Guy Fawkes' lantern, is in the Tradescant Room. There are archeological treasures from Crete, Greece and Etruria but the principal interest is in paintings. The Italian 14C and 15C are well represented, particularly by Uccello's wonderful *Hunt in the Forest* and Piero di Cosimo's dream-like *Forest Fire.* Among Italian Renaissance works are pictures by Bellini, Veronese, Tintoretto and Giorgione. There are numerous minor 17C and 18C works of the Flemish, Dutch, English and French schools, some of them on the second floor, but quite outstanding is one of Claude Lorrain's luminous landscapes, *Ascanius Shooting the Stag of Sylvia.*

Second Floor – Another high point in the collection is reached in the **Pre-Raphaelite** paintings, including Hunt's *A Converted British Family Sheltering a Christian Missionary from the Persecution of the Druids, and* Charles Collins' *Convent Thoughts.* A good selection of French Impressionists is complemented by a number of 20C British works, mainly of the Camden Town School.

The museum's collection of prints and drawings is vast, with numerous works by the pastoral visionary Samuel Palmer (1805-81).

Additional Sights

University Museum of Natural History★ (BY) – ♿⏱ *Open daily and Bank Hols, noon-5pm.* ⏱ *Closed Easter and over Christmas. Free admission. Leaflet (4 langua-ges).* ☎ *01865 270 949; Fax 01865 272 970; info@oum.ox.ac.uk; www.oum.ox.ac.uk.* "The building will shortly sink into insignificance when compared to the contents it will display and the minds it will mould", enthused its founder Sir Henry Acland in 1860. He was wrong. The museum's natural history contents (including the Oxford Dodo) tell us more about our ancestors who were Victorian than about our ancestors who were related to monkeys, and sink into insignificance beside the extraordinary building: a cast-iron neo-Gothic cathedral designed like a railway station, with 19C Decorated stone carvings of animals and plants by the Irish sculptor-mason family, the O'Sheas. A doorway at the end leads to the **Pitt Rivers Museum★ (BY)**, Oxford's bizarre anthropological collection of masks, musical instruments, jewellery, skulls, totem poles and armour, arranged by categories rather than countries and showing traditions common to different cultures.

Address Book

WHERE TO STAY

◎◎◎◎ **Chestnuts**, *45 Davenant Road*. ☎/Fax 01865 553 375; stay@chestnutsguesthouse.co.uk; chestnutsguesthouse.co.uk. This small (six-room) guest house is under friendly personal management with touches such as bath robes and mineral water in bedrooms, and is just a short walk to the town's water meadows and centre.

◎◎◎ **Marlborough House,** *321 Woodstock Road*. ☎ 01865 311 321; Fax 01865 515 329; marlboroughhouse@btconnect.com. This modern three-storey houses offers 16 simple yet spacious rooms, each with its own kitchenette, a short bus ride from the town centre.

WHERE TO EAT

◎◎◎ **White Hart,** *Wytham*. ☎ 01865 244 372; Fax 01865 812 950; whitehartwytham@yahoo.co.uk. Pretty 18C village pub 3 mi/5km north west of city centre, serving modern British food on a delightful courtyard terrace or in a flagstoned dining room with scrubbed tables and roaring fires.

◎◎◎ **Branca,** *111 Walton Road*. ☎ 01865 556 111; Fax 01865 556 501; info@branca-restaurants.com; www.branca-restaurants.com. Stylish modern restaurant serving vibrant contemporay Italian cooking offering plenty more besides pizzas and pastas.

◎◎◎ **Mole Inn,** *Toot Baldon* ☎ 01865 340 001; Fax 01865 343 011; info@themoleinn.com; www.themoleinn.com. The standard of cuisine at this immaculately refurbished inn is several notches higher than standard Oxfordshire pub fare, running from earthy classics to modern globally influenced dishes, all prepared with assurance and care.

University College (BZ) – ⏱ *Open certain days throughout the year; telephone for details.* ☎ 01865 276 602; www.univ.ox.ac.uk. Founded in 1249, with a Jacobean-Gothic curved front, the western of its two vaulted gateways leads to the large mid-17C quad with the hall and chapel (note the 17C painted glass by Van Linge), and the eastern gateway to the smaller early 18C quad. Under a domed chamber in the northeast corner of the main quad is Onslow Ford's neo-Classical nude statue of the drowned poet Shelley.

Hertford College (BZ) – ♿ *Catte Street.* ⏱*Open daily except during examination periods, 10am-6pm/dusk.* ⏱ *Closed Easter, 24 Dec to 2 Jan. Wheelchair access to quadrangles.* ☎ 01865 279 400; Fax 01865 279 466; www.hertford.ox.ac.uk. Founded as Hart Hall in 1282 and refounded as Hertford College in the 19C, its bridge over New College Lane was built in 1913 to link the two quads.

Exeter College (BZ) – ♿ *Open daily, 2-5pm (subject to change).* ⏱ *Closed Easter, 25-26 Dec, 1 Jan.* ☎ 01865 279 600; Fax 01865 279 630; postmaster@exeter.ox.ac.uk; www.exeter.ox.ac.uk. Founded 1314, combining Jacobean profuseness and Victorian values, its oldest part is **Palmer's Tower** (1412); in Gilbert Scott's 1857 chapel (modelled on the Sainte Chapelle in Paris) is a tapestry by Morris and Burne-Jones, both of whom were undergraduates at Exeter.

Jesus College (BZ) – ⏱*Open daily, 2-4.30pm.* ⏱ *Closed 1 week at Easter and Christmas.* ☎ 01865 279 700; Fax 01865 279 687; enquiries@jesus.oxford.ac.uk; www.jesus.ox.ac.uk. Founded 1571, its east front is very late Perpendicular, the Front Quad, Hall and Chapel Jacobean-Gothic and the Inner Quad 17C-18C Classicism.

St Michael at the Northgate (BZ) – The oldest building with a Saxon tower in Oxford, and 13C interior. Oxford's earliest stained glass (c 1290) is in the east window, depicting St Nicholas, St Edmund of Abingdon, St Michael, and the Virgin and Child.

Worcester College (BY) – ♿⏱*Open daily, 2-5pm/dusk.* ☎ 01865 278 300; Fax 01865 278 387; www.worcester.ox.ac.uk. Founded in 1714, from the medieval foundation of Gloucester College, a relic of the foundation exists in the five monastic houses on the south side of the main quadrangle. The rest of the buildings are 18C Classical, though the interior of the chapel was melodramatised in the 19C by William Burges. The **gardens** are graced by a lake and are among the most serene in Oxford.

Keble College (BY) – ♿⏱ *Open all year, daily, 2pm-5pm.* ⏱ *Closed bank holidays, 25-26 Dec.* 🎫 *No charge.* ☎ 01865 272 727. Founded 1870 and built of brick by William Butterfield in strident Victorian Gothic, Keble is a monument to the Oxford Movement and the Gothic Revival, reaching its highest expression in the ecclesiastical engineering of the **chapel**, where a copy of Holman Hunt's *The Light of the World* hangs in the Liddon Memorial Chapel.

PEAK DISTRICT★★

S. Yorkshire, Derbyshire, Staffordshire: ENGLAND

MICHELIN ATLAS P 35 OR MAP 502 O, P 23 AND 24

The teeming northen industrial areas of Sheffield, Manchester, the Potteries and West Yorkshire have on their doorstep the unspoiled landscape of the **Peak District National Park** (542sq mi/approx 1 400km2), which extends from Holmfirth in the north to Ashbourne in the south and from Sheffield in the east to Macclesfield in the west. The underlying rock is limestone of two very different kinds: to the north gritstone, which gives rise to the sombre moorlands and precipitous outcrops of the **Dark Peak**, culminating in **Kinder Scout** (2 088ft/636m); to the south, the lighter stone of the more pastoral **White Peak**, a plateau divided up by drystone walls and by spectacular steep-sided dales.

It was on Kinder Scout, on 24 April 1932, that a mass trespass by ramblers was organised. They were anxious to establish a right of access to these wild spots. The "trespass" resulted in the imprisonment of five of their number. In the end, however, it helped lead to the establishment of National Parks. Today, disused railway lines have been turned into footpaths; there are rock faces to be climbed and pot-holes to be explored, particularly around Castleton, where the caves can be visited by the less energetic as well. ▯ *13 Market Place, Ashbourne* ☎ *01335 343 666; ashbourneinfo@derbyshiredales.gov.uk* ▯ *Old Market Hall, Bridge Street, Bakewell* ☎/Fax *01629 813 227; bakewell@peakdistrict-npa.gov.uk* ▯ *The Crescent, Buxton* ☎ *01298 25106; tourism@highpeak.gov.uk* ▯ *Buxton Road, Castleton* ☎ *01433 620679; castleton@ peakdistrict-npa.gov.uk* ▯ *Main Street, Edale* ☎ *01433 670207; edale@peakdistrict-npa. gov.uk* ▯ *Crown Square, Matlock* ☎ *01629 583388; matlockinfo@derbyshiredales.gov. uk* ▯ *The Pavilion , Matlock Bath* ☎ *01629 55082; matlockbathinfo@derbyshiredales. gov.uk.* **All offices:** *www.visitpeakdistrict.com.*

▶ **Orient Yourself**: You will need a car to get around. Buxton and Matlock are good touring bases.

Don't Miss: Chatsworth; Hardwick Hall; Dovedale.

Organizing Your Time: Allow a day at Chatsworth plus at least another 2 days for the best of the rest.

Especially for Kids: A cave visit; the cable cars at the Heights of Abraham; Gulliver's Kingdom.

Walking Tours and Trails: The Peak District is a mecca for walkers with an annual two-week Walking Festival *(third week April through second week May)* and a weekly programme of walks often led by National Park Rangers departing from various points: click on *www.visitpeakdistrict.com* for details.

Northern Section

In alphabetical order

Buxton – The Romans discovered the warm springs and built baths here in about AD 79. In the 16C Mary Queen of Scots was occasionally permitted, during her long captivity at Sheffield Manor, to come to "take the waters" for her rheumatism at the Old Hall, now the Old Hall Hotel in the Crescent. Buxton did not however begin to take on the aspect of a spa town, such as Bath or Cheltenham, until 1780 when the 5th Duke of Devonshire commissioned John Carr of York to build **The Crescent** which, with the nearby **Opera House**, is still the centre of activity. The town grew in the 1860s with the advent of locomotives capable of coping with the steep gradients.

Castleton Caves – The village of Castleton is still dominated by the ruined keep (mostly 12C) of the castle which was begun by William Peveril soon after the Norman Conquest.
The local caves are natural cavities or lead-mining workings or a mixture of both. This important range of caverns presents lofty chambers with attractive mineral colourings and a variety of limestone formations, rippling draperies, stalactites, stalagmites and columns.

Peak Cavern – ⏱ *Open Apr-Oct, daily, 10am-5pm; Nov-Mar, Sat-Sun, 10am-5pm.* ▱ *£6.* ⤳ *Guided tour (60min). Parking. Refreshments.* ☎ *01433 620 285; info@peakcavern. co.uk; www.devilsarse.com.* is entered at the foot of the hill below the castle. Near the

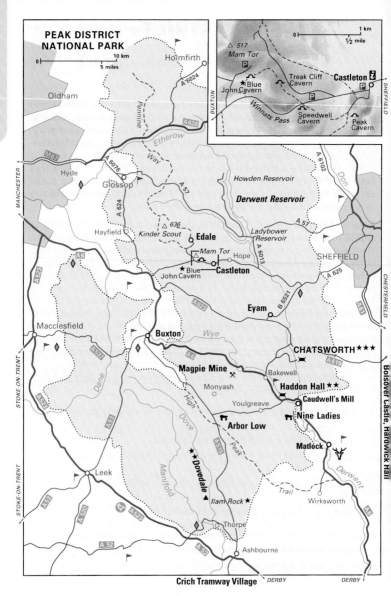

PEAK DISTRICT NATIONAL PARK

Crich Tramway Village

impressive entrance of the cave the roof is still blackened by soot from the chimneys of a community of ropemakers, who occupied the cave for 300 years until 1974 and built their houses within the cave.

Speedwell Cavern *(west by B 6061* 🕐 *Open daily, 9.30am-5pm (4pm winter).* 🎫 *£6.50.* 🚶 *Guided tour (45min). Brochure (3 languages). Parking. Refreshments. 105 steps down to boat.* ☎ *01433 620 512; Fax 01433 621 888; info@speedwellcavern.co.uk; www. devilsarse.com)* is reached by boat along an underground canal. **Winnats Pass** *(farther west)* is a steep ravine with high limestone cliffs, probably a collapsed cave system.

Blue John Cavern★ *(off A 625* 🕐 *Open daily, 9.30am-5.30pm/dusk (Jan times available by telephone).* 🕐 *Closed 25-26 Dec.* 🎫 *£7.* 🚶 *Guided tour (50min).* ☎ *01433 620 642 or 620 638; lesley@bluejohn-cavern.co.uk; www.bluejohn-cavern.co.uk)* is the source of a purplish-blue form of fluorspar, called Blue John, a semi-precious mineral which has been worked into jewellery and larger pieces for many years (vases containing Blue John were found in the ruins of Pompeii). There are several distinct veins, each with its own patterns and colouring, in which buff, purple and black predominate.

Treak Cliff Cavern *(*🕐 *Open daily at 10am. Last tour times: Mar-Oct 4.20pm (4.45pm Aug); Nov-Feb 3.20pm.* 🕐 *Closed 24-26 Dec, 1 Jan.* 🎫 *£6.* 🚶 *Guided tour (40min).*

Brochure (5 languages). Video. Parking. Refreshments. ☎ *01433 620 571; www.bluejohnstone.com)* is where in 1926 the skeletons of Bronze Age miners with their flint implements beside them were found.

There may be dozens of caverns as yet undiscovered in the fissured limestone below the summit of **Mam Tor**, which is the site of an Iron Age fort.

Derwent Reservoir – Created to supply water to the nearby cities, **Derwent, Howden** and **Ladybower Reservoirs** are today a "Lake District" to be enjoyed by yachtsmen, cyclists and walkers alike. It was here that 617 Squadron, the "Dambusters," trained with the "bouncing bomb", for the 1943 raid on the Ruhr dams.

Edale – Starting point of the Pennine Way, the first long-distance footpath in Britain, established on 24 April 1965, the anniversary of the Kinder Scout trespass. It runs along the Pennines, backbone of northern England, from Edale, across Hadrian's Wall to Kirk Yetholm in the Cheviots (250mi/402km). Its course is mostly through rugged upland country, unforgiving to the ill-prepared walker. It crosses motorways and skirts industrial areas but takes the walker through outstanding natural landscapes; many villages, buildings of note and archeological sites are scattered along its route or can be reached by short detours. Walk eastwards to the Packhorse Bridge which is one of the best of the Peak District bridges, with their narrow and low parapets to avoid the swinging panniers.

Eyam – Eyam (pronounced Eem) is known as the plague village because in the autumn of 1665 the inhabitants, who were stricken by the disease, cut themselves off from the outside world in self-imposed quarantine; twelve months later only a quarter of them had survived. The story is told in the **Eyam Museum** (*Hawkhill Road;* ◷*Open late-Mar to early-Nov, Tue-Sun and Bank Hols, 10am-4.30pm;* ⊛ *£1.75.* ☎/*Fax 01433 631 371; www. eyammuseum.demon.co.uk)* which also contains a model of a local lead mine.

Eyam Hall (⸂ *Hope Valley; House:* ◷*Open end-Jun to early-Sep, Wed-Thu, Sun and Bank Hol Mon, 11am-4pm.* ⊛ *£4.75. Craft centre, buttery and shop.* ☎ *01433 631 976, 01433 631 603; www.eyamhall.com)* a modest gentleman's residence, is still owned by the Wright family who built it in 1671. Since then it has changed little: the rooms are furnished with family portraits, costumes, silver and porcelain, 15C and 16C tapestries, a typical country gentleman's library, two 17C bacon settles in the hall, an 18C housekeeper's cupboard in the kitchen passage and a selection of utensils, some copper, in the 18C kitchen.

Southern Section
In alphabetical order

Arbor Low – *Just off the High Peak Trail*, one of the disused railway tracks, is Arbor Low, the best known of the Peak's prehistoric monuments. A circle of stones lies within a surrounding bank and ditch.

Bolsover Castle★ – *16mi/26km east of Matlock via Chesterfield by A 632.* ⸂◷ *Open daily, Apr-Oct, 10am-6pm (5pm Oct), Nov-Mar, Wed-Sun, 10am-4pm; last admission 1 hr before closing; may close earlier due to events.* ◷ *Closed 24-26 Dec, 1 Jan.* ⊛ *£6.60. Parking. Tearoom, picnics.* ☎ *01246 822 844; Fax 01246 241 569; bolsover.castle@english-heritage. org.uk; www. english-heritage.org.uk.* Bolsover is a Gothic folly of a castle perched on a hill above the coal mines and pitheads. It was commissioned by the Earl of Shrewsbury, who was married to Bess of Hardwick, and designed by her builder Robert Smythson, whose son John and grandson Huntingdon added the **Terrace Range** and **Riding School**. Completed in 1633, it provided the magical setting for Ben Jonson's masque, *Love's Welcome to Bolsover*, performed the next year before Charles I at a cost of £15 000. The interior is rich in carved Jacobean fireplaces, panelling, strapwork and ceiling paintings, particularly the **Elysium** and **Heaven Rooms**, a foretaste of Baroque.

Caudwell's Mill – *6mi/10km north of Matlock by A 6 to Rowsley (signs).* ◷ *Shop: Open daily. Mill: Open Mar-Oct, daily, 10am-6pm (4.30pm Mar); Nov-Feb, Sat-Sun, 10am-4.30pm.* ⊛ *£3. Parking. Refreshments.* ☎/*Fax 01629 734 374; www.peakdistrictproducts. co.uk.* This working Victorian flour mill, astride the River Wye, is a unique example of a water-driven roller mill, a fascinating process of clattering pulleys and sifters still producing wholemeal flour which can be bought from the shop. The mill outbuildings house several craft workshops.

Chatsworth House★★★ – ⸂ *See CHATSWORTH.*

Dovedale★★ – A dramatic two-mile gorge in the Derbyshire hills where the River Dove has washed away the soft limestone, exposing cliffs, caves and crags. Ruskin called it "an alluring first lesson in all that is admirable and beautiful."

From its entrance between Thorpe Cloud (942ft/287m) and Bunster Hill (1 000ft/305m), it meanders below the rocky outcrops of Lovers' Leap, The Twelve Apostles and **Ilam Rock**★. Upstream of Dovedale it continues to Beresford Dale, forever associated with Izaak Walton and John Cotton, authors of *The Compleat Angler*. The 1674 Fishing Temple built by Cotton still stands as a celebration of their friendship.

Haddon Hall★★ – ⏰ *Open Apr-Sep, daily, 10.30am-5.15pm; Oct, Thu-Sun, 10.30am-4.45pm.* ⬭ *£7.25, parking £1. Refreshments.* ☎ *01629 812 855; Fax 01629 814 379; info@ haddonhall.co.uk; www.haddonhall.co.uk.* Overlooking the River Wye since the 12C, rambling and very English, Haddon Hall was continually enlarged until the early 17C. It was lovingly restored by the 9th Duke of Rutland in the early 20C.

The **interior**, like the exterior, is in a multitude of styles; the Hall (1370) is medieval, the Dining Room and Great Chamber are Tudor and the Long Gallery (note Rex Whistler's painting of Haddon) is Elizabethan. The rooms are matched in splendour by the Mortlake **tapestries** of Aesop's *Fables (Feeling, Hearing, Seeing, Tasting and Smelling)*. The glory of the minuscule chapel is its **murals**.

The terraced **gardens** date from the 17C, perhaps even earlier. Lavishly planted with roses they tumble prettily to the river with its venerable stone packhorse bridge.

Hardwick Hall★★ – *2mi/32km east of Matlock via Alfreton by A 615 and A 61 north; turn right into B 6025; past Tibshelf and after having crossed M 1, turn left into a minor road north.* ♿ *Doe Lea. Hall:* ⏰*Open late-Mar to Oct, Wed-Thu, Sat-Sun, Good Friday and Bank Hol Mon, noon-4.30pm. Gardens: Open late-Mar to Oct, Wed-Mon, 11am-5.30pm. Park: Open daily, dawn-dusk. Hall and gardens* ⬭ *£7.20; gardens only, £3.90. Braille guide. Parking. Licensed restaurant. Wheelchair available if booked.* ☎ *01246 850 430; Fax 01246 854 200; hardwickhall@nationaltrust.org.uk; www.nationaltrust.org.uk.* Directly after building Chatsworth and abandoning her husband, the Earl of Shrewsbury, **Bess of Hardwick** returned to the modest manor house where she was born and rebuilt it. At the age of 70, still dissatisfied, she built another Hardwick Hall "more glass than wall" designed by **Robert Smythson**. Her descendants preferred to live at Chatsworth so the Old Hall fell into ruins and the New Hall was left unoccupied, frozen in time, one of the purest examples of 16C design and decor in the country.

The **interior** is famous for its stupendous late Elizabethan fireplaces, friezes, tapestries and **embroideries** on its walls; an embroidery in the Paved Room is by Mary Queen of Scots. Note also the *Fancie of a Fowler*. The three embroideries in the Drawing Room, *Diana and Actaeon*, the *Fall of Phaeton* and *Europea and the Bull* are by Bess herself. Portraits of her hang in the Hall and the Long Gallery.

Magpie Mine – The deep, steep-sided dales gave easy access to veins of lead, the rivers provided the power to drain the mine tunnels and the metal has been mined in the Peak District since Roman times. Magpie Mine was continuously worked for 200 years from the 1740s. Today engine houses and spoil heaps are reminders of this past activity. Old workings and shafts can still be a danger for the unwary, so do not wander into spots where you might put yourself – and your rescuers – in danger.

Matlock – From the end of the 18C, the cliffs and woods of the deep gorge carved by the River Derwent through the limestone of the southeastern part of the Peak District formed a picturesque setting for the development of modest spa facilities. The former Matlock Bath Hydro, a Victorian building with a thermal pool, now houses a **fresh-water aquarium** (*10 North Parade; Open Easter-Oct, daily, 10am-5.30pm (later in summer); Nov-Easter, Sat-Sun and Christmas Hols, 10am-5pm.* ⬭ *£1.80.* ☎ *01629 583 624, 01629 582 350 (office); Fax 01629 760 793; www.matlockbathaquarium.co.uk).* A far older Peak District industry, lead mining, is celebrated in the fascinating **Peak District Mining Museum** (*The Pavilion.* ♿⏰*Open daily, 10am (11am Oct-Mar) to 5pm (3pm Oct-Mar).* ⬭ *Museum and mine £5. Parking (charge). Refreshments. Gift shop.* ☎ *01629 583 834; mail@peakmines.co.uk; www.peakmines.co.uk*) housed in the early 20C Pavilion which was once the centre of social life in Matlock Bath. A cable car runs from Matlock over the river gorge to the **Heights of Abraham**, where you can take a tour of the Masson Cavern and expore hilltop trains (*Matlock Bath.* ♿⏰*Open late-Mar to late-Oct, daily, 10am-5pm; mid-Feb to late-Mar, Sat-Sun, 10am-5pm.* ⬭ *£9. Play areas. Restaurant, coffee shop, bar.* ☎ *01629 582 365 (24hr); Fax 01629 580 279; enquiries@h-of-a.co.uk; www. heights-of-abraham.co.uk*).

High Peak Junction Workshops and Visitor Centre – *Cromford Canal;* ⏰*Open Apr-Oct, daily, 10.30am to 5.30pm; Nov-Mar, Sat-Sun and Christmas and half term Hols, 10.30am-4pm.* ⬭ *70p museum, audio tour £1.50. Leaflets. Refrshments; picnic area. Parking.* ☎ *01629 822 831; www.derbyshire-thepeakdistrict.co.uk.* These are some of the oldest surviving railway workshops, virtually unchanged with tools and artefacts.

Crich Tramway Village★ – *15miles/ 24km south of Matlock by A 6 and B 5036 to Crich.* Open daily, early to late-Feb 10:30am-4pm; Mar Sat-Sun 10.30am-4pm, late-Mar to early-Nov, daily 10am-5.30pm; early-Nov to early-Dec, Sat-Sun 10.30am-4pm, daily. £8.50. 01773 854 321; Fax 01773 854 320; info@tramway.co.uk; www.tramway.co.uk. At their zenith in the 1920s, Britain's trams carried 4 800 billion passengers a year, but in the postwar period most of the country's 2 600mi of tramways were ripped up and only recently has there been a modest revival of this efficient mode of mass urban transport. The Tramway Museum Society has been preserving trams since 1955 and today proudly displays many of its much-loved and beautifully restored specimens at Crich. Visitors can admire the array of machines on display in the depot and Exhibition Hall, then take a trip along a reconstructed street with many fascinating features of the tramway age into more open countryside high above the Derwent Valley. While the trams include a Prague *Elektricka*, a streamliner of American design from The Hague and a horse-drawn four-wheeler from Portugal, the majority are of British origin and range from such oddities as a Blackpool toast-rack and box-like steam locomotive to more conventional double and single-deckers in the handsome liveries of their once-widespread municipal networks.

Nine Ladies – A stone circle surrounded by many barrows indicates the importance of the area to Neolithic man.

Red House Stables – *2.5mi/4km north of Matlock by A 6 (signs).* – Old Road, Darley-dale. Open daily, 10am-5pm (4pm winter). £2.75. Parking. 01629 733 583; www.workingcarriages.com. The collection of working carriages housed at this family-run stables have together garnered a formidable list of film and television credits, including *Pride and Prejudice, Jane Eyre* and *Sense and Sensibility*. Regular tours by liveried coach-and-four can be booked to Haddon Hall or Chatsworth Park.

Well Dressing

The annual Well Dressing is a unique Peak District tradition. Pagan thanks-givings to local water spirits have been transformed into Christian ceremonies, in some 20 Peak District villages. Eyam, Youlgreave, Wirksworth and Monyash are just some of the villages where the dressing takes place from early May to August each year. A large board is covered in clay, a design pricked out on it and then flowers, seeds, bark, lichens and grasses are used to fill out the design in colours. The board is then placed by the well or spring and blessed at a special open-air church service.

PEMBROKESHIRE COAST★★

Pembrokeshire, WALES

MICHELIN ATLAS P 14 OR MAP 503 E, F 27, 28 AND 29

The Pembrokeshire Peninsula, most western part of Wales and part of the old Kingdom of Dyfed, "land of magic and enchantment," abounds not only in the dolmens and megaliths of prehistory but also in the splendid stone crosses of Celtic Christianity. Unit 2, Upper Park Road, Tenby SA70 7LT. 01834 842402/04 ; Fax 01834 845 439; tenby.tic@pembrokeshire.gov.uk. The Barbecue, The Harbour, Saunder-sfoot, SA69 9HE 01834 813672; Fax 01834 813673; saundersfoot.tic@pembrokeshire. gov.uk. 19, Old Bridge, Haverfordwest. SA61 2EZ. 01437 763110; Fax 01437 767738; haverfordwest.tic@pembrokeshire.gov.uk. The Square, Fishguard, SA65 9HA. 01348 873484; Fax 01348 875246; fishguard.tic@pembrokeshire.gov.uk. Commons Rd, Pembroke. SA71 4EA 01646 622388 Fax: 01646 621396; pembroke.tic@pembrokeshire. go.uk. All offices: www.visitpembrokeshire.com.

A Bit of History

From the late 11C the native Welsh were largely displaced from south Pembrokeshire by Anglo-Normans, bent on colonisation and settlement; even today the linguistic boundary known as the **Landsker** follows the old military frontier separating the northern "Welshry" of distinct Celtic character from the southern "Englishry" with its anglicised place-names and square-towered churches.

Geological Notes

in 1952 the coastline was designated the **Pembrokeshire Coast National Park**, the smallest and, as it comprises mostly coastal scenery, the least typical of the National Parks of Wales and England; its wonderful variety of beaches is backed by a cliffline revealing a complex and sometimes spectacular geology and harbouring a rich bird-life.

From Amroth in the south to Poppit Sands in the north, the coastline's myriad delights are linked together by the Pembrokeshire Coast Path (180mi/290km long). Enquire at any of the National Park information centres *(see 🛈 on map)* for details of walks (the coast near Castlemartin in the south serves as a firing range).

Surfers, water skiers, yachtsmen, power-boat enthusiasts and sea anglers have a wide variety of sandy or pebble beaches, coves, inlets and creeks to choose from on this varied coastline. For some areas access is more difficult, while for others there are parking facilities within a few yards of the beach.

▸ **Orient Yourself**: Pembokeshire is a large area to cover in a few days. Most places of interest lie in the south and west of the county. Tenby is a popular seaside base. Haverford West is a good base for exploring the south and the west.

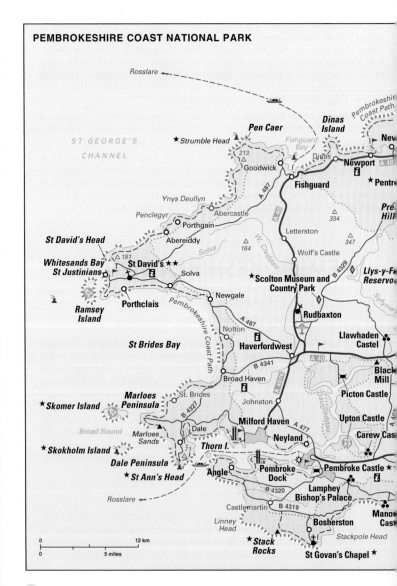

PEMBROKESHIRE COAST NATIONAL PARK

Parking: Try to leave your car behind and use the Puffin Shuttle bus service which operates Jun to late-Sep, daily, 9am-6.30pm approx. Hail-and-ride- service between St David's and Milford Haven stopping at points along the coast for walkers to access the Coast Path National Trail. *Adult Day Explorer Fare £4;* ☎ *01437 764 636 (National Park Authority); 01437 776 313 (Pembrokeshire Greenways); www.pembrokeshiregreenways.co.uk.*

Don't Miss: St David's; Tenby; a trip on a high-speed inflatable.

Organizing Your Time: allow at least three days to see the highlights of the south and west of the county.

Especially for Kids: there are excellent beaches (see below) all around the coast.

Beaches: Also click on www.visitpembrokeshire.com/beaches.asp.

Walking Tours: See www.visitpembrokeshire.**com** for other walks.

Bicycle Trails: Pembrokeshire is a great place for cyclists: click on www.cyclepembrokeshire.com for details.

Boat Trips: There are several conventional boat trips plus exciting high-speed inflatable rides, for example, from Solva to Ramsey Island.

Excursions

From Tenby to St David's

85mi/135km – see map

Beginning at the delightful resort of Tenby and ending in the far west at St David's, this tour introduces some of the important sights of **Pembrokeshire Coast National Park**.

Tenby (Dinbych-y-pysgod)★★ – See TENBY.

▶ *Go west on A 4139 and after 4mi/6km, turn left into B 4585.*

Manorbier (Maenorbyr) – "The most delectable spot in Wales," according to Giraldus Cambrensis, traveller and historian born here c 1146. When seen from the bay, the mighty walls of **Manorbier Castle**, (*Open Easter-Sep, 10.30am-5.30pm. £3.50. Parking.* ☎ *01834 871 394; www.manorbier-castle.co.uk*) which belonged to his family, recall the great Crusader strong-holds of the Levant.

▶ *Take a succession of local roads round the coast to Bosherston and if possible continue on down to the coast near St Govan's Head.*

The stretch of coastline between St Govan's Head and Linney Head to the west has some spectacular limestone features: high cliffs, arches, stacks, sea caves and blow holes. On this indented coastline are two impressive pillars, **Stacks Rocks**★ (Elegug Stacks) and a natural arch known as the Green Bridge of Wales. Near Bosherston, the **chapel**★ first established as a hermit's cell by St Govan in the 6C seems almost a part of the cliff face. (*Note: this area is part of the Castlemartin artillery range and beyond this point the path leaves the coast. Check locally in advance to see if it is accessible).*

▶ *Return inland to Pembroke.*

Pembroke Castle★★ – *Open daily, 9.30am (10am Oct-Mar) to 6pm (5pm Oct and Mar; 4pm Nov-Feb).* *Closed 24-26 Dec, 1 Jan.* *£3. Guided tour (1hr) summer, Sun-Fri. Brochure (5 languages). Refreshments (in summer).* ☎ *01646 681 510; Fax 01646 622 260; www.pembrokecastle.co.uk.* The powerful and ancient castle has for centuries guarded the strategically sited town of Pembroke, which rises on a ridge, and its safe anchorage. The original fort, a palisaded enclosure at the end of the ridge (now the inner ward), was built in the late 11C; it was replaced by a stone castle in the 1190s and enlarged a century later. The massive **keep**, 70ft/21m high with walls 19ft/6m thick at the base, is the crowning glory of the castle today. Access to the 13C outer ward is through the great gatehouse; beyond, immediately to the left, stands the Henry VII Tower, one of the five projecting round towers that protect the curtain wall. Margaret Beaufort, young wife of Edmund Tudor, was sent for safety during the Wars of the Roses to her brother-in-law Jasper at Pembroke. It was most probably in this tower, in 1457, that the young Margaret, a widow at nineteen, gave birth to Henry Tudor, later King Henry VII.

The **Wogan Cavern**, below the Norman Hall, is unparalleled in British castles. It is a natural vaulted cavern, some 60ft/18m by 80ft/24m, and was probably used as a store and boathouse.

▷ *Take A 4139 north to join A 477.*

From the modern tollbridge there is a good **view** of the magnificent anchorage of **Milford Haven** described by Nelson as one of the best in the world. Sir William Hamilton set about building a town, a naval dockyard and navigation school here in 1790, an ambitious plan encouraged by Lord Nelson. By 1814, the Admiralty had founded their own dockyard at Pembroke Dock. Despite a more recent oil terminal development, commercial activity in the Haven has dwindled this century; the port ceded its supremacy to Sullom Voe in the Shetlands with the development of North Sea oil in the 1970s. The whole waterway, together with the Daugleddau estuaries, has been developed as a centre for sailing, windsurfing and waterskiing.

▷ *Continue to Johnston, then turn left onto local roads to Dale on the peninsula; continue south to the tip.*

The lighthouse and coastguard station on the red sandstone cliffs of **St Ann's Head** survey the entrance to the waterway. The rugged western shores where Atlantic rollers crash onto the sands contrast with the sheltered bays and anchorages of the eastern shores. It was in the small cove of Mill Bay that Henry Tudor (Harri Tudur) landed on 7 August 1485 on his way to victory at Bosworth Field (🔊 see LEICESTER) and the crown of England.

▷ *Go north to Marloes then west to the car park at Marloes Mere.*

The wide expanse of sand known as **Marloes Sands** separates the Dale and Marloes Peninsulas. On the beach note the **Three Chimneys**, Silurian rocks up-ended by powerful earth movements. The names of the offshore islands, Skokholm and Skomer, are the heritage of the Norse incursions. Visits can be made to the nearby bird sanctuary islands of **Skomer**★, Skokholm and Grassholm, with their colonies of sea birds, including the charming puffin, the emblem of this national park.

▷ *Return inland to Haverfordwest by B 4327.*

Haverfordwest (Hwlffordd) – The former county town with its hilltop castle ruin is of ancient origin and is still the urban centre for a wide area.

▷ *Take A 487 west to the coast.*

Newgale – One of several holiday villages on this coast, its splendid two-mile stretch of sand, backed by a storm ridge of shingle, makes this a favourite family holiday spot. Newgale marks the western end of the Landsker (🔊 see above).

▷ *Take A 487 to Solva.*

Solva (Solvach) – The pretty harbour at Lower Solva was built to be out of sight of sea-raiders. Today it shelters pleasure boats as well as fishing craft.

St David's (Ty Ddewi)★★ – 🔊 See ST DAVID'S.

From St David's to Cardigan
55mi/85km – The coastal road leads round to Strumble Head.

St David's (Ty Ddewi)★★ – 🔊 See ST DAVID'S.

▷ *From St David's take A 487; 2mi/3km beyond Croes-goch turn left.*

Beyond is **Strumble Head**★ and its light, the nearest point to Ireland.

Fishguard (Abergwaun) – The lower town offers a pretty haven for pleasure craft. Brunel planned to make Fishguard a transatlantic port to rival Liverpool. For a brief period great liners like the *Mauretania* did berth here, but today it is only the ferries that sail from the eastern side of the bay towards Rosslare.

▶ *Take A 487 which turns eastwards to skirt Fishguard Bay and Newport Bay.*

East of Fishguard the landscapes are wilder and the cliffs more precipitous.

▶ *Follow the A 487; at the turn-off for Nevern, branch right into minor roads leading inland to an imposing megalithic monument.*

Pentre Ifan★ – This massive cromlech, overlooking Newport Bay, consists of four great upright stones, three of which support a massive capstone. It stands on the lower slopes of the rounded, heather-clad **Presely Hills** (Mynydd Preseli), from whose eastern crests came the bluestones of Stonehenge, which were probably transported by water from Newport Bay.

▶ *Return to Nevern.*

Nevern – Among the yews in the churchyard of St Brynach's Church stands a splendid 11C Celtic wheelhead **cross** (13ft/4m high), richly carved in interlacing patterns.

▶ *Return to A 487.*

Castell Henllys – ♿🕐*Meline. Open Apr-Oct, daily, 10am-5pm.* 🎫 *£3.* *Guided tour available. Guide book (2 languages for children). Leaflet (English/Welsh). Parking (5min on foot from ticket office to site). Refreshments. Gift shop. Partial access for wheelchairs to site; ramp to shop.* ✆*/Fax 01239 891 319; celts@castellhenllys.com; www.castellhenllys.com.* This hilltop fort is the setting for a conscientious attempt to recreate the environment of the Iron Age; storage pit, cultivated areas and a fine trio of conical thatched huts with smoky interiors make a memorable impression.

▶ *Continue north on A 487; just south of Cardigan, before crossing the river, turn left into B 4546.*

Poppit Sands – Here the coastal footpath ends by a broad sandy beach on the south shore of the Teifi Estuary.

▶ *Return to A 487 and continue north to Cardigan.*

Cardigan (Aberteifi) – ♿ *See CARDIGAN.*

PERTH ★

Perthshire and Kinross, SCOTLAND

POPULATION 41 916

MICHELIN ATLAS P 62 OR MAP 501 J 14

TOWN PLAN IN THE MICHELIN GUIDE GREAT BRITAIN AND IRELAND

This former Royal Burgh retains the atmosphere of a country town and is an ideal touring centre, 43 mi/67km north of Edinburgh. It is situated on the River Tay, noted for salmon fishing and for freshwater mussels which produce beautiful pearls. Some of the finest specimens are incorporated in the Honours of Scotland (on display in Edinburgh Castle). 🛈 *Lower City Mills, West Mill Street, Perth PH1 5QP;* ✆ *01738 450600; perthtic@visitscotland.com; www.perthshire.co.uk.*

A Bit of History

The "Fair City" has played a prominent role in Scottish history and might well have become the capital had not James I been assassinated here in 1457. Other stirring events included the murderous Clan Combat of 1396 and the destruction of the town's monasteries following John Knox's inflammatory sermon of 1559.

On completion of the elegant Perth Bridge in 1772, the town broke out of its medieval limits. There are good examples of **Georgian architecture★** in Charlotte Street, Atholl Crescent, Rose Terrace and Barossa Place to the north of the centre.

Sights

Black Watch Regimental Museum★ – *Hay Street.* 🕐*Open May-Sep, Mon-Sat, 10am-4.30pm; Oct-Apr, Mon-Fri, 10am-3.30pm.* 🕐 *Closed Jun (last Sat) and 23 Dec to 6 Jan. Free admission. Audio tour (charge). Parking.* ✆ *0131 310 8530; www.theblackwatch. co.uk.* Balhousie Castle houses the museum tracing the history of the Regiment and

The Stone of Destiny

According to legend, the stone was Jacob's pillow which eventually reached Ireland by way of Egypt and Spain and is believed to have served as a coronation stone for the High Kings at Tara. The stone was taken to Iona in the 6C where it was presented to St Columba. It was later moved to Dunadd, Dunstaffnage and Dunkeld. After the merger of the kingdoms of the Picts and Scots, who originally came from Ireland, Kenneth MacAlpine was the first king to be crowned on the stone at Scone. Subsequently it served for the coronation of all Scottish kings until 1296 when the Scots were defeated by Edward I. He carried off the stone, which was placed beneath the Coronation chair in Westminster Abbey, where for 700 years it played an integral part in the Coronation rituals. It was stolen in 1950 but was later recovered in Arbroath Abbey. From early days controversy has raged about the authenticity of the stone. Some believe the original stone never left Scotland. Historians have examined the seals of various kings which show a larger stone while early descriptions mention a large block of black marble with a hollowed-out seat. In 1996 the people of Scotland greeted the return of the Stone of Destiny, which is the symbol of Scottish nationhood, with great emotion. It is now on display with the Honours of Scotland in Edinburgh Castle and will be returned to Westminster Abbey for future coronations.

presenting a collection of silver, battle honours, medals and Colours. In the early 18C General Wade enlisted and armed independent companies of Highlanders which became known as the **Black Watch**, for the "Watch" they kept on the Highlands and for their dark tartan, in sharp contrast to the red of Government troops. The Black Watch became a regiment in 1739 and is still in the service of the Crown.

Museum and Art Gallery★ – 78 George Street. Open Mon-Sat, 10am-5pm. Closed Christmas to New Year. Free admission. ☎ 01738 632 488; Fax 01738 443 505; museum@pkc.gov.uk; www.perthshire.com. There are interesting displays of the local glass, silver and clock-making industries in addition to the natural history section. In the art gallery hang evocative works by Scottish artists (H McCullough, the Glasgow School) and by **John Millais** (Chill October) who owed his Perthshire connections to his wife Effie Gray.

Fergusson Gallery – Marshall Place. Open Mon-Sat, 10am-5pm. Free Admission. ☎ 01738 441 944; Fax 01738 621152; jckinnear@pkc.gov.uk; www.perthshire.com. A handsome circular building, the former Water Works, houses the gallery which displays the luminous and colourful canvases of the Scottish Colourist **JD Fergusson** (1874-1961).

Excursions

Scone Palace★★ – 2mi/3km northeast by A 93. Open Apr-Oct, daily, 9.30am-5.30pm (5pm last admission); Nov-Mar, by appointment. Palace £6.95, grounds only, £3.50. Guides in State Rooms. Guide book (7 languages). Children's playground. Maze. Parking. Restaurant, picnic area. ☎ 01738 552 300; Fax 01738 552 588; visits@scone-palace.co.uk; www.scone-palace.co.uk. One of Scotland's most hallowed historic sites, Scone was the centre of Kenneth MacAlpine's Scoto-Pictish kingdom from the mid-9C and, from 1120, the first Augustinian priory in Scotland. **Moot Hill** (now occupied by a 19C chapel) was where Scottish kings were enthroned on the **Stone of Destiny** (Stone of Scone). Wrecked in the wave of destruction of 1559, the abbey eventually became the seat of the Earls of Mansfield. The present neo-Gothic palace dates from 1808. Its richly furnished apartments contain a splendid array of porcelain and ivories, unusual timepieces, busts and portraits, and a unique collection of papier-mâché objets d'art. In the 50-acre pinetum are examples of the Douglas fir, named after the botanist David Douglas, born here in 1799.

Dunkeld★ – 14mi/23km north by A 9. Dunkeld was the site of a monastic establishment from AD 700 and later of a majestic Gothic cathedral (14C-16C). It now consists of the tiny cathedral "city" and the partly ruined **cathedral** (Cathedral Street; Open Apr-Sep, daily, 9.30am-6.30pm; Oct-Mar, daily, 10am (2pm Sun) to 4.30pm. ☎ 01350 727 601; www.dunkeldcathedral.org.uk) in its attractive riverside precinct. The 15C nave is roofless but the 14C choir was restored in 1600 to serve as the parish church; the chapter house contains the Atholl mausoleum and a small museum.

Cathedral Street★ and **The Cross** were rebuilt after Dunkeld was sacked following the Battle of Killiecrankie (see PITLOCHRY) in 1689. Many 17C-18C houses have been attractively restored.

Drummond Castle Gardens★ – *20mi/32km west by A 85 and A 822 South. Muthill, Creiff.* 🕐 *Open Easter and May-Oct, daily, 1-6pm (5pm last admission).* ⚷*Castle is not open to public.* 👁 *£4. Parking.* ☎ *01764 681 433; Fax 01764 681 642; info@drummondcastle.sol.co.uk; www.drummondcastlegardens.co.uk.* The Gardens of Drummond Castle were originally laid out about 1630 by John Drummond, 2nd Earl of Perth. In about 1830, the parterre was Italianised and embellished with fine figures and statues from Italy. One of the most interesting pieces of statuary is the Sundial, designed and built by John Mylne, Master Mason to King Charles I.

PETERBOROUGH

Cambridgeshire, ENGLAND

POPULATION 134 788

MICHELIN ATLAS P 29 OR MAP 504 T 26

TOWN PLAN IN THE MICHELIN GUIDE GREAT BRITAIN AND IRELAND

Peterborough began life as a village around a monastery, some 25 miles/40km north of Cambridge. It became a town around a cathedral and then a city dominated by brickworks, and is now a high-tech centre for financial institutions with engineering and brick industries; its population has doubled in the last 20 years. A pedestrian zone has replaced the ancient city centre but the developers spared the Cathedral, the pretty 17C arcaded Guildhall, the Perpendicular church of St John the Baptist in Cowgate and some Georgian houses in Priestgate. Wooded Nene Park (4mi/6km west) provides golf courses and lakes and space for outdoor pursuits. 🛈 *45 Bridge Street* ☎ *01733 452 336; Fax 01733 452 353.*

Sights

Cathedral★★ – ♿🕐 *Open Mon-Fri, 9am-6.30pm, Sat 9am-5pm, Sun 7.30am-5pm. Sun services: 8.15am, 9.30am, 3.30pm.* 👁 *Suggested donation £3.50.* 👓 *Guided tour (1hr) daily at 2pm £3.50. Brochure (5 languages). Restaurant. Parking permits for wheelchair users; touching and hearing model.* ☎ *01733 343 342; Fax 01733 355 316; info@peterborough-cathedral.org.uk; www.peterborough-cathedral.org.uk.* Peterborough and Ely were the two great monasteries of the Fens. The Saxon monastery, founded c 655, was sacked by the Danes in 870. A second Saxon church, built in the 10C as the Minster of a Benedictine Abbey, was burnt down in 1116. The present building was started in 1118 and consecrated in 1238. A frenzied attack in 1643 by Cromwell's men destroyed the stained glass, the high altar, the cloisters and statues.

The Early English **west front** is most memorable and fascinating with its three giant arches and its rich incongruous early Perpendicular (14C) porch. The interior is a superb example of Norman architecture. The nave, with its uninterrupted vista towards the altar, the transepts and choir with their **Norman elevations** are a robust uncomplicated expression of structure and faith. The 13C **nave ceiling** is a wonderful example of medieval art with

Peterborough Cathedral

A. Williams/MICHELIN

427

figures of bishops, saints and mythical beasts painted in the lozenges. The modern (1975) addition of a large hanging crucifix is eye-catching. The 15C wooden ceiling in the sanctuary is decorated with bosses and the superb fan vaulting at the east end (in the New or Eastern Building) is late 15C Perpendicular. In this area is an 8C Saxon sculpture (Monks' or Hedda Stone). 17C Flemish tapestries hang in the apse and this ceiling was painted by Sir George Gilbert Scott in the 19C. In the north choir aisle Catherine of Aragon is buried and in the south choir aisle Mary Queen of Scots was temporarily laid to rest (1587-1612). Several fine Benedictine effigies rest in niches. The 14C Almoner's Hall *(south of the Cathedral)* houses the Visitor Centre where the history of the cathedral and the life of the monks is refreshingly described by means of models and display boards.

Railworld –   *Nene Valley Railway Station.* Open daily (except Sat-Sun, Nov-Feb), *11am-4pm.* Closed Dec 25 and Jan 1. £4. ☎ 01733 344 240; www.railworld.net. This exhibition on railways which focusses on modern trains and the future, contrasts with the adjoining eastern terminus of the Nene Valley Railway (*see below*).

Excursions

Flag Fen Bronze Age Excavation★★ – *3mi/4.8km east by A 47 and A 1130 (signs).*   *the Droveway, Northey Road.* Open daily, 10am-5pm (4pm last admission). *Closed 24 Dec-2 Jan.* £4.25. No dogs. Parking. Refreshments; picnic areas. ☎ 01733 313 414; Fax 01733 349 957; office@flagfen.com; www.flagfen.com. This fenland site in a modern industrial area is still being excavated to reveal finds over 3 000 years old. At the compact Museum in the Visitor Centre is an excellent display of bronze spearheads, rings from harnesses, bracelets and pots. The outdoor trail leads to a reconstructed turf-roofed Bronze Age round-house (from 1500 BC), past a cross-section of Roman Road and into a shed with planks and joints preserved in water tanks. In the Exhibition Hall vast piles of timber from 1350 BC are submerged in muddy peat and kept damp. Old breeds of sheep and pigs roam outside.

Nene Valley Railway★ – *8mi/13km west on A 47 and south on A 1.*   *Operates Feb-Mar, Sun; Easter to Apr, Sat-Sun; May-Jul, Wed, and Sat-Sun, Aug-Oct Sat-Sun, plus events throughout the year.* £10. Yard and Station open for viewing all year; Museum open service days only. Cafe. ☎ 01780 784 4404 (timetable), 01780 784 444 (general enquiries); www.nvr.org.uk. Steam locomotives puff along the track through Nene Park via a tunnel and Yarwell Junction between Wansford and Peterborough *(15mi/24km – 90min return)*. The carriages are fitted out with shiny wooden fascia and the smoke billowing over the flat landscape makes the ride a nostalgic one for the older generation and like something out of a school history book for children. At Peterborough the train halts while the engine changes ends. The **museum** at Wansford displays one carriage with railway memorabilia and an engine shed with **Thomas the Tank Engine** (the subject of a highly successful series of children's books by the Reverend Audry) and old rolling stock, some from abroad.

PITLOCHRY★

Perthshire and Kinross, SCOTLAND

POPULATION 3 126

MICHELIN ATLAS P 61 OR MAP 501 I 13

This attractive town, set in the Tummel Valley, 28 mi/45km north east of Perth-makes a fine touring centre to enjoy the magnificent scenery of mountains, lochs and moors. It hosts a festival of drama, music and art in summer. *22 Atholl Road, PH16 5BX ☎ 01796 472215, 01796 472751; pitlochrytic@visitscotland.com; www. perthshire.co.uk.*

Visit

Pitlochry Power Station Visitor Centre– *200 Dunkeld Road. &.© Open Apr-Oct, daily, 10am-5.30pm. ⌐ £2 (no charge to view salmon observation window). Parking. ☎ 01796 473 152; www.scottish-southern.co.uk.* A dam *(54ft/16m high and 475ft/140m long)* has created Loch Faskally. A salmon ladder – with an observation window – enables salmon to move upstream to their spawning grounds. The visitor centre presents an exhibition on hydro-electric power.

Excursions

Queen's View★★ – *10mi/16km west by B 8019.* This beauty spot was named after Queen Victoria's visit in 1866, and commands a wonderful view up Loch Tummel, with the cone shape of Schiehallion (3 547ft /1 083m) to the left.

Killiecrankie – *5mi/8km north by B 8019 and local road. &.© Site: Open daily. Visitor Centre: late-Mar to Oct, daily, 10am-5.30pm. Guide book (3 languages). Exhibition boards (8 languages). Free Admission. ⌐ Parking £1.60 Refreshments, picnic area.☎/Fax 01796 473 233; killiecrankie@nts.org.uk; www.nts.org.uk.* The visitor centre offers a dramatic exhibition of the **Battle of Killiecrankie** (27 July 1689) fought on high ground to the north of the narrow pass of Killiecrankie. John Graham (Viscount Dundee) and his Highlanders soundly defeated the government troops of William and Mary but Dundee was mortally wounded. A month later the leaderless Highlanders were wiped out at Dunkeld *(© see PERTH).* The end of the Jacobite saga, however, did not come until Culloden *(© see INVERNESS)* in 1746. A path leads to the **Soldier's Leap** where an English soldier is said to have jumped to safety.

Blair Castle★★ – *7mi/12km north by A 9. Blair Atholl. &.© Open late-Mar to late-Oct, daily, 9.30am-4.30pm. Nov-Mar Tues and Sat 9.30am-12.30pm. ⌐ £6.90. Brochure (4 languages). Deer park. Nature trails. Play area. Licensed restaurant, picnic area. Wheelchair access to ground floor and grounds. Parking. ☎ 01796 481 207; Fax 01796 481 487; bookings@blair-castle.co.uk; www.blair-castle.co.uk.* Blair Castle was the centre of the ancient kingdom of Atholl and the home of the Duke of Atholl until the death of the last of the line in 1996. A large part of the tower built here in 1269 still remains, and the castle with its turrets, crenellations and parapets continues to command a strategic route into the Central Highlands. The Duke of Atholl retains the only private army left in the British Isles, the **Atholl Highlanders**, sole survivor of the clan system.

The closely interwoven histories of the family and castle are highlighted by family **portrait**s (Lely, Jacob de Wet, Honthorst, Hoppner, Zoffany, Landseer) cross-referenced to genealogical tables, interesting collections (armour and porcelain), Jacobite and other historic relics (one of the original copies of the National Covenant). The 18C interiors are of particular interest, especially those with sumptuous stucco ceilings (Picture Staircase, Dining and Drawing Rooms) by Thomas Clayton.

PLYMOUTH★

Devon, ENGLAND

POPULATION 245 295

MICHELIN ATLAS P 3 OR MAP 503 H 32 – LOCAL MAP SEE TINTAGEL

Plymouth, the principal town of the Southwest, lies on the border between Devon and Cornwall. It has a spacious, airy feel to it and is arranged in three distinct areas: the Hoe and its environs, adorned with the splendour of Victorian and Edwardian buildings; the older, bustling Barbican district by the harbour with its fish markets and narrow streets; and the commercial centre, rebuilt after the war, with its wide shop-lined avenue. *Plymouth Mayflower, 3-5 The Barbican ☎ 01752 306 330; Fax : 01752 257 955; www.visitplymouth.co.uk*

▶ **Orient Yourself**: The Plymouth Dome is a good starting point for exploring the city. All the main sights are in or near The Hoe and the Barbican areas, which are easily covered on foot.

😀 **Don't Miss**: Buckland Abbey; a boat trip *(for details, contact the tourist office)*.

🕐 **Organizing Your Time**: Allow 2 days to see the city and an excursion.

🧒 **Especially for Kids**: National Marine Aquarium; beaches close by (Cawsand and Whitesands); Dockyards and Warships boat trip.

A Bit of History

Plymouth developed from the amalgamation of three towns: **Sutton**, **Devonport** and **Stonehouse**. The Plantagenet period brought trade with France and by the Elizabethan period trade had spread worldwide, so that for a time it was the fourth largest town in England after London, Bristol and York. From the 13C Plymouth also played a prime role as a naval and military port, from which warriors and explorers such as Drake, Raleigh, Hawkins and Grenville (all Devonians), Cook and the Pilgrim Fathers set sail.

The Royal Naval Dockyard was founded by William III in 1691 on Bunkers Hill, Devonport, its initial five acres being much increased to the north. In the Second World War the city suffered serious bomb damage.

Naval and Military Plymouth

The Hoe (Z) – On "that loftie place at Plimmouth call'd the Hoe" (Drayton), **Sir Francis Drake** (1540-96) is said to have seen the "invincible" Spanish Armada arriving one day in 1588 and decided to finish his game of bowls (or wait for the tide to turn?) before going to battle. It remains an ideal point from which to **view** the maritime traffic on the Sound, the natural harbour at the mouth of the Rivers Tamar and Plym. The modern **Plymouth Dome**★ *(&🕐 Open Mar-Sep, daily; Oct-Feb, Tue-Sun; 10am-5pm. ☜ £4.75. Combined ticket with Smeaton's Dome £6.50. Café. Facilities for people with mobility or sensory impairment. ☎ 01752 600 608 (Infoline); 01752 603 300 (administration); enquiries@plymouthdome.info, www.plymouthdome.info)* visitor centre explains the city's rich heritage. **Smeaton's Tower,** *(🕐 Open Mar-Oct, daily, 10.30am-4.30pm. ☜ £2.25; joint ticket with Plymouth Dome £6.50. ☎ 01752 600 608 (Infoline), 01752 603 300 (administration); enquiries@plymouthdome.info, www.plymouthdome.info)* a red and white painted lighthouse, was erected on the Hoe in 1884 after 123 storm-battered years on Eddystone Rocks about 14mi/23km southwest of Plymouth. The present **Eddystone Lighthouse**, built in 1878-82, can be seen from the Hoe and even better from the top of Smeaton's Tower, from where there is a splendid **view**★★. Other monuments testifying to Plymouth's role in history include Boehm's 1884 **Drake Statue (A)**, the **Armada Memorial (B)** and the **Naval War Memorial (D)** bearing the names of 22 443 men.

The southern limit of the Sound is marked by the mile-long **Breakwater** constructed by **John Rennie** from 1812 to 1841 to counter heavy sea swell from the southwest.

Royal Citadel (Z) – *☜ Guided tour only. May–Sep 2.30pm Tue, Thu. ☜ £3.50. ☎ 01752 775 841; www.english-heritage.org.uk.* From the early 15C the land to the east of the Hoe served as the site for a stronghold. In 1590-91 Drake began a fort intended to protect the Sound against marauding Spaniards and it was in this place that Charles II had the present castle built in 1666-71. The **ramparts** command **views**★★ of the Sound, the Barbican and the mouth of the Tamar. The 1670 **Main Gate** of Portland stone

PLYMOUTH

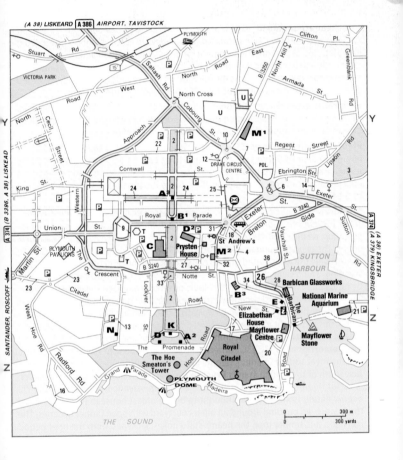

originally contained a bust of Charles II with the royal arms and inscription, but this was tactfully replaced by four cannon balls when the citadel was surrendered personally to William III in 1688! The 17C Guard House, Governor's House and Storeroom have all been rebuilt and the small **chapel of St Katherine,** (🕐 *Open all year. Sun service at 11.15am*) built in 1688, was enlarged in the 19C. The frescoes on the east wall were painted by an NCO in the Royal Engineers who died in the First World War.

Barbican and City Centre

Barbican (Z) – Old Plymouth survives in the Barbican, an area extending a quarter of a mile inland from Sutton Harbour, combining modern amenities with medieval houses, Jacobean doorways, cobbled alleys and the **Mayflower Stone** on the pier commemorating the voyage of the **Pilgrim Fathers**, who set sail in 1620 in their

90ft/27m ship, the *Mayflower*. Many other famous voyages are commemorated in the numerous stones and plaques on the pier.

National Marine Aquarium – *Rope Walk, Coxside.* ♿ 🕐 *Open daily, 10am-6pm (5pm Nov-Mar); last admission 1hr before closing.* 🕐 *Closed 25 Dec.* 💷 *£8.75.* ☎ *01752 600 301 (switchboard); 01752 220 084 (info line); marketing@national-aquarium.co.uk; www. national-aquarium.co.uk.* The tanks represent different environments, such as fresh stream, shallow sea, coral reef, etc. with an array of fish, from delicate sea horses to the mighty shark.

Plymouth Mayflower Centre – *3-5 The Barbican.* 🕐 *Open Apr-Oct, daily, 10am-4pm (Nov-Apr Mon-Sat, 10-4).* 💷 *£4; joint ticket with Aquarium available.* ☎ *01752 306 330; www.visitplymouth.co.uk.* This exhibit is interactive and informative.

The Elizabethan House *(32 New Street.* 🕐*Open Apr-Oct, Wed-Sun, 10am to 5pm.* 💷 *£2. Shop.* ☎ *01493 855 746; museum@plymouth.gov.uk)* and its neighbour were built in the late 16C as part of a development for merchants and sea-captains prosperous from trade and booty. The timber-framed and limestone houses are distinguished by their windows extending across the full width of the ground and first floors, exposed beams, large fireplaces and stout 16C-17C carved oak furniture.

Barbican Glassworks *(the Old Fishmarket.* 🕐*Open Mon-Sat, 9am-6pm, Sun 11am-5pm.* ☎ *01752 224 777; info@dartington.co.uk; www.devon-connect.co.uk)* showcases glass-blowers at work dipping long blowpipes into a furnace of red-hot glass.

Plymouth Gin Distillery (Z) – *60 South Side Street.* ♿ 👣 *Guided tour (50min), Mon-Fri, 9.30am-5.30pm; (Sat 10am, Sun 11am). Cafe.* 💷 *£2.75.* ☎ *01752 665 292; rose@plymouthgin.com; www.plymouthgin.com.* The distillery is housed in what was once a Dominican Friary founded in 1425. Today it is possible to take a guided tour to see how gin is made.

St Andrew's (Z) – ♿ 🕐 *Open daily, 9am-4pm. Sun services: first Sun in the month at 8am, 10am, 6.30pm, other Sun at 8am, 9.30am, 11.15am, and 6.30pm. Guide book (4 languages). Shop.* ☎ *01752 661 414 (Administrator, Mon-Fri, 9am-2pm); www.standrewschurch. org.uk.* The church, founded in 1050 and rebuilt in the 15C, was firebombed in 1941; this left only the walls, fluted granite piers, chancel arches and the 136ft/41m tower standing. The rebuilt church, re-consecrated in 1957, has six distinctive **windows** by John Piper (1904-92), their vivid colours offset by a patinaed Delabole slate floor. On a window ledge *(first window west of the south door)* is the so-called **Drake crest scratching** showing the *Golden Hinde* with a cord from her bow partly encircling a globe; this is thought to have been carved by a mason working in the church at the time of Drake's return from circumnavigating the world (3 November 1580). Among the **memorials** are a 12C-13C Purbeck marble effigy, tablets to Frobisher and Drake and the royal arms of Charles I, George III and George IV.

Just south of the church stands **Prysten House**, *(Finewell Street;* 🕐*Open Apr-Oct, Mon-Sat, 10am-3.30pm.* 💷 *£1.* ☎ *01752 661 414; prystenhouse@standrewschurch. org.uk)* dating from 1490 and thought to be the oldest house in Plymouth. It is a three-storeyed building around an inner courtyard with open timber galleries. The hall has a fine timber roof, the beams still smoke-blackened from the brief period after the Dissolution when the house was used for bacon-curing, and fine mullioned windows and stone fireplaces.

Merchant's House Museum (Z) – *33 St Andrew's Street.* 👣 *Guided tour Apr-Oct, daily, 10am-5pm, on the hour.* 💷 *£2.40.* ☎ *01493 857 900; www.visitplymouth.co.uk.* This mid-16C timbered house, its upper floors supported on stone corbels and with windows the full width and height of the front, owes its present style to William Parker, Mayor of Plymouth in 1601-02, a merchant and successful buccaneering sea-captain. It houses the Museum of Old Plymouth, including among the exhibits a reconstruction of one of Plymouth's old pharmacies.

City Museum and Art Gallery★ (Y) – *Drake Circus.* ♿🕐*Open Tue-Sat and Bank Hol Mon, 10am-5.30pm (5pm Sat and Bank Hol Mon).* 🕐 *Closed Good Friday, 25-26 Dec. Free admission. Refreshments.* ☎ *01752 304 774; Fax 01752 304 775; enquiry@plymouthmu-seum.gov.uk; www.plymouthmuseum.gov.uk.* The spacious Victorian building displays a mere fraction of its rich and splendid collections relating to the city's **maritime history** in terms of its mercantile associations and naval dockyard, local industries, regional history and contemporary arts scene. On permanent display upstairs is a selection from the **Cottonian Collection,** comprising paintings, old master drawings, prints and engravings, books, manuscripts, furniture and various objets d'art amassed by several generations of collectors (particularly strong representations of **Joshua Reynolds,** born in Plympton St Maurice).

Plymouth became the home of **William Cookworthy,** discoverer of the Cornish kaolin which made the production of **hard paste porcelain** a reality in this country from 1768; an excellent display relates the development of this new material.

Excursions

Buckland Abbey★★ – *Yelverton, 9mi/15km north.* ♿⏲ *Open late-Mar to early-Nov, Fri-Wed, 10.30am-5.30pm; early-Nov to late-Dec and late-Feb to late-Mar, Sat-Sun, 2-5pm; last admission 45min before closing.* 🎟 *£6; grounds only, £3.20. Leaflet (5 languages). Parking. Licensed restaurant; tearoom; picnics in car park. Wheelchairs and motorised buggy available; Braille guide.* ☎ *01822 853 607; Fax 01822 855 448; bucklandabbey@ nationaltrust.org.uk; www.nationaltrust.org.uk.* Buckland was founded in 1278, the last Cistercian abbey built in England and Wales. At the Dissolution, the property was sold to Sir Richard Grenville, Marshal of Calais. His grandson, the famous naval commander Sir Richard Grenville (1541-91), converted the abbey into an Elizabethan mansion before his rich and famous cousin, **Sir Francis Drake**, purchased the estate from him in 1581. The property has since been transformed from Tudor mansion to Georgian family home – the impression it largely still exudes – then restored after a devastating fire in 1938 and finally assigned to the National Trust in 1946. It is used by Plymouth City Council as a branch of the City Museum and Art Gallery. The garden is largely 20C, and the herb garden is said to have been established following a visit by Vita Sackville-West.

The **Great Barn,** buttressed and gabled, dates back to the 14C and was built to store the abbey's tithes and dues; its size reflects the prosperity enjoyed by the Cistercians at that time. The house, accommodating elements of the original church in its domestic context in a fascinating way, is approached from the south. To the left is Grenville's kitchen wing incorporating the retaining arches of the chapels arranged along the east wall of the abbey's former transept. Inside the house, a panelled corridor leads to the main staircase hung with topographical prints. The **Four Lives Gallery,** running the full length of the original nave, outlines the phases in the history of the abbey from 1278 to 1988. Drake's coat of arms is set into the plaster overmantel in the north crossing arch. The south wing was added in the 1790s to accommodate a practical entrance; the glass panels in the window on the stairs were engraved by Simon Whistler to commemorate the 400th anniversary of Drake's defeat of the Spanish Armada (1588). The **Drake Gallery,** which dominates the first floor, was added in the 1570s and currently houses an exhibition on the great seaman and explorer (portraits, the Drake Cup, the Armada Medals, and a late 16C side drum known as

Sir Joshua Reynolds (1723-92)

Undoubtedly, Reynolds was the most important English painter of the 18C. Not only was he accomplished, intelligent and versatile as a painter of Society portraits, he compounded a body of ideas on art, which he delivered through a series of 15 *Discourses on Art* (1769-90), against which critics, commentators and artists could measure their opinions for generations to come. As the founding President of the Royal Academy, Reynolds combined the philosophical ideals of the Age of Reason with the aesthetics and sensitivity of the emerging Romantic movement to establish a truly English School of painting. He confirmed portraiture, appreciated by the growing ranks of military leaders, successful businessmen and leading intellectuals (Dr Johnson, Horace Walpole), as the most highly regarded art form after History painting. He respected landscape and sporting pictures, preferred by the country gentry, as a medium worthy of merit in its own right.

Reynolds was the son of a Devon clergyman-schoolmaster; he served his apprenticeship in London (1740-43) under the fashionable portraitist Thomas Hudson, before travelling to Italy to assimilate the examples of Renaissance and Baroque art, notably in Rome. There, he came to understand the value of History painting whereby the artist must study Nature and then improve on it so as to formulate an expression of drama and poignancy in the grand style. Despite his theories, Reynolds's most enduring works are his portraits, a genre at which he excelled. He was astute enough to appreciate the powerful image that portraiture might project for his patron: by representing his sitters in a pose borrowed from Classical sculpture (the Apollo Belvedere, for example), and surrounding him with allegorical attributes in the manner of Rubens and Van Dyck, Reynolds could impart some of the spirit of History painting in the grand manner in his portraits. His success as an artist rested largely in his resourceful ability to vary gesture, texture and detail so as best to flatter his sitter and capture each personality's spirit of individuality.

Address Book

WHERE TO STAY

⊜⊜ **Ashgrove,** *218 Citadel Road, The Hoe.* ☎ *01752 664 046; Fax 01752 252 112; ashgrovehoe@aol.com.* This pretty terraced house right on the Hoe has hospitable owners, a bright lounge-breakfast room and 10 immaculate rooms.

⊜⊜⊜ **Athenaeum Lodge,** *4 Athenaeum Street, The Hoe.* ☎/*Fax 01752 665 005; info@athenaeumlodge.com; www. athenaeumlodge.com.* Rooms are neat and tidy in this family- owned Georgian Grade II Listed building on The Hoe and offer good value.

WHERE TO EAT

⊜⊜⊜ **Ship Inn,** *Noss Mayo.* ☎ *01752 872 387; Fax 01752 873 294; ship@nossmayo. com; www.nossmayo.com.* It's worth the 10 mi/16km drive south to this 18C inn for the location alone on a picture-postcard creek, though the food - nautically flavoured, naturally - and the atmosphere also make this a delightful outing.

⊜⊜⊜ **Artillery Tower,** *Firestone Bay.* ☎ *01752 257 610; www.artillerytower.co.uk.* Modern European fare with flair and care - breads, pasta and chocolates are all home-made - is served up in the unique and atmospheric location of a 500-year-old sea-facing circular gun emplacement.

Drake's Drum). The panelled **Drake Chamber** is hung with a series of 16-17C portraits -and contains English and continental furniture of the same period. At the opposite end of the Drake Gallery is the **Georgian Room** which reflects a completely different taste (portraits and marine scapes, 18-19C furniture). The **Pym Gallery** contains four murals commissioned by Lord and Lady Astor for the Festival of Britain celebrations of 1951 and legends associated with Drake. The **Great Hall**, at the heart of the old abbey beneath the tower, is paved in pink and white tiles (possibly Dutch) and lined with oak panelling. Its most striking feature is the fine plasterwork, much of which is original. The furniture is predominantly 16-17C. The **chapel**, initially re-created in 1917 on the site of the abbey church high altar, houses several empty graves. The kitchen, with French style brick charcoal ovens and a range of old-fashioned kitchen utensils, was added in the 17C.

Saltram House★★ – *3.5mi/5.5km east on A 374* **(Z)** *then south on A 38 to Plympton.* ♿🕐 *House: Open late-Mar to Sep, Sat-Thu and Good Friday, noon-4.30pm; Oct to early-Nov, Sat-Thu, 11.30am-3.30pm. Garden and Chapel Art Gallery: Open late-Mar to mid-Dec, Sat-Thu and Good Friday, 11am-5pm (4pm early-Nov to mid-Dec); also Jan-Mar, Sat-Thu, 11am-4pm (garden only), Sat-Sun (gallery only).* 🎫 *House and garden £7; garden only, £3.50. Information sheet (5 languages). Braille guide; audio tape; wheelchairs available; lift to first floor. Parking. Licensed restaurant, tearoom.* ☎ *01752 333 500; Fax 01752 336 474; saltram@nationaltrust.org.uk; www.nationaltrust.org.uk.* In 1712 the Parker family of Boringdon bought the Tudor mansion at Saltram and in 1750 John Parker's wife, Lady Catherine, set about improving it, but she died in 1758.

In 1768 her son John Parker II, an MP, inherited the house; through his lifelong friend **Joshua Reynolds**, born locally at Plympton in 1732, he met the architect **Robert Adam,** who was then working with **Thomas Chippendale**. Following a fire, Adam, Chippendale, Reynolds and Angelica Kauffmann all worked at Saltram, with the result that the house contains some of the finest 18C rooms in the country. In 1818 the local architect John Foulston added a music room to the library, designed a balustraded porch with Doric columns at the front and enlarged the windows above it.

The house however remains much as it was in the 18C – a happy blend of Adam's architecture, Chippendale's furniture, Reynolds' portraits, Kauffmann's paintings and an outstanding collection of porcelain.

South Cornish Coast between Plymouth and Truro – *West.* ♿ *See TRURO.*

PORTMEIRION★★★

Gwynedd, WALES

MICHELIN ATLAS P 32 OR MAP 503 H 25

Built on a wooded peninsula, with wonderful views over the shining waters and sweeping sandbanks of Traeth Bach, and with the mountains of Snowdonia as a backdrop, this dream village was the creation of the ever-fertile imagination of the long-lived architect and pioneer preservationist, Sir Clough Williams-Ellis (1893-1978). It has often been used as the setting for films and television programmes, the most famous of which was *The Prisoner* (1966-67), a TV series which gained cult status, starring Patrick McGoohan. 🚹 *High Street, Harlech* ☎ *01766 780 658 (seasonal); Fax 01766 780 658; tic.harlech@eryri-npa.gov.uk; www.gwynedd.gov.uk.* 🚹 *High Street, Porthmadog* ☎ *01766 512 981; Fax 01766 515 312; porthmadog.tic@gwynedd.gov.uk. Portmeirion Village has its own information centre* (*see below for contact details*)**.**

Visit *30min*

♿🕐 *Open daily, 9.30am-5.30pm.* 👓 *£6. Brochure (2 languages). Audio visual presentation. Audio tour. Parking. Refreshments.* ☎ *01766 770 000; Fax 01766 771 331; info@portmeirion-village.com; www.portmeirion.com.* The village is an extraordinary mixture of fantasy, theatrical effects and visual tricks, all designed to celebrate life as festival and architecture as fun. Sir Clough claimed that it was to serve "no useful purpose save that of looking both handsome and jolly", sufficient incentive to attract the large number of visitors who come for the day or to stay in the hotel or in one of the array of delightful buildings, most of them with a Baroque, Rococo or Mediterranean flavour. Archways lead to **Battery Square** with some of Portmeirion's earliest buildings, while the Citadel area is dominated by the **Campanile**, which looks much taller than its actual height (80ft/24m) because of Sir Clough's mastery of illusionism. In the valley leading down to the shoreline is the **Piazza**, the green heart of the village, with shops and restaurants and views to the Pantheon and the Bristol Colonnade, one of the many structures rescued from demolition and lovingly re-erected here. There is a Gothic Pavilion, a Triumphal Arch, a Gloriette, as well as an endless array of decorative details and masterly landscaping. A final touch of wizardry is the **Stone Boat** at the quayside.

Portmeirion

Wales Tourist Board

Excursions

Harlech Castle★★ – *18mi/29km east by A 487 to Maentwrog then south by A 496 or by toll-road (8mi/13km) across the estuary marshes.* Open late-Mar to late-Oct, *daily, 9.30am-5pm (6pm Jun to late Sep); late-Oct to late-Mar, daily, 9.30am (11am Sun) to 4pm.* Closed 24-26 Dec, 1 Jan. £3. 01766 780 552; www.harlech.com. Harlech Castle was started in 1283, during Edward I's second campaign in Wales, and completed in 1289. Its impressive outline rises on a rocky crag, 200ft/60m above the plain; from the castle battlements the panoramic views stretch to the high peaks of Snowdonia, across Tremadog Bay to the Lleyn Peninsula and, to the southwest, out to the open sea.

The castle's position with the fortified seaward side protected by walls and artillery platforms ensured its defences. The military architect **James of St George,** master mason of most of Edward's castles in Wales, was rewarded by being appointed Constable of Harlech, from July 1290.

The song *Men of Harlech* commemorates the holding of the castle for the Lancastrians, for eight years, during the Wars of the Roses, when it gave shelter to Henry VI's Queen, Margaret of Anjou. The garrison was permitted to march out in triumph in 1468, rather than being put to the sword or hanged – a more usual treatment for losers in those times.

Before entering, pause to look at the massive east front with its **Gatehouse**, and solid drum towers – the daunting sight which confronted would-be attackers. Enter by the modern wooden stairs, at the spot where a second, inner drawbridge pivoted to come down on bridge towers behind, of which only the foundations now remain. Inside the castle, the strength and importance of the gatehouse becomes apparent. Traceried windows, facing the Inner Ward, gave ample light to self-contained suites with fireplaces and a chapel. Here, in contrast to the purely military character of towers and curtain wall, is one of the finest examples of the fortified domestic architecture of the time.

Lleyn (Llyn) Peninsula★★ – *West by A 487 and A 497.* Geologically a continuation of the mountains of Snowdonia, this remote peninsula with its wild scenery and splendid coastline with many fine golden sandy beaches, is one of the strongholds of Welshness. At the base of the peninsula is the charming Victorian seaside resort of **Criccieth** with the ruins of its 13C Welsh **castle,** (*Site: Open daily. Visitor Centre: Open late-Mar to late-Sep, daily, 10am-5pm (6pm Jun to late-Sep).* Closed 24-26 Dec, 1 Jan. £2.90. 01766 522 227; www.porthmadog.com/cricc.html) and a little farther west the popular resort of **Pwllheli**, both possible starting points for exploring the Lleyn, which has no major towns.

In the village of **Llanystumdwy** *(2mi/3km west of Criccieth)* is the **Lloyd George Museum** (*Open Jul-Sep, daily, 10.30am-5pm. Jun, Mon-Sat and Bank Hol Sun, Easter and May, Mon-Fri, 10.30am-5pm. Oct, Mon-Fri, 11am-4pm.* £3. *Leaflet (3 languages). Guide book (2 languages). Parking. Picnic area. Guide dogs permitted. Wheelchair access to Museum and to ground floor of Highgate Cottage and Shoemaker's Workshop; induction loop in the reception, theatre and Shoemaker's workshop.* /Fax 01766 522 071; amgueddflydd-museums@gwynedd.gov.uk; www.gwynedd.gov.uk), the boyhood home of David Lloyd George (1863-1945), Liberal Member of Parliament for Caernarfon for 55 years and Prime Minister from 1916 to 1922.

Near the end of the peninsula, sheltered from the winds among the trees of the westernmost woodland, are the delightful gardens of **Plas-yn-Rhiw**★, *(Rhiw.* Open mid-May to Sep, Wed-Mon and Bank Hol Mon; Oct, Sat-Sun and 21-25; late-Mar to mid-May, Thu-Mon, noon-4.30pm. *House and garden £3.40; garden only, £2.20. Braille guide. Picnic area. Parking.* 01758 780 219, Fax 01758 780 219; plasynrhiw@ nationaltrust.org.uk; www.nationaltrust.org.uk.) an endearing little country house, part Tudor, part Georgian.

The other attractions of the peninsula are mostly natural ones, ranging from the strangely shaped trio of hills named Tre'r Ceiri, to wonderful sandy beaches and, in the far southwest, the rugged height of **Mynydd Mawra**, overlooking the pilgrims' island of **Bardsey**★.

PORTSMOUTH★

Hampshire, ENGLAND

POPULATION 174 690

MICHELIN ATLAS P 10 OR MAP 504 Q 31

Britain's premier naval base, 81 mi/130km south of London, is set on **Portsea Island** between two almost landlocked harbours, Portsmouth and Langstone. There was no significant settlement on the island until the 12C but the early 15C saw the development of the naval base and in 1495 the first dry dock in the world was built. By the end of the 17C Portsmouth had become the principal naval base in the country. In the 18C when France was Britain's major enemy, the fortifications were strengthened. After heavy bombing in the Second World War the city was rebuilt and expanded all over Portsea Island and onto the mainland between Portchester and Farlington. ⊡ *The Hard, entrance to Historic Dockyard ☎. 023 9282 6722; Fax 023 9282 7519; vis@portsmouthcc.gov.uk;www.visitportsmouth.co.uk*

▶ **Orient Yourself**: The main sights are spread out over quite a wide area (*see the map*).

🕭 **Don't Miss**: the Historic Dockyard *(the Historic Dockyard passport ticket includes a harbour boat tour; otherwise £4)*; the Spinnaker Tower on a clear day.

🕐 **Organizing Your Time**: Allow 1 to 2 days.

Especially for Kids: HMS *Victory*; Explosion!; Blue Reef Aquarium; the beach and seaside amusements at Southsea.

🖝 **Walking Tours**: information available from tourist information centre.

Historic Dockyard *3hr*

Victory Gate, Queen Street and the Hard; ♿🕐 Open daily, 9.45am-5.30pm (10am-5pm Oct-Mar); last admission 1hr before closing. 🕐 Closed 25 Dec. ☎ Passport ticket £15.50 (includes one entry to each attraction on site, plus harbour boat tour, valid one year) , single attraction £9.70. Guide book (4 languages). HMS Victory: 🖝 Guided tour (45min) subject to availability. The Mary Rose: Audio guide (6 languages); touch case and induction loop for the disabled. HMS Warrior 1860 (1hr): Deck plan available (7 languages). Royal Naval Museum (90min): Audio-visual presentation (2 languages). Restaurant, Maritime and Specialist Gift Shop. Parking £5. ☎ 023 9286 1533; Fax 023 9229 5252; mail@historicdockyard.co.uk; www.historicdockyard.co.uk.

HMS Victory★★★ – On 21 October 1805, Admiral Horatio Nelson's splendid 3-masted flagship (laid down at Chatham in 1759) led the victorious attack on a combined French and Spanish fleet off Cape Trafalgar in Spain – at the cost of her admiral's life. In the 1920s the *Victory* was brought into dry dock after 150 years at sea and she continues to serve as the flagship of the Commander in Chief, Naval Home Command and is still manned by serving Royal Naval and Royal Marines personnel. She is being restored to the configuration she held at the battle of Trafalgar.

The Mary Rose★★ – On 19 July 1545, the 4-masted *Mary Rose* (built 1509), vice flagship of the English fleet, keeled over and sank while preparing to meet a French attack. Henry VIII and his army on Southsea Common could hear the cries of the drowning men. In the 1960s the wreck was found, preserved in the Solent silt; in 1982 the hull was raised and it is now a unique Tudor time-capsule remarkably preserved after 437 years on the seabed. The **exhibition** of the many objects recovered – treasures and possessions of her crew – gives an insight into Tudor nautical life. An audio-visual presentation describes the dramatic salvage operation.

HMS Warrior 1860 – Once the pride of Queen Victoria's Navy, Britain's first iron-clad battleship was commissioned in the 1860s. After 100 years of use for various purposes she has been superbly restored and now displays a living exhibition of life in the Victorian Navy.

Royal Naval Museum★★ – The museum stands alongside HMS *Victory* and the *Mary Rose* in the heart of the historic naval base and is devoted to the overall history of the Royal Navy. The galleries are packed with mementoes of those who have served their country at sea through a thousand years of peace and war. The ghosts of past seamen are brought vividly to life in a series of exciting modern displays.

In the Victory Gallery there is a panoramic painting by WL Wyllie and a model evoking the Battle of Trafalgar.

Old Portsmouth ★ *1hr 30min*

Harbour Ramparts – The original town which grew up around the **Camber** south of the dockyard was once entirely enclosed by ramparts; today only those on the harbour side are complete, forming a pleasant promenade with **views** of Gosport and Spithead. At the end of Broad Street the **Point (BY)** affords fine **views**★★ of ships entering and leaving the port. The **Round Tower (BZ)**, built on the orders of Henry V, was modified in Henry VIII's reign and again in the 19C. The **Square Tower (BZ)**, built in 1494 and also much modified, contains, in a small recess, a gilded bust of **Charles I** by **Le Sueur.**

St Thomas Cathedral★ **(BZ)** – It was built c 1180 as a chapel to honour **Thomas Becket**, martyred in 1170. Only the Early English **choir** and **transepts** survived the Civil War; in around 1690 the nave and tower were rebuilt and the attractive octagonal wooden **cupola** – a landmark from the sea – was added in 1703. In the south chancel aisle is a **monument** to the notorious Duke of Buckingham, murdered in 11 High Street in 1628. After the church was elevated to cathedral status in 1927, extensions were made in 1938-39.

Royal Garrison Church (BZ) – This was part of a hospital founded c 1212; it was demolished in 1827. The church was bombed in 1941 and today only the beautiful Early English chancel with leafy bosses and capitals retains its roof.

City Museum and Records Office (CY) – *Museum Road.* 🔷🕐 *Open daily, 10am-5.30pm (5pm Nov-Mar).* 🕐 *Closed 24-26 Dec. Parking. Ramp; lift; induction loop. Free admission.* ☎ *023 9282 7261; Fax 023 9287 5276; searchroom@portsmouthcc.gov.uk; www.portsmouthmuseums.co.uk.* The displays are devoted to local history and arts from the 17C to the 20C.

Southsea (CZ) – The strip of land at the south of Portsea Island was rough marshland until the 19C when an elegant suburb of Portsmouth and a coastal resort began to grow and the Common became a pleasure area. At the southernmost tip of the island stands the **Castle**★ *(Clarence Esplanade.* 🔷🕐 *Open Apr-Oct, daily, 10am-5.30pm.* ⊜ *£2.50.* ☎ *023 9282 7261; Fax 023 9287 5276; cspendlove@portsmouthccgov.uk; www. portsmouthmuseums.co.uk),* built by Henry VIII in 1544-45 as part of the chain of forts protecting the ports along the south and east coast. The central **keep**, surrounded by a dry moat, is still mainly Tudor; inside are displays of the growth of Portsmouth's fortifications.

The **D-Day Museum and Overlord Embroidery (CZ)** *(Clarence Esplanade.* 🔷🕐*Open daily, 10am-5.30pm (5pm Nov-Mar).* 🕐 *Closed 24-26 Dec.* ⊜ *£5.50. Film (14min). Audio guide (30min). Refreshments. Parking for disabled visitors; sound guide; induction loop.* ☎ *023 9282 7261; Fax 023 9285 5276; info@ddaymuseum.co.uk; www.portsmouthmu-seums.co.uk)* near the castle illustrates the major events of the Second World War. The centrepiece is the Overlord Embroidery with 34 panels recounting the story of the D-Day operation.

Blue Reef Aquarium *(Clarence Esplanade.* 🔷🕐 *Open daily, 10am-5pm; 10-4pm Nov - Feb.* 🕐 *Closed 25 Dec.* ⊜ *£6.95. Cafe, picnic. Shop.* ☎ *023 92 875 222; Fax 023 92 294 443; portsmouth @ bluereefaquarium.com; www.bluereefaquarium.com)* is one of the country's burgeoning number of new-wave aquaria with large high-visibility tanks and special viewing features which take visitors on an undersea safari through the world's oceans. Highlights include a spectacular underwater walk-through tunnel, the otter hole and a frogs and nursery feature.

Additional Sights

The Spinnaker Tower – *Gunwharf Quays.* 🔷🕐*Open Mon-Wed 10am-6pm, Thur-Sat 10am- 8pm, Sun 11am-5pm.* 🕐 *Closed 25 Dec.* ⊜ *£4.95 (additional £2 for external lift). Cafe.* ☎ *023 9285 7520 (Disabled visitors* ☎ *023 9285 7520); Fax 023 9229 8726; www.spinnakertower.co.uk.* Soaring 558ft/170 metres into the sky above the historic harbour, the Spinnaker Tower, completed 2005, is the tallest public viewing tower in Great Britain with panoramic views which stretch as far as the Isle of Wight. There are observation decks at the 100m mark or you can go right to the top. Take your pick from a 572-step trek, a high speed internal lift or a glass external lift with panoramic views (additional charge).

PORTSMOUTH AND SOUTHSEA

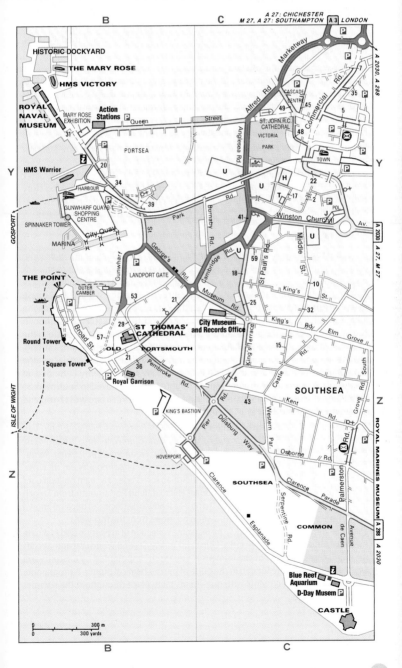

Charles Dickens' Birthplace – *393 Old Commercial Road.* ⏱*Open Apr-Oct, daily, 10am-5.30pm (5pm Oct); also 7 Feb, 10am-5pm.* ⌨ *£2.50.* ☎ *023 9282 7261; info@ charlesdickensbirthplace.co.uk; www.portsmouthmuseums.co.uk.* The small neat city centre terrace house where Dickens was born in 1812 and spent the first four months of his life has been restored and furnished in the style of the period. Across the landing from the bedroom a small exhibition includes the green velvet couch on which he died at Gad's Hill Place in Kent.

Royal Marines Museum★ – *Eastney. Leave by Clarence Parade, A 288* **(CZ)**. ♿⏱ *Open daily, 10am-5pm (4.30pm Sep-Whitsun).* ⏱ *Closed Dec 15.* ⌨ *£4.75.* ☎ *023 9281 9385; Fax 023 9283 8420; info@royalmarinesmuseum.co.uk; www.royalmarinesmuseum. co.uk.* Set in the original 19C officers' mess, this imaginative display describes the creation, history and modern-day work of the Royal Marine Corps. Also of note are the presentations on the Marines' work in Arctic and jungle conditions, the D-Day landings, the Marines' service in the UN and the "talking head" of Hannah Snell, who joined the Marines disguised as a man. There are collections of medals, silver, uniforms and portraits associated with the corps.

Royal Navy Submarine Museum – *Haslar Jetty Road.* ♿ ⏱ *Open daily, 10am-5.30pm (4.30pm Sept-May) last admission 1hr before closing.* ⏱ *Closed 24 Dec-1 Jan.* ⌨ *£5.50, combined ticket with Explosion! available. Parking. Cafe.* ☎ *023 9252 9217; Fax 023 9251 1349. www.rnsubmus.co.uk.* The museum is devoted to the history of submaries and their role in peace and war. Highlights include torpedoes, a Polaris missile and hands-on exhibits of periscopes and diving equipment.

Explosion! – *Priddy's Hard.* ♿ ⏱*Open daily, 10am-5.30pm (4.30pm Nov-Mar) last admission 1hr before closing.* ⏱ *Closed 1 Jan, 25-26 Dec.* ⌨ *£5.50, combined ticket with Royal Navy Submarine Museum available. Parking. Cafe. Shop.* ☎ *020 9250 5600; Fax 020 9250 5605; info@explosion.org.uk; www.explosion.org.uk.* The gripping story of naval firepower is traced through audio visual presentation, workers' testimonies and awesome exhibits on such topics as mines, torpedoes and modern missiles.

Excursions

Portchester Castle★ – *5mi/8km north on A 3* **(CY)**. ♿⏱ *Open daily, 10am-6pm (4pm Oct-Mar).* ⏱ *Closed 24-26 Dec.* ⌨ *£3.70. Parking. Wheelchair access to grounds and lower levels.* ☎ *023 9237 8291; www.english-heritage.org.uk.* At the north end of Portsmouth harbour stands a castle all but surrounded by the sea. The first phase of its construction was in the late 3C when the Romans built defence walls 10ft/3m wide and 20ft/6m high enclosing 9 acres/3.5ha of land; the walls still stand although the fort was used by the Saxons in the 5C-6C and became a medieval castle in the early 12C in the reign of Henry I. An inner bailey with a moat was built and a strong, austere **keep** which was heightened in the mid 12C. Richard II built a palace in the inner bailey in the late 14C, though it is now in ruins. In 1133 Henry I founded an Augustinian priory within the walls and although the priory moved to Southwick 20 years later the church of St Mary has remained – Norman with a fine **west front** and ornate **doorway** and, inside, a 12C **font**.

Royal Armouries Museum of Artillery – *Fort Nelson, Portsdown Hill Road; 9mi/14km northwest on M 27* **(CY)**. ♿⏱ *Open daily, Apr-Oct, 10am-5pm; Nov-Mar, 10.30am-4pm; last admission 1hr before closing.* ⏱ *Closed 25-26 Dec. Free admission. Parking. Refreshments. Handheld audio guide.* ☎ *01329 233 734; fnenquiries@armouries.org.uk; www. armouries.org.uk..* This superbly restored Victorian fort is one of a chain built on Lord Palmerston's orders high across Portsdown Hill to defend Portsmouth from French invasion. The forts faced "backwards" to repel a landward attack and became known as **"Palmerston's Folly."** There are sweeping **views** from the fort walls.

Together with re-created barracks, the fearsome collection of artillery includes ornate medieval bronze cannon from India, China and Turkey, Second World War anti-aircraft guns and three sections of the immense "Supergun" impounded by Customs and Excise in 1990, en route for Iraq in the guise of petro-chemical piping. A programme of events and re-enactments with gun-firings takes place throughout the summer and autumn.

RICHMOND★

North Yorkshire, ENGLAND

POPULATION 7 862

MICHELIN ATLAS P 45 OR MAP 502 O 20

Richmond is an attractive country market town set at the foot of Swaledale on the northwest edge of the **Yorkshire Dales National Park**. It was the home of Frances l'Anson, the sweet lass who in 1787 married the writer of the 18C song "Sweet Lass of Richmond Hill." *Friary Gardens, Victoria Road ☎ 01748 850 252; Fax 01748 825994; richmond@ytbtic.co.uk; www.yorkshiredales.org.*

Sights

Richmond Castle★ – *Open daily, late-Mar to Sept 10am-6pm, Oct to late-Mar (Thu-Mon) 10am-4pm. Closed 24-26 Dec, 1 Jan. £3.60. Wheelchair access to grounds. ☎ 01748 822 493; www.english-heritage.org.uk.* The castle stands on a cliff edge high above the river. It was begun by Alan the Red in 1071, the probable date of the masonry of the curtain walls. It has played a small part in the history of England, as it was left untouched by the Wars of the Roses and the Civil War. The entrance is through the **keep**, built of grey Norman masonry (100ft/30m), stout enough to stand comparison with Rochester and the White Tower in the Tower of London. An 11C arch leads into the courtyard. **Scolland's Hall**, built in 1080, is, after the hall-keep at Chepstow, the oldest such building in England. From the roof of the keep there is a splendid **view** across the cobbled marketplace and over the moors.

Georgian Theatre Royal and Museum★ – *Through Friar's Wynd from Market Place. Victoria Road. Museum: Open 10.30am-3.30pm (last tour). £2.50. ☎ 01748 823 710; 01748 823 021 (box office); www.georgiantheatreroyal.co.uk.* The only Georgian theatre in the country with its original form and features, it was opened on 2 September 1787, and was used for many years from the 1840s as an auction room and restored in 1963.

Green Howards Regimental Museum – *Trinity Church Square. Open Apr to mid-May, Mon-Sat, 9.30am (2pm Easter Sun) to 4.30pm; mid-May to Oct, daily, 9.30am (2pm Sun) to 4.30pm; Nov and Feb-Mar, Mon-Fri, 10am-4.30pm. Closed Dec-Jan. £3. Audio guide. Interactive video. ☎ 01748 826 561; Fax 01748 826 561; www.green-howards.org.uk.* The museum, which is housed in the 12C Holy Trinity Church, was opened in 1973 by the Colonel in Chief, the late King Olaf V of Norway; displays include uniforms, medals, campaign relics, weapons, badges and pictures from 1688 to the present day.

Excursions

Barnard Castle – *15mi/24km northwest by B 6274, A 66 and minor road (right). Open late-Mar to Oct, daily, 10am-6pm (4pm Oct); Nov-Mar, Thu-Mon, 10am-4pm. Closed 24-26 Dec, 1 Jan. £2.50. Audio guide. Picnic site. ☎ 01833 638 212; www.english-heritage.org.uk.* The ruined castle stands high up on the steep left bank of the River Tees, overlooking the town that has grown up beneath it. It was built early in the 11C, on land given by William II to the Baliols, who founded Balliol College, Oxford in 1263, and Sweetheart Abbey in Scotland. Of the original four wards, only the town, the middle and inner ward survive, the **Baliol Tower**, c 1250, straddling the curtain wall of the inner ward, being the best-preserved part.

The Bowes Museum★ – *Barnard Castle (signposted). Open daily, 11am-5pm. £7. Guided tours late-May to Oct. Closed 24-26 Dec and 1 Jan. Parking. Refreshments. Shop. Gardens. ☎ 01833 690 606; Fax: 01833 637 163; info@bowesmuseum.org.uk; www.bowesmuseum.org.uk.* A French-designed château, set in landscaped gardens (20 acres/9ha) is an unexpected surprise in this area. It was built, from 1869 onwards, to house the extraordinary array of ceramics, pictures, tapestries, furniture and other objets d'art amassed by John Bowes and his French wife, Josephine. Their treasures include novelties like an automated silver swan *(demonstrations once or twice a day; times displayed in the foyer)*; its rippling neck, as it swoops to catch a wriggling fish in its beak, is remarkably lifelike. There are also paintings of the first rank: a magnificent **St Peter** by El Greco, part of an extensive collection of 15C-19C Spanish work; two

Goyas, two Canalettos and works by Boudin and Courbet. One gallery is devoted to the paintings of Josephine Bowes.

Raby Castle★ – *6mi/10km northeast of Barnard Castle by A 688.* &⏱ *Castle: Open Jul-Aug, Sun-Fri, 1-5pm; May, June and Sep, Wed, Sun, 1-5pm, Bank Hol weekends, Sat-Wed, 1-5pm. Park and gardens: Open 11am-5.30pm. Gardens May-Sep Sun-Fri 11am-5.50pm.* ☜ *Castle, park and gardens £9; park and gardens only, £4. Parking. Refreshments.* ☎ *01833 660 202, 01833 660 207; Fax 01833 660 169; admin@rabycastle.com; www.rabycastle.com.* The castle, which was built in the 14C by the Nevill family, was forfeit to the Crown after the "Rising of the North" against Queen Elizabeth in 1569. In 1626 it was sold to Sir Henry Vane, Treasurer to Charles I, and his descendants, now the Lords Barnard, live there still. Though it appears to be a moated 14C castle, the interiors date mainly from the 18C and 19C. The house contains a good collection of paintings and furniture, and some excellent Meissen porcelain. The graceful statue of a manacled **Greek Slave** is by Hiram Powers, an American sculptor who caused a sensation when he exhibited it at the Great Exhibition of 1851.

There is a fine **Walled Garden**, where a 200 year-old fig and ancient yews blend with more recent features.

Sion Hill Hall – *Kirby Wiske; 20mi/32km south of Richmond, off A 167.* &⏱ *Open Easter Sun and Mon, and Bank Hol Mon; Jun-Sep, Wed 1-5pm (last admission 4pm). May-Oct:* ☜ *Guided tours by prior arrangement.* ☜ *£4.50. Parking. Tearoom. Gift shop.* ☎ *01845 587 206; Fax 01845 587 486; sionhall@virgin.net; www.sionhillhall.co.uk.* Walter Brierley, "the Lutyens of the north", designed this red-brick house for the Stancliffe family in 1913. Tours cover virtually the whole building, including the boudoir, the nursery (doll collection) and the butler's pantry. An eclectic collection of china, art, furniture and clocks was assembled by the last owner, Herbert Mawer. In the grounds is the **Birds of Prey Centre** which gives flying displays of its eagles, hawks and owls and runs courses.

Bolton Castle – *12mi/19km southwest by A 6108 and a minor road (right).* &⏱ *Open daily, 10am-5pm (4pm Dec-Feb).* ⏱ *Closed 24-25 Dec.* ☜ *£5. Parking. Tearoom.* ☎ *01969 623 981; Fax 01969 623 332; harry@boltoncastle.co.uk; www.boltoncastle.co.uk.* Richard Scrope started building his castle in 1379. It is basically a comfortable house of the period, built round a courtyard. For defence the castle has massive corner towers, turrets and portcullises and the whole southeast corner could be sealed off as a self-contained keep. Bolton served as prison for Mary Queen of Scots in 1568-69. Despite being "slighted" after the Civil War, it is well preserved and parts are still roofed.

RIPON★

North Yorkshire, ENGLAND

POPULATION 13 806

MICHELIN ATLAS P 40 OR MAP 502 P 21

At nine o'clock every night of the year, a horn is blown in the Market Square of this small cathedral city on the southern edge of the North York Moors. It is to "set the Watch", a custom which commemorates the responsibility of the medieval **Wakeman** for the safety of the citizens at night. A toll of two pence per house door was paid to him annually; from this "insurance premium," he made good any losses suffered. ⏺ *Minster Road* ☎*Fax 01765 604 625 (seasonal); ripontic@harrogate.gov.uk; www.yorkshiredales.org.*

Sights

Ripon Cathedral★ – *Minster Road.* &⏱ *Open daily, 7.30am (8am Sat-Sun) to 6.30pm.* ☜ *Donation £3.* ☜ *Guided tour (1hr; 5 languages), bookable in advance. Leaflet (9 languages). Parking.* ☎ *01765 604 108; www.riponcathedral.org.uk.* The cathedral was started in 1254 on the Saxon crypt of St Wilfrid's Church (AD 672). The imposing Early English west front is "the finest in England" (Pevsner).

The medieval font stands near the west door in the south aisle. Above it are roundels of 14C glass, the remains of the great east window which was shot out in 1643 by

Parliamentary troops. They also destroyed the "idolatrous images" on the **choir screen**, which were replaced by one carver during the Second World War.

The tiny **Saxon Crypt** (11ft/3.5m x 8ft/2.5m x 9ft/3m high) *(access by steps on the south side of the nave altar)* was built by St Wilfrid on his return from Rome. The reconstruction of the tower, following its collapse in 1450, resulted in a contrast between the Transitional style of the older north and west walls and the Perpendicular of the later south and east walls.

Misericords and exquisite **choir stalls** were carved over five years by William Bromflete and a handful of craftsmen, the "Ripon school", who worked here and at Beverley at the end of the 15C. On one is an "Elephant and Castle", often said to be the English misinterpretation of "Infanta of Castile" – Eleanor, Queen of Edward I – which has since been widely used as a name for public houses throughout the country. The **Chapel of the Holy Spirit** has a striking modern metal screen, symbolising the Pentecostal "tongues of flame."

The **Treasury** displays silverware given to the Cathedral, as well as the "Ripon jewel," a Saxon gold brooch set with amber and garnets, found nearby in 1976.

Market Square – It is one of the largest (2 acres/almost 1ha) in the north of the country. The **Obelisk**, at the four corners of which the horn is blown, dates from 1781 and commemorates the 60-year term as Member of Parliament of William Aislabie, of nearby Studley Royal.

The **Town Hall**, built by Wyatt in 1801, has an Ionic portico and carries along its frieze the motto "Except ye Lord Keep ye Cittie ye Wakeman Waketh in Vain". The four Town Horns, including the **Charter Horn**, many centuries old and symbolising the granting of the first Charter to Ripon in AD 886, can be seen in the Mayor's Parlour. The latest horn was presented in 1886, marking the 1000th anniversary of the Charter, and came from the Chillingham herd of wild cattle (*see ALNWICK*).

The **Wakeman's House**, a 14C two-storeyed, timber-framed house, was the home of the last holder of the office, Hugh Ripley, who in 1604, under the Charter granted by James I, became first Mayor of Ripon.

Ripon Workhouse Museum of Yorkshire Poor Law – *Allhallowgate. Open daily, late-Mar to Oct 11am-4pm; last admission 30 min before closing. £5 joint ticket with Prison and Police Museum. 01765 690 799; ripon.museums@btclick.com; www.ripon. co.uk/museums.* This 1854 building demonstrates the grim alternatives of desperate squalor (shown in a display of 19C photographs) and the harsh workhouse regime, which was often the only option for those on the margins of Victorian society – the unemployed, orphans, geriatrics and lunatics. Tramps were deloused in the coffin-like baths and put to bed in tiny night cells; in return they chopped wood or broke stones.

Prison and Police Museum – *St Marygate. Open daily, late-Mar to Oct, 11am-4pm; last admission 30 min before closing. £5 joint ticket with Workhouse Museum. 01765 690 799; ripon.museums@btclick.com; www.ripon.co.uk/museums.* In the old prison two centuries of policing are traced with exhibits including a pillory and whipping posts.

Excursions

Fountains Abbey and Studely Royal★★★ – *See FOUNTAINS ABBEY.*

Lightwater Valley – *North Stainley, 3mi/5km north of Ripon off A 6108. Open second weekend Apr- end Oct. Weekends only Apr-May and Sep-Oct; weekends and some weekdays Jun; daily school hols. Call to confirm. Park open 10am, rides 10.30am; closes from 4:30pm, depending on time of year. £15.50. 0870 458 0070, 0040; Fax 01765 635 359; leisure@lightwatervalley.co.uk; www.lightwatervalley.net.* Set in a country park of 175 acre/71ha this is one of the biggest theme parks in the north of England, with rides for all ages. Lightwater Country Village is a complex of factory outlet shops which sell gifts, clothes and household goods.

Black Sheep Brewery – *Masham, 8mi/13km north of Ripon by A 6108. Open Jul-Aug, daily, 11am-11pm (5.30pm Tue and Sun); Mar-Jun and Sep-Dec, Tue-Sun, 11am-11pm (5.50pm Tue and Sun); Jan-Feb telephone for times. Closed 25-26 Dec. Telephone for tour times/prices. 01765 680 100; 01765 689 227; sue.dempsey@blacksheep.co.uk; www.blacksheep.co.uk.* The Theakston family has maintained a long brewing tradition in Masham, and when the firm was taken over in 1989 Paul Theakston built this brewhouse in a former kiln. The tour shows the "tower" system, whereby the raw materials enter at the top and progress by gravity to the brew itself, at the bottom. A shop sells woollens, stationery and gifts on the black sheep theme.

The World of James Herriot – *23 Kirkgate in Thirsk. 12mi/20km northeast by A 61.* 🕐 *Open daily, 10am-6pm (5pm Nov-Feb).* 🎫 *£4. Parking. Shop.* ☎ *01845 524 234, Fax 01845 525 333; www.hambleton.gov.uk.* A tour of the house and surgery reveals the dedication of the veterinarian turned author, who won the hearts of the many viewers of the popular television series *All Creatures Great and Small*.

Newby Hall★ – *4mi/6km southeast by B 6265 and a minor road.* ♿🕐 *House: Open Apr-Sep, Tue-Sun and Bank Hols (Jul-Aug daily), noon-4.30pm (last admission). Garden: as for house, 11am-5pm (last admission).* 🎫 *House and garden £8.20; garden only, £6.70. Guidebook. Parking. Licensed garden restaurant. Wheelchairs available; ramps.* ☎ *01423 322 583; info@newbyhall.com; www.newbyhall.com.* The original 17C mellow brick mansion, which was extended and remodelled during the 18C by John Carr and Robert Adam, is renowned for its Adam interiors, including the Gobelins **Tapestry Room** with the *Loves of the Gods* **tapestries★** on an unusual dove-grey background and the Gallery designed for a rare collection of Classical sculpture brought from Italy by William Weddell in 1765. Additional features of interest include the Chippendale furniture and a collection of chamber pots (16C-19C).

From the south front of the house **gardens** descend to the River Ure; the main axis is a broad grass walk, flanked by herbaceous borders; on either side extend compartmented gardens planned to come into flower at different seasons. There are many rare plants, trees and shrubs and the National Collection of Cornus. A miniature passenger railway runs beside the river from the Lime Avenue to the Adventure Gardens for children. The woodland walk explores the park. The Church of Christ the Consoler, near the park gates, is a memorial to Frederick Vyner, who was killed by brigands in Greece in 1870; it was commissioned by his mother and designed by William Burges in the Early English style.

ROCHESTER

Kent, ENGLAND

POPULATION 23 971

MICHELIN ATLAS P 12 OR MAP 504 V 29

The Romans built Durobrivae to dominate the point where Watling Street crossed the River Medway some 35 mi/53 km east of the City of London. The 12C Norman castle still does, and it also dominates the cathedral and the town, a walled town cut in two by "the silent High Street, full of gables with old beams and timbers" (Charles Dickens).

Rochester and the Medway area are the scene of several of Dickens' novels *(Pickwick Papers, Great Expectations, The Mystery of Edwin Drood)* **and the Tudor Poor Travellers house, or Watts' Charity** (🕐 *Open Mar-Oct, Tue-Sat, 2-5pm.* 🕐 *Closed Bank Hols. Donation.* ☎ *01634 845 609)* on High Street also appears in one of his short stories. 🔼 *95 High Street* ☎ *01634 843 666; Fax: 01634 847891; visitor. centre@medway.gov.uk; www.medway.gov.uk/index/leisure/tourism.*

The Roman Conquest

The Medway area is rich in prehistoric and Roman sites. During Emperor Claudius's invasion of Britain, Roman legions landed near Richborough in Kent and moved westwards. An unhewn stone (15ft/5m high), erected near a ford on the Medway at Snodland, south of Rochester, in 1998, is a belated **memorial** to a decisive Roman victory in AD 43 over the army of the Celtic king Cunobelinus – Shakespeare's Cymbeline. This event sealed the fate of Britain which became part of the Roman Empire. The battle, which is described by the Greek historian Dio Cassius, probably took place near a fordable point on the Medway – near Snodland according to modern historians.

Sights

Castle★ – ⏰ *Open daily, 10am-6pm (4pm Oct-Mar).* ⏰ *Closed 24-26 Dec, 1 Jan. Audio guide (additional charge).* ☎ *£4.* ☎ *01634 402 276; www.english-heritage.org.uk.* The early **curtain walls** were built by Gundulf, Bishop of Rochester and architect of Rochester Cathedral and the Tower of London. The present massive **keep** was built by William de Corbeil, Archbishop of Canterbury, in 1127 and its ruins are an outstanding example of Norman military architecture. The dogtooth decoration on the arches, the great hall and the 13C bastions on the curtain wall are noteworthy.

Cathedral★ – ♿⏰ *Open daily, 7.30am-6pm (5pm Sat).* ⏰ *Donation £3. Guide books available. Leaflets (3 languages). Refreshments.* ☎ *01634 401 301; Fax 01634 401 410; cathedral@rochester.anglican.org; www.rochester.anglican.org.* Bishop Gundulf (1024-1108) followed Lanfranc (⏰ *see CANTERBURY*) to England and held England's second episcopal see from 1077 to his death in 1108. The cathedral was subsequently extended on two main occasions and is mostly 12C and 13C. Of particular interest is the Norman west front, rich in blind arcading, and its centrepiece, the exuberantly sculptured **west doorway** (1160) showing a strong French influence. Beyond the six Norman **nave bays** the cathedral is essentially Early English. The painting on the choir wall is the *Wheel of Fortune* and dates from the 13C when the whole of the cathedral walls were similarly painted. Note the carvings on the chapter room doorway (c 1350) and the west end of the crypt which is part of Gundulf's original work.

On the north side between the two transepts is Gundulf's **tower** (c 1100) and to the south, the ruins of the 12C cloisters.

Guildhall – *Strood.* ♿⏰ *Open daily, 10am-4.30pm (4pm last admission).* ⏰ *Closed Christmas. Wheelchair access ground floor.* ☎ *01634 848 717; Fax 01634 832 919; guildhall.museum@medway.gov.uk; www.medway.gov.uk.* In this handsome Renaissance building with its 18C gilded ship weather-vane, the museum describes the infamous Medway hulks or prison ships, with more genteel Victorian life displayed in the adjoining Conservancy wing.

Charles Dickens Centre – ⏰ *Closed for refurbishment.* ☎ *01634 844 176; Fax 01634 844 676.* At the Elizabethan Eastgate House 20C technology brings new life to the often dark world of Dickens and his characters. In the gardens outside stands the author's **Swiss Chalet** from Gads Hill Place, his last home.

Excursion

World Naval Base, Chatham★★ – *2mi/3km northeast of the Cathedral.* ♿⏰ *Open Easter to early-Nov, daily, 10am-6pm (4pm last admission); early Nov-early Dec and Feb-Easter, Wed, Sat-Sun, 10am-4pm.* ⏰ *Closed early Dec to Jan.* ⏰ *£10. Parking. Licensed restaurant, tea shop, picnic areas.* ☎ *01634 823 800; www.thedockyard.co.uk.* Established in the reign of Henry VIII, this cradle of British sea power built nearly 500 ships, including HMS *Victory*, before the Royal Navy finally left in 1984. The splendid complex (80 acres/32ha) of historic maritime buildings and docks now reinterprets the life of the dockyard through exhibits and demonstrations, from the making of flags and sails in the **Sail and Colour Loft** to the ropery (1 140ft/347m long). In the award-winning **Wooden Walls** the 18C dockyard comes to life as the visitor follows the construction of the warship *Valiant* and at **Lifeboat!** a tour aboard several of the historic boats of the Royal National Lifeboat Collection gives an insight into shipbuilding crafts and maritime history. The imposing Main Gate, bearing the arms of George III, the Commissioner's House and the church are also of interest.

Leeds Castle★ – *Maidstone, 11mi/18km southeast by A 229 and M 20.* ♿⏰ *Castle: Open 11am-5pm (10.15am-3.30pm Nov-Feb). Park: Open daily, 10am-5pm (3pm Nov-Feb).* ⏰ *Closed last Sat Jun, first Sat Jul, 25 Dec.* ⏰ *£13; park and garden only, £10.50. Brochure, illustrated guide book and pre-booked guided tour (8 languages). Parking. Restaurant and outdoor kiosks. Wheelchairs available; minibus from car park to castle; lift; induction loops; Braille guide.* ☎ *01622 765 400; Fax 01622 735 616; enquiries@leeds-castle.co.uk; www.leeds-castle.com.* Originally Norman, built on two islands in a lake, it was described by Lord Conway as "the loveliest castle in the world." A romantic stone **bridge** links the keep which rises sheer from the lake and the turreted and battlemented main building. The interior is graced by splendid **works of art** (14C-19C): statues, carvings, tapestries. Part of the castle serves as an international conference centre.

The glorious **park** and **gardens** include a duckery, aviary, secret grotto and maze.

ROYAL TUNBRIDGE WELLS

Kent, ENGLAND

POPULATION 60 272

MICHELIN ATLAS P 12 OR MAP 504 U 30

TOWN PLAN IN MICHELIN GUIDE GREAT BRITAIN AND IRELAND

A graceful combination of Georgiana and Victoriana amid parks, vistas and with a vast semi-wild common, Tunbridge Wells owes its good fortune to the accidental discovery of its mineral springs in 1606 by Lord North; it soon became a magnet for the fashionable. Queen Henrietta Maria spent six weeks there, in a tent, after the birth of her son, Charles II. Queen Anne provided the tiled paving after which the **Pantiles** are named and Queen Victoria who spent holidays here commented "Dear Tunbridge Wells, I am so fond of it." ▯ *Old Fish Market, The Pantiles TN2 5TN* ☎ *01892 515 675; Fax 01892 534 660; touristinformationcentre@tunbridgewells.gov.uk; www.visittunbridgewells.com.*

Visit

The Pantiles★ – This perfect pedestrian precinct is on two levels with an Upper Walk and a Lower Walk. The **Bath House** (1804) still shows off its chalybeate spring; the **Corn Exchange** (1802), once a theatre, displays Doric columns and Ceres, Goddess of the Harvest, on the roof; and the **Music Gallery** remains a reminder of the town's past elegance. **Union House** (1969, by Michael Levell) at one end of the Pantiles is an object lesson on how old and new can stand together in dignity. The **Church of King Charles the Martyr** at the other end is a lesson in modesty and adaptability. The 1678 church was squared in 1696, the interior turned round and given a ceiling by Wren's plasterer, Henry Doogood.

Calverley Park★ – Not so much a park as a neo-Classical new town by Decimus Burton. Inspired by Bath, it is always homogenous but never repetitive, lavish in space but spare in idiom; the ensemble is best seen around Calverley Park Crescent.

Excursions

North of Tunbridge Wells

Knole★★

15mi/24km by A 26, A 21 and A 225. Sevenoaks. House: ♿ ⏰*Open late-Mar to Oct, Wed-Sun, Good Friday and Bank Hols, noon-4pm. Garden: Open May-Sep, Wed-Sun 10.30am-5pm. Park: Open daily to pedestrians.* ⛔ *House £6.40, garden only, £2. Parking. Braille Guide. Tearoom.* ☎ *01732 462 100, 01732 450 608 (infoline), Fax 01732 465 528, knole@nationaltrust.org.uk; www.nationaltrust.org.uk.* This great late-medieval, Tudor and Jacobean mansion, standing on its knoll (hence its name) in a vast deer park, is one of the finest in England.

The house built c 1456 by Thomas Bourchier, Archbishop of Canterbury and later enlarged by Henry VIII, passed to the Sackville family who extended it in c 1603. It was the childhood home of **Vita Sackville-West**. With seven courts (the days of the week), 52 staircases (weeks of the year) and 365 rooms (days of the year), she likened it to a "medieval village". Horace Walpole, looking through different eyes, spoke of its "beautiful, decent simplicity".

Exterior – The roofline bristles with gables, pinnacles, chimneystacks and battlements, and austere gatehouses open into the Green and Stone Courts.

Interior – The **Great Hall** with its exquisite Jacobean screen is impressive. The elaborate grisaille decor of the **Great Staircase** sets off a life-size nude of the beauty Gianetta Baccelli in the lobby; the second-oldest harpsichord case made in England in 1622 is displayed in the **Spangle Dressing Room**. The rooms are ornamented with splendid friezes, ceilings, panelling and chimneypieces, in particular the **Ballroom, Crimson Drawing Room** and **Cartoon Gallery** where are displayed ornate furnishings and fine paintings (17C-18C family portraits, works by Lely, Reynolds, copies of Raphael's Cartoons).

The highlight of the tour of Knole is the **King's Room**, with its gaudy grisailles, ostrich feathers, expensive embroidery and silver ornamentation; it is "the only vulgar room in the house" (Vita Sackville-West).

Ightham Mote★★

10mi/16km on A 26 and A 227. Ivy Hatch. ♿🕐 *Open late-Mar to early-Nov, Sun-Mon and Wed-Fri, 10.30am-5.30pm (last admission 5pm), Garden 10am-5.30pm.* ⌨ *£7. Braille guide. Parking. Tea pavilion.* ☎ *01732 810 378, 01732 811 145 (infoline); Fax 01732 811 029; ighthammote@nationaltrust.org.uk; www.nationaltrust.org.uk.* Ightham (pronounced "item"), built of stone and timber in 1340, is the best preserved moated manor house in England, its survival probably largely due to its secluded site.

The crenellated Gatehouse leads into the Courtyard, where the atmosphere is immediately one of calm and privacy. Opposite is the **Great Hall**, built in the 1340s, featuring a fine Perpendicular window (c 1480) with five coats of arms in stained glass and three roof arches, one in stone and two in timber, supported on amusing sculpted corbel figures. The carved **frieze** above the fireplace and the **panelling** were designed by Norman Shaw in the 1870s. In the stairwell beyond, the **Jacobean staircase** has a Saracen's head, the Selby family crest, carved on the newel post.

The visit leads past the Servants' Passage, the Housekeeper's Room, the Crypt (the least altered part of the 14C building), and upstairs to the Oriel Room, the Old Chapel, a suite of bedrooms and past the Chapel Corridor (note the imaginative repairs to the woodwork beneath the window) to the **New Chapel**, historically the most interesting room, with the Great Hall, in the house. It has a unique **barrel-vaulted roof**, dating from 1470-80 and restored in 1890 and 1997, with early 16C painted panels decorated with tributes to the sovereign (pomegranate of Aragon, roses of York, Lancaster and the Tudors). Further rooms open to visitors include the Drawing Room (18C handpainted Chinese wallpaper, restored), the Billiards Room (unusual collection of meat drainers) and the Library.

East of Tunbridge Wells

Scotney Castle Garden – *6mi/9km by A 264, A 21 and local road. Lamberhurst. Garden:* ♿🕐 *Open late-Mar to Oct, Wed-Sun and Bank Hol Mon, 11am-6pm; last admission 1hr before closing. Old castle: open May to mid-Sep, same days and times as garden.* 🕐 *Closed Good Friday. Wheelchairs available; paths very steep in places.* ⌨ *£4.80. Braille guide. Parking.* ☎ *01892 891 081; Fax 01892 890 110; scotneycastle@nationaltrust.org.uk; www. nationaltrust.org.u.k* From a bastion near the Victorian stone mansion the eye is led sharply downwards into an enchanting scene – the steep valley sides, the moated ruin of Roger Ashburnam's 14C castle and the 17C house built into it, luxuriant trees and shrubs, all drawn together in the 19C to form a picturesque landscaped composition.

Sissinghurst Castle Garden★ – *13mi/21km by A 264, A 21 and A 262 near Cranbrook.* ♿🕐 *Open late-Mar to early-Nov, Fri-Tue, 11am to 6.30pm/dusk; last admission 1hr before closing.* ⌨ *£7.50. Braille guide. Parking. Licensed restaurant.* ☎ *01580 710 700; 01580 710 701 (infoline); Fax 01580 710 702; sissinghurst@nationaltrust.org.uk; www.nationaltrust.org.uk.* The road passes through the pretty village of **Goudhurst**. The main street rises steeply to the parish church on the hilltop. All around are the orchards and hopfields of the "Garden of England."

In 1930 **Vita Sackville-West** and her husband Harold Nicolson discovered the Sissinghurst estate. She commented enthusiastically: "I fell in love; love at first sight. I saw what could be made of it... a castle running away into sordidness and squalor, a garden crying out for rescue." The **Tower** (view) became her study and the **garden** their monument. It combines "the strictest formality of design with the maximum informality in planting". Axial walks with gardens opening off – each with a separate colour scheme – culminate in arches and statues. The result is a glorious synthesis of architectural and natural forms and colours.

West of Tunbridge Wells

Penshurst Place★

8mi/12km by A 26 and B 2176. ♿🕐 *Open late Mar-Oct, daily, noon-4pm (10.30am-6pm grounds); Mar, Sat-Sun.* ⌨ *Grounds £5.50; house and grounds £7.* 📷 *Guided tours (45min; 3 languages) mornings only by appointment; house £7; garden £8; house and garden £10. Room guides (7 languages). Parking. Refreshments. Wheelchairs (no charge).* ☎ *01892 870 307; Fax 01892 870 866; enquiries@penhurstplace.com; www. penshurstplace.com.* The mansion, which was the home of the Elizabethan poet **Sir Philip Sidney** (1554-86), is set in a pretty neo-Tudor village, clustering around the 13C church of St John the Baptist, with its Sidney Chapel. The original Great Hall (1346), built of coarse sandstone, has been added to with early Tudor, Jacobean and neo-Gothic wings.

Interior – Inside the Hall, the chestnut **timber roof** is held up by unusual life-size carvings of humble peasants. The open hearth is a rare feature and the screens are decorated with tracery. The elegant **furnishings** of the formal rooms include rare furniture, tapestries and family portraits.

The great terrace is the focus of the formal **gardens** with their clipped hedges. There is a nature trail, a farm museum and an enchanting **Toy Museum** with puppets, rocking horses and 19C dolls.

Chiddingstone

16mi/24km by A 26, B 2176, B 2027 and local road. The delightful 16C-17C dwellings, timber-framed, tile-hung, pargeted and gabled, clustered around St Mary's Church, present a rare combination of 14C Gothic and Jacobean Gothic styles. "In its way, Chiddingstone is perfect" (Pevsner).

To the west stands **Chiddingstone Castle,** *(Nr. Edenbridge. & Open (functions permitting) Jun-Sep, Thu, (Sun and Bank Hol 11am) 2pm to 5.30pm; also Good Friday, Easter Sun and Easter Mon and Spring Bank Hol. £5. Guide book (2 languages). Parking. Refreshments. No wheelchair access to castle. 01892 870 347; www.chiddingstonecastle.org.uk)* a 19C rebuilding with castellations of an earlier mansion. It is the setting for works of art amassed by the eccentric Denys Eyre Bower, a bank clerk with a remarkable eye and great enthusiasm. The collection includes portraits (Nell Gwynn), miniatures, mementoes of the Stuarts, Japanese armour and lacquerware.

Hever Castle★

13mi/21km by A 264, B 2026 and local road. & House: Open Mar-Nov, daily, noon-6pm (5pm last admission). Gardens: Open 11am-6pm (5pm last admission). Castle and gardens: £9.20; gardens only, £7.30. Historical fact sheet (7 languages). Leaflet (4 languages). Parking. Restaurants. Wheelchair access to gardens and ground floor of castle. 01732 865 224; Fax 01732 866 796; mail@hevercastle.co.uk; www.hevercastle.co.uk. This fortified manor house protected by a moat and the drawbridge and portcullis of the massive gatehouse stands in an idyllic countryside setting. It has close associations with the romantic, then tragic story of **Anne Boleyn** and King Henry VIII. In 1903 William Waldorf Astor, a rich American, acquired the manor and lavishly restored the neglected castle and landscaped the grounds.

Interior – The decor of the rooms around the intimate courtyard are more opulent than in the Boleyns' time. Much of the **woodwork** is a triumphant re-creation of the finest Renaissance craftsmanship. There are portraits of Anne, and one, by Holbein, of Henry; in her little room is the Book of Hours the young queen took to her execution on 19 May 1536. A costumed figure exhibition "Henry VIII and his Six Wives" and tableaux representing scenes from the life and times of Anne Boleyn have been set up in the Long Gallery.

Hever Castle

A. F. Kersting/MICHELIN

Gardens – The main focus is the artificial lake (38 acre/15ha), approached via an elaborate loggia and an **Italian garden** which is the frame for Astor's important collection of **antique statuary and sculpture** from Italy. Topiary, a maze and, leading through fine parkland, Anne Boleyn's Walk round out the gardens' features.

Chartwell

15mi/24km by A 264, B 206 and local road. Mappleton Road. ♿🕐*House, gardens and studio: Open Jul-Aug, Tue-Sun and Bank Hol Mon, 11am-5pm; late-Mar to Jun and Sep to early-Nov, Wed-Sun and Bank Hol Mon, last admission 4.15pm.* ⊜ *£8; garden and studio £4. Parking. Licensed restaurant.* ☎ *01732 868 381, Infoline 01732 866 368; Fax 01732 868 193; chartwell@nationaltrust.org.uk; www.nationaltrust.org.uk.* The restored Tudor house was the home of **Sir Winston Churchill** (1874-1965). It is packed with Churchilliana including many of his paintings and reflects the comfortable domestic life of the great man. The **walls** of the fine gardens were partly built by Churchill himself; there is a splendid southward prospect over rolling countryside.

Westerham

The trim former market town perched on a hill was the birthplace of General Wolfe, conqueror of New France in 1759. His residence, **Quebec House,** *(Quebec Square.* 🕐 *Open early-Apr to Oct, Tue and Sun, 2-5.30pm.* ⊜ *£3.20. Public car park 120m east of house.* ☎ *01372 868 381; www.nationaltrust.org.uk)* has interesting mementoes and his statue, sword aloft, shares the sloping green with a seated figure of Churchill.

Ashdown Forest

15mi/24km by A 264, B 2188 and B 2110 towards Wych Cross. The road runs through the picturesque villages of **Groombridge** and **Hartfield**; both have pretty weather-boarded and tile-hung houses.

A short distance before Wych Cross is the **Ashdown Forest Centre** (♿🕐 *Open Apr-Sep, daily, 2pm (11am Sat-Sun and Bank Hol) to 5pm; Oct-Mar, Sat-Sun and Bank Hol, 11am-5pm.* 🕐 *Closed 25-26 Dec. Parking. Access for wheelchair users ground floor. 01342 823 583; conservators@ashdownforest.org; www.ashdownforest.org)* housed in three rebuilt thatched barns, which explains the area's natural history.

The **Weald**, a wooded tract of sandy hills and clay vales, extends between the bold escarpments of the North and South Downs. In former times the dense forest provided timber for shipbuilding and wood for charcoal production associated with the exploitation of the local ironstone. The "hammer ponds", which supplied water-power for the many forges, are the most visible traces of the local iron industry which flourished in the 16C and 17C (🕯 *see LEWES: Anne of Cleves Museum).* This was the scene of AA Milne's books about Christopher Robin and Winnie-the-Pooh.

The core of the Weald is formed by the heaths and pine and birch woodlands of the sandy upland where Ashdown Forest survives. Parking and picnic spots invite visitors to enjoy the fine **views** and discover the countryside on foot.

RYE

East Sussex, ENGLAND

POPULATION 3 708

MICHELIN ATLAS P 12 OR MAP 504 W 31

A multitude of red-roofed houses building up to a massive squat-towered church, this exquisite small hill town is visible far off across the vast expanse of eastward-stretching levels. Its early history was one of struggle both on and with the sea. it lies just 40 mi/64km northwest of Boulogne and from 1191 was one of the **Cinque Ports**, the maritime league of Kent and Sussex towns established by Edward the Confessor to supply ships and men for the defence of the realm; despite this it suffered repeated sackings by the French. It was also battered by storms which violently changed the course of the River Rother in the 13C and later destroyed many of its buildings. The town is still a minor port, though the sea's retreat has left it two miles inland.

Tranquil centuries of decline and its former remoteness preserved Rye's charming townscape, though much of its medieval fabric wears a Georgian exterior. Artists and writers, among them Henry James, have lived here, drawn by its antique air or by the lonely landscapes and strange light of the surrounding marsh. ▯ *Heritage Centre, Strand Quay TN31 7AY ☎ 01797 226 696; Fax 01797 223460; ryetic@rother.gov. uk; www.visitrye.co.uk* ▯ *Queens Square, Priory Meadow, Hastings, TN34 1TL b 01424 781111; Fax 01424 781186; hic@hastings.gov.uk; www.1066country.com.*

Don't Miss: A drink in the Mermaid Inn; Bodiam Castle; Battle Abbey and battle-field.

Organizing Your Time: allow half a day to a full day for Rye, stay overnight and allow one to two days for excursions.

Old Town★★

With its steep and intricate streets, a wealth of different building materials and sudden glimpses of the countryside, the whole of Rye between ruined walls and former cliff-line repays careful exploration on foot.

From the riverside warehouses of Strand Quay, where the **son et lumière** accompanying the meticulously crafted **The Story of Rye**, (*Strand Quay.* ♿⊙*Open Mar-Oct, 9am-5.30pm; Nov-Feb, 10am-4pm. ☜ £2.50 Show (30min; 4 languages) every 30min. ☎ 01797 226 696; Fax 01797 223 460; ryetic@rother.gov.uk; www.rye.org.uk/heritage)* effectively evokes the past, the cobbled **Mermaid Street**★ rises sharply. Its varied buildings include the 15C **Mermaid Inn**, reputed haunt of ruthless smuggler gangs. Looking towards Church Square is the handsome Georgian façade of Lamb House, home of Henry James from 1897 and later of the satirical novelist EF Benson.

St Mary's Church – ♿⊙ *Open daily (except during services) 9am-6pm (4.30pm winter). ☜ Tower donation £2. Brochure. ☎ 01797 224 935.* This large and impressive building, which was begun in the 12C, has a famous 16C clock, its pendulum (18ft/5.5m) swinging inside, its elaborate face on the outside of the north transept, flanked by jolly painted quarter boys who strike the quarters but not the hours. From the tower there is an incomparable **view**★ of Rye's red-tiled roofs and all the country around.

Ypres Tower – This sturdy little 13C citadel on its clifftop perch, long used as a prison, now houses **Rye Castle Museum** (⊙ *Open Apr-Oct, Thu-Mon, 10.30am-1pm and 2-5pm; Nov-Mar, Sat-Sun, 10.30am-12.30pm and 1.30-3.30pm; last admission 30min before closing. East Street site 2-5pm weekdays, Sat-Sun same hours as other; ☜ £2.90 (both sites); £1.90 (single site). ☎ 01797 226728; www.ryemuseum.co.uk),* which has an annexe in East Street.

High Street – Among the many delights of the long and gently winding street is the Dutch gabled **Old Grammar School** of 1636. The round towers of the Landgate mark the point at which an isthmus connected the island port with the mainland.

Excursions

Bodiam Castle★★

13mi/21km northwest by A 268. After 11mi/18km turn left at Sandhurst and follow minor roads to Bodiam. ♿⊙ *nr. Robertsbridge. Open early-Feb to Oct, daily, 10am-6pm; early-Jan to early-Feb and Nov to mid-Feb, Sat-Sun, 10am-4pm; last admission 1hr before closing. ☜ £4.40. Parking £2. Braille guide. Tearoom. 01580 830 436; Fax 01580 830 398; bodiamcastle@nationaltrust.org.uk; www.nationaltrust.org.uk.* In a pretty landscaped setting among low hills, overlooking the levels of the River Rother, this archetypal medieval castle sits four-square within its protecting moat. It was built in 1385-88 to block movement inland by marauding Frenchmen up the then navigable river, and it retains its great gatehouse, massive curtain walls and drum towers (60ft/18m high) at each corner. A brick and concrete blockhouse, a "pillbox" of the Second World War, confirms the site's strategic importance.

Romney Marsh

East by A 270 and A 259 or B 2075 and local roads. Eastwards from Rye stretches the "Sixth Continent", the seemingly infinite levels of Walland, Denge and Romney Marshes. This once isolated land was won over bit by bit from the sea over a thousand years, yielding rich pasture for its famous sheep.

On its east coast the little resorts with magnificent beaches of sand and pebbles, linked by the miniature mainline **Romney, Hythe and Dymchurch Railway** (15mi/24km *New Romney Station.* ⊙*Open Easter to Sep, daily; Mar and Oct, Sat-Sun. ☜ £10.50 maximum fare. Children's playground (New Romney). Buffet (New Romney and Dungeness). Station shops. ☎ 01797 362 353; Fax 01797 363 591; enquiries@rdhr.org.uk; www.rhdr. org.uk),* are busy in the summer. A giant nuclear power station now stands on the shingle spit at Dungeness which is also a nature reserve.

Inland is a quiet landscape of remote churches and ancient hamlets (Old Romney, Brookland, Fairfield, St Mary in the Marsh) lost in a web of meandering lanes and watercourses. Along the foot of the old cliff from Rye to Hythe (🕯 *see DOVER*) runs the **Royal Military Canal,** dug to facilitate the transport of troops and heavy munitions between the Martello towers and coastal batteries.

Winchelsea★

2.5mi/4km west by A 259. Planted in the late 12C by **Edward I** on a sandstone bluff, to replace its storm-wracked namesake three miles away, Winchelsea never prospered in its role as a port for the Gascon wine trade. Repeatedly attacked by the French and abandoned by a receding sea, some of its chequer-board plan remained unbuilt, though three gateways remain, the Pipewell Gate, the New Gate lost in the countryside to the south, and the **Strand Gate** looking forlornly from the old clifftop to the distant sea. Some of the 18C and 19C houses in the quiet grass-verged streets have vaulted medieval cellars, a reminder of the early wine trade. All that remains of the grand town church of **St Thomas** is an impressive chancel, its side chapels containing fine 14C **effigies**★.

Hastings Castle

12mi/19km southwest by A 259. 🕐 *Castle Hill Road. Open Easter-Oct, 10am-5pm; Oct-Easter, 11am-3pm.* ✆ *£3.40.* ☎ *01424 781 111; www.discoverhastings.co.uk.* The ruins of William the Conqueror's first English castle (originally a wooden structure) stand high above the Old Town and seaside resort below. The history of the castle and of the battle are told in an informative audio-visual presentation, **The 1066 Story**.

The Victorian funicular **West Hill Cliff Railway** (🕐 *Open daily, 10am (11am Oct-Mar) to 5.30pm (4pm Oct-Mar).* ✆ *80p.* ☎ *01424 781 030)* provides an easier alternative to the steep climb.

Battle★

18mi/29km southwest by A 259, B 2093 and A 2100. The momentous victory, on 14 October 1066, of the Normans over King Harold's English army is marked by the remains of the great commemorative abbey built on its hilltop site by William the Conqueror, and also in the name of the little town which grew up to serve it.

Abbey★ – (EH) ♿🕐 *Open daily, 10am-6pm (Oct-Mar 4pm).* 🕐 *Closed 1 Jan and 24-26 Dec.* ✆ *£5.30. Audio-visual presentation (10min). Audio guide (4 languages). Braille guides. Parking (charge).* ☎ *01424 773 792; www.english-heritage.org.uk.* Following an audio-visual introduction in the **visitor centre**, an audio-tour allows visitors to follow the individual stories of three characters around the battlefield as the fighting progresses (or view the battlefield from the terrace), before visiting the abbey buildings.

Over the humble buildings of the town's marketplace rises the imposing but graceful mass of the 14C **gatehouse**, battlemented and richly decorated. Most of the great Benedictine abbey beyond was systematically dismantled at the Dissolution, though its outlines may be traced among the remaining fragments. The abbey church's high altar, erected at William's command over the spot where Harold fell, is identified by a plaque.

Stepped down the steep slope are the impressive remains of the **monks' dormitory,** its high gable with three rows of lancet windows staring blankly south towards the battlefield. The most complete survival is the west range of the cloister, now part of a private school.

A **museum** in the gatehouse presents an exhibition on monastic life and the history of the abbey.

Battlefield★ – From the **terrace walk** there is a commanding view of the tranquil scene over which this most decisive of English battles was fought. It was on this ridge that Harold deployed his men after their exhausting forced march from York. On the far side of the swampy valley were ranged their Norman adversaries with their French and Breton allies, fresh from their nearby beachhead at Hastings. The day-long battle was fierce and bloody; a pathway with topographical models at intervals follows its course up and down the fateful slopes.

ST ALBANS ★

Hertfordshire, ENGLAND

POPULATION 80 376

MICHELIN ATLAS P 19 OR MAP 504 T 28

The Romans built Verulamium on the south bank of the River Ver, 27mi/43km northwest of London. Following their departure the town's building blocks were transferred to the other bank to build an abbey, beside which a new town soon developed. After the Dissolution (16C) the abbey church became the parish church and in 1877 it was raised to the status of a cathedral. 🏛 *Town Hall, Market Place, AL3 5DJ* ☎ *01727 864 511; Fax 01727 863 533; tic@stalbans.gov.uk; www.stalbans.gov.uk/tourism*

- 🕙 **Don't Miss**: Verulamium Museum; Cathedral; Woburn Abbey; Hatfield House.
- 🕐 **Organizing Your Time**: Allow half a day in St Alban's.
- **Kids** **Especially for Kids**: Woburn Safari Park or Whipsnade Animal Park.
- 🚶 **Walking Tours**: City Walks start outside the Old Town Hall in Market Place. ✆ £2. Details and tickets from tourist information centre.

Verulamium ★

Verulamium, the third-largest city in Roman Britain, was established in AD 49 on the Watling Street and rebuilt at least twice – once after being sacked by Boadicea in AD 61 and c 155 after a major fire. When the Romans withdrew, Verulamium declined. By 940 its ruins "were hiding places for robbers, body snatchers and evil women", according to the Saxon abbot. By 1591 Edmund Spenser wrote of the Roman town "Of which there now remains no memorie, Nor anie little moniment to see." The Roman site was excavated by Sir Mortimer Wheeler in the 1930s and by Professor Sheppard Frere in the 1950s and is now a public park, Verulamium Park, beside the river.

Verulamium Museum ★ – ♿ *St Michael's Street.* 🕐 *Open daily, 10am (2pm Sun) to 5.30pm.* ✆ *£3.30. Parking.* ☎ *01727 751 810; Fax 01727 859 919; museums@stalbans.gov.uk; www.stalbansmuseums.org.uk.* The museum displays some of the most impressive Roman works to be unearthed in Britain, which provide a fascinating glimpse of Roman life – ironwork, jewellery, coins, glass, pottery and **exceptional mosaics** of the Sea God and the Lion.

Roman Theatre – *Northwest of the museum, on the other side of the main road. Bluehouse Hill.* 🕐 *Open daily, 10am-5pm (4pm Nov-Mar);* 🕐 *Closed 1 Jan and 25-26 Dec.* ✆ *£1.50.* ☎ *01727 835 035; www.romantheatre.co.uk.* Orignally it was almost round and was probably used for public and religious festivals. Later the stage was enlarged and a row of columns was erected behind it in imitation of a conventional Roman theatre. It was again enlarged c AD 300. In front of it there was a temple; nearby in St Michael's churchyard were the basilica and forum.

Hypocaust – *Southwest of the museum in Verulamium Park.* The bath suite of a large villa has been preserved in situ with the central heating system – hot air, heated by a fire, passed through flues and underfloor channels.

Town walls – *South of the museum in Verulamium Park.* The walls of brick and flint (6ft/2m thick and 16ft/5m high) were reinforced by bastions, of which two remain, together with the foundations of the London Gate.

Cathedral ★ *1hr*

♿🕐 *Open daily, 9am-5.45pm.* ✆ *Donation £2.50.* 🚶 *Guided tour (1hr; ✆ £3; by appointment) Sun at 2.30pm, Mon-Fri at 11.30am and 2.30pm, Sat at 11.30am and 2pm. Restaurant. Ramps; touch and hearing centre.* ☎ *01727 890 208, 01727 860 780; Fax 01727 850 944; admin@stalbanscathedral.org.uk; www.stalbanscathedral.org.uk.* The original abbey was Saxon, a shrine to St Alban, England's first Christian martyr. The present building, dominated by its Norman central tower, was started in 1077 by Paul of Caen, a Norman and possibly the illegitimate son of Lanfranc, Archbishop of Canterbury. Lanfranc built an abbey with five apses; Paul's abbey had seven.

A hundred years later the impressive Norman nave was lengthened in the Early English style. When five piers on the south side collapsed they were replaced by Decorated ones. The very Victorian west front dates from 1879 and the chapter house from 1982.

Interior – "There is nothing to attract, though much to respect and much to investigate" (Pevsner). The beauty lies not in the structure but in the furnishings – the exquisite medieval wall paintings and ceiling panels, the nave screen (1350), the reredos (1484), the Lady Chapel (1320), the **shrine** of St Alban.

Excursions

Hatfield House★★ – *6mi/10km east of St Albans by A 414.* ♿ *House.* ◷ *Open Easter Sat to Sep, daily, noon-5pm.* ☞ *Guided tour of house, weekdays only. Park and gardens open daily, 11am-5.30pm.* ☞ *House, park and gardens £8; park and gardens only, £4.50; park only, £2. Brochure (7 languages). Parking. Licensed restaurant.* ☎ *01707 287 010; Fax 01707 287 033; curator@hatfield-house.demon.co.uk; www.hatfield-house.co.uk.* This is one of the finest and largest Jacobean houses in England, which has been the home of the Cecil family since Henry VIII invited them to accept it in exchange for their previous property Theobalds.

The present house was commissioned by Robert Cecil from Robert Lyminge, architect of Blickling Hall (♿ *see NORWICH*), who adopted the traditional E-plan. He used the bricks from the earlier palace, adding decorative detail with the use of stone quoins and openwork balustrades; the south front has a striking façade of Caen stone.

The **Interior** of the house has several characteristic features of the period, notably the hall, staircase and long gallery. In the **Marble Hall** the magnificently carved screen, minstrels' gallery and panels are Jacobean, the gigantic 17C allegorical tapestry from Brussels and the ceiling and gallery panels by Taldini. The **Ermine Portrait** of Elizabeth I is attributed to Nicholas Hilliard while the one of her cousin Mary Queen of Scots is said to be by Rowland Lockey. The **grand oak staircase** is Jacobean carving at its best. Note the relief of the horticulturist John Tradescant, gardener to Charles I, on one of the newels at the top of the stairs, and the *Rainbow Portrait* of Elizabeth I.

Extended the length of the range in the 19C, the **long gallery** has the crystal Posset Set (believed to be a betrothal gift to Queen Mary and King Philip of Spain) by Cellini at one end, Queen Elizabeth's silk stockings, hat and gloves at the other. In the library amid the 10 000 volumes and the mosaic portrait of the builder, Robert Cecil, are displayed a letter from Mary Queen of Scots and her execution warrant, signed by Lord Burghley, Cecil's father. In the chapel the biblical stained glass with its wonderful clarity is Flemish.

An Elizabethan **knot garden** and a traditional **herb garden** are recent additions to the grounds.

Knebworth House★ – *5mi/8km north by A 1 junction 7.* ♿◷ *Open first week Apr-Easter Mon, late-May to early-Sep, weekends, 11am (noon house) to 5.30pm (5pm house).* ☞ *£9; playground and gardens only, £7. Brochure (4 languages).* ☞ *Guided tour (55 min). Parking. Refreshments.* ☎ *01438 812661, Fax 01438 811908; info@knebworthhouse.com; www.knebworthhouse.com.* The great hall with its richly carved screen and minstrels' gallery has hardly changed since the house was built in the 15C. The Gothic style was introduced by **Bulwer-Lytton**, the writer of historical fantasies; it is best seen in the **State Drawing Room** – turreted fireplace, painted panels and stained-glass windows. Lytton's favourite room was his study; on visiting him there in the company of Charles Dickens, Edward Fitzgerald recalled "We saw an Eastern potentate sitting on luxurious cushions, with dreamy eyes and reposeful manner, smoking a chibouk."

Whipsnade Wild Animal Park★ – *Dunstable* ◷ *Open late-Mar to Sep, daily, 10am-6pm (7pm Sun and Bank Hols); Oct to late-Mar, daily at varying times; last admission 1hr before closing.* ◷ *Closed 25 Dec. Safari tour by bus and Great Whipsnade Railway (£2) at 1pm, 2pm, 3pm and 4pm.* ☞ *£14.50. £11 per car.* ☎ *01582 872 171; www.whipsnade.co.uk.* On the top of Dunstable Downs, this park has played a major role in animal conservation adn welfare. On hand are larger species such as elephants, rhinos, lions and giraffes and a collection of smaller creatures, birds, and aquatic mammals.

Elizabeth I at Hatfield

It was at Hatfield under an oak tree that Elizabeth I heard of her succession – "It is the Lord's doing and it is marvellous in our eyes." All that remains of her childhood home, a palace built by Cardinal Morton, is the Hall – "one of the foremost monuments to medieval brickwork in the country" according to Pevsner. The Cecils have played an important role in national politics – William Cecil, Lord Burghley, was chief minister to Elizabeth I; he was succeeded by Robert Cecil who also served James I (VI of Scotland). In the 19C Lord Salisbury (1830-1903) was three-times Prime Minister.

The Armada Portrait by George Gower

Woburn Abbey★★ – *22mi/35km north of St Albans by M 10, M 1 to junction 12 and minor road west. House and Grounds* &🕐 *Open late-Mar to Sep, daily, 11am (10am deer park) to 4pm (5pm Sun and Bank Hol).* ⌕ *£5. Deer Park £3 per car.* ⌕ *Guided tour (75min) by appointment. Parking. Refreshments. Wheelchair access (telephone in advance).* ☎ *01525 290 666; Fax 01525 290 271; enquiries@woburnabbey.co.uk; www. woburnabbey.co.uk.* Woburn was a Cistercian abbey for 400 years before becoming a private mansion. The north range was refurbished in 1630 but the more magnificent changes date from the 18C. In 1747 the west range was rebuilt by **Henry Flitcroft** (1697-1769) and in 1787 **Henry Holland** rebuilt the south and east ranges, although the latter was demolished in 1950.

The **interior** contains many sumptuously furnished apartments. The 4th Duke's bedroom contains the **Mortlake Tapestries** (1660s), which are based on Raphael's *Acts of the Apostles*, a white mid-18C ceiling, depicting the Four Seasons, and a sculpture of Hermaphroditus and Salmacis by Delvaux.

The **State Rooms** in the Flitcroft range include **Queen Victoria's Bedroom** with etchings by Victoria and Albert; **Queen Victoria's Dressing Room** in which the walls are covered with superb 17C Dutch and Flemish paintings including *Nijmegen on the Vaal* and *Fishermen on Ice* by Aelbert Cuyp, and *Jan Snellinck* by Van Dyck; the **Blue Drawing Room** with its ceiling (1756) and its fireplace by Duval and Rysbrack; the **State Saloon** with its ornamental ceiling and Rysbrack chimneypiece; the **State Dining Room** graced by a Meissen dinner service and a portrait by Van Dyck; the **Reynolds Room** displaying 10 of his portraits; and the **Canaletto Room** hung with 21 Venetian views. The **Library**, the finest room in the Holland range, is divided into three parts by fluted Corinthian columns; on the walls hang *Self-Portrait* and *Old Rabbi* by **Rembrandt**. The **Long Gallery,** also divided by columns, by Flitcroft, is hung with 16C paintings including the *Armada Portrait* of Elizabeth I.

In the **grounds** are two stable courtyards by Flitcroft and the pretty Chinese dairy by Holland. The park (3 000 acres/1 200ha) was landscaped by Humphry Repton and contains nine different species of deer (1 000 head), including Milu, originally the Imperial herd of China, which is preserved here.

Woburn Safari Park – *Entrance 1mi/1.5km from the house.* &🕐 *Open early-Mar to late-Oct, daily, 10am-5pm/dusk; late-Oct to early-Mar (weather permitting), Sat-Sun, 11am-3pm/dusk.* ⌕ *£14.50. Parking. Restaurant.* ☎ *01525 290 407; Fax 01525 290489; info@woburnsafari.co.uk; www.woburnsafari.co.uk.* There is nothing new about elephants, tigers, lions, zebras, bison, rhinos and wildebeest grazing in the park at Woburn. As early as 1894 it was said there was no better animal collection outside London Zoo.

ST ANDREWS★★

Fife, SCOTLAND

POPULATION 11 136

MICHELIN ATLAS P 56 OR MAP 501 L 14

This Fife coast resort, with its cathedral, castle and long-established university, is also famous as the home of golf. *70 Market Street, KY16 9NU ☎ 01334 472 021; Fax 01334 478 422; standrews@visitfife.com; www.visitstandrews.co.uk*

A Bit of History

There was an early religious settlement of St Mary, associated with relics of St Andrew. In the 12C a priory, and later a cathedral were established, leading to the foundation of the University. By 1472 St Andrews was the ecclesiastical capital of Scotland. Its importance declined in the 17C, owing to the switch in trade from the Baltic to the American colonies, and after the Act of Union in 1707. The 19C, however, saw St Andrews return to prominence as a tourist and golfing centre, an importance it has kept to this day.

Sights

Cathedral★ – *(HS) Open daily, 9.30am-6.30pm (4.30pm Oct-Mar). Combined ticket with castle £5. ☎ 01334 472 563; www.historic-scotland.gov.uk.* The imposing **St Regulus Church** may have been built originally to house the relics of St Andrew. Robert of Scone built the church, with its lofty tower, between 1127 and 1144. The tower *(151 steps)* affords a magnificent **panorama★★** across St Andrews and its main monuments. St Regulus's was replaced from 1160 by the later cathedral, the largest church ever built in Scotland. After the Reformation this once-noble building was used as a stone quarry, and reduced to the ruin on view today. The **museum** has a good collection of early Christian sculptured stones. The ruined 13C **castle,** *(HS Open same hours as cathedral. Combined ticket with cathedral £5. ☎ 01334 477 196; www.historic-scotland.gov.uk)* overlooking the foreshore, was once a part of the palace of the archbishop.

St Andrews University – *Guided tour Jun-Aug, Mon-Fri at 11am, 2.30pm from St Salvator's Chapel Tower. £4. ☎ 01334 462 245; Fax 01334 463 330; histours@st-and.ac.uk; www.st-and.ac.uk.* Founded in 1410 and granted a Papal Bull in 1413, it was the first in Scotland, and third only after Oxford and Cambridge. It became in the 16C a centre for reformist doctrines and thus involved in struggles with both the established Church and the Crown. This had some bearing on the plan to move the

R. Lees/Still Moving

Golf course, St Andrews

University to Perth in the 17C. **St Salvator's College,** founded in 1450 by Bishop James Kennedy, remains the nucleus of the Faculty of Arts; the Gothic chapel is the only remaining 15C building.

Excursions

Scotland's Secret Bunker – *10mi/16km southeast by B 9131 and B 940.* ⚄ *Crown Buildings Troywood.* ⏱ *Open Apr-Oct, daily, 10am-6pm (last admission 5pm).* ⚄ *£7.50. Audio-visual presentation. Parking. Café.* ☎ *01333 310 301; mod@secretbunker.co.uk; www.secretbunker.co.uk.* Deep below the surface of Fife's smiling farmlands, the bunker (130ft/40m deep, protected by 10ft/3m of reinforced concrete) built as an early warning radar station and converted to a nuclear command centre, evokes all the menace of the Cold War era. All stages of operational life are brought hauntingly to life with audio-visual displays.

East Neuk★★ – *Leave St Andrews by A 917.* The East Neuk, or East Corner, is a stretch of coastline dotted with picturesque fishing villages, each clustered around its harbour and with a wealth of vernacular architecture. These were the ports to which once came the wealth and prosperity of the fisheries and the Baltic and Dutch trade. With Dunfermline as the political capital and St Andrews as the ecclesiastical and the rich coastal burghs, Fife was aptly described by James VI as the "beggar's mantle with a fringe of gold."
Crail is the most attractive village; in **Anstruther** is the **Scottish Fisheries Museum**★★, (⚄ *St Ayles Harborhead.* ⏱ *Open daily, 10am (11am Sun Apr-Sep; noon Sun Oct-Mar) to 5.30pm (4.30pm Oct-Mar; 5pm Sun Apr-Sep).* ⚄ *£4.50. Parking. Tearoom. Shop.* ☏/*Fax 01333 310 628; enquiries@scotfishmuseum.org; www.scotfishmuseum.org)* and in **Pittenweem** Kellie Lodge, the corbelled, pantiled and crow-stepped town house of the Earls of Kellie Castle (⚄ *see below*).

★**Kellie Castle** – *(NTS) 10mi/16km south by B 9131 and B 9171.* ⚄ *Pittenweem. Castle:* ⏱ *Open late-Mar to late-Sep, daily 1-5pm; last admission 4.15pm. Gardens and grounds: Open daily, 9.30am-dusk.* ⚄ *£8. Leaflet (7 languages). Children's adventure trail. Parking. Tearoom.* ☎ *01333 720 271; Fax 01333 720 326; www.nts.org.uk.* Just inland behind this "fringe of gold" is Kellie Castle. It is in fact a laird's house, an example of unspoilt 16C-17C traditional Scottish architecture: corbelled turrets with conical roofs, pedimented dormers, crow-stepped gables, pitched roofs and string courses. A period of neglect from 1830 was, happily, followed by the castle being leased by the architect **Sir Robert Lorimer.** With the help of his brother, an artist, and in the next generation, Hew Lorimer, the sculptor, Kellie Castle was restored to its former glory. The 17C **plasterwork ceilings** are notable, in particular that of the Vine Room.

Golf: A Royal and Ancient Game

St Andrews links – with swards of springy turf and sand bunkers - have, since the 15C, been a place for playing golf or the early ball and stick version of this sport. So popular was the game that by 1457 an Act of Scottish Parliament was passed requiring that "futeball and the golfe be utterly cryit down" in favour of kirk attendance and archery practice. Mary Queen of Scots was an occasional player, her son James VI popularised the game in England.

Founded in 1754, the Society of St Andrews Golfers had the title **Royal and Ancient** conferred on it by William IV in 1834 and is now recognised as the ruling body. To meet the increasing popularity of the sport, new courses were laid out supplementing the **Old Course**, established several centuries ago.

By the beginning of the 20C St Andrews was firmly established as the Golfing Mecca and the town now regularly hosts the British Open and Amateur Championships, Walker Cup Matches and other tournaments which draw the stars of the professional circuit, bringing record-breaking crowds. Two of the greatest names in golfing history are immortalised by hole names on the Old Course : Tom Morris (18th) and Bobby Jones (10th). The **British Golf Museum** (⚄ *Bruce Embankment;* ⏱ *Open Mar to Oct, daily, 9.30am-5.30pm (5pm Sun); Nov to Mar, daily, 10am-4pm.* ⚄ *£5. Parking (charge).* ☎ *01334 460 046; Fax* ☎ *01334 460064; hilarywebster@randagc.org; www.britishgolfmuseum.co.uk.)* traces 500 years of golfing history.

Leuchars – *Population 2 203. 6mi/10km northwest by A 91 and A 919.* The village is known for its Junction, the railway station for St Andrews, and for the RAF base nearby. The **church**★, (🕐 *Open Apr-Oct, daily, 9am-6pm. Services: 11am. Guide book.* ☎ *01334 839 709)* which dominates the village from its elevated position, has a 12C chancel and apse, exceptionally fine examples of Norman work, with grotesque heads over arcading on the outside walls.

ST DAVID'S★

TYDDEWI – Pembrokeshire, WALES

POPULATION 1 428

MICHELIN ATLAS P 14 OR MAP 503 E 28 – LOCAL MAP PEMBROKESHIRE COAST

The cathedral, not unnaturally, is the centrepiece of this tiny city. Since the decree of Pope Callixtus II in the 12C, two pilgrimages to St David's are the equivalent of one to Rome – a privilege shared only with Santiago de Compostella in Spain. There has been a Christian community and daily worship on this site for more than fourteen centuries. St David's today is a thriving tourist-oriented community, set at the westernmost point of the **Pembrokeshire Coast Path** (👣 *see PEMBROKESHIRE COAST).* 🚩 *The Grove, St. Davids SA 62 6NW* ☎ *01437 720392 ; Fax: 01437 720099; enquiries@stdavids.pembrokeshire.org.uk; www.visitpembrokeshire.com.*

Sights

Cathedral★★ – 👤🕐 *Open all year, daily, 7.30am (12.45pm Sun)-6pm.* 💰 *Donation £2.* 👥 *Guided tour (1hr 30min;* 💰 *£2.50, 16 and under: £1) July-Aug: Mon-Tue and Thurs-Fri, at 2.30pm. Brochure (4 languages). Parking. Wheelchair access.* ☎ *01437 720 691; Fax 01437 721 885.* Wales' greatest church, built in lichen-encrusted purple stone, sits in a secluded hollow, revealing itself with dramatic suddenness to the visitor passing through the gatehouse into the precinct containing both Cathedral and Bishop's Palace.

The original church, built on the banks of the Alun by St David (c AD 462-520), was burnt down in 645 and again, by the Danes, in 1078. The present building was started in 1180 by Peter de Leia (1176-98), Florentine monk and third Norman bishop. Up to the wall behind the high altar, what we see today is substantially his cathedral, though the tower fell in 1220 and an earthquake in 1248 left the westernmost pillars of the nave leaning alarmingly outwards. The whole building slopes upwards from

Bishop's Palace, St David's

CADW: Welsh Historic Monuments©Crown

west to east (approx 14ft/3.5m) and presents a unique and striking impression to a visitor entering the south porch, at the western end of the nave. The late 15C **nave roof** is a magnificent piece of work, in Irish oak, incorporating the dragon of Wales on the pendants. In the south choir aisle is the tomb of the historian **Gerald of Wales,** known in Latin as Giraldus Cambrensis (1146-1223). Before the high altar is the table tomb of **Edmund Tudor**, grandfather of Henry VIII, who ordered it to be moved here from Grey Friars at Carmarthen after the Dissolution. The remains of St David's shrine, built in 1275, are on the north side of the Presbytery. During restoration work in 1886 bones found in an oak and iron reliquary, at the back of the Holy Trinity Chapel, were declared by the Dean to be those of St David and his confessor, Justinian, but carbon dating proved they are 11C or 12C relics and medical evidence points to St Caradog, who lived on fish on Newgale Beach.

Bishop's Palace★ – ⏱ *Open late-Mar to late Oct, daily, 9.30am-5pm (6pm Jun to late Sept); rest of the year, Mon-Sat, 9.30am (11am Sun)-4pm.* 🎫 *£1.70, £4.60 (family 2Adults+3Children), £1.20 (concession).* ☎ *0437 720 517.* The close wall surrounding cathedral and palace probably dates from c 1300. The Palace we see today was built mainly by Bishop Gower (1328-47), who also added the south porch and the Decorated windows to the cathedral. His palace consists of three long buildings, surrounding a courtyard, which is completed by a wall pierced by a buttressed gateway. The **Bishop's Hall** and **Solar**, with kitchen and chapel, appear to have been the main residence, the **Great Hall** to the south, with its elaborate porch and stairs from the courtyard, being reserved for the entertainment of important guests. After the Reformation the decay of palace and cathedral began. Bishop Barlow (1536-48) wished to remove the See to Carmarthen and stripped the palace roof of its lead – ostensibly for re-use on his new palace, though it was said in St David's that the sale of the lead provided generous dowries for his five daughters, each of whom married a bishop!

St Non's Chapel – Immediately south of the city are the cliffs and coves of the Pembroke coast. Here can be found a number of sites associated with the saint: the ruined chapel dedicated to his mother, St Non, where he is held to have been born; St Non's Well and, to the west, the tiny harbour inlet at Porthclais, where, by tradition, David was baptised.

There are several boat excursions that depart from St Justinian, a few minutes drive from St David's in search of the local wildlife. There is usually a choice of taking a conventional boat or a ride in a jet-powered rigid inflatable which can be a bit bumpy but is also a great thrill.

Thousand Islands Expeditions operate from St Justinian or Whitesand Bay according to season. *Around Ramsey Island and into sea-caves (2hr)* 🎫 *£22.50. Jet-powered white-water rafting (45 mins, unsuitable for young children)* 🎫 *£25. Trip to Ramsey Island by conventional boat: landing (half/all-day)* 🎫 *£10; landing and around the island (3hr on the island and 1hr 30min cruising)* 🎫 *£18; round trip only* 🎫 *£12. Puffin Watch (with RSPB guide) Apr to end-Jul* 🎫 *£15. Sunset Shearwater Watch (with RSPB guide) May to end-Aug,* 🎫 *£15; Grassholm Island (with RSPB guide)* 🎫 *£35 (half day). Booking Office: Cross Square, St David's* ☎ *01437 721 721, 0800 163 621; Fax* ☎ *01437 720 747; info@ tiex.co.uk; www.tiex.co.uk.*

Voyage of Discovery operates daily according to demand and season from St Justinian with trips around Ramsey Island *(1hr 30min; no landing)* and to the outer islands to include whale and dolphin watching. *Booking office: 1 High Street, St David's.* ☎ *01437 720 285; john@ramseyisland.co uk; wwwramseyisland.co.uk.*

ST IVES★★

Cornwall, ENGLAND

POPULATION 10 092

MICHELIN ATLAS P 2 OR MAP 503 D 33

This picturesque fishing harbour on the north Cornish coast is a much-visited summer resort and has been a favourite with artists since the 1880s when Whistler and Sickert followed in the footsteps of Turner; it is still a working artists' centre today.

Areas of interest include the small headland known as the **Island**, a network of stepped and winding alleys, and hillside terraces, all lined by colour-washed, slate-roofed fishermen's houses, crowded shoulder to shoulder. ⊞ *The Guildhall, Street-an-Pol, TR26 2DS ☎ 01736 796 297; Fax 01736 798 309; ivtic@penwith.gov.uk; www.go-cornwall.com.*

🅿 **Parking**: Park on the edge of St Ives (and Mousehole) as the streets are very narrow.

⊘ **Don't Miss**: Tate St Ives; Land's End cliff scenery; Minack Open-Air Theatre; St Michael's Mount.

🕐 **Organising Your Time**: aAlow a day in St Ives, at least two days for excursions.

🄺🄸🄳 **Especially for Kids**: There are excellent beaches all around this part of Cornwall; Land's End attractions; Geevor Tine Mine.

Sights

Tate St Ives★★ – (NACF) ♿ *Porthmeor Beach.* 🕐 *Open Mar-Oct, daily, 10am-5.30pm; Nov-Feb, Tue-Sun, 10.30am-4.30pm.* 🕐 *Closed 24-26 Dec.* 👓 *£5.50. Restaurant. ☎ 01736 796 226; Fax 01736 794 480; information@tate.org.uk; www.tate.org.uk.* This splendid building (1973), erected on the site of a gas works, enjoys a **view**★★ over the sands of Porthmeor Beach. Designed by Eldred Evans and David Shalev, the asymmetrical gallery consists of swirling forms spiralling upwards: shallow steps lead up to the entrance as a wheelchair ramp turns elegantly down between high walls.

R. Besse/MICHELIN

Penwith coastline

Artists in St Ives

The **St Ives Society of Artists** was founded by John Park and Borlase Smart, students of Julius Olsson, 1926-1927. During the following decade, the sculptors Ben Nicholson, **Barbara Hepworth** and Naum Gabo moved there from London; they befriended the local self-taught artist **Alfred Wallis**, who painted naive marine pictures that have as much charisma as those of Theodore Rousseau. Typical subjects include the sea, the coastal landscape and boats, although later the figurative element dissolved into abstraction. The 1950s witnessed the arrival of a new generation of painters inspired by the local landscape but influenced by trends from New York. Since then, painters have continued to come to St Ives to capture the light and the movement of the sea, including **Patrick Heron**, Terry Frost and Peter Lanyon.

Inside, stairways climb through airy space for access to the changing exhibitions of post-war modern works from the London Tate collection. These concentrate particularly on artists associated with St Ives including Alfred Wallis, Ben Nicholson, Barbara Hepworth, John Wells, Terry Frost, Patrick Heron (who designed the stained glass window on the ground floor). A number of works by Bernard Leach are also on display (ceramics fusing eastern and western traditions).

Barbara Hepworth Museum★★ – ⏰ *Open Mar-Oct, daily, 10am-5.30pm; Nov-Feb, Tue-Sun, 10.30am-4.30pm; restricted admission occasionally during the high season.* ⏰ *Closed 24-26 Dec.* ⚲ *£4.50.* ☎ *01736 796 226; Fax 01736 794 480; www.tate.org.uk.* Barbara Hepworth (1903-75) came to St Ives with Ben Nicholson in 1943, decided to settle, and stayed here until her death.

The house she lived in, filled with sleek, polished wood and stone abstract **sculptures** spanning a life's work, and workshops with unfinished blocks of stone, left pretty much as they were at the artist's death, contrast with the small white-walled garden which provides a serene setting for some twenty abstract compositions in bronze and stone.

Parish Church★ – The church dates – except for the 20C baptistery – from the 15C and is dedicated to the fishermen-Apostles St Peter and St Andrew, and St Ia, the early missionary who arrived in the area from across the sea on a leaf and after whom the town is named. It stands by the harbour, distinguished by its pinnacled 85ft/26m tower of Zennor granite. Note the **wagon roof**, carved **bench ends** and stone **font**. The **Lady Chapel** contains the tender *Mother and Child* (1953) by Barbara Hepworth who also designed the stainless-steel Christmas rose candlesticks.

Smeaton Pier – The pier and its octagonal domed lookout were constructed in 1767-70 by the builder of the third Eddystone lighthouse, John Smeaton. At its shore end is the small St Leonard's sailors' chapel.

St Nicholas Chapel – The chapel on the "Island" is the traditional seamen's chapel built as a beacon. It commands a wide **view★★** across the bay.

Excursion

Penwith★★

St Ives to St Michael's Mount 35mi/58km – local map ⚲ *see TINTAGEL.* Penwith is the most westerly headland in England. This sparsely populated region has its own bleak beauty deriving from its granite foundation, the wind, the blue of the ocean and its small granite churches and Celtic wayside crosses. Take any opportunity to leave the coast road to admire the views from the cliffs.
Take B 3306 west from St Ives.

Zennor – The outdoor **Wayside Folk Museum**, (⏰ *Open Apr-Oct, Sun-Fri, 11am (10.30am May-Sep) to 5pm (5.30pm May-Sep); also Sat during summer school and Bank Hols.* ⚲ *£2.25. Parking.* ☎ *01736 796 945*) set in an old miller's house, shows the evolution of implements from stone to iron. The 12C-13C granite **church★**, on a 6C site, was enlarged in the 15C and restored in the 19C. Inside are a tithe measure, now serving as a holy water stoup, two fonts of Hayle limestone and, on a bench-end, the 16C carving of the pretty **Mermaid of Zennor**.

Chysauster Prehistoric Village★ – ⏰ *Open late-Mar Oct, daily, 10am-6pm (5pm Oct).* ⚲ *£1.80. Parking.* ☎ *07831 757 934.* The best-preserved **prehistoric Cornish village**, inhabited probably from 100 BC to AD 250, consists of at least eight circular stone houses, which would originally have been roofed with turf or thatch, in two lines of four just below the crest of the hill.

Geevor Tin Mine

Near Pendeen lighthouse. Pendeen. ◷ *Open Sun-Fri and Bank Hol Sat, 10am-4pm (3pm late-Oct to early-Apr); Christmas, telephone for times.* ⊚ *£7. Tour of mine and museum (2hrs). Some areas wheelchair accessible.* ☎ *01736 788 662; Fax 01736 786 059; pch@ geevor.com; www.geevor.com.* The tour and museum of what was one of Cornwall's last working mines and its museum demonstrate the process by which tin, copper, iron and arsenic were separated from the bedrock.

St Just-in-Penwith

The prosperity enjoyed by this 19C mining town is reflected in the substantial buildings lining the triangular square, the fine terraces of cottages and the large Methodist Chapel. The **church**★ features a 15C pinnacled tower, dressed granite walls, an elaborate 16C porch, wall paintings and a 5C tomb in the north aisle.

A mile to the west (partly on foot), the hillock of **Cape Cornwall**★ rises 230ft/70m, giving **views**★★ of Brisons Rocks, Land's End and the Longships lighthouse.

Just before reaching Land's End, the road passes through the little village of Sennen, home to the most westerly church in England (walk down to **Sennen Cove**★, 20min there and back, for a good **view**★ of Whitesand Bay, Brisons Rocks and Cape Cornwall).

Land's End★

The attraction of Land's End is less its physical beauty (and much less its visitor attractions) than its position at the westernmost point of England, overlooking some of the finest local cliff **scenery**★★★ perpetually assailed by the surging swell of the Atlantic. For a peaceful view, come early and walk along the coastal path, or come at sunset and wait for the beams from the lighthouses to add a magical touch. Ramblers and walkers can approach along the Cornwall Coastal Path.

Somewhat confusingly, part of Land's End has been commandeered by a mini-theme park, also known as **Land's End** (or "Legendary Land's End, the Ultimate Destination" – ♿. *Sennen.* ◷ *Open daily, 10am-dusk.* ◷ *Closed 24-25 Dec.* ⊚ *Inclusive ticket or separate charge for each attraction. Parking charge £3. Right of way for walkers, free of charge, over site. Restaurant; hotel.* ☎ *0970 4580099; Fax* ☎ *01736 871 812/719; info@landsend-landmark.co.uk; www.landsend-landmark.co.uk).* This comprises six visitor attractions dealing with Cornish mythology and local matters plus shops and cafes.

Carry on along the B 3315, leaving the road to view the idyllic sheltered cove of **Porthcurno**★, the nearby famous **Minack Open-Air Theatre**, *(*◷ *Performances May to late-Sep, Mon-Fri at 8pm; also Wed and Fri at 2pm.* ⊚ *£7.50.* ☎ *01736 810 181; info@minack.com; www.minack.com)* founded in 1929 with its stunning ocean backdrop and views over Lamorna Cove. The theatre's fascinating history is recounted in the **Rowena Cade Exhibition Centre** *(*◷ *Open Apr-Oct, 9.30am-5.30pm; Oct-Mar, 10am-4pm.* ⊚ *£3. Parking. Refreshments.* ☎ *01736 810 181; info@minack.com; www. minack.com)* which gives access to the theatre.

Mousehole★

Mousehole ("Mowzel") is an attractive – and often crowded – village. Its **harbour** is protected by a quay of Lamorna granite and a **breakwater** dating from 1393. Set back from the low granite fishermen's cottages at the water's edge is the half-timbered Keigwin Arms, the only house left standing after a Spanish raid in 1595. A mile south of Mousehole is **Spaniards' Point** where the raiders landed to pillage the country for miles around.

Newlyn★

Newlyn is the major fishing village in the southwest (mackerel, whitefish, lobster, crab). The beautiful light and the charm of the cottages clustered round the harbour and on the hillside attracted a group of painters who founded the **Newlyn School** in the 1880s. The **Pilchard Works**★ *(*◷ *Open Easter-Oct, Mon-Fri, 10am-6pm (5.15pm last admission).* ☎ *01736 332 112; nick@pichardworks.co.uk; www.chycor.co.uk/tourism/ cata-guest/pilchard-works/pilchard-works.htm)* are reminders of this once thriving local trade.

Penzance★

🛈 *Station Road, Penzance* ☎ *01736 362 207.* The busy market town, badly damaged in the Spanish raid of 1595 and now largely post-1800, has been a popular holiday resort for over 150 years (since the arrival of the Great Western Railway). The half-mile long **Western Promenade** reflects 19C Penzance's importance as a resort. The harbour area has a wonderful **outlook**★★★ over Mount's Bay and St Michael's Mount. It is from here that the MV **Scillonian III** sails to the **Isles of Scilly** (also served by Penzance Heliport, weather permitting). The **National Lighthouse Centre**★, *(Wharf Road. ⏰ Open Easter-Oct, daily, 10.30am-4.30pm. ⏰ Closed some Sat. Telephone in advance to check opening times. ☞ £3. Leaflet (4 languages). ☎ 01736 360 077)* housed in an old buoy store, contains a fascinating collection of lights and artefacts relating the history of the lighthouse service. The town centre, particularly **Market Jew Street** and **Chapel Street**★, boasts some attractive 17C, 18C and 19C buildings including Market House, the surprising Egyptian House (1835), Abbey House and The Admiral Benbow. Closeby, the **Penlee House Gallery and Museum**★ *(NACF ♿ Morrab Road. ⏰ Open Mon-Sat, 10am (10.30am Oct-Apr) to 5pm (4.30pm Oct-Apr). ☞ £2. Leaflet. Parking. Café. ☎ 01736 363 625; info@penlee-house.demon.co.uk; www.penleehouse. org.uk)* is a centre of art and heritage for West Cornwall including a fine collection of art from 1750 to the present with works by the Newlyn School.

Trengwainton Garden★★

2mi/3km northwest of Penzance. ♿⏰ Open mid-Feb to Oct, Sun-Thu and Good Friday, 10.30am-5.30pm (5pm Feb-Mar and Oct). ☞ £4.50. Braille guide. Refreshments. ☎01736 363 148; Fax 01736 362 297 (during opening hours); trengwainton@nationaltrust.org. uk; www.nationaltrust.org.uk. The garden lies along the half-mile drive to the house, beyond which a second garden of azaleas and rhododendrons gives a fine **view**★★ of Mount's Bay. In the early 20C, with the owners of Trewithen and Hidcote in Gloucestershire, Sir Edward Bolitho financed Kingdon Ward's plant collecting expeditions of 1927-28 to bring back specimens from Burma, Assam and China from which the rhododendron and azalea collections have been built up and hybridised. The series of walled gardens contains magnolias and a host of other flowering trees.

St Michael's Mount★★

(NT) Causeway from Marazion. ♿ Access: at high tide by ferry; at low water on foot across the sands and causeway. Castle: ⏰ Open mid-Mar-Oct, Mon-Fri, 10.30am-5.30pm (4.45pm last admission). Garden May – Oct 10am-5:30pm; Nov-Mar, telephone for times. ☞ £5.50. Audio tour. Video introduction. Leaflet (6 languages). Braille guide. Café, restaurant. ☎ 01736 710 507 or 01736 710 265; Fax 01736 711 544; godolphin@manoroffice.co.uk; www.stmichaelsmount.co.uk. Mediterranean tin traders are said to have settled on what they called the island of Ictis in 4 BC. According to Cornish legend, in AD 495 fishermen saw the archangel Michael on the granite rock rising out of the sea. The island became a place of pilgrimage and a Celtic monastery is said to have stood on the rock from the 8C to 11C. In c 1150 Abbot Bernard of Mont-St-Michel off the coast of Normandy built a Benedictine monastery here which, as alien property, was appropriated by the Crown in 1425 and finally dissolved in 1539.

The rock frequently served as a strongpoint from the Middle Ages to 1647, when its last military commander, Colonel John St Aubyn, bought the **castle** as a family residence. It is now a hybrid of 14C-19C styles, with a Tudor doorway bearing the St Aubyn arms, a 14C entrance hall, a restored 14C church with 15C windows, and an 18C Rococo-Gothic drawing room.

SALISBURY★★

Wiltshire, ENGLAND

POPULATION 39 268

MICHELIN ATLAS P 9 OR MAP 503 O 30

The new town of Salisbury came into existence with the new cathedral, was granted a charter in 1227 and was controlled by the bishops until 1611. The earlier city of **Old Sarum**★ *(2mi/3km north)*, an Iron Age hilltop fort (28 acres/11ha), had been modified by the Romans and Saxons and finally became a Norman strongpoint where two successive cathedrals were built. From 1078-99 **St Osmund** was bishop of the first cathedral which was destroyed by lightning and then rebuilt and enlarged by **Bishop Roger**, who also converted the castle into an episcopal palace. His fall from power in 1139 marked the beginning of prolonged friction between the clergy and the king's men over possession of the castle-palace.

By the beginning of the 13C the inadequate water supply and the fact that they no longer needed a hilltop fort decided the citizens and clergy of Old Sarum to build their third cathedral on the banks of the River Avon. The buildings on the hilltop fell into ruin and today only the castle ruins and the ground plan of the cathedral can be seen within the earthworks, with a fine view over Salisbury Plain and New Sarum, now Salisbury. ⓘ *Fish Row, SP1 1EJ* ☎ *01722 334 956; Fax 01722 422 059; visitorinfo@salisbury.gov.uk; www.visitsalisburyuk.com*

▶ **Orient Yourself**: Salisbury is a small city centre and can be covered on foot.

🅿 **Parking**: There is a park-and-ride scheme operating; look for signs as you approach the city centre.

⊛ **Don't Miss**: Cathedral; Wilton House; Old Sarum.

🕓 **Organizing Your Time**: Allow 1-2 days for city centre and excursions.

Kids **Especially for Kids**: Large adventure playground at Wilton House.

Cathedral★★★

For many people, Salisbury epitomises the Early English style at its best, medieval Gothic in its purest, most ascetic form. It is unique among England's older cathedrals having been built in a single style, with the tallest spire (404ft/123m) conceived largely by Elias de Derham. Construction spanned two phases: foundation stone to consecration and completion of the west screen (1220-58-65); heightening of the tower and construction of the spire (1334-80). The materials used included silver-grey limestone from Chilmark *(12mi/19km west)* and Purbeck marble.

Exterior – The ornate **west screen** extends from the gabled portals up through lines of statue-filled niches, lancet windows and arcading to the pointed gable and corner towers with their miniature angel pinnacles and ribbed spires. The most spectacular feature of the cathedral, the **spire** over the heightened tower, was added almost a century later but harmonizes perfectly with the rest of the church.

Interior – ♿🕓 *Open daily, 7.15am-6.15pm (8.15pm, Mon-Sat, Jun-Aug).* 💬 *Guided tour (several languages): Sun,*

Salisbury Cathedral spire

A. Taverner?MICHELIN

4pm-6.15pm (Apr-Sep only), Mon-Sat, 10am-4pm, 6.30pm-8.15pm (Jun-Aug only). Tower tour ($4.50): Jan-Nov, Mon-Sat at 2.15pm, 11.15am (Mar-Oct only), 3.15pm (Apr-Sep only), 6.30pm (Jun-Aug only); also May-Sep, Sun, at 4.30pm. Magna Carta (in Chapter House): On display daily except 25 Dec. Services: Sun, 8am (Holy Communion), 10am (Sung Eucharist), 11.30am (Matins), 3pm (Evensong). Guide book (6 languages). Leaflet (9 languages). Donation £4. ☎ 01722 555 120; Fax 01722 555 116; visitors@salcath. co.uk; www.salisburycathedral.org.uk. The interior of the west screen exemplifies the beauty of pure line; nothing remains of the medieval colour. The **nave** (229.5ft/70m) extends over half the length of the whole building (449ft/137m), its vault towering to a height of 84ft/25m. Along the arcade, piers of Purbeck marble reach up to quatrefoils of grey, unpolished stone, canted by polished black shafts capped with moulded capitals, then up again through galleries marked by clusters of black colonnettes to the tall lancets of the clerestories. Between the arcade pillars on the south side are the tomb chests of **Bishops Roger** (d 1139) and **Joscelin** (d 1184), the shrine of **St Osmund** (d 1099) and the chain-mailed **William Longespée** (d 1226), half-brother of King John and husband of Ela, the founder of Lacock Abbey. Giant piers of clustered black marble columns mark the **crossing**, intended to support the original tower, but since the 14C required to bear the additional 6 500 tons of the heightened tower and spire. The piers have in fact buckled a noticeable 3.5in/9cm, despite reinforcing internal and external buttresses, massive 15C tie-beam arches across the transepts and a Decorated stone vault over the crossing. A brass plate in the crossing marks the spot where a plumb-line let down from the spire point by Sir Christopher Wren in 1668 reached the floor – 29.5in/75.5cm off-centre to the southwest. In the north aisle is the oldest working clock in England (c 1386), restored in 1931 *(new parts painted green)*. The altar-frontal and hangings in the Mothers' Union chapel *(south transept)* are made of material from the 1953 coronation. The blue window dedicated to *Prisoners of Conscience* (1980) in the **Trinity Chapel** is by Gabriel Loire, a stained-glass craftsman from Chartres. This chapel also contains beautiful, very slim, black Purbeck marble shafts rising to the vaulting. A **roof tour** leads up to the Parvis Room and triforium *(120 steps)* and, restoration work permitting, up the tower through the clock and bell chambers to the external gallery at the base of the spire, otherwise to the gutters of the nave roof.

Cloisters and Chapter House – Construction of the Decorated Gothic style chapter-house and cloisters was begun c 1263, making the latter the earliest in any English cathedral; they are also the longest (181ft/55m). The vault of the octagonal chapter-house (58ft/18m across) is supported on a central column, surrounded by eight ringed Purbeck marble shafts which continue to rise from their foliated capitals as ribs to ceiling bosses, before dropping to clusters of slim columns framing the windows. An Old Testament frieze (restored in the 19C) fills the spandrels between the niches on either side of the canons' seats. The main floor display is dedicated to one of the four original copies of the **Magna Carta.**

Cathedral Close★

The Close, spacious and mellow with the ancient stone and terracotta bricks of its 16C-18C houses, was enclosed in the 1330s against the "riotous citizenry." The walls are of stone from the abandoned cathedral and castle of Old Sarum. In the northwest corner is a secondary close, known as the **Choristers' Close**. There are four entries to the Close.

St Ann's and Bishop's Gates – The gates in the east wall abut the 18C Malmesbury House and the old Bishop's Palace, an island building (c 1220), now the Cathedral School.

Harnham or South Gate – The distant south gate leads to the dissolved De Vaux College and St Nicholas Hospital, the latter the source of Trollope's *The Warden*.

Salisbury and South Wiltshire Museum★ – *(NACF) West side of the Close.* ♿ ⏰ Open Mon-Sat, 10am-5pm; also Jul-Aug, Sun, 2-5pm. ⏰ Closed 24-27 Dec. £4. Leaflet (3 languages). ☎ 01722 332 151; Fax 01722 325 611; museum@salisburymuseum.freeserve. co.uk; www.salisburymuseum.org.uk. This medieval flint and brick **King's House**, named after the visits of James I, contains a **Stonehenge** collection, a model of and relics from Old Sarum as well as sections on porcelain and pottery.

Redcoats in the Wardrobe★– *West side of the Close.* ♿ ⏰ Open Apr-Oct, daily, 10am-5pm; Nov to mid-Dec and Feb-Mar, Tue-Sun. £2.75. Parking. Refreshments. ☎ 01722 414 536; www.wardrobe.org.uk. The museum of the **Royal Gloucestershire, Berkshire and Wiltshire Regiment** is housed in the Wardrobe, one of the first houses to be built in the Close (1254) as the Bishop's document storehouse and wardrobe; it was altered in the 15C and later converted into a dwelling. Epic moments in the regiments' histories are illustrated through displays of uniforms, weapons, despatches, maps, medals, silver, snuffboxes.

Mompesson House★ – *(NT)* ♿ *Choristers' Close.* ⏰ *Open late-Mar to late-Sep, Sat-Wed and Good Friday, noon-5.30pm.* ⊕ *£4.20. Leaflet (7 languages and Braille). Parking in city centre nearby (charge). Tearoom.* ☎ *01722 335 659; Fax 01722 321 559; wmpkxr@smtp.ntrust.co.uk; www.nationaltrust.org.uk.* Through a fine 18C wrought-iron gateway and the front door, above which stands the stone-carved coat of arms of Charles Mompesson, who built the house in 1701, is a well-furnished interior set against ornate **Baroque plasterwork.** The oak **staircase**, inserted in the 1740s at the back of the hall, is the principal architectural feature, rising by shallow flights with three crisply turned banisters to each tread. Also of note is the collection of **English drinking glasses** dating from 1700, with 370 different types of glass displayed in period cabinets in the Dining and Little Drawing Rooms.

North or High Street Gate – The gate, with a statue of **Edward VII**, opens from Choristers' Close into the town by way of an alleyway of old houses and the **Matrons' College** built in 1682 as almshouses for canons' widows.

Additional Sights

Medieval Streets – Between the cathedral and the 19C **Market Square** to the north extends a network of medieval streets, lined by gabled half-timbered houses dating from the 14C-17C. The alley names indicate the trades which once flourished there – Fish Row, Butcher Row, Silver Street. At the centre in a small square stands the 15C hexagonal **Poultry Cross.**

Sarum St Thomas Church★ – *Northeast end of the High Street.* A Perpendicular church dating from 1220 with a low square tower of 1390. It has a **doom painting** (c 1475, the largest in England) above the chancel arch, featuring Christ in Majesty and the New Jerusalem – perhaps a representation of 15C Salisbury. The **Lady Chapel**, decorated with very small 15C frescoes, has splendid wrought-iron railings and finely carved **woodwork**, both dating from 1725. Admire also the roof (1470) with angel musicians on the beams.

Excursions

Wilton House★★

♿⏰ *Open Easter-Oct, daily, 10.30am-5.30pm (4.30pm last admission).* ⊕ *£9.75; grounds only, £4.50. Leaflet. Parking. Adventure Playground. Refreshments.* ☎ *01722 746 729 (24hr information line); tourism@wiltonhouse.com; www.wiltonhouse.com.* William Herbert, soon to become the first Earl of Pembroke, was given the property of the dissolved Benedictine convent at Wilton by Henry VIII in 1544 and built a house on the site. Successive generations have left their mark: the 4th Earl commissioned **Inigo Jones** to design the house anew in 1630, incorporating a stateroom for his collection of portraits by Van Dyck – the work was completed by his nephew John Webb following a fire in 1647; the 8th Earl, founder of the Royal Wilton Carpet Factory (King Street) and collector (Wilton Diptych, now in the National Gallery, London), appointed agents to find new pictures and marbles; the 9th Earl built the **Palladian bridge** (1737) and redesigned the **garden**; the 11th Earl called in **James Wyatt** in 1801, who greatly altered the house, rebuilding the west and north fronts and adding the two-tier Gothic cloister in the original inner court. More recently, the house has been featured in the films *The Madness of King George* (1994) and *Sense and Sensibility* (1995).

Tour – *1hr.* In the Visitor Centre in the **Old Riding School**, a short video provides an introduction to the house, before visitors are ushered through the Victorian kitchens and laundry. The raised entrance hall and **cloisters**, remodelled from the original inner courtyard, are decorated with a number of Classical sculptures, paintings, fine furniture, Oriental porcelain, and display cases of medals and mementoes of famous people. A staircase leads down to the ground floor. The 19C **Gothic Hall** includes portrait busts of Sidney Herbert and Florence Nightingale. The two **smoking rooms** are hung with equestrian portraits in oil and Spanish Riding School gouaches commissioned by the 10th Earl, soldier and authority on riding. Note the typical Inigo Jones moulded detail in cornices, doorways and chimneypieces, and the beautiful furniture. The suite of formal **State Apartments** by Inigo Jones is characterised by a wealth of Classical enrichment, with many details picked out in gold leaf. The furniture includes pieces by William Kent and the younger Chippendale and 18C French items. The Little Ante Room is hung mainly with small French and Dutch scenes. The **Corner Room**, overlooking the vast lawn with cedars of Lebanon to the east and the Palladian bridge to the south, is decorated with pictures by Andrea del Sarto, Parmigiano, Rubens and Frans Hals. The ceiling of the **Colonnade Room**, intended as the State Bedroom, is painted with fantastical 17C monkey motifs *(singerie)* and fine portraits adorn the walls. In the **Great Ante Room** are portraits by Rembrandt, Van Dyck and Clouet. The white and gold **Double Cube Room**, measuring 60ft x 30ft x 30ft (18m x 9m x 9m), was specially designed by Inigo Jones to house the 4th Earl's unique collection of splendid Van Dyck portraits and completed by Webb in 1653. It was in this room that many strategic plans were laid by the likes of Eisenhower and Churchill (a frequent visitor) during the Second World War, when Wilton House was the headquarters of the Southern Command. The 30ft x 30ft x 30ft **Cube Room** (9m x 9m x 9m) is also decorated in white and gold, the ornament delicate in keeping with the size of the room.

The house sits square on a flat lawn which stretches south to the river, marked by the Palladian bridge and a few trees, before becoming pasture beyond.

Shaftesbury

The town is perched on the crest of a 700ft/213m spur, an excellent **vantage point**★, which accounts for King Alfred's choice of the site as a strong-point in his struggle against the Danes.

The **abbey** (🕐 *Open Apr-Oct, daily, 10am-5pm.* 🎫 *Tour and audio tour £2.* ☎ *01747 852 910; Fax 01747 852 910; user@shaftesburyabbey.fsnet.co.uk; www.shaftesburyabbey. co.uk)*, founded in 888 by King Alfred for his daughter, became the wealthiest nunnery in England. In the 15C-16C the saying went that if the Abbess of Shaston (Shaftesbury) were to marry the Abbot of Glaston (Glastonbury) their heirs would own more land than the king. In 1539 Henry VIII dissolved both abbeys and now only the ground plan of Shaston remains visible. Shaftesbury town's most attractive street is the steep and cobbled **Gold Hill**★, lined on one side with small 16C, 17C and 18C houses and on the other by a massive buttressed 13C ochre-coloured wall.

SCARBOROUGH

North Yorkshire, ENGLAND

POPULATION 38 809

MICHELIN ATLAS P 47 OR MAP 502 S 21

TOWN PLAN IN THE MICHELIN GUIDE GREAT BRITAIN AND IRELAND

Scarborough, on the chilly northeast coast, claims to be Britain's first seaside resort. Its two sweeping beaches are separated by a headland which is crowned by a 12C castle built around a Roman signal station; on one side are the medieval town, the old fishing harbour and the popular beaches of South Bay; on the other are the rocks and sand of North Bay, backed by gardens.

A Bit of History

The town's development as a resort can be traced back to the discovery of a medicinal spring in 1626; by 1676 the waters were claimed to cure any number of ailments, including "The Hypochondriac Melancholy." It reached its fashionable zenith in the late 19C and early 20C, and despite the recent transformation of part of the South Bay seafront by garish amusement arcades, Scarborough remains one of the very best places in Britain in which to savour the atmosphere of the Victorian seaside.

▸ **Orient Yourself**: Summer open-top bus tours, ask at tourist office for details.

🙈 **Don't Miss**: Robin Hood's Bay; Whitby.

🕐 **Organizing Your Time**: Allow 1-2 days for Scarborough and excursions.

🧒 **Especially for Kids**: Sea Life Centre; Atlantis Water Park; Kinderland Children's Fun Park; North Bay and South Bay beaches.

Address Book

OUT AND ABOUT IN SCARBOROUGH

Tourist Information Centre –
Brunswick Shopping Centre,Westborough,
Scarborough, YO11 1UE; 01723 383637;
Fax 01723 507302; scarboroughtic@
scarborough.gov.uk; www.scarborough.
gov.uk, www.discoveryorkshirecoast.com

Pubs and Restaurants – Fish and chips,
seafood stalls and restaurants.

Entertainment – Variety shows, musicals
and drama (Spa Theatre, Steven Joseph
Theatre); Tea and Coffee dances; yachting
events; Cricket Festival; Motorcycle
fixtures and International Bike Week
(at Oliver's Mount Circuit); Scarborough
Fair and Filey's Edwardian Festival.
Pony rides for children, fun fairs, llama
trekking, bowling, rambling and
watersports.

Visit

Along the **seafront**, there are promenades, cliff railways, bridges spanning deep denes, pavilions, cafés, chalets, pretty little shelters and the great bulk of the expensively refurbished **Spa**, now an entertainment and conference centre. The elegant **Crescent** (in fact, a one-way oval), in the centre of town overlooking South Bay, begun in 1833 incorporates a number of fine stone-built villas, one of which was the home of the Sitwell family; this is now the **Wood End Museum**, (⊙ *Open Spring Bank Hol to Sept, Tue-Sun, 10am-5pm; Oct to Spring Bank Hol, Wed, Sat-Sun, 11am-4pm.* ⊜ *£2.50, combined ticket with Art Gallery and Rotunda Museum.* ☎ *01723 367 326)* with natural history exhibits as well as Sitwelliana; its neighbour has become the **Art Gallery**, (⊙ *Open Jun-Sep, Tue-Sun and Bank Hols, 10am-5pm; Oct-May, Thu-Sat, 11am-4pm.* ⊜ *£2.50, combined ticket with Wood End and Rotunda Museum.* ☎ *01723 374 753)* whose pictures include a number of paintings by the popular Victorian artist John Atkinson Grimshaw (1836-93). The **Rotunda** (⊙ *Open Jun-Sep, Tue-Sun 10am-5pm; Oct-May, Tue and Sat-Sun, 11am-4pm.* ⊜ *£2.50, combined ticket with Wood End and Art Gallery.* ☎ *01723 374 839)* of 1828-29 is a fine example of a purpose-built Georgian museum (temporary exhibitions), still with the original circular panorama of the geology of the Yorkshire coast adorning the inside of its dome.

On North Bay beach the **Sea Life and Marine Sanctuary** (⚭⊙ *Open daily, 10am-5pm (4pm Oct-Apr).* ⊙ *Closed 25 Dec.* ⊜ *£6.25. Parking (charge). Restaurant. Leaflet.* ☎ *01723 373 414; www.sealife.co.uk)*, an underwater safari plus rescued animals, such as seven endangered Humboldt Penguins, is one of the town's more interesting and educational family diversions.

A. Williams/MICHELIN

Scarborough

Two Churches – The ancient parish church is **St Mary's**, (&🕐 *Open mid-Apr to mid-May; Mon-Fri, 2pm-4pm; end-May to mid-Sep, Mon-Fri, 10am-4pm, Sun, 1-4pm; www. stmarys.holyapostles.btinternet.co.uk*) a Cistercian foundation, dating from around 1180. **Anne Brontë** (1820-49) is buried in the churchyard. The influx of 19C residents and holiday-makers was served by **St Martin-on-the-Hill,** one of the finest structures designed by the church architect George Frederick Bodley (1827-1907), with an interior containing a remarkable collection of pre-Raphaelite religious art.

Theatre in the Round – The Stephen Joseph Theatre enjoys a national reputation, not least because of its association with playwright **Alan Ayckbourn**, many of whose plays have been performed here before moving to London. The theatre is housed in a splendid Art Deco former cinema.

Excursions

Sledmere House★
21mi/34km south on A 645, B 1249 and B 1253 (right). &🕐 *Open first Sun in May to last Sun in Sep, Tue-Fri, Sun and Bank Hol Mon, 10.30am (11.30am house) to 4.30pm (4pm last entrance to house); also Good Friday to Easter Monday and Apr, Sun only.* 👓 *£4.50; park and gardens only, £2. Parking. Café. Ramp, lift.* ☎ *01377 236 637; Fax 01377 236 500; www.driffield.co.uk.*
The house was begun in 1751 but the present exterior is the work of Sir Christopher Sykes, who died in 1801. According to existing drawings he was his own architect and draughtsman. The park was laid out by Capability Brown; the plasterwork is by Joseph Rose, who was employed by Adam and Wyatt to execute their own designs. Residents here included **Sir Tatton Sykes** (1772-1863), fourth baronet, famous for his breeding of sheep and horses, his racehorses and skill at riding (he was master of foxhounds for over 40 years). Following a fire in 1911, the house was rebuilt to look much as it would have done in the early 1800s. The **Staircase Hall**, the **Grand Staircase** and the **Library** are decorated in colours which harmonise with the architectural style. Chippendale and Sheraton furniture, French furnishings and paintings, exquisite porcelain and antique statuary are displayed in the many fine rooms of this "lived-in" house.

Filey Bay
21mi/34km south on A 165 and a minor road left.

Filey – *Population 6 619.* The projecting headland, **Filey Brigg**, protects the charming Victorian town from the North Sea. Two cottages dating from 1696 house the **Filey Museum** (*Queen Street.* &🕐 *Open Easter-Oct, daily, 11am (2pm Sun) to 5pm; also Jul-Aug, Tue, 7pm-9pm.* 👓 *£1.50. Wheelchair access to ground floor and museum garden.* ☎ *01723 515 013).* The sandy beach stretches south along the coast right down to Flamborough Head.

▶ *Continue south (for another 13.5mi/22km) towards Bridlington on A 165, B 1229 and B 1259 via Flamborough.*

Flamborough Head★ – The headland (215ft/66m), from which there are spectacular **views** out to sea and along the coast, is marked by a lighthouse. The area is a nature reserve.

North along the coast (*Cleveland Way footpath*) is some outstanding chalk cliff scenery, particularly near **Bempton**, where the cliffs soar to 427ft/130m.

▶ *Proceed 2.5mi/4km southeast on the Great Driffield road at Garton Hill.*

The Gothic style of **Sir Tatton Sykes Memorial** (1865, & *see Sledmere House above*) (120ft/37m high) is stranger than any genuine Gothic tower.

Robin Hood's Bay★
16mi/26km north of Scarborough on A 171, then a minor road to the right (signposted). The little village tucked in this picturesque bay was once the haunt of smugglers.

Whitby Abbey★
21mi/34km north of Scarborough on A 171. & *See WHITBY.*

Isles of **SCILLY**★

Cornwall, ENGLAND

POPULATION 2 048

MICHELIN ATLAS P 2 OR MAP 503 A, B 34 – 28 MILES SOUTHWEST OF LAND'S END

ACCESS FROM PENZANCE AND EXETER

This wind-battered archipelago off England's southwesterly tip is designated an Area of Outstanding Natural Beauty, a Heritage Coast, and its waters a Marine Park, managed by the Isles of Scilly Environmental Trust in collaboration with the Duchy of Cornwall; additional sites are further protected under English Nature's conservation scheme for Sites of Special Scientific Interest. The approach by sea or air gives a partial **view**★★★ of the five inhabited, 40 uninhabited and 150 or so named rocks set in a close group in the clear blue-green ocean. *Hugh Town, St Mary's, TR21 0LL ☎ 01720 422 536; Fax 01720 423782; tic@scilly.gov.uk; www. simplyscilly.co.uk*

▶ **Orient Yourself**: The main islands are St Mary's and Tresco.

Don't Miss: Tresco Abbey Gardens.

Organizing Your Time: Allow at least two nights.

Especially for Kids: Superb beaches.

A Bit of History

The Scilly Isles shows evidence of Bronze Age culture in the 50 or so **megalithic passage graves** dating from c 2000-1000 BC. They have been associated with a culture from Brittany which left other traces in West Cornwall and County Waterford, Eire. From AD 400-1000 there were Christian hermits on the isles and monks on Tresco. In AD 930 Athelstan dispatched the Danes from the isles and in 1114 Henry I granted Tresco to Tavistock Abbey to establish a Benedictine priory. In the 1830s Squire Augustus Smith became Lord Proprietor; the islands knew 40 years of prosperity during which houses, churches and schools were built, five shipbuilding yards were established on St Mary's and the **flower industry** was begun.

GETTING THERE

The *Scillonian III* operates a summer boat service from Penzance to St Mary's. Fixed-wing aircraft services operate from Southampton, Bristol, Exeter, Newquay and Land's End. Timetable and booking information for travel by fixed-wing flight and sea ☎ *0845 710 555; www.islesofscilly-travel. co.uk.*

Helicopter flights take 20 minutes from Penzance to St Mary's and operate six days a week with regular flights throughout the day. Timetable and booking information from British International ☎ *01736 363 871: www. islesofscillyhelicopter.com*

Visit

St Mary's – 3mi/5km across at its widest, with a coastline of 9mi/15km, St Mary's is the largest and principal island on which all but a few hundred Scillonians live. The main town, **Hugh Town**, runs the length of the sand bar between the main part of the island and the hill to the west, the **Garrison**. The **Guard Gate**, built in the mid-18C, gives access to the eight-pointed **Star Castle (Museum**★ *Open Easter-Oct, daily, 10am-noon and 1.30-4.30pm (also Jun-Aug, 7.30-9pm); Nov-Easter, Wed, 2-4pm. £1. ☎/Fax 01720 422 337; info@iosmuseum.org; www.iosmuseum.org)* built in 1594 at the time of Elizabeth I's feud with Spain. The **Garrison Walk**★ *(2hr)* inside the rampart walls circles the headland and affords excellent **views**★★ of the islands. Fifteen minutes walk from the **Telegraph Tower** on the island's highest point (158ft/48m) is a 3C BC stone burial chamber, **Bants Carn**. The large inlet, **Porth Hellick,** has a 4000-year-old passage grave. Eroded granite rocks with names such as Monk's Cowl and Kettle and Pans make **Peninnis Head**★ a spectacular sight.

Tresco★ – From the western landing point (New Grimsby), the path leads up past **Cromwell's Castle,** a 60ft/18m tower built in 1651 as a defence against a possible Dutch invasion, and the ruins of **King Charles' Castle**, which dates from 1550-54.

Gig Racing★★

🕐 *Apr-Sep, Wed and Fri at 8pm. To follow the race by boat consult the blackboards on the quay for departure times and costs.* The gigs of elm planking 0.25in/0.6cm thick, 28-30ft/8.5-9m long with 5ft/1.5m beam and less than 2ft/0.6m draught were built as rival pilot launches and smuggling craft – they were banned from having more than six oars so as not to have an advantage over the excise cutters. On Wednesday and Friday evenings throughout the summer the six-oared island gigs race in the St Mary's roadstead, starting from Nut Rock off Samson at 8pm sharp and finishing at the Quay. Traditional favourites built by perhaps the most eminent Peters boatyard at St Mawes include *Bonnet* (built 1830) and *Golden Eagle* (1870) which are manned by St Mary's crews and St Agnes's *Shah* (1873); the *Islander* (1989), built in Scilly from Cornish elm, is arguably the fastest and most beautiful. Latterly the sport has enjoyed such a revival as to warrant a World Championships event held in May.

On being appointed Lord Proprietor in 1834, Augustus Smith chose to settle on Tresco, where he built a Victorian-medieval castle mansion using island stone and wrecked ships' timbers near the ruins of a priory dedicated to St Nicholas, patron saint of sailors, which had fallen victim to fire at the hands of marauding pirates. Around the ruins he created the now famous subtropical **Abbey Gardens**★★, (&🕐 *Open daily, 10am-4pm.* 🎫 *£7.50. Café.* ☎ *01720 424 105; mikenelhams@tresco.co.uk; www. tresco.co.uk)* from seeds and plants (succulents and hard-leaved salt-resistant plants from the Mediterranean and Canary Islands) brought back by Scillonian sailors and professional plant collectors. His successors extended the range of exotic plantings in the gardens, which continue to enthrall horticulturists and amateur gardeners alike. From the terraces, there are fine **views**★★ over the gardens and beyond. On the edge of the gardens is **Valhalla**, an extraordinary collection of figureheads and other carved ornaments from the thousand ships wrecked off the islands in the past two centuries.

Other islands to visit include **Bryher, St Agnes, St Martin's** and **Samson** – a deserted island with many megalithic remains and the ruins of 19C cottages.

SHEFFIELD

South Yorkshire, ENGLAND

POPULATION 431 607

MICHELIN ATLAS P 35 OR MAP 502 P 23 – LOCAL MAP PEAK DISTRICT

TOWN PLAN IN THE MICHELIN GUIDE GREAT BRITAIN AND IRELAND

The fourth largest provincial city in England has been known since the 14C for the production of fine cutlery. The essential ingredients were to hand – the hills were rich in iron ore and thickly clad in woods for charcoal, grindstones were made of local stone and five rivers provided water power. Sheffield plating, the coating of copper items with silver by fusion, was a process invented in 1742 by Thomas Bolsover. Though some of its traditional industry has declined, Sheffield remains an important manufacturing centre and the commercial and cultural focus of a wide region. Its air is clean, its river valleys greener than in past centuries and its suburbs touch the boundary of the **Peak District National Park** (& *see PEAK DISTRICT).*

Sights

Cutlers' Hall★ – & *Church Street.* 🕐 *Open by appointment only for groups.* 🎫 *£3.* ☎ *0114 272 8456.* The third hall on this site, built in 1832 in a dignified Grecian style, houses the Company's silver and is the setting for their annual banquet.

Cathedral Church of St Peter and St Paul – & *Church Street.* 🕐 *Open daily, 7.30am (9.45am Sat) to 6.30pm.* 🎫 *Donation.* 🔈 *Guided tour (1hr) by appointment (5 languages). Leaflet. Bookshop:* 🕐 *Open 9.30am-5pm except Sun.* ☎ *0114 275 3434; Fax 0114 278 0244; enquiries@sheffield.cathedral.org.uk; www.sheffield.cathedral.org.uk.* The

Address Book

OUT AND ABOUT IN SHEFFIELD

Tourist Information Centre – *Winter Garden, Surrey Street* ☎ *0114 221 1900: visitor@sheffield.gov.uk. www.sheffieldcity.co.uk.*

Pubs and Restaurants – There is a wide choice of places to eat, with many restaurants concentrated on **Ecclesall Road, Abbeydale Road**, in the city centre and Broomhill. Other areas of note are **Division Street, West Street** and **Devonshire Street,** offering both restaurants and a good choice of pubs.

Shopping – The **Moor** is a pedestrianised shopping precinct with many of the larger stores, and a market (*open daily except Thu and Sun*). **Fargate**, **Pinstone Street** and **Barkers Pool** are lined with fashion stores. In the bohemian **Devonshire Quarter** is The Forum,(over 20 boutiques, mostly for the young). The **Castlegate Quarter** boasts three traditional markets (*open daily except Thu and Sun*), and **Orchard Square** in a courtyard setting

offers department and independent stores.

Outside the city centre there are two shopping malls: **Meadowhall** (*off Junction 34 of the M1)* and **Crystal Peaks** (*off Junction 30/31 of the M1)* Ecclesall Road – gift, clothes and antiques shops – and Abbey Road, are also worth a visit.

Entertainment – Sheffield boasts a wide range of nightclubs. For details see the *Dirty Stopout's Guide*, available free from the Tourist Information Centre. Details are also published in the weekly Sheffield Telegraph. Meadowhall and Crystal Peaks shopping centres both boast multi-screen cinemas; the Showroom cinema complex and the multi-screen Odeon cinema (*Arundel Gate*) are in the city centre.

Sheffield Ski Village and **IceSheffield,** golf courses, greyhound and stock car racing, rambling are available to sports enthusiasts. The Hallam FM Arena hosts rock concerts, ice shows, ice hockey fixtures. The **Don Valley Stadium** and **City Hall** are also major venues.

---

originally cruciform building probably dates from the 12C. Most of what is visible today is in the Perpendicular style, much altered in the restoration of 1880, with extensions in the 1930s and 1960s. The **Shrewsbury Chapel** now forms the sanctuary of the Lady Chapel in the southeast corner and was added by the fourth Earl of Shrewsbury (d 1538). His **tomb**★ shows him in armour and wearing the robes of the Order of the Garter. **St George's Chapel**, now the Chapel of the York and Lancaster Regiment, has an unusual screen of Sheffield-made swords and bayonets – the swords placed point uppermost denote service still being offered; bayonets, point down, signify weapons of war laid aside. The church was elevated to cathedral status in 1914.

Millennium Galleries – ⏰ *Open daily, 10am (11am Sun) to 5pm. (Parking Arundel Gate NCP (3min walk).* ☎ *0114 278 2600; Fax 0114 278 2604; info@sheffieldgalleries.org.uk; www.sheffieldgalleries.org.uk.* These galleries put on temporary and permanent exhibitions.

Ruskin Gallery – *Norfolk Street.* Art critic, essayist and poet John Ruskin (1819–1900) set up the Guild of St George to fight social injustice; its first museum, founded in Walkley in 1875, aimed to give ironworkers a chance to enjoy "what is lovely in the life of nature, and heroic in the life of men." This small gallery displays the Guild's permanent collection of work by a team of "colour copyists", whose skills brought great art and architecture to the masses in pre-television days. These include intricate copies of art by Titian, Botticelli and Carppaccio, many pieces by Charles Fairfax Murray and some work by Ruskin himself.

Graves Art Gallery – ♿ *Top floor of library, Surrey Street.* ⏰ *Open Mon-Sat, 10am-5pm. Wheelchair access by arrangement.* ☎ *0114 278 2600; Fax 0114 273 4705; info@sheffieldgalleries.org.uk; www.sheffieldgalleries.org.uk.* This attractive suite of galleries is known for its holding of Old Masters as well as 19C and 20C French and British art, and a particularly good selection of British watercolours.

Mappin Art Gallery and City Museum – ♿ *Weston Park.* ⛔ *Closed for renovation.* ☎ *0114 278 2600; info@sheffieldgalleries.org.uk; www.sheffieldgalleries.org.uk.* The gallery presents a collection of Victorian paintings and 18C and 19C English art, including Constable and Turner.

The museum presents the world's largest collection of old Sheffield plate and of cutlery representing European and Asian craftsmanship from the Bronze Age to the present day. There are also fine collections of silver, clocks, ceramics and glass. Local archaeology exhibits include outstanding material from the Peak District and the unique Anglo-Saxon boar-crested Benty Grange Helmet.

Kelham Island Museum – ◷ *Open Mon-Thu, 10am-4pm; Sun, 11am-4.45pm.* ⌷ *£3.50. Parking. Café.* ☎ *0114 272 2106; Fax 0114 275 7847; postmaster@simt.co.uk; www. simt.co.uk.* This museum celebrates the proud history of Sheffield's dependence on the steel industry.

Sheffield Manor – *Manor Lane.* ◷ *Open by appointment only.* ☎ *Contact the City Museum (& see above).* Originally the manor was the southern annexe of Sheffield Castle, where Mary Queen of Scots spent nearly fourteen of the nineteen years of her captivity, in the custody of the sixth Earl of Shrewsbury and his Countess, Bess of Hardwick, before being tried and executed in 1587. The Turret House, built in 1574, still has fine plaster ceilings and houses a small museum of exhibits connected with the manor and the captive Queen.

Bishops' House – . &◷ *Meersbrook Park. Open Sat-Sun, 10am (11am Sun) to 4.30pm.* ☎ *0114 278 2600; info@sheffieldgalleries.org.uk; www.sheffieldgalleries.org.uk.* The timber-framed yeoman's house (c 1500), little changed since last altered in 1753, now houses a small museum of Sheffield life in Tudor and Stuart times.

Excursions

Abbeydale Industrial Hamlet – *4mi/6km southwest of Sheffield by A 621.* &◷ *Open Mon-Thu: 10am-4pm, Sun: 11am-4.45pm.* ⌷ *£3.50. Parking. Café.* ☎ *0114 236 7731; Fax 0114 235 3196; simt@argonet.co.uk; www.simt.co.uk.* By 1714, and possibly earlier, scythes were being forged here, under water-powered tilt hammers. The steel furnace was installed early in the 19C and the clay crucibles were made on site. The Abbeydale Works ceased production in 1933 and in 1970 became a museum – manager's house and workmen's cottages, forge, grinding hull, water wheels and riveting shop.

Elsecar – *11mi/18km north of Sheffield by M 1 to Junction 36 and A 6135; follow signs to Elsecar Heritage.* ◷ *Open daily, 10am-5pm (subject to change in winter).* ⌷ *Powerhouse £3.25; Living History Centre £1.* ☎ *01226 740 203.* Originally built as industrial workshops by the local Earls Fitzwilliam, this complex of gritstone units has been converted into a crafts, science and history centre. Interactive displays in the Powerhouse illustrate the principles of energy and technology; ceramics and furniture are made and sold in the craft workshops; the Living History Centre explores life above and below stairs in the days of the Earls Fitzwilliam.

Magna★ – ◷ *Open daily, 10am-5pm; Nov-Feb, Tue-Sun, 10am-5pm (open Mon in school holidays).* ◷ *Closed 24-25 Dec.* ⌷ *£6.99. Parking. Cafeteria.* ☎ *01709 720 002; info@magnatrust.co.uk; www.magnatrust.org.uk.* This exhibition is based on the four elemens associated in the steelmaking process - earth, air, fire and water - each in its own pavilion linked by walkways suspended in the darkened interior of the Templeborough melting shop.

Conisbrough Castle – &◷ *Open daily, 10am-5pm (4pm Oct-Mar); last admission 40mins before closing.* ◷ *Closed 24-26 Dec, 1 Jan.* ☎ *01709 863 329; Fax 01709 866 773; info@conisbroughcastle.org.uk; www.conisbroughcastle.org.uk.* Only the circular keep (90ft/27m high, 52ft/16m in diameter) with its massive buttresses (9ft/3m thick) remains of the oldest Norman castle in England. The roof and two floors have been recently restored.

Earth Centre – ◷ *Open daily, 10am-5pm (4pm Nov-Easter).* ☎ *£4.50. Parking. Restaurant.* ☎ *01709 513 933; Fax 01709 512 010; info@earthcentre.org.uk; www.earthcentre. org.uk.* The slagheaps of two former coal mines have been transformed into an environmental theme park on the banks of the River Don.

Abbeydale Industrial Hamlet – &◷ *Open Easter-Oct, Mon-Thu, 10am-4pm, Sun, 11am-4.45pm.* ⌷ *£3. Parking. Café.* ☎ *0114 236 7731; Fax: 0114 235 3196; simt@argonet. co.uk; www.simt.co.uk.* The Abbeydale Works ceased production in 1933 and became a museum depicting the industrial life of the mill in 1970.

SHERBORNE★

Dorset, ENGLAND

POPULATION 7 606

MICHELIN ATLAS P 8 OR MAP 503 M 31

The busy centre of the district's dairy-farming industry, Sherborne, with its imposing abbey church, public school and fine warm **Ham Hill stone** buildings, has the charm of a small cathedral city. *3 Tilton Court, Digby Road, Sherborne DT9 3NL ☎ 01935 815 341 Fax : 01935 817 210; tourism@westdorset-dc.dove.uk.*

Sights

Abbey★★ – *Open daily, 8.30am-6pm (4pm winter). Guided tour by appointment. Brochure (7 languages). ☎ 01935 812 452; Fax 01935 812 206; abbey@sherborne.netkonect. co.uk.* The abbey church, rebuilt during the 15C, contains elements which date back to Saxon times when Sherborne was made the See of the Bishop of Wessex, **St Aldhelm,** in 705. The Norman church extended as far west as the Saxon church, as the late Norman **south porch** proves. The 15C **crossing tower,** on massive Saxon-Norman piers and walls, has paired bell openings and twelve pinnacles; the two-tiered Perpendicular windows along the south front are divided midway by the eight-light transept window.

Inside, the **chancel** shafts rise directly from the floor up to the earliest large-scale **fan vault** in the country, and the effect is breathtaking. Despite flying buttresses the almost flat vault had dropped 7in/17.5cm over 400 years and both had to be exactly rebuilt in 1856. Even more impressive is the late 15C **nave vault**, which is slightly arched, unlike the choir vault. Here a shortage of funds meant that the Norman aisle walls, Saxon west wall and arcade piers were retained; however, as the north file of piers was 14in/35cm to the west, a string course, emphasised by angel corbels, had to be inserted and a regular clerestory above it (the windows are out of line with the arcades) and the shafts sent from on high to sweep up to a cobweb of ribs with coloured bosses. A splendid, unadorned Norman **tower arch** divides the nave from the chancel. One of the original **Saxon doorways** can be seen at the end of the north aisle.

Sherborne Castle★ – *Castle and gardens: Open Apr-Oct, Tue-Thu, Sat-Sun and Bank Hol Mon, 12.30pm (2.30pm Sat) to 4.30pm ((last admission). £6; grounds only £3.20 Tearoom. ☎ 01935 813 182; enquiries@sherbornecastle.com; www.sherbornecastle.com* The Old Castle, now a ruin (model and explanation in the town **museum**, Abbey Gate), was built in 1107-35. In 1592 it was acquired by **Sir Walter Raleigh**, who then decided to build a new house, known as Sherborne Lodge, which forms the nucleus of the present house, commonly known as Sherborne Castle, on the far bank of the River Yeo. He created a four-storey house beneath a Dutch gable and balustrade, built of Ham stone with rendered walls. Sir John Digby, who was sold the property by James I following Raleigh's imprisonment, enlarged the castle in 1620-30, keeping faithfully to Raleigh's style, and it has remained in the Digby family ever since.

The house, set in parkland modelled by **Capability Brown** in 1776-79, contains fine collections of paintings, furniture and porcelain. Particularly noteworthy are the famous historic painting (1600) of Queen Elizabeth I in procession, the 17C plaster ceiling in the Red Drawing Room, and the heraldic chimney-piece in the Solarium. The Oak Room has 1620 **panelling** and a remarkable pair of **Jacobean inner porches.**

Excursions

Cadbury Castle – *7mi/11km north on B 3148 and a minor road to the right.* Excavations give evidence of occupation in prehistoric times and of the construction of an Iron Age hilltop fort c 600 BC. The Romans occupied the castle after the AD 43 invasion and the Saxons re-fortified it late in the 5C. The site, with its commanding **views★★**, is also reputed to be that of King Arthur's castle, **Camelot.**

Yeovil – *5mi/8km west on A 30. See YEOVIL.*

Fleet Air Arm Museum, Yeovilton★★ – *See YEOVIL: Excursions.*

Crewkerne –*14mi/23km west on A 30.* The parish churcha is a Perpendicular rebuilding with immense windows from an older church. The 80ft/24m tower has Somerset tracery bell openings on two levels topped by gargoyles, pinnacles and a stair-turret. The west front is marked by twin octagonal turrets fringed by more gargoyles. The interior has a fan vault beneath the tower and a square Norman Purbeck marble font.

SHETLAND ISLANDS⋆

Shetland, SCOTLAND

POPULATION 22 522

MICHELIN ATLAS P 75 OR MAP 501 P, Q, R 1 TO 4

ACCESS: SEE THE MICHELIN GUIDE GREAT BRITAIN AND IRELAND

Of the 100 Shetland Islands, lying some 60 miles north of Orkney, less than 20 are inhabited. The capital, Lerwick, is on the east coast of Mainland which is 50mi/81km long north to south, and 20mi/32km across at its widest. In contrast to Orkney, Shetland has few tracts of flat land and many inlets called **voes**. The economy was dominated by fishing and crofting until the oil boom of the 1970s. Although **Sullom Voe** is Europe's largest oil port, the oil industry still takes second place to fishing in importance, and the area directly affected by it is limited. Elsewhere the visitor will still find the attractions of wild beauty and empty spaces. Archaeological finds including an Iron Age village near Sumburgh provide interesting evidence of early human settlement.

Visit

Lerwick – *Market Cross, Lerwick* ☎ *01595 693 434.* The natural harbour is sheltered by the Island of Bressay. The attractions of Shetland's capital include the ruined **Clickhimin Broch**⋆, Fort Charlotte (17C) and a local museum.

Excursions

Jarlshof★★ – *Mainland. 25mi/40km south of Lerwick by A 970.* 🕙 *Open Apr-Sep, daily, 9.30am-6.30pm.* 🎟 *£2.50. Parking.* ☎ *01950 460 112.* The site of Jarlshof has been occupied from the middle of the 2nd millennium BC until the 17C. There are six Bronze Age houses, and a late Iron Age broch with other dwellings clustered around it. Numerous Viking longhouses tell of several centuries of occupation and there was a farmstead here in the 13C. In the 16C New Hall was built for Earl Robert Stewart.

Mousa Broch★★★ – *(HS) Mousa Island. 12mi/19km south by A 970. Motor boat (15min) from Sandwick jetty, by appointment with the proprietor.* ☎ *01950 431 367.* Small fortified farms, brochs, were peculiar to Scotland, the culmination of a tradition stretching back to 500 BC. Most have crumbled, but Mousa, probably dating from the first or second century AD, still stands.

A staircase, chambers and galleries were built into the thickness of the walls of the imposing kiln-shaped **tower** which is more than 40ft/15ft across at its base. In the courtyard are a hearth and lean-to structures.

Mousa Broch

B. Kaufmann/MICHELIN

Up Helly Aa★★★

This colourful and rousing fire festival is the most colourful reminder of the Viking heritage. Explanations for the pageant held on the last Tuesday in January are various, from spring rites to placating the Norse gods, or up-ending of the holy days. The principal figure, the **Guizer Jarl** (earl) and his warriors, all clad in the finery of Viking war dress, head the great torch-lit procession in their Viking longship. A thundering rendering of the *Galley Song* precedes the burning of the galley and the final song, *The Norseman's Home*. Celebrations continue throughout the night.

SHREWSBURY

Shropshire, ENGLAND

POPULATION 64 219

MICHELIN ATLAS P 26 OR MAP 503 L 25

TOWN PLAN IN THE MICHELIN GUIDE GREAT BRITAIN AND IRELAND

Once the capital of the mid-Welsh dominions of Powys, the medieval border town of Shrewsbury grew up around its Norman castle, which commanded the loop in the Severn. The town today has elegant Queen Anne and Georgian buildings, a wealth of "black and white" houses and fascinating "shuts" – medieval short cuts and alleyways. The two main bridges over the Severn are still, after centuries of border unrest, known as English Bridge and Welsh Bridge. Charles Darwin (1809-82), the naturalist, was born here and a statue to him stands outside his old school, now the Library. Another famous townsman, Clive of India (1725-74), is commemorated with a statue in The Square. 🖪 *The Music Hall, The Square SY1 1LH ☎ 01743 281200; Fax 01743 218213; tic@shrewsburytourism.co.uk; www.shrewsburytourism.co.uk.*

Sights

Abbey★ – ♿🕐 *Open daily, 9.30am (10.30am late-Oct to late-Mar) to 5.30pm (3pm late-Oct to late-Mar). 🕐 Closed 1 Jan and 25-26 Dec. ☜ Guided tour by appointment. Leaflet (7 languages). ☎ 01743 232 723; Fax 01743 240 172; shrewsburyabbey@netscapeonline.com.uk; www.shrewsburyabbey.com.* The Benedictine Abbey, founded in 1083, stands just outside the town, across the English Bridge. The 14C tower carries a statue of Edward III, in whose reign it was built, and there are Norman pillars in the nave dating from the 11C.

Castle – ♿🕐 *Open Feb to Dec, daily, 10am-4pm (times may vary so phone to confirm). 🕐 Closed 18 Dec to 13 Feb. Leaflet and brochure. Parking for disabled visitors by arrangement. ☎ 01743 358 516 , 01743 262 292; Fax 01743 270023; shropsrm@zoom.co.uk; www.shrewsburymuseums.com.* The castle was built by Roger de Montgomery in 1083 and restored in the 14C. In 1787 it was converted into a home for Sir William Poultney, Member of Parliament for Shrewsbury (1776-1805) by Thomas Telford. In 1926 the building became the Council Chambers and the Mayor's parlour was all that survived of Telford's work. The building now houses the **Shropshire Regimental Museum.**

Shropshire Regimental Museum – ♿🕐 *Open same hours as castle above.* This fine example of a three-storey Tudor merchant's timber-framed house, built in the late 16C, is now used as a local and social history **museum**. There is a collection of Roman artefacts from the city of Viroconium.

Excursions

Ironbridge Gorge Museum★★ – ♿ *See IRONBRIDGE GORGE.*

Weston Park★★ – *17mi/27km east of Telford by A 5. ♿ House: 🕐 Open Jul-Aug, daily, 11am-7pm; Apr-Jun and mid-Sep, Sat-Sun; also Easter weekend. Park and Gardens: Open same days as house, 1-4.30pm. ☜ House, park and garden £4.50; park and garden £2.50. Parking. Restaurant. Wheelchair route available. ☎ 01952 852 100; Fax 01952 850 430; enquiries@weston-park.com; www.weston-park.com.* The red brick house of 1671 is unusual in having been built by a woman, Lady Elizabeth Wilbraham; evidence of her architectural enthusiasm can be seen in her annotations to Palladio's First Book of Architecture in the library.

The splendidly furnished interior is remarkable for the quality of the portraits, which include works by most of the masters of this art from Holbein onwards – Lely's likeness of Lady Wilbraham in the Drawing Room and that rarity, a portrait by Constable (of the Hon and Revd George Bridgeman).

Beyond the formal gardens is the park, designed by Capability Brown; it is grazed by deer and rare breeds of sheep and contains many family attractions – a miniature railway, pets corner, adventure playground, picnic area.

Royal Air Force Museum, Cosford – *23mi/37km east by A 5, M 54 and south by A 41 from junction 3. ♿ Cosford. 🕐 Open daily, 10am-6pm (4pm last admission). 🕐 Closed*

1 Jan and 23-26 Dec. ⚬⚬ *Flight simulator. £2 Parking. Licensed restaurant.* ☎ *020 8205 2266 or* ☎ *01902 376 200; Fax 01902 376 211; cosford@rafmuseum; www.rafmuseum.com* Together with the more familiar passenger airliners and Second World War aircraft, the collection of over 80 aeroplanes and missiles includes some unusual prototype planes and a fascinating insight into the development of technology such as the Martin-Baker ejector seat.

Wenlock Priory★ – *(EH) 12mi/19km southeast by A 458.* ⊙ *Open late-Mar to Oct, daily, 10am-6pm (5pm Oct); Nov-Mar, Wed-Sun, 10am-1pm, 2-4pm.* ⊙ *Closed 1 Jan and 24-26 Dec.* ⚬⚬ *£3. Audio guide (3 languages). Parking.* ☎ *01952 727 466; wenlock@ english-heritage.org.uk; www. english-heritage.org.uk.* The Cluniac priory was founded c 690, pillaged by the Danes and later refounded. The church, one of the longest monastic churches in England (the nave is 350ft/106m long), was built in the 1220s by Prior Humbert.

The delicate interlaced arcading of the chapter house is the work of the Normans. So too is the magnificent **lavatorium** (1180), where the monks washed before meals; the elaborately carved panels in "Wenlock marble" depict Christ with St Peter and two Apostles. The Prior's Lodging (12C) is a fine medieval building, which was much extended in the 1490s, has been a private dwelling since the Dissolution (16C).

Wenlock Edge★ – *Southwest of Much Wenlock by B 4378 and B 4368.* The massive limestone escarpment, which was celebrated by the poet AE Housman, provides magnificent **views** over Shropshire.

Montgomery (Trefaldwyn) – *15mi/24km southwest by B 4386.* A medieval "new town" granted a Charter by Henry III in 1227, Montgomery grew up beneath the **castle★** (⊙ *Open daily 9am-5pm*) on the ridge above. The town has expanded little and the original rectangular layout is intact, though it now has the character of a Georgian market town. In the parish church of **St Nicholas** is the **canopied tomb** of Richard Herbert, his wife Magdalen, and their eight children, one of whom was the poet George Herbert (1593-1633).

Powis Castle★★ – *20mi/32km west to Welshpool by A 458* – ♿ *Castle and museum:* ⊙ *Open Jul-Aug, Tue-Sun; late-Mar to Jun and Sep to early Nov, Wed-Sun and Bank Hol Mon, 1-5pm. Garden: Open as castle, 11am-6pm.* ⚬⚬ *£7.50; garden only, £5. No dogs. Parking. Licensed restaurant.* ☎ *01938 551 920; 01938 551 944 (infoline); Fax 01938 554 336; powiscastle@nationaltrust.org.uk; www.nationaltrust.org.uk.* The town of Welshpool (Y Trallwng) lies at the northern end of the ridge on which is built Powis Castle. The barony of the la Pole was granted to Gruffyd ap Gwenwynwyn in 1277 on condition that his son renounce all Welsh princely titles. The massive twin towers of the gateway date from the decades prior to 1300. In 1587 the castle was bought by Sir Edward Herbert who quickly adapted it to Elizabethan standards of comfort. The Long Gallery, with its mid-17C *trompe-l'œil* panelling, is dated 1592-93 while the Dining Room and Oak Drawing Room were remodelled in the early 20C. The castle houses the collections of the first **Lord Clive** (1725-74) victor of Plassey and founder of British India, and many fine paintings.

The **gardens**, their Italianate terraces enhancing the castle's craggy site, were created towards the end of the 17C. They were not later subjected to the fashionable attentions of Capability Brown and are one of the rare remaining masterpieces of the period.

Isle of **SKYE** ★★

Highland, SCOTLAND

POPULATION 8 868

MICHELIN ATLAS P 65 OR MAP 401 A, B 11 AND 12

All the mystery and enchantment of a Hebridean isle are to be found on Skye, the largest of the Inner Hebrides group, just off the north west mainland. In Norse and Gaelic tales, Skye is the Island of Cloud or the Winged Isle. Crofting, tourism and forestry are the principal occupations of the islanders, 85 percent of whom are still Gaelic speakers. In 1995 the ferries were replaced by a **bridge**. 🛈 www.visitscotland.com.

The Cuillins

Visit

The Cuillins★★★ – The scenic splendour of the Cuillins makes these peaks the isle's most famous feature. The **Black Cuillins**, a six-mile arc of sharp peaks, encircle Loch Coruisk; many of these peaks are over 3 000ft/914m in height, with Sgurr Alasdair (3 309ft/993m) the highest. On the other side of Glen Sligachan the softly-rounded forms of the pink granite **Red Cuillins** contrast with their neighbours.

Portree★ – Skye's pleasant little capital, arranged around a sheltered bay, is a popular yachting centre.

Kilmuir – The town stands on the north coast of **Trotternish Peninsula★★** (lovely seascapes, basaltic rock pinnacle). The small churchyard has a monument to **Flora MacDonald** (1722-90), known for her part in the escape of Bonnie Prince Charlie after the collapse of the Jacobite cause at Culloden. She brought the Prince, disguised as her maid, from Benbecula in the Outer Hebrides to Portree. From here he left for France and lifelong exile.

Skye Museum of Island Life★ – ♿ ○ *Open Apr to mid-Oct, Mon-Sat, 9.30am-5.30pm.* ⬿ *£1.75. Parking. Gift shop.* ☎/*Fax 01470 552 206.* A typical crofter's house, a weaver's house, a smithy and a ceilidh house give some idea of crofting life in the 19C.

Dunvegan Castle – ♿ ○ *Open daily, 10am (11am Nov to mid-Mar) to 5.30pm (4pm Nov to mid-Mar).* ⬿ *Castle £6; gardens £4. Seal boats (£4). Information cards (several languages). Parking. Licensed restaurant.* ☎ *01470 521 206; Fax 01470 521 205; info@dunvegancastle. com; www.dunvegancastle.com.* Until 1748 the only entrance to this Hebridean fortress, the seat of the MacLeods, was by a sea gate. The castle is set on a rocky platform overlooking Loch Dunvegan. Most notable of the treasures kept here is the fragment of silk, known as the **Fairy Flag**. Legend has it that the flag given to the 4th Chief by his fairy wife has the power to ward off disaster to the Clan; this has been twice invoked. Other relics include the broadsword of the 7th Chief, the Dunvegan Cup and the Horn of Rory Mor, the 15th Chief.

Armadale Castle Gardens and Museum of the Isles – ♿ ○ *Open Apr-Oct, daily, 9.30am-5.30pm.* ⬿ *£4. Leaflet (6 languages). Parking. Licensed restaurant.* ☎ *01471 844 305; Fax 01471 844 275; office@cland.demon.co.uk; www.cland.demon.co.uk.* Part of Armadale Castle houses a museum-cum-exhibition featuring the "Sea Kingdom", the story of the Lords of the Isles and the Gaelic culture. The grounds offer walks and scenic **viewpoints** overlooking the Sound of Sleat.

SNOWDONIA★★★

Gwynedd, WALES

MICHELIN ATLAS P 32 OR MAP 503 I 24

Snowdonia was designated a National Park in 1951; it covers 840 sq mi/2 180km2 of wild beauty amongst the scenic mountains of North Wales and is the second largest of such parks in England and Wales. Yr Wyddfa Fawr, The Great Tumulus, or Snowdon (3 560ft/1 085m), as it is called in English, dominates the northern sector, Cader Idris (2 930ft/830m) the south. There are 96 peaks of over 1 970ft/600m in the park. *Snowdonia National park Headquarters: ☎ 01766 770 274. Gwynedd Council: ☎ 01286 672 255.*

🅿 **Parking**: Operates Jun-Oct; limited service in winter. Timetable available from local Information Centres. ☎ 01766 770 274 (Snowdonia National Park Headquarters); ☎ 01286 672255 (Gwynedd Council).

🕑 **Don't Miss**: Snowdon Mountain railway and the vew from the summit; Llechwed Slate Caverns; Machynlleth Centre for Alternative Technology.

🕐 **Organizing Your Time**: Allow at least three days

Kids **Especially for Kids**: Either of the mountain railways; Celtica.

🏃 **Mountaineering**: National Mountain Centre 🕐 *Open mid-Jul to early-Sep, daily, 9.30am-5.30pm; courses (2hr) at 9.30am, noon and 3pm in abseiling, climbing, canoeing (participants must be able to swim; change of clothes advisable) and skiing (long trousers, long sleeves and gloves); ⊗ £10 per course. Booking available. Equipment provided. ☎ 01690 720 214; Fax 01690 720 394; info@pyb.co.uk; www. pyb.co.uk.*

🎿 **Skiing**: Rhiw Goch Ski and Mountain Bike Centre.

🚴 **Mountain Biking**: Rhiw Goch Ski and Mountain Bike Centre. Also Coed-y-Brenin Forest Park and Gwydir Forest.

🚶 **Walking**: Ask about park ranger-guided walks at any tourist office; Coed-y-Brenin Forest Park and Gwydir Forest are good locations.

In and Around the National Park

Beddgelert – Three valleys meet here and the village looks south to the Pass of Aberglaslyn. The dramatic scenery is enough to attract the tourist, but in the 18C the local innkeeper, anxious to encourage trade, embroidered an old legend, and created "Gelert's Grave". The tale has it that Llywelyn the Great had a hound called Gelert. He left Gelert guarding his baby son and returned to find the child missing and the dog covered in blood. Llywelyn, believing Gelert had killed his son, slew the poor beast before he discovered that it had in fact saved the boy from a wolf, whose body was discovered nearby.

Betws-y-Coed★ – Beautifully set amid tree-clad slopes at the junction of the Rivers Conwy and Llugwy, Betws-y-Coed (Chapel in the Woods) has been the gateway to Snowdonia since Telford's great London-Holyhead road (A 5) was driven through North Wales in the early 19C. The huge stables of the hotel are today the **National Park Visitor Centre** (⌖ *see above*). A sturdy stone bridge, Pont y Pair, spans the Llugwy downstream from its romantically wooded ravine, where cascades form the famous **Swallow Falls**. Telford's ornate cast-iron bridge over the Conwy proclaims that it was "Constructed in the same year the Battle of Waterloo was fought."

Llanberis★ – This little slate-quarrying town is best known as the starting point for the ascent of Snowdon by the **Snowdon Mountain Railway** (⌖ *see below*) but has attractions of its own such as the **Welsh Slate Museum★** (⌖ 🕐 *Open Easter-Oct, daily, 10am-5pm; Nov-Mar, Sun-Fri, 10am-4pm. ⊗ £3.50. 3-D audio-visual show (4 languages). Children's play area. Café; picnic areas. ☎ 01286 870 630; Fax 01286 871 906; wsmpost@btconnect.com; www.nmgw.ac.uk),* a branch of the National Museum appropriately housed in the engineering workshops of the great Dinorwig Quarry. Visitors can penetrate far into the depths of the mountain, where the turbines of the **Dinorwig Power Station** are housed in great man-made caverns, or ride on another narrow-gauge railway along the lakeside of Llyn Padarn. Presiding over the scene from its crag-top is the early 13C round tower of **Dolbadarn Castle**, that rarity in North Wales, a purely Welsh stronghold.

Snowdon★★★ – The easiest ascent of the highest mountain in England and Wales is from Llanberis, by the trains of the **Snowdon Mountain Railway★★** (♿🕐 *Operates (weather permitting) mid-Mar to early-Nov, daily, 9am-5pm every 30min. Before mid-May and when summit is inaccessible by train, trains terminate at Clogwyn or Rocky Valley. Duration: 2hr 30min including 30min at summit. ⌨ Return £18; Earlybird train at 9am, 9.30am, 10am £15; single fares available; reduced fares when trains terminate at Clogwyn or Rocky Valley. Parking. Licensed bar; cafeteria at summit; cafeteria at station. Ramps. ☎ 0870 458 0033; Fax 01286 872518; info@snowdon-*

Nant Ffrancon, Snowdonia

R. O. Eames/The National Trust

railway.co.uk; www.snowdonrailway.co.uk), a rack-and-pinion line built in 1896 and the only one of its type in Britain; its centenarian steam locomotives are occasionally supplemented by diesels. For the more energetic, five main footpath routes are fully described in the leaflets and maps published by the Park Authority; the most straightforward follows the ridge used by the railway, while the most scenic begins at the Pen-y-Pass car park on Llanberis Pass. For experienced walkers, the scramble along the knife edge of Crib Goch can serve as an exhilarating prelude to completing the whole of the Snowdon Horseshoe, the great crescent of peaks and ridges looking down on Llyn Glaslyn and Llyn Llydaw. Given fine weather, the **panorama★★★** from the summit of Snowdon takes in the whole of Anglesey, the Isle of Man, and the Wicklow Mountains in Ireland.

Blaenau Ffestiniog★ – Slate is still quarried here but on a lesser scale than in the past. In the **Llechwedd Slate Caverns★** (♿🕐 *Open daily, 10am-5.15pm, (4.15pm Oct-Feb); last admission 1 hr before closing. 🕐 Closed 1 jan and 25-26 Dec. ⌨ £7.50. Audio guide (4 languages). No dogs. Parking. Licensed restaurant; café; Victorian pub. Partial wheelchair access to tramway tour and most surface attractions. ☎ 01766 830 306; Fax 831 260; llechwedd@ aol.com; www.llechwedd.co.uk)*, the story of Welsh slate is told on film and visitors are carried by train through caverns, where tableaux depict the working conditions. A pub and shop and houses above ground replicate mid- and early-20C village life too. Blaenau Ffestiniog is linked to Porthmadog on the coast by the **Ffestiniog Railway★★** (♿🕐 *Operates daily (certain days only late-Nov to early-Mar), 9am-5pm. Porthmadog-Blaenau Ffestiniog-Porthmadog (2hr 15min). ⌨ £14 maximum. Parking. Refreshments. ☎ 01766 516 073 (for timetable); Fax 01766 516 006; info@festrail.co.uk; www.festrail.co.uk)*, built in 1836 to haul slate from quarry to port, the narrow-gauge line (13mi/21km) now takes tourists through the splendidly wooded scenery of the Vale of Ffestiniog, past lakes and waterfalls, to this extraordinary "city of slate" among the mountains.

Cadair Idris – The great "Chair of the Giant Idris" (2 927ft/893m), one of the most challenging mountains in Britain, looms above the beautiful valley of the Mawddach and the little town of **Dolgellau★**, where dark stone buildings cluster around the market square. The mountain is best climbed by the Minffordd Path which starts on the far southeastern flank; its majestic presence can also be appreciated from the **Precipice Walk★**, one of a number of waymarked footpaths laid out around Dolgellau in the late 19C.

Harlech Castle★★ – 🎧 *See PORTMEIRION.*

Machynlleth★ – This little town just beyond the southern boundary of the National Park is famous as the place where Owain Glyndwr was crowned Prince of Wales in 1404. It is also the home of the multi-media experience called **Celtica★**, (♿🕐 *Open daily, 10am-6pm. £4.95. Audio visual (5 languages). Indoor safe play area. Tearoom. 01654 702 702; Fax 01654 703 604; bryn@celtica.wales.com; www.celtica.wales.com)* a sophisticated and highly enjoyable evocation of the world of the Celts. Located in a former slate quarry, the **Centre for Alternative Technology★★** (3mi/5km north by A 487 ♿🕐 *Open daily, 10am (9.30am mid-Jul to Aug) to 5.30pm (5pm Nov-Mar). 🕐 Closed 25 Dec and mid-Jan. ⌨ £7 (Mar-Oct); £5 (Jan-Mar). ☎ 01654 705950; Fax 01654 702782; info@cat.org.uk; www.cat.org.uk)*, is a pioneering establishment that has been inventing, testing and promoting "green" ideas since its inception in 1973. Reached by water-powered cliff railway, its array of installations demonstrating the virtues of wind, solar and water power are both convincing and entertaining, while the organically maintained parkland in which they are set owes nothing to picturesque ideals but rather proclaims the beauty of an earth-friendly aesthetic.

SOUTHAMPTON

Hampshire, ENGLAND

POPULATION 210 138

MICHELIN ATLAS P 9 OR MAP 504 P 31

This great south coast port, naturally favoured with a double tide, began as a Roman coastal garrison, Clausentum, on the east bank of the Itchen. By the 8C the Saxon port of **Hamwic** was already serving the royal city of Winchester and it has continued to grow, becoming one of Britain's major container ports. After severe bombing in the Second World War, the town began a successful recovery in the fifties and alongside medieval remains a modern city has grown up, with a lively university and renewed industry. *9 Civic Centre Road SO14 7FJ ☎ 023 8083 3333; Fax 023 8083 338; tourist.information@southampton.gov.uk; www. visit-southampton.co.uk*

Old Town

A good deal of the medieval defences and town buildings can still be seen today. The impressive northern gate to the town, the **Bargate★ (Y)**, built c 1180, was given its large towers c 1285 and its forbidding north face in the 15C. The **west wall** of the early defences rises spectacularly above the **Western Esplanade (YZ)**, where Southampton Bay once lapped the shore. Note the 15C **Catchcold Tower (Y)** and the **Arcade (Z)** running from the site of **Biddlesgate** to the **Blue Anchor Postern (Z)**. At the top of Blue Anchor Lane the large early 16C **Tudor House★ (Z)** incorporating an earlier banqueting hall which houses a museum (closed for refurbishment); outside, a 16C **garden** of flowers and herbs and a "knot garden" have been re-created.

At the far end steps lead down to the shell of the **Norman House (Z A)**, a fine example of a 12C merchant's house which was incorporated into the town wall defences in the 14C.

St Michael's Church (Z) – ⓢ *Open Easter-Sep, daily, 11am-1pm (except Sun) and 2-4.30pm. Sun service 10.30am. ☎ 023 8033 0851.* This is the oldest building in the medieval town, built soon after the Norman conquest and enlarged throughout the Middle Ages and in the 19C. A distinctive feature is the elegant 18C stone spire rising from the squat 11C **tower**. The furnishings of excellent quality include a black **Tournai marble font** of c 1170, two 15C brass **lecterns** and the 1567 **tomb** of Sir Richard Lyster, who occupied Tudor House.

Back on the Western Esplanade, just beyond the 14C **West Gate (Z)** and the 1428 **Merchants' Hall (Z)** stands the **Mayflower Memorial (Z)**, erected in 1913 to commemorate the sailing of the Pilgrim Fathers in 1620. The **Wool House (Z)** (ⓢ *Open Tue-Fri, 10am-1pm and 2-5pm (4pm Sat), Sun, 2-5pm. Closed Bank Hols. Wheelchair access to ground floor. ☎ 02380 635 904 or 02380 223 941; www.southampton.gov. uk/leisure/heritage)*, a beautifully restored 14C stone warehouse, now the **Maritime Museum**, displays models of ships and exhibits from the history of this great port.

God's House (Z) was founded c 1185 as an almshouse and hostel for travellers. To its east stand the early 14C **God's House Gate (Z)**, and the early 15C **God's House Tower (Z)** (ⓢ *Open all year, Tues-Fri, 10am-noon and 1pm- 5pm (4pm Sat), Sun, 2pm-5pm. Closed public holidays. Time 1hr. No charge. ☎ 01703 635 904.)*, containing the local archeological museum.

Additional Sights

City Art Gallery★ – ⓢ *Open Tue-Sun, 10am (1pm Sun) to 5pm (4pm Sun). Guided tour available; telephone for times. Parking. Refreshments. Signed tour for the deaf for some temporary exhibitions. ☎ 02380 832 277; art.gallery@southampton.gov.uk; www. southampton.gov.uk/leisure/arts.* The gallery has an excellent collection of modern art, including works by Spencer, Sutherland and Lowry.

Howard's Way Cruise – ⓢ *Cruise (2hr) down Southampton Water, all year. £7.50. Parking (charge). Brochure. Refreshments, bar. ☎ 02380 223 278; Fax 02380 571 471; www.bluefunnel.co.uk.* From Ocean Village (X). The tour gives an impression of the immensity of the port, though its interest depends on which vessels are in dock.

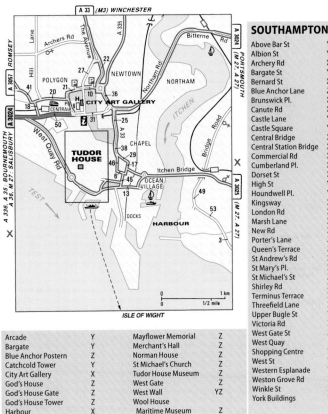

Excursions

New Forest★★ –   *See NEW FOREST.*

Broadlands★ – *8mi/13km northwest on A 3057 (X), or 1mi/2km short of Romsey.*   *Open mid-Jun to Aug, daily, noon-5.30pm (4pm last admission). £5.95. Parking. Refreshments. ☎ 01794 505 010; admin@broadlands.net; www.broadlands.net.* In 1736 the 1st Viscount Palmerston bought a small Tudor manor near Romsey and set about transforming its grounds. His son the 2nd Viscount commissioned **Capability Brown** to continue this work and rebuilt the house in the Palladian style. He added the pedimented three-bay portico to produce a noble **west front,** overlooking the beautiful River Test. **Henry Holland** created the east entrance front and the elegant dining room – the setting for three splendid **Van Dyck** paintings. The house is notable for the **Wedgwood Room** with its friezes and mouldings, a fine collection of 18C Wedgwood pieces and four portraits by Sir Peter Lely of ladies at Charles II's court. The white and gold plasterwork of the **Saloon** and the painted medallions in the drawing room ceiling are exquisite. In the 20C the house became the residence of Lord Mountbatten of Burma (1900-79). An exhibition and an audio-visual presentation are on view in the stable block.

Romsey Abbey★ – *9mi/15km northwest on A 3057 (X). Open daily, 8.30am-5.30pm (excluding services). ☎ 01794 513 125, Fax 01794 523 806; parishoffice@romseyabbey. org.uk; www.romseyabbey.org.uk.* The town of Romsey grew up around a nunnery founded by Edward the Elder, son of Alfred the Great, in 907 and largely rebuilt from c 1120-1230. At the Dissolution the convent was suppressed and the buildings destroyed but the abbey church survived to serve as the parish church. The purity and simplicity of the **interior★★** make this an excellent example of late Norman architecture. The elevation of the south choir aisle is of special interest. In the east chapel of the south choir aisle is a **Saxon crucifix** of c 1100, depicting Christ crucified, with two angels, the Virgin and St John. A second Saxon sculpture, the 11C **rood**, is outside on the south side, next to the finely decorated Abbess's Doorway.

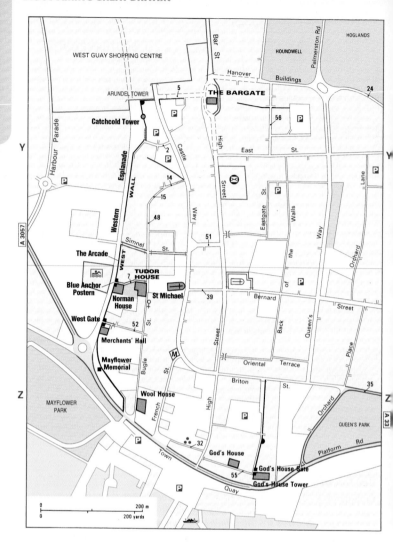

Sir Harold Hillier Gardens and Arboretum – ♿🕐 *Open daily, 10.30am-6pm (or dusk if earlier).* ⊗ *£4.25. Parking. Restaurant, café.* ☎ *01794 368 787; Fax 01794 368 027; Hillarb@ compuserve.com; www.hillier.hants.gov.uk.* Set in the rolling Hampshire countryside, the magnificent landscaped gardens and woodlands are a delight in all seasons.

Mottisfont Abbey – *(NT)* ♿ *House (Whistler Room and cellarium), garden and grounds:* 🕐 *Open late-Mar to early-Nov, Sat-Wed (also Good Friday and Thu, Jun-Aug), 11am-6pm (dusk if earlier); special opening of Rose Garden in Jun, 11am-8.30pm. Picture collection: Sun-Tue, 11am-6pm (last admission 5pm); otherwise telephone for confirmation.* ⊗ *£6. Parking. Refreshments.* ☎ *01794 341 220 (infoline), 01794 340 757; Fax 01794 341 492; mottisfontabbey@ntrust.org.uk; www.nationaltrust.org.uk.* Formerly a 12C Augustinian priory, the charming house boasts a drawing room decorated by Rex Whistler and a collection of 19C-20C paintings.

Andover Museum and Museum of the Iron Age – ♿🕐 *Open Tue-Sun 10am (2pm Sun and Ban Hol Mon) to 5pm.* ⊗ *No charge. Parking. Coffee shop.* ☎ *01264 366 283.* Archaelogical finds and tableaux re-create a prehistoric Celtic way of life.

Hawk Conservancy Trust, *Andover* – ♿🕐 *Open early-Feb to Oct, daily, 10.30am-5.30pm (last admission 4pm). Flying demonstartions at noon, 2pm and 3.30pm.* ⊗ *£6.25. Parking. Coffee shop. Picnic Area.* ☎ *01264 773 850; Fax 01264 773 772; info@ hawk-conservancy.org; www.hawk-conservancy.org.* A close encounter with majestic birds of prey kept in large enclosures on the wooded grounds. There are free-flying demonstrations with an opportunity for visitors to hold a bird of prey.

STAMFORD★★

Lincolnshire, ENGLAND

POPULATION 17 492

MICHELIN ATLAS P 29 OR MAP 504 S 26

Stamford has a long history, being one of the five Danelaw towns. "As fine a built town all of stone as may be seen" was the opinion of Celia Fiennes, late 17C traveller and writer. Located half-way between the Midlands and East Anglia, it has maintained its elegance and was the first town in England to be designated a Conservation Area. *Arts Centre, 27 St Mary's Street PE9 2DL ☎/Fax 01780 755 611; stamfordtic@skdc.com; www.southwestlincs.com/stamford.html.*

Sights

St Martin's Church★ – *High Street St Martin's.* 🕐 *Open daily, 10am-4pm. Sun service 9.30am.* 👐 *Donation. Brochure.* The church was rebuilt c 1480 in the Perpendicular style. The north chapel is dominated by the imposing alabaster monument to **William Cecil, Lord Burghley** (1520-98). In the nearby churchyard is the grave of Daniel Lambert (1770-1809), reputed to be the fattest man in England, who, in spite of his size, was a keen horseman and "very partial to the female sex." He weighed 52st 11lb when he died.

Lord Burghley's Hospital★ – *Corner of Station Road and High Street St Martin's.* The charming late Elizabethan almshouses were built on the site of the medieval hospital of St John the Baptist and St Thomas the Martyr in 1597.

Brazenose Gate – *St Paul's Street.* The 14C gate, which was rebuilt here c 1688, was originally part of Brazenose College *(demolished)*, set up in 1333 by students seceding from Brasenose College in Oxford.

Browne's Hospital★ – *Broad Street.* 🕐 *Open May-Sep, Sat-Sun and Bank Hol Mon; Oct-Apr by appointment.* 👐 *£1.50.* ☎ *01760 763 746.* One of the best-preserved medieval hospitals in England, Browne's was built c 1475, with cubicles for "ten poor men" in what is now the Board Room. Both the chapel and the audit room are lit by unforgettable c 1480 stained glass.

Stamford Museum – *Broad Street.* 🕐 *Open Mon-Sat, 10am-5pm; also Apr-Sep, Sun, 2-5pm.* 🕐 *Closed 1 Jan and 24-26 and 31 Dec.* ☎ *01780 766 317; Fax 01780 480 363; www.lincolnshire.gov.uk* The story of Stamford embraces its Saxon origins and its starring role as Middlemarch in the BBC television serial of the eponymous novel by George Eliot. Most odd is the lifesize model of Daniel Lambert, 52st 11lb (see above), who died on a visit here in 1809 and whose clothes have been displayed in the town ever since; beside is a diminuitive model of Charles Stratton, "General Tom Thumb", dressed in a suit he donated after viewing Lambert's clothes in 1846.

Excursions

Burghley House★★ – *Southeast of Stamford.* ♿🕐 *Open late-Mar to late-Oct, daily, 11am-5pm (4.30pm last admission).* 🕐 *Closed 31 Aug.* 👣 *Guided tour (80min). Parking. Restaurant.* 👐 *£7.10.* ☎ *01780 752 451; Fax 01780 480 125; burghley@burghley.co.uk; www.burghley.co.uk.* It is one of the finest Elizabethan mansions, built by **William Cecil, Lord Burghley**, "the greatest, gravest and most esteemed Councillor that ever Your Majesty had" (Essex). The extensive late 17C redecorations include the Baroque ceilings painted by **Laguerre** and **Verrio** which are at their most exuberant in the **Heaven and Hell Rooms.**

The distinguished collection of **paintings** includes works by Paolo Veronese, Jean Tassel and Francesco Bassano in the **Chapel**; Gainsborough, Kneller and Lawrence in the **Billiard Room**; and Brueghel the Younger in the **Marquetry Room**. Most fascinating of all is the Pagoda Room – here are Henry VIII (by Van Cleve), William Cecil (by Gheeraerts the Elder), Elizabeth I (by Gheeraerts the Younger) and Oliver Cromwell (by Robert Walker); Capability Brown (by Nathaniel Dance) looks out over the grounds he created.

Deene Park – *11mi/18km southwest by A 43 and minor road (right-signs).* ♿🕐 *Open Jun-Aug, Sun, 2-5pm; Easter Sun-Mon and May Day Hol and previous Sun, Spring and Summer Bank Hol Mon and previous Sun, 2-5pm; otherwise by appointment.* 👐 *House*

Burghley House

and Gardens £5.50; gardens £3. Guided tour (90min) by appointment. Parking. Teas. Ramps. ☎ 01780 450 278 or 450 223; Fax 01780 450 282; admin@deenepark.com; www. deenepark.com. The ancestral home of the Brudenell family, whose most famous son is remembered for having led the Charge of the Light Brigade in 1854 during the Crimean War, is 16C and 17C, ranged around a central courtyard, with 18C and 19C additions.

The most important part of the interior is the Great Hall of 1571 with its splendid Renaissance decoration and miraculously well-preserved alternate single and double hammerbeam roof. More intimate is the miniature **Oak Parlour** with 1630 panelling and portrait of Louise de Kerouaille and the **Drawing Room** with 12 charming Jacobean portraits of women and children.

Kirby Hall – (EH) 13mi/21km southwest by A 43 and minor road (right). ♿ 🕐 Open late-Mar to Oct, daily, 10am-6pm (5pm Oct); Nov to late-Mar, Sat-Sun, 10am-4pm. 🕐 Closed 1 Jan, certain days mid Aug (call for dates) and 24-26 Dec. ⬡ £3.30 Audio guide. Parking. Wheelchair access to ground floor, grounds and garden. ☎ 01536 203 230. Kirby Hall is a fine example of a large stone-built Elizabethan mansion, begun in 1570 with 17C alterations. Bought and completed in 1757 by Sir Christopher Hatton, a favourite of Elizabeth I, it was further extended into one of the most magnificent mansions of the Elizabethan era. Now mostly ruins, a few rooms still survive, such as the great hall with its canted ceiling.

The great garden, laid out in the late 17C, is currently being restored to its former glory.

STIRLING★★

Stirling, SCOTLAND

POPULATION 30 515

MICHELIN ATLAS P 55 OR MAP 501 I 15

TOWN PLAN IN THE MICHELIN GUIDE GREAT BRITAIN AND IRELAND

Controlling the route between Edinburgh and the Highlands and the **crossing of the Forth at its tidal limit**, Stirling has been strategically important from time immemorial, and its long history has been essentially that of the castle and former royal residence perched on its well-nigh impregnable crag. Today it is an ideal touring centre, with a variety of possible day trips, into the Trossachs, Rob Roy country, Fife or the Ochils, to name but a few. *41 Dumbarton Road FK8 2QQ ☎ 08707 200 620; Fax 01786 450039; stirlingtic@aillst.ossian.net; www.visitscottishheartlands.com*

A Bit of History

From its magnificent site Stirling has seen many battles, the most important being Stirling Bridge in 1297 and Bannockburn in 1314. Royal association began with David I, who in 1126 granted the burgh royal status. Stirling became a permanent royal residence with the accession of the **Stewarts**, and its Golden Age came under **James IV**, a true Renaissance prince. After his death at Flodden (1513), his Queen Margaret brought her son to Stirling, where he was crowned as James V. His daughter **Mary Queen of Scots** was crowned in the Chapel Royal, and her infant son, the future **James VI** of Scotland and I of England, was baptised here in 1566.

It was with his departure to Whitehall that Stirling's role as a royal residence ended.

Sights

Stirling Castle★★

🕐 *Open daily, 9.30am-6pm (5pm Oct-Mar); last admission 45min before closing.* 👣 *Guided tour available. 🎧 £7 (joint ticket witih Argyll's Lodging). Visitor Centre: Parking £2 (maximum stay 3hr). Refreshments. ☎ 01786 450 000.* The approach to the castle is up through the old town. A statue of Robert the Bruce stands guard on the esplanade. In the **Casemates** there is an interesting exhibition with models and life-size figures.

Palace – Begun by James IV in 1496 it was completed by his son in 1540. A masterpiece of Renaissance ornamentation, it had little effect on Scottish architecture in general.

Stirling Castle

Its outstanding feature is the elaborate design of the **external elevations**★★★ – best admired from the Upper Square – showing clearly the evolution of style over a period of 150 years. The façade of the **Great Hall** (1460-88) is lit by four pairs of embrasured windows below a crenellated parapet with wall-walk above the cornice; the noble interior is notable for its **hammerbeam oak roof**, minstrels' gallery and dais flanked by oriel windows. In contrast the **Palace** itself (1496-1540) is decorated with original figure carvings in recessed arches and above the cornice; the **royal apartments** boast fine 16C oak medallions known as the **Stirling Heads**★★. The early Renaissance **Chapel** (1594) features round-headed windows framing the elaborate doorway and an ornate interior. The King's Old Building houses the **Regimental Museum**★ (⏱ *Open Easter-Sep, Mon-Sat, 10am-5.45pm, Sun, 11am-4.45pm; Oct-Easter, daily 10am-4.15pm; last admission 15min before closing. Donation. Parking.* ☎ *01786 475 165; museum@ argylls.co.uk; www.argylls.co.uk), of the Argyll and Sutherland Highlanders which presents 200 years of heroic regimental history.

Old Town – The medieval town, with its narrow wynds and steep streets spills downhill from the castle. It is best explored on foot.

The splendid mansion, **Argyll's Lodging**★ (⏱ *Open Apr-Sep, daily, 9.30am-6pm (5pm Oct-Mar); last admission 45min before closing.* ☒ *£3; joint ticket with Stirling Castle £7.* ☎ *01786 450 000)* was built in 1632 by Sir William Alexander, founder of Nova Scotia. Everywhere are examples of fine **Scottish Renaissance decoration**★.

Only a ruined façade remains of **Mar's Wark**, the palace started in 1570 for John Erskine, Regent and Hereditary Keeper of the castle, and guardian of the young Prince James.

In the **Church of the Holy Rude**★, (⏱ *Open May-Sep, Mon-Sat, 10am-5pm. Services: Sun at 11.30am (Jan-Jun), 10am (Jul-Dec).* ☎ *01786 475 275; www.stir.ac.uk/town/facilities/holyrude/index.html)* the infant James VI was crowned, in 1567, with John Knox preaching the sermon. It retains its 15C oak **timberwork roof**. Beyond Bothwell House *(39 St John's Street)* with its projecting tower, stands the **Old Town Jail**, (♿ *Open daily, 9.30am-5pm (6pm Apr-Sep; 5pm Mar, Oct; 4pm Nov-Feb); last admission 30min before closing.* ⏱ *Closed 1 Jan and 25-26 Dec.* ☒ *£3.95.* 👥 *Guided tour (5 languages). Audio tour in winter. Scripts for hearing-impaired visitors. Parking.* ☎ *01786 450 050; otjva@aillst.ossian.net)* where the harshness of prison life can be experienced.

At the bottom of Broad Street, formerly the centre of burgh life, with its mercat cross and tolbooth, is **Darnley's House**, a town house where Mary's husband, Lord Darnley, is said to have stayed while the queen attended to affairs of state at the castle.

Excursions

Dunblane★ – *6mi/10km north by A 9.* A mainly residential town of some 6 000 inhabitants, Dunblane is grouped round its beautiful 13C Gothic **cathedral**★★ *(HS* ⏱ *Open daily, 9.30am (2pm Sun Oct-Mar) to 6.30pm (4.30pm Oct-Mar).* ☎ *01786 823 388).* An ecclesiastical centre since Celtic times, the cathedral dates from David I's creation of the bishopric in 1150. It was neglected, but not pillaged, following the Reformation, and so remains today a fine example of 13C Gothic architecture. The vigorous carving of the canopied 15C **Chisholm stalls** and their misericords (below the west window) is remarkable. In the glorious **choir** with its soaring lancet windows are the ornate **Ochiltree stalls**. The **Lady Chapel**, the oldest part of the building, has ribbed vaulting and carved bosses. Adjoining the south side of the nave is a 12C tower, and the magnificent **west front**★★, overlooking the Allan Water, is a masterpiece.

The Dean's House contains a museum of both cathedral and town.

Doune★ – *8mi/13km by A 84.* The late 14C **castle**★, *(HS* ♿ ⏱ *Open Apr-Sep, daily, 9.30am-6.30pm; Oct-Mar, Sat-Wed, 9.30am to 4.30pm;* ☒ *£2.80. Parking. Picnic area.* ☎ *01786 841 742)* with its four-storey **keep-gatehouse** (95ft/29m-high), stands apart from the village. With elaborate accommodation on a semi-royal scale, it is an example of a truly self-contained, secure residence of its period.

In the 17C and 18C the village was famous for the manufacture of fine **pistols**, made entirely of metal. They are highly decorated and were used mainly by Highland cattle drovers.

The **Doune Hill Climbs** take place each year, in June, on a course laid out on the estate.

Bannockburn Heritage Centre – *(NTS) 2mi/3km south by A 9.* ♿ *Site:* ⏱ *Open daily. Visitor Centre: Open Apr-Oct, daily, 10am-6pm; Mar and Nov to late-Dec, daily, 10.30am-4pm.* ☒ *£3.50. Guide book (3 languages). Audio-visual presentation. Parking. Refreshments.* ☎ *01786 812 664; Fax 01786 810 892; www.nts.org.uk.* An equestrian statue of

Robert the Bruce marks the king's command post on the eve of the battle. By 1313 Bruce had retaken most of the kingdom lost to Edward I, who had died in 1307. On 24 June 1314, he routed a numerically superior English army, ineptly led by Edward II. After Bannockburn, independence for Scotland was assured, though not formalised until the Declaration of Arbroath (1320) and the Treaty of Northampton in 1328. An audio-visual presentation tells the dramatic story.

National Wallace Monument – *1mi/1.5km northeast by A 9 and, at the Causewayhead roundabout, B 998.* ○ *Open (weather permitting) daily, 10am (9am Jul-Aug) to 5pm (6.30pm Jul-Aug).* ○ *Closed 1 Jan and 25-26 Dec.* ○ *£3.95. Audio-visual presentation. Parking. Wheelchair access to the grounds. Limited access to the monument. Refreshments.* ☎ *01786 472 140; www.nationalwallacemonument.com.* **Sir William Wallace** (1270-1305) rallied Scottish forces against English rule. He recaptured the castle from Edward I's forces after his victory at Stirling Bridge in 1297. Following the Scots' submission in 1304, Wallace was captured and died a traitor's death in London in 1305. An audio-visual presentation depicts Wallace and his place in Scottish history. From the viewing platform (246 steps) atop Abbey Craig (362ft/110m) there is a **panorama**★★ of Stirling and all the country around.

STOKE-ON-TRENT

Staffordshire

POPULATION 266 543

MICHELIN ATLAS P 35 OR MAP 403 N 24

TOWN PLAN IN THE MICHELIN GUIDE GREAT BRITAIN AND IRELAND

Despite over 50 years of unification, the six towns known as the Potteries – Stoke, Tunstall, Burslem, Hanley, Fenton and Longton – remain separate entities, each maintaining an identity of its own. **Arnold Bennett** immortalised them in his novels as the Five Towns.

The potteries existed long before the time of England's most distinguished potter, **Josiah Wedgwood** (1730-95). Kilns dating c 1300 have been found at Sneyd Green and there were Adams and Wedgwood potters in the 1600s; but it was the opening of Josiah Wedgwood's Etruria factory (1769), the exploitation of Staffordshire's coalfields and the digging of the Trent-Mersey Canal that turned a local industry into a national one and an industry into an art.

Most of the great brick kilns (bottle, conical, squat, swollen, slender) have now disappeared. A few remain, particularly in Longton, standing out on the horizon, as monumental as Stonehenge. ▯ *Victoria Hall, Cultural Quarter, ST1 3AD* ☎ *01782 236 000; Fax 01782 236005; stoke.tic@stoke.gov.uk; www.visitstoke.co.uk*

- ⊙ **Don't Miss**: The Wedgwood Story; Little Moreton Hall.
- ○ **Organizing Your Time**: Allow 1-2 days including an excursion.
- **Especially for Kids**: Alton Towers; Trentham.

Museums

Gladstone Pottery Museum★ – *Uttoxeter Road, Longton.* ♿○ *Open daily, 10am-5pm (4pm last admission).* ○ *£4.95. Leaflet (5 languages). Video (6 languages; English subtitles for hearing impaired). Parking. Licensed restaurant; picnics.* ☎ *01782 319 232; Fax 01782 598 640; gladstone@stoke.gov.uk; www.stoke.gov.uk/gladstone.* This unique surviving pottery factory or "potbank" retains its original workshops, cobbled yard and distinctive bottle ovens. In its early years the Gladstone Works (founded 1850) employed 41 adults and 25 children. It produced bone china until the 1960s when it was converted into a museum of British pottery. Displays illustrate the growth of the Staffordshire pottery industry, the various products, the art of colouring and decorating them, and the potter at home. The potters' traditional skills are demonstrated in the workshops.

The Potteries Museum and Art Gallery★ – *Bethesda Street, Hanley.* ♿○ *Open Mar-Oct, daily, 10am (2pm Sun) to 5pm; Nov-Feb, 10am (1pm Sun) to 4pm.* ○ *Closed 1 Jan* *and 25 Dec. Refreshments.* ☎ *01782 232 323; Fax 01782 232 500; museums@stoke.gov. uk; www.stoke.gov.uk/museums*. The city museum houses one of the finest ceramics collections (in the Potteries), starting with English pottery c 1350, through the beginning of earthenware as an English art (Thomas Toft's Charles II plate), to the glorious years of the 18C and the prosperous years of the 19C (Spode and Copeland's View of Naples and **Minton's bone china vases**), finishing with the Art Deco follies of Clarice Cliff, the modern studio movement and examples of current industrial production.

Excursions

Biddulph Grange Garden★ – ◷ *Open late-Mar to early-Nov, Wed-Sun and Bank Hol Mon, 11am (noon Wed-Fri) to 6pm; early-Nov to mid-Dec, Sat-Sun, noon-4pm/dusk; last admission 5.30pm/dusk.* ⊗ *Mid-March to 30 Oct: £5.00, early Nov to mid-Dec: £2.00* ☎ *01782 517 999; Fax 01782 510 624; biddulphgrange@nationaltrust.org.uk; www. nationaltrust.org.uk*. This unusual and exciting garden was designed in the mid-19C by James Bateman to display specimens from his extensive plant collection.

Little Moreton Hall★★ – *(NT) 10mi/16km north on A 500 and A 34.* ♿◷ *Open late-Mar to early-Nov, Wed-Sun, Good Friday and Bank Hol, 11.30am-5pm/dusk; early-Nov to late-Dec, Sat-Sun, 11.30am-4pm (⊗ Dec restricted access).* ⊗ *£5.25.* 🍽 *Guided tour (50min) most afternoons. Guide book. Mini guide (5 languages). Parking. Licensed restaurant; picnic area. Wheelchair; access to ground floor and gardens.* ☎ *01260 272 018; littlemoretonhall@ntrust.org.uk; www. nationaltrust.org.uk*. The beautiful moated half-timbered manor house is characterised by rich and intricate patterns on square panels, elaborate joinery and window tracery and 16C glass.

It was begun in the 1440s with the building of the Great Hall and completed some 140 years later with the addition of John Moreton's Long Gallery. Note the tracery in the bay window of this Great Hall, the painted panelling frieze in the Parlour which tells the story of Susanna and the Elders, the arch-braced roof trusses and plaster figures of Destiny and Fortune in the Long Gallery.

The Wedgwood Story★ – *7mi/11km south on A 500, A 34 and a minor road (left) to Barlaston.* ♿◷ *Open daily, 9am (10am Sat-Sun) to 5pm.* ⊗ *£6.95. Self-guided tour (2hr). Audio-guide (2 languages). Parking. Restaurant, bistro. Wedgwood Shop.* ☎ *01782 204 218; booking@wedgwood.com; www.thewedgwoodstory.com*. At the 1938 Wedgwood Factory (set in parkland and a model in its day) are full displays of the pottery-making process, an excellent collection of Wedgwood ware (neo-Classical, Victorian, Art Nouveau, Art Deco and modern), and Wedgwood portraits by Stubbs, Reynolds, Lawrence and Wright of Derby.

Alton Towers – *12mi/19km east on A 50, A 521 and B 5032. Rides and attractions:* ♿ *Rides and attractions:* ◷ *Open mid-Mar to early-Nov, daily, 9.30am-7pm, 6pm or 5pm according to season.* ⊗ *Premium £25; peak £23.50; off-peak £18.50. Parking. Restaurants. Wheelchairs available, most rides accessible.* ☎ *0990 204 060; Fax 01538 704 097; www. alton-towers.com; www.alton-towers.co.uk*. This famous theme park offers a great variety of spectacular rides as well as tranquil gardens. It is set in the grounds of Alton Towers, a 19C neo-Gothic mansion, now in ruins, designed by Anthony Salvin for Charles Talbot, 15th Earl of Shrewsbury.

Trentham – *5 mi/8km south of Hanley* ♿◷ *Italian Garden and Parkland 10am to 6pm or dusk* ⊗ *£4. Lakeside and Woodland Walks 8am until dusk, free entry. Monkey Forest 10am-4pm.* ⊗ *Italian Garden and Parkland £4; Monkey Forest £5. dventure playground* ☎ *01782 657341; Fax 01782 644536; enquiry@trenthamleisure.co.uk; www. trenthamleisure.co.uk*. The 750-acre site formerly known as Trentham Gardens is undergoing a £100 million regeneration project to restore Britain's most spectacular Italian Garden. Aside from the landscaped gardens and lake a huge Garden Centre, a speciality shopping Village, restaurants and a Monkey Forest featuring 100 Barbary Macaque monkeys roaming freely through the trees, are its principal attractions to date with many more outdoor attractions planned including a Treetops Activity Trail and a Butterfly Jungle.

STONEHENGE★★★

Wiltshire, ENGLAND

MICHELIN ATLAS P 9 OR MAP 503 O 30

Stonehenge, Britain's most celebrated prehistoric monument, is 4 000 years old; radiocarbon dating indicates that its construction was begun in c2950 BC and completed in three phases by c 1550 BC. In context with other comparable feats of civil engineering, it is several centuries later than the Great Pyramid in Egypt, contemporary with Minoan culture in Crete, a millennium earlier than the first Great Wall of China, 2 000 years earlier than the Aztec constructions (and carved stone calendars) of Mexico and 3 500 years older than the figures on Easter Island. For centuries it has sent writers, painters and every sort of visitor into flights of fancy, for its purpose remains an enigma. Although many of the stones have fallen or disappeared it is still possible, from the centre of the circle, to see the sun rise over the Heel Stone *(at the entrance)* on midsummer's day; there are suggestions that it was constructed as an astronomical obser-vatory or a sanctuary for a sun-worshipping cult, or even a combination of the two. The main axis has always been aligned with the midsummer sunrise and Stonehenge must have been a ceremonial centre celebrating the sun and marking the seasons. Certainly it was not "built by the Druids", the priesthood of the Celtic peoples who reached Britain in 250 BC, long after the completion of the final phase of the building.

Visit

&♿🕐 *Open daily, 9.30am (9am Jun-Aug) to 6pm (7pm Jun-Aug; 5pm mid-Oct to late-Oct; 4pm late-Oct to mid-Mar).* 🕐 *Closed 1 Jan and 24-26 Dec. £4.40 Audio tour (9 langua-ges). Parking. Refreshments.* ☎ *01980 624 715; www.stonehengemasterplan.org; www. english-heritage.org.uk.*

The Period – When work began the area was inhabited by nomadic hunters and early farming settlers who had crossed the Channel and North Sea in skin boats. By 2000 BC the Beaker Folk spread into Wessex along the chalk upland tracks, grow-ing into a community of 12-15 000, ruled by the cattle-barons of Salisbury Plain, who also controlled the metal industry. There was a growing priesthood who, at peak periods in the construction of Stonehenge, could call on the population to provide the 600 men needed to haul a sarsen stone up the Vale of Pewsey, or 200 to erect it on site.

Aerial view of Stonehenge

The Building Design – Like many a medieval cathedral Stonehenge was much remodelled after its foundation. In the **first phase**, 2950-2900 BC, a ditch with an inner bank of chalk rubble (6ft/nearly 2m high) was dug. This, with a ring of 56 holes, known as the Aubrey Holes, after the 17C pioneer of field archeology John Aubrey (1626-97), encloses an area 300ft/91m in diameter. To the northeast the bank and ditch were cut to make an entrance marked inside by two upright stones and outside by the **Heel Stone** (near the road). Inside the enclosure four **Station Sarsens** were set up at the cardinal points of the compass.

In the **second phase,** c 2100 BC, a double ring of undressed **bluestones** was set up toward the centre; these stones, weighing up to 4 tons each, were transported 240mi/386km from the Presely Hills in southwest Wales, mainly by water and finally along the wide **Avenue** which was built from the River Avon to the entrance of the henge.

In the **third phase**, c 2000 BC, the structure was transformed. The bluestone rings were replaced by a circle of tall trilithons. These standing stones were tapered at one end and tenoned at the top to secure the curving mortised lintels, which were linked to each other by tongues and grooves, having been levered gradually into position. Inside the circle five separate giant trilithons rose in a horseshoe, opening towards the Heel Stone. The entrance was marked by new uprights, one of which, the Slaughter Stone, now fallen, remains. By the end of this **final phase**, c 1550 BC, the dressed bluestones were reintroduced in their present horseshoe formation, within the sarsen horseshoe.

STOURHEAD★★★

Wiltshire, ENGLAND

MICHELIN ATLAS P 8 OR MAP 403 N 30

The garden at Stourhead is one of the supreme examples of English landscape style.

Visit

Garden – ♿ *Garden:* ⏱ *Open daily, 9am-7pm/dusk. House: Open late-Mar to early-Nov, Sat-Wed and Good Friday, noon-5.30pm/dusk. Garden and house ⊜ £8.70; garden or house £4.90; garden only, Nov-Feb £3.80. Restaurant. Refreshments. Parking.* ☎ *01747 841 152; Fax 01747 842 005; stourhead@ntrust.org.uk; www.nationaltrust.org.uk.* This idyllic scenery was created by the banker Henry Hoare II (1705-85), whose father had built a Classical house here in 1721, designed by the architect Colen Campbell,

Autumn colours at Stourhead

pioneer of English Palladianism. Henry Hoare was influenced in his garden design by the landscapes he saw on his travels and even more by the paintings of Claude Lorraine and Nicholas Poussin, in which nature is presented in luminous shades and focal points are provided by statuary or Classical buildings.

He first had the great triangular lake formed, then began the planting of deciduous trees and conifers, "ranged in large masses as the shades in a painting." In collaboration with his architect, Henry Flitcroft, he began to build those gems of garden architecture which, on an anti-clockwise tour of the lake, may be pinpointed from across the water as the Temple of Flora (1744-46) and the Grotto, the Gothic Cottage, the Pantheon (1753-54), the Temple of Apollo, high among the trees, and the Palladian Bridge.

In 1765 Hoare acquired the 1373 Civic High Cross from Bristol, enabling him to create an entirely English vista of lake, Turf Bridge, Cross, and, in the background, Stourton church and village. His planting, now wonderfully mature, has been added to by his successors to give a wealth of exotic specimens and of ever-changing seasonal effects.

At the far end of the "outer circuit" stands **Alfred's Tower** (🕐 *Open late Mar-Oct, Tues-Fri, 2pm-5.30pm; Sat-Sun, Good Friday and bank holiday Mondays 11.30am-5.30pm/ dusk if earlier.* 💷 *£1.50, children: 70p)*, a triangular brick folly built on the spot where Alfred allegedly raised his standard when resisting the Danes, but more probably commemorating the succession of George III and peace with France (1762). At the top of the narrow tower is a viewing balcony (206 steps).

House – Campbell's house of 1721 consisted of the central block; the flanking pavilions containing the picture gallery and library were added by Henry Hoare II's heir, Sir Richard Colt Hoare (1758-1838). A large proportion of the house contents were sold in 1883, and in 1902 a fire destroyed the early 18C interiors, although the contents of the ground floor staterooms were largely saved.

The **hall**, a perfect 30ft/9m cube, is hung with portraits of the Hoare family. The long barrel-vaulted **library**, considered a particularly fine Regency interior, contains some splendid pieces of **Chippendale** furniture and **Canaletto** pen and wash drawings of Venice. Further treasures are to be found in the South Wing (furniture) and **Picture Gallery**: landscapes by **Claude** and **Poussin** which inspired Henry Hoare II's design for the gardens.

STRATFORD-UPON-AVON★★

Warwickshire

POPULATION 22 231

MICHELIN ATLAS P 27 OR MAP 403 P 27

Stratford is Arden country; its timber frames were hewn from the surrounding Forest of Arden and its favourite son's mother was called Mary Arden. **William Shakespeare** (1564-1616) forsook his home town and his wife, Anne Hathaway, for London, where success came to him as a jobbing playwright, who was able to distil sex and violence, farce and philosophy into the most potent lines in the language. He returned to Stratford in 1611, rich and famous enough to acquire a coat of arms, and lived at New Place until his death. Stratford is now one of England's most popular tourist destinations and as a result can be very congested, especially during the summer months.

▶ **Orient Yourself**: The centre is small enough to comfortably cover most attractions on foot. A hop-on, hop-off City Sightseeing Bus covers the rest. ☎ 01789 299 866; www.citysightseeing.co.uk.

🅑 **Don't Miss**: Hall's Croft; a night at the Royal Shakespeare Theatre; Mary Arden's House and the Shakespeare Countryside Museum.

🕐 **Organizing Your Time**: Allow two days plus time for excursions.

🥾 **Walking Tours**: *Town Walk Mon- Wed 11am, Thur- Sun 2pm. (Times vary Christmas and New Year).* 💷 *£5. Meet at the Swan Fountain, Waterside (opposite Sheep Street), near The Royal Shakespeare Theatre. Booking not necessary.* ☎ *01789 292 478, 07855 760 377. Ghost Walk Thur and Friday 7:30pm. Booking necessary.* ☎ *01789 292 478, 07855 760 377.*

A. Williams/MICHELIN

Mary Arden's House

Sights

Shakespeare's Birthplace★ (A) – ♿🕐 *Open daily, Jun-Aug 9am (9.30am Sun) - 5pm; Apr-May, Sep-Oct, 10am (10.30am Sun) - 5pm; Nov-Mar, 10am (10.30 Sun) - 4pm.* 🕐 *Closed 23-25 Dec.* 👁 *£6.50; joint ticket to 3 Shakespearean Properties in town £8.50; joint ticket to 5 Shakespearean Properties £12. Brochure (4 languages).* ☎ *01789 204 016; info@shakespeare.org.uk; www.shakespeare.org.uk.* The half-timbered house where the dramatist was born is part museum (including a First Folio), part shrine. Note the graffiti on the upstairs windows (Scott, Carlyle, Ellen Terry and Henry Irving). In the same complex is an exhibition illustrating Shakespeare's life and times.

Harvard House – ♿🕐 *Open May-Oct, Tue-Sat and Bank Hol Mon, 10am (10.30am Sun) to 4.30pm.* ☎ *01789 204 016.* This ornately carved half-timbered house bears the

---

Address Book

**OUT AND ABOUT
IN STRATFORD-UPON-AVON**

Tourist Information Centre – *Bridgefoot CV37 6GW b 0870 160 7930; stratfordtic@ shakespeare-country.co.uk; www. shakespeare-country.co.uk.*

Public Transport – For details of local buses ☎ 01788 535 555 (Busline), or call in at the Midland Red Travel Shop located inside the Stratford TIC. An "Explorer" ticket giving a day's unlimited travel on all Midland Red journeys can be purchased from the driver. For details on buses and trains apply to the Passenger Transport Authority for the West Midlands ☎ 0121 200 2700. Visitors travelling to Stratford-upon-Avon by train from London can purchase a **Shakespeare County Explorer** valid for 1, 3 or 5 days, and entitling travellers to a return train journey plus unlimited travel on local Midland Red Buses. ☎ 01789 267 522 or 01926 311 470.

Pubs and Restaurants – A list of pubs, restaurants and cafés is available from the **Tourist Information Centre** (👁 *see above*).

Shopping – Shopping arcades include the **Minories**, the **Mulberry Centre**, **Bards Court**, **Red Lion Court** and **Bell Court**. The main shops are in **High Street** and **Henley Street**. **Sheep Street** is worth a visit for shoppers in search of something a bit different; a street market is held every Friday in **Rother Street**.

Entertainment – A visit to the theatre is a must. The **Royal Shakespeare Theatre** is the largest of all the RSC theatres in Stratford, and its two restaurants overlook the River Avon. The **Swan Theatre's** interior design reflects an Elizabethan theatre, with plays by Shakespeare and Ben Jonson among others. For more contemporary plays, visit The Other Place Theatre. Stratford has two nightclubs, **Celebrities Nightclub** (open Mondays and Wednesdays to Saturdays) ☎ 01789 293 022.

date 1596 when it was home to Katharine Rogers. The American flag flies in honour of her son, **John Harvard** (b 1607), founder of Harvard University, which owns the building today. Inside the house is displayed the Neish Collection of Pewter which includes pieces ranging from Romano Britain to the 19C.

Nash's House and New Place – 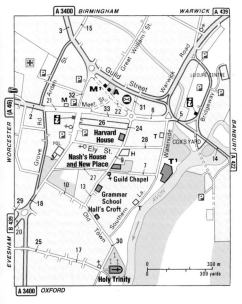 *Open mid-Mar to mid-Oct, daily, 9.30am (10am Sun) to 5pm; mid-Oct to mid-Mar, daily, 10am (10.30am Sun) to 4pm.* £3; *joint ticket to 3 Shakespearean Properties £8.50; joint ticket to 5 Shakespearean Properties £12. Brochure (4 languages).* 01789 204 016; info@shakespeare. org. uk; www.shakespeare. org.uk. Of Shakespeare's retirement home, built in 1483, only the foundations remain but next door in **Nash's House,** home of Shakespeare's granddaughter, behind the much-restored frontage, is an exhibition about the history of Stratford.

Hall's Croft★ – *Open mid-Mar to mid-Oct, daily, 9.30am (10am Sun) to 5pm; mid-Oct to mid-Mar, daily, 10am (10.30am Sun) to 4pm. Closed 25 Dec.* £3; *joint ticket to 3 Shakespearean Properties £8.50; joint ticket to 5 Shakespearean Properties £12. Brochure (5 languages).* 01789 204 016; info@shakespeare. org. uk; www.shakespeare.org. uk. Shakespeare's eldest daughter, Susanna, married physician John Hall and the couple lived here until some time after 1616. The restored house, part 16C-part 17C, contains furniture and paintings from Hall's time, notes about his patients and a small exhibition on medicine in his day.

Guild Chapel – *Open daily, 10am-4.30pm.* 01789 204 671; Fax 01789 297 072. The Chapel of the Guild of the Holy Cross (founded 1269), the ruling body of Stratford before the Reformation, is predominantly Perpendicular, with wall-paintings of Christ, Mary, St John, St Peter and the Last Judgement in the **chancel**.

Grammar School – *Exterior only.* Built c 1417 as the Holy Cross Hall and turned into a school after the Reformation; amongst its pupils was William Shakespeare.

Holy Trinity Church – *Open (special services permitting) Mon-Sat, 8.30am (9am Nov-Feb) to 6pm (4pm Nov-Feb), Sun, 2-5pm; last admission 20min before closing.* £1. *Leaflet (17 languages).* 01789 266 316; www.stratford-upon-avon.org. With an Early English tower and transepts and early Perpendicular nave and aisle, Holy Trinity would be notable even without **Shakespeare's grave** on the north side of the chancel. "Blessed be the man who spares these stones / And cursed be he that moves my bones." No one has touched them.

Royal Shakespeare Theatre (T¹) – *Royal Shakespeare Company Collection: Open daily, Mon-Sat, 2-6.30pm, Sun, noon-4pm. Guided Theatre Tour (1hr) from the Royal Shakespeare Theatre at 1.30pm, 5.30pm and after the evening performance, from the Swan Theatre Sun at noon, 1pm, 2pm, 3pm (pre-booking essential). Closed 24-25*

Address Book

For coin ranges, see Legend at the back of the guide.

charming breakfast room and 6 Laura Ashley-style bedrooms.

WHERE TO STAY

Victoria Spa Lodge, *12 Evesham Place* ☎ *01789 227 985; Fax 01789 204 728; www. victoriaspa.co.uk.htm. This beautiful Victorian lodge, a 20-minute rural walk from the town centre, originally built as a spa (and where the future Queen Victoria once stayed) offers pretty public rooms and 7 bedrooms in country cottage style.*

Virginia Lodge, *12 Evesham Place* ☎ *Fax 01789 292 157 enquiries@ virginialodge.co.uk www.virginialodge.co. uk. A family-friendly Victorian house, a 5-minute walk to the town centre with a*

WHERE TO EAT

Golden Cross, *Wixford Road, Ardens Grafton* ☎ *01789 772420; Fax 01789 773 697. Modern British food is on offer at this slickly run pub 5 mi/8km south of the town centre; the large garden and terrace is ideal for summer dining with a distinctly rural interior for less clement weather.*

Hamiltons Brasserie, *8 Waterside.* ☎ *01789 209109; Fax 01789 295 981. Next to the Royal Shakespeare Theatre this smart contemporary restaurant offes an eclectic menu featuring modern and classic dishes.*

Dec. ☎ *£4. Refreshments at The Royal Shakespeare Theatre and during performances at the Swan Theatre. Wheelchair access to ground floor only; Sign and Touch Theatre tours available.* ☎ *01789 403 405; enquiries@rsc.org.uk; theatretours@rsc.org.uk; www. rsc.org.uk.* It opened in 1932 as the Shakespeare Memorial Theatre and is now the headquarters of the **Royal Shakespeare Company**. Adjoining it is the **Swan Theatre**, built in 1986 with a Jacobean-style apron stage and galleried seating within the shell of an earlier theatre largely destroyed by fire in 1926. The Royal Shakespeare Company Collection includes paintings, sculpture and historical theatre material (backstage tours).

Excursions

The Cotswolds★★★ – ♿ *See The COTSWOLDS.*

Mary Arden's House and the Shakespeare Countryside Museum★ – *4mi/6km north, off A 3400 in Wilmcote.* ♿ ⏱ *Open daily. Jun-Aug, 9.30am (10am Sun) - 5pm, Apr-May, Sep-Oct, 10am (10.30am Sun) to 5pm, Nov-Mar, 10am (10.30am Sun) to 4pm.* ⏱ *Closed 23-25 Dec.* ☎ *£5.50; joint ticket to 3 Shakespearean Properties £8.50; joint ticket for all 5 Shakespearean Properties £12. Brochure (4 languages).* ☎ *01789 204 016; info@shakespeare.org.uk; www.shakespeare.org.uk.* Home of Shakespeare's mother, Mary Arden, featuring herring-bone timber framing and, mercifully, unrestored. Between the house and neighbouring **Glebe Farm** (preserved as a c 1900 farmhouse) are dovecots, cowsheds, barns and outbuildings.

Anne Hathaway's Cottage – *1mi/2km west via Shottery Road.* ⏱ *Open mid-Mar to mid-Oct, daily, 9am (9.30am Sun) to 5pm; mid-Oct to mid-Mar, 9.30am (10am Sun) to 4pm.* ⏱ *Closed 23-26 Dec.* ☎ *Joint ticket to 3 Shakespearean Properties. £8.50; joint ticket to 5 Shakespearean Properties £12. Brochure (4 langugages).* ☎ *01789 204 016; info@ shakespeare. org. uk; www.shakespeare.org.uk.* It is more a farmhouse than a cottage, and the rear was rebuilt after a fire in 1969. Upstairs are some dramatic tie-beams and the Hathaway bed. The grounds contain a herb-scented garden, orchard and Shakespeare tree garden.

Ragley Hall★ – *10mi/16km west off A 46, 2mi/3km beyond Alcester.* ♿ *House:* ⏱ *Open Apr-Oct, Thur-Sun and Bank Hol Mon. Park and garden: Open as for house and daily in school summer holidays; telephone for details of times and charges.* ☎ *01789 762 090; Fax 01789 764 791; info@ragleyhall.com; www.ragleyhall.com.* Noble rather than stately Ragley was designed and built by Robert Hooke in Palladian style for the Marquess of Hertford, between 1679 and 1683. James Gibbs added some of the most perfect plasterwork **ceilings** he ever conceived around 1750, and thirty years later Wyatt built the gigantic portico. The walls are hung with paintings by Wootton, Van Loo, Reynolds, Hoppner, Lely and Cornelius Schut. The surprise is the **South Staircase Hall** decorated by Graham Rust between 1969 and 1983, with its ceiling of *The Temptation* and murals portraying classical gods, monkeys, birds and contemporary members of the Seymour family, all in a post-Realist Baroque style.

"If music be the food of love, play on"

Although the most popular of dramatists in England already in his own day, Shakespeare long remained problematic for audiences abroad not only because of the language barrier, but also because of the dominance of French culture and its classical conceptions of theatre. Once Romanticism swept through France, however, the cult of Shakespeare began to flourish, championed initially by Berlioz (fantasia on *The Tempest, King Lear* overture, *Romeo and Juliet* symphony, pieces inspired by *Hamlet* and the opera *Béatrice et Bénédict* from *Much Ado About Nothing*) and Delacroix (paintings of Lady Macbeth in 1825 and 1849, lithographs and paintings of scenes from *Hamlet*, paintings of *Cleopatra*, and *Othello* and *Desdemona*). Adaptations of his works were made by Alfred de Vigny *(Othello, The Merchant of Venice)* and George Sand *(As You Like It)*, and Victor Hugo's son produced the best of numerous translations of Shakespeare's complete plays which appeared at this time (late 19C). Elsewhere in Europe, operas based on Shakespeare's plays were written by, for example, Rossini *(Elizabetta d'Inghilterra, Otello)* and Verdi *(Macbeth, Otello, Falstaff)*, while Mendelssohn composed his *A Midsummer Night's Dream* overture. Later in the 19C Tchaikovsky produced his fantasia on *The Tempest*, a symphonic poem on *Romeo and Juliet*, and a *Hamlet* overture.

In the 20C, the spirit of Shakespeare and his age has continued to inspire English composers such as Elgar *(Falstaff)*, Vaughan Williams *(Serenade to Music*, from *The Merchant of Venice)*, Holst *(At the Boar's Head Opera)* and Britten *(A Midsummer Night's Dream* opera).

Upton House★ – *(NT) 14mi/22km southeast on A 422.* ♿ *House:* 🕐 *Open late-Mar to early-Nov, Sat-Wed, Good Friday and Bank Hol Mon, 1-5pm. Garden: late-Mar to early-Nov, Sat-Sun and Bank Hol Mon, 11am-5pm; other Mon-Wed, 12.30-5pm; early-Nov to mid-Dec, Sat-Sun, noon-4pm.* 📷 *House and garden £6; garden £3. Braille guide. Parking. Licensed restaurant. Wheelchair access to ground floor; motorised buggy for access to lower garden.* ☎ *01295 670 266; 0870 609 5390 (Infoline) uptonhouse@ntrust.org.uk; wwwnationaltrust.org.uk.* A late 17C house, bought by Viscount Bearsted, son of the founder of the Shell company and exhibiting his spectacular collection of porcelain and paintings. In the **Hall** is a view of Venice by Canaletto and a landscape by Wootton. In the **Long Gallery** are Dutch paintings – note Jan Steen's Four Senses as well as the Chelsea and Bow porcelain. The **Boudoir** is reserved exclusively for French 18C and 19C works, including Boucher's *Venus and Vulcan*. The **Porcelain Lobby** is packed with Sèvres, Chinese, Chelsea and Derby china and porcelain. In the Games Room are Hogarth's *Morning* and *Night* and in the **Billiard Room** Hondecoeter's *Turkey Cock*. The pride of the collection is in the **Picture Gallery**, where among works by Holbein, Hogarth, Guardi, Rembrandt – an attribution, Tintoretto, Bruegel the Elder and Bosch hangs El Greco's *Christ taken in Captivity*, believed to be the model for his altarpiece in Toledo Cathedral.

Broughton Castle – *22mi/35km southeast on A 422 to Banbury, then southwest on B 4035.* 🕐 *Open mid-May to mid-Sep, Wed, Sun and Bank Hols, 2-5pm; also Thur in Jul-Aug, 2-5pm.* 📷 *£5. Parking. Refreshments. Wheelchair access to ground floor and gardens.* ☎*/Fax: 01295 276 070; www.broughtoncastle.demon.co.uk.* The moated manor house of c 1300, extended in 1554 and 1599, became the centre of Parliamentary opposition to Charles I, where the leaders Hampden, Pym, Warwick and the owner, Lord Saye and Sele met in the Council Chamber. The Great Hall, dining room and chapel show the 1300 interior at its best, while the King's Chamber chimneypiece and the Great Parlour ceiling show the best of the Elizabethan extension work. The 18C Gothick Gallery, with busts of Inigo Jones and Ben Jonson, by Rysbrack, fits admirably with the 1300s through its simplicity and restraint.

SWANSEA ★

Abertawe – Swansea, WALES

POPULATION 172 433

MICHELIN ATLAS P 15 OR MAP 503 I 29

TOWN PLAN IN THE MICHELIN GUIDE GREAT BRITAIN AND IRELAND

Swansea is the lively urban centre for southwest Wales, after Cardiff the country's second city, and a commercial and pleasure port with a ferry service to Cork. Three centuries of industrial activity in the **Lower Swansea Valley** created one of Britain's most spectacularly derelict landscapes. Since the late 1960s a thoroughgoing programme of reclamation has succeeded in transforming the area, which now consists of parkland, light industrial units, and commercial and retail developments, with few traces left of its industrial past. Part of the fortune from copper-smelting made here by the Vivian family was spent in building the **Glynn Vivian Art Gallery**★ (& ⏱ *Open Tue-Sun and Bank Hol Mon, 10am-4.45pm. Shop.* ☎ *01792 651 738 and 655 006; Fax 01792 651 713; glynn.vivian.gallery@swansea.gov.uk; www.swansea.gov.uk),* in the city centre, which, apart from its collection of Swansea pottery, is one of the best places in which to survey the variety of Welsh art.

- 🚫 **Don't Miss**: The Maritime Quarter; the Gower Peninsula especially Rhossili and its views.
- ⏱ **Organizing Your Time**: Allow one day to see Swansea.
- 🧒 **Especially for Kids**: there are lots of children's activities and seaside attractions at The Mumbles; the beaches of the Gower Peninsula.

Visit

Maritime Quarter★ – The mid-19C South Dock has been renovated as a marina, the centrepiece of a new "inner-city village" of spruce apartments, public squares and quayside walks, on one of which sits the statue of Swansea-born poet **Dylan Thomas** (1914-53). The varied exhibits of the **Maritime and Industrial Museum**★ (& ⏱ *Open Tue-Sun and Bank Hol Mon, 10am-5pm. Historic vessels and tramshed: Open Apr-Sep.* ⏱ *Closed 1 Jan and 25-26 Dec. Parking nearby. Café.* ☎ *01792 650 351 or 470 371; swansea.maritime.museum@swansea.gov.uk; www.swansea.gov.uk),* are housed in a brightly-converted former warehouse and include a complete, re-erected woollen mill; several retired vessels, among them a lightship, are moored at the quayside, and historic vehicles of the Mumbles Tramway can be seen in the tramshed.

Address Book

OUT AND ABOUT IN SWANSEA

Tourist Information Centre – *Plymouth Street SA1 3QG b 01792 468 321; Fax 01792 464 602; tourism@swansea.gov.uk; www. visitswanseabay.com.*

Entertainment – Nightclubs, bars and restaurants are to be found in the Maritime Quarter on the waterfront. Some pubs offer live music.

Concerts by international orchestras and soloists are held at the **Brangwyn Hall,** opera and ballet at the **Grand Theatre**. Other venues include **Dylan Thomas Theatre,** the **Taliesin Theatre** and the **Cwmtawe Theatre** and **Penyrheol Theatre.**

In addition to the local festivals – the **Swansea Summer Show** (August), **Swansea Festival of Music** (autumn), the **Margam Festival** (July-August) and

the **Llanelli Festival** (September-October), the **Gower Festival** of small concerts takes place in the churches of the area (July); except in summer visitors may attend the rehearsals of the famous **Male voice choirs.**

Outdoor activities include canoeing, sailing, surfing (Bay Caswell and Langland Bay or Llangennith for the Atlantic rollers), windsurfing (Oxwich, Port Eynon), waterskiing (Swansea Bay, Oxwich Bay), hang-gliding and parascending (Rhossili Bay).

The Swansea Leisure Centre provides for many **indoor activities** – swimming (water slide and diving tank), roller skating, squash, badminton, trampoline, volleyball, martial arts, table tennis, bowling, sauna, steam room, sunbeds.

Excursions

Gower Peninsula★★ – West of Swansea a chain of superb beaches and magnificent cliffs extends along the south coast of the peninsula (14mi/22km), Britain's first designated Area of Outstanding Natural Beauty.

The Mumbles, Swansea's own seaside resort overlooked by Oystermouth Castle, was the terminus of the Mumbles Railway, the world's first scheduled passenger railway, which opened for horse-drawn traffic in 1804 and closed only in 1960.

Further west, near Reynoldston, the moorland ridge of **Cefn Bryn** offers a **panorama** which extends, in clear conditions, far across the Bristol Channel to Hartland Point on the Devon coast, to the Brecon Beacons and westward to the Presely Hills.

The approach to the tiny village of **Rhossili**★★ in the far southwestern corner of the peninsula does not prepare the visitor for the breathtaking **views** which open up from the coastguard cottages housing the National Trust visitor centre. The cliffs fall dramatically away to the great arc (3mi/5km) of **Rhossili Bay** with the surf crashing on its wonderful sandy beach. High above is Rhossili Down (633ft/193m); to the south is **Worms Head**, a mile-long sea-serpent in rock, accessible only at low tide.

Aberdulais Falls★ – *(NT) 11mi/17km northeast by A 483, A 48 and A 465.* ♿🕐 *Open late-Mar to early-Nov, daily, 10am-5pm (11am-6pm Sat-Sun and Bank Hol Mon); early-Nov to late-Dec Fri-Sun, 11am-4pm.* ⬚ *£3.* ⬚ *Guided tour: Jul-Aug, daily. Audio tour. Parking. Dogs must be on lead. Lift to falls.* ☎ *01639 636 674; Fax 01639 645 069; gaberd@ smtp.ntrust.org uk; www.nationaltrust.org.uk.* In a pretty wooded gorge, the waters of the River Dulais crash down among huge boulders and past the remains of the works of the Aberdulais Tinplate Co, founded 1830. The site's industrial history goes back to 1584, when copper smelting began; in the late 18C-early 19C it was frequented by artists (including Turner) who found it an appropriately picturesque subject.

Kidwelly★ **(Cydweli)** – *(CADW) 21mi/34km northwest by A 483, A 4070 and A 484.* ♿🕐 *Open late-Mar to late-Oct, daily, 9.30am-5pm (6pm Jun to late-Sep); late-Oct to late-Mar, daily, 9.30am (11am Sun) to 4pm.* 🕐 *Closed 1 Jan and 24-26 Dec.* ⬚ *£2.50. Parking. Ramps.* ☎*/Fax 01554 890 104.* Bishop Roger of Salisbury's first ringwork was certainly complete by the foundation of the priory about 1130, though the present **castle** dates from the 1280s. The walls enclosed the Norman town to form a 'bastide' such as are found in North Wales at Conwy and Caernarfon. St Mary's Church, built c 1320, in Decorated style, originally served a Benedictine monastery.

National Botanic Garden of Wales★ – ♿🕐 *Open daily, 10am-6pm (4.30pm Nov to mid-Apr).* ⬚ *£6.95. Parking. Restaurant, cafeteria, open-air picnic areas.* ☎ *01558 668 768; Fax 01558 668 933; info@gardenofwales.org.uk; www.gardenofwales.org.uk.* The **Great Glasshouse**, the largest single span glass house in the world, creates a perfect Mediterranean landscape in miniature where 10 000 plants, numbering 1 000 species, can flourish in their native environment. The surrounding grounds were laid out in the Regency period with five lakes, herbaceous borders and a double walled garden, which have been rescued from dereliction as a Millennium project. The house, **Middleton Hall** (destroyed by fire in 1931), was designed by Samuel Cockerell for Sir William Paxton.

TAUNTON★

Somerset, ENGLAND

POPULATION 55 855

MICHELIN ATLAS P 7 OR MAP 504 K 30

The county town of Taunton, gateway to the West Country, is an agricultural and commercial centre at the heart of the fertile Vale of Taunton (Taunton Deane), famous for its cider apples. ▯ *The Library, Paul Street, TA1 3XZ.* ☎ *01823 336344; Fax 01823 340308; tauntontic@tauntondeane.gov.uk; www.heartofsomerset.com.*

Sights

Castle – The castle, dating from the 11C-12C, is especially known for its ownership by successive bishops of Winchester. The Civil War put Taunton, and the castle in particular, under siege three times. Part of it now houses the **Somerset County Museum**★ (&⃝ *Open Tue-Sat and Bank Hol Mon, 10am-5pm (3pm Nov-Mar).* ⃝ *Closed 1 Jan, Good Friday and 25-26 Dec.* ⃝ *£2.50.* ☎ *01823 320 200; Fax 01823 320 229; county-museums@somerset.gov.uk; www.somerset.gov.uk/museums).*

After his unsuccessful rebellion against Henry VII in 1497 **Perkin Warbeck** was brought to trial in the great hall. Following defeat at Sedgemoor in 1685 Charles II's natural son, the **Duke of Monmouth,** and many of his followers were tried by **Judge Jeffreys** in the great hall; 508 of them were condemned to death in the notorious **Bloody Assizes**, although it is not known exactly how many actually died (an estimated 300-500, with 800-1 000 transported to the West Indies). Monmouth himself was executed on Tower Hill a month later.

St Mary Magdalene★ – ⃝ *Open Mon-Fri, 8.30am-5.15pm, Sat, 9am-4pm. Services: Sun at 8am, 10.30am, 6.30pm.* In the true Somerset tradition, this splendid medieval church culminates in a soaring tower (1488-1514) built of lovely red and tawny-gold Ham Hill stone. Inside, the roof carvings (bosses and angels) are typical examples of Somerset craftsmanship.

St James'★ – This 14C-15C (except north arcade and aisle) church features a 120ft/37m tower of Quantock red sandstone with Ham stone decoration.

Excursions

Ilminster★ – *9.5mi/16km southeast.* This Ham stone market town, which flourished from the wool trade in the 15-16C, was listed as having a **Minster**★★ in Domesday. St Mary's most impressive feature is its 90ft/27m crossing tower, modelled on that of Wells Cathedral. It has two levels of bell openings up to a crest of gargoyles, pinnacles and a spirelet on the stair turret. The 15C Perpendicular building with nave, transepts, chancel and tower was extended with aisles in the 16C. Galleries were added above the nave and aisles in 1824-25 to accommodate larger congregations. Note the fan vaults inserted at the crossing and Wadham chapel *(north transept)*, built in 1452 to house the tomb chests of Sir William Wadham (d 1452) and Nicholas (d 1618) who founded Wadham College, Oxford.

Somerset Levels – *10-15mi/15-25km northeast.* This wide, flat area south of the Mendip Hills and east of the Quantocks has been used since ancient times as summer pasture and fertile arable land, when the banks of the water-filled rhines are bright with wild flowers. In winter much of the area is waterlogged, providing rich feeding ground for golden plovers, lapwings, snipe and many other species of bird. The busiest bird season is April and early May. Among the best places to go birdwatching are Shapwick Heath, Tealham and Tadham Moors *(off B 3151 between Westhay and Wedmore)*, West Sedgemoor RSPB reserve *(off A 378 between Fivehead and Langport)*. Further information available from the Willows and Wetland Visitor Centre, Meare Green, Stoke St Gregory.

The 14C Abbot's Fish House at Meare was used for drying, salting and storing fish for Glastonbury Abbey *(to view the interior, apply at the house next door)*. The village of Wedmore is historic as the place of the signing of the treaty between King Alfred and the Danes in AD 878.

TENBY★★

DINBYCH-Y-PYSGOD – Pembrokeshire, WALES

POPULATION 5 226

MICHELIN ATLAS P 14 OR MAP 503 F 28

This little medieval town on its rocky promontory, near the country's south-western most point, combines all the ingredients of a seaside resort in a compact and pleasing pattern. Dinbych-y-Pysgod – little fort of the fishes – originated in a tiny Welsh fortress on Castle Hill. Later it became a satellite of the main Norman stronghold at Pembroke, was sacked by the Welsh and on its rebuilding surrounded by sturdy ramparts. Its popularity as a watering-place dates from the Napoleonic wars. ▯ *Unit 2, Upper Park Road, SA70 7LT. ☎ 01834 842402/04; Fax 01834 845439; tenby.tic@pembrokeshire.gov.uk; www.visitpembrokeshire.com.*

Visit

Harbour and Seafront★★ – A perfect composition of jetty, massive retaining walls, Fishermen's Chapel and rugged warehouses, backed by Georgian and Regency houses crowded prettily together and rising to crown the low cliff. Superb sandy beaches extend north and south. Castle Hill has a local museum with paintings by Augustus and Gwen John and other Tenby artists, and is topped by a statue of Prince Albert waiting patiently for a Victoria who in fact never came here. Cut off at high tide is St Catherine's Island with its Victorian fort (1869).

Town – Landward is a good stretch of the **town walls**, enclosing a characteristically intricate web of medieval streets, widening out at **St Mary's**, (☉ *Open daily, 9am-5pm. Services: see notice in main porch. ☎ 01834 842 068 (Rectory); stmary_tenby@freenet co.uk; www.angelfire.com/mt/TenbyStMarys)* one of Wales' most substantial parish churches, with a spire (152ft/46m). The **Tudor Merchant's House** *(NT ☉ Open Mar-Nov, Mon-Tue, Thu-Sun, 10am (noon Sun) to 5pm (Oct-Nov, Sun 3pm). ☜ £2. ☎/Fax 01834 842 279)*, is a late 15C town dwelling, virtually unchanged externally and well preserved inside, with Flemish chimneys and period furniture.

WHERE TO STAY

☺☺☺☺ **Gower,** *Milford Terrace, Saundersfoot ☎ 01834 813 452; Fax 01834 810 242; tim.rowe@rotels.com; www. rotels.com.* This smart four-storey hotel, refurbished in 2004 is close to the beach with immaculate rooms and a bright spacious Orangery-style restaurant.

Wales Tourist Board

Tenby

Excursions

Caldey Island★ – *Access by boat from Tenby harbour.* ♿🕐 *Operates (weather permitting) Easter-Oct, Mon-Fri, from 10am, every 20-30min; also Jun-Aug, Sat, from 10.45am. Time 20-30min.* ♿ *£7. Access for disabled passengers easier at high tide.* ☎ *01834 844 453 (John Cattini); caldeyisland@supanet.com; www.caldey-island.co.uk.* In 1136 Caldey was given to the Benedictine order and a monastery established, replacing the original 6C settlement. Today a self-sufficient Cistercian community with a score or so of helpers runs a dairy and perfumery on the island.

Carew Castle★ – *5mi/8km west of Tenby just off A 477.* ♿🕐 *Open Easter-Oct, daily, 10am-5pm.* ♿ *Castle and mill £2.80; castle or mill £1.90. Guided tour (1hr). Leaflet (2 languages). Wheelchair access to the ground floor.* ☎ *01646 651 782, 651 657; Fax 01646 651 782; enquiries@carewcastle.com; www.carewcastle.com.* Much of the castle standing today dates from the late 13C-early 14C. The most striking feature, however, is the North Range, started about 1558. The magnificent Elizabethan architecture, with rows of tall mullioned windows, reflected in the mill pool, recaptures some of the elegance of the period.

The nearby **tidal mill**, the only one of its kind remaining in Wales, is a restored late 18C building and has an audio-visual presentation to explain its workings to visitors. The **Celtic Cross** near the entrance to the castle is one of the earliest Christian monuments in Wales. Heavily ornamented with Celtic and Scandinavian designs, it was erected as a memorial to the ruler Maredudd ap Edwin, killed in battle in 1035.

Pendine – *17mi/27km east by A 478, A 477 and B 4314.* The stretch of **Pendine Sands** offers excellent bathing and angling. In 1924-26 Sir Malcolm Campbell and Parry Thomas established world land-speed records here, Parry Thomas being killed in his 1927 attempt to beat the existing record of 174.8mph/281.3kph.

Laugharne (Talacharn) – *21mi/33km east by A 478, A 477 and B 4314.* The controversial poet **Dylan Thomas** (1914-53) lived in this small town on the Taf estuary from 1938, latterly in **The Boathouse**, (🕐 *Open May-Oct, daily, 10am-5pm; Nov-Apr, daily, 10.30am-3pm.* ♿ *£3. Audio-visual presentation (25min). Bookshop. Tearoom.* ☎ *01994 427 420; tourism@carmarthenshire.gov.uk; carmarthenshire.gov.uk)* now a museum of his life and work. He is buried in St Martin's churchyard. The character – and characters – of Laugharne are reflected in his "play for voices" *Under Milk Wood*.

THAMES VALLEY★★

MICHELIN ATLAS P 18 OR MAP 504 Q, R 28 AND 29

FOR A DESCRIPTION OF THE LOWER THAMES, SEE UNDER LONDON

"Sweet Thames! run softly, till I end my song" – this much-quoted refrain from Edmund Spenser's Prothalamion (1596) still captures the nature of England's most famous river; its gently winding course between Kew and its source in the Cotswolds, offers many varied pleasures as it passes through typically English countryside of low hills, woods, meadows, country houses, pretty villages and small towns. Reading is the only industrial centre.

For long sections no road follows its course but there is usually a towpath. The result is that while the motorist may admire the river in towns along its route, the Thames' quiet beauty can be fully appreciated only from a boat or on foot. In the summer months many Thames-side towns and villages offer boat trips or the chance to hire a boat – and such an experience need not be as full of mishaps as the journey described in Jerome K Jerome's amusing idyll Three Men in a Boat – essential reading for any traveller on the Thames. *King's Arms Barn, Kings Road, Henley-on-Thames RG9 2DG ☎ 0149 578 034; Fax 01491 412 703; henleytic@hotmail.com; www.visit-henley.org.uk* *Abbey House, Abingdon, OX14 3JE ☎ 01235 520 202, 01235 547 614; Fax 01235 547 612; tourism@whitehorsedc.gov.uk; www.whitehorsedc.gov.uk/Tourism/abingdon.asp.*

- **Don't Miss**: Abingdon, Mapledurham, Basildon Park, Henley-on-Thames if it's regatta time (but very crowded).
- **Organizing Your Time**: Allow 2-3 days.
- **Especially for Kids**: Wind in the Willows Gallery at The River and Rowing Museum.
- **Bicycle Trails**: Some sections of the Thames Path are suitable for cycling.

Special Feature

Swan-Upping – Every July a colourful procession mounts the river, from Sunbury-on-Thames to Whitchurch Lock. Her Majesty's Swan Keeper and representatives of two City Livery Companies, the Worshipful Company of Dyers and the Worshipful Company of Vintners, take "up" out of the water the new cygnets and nick their bills to denote ownership. Swans with no nicks belong to the Crown, those with one nick to the Dyers' Company and those with two nicks to the Vintners' Company. The ceremony dates back to the 12C. Swans have always been indigenous to England and claimed as the property of the Crown and a very few nobles. Today only the two Livery Companies share the privilege with the Crown but the tradition of "Swan Upping" continues.

Henley Regatta

Lower Thames

*For a local map and a description of the main sights west of Central London (**Hampton Court**★★★, **Richmond**★★★ and **Kew Gardens**★★★) see London.*

FROM WINDSOR TO OXFORD

71mi/114km – allow at least a whole day

Windsor Castle★★★ – See WINDSOR CASTLE.

Eton College★★ – See WINDSOR CASTLE : Excursion.

Cookham – This pretty village has been immortalised by the artist **Sir Stanley Spencer** (1891-1959). The former Wesleyan Chapel which Spencer attended as a boy is now the **Stanley Spencer Gallery**★ (Open Good Friday-Oct, daily, 10.30am-5.30pm; Nov-Easter, Sat-Sun and Bank Hols, 11am-5pm. £1. Leaflet (8 languages). Guided tour (60min). ☎ 01628 471 885; www.stanleyspencer.org). Cookham features in many of his paintings, notably *Christ Preaching at Cookham Regatta* and *The Betrayal*.

Henley-on-Thames – In the first week of July oarsmen come from all over the world to this charming town for the **Henley Royal Regatta**, England's premier amateur regatta.

The elegant 5-arched **bridge**, designed in 1786, bears carved heads of Father Thames and the goddess Isis. It is overlooked by the 1550 tower of the 13C **St Mary's Church,** (Open Mon-Sat, 9am-5pm. Leaflet, guide book (4 languages). ☎ 01491 577 340; Fax 01491 577 340; rector.hwr@lineone.net) enlarged c 1400. Inside, is an early 17C monument to Lady Periam; in the churchyard stand almshouses and the timber-framed Chantry House. The town has a good number of Georgian and earlier timber-framed inns and houses.

The **River and Rowing Museum** (Mill Meadows Open daily, 10am-5.30pm (5pm Sep-Apr). Closed 1 Jan and 24-25, 31 Dec. £3 (including Wind in the Willows £6). Parking. Café. ☎ 01491 415 600; Fax 01491 415 601; museum@rrm.co.uk; www.rrm.co.uk), is set in an award-winning building of exposed concrete and glass with a terne coated steel roof, clad in green oak. Its innovative galleries illustrate three main themes: the evolution of rowing from the Greek trireme to the latest in racing craft; the River Thames as a habitat for wildlife and a means of trade and source of pleasure; the history of Henley-on-Thames and the world-famous Royal Regatta - using touch-screens, interactive models and audio-visual presentations. The exhibits include archeological finds, a dug-out, a Thames skiff (1909) and a steam launch (1876) used by the Regatta umpires. There is also a walk through Wind in the Willows gallery celebrating Kenneth Grahame's famous story set on the Thames (see below). A hand held audio guide tells you the story as you walk through the exhibition.

Mapledurham★ – Open from Easter-Sep, Sat-Sun and Bank Hols, 2-5pm. House £4; water mill £3; combined ticked £6. Car park. Tearoom. ☎ 0118 972 3350; Fax 0118 972 4016; Mtrust.1997@aol.com; www.mapledurham.co.uk. An Elizabethan **manor house** beside a 14C church and a fully operational **watermill** dating back to the 15C form an almost perfect riverside picture. The house was completed c 1612 by Sir Richard Blount (pronounced Blunt). Though many changes were made over the centuries there is still much to admire, notably the great oak staircase, fine Jacobean plasterwork, many portraits and the chapel, an imaginative piece of Strawberry Hill Gothic.

Pangbourne – The River Pang joins the Thames at this village where **Kenneth Grahame** lived from 1922-32 and wrote his children's book *The Wind in the Willows*. At the Swan Inn, built in 1642, rain finally caused Jerome K Jerome's *Three Men* to abandon their boat and return to London.

Basildon Park★ – House, park, garden and walks: Open late-Mar to early-Nov, Wed-Sun, Bank Hol Mon, 1pm (noon, park, garden and walks) to 5.30pm. House £4.40; park, garden and walks only, £2. Parking. Restaurant. ☎ 0118 984 3040; Infoline 01494 755 558; Fax 01189 841 267; tbdgen@smtp.ntrust.org.uk; basildonpark@ntrust. org.uk; www.nationaltrust.org.uk. The splendid Palladian villa of mellow Bath stone, overlooking a lush part of the Thames valley, was built by John Carr in 1776. In the early 20C it was planned to have it moved to the United States, but fortunately only some of the fittings were sold and are now in New York's Waldorf Astoria Hotel. The house was saved from demolition in 1952 by Lord and Lady Iliffe, who restored it and donated it to the National Trust.

The **west front** is dominated by a giant recessed portico of four Ionic columns rising from the first floor to the pediment at roof level. The house is entered through low ground-floor arches and narrow twin staircases which climb to the portico and the entrance to the hall. The beautifully restored house is rich in exquisite **plasterwork** on ceiling and walls, notably in the blue and gold dining room, green drawing room and the pink, lilac, green and grey hall. The sumptuous Octagon Room, overlooking the Thames, was decorated c 1840. There is a fine collection of 18C paintings and a portrait of Lord Iliffe by Graham Sutherland in the Library.

Goring and Streatley – The villages, with the weir and Goring Lock, are set in what is acknowledged as one of the most beautiful parts of the Thames, offering enjoyable riverside walks.

Dorchester ★– This historic village on the Thame, a tributary of the Thames, dates back to the Bronze Age. The Romans built their own town Dorocina on the site. In AD 635 St Birinus baptised king Cynegils of Wessex in the river; a Saxon church was built, on the site of which the Norman **abbey church,** (🕐 *Open daily, 9am-7pm/ dusk. Museum Tues-Fri 1-5pm (Sat 11am, Sun and Bank Hols 2pm). Tea Room.* ☎ *01865 340 007 (Rectory); enquiries@dorchester-abbey.org.uk; www.dorchester-abbey.org.uk)* now stands. Most of the church is in fact Decorated, its crowning glory being the enormous six-light **east window** of 1340. The north wall has an equally spectacular **Jesse Window**, depicting in its tracery Christ's lineage back to Jesse. Opposite are the flamboyantly pinnacled sedilia and piscina. In the village several great coaching inns have survived as well as many fine houses and thatched cottages.

Abingdon★ – The town grew up around an abbey founded in the 7C, though the only remaining abbey buildings are the 13C **Chequer** with its tall chimney, the c 1500 **Long Gallery** with an oak-beamed roof and the 15C **gateway** beside the medieval church of St Nicholas. A notable feature is the 17C **County Hall★** by Christopher Kempster, who assisted Wren in the construction of the dome of St Paul's Cathedral. (🕐 *Open daily, 10.30am-4pm.* 🚫 *Closed 25-26 Dec and Bank Hols. Roof visit Apr-Sep, Sats by appointment.*☎ *01235 523 703; enquiries@abingdonmuseum.free-online.co.uk; www.abingdon.angle.uk.com).* Abingdon's skyline is characterised by the 15C spire of the wide 5-aisled **St Helen's Church**, (🕐 *Open summer, Mon-Sat, 9.30am-4pm, Sun, 8am-3pm.* 👝 *Donation.* ☎ *01235 520 144)* mostly rebuilt in the 15C; there are 14C paintings on the roof of the inner north aisle and a painted medieval ceiling (*Tree of Jesse*) in the Lady Chapel. Delightful 15C **almshouses**★ border the churchyard.

Iffley Church★ – *Church Way.* 🕐 *Open daily, 8am-5pm/dusk. Key available from the Rectory.* ☎ *01865 773 516; richard.lea@lineone.net; www.iffley.co.uk.* Iffley, now one of Oxford's suburbs, has one of the best preserved Norman village churches in England, with a central tower and a profusion of zigzag moulding, typical of the late 12C.

Oxford★★★ – 👝 *See OXFORD.*

TINTAGEL

Cornwall, ENGLAND

POPULATION 1 721

MICHELIN ATLAS P 3 OR MAP 503 F 32

Tintagel especially and the West Country in general are associated with the elusive legend of **Arthur**, "the once and future king", which has been passed down by word of mouth since the 8C and in written form since the 12C, inspiring poets and authors through the ages: William of Malmesbury, Geoffrey of Monmouth, the 12C chronicler Wace, Sir Thomas Malory, Spenser, Tennyson, Swinburne and TH White. The legend lives on, perpetuated by tourism and the New Age movement. Tintagel is also the site of the largest find of 5-6C eastern Mediterranean pottery sherds in the British Isles, suggesting once thriving trade links.

🙈 **Don't Miss**: Spectacular coastal and cliff scenery (Tintagel Castle, Morwenstow, Bedruthan Steps, Hell's Mouth, Trevose Head); Padstow, particularly for its fish restaurants and traditional celebrations.

🕐 **Organizing Your Time**: Allow 2-3 days.

Kids **Especially for Kids**: Excellent beaches all along this coast; lots of seaside amusements at Newquay, plus Newquay Zoo.

🐟 **Walking Tours/Trails**: The Cornwall Coast Path, particularly from Trevone to Padstow.

N. Benavides/MICHELIN

Old Post Office

Visit

Tintagel Castle – *(EH)* 🕐 *Open daily, 10am-6pm (5pm Oct; 4pm Nov-Mar).* 🕐 *Closed 1 Jan and 24-26 Dec.* ⊚ *£3.90.* ☎/*Fax 01840 770 328; customers@english-heritage.org. uk; www.english-heritage.org.uk.* Access by a steep road from the main street; 30min on foot there and back, or by four-wheel drive.

The **site**★★★ overlooking the sea from precipitous rocks is more dramatic than the fragmentary **castle ruin**, which includes walls from the 1145 chapel and great hall, built on the site of a 6C Celtic monastery, and other walls dating from the 13C – all centuries after Arthur's time.

Old Post Office★ – This small manor house with 3ft/just under 1m thick walls and undulating slate roofs dates from the 14C. The atmospheric, compact little house contains simple country furniture.

Excursions

North Cornish Coast (east of Tintagel)

🛈 *Crescent Car Park, Bude, EX23 8LE* ☎ *01288 354240; Fax 01288 355769; budetic@ visitbude.info; www. visitbude.info, www.north-cornwall.com.*

Boscastle★ – *Off B 3263.* This pretty village straggles downhill to a picturesque inlet between 300ft headlands; it is the only **natural harbour** between Hartland Point and Padstow.

Poundstock★ – The 13-15C **church**★, with its square unbuttressed tower and square 14C font, the lychgate and the unique, sturdily built 14C **guildhouse**★ form a secluded group in a wooded dell.

Bude – This harbour town in the cliffs, which stand tall against the incoming Atlantic, is a very popular holiday resort with golden sandy beaches and breakers ideal for surf-

---

Situating the King Arthur Story

Arthur, son of Uther Pendragon, was either born or washed ashore at Tintagel; there he had his castle and lived with his queen, **Guinevere**, and the **Knights of the Round Table**, including **Lancelot du Lac**, who had an affair with Guinevere, Lancelot's son by Elaine Galahad, the only knight to succeed in the quest for the Holy Grail, and **Tristan**, the nephew or son of King Mark whose fort was Castle Dore, near Fowey on the south Cornish Coast. **Merlin**, the magician, lived in a cave beneath Tintagel Castle and on a rock off Mousehole. The sword **Excalibur**, forged in Avalon, was drawn from the stone by Arthur and eventually thrown into **Dozmary Pool** on Bodmin Moor. **Camelot** is believed by some to be Cadbury Castle (🕮 *see SHERBORNE*).

The Battle of Mount Bladon (c 520), when Arthur defeated the pagan Saxons, was possibly fought at Liddington Castle near Swindon, or Badbury Rings, Dorset; the **Battle of Camlan**, the final struggle against Mordred, the king's usurping stepson or bastard son, took place on the banks of the River Camel on Bodmin Moor. Mortally wounded, Arthur sailed into the sunset to the Islands of the Blest (Scilly), or to Avalon, held by some to be close to Glastonbury, where his tomb was "discovered" with that of Guinevere in the 12C.

ing. The **breakwater**★★ beyond the 19C Bude Canal offers a good view of the sea at high tide. The local **museum,** *(Lower Wharf.* ○ *Open Easter-Sep, daily, 11am-4.30pm.* ⬟ *50p. the.clerk@budestratton. gov.uk)* gives information on the history of the canal, Bude and Stratton.

Stratton – The narrow streets of this old market town climb to the **church**★ begun in 1348 (north arcade), the granite south arcade being added in the mid-15C, the chancel and 90ft/27m pinnacled tower in the 16C. The font is Norman, the pulpit Jacobean. The east window is by Burne-Jones.

Morwenstow – Cornwall's northernmost parish boasts a fine **church**★ with a Norman south door featuring zig-zag moulding on small columns, two interior arcades, one with Norman and Early English piers. Beneath the original bossaged wagon roof are a Saxon font with cable moulding (c800) and mid-16C bench-ends.

The spectacular **cliffs**★★ (450ft/133m high) reach out to offshore rocks.

Clovelly★★ – ⬤ *See ILFRACOMBE: Excursions.*

North Cornish Coast (west of Tintagel)

⬛ *Municipal Offices, Marcus Hill, Newquay TR7 1BD* ☎ *01637 871 345; Fax 01637 852 025: info@newquay.co.uk; www. newquay.co.uk, www.north-cornwall.com* ⬛ *North Quay, Padstow* ☎ *01841 533449 Fax 01840 532356; padstowtic@visit.org.uk; www. north-cornwall.com.*

Padstow★ – In the 6C St Petroc, landing from Wales, founded a Celtic minster at the mouth of the Camel estuary. In 981, minster and town were destroyed by the Vikings. The town recovered, developing into an important port until the 19C when ships became too large to pass the sand bar, known as Doom Bar, at the estuary mouth. The harbour is enclosed by quays lined with attractive old houses, while a network of narrow streets behind the quay ends at St Petroc's Church and **Prideaux Place**★, *(*○ *Open Easter Sun - 31 Mar, 8 May - 6 Oct: Sun-Thur, 1.30 - 4pm (last tour). Grounds & Tearoom: Easter Sun - 6 Oct: Su -Thur, 12.30 - 5pm. Opera performances, exhibitions.* ☎ *01841 532 411; Fax 01841 532 945; office@prideauxplace.fsnet.co.uk; www.hha.org.uk)* an Elizabethan house with 18C battlements set in gardens and landscaped parkland, still in the Prideaux family. The church, with its embattled west tower dating from the 13C, contains an octagonal 15C font of Catacleuse stone. In the churchyard stands a Celtic cross-shaft.

There are **boat trips** *(contact the Tourist Information Centre for details)* from the harbour to view the spectacular cliffs, rocks and caves beyond the Camel Estuary (frequently quite choppy, despite what the boatmen say).

Trevone – For those feeling energetic, the **Cornwall Coast Path**★★ (5mi/8km on foot) is a spectacular way of reaching Trevone from Padstow, circling the 242ft/74m Stepper Point and passing the natural rock arches of Porthmissen Bridge. The village and chapel with a slate spire stand in a small, sandy cove guarded by fierce offshore rocks.

Trevose Head★ – *6mi/9km west on B 3276 and by-roads; last half a mile on foot.* From the 1847 lighthouse on the 243ft/74m head, it is possible to see that of Hartland Point, 40mi/64km northeast, and that of Pendeen on West Penwith. By day the **views**★★ are of bay after sandy cove after rocky island.

Bedruthan Steps★ – *Cliff staircase;* ○ *Open Easter-Oct. Telephone for details.* ☎ *01208 74281.* The arc of sand (1.5mi/1km) spectacularly scattered with giant rocks worn to the same angle by waves and wind is visible over the cliff edge. Legend has it that the rocks were the stepping stones of the giant Bedruthan.

Newquay – This popular resort with sandy beaches at the foot of cliffs in a sheltered, north-facing bay takes its name from the new quay, built in 1439 to protect the port. By the 18-19C Newquay was a pilchard port, exporting salted fish to Italy and Spain. The **Huar's House** on the headland, from which the huar summoned the fishermen when he saw shoals of fish enter the bay, dates from this period. Newquay has recently enjoyed a revival led by surfers and hosts world class surfing competitions. Its **Zoo**, (♿ Trenance Gardens. 🕐 Open Nov-Mar 10am-5pm: Apr-May 10am-6pm. 💷 £9.45 summer; £5.75 winter. Restaurant, shop, childrens play areas, maze. ☎ 01637 873342; Fax 01637 851318; info@newquayzoo.org.uk; www.newquayzoo.co.uk) is one one of the best wildlife parks in the country.

Trerice★ – (NT) ♿ Kestle Mill. 🕐 Open Mar – Sept 11am-5.30pm (5pm Oct). 💷 £5.50. Braille guide. Restaurant. ☎ 01637 875 404; Fax 01637 879 300; trerice@ntrust.org.uk; www.nationaltrust.org.uk. This small, silver-grey stone Elizabethan **manor house** was rebuilt to an E-shaped plan in 1572-73. The east front is highly ornate with scrolled gables and a beautiful stone-mullioned window onto the great hall with 16C glass. The interior is particularly notable for the quality of its 16C **plasterwork** and fine furniture.

St Agnes Beacon★★ – The beacon, at 628ft/191m, affords a panorama★★ from Trevose Head to St Michael's Mount, with in the foreground the typical north Cornish landscape, windswept and speared by old mine stacks.

Hell's Mouth★ – From the cliff-edge, the blue-green-black sea breaks ceaselessly against the sheer, 200ft/60m cliff-face; the only sounds are the screaming of the sea-birds and the endless wash of the waves.

Hayle – This estuary town, once an important centre for copper, tin and iron smelting, is now popular for its miles of sandy beaches.

St Ives★★ – ♿ See ST IVES.

TOTNES★

Devon, ENGLAND

POPULATION 7 018

MICHELIN ATLAS P 4 OR MAP 503 – I, J 32

The ancient town of Totnes, "one of the most rewarding small towns in England" (Pevsner, The Buildings of England: Devon), stands at the highest navigable and lowest bridging point on the River Dart on the south Devon coast. The narrow main street runs steeply between 16-17C wealthy merchants' houses built of brick and stone or colour-washed. As **Fore Street**, it climbs as far as **East Gate**, a reminder that Totnes was once a walled town; beyond this it becomes **High Street**. Totnes's most prosperous period was 1550-1650, when it controlled ships carrying cargoes of cloth and tin to Spain and France. ℹ Town Mill, The Plains ☎ 01803 863 168; Fax 01803 86577; enquire@totnesinformation.co.uk; www.totnesinformation.co.uk.

Sights

Fore Street – The half-timbered **Elizabethan Museum**★ (70 Fore Street. 🕐 Open Apr-Oct, Mon-Fri and Bank Hol Mon, 10.30am-5pm. 💷 £1.50. 🎧 Guided tour (45min) by appointment. ☎ 01803 863 821; totnes.museum@virgin.net; www.devonmuseums. net/totnes), the dark red brick **Mansion** (now a community education centre), a late 18C Gothic house (in Bank Lane), and other attractive buildings (nos 48 and 52) testify to Totnes's former prosperity.

Rampart Walk – Just beyond the Arch at the top of Fore Street turn right up a flight of steps. The cobbled path of the old ramparts leads past cottages fronted with magnificent displays of flowers in tubs, troughs and pots.

High Street – Interesting features include the **Guildhall**,(🕐 Open Apr-Oct, Mon-Fri, some Bank Hols,10.30am-4.30pm. 💷 £1. Brochure (6 languages). 🎧 Guided tour (20min). ☎ 01803 862 147; Fax 01803 864 275) which occupies the site of an earlier Benedictine priory although the present building largely dates from 1553, the house at no 16, now a bank, which was built in 1585 by a local pilchard merchant (whose initials are on the façade), and the granite pillared **Butterwalk**★, which has protected shoppers from the rain since the 17C.

St Mary's★ – The 15C parish and priory church with its red sandstone tower adorned with gruesome gargoyles contains a beautiful Beer stone rood screen dating from 1459, which stretches across the entire width of the church.

Castle – (EH) ◷ *Open late-Mar to Oct, daily, 10am-6pm (5pm Oct).* 🖾 *£1.80. Parking.* ☎ *01803 864 406.* High on a mound sits the castle, encircled by 14C ramparts built to strengthen the late 11C motte and bailey earthworks. The castle walls command excellent **views**★★★ of the Dart River valley.

British Photographic Museum★ – *In Bowden House on the outskirts of town (southwest).* ◷ *Open May-Sep, Mon-Fri, noon-5pm.* 🖾 *Guided tour at 2pm, 3pm, 4pm.* 🖾 *£4.95. Parking. Café.* ☎ *01803 863 664.* This museum contains an extensive and fascinating collection of cameras and photographic equipment dating from the very earliest models to more recent examples.

Excursion

Dartington Hall – *2mi/3km northwest on A 385 and A 384.* ♿◷ *Open daily, dawn-dusk.* 🖾 *Donation £2.* 🖾 *Guided tour available £4. Parking.* ☎ *01803 866 688; graham@dartingtonhall.org.uk; www.dar-tington.u-net.com.* Seventy five years after its foundation, Dartington flourishes, ever expanding the concepts of its founders: **Leonard** (1893-1974) and **Dorothy** (1887-1968) **Elmhirst**, who believed in the encouragement of personal talent and responsibility through progressive education and rural regeneration. In practical terms, this meant the establishment of a working community where people would find scope for their personal development while earning a living. Within relatively

> ### Dartington International Summer School
>
> The great music festival which is held annually has its roots in the dynamic interaction of such figures as Imogen Holst, Artur Schnabel, Elizabeth Lutyens, Igor Stravinsky (1957), Benjamin Britten (who wrote his *Rape of Lucretia* for Dartington), the Amadeus String Quartet (formed at Dartington), Peter Maxwell Davies, Mark Elder, Harrison Birtwhistle, Michael Flanders and Donald Swann (who perfected their evening cabarets entitled *At the Drop of a Hat* there).

few years of the Elmhirsts' purchase of the long-desolate house and 800 acres of land around it, the name Dartington had become synonymous with "advanced" co-education, summer schools, art courses, exhibitions and concerts. Dartington school closed in 1987 but the **Dartington Hall Trust** continues to provide conference and educational facilities, and a varied educational programme.

The Great Hall, set in fine gardens, was begun 1388-1400. The Elmhirsts purchased it, derelict, in 1925 and had it restored under the then most eminent exponent of "conservative restoration," **William Weir**. In stark contrast with the older buildings is **High Cross House**★ (1931-32 ♿◷ *Open Apr-Oct, Tues-Fri, 10.30am-4.30pm, Sat-Sun 2pm-5pm; otherwise by appointment.* 🖾 *£2.50, £1.50 (concession). Parking. Terrace café.* ☎ *01803 864 114.*), William Lescaze's International Modernist style building painted blue and white, intended as the residence for the headmaster of Dartington school before it closed. It now houses the Trust archives, a study centre and temporary exhibitions.

The **TROSSACHS**★★★

Stirling, SCOTLAND

MICHELIN ATLAS P 55 OR MAP 501 G 15

Occupying Scotland's midriff area, the Trossachs is one of the country's most famous scenic areas, with rugged mountains and wooded slopes reflected in the waters of many lochs. From Callander and Loch Venachar in the east, to Loch Katrine and even to the shores of Loch Lomond in the west, this whole area of great scenic beauty is easily accessible. *Ancester Square,Callander* ☎ *08707 200 628; www.lochlomond-trossachs.org, www.trossachs.org.uk National Park Headquarters, The Old Station, Balloch Road, Balloch G83 8BF* ☎ *01389 722600; Fax 01389 722633; info@lochlomond-trossachs.org; www.lochlomond-trossachs.org.*

▸ **Orient Yourself**: Callander is a good base. Outdoor explorers should make the National Park Headquarters their first stop.

Don't Miss: Loch Katrineand the panorama closeby; Loch Lomond; Ben Lomond.

Organizing Your Time: Allow 2-3 days.

Also See: Perth, Stirling.

Walking: Callander is a centre for hill walking with several "Munros" (peaks over 3,000 feet/914m) close by, go to *www.trossachs.org.uk* for more details; Queen Elizabeth Forest Park.

Bicycle Trails: Cycle hire from Loch Katrine Visitor Centre and Queen Elizabeth Forest Park. Go to the Activities page on *www.trossachs.org.uk* for more details.

Fishing: Lake of Menteith, Queen Elizabeth Forest Park.

Loch Katrine

Queen Elizabeth Forest Park – Planned forestry was practised in the Loch Ard area as early as 1794, supplying building materials, fuel and an associated tanning industry. The Forestry Commission purchased land in 1928; and some 42 000 acres/17 000ha were designated the Queen Elizabeth Forest Park in 1953. Details of leisure opportunities (forest drives, walking, cycling, picnics and fishing) within the forest park boundaries are available from the Queen Elizabeth Forest Park **visitor centre** (& *Open Mar-Dec daily. Parking (charge). Café, picnic area.* ☎ *01877 382 258; Fax 01877 382 120) north of Aberfoyle.*

Rob Roy MacGregor (1671–1734)

Much of the rugged terrain of the Trossachs is closely associated with the daring exploits of the outlawed clan leader and hero of Sir Walter Scott's novel, Rob Roy (1818). Rob, his wife and two of their sons lie in the churchyard of Balquhidder on Loch Voil to the north. The **Rob Roy Story** (&🏛 *Tourist Information Centre, Callander, ⏰Open Jul-Aug, daily, 9am-8pm; Jun and Sep, daily, 9.30am-6pm; Mar-May and Oct-Dec, daily, 10am-5pm; Jan-Feb: Phone for details. Last admission 45 mins before closing. ☜ £3.25. Translation (4 languages). ☎ 01877 330 342; Fax 01877 330 784; robroyst@aillst.ossian.net)* presents a vivid account of the life of the noted freebooter. & *See also Aberfoyle.*

In and Around the Trossachs

Callander★ – This busy summer tourist centre became known to millions as the Tannochbrae of television's *Dr Finlay's Casebook*. Callander has been popular with visitors for over a century and is the main eastern gateway to the Trossachs.

Loch Venachar – The Trossachs road (*A 821*), skirts the lower slopes of **Ben Ledi** (2 882ft/879m) overlooking the banks of Loch Venachar, before reaching the scattered settlement of **Brig o'Turk** at the mouth of Glen Finglas.

The village has associations with the Ruskins and Millais, whose holiday here in 1853 was followed by an annulment of the Ruskins' marriage and Effie's remarriage to Millais. This spot later became a favourite haunt of the **Glasgow Boys** (& *see GLASGOW*).

Loch Katrine★★ – *1mi/1.5km from A 821 to the pier, visitor centre and car park. There is no access round the loch for vehicles.* For those who do not relish hill walking, the only, but very rewarding, way to see this lovely loch, source of Glasgow's water supply since 1859, is to take a **boat trip** (& ⏰ *Operates from Trossachs Pier, Apr-Oct, daily, at 11am (except Wed), 1.45pm, 3.15pm; ☜ return £5-5.50. ☎ 01877 376 316; Fax 01877 376 317; lochkatrine@scottishwater.co.uk; www.lochkatrine.org.uk)* on the *SS Sir Walter Scott*. Ellen's Isle and Factor's Isle figure respectively in works by Sir Walter Scott, the poem *The Lady of the Lake* and the novel *Rob Roy*. Scott's romantic poem did much to popularise the Trossachs, and the Wordsworths and Coleridge followed in his footsteps in 1830. The boat turns at Stronachlachar, from where a road leads west to Loch Lomond. Glen Gyle at the head of the loch was the birthplace of Rob Roy.

To the south of Loch Katrine looms the twin-peaked form of **Ben Venue** (2 393ft/727m). Beyond, a hilltop viewpoint affords a magnificent **panorama**★★★ across the Trossachs, with Ben Venue, Loch Katrine with its ring of mountains, Ben An, Finglas Reservoir, Ben Ledi with Brig o'Turk at its foot and Loch Venachar.

Aberfoyle – The attractive village, busy now with tourists every summer, was made famous as the place from where Rob Roy abducted Baillie Nicol Jarvie, factor to the Duke of Montrose. Jarvie had evicted Rob's family, and in reprisal was held captive on what is today known as Factor's Isle in Loch Katrine.

A road leads west through the forest park to Loch Lomond.

Loch Lomond★★ – The blue waters of this loch (653ft/200m deep) are flanked by rugged mountains in the north and pastoral woodlands in the south. Rising on the far side of the loch from the pier at Inversnaid are the rugged forms of the Cobbler, Bens Vorlich, Vane and Ime. **Loch Lomond Shores,** a state-of-the-art visitor centre (& ⏰ *Open daily, 10am-5pm. ☜ £5.95 combined ticket for audiovisual presentations and access to rooftop terrace or separate charge for each. Parking. Café. Restaurant. ☎ 01389 721 500; Fax 01389 720 603; loch.lomond@scotent.co.uk; www.lomondshores.co.uk).*

The **West Highland Way**, starting from Milngavie, north of Glasgow follows the east shore northwards to Fort William passing on the way the lower slopes of **Ben Lomond**★★ (3 192ft/974m). This shapely peak is the most southerly of the Highland Munros (mountains over 3 000ft/912m).

To enjoy the charm of Loch Lomond take a boat trip calling at the attractive village of **Luss★** with its mellow stone cottages, Tarbet, Inversnaid and Rowardennan.

Lake of Menteith – This stretch of water is one of the venues for the Grand Match between north and south, organised by the Royal Caledonian Curling Club and is also popular with fishermen.

The remains of **Inchmahome Priory** (HS ⏰ *Open Apr-Sep, daily, 9.30am-6.30pm (last sailing 5.15pm). ☜ £3.30 (including ferry). Parking. Picnic area. ☎ 01877 385 294)* on one of the tiny islands include the mid-13C ruins of the church and chapter house. The infant Mary Queen of Scots was brought here for safety for a while in 1547, before embarking for France and her marriage to the Dauphin.

TRURO

Cornwall, ENGLAND

POPULATION 16 522

MICHELIN ATLAS P 2 OR MAP 503 E 33

By the 18C Truro, once a river port and mining centre, was considered the county "metropolis", with a theatre and assembly rooms, county library (1792) and the cathedral (1850). It had developed into the most notable Georgian town west of Bath, with 18C houses in Boscawen, Lemon and other streets. Repeated requests for Cornwall once more to become an independent see were finally granted and in 1880 the cathedral foundation stone was laid. Completed by 1910, Truro Cathedral is a mixture of Normandy Gothic with upswept vaulting, vistas through tall arcades and, outside, three steeple towers which give the building its characteristic outline. The **Royal Cornwall Museum**★★ *(NACF ○ Open Mon-Sat, 10am-5pm. Closed Bank Hols. Free Admission. ⌐ Guided tour (60min). Printed guide (5 languages). Courtney Library: Open Mon-Sat, 10am-1pm and 2-5pm. Café. ☎ 01872 272 205; Fax 01872 240 514; enquiries@royal-cornwall-museum.freeserve.co.uk; www. royalcornwallmuseum.org.uk),* in River Street is the learned and vibrant showplace of the Royal Institution of Cornwall (f 1818) and the repository for a variety of artefacts relating to the geology, archeology and social history of Cornwall as well as a collection of fine and decorative arts. *Pydar House, Pydar Street, Truro, TR1 1EA ☎ 01872 322900; Fax 01872 322895; tourism@cornwallenterprise.co.uk; www. visitcornwall.co.uk.*

- ☺ **Don't Miss**: Eden Project; Trewithen Garden; Fowey.
- ○ **Organizing Your Time**: Allow 4 days.
- ⊞ **Especially for Kids**: Gweek Seal Sanctuary; beaches at Kynance Cove and Mullion Cove.

Excursions

South Cornish Coast between Truro and Plymouth

Trelissick Garden★★ – ♿○ *Open mid-Feb to early-Nov, daily, 10.30am (12.30pm Sun) to 5.30pm/dusk. Woodland walks daily. ⌐ £5. Arts and crafts gallery. Parking. Licensed restaurant. Braille guide; wheelchairs and electric buggy for hire. ☎ 01872 862 090; Fax 01872 865 808; trelissick@nationaltrust.org.uk; www.nationaltrust. org.uk.* From the gardens beyond the Classical, porticoed house (built 1750, remodelled 1825), there are superb **views**★★ over the park, Falmouth and out to sea. The woodland dropping down to the river has a variety of trees, shrubs, exotics and perennials. Spacious areas of lawn feature summer-flowering shrubs; particular highlights include the hydrangeas (over 130 varieties), azaleas and rhododendrons. The Cornish Apple Orchard has been created to preserve as many traditional varieties of apple as possible.

▸ *Take the B 3289 and the* **King Harry Ferry** *(○ Operates daily. ○ Closed 1 jan, 1 week mid-Mar and 25-26 Dec. ⌐ Single £4 per car. Feock to Philleigh (5min); telephone for timetable. ☎ 01872 862 312; www.kingharryferry.co.uk.) across the Carrick Roads.*

St Just-in-Roseland★★ – The **church** here, built on a 6C Celtic site in the 13C and restored in the 19C, has a remarkable setting in an enchanting, steep churchyard garden. The church stands so close to the creek and little harbour that at high tide it is reflected in the water.

St Mawes★ – In 1539-43 Henry VIII constructed this cloverleaf-shaped **castle**★ ○ *Open late-Mar to Oct, daily, 10am-5pm (6pm Jul-Aug, 4pm Oct - Mar); ○ Closed 1 Jan and 24-26 Dec. ⌐ £3.60. Parking ☎ 01326 270 526; keith.robson@english-heritage.org.uk; www.english-heritage.org. uk),* with motte and bailey, as a pair with Pendennis Castle on the opposite bank of

Traditional Cornish dishes include the renowned Cornish pasty, Muggety Pie (sheep's innards), Kiddley Broth (bread soaked in boiling water: the staple fare of poor tin-mining families) and Stargazy Pie (so-named because of the pilchards' heads poking up through the crust).

the Fal (the Carrick Roads), to safeguard the mile-wide entrance to the estuary. The castle, situated in pleasant gardens, affords excellent **views**★ right out to Manacle Point (see below) 10mi/16km south.

Veryan★ – Four curious little white-walled **round houses** with Gothic windows and a conical thatched roof surmounted by a cross lend this village its unique charm.

Probus★ – The granite church **tower**★ here is the tallest in Cornwall (125ft 10in/38m). There is also the interesting and informative **Probus County Demonstration Garden** ★ (♿⏰ *Open Mar-Nov, daily, 10am-5pm; Dec-Feb, Mon-Fri, 10am-4pm.* ✏ *£3. Parking. Refreshments. Plant sales.* ☎ *01726 882 597; Fax 01726 883 868; enquiries@ probuscardens.org.uk; www.probusgardens.org.uk).*

Trewithen★★★ – *Grampground Road. Garden:* ♿⏰ *Open Mar-Sep, Mon-Sat (also Sun, Apr-May), 10am-4.30pm. House:* 🚶 *Guided tour (35min) Apr-Jul, Mon-Tue and Aug Bank Hol Mon, 2-4pm.* ✏ *Garden £3.75; house £4. Dogs on leads. Parking. Refreshments.* ☎ *01726 882 764 (gardens), 01726 883 647 (estate office); Fax 01726 882 301; gardens@ trewithen-estate.demon.co.uk; www.trewithengardens.co.uk.* The estate is noted for its 28 acres/11ha of beautiful landscape and woodland **gardens** which include, in season, magnificent banks of rhododendron, camellia and magnolia, several of which are house hybrids. The gardens provide an elegant setting for a fine Georgian **country house** (1715-55) containing period furniture, paintings and porcelain.

Mevagissey★★ – This picturesque old fishing village, with its old quayside boathouses and sail lofts, maze of twisting backstreets and nets of all shapes and colours drying on walls, attracts crowds of visitors all summer. It boasts an unusual double harbour with a 1770s pier.

Lost Gardens of Heligan★ – *Pentewan.* ♿⏰ *Open daily, 10am-6pm (5pm Nov – Feb)).* ⏰ *Closed 24-25 Dec.* ✏ *£7.50. Parking. Refreshments. Plant sales. Wheelchair loan.* ☎ *01726 845 100; Fax 01726 845 101; info@heligan.com; www.heligan.com.* These 57 acre/23ha gardens, originally laid out in the 18C by Thomas Gray but left to grow wild by the 20C, have been painstakingly recovered from dereliction since 1991. They include Flora's Garden (rhododendrons), a walled vegetable garden, fruit orchards, "The Jungle" (exotic trees planted in the 19C) and "The Lost Valley" (indigenous species and a water-meadow).

▶ *The road follows the wide sweep of St Austell Bay*★★.

Fowey★★ – 🛈 *5 South Street, Fowey PL23 1AR* ☎ *01726 833 616; Fax 01726 834 939; info@fowey.co.uk; www.fowey.co.uk.* This small town (pronounced Foy), on the hillside above an excellent natural harbour at the mouth of the river Fowey, was once one of England's busiest ports. It is well worth walking out to **Gribbin Head,** from which there are **views**★★ for miles around. We also recommend taking a **boat trip** round the harbour and coast where the cliffs rise dark and sheer from the water, or upriver between wooded hillsides. In town, walk along **Fore Street**, lined with picturesque old houses, and visit the 14-15C **church of St Nicholas** (on the site of a Norman church dedicated to St Fimbarrus), with its tall, pinnacled tower, two-storey porch in Decorated style, fine wagon roof and Norman font of Catacleuse stone.

Polperro★ – The closely packed cottages and winding alleys of this attractive old fishing village (closed to vehicles) lie at the bottom of the steep road which follows the stream down to the double harbour in the creek. A converted pilchard factory on the waterfront houses a small **museum** (⏰ *Open Easter-Oct, daily, 10am-6pm.* ✏ *£1.50.* ☎ *01503 272 423; www.polperro.org)* of photographs by Lewis Harding (1806-93) and 18C memorabilia of the area's prosperity long dependent on fishing and smuggling.

St Germans – Attractive almshouses, built in 1583, stand at the centre of this old village. The **church**★ (*0.5mi/just under 1km east of the village Star Street/Orbit Street.* ⏰*Open daily, 10am-4pm. Services: 1st and 3rd Sun at 10.30am (Holy Communion); 2nd and 4th at 6pm (Worship).* ☎ *01503 230 690; info@churchestogetherinstar.co.uk ; www.afwy61.ukgateway.net/index.html)* is one of the finest examples of Norman architecture in Cornwall. Dissimilar towers frame a majestic west front with a splendid Norman doorway, encircled by seven richly decorated orders carved in the local blue-grey-green Elvan stone. The east window has glass by William Morris.

Antony House★ – ♿⏰ *Open Apr-Oct, Tues-Thur and bank holiday Mondays, 1.30pm-5.30pm; also Jun-Aug, Sun, 1.30pm-5.30pm.* ✏ *£4. No dogs. Tea room. Wheelchair access to garden but not house.* ☎ *01752 812 191.* Sir William Carew built this Classical grey stone house extended by red brick wings in 1721. It contains a varied collection of 18C furniture and distinguished portraits, including three by Reynolds in the panelled salon and one of Edward Bower's memorable portraits of King Charles I at his trial.

Plymouth★★ – 👣 *See PLYMOUTH.*

South Cornish Coast between Truro and St Michael's Mount

Trelissick Garden★★ – 👣 *See above.*

Falmouth★ – 🏠 *28 Killigrew Street, Falmouth* ☎ *01326 312 300; Fax 01326 313 457.* From **Pendennis Castle**★ (👣🕐 *Open daily, 10am-6pm (5pm Oct; 4pm Nov-Mar).* 🕐 *Closed 1 Jan and 24-26 Dec.* 👛 *£4.60 Parking. Refreshments (Apr-Oct).* ☎ *01326 316 594; www. english-heritage.org.uk),* on the point, a low ridge runs inland, dividing the town in two: the hotel-residential district looks south over Falmouth Bay, while the old town with its **waterfront** faces north up the Fal estuary (known by its Cornish name of Carrick Roads). The waterfront stretches for over half a mile from Greenbank Quay to Prince of Wales Pier. The various quays and slips can be accessed from the main street which runs parallel to it. The river is overlooked by 18C houses and warehouses standing on the 17C harbour wall. Falmouth's **Municipal Art Gallery** (👣🕐 *Open Mon-Sat, 10am-5pm.* 🕐 *Closed 1 Jan, winter Bank Hols and 25-26 Dec.* ☎ *01326 313 863; Fax 01326 312 662; www.falmouthartgallery.com; info@falmouthartgallery.com),* contains a good selection of maritime, Victorian and early 20C paintings, and the **National Maritime Museum** (🕐 *Open daily, 10am-5pm (6pm Easter-Aug).* 🕐 *Closed 25 Dec and 6-31 Jan.* 👛 *£6.50. Parking. Cafe.* ☎ *01326 313 388; Fax 01326 317 878; enquiries@ nmmc.co.uk; www.nmmc.co.uk),* documents local maritime history (smuggling, myths and superstition, ship-building industry).

Glendurgan Garden★★ – 👣🕐 *Open mid-Feb to early-Nov, Tue-Sat and Bank Hol Mon, 10.30am-5.30pm (4.30pm last admission).* 🕐 *Closed Good Friday.* 👛 *£4.50. Guide (Braille, 3 languages). Parking. Refreshments.* ☎ *01326 250 906 (opening times), 01872 862 090; Fax 01872 865 808; glendurgan@nationaltrust.org.uk.* This beautiful garden, richly planted with subtropical trees and shrubs, drops down to Durgan hamlet on the Helford River. It is home to an interesting laurel maze and a Giant's Stride (maypole).

Lizard coastline

Lizard Peninsula★ – There is no coastal road running round this southernmost part of England, the source of Serpentine rock, so it is advisable to be selective when exploring, choosing from the following: **Gweek Seal Sanctuary**★(& ⏱ *Open summer, daily from 10am; winter, telephone for opening times.* ⏱ *Closed 25 Dec.* ☞ *£9.95. Children's play area. Parking (no charge). Shop. Café, barbecue and picnic area.* ☎ *01326 221 361; www.sealsanctuary.co.uk;* the south side of the **Helford estuary**; the **Manacles** off Manacles Point (an underwater reef responsible for many a shipwreck); the famous old fishing and smuggling village of **Coverack**★; **Landewednack**★ with its thatched roofs and **church**★ decorated with glossy green and black-velvet serpentine stone; the Lizard and its 1751 lighthouse (altered in 1903) on the southernmost tip of England; and the popular **Kynance Cove**★★ and **Mullion Cove**★★.

Helston – Helston is the market town for the Lizard peninsula. On 8 May (or the previous Saturday if this falls on a Sunday or Monday), the town is closed to traffic for the famous **Flora Day Furry Dance**★★ (⏱ *Performed on 8 May, or the previous Sat if the 8th falls on a Sun or Mon, at 7am, 8.30am (Hal-an-Tow procession from St John's), 10am (Children), noon (Ladies and Gentlemen) and 5pm.).* Five processional dances are performed along a 3-4mi/2-2.5km route (beginning and ending at the Guildhall), including the Hal-an-Tow at 8.30am, the children's procession at 10am and the Invitation Dance for couples at noon.

St Michael's Mount★★ – & *See ST IVES.*

TWEED VALLEY★★

Borders, SCOTLAND

MICHELIN ATLAS P 50 OR MAP 501 K, L AND M 17

On its long and beautiful course the Tweed flows past several famous landmarks – castles, abbeys, great houses – making the exploration of its banks a delight. 🏛 *Town House, The Square, Kelso TD5 7HF. Peebles.High Street, Peebles EH45 8AG. Abbey House, Abbey Street, Melrose TD6 9LG.* **All offices** ☎ *0870 608 0404 Fax 01750 21886; bordersinfo@visitscotland.com; www.scot-borders.co.uk*

▸ **Orient Yourself**: Moffat and Melrose are good bases for exploring the area.

◉ **Don't Miss**: Abbotsford; the decorative sculpturework at Melrose Abbey; the setting of Dryburgh Abbey; Traquair House; the library at Mellerstain; the Grey Mare's Tail waterfall.

⏱ **Organizing Your Time**: allow three days.

⊙⊙ **Bicycle Trails**:The forests of the Scottish Borders provide some of the best mountain biking in the country and there are many waymarked cycling routes

⤳ **Fishing**: The River Tweed is one of the foremost salmon rivers in Scotland, though its tributaries teeming with many other species of fish also attract the angler.

Geological Notes

River and landscape – The Tweed, third longest river in Scotland after the Tay and the Clyde, rises in the Tweedsmuir Hills and reaches the sea at Berwick-upon-Tweed; for the last part of its course it serves as the border between England and Scotland.
It is ringed by hills in its upper reaches – the Cheviots to the south and the **Lammermuir Hills** to the north – and its valley is constricted and irregular. In its middle reaches it is broad with majestic curves, overlooked by ruined abbeys and prosperous Border towns.
The Tweed Valley has long been a favoured area of settlement. Iron Age and Roman forts, and monastic houses are found all over the region. It was much fought over and the troubled times are remembered in many a Border ballad and poem.
Today, the valley is primarily agricultural, though the traditional woollen and knitwear industries are the mainstay of the towns.

Excursion

130mi/210km – ⏱ *See map below.*

Moffat

A small town at the head of Annan Valley, Moffat makes a good base from which to explore the Tweedsmuir Hills, where the River Tweed has its source.

▷ *Take A 708 Selkirk road.*

Grey Mare's Tail★★

At the head of Moffat Water Valley is the Grey Mare's Tail, a spectacular waterfall (200ft/60m drop). The road leads on up the now narrow V-shaped valley to cross the pass and then descends the valley of the Little Yarrow Water. Here, by St Mary's Loch, is Tibbie Shiel's Inn, meeting place of **James Hogg** (1770-1835), "the Ettrick Shepherd" and his friends.

▷ *Take the road to the left, signposted Tweedsmuir, past Megget Water; turn right into A 701.*

Broughton

In this trim roadside village is the **John Buchan Centre** (Old Church ⏱ *Open Easter and May-Sep, daily, 2-5pm.* ⏱ *£1.50. Parking.* ☎ *01899 221 050*), a tribute to the author and statesman **John Buchan**, Lord Tweedsmuir (1875-1940).

▷ *Take B 7016 east and B 712 north, running parallel to the Tweed. At the junction, turn right into A 72.*

One mile short of Peebles, on a rocky outcrop overlooking the river is **Neidpath Castle,** (♿⏱ *Open mid-Jun to early-Sep, daily, 10.30am (12.30 Sun) to 4.30pm; also Easter and May Bank Hols.* ⏱ *£3.* ↝ *Guided tour (30min) by appointment. Guide book. Parking.* ☎/*Fax 01721 720 333; keith.roxburgh@eidos.net; www.scot-borders.co.uk*) a 14C L-plan tower house. It is typical of the fortified dwellings needed for safety in the days of border and clan warfare.

Peebles

The former spa town is a good centre from which to explore the Tweeddale countryside, or to fish for salmon. The author **Robert Louis Stevenson** and the explorer **Mungo Park** lived in the town. **William Chambers,** publisher of the famous Dictionary, who was born here, donated the Chambers Institute, a library and a museum to the town.

▷ *6mi/10 km down river, by A 72. Cross the Tweed at Innerleithen.*

Traquair House★★

♿⏱ *Open Easter-Oct, daily, 12.30pm (10.30am Jun-Aug) to 5.30pm.* ⏱ *£5.50. Leaflet (5 languages). Parking. Refreshments.* ☎ *01896 830 323; Fax 01896 830 639; enquiries@traquair.co.uk; www.traquair.co.uk.* There was a royal hunting lodge here as early as 1107, which was transformed into a Border "peel", or fortified tower house, during the Wars of Independence. The wings were added in late 17C. This typical tower house has a wealth of relics, treasures and traditions and many Jacobite associations and personal belongings of Mary Queen of Scots. Also of interest are the **vaulted chamber** where cattle used to be herded in times of raids, a priest's room *(third floor)*, carved 16C **wood panels** in the chapel and a **brew-house** – the ale is highly regarded by enthusiasts.

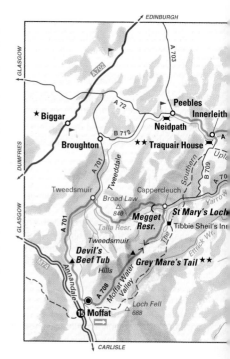

▷ *Return to A 72 and continue eastwards by B 7060 then A 7 to the left towards Abbotsford.*

Abbotsford★★

⌖⏲ *Open mid-Mar to Oct, daily, 9.30am (2pm Sun, mid-Mar to May and Oct) to 5pm. ⌾ £4. Guide book (3 languages). Tearoom. ☎ 01896 752 043; Fax 01896 752 916; abbotsford@melrose.bordernet.co.uk; www.melrose.bordernet.co.uk/abbotsford.* A fantasy in stone, typical of **Sir Walter Scott** (1771-1832), the man who did so much to romanticise and popularise all things Scottish. When in 1799 he became sheriff of Selkirkshire, he bought a house at Achiestiel, and later, in 1812, the farmhouse which he renamed and transformed into Abbotsford. In the study is preserved his massive writing desk; following a financial crisis in 1826 Scott wrote a staggering three novels a year whilst he repaid his creditors; he died here at Abbotsford, overlooking his beloved River Tweed, on 21 September 1832. There is in the house a collection of some 9000 rare books and some of the many items relating to Scotland and its history collected by Sir Walter throughout his life.

▷ *Take A 7 to return to A 72 then turn right.*

Melrose★

The pleasant town, grouped around the abbey ruins, is overshadowed by the **Eildon Hills**. Their strange triple peak – of volcanic origin – was once believed to have been the work of Michael Scott, a 13C wizard, who is buried in the abbey.

David I founded **Melrose Abbey★★** (⏲ ⌖ *Open daily, 9.30am (2pm Sun Oct-Mar) to 6.30pm (4.30pm Oct-Mar). Audio tour. ⌾ £3.30 Parking. Picnic area. ☎ 01896 822 562)* in 1136. The original buildings were damaged in the 14C, notably in 1322 by Edward II's retreating army. Robert the Bruce, whose heart is buried here (commemorative plaque with stylised design 1998), ensured their rebuilding. The ruins date from the late 14C to the early 16C and, uncharacteristically for a Cistercian foundation, are distinguished by a profusion of **decorative sculpture★★★**: delicate tracery, canopied niches, intricate vaulting and ornate gables. The remains of what was perhaps the richest abbey in Scotland were restored in the 1820s on the initiative of Sir Walter Scott.

▷ *Leave Melrose by B 6361 running along the Tweed. Past the viaduct, turn left onto A 68, then, once over the river, right on a minor road to Leaderfoot, then up Bemersyde Hill and turn right onto B 6356.*

Scott's View★★

The viewpoint (593ft/181m) faces west across the winding Tweed to the three conical peaks of the Eildons. In the near foreground is Bemersyde House, the home presented

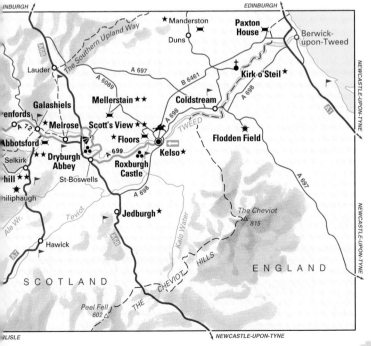

in 1921 by the nation to **Earl Haig,** who is buried in Dryburgh Abbey. Old Melrose, the original site of the Cistercian settlement, nestles below in a graceful meander of the Tweed.

▷ *Continue by the local road to Dryburgh Abbey.*

Dryburgh Abbey★★

  Open daily, 9.30am (2pm Sun) to 6.30pm (4.30pm Oct-Mar).   *£2.80. Parking. Picnic area.* ☎ *01835 822 381.* It is one of the group of Border abbeys founded by David I, and it was begun in 1150. It was repeatedly attacked by the English in the 1300s and was badly damaged when the town of Dryburgh was razed in 1544. A sheltered meander of the Tweed provides a splendid **setting**★★★ for the majestic ruins of the abbey in mellow red stone. Note the night stair leading to the dormitory. Sir Walter Scott's final resting-place is in the east chapel. The **conventual buildings** are among the best preserved groups.

▷ *Return to B 6356 then take B 6004 to St Boswells and turn left onto A 699 alongside the Tweed.*

Kelso★

Standing at the confluence of the Tweed and its main tributary, the Teviot, Kelso grew from a fording place into a thriving market town. Here again are the ruins of a fine **abbey**, founded in 1128, but many times destroyed, the latest being in 1545, despite a desperate resistance put up by the monks to the "Rough Wooing" by the English army. The town has some remarkable Georgian architecture – parapeted hipped roofs with dormers, straight-headed windows with hoods on scroll brackets – and the cobbled town **square**★★, originally the market place, features the elegant 19C **Town Hall**. The graceful bridge was built in 1803 by John Rennie.

Floors Castle★

On the outskirts of Kelso. *Open Good Friday to Oct, daily, 10.30am-4.30pm.*   *£5.50 Guide book (5 languages). Parking. Licensed restaurant; coffee shop; picnic area; walks; adventure playground.* ☎ *01573 223 333; Fax 01573 226 056; marketing@floorscastle. com; www.floorscastle.com.* The distinctive pinnacled silhouette stands on a terraced site overlooking the Tweed. The main block, built to the designs of William Adam, was extended in the 19C when William Playfair added the wings. Many of the rooms were refurbished early this century by the American wife of the 8th Duke of Roxburghe, to accommodate her outstanding **collection of tapestries** and **furniture**.

Mellerstain★★

6mi/10km northwest of Kelso by A 6089. *Open Easter and May-Sep, Sun-Fri, 12.30-5pm; Oct, Sat-Sun, 12.30pm-5pm; (4.30pm last admission).*   *£5.50.* *Guided tour (2hr). Leaflet (5 languages). Parking. Tearoom.* ☎ *01573 410 225; Fax 01573 410 636; enquirires@mellerstain.com; www.mellerstain.com.* The glory of this attractive 18C mansion is the delicacy of Robert Adam's interior decoration (*see also Culzean and Hopetoun House).* Mellerstain *(view from the forecourt)* is unique as the renowned architect rarely planned a house from beginning to end and it has the added distinction of being a combined effort by father and son. William Adam's wings (1725) in the vernacular style is in striking contrast to Robert's severe castellated central section in mellow stone.

Interior – Adam's skill and craftsmanship are evident throughout the house. The exquisite **ceilings**★★★ in delicate pastel colours are complemented by matching fireplaces, woodwork and furniture.

The **Library**★★★ is a masterpiece: the eye moves from the centrepiece of the delicate ceiling with Zucci roundels to the unifying patterns echoed on the friezes, bookcases, doors and fireplace. There is a fine collection of paintings including many family portraits.

▷ *Return to Kelso and continue down river on A 698.*

Coldstream

A busy market town grew up at this fording place of the Tweed. Here General Monck raised his regiment of Northumbrian troops, having been given the task by Cromwell of policing Scotland's east coast. On 1 January 1660 the General and his regiment set out for London on the march which eventually led to the Restoration of Charles II. The small local **museum** has an excellent section on the **Coldstream Guards**, (*Open Apr-Oct, Mon-Sat, 10am (2pm Sun; 1pm Oct) to 4pm. Parking. Wheelchair access to ground floor.* ☎ *01361 883 960)* the regiment's name after 1670.

▷ *Follow A 697 across the Tweed to Cornhill-on-Tweed then Branxton.*

Flodden Field

A monument inscribed "To the brave of both nations" marks Pipers Hill, the centre of the English positions. In two hours, on 9 September 1513, the smaller English army slaughtered the flower of Scotland's chivalry and their King, James IV, who had led them into battle in support of his recently renewed "Auld Alliance" with the French.

▶ *Return to A 698; take a local road to Norham Castle on its riverside site.*

Norham Castle

Open late-Mar to Sep, daily, 10am-6pm. *£1.90 No access to keep for wheelchairs.* *01289 382 329.* Hugh Puiset, Bishop of Durham, completed the massive stone keep of his castle about 1174. From the 12C to 16C, Norham guarded one of the main crossings of the Tweed. It was in Norham Church on 20 November 1292 that John Balliol swore fealty to Edward I, after being chosen as King of Scotland three days previously, at Berwick.

▶ *Continue east beside the river via Horncliffe; beyond Horncliffe turn left and cross the river; turn right into B 6461.*

Paxton House

House and Gallery: Guided tour Apr-Oct, daily, 11.15am-5pm (4.15pm last tour). Grounds: Open Apr-Oct, daily, 10am-dusk. House and grounds £5; grounds only, £2.50. Parking. Tearoom; picnic areas. 01289 386 291; Fax 01289 386 660; info@ paxtonhouse.com; www.paxtonhouse.com. The perfect Palladian mansion, built in the 1750s, designed by the Adam family (delicate plasterwork) and furnished by **Chippendale** and Trotter; the Regency **picture gallery** acts as an outstation of the National Galleries of Scotland.

▶ *Take B 6461 east to Berwick-upon-Tweed.*

Berwick-upon-Tweed★★ – *See BERWICK-UPON-TWEED.*

WARWICK★

Warwickshire, ENGLAND

POPULATION 22 476

MICHELIN ATLAS P 27 OR MAP 403 P 27

TOWN PLAN IN THE MICHELIN GUIDE GREAT BRITAIN AND IRELAND

"This perfect county town" (Pevsner), at the heart of the English Midlands is mostly in the Queen Anne style; it contrasts with but does not detract from its 14C castle "the most perfect piece of castellated antiquity in the kingdom" (Lord Torrington). *The Court House, Jury Street, CV34 4EW ☎ 01926 492 212; www.warwick-uk.co.uk.*

Sights

Warwick Castle★★ – ♿🕐 *Open daily, 10am-6pm (5pm Oct-Mar). 🕐 Closed 25 Dec. 👓 £10.75 (Mar to mid-May and mid-Sep to Feb); £12.50 (4 May to 8 Sep); £13 (weekends and Bank Hol, 4 May to 8 Sep). Guide books (6 languages). Audio guide (4 languages). Parking. Restaurants, summer barbecue. Wheelchairs available for grounds: telephone in advance. ☎ 0870 442 2000 (information); Fax 01926 401 692; customer.information@warwick-castle.com; www.warwick-castle.co.uk.* The castle stands beside the River Avon on the site of a Norman motte and bailey and possibly a Saxon stronghold before that. The mound is now incorporated into the elegant grounds, landscaped by Capability Brown in the 1750s; the Victorian landscape gardener Robert Marnock added the Peacock Garden and the recently restored formal Rose Garden.

The curtain walls and gatehouse are 14C, the Bear Tower and Clarence Tower date from the 15C. The castle was begun by Thomas de Beauchamp, 11th Earl of Warwick (1329-69), and was also the residence of Richard (1382-1439), the 13th Earl, who executed Joan of Arc. Now part of the Tussauds Group, the castle has been "brought to life" using tableaux of wax figures recreating characters and events in the castle's history, beginning with *"Kingmaker"*, Richard Neville Earl of Warwick's preparations for his final battle in 1471 amid the sounds and smells of the medieval castle. Jacobean Warwick is represented by the Ghost Tower and Victorian life is recreated in Frances, Countess of Warwick's *"Royal Weekend Party"*, held in 1898 with guests including the Prince of Wales and a young Winston Churchill.

Collections of paintings and furniture are displayed in the 17C and 18C **State Rooms** including the magnificent Red, Green and Cedar Drawing Rooms with works by Lely, Van Dyck and furniture by Boulle, and the Blue Boudoir with its portrait of Henry VIII after Holbein. Other attractions include the armoury, dungeons and torture chamber.

Lord Leycester Hospital, Warwick

A. F. Kersting/MICHELIN

Lord Leycester Hospital★ – *High Street.* ○ *Open Tue-Sun, 10am-5pm (4pm Oct-Mar) and Bank Hols.* ○ *Closed Good Friday, 25 Dec.* ◎ *£3.20. Brochure (3 languages).* ☎ *01926 492 797.* This was founded in 1571 by Queen Elizabeth's favourite, Lord Leicester. The oldest parts of the timber-framed building, which surrounds a charming partly-cloistered courtyard, are the chapel (1383) and the guildhall (1450), built by Warwick the "king-maker."

Collegiate Church of St Mary★ – *Church Street.* ○ *Open daily, 10am-6pm (4.30pm winter).* ☎ *01926 403 940; Fax 01926 402 118; terry@powo.spacomputers.com; www. saintmaryschurch.co.uk .* Although the church was rebuilt after a fire in 1694, it dates from 1123 and its glory is the Beauchamp (pronounced *beecham*) Chapel (15C) containing the **tomb**★ and superb gilded bronze effigy of Richard de Beauchamp, Earl of Warwick, and also the tomb of Robert Dudley, Earl of Leicester.

Excursion

Kenilworth Castle★ – *(EH) 5mi/8km north on A 46 and A 429.* ♿○ *Open daily, 10am-6pm (5pm Oct; 4pm Nov to late-Mar).* ○ *Closed 1 Jan and 24-26 Dec.* ◎ *£4.40 Audio guide (4 languages). Parking. Refreshments, picnic areas.* ☎ *01926 852 078; Fax 01926 851 514; www.english-heritage.org.uk.* The castle was the home (13C) of Simon de Montfort; in its **Great Hall** Edward II (1307-27) stood as a prisoner in a black dress before being taken to his death at Berkeley Castle. Kenilworth was strengthened by John of Gaunt (14C) and became the seat of the Earl of Leicester (late 16C). It was wrecked after the Civil War and the immense awe-inspiring sandstone ruins, by then overgrown with ivy, became the inspiration for *Kenilworth* (1862), a historical novel by Sir Walter Scott.

WELLS★★

Somerset, ENGLAND

POPULATION 9 763

MICHELIN ATLAS P 16 OR MAP 503 M 30

The calm of the cathedral within its precinct contrasts majestically with the bustle of the Market Square in England's smallest cathedral city. Together with the other Mendip towns (Frome, Glastonbury, Shepton Mallet and Street), Wells prospered as a centre of the wool trade in the Middle Ages. The social history of Wells and the Mendip area are outlined in the Wells Museum (♿○ *Open Apr-Oct, daily, 10am-5.30pm (8pm mid-Jul to mid-Sep); Nov-Mar, Wed-Mon, 11am-4pm.* ○ *Closed 24-25 Dec. Room guide (4 languages).* ◎ *£2.50.* ☎ *01749 673 477)* in the Chancellor's House on the Cathedral Green. ⓘ *Town Hall, Market Place* ☎ *01749 672 552; Fax 01749 670 869; touristinfo@wells.gov.uk; www. wells.gov.uk.*

- ⊙ **Don't Miss:** The Cathedral, particularly its West Front; Cheddar Gorge and Caves.
- ○ **Organizing Your Time:** Allow half a day in Wells.
- ⒦ **Especially for Kids:** Wookey Hole.
- ⓢ **Also See:** Bath, Bristol, Glastonbury, Laycock.
- ⌇ **Walking Tours:** During the summer season there are guided walks of Wells departing from the tourist information centre.

Cathedral★★★

○ *Open daily, 9am-7pm, (6.15pm Oct-Mar). Services: Sun at 8am (Holy Communion), 9.45 (Sung Eucharist), 11.30am (Matins), 3pm (Evensong); Mon-Sat at 7.30am (Matins), 8am (Holy Communion), 5.15pm (Evensong); Tue and Thu at 12.25pm (Holy Communion).* ☎ *01749 674 483; Fax 01749 832 210; visits@wellscathedral.uk.net; www.wellscathedral. org.uk). Audio guide for visually impaired visitors.* Wells was the first cathedral church in the Early English style; it took more than three centuries to plan and build, from c 1175 to 1508.

Wells Cathedral

Exterior – Despite weathering and much destruction by the Puritans, the **west front** is one of England's richest displays of 13C sculpture. Long ago, with its figures coloured and gilded, it would have resembled an illuminated manuscript or a sumptuous tapestry. Although now monochrome, it is tinted at sunset and gilded by floodlight at night. The screen front is nearly 150ft/46m across, twice as wide as it is tall, extending round the bases of the west towers – strange constructions which continue the gabled lines of the screen in slim and soaring pinnacled buttresses and tall paired lancets, only to stop abruptly. The 300 statues, half of them life-size, rise to a climax in the centre gable with a frieze of the Apostles and Our Lord flanked by two six-winged cherubim. The figure of Christ in Majesty was sculpted by David Wynne as part of the 20C restoration.

The **north porch** leads to a twin doorway flanked by some delightful tiers of 13C blank arcading. Set into the west wall of the north transept is a **quarter-jack** – 15C knights strike the bells with their pikes at the quarters.

Interior – Viewed from the west to the east end the most striking feature of the **nave** is the **scissor arch**, constructed together with similar arches at the north and south sides of the crossing in 1338-48, when the west piers of the crossing tower began to subside. The nave itself was completed in 1239. Note the stiff leaf **capitals** at the top of the piers, the stone pulpit dating from c 1547 at the east end of the nave and the adjoining Sugar Chantry (1489) enriched with fan vaulting, angel figures in the frieze and an ogee doorway. The constant features, the **roof vaulting** and **pier shafting**, are subtly varied in each sector of the cathedral; the vaulting reaches its climax in the star in the Lady Chapel, and the piers in the slender clustered column in the chapter-house. Note, in the **chancel**, the Jesse or **Golden Window** of medieval glass and the embroidered stall backs.

There are interesting carvings in the **south transept**: the capitals portray men's heads, animal masks hidden among leaves and everyday scenes such as a man with toothache and even two men caught in the act of stealing apples from an orchard; the **corbels** also portray figures, including an angel. The circular font, with Jacobean cover, is the only relic of an earlier cathedral on an adjacent site. Other features in the cathedral include the **piers** in the retro-choir which produce a forest of ribs to support intricate **tierceron vaulting**, and the 13C cope chest and medieval **misericords** showing a man killing a wyvern and Alexander the Great being lifted to heaven by two griffins; the **star vault** in the Lady Chapel, an unequal octagon crowned by a finely painted boss and retaining original c 1315 glass.

In the north transept is an **astronomical clock** of 1390, with the sun and a star revolving round the 24-hour dial and, above, a **knights' tournament** in which one knight is struck down at every quarter hour.

Chapter-house – A wide curving flight of **steps**, laid c 1290, leads to the splendid octagonal chapter-house, the building of which was completed by 1306. From its slender clustered centre pier 32 ribs fan out to meet those rising from each angle in an encircling octagonal rib.

Cathedral Precinct – Three 15C **gates** lead from the city streets to the calm of the Green and the spectacular view of the cathedral exterior: Brown's Gate *(from Sadler Street)*, Penniless Porch *(northeast corner)* and Bishop's Eye *(east side)*. The 1459 **Chain Gate** at the north east of the Green gives access to **Vicars' Close**, a 150yd/137m long street of identical cottages built in c 1348 for members of the cathedral in minor orders. On the south side of the cathedral stands the 700-year-old **Bishop's Palace**★, (&🕐 *Open Apr-Oct, Sun, Tue-Fri and Bank Hol Mon, 10.30am (1pm Sun) to 5pm (last admission); also Aug, Sat (weddings permitting) 10.30am-5pm (last admission).* ⊜ *£3.50. Refreshments.* ☎ *01749 678 691)* stoutly walled and encircled by a moat. Inside are walled gardens and the welling springs from which the city gets its name – 3 400 000 gallons a day, or 40 gallons a second (c 15 million litres a day, 180 litres a second). There are also the ruins of the old banqueting hall, the present palace and a beautiful **view**★★ of the east end of the cathedral.

Additional Sight

St Cuthbert★ – 🕐 *Open daily, 9am-4pm. Services: Sun at 8am, 10am, 6.30pm.* ☎ *www. stcuthbertwells.co.uk.* This magnificent Perpendicular parish church, overshadowed by its famous neighbour at the other end of town, stands on the site of earlier churches dating back to a Saxon building. The elegant **tower** (122ft/37m) has slender stepped buttresses framing enormously tall bell openings. The inside features a typical 16C

A. Taverner/MICHELIN

Cheddar Gorge

Somerset-style wooden **roof** (restored in 1963), with tie-beams, cresting, coffering and ornamentation, a superb late Jacobean **pulpit** (1636) and two much mutilated early **altarpieces**, commissioned in 1470 (the contract is also in the church).

Excursions

Wookey Hole★ – *2mi/3km northwest of Wells on a minor road.* The approach is through wooded pastureland at the foot of the Mendip plateau. The hole is in a 200ft/61m cliffside from which the River Axe gushes in a torrent.

The **caves**★ (🕑 *Open Mar-Oct, daily, 10am-5pm; Nov-Feb, 10.30am-4.30pm.* 🕑 *Closed 17-25 Dec. ⌂⌂ Guided tour (2hr) of caves and paper mill (paper mill accessible by wheelchair). Leaflet (5 languages). ⊜ £7.60. Parking. Restaurant; picnic area. ☎ 01749 672 243; Fax 01749 677 749; witch@wookeyhole.co.uk; www.wookey.co.uk)* contain six chambers through which the river flows, always present, in echoing cascades and deep blue-green pools. The tour leads through some 350yd/320m of caverns containing **stalactites, stalagmites**, "frozen" waterfalls and translucent pools. There is no evidence of Stone Age occupation, but the caves were inhabited by Iron Age man in 300 BC and later by Romano-British and Celtic peoples. The **Witch's Magic Cavern** concludes the tour with the unfurling of history and legend in times past, present and future.

Visitors should also make time to visit the **papermill**★; paper was first made at Wookey Hole c 1600.

Cheddar Gorge★★ – *9mi/14km northwest on A 371.* The gorge is 2mi/3km long with a 1:6 gradient, twisting and turning in its descent from the Mendips. The cliffs are of limestone, gaunt and grey where the fissured walls and pinnacles rise vertically 350-400ft/107-122m. From near the foot of the gorge **Jacob's Ladder**, a staircase of 274 steps (rest benches), leads up to a panoramic **view**★ of the Mendips, the Somerset Levels and the Quantocks.

Caves★★ – 🕑 *Open daily, 10am-5pm (10.30am-4.30pm mid-Sep to May).* 🕑 *Closed 24-25 Dec. Jacobs Ladder, Gough's Cave, Cox's Cave, Heritage Centre, Crystal Quest, Lookout Tower, Gorge Walk ⊜ £7.90. Parking. Refreshments. ☎ 01934 742 343; Fax 01934 744 637; www.cheddarcaves.co.uk.* The caves are near the gorge bottom on the south side *(left, going down).* **Cox's Cave** was discovered in 1837 and **Gough's Cave** in 1890. The series of chambers follows the course of underground streams through the porous limestone. The stalagmites and stalactites, petrified falls, lace curtains and pillars are coloured according to the minerals in the limestone – rust red (iron), green (manganese) and grey (lead). In the **heritage centre** the weapons, utensils in flint, bone and antler horn, iron and bronze, pottery and the skull of Cheddar Man indicate that the caves were inhabited intermittently from the Paleolithic to the Iron Age (20 000-500BC) and in Roman times.

The village of **Cheddar**, which extends from the foot of the gorge to the parish church at the south end of the main street, gave its name to the English national cheese: in 1170, Henry II bought 80cwt of Cheddar, declaring it the "best cheese in England".

West Country Cheese

According to one fanciful legend, the history of West Country cheese began when monks on a pilgrimage to Glastonbury took shelter from a terrible storm in the Cheddar caves and found that the milk they were carrying in leather pouches had turned into a delicious cheese: Cheddar has since become synonymous with English cheese, notably abroad. The fanciful element in the story lies in the fact that the Cheddar Caves remained inaccessible to all but climbers until the 19C. The truth of the tale is that itinerant holy men, especially early Celtic monks from Ireland, were instrumental in developing the art of cheese-making not only as a means of saving what otherwise might be wasted milk but also for eating on days of fasting when meat was forbidden: hence the reason for dairy products (and sometimes eggs) being referred to as "white meat." During the times when the wool trade prospered, certainly up to the 16C, cheeses throughout England must predominantly have been made with ewes' milk (examples of those which still are include Wensleydale and Caerphilly).

There are many places in the West Country at which to buy excellent cheeses; visitors to Wells should look out for The Fine Cheese Co.

WESTERN ISLES
SCOTLAND

POPULATION 23 224

MICHELIN ATLAS P 71 OR MAP 501 Z, A 8, 9 AND 10

ACCESS: SEE THE MICHELIN GUIDE GREAT BRITAIN AND IRELAND

The chain of islands known as the Western Isles extends some 130mi/more than 200km from Barra Head in the south to the Butt of Lewis in the north. Buffeted by Atlantic waves, they are treeless and windswept, but rejoice in glistening lochans, superb sandy beaches, and crystal-clear waters.

Gaelic culture flourishes in the islands; special events and festivals of Gaelic art and music (Mods) are held all year round. Gatherings (ceilidhs), concerts, highland games and agricultural shows are joyful community occasions with music, dance, poetry among other performances. *Isle of Lewis: 26 Cromwell Street, Stornoway, , HS1 2DD, ☎ 01851 703 088; Fax: 01851 705 244; www.visithebrides.com* *Isle of Harris: Pier Road, Tarbert, HS3 3DJ ☎ 01859 502 01; Fax 01859 502011; www.visithebrides.com*

▶ **Orient Yourself: Lewis and Harris** – They are in effect one island, which is almost cut in two by West and East Loch Tarbert. Lewis consists largely of rolling moorlands, while Harris is altogether more mountainous. Traditional activities include peat working and the weaving of **Harris tweed** (the orb trademark is a guarantee of quality).

Visit

Stornoway – *Lewis.* Stornoway, the capital and only sizeable town, is the base for excursions inland where hotels and petrol stations are scarce. The land-locked harbour is overlooked by a 19C castle. Eye peninsula to the northeast has some fine sandy beaches.

Callanish Standing Stones★★ – *Lewis. 16mi/26km west of Stornoway, well signposted off A 858.* Over 4 000 years old and contemporary with Stonehenge, the stones, of Lewisian gneiss, form a circle plus alignments with the points of the compass and it is generally assumed that they were used for astronomical observations. A central burial chamber is a later Neolithic addition (2500-2000 BC).

Carloway Broch★ – *Lewis. 5mi/8km beyond Callanish Standing Stones, signposted off A 858.* Although it is not a complete example of a broch (small fortified farm going back to 500BC), enough remains of the galleried walls and entrance chamber for the builders' skill to be admired.

Arnol Black House – *Lewis. 6mi/10km beyond Carloway, signposted off A 858.* ♿ �◷ *Open Mon-Sat, 9.30am-6.30pm (4.30pm Oct-Mar).* ⊙ *£2.80. Parking.* ☎ *01851 710 395.* A typical island dwelling (living area, sleeping area, kitchen and stable-cum-barn all under one thatched roof), called a black house because of its open hearth, Arnol Black House has been preserved as a reminder of island life as it was until half a century ago.

St Clement's Church – *Harris. 60mi/97km southeast of Stornoway by A 859.* �◷ *Open at all reasonable times; key available from key-holder.* ☎ *0131 668 8800 (Historic Scotland, Edinburgh).* In the town of Rodel near the southern tip of Harris stands a church famous for the outstanding **tomb★** of its 16C builder, Alexander MacLeod (d 1546), decorated with carvings, including the Twelve Apostles, the Virgin and Child and the galley emblem of the Lord of the Isles.

Uist and **Benbecula** – Bridges and causeways link the islands which offer spectacular land and seascapes: rolling hills and moorland, white sand dunes and beaches, sparkling sea lochs and pounding waves. The chambered cairns and stone circles, castles and chapels attest to the islands' rich history. Nature lovers will delight in the many nature reserves and wildfowl sanctuaries including swans, ducks, greylag geese and the elusive corncrake. In summer there is also a profusion of wild flowers and good walking and fishing. The local people earn their living from crofting and fishing.

Barra – *Caledonian McBrayne passenger and car ferry services from South Uist. For ferry times and reservations* ☎ *08705 650 000, 01851 702361; www.calmac.co.uk. Highland Airways operates flights between Stornoway and Benbecula Monday to Friday* ☎ *01851 701828; www.highlandairways.co.uk . British Airways flies between Stornoway to Barra Mon-Sat.* ☎ *www.british-airways.com).* The romantic small island, which takes great pride in its Norse heritage, is famous for its fine beaches.

WESTER ROSS★★★

Highland, SCOTLAND

MICHELIN ATLAS P 66 OR MAP 501 D, E 10, 11 AND 12

The Atlantic seaboard of Wester Ross is wild and dramatic, with magnificent mountains and placid lochs. The main touring centres are Kyle of Lochalsh, Gairloch and Ullapool, and from these the visitor may drive, walk, climb, fish or sail, to enjoy to the full this glorious area. ☐ *Auchtercairn, Gairloch ☎ 01445 712 130.* ☐ *Car Park, Kyle of Lochalsh DD8 4EF ☎ 01599 534 276; Fax 01599 534 808* ☐ *Argyle Street, Ullapool ☎ 01854 612135; www.ullapool.com.*

- **Don't Miss**: Inverewe Garden; Loch Maree; Eilean Donan Castle.
- **Be Careful**: Do not underestimate distances. Single track and winding lochside roads need time. Remember to keep the gas tank well topped-up.
- **Organizing Your Time**: Allow 2-3 days.
- **Also See**: Inverness, Oban, Isle of Skye, Western Isles.

From Kyle of Lochalsh to Gairloch★★★ 1

120mi/192km if visiting Eilean Donan Castle – allow a whole day

The route covers some of the finest scenery in the Wester Ross region – Loch Maree studded with islands, the Torridon area and the Applecross peninsula.

Some of the roads will be busy in the height of the tourist season, but many stretches will allow the luxury of enjoying the scenery in solitude. **Kyle of Lochalsh** – *Population 803.* This is the ferry port for Skye and a busy place in summer.

Eilean Donan Castle★ – *9mi/15km east of Kyle of Lochalsh by A 87.* ☼ *Open Apr-Oct, daily, 10am-5.30pm (4pm Nov and Mar).* ☞ *£4.* ☞ *Guided tour (7 languages). Parking. Tearoom.* ☎*/Fax 01599 555 202, 291; info@donan.f9.co.uk; www.eileandonancastle.com.* The castle enjoys an idyllic **setting**★★ on an island in the loch, with the mountains behind. It is now linked to the shore by a bridge and was completely reconstructed in the 20C, as it was abandoned for 200 years following an abortive Jacobite landing, with Spanish troops in support, in 1719.

The two rooms open to the public display a variety of mementoes relating to the MacRaes who were the guardians of the castle and hereditary bodyguards to the MacKenzies. The ramparts afford fine **views** of three lochs.

▸ *Return to Kyle and leave by the road running along the coast to the north, with its views across to Skye and the Cuillins.*

Plockton★ – Once a "refugee" settlement at the time of the Highland clearances, Plockton, with its palm-lined main street and sheltered bay is a centre for yachtsmen and wind-surfers.

▸ *At Achmore, take A 890 to the left, and at the junction with A 896, go left again, towards Lochcarron. At Tornapress, the visitor can elect to continue on A 896 to Shieldaig, but the minor road across the peninsula, via Bealach-na Bo well repays the effort. It has hairpin bends and 1:4 gradients, and is not recommended for caravans or learner drivers.*

Bealach-na-Bo – *2 053ft/626m.* On the way up to the pass the hanging valley frames spectacular vistas of lochs and mountains, while from the summit car park, the **views**★★★ westward of Skye and its fringing islands are superb.

Applecross – Site of the monastery founded in the 7C by St Maelrubha, now a holiday centre with a red sandy beach.

▸ *Either continue north along the coast, via Fearnmore, to Torridon, or return to Tornapress and proceed to Torridon by A 896.*

Torridon – There is a countryside **centre** (NTS. ☼ *Open May to late-Sep, daily, 10am-6pm. Deer museum and park: Open daily.* ☞ *£2 Audio-visual presentation. Parking.* ☎ *01445 791 221; Fax 01445 791 378; smacnally@nts.org.uk; www.nts.org.uk)* here with an audio-visual introduction to the area. Information is available on walking and climbing routes.

Glen Torridon – A flat-bottomed glacial valley, overlooked by the seven summits of "The Grey One" **Liathach** (3 456ft/1 054m) on the left, with Beinn Eighe (3 309ft /1 010m), a long ridge of seven peaks, to its northeast.

▸ *At Kinlochewe, take A 832 to the left.*

Aultroy Visitor Centre – ⏰ *Open early-May to early-Sep, daily, 10am-5pm.* ☎ *01445 760 254* The centre explains the fascinating ecology of the **Beinn Eighe National Nature Reserve** (11 757 acre/4 758ha) Britain's first, with its splendid remnants of the native Scots pine forest.

Loch Maree★★★ – Loch Maree epitomises the scenic beauty and grandeur of the west coast. It lies between a shoulder of Beinn Eighe and the towering **Ben Slioch** (3 217ft/980m) to the north, and is studded with islands, on one of which, Isle Maree, St Maelrubha set up his cell in the 7C.

Victoria Falls★ – A platform and the riverside path give good views of these falls, named after Queen Victoria's visit in 1877.

Gairloch – The ideal centre for touring the Torridon area, exploring the hills and enjoying the sandy beaches of this part of the west coast, and admiring the splendid views of the Hebridean Islands.
The pier at the head of the loch still has all the bustle of a fishing port.

The **Gairloch Heritage Museum** (♿⏰ *Open Apr-Sep, Mon-Sat, 10am-5pm; Oct, Mon-Fri, 10am-1.30pm; Nov-Mar, by appointment.* ☎ *£2.50. Guide book (4 languages). Parking. Restaurant.* ☎ *01445 712287; info@GairlochHeritageMuseum.org.uk)* illustrates a way of life that has now gone from these parts, including a croft house room, shop, schoolroom, the ironworks of the 17C and illicit whisky distilling.

From Gairloch to Ullapool★★ [2]

56mi/90km – about 4hr

This route runs along the coastline with its bays, beaches and headlands all backed, inland, by breathtaking mountain scenery.

▷ *Take A 832 across the neck of the Rubha Reidh peninsula.*

Stop, before descending to the River Ewe, and look back from the roadside **viewpoint★★★**, at the superb view of Loch Maree with its forested islands.

Inverewe Garden★★★ – ♿⏰ *(NTS) Open daily, late-Mar-Oct, 9am-9pm; Nov to late-Mar, 9.30am-5pm.* ☎ *£7 Guide book (3 languages). Visitor Centre: Open late-Mar to Oct, daily, 10am-5pm. Parking. Licensed restaurant.* ☎ *01445 781 200; Fax 01445 781 497; inverewe@nts.org.uk; www.nts.org.uk.* These outstanding gardens, in a magnificent coastal setting, show many sorts of plants to their best advantage. The gardens (64 acres/26ha) are made possible so far north, on the same latitude as Leningrad, by the influence of the Gulf Stream. The property, a barren peninsula with an acid peat soil exposed to the Atlantic gales, was bought for Osgood Mackenzie in 1862. A rabbit-proof fence was erected, Scots and Corsican pines were planted as wind-breaks and soil was imported. A lifetime of planning and planting, continued after his death

by his daughter, has created this memorial to him. Colour is found at most seasons, with azaleas and rhododendrons in May, the rock garden in June, herbaceous borders in midsummer and heathers and maples in the autumn.

▷ *Continue along A 832, following the shoreline of Loch Ewe and across the neck of the Rubha Beag peninsula.*

The island in Gruinard Bay was the scene of an anthrax experiment during the Second World War. As the road hugs the southern shore of Little Loch Broom, straight ahead is the majestic **An Teallach** (3 484ft/1 062m); to the north rise the twin peaks of Beinn Ghobhlach, the Forked Mountain.

▷ *Continue on A 832, turning left at its junction with A 835.*

Inverewe

NTS Edinburgh

Falls of Measach★★ – The waters of the River Droma make a spectacular sight as they drop over 150ft/45m in the wooded cleft of the **Corrieshalloch Gorge**★.

▶ *Continue northwest on A 835.*

The road follows the north shore of **Loch Broom**★★, with its scattered houses and traces of former field patterns, lying in a particularly attractive setting.

Ullapool★ – The village was laid out in the 18C by the British Fisheries Society and flourished as a fishing port during the herring boom. Fishing still plays an important part in the local economy and factory ships can usually be seen, in season, anchored at the mouth of the loch. Ullapool is an ideal touring centre for the Wester Ross area. It is the car ferry terminal for Stornoway, a haven for yachtsmen and an unrivalled centre for sea angling. Various boats sail to the **Summer Isles** (⏱ *Operates, weather permitting, Apr-Oct, daily, 10am-4.15pm. Information about operators, times and charges from TIC or Summer Queen Cruises ☎ 01854 612 472),* where seals and sea birds are the principal attraction.

WHITBY

North Yorkshire, ENGLAND

POPULATION 13 640

MICHELIN ATLAS P 47 OR MAP 502 S 20

Whitby was formerly a centre for ship-building and whaling and is now a fishing port and holiday resort at the mouth of the River Esk in the north east of England. It is divided into a relatively modern west side and an east side, steeped in history, overlooked by the abbey ruins on the headland, a stark skeleton etched against the sky. The beaches, which are popular for bathing and wind-surfing, range from **Robin Hood's Bay**★ *(south,* 👓 *see SCARBOROUGH: Excursions)* to **Staithes** and **Saltburn** *(north).* It was in Whitby that the explorer **Captain James Cook** (1728-79, 👓 *see below),* served his seafaring apprenticeship. The more ghoulishly inclined may be interested to know that the first few chapters of **Bram Stoker's** *Dracula* are set in Whitby. ⓘ *Langborne Road, YO21 1YN ☎ 01947 602674*

Sights

Whitby Abbey★ – ⏱ *Open daily, 10am (9.30am mid-Jul to Aug) to 6pm (5pm Oct, 4pm Nov to late-Mar, 5pm 15-23 Feb).* ⏱ *Closed 1 Jan and 24-26 Dec, 30 Mar until 2pm.* ⏳ *£3.60 Parking. ☎ 01947 602 674.* A double monastery was founded in AD 657 by **St Hilda,** Abbess of Hartlepool, on the probable site of a Roman signal station, on land given to her by Oswy, King of Northumbria. Much of what we know about Hilda is from the writings of the Venerable Bede. This godly noblewoman, a pioneer of Anglo-Saxon conversion to Christianity, established her community under the Rule of St Benedict, earning Whitby an outstanding reputation as a holy place. The abbey was the setting for the **Synod of Whitby** in AD 664, a turning point in the history of the English Church, at which the Roman, rather than the Celtic, method of dating Easter was chosen. Under Hilda's leadership, the abbey also became renowned as a seat of learning; numerous early bishops were schooled here. It was at Whitby that the poet **Caedmon**, who worked on the abbey lands, "sang the Creation of the world" as Bede puts it – the first known poet to do so in his native English tongue.

In 867 the abbey was sacked by the Danes, bringing monastic life there to an end for two centuries. In 1078 it was re-founded by one of William the Conqueror's knights Reinfrid, who gave up the sword to devote himself to a life of religion; the present ruins belong to a second rebuilding which took place between 1220 and 1320. The high quality of the Early English style is typical of other abbeys in the north, particularly at Rievaulx, which is contemporary with Whitby. The abbey was finally suppressed under Henry VIII – one of the last great houses to be so – in 1539.

All that now remains to be seen of this once great abbey is the east front with typical early Gothic lancet windows, the grand Early English aisled presbytery, the north transept and north wall of the nave with a door and windows in ornate 14C Decorated style and part of the west front, once surmounted by a large Perpendicular window. The plan of the domestic abbey buildings can be seen, although hardly anything

Paschal Controversy

The question of how to set the date for Easter, the Christian Passover, provoked considerable dispute in the early Church, largely due to the many different traditions – Jewish, Roman, Antiochene, Alexandrine – to which the members of this new congregation variously adhered. Trouble arose in the British Isles after the arrival of the Roman missionaries because the Celtic Churches had their own method of computation, which they believed they followed that of St John. This threatened to split the English church, with the Christians of Northumbria led by **King Oswy** and the bishops St Colman and St Chad adopting the Celtic system, and the Christians of the south led by St Wilfrid preferring the Roman. At the **Synod of Whitby**, the controversy was finally settled by King Oswy who, having heard St Wilfrid's arguments that the Roman system was founded on the authority of St Peter, decided to follow the Keeper of the Keys of Heaven.

survives of the buildings themselves (much of the medieval stonework was re-used in the impressive 17C Abbey House to the southwest).

St Mary's Church – &⏲ *Open daily, 10am-5pm (noon Oct-Mar; 4pm Mar-May).* ⚭ *Donation £1. Services: Sun (except 1st Sun each month) at 11.15am (Matins); 1st Sun each month at 11am (Holy Communion). Parking. Brochure available (charge).* ☎ *01947 603 421.* 199 steps lead up from the town to this basically Norman church, which shares the clifftop with the abbey. It was modified in Stuart and Georgian times, leaving a charming mixture of white-painted galleries, box pews and "barley sugar" columns. It features a fine three-decker pulpit. The church graveyard contains a memorial to the poet Caedmon.

Captain Cook Memorial Museum – *Grape Lane.* ⏲ *Open Apr-Oct, daily, 9.45am-5pm (4.30pm last admission); Mar, Sat-Sun, 11am-3pm.* ⚭ *£2.80. Brochure.Open Apr-Oct, daily, 9.45am-5pm (4.30pm last admission); Mar, Sat-Sun, 11am-3pm.* ⚭ *£2.80. Brochure.* ☎/Fax *01947 601 900; captcookmuseumwhitby@ukgateway.net; www.cookmuseumwhitby. co.uk.* In the late 17C house of shipowner John Walker, where James Cook served as an apprentice, is a museum celebrating the years Cook spent in Whitby and his achievements as one of the world's greatest navigators. The exhibition includes a tour of the rooms of the house, furnished to give an impression of life in the mid 18C, and containing letters, documents and artefacts reflecting Cook's naval life and expeditions. The visit ends in the attic where the young apprentice seaman would have had his quarters when ashore *(special exhibitions).*

Excursions

Goathland – *8mi/13.5km southwest on A 171 west towards Middlesbrough, then A 169 south and a minor road to right (signposted).* ⏲ *Open all year, daily, 10.30am-5.30pm.* ☎ *01947 896 483.* The road leads across some spectacular Yorkshire Moors scenery to this typical local village, which has risen to fame as the fictitious "Aidensfield" in which the popular British television series *Heartbeat* is set. An exhibition centre contains all the information on the series and its stars that avid fans could hope to find.

Captain Cook Birthplace Museum★ – *28mi/45km west, on A 171 and in Ormesby left on B 1380 (signs) to Stewart Park, Marton, near Middlesbrough.* &⏲ *Open Tue-Sun, Bank Hol Mon and all week in school holidays, 10am (9am winter) to 5.30pm (4pm winter); last admission 45min before closing.* ⏲ *Closed 1 Jan and 25-26 Dec.* ⚭ *£2.40. Parking. Cafe. Lift.* ☎ *01642 311 211; www.middlesbrough.gov.uk.* An excellently appointed museum, recently refurbished to include the latest in interactive displays, near the site of the cottage where Captain James Cook was born, traces his early life, his naval career and exploratory voyages to Canada and Australia, as well as his three Pacific voyages of discovery 1768-89.

A **Captain Cook Heritage Trail**, signposted by ships, runs between Middlesbrough and Whitby for those interested in following in some of the great navigator's footsteps. Details from the local tourist office.

WICK

Highland, SCOTLAND

POPULATION 9 713

MICHELIN ATLAS P 74 OR MAP 501 K 8

Near the north easternern tip of the Scottish mainland Wick stands close to the mouth of the river of the same name – after the Norse term Vik, meaning a bay. It is a thriving market town and was once the country's premier herring port with two good harbours – one designed by Thomas Telford and later improved by Stephenson. **The Wick Heritage Centre** *(Open Jun to mid-Sep, Mon-Sat, 10am-5pm. £2. Guide book (10 languages). Parking. ☎ 01955 605 393)* **presents the town's history by means of an attractive series of tableaux.** *Whitechapel Road Caithness ☎ 01955 602 596; www.visitjohnogroats.com*

Excursions

Duncansby Head★ – *19mi/31km north by A 9.*

John o'Groats – Traditionally this is the northeasternmost point in mainland Britain, some 876mi/1 410km from the southeastern most point, Land's End. The settlement takes its name from a Dutchman, Jan de Groot, who started a ferry service to the Orkneys in the 16C. The eight-sided tower of the hotel recalls the tale of this ferryman who, to settle disputes amongst his seven descendants, built an octagonal house, with eight doors and an octagonal table.

▶ *Take the local road eastwards.*

The northeastern headland of mainland Scotland, **Duncansby Head**★, overlooks the treacherous waters of the Pentland Firth, a seven-mile-wide channel. The **scenery** is spectacular: sheltered coves, sandy bays, narrow inlets, steep cliffs and rock arches. Standing just offshore, the **Stacks of Duncansby**★★, pointed sea stacks, rise a spectacular 210ft/64m up from the water. A variety of sea birds flock to the rock ledges.

Prehistoric Monuments – *18mi/29km south by A 9.*

Hill o'Many Stanes★ – This fan-shaped arrangement of 22 lines of stones was laid out in the Bronze Age, perhaps for some astronomical purpose. Similar settings exist elsewhere in northern Scotland.

▶ *Continue on A 9 and turn right at West Clyth onto a local road.*

Grey Cairns of Camster★ – The cairns date from the Neolithic period (4000 – 1800 BC). The **Long Cairn**★★ (195ft/60m long by 33ft/10m wide) incorporates two earlier beehive cairns. Both the **Long** and smaller **Round Cairn** can be viewed from the outside but access to the inner chambers is for the agile only, as the entrance passageways must be negotiated on hands and knees.

Isle of **WIGHT**★★

ENGLAND

POPULATION 124 577

MICHELIN ATLAS P 9 OR MAP 504 P, Q 31 AND 32

ACCESS: SEE THE MICHELIN GUIDE GREAT BRITAIN AND IRELAND

The island (147sq mi/380km2) has been a holiday destination since Queen Victoria chose Osborne for her country retreat. Visitors attracted by the mild sunny climate and varied scenery can choose the popular sandy beaches of the eastern coastal resorts, notably **Sandown**, the more elegant **Shanklin**, and **Ventnor** with its **botanic gardens** on the sunny ledge of the Undercliff; or the rolling hills of the ridge of chalk downs running east from Culver Cliff through the quieter western part to The Needles. **Cowes** is the premier yachting centre in Britain; it hosts regattas as well as the famous Cowes Week in August. On the west coast at the mouth of the

Regatta

River Yar, Henry VIII's castle *(EH ♿ ⏲ Open late-Mar to Oct, daily, 10am-6pm (5pm Oct); last admission 30 min before closing. 💷 £2.30. Wheelchair access ground floor. ☎ 01983 760 678)* **overlooks the sea on two sides at Yarmouth**, an attractive port popular with yachtsmen. *Island website: www.islandbreaks.co.uk.*

⊙ **Don't Miss**: Osborne House.

Kids Especially for Kids: There are several fine sandy beaches and various family seaside attractions including a large amusements attraction at the Needles; Dinosaur Isle; Brading The Experience.

⚲ **Also See**: Bournemouth, Portsmouth, Southampton.

🚶 **Walking Tours and trails**: A 65mi/105km coastal path around the island connects with cross-country trails offering spectacular views of downs, cliffs and sea. In total there are 500 miles of well-maintained and signposted footpaths, and in May the island hosts the largest Walking Festival in the UK.

🚲 **Bicycle Trails**: There is a cycling festival in late September and over 200 miles of cycle routes. *www.sunseaandcycling.com.*

Getting to the Isle of Wight

Ferries - There are three operators servicing the island. The fastest route takes about 15 minutes, the slowest about 35 minutes. Red Funnel runs a passenger and vehicle ferry and a high speed passenger only ferry, both between Southampton and Cowes ☎ *0870 444 8898; post@redfunnel.co.uk; www.redfunnel.co.uk.* Hovertravel operate a hovercraft service (passenger only) between Southsea and Ryde ☎ *01983 811 000; Fax 01983 562 216; info@hovertravel.co.uk; www.hovertravel.co.uk.* Wight Link operate a passenger and vehicle ferry between Portsmouth and Fishbourne, a passenger and vehicle ferry between Lymington and Yarmouth, and a foot-passenger only catamaran between Portsmouth and Ryde. ☎ *0870 582 7744; info@wightlink.co.uk; www.wightlink.co.uk.*

Sights

Alum Bay – The westernmost bay of the island, where alum was mined, is a remarkable geological phenomenon, with its sandstone cliffs richly coloured with more than 20 mineral hues. In the afternoon sun a boat trip to the **Needles**, sea stacks 100ft/30m offshore, gives fine views of the colourful slopes framed by chalk cliffs.

Tennyson Down was one of Alfred, Lord Tennyson's (1809-92) favourite walks during the years he lived at Farringford; a granite cross (38ft/12m high) commemorates the great poet.

Arreton – The handsome stone **manor house** bears the date 1639 on the front porch; among the period furnishings note the fine panelling in the hall and dining parlour. The upper floors now house a museum of childhood, a collection of toys and dolls from the past. **St George's Church** contains elements of Early Norman and Early English work and a radio museum.

Brading★ – The remains of the 3C **Roman Villa**★ (♿ ⏱ *Open Apr-Oct, daily, 9.30am-5pm; Nov-Mar by appointment.* ♾ *£2.75.* *Guided tour by appointment. Guide book. Parking. Picnic area.* ☎ *01983 406 223; Fax 01983 406 223*) southwest of the village comprise the ground plan of the west wing – with good 4C **mosaics** of figures from Classical mythology – and a display of artefacts. **St Mary's Church**★, (⏱ *Open daily, 9am-5pm*) built c 1200, has a late 13C west tower with a recessed spire; in the Oglander Chapel are impressive family tombs, notably that of the diarist Sir John Oglander (d 1655), represented as a recumbent medieval knight. **Brading, The Experience** began life as a simple wax museum illustrating the history of the island, but has extended to encompass Great British Legends, Animal World, World of Wheels collection of vintage cars and traction engines, as well as the usual famous faces and Chamber of Horrors (♿ ⏱ *Open daily, 10am-5.30pm.* ♾ *£6.50. Factory discount shops. Cafe. Parking.* ☎ *01983 407 286; Fax 01983 402 112; info@bradingtheexperience.co.uk; www. bradingtheexperience.co.uk*). In 1607 Sir John Oglander took over **Nunwell House**★ (*1mi/2km west* ⏱ *Open Jul-Sep, Mon-Wed, 1-5pm; also Spring Bank Hol Sun and Mon, 1-5pm.* ♾ *£4; garden only, £2.50.* *Guided tour of house (1hr) starting at 30min past the hour until 3.30pm. Brochure (2 languages). Parking. Refreshments; picnic area.* ☎ *01983 407 240*) which stayed in the family until recently. Charles I's last night of freedom was probably spent here.

Carisbrooke Castle★★ – (EH) ♿ ⏱ *Open daily, 10am-6pm (5pm Oct; 4pm Nov-Mar).* ⏱ *Closed 24-26 Dec, 1-2 Jan.* ♾ *£4.60.* *Guided tour £1. Parking. Refreshments (summer only). Wheelchair access to grounds and lower levels only.* ☎ *01983 522 107; www.english-heritage.org.uk.* In 1100 Richard de Redvers built the keep and curtain walls on the site of a Roman stronghold. Carisbrooke was the family's powerbase until the death of the ambitious Countess Isabella in 1293 when Edward I bought the troublesome castle and installed Crown-appointed governors of the island. The last resident governor, Queen Victoria's daughter Princess Beatrice, died there in 1944. The castle withstood French attack in the 14C and was further fortified against the Spanish in the late 16C. During the imprisonment of King Charles I in 1647-48 prior to his trial in London the **bowling green** was created for his entertainment and he is said to have walked daily around the **battlements**. He also made two attempts to escape through the castle windows.

After passing through an Elizabethan gateway dated 1598 the visitor crosses a bridge to the massive 14C **gatehouse** with twin drum towers. The Norman curtain wall encloses the high motte and 12C shell **keep** (with **views**★ for miles around), the 13C St Nicholas Chapel rebuilt in 1904 and a range of private apartments around the late12C **Great Hall** which houses a museum of island history. An interactive exhibit in the Old Coach House explores life in the castle and the new donkey centre houses the famous Carisbrooke donkeys who give regular demonstrations in the **well-house** of the unique 1587 treadmill used to draw water from the 161ft/49m well.

Godshill – Above this much-visited village stands the 14C-15C church of **All Saints** (⏱ *Open daily, 9am (12.15pm Sun) to 5pm (dusk Nov-Mar). Guide book.* ☎ *01983 840 895; rfrjohn@aol.com*), notable for its unique mid-15C **Lily Cross mural** (south transept) under a wagon roof, the fine early 16C monument to Sir John Leigh and a double nave plan. West of the church stands a group of attractive thatched cottages.

Osborne House★★ – (EH) ♿ ⏱ *Open late-Mar-Oct, daily, 10am-5pm (4pm last admission to house).* ♾ *£7.50; grounds only (Apr-Oct) £4. Parking. Cafeteria. Wheelchair access to exterior and ground floor; ramp.* ☎ *01983 200 022; www.english-heritage.org.uk.* In a delightful position with views of the sea which reminded him of Naples, Prince Albert worked with Thomas Cubitt to create this enormous Italianate villa with six-storey campanile and terraced gardens, completed in 1851. For Queen Victoria, Osborne was "a place of one's own, quiet and retired," a favourite home for family vacations with her children, grandchildren and great-grandchildren.

After Albert's death in 1861 Queen Victoria spent much of her 40 years of widowhood at Osborne, dying there in 1901. Her insistence that everything should be kept exactly as it had been during Albert's life gives a remarkable picture of royal family life, from the richly furnished state rooms to the intimacy of the **Queen's Sitting Room** where Victoria worked side by side with her husband at **twin desks**, the Queen's being very slightly shorter. Family photographs and a family tree trace the extensive network of descendants, many of whom stayed in the royal **nursery** above Victoria and Albert's rooms. The only major addition to the house after Albert's death was the **Durbar Wing** built in 1890; its amazing principal room celebrating Victoria's role as Empress of India was created by Bhai Ram Singh and John Lockwood Kipling, Rudyard's father.

A carriage ride through the **grounds** takes visitors to the **Swiss Cottage**, imported from Switzerland and erected in 1853, where the royal children learned to cook on small ranges and entertained their parents. Their natural history collections are displayed in a smaller chalet **museum**, near to the miniature **fort** with cannon, the Queen's bathing hut and a delightful collection of miniature wheelbarrows, each bearing the initials of its royal owner.

Fossils and Dinosaurs

Many important dinosaur discoveries have been made on the Isle of Wight including the carnivorous **Neovenator**, a relative of the Allosaurus from the American land mass, which was much closer to Britain 115 million years ago. The crumbling chalk cliffs have revealed fossilized skeletons of unknown species. The excellent new **Dinosaur Isle** (see opposite) is the island's main centre for all things palaeontological and you may also wish to visit **Dinosaur Farm Museum** *(on the coast road, A 3055, near Brighstone   Open: Jul-Aug, daily; Easter-Jun and Sep, Tue, Thu, Sun; 10am-5pm.   £2.30. Guided fossil hunt book in advance, £3.50. 01983 740 844, 07970 626 456)* where many other finds are displayed.

Sandown Dinosaur Isle –   *Open daily, 10am-6pm (4pm Nov-Mar).   Closed 25-26 Dec.   £4.60. 01983 404 344; Fax 01983 407 502; www.dinosaurisle.com.* Adults and children alike will have a thrilling encounter with roaring dinosaurs and discover many prehistoric plants and animals. The impressive Brachiosaurid skeleton has pride of place. There are also dinosaur footprints and huge ammonites found in the Lower Greensand near Whale Chine.

Shorwell – This peaceful village nestling below the downs is notable for **St Peter's Church**★; it is mainly Perpendicular except for the early 13C south doorway and late 12C north chapel containing **monuments** to members of the Leigh family of Northcourt, just north of the church. Over the door is a large c 1440 **wall painting**★ of St Christopher wading through the water. Other treasures are a 1541 Cranmer Bible, a 1579 "Breeches" Bible, a Jacobean font cover and a pulpit canopy with hour-glass and a Dutch wooden panel.

Quarr Abbey – In 1907 French Benedictine monks from Solesmes in the Loire Valley bought the Victorian Quarr House; the abbey church was built in 1911-12. This masterpiece of construction in brick is the most impressive modern building on the island.

At the east end of the **Abbey Church** *(Open daily, dawn-8.45pm. Services: daily. Parking. Refreshments (Easter-Oct). 01983 882 420)* stands a solid square tower; the high cylindrical south tower rises from an enormous plain wall. The entrance at the west end through a huge brick arch topped by steep gables leads into the low short nave, which opens out to a long high choir without aisles or transepts. The church is bathed in yellow light from the tall east windows, by the superb soaring arches inside the east tower.

WINCHESTER★★

Hampshire, ENGLAND

POPULATION 36 121

MICHELIN ATLAS P 9 OR MAP 504 P, Q 30

TOWN PLAN IN THE MICHELIN GUIDE GREAT BRITAIN AND IRELAND

This ancient cathedral city was the capital of **Wessex** and of England, from the early 9C to about 100 years after the Norman conquest. There are signs of early habitation in the area (notably the Iron Age hilltop fort on St Catherine's Hill). *Guildhall, The Broadway ☎ 01962 840 500.*

▶ **Orient Yourself**: Winchester is a small city and can easily be covered on foot.

☺ **Don't Miss**: The Cathedral; St Cross Hospital; Winchester College.

🕓 **Organizing Your Time**: Allow 1 day in Winchester.

Especially for Kids: Mid-Hants Watercress Line specials (such as Thomas the Tank Engine and Chrsitmas time); Marwell Zoo.

Walking Tours: Guided tours take place throughout the year, departing from the Tourist Information Centre, at 11am and/or 2.30pm.

A Bit of History

It was only after the Roman invasion of AD 43 that the city known as **Venta Bulgarum** was founded. After the Romans withdrew, the city declined until the Saxon king, Cenwall of Wessex, built a church there in 648 and created a bishopric in 662. After 878 **Alfred the Great** consolidated his defence of Wessex against Danish attacks by setting up a series of fortified **burghs**, of which Winchester was the largest.

At the time of the Norman conquest the city was already of such importance that **William I** was crowned there as well as in London. He built a castle in the southwest angle of the city walls and established a new cathedral in 1070. After the 12C Winchester yielded to London as the preferred royal residence. During the Civil War the Norman castle was largely destroyed, the cathedral damaged and the city looted by Parliamentary troops. After the Restoration the city recovered and in 1682 Charles II commissioned Wren to design a great palace, though work stopped on the monarch's death in 1685.

Cathedral★★★ *2hr*

🚻🕓 *Open (services permitting) daily, 8.30am-6pm.* ☺ *Donation £3.50; Gallery and library £1; Guided tour Mon-Sat at 10am, 11am, noon, 1pm, 2pm, 3pm; Guided tour by appointment £3.50 per person; Crypt tour (conditions permitting); viewing platform. Brochure (8 languages). Refectory. Wheelchair access; chair lift; induction loop. ☎ 01962 857 225 (adult bookings), 01962 857 224 (under 18 bookings); Fax 01962 847 201; cheryl.bryan@winchester-cathedral.org.uk; www.winchester-cathedral.org.uk.* The cathedral stands surrounded by lawns on the same site as the 7C Saxon minster, the foundations of which were located in the 1960s. An early bishop of Winchester, **St Swithin,** was buried outside the west end of the minster in 862. There was torrential rain on the day in 1093 when his grave was transferred inside the new church, though he had expressly asked to be buried in the open air; this gave rise to the legend that if it rains on St Swithin's Day (July 15) it will rain for forty days.

William Walkelyn, appointed bishop by William I, began building the new cathedral in 1079. In 1202 the east end was reconstructed, in the early 14C the Norman choir was rebuilt in the Perpendicular style and the nave and west front were rebuilt between 1346 and 1404. After further remodellings of the nave, Lady Chapel and chancel from 1486-1528, the longest Gothic church in Europe (556ft/169m) was complete.

When, in 1652, Parliament ordered the cathedral (ransacked in the Civil War) to be destroyed, it was saved only by a petition of the citizens. Early in the 20C the east end, built on marshland and supported on a 13C beech tree raft, began to sink, causing the walls to crack and the roof to fall; the cathedral was saved by a diver, William Walker, who worked alone from 1906-12 replacing the rotting rafts with cement.

Exterior – Built largely of stone from the Isle of Wight, the cathedral's exterior with its squat Norman **tower** is impressive, though less exciting than the interior.

Interior – **Bishop William of Wykeham** (1324-1404) rebuilt the Norman pillars in the lofty twelve-bay nave, with its bosses and **stone lierne vault**, to support the graceful Perpendicular arches surmounted by balconies with clerestory windows. Of special note are the **west window**, the ornate William of Wykeham's Chantry, Jane Austen's tomb, window and brass, the 12C black Tournai marble **font** and the Jacobean pulpit. In the Norman transept the rounded arches are surmounted by twin-arched galleries below irregular clerestory windows. The **Holy Sepulchre Chapel** (north transept) has exquisite 13C wall paintings.

In the chancel the **choir stalls** (1308) are ornamented with remarkable **misericords**; the marble tomb of the "ungodly" King William Rufus (d 1100) stands under the tower. The **stone reredos** with three tiers of statues above the altar is early 16C; the early Tudor **vault** has outstanding **bosses**.

In the Early English retro-choir (13C) the chapels and chantries are dedicated to 15C-16C bishops. The early 13C Lady Chapel lit by seven-light windows is adorned with fine Tudor woodwork and **wall paintings**.

The 12C **Winchester Bible** is the jewel of the rich collection of manuscripts and books in the 12C Library *(access from south transept)*.

In the north aisle of the nave is the grave of **Jane Austen** (1775-1817), most famous as the author of *Pride and Prejudice, Emma* and *Mansfield Park*, who moved to Winchester for treatment in her last illness.

Cathedral Close – The few remaining monastic buildings south of the cathedral include the **Deanery**, formerly the Prior's Lodging, with a three-arched porch and a 15C hall. The 14C **Pilgrims' Hall**, *(3, The Close. ◷ Open daily, call for opening times, ☎ 01962 854 189 (Pilgrims Hall); pilgrimssecretary@btinternet.com)* now part of the choir school, has possibly the oldest **hammerbeam roof** in existence. Beside the sturdy **St Swithin's Gate** stands the 15C timber-framed **Cheyney Court** and early 16C stables, also timber-framed and now part of the Pilgrims' School.

Additional Sights

Winchester College★ – ♿ ☞ *Guided tours for individuals and small groups (up to 10 people) daily, telephone for details.* ☞ *£2.50. Guide book.* ☎ *01962 621 209; Fax 01962 621 166; enterprises@wincoll.ac.uk; www.winchestercollege.org.* The college was founded in 1382 by **Bishop William of Wykeham** (pronounced *wickham*), to provide an education for 70 poor scholars, 16 choristers and 10 "commoners" (now 500) from wealthy families, to be continued at New College, Oxford, which Wykeham had already founded in 1379. Pupils are still known as "Wykehamists".

The school is entered by the 14C **Outer Gate** in College Street. Through the Middle Gate is **Chamber Court**, the centre of college life, surrounded by Wykeham's original late 14C buildings. The **Hall** on its south side (1st floor) has fine 16C wooden panelling on which hang portraits of former pupils and a 16C portrait of the founder. The **Chapel**, with its prominent 15C pinnacled tower was heavily restored in the 19C, but retains its medieval **wooden vault**, one of the first attempts at fan vaulting in England and the original 14C **choir stalls** with fine misericords. In the centre of Wykeham's 14C cloister stands the early 15C **Fromond's Chantry,** the only example in England of a chapel so placed. The red-brick and stone **School** (west of cloister), was built in 1683-87 for the increasing number of "commoners". Sir Herbert Baker's simple peaceful **War Cloister**, built in 1924, commemorates Wykehamists who fell in two World Wars.

Castle Great Hall★ – ◷ *Open daily, 10am-5pm (4pm Sat-Sun winter). ◷ Closed 25-26 Dec. Brochure (3 languages). ☞ Guided tour in summer by appointment. ☎ 01962 846 476; the.great.hall@hants.gov.uk; www.hants.gov.uk/discover/places/great-hall.html.* The Hall is the only surviving part of the castle, built in Norman times and slighted by order of Parliament in the Civil War. The room (110 x 55 x 55ft/34 x 17 x 17m) dating from 1222-36, is a splendid example of a medieval hall, with its timber roof supported on columns of Purbeck marble. On the west wall hangs the oak **Round Table** (18ft/5m diameter) which dates from the 14C; it is decorated with paintings of the Tudor Rose in its centre, King Arthur and a list of his knights around the edge.

High Street – At the east end *(The Broadway)* stands a bronze statue to Alfred the Great, erected in 1901. Among the buildings in the pedestrian street are the former **Guildhall** (now a bank), built in 1713, opposite the timber-framed **God Begot House★** dating from 1558. Note also the 15C stone carved **Butter Cross**, around which markets were held.

St Cross Hospital★★ – *1mi/2km south. A beautiful walk across the meadow.* ♿ 🕐 *Open Apr-Oct, Mon-Sat, 9.30am-5pm; Nov-Mar, 10.30am-3.30pm.* 🕐 *Closed Good Friday, 25 Dec.* 👁 *£2.* 🔍 *Guided tour (1hr) by appointment. Brochure (4 languages). Refreshments (Apr-Oct).* ☎ *01962 851 375; Fax 01962 878 221* The oldest charitable institution in England was founded by Bishop Henry de Blois in 1136. In 1445 Cardinal Beaufort added his Almshouses of Noble Poverty. The cruciform **Chapel**, built from around 1160 to the late 13C, is a fine example of transitional Norman architecture and is rich in zig-zag stone carving on the arches and chancel vaulting. In the **Lady Chapel** is a **Flemish triptych** of c 1530. The **Brethren's Hall** has a minstrels' gallery and an impressive open-timbered late 15C roof. A range of two-storey **15C cottages** forms the west side of the close.

Excursions

Mid-Hants Watercress Line – *Alresford. 8mi/13km northeast by A 31 and B 3046.* ♿ 🕐 *Operates May-Sep, Tues-Thu; Oct-Jan, Sat-Sun.* 👁 *£9. Parking. Refreshments. Wheelchair access to trains at Alresford.* ☎ *01962 734 866 (recorded timetable information); 01962 733 810 (general information); info@watercressline.co.uk; www.watercressline.co.uk.* Named for the watercress beds which can still be seen in and around the handsome small Georgian town of Alresford (pronounced Arlsford), the old-fashioned steam engines run for 10 miles/16km over the hills to the market town of Alton. Special events throughout the year include Friends of Thomas the Tank Engine and Santa Specials *(advance booking advisable).*

Jane Austen's House – *Chawton. 18mi/29km northeast by A 31 and B 3006.* ♿ 🕐 *Open Mar-Nov, daily (Sat-Sun, Dec-Feb), 11am-4.30pm.* 🕐 *Closed 25-26 Dec.* 👁 *£4.* ☎ *01420 83262; www.janeaustenmuseum.org.uk.* Her eight years sharing this peaceful red-brick house with her mother and sister Cassandra were some of Jane Austen's happiest and most productive. The tiny table at which she wrote and revised her novels stands in the dining parlour with its creaking door that helped preserve the secrecy of her writing. Early editions are displayed alongside letters, family portraits and pieces of needlework.

Gilbert White's House – *Selbourne. 22mi/36km northeast by A 31 and B 3006.* 🕐 *Open daily, 11am-5pm; last admission 30min before closing.* 🕐 *Closed 25-31 Dec.* 👁 *£4.50. Tearoom. Parking nearby. Wheelchair access to garden and ground floor.* ☎ *01420 511 275; Fax 01420 511 040; gilbertwhite@btinternet.com.* The long garden at Rev Gilbert White's home "The Wakes" runs down to the foot of Selbourne Hill where the 18C naturalist made his detailed ecological study, later published as *The Natural History and Antiquities of Selbourne*. The original manuscript, written as a series of letters to two friends, can be seen inside "The Wakes" which also houses the **Oates Museum** commemorating Captain Lawrence Oates, a member of Scott's expedition to the South Pole.

Marwell Zoo – *6mi/10km southeast on B 2177.* ♿ 🕐 *Open daily, 10am-6pm (4pm in winter).* 🕐 *Closed 25 Dec.* 👁 *£10 Jul-Sep; £9.50 Oct-Jun. Parking. Refreshments.* ☎ *01962 777 407, 07626 943 163 (recorded information); marwell@marwell.org.uk; www.marwell.org.uk.* The grounds of 16C Marwell Hall are home to a wide variety of animals and birds, including large cats, primates, giraffes and rhinos, with an emphasis on conservation.

WINDSOR★

Berkshire, ENGLAND

POPULATION 30 136 (INCLUDING ETON)

MICHELIN ATLAS P 20 OR MAP 504 S 29

TOWN PLAN IN THE MICHELIN GUIDE GREAT BRITAIN AND IRELAND

Windsor is synonymous with its **castle** (♿ *see WINDSOR CASTLE*), **home to English monarchs for over nine centuries.** 🏛 *24 High Street* ☎ *01753 743 900; Fax 01753 743 904.*

▶ **Orient Yourself**: Windsor town centre is small and can easily be covered on foot. For farther afield use the City Sightseeing hop-on hop-off open-top bus tour. *www.citysightseeing.co.uk.*

⊙ **Don't Miss**: Windsor Castle, particularly St George's Chapel; Eton College, particularly the College Chapel; Savill Gardens and Valley Gardens in spring.

🕐 **Organizing Your Time**: Allow one day for Windsor town centre, including Eton.

Kids **Especially for Kids**: Legoland.

🕭 **Also See**: Chiltern Hill, Guildford, London, Oxford, St Albans.

🚶 **Walking Tours/Trails**: Fortown centre guided tours ☎ www.windsor.gov.uk/attractions/tours.htm.

🚲 **Bicycle Trails**: Cycling is allowed inside Windsor Great Park, as long as you remain on the tarmac roads. As there are few vehicles travelling within the Great Park this is suitable for all ages.

💧 **Boat Trips**: For details ☎ www.windsor.gov.uk/attractions/boat_trips.htm.

Visit

The old town, extending round two sides of the castle walls, comprises one main street, **Thames Street**, which is intersected by the road leading down from the castle gate and then continues as High Street and Sheet Street. The network of old **cobbled streets** bordered by High Street, Castle Hill, Church Lane and Street and Albans Street contains a number of fine 16C-18C timber-framed houses with oversailing upper floors rising to pointed gables.

The short High Street is distinguished by St John's parish **church**, re-built in 1822, and the **Guildhall**, begun by Sir Thomas Fitch c 1637 and completed by Sir Christopher Wren in 1690. In the niches of the pilastered upper floor are statues of Queen Anne and Prince George of Denmark.

Excursion

Eton College★★

10 min on foot across Windsor Bridge. 🕐 *Open during term time. Chapel.* 🕐 *Closed Mon-Sat, 1-2pm, Sun, 12.30-2pm.* 🎟 *£4.* 🚶 *Guided tour £5, daily at 2.15pm, 3.15pm.* ☎ *01753 671 177; Fax 01753 671 265; visits@etoncollege.org.uk; www.etoncollege.com.*
The College, perhaps the best known of all British schools, was founded in 1440 by the young Henry VI. It comprised a church, almshouses and a community of secular priests giving free education to 70 poor Scholars and choristers. The following year Henry founded King's College, Cambridge, where the boys could continue their education (🕭 *see WINCHESTER*). As it became fashionable for the nobility to send their sons to Eton, pupil numbers greatly increased.

Visit – The paved **School Yard,** centre of college life, is dominated by the 16C red-brick **Lupton's Tower** on the east side. To the north is **Lower School**, the 15C brick building originally constructed by Henry VI to house the Scholars. **Upper School** on the west side was built in the 17C to accommodate the increasing number of boys. In the centre of the yard stands a 1719 bronze statue of the founder.

The **College Chapel★★**, built from 1449-82, is one of the best examples of Perpendicular architecture in England, even though the fan vaulting was completely reconstructed in 1957. The 15C **wall paintings★** are the finest of their kind in England. The modern stained glass (Evie Holme, John Piper), and the tapestry reredos and panelling by William Morris from designs by Burne-Jones are notable.

The brick **Cloister Court** dates back to Henry VI's time, although the second floor on the north and east sides and the College Library on the south are 18C. Below this is the 15C College Hall where the collegers eat; in the undercroft is the **Museum of Eton Life.**

Legoland Windsor

2mi/3km southwest of Windsor on B 3022. Shuttle bus from Windsor town centre. 🕐 *Open mid-Mar to early Sep, daily; early-Sep to mid-Oct, Thu-Mon; mid-Oct-early Nov, daily; mid-Dec to early Jan; 10am-5pm (6pm in school holidays).* 🎟 *£26. Parking. Restaurants.* ☎ *08705 040 404 (information and booking); www.legoland.co.uk.* Millions of Lego building blocks are used to impressive effect in this beautifully landscaped park. Moving models and miniature European towns show the skills of professional Lego-builders; children can have a go in the Imagination Centre. Rides and live shows are geared for children up to the age of 12.

WINDSOR CASTLE★★★

England's largest castle is also the largest inhabited stronghold in the world and has been a favourite royal residence, frequently extended and rebuilt, since William the Conqueror first built a motte and bailey on the site c 1080.

A Bit of History

By 1110, the Castle had become a royal lodge where Henry I held his first court. Henry II erected the first stone buildings between 1165 and 1179, constructing one range of royal apartments in the Upper Ward (to the east of the Round Tower) and one in the Lower Ward. Faced with rebellion by his sons he modernised the defences, rebuilding the earthen walls and wooden Round Tower in stone. Under Henry III (1216-72) this work was virtually completed. Edward III (1327-77) reconstructed the royal apartments for his newly-founded Order of the Garter. Under Charles II the State Apartments were rebuilt in an ambitious renovation project which included the reconstruction of St George's Hall and the King's Chapel, in which the architect Hugh May concentrated on fitting out the interior in a manner fit for a king, insulating the rooms with oak panelling festooned with Grinling Gibbons carvings. However, the principal changes were made in the early 19C when George IV commissioned Sir Jeffry Wyatville as his architect; he built the machicolated walls and several towers, raised the massive Round Tower, giving the castle its famous outline, and remodelled the State Apartments, adding the Waterloo Chamber. This section was badly damaged by fire in 1992. The principal change under Queen Victoria was the addition of a private chapel in memory of Prince Albert, who died here on 14 December 1861. Queen Mary, wife of George V, carried out careful restoration work on the castle at the turn of the century, and it became the childhood home of HRH the Princesses Elizabeth and Margaret during the Second World War, since which it has remained the royal family's principal home. The Court is in official residence throughout April and for Ascot Week in June when the annual Garter Day ceremonies are held.

Visit

🕐 *Open daily, 9.45am-5.15pm (4.15pm Nov-Feb); subject to change on short notice; last admission 1hr15min before closing.* 🕐 *Closed Good Friday, 17 Jun and 25-26 Dec.* 🎟 *Ticket £12.50; £6 during closure of State Apartments; re-entry ticket valid for day of purchase available to those leaving the precincts for refreshment.* ☎ *01753 868 286 or* ☎ *01753 831 118 (24hr information line). windsorcastle@royalcoolection.org.uk; www. royalresidences.com.*

Access to the Castle is in Castle Hill, past **Henry VIII's Gateway** *(left)*, built in 1511 and bearing the king's arms, the Tudor rose and the Spanish pomegranate of Catherine of Aragon, through the Advance Gate and into the Moat Road.

The impressive **Round Tower**, in fact oval, stands on the site of William I's original fortress and was raised to its present height by Wyatville in the 19C; it houses the Royal Archives (☛ *not open to the public).* An opening in the outer wall northwest of the tower leads to the **North Terrace** (c 1570), which affords **views**★★ of Eton College and London *(east).* Between the outer wall and the tower mound stands the twin-towered **Norman Gateway (B)**, which was built by Edward III in 1359; its portcullis is still in position.

Downhill to the west, in the **Lower Ward**, are the **Military Knights' Lodgings (A)** *(right of Henry VIII's Gateway)* for retired army officers who wear scarlet uniforms dating from William IV. An archway *(north side)* leads into the **Horseshoe Cloister** (c 1480) of brick and half-timbered houses built by Edward IV for the minor clergy, which, though heavily restored in the 19C, retains great charm. The **Curfew Tower** was built by Henry III, its conical roof being added in the 19C.

20 November 1992

The devastating fire which broke out in the Queen's Private Chapel at the northeast angle of the upper ward is thought to have been caused by a spotlight on a curtain high above the altar. Major losses included the wooden ceiling of St George's Hall and Grand Reception room. Restoration work was completed in November 1997, six months ahead of schedule, to coincide with the Queen's 50th wedding anniversary. It was the largest project of its kind this century, costing in excess of £37 million and calling on the skills of some of the finest craftsmen in the country.

St George's Chapel★★★ *45min*

This great Perpendicular chapel was begun by Edward IV to replace Henry III's chapel to the east which Edward III had enlarged and dedicated to his **Most Noble Order of the Garter.** The **Royal Beasts** (modern replacements) above the flying buttresses of the west end trace the royal descent from Edward III, the Lancastrians on the south side, the Yorkists on the north. The chapel is the final resting place of ten sovereigns. On Garter Day each year, the Queen and Knights of the Garter process here from the Upper Ward.

Nave – Although the nave is wide for its height, the slender clustered piers lead the eye uninterruptedly to the crowning glory of the chapel, the almost flat **lierne vault,** rich with coloured bosses – completed in 1528. The blank panelling between the tall arcades and the clerestory windows is topped with crowned and smiling angels. The aisles are notable for their **fan vaulting.** The impressive Perpendicular **west window** depicts 75 figures mainly in early 16C glass, the remainder being 19C.

Quire – Beyond the beautifully fan-vaulted crossing, the Quire (chancel) is overlooked by two **oriels**, one, in stone, belonging to Edward IV's chantry chapel, the other a wooden Renaissance structure built by Henry VIII. The **iron grille** below it was made in 1482 by John Tresilian. The ornate **stalls★★★**, abounding in misericords and other carvings, were built in 1478-85; the top tier, surmounted by a richly carved canopy, is for the Knights of the Garter. The banners, crests, helmets, mantling and swords of the living Knights mark their places. The stall plates are of the living and deceased since the foundation of the Order in 1348 (about 700 Knights in all). The middle tier is for the Military Knights, minor canons and choirmen; and the lowest tier is for the choirboys. The reredos was rebuilt in 1863 as a memorial to Prince Albert, as was the former **Lady Chapel** decorated with marbles and wall paintings, all highlighted in gold. Edward III's **battle sword** (6ft 8in/2m) is in the south chancel aisle. The glorious **east window** (30ft/9m high and 29ft/8.8m wide; 52 lights) commemorates Prince Albert (incidents from his life illustrated in the lower tier, below the Resurrection and the *Adoration of the Kings*).

St George's Chapel, Windsor

A. F. Kersting/MICHELIN

Albert Memorial Chapel – The original chapel (1240) was given its magnificent Victorian embellishment by Sir George Gilbert Scott after the death of Albert, the Prince Consort, and is a supreme example of the 19C revivalist age with Venetian mosaics, inlaid marble panels and statuary. Prince Albert's tomb was later removed to Frogmore (☾ see below).

State Apartments★★ 1hr 30min

Only the north range can be visited, the east and south being the present royal apartments. From the North Terrace the tour begins at the **Grand Staircase**, built for Queen Victoria in 1866, with its display of arms and armour including that of Henry VIII, below Sir Francis Chantrey's full-size statue of George IV. It leads to the **Grand Vestibule** (trophies, arms and armour) where Sir James Wyatt's lively fan vaulting and lantern contrast with the heaviness of the staircase. The marble statue of Queen Victoria, seated, was made in 1871.

Public Rooms – These rooms provide examples of the work done for George IV by Wyatville (Wyatt's nephew) from 1820-30, in which he used Gothic style for processional spaces and an eclectic form of Classicism for the main reception rooms. In the **Waterloo Chamber** hangs a series of portraits by Sir Thomas Lawrence, of the monarchs and leaders, both military and political, involved in Napoleon's final defeat. The chamber is now used for the annual luncheon given by the Queen for the Knights of the Garter, and for balls, receptions and concerts. The Grinling Gibbons limewood panels (c 1680) were retrieved from the King's Chapel. The **Garter Throne Room**, created on older foundations, and Ante Throne Room are the rooms in which the Knights Companion assemble and the monarch invests new knights before the annual service in St George's Chapel. Both rooms boast panels and carvings by **Grinling Gibbons** (1648-1721).

The **Grand Reception Room** (restored after the 1992 fire) is Wyatville at his most exuberant – ornate French Rococo hung with Gobelins tapestries and decorated with gilt plasterwork, massive chandeliers and bronze busts. The same artist created the long, sober **St George's Hall** (restored) out of the hall built by Edward III for the Knights of the Garter and the Baroque chapel which Hugh May had built for Charles II. The 700 past Garter Knights' escutcheons are set in the panelling of the plaster ceiling, made to look like wood.

The new octagonal **Lantern Lobby**, created after the fire on the site of the previous Private Chapel and designed by Giles Downes, with

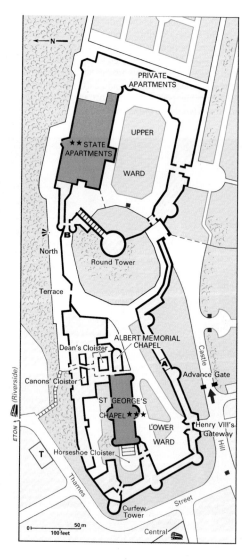

a virtuoso neo-Gothic umbrella vault surrounded by a gallery, was joint winner of the 1998 Building of the Year award (with Norman Foster's American Air Museum at Duxford in Cambridgeshire).

Newly open to the public *(from October to March each year)* are the **Crimson Drawing Room**, the **State Dining Room** and the **Octagon Dining Room**.

The Queen's Rooms – The **Queen's Guard Chamber**, remodelled under George IV as a museum of British military achievement, containing busts of Sir Winston Churchill and the Dukes of Marlborough and Wellington, leads into the panelled Queen's Presence Chamber which, with the adjoining **Queen's Audience Chamber,** is essentially unchanged since the time of Charles II; Hugh May planned them with ceilings painted by Verrio and superb carvings by Gibbons; the Gobelins tapestries are late 18C additions. The white marble Adam fireplace in the Presence Chamber was brought from Buckingham Palace by William IV.

Wyatt and his nephew share responsibility for the blue silk **Queen's Ballroom**; the elder architect remodelled the room and Wyatville designed the ceiling as well as that of the red **Queen's Drawing Room**, which also contains some of the earliest plate glass in England. Eight Van Dyck portraits hang in the Ballroom while the Drawing Room contains a variety of paintings including Holbeins.

The King's Rooms – The **King's Drawing Room**, once used by Queen Victoria for private theatrical performances, contains five paintings by Rubens and his followers, some fine fittings and Chinese porcelain. The **King's Bedchamber** has undergone considerable modification over the centuries; note the grandiose "polonaise" bed attributed to French furniture designer George Jacob and furnished for the occasion of a visit from Emperor Napoleon III and his wife Eugénie in 1855 (their initials appear at the foot of the bed). On the walls of the red-damask-lined **King's Dressing Room** are a number of **masterpieces**★★ by Dürer, Memling, Clouet, Holbein, Rembrandt, Rubens and Van Dyck, among others. The **King's Closet** is similarly furnished with fine pieces, mainly French, made of exotic woods set with Japanese lacquer panels and bronze mounts. The **King's Dining Room** retains much of the character it had under Charles II: Verrio ceiling depicting a Banquet of the Gods, panelling decorated with carvings by Gibbons and Henry Philips.

Queen Mary's Dolls' House – The Dolls' House, designed by Sir Edwin Lutyens, was presented to Queen Mary in 1924. The fascination of this piece is that everything is exactly on a 1:12 scale – not only the furniture, but even the printed leatherbound books in the library, paintings, the garden designed by Gertrude Jekyll and the vintage cars in the garage.

Windsor Park★

In the mid 18C George II charged his son, William Duke of Cumberland, with the task of organising the vast Windsor Forest, hunting ground of Saxon leaders and medieval knights. 4 800 acres/1 942ha of overgrown woodland were cleared, streams were

The Order of the Garter

The highest order of chivalry in the land is also the oldest to survive in the world. It was established by Edward III in 1348 when England was engaged in the Hundred Years War with France and may have been modelled on the legendary story of 5C King Arthur and his Knights of the Round Table; not only was the order to reward men who had shown valour on the battlefield, but also to honour those who manifested the idealistic and romantic concept of Christian chivalry. Tradition relates how at a ball fêting the conquest of Calais in 1347, the king retrieved a fallen garter and returned it to its rightful owner, the young and beautiful Joan of Kent, Countess of Salisbury, with the words, "Honi soit qui mal y pense" *(Shame on him who thinks evil of it)* – the emblem and motto of the Order. A more likely derivation is a strap or sword-belt from a suit of armour to denote the bond of loyalty and concord. At its initiation, Edward III nominated 25 Companion Knights, including the Heir Apparent (the Black Prince), thereby providing himself with his own jousting team as well as one with which to do battle! Nowadays, there are still 25 **Companion Knights**, including the Prince of Wales and at least one representative of each of the armed forces (Army, Navy, Air Force). Additional **Royal Knights** may be appointed by the sovereign following amendments made to the statutes by George I, and since 1905 Stranger, Foreign or **Extra Knights**, a status conferred upon regents or monarchs only (not necessarily Christian, as they have included two Sultans of Turkey, two Shahs of Persia and four Emperors of Japan).

diverted to drain the marshes into newly dug ponds, which eventually flowed into the especially created 130 acres/53ha of Virginia Water. George III continued this land reclamation work and established two farms.

The park is now divided into **Home Park,** which is private, and **Great Park,** most of which is public. A significant feature of the park is the **Long Walk,** a 3mi/5km avenue running south as far as the **Copper Horse,** an equestrian statue of George III in Great Park. Under Charles II the avenue was planted with elm trees, in 1685, the year in which he died, but in 1945 the trees, which had fallen victim to Dutch Elm disease, had to be replaced by chestnuts and planes. Two former royal residences are tucked away in the park: Royal Lodge, used as a retreat by George IV and now by Queen Elizabeth the Queen Mother, and Cumberland Lodge, where William Duke of Cumberland resided while redesigning the park. Smith's Lawn is an area reserved for polo matches, and beyond it stretch the **Valley Gardens** (⏱ *Open daily, 8am-7pm (4pm/dusk in winter) via local (paying) car park.* ☎ *01753 847 518; Fax 01753 847 536; savillgarden@crownestate.org.uk; www.savillgarden.co.uk),* as far as Virginia Water.

Savill Gardens (♿ *Near Englefield Green, off the A 30.* ⏱ *Open daily, 10am-6pm (dusk Oct; 4pm Nov-Feb).* ⏱ *Closed 25-26 Dec.* ⊕ *£5 Apr-May; £4 Jun-Oct; £3 Nov-Mar. No dogs. Parking. Licensed restaurant, picnic area. Plant shop.* ☎ *01753 847 518; Fax 01753 847 536; savillgarden@crownestate.org.uk; www.savillgarden.co.uk)* are another, independent set of landscaped wooded gardens laid in 1932 and endowed with a fine Temperate House in 1995. In spring, rhododendrons, azaleas, camellias and magnolias put on a fabulous show and in summer numerous varieties of lilies and roses burst into colour.

The **Royal Mausoleum,** Frogmore Garden, in Home Park was begun in 1862, the year after Prince Albert's death, specifically so that Queen Victoria and Albert could be buried side by side. The Romanesque-style exterior is topped with a dome, while the rich interior reflects the Consort's passion for the Italian Renaissance. Frogmore House (1684) is furnished largely with possessions accumulated by Queen Mary (black *papier maché* furniture, wax and silk flowers).

At Runnymede a circular temple (1957) commemorates the signing of Magna Carta by King John in 1215. Nearby are the austere John F Kennedy Memorial (1965) and the dignified Commonwealth Air Forces Memorial (1953).

WORCESTER ★

Worcestershire, ENGLAND

POPULATION 82 661

MICHELIN ATLAS P 27 OR MAP 503 N 27

TOWN PLAN IN THE MICHELIN GUIDE GREAT BRITAIN AND IRELAND

The great red sandstone cathedral rising above the bend in the River Severn, the wealth of timber-framed buildings and the Georgian mansions make Worcester (pronouced Wuster) one of the most English of English cities. The city name is also synonymous with its Royal Worcester porcelain and Worcester(shire) sauce. 🛈 *Guildhall, High Street WR1 2EY*☎ *01905 726 311; 01905 722481; touristinfo@cityofworcester.gov.uk; www.visitworcester.com.*

▶ **Orient Yourself**: The city centre is small and easily covered on foot.

☺ **Don't Miss**: The Cathedral, the Royal Worcester Porcelain Works.

➳ **Walking Tours**: Depart from the Guidhall ⏱ *Apr - Sept, Mon - Fri 11am. Wed 11am, 2.30pm.* ☎ *07890 222117; www.worcesterwalks.co.uk.* Great Malvern is a perfect base for some wonderful hill walking in the Malvern Hills.

Cathedral★★ – ♿⏱ *Open daily, 7.30am-6pm.* ⊕ *Donation £3.* ➳ *Guided tour (1hr), booking essential. Brochure (8 languages). Tearoom. Induction loop; touch and hearing centre.* ☎ *01905 28854; Fax 01905 611 139; info@worcestercathedral.org.uk; www.cofe-worcester.org.uk.* In the late 11C an earlier church was rebuilt by Wulstan, the Saxon Bishop of Worcester, who thrived under his new Norman masters and was later canonised. His superb **crypt** survives but the greater part of his building, including the tower, was reconstructed in the 14C. The **choir** is an outstanding example of the

Early English style. There are many monuments – **King John's tomb** in the choir, the **Beauchamp tomb** (14C) in the nave, the alabaster effigy (c 1470) of the Virgin and Child in the southeast transept. **Prince Arthur's Chantry** and its delicate tracery are late Perpendicular work.

The Cloisters were rebuilt in 1374 with wonderful medieval bosses. The east walk leads to the **chapter house** (c 1150), a very early example of central shaft vaulting. The **Edgar Tower**, once the main entrance to the medieval monastery and fortified against anticlerical rioters, now opens into the serene cathedral precincts.

Every third year the choirs of Worcester, Gloucester and Hereford meet at the cathedral in the Three Choirs Festival (next in Worcester in 2008).

Royal Worcester Porcelain Works★ – *Severn Street, south of the Cathedral.* ⏱ *Open Mon-Sat, 9am-5.30pm, Sun, 11am-5pm.* ⏱ *Closed 25-26 Dec and Easter Sun.* 🎫 *Factory/ film £2.25; museum £3; combined ticket £8. Factory tour (1hr; £5) Mon-Fri from 10.25am. Connoisseurs' tour (2hr) by appointment. Parking. Refreshments. Factory seconds on sale.* ☎ *01905 21247; Fax 01905 617 807; rwgeneral@royal-worcester.co.uk; www.royal-worcester.co.uk.* The factory tour presents an opportunity to see how the famous **Royal Worcester** porcelain is made. The success of the factory, founded in 1751, was due to the use of Cornish soaprock to simulate Chinese porcelain and the ability to adapt to changing fashions (Chinoiserie, Classicism, Romanticism).

The **Museum of Worcester Porcelain** (♿⏱ *Hours and charges as above.* ☎ *01905 746000; Fax 01905 617 807; museum@royal-worcester.co.uk; www.royal-worcester.co.uk.)* displays some of the finest Royal Worcester products – the *vase of Wellington and Blucher* by Humphrey Chamberlain, *the veiled Lady* and *Chicago Exhibition Vase* by James Hadley, honeycombed masterpieces by George Owen and the bird series by Dorothy Doughtey.

The Commandery – *Sidbury.* ♿⏱ *Open Mon-Sat, 10am-5pm, Sun, 1.30-5pm.* ⏱ *Closed 1 Jan and 25-26 Dec. Admission charge. Guide book (3 languages). Refreshments.* ☎ *01905 361 821; Fax 01905 361 822; thecommandery@cityofworcester.gov.uk.* The building, originally St Wulstan's Hospital (11C), is mostly 16C. It was Charles II's headquarters at the Battle of Worcester (1651) and houses a museum devoted to the Civil War – video of the Battle of Worcester.

Greyfriars – *(NT) Friar Street.* ⏱ *Open Apr-Oct, Wed-Thu and Bank Hol Mon, 2-5pm.* 🎫 *£3. Information sheet (5 languages). Public car park in Friar Street.* ☎ *01905 23571; greyfriars@smtp.ntrust.org.uk; www.nationaltrust.org.uk.* The house (c 1480) is the most impressive timberframed building in the street; the interior is hung with tapestries and crewel work and there is an enchanting garden.

Guildhall – *High Street.* ⏱ *Open (functions permitting) Mon-Sat, 9am-4.30pm.* ⏱ *Closed 25 Dec.* ☎ *01905 722 480.* The building was completed in 1724 in red brick with stone dressings; the niches contain statues of Charles I, Charles II and Queen Anne; on the parapet are Labour, Peace, Justice, Plenty and Chastisement. The splendid **Assembly Room** has an Italianate ceiling which contrasts with the simple Classicism beneath.

Excursions

Elgar Trail★ – *Circuit of 40mi/65km signposted with "violins".* Much of the music of **Sir Edward Elgar** (1857-1934), most "English" of composers, evokes this countryside of broad, tranquil vale and soaring hills. The circular route links the Elgar **Birthplace Museum** (♿⏱ *Open daily, 11am-5pm (4.15pm last admission).* ⏱ *Closed 25 Dec-Jan 1.* 🎫 *£3.50. Wheelchair access to Elgar Centre and ground floor of cottage.* ☎ *01905 333 224; Fax 01905 333 426; birthplace@elgar.org; www.elgar.org)* at Lower Broadheath near Worcester with his grave in the Roman Catholic churchyard in Little Malvern at the foot of the hills that so inspired him.

Great Malvern – *8mi/13km south on A 449.* In the late 18C the small settlement which had grown up round the priory became fashionable owing to the medicinal properties of the local water; a **Pump Room** and Baths were built in the Greek Revival style in 1819-23.

Priory Church (♿⏱ *Open Apr-Sep, Mon-Sun, 9am-6.30pm (4.30pm Oct-Mar).* 🎫 *Donation. Leaflet (3 languages). Guide book. Refreshments (Mon-Sat Lyttelton Well, church yard entrance).* ☎ *01684 561 020; Fax 01684 561 020 (Parish Office, weekday mornings only); gmpriory@hotmail.com; www.greatmalvernpriory.org.uk)* contains some of the finest stained glass in the country.

The highest of the Malvern Hills, which rise steeply above the town, is **Worcestershire Beacon** (1 395ft/426m), from which there is claimed to be a **view** of 15 counties and three cathedrals – Worcester, Hereford and Gloucester.

WYE VALLEY ★

Herefordshire, Worcestershire, Gloucestershire (ENGLAND), Monmouthshire (WALES)

MICHELIN ATLAS P 16 OR MAP 503 L, M 28 AND 29

The River Wye twists and turns through changing landscapes on its course (135mi/220km) from Plynlimon (east of Aberystwyth, on the west coast of mid Wales) to the Bristol Channel. The final stretch, between Ross and Chepstow, has been popular since the late 18C and early 19C when it became one of the resorts of connoisseurs of Romantic scenery. The steep slopes of the deep and narrow valley are clothed in magnificent woodlands of oak, beech, yew and lime, which are pierced occasionally by limestone crags. *Castle Car Park, Bridge Street, Chepstow, NP16 5EY ☎ 01291 623 772; Fax 01291 628004; chepstow.tic@monmouthshire.co.uk; www. visitwyevalley.com Shire Hall, Agincourt Square, NP25 3DY ☎ 01600 713 899; Fax 01600 772 794; monmouth.tic@monmouthshire.gov.uk; www.visitwyevalley.com.*

- **Don't Miss:** Chepstow Castle, Tintern Abbey, view at Symonds Yat.
- **Organizing Your Time:** Allow 1-2 days.
- **Walking Tours and Trails:** Between Monmouth and Chepstow, **Offa's Dyke Path** follows the high east bank, providing glimpses through the trees of the river winding far below. The **Wye Valley Walk** (waymarked) is a less strenuous path that follows the river bank between Hereford and Chepstow.

Ross-on-Wye to Chepstow 32mi/52km

Ross-on-Wye – The **Market House**★, built in sandstone in the 1670s, bears a medallion of Charles II placed by John Kyrle, "Man of Ross", a benefactor of many of the buildings in the town. His generosity paid for the reconstruction in 1721 of the top of the spire (208ft/63m) of **St Mary's Church** (mainly 13C). A cross in the churchyard is a memorial to the 315 plague victims "buried nearby by night without coffins" during 1637. Tudor almshouses in Church Street were restored in 1575 by the Rudhall family, some of whose tombs are in the church.

▶ *Take B 4228 south; after 3mi/5km turn right at the Wye bridge and follow signs to Goodrich Castle.*

Goodrich Castle★ – (EH) ◷ *Open late-Mar to Oct, daily, 10am-6pm (5pm Oct); Nov to late-Mar, Wed-Sun, 10am-1pm and 2-4pm.* ◷ *Closed 1 Jan and 24-26 Dec.* ☞ *£2.70. Free audio guide. Parking.* ☎ *01600 890 538.* The picturesque sandstone ruin stands on a high spur commanding an ancient crossing of the Wye. Most of the castle dates from c 1300 but the keep is Norman and the original entrance, now a window, was at first floor level. During the Civil War the Royalist garrison was forced into surrender by the use of a large mortar, "Roaring Meg", which was specially cast by the besiegers nearby and is now to be seen in Churchill Park in Hereford.

▶ *Continue south on B 4228 and B 4229; turn left into a steep and narrow road to Symonds Yat and Yat Rock; park in the Forestry Commission car park.*

Symonds Yat★ – From **Yat Rock** (473ft/144m) there is a famous and vertiginous **view**★ of the extraordinary loop in the river and a fine prospect of the rich farmland of Herefordshire to the north.

▶ *Continue south on B 4432 and B 4228. At the crossroads EITHER turn left into A 4136 to Monmouth OR continue south; in Coleford take B 4226 east and B 4227 south to Soudley.*

Forest of Dean – *Picnic sites, camping grounds and signed footpaths.* The **Dean Heritage Museum** (& *Camp Mill, Soudley.* ◷ *Summer 10am-5.30pm, winter 10am-4pm.* ◷ *Closed 1 Jan and 24-26 Dec.* ☞ *£4.50 Guide (4 languages). Parking. Refreshments.* ☎ *01594 822 170; Fax: 01594 823 711; deanmuse@btinternet.com; www.deanheritage-museum.com)* presents an exhibition about the Royal Forest of Dean – natural and man-made woodlands, charcoal burning, an overshot waterwheel and a reconstruction of a cottage and the type of coal mine still being worked by the "Free Miners" of the Forest.

The forest, a royal hunting preserve since Canute's day, described by Drayton as "Queen of Forests All", is a district of wooded hills, bounded by the Severn (south and east) and the Wye (west); it has supplied timber for the navy as well as being worked for coal and iron. In 1938 it became the first Forest Park in England and Wales, administered by the Forestry Commission.

▶ *Return to Coleford; take B 4431 and A 4136 west to Monmouth.*

Monmouth★ – The 13C fortified **bridge-gate,** the emblem of Monmouth, leads into wide Monnow Street. The town has retained much of its medieval street plan but little remains of the castle where **Henry V** (1387-1422) was born. His statue is set in a recess in the handsome Georgian **Shire Hall** (1724) which replaced the Elizabethan Market Hall. Below him stands another local notable, the Hon CS Rolls, co-founder of Rolls-Royce and a pioneer of flying. The **museum** nearby recalls the visits paid by Nelson. **Great Castle House,** a splendid stone building (1673), is the headquarters of the Royal Monmouthshire Royal Engineers.

▶ *Make a detour west for 8mi/13km by A 40.*

Raglan Castle★ – (CADW) 🕐 *Open late-Mar to late-Oct, daily, 9.30am-5pm (6pm Jun to late-Sep); late-Oct to late-Mar, daily, 9.30am (11am Sun) to 4pm.* 🕐 *Closed 1 Jan and 24-26 Dec.* 💷 *£2.50.* ☎ *01291 690 228.* The striking silhouette is composed of a fortress within a fortress. The great tower, known as the "Yellow Tower of Gwent," begun in 1435, reflects the insecurity of an age when a lord had to be able to isolate himself from even his own liveried men, in case they should decide to change their allegiance.

▶ *From Monmouth take A 466 south.*

Tintern Abbey★★ – (CADW) ♿🕐 *Open late-Mar to late-Oct, daily, 9.30am-5pm (6pm Jun to late-Sep); late-Oct to late-Mar, daily, 9.30am (11am Sun) to 4pm.* 🕐 *Closed 24-26 Dec.* 💷 *£3.25.* ☎ *01291 689 251; cadw@wales.gsi.gov.uk; www.cadw.wales.gov.uk.* The steep wooded slopes of the winding valley provide a picturesque setting for this Romantic ruin. In the latter part of the 18C the Abbey became a favoured destination of sentimental tourists, among them William Wordsworth, who here *"felt / A presence that disturbs me with the joy / Of elevated thoughts."*

Much of the 13C abbey church still stands; the full length of the building (236ft/72m) was revealed in the 19C by the removal of the remains of the stone screen which formerly divided the nave from the choir. The foundations, set in the turf, are all that is visible of the cloisters, chapter house, dining hall, kitchen, infirmary, abbot's lodging and guest house.

Monnow Bridge, Monmouth

The abbey was founded in 1131 by Walter de Clare, Anglo-Norman Lord of Chepstow, for a community of Cistercians, who followed a rule of silence and settled in simple houses devoid of ornament "far from the habitations of men". In the late 13C under the patronage of Roger Bigod the original modest church was replaced by a much more lavish structure. In 1536 the abbey was surrendered to the King's commissioners by the abbot, Richard Wyche.

▶ *Continue south on A 466 for about 2.5mi/4km; turn right to viewpoint.*

Wyndcliff – *Access to the viewpoint either by 365 steps or by a less steep approach from a car park 0.5mi/0.75km further south by A 466.* From the **Eagle's Nest Viewpoint**★ on top of the limestone cliff (800ft/240m), which dominates the loop in the river, the eye is led down the final reaches of the Wye to the mighty span of the Severn Suspension **Bridge**, (⌂ *Toll £4.80 per car, charged westwards only.* ☎ *01454 632 436; www.severnbridge.co.uk*) which was completed in 1966. Farther downstream is the **Second Severn Crossing** (nearly 3mi/5km long) consisting of a cable-stayed bridge (1 500ft/450m) approached by viaducts with spans of varying length; it was opened in 1996 to carry the increasing volume of traffic between Wales and England.

▶ *Continue south on A 466 to Chepstow.*

Chepstow★ – The partly walled town slopes down from the great Town Gate to the ancient crossing of the Wye, bridged by an elegant cast-iron structure (1816) designed by John Rennie, which provides the best view of the castle.

Chepstow Castle★★ (CADW ♿ ⏱ *Open late-Mar to late-Oct, daily, 9.30am-5pm (6pm Jun to late-Sep); late-Oct to late-Mar, daily, 9.30am (11am Sun) to 4pm.* ⏱ *Closed 24-26 Dec.* ⌂ *£3.* ☎ *01291 624 065; cadw@wales.gsi.gov.uk; www.cadw.wales.gov.uk*) was begun in 1067 by William FitzOsbern, one of William the Conqueror's closest associates, then engaged in securing the western boundary of his domain. The site has excellent natural defences – a long narrow ridge, protected by cliffs dropping sheer into the river to the north and a deep declivity to the south. At the east end is the 13C Lower Bailey, guarded by the Outer Gatehouse and Marten's Tower. Beyond the Middle Ward rises the heart of the original castle, FitzOsbern's Great Tower, a hall-keep which is probably the earliest secular stone building in Britain. The Upper Ward leads to the castle's western extremity and highest point, the outer defence works of the Barbican.

YEOVIL

Somerset, ENGLAND

POPULATION 28 317

MICHELIN ATLAS P 8 OR MAP 403 M 31

Archeological finds suggest that this bustling West Country town has been settled since the Bronze Age. Yeovil was an important leather and glove centre from the 14C, and later became known for its flax. The opening of the railway link with Taunton in 1853 broadened the town's horizons. The population increased and the buildings now in evidence are principally 19-20C with a few scattered 18-19C Georgian houses and older inns (Princess Street, High Street, Silver Street). 🛈 *Hendford, BA20 1UN ☎ 01935 845946; Fax 01935 845940; yeoviltic@southsomerset. gov.uk; www.visitsouthsomerset.com.*

Sights

St John the Baptist★ - ⏱ *Open daily, 10am-3pm. Services: Sun at 8am, 10.30am, 6.30pm.* ☎ *01935 475 396.* This parish church is early Perpendicular, bristling with pinnacles and built of grey lias with Ham Hill stone dressings (1380-1400). The stoutly buttressed 90ft/27m tower dates from the late 14C. Other interesting features are its 18 large windows, roof bosses carved as faces and masks, crypt supported by a central octagonal pier, and 15C lectern and font (the former one of only four remaining from 1450).

Museum of South Somerset - ⏱ *Open Tue-Fri, 10am-4pm (also Sat in summer), Mon by appointment.* ☎ *01935 424 774; heritage.services@southsomerset.gov.uk;*

www.southsomersetmuseums.org.uk. Located in an 18C coach house, this museum contains a display of tableaux on local industries, miscellaneous archeological artefacts discovered in the area and a bequest of 18C-19C glassware, costume and firearms.

Excursions

Fleet Air Arm Museum★★

Yeovilton. 6mi/10km north, signposted off the B 3151. (NACF) ♿🕐 *Open Mar-Nov, daily, 10am-4.30pm (5.30pm Apr-Oct); last admission 1hr 30min before closing.* 🕐 *Closed 24-26 Dec.* 🎫 *£8. Parking. Refreshments.* ☎ *01935 840 565; Fax 01935 842 630; info@ fleetairarm.com; www.fleetairarm.com.* This museum, next to the Royal Naval Air Station where Sea Harriers and Sea Kings are daily put through their paces, is dedicated to aviation in the Royal Navy from its earliest days to the present. The display includes over 40 aircraft, paintings, photographs, medals, uniforms, models, artefacts and memorabilia. There are four halls, with recommended routes indicated, covering the First World War, the Fleet Air Arm Second World War campaign and Pacific War, the story of the aircraft carrier, and local contributions to aeronautical technology (Concorde, Harrier jump-jet). Peripheral displays illustrate the ongoing role of the Royal Navy's airborne section.

Montacute House★★

5m/8km west. (NT) ♿ *House:* 🕐 *Open late-Mar to early-Nov, Wed-Mon, 11am-5pm. Garden and park: Open same hours as house; also early-Nov to Mar, Wed-Sun, 11.30am-4pm. House, garden and park* 🎫 *£6.20; garden and park only, £3.40 (£2 early Nov to late-Mar). Parking. Licensed restaurant.* ☎ *01935 823 289; wmogen@smtp.ntrust.org. uk; montacute@nt.org.uk; www.nationaltrust.org.uk.* Ham Hill provided the warm tawny-ochre and grey-brown stone used for Montacute House, the village and the Perpendicular parish church. The handsome Elizabethan three-storey H-shaped mansion was built in 1597-1601 for Sir Edward Phelips, a successful lawyer, Speaker of the House of Commons (1604) and Master of the Rolls (1611), probably by William Arnold (Cranborne Manor and Dunster Castle). In 1786, a later Sir Edward reversed the house, making the main entrance the **west front** which he altered by incorporating the porch, pillars and ornamental stone from the demolished Clifton House. The original east front, overlooking the balustraded forecourt and attractive gardens, is flanked by twin pavilions with ogee roofs crowned by open stone spheres. Montacute's fortunes fluctuated with those of the Phelips family, and from 1911 it was let – the most famous tenant was Lord Curzon (1915-25), who entrusted the redecoration to the novelist Elinor Glyn. In 1931 the house, in a sad state of dereliction, was purchased by the National Trust.

Interior – Entrance to the house is through the original east doorway into the screens passage. The **Dining Room** *(left)* was created by Lord Curzon out of the old Buttery from which dishes were carried through the **Great Hall** to the formal dining room (♿ *see Library below*). The Elizabethan chimney-piece bears the Phelips coat of arms of 1599. The tapestry of a knight against a millefleurs background is Flemish; the walnut refectory table 16C Italian; and there are some fine Tudor portraits. The Great Hall, the communal living room until after the Restoration, retains from the 16C its panelling, the ornate stone screen with arches and pillars, and the heraldic glass in the window. At the far end of the hall is the charming **Skimmington Frieze**, a 17C plaster relief depicting the ordeals of a hen-pecked husband.

The **Parlour**, with its original Ham stone fireplace, Elizabethan panelling and frieze of nursery animals, contains some fine 18C furniture (beautiful centre table by Thomas Chippendale the Younger), as does the **Drawing Room** (red damask covered chairs by Walter Linnell, 1753). The staircase, each tread a single 7ft/2m block of stone, rises in straight flights around a solid stone pier. The tapestries are 15-16C.

Lord Curzon's Room (first floor) contains his lordship's bath stowed in a "Jacobean" cupboard, a 17C overmantel of King David at Prayer, an 18C bed, a Dutch oak drop-leaf table and an 18C japanned skeleton mirror. The **Crimson Room**, so-called since the 19C when red flock wallpaper replaced the tapestries below the plaster frieze, contains a sumptuous oak four-poster bed carved with the arms of James I. The **Library**, once the formal dining room and destination of the dishes brought from the distant kitchens, features some remarkable heraldic glass – a tourney of 42 shields displaying the Phelips arms, those of the sovereign and of some of Phelips's neighbours and friends. Other interesting features in this former state room are the Portland stone mantelpiece, plaster frieze, Jacobean inner porch, 19C moulded plaster ceiling and bookcases.

The Long Gallery (172ft/52m), lit with oriels at either end, occupies the entire top floor; it is the longest in existence. It now provides the perfect setting for a panoply of Tudor and early Jacobean England through 90 portraits (on loan from the National Portrait Gallery).

The formal layout of the gardens is designed to enhance that of the house, with green lawns and yew hedges providing a fine foreground to the warm hues of Ham stone. Changing borders and the rose garden add colour.

YORK★★★

North Yorkshire, ENGLAND

POPULATION 123 126

MICHELIN ATLAS P 40 OR MAP 502 Q 22

Formerly an economic centre based on the wool trade, York is marked by many elegant Georgian buildings that reflect the wealth of those moving from the north into what has become an important centre of social and cultural life.

▶ **Orient Yourself**: Most of the city's attractions are within the old walls and is best explored on foot. There are lots of guided walks (*see www.york-tourism.co.uk*) but for a general introduction try Yorkwalk (🕐 *daily Feb-Nov 10.30am, 2.15pm; Sat-Sun only 10.30am, 2.15pm Dec-Jan* ☎ *01904 622 303; www.yorkwalk.co.uk*). Just turn up at their Museum Street office. City Sightseeing operate hop-on, hop-off open top bus tours (🕐 *daily Easter-September, Sat-Sun Oct* ☎ *01904 655 585; www. yorktourbuses.co.uk*) buy your ticket on the bus.

🙈 **Don't Miss**: The stained glass in York Minster; National Railway Museum; The Shambles; Castle Howard, particularly its park.

🕐 **Organizing Your Time**: Allow 2-3 days for the city centre alone.

🄺🄸🄳 **Especially for Kids**: National Railway Museum; Jorvik Viking Centre.

🚲 **Bicycle Trails**: York is a cycle-friendly city; for cycle routes and information go to www.york.gov.uk/cycling/index.html.

A Bit of History

In AD 71 the Roman Ninth Legion built a fortress, **Eboracum**, later capital of the northern province. Here in AD 306 Constantine the Great was proclaimed Emperor. After the departure of the Roman legions the Anglo-Saxons made **Eoforwic** the capital of their Kingdom of Northumbria. In AD 627 King Edwin was baptised by Paulinus here. In AD 866 the Vikings captured the city, which became **Jorvik**, one of their chief trading bases. Viking rule lasted until AD 954 but Scandinavian influence and custom, as well as street names, continued long after the Norman conquest.

Medieval York, its prosperity based on wool, was a city of 10 000 people and forty churches, the richest city in the country after London. With the decline of the wool trade after the Wars of the Roses (1453-87) and following the Dissolution of the Monasteries the city's prosperity waned.

York Minster★★★ *1hr 30min*

(BY) 🚹🕐 *Open (services permitting) daily, 9am-6pm (later in summer).* 🚌 *Minster £5.00. Undercroft, Treasury and Crypt £3.50 . Combined ticket (Minster, Undercroft, Treasury, Crypt). Tower £7.00.* 🚶 *Guided tour (1hr). Leaflet (16 languages). Restaurant in St William's College. Ramps.* ☎ *01904 557 216; Fax 01904 557 218; vistors@yorkminster. org; www.yorkminster.org.* The dedication of the Cathedral Church to St Peter emphasises the close links with Rome after the union of the Celtic and Roman traditions at Whitby in AD 664 (🕯 *see WHITBY*). The Minster is the largest Gothic church north of the Alps (534ft/160m long; 249ft/76m wide across the transepts; 90ft/27m from floor to vault; 198ft/60m to the top of the towers). The west front, completed by the additions of the towers in 1430-70, presents an almost 13C "French" outline. It is curious that such a design caught on so late in England, which has its own glorious "screen" façades in Lincoln and Wells.

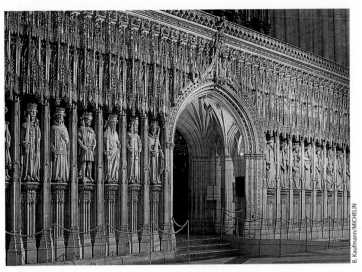

York Minster

B. Kaufmann/MICHELIN

Interior

The nave, built between 1291 and 1350, is in Decorated style; the transepts of the mid 13C are the oldest visible parts of the present building. The **Chapter House★★**, octagonal with a magnificent wooden vaulted ceiling, can be dated to just before 1300. The **Choir Screen★★** is by William Hyndeley, late 15C. Its central doorway is flanked by statues of English kings from William the Conqueror. The finest monument in the Minster is the **tomb** (1) of the man whose initiative began the present building, **Archbishop Walter de Gray**, Archbishop from 1215 until his death in 1255; his crozier, paten, chalice and ring are displayed in the Treasury.

Stained Glass★★★ – The Minster contains the largest single collection of medieval stained glass to have survived in England. The **West Window** (2) with its curvilinear heartshaped tracery was painted in 1339 by Master Robert for Archbishop William de Melton. It was the largest in the Minster at the time but was surpassed by the **East Window** (3) in the Lady Chapel, painted by John Thornton of Coventry between 1405 and 1408.

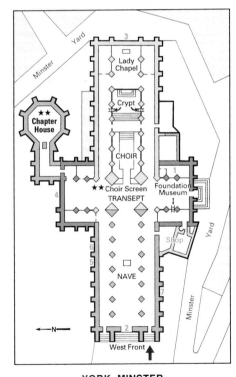

YORK MINSTER

1220-1260 Early English

1280-1350 Decorated

1361-1472 Perpendicular

Address Book

OUT AND ABOUT IN YORK

Tourist Information Centre – *York Tourism Bureau, George Hudson's Street,* ☎ *01904 554 491; York Tourist Information Centre, De Grey Rooms, Exhibition Square,* ☎ *01904 621 756.*

Pubs and Restaurants – Micklegate Bar, Stonegate Walk, Swinegate are worth exploring. The booklet *Days and Nights*

lists establishments.

Shopping – Elegant Edwardian shops (Mulberry Hall) in Stonegate, Swinegate (courtyard setting).

Entertainment – The Grand Opera House, the Theatre Royal and the Barbican Centre host dance, opera, musicals and drama.

It is the largest expanse of medieval glass in the country and revitalised the already well-established York school of glass painting. The **Five Sisters Window** (4), lancets of grisaille glass from c 1250, is the oldest window still in its original place in the Minster.

The **Pilgrimage Window** (5), c 1312, shows grotesques, a monkey's funeral and scenes of hunting, reminiscent of some of the misericord carvings of the time. Next to it is the **Bellfounders Window** (6), given by Richard Tunnoc, who was buried in the Minster in 1330. He is depicted presenting his window to the Archbishop, amongst scenes of casting and tuning a bell. The **Jesse Window** (7), depicting Jesus' family tree, dates from 1310.

Foundation Museum – In 1966-67 the foundations of the east wall, west towers and the 16 000 ton Central Tower were found to be yielding. A programme of reinforcement was begun which lasted five years. Thousands of tons of soil and rubble were removed, exposing walls both of the Roman headquarters building and the early Norman cathedral (c 1080-1110), with its remarkable oak reinforced foundations. New concrete foundations, tied to the old by stainless steel rods, were poured into place and today's visitor can see the clearly indicated lines of the Roman and Norman buildings.

The **Treasury** *(access via the Foundation Museum)* displays a collection of York domestic silver, from 1485 to 1858, and church plate belonging to the Minster and on loan from churches all over the north of England.

National Railway Museum★★★

(AY) ♿🕐 *Open daily, 10am-6pm.* 🕐 *Closed 24-26 Dec. Parking (charge). Restaurant.* ☎ *01904 621 261; 01904 686 286 (Infoline); Fax 01904 611 112; nrm@nmsi.ac.uk; www.nrm.org.uk.* Part of the National Museum of Science and Industry, this magnificent collection presents in an exemplary way the history of railways in the country of their invention. The Great Hall, a wonderfully spacious former locomotive shed, houses an array of locomotives which range from the crudely engineered *Agenoria* of 1829 to near-contemporary diesel and electric locomotives and a mock-up of a Channel Tunnel locomotive. Stealing the show, however, are railway icons like the *Stirling 4-2-2* of 1870 with its single great driving wheel, the elegant Great Western *Lode Star* of 1907, or the superbly streamlined London and North Eastern Railway's *Mallard*, which achieved a speed of 126mph/203kph in 1938 and has held the world's speed record for steam ever since. *Mallard's* Art Deco allure contrasts with the functional lines of British Railways' last steam locomotive, *Evening Star*, built in 1960 and retired by 1968, the date of British steam's final displacement by diesel and electric power.

Constantine the Great

A bronze **statue** (5ft/1.6m high) by Philip Jackson (1998) near the south door of York Minster, marks the probable spot where Constantine was proclaimed Emperor by the army in 306 on the death of his father, a general in the Roman army, in York. After Constantine had gained control of the Western Empire in 312 and become sole ruler in 324, he extended toleration to all religions. His mother, Helena, was a Christian convert and, although the Emperor himself was baptised only on his deathbed in 337, he took an interest in religious matters and opened the council at Nicaea in 325 which laid down the creed that still forms the basic statement of faith of Christian churches. Christianity became the officially established religion of the Empire and later spread to all corners of the world.

The museum's concern extends beyond the glamour of machines like these to the whole technology and culture of the railway, demonstrated by an extraordinarily rich and varied array of other objects displayed in the South Hall as well as in the Great Hall. Ranging from a late medieval German miner's *Hund*, a crude truck running on wooden rails, to the sumptuous interior of a royal coach, they also include fascinating works of art, decorative articles, posters and any amount of railway paraphernalia as well as an extensive "O" gauge model railway layout of a size and realism beyond a schoolboy's wildest dreams.

The South Hall recreates something of the atmosphere of a mainline station from the middle years of the 20C, allowing from its platforms close inspection of engine cabs, the interiors of coaches, primitive or luxurious, dining and sleeping cars, goods wagons and road vehicles. On view in the yards outside are more treasures undergoing or awaiting restoration as well as a miniature railway.

The Walled Town

The Walls★★ – The walls (3mi/5km) embrace the whole of medieval York. The **Multangular Tower (BY)**, western corner of the Roman fort, still stands in the Yorkshire Museum Gardens, near the ruins of St Mary's Abbey (see below). The 13C walls follow the course of the Roman wall to the north of the Minster and are built atop the earthen bank raised by the Anglo-Danish kings. Where roads entered the city through the earthen bank the Normans built fortified gateways, now known as "bars". **Bootham Bar (BY)** is on the site of the Roman gateway. The walls lead around the Deanery Garden to **Monk Bar (BY)** and on to Aldgate; here a swampy area and the River Foss constituted the defences. Brick-built walls, c 1490, run from **Red Tower (CY)**, pass **Walmgate (CZ)** around the south of York Castle to **Fishergate Postern (CZ)**, built in 1505 on what was then the riverbank. Here York Castle took up the defences. Beyond Skeldergate Bridge and **Baile Hill (BZ)**, the walls resume to **Micklegate Bar (AZ)**, traditional point of entry of the monarch into York, and where the severed heads of traitors were exposed after execution. From here the walls turn northeast and lead to the North Street Postern (BY), where the ferry crossed the Ouse before the building of Lendal Bridge.

York Castle Museum★ **(BZ)** – *Open daily, 9.30am-5pm; (4.30pm Nov-Mar). Closed 1 Jan and 25-26 Dec. £5.95. Leaflet (5 languages). Exhibition. Coffee bar. Wheelchair access to ground floor (no charge). 01904 653 611; Fax 01904 671078; www. york.gov.uk*. In what was the **Debtors Prison** and the **Female Prison,** two striking buildings from 1705 and 1777 respectively, there is now a museum of everyday life. "Kirkgate" is an authentic reproduction of a Victorian street, with a **Hansom cab**, a design perfected by a York architect, **Joseph Aloysius Hansom** (1803-82). The **Coppergate Helmet**, a Saxon helmet (c AD 750) found in 1982 during the Jorvik Centre excavations, is displayed here; it is made of iron with brass fittings and it probably belonged to a Northumbrian noble. There are costumes, period rooms, pubs and shops as well as the actual cell in which Dick Turpin was held before his execution on 7 April 1739. The famous "Ride to York" which Ainsworth attributed to Turpin in his novel *Rookwood* was not, in fact, made by Turpin but by John Nevinson, a highwayman who was hanged in York in 1685.

Clifford's Tower (BZ) – Built 1250-75 by Henry III, to replace the Conqueror's timber fort, burnt down by a mob attacking besieged Jews there in 1190. The name commemorates Roger de Clifford who was captured during a battle at Boroughbridge and hanged in chains from this tower on 16 March 1322.

Fairfax House★ **(BZ)** – *Open mid-Feb to Dec, Sat-Thu, 11am (1.30pm Sun) to 5pm; last admission 4.30pm. Guided tour Fri, 11am, 2pm. £4.50. Brochure (3 languages). 01904 655 543; Fax 01904 652 262; www.fairfaxhouse.co.uk*. This Georgian house was built by Viscount Fairfax for his daughter Anne, in 1755. The ceilings by Cortese and carved wooden mouldings have been restored or replaced. It houses a collection of Georgian furniture, paintings, clocks and porcelain, and there are displays of eating and dining in 18C England.

Jorvik Viking Centre★ **(BZ)** – *Open daily, 9am-5.30pm (last admission); Nov-Mar, telephone to check times. Closed 25 Dec. £6.95. Audio tour (5 languages). 01904 643 211 (24hr information), 01904 543 403 (advance booking); Fax 01904 627 097; marketing.jorvik@lineone.net; www.vikingjorvik.com*. During building operations between 1976 and 1981, archeologists uncovered four rows of buildings from the Viking town, with remarkably well preserved items, including boots and shoes, pins, plants and insects. Two rows now illustrate an archeological 'dig' and two have been

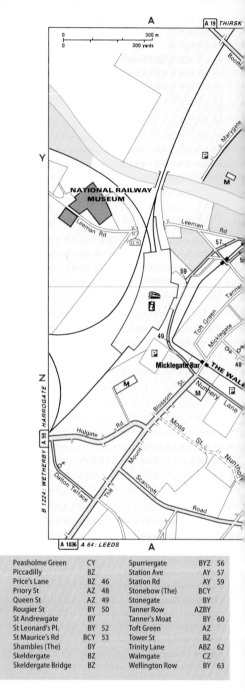

accurately reconstructed. "Time Cars" take the visitor on a journey back into Jorvik, with sights sounds and smells as they would have been on an October day in AD 948. In February each year the York Archeological Trust stages the **Jorvik Viking Festival**, with longship races, feasting and fireworks.

Merchant Adventurers' Hall (BZ) – ♿🕐 *Open Mon-Thu, 9am-5pm (3.30pm winter), Fri-Sat 9am-3pm; Sun (except in winter), noon-4pm. Closed 2 weeks at Christmas. ⊙ £2. Leaflet and guide book (9 languages). Ramps, partially accessible. ☎/Fax 01904 654 818; The.clerk@mahall-york.demon.co.uk; www.theyorkcompany.sagenet.co.uk.* A brick undercroft, with a Chapel first consecrated in 1411, is crowned by a timber-framed Great Hall, built c 1357.

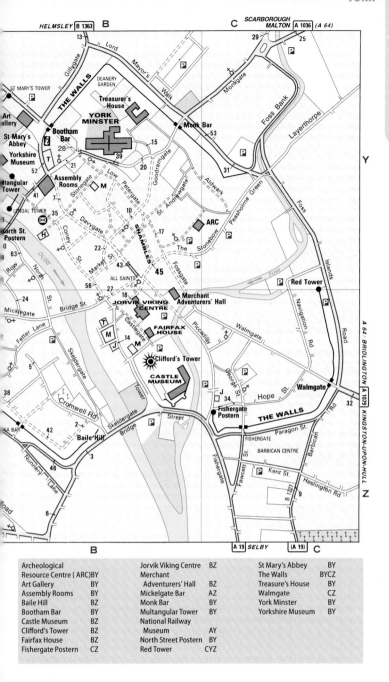

Archeological		Jorvik Viking Centre	BZ	St Mary's Abbey	BY
Resource Centre (ARC)BY		Merchant		The Walls	BYCZ
Art Gallery	BY	Adventurers' Hall	BZ	Treasure's House	BY
Assembly Rooms	BY	Mickelgate Bar	AZ	Walmgate	CZ
Baile Hill	BZ	Monk Bar	BY	York Minster	BY
Bootham Bar	BY	Multangular Tower	BY	Yorkshire Museum	BY
Castle Museum	BZ	National Railway			
Clifford's Tower	BZ	Museum	AY		
Fairfax House	BZ	North Street Postern	BY		
Fishergate Postern	CZ	Red Tower	CYZ		

Shambles★ (BY) – The most visited amongst the many picturesque streets of the city, with overhanging timber-framed houses. Nearby **Pavement (BY 45)**, with the Guild Church of All Saints, is so called because it was the first street in medieval York to be paved.

Assembly Rooms (BY) – The rooms (now a restaurant), which were designed by Richard Boyle, 3rd Earl of Burlington, and built in 1731, include a finely proportioned **Egyptian Hall** with Corinthian columns and clerestory lighting. The Rooms were needed for dancing and for gaming following the growing social life of York, which by this time had three stage-coach services a week to and from London.

Yorkshire Museum (BY) – ♿🕐 *Open daily, 10am-5pm. Exhibitions all year.* 🕐 *Closed 1 Jan and 25-26 Dec.* ✆ *£3.95.* ☎ *01904 551 800; yorkshiremuseum@york.gov.uk; www. york.gov.uk.* The museum traces the history of York and its surroundings from the time of the Roman invasion, through the Viking period and the Middle Ages; the highlights of the latter period are the Middleton Jewel and the Middleton Ring, both of which were probably connected with the Neville family of Middleham Castle (south of Richmond). The section on **St Mary's Abbey**, a Benedictine house, founded in 1088 by William Rufus, incorporates some of the actual ruins which are mostly late 13C; every 4 years in June and July they are the setting for the **York Cycle of Mystery Plays**, the life of Christ told in a series of plays dating from around 1340.

York City Art Gallery (BY) – ♿🕐 *Open daily, 10am-5pm. Last admission 4.30pm* 🕐 *Closed 1 Jan and 25-26 Dec.* ✆ *£2. Shop.* ☎ *01904 551 861; 01904 551 864 (24hr answerphone); Fax 01904 551 866* An extensive collection of paintings, from 1350 to the present day, including many portraits and nude studies by the York painter **William Etty** (1787-1849), who is buried in St Olave's churchyard, Marygate.

Treasurer's House (BY) – *(NT)* ♿🕐 *Open late-Mar to early-Nov, Sat-Thu, 11am-4.30pm.* ✆ *£3.80. Guide book. Licensed tearoom. Braille guide.* ☎ *01904 624 247; Fax 01904 647 372; treasurershouse@ntrust.org.uk; www.nationaltrust.org.uk.* Rebuilt in the 17C and 18C, this was the house of the Treasurers of York Minster and has a magnificent series of rooms with furniture and pictures from many periods. The **Great Hall** has had its false ceiling removed, and has an unusual staircase c 1700. The early 18C ceiling in the **Dining Room** has decorated beams and panels.

The fascinating collection of 18C drinking vessels illustrates the skill and ingenuity of the glassmaker. Stems, bowls and feet were variously fashioned: twisted, fluted, folded, engraved, cut and faceted.

Excursions

Sutton Park – *8mi/13km north by B 1363 (BY).* ♿ *House:* 🕐 *Open Apr-Sep, Wed, Sun and Bank Hol Mon, 1.30pm-5pm; also Good Friday to Easter Mon. Gardens: Open Apr-Sep, daily, 11am-5pm.* ✆ *£6; garden only, £3.50. Parking. Wheelchair access to garden.* ☎ *01347 810 249/239; Fax 01347 811 251; suttonpark@fsbdial. co.uk; www. statelyhome. co.uk.* A house by Thomas Atkinson, c 1750, it contains beautiful 18C panelling and furniture, as well as a fine collection of Meissen and Imari porcelain. The gardens contain many unusual and interesting plants.

Castle Howard★★ – *15mi/24km northeast by A 64 and minor road north.* ♿🕐 *Open mid-Mar to early-Nov, daily, 10am (11am house) to 4.30pm (last admission); grounds close 6.30pm.* ✆ *£8 Guide book. Parking. Licensed cafeteria.* ☎ *01653 648333; Fax 01653 648 501; house@castlehoward.co.uk; www.castlehoward.co.uk.* Castle Howard, **Sir John Vanbrugh's** great piece of architectural theatre, was the first building he had ever designed. Soldier, turned dramatist on his return to England in 1692, Vanbrugh attracted the attention of the Whig nobility of his day – perhaps owing to his popular, if bawdy, plays – and came to the notice of **Charles Howard**, 3rd Earl of Carlisle, through the Kit-Cat Club. Vanbrugh was assisted by **Nicholas Hawksmoor,** already an established architect, who was responsible for the realisation of the design and much of the detail. When Vanbrugh, enthusiastic amateur, was chosen to build a house fitted to the position of the Earl, Jonathan Swift commented: "Van's genius, without thought or lecture, is hugely turned to Architecture." "Genius" was assuredly there. The landscaping of the surrounding **park**★★★ is one of the most grandiose projects of the great age of landscaping; it consists of a series of compositions focused on some of the most ambitious and beautiful garden structures ever built, notably the **Temple of the Four Winds**, Vanbrugh's last work and, crowning a distant rise, a colossal colonnaded **Mausoleum** by Hawksmoor. The specialist woodland garden presents rare trees, shrubs, rhododendrons and azaleas.

The striking entrance to the house, topped by a painted and gilded dome (80ft/24m), is familiar to many as the castle was used as the principal location for the television series *Brideshead Revisited*.

House – The **statuary** in the **Grand Entrance** and elsewhere is from but two of the three ship-loads collected by the 4th Earl in Italy, the third vessel having been lost at sea. A remarkable piece is the **altar** from the Temple of Delphi, its top slotted to receive the tripod which held the sacred flame. On the **China Landing**, among portrait busts, are displayed services of Meissen, Crown Derby and Chelsea, together with a Dutch **tulip vase**, from c 1704.

The heart of the house is the **Great Hall**, which rises through two storeys into the painted dome, a most light-hearted but impressive concept of English architecture.

The columns and capitals were carved by Samuel Carpenter, a Yorkshire mason; the cupola is by Nadauld, a Huguenot refugee; both worked on the flowing pinewood swags in the **Music Room** and **Tapestry Room**.

In the **Long Gallery** and its **Octagon** are pictures by Lely, Kneller and Van Dyck. The finest are probably the two **Holbeins** – a portrait of **Henry VIII**, showing a disillusioned and stricken monarch, painted in 1542, just after the execution of Catherine Howard; 1538 is the date of his portrait of Thomas Howard, 3rd Duke of Norfolk, Catherine's uncle, who escaped the block himself only because the King died on the day appointed for the execution. The magnificent stained-glass windows in the **Chapel** are by the 19C artist Sir Edward Burne-Jones.

The **Stable Court** presents a display (changed annually) of period costume from the 17C onwards drawn from the largest private collection in Britain.

Eden Camp – *Near Malton, 20mi/32km northeast by A 64 and A 169.* ⊙ *Open mid-Jan to late-Dec, daily, 10am-5pm (4pm last admission).* ⊛ *£4. Assault Course. Parking. Prisoners' Canteen, Officers' Mess tearooms, Garrison Cinema Bar.* ☎ *01653 697 777; Fax 01653 698 243; admin@edencamp.co.uk; www.edencamp.co.uk.* The bleak huts of a Second World War prisoner of war camp now house an extensive range of exhibits and displays which, despite some questionable interpretation of history, succeed in recreating the atmosphere of the "People's War."

Selby Abbey★ – *14mi/22km south by A 19.* ♿ ⊙ *Open daily, 9am-5pm (4pm Oct-Mar).* ⊙ *Closed 26-27 Dec.* ⊛ *Donation.* ⊶ *Guided tour (45min) by appointment.* ☎ *01757 703 123; Fax 01757 708 878; selbyabbeyyorks@aol.com.* The abbey was probably founded by the Benedictines in 1069, thus pre-dating both Durham and St Mary's Church in York. The present church was begun by Abbot Hugh de Lacey c 1100. The **west front** contains the three main styles of the building, which combines earlier strength and simplicity with later elegance. The doorway is Norman (c 1170); above is Early English work pierced by a Perpendicular window and small Early English lancets in the side bays. The **nave** with its gigantic circular piers is mid-Norman, a reflection of Durham. The spectacular distortion of the easternmost arches is due to a high water table. The **Jesse Window** (c 1330) at the east end is a remarkable piece of work, though much restored. High above the south side of the choir is a **14C window** depicting the arms of the Washington family – the "Stars and Stripes" motif of the American flag. The **Norman font** at the west end of the north aisle has a magnificent 15C wooden cover, one of the few pieces saved from the disastrous fire of 1906.

Samuel Smith Old Brewery, Tadcaster – *7mi/11km southwest by A 64 (AZ).* ⊶ *Guided tour (approx 60min) by appointment mid-Jan to mid-Dec, Mon-Thur at 11am, 2pm, 7pm.* ⊙ *Closed Bank Hols.* ⊛ *£4 including sample drink.* ☎ *01937 839 201.* The brewery, which was established in 1758, still preserves the old-fashioned methods of brewing, makes its own casks and uses shire horses for local deliveries.

Address Book

For coin ranges, see Legend at the back of the guide.

WHERE TO STAY

Curzon Lodge, *23 Tadcaster Rd, Dringhouses.* ☎ *01904 703157; Fax 01904 703157.* This 17C house sits on the dge of the city and features quiet rooms in its converted 18C stable which are furnished and decorated in homely flowery style.

Acer, *52 Scarcroft Hill.* ☎ *01904 653839; Fax 01904 653839; info@ acerhotel.co.uk; www. acerhotel.co.uk.* This pretty, terraced Victorian house a few minutes walk from the city centre offers immaculate traditional rooms and a warm welcome.

WHERE TO EAT

The Tasting Room, *13a Swinegate Court East.* ☎ *01904 627 879; bookings@thetastingroom.co.uk; www. thetastingroom.co.uk.* Nestled in a quaint courtyard, choose from the bistro or restaurant menu to enjoy fresh home-prepared food within a spacious and contemporary funky, chatty environment.

Rish, *7 Fossgate* ☎ *01904 622 688; 01904 671 931; www.rish-york.co.uk.* The exterior is art deco, the interior is contemporary and elegant, which mirrors the food - a fusion of English essentials with European and Oriental tastes (and Rish? - its Arabic for feathers!). Good value lunch

Rose & Crown, *Main Street, Sutton-on-Forest (12 mi/19 km north of York).* ☎ *01347 811 333; Fax 811 444; mail@ rosecrown.co.uk; www.rosecrown.co.uk.* Worth the journey for the rustic yet relaxed and stylished bar ambience and the exceptional pub cooking featuring a Modern English menu that has imaginative twists. Excellent value.

YORKSHIRE DALES★

North Yorkshire, ENGLAND

MICHELIN ATLAS PP 39 OR MAP 502 N, O 21 AND 22

Northwest of the great northern manufacturing towns of Leeds and Bradford lie the Yorkshire Dales, presenting many of the dramatic features of limestone scenery, crags, caves, "limestone pavements" and swallow holes in which streams disappear. In the broad dales such as Airedale, Wensleydale and Wharfedale the stone-built villages are set harmoniously in an ancient pattern of stone-walled fields. The **Pennine Way** passes through the region via Malham, Horton-in-Ribblesdale, Pen-y-ghent, Hawes and Hardrow. Most of this country is preserved in the **Yorkshire Dales National Park** (680sq mi/ 760km2 which is skirted on the east and south by an arc of pleasant towns – Richmond, Ripon, Harrogate and Skipton. ⬚ *National Park Information Centres: ☎ 01969 663424 (Aysgarth Falls); aysgarth@ytbtic.co.uk; ☎ 01524 251419 (Clapham); clapham@ytbtic.co.uk; ☎ 01756 752774 (Grassington); grassington@ytbtic.co.uk; ☎ 01969 667450 (Hawes); hawes@ ytbtic.co.uk; ☎ 01729 830 363 (Malham); malham@ytbtic.co.uk; ☎ 01539 620125 (Sedbergh); sedbergh@ytbtic.co.uk.*

Town/village Information Centres: ⬚ 8 Station Road, Bentham ☎ 01524 241 049. ⬚ Pen-y-Ghent Cafe, Horton-in-Ribblesdale ☎ 01729 860 333. ⬚ Community Centre car park, Ingleton ☎ 01524 241 049 (Easter-Oct). ⬚ Town Hall, Cheapside, Settle ☎ 01729 825 192. ⬚ 9 Sheep Street, Skipton ☎ 01756 792 809. Website for area: www.yorkshirevisitor. com

Skipton

The town is a good base from which to explore the **Yorkshire Dales** by car or by boat (🕐 *Operates daily Easter-Oct, call for times ☎ and Fax 01756 790829; info@ canaltrips.co.uk; www. canaltrips.co.uk*) on the Leeds-Liverpool Canal which crosses the Pennines. The broad High Street, where a traditional market is held four times a week, leads up to the castle.

Skipton Castle★ – 🕐 *Open daily, 10am (noon, Sun) to 6pm (4pm Oct-Feb). 🕐 Closed 25 Dec. ▣ £4.60. Tour sheet (8 languages). Parking nearby. ☎ 01756 792 442; Fax 01756 796 100; www.skiptoncastle.co.uk.* The castle was substantially strengthened by Robert de Clifford in the early years of the 14C before his death at Bannockburn in 1314. The beautiful **Conduit Court** was built by the 10th Earl, before the castle suffered the ravages of the Civil War. Its present appearance owes much to the restorations made by Lady Anne Clifford (1589-1676), who in 1657-58 added the parapet with the Clifford motto *Desormais* over the main gate and recorded the work of restoration on a tablet over the Tudor entrance to the castle itself. The natural defences on the north side are best seen from the canal towpath from Eller Bridge.

Holy Trinity Church – ♿🕐 *Open daily, 10am-4.30pm (dusk in winter). Leaflet. Visitor board (6 languages). Refreshments (most Sat, 10am-4pm, Fri, 10am-2pm). ☎ 01756 700 773 (Mon-Fri, 9.30-11.30am); office@holytrinityskipton.org.uk; www.holytrinityskipton. org.uk.* The church was enlarged in the 15C; its fine roof dates from 1488 and the **rood screen** from 1533. After the Dissolution, the Clifford family were buried here in the parish church rather than as before in Bolton Priory.

Craven Museum – Town Hall. ♿🕐 *Open Apr-Sep, Wed-Mon, 10am (2pm Sun) to 5pm; Oct-Mar, Mon and Wed-Fri, 1.30-5pm, Sat, 10am-4pm. ☎ 01756 706 407; Fax 01756 706 412; museum@cravendc.gov.uk.* Displays on history, archeology, lead mining, costume, local wildlife.

The Dales

Bolton Priory★ – *5mi/8km east of Skipton by A 59 and B 6160. Access to The Strid (♿ see below) and Barden Bridge by footpaths on both banks of the river. ♿🕐 Open Mon-Sun, 8am-6pm (4pm winter). ⬚ Guided tour (30min) by appointment. Leaflet (8 languages). Induction loop. ☎ 01756 710 238.* Bolton Priory was founded by the Augustinians c 1154, in a setting of great beauty on a bend of the River Wharfe. At the Dissolution, the lead was stripped from all the roofs except for the gatehouse and the nave of the church. The west front of the church is an outstanding example of Early English architecture.

The Strid – *5mi/8km east of Skipton by A 59 and B 6160.* Access on foot from Bolton Priory (♾ *see above*). ⚠ *It is dangerous to attempt to jump from one bank to the other.* Here the river Wharfe hurtles through a very narrow channel. The son of the founder of Bolton Priory, Alicia de Rumilly, is thought to have died in attempting to jump from one bank to the other.

Malham – *10mi/16km north east of Skipton by A 65 and north by a side road.* The village contains an information centre about the National Park. To the north is **Malham Cove**, a natural amphitheatre of awesome grandeur. The lime-rich waters of **Malham Tarn** support a unique collection of plants and animals.

White Scar Caves – *20mi/32km northwest of Skipton by A 65 and B 6255.* ⏱ ⛴ *Guided tour (80min; weather permitting) daily, 10am-5.30pm.* ⏱*Closed 25 Dec.* ✈ *£6.95. Guide book and leaflet. Parking. Café, picnic areas.* ☎ *01524 241 244; Fax 01524 241 700; info@ whitescarcave.co.uk; www.whitescarcave.co.uk.* This vast showcave presents a massive ice-age cavern, underground waterfalls and streams and stalactites galore.

Three Peaks – *20mi/32km northwest of Skipton by A 65.* Walkers are attracted by the relatively easy gradients and fine views provided by the summits of **Ingleborough** (2 373ft/722m), **Great Whernside** (2 419ft/738m) and **Pen-y-ghent** (2 273ft/693m).

Yorkshire Dales Falconry and Conservation Centre – *Crows Nest, near Giggleswick; northwest of Skipton by A 65 via Settle.* ♿ ⏱ *Open daily, 10am-5pm. Flying demonstrations at noon, 1.30pm, 3pm, 4.30pm.* ✈ *£4.15. Bird Handling courses; adventure playground. Parking. Tearoom.* ☎ *01729 822 832.* This bird-of-prey centre is set in converted stone farm buildings looking back over dramatic dales scenery. Among the breeds giving regular flying demonstrations are eagles, vultures, hawks, falcons, owls and kites.

Hardrow Force – *35mi/56km north of Skipton by B 626 and B 6160; in Hawes turn left into A 684.* This is the highest single-drop waterfall in England, where Blondin once walked a tightrope, cooking an omelette as he went.

YORKSHIRE MOORS★

North Yorkshire, ENGLAND

MICHELIN ATLAS PP 46 AND 47 OR MAP 502 Q, R, S 20 AND 21

The beauty of this expanse of open moorland lies in its unforgettable wildness. The heather-covered high ground stretches southeast from industrial Middlesbrough to Whitby and Scarborough on the coast and to Pickering (♾ *see below*) and Helmsley (♾ *see below*) in the south. Most of the land from the Cleveland Hills east to the rugged cliffs of the Yorkshire coastline is embraced by the **North York Moors National Park** (553sq mi/1 432 sq km). ⚑ *Area website: www.yorkshi-revisitor.com.*

Sights

Rievaulx Abbey★★ – *3mi/5km northwest of Helmsley by B 1257.* ⏱ *Open daily, 10am (9.30am mid-Jul to mid-Aug) to 6pm (5pm Oct; 4pm Nov-Mar).* ⏱ *Closed 1 Jan and 24-26 Dec. Museum and exhibition.* ✈ *£3.60. Parking. Audio tour (3 languages).* ☎ *01439 798 228.* Rievaulx, the first major monastery built by the Cistercians, was founded c 1132 and the monastic buildings must have been completed in the late 12C. The least ruined part is the austere **nave** which dates from c 1135-40. The walls of the Early English, 13C **presbytery** still rise to three tiers, showing little of the severity of design of the nave. The shrine of the first Abbot, William, is set in the west wall of the **chapter house**. A complex of monastic buildings – infirmary, chapel, kitchens and a warming house – give an idea of the activities and work of the community.

Rievaulx Terrace – *2.5mi/4km northwest of Helmsley by B 1257. (NT)* ♿ ⏱ *Open late-Mar to early-Nov, daily, 10.30am-6pm (5pm Oct-Nov); last admission 1hr before closing. Ionic Temple closed 1pm-2pm.* ✈ *£3.30.* ☎ *01439 798 340, 01439 748 283; Fax 01439 748 284; yorknu@smtp.ntrust.org.uk; www.nationaltrust.org.uk.* The natural feature of the escarpment was landscaped in the picturesque style favoured in the 18C into a long curving grass terrace providing a series of views of Rievaulx abbey ruins and a stretch of the River Rye. The south end is marked by a circular Tuscan temple and

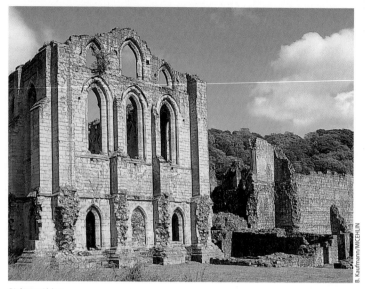

B. Kaufmann/MICHELIN

Rielvaux Abbey

the north by an Ionic temple, which was used for taking refreshment. The basement service rooms now present an exhibition about the owners of Duncombe Park who commissioned the terrace.

Duncombe Park – *On the edge of Helmsley.* ⏱ *Garden: Open late-Apr to late-Oct, Sun-Thu, 11am-5.30pm/dusk. House:* 🚶 *Guided tour Apr-Oct, Sun-Thu, noon-5pm (tours 12.30-3.30pm).* 🎫 *£6; garden and park only, £3. Nature reserve. Walks. Orienteering. Restaurant.* ☎ *01439 770 213; Fax 01439 771 114; sally@duncombepark.com; www. duncombepark.com.* The house, built in the Baroque style with Palladian elements, was designed by William Wakefield, probably with the collaboration of Sir John Vanbrugh; the wings (1843) are by Sir Charles Barry. The principal rooms, which are decorated in the grand Edwardian manner, display family portraits, English and French furniture, a Wedgwood shell dessert service decorated with a rare moonlight lustre glaze. The bedrooms display French and Italian furnishings. An archive room on the history of the house is in the servants' quarters in the basement.

The site was chosen when interest in landscape gardens was at its height. The garden is therefore essentially green with the only touch of colour in the parterres north and south of the house. The outstanding feature is the curving **grass terrace** looking eastwards over the winding course of the Rye; each end is marked by a Greek rotunda – Ionic at the north end and Doric at the south. The south terrace, which provides an ideal habitat for wild flowers, is backed by woods in which stands the Conservatory, designed in 1851 by Barry, to stand in a clearing.

Helmsley Walled Garden, (♿⏱ *Open Apr-Oct, daily, 10.30am-5pm.* 🎫 *£2.50. Café (closed most Mon).* ☎*/Fax 01439 771 427; info@helmsleywalledgarden.co.uk; www. helmsleywalledgarden.co.uk) below the south wall of Helmsley Castle (entrance from the village),* is being restored to its original layout, with fruit trees and herbaceous borders against the walls, a herb garden and ornamental garden near the glasshouses, the pond and fountain at the centre and fruit bushes and vegetables beyond.

Helmsley – The southern gateway to the North York Moors is an attractive village, which centres on a spacious square. On the north side of the village stands **Helmsley Castle** (EH ⏱ *Open late-Mar to Oct, daily, 10am-6pm (5pm in Oct); Nov-Mar, Wed-Sun, 10am-1pm, 2-4pm.* ⏱*Closed 1 Jan and 24-26 Dec.* 🎫 *£2.60. Parking (charge).* ☎ *01439 770 442; www.english-heritage.org.uk)* protected by massive rings of banks and ditches; its keep, originally D-shaped, was slighted after the Civil War. The west range and tower, built on 12C foundations, survive as 16C domestic buildings, roofed and glazed with oak panelling and plaster ceilings.

Hutton-le-Hole – Sheep nibble the grass verges in this charming village. The **Ryedale Folk Museum** (♿⏱ *Open mid-Mar to early-Nov, daily, 10am-5.30pm (4.30pm last admission).* 🎫 *£3.25. Guide book (3 languages).* ☎ *01751 417 367; info@ryedalefolkmuseum.co.uk;*

www.ryedalefolkmuseum.co.uk) presents a large collection of rural memorabilia.
The ruins of **Rosedale Abbey (12C)** lie at the bottom of the steep north slope *(road gradient 1:3)* which gives a magnificent panoramic **view**★ across the moors.

Pickering – *Population 5 316.* This pleasant market town is poised on a limestone bluff on the southern edge of the National Park at an important crossroads. The town is noted for its **castle** *(EH &🕐 Open late-Mar to Sep, daily, 10am-6pm; Oct, daily, 10am-1pm, 2-5pm; Nov-Mar, Wed-Sun, 10am-1pm, 2-4pm. 🕐Closed 1 Jan and 24-26. ⊕ £2.50. Parking. ☎ 01751 474 989; www.english-heritage.org.uk)* which is built of the rock on which it stands; the high steep motte carries a 13C keep which probably replaced an earlier structure.

The **Church of St Peter and St Paul,** mostly Norman built on a Saxon site, contains wall paintings depicting the lives and deeds of the saints *(north and south walls);* they were discovered in 1851 and restored.

North York Moors Railway – *Pickering to Grosmont &🕐early-Mar to early-Nov, daily. ⊕ £10 (return ticket/round trip. Parking. Refreshments. ☎ 01751 472 508; Fax 01751 476 970; admin@nymrpiccenng.fsnt.co.uk; www.northyorkshiremoorsrailway.com.* Steam locomotives still haul trains between Grosmont and Pickering *(18mi/29km),* part of the line laid in 1836, when Stephenson opened the Pickering-Whitby Railway.

INDEX

MAPS AND PLANS

COMPANION PUBLICATIONS

MAPS OF GREAT BRITAIN

Michelin maps 501, 502, 503, 504 – Scotland; Northern England, The Midlands; Wales, The Midlands, South West England; South East England, The Midlands, East Anglia (Scale 1: 400 000 - 1cm = 4km - 1in: 6.30miles) cover the main regions of the country, the network of motorways and major roads and some secondary roads. they provide information on shipping routes, distances in miles and kilometres, major town plans, services, sporting and tourist attractions and an index of places; the key and text are printed in four languages.

COUNTRY MAPS

The Michelin Tourist and Motoring Atlas - Great Britain & Ireland (Scale 1: 300 000 - 1cm = 3km - 1in: 4.75 miles) covers the whole of the United Kigdom and the Republic of Ireland, the national networks of motorways and major roads. It provides information on route planning, shipping routes, distances in miles and kilometre, over 60 town plans, services, sporting and tourist attractions and an index of places; the key and text are printed in six languages.

ROUTE PLANNING VIA INTERNET

Michelin is pleased to offer a route-planning service on the Internet: www. ViaMichelin. com. Choose the shortest route, a route without tolls, or the Michelin recommended route to your destination; you can also access information about hotels and restaurants from The Red Guide, and tourist sites from The Green Guide.

Bon voyage!

Legend

★★★ **Highly recommended**

★★ **Recommended**

★ **Interesting**

Tourism

Sightseeing route with departure point indicated	Map co-ordinates locating sights
Ecclesiastical building	Tourist information
Synagogue – Mosque	Historic house, castle – Ruins
Building (with main entrance)	Dam – Factory or power station
Statue, small building	Fort – Cave
Wayside cross	Prehistoric site
Fountain	Viewing table – View
Fortified walls – Tower – Gate	Miscellaneous sight

Recreation

Racecourse	Waymarked footpath
Skating rink	Outdoor leisure park/centre
Outdoor, indoor swimming pool	Theme/Amusement park
Marina, moorings	Wildlife/Safari park, zoo
Mountain refuge hut	Gardens, park, arboretum
Overhead cable-car	Aviary, bird sanctuary
Tourist or steam railway	

Additional symbols

Motorway (unclassified)	Post office – Telephone centre
Junction: complete, limited	Covered market
Pedestrian street	Barracks
Unsuitable for traffic, street subject to restrictions	Swing bridge
Steps – Footpath	Quarry – Mine
Railway – Coach station	Ferry (river and lake crossings)
Funicular – Rack-railway	Ferry services: Passengers and cars
Tram – Metro, underground	Foot passengers only
Main shopping Bert (R.)... street	Access route number common to MICHELIN maps and town plans

Abbreviations and special symbols

C	County council offices	T	Theatre
H	Town hall	U	University
J	Law courts		Park and Ride
M	Museum	M3	Motorway
POL.	Police	A2	Primary route

Manufacture française des pneumatiques Michelin

Société en commandite par actions au capital de 304 000 000 EUR
Place des Carmes-Déchaux – 63000 Clermont-Ferrand (France)
R.C.S. Clermont-Fd B 855 200 507

© Michelin et Cie, Propriétaires-éditeurs
Dépot légal mars 2006 – ISSN 0763-1383

Pre-Press : Nord Compo à Villeneuve-d'Ascq
Printing and Binding: Aubin à Ligugé
Printed in France, janvier 2006

Made in France